ENCYCLOPEDIA OF
GOVERNMENT AND POLITICS

ENCYCLOPEDIA OF GOVERNMENT AND POLITICS

Volume 1

Second Edition

Edited by
Mary Hawkesworth
and Maurice Kogan

Routledge
Taylor & Francis Group

LONDON AND NEW YORK

First published 1992
by Routledge
11 New Fetter Lane, London EC4P 4EE

Simultaneously published in the USA and Canada
by Routledge
29 West 35th Street, New York, NY 10001

Reprinted in 2004

Routledge is an imprint of the Taylor & Francis Group

Selection and editorial matter
© 2004 Mary Hawkesworth and Maurice Kogan
The chapters © 2004 Routledge

Typeset in Sabon by Taylor & Francis Books Ltd
Printed and bound in Great Britain by TJ International Ltd, Padstow, Cornwall

British Library Cataloguing in Publication Data
A catalogue record for this book is available from the British Library

Library of Congress Cataloging in Publication Data
Encyclopedia of government and politics/edited by
Mary Hawksworth and Maurice Kogan – 2nd ed.
p. cm.
Includes bibliographical references and index.
1. Political science – Encyclopedias. I. Hawksworth, M. E.,
952– II. Kogan, Maurice.
JA61. C66 2003
320'.03 – dc21
2003046669

ISBN 0–415–27622–5 (set)
ISBN 0–415–27623–3 (volume 1)
ISBN 0–415–27624–1 (volume 2)

CONTENTS

CONTENTS

CONTENTS

CONTENTS

CONTENTS

CONTENTS

CONTENTS

CONTENTS

CONTRIBUTORS

Jeffrey Anderson is Graf Goltz Professor and Director of the BMW Center for German and European Studies of the Edmund A. Walsh School of Foreign Service, Georgetown University. He is the author of *German Unification and the Union of Europe* (Cambridge University Press, 1999) and *The Territorial Imperative* (Cambridge University Press, 1992), and edited *Regional Integration and Democracy* (Rowman and Littlefield, 1999). His current research examines the 'Europeanization' of the polity and political economy regimes of the member states in the European Union.

Anthony Clark Arend is Professor in the Department of Government and the Walsh School of Foreign Service and Director of the Institute for International Law and Politics at Georgetown University. He is also an adjunct professor of law at the Georgetown University Law Center. His publications include *Legal Rules and International Society* (Oxford University Press, 1999), as co-editor, *International Rules: Approaches from International Law and International Relations* (Oxford University Press, 1996) and, as co-author, *International Law and the Use of Force: Beyond the United Nations Charter Paradigm* (Routledge, 1993). His main research interests are in the areas of international law, international organization, and constitutional law of US foreign relations.

Peter R. Baehr is Professor Emeritus of Human Rights at the University of Leiden and of Utrecht and was formerly Professor of International Relations at the University of Amsterdam. He was Executive Secretary of the Scientific Council for Government Policy in The Hague, and was Chair of the Dutch Advisory Committee on Human Rights and Foreign Policy. Publications in English include (with Leon Gordenker) *The United Nations at the End of the 1990s* (3rd edition, St. Martin's Press, 1999) and *Human Rights: Universality in Practice* (Palgrave, 2001).

Kate Bedford is a doctoral candidate in the Department of Political Science at Rutgers University. Her teaching and research interests include gender and politics, comparative politics, international political economy, and sexuality studies. Her current research focuses upon the assumptions about race, class, and heteronormativity embedded in the World Bank's advocacy of women's employment as a development strategy.

Ivar Bleiklie is Professor of Administration and Organization Theory at the University of Bergen and the Rokkan Centre for Social Studies, Norway. His publications include: *Comparative Biomedical Policy*, as co-editor (Routledge, forthcoming), *Transforming Higher Education. A Comparative Study*, as co-editor (Jessica Kingsley, 2000), *Policy and Practice in Higher Education*, as co-author (Jessica Kingsley, 2000), and *Service Regimes in Public Welfare Administration* (Tano Aschehoug, 1997). He heads the national Norwegian research programme on Knowledge, Education and Learning, is a board member of the Consortium of Higher Education Researchers, and is currently working on a study of reform and change in higher education and health care organization.

Jean Blondel is Professorial Fellow at the European University Institute, Florence, and Visiting Professor at the University of Siena. He was formerly Professor of Government at the University of Essex and first Director of the European Consortium for Political Research. He was Visiting Scholar at the Russell-Sage Foundation in New York in 1984–5. His publications include *Comparative Legislatures* (Prentice-Hall, 1973), *World Leaders* (Sage, 1980), *The Discipline of Politics* (Butterworth, 1982), *Comparative Government* (2nd edition, Philip Allan, 1995) and *The Nature of Party Government* (Palgrave, 2000).

G. R. Boynton is Professor of Political Science at the University of Iowa. His publications include *Video Rhetorics* (University of Illinois Press, 1997), *Mathematical Thinking About Politics* (Longman, 1980), *Representatives and Represented* (Wiley, 1975) and *Legislative Systems in Developing Countries* (Duke University Press, 1975). His primary research interests include political communication, analytical political theory, and the comparative study of legislatures.

Naomi Caiden is Professor and Chair of the Department of Political Science, California State University, Los Angeles. She was editor of *Public Budgeting and Finance* (1988–94). Among her many publications are *Planning and Budgeting in Poor Countries*, with Aaron Wildavsky (Transaction Publishing, 1980), and the past three revisions of Aaron Wildavsky's *The New Politics of the Budgetary Process* (5th edition, Addison Wesley Longman, forthcoming). She has consulted with various international bodies, including the World Bank and United Nations, and was awarded the Aaron B. Wildavsky Award for Lifetime Scholarly Achievement in Public Budgeting from the American Society for Public Administration.

Kenneth J. Campbell has taught international relations at the University of Delaware since 1990 and is the director of its international relations programme. He is the author of *Genocide and the Global Village* (Palgrave, 2001) and is currently writing a book on global leadership in twenty-first-century international relations.

Ronald H. Chilcote is Professor of Political Science and Economics at the University of California, Riverside. He is founder and currently Managing Editor of the journal *Latin American Perspectives*, and his many publications include *Power and the Ruling Classes in Northeast Brazil* (Cambridge University Press, 1990) and *The Portuguese Revolution of 25 April 1974* (University of Coimbra, 1987). His research has focused on Portuguese-speaking Africa, Brazil and Portugal.

Catharin E. Dalpino teaches Political Development in Asia at Georgetown University and at the School of Advanced International Studies at Johns Hopkins

University. She is concurrently a Fellow at the Brookings Institution. Her books include *Deferring Democracy: Promoting Opennesss in Authoritarian Regimes* (Brookings Institution Press, 2000) and *Watersheds and Wakeup Calls: The Politicial Consequences of the Asian Economic Crisis* (Brookings, 2003). She co-edits the Georgetown Southeast Asia Survey and is currently working on a book about US policy in Southeast Asia after September 11, to be published by the Georgetown University Press.

Lori Fisler Damrosch is Professor of Law at Columbia University, where she holds the Henry L. Moses Chair in Law and International Organization. She has served as counsel for the United States before the International Court of Justice and other international tribunals. She is the editor of *The International Court of Justice at a Crossroads* (Transnational, 1987) and *International Law: Cases and Materials* (West, 2001, with co-editors). She has served as a Vice President of the American Society of International Law and began a five-year term as co-editor in Chief of the *American Journal of International Law* in April 2003. Her current research interests include the settlement of international disputes and control of the use of military force under constitutional and international law.

Mattei Dogan is Senior Fellow at the National Centre for Scientific Research in Paris and Professor Emeritus at the University of California at Los Angeles. He has been Visiting Professor at the University of Trento, Indiana University, Yale University, Institute of Statistical Mathematics in Tokyo and the University of Florence. He is co-founder of the Society for Comparative Research and was a member of the editorial board of the *Revue Française de la Sociologie*. His most recent publication is *Elites, Crises and the Origins of Regimes* (Rowman & Littlefield, 1998). Formerly chair of the IPSA research committee on political elites, he is currently chair of the ESA research committee on comparative sociology.

R. Bruce Douglass teaches political theory at Georgetown University in Washington, DC. His most recent book is *A Nation under God?* (Rowman & Littlefield, 2000), which he edited with Joshua Mitchell. He is an editor of the journal *The Responsive Community*, and his current research includes a study of the relevance of Max Weber's view of the fate of modern societies (particularly as elaborated in *The Protestant Ethic and the Spirit of Capitalism*) to current conditions.

Leela Fernandes is Associate Professor of Political Science and Women's/Gender Studies at Rutgers University. She is the author of *Producing Workers: The Politics of Gender, Class and Culture in the Calcutta Jute Mills* (University of Pennsylvania Press, 1997) as well as numerous articles on labour politics, gender and politics and globalization in India. She is currently writing a book entitled *Inventing the New Indian Middle Class: Culture, Nation and the Politics of Economic Reform in India*.

Elizabeth G. Ferris is currently serving as Coordinator of the Diakonia and Solidarity team of the World Council of Churches (WCC), Geneva, responsible for the WCC's programmes in development, service and humanitarian response. She taught Political Science for 10 years at various US universities and was a Fulbright Professor at the National Autonomous University of Mexico. She was also Study and Interpretation Secretary for Refugees of the WCC, Research

Director at the Life & Peace Institute, Uppsala, and Director of the Church World Service Immigration and Refugee Program of the National Council of Churches, New York. She has written extensively on humanitarian, development and peace issues.

Lawrence Freedman is Professor of War Studies at King's College, University of London. His publications include *The Evolution of Nuclear Strategy* (3rd edition, Palgrave, 2003).

David Galbreath is a Ph.D. candidate at the Institute for Politics and International Studies, University of Leeds. His doctoral dissertation is entitled 'Nation-building and Minority Politics: a comparative case study of Estonia and Latvia'. In addition, his research interests are the effects of European integration on public policy and the evolution of party systems in Eastern Europe. He is currently a J. William Fulbright Fellow to Latvia.

Jack A. Goldstone is Professor of Sociology and International Relations at the University of California, Davis. He is the author of *Revolution and Rebellion in the Early Modern World* (University of California Press, 1991) and editor of *The Encyclopedia of Political Revolutions* (Congressional Quarterly Press, 1991).

Guy S. Goodwin-Gill is a Fellow of All Souls College, Oxford. He was formerly Professor of International Refugee Law in the University of Oxford and is the Founding Editor of the *International Journal of Refugee Law*. His publications include *The Refugee in International Law* (2nd edn, Clarendon Press, 1996) and *International Law and the Movement of Persons Between States* (Clarendon Press, 1978), as well as articles on the international law aspects of asylum, migration, elections, and children in armed conflict.

Fred I. Greenstein is Professor of Politics at Princeton University, and has published numerous books and articles on personality and politics, children and politics, American political parties and the American Presidency. His publications include *Children and Politics* (Yale University Press, 1965), *Personality and Politics: Problems of Evidence, Inference and Conceptualization* (Markham, 1969), *The Hidden-Hand Presidency: Eisenhower as Leader* (Basic Books, 1982), *How Presidents Test Reality: Decisions on Vietnam, 1954 and 1965* (Russell Sage, 1989) and *The Presidential Difference: Leadership Style from FDR to Clinton* (The Free Press, 2000).

Jean Grugel is Reader in Politics at the University of Sheffield. She is an editor of the *Bulletin of Latin American Research*. Her publications include *Democratization: A Critical Introduction* (Palgrave, 2002), *Democracy without Borders*, as editor (Routledge 1999) and *Regionalism Across the North–South Divide*, as co-editor with W. Hout (Routledge 1999). She is currently working in the areas of globalization and democracy, inter-regionalism and citizenship and new regionalism.

John A. Guidry is Visiting Assistant Professor of Political Science at Macalester College in St. Paul, Minnesota. He has published several articles on social movements and citizenship in Brazil, and his research interests include the politics of Latin America and the developing world. He edited, along with Michael D.

Kennedy and Mayer N. Zald, *Globalizations and Social Movements: Culture, Power, and the Transnational Public Sphere* (University of Michigan Press, 2000). He is currently completing a book manuscript on citizenship in Brazil during the consolidation of democracy in the 1990s.

Jeffrey W. Hahn is Professor of Political Science and Director of the Russian Area Studies Concentration (RASCON) at Villanova University. He is the author of *Soviet Grassroots: Citizen Participation in Local Soviet Government* (Princeton University Press, 1988), the co-editor of *Local Power and Post Soviet Politics* (M.E. Sharpe, 1994), and the editor of *Democratization in Russia: The Development of Legislative Institutions* (M. E. Sharpe, 1996) and *Regional Russia in Transition: Studies from Yaroslavl* (Johns Hopkins University Press, 2001). His articles have appeared in many journals, including the *British Journal of Political Science*, *Slavic Review*, *Post-Soviet Affairs*, *Problems of Communism* and *Polity*. He is currently working on a project dealing with public policy at the regional level in Russia.

Grant Harman is Emeritus Professor of Educational Management at the University of New England. His research interests are mainly in higher education management and policy, inter-governmental relations, science policy, and comparative higher education studies. He is coordinating editor of the journal *Higher Education*, published by Kluwer Academic Publishers.

Robert Harris is Professor in the Department of Politics and International Studies at the University of Hull, UK, and has held visiting professorships in Hong Kong, Japan and Malaysia. The majority of his numerous publications are in criminology and criminal justice. He has recently completed work on his latest book, *Political Corruption: In and Beyond the Nation State* (Routledge, 2003).

Stephen Harrison is Professor of Social Policy at the University of Manchester. He was previously Professor of Health Policy and Politics at the University of Leeds. He has written widely on the politics of health care and medicine, and his books include *The Dynamics of British Health Policy*, with David Hunter and Christopher Pollitt (Unwin Hyman, 1990), *Just Managing: Power and Culture in the National Health Service*, with Christopher Pollitt *et al.* (MacMillan, 1992) and *Controlling Health Professionals*, with Christopher Pollitt (Open University Press, 1994). He is currently studying the politics of the 'evidence-based medicine' movement and attempts to democratize the UK National Health Service.

Mary Hawkesworth is Professor of Political Science and Women's Studies and Senior Scholar at the Center for American Women and Politics at Rutgers University. Her teaching and research interests include feminist theory, women and politics, contemporary political philosophy, philosophy of science, and social policy. She is the author of *Beyond Oppression: Feminist Theory and Political Strategy* (Continuum Press, 1990), *Theoretical Issues in Policy Analysis* (State University of New York Press, 1988), editor of *The Encyclopedia of Government and Politics* (Routledge, 1992; 2nd edition, 2003), and *Feminism and Public Policy* (*Policy Sciences* 27(2–3), 1994), and co-editor of *Gender, Globalization and Democratization* (Rowman and Littlefield, 2001). Her articles have appeared in the leading journals of feminist scholarship including *Signs, Hypatia, Women and Politics, Journal of Women's History, NWSA Journal, International Journal of Women's Studies*, and the *Women's Studies International Forum*. She has served on the Editorial Boards of *Signs: A Journal of Women in Culture and Society, Women and Politics* and the *International Feminist Journal of Politics*.

Ferrel Heady is Professor Emeritus of Public Administration and Political Science at the University of New Mexico, Albuquerque. He has served as Academic Vice-President and President of the University of New Mexico. He was Professor of Political Science at the University of Michigan, Ann Arbor, and was President of the American Society for Public Administration. His publications include *Public Administration: A Comparative Perspective* (6th edition, Marcel Dekker, 2001).

Renee Heberle teaches Political Theory and Feminist Theory and Politics at the University of Toledo, USA. Her research interests are in the areas of Critical Theory, gender and violence, and law and society. She is currently working on an edited volume of essays titled *Feminist Interpretations of Theodor Adorno*.

Marie T. Henehan is Senior Lecturer and Research Associate in Political Science at Colgate University. She is author of *Foreign Policy and Congress: An International Relations Perspective* (University of Michigan Press, 2000) and co-editor (with J. Vasquez) of *The Scientific Study of Peace and War: a text-reader* (Lexington Books, 1992).

Mary Henkel is Associate Professor in the Centre for the Evaluation of Public Policy and Practice, Brunel University, UK. Her research interests are in higher education, research and science policies, in particular their implications for academic cultures and structures. Publications include *Government and Research: The Rothschild Experiment in a Government Department*, as co-author with Maurice Kogan (Heinemann Educational Books, 1983), *Government, Evaluation and Change* (Jessica Kingsley Publishers, 1991), and *Academic Identities and Policy Change in Higher Education* (Jessica Kingsley Publishers, 2000).

Barry Hindess is Professor of Political Science in the Research School of the Social Sciences, Australian National University. His publications include *Discourses of Power: from Hobbes to Foucault* (Blackwell, 1996) and *Governing Australia: studies in contemporary rationalities of government*, edited jointly with Mitchell Dean (Cambridge, 1998). He is currently preparing a book on democracy to be published by Routledge.

Leslie Holmes is Professor of Political Science and Deputy Director of the Contemporary Europe Research Centre at the University of Melbourne. He has taught at the Universities of Essex, Kent and Aberystwyth, and has been on the Executive Committee of both the British National Association for Soviet and East European Studies and the Political Studies Association of the UK. He has been President of the International Council for Central and East European Studies since 2000, and is a former President of the Australasian Political Studies Association. His publications include *The Policy of Process in Communist States* (Sage, 1981), *Politics in the Communist World* (Oxford University Press, 1986), *The End of Communist Power* (Polity, 1993), *Post-Communism* (Polity, 1997), and, as co-author with John Dryzek, *Post-Communist Democratization* (Cambridge University Press, 2002). His principal research interests are corruption in post-communist states and Western Europe, political party financing, post-communist democratization, and legitimation.

Ole R. Holsti is George V. Allen Professor of International Affairs in the Political Science department at Duke University and has taught at Stanford University, the University of California, Davis, and the University of British Columbia. He has won many awards, including the Nevitt Sanford Award for Distinguished Contributions to Political Psychology in 1988. He was President of the International Studies Association from 1979 to 1980, and served on the council of the American Political Science Association as well as on the Advisory Board of the University Press of America. He has written numerous articles and his publications include *American Leadership in World Affairs: The Breakdown of Consensus* (Allen & Unwin, 1984), as co-editor, *Change in the International System* (Westview Press, 1980), and *Public Opinion and American Foreign Policy* (University of Michigan Press, 1996, 2nd edition forthcoming).

Kenneth R. Hoover is Professor of Political Science at Western Washington University. Recently, he has been an Academic Visitor at Nuffield College, Oxford, and the London School of Economics, as well as Chair of the Department of Political Science at Western Washington University. His publications include *Economics as Ideology: Keynes, Laski, Hayek and the creation of contemporary politics* (Rowman and Littlefield, 2003), *The Elements of Social Scientific Thinking* (8th edition, Thompson/Wadsworth, 2003), *Ideology and Political Life* (3rd edition Thompson/ Wadsworth, 2001), *The Power of Identity: Politics in a New Key* (Chatham House, 1997) and, with Raymond Plant, *Conservative Capitalism in Great Britain and the United States: a critical appraisal* (Routledge, 1989). His current research interests involve the interplay of identity and ideology.

Denise M. Horn is a doctoral candidate in Political Science at Rutgers University. She is the Senior Research Associate for the Center for Global Security and Democracy, where she has specialized in examining the impact of American foreign policy on the lives of women, particularly in the Baltic region. Her doctoral research explores the connections between American civil society, US foreign policy, and transnational efforts to resolve security issues in the former Soviet states.

Shiping Hua teaches East Asian Politics at Eckerd College, Florida, and at the University of Louisville, Kentucky. His publications include *Scientism and Humanism: Two Cultures in Post-Mao China, 1978–1989* (The State University of New York Press, 1995) and, as editor, *Chinese Political Culture, 1989–2000* (M.E. Sharpe, 2001). He is working on his next book: *Utopianism in Chinese Political Culture, 1898–2000*, to be published by Rowman & Littlefield.

Helen Ingram holds the Warmington Endowed Chair in the School of Social Ecology and is Professor in the Department of Society and Politics, University of California, Irvine. Previously she was Director of the Udall Center for Studies in

Public Policy at the University of Arizona. In addition to co-authoring *Policy Design for Democracy* with Anne Schneider (University Press of Kansas, 1997) she has published extensively on public policy issues in natural resources, water, and environment.

Jeffrey Isaac is Associate Professor of Political Science at Indiana University, Bloomington. His publications include *Power and Marxist Theory: A Realist View* (Cornell University Press, 1987) and articles in such journals as *Polity, Political Theory, History of Political Thought* and *Praxis International*. He has just completed a book on the political writings of Hannah Arendt and Albert Camus.

Kanishka Jayasuriya is Associate Professor in the Department of Politics and Social Administration, City University of Hong Kong. His publications include *Towards Illiberal Democracy in Pacific-Asia*, as co-author (Macmillan, 1995), *Law, Capitalism and Power in Asia: The Rule of Law and Legal Institutions*, as editor (Routledge, 1998) and *Politics and Markets in the Wake of the Asian Crisis*, as co-editor (Routledge, 1999). He is currently completing a volume entitled *Globlisation and Law: regulatory state and constitutionalisation beyond the state* (forthcoming). His research focuses on the political and social dynamics of domestic and transnational legal, judicial and regulatory institutions.

Robert O. Keohane is James B. Duke Professor of Political Science, Duke University. He is the author of *After Hegemony: Cooperation and Discord in the World Political Economy* (Princeton University Press, 1984), for which he received the second annual Grawemeyer Award for Ideas Improving World Order, co-author of *Power and Interdependence: World Politics in Transition* (3rd edition, Little, Brown & Co., 2001) and *Designing Social Inquiry: Scientific Inference in Qualitative Research* (Princeton, 1994) and is also author of *Power and Governance in a Partially Globalized World* (Routledge, 2002) and *International Institutions and State Power: Essays in International Relations Theory* (Westview, 1989). He was editor of the journal *International Organization* and has served as the president of the International Studies Association and the American Political Science Association.

Muqtedar Khan is Director of International Studies, Chair and Assistant Professor in the Department of Political Science at Adrian College, Michigan. He is the author of *American Muslims: Bridging Faith and Freedom* (Amana, 2002). His work on Islamic political philosophy and US foreign policy has appeared in journals such as *Cultural Dynamics, Security Dialogue, Middle East Policy, The Muslim World, Islam and Christian-Muslim Relations, Islamica, American Journal of Islamic Social Sciences, Middle East Affairs, Middle East Insight, Diplomat,* and *Intellectual Discourse*. His political commentaries have appeared in the *Washington Post, Wall Street Journal* and *Daily Telegraph*.

Abraham Kim is a Ph.D. Candidate in the Political Science department at Columbia University. He was a research associate in the political-military department at the Center for Strategic and International Studies in Washington, DC and wrote extensively on Asian security issues. He is currently writing a dissertation, entitled

Healing Divided Nations, that compares the reunification experience of the two Koreas, China-Taiwan, Vietnam, Germany and Yemen.

Samuel S. Kim is Adjunct Professor of Political Science and Senior Research Scholar at the East Asian Institute, Columbia University. His publications include *China, the United Nations, and World Order* (Princeton University Press, 1979), *The Quest for a Just World Order* (Westview Press, 1984), as co-editor, *The War System: An Interdisciplinary Approach* (Westview Press, 1980), *The United Nations and a Just World Order* (Westview Press, 1991), *The Constitutional Foundations of World Peace* (State University of New York Press, 1993), *China's Quest for National Identity* (Cornell University Press, 1993) and as editor, *Korea's Globalization* (Cambridge University Press, 2000); *East Asia and Globalization* (Rowman & Littlefield Publishers, 2000) and *The International Relations of Northeast Asia* (Rowman & Littlefield Publishers, forthcoming).

Peter Knoepfel is Professor of Policy Analysis and Environmental Policy at the Institute for Advanced Studies in Public Administration, University of Lausanne. He was Director of the Institute from 1994 to 2002. He was previously scientific project director at the Berlin Centre for Social Sciences, President of the Swiss Association for Political Science and a member of several Swiss governmental commissions. His publications include more than two dozen books and 150 articles, in German, French and English, on theoretical and practical aspects of public policy analysis, environmental and related policy. His research interests concern comparative environmental policies, natural resources, urban development and cultural policy.

Maurice Kogan is Professor Emeritus of Government and Director of the Centre for the Evaluation of Public Policy and Practice at Brunel University. He is the author or joint author of several works on educational, health, higher education, social services and science policy and on the struggle for power in the British Labour Party and editor of *Encyclopedia of Government and Politics* (Routledge 1992).

David Kowalewski is Professor of Political Science at Alfred University, Alfred, New York, and has taught as a Fulbright Professor in Kenya and the Philippines. His publications include *Global Establishment: The Political Economy of North-Asian Networks* (Macmillan, 2000), and his articles on international organizations have appeared in journals including *Comparative Political Studies* and the *Journal of Political and Military Sociology*.

Joseph LaPalombara is the Arnold Wolfers Professor Emeritus of Political Science and Management at Yale University, where he has also directed the Institution for Social and Policy Studies. His publications include *Political Parties and Political Development*, as co-editor with M. Weiner (Princeton University Press, 1966), as co-author, *Crises and Sequences in Political Development* (Princeton University Press, 1971), *Politics within Nations* (Prentice-Hall, 1974), *Democracy Italian Style* (Yale University Press, 1987) and, with others, *Organizational Learning and Knowledge* (Oxford University Press, 2001).

J. A. Laponce is Professor of Political Science at the University of British Columbia; he also chairs the Research Committee on Language and Politics of the International

Political Science Association. He was President of the Academy of Humanities and Social Services of the Royal Society of Canada and co-editor of the *International Political Science Review*. He has contributed articles to numerous journals, and his publications include *The Protection of Minorities* (University of California Press, 1961), *People vs Politics* (Toronto University Press, 1970), *Languages and Their Territories* (Toronto University Press, 1987) and *Left and Right* (Toronto University Press, 1981).

Gary Lehring is Associate Professor in the Department of Government at Smith College. His research focuses on the way that public policies help shape and change public understandings of lesbian and gay identity. He is the author of *Officially Gay: The Political Construction of Gay Identity* (Temple University Press, 2003), as well as a number of articles on lesbian and gay politics including pieces about gay liberation, the political history of the gay movement, Queer Nation, and gays in the military. His current research project examines the intersection between globalization and identity politics, focusing on the emergent gay liberation movements in central America.

Robin Lovin is Cary Maguire University Professor of Ethics at Southern Methodist University in Dallas, Texas. He has been a member of the faculty since 1994 and served as Dean of the School of Theology from 1994–2002. He previously taught at the University of Chicago and Emory University. His publications include *Reinhold Niebuhr and Christian Realism* (Cambridge University Press, 1994) and *Christian Ethics: An Essential Guide* (Abingdon Press, 2000).

Timothy W. Luke is University Distinguished Professor of Political Science at Virginia Polytechnic Institute and State University in Blacksburg, Virginia. He is also Executive Director of the Institute for Distance and Distributed Learning, and he serves as Co-Director of the Center for Digital Discourse and Culture in the College of Arts and Sciences at Virginia Tech. His most recent books are *Capitalism, Democracy and Ecology: departing from Marx* (University of Illinois Press, 1999), *The Politics of Cyberspace*, edited with Chris Toulouse (Routledge, 1998), and *Ecocritique: contesting the politics of nature, economy and culture* (University of Minnesota Press, 1997). His latest book, *Museum Politics: powerplays at the exhibition* was published in 2002 with the University of Minnesota Press.

Eithne McLaughlin is Professor of Social Policy at Queen's University, Belfast. She was the commissioner and editor of a three volume series on equality in Northern Ireland published in 1996 by The Standing Advisory Commission on Human Rights, of which she was a Vice Chair. She was a member of the influential Commission on Social Justice in the UK in the mid 1990s. She is currently a Co-Director of the Northern Ireland Poverty and Social Exclusion Study, and a fellow of the UK's Academy of the Learned Societies of the Social Sciences.

Denis McQuail is Professor Emeritus at the University of Amsterdam and Visiting Professor in the Department of Politics at the University of Southampton. He is a member of the editorial board of *Political Communication* and an editor of the *European Journal of Communication*. His teaching and research focuses on numerous aspects of mass communication. Recent and forthcoming publications include *Media Policy*, edited with Karen Siune, (Sage, 1998), *The Politics of News: News of Politics*, edited with Doris Graber and Pippa Norris (Congressional Quarterly, 1998), *McQuail's Mass Communcation Theory* (Sage, 2000), *The Media in Europe*, edited with Mary Kelly and Gianpietro Mazzoleni (Sage 2003) and *Media Accountability and Freedom of Publication* (Oxford University Press, 2003).

Talukder Maniruzzaman is Professor of Political Science at the University of Dhaka, where he was Head of Department from 1975 to 1978. He has won several scholarships and fellowships including the Nuffield Foundation Fellowship at the University of London, a fellowship at the Woodrow Wilson International Center for Scholars, Washington DC and the Japan Foundation Fellowship. He has published many articles in international journals and has contributed to several edited volumes. His publications include *Japan's Security Policy for the Twenty-First Century* (Dhaka University Press, 2000), *Military Withdrawal from Politics: A Comparative Study* (Ballinger Publishing Company, 1987), *The Security of Small States in the Third World* (Austrialian National University Press, 1982) and *The Bangladesh Revolution and Its Aftermath* (Bangladesh Books International, 1980). He is currently working on a book entitled *A Comparative Study of the Atomic Policy of Major Asian Powers*.

Luigi Manzetti is Associate Professor of Political Science and Director of Latin American Studies at Southern Methodist University and a Senior Fellow at the North–South Center of the University of Miami. He has been a consultant for the US Agency on International Development, the United States Information Agency, the World Bank, and the Italian Foreign Ministry. He specializes in corruption, economic integration, privatization, and regulatory policy in Latin America. He is the author of *The IMF and Economic Stabilization* (Praeger, 1991), *Political Forces in Argentina* (with Peter G. Snow, Praeger, 1993), *Institutions, Parties and Coalitions in Argentine Politics* (Pittsburgh University Press, 1993), *Privatization South American Style* (Oxford University Press 1999), and the editor of *Regulatory Policy in Latin America: Post-Privatization Realities* (North–South Center Press at the University of Miami, 2000).

Martin Marger is Adjunct Professor of Social Science at Michigan State University. He taught previously at Waynesburg College and Northern Kentucky University. His publications include *Elites and Masses* (2nd edn, Wadsworth, 1987), *Social Inequality: patterns and processes* (2nd edn, McGraw-Hill, 2002), *Race and Ethnic Relations: American and global perspectives* (6th edn, Wadsworth, 2003), and *Power in Modern Societies*, with Marvin Olsen (Westview, 1993). His current research interests focus on the processes of immigrant economic and social adaptation.

Geoffrey Marshall is an Honorary Fellow of Queen's College, Oxford, where he was a Fellow and Tutor in Politics and a University lecturer in Politics from 1957–93 and Provost of Queen's College from 1993–9. He has been Assistant Editor of *Public Law* since 1960. His publications include *Parliamentary Sovereignty* (Oxford University Press, 1957), *Police and Government* (Methuen, 1965), *Constitutional Theory* (Oxford University Press, 1971), *Constitutional Conventions* (Oxford University Press, 1984) and, as editor, *Ministerial Responsibility* (Oxford University Press, 1989).

T. David Mason is the Johnie Christian Family Professor of Peace Studies at the University of North Texas. His research on the politics of reform, repression, civil wars and ethnic conflicts has appeared in the *American Political Science Review*, *Journal of Politics*, *Social Science Quarterly*, *International Studies Quarterly*, *Public Choice*, *Journal of Conflict Resolution* and other journals. He is the co-editor of two anthologies on US–Japanese relations and the author of several book chapters in anthologies dealing with conflict processes. His book *Caught in the Crossfire: Revolution, Repression, and the Rational Peasant* will be published by Rowman & Littlefield in 2003.

Toivo Miljan is Professor in the Department of Political Science at Wilfrid Laurier University, Ontario, and has been Adjunct Professor of Political Science at the Swedish School of Business and Economics, Helsinki, since 1988. He was co-director of the Centre of Foreign Policy and Federalism (1982–92) and until 1998 he served as the founding Director of the EuroFaculty in Riga. His publications include the *Estonian Historical Dictionary* (Scarecrow Press, 2003), *The Reluctant Europeans* (C. Hurst, 1977), *Food and Agriculture in Global Perspective* (Pergamon Press, 1980) and, as editor, *The Political Economy of North-South Relations* (Broadview Press, 1987). He has recently been studying transitions to democratic capitalism, mainly in East Central Europe, Latin America and Asia.

W. L. Miller holds the Edward Caird Chair of Politics at the University of Glasgow. He has directed or co-directed election survey studies in Britain, Russia and Poland. His publications – as author or co-author – include *Elections and Voting* (Macmillan, 1987), *Media and Voters* (Oxford University Press, 1991), *Political Culture in Contemporary Britain* (Oxford University Press, 1996), and most recently *A Culture of Corruption? Coping with Government in Postcommunist Europe* (Central European University Press, 2001). He is currently researching public attitudes to globalization, national identities and ethnic minorities in various parts of Eastern Europe, East Asia, and Britain.

Helen V. Milner is James T. Shotwell Professor of International Relations at Columbia University. Her publications include *Interests, Institutions and Information: Domestic Politics and International Relations* (Princeton, 1997), *Resisting Protectionism: Global Industries and the Politics of International Trade* (Princeton, 1988); as co-editor they include *The Political Economy of Economic Regionalism* (Columbia Univeristy Press, 1997), *Internationalization and Domestic Politics* (Cambridge University Press, 1996), and *Political Science: The State of the Discipline* (Norton, 2002). Her current interests concern international politics, international and comparative political economy, West European politics and globalization and development.

Gwen Moore is Associate Professor of Sociology at the University at Albany, State University of New York. Recent publications include 'Elite Studies at the Year 2000', edited with John Higley in the *International Review of Sociology*, and *Gendering Elites: Economic and Political Leadership in 27 Industrialised Nations* (Macmillan, 2000), edited and coordinated with Mino Vianello. Her research focuses on comparative elite studies, analyses of gender and authority, and investigations of personal, community and national network structures.

Craig N. Murphy is Professor of Political Science at Wellesley College, Massachusetts. His recent publications include *International Relations and the New Inequality* (Blackwell, 2002) and *Egalitarian Politics in an Age of Globalization* (Palgrave, 2002). He is Chair of the Academic Council on the UN System, past president of the International Studies Association, and is one of the founding editors of *Global Governance*.

Mark Neocleous teaches politics at Brunel University, UK, and is editor of the journal *Radical Philosophy*. His publications include *Administering Civil Society: Towards a Theory of State Power* (Macmillan, 1996), *Fascism* (Open University Press, 1997), *The Fabrication of Social Order: A Critical Theory of Police Power* (Pluto Press, 2000). His book *Imagining the State* is forthcoming with Open University Press. He is currently working on the monstrous and the dead in political thought.

Kai Nielsen is Emeritus Professor of Philosophy at the University of Calgary and Adjunct Professor of Philosophy at Concordia University. He is a past President of the Canadian Philosophical Association, and is a member of the Royal Society of Canada. His publications include *Equality and Liberty: A Defense of Radical Egalitarianism* (Rowman & Allenheld, 1985), *Marxism and the Moral Point of View* (Westview Press, 1989), *Naturalism without Method* (Prometeus Books 1996) and *Globalization and Justice* (Humanities Books, 2003).

Øyvind Østerud is Professor of International Conflict Studies in the Department of Political Science, University of Oslo. His publications include *Agrarian Structure and Peasant Politics* (1978) and, as editor, *Studies of War and Peace* (Norwegian and Oxford University Press, 1986) and *Power and Democracy* (Ashgate, 2003). His current research interests include sovereign statehood and nationality conflicts, power and democracy, and post-Cold War geopolitics.

Michael Pacione holds the Chair of Geography at the University of Strathclyde, Glasgow. He has held academic positions at Queen's University, Belfast, at the University of Guelph, Ontario, and at the University of Vienna. He has published twenty-five books and more than 100 research papers in an international range of academic and professional journals. His most recent books include *Glasgow: the Socio-Spatial Development of the City* (Wiley, 1995); *Britain's Cities: Geographies of Division in Urban Britain* (Routledge,1997); *Applied Geography: Principles and Practice* (Routledge, 1999); and *Urban Geography: A Global Perspective* (Routledge, 2001). His principal research interest is urban geography and an applied or problem-orientated perspective informs much of his work.

Dennis Palumbo is Emeritus Professor of Justice Studies at Arizona State University. He has also taught at the University of Kansas and has been principal and co-principal investigator on several large research grants from the National Institute of Justice, National Institute of Health and the National Traffic and Highway Safety Administration. He has authored, co-authored and edited numerous books and articles on public policy implementation and evaluation, and was founding editor and co-editor of the *Policy Studies Review*.

CONTRIBUTORS

Stanley Payne is Hilldale-Jaime Vicens Vives Professor of History at the University of Wisconsin-Madison. He is the author of *A History of Fascism, 1914–1945* (University of Wisconsin Press, 1995) and of numerous other books on fascism and the history of Spain and Portugal, including *A History of Fascism in Spain, 1923–1977* (University of Wisconsin Press, 2000) and *The Franco Regime, 1936–1975* (University of Wisconsin Press, 1987).

George Philip is Professor of Comparative and Latin American Politics at the London School of Economics and Political Science. He is the author of *Oil and Politics in Latin America* (Cambridge University Press, 1982), *The Military in Latin American Politics* (Croom Helm, 1985) *The President in Mexican Politics* (Macmillan, 1992) and *Democracy in Latin America* (Polity, 2003).

Adamantia Pollis is Professor Emerita of Political Science in the Graduate Faculty at the New School University, New York and Visiting Professor at the Graduate Center, CUNY, New York. She has been a Visiting Professor at the University of the Aegean, Columbia University and Essex University. She has written extensively on various aspects of human rights and the politics of Greece, Turkey and Cyprus. Her publications include, as editor, *The Contemporary Mediterranean World* (Praeger, 1983), and as co-editor with Peter Schwab, *Human Rights: Cultural and Ideological Perspectives* (Praeger, 1979), *Towards a Human Rights Framework* (Praeger, 1982) and *Human Rights: New Perspectives, New Realities* (Lynne Rienner, 2000).

G. Bingham Powell is Marie C. and Jospeh C. Wilson Professor of Political Science at the University of Rochester, New York. He is the author of *Contemporary Democracies: Participation, Stability and Violence* (Harvard University Press, 1982), which in 1983 won the American Political Science Association's Woodrow Wilson Prize for the best book in Political Science in the previous year. His recent book, *Elections as Instruments of Democracy* (Yale University Press, 2000), was co-winner of the Mattei Dogan Award, 2002, for the Best Comparative Book of the Year by the Society for Comparative Research. He is also a former editor of the *American Political Science Review*.

David C. Rapoport has taught Political Theory at the University of California at Los Angeles since 1961. He is the founding co-editor of the *Journal of Terrorism and Political Violence*, founding director of the Center for the Study of Religion, UCLA, and in 1970 he developed the first American course on terrorism. His many publications include *Assassination and Terrorism* (CBC, 1971), *The Morality of Terrorism* (2nd edn, Columbia, 1989), *Inside Terrorist Organizations* (2nd edn, Frank Cass, 2000) and *The Democratic Experience and Political Violence* (Frank Cass, 2001). He is currently writing a book entitled *The Four Waves of Modern Terror*.

Bernard Reich is Professor of Political Science and International Affairs and Chair of the Department of Political Science at George Washington University, Washington, DC. He has lived in the Middle East on Fulbright and National Science Foundation Fellowships and has visited there often for research and conferences. He is the author, editor or co-editor of more than fifty books, book chapters or articles on the Middle East.

Stanley Renshon is Professor of Political Science at the City University of New York and a certified psychoanalyst. He is the author of over seventy articles and ten books in the field of political psychology. His 1998 book *High Hopes: The Clinton Presidency and the Politics of Ambition* (Routledge) won the Richard E. Neustadt Award for the best book on the presidency and the National Association of Psychoanalysis' Gravida for the best biography. He is at work on a psychological portrait of the George W. Bush presidency.

J. Magnus Ryner is Lecturer in the Department of Political Science and International Studies at the University of Birmingham. His research is on transnational relations, European integration and the restructuring of welfare states. His publications include *Capitalist Restructuring, Globalisation and the Third Way: Lessons from the Swedish Model* (Routledge, 2002) and, as co-editor with Alan Cafruny, *A Ruined Fortress: Neoliberal Hegemony and Transformation in Europe* (Rowman & Littlefield, 2003).

Shamit Saggar is Reader in Electoral Politics at Queen Mary, University of London. He is currently on secondment to the Prime Minister's Strategy Unit, Cabinet Office, where he works as a Senior Policy Advisor. He has held posts at the Universities of Essex and Liverpool and visiting academic appointments at the University of California, Los Angeles, the Australian National University, the University of Western Australia, and New York University. His publications include four book-length studies, two edited books, and more than thirty book chapters and refereed journal articles. His most recent book is *Race and Representation* (Manchester University Press, 2000).

Saskia Sassen is Ralph Lewis Professor of Sociology at the University of Chicago, and Centennial Visiting Professor at the London School of Economics. She is currently completing her forthcoming book *Denationalization: Territory, Authority and Rights in a Global Digital Age* (under contract with Princeton University Press, 2003) and has recently completed for UNESCO a five-year project on sustainable human settlement. Her most recent books are *Guests and Aliens* (New Press 1999), the edited *Global Networks, Linked Cities* (Routledge, 2002) and *The Global City* (2nd edn, Princeton University Press, 2001). She serves on several editorial boards and is an advisor to several international bodies. She is a Member of the Council on Foreign Relations, and Chair of the new Information Technology, International Cooperation and Global Security Committee of the Social Science Research Council (USA).

Anne Larason Schneider is Dean of the College of Public Programs at Arizona State University and Professor, School of Justice Studies. She has also held academic positions at Yale University and Oklahoma State University. She is the co-author (with Helen Ingram) of *Policy Design for Democracy* (University Press of Kansas, 1997) and other books and articles on public policy and democracy.

Martin Shaw is a sociologist and Professor of International Relations and Politics at the University of Sussex. His books include *War and Genocide* (Politym 2003), *Theory of the Global State* (Cambridge University Press, 2000) and *Civil Society and Media in Global Crises* (Pinter, 1996). He is currently working on a new book on the theory of genocide and a study of 'risk-transfer war'. He edits www.theglobalsite.ac.uk.

Timothy M. Shaw is Professor of Commonwealth Governance and Development and Director of the Institute of Commonwealth Studies in the School of Advanced Study at the University of London. He taught at Dalhousie University in Nova Scotia for three decades and is continuing Visiting Professor at Mbarara University in Uganda and at Stellenbosch University in South Africa. He has taught at universities in Denmark, Japan, Nigeria, Zambia and Zimbabwe, and continues to edit book series for Ashgate and Palgrave Macmillan.

Michael Sheehan is Professor of International Relations at the University of Aberdeen and Director of the Scottish Centre for International Security. His publications include *The Arms Race* (Basil Blackwell, 1983), *Arms Control: Theory and Practice* (Basil Blackwell, 1988), *The Balance of Power: History and Theory* (Routledge, 1996) and, as editor, *National and International Security* (Ashgate, 2000). He is currently researching critical security theory and Korean security issues.

Anthony D. Smith is Professor of Ethnicity and Nationalism at the London School of Economics and Political Science. He is the editor of *Nations and Nationalism* and Vice-President of the Association for the Study of Ethnicity and Nationalism. His publications include *The Ethnic Origins of Nations* (Basil Blackwell, 1986), *National Identity* (Penguin, 1991), *Nationalism and Modernism* (Routledge 1998) and *The Nation in History* (University Press of New England, 2000). His current interests include the relationship between the visual arts and nationalism, myths of ethnic election and the relationship of social class to nations.

Leslie Stevenson is Honorary Reader in Philosophy at the University of St Andrews, having retired after over 30 years of teaching philosophy there. His publications include *Ten Theories of Human Nature*, with David Haberman (3rd edn, Oxford University Press, 1998, 4th edn forthcoming), *The Many Faces of Science: an introduction to scientists, values and society*, with Henry Byerly (2nd edn, Westview Press, 2000) and, as editor, *The Study of Human Nature* (2nd edn, Oxford University Press, 2000).

Aleks Szczerbiak has been lecturer in Contemporary European Studies at the Sussex European Institute, University of Sussex, since 1998. His numerous publications on Central and East European comparative politics include *Poles Together? The Emergence and Development of Political Parties in Post-communist Poland* (Central European University Press, 2001). His current research interests include electoral and party politics, the impact of the EU on domestic politics and the politics of dealing with the communist past. He is Associate Editor and Reviews Editor of *Party Politics*.

Bassam Tibi is Professor of International Relations and Director, University of Göttingen. He has held numerous visiting professorships, in Europe, Asia, Africa, and the USA, including Harvard, Princeton, Ann Arbor (Michigan), and University of California-Berkeley. He was a member of the Fundamentalism Project for the American Academy of Arts and Sciences and is currently participating in the Culture Matters project for Harvard Academy for International Studies and Tufts University. His recent publications include *The Challenge of*

Fundamentalism. Political Islam and the New World Disorder (2nd edn, University of California Press, 2002) and *Islam between Culture and Politics* (Palgrave, 2001).

Jim Tomlinson is Professor of Economic History in the School of International Studies at Brunel University, where he has taught since 1977. His recent publications include *Democratic Socialism and Economic Policy: the Attlee Years, 1945–1951* (Cambridge University Press, 1997) and *The Politics of Decline: Understanding Post-war Britain* (Longman-Pearson, 2001). He is currently working on the impact of the rise of national economic management on popular economic understanding and behaviour.

John Vasquez holds the Harvey Picker Chair in International Relations at Colgate University. He has published twelve books, including *The Power of Power Politics: From Classical Realism to Neotraditionalism* (Cambridge University Press, 1998), *The War Puzzle* (Cambridge University Press, 1993), *What Do We Know about War?* (Rowman and Littlefield, 2000), and most recently *Realism and the Balancing of Power: A New Debate*, co-edited with Colin Elman, (Prentice Hall, 2003). He has taught previously at Rutgers University, Vanderbilt University, and Earlham College. He has been president of the International Studies Association and the Peace Science Society (International).

Andrew Vincent is Professor of Political Philosophy at Sheffield University. He was formerly Professor in the School of European Studies at Cardiff University, a senior research fellow at the Australian National University and co-director of the Collingwood and British Idealism Centre, Cardiff University. He is author of *Theories of the State* (Basil Blackwell, 1987), *Modern Political Ideologies* (2nd edn, Basil Blackwell, 1995), and *Nationalism and Particularity* (Cambridge University Press, 2002), co-author of *A Radical Hegelian: The Social and Political Philosophy of Henry Jones* (University of Wales and St Martin's Press, 1993) and *British Idealism and Political Theory* (Edinburgh University Press, 2001). He is also editor of *Political Theory: Tradition and Diversity* (Cambridge University Press 1997).

Dagmar von Walden Laing is a researcher in health policy. She previously worked as an educator and administrator within the Swedish health care system. Her publications include 'HIV/AIDS in Sweden and the United Kingdom. Policy Networks 1982–1992' (*Stockholm Studies in Politics*, 81, 2001) and 'The Role of Non-Profit Organizations in Managing HIV/AIDS in Sweden', in Kenis and Marin (eds) *Managing AIDS: Organizational Responses in Six European Countries* (Ashgate, 1997). She has also contributed to publications on Academic Responses to the UK Foresight Programme and on Assessing Payback from Department of Health R&D for the Centre for the Evaluation of Public Policy and Practice, Brunel University.

Paul Webb is Professor of Politics at the University of Sussex. His research interests focus on representative democracy, particularly party and electoral politics. His recent books include *Political Parties in Advanced Industrial Democracies* (Oxford University Press, 2002) and *The Modern British Party System* (Sage Publications, 2000). He is co-editor of the journals *Party Politics and Representation*.

Ngaire Woods is Fellow in Politics and International Relations at University College, Oxford University. She has just completed a book on the IMF and World Bank (forthcoming) and has previously published *The Political Economy of Globalization* (Palgrave, 2000), *Inequality, Globalization and World Politics* (Oxford University Press, 1999) and *Explaining International Relations since 1945* (Oxford University Press, 1996). She has recently established a Global Economic Governance programme at Oxford University focused on managing globalization through international economic institutions and global private sector regulation.

William Zartman is the Jacob Blaustein Distinguished Professor of International Organization and Conflict Resolution at the School of Advanced International Studies of the Johns Hopkins University. He is author of *The Practical Negotiator* (Yale University Press, 1982), *Ripe For Resolution* (Oxford University Press, 1989) and editor of *Preventive Negotiations* (Rowman & Littlefield, 2000) and *Power and Negotiation* (University of Michigan Press, 2001). He is a member of the Processes of International Negotiation (PIN) Group at the International Institute for Systems Analysis, and has been a Distinguished Fellow of the US Institute of Peace, Olin Professor at the US Naval Academy, and Halévy professor at Sciences Pô, Paris.

PREFACE

Any effort to inventory the state of knowledge within an academic discipline is a daunting task. In this instance the task was further complicated by our desire to demonstrate the critical role played by theoretical assumptions and methodological techniques in the production of knowledge about the political world. We are grateful to all of our colleague contributors who have taken this challenge seriously and worked so well to produce interesting and distinguished accounts of the main themes and subjects which constitute the study of politics and government.

We owe particular thanks to Frances Parkes, Stephanie Rogers, Gerard Greenway, and Aileen Harvey at Routledge who have provided invaluable editorial assistance at various stages in the production of the second edition of the Encyclopedia.

To Ulla Kogan and Philip Alperson heartfelt thanks for gracing our lives through prolonged periods of seemingly unending intellectual labour.

Mary Hawkesworth
Maurice Kogan

PART I

INTRODUCTION

1

POLITICAL SCIENCE IN A NEW MILLENNIUM: ISSUES OF KNOWLEDGE AND POWER

Mary Hawkesworth

While the first edition of the *Routledge Encyclopedia of Government and Politics* was in press, the Berlin Wall came down. Over the past decade, the Soviet empire collapsed and the Cold War has ended, giving rise to systemic economic and political transformations. Globalization and democratization have been transforming domestic and international politics around the world. Neo-liberalism has had complex effects even in social-democratic and socialist states. European economic and political integration has transformed political relations among member states as well as among aspiring member states. Modeling itself on the European Union, the African Union aspires to comparable benefits from economic integration and military coordination. Regional wars in the Balkans and in Rwanda and Burundi have raised new charges of genocide. Apartheid in South Africa was finally defeated and a new multi-racial, multi-ethnic democracy launched. Global civil society has mobilized through the internet and the proliferation of non-governmental organizations. Fast-breaking developments in information technology and communication technology are opening new possibilities and challenging traditional relations in homes, schools, cities, businesses, states, and international affairs. Terrorism has reemerged on the global scene and generated unprecedented international assent to a 'war' that is not between states, but pits a coalition of Western military forces operating under executive order against non-state actors, the al-Qaida network, which moves clandestinely within and across national boundaries of multiple states.

Political scientists' understandings of the world have been challenged by dramatic political developments such as these, which they neither predicted nor possessed knowledge to prevent or control. Despite continuing methodological debates within the discipline of political science over the best means to produce knowledge of the political world (rational choice and formal mathematical models, quantitative techniques vs qualitative analysis, inductive inferences, 'large-n' vs 'small-n' studies, case studies, ethnography, historical analysis, hermeneutics, discursive analysis), none of the contending methodologies enabled political scientists to anticipate the major political events of the past decade. Debate is on-going about how best to explain such political events after the fact – a debate, which according to some critics, may have more to do with legitimating the scientific image of the discipline than with adequate explanation of the changing political world (Blyth and Varghese 1999; Brown 1998; Gunnell 1995).

What, then, do political scientists know? What is the relation between disciplinary claims to knowledge and the production of particular kinds of politics? Do political scientists as knowledge producers merely describe and explain independent political events or do they generate paradigms that help shape the political world?

The second edition of the *Encyclopedia of Government and Politics* is designed to answer such questions. The substantive chapters provide an overview of the state of political studies in the new millennium. In the following sections, the Introduction 1) situates this effort to systematize political knowledge in a long tradition of Encyclopedia making; 2) traces debates within the discipline about the nature of political knowledge in relation to larger epistemological questions within the philosophy of science; and 3) examines the way that political scientists shape politics, often unintentionally, through the deployment of basic definitions of politics and categories of political analysis.

Systematicity and the politics of knowledge

The very idea of an *Encyclopedia of Government and Politics* raises important questions about the relationship between knowledge and politics. Although the concept originates from the Greek *egkuklios paideia* or general education, the notion of an encyclopedia in contemporary parlance invokes a far more ambitious and political project. The transition from ancient to modern conception involves a shift from the classical objective of initiating the student into the modes of analysis and domains of inquiry characteristic of an educated person to the radical eighteenth-century objective of systematizing all human knowledge. Even in ancient times cultivating the intellect was acknowledged to pose a threat to established institutions, for education entails a distancing from tradition and the possibility of a sustained challenge to prevailing conventions and norms. The eighteenth-century experience of the French *encyclopédistes*, however, dramatically reinforced the association between the acquisition of knowledge and the threat to the *status quo*. When the *encyclopédistes'* determination to chart the branches of human knowledge met with the recurrent efforts by church and state to censor and suppress the resulting *Encyclopédie*, the dynamic of liberation/subversion was irrevocably appended to the concept of knowledge. The first major effort to produce an encyclopedia thus proved itself to be a profoundly political affair.

Confronted with the rapid development of scholarly fields, the *encyclopédistes* believed that a general inventory of knowledge was both possible and imperative. Convinced of the solidarity of the sciences, the *encyclopédistes* undertook the careful organization and classification of seemingly diverse material in order to reveal the underlying unity of knowledge. They heralded the discovery of unifying principles in the three faculties of the human mind – reason, intellect, and imagination – as the means not only to explode vulgar errors and weaken propensities toward dogmatism, but also to lay the foundation for change in the general way of thinking. Central to this change was a repudiation of medieval metaphysics and a commitment to empiricism, understood as a reliance upon the senses as the principal sources of knowledge, and upon experience and experiment as the grounds upon which to test knowledge claims. Empiricist techniques were considered the key to liberating the mind from superstition and providing the means for objective knowledge of the natural and social worlds (Diderot *et al.* 1751–65).

The epistemological emphasis upon the human senses had a number of social, political and ethical corollaries. When the senses were accredited as the sole source of evidence, the doctrine of *homo mensuris* – the human being as measure of all things – subtly shifted the focus of human attention to the conditions and rewards in this world and away from those promised in a putative afterlife. This doctrine, brazenly egalitarian, empowered the individual knower by insisting that each individual possessed the capacity to judge truth and falsity without reference to any higher authority. The promotion of individual happiness and the elimination of human misery were validated as legitimate criteria against which to measure existing institutions. Informed by individualist assumptions and inspired by utilitarian objectives, the *encyclopédistes*' 'general way of thinking' posed a radical threat to a social order dependent upon hierarchy, religion and deference. Their science sustained standards of evaluation that warranted collective action to transform social relations. Progress was said to be the concomitant of knowledge because science was believed to be inherently liberating. It could free the individual from slavish obligations to king and collective precisely because it freed the mind from unsupportable superstitions, supplanting prejudice and dogma with humane standards for assessing the merits of existing institutions, thereby providing both motive and legitimation for action to change any institutions found to be markedly deficient. The threat posed by the *Encyclopédie* was not overlooked by the authorities of the *ancien régime*. In 1751, the Archbishop of Paris issued a *mandement* against the *Encyclopédie*; in 1752 the Royal Council of State issued an order prohibiting further publication of the work. In 1759, the *Parlement de Paris* condemned the project and a decree in *Conseil du Roi* revoked the *Encyclopédie*'s 'privilege', effectively suppressing the work until 1766.

To promote their transformative objectives, the *encyclopédistes* devised a methodology to ensure that their science would be accessible to the literate public. The *Encyclopédie* was designed to be both 'dictionary and treatise of everything the human mind might wish to know' (Diderot *et al.* 1751–65). As dictionary, the seventeen volumes emphasized careful definitions of topics, arranged alphabetically. As treatise, each entry sought to view its topic from every possible angle, 'transcending the general movement of contemporary thought in order to work for future generations'. In delving into the details of the topic, the analyst sought to illuminate the depth and complexity of issues and the means by which apparently disparate dimensions of a problem could be brought into synthesis. In addressing a topic, each author was asked to consider '*genre, differencia specifica*, qualities, causes, uses and the elaboration of method'. On the conviction that knowledge depended upon correct use of language, special effort was made to be as precise as possible in the use of terms and to integrate the exact scientific explanation of phenomena into the accepted language of the day. Excessive recourse to jargon and mystification through the introduction of obfuscating terminology was shunned. Because the *Encyclopédie* incorporated the works of some of the most renowned authors of the day, no effort was made to correct the mistakes of the contributors. Indeed, in later editions, certain controversial essays were published intact, but immediately followed by refutations of central claims and arguments. Such a tolerance for intellectual debate was supported by the *encyclopédistes'* belief that a key element in the 'revolution of the human mind' to which they aspired was a heightened capacity for scepticism and critique (Lough 1968; Wade 1977).

The legacy of the *encyclopédistes* is rich and varied. Their convictions about the unity of the sciences and the progressive nature of scientific inquiry have had a profound influence upon subsequent developments in the social sciences. Their contention that empiricism constituted the sole method for the acquisition of knowledge remained largely unchallenged among social scientists for two centuries. The individualist premises that undergird their work have shaped the intellectual investigations and the political aspirations of subsequent generations. Their appeal to social utility as the principal criterion for assessing social and political institutions has shaped political discourse and research methodologies in both the nineteenth and twentieth centuries. Moreover, their attention to the political consequences of particular modes of knowledge resonates in the recent arguments of critical theorists and postmodernists, who examine the relation between social science and prevailing regimes of power.

This *Encyclopedia of Government and Politics* stands in complex relation to the *Encyclopédie*, incorporating certain of its norms and strategies, while implicitly or explicitly repudiating others. Its format is modelled upon the revised version of the *Encyclopédie methodique* (1782–1820), organized topically with a specialized focus rather than alphabetically. Leading scholars in the field were commissioned to write articles that would provide both an overview of a designated topic and a critique of alternative methodological approaches to that topic. Avoidance of unnecessarily technical jargon, precision in definition, and clarity in presentation constituted guiding principles. While the *encyclopédistes'* goal to systematize all human knowledge was intentionally abandoned, efforts were made to provide comprehensive coverage of political studies at the beginning of the twenty-first century. Specific inclusions and omissions reflect compromises necessitated by the uneasy coexistence of aspirations to timeliness and to timelessness.

Perhaps the major break with the *Encyclopédie* involves the rejection of commitments to the unity of the sciences, naïve assumptions about the self-evidence of empirical data, and the optimistic equation of 'knowledge' with 'progress'. In contrast to the notion that the fundamental capacities of the human mind fix a simple strategy for the acquisition of knowledge in the natural and the social sciences, this encyclopedia begins with the assumption that research strategies and methodological techniques have far more to do with debates within scholarly disciplines than with fundamental faculties of the human mind. As a consequence, diversity in issues investigated, methodologies adopted, and strategies of analysis and argumentation accredited are expected as the norm, not only with respect to demarcating the natural sciences from the social sciences, but also within the social sciences themselves. Thus it is taken as given that various scholars committed to behavioural, institutional, statistical, theoretical, structural, functionalist, psychological, semiotic, hermeneutic and genealogical methods will construe the political world differently. To assume unity of knowledge only serves to mask the discrepancies illuminated by various research strategies, pre-emptively precluding consideration of important dimensions of the politics of knowledge.

To conceive of the 'politics of knowledge' in this sense requires a break with an overly simplistic notion of empiricism, which posits a simple and direct relation between knower and known. According to certain versions of empiricism, the senses function as faithful recording mechanisms, placing before the 'mind's eye' exact replicas of that which exists in the external world, without cultural or linguistic mediation. Precisely because observation is understood as exact replication, such empiricist strategies for the acquisition of knowledge are said to be 'neutral' and 'value-free'. From the empiricist view, scientific investigations can grasp objective reality, because the subjectivity of individual observers can be controlled through rigid adherence to neutral procedures in the context of systematic experiments and logical deductions.

Empiricist assumptions have been central to the development of the discipline of political science and to the scientific study of politics in the twentieth century (Tanenhaus and Somit 1967; Greenstein and Polsby 1975; Finifter 1983; Seidelman and Harpham 1985; King, Keohane and Verba 1994). (In this case, as in numerous cases throughout the essay, hundreds of texts could be cited to support this claim. For the sake of brevity, a few well-known examples have been chosen. Except in cases of direct quotation then, references should be taken as representative rather than exhaustive.) A break with empiricism then requires careful justification. Towards that end, the following section will explicate and critique the positivist and Popperian conceptions of science that have profoundly influenced the recent practice of political science. An alternative conception of science will then be advanced and its implications for the understanding of politics and for the structure of this encyclopedia will be explored.

Although such an excursion into the philosophy of science may at first appear far removed from the central concerns of political scientists, a clear understanding of the assumptions about science that inform disciplinary practices is important for a variety of reasons. Not only will a brief review of contending conceptions of science clarify the methodological presuppositions of political scientists, but it will also lay the foundation for challenging the myth of methodological neutrality. In so doing it will identify new areas for investigation concerning the political implications of particular modes of inquiry and thereby foster theoretical self-consciousness about the relation of political science to contemporary politics.

Contending conceptions of science

Within the social sciences, empiricist commitments have generated a number of methodological techniques to ensure the objectivity of scientific investigations. Chief among these is the dichotomous division of the world into the realms of the empirical and the non-empirical. The empirical realm, comprising all that can be corroborated by the senses, is circumscribed as the legitimate sphere of scientific investigation. As a residual category, the non-empirical encompasses everything else – religion, philosophy, ethics, aesthetics and evaluative discourse in general, as well as myth, dogma and superstition – which is relegated beyond the sphere of science. Within this frame of reference, social science, operating within the realm of the observable, restricting its focus to descriptions, explanations and predictions that are intersubjectively testable, can achieve objective knowledge. The specific techniques requisite to the achievement of objective knowledge have been variously defined by two conceptions of science which have shaped the practice of political science – positivism and critical rationalism.

On the grounds that only those knowledge claims founded directly upon observable experience can be genuine, positivists adopted the 'verification criterion of meaning' (which stipulates that a contingent proposition is meaningful, if and only if it can be empirically verified) as their core concept (Joergenson 1951; Kraft 1952; Ayer 1959). The verification criterion was deployed to differentiate not only between science and non-science, but between science and 'nonsense'. In the positivist view, any statement which could not be verified by reference to experience constituted nonsense: it was literally meaningless. The implications of the verificationist criterion for a model of science were manifold. All knowledge was believed to be dependent upon observation, thus any claims, whether theological, metaphysical, philosophical, ethical, normative or aesthetic, which were not rooted in empirical observation were rejected as meaningless. The sphere of science was thereby narrowly circumscribed and scientific knowledge was accredited as the only valid knowledge. In addition, induction, a method of knowledge acquisition grounded upon observation of particulars as the foundation for empirical generalizations, was taken to provide the essential logic of science.

The task of science was understood to comprise the inductive discovery of regularities existing in the external world. Scientific research sought to organize in economical fashion those regularities which experience presents in order to facilitate explanation and prediction. To promote this objective, positivists endorsed and employed a technical vocabulary, clearly differentiating facts (empirically verifiable propositions) and hypotheses (empirically verifiable propositions asserting the existence of relationships among observed phenomena) from laws (empirically confirmed propositions asserting an invariable sequence or association among observed phenomena) and theories (interrelated systems of laws possessing explanatory power). Moreover, the positivist logic of scientific inquiry dictated a specific sequence of activities as definitive to 'the scientific method'.

According to this model, the scientific method began with the carefully controlled, neutral observation of empirical events. Sustained observation over time would enable the regularities or patterns of relationships in observed events to be revealed and thereby provide for the formulation of hypotheses. Once formulated, hypotheses were to be subjected to systematic empirical tests. Those hypotheses which received external confirmation through this process of rigorous testing could be elevated to the status of 'scientific laws'. Once identified, scientific laws provided the foundation for scientific explanation, which, according to the precepts of the 'covering law' model, consisted in demonstrating that the event(s) to be explained could have been expected, given certain initial conditions (C1, C2, C3,...) and the general laws of the field (L1, L2, L3,...). Within the framework of the positivist conception of science, the discovery of scientific laws also provided the foundation for prediction which consisted in demonstrating that an event would occur given the future occurrence of certain initial conditions and the operation of the general laws of the field. Under the covering law model, then, explanation and prediction have the same logical form, only the time factor differs: explanation pertains to past events; prediction pertains to future events.

Positivists were also committed to the principle of the 'unity of science', i.e. to the belief that the logic of scientific inquiry was the same for all fields. Whether natural phenomena or social phenomena were the objects of study, the method for acquiring valid knowledge and the requirements for explanation and prediction remained the same. Once a science had progressed sufficiently to accumulate a body of scientific laws organized in a coherent system of theories, it could be said to have achieved a stage of 'maturity' which made explanation and prediction possible. Although the logic of mature science remained inductive with respect to the generation of new knowledge, the logic of scientific explanation was deductive. Under the covering law model, causal explanation, the demonstration of the necessary and sufficient conditions of an event, involved the deductive subsumption of particular observations under a general law. In addition, deduction also played a central role in efforts to explain laws and theories: the explanation of a law involved its deductive subsumption under a theory; and explanation of one theory involved its deductive subsumption under wider theories.

The primary postulates of positivism have been subjected to rigorous and devastating critiques (Popper 1959, 1972a, 1972b). Neither the logic of induction nor the verification criterion of meaning can accomplish positivist objectives; neither can guarantee the acquisition of truth. The inductive method is incapable of guaranteeing the validity of scientific knowledge owing to the 'problem of induction' (Hume 1739, 1748). Because empirical events are contingent, i.e. because the future can always be different from the past, generalizations based upon limited observations are necessarily incomplete and, as such, highly fallible. For this reason, inductive generalizations cannot be presumed to be true. Nor can 'confirmation' or 'verification' of such generalizations by reference to additional cases provide proof of their universal validity. For the notion of universal validity invokes all future, as well as all past and present, occurrences of a phenomenon; yet no matter how many confirming instances of a phenomenon can be found in the past or in the present, these can never alter the logical possibility that the future could be different, that the future could disprove an inductively derived empirical generalization. Thus, a demonstration of the truth of an empirical generalization must turn upon the identification of a 'necessary connection' establishing a causal relation among observed phenomena.

Unfortunately, the notion of necessary connection also encounters serious problems. If the notion of necessity invoked is logical necessity, then the empirical nature of science is jeopardized. If, on the other hand, positivism appeals to an empirical demonstration of necessity, it falls foul of the standard established by the verification criterion of meaning, for the 'necessity' required as proof of any causal claim cannot be empirically observed. As Hume pointed out, empirical observation reveals 'constant conjunction' (a 'correlation' in the language of contemporary social science); it does not and cannot reveal necessary connection. As a positivist logic of scientific inquiry, then, induction encounters two serious problems: it is incapable of providing validation for the truth of its generalizations and it is internally inconsistent, for any attempt to demonstrate the validity of a causal claim invokes a conception of necessary connection that violates the verification criterion of meaning.

The positivist conception of the scientific method also rests upon a flawed psychology of perception. In suggesting that the scientific method commences with 'neutral' observation, positivists invoke a conception of 'manifest truth' which attempts to reduce the problem of the validity of knowledge to an appeal to the

authority of the source of that knowledge (for example, 'the facts "speak" for themselves'). The belief that the unmediated apprehension of the 'given' by a passive or
receptive observer is possible, however, misconstrues both the nature of perception
and the nature of the world. The human mind is not passive but active; it does not
merely 'receive' an image of the given, but rather imposes order upon the external
world through a process of selection, interpretation and imagination. Observation is
always linguistically and culturally mediated. It involves the creative imposition of
expectations, anticipations and conjectures upon external events.

Scientific observation, too, is necessarily theory-laden. It begins not from
'nothing', nor from the 'neutral' perception of given relations, but rather from
immersion in a scientific tradition which provides frames of reference or conceptual
schemes that organize reality and shape the problems for further investigation. To
grasp the role of theory in structuring scientific observation, however, requires a
revised conception of 'theory'. Contrary to the positivist notion that theory is the
result of observation, the result of the systematization of a series of inductive generalizations, the result of the cumulation of an interrelated set of scientific laws, theory
is logically prior to the observation of any similarities or regularities in the world;
indeed, theory is precisely that which makes the identification of regularities
possible. Moreover, scientific theories involve risk to an extent that is altogether
incompatible with the positivist view of theories as summaries of empirical generalizations. Scientific theories involve risky predictions of things that have never been
seen and hence cannot be deduced logically from observation statements. Theories
structure scientific observation in a manner altogether incompatible with the positivist requirement of neutral perception, and they involve unobservable propositions
that violate the verification criterion of meaning: abstract theoretical entities cannot
be verified by reference to empirical observation.

That theoretical propositions violate the verification criterion is not in itself
damning, for the verification criterion can be impugned on a number of grounds. As
a mechanism for the validation of empirical generalizations, the verification criterion
fails because of the problem of induction. As a scientific principle for the demarcation of the 'meaningful' from the 'meaningless', the verification criterion is
self-referentially destructive. In repudiating all that is not empirically verifiable as
nonsense, the verification criterion repudiates itself, for it is not a statement derived
from empirical observation nor is it a tautology. Rigid adherence to the verification
criterion then would mandate that it be rejected as metaphysical nonsense. Thus the
positivist conflation of that which is not amenable to empirical observation with
nonsense simply will not withstand scrutiny. Much (including the verification criterion itself) that cannot be empirically verified can be understood and all that can be
understood is meaningful.

As an alternative to the defective positivist conception of science, Karl Popper
advanced 'critical rationalism' (1972a, 1972b). On this view, scientific theories are
bold conjectures which scientists impose upon the world. Drawing insights from
manifold sources in order to solve particular problems, scientific theories involve
abstract and unobservable propositions which predict what may happen as well as
what may not happen. Thus scientific theories generate predictions that are incompatible with certain possible results of observation, i.e. they 'prohibit' certain
occurrences by proclaiming that some things could not happen. As such, scientific

theories put the world to the test and demand a reply. Precisely because scientific theories identify a range of conditions that must hold, a series of events that must occur and a set of occurrences that are in principle impossible, they can clash with observation; they are empirically testable. While no number of confirming instances could ever prove a theory to be true due to the problem of induction, one discon-firming instance is sufficient to disprove a theory. If scientific laws are construed as statements of prohibitions, forbidding the occurrence of certain empirical events, then they can be definitively refuted by the occurrence of one such event. Thus, according to Popper, 'falsification' provides a mechanism by which scientists can test their conjectures against reality and learn from their mistakes. Falsification also provides the core of Popper's revised conception of the scientific method.

According to the 'hypothetico-deductive model', the scientist always begins with a problem. To resolve the problem, the scientist generates a theory, a conjecture or hypothesis, which can be tested by deducing its empirical consequences and measuring them against the world. Once the logical implications of a theory have been deduced and converted into predictions concerning empirical events, the task of science is falsification. In putting theories to the test of experience, scientists seek to falsify predictions, for that alone enables them to learn from their mistakes. The rationality of science is embodied in the method of trial and error, a method which allows error to be purged through the elimination of false theories.

In mandating that all scientific theories be tested, in stipulating that the goal of science is the falsification of erroneous views, the criterion of falsifiability provides a means by which to reconcile the fallibility of human knowers with a conception of objective knowledge. The validity of scientific claims does not turn on a demand for an impossible neutrality on the part of individual scientists, on the equally impos-sible requirement that all prejudice, bias, pre-judgement, expectation or value be purged from the process of observation or on the implausible assumption that the truth is manifest. The adequacy of scientific theories is judged in concrete problem contexts in terms of their ability to solve problems and their ability to withstand increasingly difficult empirical tests. Those theories which withstand multiple inter-subjective efforts to falsify them are 'corroborated', identified as 'laws' which with varying degrees of verisimilitude capture the structure of reality, and for that reason are tentatively accepted as 'true'. But in keeping with the critical attitude of science even the strongest corroboration for a theory is not accepted as conclusive proof. For Popperian critical rationalism posits that truth lies beyond human reach. As a regulative ideal which guides scientific activity truth may be approximated, but it can never be established by human authority. Nevertheless, error can be objectively identified. Thus informed by a conception of truth as a *regulative ideal* and oper-ating in accordance with the requirements of the criterion of falsifiability, science can progress by the incremental correction of errors and the gradual accretion of objective problem-solving knowledge.

Most of the research strategies developed within political science in the twentieth century draw upon either positivist or Popperian conceptions of the scientific method. The legacy of positivism is apparent in behaviouralist definitions of the field which emphasize data collection, hypothesis formulation and testing, and other formal aspects of systematic empirical enterprise, as well as in approaches which stress scientific, inductive methods, statistical models and quantitative research designs. It surfaces in conceptions of explanation defined in deductive terms and in commitments to the equivalence of explanation and prediction. It emerges in claims that political science must be modelled upon the methods of the natural sciences for those alone are capable of generating valid knowledge. It is unmistakable in the assumption that 'facts' are unproblematic, that they are immediately observable or 'given', and hence their apprehension requires no interpretation. It is embodied in the presumption that confirmation or verification provides a criterion of proof of the validity of empirical claims. And it is conspicuous in the repudiation of values as arbitrary preferences, irrational commitments or meaningless propositions which lie altogether beyond the realm of rational analysis (Storing 1962; Eulau 1963; Kaplan 1964; Meehan 1965; Eulau and March 1969; Welsh 1973).

Popper's insistence upon the centrality of problem solving and incrementalism in scientific activity resonates in the works of those committed to a pluralist approach to political analysis. Popperian assumptions also surface in the recognition that observation and analysis are necessarily theory-laden, as well as in the commitment to intersubjective testing as the appropriate means by which to deflect the influence of individual bias from substantive political analyses. They are manifest in the substitution of testability for verifiability as the appropriate criterion for the demarcation of scientific hypotheses and in the invocation of falsification and the elimination of error as the strategy for the accumulation of political knowledge. They are reflected in the pragmatic notion that the existing political system constitutes the appropriate 'reality' against which to test political hypotheses. They are obvious in the critique of excessive optimism concerning the possibility of securing truth through the deployment of inductive, quantitative techniques, in the less pretentious quest for useful knowledge and in the insistence that truth constitutes a regulative ideal rather than a current possession of political science. They are conspicuous in arguments that the hypothetico-deductive model is applicable to political studies and in appeals for the development of a critical, non-dogmatic attitude among political scientists. Moreover, Popperian assumptions are apparent in a variety of strategies devised to bring reason to bear upon normative issues, while simultaneously accepting that there can be no ultimate rational justification of value precepts. Popperian presuppositions about the fundamental task of social science are also manifest in the pluralists' commitment to a conception of politics premised upon a model of the market that focuses research upon the unintended consequences of the actions of multiple actors rather than upon the particular intentions of political agents (Cook 1985; Lindblom and Cohen 1979; MacRae 1976; Wildavsky 1979).

Popperian critical rationalism provides ample justification for abandoning methodological strategies informed by defective positivist precepts. It does not, however, provide either a satisfactory account of science or a sufficiently sophisticated foundation for political inquiry. Although Popper's critical rationalism is a significant improvement over early positivist conceptions of science, it too suffers from a number of grave defects. The most serious challenge to critical rationalism has been raised by post-positivist presupposition theories of science (Polanyi 1958; Humphreys 1969; Suppe 1977; Brown 1977; Bernstein 1978, 1983; Hesse 1980; Longino 1990; Stockman 1983; Gunnell 1986, 1995, 1998). Presupposition theories of science concur with Popper's depiction of observation as 'theory-laden'. They agree that 'there is more to seeing than meets the eye' (Humphreys 1969: 61) and that perception involves more than the passive reception of allegedly manifest sense-data. They suggest that perception depends upon a constellation of theoretical presuppositions that structure observation, accrediting particular stimuli as significant and specific configurations as meaningful. According to presupposition theories, observation is not only theory-laden but theory is essential to, indeed, constitutive of all human knowledge.

Within recent work in the philosophy of science, the epistemological and ontological implications of the post-positivist understanding of theory have been the subject of extensive debate. Arguing that the theoretical constitution of human knowledge has ontological as well as epistemological implications, 'anti-realists' have suggested that there is no point in asking about the nature of the world independent of our theories about it (Laudan 1990). Consequently the truth status of theories must be bracketed. But anti-realists have insisted that theories need not be true to be good, i.e., to solve problems (van Fraassen 1980; Churchill and Hooker 1985). Metaphysical 'realists', on the other hand, have emphasized that even if the only access to the world is through theories about it, a logical distinction can still be upheld between reality and how we conceive it, between truth and what we believe (Harre 1986). Hilary Putnam (1981, 1983, 1988, 1990) has advanced 'pragmatic' realism as a more tenable doctrine. Putnam accepts that all concepts are theoretically constituted and culturally mediated and that the 'world' does not 'determine' what can be said about it. Nonetheless, it makes sense on pragmatic grounds to insist that truth and falsity are not merely a matter of decision and that there is an external reality that constrains our conceptual choices. Following Putnam's lead, 'scientific realists' have argued that scientific theories are referential in an important sense and as such can be comparatively assessed in terms of their approximations of truth (Glymour 1980; Newton-Smith 1981; Miller 1987).

While the debates among realists and anti-realists about the criteria of truth and the nature of evidence are intricate and complex, both realists and anti-realists share convictions about the defects of positivism and accept the broad contours of what is called below 'presupposition theories of science'. On this view, science, as a form of human knowledge, is dependent upon theory in multiple and complex ways. Presupposition theories of science suggest that the notions of perception, meaning, relevance, explanation, knowledge and method, central to the practice of science, are all theoretically constituted concepts. Theoretical presuppositions shape perception and determine what will be taken as a 'fact'; they confer meaning on experience and control the demarcation of significant from trivial events; they afford criteria of relevance according to which facts can be organized, tests envisioned and the acceptability or unacceptability of scientific conclusions assessed; they accredit particular models of explanation and strategies of understanding; and they sustain specific methodological techniques for gathering, classifying, and analysing data. Theoretical presuppositions set the terms of scientific debate and organize the elements of scientific activity. Moreover, they typically do so at a tacit or preconscious level and it is for this reason that they appear to hold such unquestionable authority.

The pervasive role of theoretical assumptions upon the practice of science has profound implications for notions such as empirical 'reality', and the 'autonomy' of facts, which posit that facts are 'given', and that experience is ontologically distinct from the theoretical constructs that are advanced to explain it. The post-empiricist conception of a 'fact' as a theoretically constituted entity calls into question such basic assumptions. It suggests that 'the noun, "experience", the verb, "to experience" and the adjective "empirical" are not univocal terms that can be transferred from one system to another without change of meaning.... Experience does not come labelled as "empirical", nor does it come self-certified as such. What we call experience depends upon assumptions hidden beyond scrutiny which define it and which in turn it supports' (Vivas 1960: 76). Recognition that 'facts' can be so designated only in terms of prior theoretical presuppositions implies that any quest for an unmediated reality is necessarily futile. Any attempt to identify an 'unmediated fact' must mistake the conventional for the 'natural', as in cases which define 'brute facts' as 'social facts which are largely the product of well-understood, reliable tools, facts that are not likely to be vitiated by pitfalls.... in part [because of] the ease and certainty with which [they] can be determined and in part [because of] the incontestability of [their] conceptual base' (Murray 1983: 321). Alternatively, the attempt to conceive a 'fact' that exists prior to any description of it, prior to any theoretical or conceptual mediation, must generate an empty notion of something completely unspecified and unspecifiable, a notion that will be of little use to science (Williams 1985: 138).

Recognition of the manifold ways in which perceptions of reality are theoretically mediated raises a serious challenge not only to notions of 'brute data' and the 'givenness' of experience, but also to the possibility of falsification as a strategy for testing theories against an independent reality. For falsification to provide an adequate test of a scientific theory, it is necessary that there be a clear distinction between theoretical postulates and independent correspondence rules that link theoretical principles to particular observations. Embodying the idea of theory-independent evidence, neutral correspondence rules are essential to the very possibility of refutation, to the possibility that the world could prove a theory to be wrong. If, however, there is no tenable distinction between theoretical assumptions and correspondence rules, if what is taken to be the 'world', what is understood in terms of 'brute data' is itself theoretically constituted (indeed, constituted by the same theory that is undergoing the test), then no conclusive disproof of a theory is likely. For the independent evidence upon which falsification depends does not exist; the available evidence is preconstituted by the same theoretical presuppositions as the scientific theory under scrutiny (Moon 1975: 146; Brown 1977: 38–48; Stockman 1983: 73–6).

Contrary to Popper's confident conviction that empirical reality could provide an ultimate court of appeal for the judgement of scientific theories and that the critical, non-dogmatic attitude of scientists would ensure that their theories were constantly being put to the test, presupposition theorists emphasize that it is always possible to 'save' a theory from refutation. The existence of one disconfirming instance is not sufficient to falsify a theory because it is always possible to evade falsification on the grounds that future research will demonstrate that a counter-instance is really only an 'apparent' counter-instance. Moreover, the theory-laden character of observation and the theory-constituted character of evidence provide ample grounds upon which to dispute the validity of the evidence and to challenge the design or the findings of specific experiments which claim to falsify respected theories. Furthermore, post-positivist examinations of the history of scientific practice suggest that, contrary to Popper's claim that scientists are quick to discard discredited theories, there is a great deal of evidence that neither the existence of counter-instances nor the persistence of anomalies necessarily lead to the abandonment of scientific theories. Indeed, the overwhelming evidence of scientific practice suggests that scientists cling to long-established views tenaciously, in spite of the existence of telling criticisms, persistent anomalies and unresolved problems (Ricci 1984; Harding 1986). Thus it has been suggested that the 'theory' that scientists themselves are always sceptical, non-dogmatic, critical of received views and quick to repudiate questionable notions has itself been falsified and should be abandoned.

The problem of falsification is exacerbated by the conflation of explanation and prediction in the Popperian account of science. For the belief that a corroborated prediction constitutes proof of the validity of a scientific explanation fails to recognize that an erroneous theory can generate correct predictions (Moon 1975: 146–7; Brown 1977: 51–7). The logical distinction between prediction and explanation thus provides further support for the view that no theory can ever be conclusively falsified. The problem of induction also raises doubts about the possibility of definitive refutations. In calling attention to the possibility that the future could be different from the past and present in unforeseeable ways, the problem of induction arouses the suspicion that a theory falsified today might not 'stay' falsified. The assumption of regularity which sustains Popper's belief that a falsified theory will remain falsified permanently is itself an inductionist presupposition which suggests that the falsifiability principle does not constitute the escape from induction which Popper had hoped (Stockman 1983: 81–2). Thus despite the logical asymmetry between verification and falsification, no falsification can be any stronger or more final than any corroboration (Brown 1977: 75).

Presupposition theorists acknowledge that 'ideally, scientists would like to examine the structure of the world which exists independent of our knowledge – but the nature of perception and the role of presuppositions preclude direct access to it: the only access available is through theory-directed research' (Brown 1977: 108). Recognition that theoretical presuppositions organize and structure research by determining the meanings of observed events, identifying relevant data and significant problems for investigation and indicating both strategies for solving problems and methods by which to test the validity of proposed solutions, raises a serious challenge to the correspondence theory of truth. For it both denies that 'autonomous facts' can serve as the ultimate arbiter of scientific theories and suggests that science is no more capable of achieving the Archimedean point or of escaping human fallibility than is any other human endeavour. Indeed, it demands acknowledgement of science as a human convention rooted in the practical judgements of a community of fallible scientists struggling to resolve theory-generated problems under specific historical conditions. It sustains an image of science that is far less heroic and far more human.

As an alternative to the correspondence theory of truth, presupposition theorists suggest a coherence theory of truth premised upon the recognition that all human knowledge depends upon theoretical presuppositions whose congruence with nature cannot be established conclusively by reason or experience. Theoretical presuppositions, rooted in living traditions, provide the conceptual frameworks through which the world is viewed; they exude a 'natural attitude' which demarcates what is taken as normal, natural, real, reasonable or sane, from what is understood as deviant, unnatural, utopian, impossible, irrational or insane. In contrast to Popper's conception of theories as conscious conjectures which can be systematically elaborated and deductively elucidated, the notion of theoretical presuppositions suggests that theories operate at the tacit level. They structure 'pre-understandings' and 'pre-judgements' in such a way that it is difficult to isolate and illuminate the full range of presuppositions which affect cognition at any given time (Bernstein 1983: 113–67). Moreover, any attempt to elucidate presuppositions must operate within a 'hermeneutic circle'. Any attempt to examine or to challenge certain assumptions or expectations must occur within the frame of reference established by the other presuppositions. Certain presuppositions must remain fixed if others are to be subjected to systematic critique. This does not imply that individuals are 'prisoners' trapped within the framework of theories, expectations, past experiences and language in such a way that critical reflection becomes impossible (ibid.: 84). Critical reflection upon and abandonment of certain theoretical presuppositions is possible within the hermeneutic circle; but the goal of transparency, of the unmediated grasp of things as they are, is not. For no reflective investigation, no matter how critical, can escape the fundamental conditions of human cognition.

A coherence theory of truth accepts that the world is richer than theories devised to grasp it; it accepts that theories are underdetermined by 'facts' and, consequently, that there can always be alternative and competing theoretical explanations of particular events. It does not, however, imply the relativist conclusion that all theoretical interpretations are equal. That there can be no appeal to neutral, theory-independent facts to adjudicate between competing theoretical interpretations does not mean that there is no rational way of making and warranting critical evaluative judgements concerning alternative views. Indeed, presupposition theorists have pointed out that the belief that the absence of independent evidence necessarily entails relativism is itself dependent upon a positivist commitment to the verification criterion of meaning. Only if one starts from the assumption that the sole test for the validity of a proposition lies in its measurement against the empirically 'given' does it follow that, in the absence of the 'given', no rational judgements can be made concerning the validity of particular claims (Bernstein 1983: 92; Brown 1977: 93–4; Stockman 1983: 79–101; Gunnell 1986: 66–8).

Once the 'myth of the given' (Sellars 1963: 164) has been abandoned and once the belief that the absence of one invariant empirical test for the 'truth' of a theory implies the absence of all criteria for evaluative judgement has been repudiated, then it is possible to recognize that there are rational grounds for assessing the merits of alternative theoretical interpretations. To comprehend the nature of such assessments it is necessary to acknowledge that although theoretical presuppositions structure the perception of events, they do not create perceptions out of 'nothing'. Theoretical interpretations are 'world-guided' (Williams 1985: 140). They involve both the pre-understanding brought to an event by an individual perceiver and the stimuli in the external (or internal) world which instigate the process of cognition. Because of this dual source of theoretical interpretations, objects can be characterized in many different ways, 'but it does not follow that a given object can be seen in any way at all or that all descriptions are equal' (Brown 1977: 93). The stimuli that trigger interpretation limit the class of plausible characterizations without dictating one absolute description.

Assessment of alternative theoretical interpretations involves deliberation, a rational activity which requires that imagination and judgement be deployed in the consideration of the range of evidence and arguments that can be advanced in support of various positions. The reasons offered in support of alternative views marshal evidence, organize data, apply various criteria of explanation, address multiple levels of analysis with varying degrees of abstraction and employ divergent strategies of argumentation. This range of reasons offers a rich field for deliberation and assessment. It provides an opportunity for the exercise of judgement and ensures that when scientists reject a theory, they do so because they believe they can demonstrate that the reasons offered in support of that theory are deficient. That the reasons advanced to sustain the rejection of one theory do not constitute absolute proof of the validity of an alternative theory is simply a testament to human fallibility. Admission that the cumulative weight of current evidence and compelling argument cannot protect scientific judgements against future developments which may warrant the repudiation of those theories currently accepted is altogether consonant with the recognition of the finitude of human rationality and the contingency of empirical relations.

Presupposition theorists suggest that any account of science which fails to accredit the rationality of the considered judgements that inform the choice between alternative scientific theories must be committed to a defective conception of reason. Although the standards of evidence and the criteria for assessment brought to bear upon theoretical questions cannot be encapsulated in a simple rule or summarized in rigid methodological principles, deliberation involves the exercise of a range of intellectual skills. Conceptions of science that define rationality in terms of one technique, be it logical deduction, inductive inference, or empirical verification, are simply too narrow to encompass the multiple forms of rationality manifested in scientific research. The interpretive judgements that are characteristic of every phase of scientific investigations, and that culminate in the rational choice of particular scientific theories on the basis of the cumulative weight of evidence and argument, are too rich and various to be captured by the rules governing inductive or deductive logic. For this reason, *phronesis*, practical reason, manifested in the processes of interpretation and judgement characteristic of all understanding, is advanced by presupposition theorists as an alternative to logic as the paradigmatic form of scientific rationality (Brown 1977: 148–52; Bernstein 1983: 54–78).

Presupposition theorists suggest that a conception of practical reason more accurately depicts the forms of rationality exhibited in scientific research. In contrast to the restrictive view advanced by positivism which reduces the arsenal of reason to the techniques of logic and thereby rejects creativity, deliberative judgement and evaluative assessments as varying forms of irrationality, *phronesis* constitutes a more expansive conception of the powers of the human intellect. Presupposition theorists suggest that a consideration of the various processes of contemplation, conceptualization, representation, remembrance, reflection, speculation, rationalization, inference, deduction and deliberation (to name but a few manifestations of human cognition) reveals that the dimensions of reason are diverse. They also argue that an adequate conception of reason must encompass these diverse cognitive practices. Because the instrumental conception of rationality advanced by positivists is clearly incapable of accounting for these various forms of reason, it must be rejected as defective. Thus presupposition theorists suggest that science must be freed from the parochial beliefs that obscure reason's diverse manifestations and restrict its operation to the rigid adherence to a narrow set of rules. The equation of scientific rationality with an infallible formal logic must be abandoned not only because there is no reason to suppose that there must be some indubitable foundation or some ahistorical, invariant method for scientific inquiry in order to establish the rationality of scientific practices, but also because the belief that science can provide final truths cannot be sustained by the principles of formal logic, the methods of empirical inquiry or the characteristics of fallible human cognition. *Phronesis* constitutes a conception of rationality that can encompass the diverse uses of reason in scientific practices, identify the manifold sources of potential error in theoretical interpretations, and illuminate the criteria of assessment and the standards of evidence and argument operative in the choice between alternative theoretical explanations of events. As a conception of scientific rationality, then, *phronesis* is more comprehensive and has greater explanatory power than the discredited positivist alternative.

Presupposition theorists offer a revised conception of science which emphasizes the conventional nature of scientific practices and the fallible character of scientific explanations and predictions. Confronted with a world richer than any partial perception of it, scientists draw upon the resources of tradition and imagination in an effort to comprehend the world before them. The theories they devise to explain objects and events are structured by a host of presuppositions concerning meaning, relevance, experience, explanation and evaluation. Operating within the limits imposed by fallibility and contingency, scientists employ creative insights, practical reason, formal logic and an arsenal of conventional techniques and methods in their effort to approximate the truth about the world. But their approximations always operate within the parameters set by theoretical presuppositions; their approximations always address an empirical realm which is itself theoretically constituted. The undetermination of theory by data ensures that multiple interpretations of the same phenomena are possible.

When alternative theoretical explanations conflict, the judgement of the scientific community is brought to bear upon the competing interpretations. Exercising practical reason, the scientific community deliberates upon the evidence and arguments sustaining the alternative views. The practical judgement of the practitioners in particular fields of science is exercised in weighing the evidence, replicating experiments, examining computations, investigating the applicability of innovative methods, assessing the potential of new concepts and considering the validity of particular conclusions. Through a process of deliberation and debate, a consensus emerges among researchers within a discipline concerning what will be taken as the valid theory. The choice is sustained by reasons which can be articulated and advanced as proof of the inadequacy of alternative interpretations. The method of scientific deliberation is eminently rational: it provides mechanisms for the identification of charlatans and incompetents, as well as for the recognition of more subtle errors and more sophisticated approximations of truth. But the rationality of the process cannot guarantee the eternal verity of particular conclusions. The exercise of scientific reason is fallible; the judgements of the scientific community are corrigible.

The revised conception of science advanced by presupposition theorists suggests that attempts to divide the world into ontologically distinct categories of 'facts' and 'values', or into dichotomous realms of the 'empirical' and the 'normative', are fundamentally flawed (Hawkesworth 1988). Such attempts fail to grasp the implications of the theoretical constitution of all knowledge and the theoretical mediation of the empirical realm. They fail to come to grips with valuative character of all presuppositions and the consequent valuative component of all empirical propositions. The theoretically mediated world is one in which description, explanation and evaluation are inextricably linked. Any attempt to impose a dichotomous relation upon such inseparable processes constitutes a fallacy of false alternatives which is as distorting as it is logically untenable. For the suggestion that 'pure' facts can be isolated and analysed free of all valuation masks the theoretical constitution of facticity and denies the cognitive processes through which knowledge of the empirical realm is generated. Moreover, the dichotomous schism of the world into 'facts' and 'values' endorses an erroneous and excessively limiting conception of human reason, a conception which fails to comprehend the role of practical rationality in scientific deliberation and which fails to recognize that science is simply one manifestation of the use of practical reason in human life. Informed by flawed assumptions, the positivist conception of reason fails to understand that *phronesis* is operative in philosophical analysis, ethical deliberation, normative argument, political decisions and the practical choices of daily life as well as in scientific analysis. Moreover, in stipulating that reason can operate only in a naïvely simple, 'value-free', empirical realm, the positivist presuppositions that inform the fact/value dichotomy render reason impotent and thereby preclude the possibility that rational solutions might exist for the most pressing problems of the contemporary age.

Although the arguments that have discredited positivism are well known to philosophers, they have had far too little impact in the discipline of political science. This is especially unfortunate because the critique of positivism has wide-ranging implications for the discipline of political science. The post-positivist conception of knowledge suggests that divergent theoretical assumptions should have a pervasive influence upon the understanding of the political world, sanctioning contentious definitions of politics and focusing attention upon disparate variables, while simultaneously masking the controversial character of evidence adduced and the contestability of accredited strategies of explanation. Thus the post-positivist conception of science opens new areas of investigation concerning disciplinary presuppositions and practices: What are the most fundamental presuppositions of political science? What limitations have been imposed upon the constitution of knowledge within political science? By what disciplinary mechanisms has facticity been accredited and rendered unproblematic? How adequate are the standards of evidence, modes of analysis, and strategies of explanation privileged by the dominant tradition? Have methodological precepts subtly circumscribed contemporary politics?

Questions such as these focus attention upon the political implications of determinate modes of inquiry. The politics of knowledge emerges as a legitimate focus of analysis, for the analytical techniques developed in particular cognitive traditions may have political consequences that empiricist precepts render invisible. In circumscribing the subject matter appropriate to 'science', restricting the activities acceptable as 'empirical inquiry', establishing the norms for assessing the results of inquiry, identifying the basic principles of practice, and validating the ethos of practitioners, methodological strictures may sustain particular modes of political life. For this reason, the empiricist myth of methodological neutrality must be supplanted by an understanding of methodology as 'mind engaged in the legitimation of its own political activity' (Wolin 1981: 406). Such a revised conception of methodology requires detailed examination of the complex relations among various conceptions of politics, various techniques of political analysis and various forms of polity. The next section briefly considers the stakes involved in such investigations in the context of competing definitions of politics.

Politics: constitutive definitions

Within the field of political science there is no one definition of politics that holds the allegiance of all political scientists. The lack of a universally agreed upon definition does not imply that the topic is indefinable, that politics is a simple concept that admits of no further definition and, hence, must be grasped intuitively (Moore 1903). Nor does it imply that political scientists do not know what they are doing. On the contrary, contending definitions reflect important epistemological and methodological disagreements within the discipline. Alternative conceptions of politics construe the political world differently, in part because they derive from different understandings of reason, evidence and explanation, and in part because they are informed by radically different understandings of human possibility. As a consequence, the stakes in these conceptual disputes involve not just disciplinary politics, but also the shape of politics in the contemporary world. To explore these stakes, it is helpful to compare a classical definition of politics with a range of definitions advanced by contemporary political scientists.

In the classical conception advanced by Aristotle (1958) in *The Politics*, the activities of ruling and of politics were not equivalent. While ruling typically involved hierarchical relations of domination and subordination, politics was possible only as a relation among equals. In contrast to endeavours related to subsistence, production and reproduction that occurred in a sphere governed by necessity, politics existed only in a realm of freedom. On Aristotle's view, the participation of equals in collective decision making concerning the content and direction of public life constitutes the essence of politics. If the participation of equal citizens in an interchange of ruling and being ruled comprises the activity of politics, the citizens' achievement of a mode of life characterized by human excellence is its aim. To achieve this end, Aristotle noted that citizens must share a common system of values, they must be united in their perceptions of the just and the unjust. Only under such conditions could citizens escape the mire of conflicting wills and act co-operatively to achieve their common objectives. Thus political life is a testament to human freedom: within the political community, equal citizens identify the values they wish to live by and create rules and institutions to instantiate those values.

When Aristotle dubbed politics the master art, he suggested that politics necessarily involves a form of practical knowledge concerning both what is good for the community and how to attain that good. Political knowledge provides answers to questions such as: How ought people to live? What rules should govern collective life in order to enable citizens to achieve human excellence? What practices and institutions are most conducive to the achievement of the human *telos* – the highest and best form of human existence?

As a person interested in the comparative study of politics, Aristotle knew full well that such questions could be answered at two markedly different levels: at the first level, by citizens within a political community who were actively shaping their collective life; at the second level, by a political observer comparing the responses of various political communities to the same questions. In collecting hundreds of constitutions, Aristotle gained impressive evidence of the extent to which engagement in politics enabled determinate peoples to express their freedom. Reflecting the varying values of particular politics, diverse constitutions embodied alternative conceptions of the good life.

Aristotle did not believe that documenting alternative forms of political organization required a relativist endorsement of differing modes of life as equally beneficial. On the contrary, he was convinced that systematic political inquiry could provide an authoritative and final answer to the question of the highest form of human existence. Operating at the second level, political knowledge could afford definitive answers to the central political questions. Investigation of particular constitutions would make it possible to extract the essence of politics.

Aristotle's conceptions of politics and of political knowledge are intimately connected to a specific research strategy and a particular model of explanation. His strategy requires a preliminary gathering of diverse instances of a phenomenon and particular attention to received views about that phenomenon. Examination of similarities and differences then allows careful classification according to essential properties, which are inherently teleological. Methodologically,

> political inquiry requires a move from partial perspectives to an integral view, from opinions to a grasp of the thing in its wholeness. It proceeds by taking a variety of viewpoints into account, weighing them against each other and seeking the comprehensive view that can withstand criticism. In the course of inquiry, there is a growing awareness of the shape of things as a whole and this awareness gradually reveals the partiality and distortion of the original perspectives.
>
> (Miller 1979: 167)

Comprehension emerges from a sustained engagement with experiences whose meaning initially appears vague or inchoate. Use of this method produces *aletheia*, truth, that which remains when all error is purged.

Aristotle's technique for the acquisition of political knowledge presupposes that reason can distinguish essence from appearance, and actuality from potentiality. His research methodology suggests that the attainment of truth is possible, even if the process is arduous and demanding. His distinction between the activity of politics and the second order activity of political theory also illuminates a critical disjuncture between freedom, power and truth. For it acknowledges that citizens may exercise their freedom, act in good faith and use their power to institutionalize values that fall short of the achievement of the human *telos*. Within politics, freedom and the power of people to realize their shared values may eclipse truth. Political theorists who systematically investigate the nature and purposes of political life may grasp the truth about human possibility. But the possession of truth remains at a great remove from the power to institutionalize its precepts.

21

In contrast to the Aristotelian conception, twentieth-century definitions of politics have intentionally eschewed any reference to the human *telos*. Informed by empiricist assumptions, political scientists abandoned consideration of what might be in order to concentrate upon description and explanation of what is. Thus, they attempted to devise value-free definitions of politics grounded squarely upon the empirically observable. A brief examination of the definitions most frequently invoked by political scientists suggests, however, that each definition subtly structures the boundaries of the political in a thoroughly value-laden fashion.

For the first half of the twentieth century, the 'institutional definition' of politics dominated the discipline of political science. On this view, politics involves the activities of the official institutions of state (Goodnow 1904; Hyneman 1959). Established by tradition and constitution, existing governmental agencies constitute the focal point of empirical political research. Typically adopting a case-study approach, political scientists examine constitutional provisions to identify the structures of governance and the distribution of powers within those structures in particular nations. Great effort is devoted to the interpretation of specific constitutional provisions and to the historical investigation of the means by which such provisions are subtly expanded and transformed over time. This approach often tends to be heavily oriented towards law, investigating both the legislative process and the role of the courts in interpreting the law. Foreign policy is typically conceived in terms of the history of diplomacy, and domestic policy is understood in relation to the mechanisms by which governments affect the lives of citizens.

While the focus on the official institutions of state has a certain intuitive appeal, the institutional definition of politics can be faulted for sins of omission. If politics is to be understood solely in terms of the state, what can be said of those societies in which no state exists? If the constitution provides a blueprint for the operations of the state, how are states that lack constitutions to be understood? What can be known about states whose constitutions mask the real distribution of power in the nation? If governments are by definition the locus of politics, how are revolutionary movements to be classified? The institutional definition of politics provides neither a neutral nor a comprehensive account of political life. It accredits a particular mode of decision making within the nation-state by stipulative definition. In so doing, it subtly removes important activities from the realm of the political.

Concerns such as these led many scholars to reject the institutional definition of politics as underinclusive. By structuring the focus of political analysis exclusively on the institutions of state governance, this definition fails to encompass the full range of politics. It cannot account for political agents such as political bosses, political parties and pressure groups operating behind the scenes to influence political outcomes. It excludes all modes of political violence, except those perpetrated by states, from the sphere of the political. It thereby delegitimizes revolutionary activity, regardless of precipitating circumstances. And in important respects the institutional definition of politics narrowly construes the range of human freedom, identifying constitutionally designated mechanisms for social transformation as the limit of political possibility. In addition, the institutional definition of politics fails to do justice to international relations, leaving altogether unclear the political status of a realm in which there exist no binding law and no authoritative structures capable of applying sanctions to recalcitrant states.

To avoid the limitations of the institutional definition, many political scientists have argued that politics is better understood as a struggle for power (Mosca 1939; Lasswell 1950; Catlin 1964; Morgenthau 1967). Within this frame of reference, individuals participate in politics in order to pursue their own selfish advantage. The central question for political research then is 'who gets what, when, how' (Lasswell 1950). Such a research focus necessarily expands political inquiry beyond the bounds of governmental agencies, for although the official institutions of state constitute one venue for power struggles, they by no means exhaust the possibilities. Within the struggle-for-power conception, politics is ubiquitous.

In an important sense, the struggle-for-power definition of politics not only expands the sphere of political research beyond the institutions of state, it also extends political analysis beyond the realm of the empirically observable. The exercise of power often eludes direct observation and the effects of power are more easily inferred than empirically documented. Thus it is not surprising that many political researchers working with the conception of politics as power-struggle ground their investigations upon a number of contentious assumptions. Perhaps the most fundamental of these is a conception of the person as a being actuated primarily by the *libido dominandi*, the will to power. Precisely because individuals are taken to be governed by an unquenchable desire for power, politics is said to be essentially a zero-sum game in which competition is unceasing, and domination for the sake of exploitation is the chief objective. But the posited will to power, which constitutes the explanatory key to the inevitable nature of political life, is lodged deep in the human psyche – wholly unavailable for empirical observation. Although proponents of the struggle-for-power definition have claimed simply to be 'political realists', it is important to note the circularity that informs their cynical 'realism'. Politics is defined as a struggle for power 'because' human beings are driven by the *libido dominandi*; but the evidence that people are driven by the *libido dominandi* is inferred from their involvement in politics.

An unacceptable degree of circularity also infects the response of political 'realists' to their critics. Critics have objected that the struggle-for-power definition fails to explain the full range of political phenomena: If politics is merely a competition through which individuals seek to impose their selfish objectives on others, why have values such as equality, freedom and justice played such a large and recurrent role in political life? With its relentless emphasis upon the pursuit of selfish advantage, the struggle-for-power conception of politics seems unable to account for this dimension of politics. Political 'realists', such as Gaetano Mosca, have suggested that appeals to noble principles constitute various forms of propaganda disseminated to mask the oppressive character of political relations and thereby enhance the opportunities for exploitation. According to Mosca (1939), no one wants to confront the naked face of power. Political leaders do not wish to have their selfish objectives unmasked because it will make their achievement more difficult. The masses do not wish to confront their own craven natures. So rulers and followers collude in the propagation of 'political formulae' – noble phrases that accord legitimacy to regimes by masking the ruler's self-interest. Whether the appeal be to 'divine right of kings', 'liberty, fraternity and equality', or 'democracy of the people, by the people and for the people', the function of the political formula is the same: a noble lie that serves as legitimating myth. Thus political realists discount the role of substantive values in politics by unmasking them as additional manifestations of the will to power, a will that is posited and for which no independent evidence is adduced.

Although such a degree of circularity may impugn the logical adequacy of the struggle-for-power conception of politics, it does not mitigate the unsavoury consequences of the widespread dissemination of the definition by political scientists. When 'science' asserts that politics is nothing more than the struggle for power, the moral scope of political action is partially occluded. If people are convinced that politics necessarily involves the pursuit of selfish advantage, then the grounds for evaluating political regimes is severely circumscribed. In an important sense, the distinction between a good ruler (i.e. one who rules in the common interest) and a tyrant (i.e. one who rules in self-interest) ceases to have meaning. For if all politics is by definition a struggle for selfish advantage, then what distinguishes one ruler from another cannot be the divergent ends pursued by each. All that distinguishes a 'noble statesperson' from an 'ignoble oppressor' is the nature of the political formula disseminated. A 'good ruler' is simply an excellent propagandist. What distinguishes regimes is not the values pursued, but the ability of the political leaders to manipulate popular beliefs. Within the frame of cynical 'realism', it makes no sense to denounce the systematic manipulation of images as an abuse of the democratic process, for manipulation is a constant of political life. What cynical science must denounce is the illusory notion that democracy could be anything more.

Pluralists have advanced a third conception of politics that has had an enormous influence upon the discipline of political science. Devised to avoid the shortcomings of both the institutional and the struggle-for-power definitions, pluralists conceive politics as the process of interest accommodation. Unlike the cynical insistence that power is the only value pursued in politics, pluralists argue that individuals engage in politics to maximize a wide range of values. While some political actors may pursue their selfish advantage exclusively, others may seek altruistic ends such as equality, justice, an unpolluted environment, or preservation of endangered species. Without pre-emptively delimiting the range of values that might be pursued, pluralists suggest that politics is an activity through which values and interests are promoted and preserved. In contrast to the institutional definition's focus on the official agencies of government, pluralists emphasize that politics is a process of 'partisan mutual adjustment' (Lindblom 1965), a process of bargaining, negotiating, conciliation and compromise through which individuals seeking markedly different objectives arrive at decisions with which all are willing to live. On this view, politics is a moderating activity, a means of settling differences without recourse to force, a mechanism for deciding policy objectives from a competing array of alternatives (Crick 1962).

The pluralist conception of politics incorporates a number of modernist assumptions about the appropriate relation of the individual to the state. Pervaded by scepticism concerning the power of human reason to operate in the realm of values and the concomitant subjectivist assumption that, in the absence of absolute values, all value judgements must be relative to the individual, pluralists suggest that individuals must be left free to pursue their own subjectively determined ends. The goal of politics must be nothing more than the reconciliation of subjectively defined needs and interests of the individual with the requirements of society as a whole in the most freedom-maximizing fashion. Moreover, presupposing the fundamental equality of individuals, pluralists insist that the state has no business favouring the interests of any individual or group. Thus, in the absence of rational grounds for preferring any individual or value over any other, pluralists identify coalition building as the most freedom-maximizing decision principle. Politics *qua* interest accommodation is fair precisely because the outcome of any negotiating situation is a function of the consensus-garnering skill of the participants. The genius of this procedural conception of politics lies in its identification of solutions capable of winning the assent of a majority of participants in the decision process.

Pluralists have ascribed a number of virtues to their conception of politics. It avoids the excessive rationalism of paternalist conceptions of politics that assume the state knows what is in the best interests of the citizenry. It recognizes the heterogeneity of citizens and protects the rights of all to participate in the political process. It acknowledges the multiple power bases in society (for example, wealth, numbers, monopoly of scarce goods or skills) and accords each a legitimate role in collective decision making. It notes not only that interest groups must be taken into account if politics is to be adequately understood, but also that competing interests exist within the official institutions of state; that those designated to act on behalf of citizens must also be understood to act as factions, whose behaviour may be governed as much by organizational interests, partisanship, and private ambitions as by an enlightened conception of the common good.

Despite such advantages, pluralism, too, has been criticized for failing to provide a comprehensive conception of politics. In defining politics as a mechanism for decision making which constitutes an alternative to force, the interest-accommodation definition relegates war, revolution and terrorism beyond the sphere of politics. In emphasizing bargaining, conciliation and compromise as the core activities of politics, the pluralist conception assumes that all interests are essentially reconcilable. Thus it sheds little light upon some of the most intractable political issues that admit of no compromise (for example, abortion, apartheid or racism more generally, 'holy war'). Moreover, in treating all power bases as equal, pluralists tend to ignore the structural advantages afforded by wealth and political office. The notion of equal rights of participation and influence neglects the formidable powers of state and economy in determining political outcomes. In addition, the interest-accommodation definition of politics has been faulted for ethnocentrism. It mistakes certain characteristics of political activity in Western liberal democracies for the nature of politics in all times and places.

Although the pluralist conception fails to achieve a value-neutral, comprehensive definition of politics, it too has a subtle influence upon the practice of politics in the contemporary world. When accredited by social scientists as the essence of politics, the interest-accommodation conception both legitimizes the activities of competing interest groups as the fairest mechanism of policy determination and delegitimizes revolutionary action and political violence as inherently anti-political. Even in less extreme circumstances, the pluralist definition of politics may function as a self-fulfilling prophecy, severely curtailing the options available to a political community by constricting the parameters within which political questions are considered.

The pluralist conception of politics presupposes the validity of the fact/value dichotomy and the emotivist conception of values. As a version of non-cognitivism, emotivism is a meta-ethical theory which asserts that facts and values are ontologically distinct and that evaluative judgements involve questions concerning subjective emotions, sentiments or feelings rather than questions of knowledge or rational deliberation (Hudson 1970). Applied to the political realm, emotivism suggests that moral and political choices are a matter of subjective preference or irrational whim about which there can be no reasoned debate.

Although emotivism has been discredited as an altogether defective account of morality and has been repudiated by philosophers for decades, emotivism continues to be advanced as unproblematic truth by social scientists (MacIntyre 1981; Warwick 1980). And there is a good deal of evidence to suggest that 'to a large degree, people now think, talk and act as if emotivism were true' (MacIntyre 1981: 21). Promulgated in the texts of social science and incorporated in pop culture, emotivist assumptions permeate discussions of the self, freedom and social relations (Bellah *et al.* 1985). Contemporary conceptions of the self are deeply infused with emotivist and individualist premises: the 'unsituated self' who chooses an identity in isolation and on the basis of arbitrary preferences has become a cultural ideal. Freedom is conceived in terms of the unrestrained pursuit of idiosyncratic preferences in personal, economic, moral and political realms. Moral issues are understood in terms of maximizing one's preferred idiosyncratic values, and moral dilemmas are treated as strategic or technical problems related to zero-sum conditions under which the satisfaction of one preference may obstruct the satisfaction of another preference. Thus the individual *qua* moral agent becomes indistinguishable from the 'rational maximizer' hypothesized by rational choice theory. Respect for other individuals is equated with recognition of their rights to choose and to pursue their own preferences without interference. Condemnation of the immoral actions of others is supplanted by the non-judgemental response of 'walking away, if you don't like what others are doing' (Bellah *et al.* 1985: 6). Emotivism coupled with individualism encourages people to find meaning exclusively in the private sphere, thereby intensifying the privatization of the self and heightening doubts that individuals have enough in common to sustain a discussion of their interests or anxieties (Connolly 1981: 145).

Any widespread acceptance of emotivism has important ramifications for political life. At its best, emotivism engenders a relativism which strives 'to take views, outlooks and beliefs which apparently conflict and treat them in such a way that they do not conflict: each of them turns out to be acceptable in its own place' (Williams 1985: 156). The suspension of valuative judgement aims at conflict reduction by conflict avoidance. By walking away from those whose subjective preferences are different, individuals avoid unpleasant confrontations. By accepting that values are ultimately arbitrary and hence altogether beyond rational justification, citizens devise a *modus vivendi* which permits coexistence amidst diversity.

This coexistence is fragile, however, and the promise of conflict avoidance largely illusory. For the underside of emotivism is cynicism, the 'obliteration of any genuine distinction between manipulative and non-manipulative social relations' and the consequent reduction of politics to a contest of wiles and wills ultimately decided by force (MacIntyre 1981: 22, 68). Thus when intractable conflicts arise because avoidance strategies fail, they cannot be resolved through reasoned discourse, for on this view, rational discussion is simply a façade which masks arbitrary manipulation.

Thus the options for political life are reduced by definition either to the intense competition of conflicting interests depicted in the pluralist paradigm or to the resort to violence.

The political legacy of emotivism is radical privatization, the destruction of the public realm, 'the disintegration of public deliberation and discourse among members of the political community' (Dallmayr 1981: 2). For widespread acceptance of the central tenets of emotivism renders public discussion undesirable (for it might provoke violence), unnecessary (for the real outcomes of decisions will be dictated by force of will), and irrational (for nothing rational can be said in defence of arbitrary preferences). Privatization produces a world in which individuals are free to act on whim and to realize their arbitrary desires, but it is a world in which collective action is prohibited by a constellation of beliefs which render public deliberation impotent, if not impossible. The pluralist conception of politics is not the sole disseminator of emotivism in contemporary societies, but its confident proclamation of interest accommodation as the only viable mode of politics contributes to a form of public life that is markedly impoverished. That it appeals to scientific expertise to confer the 'legitimacy of fact' upon its narrow construal of political possibility should be the cause of some alarm to members of a discipline committed to value-free inquiry.

To escape problems of ethnocentrism and devise a conception of politics that encompasses the political experiences of diverse cultures and ages, in the 1960s behavioural political scientists suggested a new approach that would be both broadly comparative and thoroughly scientific. Extrapolating from organic and cybernetic analogies, both systems analysis and structural-functionalism conceived politics as a self-regulating system existing within a larger social environment and fulfilling necessary tasks for that social environment (Easton 1971; Almond and Coleman 1960; Mitchell 1958, 1967). On this view, politics involves performance of a number of functions without which society could not exist. The task of political science was to identify these critical political functions, show how they are performed in divergent cultural and social contexts, and ascertain how changes in one part of the political system affect other parts and the system as a whole so as to maintain homeostatic equilibrium. Once political inquiry had generated such a comprehensive understanding of political processes, political scientists could then provide meaningful cross-cultural explanations and predictions. The goal of the systematic cross-cultural study of politics, then, was to generate a scientific understanding of the demands made upon political systems (for example, state building, nation building, participation, redistribution), the nature of the systems' adaptive responses, including the conversion processes which operate to minimize change, and the scope of political development in terms of structural differentiation and cultural secularization which emerge when the system confronts challenges that surpass its existing capabilities.

Despite its wide popularity, this functionalist conception of politics encountered difficulties with its effort to identify the core political functions without which societies could not survive. Although scholars committed to the functionalist approach generally concurred with David Easton that the political system involves 'those actions related to the authoritative allocation of values' (Easton 1971: 143–4); they disagreed about precisely what those actions entailed. Mitchell (1958, 1967) identified four critical political functions: the authoritative specification of system goals; the authoritative mobilization of resources to implement goals; the integration of the system (centre and periphery); and the allocation of values and costs. Easton (1971), as well as Almond and Coleman (1960), offered a more expansive list including interest articulation, interest aggregation, rule making, rule application, rule adjudication, political recruitment, political socialization and political communication.

Critics noted that neither enumeration was sufficiently precise to satisfy expectations raised by the model. Neither delineated clearly between the system and its boundaries; neither specified a critical range of operation beyond which the system could be said to have ceased to function; neither explained the requirements of equilibrium maintenance with sufficient precision to sustain a distinction between functional and dysfunctional processes. In short, critics suggested that terminological vagueness and imprecision sustained the suspicion that the putative political functions were arbitrary rather than 'vital' or indispensable (Landau 1968; Gregor 1968; Stephens 1969).

In contrast to the promise of scientific certainty that accompanied the deployment of the functionalist conception of politics, critics also pointed out that the model generated no testable hypotheses, much less identified 'scientific laws' of political life. In marked contrast to the optimistic claims advanced by its proponents, critics argued that the chief virtue of the functionalist conception was heuristic: it provided an elaborate system of classification that allowed divergent political systems to be described in the same terms of reference. A common vocabulary of analysis enabled comparison of similarities and differences cross-culturally (Dowse 1966; Gregor 1968).

Additional limitations were noted by critics of the functionalist conception of politics. The model's emphasis upon system maintenance and persistence rendered it singularly incapable of charting political change. While traditional modes of political analysis classified revolutions and *coups d'état* as fundamental mechanisms of political transformation, functionalist analyses could depict such events as adaptive strategies by which the 'system' persists. Thus the systems approach blurred important issues pertaining to the character of political regimes and the significant dimensions of regime change (Groth 1970; Rothman 1971).

If functionalist analyses tended to mask political change at one level, at another level they tended to impose an inordinate uniformity upon the scope of political development. Within the functionalist literature, the pattern of development characteristic of a few Western liberal democracies such as the USA and Great Britain was taken as paradigmatic of all political development. Succumbing to a form of 'inputism', political scientists proclaimed that certain modes of economic development rendered certain political developments inevitable. The dissemination of capitalist markets would produce strains upon traditional societies, resulting in increasing demands for political participation, which would eventually culminate in the achievement of liberal democracy. Despite the clear ideological content of this projection and despite critics' cogent repudiation of the scientific pretensions of functionalism, this model of development has been repeatedly hailed by political scientists as a matter of indisputable, empirical fact. What is important to note here is not merely that political scientists operating within this tradition have mistaken the political choices of particular political communities for the universal political destiny of the species or that their beliefs about the value-neutrality of their scientific endeavour have blinded them to the hegemonic aspects of their projections, but also that political scientists have used their leverage as 'experts' to advise developing nations to adopt strategies that produce the world prophesied by political science.

While modernization theory suffered some set-backs in the 1970s and 1980s as a number of 'modernizing' democracies in Latin America and Africa were overthrown by military dictatorships, modernization theory has been reinvigorated in the 1990s under the rubric of 'democratization'. Once again political scientists are linking capitalist markets with competitive elections as the key to 'democratic consolidation'. Like earlier proponents of modernization, consultants currently offering advice on democratic consolidation assume that modern methods of capitalist production and exchange will generate modernist belief systems, including commitments to representative democracy. Participation in a competitive market economy will promote norms of instrumental rationality, universalism, and egalitarianism, which foster mobility and individual achievement, while negating hierarchies rooted in ascriptive status. The rise of individualism will in turn foster demands for increasing political participation and the emergence of multi-party electoral contests.

The assumptions of modernization and democratization theories (i.e. the process is linear, cumulative, expansive, diffuse, and fundamentally occupied with the tradition/modernity dichotomy) offer little insight into the simultaneous emergence of various forms of ethnic nationalism and fundamentalism during the 1990s. Nor do they square well with the possibility that human freedom is compatible with more than one version of modernity. Nevertheless, they do represent yet another instance of the politics of knowledge. Armed with the assumptions of this model of economic and political development, some political scientists are again reshaping the world in their own image.

Where Aristotle advanced a conception of political knowledge that preserved the distinction between the free choices of political agents in particular nations and the truth possessed by political theorists; under the guise of value-free empirical inquiry, contemporary political scientists have used scientifically accredited 'facts' to supplant political choice. Under the rubric of realism, they have recommended action to enhance the stability of regimes by minimizing 'dysfunctional' and 'destabilizing' forces such as citizen participation. Under the precept of scientific prediction, they have promoted capitalist market relations as the substance of an inevitable political development. Although implementation of such policy advice is typically justified as another example of knowledge hastening progress, there are good reasons to challenge such optimism. When the liberation/subversion dynamic surfaces in relation to knowledge accredited by contemporary political science, there is at least as great a likelihood that scientific knowledge will subvert freedom as that it will contribute to undisputed 'progress'.

Behaviouralism in political science was committed to the belief that definitions are and must be value-free, that concepts could be operationalized in a thoroughly non-prescriptive manner and that research methodologies are neutral techniques for the collection and organization of data. Behaviouralism conceived the political scientist as a passive observer who merely described and explained what exists in the political world. Post-behaviouralism challenged the myth of value-neutrality, suggesting that all research is theoretically constituted and value permeated. But, in illuminating the means by which the conviction of value-free research masked the valuative component of political inquiry, post-behaviouralism did not question the fundamental separation between events in the political world and their retrospective analysis by political scientists. In recent years, critical theorists and postmodernists have suggested that this notion of critical distance is yet another myth. Emphasizing that every scientific discourse is productive, generating positive effects within its investigative domain, postmodernists caution that political science must also be understood as a productive force which creates a world in its own image, even as it employs conceptions of passivity, neutrality, detachment and objectivity to disguise and conceal its role (Foucault 1973, 1979). Even a cursory examination of the four allegedly value-neutral definitions of politics that have dominated twentieth-century political science suggests that there are good reasons to treat the postmodernists' cautions seriously. For each definition not only construes the political world differently, but also acts subtly to promote specific modes of political life.

Implications: the structure of the encyclopedia

If post-positivist conceptions of knowledge and science, as well as postmodernist cautions concerning the productive effects of disciplinary practices are to be taken seriously, then an encyclopedia produced in the twenty-first century must differ in important respects from its predecessors. The attempt to provide an overview of the main topics investigated within the subfields of the discipline must be matched by a strategy that allows questions concerning the constitutive components of political research to surface. Rather than succumb to myths of value-neutrality, the analysis of each topic must attempt to illuminate the substantive implications of diverse methodologies. Rather than accredit the notion of an unproblematic scientific objectivity, efforts must be made to explicate and assess the standards that inform disciplinary judgements.

Toward these ends, this encyclopedia has recruited contributors committed to a wide range of methodological approaches. Each author has been asked to provide a concise critical analysis, rather than a descriptive capsule sketch, of the topic under investigation. In particular, authors have been asked to address methodological as well as substantive issues pertaining to the subject, engaging relevant debates concerning the strengths and weaknesses of alternative research strategies and differentiating fruitful from flawed approaches.

This encyclopedia is organized by subfield. Rather than seeking methodological uniformity within each subfield, efforts have been made to recruit scholars who adopt contending approaches to related topics in the hope that the juxtaposition of competing accounts will help illuminate the theoretical presuppositions and the political implications of alternative modes of inquiry. The inclusion of alternative approaches is thus designed to enrich the portrayal of political life, to heighten understanding of the limitations of particular approaches and to increase the analytical sophistication of readers.

Structuring this encyclopedia along these lines involves a number of dangers. In attempting to provide a systematic account of the state of political studies that includes political theory, contemporary ideologies, comparative political institutions, processes and behaviour, political cleavages within the nation-state, theories of policy-making, comparative examination of a range of substantive policy areas, as well as international relations and major issues confronting the contemporary world, the encyclopedia faces the formidable danger that it will fail to provide a comprehensive and comprehensible account of such a broad array of topics. In adopting a strategy that challenges the empiricist foundation that sustains the bulk of research in contemporary political science, the volume confronts the possibility of dismissal concomitant to any effort to challenge established traditions and entrenched power, for the behaviouralists who continue to dominate the discipline of political science may choose to ignore rather than engage sustained critique. Moreover, in advancing a conception of political science that supplants claims to transcendent truth with recognition of the far more fallible foundations of human cognition, the project risks rejection by those who prefer a more heroic, albeit fictive, depiction of the discipline's authority. Such risks are as unavoidable as they are rife.

The production of the second edition of this encyclopedia, however, also affords a number of opportunities. It provides an occasion for a systematic stocktaking – for a review of the substantive research findings generated within the discipline, for a reassessment of the role of diverse analytical techniques in shaping those substantive claims, and, more generally, for an examination of the theoretical underpinnings of political inquiry. It invites a re-evaluation of the relations between knowledge and power within disciplinary discourses. It encourages renewed investigation of the extent to which solutions to the problems confronting contemporary politics are constrained by outmoded and unwarranted disciplinary assumptions. In so doing, the encyclopedia will stimulate creative thinking about the world captured in the discourses of political science. The extent to which the encyclopedia contributes to this end will be the ultimate measure of its utility.

References

Almond, G. and Coleman, J. (eds) (1960) *The Politics of Developing Areas*, Princeton: Princeton University Press.

Aristotle (1958) *The Politics*, trans. and ed. E. Barker, Oxford: Oxford University Press.

Ayer, A. J. (ed.) (1959) *Logical Positivism*, New York: Free Press.

Bellah, R., Madsen, R., Sullivan, W., Swidler, A. and Tipton, S. (1985) *Habits of the Heart: Individualism and Commitments in American Life*, New York: Harper & Row.

Bernstein, R. (1978) *The Restructuring of Social and Political Theory*, Philadelphia: University of Pennsylvania Press.

—— (1983) *Beyond Objectivism and Relativism*, Philadelphia: University of Pennsylvania Press.

Blyth, M. and Varghese, R. (1999) 'The State of the Discipline in American Political Science: Be Careful What you Wish For', *British Journal of Politics and International Relations* 1(3): 345–65.

Brown, H. (1977) *Perception, Theory and Commitment: The New Philosophy of Science*, Chicago: Precedent Publishing Company.

Brown, R. H. (1998) 'Modern science and its critics: toward a post-positivist legitimization of science', *New Literary History* 29(3): 521–50.

Catlin, G. (1964) *The Science and Method of Politics*, New York: Archon Press.

Churchland, P. M. and Hooker, C. (1985) *Images of Science*, Chicago: University of Chicago Press.

Connolly, W. E. (1981) *Appearance and Reality in Politics*, Cambridge: Cambridge University Press.

Cook, T. (1985) 'Postpositivist critical multiplism', in R. Shotland and M. Marks (eds) *Social Science and Social Policy*, Beverly Hills: Sage Publications.

Crick, B. (1962) *In Defence of Politics*, London: Weidenfeld & Nicolson.

Dallmayr, F. (1981) *Beyond Dogma and Despair*, Notre Dame: University of Notre Dame Press.

Diderot, D. *et al.* (1751–65) *Encyclopédie, ou dictionnaire raisonné des sciences, des arts et des métiers, par une société de gens de lettres*, 17 vols, Paris: Le Breton, Briasson, David & Durand.

Dowse, R. (1966) 'A functionalist's logic', *World Politics* (July): 607–22.

Easton, D. (1971) *The Political System: An Inquiry into the State of Political Science*, 2nd edn, New York: Knopf.

Encyclopédie méthodique ou bibliothèque universelle de toutes les connaissances humaines, Paris: Panckoucke, 1782–94; Agasse, 1794–1820.

Eulau, H. (1963) *The Behavioral Persuasion in Politics*, New York: Random House.

Eulau, H. and March, J. (eds) (1969) *Political Science*, Englewood Cliffs, NJ: Prentice-Hall.

Finifter, A. W. (ed.) (1983) *Political Science: The State of the Discipline*, Washington, DC: American Political Science Association.

Foucault, M. (1973) *The Order of Things: An Archaeology of the Human Sciences*, New York: Vintage Books.

—— (1979) *Discipline and Punish: The Birth of the Prison*, New York: Vintage Books.

Glymour, C. (1980) *Theory and Evidence*, Princeton: Princeton University Press.

Goodnow, F. (1904) 'The work of the American Political Science Association', *Proceedings of the American Political Science Association* 1: 37.

Greenstein, F. and Polsby, N. (eds) (1975) *Handbook of Political Science*, vols I–VII, Reading, MA: Addison-Wesley.

Gregor, A. J. (1968) 'Political science and the use of functionalist analysis', *American Political Science Review* (June): 425–39.

Groth, A. J. (1970) 'Structural functionalism and political development: three problems', *Western Political Quarterly* (September): 485–99.

Gunnell, J. (1986) *Between Philosophy and Politics*, Amherst: University of Massachusetts Press.

—— (1995) 'Realizing theory: the philosophy of science revisited', *The Journal of Politics* 57(4): 923–40.

—— (1998) *The Orders of Discourse: Philosophy, Social Science and Politics*, Lanham, MD: Rowman and Littlefield.

Harding, S. (1986) *The Science Question in Feminism*, Ithaca: Cornell University Press.

Harre, R. (1986) *Varieties of Realism*, Oxford: Basil Blackwell.

Hawkesworth, M. E. (1988) *Theoretical Issues in Policy Analysis*, Albany, NY: SUNY Press.

Hesse, M. (1980) *Revolutions and Reconstructions in the Philosophy of Science*, Brighton: Harvester Press.

Hudson, W. D. (1970) *Modern Moral Philosophy*, New York: Anchor Books.

Hume, D. (1739) *A Treatise of Human Nature*, ed. L. A. Selby-Bigge, Oxford: Clarendon Press.

—— (1748) *An Enquiry Concerning Human Understanding*, ed. L. A. Selby-Bigge, Oxford: Clarendon Press.

Humphreys, W. (ed.) (1969) *Perception and Discovery*, San Francisco: Freeman, Cooper.

Hyneman, C. (1959) *The Study of Politics*, Urbana: University of Illinois Press.

Joergenson, J. (1951) *The Development of Logical Empiricism*, vol. II, no. 9 of the *International Encyclopedia of Unified Science*, Chicago: University of Chicago Press.

Kaplan, A. (1964) *The Conduct of Inquiry: Methodology for Behavioral Science*, San Francisco: Chandler Publishing.

King, G., Keohane, R. and Verba, S. (1994) *Designing Social Inquiry: Scientific Inference in Qualitative Research*, Princeton: Princeton University Press.

Kraft, V. (1952) *The Vienna Circle*, New York: Philosophical Library.

Landau, M. (1968) 'On the use of functional analysis in American political science', *Social Research* (Spring): 44–75.

Lasswell, H. (1950) *Politics: Who Gets What, When, How*, New York: P. Smith.

Laudan, L. (1990) *Science and Relativism*, Chicago: University of Chicago Press.

Lindblom, C. (1965) *The Intelligence of Democracy: Decision-Making Through Mutual Adjustment*, New York: Free Press.

Lindblom, C. and Cohen, D. (1979) *Usable Knowledge: Social Science and Social Problem Solving*, New Haven: Yale University Press.

Longino, H. (1990) *Science As Social Knowledge: Values and Objectivity in Scientific Inquiry*, Princeton: Princeton University Press.

Lough, J. (1968) *Essays on the Encyclopédie of Diderot and D'Alembert*, London: Oxford University Press.

MacIntyre, A. (1981) *After Virtue*, Notre Dame: University of Notre Dame Press.

MacRae, D. (1976) *The Social Function of Social Science*, New Haven: Yale University Press.

Meehan, E. (1965) *The Theory and Method of Political Analysis*, Homewood, IL: Dorsey Press.

Miller, E. (1979) 'Metaphor and political knowledge', *American Political Science Review* 73 (1): 155–70.

Miller, R. (1987) *Fact and Method*, Princeton: Princeton University Press.

Mitchell, W. C. (1958) 'The polity and society: a structural functional analysis', *Midwest Journal of Political Science* 2: 403–40.

—— (1967) *Sociological Analysis and Politics*, Englewood Cliffs, NJ: Prentice-Hall.

Moon, D. (1975) 'The logic of political inquiry: a synthesis of opposed perspectives', in F. Greenstein and N. Polsby (eds) *Handbook of Political Science*, vol. 1, Reading, MA: Addison-Wesley.

Moore, G. E. (1903) *Principia Ethica*, London: Cambridge University Press.

Morgenthau, H. (1967) *Politics Among Nations: The Struggle for Power and Peace*, NewYork: Knopf.

Mosca, G. (1939) *The Ruling Class*, New York: McGraw-Hill.

Murray, T. (1983) 'Partial knowledge', in D. Callahan and B. Jennings (eds) *Ethics, The Social Sciences and Policy Analysis*, New York: Plenum Press.

Newton-Smith, W. (1981) *The Rationality of Science*, London: Routledge.

Polanyi, M. (1958) *Personal Knowledge*, Chicago: University of Chicago Press.

Popper, K. (1959) *The Logic of Scientific Discovery*, New York: Basic Books.

—— (1972a) *Conjectures and Refutations: The Growth of Scientific Knowledge*, 4th edn rev., London: Routledge & Kegan Paul.

—— (1972b) *Objective Knowledge: An Evolutionary Approach*, Oxford: Clarendon Press.

Ricci, D. (1984) *The Tragedy of Political Science: Politics, Scholarship and Democracy*, New Haven: Yale University Press.

Putnam, H. (1981) *Reason, Truth and History*, Cambridge: Cambridge University Press.

—— (1983) *Realism and Reason*, Cambridge: Cambridge University Press.

—— (1988) *Representation and Reality*, Cambridge: MIT Press.

—— (1990) *Realism with a Human Face*, Cambridge: Harvard University Press.

Rothman, S. (1971) 'Functionalism and its critics: an analysis of the writings of Gabriel Almond', *Political Science Reviewer* (Fall): 236–76.

Seidelman, R. and Harpham, E. (1985) *Disenchanted Realists: Political Science and the American Crisis, 1884–1984*, Albany, NY: SUNY Press.

Sellars, W. (1963) *Science, Perception and Reality*, New York: Humanities Press.

Stephens, J. (1969) 'The logic of functional and systems analyses in political science', *Midwest Journal of Political Science* (August): 367–94.

Stockman, N. (1983) *Anti-Positivist Theories of Science: Critical Rationalism, Critical Theory and Scientific Realism*, Dordrecht: D. Reidel.

Storing, H. J. (ed.) (1962) *Essays on the Scientific Study of Politics*, New York: Holt, Rinehart & Winston.

Suppe, F. (ed.) (1977) *The Structure of Scientific Theories*, 2nd edn, Urbana: University of Illinois Press.

Tanenhaus, J. and Somit, A. (1967) *The Development of Political Science: From Burgess to Behavioralism*, Boston: Allyn & Bacon.

van Fraasen, B. (1980) *The Scientific Image*, Oxford: Oxford University Press.

Vivas, E. (1960) 'Science and the studies of man', in H. Schoek and J. Wiggans (eds) *Scientism and Values*, Princeton: D. van Nostrand Company.

Wade, I. (1977) *The Structure and Form of the French Enlightenment*, 2 vols, Princeton: Princeton University Press.

Warwick, D. (1980) *The Teaching of Ethics in the Social Sciences*, Hastings-on-Hudson, NY: Institute of Society, Ethics and the Life Sciences.

Welsh, W. (1973) *Studying Politics*, New York: Praeger.

Wildavsky, A. (1979) *Speaking Truth to Power*, Boston: Little, Brown & Co.

Williams, B. (1985) *Ethics and the Limits of Philosophy*, Cambridge, MA: Harvard University Press.

Wolin, S. (1981) 'Max Weber: legitimation, method and the politics of theory', *Political Theory* 9 (3): 401–24.

PART II

POLITICAL THEORY
Central concepts

2

CONCEPTIONS OF THE STATE

Andrew Vincent

The state is one of the most difficult concepts in politics. For some scholars the discipline of politics is wholly concerned with the state; for others politics exists in social contexts outside the sphere of the state. One of the most intractable problems in such debates is that there is little agreement on what is being studied. Is the state a body of governing institutions; a structure of legal rules; a subspecies of society; or a body of values and beliefs about civil existence? These and many other questions plague the study of the state. This chapter will first look at the origin of the word; then at the state's problematic relation to other political concepts; the contending views of its history and its entry into the academic vocabulary; the diversity of theoretical approaches to it; and finally, arguments concerning its demise.

The word state derives from the Latin *stare* (to stand) and *status* (a standing or condition). Roman writers, such as Cicero and Ulpian, as well as later medieval lawyers, used such terms as *status civitatis* or *status regni*. This use of *status* referred to the condition of the ruler, the fact of possessing stability, or the elements necessary for stability. Standing or status was usually acquired through family, sex, profession and most importantly property. This is where we also find the subtle linkage with the word 'estate'. The English word 'state' is, in fact, a contraction of the word 'estate'. This is similar to the old French word *estat* and modern French *état*, both of which can imply a profession or social status. Groups had different status and thus estate. The term 'estates of the realm' is derived from this. The highest estate, with property, rank and family, was usually the ruling group or person. The highest estate had potentially the greatest authority and power. Such authority was often seen as the guarantee of order and public welfare. It was thus linked to stability, which derived from the same root term. Those in authority – the highest estate – had insignia, crests and so forth illustrating their stateliness or status.

Some argue that we can find an awareness of the state, in the above usage, in the twelfth century (Post 1964; Mitteis 1975; Black 1993). A popular line of interpretation stresses a more definite noun usage in which the state is understood as a 'public power' above both ruler and ruled, which constitutes the locus of political and legal authority. It is not simply a matter of standing, stability or stateliness, although this terminology is carried over into the more modern usage, but a definite new form of continuous public power which constitutes a new type of civil existence (see Vincent

1987; Skinner 1989). There are two basic positions taken on this latter noun usage of state. Both identify the origin of the state in the sixteenth century; whereas one sees Machiavelli as the prime mover (Cassirer 1946; Meinecke 1957), the other identifies heirs of Italian humanism in France, such as Guillaume Budé, Bernard du Haillan and Jean Bodin, as the real formulators of the modern idea (Hexter 1973; Church 1972; Skinner 1978; Dyson 1980).

There are a number of formal characteristics intrinsic to the state. It has a geographically identifiable territory with a body of citizens. It claims authority over all citizens and groups within its boundaries and embodies more comprehensive aims than other associations. The authority of the state is legal in character and is usually seen as the source of law. It is based on procedural rules which have more general recognition in society than other rules. The procedures of states are operated by trained bureaucracies of office holders. The state also embodies the maximal control of resources and force within a territory. Its monopoly is not simply premised on force; most states try to claim legitimacy for such a monopoly, namely, they seek some recognition and acceptance from the population. In consequence, to be a member of a state implies a specific civil disposition. Further, the state is seen as sovereign, both in an internal sense within its territory, and in an external sense, namely, the state is recognized by other states as an equal member of international society. Finally, the state is a continuous public power distinct from rulers and ruled.

The state stands in a complex relation to a number of political concepts such as society, community, sovereignty and government. Many of these concepts have senses which coincide with particular views of the state. The state can, for example, be said to create all associations within itself. In this sense, nothing is distinct from the state. Society becomes an aspect of the state. On the other hand, if sovereignty is regarded as popular, residing in the people who create the state for limited ends, then the position is reversed and society can be viewed as prior and independent of the state. Similarly, the state can be seen as synonymous with government or separate from government and giving authority to it. These issues present the student of politics with intractable problems of interpretation.

Essentially there are three general perspectives on the historical origin of the state. The first argues that the state idea dates back to the early Greek *polis* (city-state) of around 500 BC. For Aristotle, political science was the study of the *polis*. There were unquestionably conceptions of territory, citizenship, authority and law entailed in the *polis*, however, there was no conception of separate powers of government, no conception of a separate civil society and no very precise idea of a legal constitution. Furthermore, the life of the *polis* was often deeply integrated with religious, artistic, and ethical practices. It was also on such a small scale, compared to modern states, that, overall, it is stretching the imagination to call it a state in any contemporary sense. Empires, despite statelike features, are also too loose and fragmented structures to call states.

The second perspective dates the state from the early Middle Ages. Roman and canon law had established ideas of a transcendent public welfare. Public power and law were associated with the office of the sovereign, initially identified with Papal sovereignty. There were also concepts of citizenship and the rule of law in medieval political thought. The problems with this view are, first, etymological, namely, can one argue seriously about a word where it does not exist? The word state does not appear in political parlance until approximately the sixteenth century, although some would argue that the practices of state long precede the word (see Black 1993). Second, the feudal structure of the Middle Ages tended to have a fragmenting effect. Feudal life was made up of a massive subsystem of associations. Many of the larger associations, the nobility, church and guilds, had their own laws and courts. Monarchy was not in a pre-eminently sovereign position. It was often regarded as an elective office and not necessarily hereditary. The monarchs also relied heavily on the support of the nobility and other estates to help them rule. Medieval society was criss-crossed with overlapping associations and conflicting loyalties. Monarchs were reliant on the community of the realm and consequently were often regarded as subject to the law, not as its source. Finally, it is difficult to identify clearly defined territorial units with consistently loyal populations in the Middle Ages. The only loyalty that transcended local groups attachments was the Church. All were members of the *respublica christiana*. It was crucial for this vision to break down before the idea of independent political units could grow.

The third perspective dates the emergence of the state from the late Middle Ages and more specifically from the sixteenth century. This view finds support from the etymology. It is a view shared by a number of more recent authorities. However, there is still some debate as to which theorists introduced the idea (Machiavelli or Bodin), and when and where the practice of the modern state began. The contending authorities, as discussed earlier, focus their attention, respectively, on Renaissance Italy and France under the early absolutist monarchs.

Before discussing the distinct academic approaches to the state, it is important to examine briefly the actual entry of the 'concept of the state' into the academic vocabulary. Oddly, it only figures as a central concept of *academic* discussion in the later nineteenth century. There are internal and external reasons for the 'state focus' in disciplines such as political studies, history, sociology, legal and political theory during this period.

Externally, there was a symbiosis between the expansion of nation states in the nineteenth and early twentieth centuries and the concentration on the concept of the state in academic studies. Thus, in historical terms, for example, Italy was only unified as a state in 1861 and Germany in 1871. The USA was searching for a secure sense of identity throughout the nineteenth century, especially after the enormous upheaval of the civil war in the 1860s. Overall, the nineteenth and twentieth centuries encompassed a period of accelerated state-making, the enthused formation and promulgation of nationalisms, often through the development of public education systems, and the widespread creation and application of state constitutions. The language of the state was also embodied in calls for both sovereignty and self-determination – a call which increased throughout the twentieth century, especially in the period of post-1945 decolonization. The fact that the discipline of politics grew within the universities of most developing modern states during the late nineteenth and twentieth centuries, and that the initial primary focus of political studies was the concept of the state, is not fortuitous.

The 'state focus' of disciplines was also tied to educational imperatives. To focus on the state was not only to learn about the history of institutions, but was also to be inculcated with national sentiment. This was essentially embodied in the idea of citizen education. Further, with the growth of the state sector in the nineteenth and twentieth century, there was a perception of the need for trained personnel to fulfil the growing requirements of the public services. In addition, many of those who entered into the teaching and promulgation of political studies in universities were themselves often committed to the idea of the 'public service' state. To train the new recruits for state bureaucracies to carry out specialized research for governments and to be able to affect subtly the direction of governmental thinking, via institutional design, were seen as desirable aims by many in the discipline. There has therefore often been a close and productive relation in countries like France, Norway and Germany between the state and academic elites. In France, this had always been manifest in the *Grandes Écoles* tradition, and, in terms of the discipline of politics, in the original *École Libre des Sciences Politiques de France*. The same idea developed in Britain, in the early 1900s, with the setting up of the London School of Economics and Political Science, although the relation of academic and state elites has been much more fragmentary and unstructured in the context of the United Kingdom.

Having examined the main outline of its historical origin and its entry into academic vocabulary we will now turn briefly to the academic approaches to the study of the state and their respective merits. Essentially there are five approaches which often overlap. They are:

1 juristic or legal;
2 historical;
3 sociological/anthropological;
4 philosophical/normative;
5 political-scientific.

The legal approach has the oldest pedigree. It dates back to the use of Roman law vocabulary in the earliest descriptions of the state. Words like power, authority and legitimacy, when used in relation to the state from the sixteenth century, had deep roots in Roman law. The early critiques of feudal rule, initially by Papal lawyers, derived from Roman law sources (see Black 1993; Vincent 1987). These formed the background for notions of authority and law focused on centralized rule. However, the temptation to characterize the state as a hierarchical body of legal rules, linked by some sovereign authority, can be found in many theorists in the twentieth century (Kelsen 1945; Hart 1961). In fact, the intellectual tradition of legal positivism shows a marked preference for this form of interpretation. Others find this approach too limiting. They contend that there are many more factors that enter into the definition and character of the state than simply a hierarchy of legal rules.

Many historians have written detailed studies of the development of the state (Strayer 1970; Shennan 1974; Anderson 1974; Hall 1986). Some lay more emphasis on the factors which are connected to the rise of the state, as in the growth of Renaissance city-states, the Reformation, the breakup of the Holy Roman Empire, the growth of centralized salaried bureaucracies, standing armies, centralized taxation, or dynastic and religious wars (see Tilly 1975). Others emphasize the history of certain ideas accompanying the events in state growth (Skinner 1978). For many historians, the practice of the state is much more messy and haphazard than legal or philosophical theories would lead us to believe. Theory alone is too simple and abbreviated to catch all the diverse interests and pressures which accompanied state growth. The weakness of the historical approach is that the state is not just an empirical entity which can be grasped by examining historical events. Statehood involves, from its earliest manifestations in the European political vocabulary, complex and rich theories of civil and political existence. To neglect such a dimension of the state impoverishes our understanding.

Sociologists and anthropologists have tended to view the state as a way of organizing society, one that is found in certain more developed economies. In other words, 'state societies' are a subspecies of the genus of society (see Lowie 1927; Krader 1968). Another way of putting this is that the state is a subspecies of government. State organization is one form in which humans have organized their social existence. Sociologists, such as Durkheim, Duguit, Weber and MacIver, largely viewed the state in this manner. The state was explained through the broader study of the concept of society – a point later echoed in pluralist political science.

One of the difficulties in summarizing this sociological approach is that it encompasses such a diverse range of theories, whether it be Durkheim's positivism, Marxist political economy, Talcott Parsons's functionalism, or the more recent debates in historical and political sociology (Poggi 1978; Badie and Birnbaum 1983; Mann 1990). On a very general level, this approach stresses the economic and social preconditions of states, the types of states and what causes them to appear, and the factors giving rise to the responsiveness, durability and decline of states. Talcott Parsons, for example, saw the state as a unique product of the division of labour in advanced industrial societies (Parsons 1967). Specialized organizations developed in relation to this division of labour and became centred on the state. The state thus implied a certain level of industrialization. It could therefore be described as a collection of specialized agencies associated with the division of labour in advanced industrialized societies. Its function was to mediate and reduce conflict and tension between the different sectors of society.

The philosophical/normative conception of the state constitutes the main element of classical political theory, specifically from the sixteenth century onwards. Classical political theory is concerned with reflection on issues such as human nature, morality, the family and forms of constitution. It has two preeminent tasks with regard to the state: the first is to reflect on the right, best or most just order; the second is concerned with the identity of the state itself, which is intricately bound up with the values and ideas concerning civil existence. The problem with many historical and empirical theories of the state is that they usually take the identity of the state as either given or unproblematic. Classical political theory has never taken the state for granted. However, it has sometimes been in danger of losing touch with the empirical reality of the state and giving an overly abstract impression of its character.

We are often so accustomed to perceiving the state as a form of government or set of institutions that it is difficult to think of it in relation to a broader framework of normative commitments. For many normative theorists, the state concept is to be understood both as a body of values and as partly constitutive of political reality. The state forms, in other words, the ideal presupposition for any civilized life. It thus embodies a sense of the right social order within which citizens can be integrated. There are though a diversity of normative theories of the state (Dyson 1980; Vincent

1987; Hoffman 1995; Bartelson 2001). The present classification of normative theories will be:

1   absolutist;
2   constitutional;
3   ethical;
4   pluralist.

The first important landmark in normative theory was the attempt to see the state as embodied in the absolute sovereign person. This was an idea developed in the works of Bodin, Hobbes and Bossuet and in the actual practice of monarchs like Louis XIV. It can be found from the early sixteenth century onwards, initially in France. At its height, the sovereign person was seen to be characterized by divine right and ownership of the kingdom (Rowen 1980). The sovereign's interests were, in effect, the state's interests. The embodiment of the state in the sovereign illustrates the continued importance of sovereignty in the history of the state. The impersonal state of the twentieth century finds its root in the personal state of the sixteenth century. The weakness of the absolutist theory was that it was too focused on the institution and practice of absolute sovereignty which was, in practice, an absurdity. It is also doubtful that it ever existed fully in practice. It was rather an abstract legal doctrine. Limitations on sovereign power existed throughout the absolutist era. It was also often dependent on the character of the sovereign person and the economic and political circumstances of the kingdom. However, it still provided a lasting vocabulary for the discussion of the state.

The constitutional theory encapsulates the longest, most influential, and yet most tangled state idea. Essentially this theory identifies the state with a complex of institutional structures and values which, through historical, legal, moral and philosophical claims, embodies limitation and diversification of authority and a complex hierarchy of rules and norms, which, in turn, act to institutionalize power and regulate the relations between citizens, laws and political institutions. The deep roots of this theory lie in Roman law and the ideas and practices of late medieval Europe. The limitations of the constitutional theory are not imposed *on* the state, but are rather constitutive of a particular theory of the state. The priority of certain rules within the constitutional theory is premised on their seriousness. All limitation is therefore self-limitation by the state.

By the nineteenth century, constitutionalism had become most closely associated with liberalism and liberal democracy, although its origins are occasionally dated back to theorists like John Locke. Other ideologies, such as conservatism and parliamentary socialism, have also found a comfortable home within the constitutional theory. The forms of limitations employed within constitutional theories have also varied enormously, ranging across legal and historical themes, such as the ancient constitution doctrine, fundamental and common law, the rule of law, legal conventions, written documents, bills of rights; institutional devices, such as the mixed and balanced constitution, the doctrine of checks and balances, the separation of powers, or federalism; complex political and moral devices such as representative democracy, the separation between state and society, contractualism, natural and human rights doctrines, consent theories, and so forth. It would be no exaggeration to say that the agenda of much contemporary Western political theory is rooted in the constitutional state framework. The weakness of the constitutional theory is its success. Everyone is or wants to be a constitutionalist. This has led paradoxically to its trivialization. Constitutionalism can become just a series of formal procedural devices without normative significance. In addition, there has been considerable internal conflict within liberal democratic constitutionalism over the reach of the state. Some, for example, have been keen to limit its role in the economy, others to deny such limitations and to argue for a strong developmental role for the state. This latter argument has given rise to a debate between minimal and developmental state theories (see Marquand 1988).

A third normative theory has roots in the more total life of the Greek *polis*. It developed in the context of the German idealist tradition, against the backdrop of the French revolution (Hegel 1967; Vincent 1987: ch. 4). The ethical state is seen to be the result of a long historical development from the Greeks. It is not an accidental phenomenon, but rather is seen to develop out of the inner nature of humans as rational creatures. The state and citizens are seen to have a common rational substance. The state is the *modus operandi* of both citizens and institutions. It is still rooted in a constitutionalist setting, but with the crucial difference that it is directed at the maximal ethical self-development and positive freedom of its citizens. It is thus the unity of a cognitive disposition with the purposes of institutional structures and rules. The state embodies the rational customs and laws which rule individual action. The state is therefore not just a system of laws or institutions, rather it represents a rational ethical order implicit in the consciousness of individual citizens. The weaknesses of this theory are its apparent archaism and inappropriateness to the contemporary world. The idea of an ethical state (with an overarching ethical code or general will) strikes most students of politics as suspect and potentially autocratic. However, it had undeniably a key role to play in the reassessment of the state at the beginning of the twentieth century (see Vincent and Plant 1984).

The normative pluralist theory perceived the state, in the broadest sense, to be a synthesis of living groups (see Gierke 1934; Maitland 1911; Figgis 1914; Hsiao 1927; Nicholls 1975; Vincent 1987; Bartelson 2001). Groups are integrated not absorbed in the state. Narrowly focused, pluralism centres on the state as the summation of group life. It denotes all groups in totality. In representing the whole, it is distinct from all other groups. The state, as the representation of the total system of groups, prevents injustices being committed by individuals or groups, secures basic rights and regulates group behaviour. The pluralist state is not sovereign (in any conventional sense), partly because it is constituted by groups whose independence is recognized within the idea of the state. For some pluralists groups possess legal personality and only such a conception of group life can defend liberty. The weakness of the pluralist theory is that it never resolved the relation of government to groups. There is also a certain naïveté about the nature of groups. Groups can be oppressive and restrictive on liberty. Also, how can any consensus really be formed in such a society when it is peopled by such diverse interests? Pluralists fail to answer these questions.

Turning now to the political science conception of the state. The term political science was an open concept in the early 1900s, incorporating normative, empirical and historical elements. Initially, the state idea satisfied 'strategic' demands for disciplinary consolidation and provided a 'creative' leverage for academic inquiry. Strategically, the state idea provided political science with a ready-made subject matter. Thus, where economics had become progressively more technical, law validated a powerful public profession, and history had become more specialized, political science needed its own unique field of study. The state provided this uniqueness (see Collini *et al.* 1983). Creatively, the state became the linchpin for the whole narrative sequence underpinning classical political theory. The Greek *polis* was easily transposed into the 'state'. Political science was therefore 'summed up' in the science of the state.

Initial interest in the state became integral to the 'institutionalist perspective' of political science. The institutional approach, in its most direct sense, identified the function of political study as articulating the meaning of the state. The word that most adequately describes this theme is the German term *Staatslehre*. The origin of this idea can be found in philosophers such as G.W.F. Hegel and J.G. Fichte, in their various *Rechtsphilosophie*. It reached its academic zenith in nineteenth-century juristic writers in Germany, such as Otto von Gierke, George Jellinek and Johann Bluntschli. *Staatslehre* meant that to learn about politics one had to learn about the state, and to learn about the state meant both empirical and normative investigation. This was the first serious form in which the term political science was understood in both Europe, Britain and North America. The state was thus an opportune 'linking concept' for this understanding of political science.

This institutionalist approach fell into serious decline during the 1930s. The empirical dimension began to take priority. This priority reflected, to some degree, a growing commitment to 'scientism', specifically with the 1950s' behavioural revolution in the work of political scientists such as David Easton (Easton 1965; Farr and Seidelman 1993; Monroe 1997). Empirical theory was seen as the key to the future advancement of the subject. The state was increasingly viewed as social object to be explained via economic and social causation. Much twentieth-century literature on comparative politics developed along these lines. However, one should be careful of simply equating the decline of the normative and historical state idea with the rise of a more empiricist or behavioural approach. The idea of the state was still important to some political scientists well into the 1950s. Second, the state idea never fell into quite the same decline in Britain and Europe as in North America.

As a consequence of the withering of the normative component, the descriptive view of state theory expanded and diversified into a range of empirically orientated approaches during the 1960s. The most well known are: pluralism and neo-pluralism; elite theory; corporatism and neo-corporatism; various types of Marxism; and forms of political economy, particularly public or rational choice theory (Dunleavy and O'Leary 1987). Empirical pluralists and neo-pluralists view society as constituted by groups and the state as virtually synonymous with government, which is a target or location for pressure or interest group activity. Power is about the resources that groups can command in the competitive market. For some, government reflects the dominant coalition on a particular policy (Latham 1965). Other pluralists see government as an impartial umpire or neutral arbiter; this is reflected in Robert Dahl's account of polyarchy (Dahl 1971). Most pluralists incorporate a theory of democracy, viewed as a form of interest articulation and market competition. Such a notion of democracy is seen as more realistic than the older classical normative notions of democracy. For pluralists, such as Dahl and Schumpeter, democracy is concerned with the competition between groups and the selection of leaders (Schumpeter 1943). The successful group(s), from the electoral process, formulate policy through government functionaries.

Early elite theorists, such as Mosca, Pareto and Michels, argued that all societies are dominated by small minorities, a thesis most cogently encapsulated in Michels's 'iron law of oligarchy' (Michels 1959). Regardless of the type of regime, they asserted the continuity of elites in politics, maintaining that this was an empirically verifiable fact. This contrasted sharply with the pluralist vision of government. However, later elite theories were dominated by the attempt to integrate elitism and pluralism, giving rise to the term 'democratic elitism' (Bachrach 1967). The empirical studies of elite theorists concentrated on the small groups that influence and structure policy, examining the social background, recruitment and attitudes of such groups. States can thus be categorized according to the nature, unity, and diversity of elites.

Corporatist theories are, at the present moment, still in considerable flux. Some corporatists use the term state as a synonym for government; for others it represents the fusion of certain important interests into the structure of government (Schmitter 1974). In this sense, corporatism is differentiated from pluralism by the more limited number of groups competing, the nature of the groups and their status in relation to government. In Cawson's classification there are three main forms of corporatism in contemporary political science: (1) a totally new form of economy, different from capitalism and socialism; (2) a form of state within the capitalist society; and (3) a way in which interests are organized and interact with the state (Cawson 1986: 22).

In Marxism the state is related historically to certain class interests, the defence of private property and capital accumulation. The state has developed apace with capitalist economies. Two views, however, have tended to dominate Marxist thinking on the state to the present day. The first sees the state as an oppressive or coercive instrument of the dominant bourgeoisie, holding capitalism in place. This class state will either be crushed or wither away after revolution and be replaced either by the dictatorship of the proletariat or by communism. The second view (most dynamically influenced by the writings of the Italian Marxist Gramsci) is that the state is seen to have relative autonomy from the economic base and acts as a site of conflict between competing class interests. Also, in this second account, state dominance is exerted subtly through ideological hegemony (Carnoy 1984; Jessop 1983 and 1990; Miliband 1973).

Finally, the economistic approach to the state embeds it in individual choice theory, which is rooted in methodological individualism. The state basically emerges from the logic of self-interested individual choice – a clear example being public choice theory (Buchanan 1975). A resonant argument can also be found, in a very different intellectual format, in libertarian writings (Nozick 1974; Anthony de Jasay 1985 and Gauthier 1986). For rational choice theory collective action, in terms of minimal objectives such as law, order and defence, helps an individual to minimize costs and maximize benefits. It is therefore in the interests of rational self-interested individuals to create a minimal state to achieve these ends (Buchanan and Tullock 1962; Elster 1986; McLean 1987). However, rational choice type theory cannot allow too interventionary a state, since it would confer more costs than benefits on individuals. It needs, therefore, constitutional restraints premised on individual consent and rational choice. It is important to recall here that the roots of these rational choice and economistic arguments lie in empiricism.

Despite the deep scepticism over institutionalism and statism within empirical political science, there has been a partial resurrection of the state idea in the 'new institutionalism'. The differences between traditional institutionalism and the 'new institutionalism' derive largely from the fact that the new institutionalism arose from a critical reaction to empirical political science. The new institutionalism also bears the marks of long exposure to positivism and the need to appear scientifically and empirically rigorous. The basic gist of the new institutionalist argument is that pluralism has become too society-centred. Political science needs to be rebalanced with a more state-centric approach (Krasner 1978; Skocpol 1979; Nordlinger 1981; Evans *et al.* 1985). The state is thus seen to be both an important actor and relatively autonomous from societal interests. State officials and processes are consequently taken seriously as partly autonomous from societal preferences. The state must therefore be examined at the macropolitical level. In fact, the state is seen as the key factor moulding individual interests and choices. Some see this argument as part of a process of bringing the state back into political science. Political scientists, such as March and Olson (1984), thus see the new institutionalism as equivalent to a paradigm change in political science. Hardly surprisingly, critics of this view have suggested, among other things, that this position has become too state-centric and that, contrary to the views of the new institutionalists, the state always acts in some societal interest (Jordan 1990).

In summary, the empirical political science perspective – with the exception of the new institutionalism – has tended consistently to stress the informal character of political processes and has consequently played down the formal institutional side of the state.

More recent political science has retained this 'informalist bias'. For example, it is now argued, within political science, that the whole idea of the state is changing out of all recognition. Instead of the state, there is the pervasive concept of 'governance' (see Rhodes 1997). Governance implies a new process of governing wholly distinct from state activity. However, as most political science commentators agree, governance is over-burdened with meanings in current literature. It is generally said to subsist in a broad diversity of self-organizing policy networks. The state becomes, at most, a loose aggregation of inter-organizational networks, made up of both societal and central governmental actors, with no overarching sovereign authority.

The governance idea is also linked to the debate concerning 'policy communities'. The 1980s and 1990s saw a massive growth in policy studies literature focusing on 'policy communities', in some cases self-consciously directed against the claims of the 'new institutionalism' (Jordan 1990). Policies, in this context, are seen as being made between a myriad of interconnecting, interpenetrating organizations. The notion of the policy community, which derived from the work of the American political scientists Heclo and Wildavsky, has now become a conventional wisdom in current political science (Heclo and Wildavsky 1974). There has also been the emergence of the idea of different levels of governance – or 'multi-level governance'. For example, the doctrine of subsidiarity in the European Union, correlates with this theme. This kind of analysis blurs the difference between the state and civil society.

Thus, in essence, one can have governance without government, or, alternatively, governance without the state. States become centreless.

The above governance thesis is also connected to a number of other themes, for example, the 'hollowing out of the state'. 'Hollowing out' entails, as in 'governance', a loss of state functions both upwards and downwards (see Weller, Bakvis and Rhodes 1997). 'Internally' it can mean privatization or the loss of functions by the centre to different delivery systems, or, 'externally', the loss of functions to larger legal and political groupings, such as the European Union, or, alternatively, to global legal or commercial groups. There is still a need to maintain public order, however, within the 'hollowing thesis', this can be done without the state. Other mechanisms can steer and control. One of the ideas, discussed in tandem with 'hollowing out' and 'governance', is the 'new public management'. This refers to the creation of new forms of private executive agencies and the separation of policy shaping from policy performance. It also entails the increasing use of private market incentive systems within public services provision.

Some political scientists have linked this process of hollowing, governance and new public management to a wholly different form of state, namely, the 'regulatory state', which is seen to be replacing the 'welfare state' (see Majone 1996 and Bishop, Kay and Mayer 1995). States, in this reading, exercise authority and control by systems of rules within which diverse non-state agencies and delivery systems function. Such general rules control the parameters within which governance functions. Activities are thus hived off from central government, but are still bound by rules. In this scenario, future debates about public policy and state activity are seen to focus on the actual substance and extent of central regulation (Grant 1993). Another fairly recent argument has also noted the subtle move of contemporary states away from rigid legal rules towards complex evaluation and quality inspection regimes, which, in turn, has spawned a powerful industry of consultants, inspectors and evaluators. This has given rise to the conception of the 'evaluative state' (Henkel 1991; Neave 1988).

Finally, politics literature in recent years has speculated extensively on the end of the state. One of the principle areas of this debate has been globalization. There is little agreement on the concept, however, globalization loosely implies that the state has become an anachronism and its power and authority are being gradually drained away to non-state actors. Further, increasing interconnectedness between human beings is leading to a relatively borderless world. There are two broad views on globalization. One is essentially normative and links up with doctrines such as universal human rights. The other refers to large-scale economic trends where the global market is seen to be replacing the state. The real global actors are thus financial markets and international corporations. States become ciphers for global market forces.

There are stronger and weaker versions of this latter thesis. Kenichi Ohmae (1996) adopts the stronger view seeing globalization as a positive benefit for world consumers. Others see a piecemeal evolution. In this latter scenario, many aspects of life – pollution, disease, regulation of trade or environmental control – are no longer simply state issues. Further, the rapid post-1945 growth of international trade and international trade treaties (like GATT); international financial organizations (like the World Bank); international legal, political and military organizations (like the UN,

International Court of Human Rights, and NATO); international travel and migration; global communications such as the internet and email; the growth of intergovernmental and non-governmental agencies, have all constrained or changed the sphere of the twenty-first-century state. In sum, changes within international power and security, the growing influence of non-governmental transnational organizations, erosions of sovereignty in areas of state activity, have all changed the sphere of application of the state moving it toward a more globalized framework.

However, others have been uneasy with this globalization thesis. It is contended that the evidence for this decline of the state and rise of the global economy is remarkably thin (Hirst and Thompson 1996). Globalizing forces have, in fact, existed since the very inception of capitalism. Further, notions like unlimited sovereignty have always been curtailed by the needs of commerce and politics. States did not emerge individually, but rather as parts of systems of states. In addition, trade and cultural connectedness have long been part of human experience, certainly since the nineteenth century. Paradoxically, though, the movement for globalization has often been driven by states rather than market forces. In the welter of globalizing rhetoric this simple but pertinent point is often forgotten.

One other question which is often neglected in globalization argument is what actually replaces the state system? Some speculate that an immensely complex and disordered structure will result, almost a neo-feudalism (Cerny 1998). Others see that states have always been curtailed and limited in terms of the international system, thus globalization will seem just a slight acceleration of our present situation. Again, others see a much more positively integrated world. The important thing, in this latter view, is to look for new forms of 'cosmopolitan democracy' beyond the nation state model (Held 1995).

The recent emphasis on governance, hollowing out, policy communities and globalization, all in their different ways, signal the end or mutation of the formal concept of the state. However, for the foreseeable future it is highly unlikely that we will see much decisive evidence of this purported ending. The state will remain well into this next century a crucial actor in all political study. However, what is clear is that the manner in which we study the state can vary enormously. This is often forgotten in the literature. A balanced picture of the state can only be acquired if we remember that it is not just an economic, historical or sociological phenomenon, but also a tissue of values and normative aspirations about civil existence.

References

Anderson, P. (1974) *Lineages of the Absolutist State*, London: New Left Books.

Bachrach, P. (1967) *The Theory of Democratic Elitism*, London: University of London Press.

Badie, B. and Birnbaum, P. (1983) *The Sociology of the State*, Chicago: Chicago University Press.

Bartelson, J. (2001) *The Critique of the State*, Cambridge: Cambridge University Press.

Bishop, M., Kay, J. and Mayer, I. (eds) (1995) *The Regulatory Challenge*, Oxford: Oxford University Press.

Black, A. (1993) *Political Thought in Europe 1250–1450*, Cambridge: Cambridge University Press.

Buchanan, J. (1975) *The Limits of Liberty: Between Anarchy and Leviathan*, Chicago: Chicago University Press.

Buchanan, J. and Tullock, G. (1962) *The Calculus of Consent*, Ann Arbor: University of Michigan Press.

Carnoy, M. (1984) *The State and Political Theory*, Princeton, NJ: Princeton University Press.

Cassirer, E. (1946) *The Myth of the State*, New Haven: Yale University Press.

Cawson, A. (1986) *Corporatism and Political Theory*, Oxford: Basil Blackwell.

Cerny, P. (1998) 'Neo medievalism, civil war and the new security dilemmas: globalization as durable disorder', *Civil Wars*, 1, no. 1.

Church, W. F. (1972) *Richelieu and Reasons of State*, Princeton, NJ: Princeton University Press.

Collini, S., Winch, D. and Burrow, J. (1983) *That Noble Science of Politics*, Cambridge: Cambridge University Press.

Dahl, R. (1971) *Polyarchy: Participation and Opposition*, New Haven: Yale University Press.

Dunleavy, P. and O'Leary, B. (1987) *Theories of the State: The Politics of Liberal Democracy*, London: Macmillan.

Dyson, K. H. F. (1980) *The State Tradition in Western Europe: A Study of an Idea and Institution*, Oxford: Martin Robertson.

Easton, D. (1965) *A Systems Analysis of Political Life*, New York: John Wiley.

Elster, J. (ed.) (1986) *Rational Choice*, Oxford: Blackwell.

Evans, P. B., Rueschemeyer, D. and Skocpol, T. (eds) (1985) *Bringing the State Back In*, Cambridge: Cambridge University Press.

Farr, James and Seidelman, Raymond (eds) (1993) *Discipline and History: Political Science in the United States*, Ann Arbor: University of Michigan Press.

Figgis, J. N. (1914) *Churches in the Modern State*, London: Longmans, Green & Co.

Gauthier, D. (1986) *Morals by Agreement*, Oxford: Clarendon Press.

Gierke, O. von (1934) *Natural Law and the Theory of Society*, Cambridge: Cambridge University Press.

Grant, Wyn (1993) *Business and Politics in Britain*, London: Macmillan.

Hall, J. A. (ed.) (1986) *States in History*, Oxford: Blackwell.

Hart, H. L. A. (1961) *The Concept of Law*, Oxford: Clarendon Press.

Heclo, H. and Wildavsky, A. (1974) *The Private Government of Public Money*, London: Macmillan.

Hegel, G. W. F. (1967) *The Philosophy of Right*, Oxford: Oxford University Press.

Held, D. (1995) *Democracy and the Global Order*, Cambridge: Polity Press.

Henkel, Mary (1991) *Government Evaluation and Change*, London: Jessica Kingsley Publishers.

Hexter, J. H. (1973) *The Vision of Politics on the Eve of the Reformation: More, Machiavelli and Seyssel*, London: Allen Lane.

Hirst, P. and Thompson, G. (1996) *Globalization in Question*, Cambridge: Polity.

Hoffman, J. (1995) *Beyond the State*, Cambridge: Polity Press.

Hsiao, K. C. (1927) *Political Pluralism: A Study in Contemporary Political Theory*, London: Kegan Paul.

Jasay, A. de (1985) *The State*, Oxford: Basil Blackwell.

Jessop, B. (1983) *The Capitalist State*, Oxford: Martin Robertson.

—— (1990) *State Theory: Putting Capitalist States in their Place*, Oxford: Blackwell.

Jordan, Grant (1990) 'Policy community realism versus "new" institutionalist ambiguity', *Political Studies*, XXXVII.

Kelsen, H. (1945) *The General Theory of Law and State*, New York: Russell & Russell.

Krader, L. (1968) *The Formation of the State*, Englewood Cliffs, NJ: Prentice-Hall.

Krasner, S. (1978) *Defending the National Interest*, Princeton, NJ: Princeton University Press.

Latham, E. (1965) *The Group Basis to Politics*, New York: Cornell University Press.

Lowie, R. H. (1927) *The Origins of the State*, New York: Harcourt Brace.

Maitland, F. W. (1911) 'Moral and legal personality'. Appendix C in D. Nicholls, *The Pluralist State*, London: Macmillan.

Majone, G. (ed.) (1996) *Regulating Europe*, London: Routledge.

Mann, M. (ed.) (1990) *The Rise and Decline of the Nation State*, Oxford: Blackwell.

March, J. and Olson, J. P. (1984) 'The new institutionalism', *American Political Science Review*, 78.

Marquand, D. (1988) *The Unprincipled Society: New Demands and Old Politics*, London: Jonathan Cape.

McLean, I. (1987) *Public Choice: An Introduction*, Oxford: Blackwell.

Meinecke, F. (1957) *Machiavellianism: The Doctrine of Raison d'État and its Place in Modern History*, London: Routledge & Kegan Paul.

Michels, R. (1959) *Political Parties*, New York: Dover.

Miliband, R. (1973) *The State in Capitalist Society*, London: Quartet Books.

Mitteis, H. (1975) *The State in the Middle Ages: A Comparative Constitutional History of Feudal Europe*, Amsterdam: North Holland.

Monroe, K. R. (ed.) (1997) *Contemporary Empirical Political Theory*, Berkeley: University of California Press.

Neave, G. (1988) 'On the Cultivation of Quality, Efficiency and Enterprise: An Overview of Trends in Higher Education in Western Europe, 1986–1988', *European Journal of Education*, 23 (1–2).

Nicholls, D. (1975) *The Pluralist State*, London: Macmillan.

Nordlinger, E. A. (1981) *On the Autonomy of the Democratic State*, Cambridge, MA: Harvard University Press.

Nozick, R. (1974) *Anarchy, State and Utopia*, New York: Basic Books.

Ohmae, K. (1996) *The End of the Nation-State*, London: HarperCollins.

Parsons, T. (1967) *Sociological Theory and Modern Society*, New York: Free Press.

Poggi, G. (1978) *The Development of the Modern State*, London: Hutchinson.

Post, G. (1964) *Studies in Medieval Legal Thought: Public Law and the State 1100–1322*, Princeton, NJ: Princeton University Press.

Rhodes, R. (1997) *Understanding Governance: Policy Networks, Governance, Reflexitivity and Accountability*, Buckingham and Philadelphia: Open University Press.

Rowen, H. (1980) *The King's State: Proprietary Dynasticism in Early Modern France*, New Jersey: Rutgers University Press.

Schmitter, P. C. (1974) 'Still the century of corporatism?', *Review of Politics* 36.

Schumpeter, J. (1943) *Capitalism, Socialism and Democracy*, London: Allen & Unwin.

Shennan, J. H. (1974) *The Origins of the Modern European State 1450–1725*, London: Hutchinson.

Skinner, Q. (1978) *The Foundations of Modern Political Thought*, vols 1 and 2, Cambridge: Cambridge University Press.

Skinner, Q. (1989) 'The State' in T. Ball, J. Farr and Hanson (eds) *Political Innovation and Conceptual Change*, Cambridge: Cambridge University Press.

Skocpol, T. (1979) *State and Revolutions*, Cambridge: Cambridge University Press.

Strayer, J. R. (1970) *On the Medieval Origins of the Modern State*, Princeton, NJ: Princeton University Press.

Tilly, C. (ed.) (1975) *The Formation of National States in Western Europe*, Princeton, NJ: Princeton University Press.

Vincent, A. W. (1987) *Theories of the State*, Oxford: Basil Blackwell.

Vincent, A. W. and Plant, R. (1984) *Philosophy, Politics and Citizenship*, Oxford: Basil Blackwell.

Weller, P., Bakvis, H. and Rhodes, R. A. W. (eds) (1997) *The Hollow Crown*, London: Macmillan.

Further reading

Black, A. (1988) *State, Community and Human Desire*, Hemel Hempstead: Harvester Wheat-sheaf.

Bosanquet, B. (2001) *The Philosophical Theory of the State*, South Bend, IN: St Augustine's Press.

Cheyette, F. L. (1982) 'The invention of the state', in B. K. Lackner and K. R. Philp (eds) *Essays in Medieval Civilization: The Walter Prescott Webb Memorial Lectures*, Austin: University of Texas Press.

D'Entreves, A. P. (1967) *The Notion of the State*, Oxford: Clarendon Press.

Dyson, K. H. F. (1980) *The State Tradition in Western Europe: A Study of an Idea and Insti-tution*, Oxford: Martin Robertson.

Levine, A. (ed.) (1992) *The State and its Critics*, 2 volumes, Aldershot: Edward Elgar.

Lubasz, H. (ed.) (1964) *The Development of the Modern State*, New York: Macmillan.

MacIver, R. M. (1926) *The Modern State*, Oxford: Oxford University Press.

McLellan, G., Held, D. and Hall, S. (eds) (1984) *The Idea of the Modern State*, Milton Keynes: Open University Press.

Nettl, J. P. (1968) 'The state as a conceptual variable', *World Politics* 20: 559–92.

O'Connor, J. (1973) *The Fiscal Crisis of the State*, New York: St Martin's Press.

Tivey, L. (ed.) (1981) *The Nation State: The Formation of Modern Politics*, Oxford: Martin Robertson.

Vincent, A.W. (2002) *Nationalism and Particularity*, Cambridge: Cambridge University Press.

Weber, M. (1948) 'Politics as a vocation', in H. H. Gerth and C. Wright Mills (eds) *From Max Weber*, London: Routledge & Kegan Paul.

3

CONCEPTIONS OF POWER

Jeffrey Isaac

The concept of power is at the heart of political enquiry. Indeed, it is probably the central concept of both descriptive and normative analysis. When we talk about elections, group conflicts and state policies, we seek to explain events and processes in the political world by fixing responsibility upon institutions and agents. We are thus talking about power. When we ask about the constitution of the good or just society, we are contrasting present conditions with some projected alternative set of arrangements that might better enable people to conduct their lives. Here too we are talking about power. It would seem impossible to engage in political discourse without raising, whether implicitly or explicitly, questions about the distribution of power in society.

It is at least partly for this reason that social and political theorists have spent so much time arguing about the concept of power – what it means, what it denotes, how it might figure in appropriately scientific analysis or how it might be ill-suited to such analysis, and, finally, why scholars and citizens should care about any of the above. Indeed, it is a striking fact that while most political theorists would agree that power is a focal concept, they would probably agree upon little else. This has led to some awkward situations where theorists speak to each other using the same terms but meaning radically different things. Such problems of translation have never reached a point of incommensurability, and it is probably fair to say that most political theorists operate with some basic core conception of power. The core is the notion, articulated in different ways, that the concept of power refers to the abilities of social agents to affect the world in some way or other.

The word 'power' derives from the Latin *potere*, meaning 'to be able'. It is generally used to designate a property, capacity, or wherewithal to effect things. The concept has clear affinities with the concept of domination. The latter means some sort of mastery or control; derived from the Latin *dominium*, it was originally used to designate the mastery of the patriarch over his household or domain (Tuck 1979: 5–13). While the concept of power has often been interpreted as a synonym for domination, the latter connotes an asymmetry about which the former is agnostic. The concept of power also has close connections with the concept of authority. But the latter has a normative dimension, suggesting a kind of consent or authorization, about which the former is similarly agnostic. The grammars of these concepts, and their inter-relationships, are interesting and important (Pitkin 1972; Morriss 1980), but I will here concentrate upon the core notion of power as capacity to act, a genus of which the concepts of domination and authority can be seen as species.

Such a core, however, is itself quite nebulous, and it certainly admits of many different interpretations. As a consequence, a good deal of substantive inquiry and debate has been muddled by seemingly interminable and often rarefied conceptual argument. A cynical commentator would chalk up much of this disagreement to the endless methodological fixations of political theorists, who sustain subdisciplines, journals and careers by furthering meta-theoretical argument *ad infinitum* (Shapiro 1989). Such cynicism would not be unwarranted, but I think that there is more to it than this. If it is true that it is impossible to carry out political analysis without implicating the concept of power, it is also true that it is impossible to talk about power without implicating a broader set of philosophical, indeed metaphysical, questions about the nature of human agency, the character of social life and the appropriate way to study them. These broader questions are, as the history of modern social science attests, deeply contentious, and it should thus be of no surprise that this controversy has extended to the concept of power as well.

In an essay such as this it would be impossible to provide a detailed and nuanced account of such controversy. I will thus present its rough outlines. There are, I suggest, four main models of power in modern political analysis:

1   a voluntarist model rooted in the traditions of social contract theory and methodological individualism;
2   a hermeneutic or communicative model rooted largely in German phenomenology;
3   a structuralist model rooted in the work of Marx and Durkheim;
4   a postmodernist model, developed in different ways in the writing of Michel Foucault and certain contemporary feminists.

Each of these models offers not only a definition and elaboration of the concept of power, but a conception of humans, social institutions, and methods of analysis as well. Before outlining these models, I should make three things clear. First, I will treat models as no more than rough categories or general 'ideal types'. I in no way intend to suggest a kind of substantive consensus among theorists typical of each model who, despite certain similarities, often share many differences on all sorts of matters. Second, while each of these models is sufficiently distinct and autonomous to be discussed separately, it is not the case, the views of methodological ideologists notwithstanding, that these models are in all respects mutually exclusive. This is, of course, a complicated question, but I will suggest that each model in fact presents some important insights, and that theorists of power should probably think in more synthetic terms than they are accustomed to. Third, what I will discuss below are different models of the concept of power, not different theories of its distribution in particular forms of society. The discussion, in other words, will be largely meta-theoretical. Many political theorists, including participants in conceptual debates about power, have mistakenly believed that there is a one-to-one correspondence between meta-theory and theory, so that, for instance, a subscriber to Robert Dahl's arguments about the behavioural study of power is necessarily a pluralist, and vice versa. As I have argued elsewhere (Isaac 1987), this is not the case.

The voluntarist model

In referring to this model as a voluntarist one, I wish to call attention to the fact that from this view power is thought of almost exclusively in terms of the intentions and strategies of its subjects. This view is common to all of the participants in the so-called 'three faces of power' debate, and it is shared by most 'rational choice' theorists as well. Such a view is rooted in the tradition of methodological individualism, for which all claims about social life are reducible to claims about individuals (Bhaskar 1979), and it is therefore no coincidence that it can be traced back to the writing of Thomas Hobbes. Such a view, however, is capable of being extended from individual to collective subjects, so long as these are thought of as unitary aggregations of individual wills, and are treated as strategic actors seeking to maximize some kind of utility or value.

The classic statement of the voluntarist model is Robert Dahl's *International Encyclopedia of the Social Sciences* essay on power (Dahl 1968). For Dahl power is a capacity to get others to do what they would not otherwise do, to set things in motion and 'change the order of events'. As he writes: 'Power terms in modern social science refer to subsets of relations among social units such that the behaviour of one or more units (the response units, R) depend in some circumstances on the behaviour of other units (the controlling units, C)' (ibid.: 407). As Dahl's language of stimulus and response suggests, this notion of power rests upon a Newtonian analogy. We are all naturally at rest or at constant velocity, until our movements are altered by an external force. Power is such a force. For Dahl the concept of power is thus a causal concept. But Dahl, a behaviouralist, insists that his conception of causality is strictly Humean. As he writes elsewhere: 'The only meaning that is strictly causal in the notion of power is one of regular sequence: that is, a regular sequence such that whenever A does something, what follows, or what probably follows, is an action by B' (Dahl 1965: 94).

As I have argued elsewhere (Isaac 1987), this view fails to distinguish between the successful exercise and the possession of power, conceiving of power exclusively in terms of the contingent success of agents in securing their purposes. It is also empiricist in its view of causality and scientific explanation, both of which, for Dahl, are conceived in Humean terms. In this sense, appearances to the contrary, it is a view shared by Dahl's most vocal and well-known critics, Bachrach and Baratz (1970) and Lukes (1974). For all these theorists power is a behavioural relation of actual cause and effect, exhausted in the interaction between parties. While these theorists in different ways allow the importance of collective rules and resources, all also insist that these are to be sharply distinguished from, and have no necessary connection to, power. Lukes, frequently taken to be a 'radical' critic of Dahl, attests to this when he avers that all three faces of power 'can be seen as alternative interpretations and applications of one and the same underlying concept of power' (Lukes 1974: 27). For this concept power is the ability to advance one's interests in conflict with others.

This concept can be traced back to the writings of some of the 'founders' of modern political theory. Thus Thomas Hobbes defines power, in terms of the purposes of individuals, as the 'present means, to obtain some future Good' (Hobbes 1968: 63). Both Hobbes and Locke hold that 'Power and Cause are the same thing', conceiving such causation in mechanistic, Newtonian terms (quoted in Ball 1988: 83). As Locke writes:

A body at rest affords us no idea of any active power to move; and when it is set in motion itself, that motion is rather a passion than an action in it. For when the ball obeys the motion of the billiard-stick, it is not any action of the ball, but bare passion. Also when by impulse it sets another ball in motion that lay in its way, it only communicates the motion it had received from another, and loses in itself so much as the other received: which gives us [an] idea of an active power of moving.

(Locke 1961: 194–5)

It was David Hume who canonized this view, insisting that 'the idea of power is relative as much as that of cause; and both have reference to an effect, or some other event constantly conjoined with the former' (Hume 1962: 77). In this view power is nothing more than empirical causation. The formulations of Hobbes and Hume are important because they make explicit what is only implicit in many more contemporary formulations: that such a view of power presupposes an atomistic view of social relations, a Humean conception of causality, and an empiricist or 'covering law' model of scientific explanation. Hume is quite clear that any claims about underlying causes or pre-existing powers are invalid: 'the distinction...betwixt power and the exercise of it is...without foundation' (quoted in Ball 1988: 85).

A certain reading of these texts became the basis for the behavioural revolution in power research. Many of the behaviouralists also drew upon the work of Max Weber, who defined power as 'the probability that one actor in a social relationship will...carry out his own will' (Weber 1968: 53) against the resistance of others. This conception, quite influential, joins the Humean conception of causality and atomistic ontology with a phenomenological emphasis upon intentionality. The writings of Laswell and Kaplan (1950), March (1953), Simon (1953) and Dahl (1957) all treat power as a relation of empirical causation, whereby one agent prevails over another in a conflict of some sort or other. Subsequent critics, such as Nagel (1975), while they introduce sophisticated methodological arguments, clearly continue in this genre. As Nagel writes, aptly summarizing the behavioural view despite many disagreements: 'the causal version of power has achieved widespread acceptance' (Nagel 1975: 11).

This view is also shared by many rational choice theorists. While most of these theorists reject many of the more positivistic epistemological premises of behaviouralism, they share the behavioural view that social life is to be understood in terms of the contingent interactions between individuals and groups. They also share the typically behavioural aversion toward theoretical abstraction and the postulation of hidden causes and underlying structures. Unlike many behaviouralists, rational choice theorists are particularly interested in the motives, incentives and co-ordination problems involved in strategic bargaining. This interest can also be traced back to Hobbes's notions of reputation and anticipated reaction (Hampton 1986; Gauthier 1969) and Weber's concern with strategic action, but its more rigorously formalistic orientation is of more recent vintage.

Peter Blau's *Exchange and Power in Social Life* (1964) was an early effort to apply the concepts of microeconomics – self-interest, maximization, marginal cost and marginal benefit – to the conceptualization of power. For Blau power is an exchange relation between parties where an imbalance in the services exchanged (what Blau calls a 'payments deficit') is compensated for by the subordination of one party to the other. While other rational choice theorists depart from Blau on many issues, they share his interest in what Brian Barry calls 'an economic analysis' of power (Barry 1976). Barry agrees with the behaviouralists that power is a way of gaining compliance on the part of others, but, taking this concern with strategic action one step further, he writes that power is 'the possession of the means of securing compliance by the manipulation of rewards or punishments' in order to modify the behaviour of others (ibid.: 90). In this view power necessarily involves considerations of marginal cost and benefit on the part of the agents involved. Such a focus opens up many interesting game-theory questions regarding the strategic leverage of numerical minorities, the effects of procedural rules upon strategic bargaining, and the consequences of boundary conditions upon co-ordination problems affecting group bargaining (Shapley and Shubik 1954; Harsanyi 1962; Olson 1965; Shepsle and Weingast 1987).

The voluntarist model derives much of its attractiveness from its scientific pretensions. Indeed, what holds it together as much as its atomistic social assumptions is its commitment to a covering law model of scientific explanation, and its claim to be able to offer predictive and thus 'falsifiable' generalizations. To this extent the powerful barrage of criticisms of empiricist philosophy of science that have been articulated in the past twenty years cannot but serve to weaken its appeal (Isaac 1987). But the model has been confronted by other criticisms as well. Some have claimed that while the model rigorously conceptualizes problems surrounding the exercise of power, it is unable to offer theoretical explanations of how and why agents are able to exercise power as they do. Others have raised questions about the blindness of the model to questions of ideology and to the way agents' preferences and practical horizons are constituted by pre-existing normative and cultural forms that are not the *ex nihilo* creations of any maximizing individual or group. Each of these criticisms is given voice in different ways by the hermeneutic model.

The hermeneutic model

Hermeneutics is the study of meaning (Palmer 1969). The hermeneutic model of power holds that power is constituted by the shared meanings of given social communities. This approach shares with rational choice theory the idea that beliefs are the central ingredients of power relations, and that considerations of rationality necessarily come into play in social life. It differs, however, in rejecting the idea that instrumental rationality or cost–benefit thinking is a universal attribute of human beings (Wilson 1970). By contrast, hermeneutics is concerned with the varying symbolic and normative constructs that shape the practical rationalities of situated social agents. This involves an ontological belief that humans are by nature linguistic beings and that it is thus in language that the character of a society, including its forms of power, is to be found. It also involves the epistemological belief that some form of hermeneutic understanding, rather than scientific empirical generalization, is the appropriate method of studying social power.

The hermeneutic approach has acquired an increasing prominence in contemporary social theory (Bernstein 1974, 1983). Charles Taylor, for example, has argued that the first principle of any social explanation must be the uniquely linguistic and conceptual character of human social life. As he writes:

The point is that the objects of public experience – rite, festival, election, etc. – are not like the facts of nature. For they are not entirely separable from the experience they give rise to. They are partly constituted by the ideas and representations which underly them. A given social practice, like voting in the ecclesia, or in a modern election, is what it is because of a set of commonly understood ideas and meanings, by which the depositing of stones in an urn, or the marking of bits of paper, counts as the making of a social decision. These ideas about what is going on are essential to define the institution.

(Taylor 1979: 34)

An appreciation of this can be traced throughout the 'canon' of Western political philosophy – Aristotle, Machiavelli, Montesquieu, Tocqueville. None of these writers treated power as simply an empirical compliance relation, and all of them sought to account for the norms, mores and 'spirit of the laws' that constituted forms of social power.

Hegel's section on 'Lordship and Bondage' in *The Phenomenology of Mind* (1967) is undoubtedly an important ancestor of contemporary hermeneutic thinking about power. Hegel's basic point is that even relationships of extreme domination, which would appear to be entirely anomic, are sustained by the need for some kind of mutual recognition on the part of the agents. Hegel's emphasis on the centrality of consciousness and reciprocity represented a departure from the more atomistic conceptions found in Hobbes and Hume and in the English tradition more generally. This emphasis can be found in the writing of a good many nineteenth-century German social theorists, including Ranke, Dilthey, Simmel and Weber (Manicas 1987).

More recent theorists have built upon this approach. Thus Peter Winch insists that the exercise of power presupposes a normative context giving meaning to behavioural interactions, a context that the voluntaristic approach is unable to countenance:

An event's character as an act of obedience is intrinsic to it in a way which is not true of an event's character as a clap of thunder, and this is in general true of human acts as opposed to natural events.... There existed electrical storms and thunder long before there were human beings to form concepts of them.... But it does not make much sense to suppose that human beings might have been issuing commands and obeying them before they came to form the concept of command and obedience. For their performance of such acts is itself the chief manifestation of their possession of those concepts. An act of obedience itself contains, as an essential element, a recognition of what went before it as an order.

(Winch 1970: 9–10)

A command thus presumes some mode of mutual understanding, and obedience some 'uptake' of the appropriate command. While Hannah Arendt's view is both more idiosyncratic and more normative, she too insists that power cannot be understood on the voluntarist, Newtonian model: 'Power corresponds to the human ability not just to act but to act in concert. Power is never the property of the individual; it belongs to a group and remains in existence only so long as the group keeps together' (Arendt 1972: 143). According to Arendt, humans are uniquely communicative beings, and it is through their shared meanings and relationships that their capacities to act are sustained.

This view is also advanced, in a different way, by Talcott Parsons. Parsons sought to develop a comprehensive theory of 'the social system', synthesizing the insights of both the voluntaristic and phenomenological traditions. He thus emphasized the importance of both strategic interaction and the 'internalization' of social norms. According to Parsons, power is

> a generalized capacity to secure the performance of binding obligations by units in a system of collective organization when the obligations are legitimized with reference to their bearing on collective goals and where in case of recalcitrance there is a presumption of enforcement by the negative situational sanctions – whatever the actual agency of that enforcement.
>
> (Parsons 1969: 361)

What binds these various formulations together is their emphasis upon norms. For all of the proponents of the hermeneutic model, power is embedded in a system of values which constitute the very identities, as well as the possibilities for action, of social agents. While this model has much to recommend it, a number of critics have argued that its emphasis on language blinds it to the more 'material' dimensions of power, which may be real even if they are not recognized as such by social agents (Mills 1959; Gellner 1970; Habermas 1983).

The structural model

The structural model shares with the hermeneutic model an aversion to methodological individualism and an appreciation of the importance of norms. However, it avoids an exclusively normative treatment of power, contending that power has a structural objectivity that is missed by both voluntaristic and hermeneutic approaches. The structural model can be traced back to Marx's analysis of the capitalist mode of production in *Capital* (1967) and to Durkheim's *Rules of Sociological Method* (1966). Both theorists insist upon the pre-given reality of structural forms that both enable and constrain human conduct. These forms may have a normative dimension, but they are not reducible to the beliefs that social agents have about them. As Durkheim writes:

> When I fulfill my obligations...when I execute my contracts, I perform duties which are defined, externally to myself and my acts, in law and in custom.... The system of signs I use to express my thought, the system of currency I employ to pay my debts, the instruments of credit I utilize in my commercial relations...function independently of my own use of them.
>
> (Durkheim 1966: 56)

According to the structural model, power can be defined as the capacities to act possessed by social agents in virtue of the enduring relations in which they participate (Isaac 1987: 80). It does not arise *ex nihilo* in behavioural interaction, nor is it a purely normative or symbolic reality. Rather, it has a 'materiality', deriving from its attachment to structural rules, resources, positions and relationships. As I have argued elsewhere (ibid.), such a view is presupposed by a good deal of neo-Marxist analysis of class and feminist analysis of gender.

The structural model involves a relational social ontology (Bhaskar 1979). Against voluntarism it maintains that society is not reducible to the properties of individuals, and that in fact it consists of relatively enduring relations in which individuals participate. Indeed, following Marx, the model holds that 'the individual is the social being...which can individuate itself only in the midst of society' (Isaac 1987: 111–12). Such a view does not reify social structures. Rather, such structures are viewed, in the words of Anthony Giddens, as the media and outcomes of human agency. As he puts it, there is a 'duality of structure' (Giddens 1976). Social structures do not exist separate from the activities they govern and human agents' conceptions of these activities, but they are also material conditions of such activities. There would be no language, for example, without speakers speaking; and yet language is at the same time the medium without which speech would be impossible. Language thus has structural properties upon which agents draw. In this respect it is more generally paradigmatic of social structures, which provide capacities to their participants. In this view, for example, to be a capitalist is to have power. But this power does not arise from the contingent interactions of capitalists and workers, nor is it exhausted by the beliefs and normative commitments of capitalists and workers. Rather, it is a property of the structure of capitalism, one which agents draw upon and exercise in their conduct in order to achieve their specific objectives. The structural view shares much with the hermeneutic view, yet it remains committed to the project of scientific explanation and to the view that it is the task of science to hypothesize about underlying structures. In this latter belief it departs most decisively from the voluntaristic model, substituting typically realist conceptions of science for empiricist ones (Ball 1975; Bhaskar 1975; Isaac 1987).

The structural view has attained an increasing prominence in social and political science. It is contested, of course, especially by adherents to a more voluntaristic model. But it also faces a challenge from less conventional, 'postmodernist' writers. These tend to argue that the structural model remains wedded to certain typically 'modernist' beliefs in the unity of the subject and the privileged status of scientific discourse. Some of these criticisms, especially the latter one, echo the Frankfurt school's critique of instrumental reason and modern social science (Benhabib 1986). But critical theory's understanding of power is actually quite close to the structural view identified here. In common with structuralists, critical theorists tend to think of power as embedded in structured relationships and seek to deploy some kind of critical social science to identify such structures (Fay 1987).

The postmodernist model

Postmodernists, along with hermeneutic and structural theorists, reject individualism and voluntarism, and believe that language and symbols are central to power. They claim, however, that scientific discourse possesses no distinctively epistemic validity. Instead they insist that structural conceptions of power, like hermeneutic ones, unjustifiably privilege certain conceptions of knowledge and certain conceptions of human agency. As Jane Flax writes:

> Postmodern discourses are all 'deconstructive' in that they seek to distance us from and make us sceptical about beliefs concerning truth, knowledge, power, the self, and language that are often taken for granted within and serve as legitimation for contemporary Western culture.
>
> (Flax 1987: 624)

This is a view shared by many feminists (Ferguson 1987). Thus Nancy Hartsock argues that a reconceptualization of power requires 'a relocation of theory onto the epistemological terrain defined by women's lives', and that such a development would 'stress those aspects of power related to energy, capacity, and potential' rather than those connected with compliance and domination (Hartsock 1983: 151, 210). Similarly Allison Jaggar insists that there is a distinctively feminist 'epistemological standpoint' from which a more 'positive' conception of power might be articulated and justified (Jaggar 1983). What is distinctive about these theorists is their claim that conceptions of power are gender-specific and grounded not simply in philosophical differences but in radically different kinds of experience. The feminist view of power highlights certain kinds of relations – typically those involving mutuality – over others, and, like Arendt's view (1972: 62–3), it is quite explicitly normative, purporting not simply to identify but to valorize realms of experience and human possibility previously hidden by more accepted, masculinist models of power.

This is a major point of contact between feminists and the work of Michel Foucault, which, in his words, seeks to advance the 'insurrection of subjugated knowledges' that have been 'disqualified' and 'buried' by received and more accepted discourses (Foucault 1977: 81–2). Like them, Foucault claims that his genealogical analyses of power are 'anti-sciences'. His conception of power has many affinities with the structural model. He quite explicitly rejects a voluntaristic model, which views power as that 'which prohibits, which refuses, and which has a whole range of negative effects: exclusion, rejection, denial, obstruction, obfuscation, etc.' (ibid.: 183–4). As with the structural model, he views power as constituted by certain structures or 'discourses', and considers power to have a 'positive' as well as a 'negative' dimension. In other words, Foucault believes that social agents are constituted and enabled by the relations of power in which they participate, and that whatever 'resistances' power engenders they are themselves constrained by the structures in which they emerge. Foucault's writings on power have spawned an enormous critical literature. What is most important here is that, despite his affinities with the structural model, certain of Foucault's philosophical commitments decisively separate him from this model. First, he rejects any 'global' or 'totalizing' approaches to the study of social power, insisting that such discourses are 'totalitarian'. He thus favours the local analysis of 'micro-power', holding that only such knowledge can avoid becoming entrapped in modern forms of power and domination. Second, in so far as Foucault endorses a 'struggle against the coercion of a theoretical, unitary, formal and scientific discourse' (ibid.: 85), he seems to insist that even his 'local knowledges' are anti-epistemological in any sense. Third, identifying the concept of the human subject with modern forms of domination, Foucault, while talking of 'resistances', has little to say about the duality of structure and agency, and less about the way in which agents can and do transform the conditions under which they live. Finally, drawing upon Nietzsche, he seems to ontologize domination in some form or other. Rejecting the problems of freedom and justice, he maintains that 'right should be viewed...not in terms of a legitimacy to be established, but in terms of the methods of subjugation that it instigates' (ibid.: 96). In all these respects Foucault's conception of power is profoundly deconstructive. And, if it is clear that he wishes to offer some alternative, his formulations seem to defy any systematic theoretical or normative approach to social life (Taylor 1984).

It is worth noting, as a number of commentators have done, that there is a deep tension between the feminist approach to power, which valorizes feminine experience and orients itself toward some more or less genuine emancipation, and the radical anarchism, if not nihilism, of Foucault. Thus the postmodernist model constitutes substantive unity less than any other model does. Rather, what defines it above all else is a kind of suspicion of existing theoretical approaches and the claims of epistemological privilege that they support.

Conclusion

Each of the four models of power I have outlined has a point, and each fixes on some crucial dimension of social life. Each of the first three models underscores an important theme – the centrality of strategic agency, shared norms, and structured relationships to the conceptualization of power. And the fourth, postmodernist, model also offers an important insight into the fractured and problematic character of social life, insisting that power is complex, ambiguous, and located in a multiplicity of social spaces, and that traditional conceptions and methods remain insensitive to much of this.

In my view the structural alternative offers the best possibility of a creative synthesis of these insights. While it retains a commitment to certain standards of scientific explanation and criticism, it also allows for the insights provided by the alternative models. It acknowledges the importance of human agency and the self-understandings of agents. And, through Giddens's notion of the duality of structure and agency (1976: 64), it is capable of incorporating both the voluntarist insight into the importance of strategic manoeuvering and the contingency of outcomes and the Foucauldian insight into the constitutive, positive character of power, which enables as well as constrains.

In this context this can be only a suggestion, one which will undoubtedly engender critical responses. It is probably fair to say that no single model of power states everything that needs to be said about the subject, and that what is needed above all else is for these models to critically engage each other. Controversy about the concept of power would seem endemic to social theory. The best that we can hope for is that such inquiry remains wedded to real substantive theoretical and practical problems, and that it remains self-critical and continually open to contestation and revision.

References

Arendt, H. (1972) 'On violence', in *Crises of the Republic*, New York: Harcourt Brace Jovanovich.

Bachrach, P. and Baratz, M. (1970) *Power and Poverty*, New York: Oxford University Press.

Ball, T. (1975) 'Power, causation, and explanation', *Polity* 2: 189–214.

—— (1988) 'The changing face of power', ch. 4 in *Transforming Political Discourse*, Oxford: Basil Blackwell.

Barry, B. (1976) *Power and Political Theory: Some European Perspectives*, London: Wiley.

Benhabib, S. (1986) *Critique, Norm, and Utopia*, New York: Columbia University Press.

Bernstein, R. (1974) *Praxis and Action*, Philadelphia: University of Pennsylvania Press.

—— (1983) *Beyond Objectivism and Relativism*, Philadelphia: University of Pennsylvania Press.

Bhaskar, R. (1975) *A Realist Theory of Science*, Brighton: Harvester Press.

—— (1979) *The Possibility of Naturalism*, Atlantic Highlands, NJ: Humanities Press.

Blau, P. (1964) *Exchange and Power in Social Life*, New York: John Wiley and Sons.

Dahl, R. (1957) 'The concept of power', *Behavioural Science* 2: 201–15.

—— (1965) 'Cause and effect in the study of polities', in D. Lerner (ed.) *Cause and Effect*, New York: Free Press.

—— (1968) 'Power', *International Encyclopedia of the Social Sciences*, New York: Free Press.

Durkheim, E. (1966) *Rules of Sociological Method*, New York: Free Press.

Fay, B. (1987) *Critical Social Science*, Ithaca, NY: Cornell University Press.

Ferguson, K. (1987) 'Male-ordered polities', in T. Ball (ed.) *Idioms of Inquiry*, Albany, NY: SUNY Press.

Flax, J. (1987) 'Postmodernism and gender relations in feminist theory', *Signs* 12: 621–43.

Foucault, M. (1977) *Power/Knowledge*, New York: Pantheon.

Gauthier, D. (1969) *The Logic of Leviathan*, Oxford: Clarendon Press.

Gellner, E. (1970) 'Concepts and society', in B. Wilson (ed.) *Rationality*, Oxford: Basil Blackwell.

Giddens, A. (1976) *New Rules of Sociological Method*, New York: Basic Books.

Habermas, J. (1983) 'Hannah Arendt on the concept of power', in *Philosophical-Political Profiles*, Cambridge, MA: MIT Press.

Hampton, J. (1986) *Hobbes and the Social Contract Tradition*, Cambridge: Cambridge University Press.

Harsanyi, J. (1962) 'Measurement of social power, opportunity costs, and the theory of two-person bargaining games', *Behavioural Science* 7: 67–80.

Hartsock, N. (1983) *Money, Sex and Power*, New York: Longman.

Hegel, G. W. F. (1967). *The Phenomenology of Mind*, New York: Harper.

Hobbes, T. (1968) *Leviathan*, ed. C. B. Macpherson, Middlesex: Penguin.

Hume, D. (1962) *Enquiry Concerning Human Understanding*, Oxford: Clarendon Press.

Isaac, J. (1987) *Power and Marxist Theory: A Realist View*, Ithaca, NY: Cornell University Press.

Jaggar, A. (1983) *Feminist Politics and Human Nature*, Totowa: Rowman & Allanheld.

Laswell, H. and Kaplan, A. (1950) *Power and Society*, New Haven: Yale University Press.

Locke, J. (1961) *An Essay Concerning Human Understanding*, vol. 1, London: J. M. Dent & Sons.

Lukes, S. (1974) *Power: A Radical View*, London: Macmillan.

Manicas, P. (1987) *A History and Philosophy of the Social Sciences*, Oxford: Basil Blackwell.

March, J. (1953) 'An introduction to the theory and measurement of influence', *American Political Science Review* 49: 431–51.

Marx, K. (1967) *Capital*, vol. 1, New York: International Publishers.

Mills, C. W. (1959) *The Sociological Imagination*, Oxford: Oxford University Press.

Morriss, P. (1980) 'The essentially uncontestable concepts of power', in M. Freeman and D. Robertson (eds) *The Frontiers of Political Theory*, New York: St Martin's Press.

Nagel, J. (1975) *The Descriptive Analysis of Power*, New Haven: Yale University Press.

Olson, M. (1965) *The Logic of Collective Action*, Cambridge, MA: Harvard University Press.

Palmer, R. (1969) *Hermeneutics*, Evanston: Northwestern University Press.

Parsons, T. (1969) 'On the concept of power', in *Politics and Social Structure*, New York: Free Press.

Pitkin, H. (1972) *Wittgenstein and Justice*, Berkeley: University of California Press.

Shapley, L. and Shubik, M. (1954) 'A method for evaluating the distribution of power in a committee system', *American Political Science Review* 48: 787–92.

Shapiro, I. (1989) 'Gross concepts in political argument', *Political Theory* 17: 51–76.

Shepsle, K. and Weingast, B. (1987) 'The institutional foundations of committee power', *American Political Science Review* 81: 80–104.

Simon, H. (1953) 'Notes on the observation and measurement of power', *Journal of Politics* 15: 500–16.

Taylor, C. (1979) *Hegel and Modern Society*, Cambridge: Cambridge University Press.

—— (1984) 'Foucault on truth and freedom', *Political Theory* 12: 152–83.

Tuck, R. (1979) *Natural Rights Theories*, Cambridge: Cambridge University Press.

Weber, M. (1968) *Economy and Society*, Berkeley: University of California Press.

Wilson, B. (ed.) (1970) *Rationality*, Oxford: Basil Blackwell.

Winch, P. (1970) 'The idea of a social science', in B. Wilson (ed.) *Rationality*, Oxford: Basil Blackwell.

Further reading

Allen, A. (1999) *The Power of Feminist Theory: Domination, Resistance, Solidarity*, Boulder, CO and Oxford: Westview Press.

Bachrach, P. and Baratz, M. (1970) *Power and Poverty*, New York: Oxford University Press.

Barrett, M. (1980) *Women's Oppression Today*, London: Verso.

Barry, B. (1976) *Power and Political Theory: Some European Perspectives*, London: Wiley.

Bell, R., Edwards, D. V. and Harrison, R. (eds) (1969) *Political Power: A Reader in Theory and Research*, New York: Free Press.

Bourdieu, P. (2001) *Domination Masculine*, Stanford, CA: Stanford University Press.

Butler, J. (1997) *The Psychic Life of Power: Theories in Subjection*, Stanford, CA.: Stanford University Press.

Chowdhry, G. and Nair, S. (eds) (2002) *Power, Postcolonialism, and International Relations*, London and New York: Routledge.

Dahl, R. (1961) *Who Governs?*, New Haven: Yale University Press.

Dowding, K. M. (1996) *Power*, Minneapolis: University of Minnesota Press.

Foucault, M. (1977) *Power/Knowledge*, New York: Pantheon.

Giddens, A. (1979) *Central Problems in Social Theory*, Berkeley: University of California Press.

Goverde, H. (ed.) (2000) *Power in Contemporary Politics: Theories, Practices, Globalizations*, London and Thousand Oaks, CA: Sage.

Haugaard, M. (1997) *The Constitution of Power: A Theoretical Analysis of Power, Knowledge and Structure*, Manchester, UK: Manchester University Press.

Hindess, B. (1996) *Discourses of Power: From Hobbes to Foucault*, Oxford: Blackwell Publishers.

Hoffman, P. (1996) *The Quest for Power: Hobbes, Descartes, and the Emergence of Modernity*, Atlantic Highlands, NJ: Humanities Press.

Isaac, J. (1987) *Power and Marxist Theory: A Realist View*, Ithaca, NY: Cornell University Press.

Lukes, S. (1974) *Power: A Radical View*, London: Macmillan.

Newman, S. (2001) *From Bakunin to Lacan: Anti-Authoritarianism and the Dislocation of Power*, Lanham, MD and Oxford: Lexington Books.

Niebuhr, R. (1932) *Moral Man and Immoral Society*, New York: Charles Scribner's Sons.

Poggi, G. (2001) *Forms of Power*, Cambridge: Polity Press.

Polsby, N. (1980) *Community Power and Political Theory*, New Haven: Yale University Press.

Poulantzas, N. (1973) *Political Power and Social Classes*, London: New Left Books.

Wartenberg, Thomas E. (1992) *Rethinking Power*, Albany: State University of New York Press.

4

CONCEPTIONS OF LAW

Geoffrey Marshall

Law can be described in short as an ordering and regulation of human behaviour. However, this fails to distinguish it from other modes of ordering and regulation that derive, for example, from morality, religion or social convention. The exact relationships between these different forms of ordering and whether they can or cannot be clearly distinguished has perhaps been the major source of disagreement among legal theorists.

Two kinds of dispute about law have been involved: first as to its source, and second as to its elements and structure. If, as those theorists commonly described as natural lawyers believe, all law stemmed from divine law or some law of right reason immanent in the nature of things, then all human law must depend in part for its validity on compliance with that higher law. If, on the other hand, law may proceed independently from or be 'posited' by a human legislator or legislators, then it may be considered valid independently of its correspondence with divine or natural law or with justice, morality or reason. This, in brief, was the view adopted by 'legal positivists'.

In addition to disagreeing about the source and authority of law, legal philosophers have also held different theories about the way in which the elements of the legal system should be characterized. Legal philosophers, such as Thomas Hobbes, Jeremy Bentham and John Austin, depicted the operation of laws as the issue by a legislator (whether divine or human) of commands or imperatives that emphasized their collective will. On the other hand, some twentieth-century critics, such as Hans Kelsen and H. L. A. Hart, have pictured legal systems in terms of prescriptive norms and rules.

Many jurists, particularly in the USA and Europe, have devoted themselves not to formal analyses of the legal system as a whole but to studies of the judicial process or to the interplay of social and economic forces that affect legal institutions and legal decision making. The so-called realist or instrumentalist school in the USA included John Chipman Gray, Jerome Frank and Karl Llewellyn. In Scandinavia, realist and sceptical theories of law emerged in the work of Axel Hägerström, Karl Olivecrona and Alf Ross (Olivecrona 1939; Ross 1958). Within analytic legal philosophy the dispute between positivist and anti-positivist theories has continued. One modern form of non-positivist theory is seen in the writings of Ronald Dworkin (1977, 1986). It should also be added that there exists a self-denominated 'critical legal studies' movement, originating in the USA, that sees all formal legal structures as manipulated by dominant social interests, and the making of law by judges and legislators as exercises in the deployment of political power. If this conception of law is correct, the great majority of legal philosophers since Aristotle have been wasting their time.

The concept of law

In the English-speaking world a major part of the debate about the general character of law in the last thirty years has focused upon issues raised in H. L. A. Hart's work *The Concept of Law* (Hart 1961). The main purpose of Hart's book was to mount an attack on the imperative theory of law exemplified in the work of John Austin, who in 1832 in *The Province of Jurisprudence Determined* (Austin 1954) had portrayed law as consisting essentially of commands or coercive orders backed by force emanating from a sovereign legislator whom subjects were habitually accustomed to obey. Hart attacked this 'gunman theory' by arguing that the idea of orders habitually obeyed fails to capture both the variety of types and purposes of law and the idea that laws are obligatory or binding in ways that habits and practices are not. Whilst criminal laws might be analogous to commands, civil laws and rules of procedure cannot easily be so pictured. The role of legal rules is not only to command, but also to enable and to permit private arrangements (for example contracts, marriages and wills). They have a multiplicity of purposes. Besides punishing offenders, laws may distribute benefits, regulate organizations, educate law students, excite the envy of foreigners, support conventional morality and so forth. The key to the understanding of a legal system, Hart proposes, is to be found in the idea of a rule rather than in that of command. Conforming to rules differs from habitual conduct in that it involves the idea of obligation and a critical attitude to deviation by those who are subject to the rules. In any one legal system some primary rules determine duties, obligations, rights and powers. Other secondary rules will determine procedures for law making, define institutions and provide for legal change. A legal system is simply, Hart suggests, a combination of these two sorts of rules. Each system will be distinguished by a rule of recognition – a special secondary rule which lays down the standard or conditions under which valid laws may be made in the particular system. In the United Kingdom the rule of recognition will identify the Queen and both Houses of Parliament as the source of authorized law making and of change in existing laws. In the USA the notional rule of recognition will identify the constituent people of the USA acting through the procedures laid down in the Federal Constitution as the ultimate source of valid law.

The idea of such a standard-setting or pedigree rule is not dissimilar to that set out in the work of the Austrian jurist Hans Kelsen (1961, 1970, 1991). Kelsen's theory, like Hart's, is positivist in that it separates questions of morality and moral obligation from those of legal validity and legal obligation. In both systems law is valid and legally binding because it is properly made in terms of a rule which complies with criteria set out in the ultimate rule or norm of the system. In Kelsen's theory the validity of each law depends upon its ultimate derivation from a basic norm or 'Grundnorm' and upon the system of norms being efficacious and subject to general obedience. The validity of the Grundnorm itself must be presupposed.

Hart criticizes this idea as based on a misunderstanding. The basic rule of recognition in a legal system may be viewed – as may the other rules – from two viewpoints: one internal, the other external. From the internal viewpoint of those who use and work the system, the basic or pedigree rule is an operative rule of law. But as the standard of validity it cannot itself in the same sense be valid or invalid. Neither can the legal system as a whole. Validity is a relational term that determines the status of a lower rule in terms of a higher rule or standard. The existence and character of the ultimate standard or rule of recognition is a matter of social fact. From the viewpoint of an external observer it is simply the standard adopted in a particular society to regulate and identify its laws. Legal validity and legality is always in this sense relative to a particular set of legal rules. There is no legal validity floating in the air. The question of whether a legal rule is valid can only be raised when the rules in question are identified. An act may be lawful in terms of English law but not in terms of French law or international law or the law of the European Community. It is a matter of social fact which set of rules a particular community observes.

Several aspects of Hart's concept of law have met with criticism. Three issues have been:

1   the relation between law, justice and morality;
2   the idea of law as composed of rules; and
3   the application of rules in the judicial process.

Law, morality and legal positivism

Legal positivists have often been criticized for neglecting the connections between law and morality. Critics have pointed out the essential role played by such ideas as reasonableness, due process, and fairness in the common law and in the constitutional law of most developed states. These facts are not inconsistent with Hart's variety of positivism (Hart 1961), nor indeed with the views of earlier positivists such as Bentham and Austin (Bentham 1970; Austin 1954). All accepted that there are many connections between law and morality. The development of positive law, for example, is influenced by prevalent moral notions. Morality, again, may be the source of legal criticism or the inspiration for reform of the law. Third, a legal system may consciously make compliance with morality a criterion of validity for some of its laws (as does the USA, or Canada or Germany). The positivist claim would be, however, that this last possibility is a contingent fact about those particular legal systems and not a necessary feature of all systems.

In *The Concept of Law* Hart concedes that legal systems must in practice take account of certain basic features of human existence (Hart 1961). The facts of human vulnerability and limited human altruism imply that legal rules, to be effective and lasting, must make provision for certain minimum needs such as the protection of life and security, without which other rules would be pointless and short-lived. Thus there is a minimum content to human laws which is not accidental, but is not a logical requirement for the validity of laws. This is, in Hart's view, the 'core of good sense' in the natural law theorist's belief that law cannot be expounded in purely formal terms. Theorists such as the American jurist Lon Fuller, with whom

Hart had a much-discussed debate in 1956 (see Hart 1983), have argued that there are certain requirements that are inseparable from the enterprise of regulating human conduct by rules (Fuller 1964). Rules in their nature must be general, prospective not retrospective, be impartially applied, deal with like cases in a similar way and so on. Hart's reply was that these requirements did not in themselves rule out the possibility that particular laws might none the less be evil or iniquitous. For him the indisputable core of positivism is that law and morality can be separated, at least in the sense that the formal validity of a law is never conclusive as to its moral quality or as to the question of whether it deserves the citizen's obedience.

There is perhaps not a great distance between Hart and Fuller on this point. It can properly be said that if we are discussing modern civilized, and particularly liberal, systems of law, they generally do, by constitutional provisions, make the validity of laws turn not only on formal authoritative enactment but on compliance with basic substantive moral requirements. The difference seems to come only to this: that the natural lawyer wants to say that whether formally specified in the positive rules of a constitution or not, every system must be presumed to incorporate a requirement that provisions violating basic ideas of justice should be treated as invalid and be declared to be so by courts in every system. To a certain degree this view seems to be accepted in the jurisprudence of the Federal Constitutional Court in Germany. The positivist thesis which, by implication, is adopted by courts in most jurisdictions, however, is that only those substantive criteria of validity specified in the positive law of the constitution will be judicially applied. If this permits the enactment of particular unjust laws the problem raised is a moral and political one for citizens and politicians and not a judicial issue for courts of law. For a Hartian positivist, law and morality are always separable in this sense. Judges and lawyers must consider and use moral ideas in many areas of the law but only where the positive law itself imports and requires their use.

Law as rules

The view that law can be understood as a combination of different kinds of rules whose validity is specified by a rule of recognition has been contested by Professor Ronald Dworkin (1977, 1986) on the grounds, first, that law does not consist solely of rules and, second, that in modern developed legal systems there is no single rule of recognition that can act as a test for the validity of particular laws. The theory set out in *The Concept of Law* (Hart 1961) can perhaps be defended against these criticisms. It is not clear that the distinction between rules and principles is a fundamental one. In one sense it is part of a useful analysis of the rule concept. Rules in Dworkin's analysis are seen as fairly precise prescriptions that are said to be applicable in all-or-nothing fashion (Dworkin 1977: 22) whereas principles state aims or goals that may intersect and may have differing weights in accordance with which they may be balanced. Principles, in fact, appear to be rule-like statements that incorporate general or vague terms. But the primary thrust of Hart's *Concept of Law* was directed against the Austinian notion of law as command. Both rules and principles, whether or not they differ otherwise than in degree, may be contrasted with imperative commands and it may be that Hart's theory would not be fatally weakened if it were to concede that a legal system contained a combination of rules and principles.

The status of the most general rule or standard – the pedigree, basic norm or recognition rule – enters the argument at this point. A possible criticism of the rule of recognition is that there may be more difficulty in actually stating it accurately for any particular society than appears from Hart's discussion. In stating fully the basic norm of the United Kingdom legal system, for example, a long and complex proposition would need to be elaborated. Reference would perhaps need to be made to the rules and authority of common law as well as to the authority of Parliament to make statutes. Common law may be superseded by statute but it does not derive from statute and is a separate source of law. In stating or describing the ultimate sources of legal validity we might also wonder what degree of detail needs to be incorporated. Law may be made by Parliament. But do we need to specify Parliament's configuration or membership or the procedure by which it operates? And what is the force of the criticism that such a rule, whether long or short, cannot function as a test for the validity of laws? A simple answer would be that it is not intended to have that function in the sense of enabling a court or observer to decide whether a particular action or disputed rule is or is not lawful, or is a valid rule of the system. To know that it would be necessary to know a great many other things besides the rule of recognition – for example what powers, duties and obligations had been created by laws validly made under it; who had been authorized to act and in accordance with what principles; what subsidiary or delegated powers had been created; what interpretive rules had evolved or been laid down and so forth. The basic norm of a system of rules obviously could never be used as a measuring rod or test of validity in that sense – any more than knowing who had authority to make and change the rules of a game would be sufficient to allow one to act as umpire in relation to the legitimacy of particular actions in the game. That is not the function of such an identifying rule. Its job is rather to act as a signpost or identification of the ultimate source of appeal or authority as to what is legitimate or illegitimate in the system.

The judicial application of rules

Professor Dworkin's criticisms of the positivist rule model of law have been debated at length (see Raz 1979; Cohen 1984; Gavison 1987). A final element in the debate is whether the accusation that positivism is tied to a particular view of adjudication can be fairly maintained. It might certainly seem to follow from the Dworkin rules/principles distinction that if a legal system consisted solely of rules, precise answers to all legal questions would be available. But if the rule/principles distinction is rejected the idea that a legal system consists of rules does not commit its author to the view that all rules are fixed, definite or certain. Hart's discussion of adjudication (which is not a central concern of *The Concept of Law*) does not suggest a belief that rule-interpretation is a matter of mechanical application. It suggests that most legal rules or concepts have a core of meaning in which that application is uncontroversial and a penumbral area in which it is uncertain. But the Hartian model ought not to be tied to any particular thesis about the way in which uncertainty in the application of legal rules should be judicially resolved. The positivist thesis about the exclusion of morality as a necessary constituent in legal validity need not be committed to any particular theory of adjudication. Many critics of legal positivism, however, treat it as if it were synonymous with or entailed a mechanistic, inflexible or conservative view of the judicial process. A positivist model could, on the contrary, accommodate and provide for interpretive rules or codes that instructed judges to apply any theory of interpretation whatsoever, including the Dworkinian recipe that would have judges in difficult, uncertain or hard cases apply principles that would make the best sense of the system's general purposes, whatever the judges took those to be. Perhaps, though, a positivist would prefer to specify those purposes in the system's basic constitutional norms.

Positive and interpretive theory

Some of these points have been enlarged upon in the posthumously published second edition of *The Concept of Law* that appeared in 1994. In a substantial postscript to the new edition Hart set out what he took to be the difference between his own and Dworkin's approach. Hart described his own work as essentially descriptive and morally neutral, not seeking to justify or commend the processes and structures that occur in his general account of law and legal systems. Dworkin's enterprise is, he suggests, radically different, since it is evaluative and justificatory and addressed to a particular legal culture (namely that of Anglo-American law). Justification is for him 'the general part of adjudication' and is essentially interpretive or evaluative, designed to reveal the principles that provide the best moral justification for the laws of a particular system. Those laws cannot, on this view, be understood except from the internal viewpoint of a participant in the legal system. Hart's riposte is that a legal theorist must understand what it is to adopt the internal point of view, but in so doing he need not share or endorse it or surrender his descriptive stance.

Hart's work is treated by Dworkin as a representative sample of modern legal positivism, differing from earlier versions, such as those of Bentham or Austin in rejecting a command theory of law and the notion that all laws proceed from a legally unlimited sovereign authority (though it is not inconsistent with the existence of a legislative sovereign in a particular legal system whose powers are defined by the rule of recognition). Dworkin describes Hart's theory as 'plain fact positivism' in that it specifies that the criteria that provide the identification of law in a legal system must consist only of historical facts. Hart complains that this 'plain fact' label ignores his clear concession that in particular legal systems such as that of the USA (and indeed in these days many others also) the criteria of legal validity may include principles such as justice, equality and other substantive moral values. This perhaps illustrates the unclarity of the notion of a so-called 'pedigree' theory of legal validity. In the legal system as described by Hart it is, of course, a matter of plain and contingent fact what the system's criteria of valid law making are. But it is legitimate for him to object that this form of positivism does not imply that nothing other than plain facts can enter into the definition of law. One can see here also the need to keep in mind the distinction between the understanding of law in general and the criteria for the identification of laws in a particular system. Positivists, such as Hart, who have no reluctance to admit substantive moral values as contingently possible criteria for legal validity that may be adopted in a legal system are sometimes described as espousing 'soft positivism'. But one would think that 'hard positivists' who deny this possibility should be difficult to find.

In the Hart/Dworkin debate there is perhaps something characteristic of the differences between European and American approaches to the idea of law. European theorists have, from the time of Hobbes, attempted to describe the elements and structure of legal systems as a whole. The interconnections of legal theory with political philosophy, theories of the state and political obligation may have had some influence on this tradition. By contrast, American jurisprudence has concerned itself overwhelmingly, and it might even seem obsessively, with what might appear to be merely one element in a system of law, namely the judicial process. The character and overwhelming political importance of courts and adjudication in the USA may provide a partial explanation. In the writings of the American realist school and in Dworkinian anti-positivism there is almost no mention to be found of any general model of the legal system. In Professor Dworkin's *Law's Empire* (Dworkin 1986) the question 'What is Law?' becomes explicitly the question 'What is the nature of the process by which it is ascertained what the law is in a particular case?' We shall find out what law is when we know how judges should decide cases. That approach may have some value, since courts and adjudicators are to some degree assuming an increasing importance in European legal systems. Nevertheless, not all questions about law are about its application, or even its application in hard cases. There are basic questions for legislators and citizens as well as for judges that involve reflection about legal structures and about the idea and role of law in society. Not all questions of policy and morality can be resolved within the law or by judges.

The uses and limits of law

The concept of law and its relation to morality and to political obligation are not matters that concern only legal philosophers. There are times and places when individual citizens have to decide whether they are bound by, or owe allegiance to, law. Sometimes, though rarely, this question relates to the legal system in general. If Lithuania declares itself to be an independent sovereign state, or if Quebec were to secede from Canada unilaterally, as Rhodesia in 1965 rejected its existing legal subordination to the United Kingdom, the citizens of those territories need to decide what their legal and moral obligations are. Courts, also, need to apply some theory about the nature of law and the foundations of a legal system to decide cases testing the actions of the new governmental claimants to the exercise of lawful authority. In the Rhodesian case, and in other Commonwealth territories where *coups d'état* or revolutions have taken place, judges have invoked and debated theories of law – in particular Kelsen's thesis (p. 72) that the validity of laws in a system is dependent on the effective or generally efficacious operation of the system as a whole.

In liberal societies citizens also believe that there are limits to their obligation to obey particular laws. Both natural law doctrines and legal positivism permit and indeed require disobedience to law in appropriate circumstances, though adherents of natural law would in those circumstances base their rejection of obligation on the view that particular laws that clearly violate the requirements of justice cannot be valid laws, whilst legal positivists would in the same circumstances hold that legally valid and legally binding laws were not morally obligatory, since violation of basic rights was a reason for holding legal obligation to be overridden by moral obligation.

Natural lawyers perhaps do not need the concept of civil disobedience (in the sense of disobeying unjust but valid laws) since they can always claim to be exercising their legal right to disregard non-existent legal obligations, where requirements of justice are ignored by lawmakers. A Dworkinian citizen of Law's Empire also might not feel bound to treat the decisions of legislators and even of the highest appeal court as a conclusive final adjudication of what was and was not law. This may make a difference to the tactics of civil disobedience since the stage at which participants switch to or reject unlawful behaviour has often been thought important.

For the legislator and voter an understanding of the character and roles of law is an essential ingredient in decision making. In liberal societies it is believed that there are moral limits to the use of law to coerce or restrain individual action. Should law coerce individuals to prevent self-inflicted harm? Is there an area of private action (decisions involving procreation, marriage, sexual behaviour for example) which law should not penetrate? How far should law be used to restrict the freedom of communication or artistic creativity or to compel racial harmony? What law is and what it can and cannot effectively do are closely connected questions. Some modern legal theorists have attempted to generalize and analyse the technique element or functional uses of law bringing out the range of purposes beyond the coercive or penal functions. There is, for example, a grievance-remedial function; an administrative-regulatory function; a public benefit-conferring function; and a facilitation of private arrangements function (Summers and Howard 1965).

Law, perhaps it should be added, has an educative function. The study of organized society begins with it. Political, social and commercial activity is carried on within a framework whose boundaries are set by the legal and constitutional rules. Political science begins with law though it does not end with it. It is none the less not an isolated science that can stand on its own. The greatest legal scholars have always known this. Mr Justice Oliver Wendell Holmes put it this way: 'If your subject is law, the roads are plain to anthropology, the science of man, to political economy, the theory of legislation, ethics and thus by several paths to your final view of life' (Holmes 1920). Perhaps he exaggerated. But not very greatly.

References

Austin, J. (1954) 'The Province of Jurisprudence Determined', ed. H. L. A. Hart, London: Weidenfeld & Nicolson.

Bentham, J. (1970) *Collected Works*, London: Athlone Press.

Cohen, M. (ed.) (1984) *Ronald Dworkin and Contemporary Jurisprudence*, London: Duckworth.

Dworkin, R. (1977) *Taking Rights Seriously*, London: Duckworth.

—— (1985) *A Matter of Principle*, Cambridge, MA: Harvard University Press.

Fuller, L. L. (1964) *The Morality of Law*, New Haven and London: Yale University Press.

Gavison, R. (ed.) (1987) *Issues in Contemporary Legal Philosophy: The Influence of H. L. A. Hart*, Oxford: Clarendon Press.

Hart, H. L. A. (1961) *The Concept of Law*, Oxford: Clarendon Press.

—— (1983) *Essays in Jurisprudence and Philosophy*, Oxford: Clarendon Press.

Holmes, O. W. (1920) *Collected Legal Papers*, New York: Harcourt Brace & Howe.

Kelsen, (1970) *The Pure Theory of Law*, Berkeley: University of California Press.

—— (1961) *General Theory of Law and State*, New York: Russell & Russell.

—— (1991) *General Theory of Norms*, Oxford: Clarendon Press.

Olivecrona, K. (1939) *Laws as Fact*, 2nd edn, London: Stevens.

Raz, J. (1979) *The Authority of Law*, Oxford: Clarendon Press.

Ross, A. (1958) *On Law and Justice*, London: Stevens.

Summers, R. S. and Howard, C. G. (1965) *Law, Its Nature, Functions and Limits*, 2nd edn, Englewood Cliffs, NJ: Prentice-Hall.

Further reading

Allen, C. K. (1958) *Law in the Making*, 6th edn, Oxford: Clarendon Press.

Bix, B. (1993) *Law, Language and Legal Determinacy*, Oxford: Clarendon Press.

—— (1996) *Jurisprudence: Theory and Context*, London: Sweet & Maxwell.

Coleman, J. (ed.) (2001) *Hart's Postscript: Essays on the Postscript to The Concept of Law*, Oxford University Press.

Dworkin, R. (1986) *Law's Empire*, London: Collins.

Ewald, W. (1988) 'Unger's philosophy: a critical legal study', 97 *Yale Law Journal* 665.

Finnis, J. (1980) *Natural Law and Natural Rights*, Oxford: Clarendon Press.

George, R. (ed.) (1992) *Natural Law Theory*, Oxford: Clarendon Press.

—— (ed.) (1996)*The Autonomy of Law: Essays onLegal Positivism*, Oxford: Clarendon Press

Greenawalt, K. (1987) *Conflicts of Law and Morality*, Oxford: Clarendon Press.

Guest, S. (1992) *Ronald Dworkin*, Edinburgh: Edinburgh University Press.

Hacker, P. M. S. and Raz, J. (1972) *Law, Morality and Society*, Oxford: Clarendon Press.

Harris, J. W. (1979) *Law and Legal Science*, Oxford: Clarendon Press.

—— (1997) *Legal Philosophies*, 2nd edn, London: Butterworth.

MacCormick, N. (1981) *H. L. A. Hart*, London: Edward Arnold.

Marmor, A (1992) *Interpretation and Legal Theory*, Oxford: Clarendon Press

Morison, W. L. (1982) *John Austin*, London: Edward Arnold.

Patterson, D. (ed.) (1996) *A Companion to Philosophy of Law and Legal Theory*, Oxford: Blackwell.

Pennock, J. R. and Chapman, J. W. (1974) 'The Limits of Law', *Nomos* XV. New York: New York University Press.

Simmonds, N. E. (1986) *Central Issues in Jurisprudence*, London: Sweet & Maxwell.

Simpson, A. W. B. (1973) *Oxford Essays in Jurisprudence. (2nd series)*, Oxford: Clarendon Press.

Summers, R. S. (1982) *Instrumentalism and American Legal Theory*, Ithaca, NY: Cornell University Press.

—— (1984) *Lon L. Fuller*, Stanford: Stanford University Press.

Summers, R. S. and Atiyah, P. S. (1987) *Form and Substance in Anglo-American Law*, Oxford: Clarendon Press.

Unger, R. (1983) 'The critical legal studies movement', 96 *Harvard Law Review* 561.

5

CONCEPTIONS OF JUSTICE

Kai Nielsen

In thinking about justice, and about morality more generally, the traditions of both Aristotle and Locke have had a powerful influence. Both have been adapted to contemporary life in constitutional democracies. 'Sanitized' is perhaps a better description, particularly in the case of Aristotle. It would appear at first sight that Aristotle and Locke conflict but I think this is a superficial observation. Locke is indeed a severe individualist, while Aristotle stresses the social nature of the human animal: how an individual is, in her/his very identity, in her/his very humanity, a part of a greater whole. The very structure of our choices, the beings that we are, the very 'I' that is part of a 'we', are inescapably the expressions of a distinctive social ethos. And this, of course, includes the values and norms we have, our very most primitive conceptions of what is right, just and desirable. Locke, by contrast, sees individuals as independent. He views them as people capable of living in a state of nature, independent, tolerant of differences, seeking knowledge and concerned to protect their autonomy or self-ownership. A Lockean ethic will be concerned most fundamentally with the protection of individual rights. This individualist stress need not conflict with Aristotle's, or for that matter Hegel's, stress on the deep and irreversible way we are social animals through and through: how our very identity is formed by our society. Individualists, with a Lockean orientation, need not ignore their own past and how they are formed by a particular ethos with its distinctive structure of norms. We are socialized in distinctive ways that are inescapable and are a condition for our being human. But we need not be prisoners of our socialization. We are all distinctive sorts of human beings formed by a particular ethos. Sometimes, when we are a certain sort of person and fortunately situated, we can change our ethos, moving it in different directions in part as a function of our thoughts, desires, will and actions. And almost always we can by our distinctive reactions situate ourselves in patterns of our own choosing or partly of our own choosing, though set, and inescapably, in the distinctive social context in which we find ourselves. These thoughts do not, of course, come from nowhere. They are not simply the creation of the persons who think them. But they also are not unaffected by their individual thoughts. They are their own and they reflect who they distinctively are. People – or at least a not inconsiderable number of people – think of what kind of world they want and they have the ability to reflect carefully on what kind of world they have, including what distinctive kind of social creatures they and their fellows are, and they sometimes can, under propitious circumstances, forge a world a little more to their own liking, including to their own reflective and knowledgeable liking. There need be no conflict between a Lockean individualism and an Aristotelian stress on our social formation.

Where we may find conflict between Aristotle and Locke is over what is just and over how justice is to be understood. Aristotle's conception of a proper social order, a best regime, is that of a hierarchical world in which magnificent and magnanimous aristocrats rule and in which slaves do everything else. Human flourishing, so important for Aristotle, seems to be very much for the rulers alone. Locke was no egalitarian, but in the state of nature all human beings are free and their natural rights function to preserve and extend their autonomy: their self-ownership. The autonomy and self-ownership we are talking about is something that is to be sought for all human beings capable of autonomy and self-ownership. The moral import of the structure of rights is to protect the autonomy and self-ownership of all.

Classes and strata there will be, but it is Locke's conception that these divisions will not cut so deep as to undermine self-ownership and the natural rights of all human beings. People may have their stations and their duties but they are all, as creatures of God, free and stand with respect to self-ownership and the rights of humans in a condition of equality. A just social order cannot, as in an Aristotelian conception of social justice, allow a society of slaves or serfs where for some people resources external to them are properly subject entirely to communal control such that they, having no control, or very little control, of the means of life, have their autonomy undermined. *Such* class divisions are not morally tolerable for Locke. But this does not mean that no class divisions are tolerable. Locke took what we now call a class-structured society to be normal and proper.

It is true that Locke has no definite conception of human flourishing such as we have in Aristotle, but whatever human flourishing comes to, for Locke it cannot be a condition where human autonomy is undermined. Aristotle's conception of justice was unabashedly aristocratic. However, as I remarked initially, Aristotle can readily be sanitized (MacIntyre 1988; Shklar 1986: 13–33). His aristocratic conceptions could be dropped without at all touching his thoroughly social conception of human nature and its importance for a proper understanding of ethics and politics.

Marx, with clear indebtedness to Aristotle's stress on our sociality, came to stress against the ideology of the rising bourgeois order with its individualism and atomistic conception of human nature, that persons, as social creatures, could, under propitious circumstances, enhance the communal character of their lives (Miller 1981; Kain 1988; Gilbert 1990: 263–91). Moreover, a social order could, and would, come into being which would replace the extensively self-oriented individualism of the bourgeois world, with its stratification into hostile groupings, with a more egalitarian social order which would, in a way the more stratified society could not, enhance both the human flourishing and autonomy of all human beings (Marx 1962; see also Nielsen 1989a: 61–97).

The individualistic social order of which Locke's thought was an expression, as well as the aristocratic, hierarchical social order which Aristotle and the Medievals rationalized, would, as Marx saw it, gradually be replaced by this more egalitarian order. In the formation of this order the re-educative effects of public ownership and democracy, arising in a world of greater material abundance and productive power, would slowly erode the possessive individualism of the previous bourgeois order. Such individualism would gradually disappear and there would come to be a genuine social harmony in which we would acknowledge with a clarity of self-understanding both our communal natures and our self-ownership. Community and self-ownership would be linked.

Given the history of Marxism and (even more importantly) the history of actually existing socialisms claiming to be Marxist, there has been both within and without such societies considerable scepticism about the harmonious linkage of community and autonomy. What was hoped for was that deprivatized citizens would emerge under conditions of a very thoroughgoing equality of condition. They would be persons with both a firm sense of their individuality and their self-ownership, on the one hand, and of there being a 'we' on the other. This 'we' would not be an ethnocentric 'we' but a 'we' which included the whole of humanity. There would be in such socialized individuals not only a sense of distinct communities but a sense of the human community as well. However, what emerged in actually existing socialisms were authoritarian societies, thoroughly stratified, where privileges and power went to a small elite and where there was not only little autonomy but little equality as well. (Though it should also be said that in some respects these societies are more egalitarian than capitalist societies.) It should also be kept in mind that while there was much talk of community, there was in reality little in the way of community. It should be said of these societies what Marx said of medieval societies: that they were *Gesellschaften* parading as *Gemeinschaften*. They are hardly examples of where autonomy and community became uncoupled for there was little of either in such societies.

What combination of community, autonomy and equality will a thoroughly just society have and what will these things come to in a just society? Fairness seems at least to require some kind of equality but what kind and how extensive is it to be? (Rawls 1971; Hare 1978; Barry 1989). Will it, as many conservatives believe, only be a meritocratic equality of opportunity? (Bell 1979; Frankel 1971). If so, what is that to come to? Or will it, as social democrats and people on the left believe, also require equality of condition? (Barry 1989; Nielsen 1985; Cohen 1989a, 1989b). And again, if so, how is that to be understood and how extensive is it to be? If we try to stick with a conception of equality of opportunity linked with meritocratic conceptions of justice, can we actually achieve or even reasonably approximate equality of opportunity? If people come to the starting gate in the struggle of life in various conditions of advantage and disadvantage, can there be anything like a fair start at the running gate – what John Rawls calls *fair* equality of opportunity – in that struggle even if no one is constrained there by laws or regulations or discrimination? (Rawls 2001: 43–44). If everyone, advantaged and disadvantaged, were free to run, would we then actually have a condition of fair equality of opportunity? It is doubtful, to put it minimally, that we would (Nielsen 1985: 104–87). Moreover, should equality of opportunity be construed simply as, or construed at all as, everyone being able to engage, without constraint, in a competitive struggle for who is to come out on top? That is a very narrow construal of equality of opportunity. To have fair equality of opportunity it would seem at least to require equal life chances for all and that would seem at least to require something like equality of condition. But, again, how is the latter to be achieved? (Roemer 1998).

We cannot have equality of opportunity without equality of condition, or equality of condition without equality of opportunity. They require each other (Nielsen

1985: 104–87). An equality of opportunity that merely allows people an uncon-
strained start at the gate is a mockery of the very idea of equality of opportunity. In
trying to determine what fair equality of opportunity is, equality of condition is the
central thing to focus on for without it there is hardly anything like equal life
chances. But how are we to construe equality of condition? Given our (in part)
differing needs and preferences, it can hardly be simple equality where everyone in
every respect is treated exactly the same, has exactly the same stock of means and
the like (Walzer 1983: 14–16, 202–3). Not everyone needs a pacemaker or wants a
surfboard or a course in Latin. The thing to aim at is, as far as it is possible, the
equal meeting of the needs (*partly* various as they are) of everyone. This, even under
conditions of abundance or (if you will) moderate scarcity, is not possible. However,
under such conditions (say Switzerland was the world), it is something to be approximated. Where we cannot meet the needs of everyone, we must, as a second best,
and with that equal meeting of needs as a heuristic, develop fair procedures for the
unequal meeting of needs. For example, those most in need come first, or we should
give priority in the meeting of certain needs to those who in turn are the more
fruitful in satisfying the needs of others (violinist A gets the good violin rather than
violinist B because A's playing satisfies the needs of more people). Here we need to
develop ways of ascertaining what our needs are and to develop meta-procedures
(perhaps Habermas or Gauthier) for ascertaining when those particular procedures
for the unequal meeting of needs are fair (Habermas 1983; Gauthier 1985, 1986). It
is here that the stress on procedures given by Habermas is so central.

Simple equality will not do as a criterion of justice. We plainly need then a more
nuanced conception of equality of condition, for without something approximating
equality of condition we cannot achieve equality of opportunity, and without
equality of opportunity human beings will not have equal life chances, and without
an attempt to achieve that (or at least the attempt to approximate it as much as
possible), people will not stand to each other in positions of moral equality (Nagel
1979: 106–27). We cannot in such a circumstance have a society of equals
(Dworkin 1985: 181–204). Yet across the modern political spectrum there is a very
well-entrenched belief in moral equality. This belief is that the life of everyone
matters and matters equally and that politically speaking we should have a society
of equals. But it appears at least to be the case that if there is no building of a
world in which equality of condition can be approximated then there can be no
moral equality. Libertarians and other conservatives reject equality of condition as
a foolish and perhaps a dangerous bit of utopianism. Yet they are usually believers
in moral equality and they want a democratic society of equals. It looks as though,
given the soundness of the above argument, they should follow their conservative
predecessors from a more aristocratic age and reject moral equality given their
dismissal of any belief in equality of condition. Yet conservatives who are also
libertarians usually take moral equality very seriously indeed (Nozick 1974). And,
as Ronald Dworkin has pointed out, there is a sense in which contemporary conservatives as much as liberals and left wingers believe in a society of equals (Dworkin
1985). It looks at least as if such conservatives do not have their beliefs in reflective
equilibrium. It looks, that is, as if they do not have a consistent and coherent
pattern of beliefs. Without something approximating equality of condition there
can be no moral equality.

However, there are standard difficulties for the egalitarian as well, for if we seek to establish within society something approximating equality of condition, (a) can we do this without something approaching a uniformity of ethos that would undermine autonomy and individuality, and (b) would it not (*pace* what Rawls believes and argues) require state intervention in the lives of people that would also be destructive of autonomy (Rawls 2001: 189–91)? Can we, beyond the most minimal and, as we have seen, inadequate conception of equality of opportunity, have both equality and autonomy? Libertarians and other theoreticians of the right have thought that we cannot (Nozick 1974; Hayek 1960; Narveson 1988). A free society, they believe, cannot aim at an egalitarian conception of distributive justice, or for that matter any other conception of *distributive* justice, any more than it can aim at an aristocratic conception of justice where in a 'genuine community' people will have their assigned stations and duties. Caste is destructive of justice but so, libertarians claim, is equality of condition. Societies of both types are paternalistic and at least in effect, if not in intention, authoritarian.

Social justice, or, as with Friedrich Hayek and Robert Nozick, its alleged impossibility, has been at the centre of contemporary discussions of justice. John Rawls, Brian Barry, G. A. Cohen, Joshua Cohen, Thomas Scanlon, Amartya Sen, Kai Nielsen and Ronald Dworkin have been at the forefront of contemporary discussions of distributive justice and a defence of some egalitarian conception of social justice (Scanlon 1982). It is not that they deny the reality and importance of questions of individual justice (how individuals should treat one another to be fair to each other or what entitlements they should have), but, they argue, that pride of place should be given to questions of social justice: to the articulation of a correct conceptualization of how social institutions are to be arranged and to what must be done to create and sustain just institutions (Rawls 1978). Once those questions are reasonably answered – once we know what just social institutions should be like and how that is to be achieved – then it is easier to settle questions of individual justice. If we could come to understand what a just society would be like we could better understand what our individual responsibilities should be to each other and what we could rightly expect and require of each other.

The Lockean tradition, as against the liberal social democratic tradition of Rawls and Barry and the (broadly speaking) Aristotelian tradition of Alasdair MacIntyre and Charles Taylor, has, by contrast, stressed instead questions of individual justice and most particularly questions of the rights of individuals (Locke 1970; Nozick 1974; Gauthier 1988).[1] Justice from this perspective consists principally in protecting the inalienable rights of individuals: that is, with respect to all individuals, protecting their turf from boundary crossings that are illegitimate. Individuals are seen by this Lockean tradition to be self-sufficient. The principal aim of justice, and the very concept of a well-ordered society, should be to protect their self-ownership (Nozick 1974; see in opposition G. A. Cohen 1995 and Nielsen 1989d).

The Aristotelian tradition, by contrast, conceptualizes a just society, including its conception of a well-ordered society, in terms of some comprehensive theory of the good for human beings (MacIntyre 1988; Taylor 1985; Sandel 1982). As well, and again by contrast, the liberal social democratic tradition of Rawls, Barry and Scanlon, though it eschews in its conceptualization of a just society any comprehensive theory of the good, works with a minimal or thin theory of the good. In Rawls's case it comes principally to giving an account of the primary social and natural goods which any person would have to have assured to be able to realize any rational life plan they might have or any comprehensive conception of the good they might have that would similarly respect others.

For both Aristotelians and liberal social democrats, the determining of what rights we have requires a conception of the good. But only the former require a full-blown theory of the good for human beings. Both think against the Lockeans that an account of justice that approaches adequacy cannot just rely on some doctrine of inalienable rights that are recognized on reflection or in intuition to be self-evident. What rights we have and their importance in our lives is determined by conceptions of the good, for social democrats minimal ones, for communitarians a comprehensive theory of the good (Barber 1988: 54–90). As Rawls well puts it 'the just draws the limit, the good shows the point' (Rawls 2001: 141).

For theories mainly concerned with justice as a property of basic social institutions there are still two quite different stresses. One stress, as with Rawls or Barry, is that the function of justice is to provide a reasonable basis of agreement among people who seek to take due account of *the interests of all*; the other stress, as discussed by David Gauthier and Jan Narveson, sees the function of justice as the construction of social devices which enable people who are essentially egoists to get along better with one another (Gauthier 1986; Narveson 1988).[2] The first conceives of justice as *impartiality* or reciprocity, the second of justice as *mutual advantage*. Both accounts in their most powerful contemporary formulations are constructivist accounts, not relying on moral realist beliefs of either an intuitionist or naturalist variety in which moral truths are discovered as some antecedent reality not dependent on human construction. Constructivist accounts, as with Gauthier, reject such meta-ethical claims or, as with Rawls, do not rely on such claims (meta-ethical claims rejecting other sorts of meta-ethical claims) but proceed in a contractarian manner by selecting criteria for the correct principles of justice or for just social practices by ascertaining what people, bent on achieving a consensus concerning what to regard as principles of justice and just social practices, would agree on in some suitable hypothetical situation or what they actually would agree on when reasoning under certain constraints and in conditions of undistorted discourse (Habermas 1983; Rawls 1980, 1985).[3] Both accounts are contractarian and both constructivist. What Gauthier rejects, Rawls, more prudently, sets aside as unnecessary for the articulation of a theory of justice.

Historically speaking, the tradition conceiving of justice as impartiality has a broadly Kantian source and that of conceiving of justice as mutual advantage has a Hobbesian source. Brian Barry and Will Kymlicka have recently argued powerfully that these two traditions are in conflict, a conflict of such a sort that they cannot be reconciled (Barry 1989; Kymlicka 1989, 1990). They further claim that in much contemporary theorizing about justice, including most importantly that of John Rawls, these two at least arguably incompatible traditions stand in conflict. We cannot, they maintain, have it both ways, as Rawls in effect argues. The correct move, Barry and Kymlicka assert, is to reject the Hobbesian mutual advantage tradition. The way to go is to accept and clarify the tradition stressing that justice is the impartial consideration of the interests of everyone. That, they argue, is the account to be elucidated and developed.

Influential formulations of both accounts, as seen paradigmatically in the work of Rawls and Gauthier, share the belief, a belief also held by Habermas, that 'justice is what everyone could in principle reach a rational agreement on' (Barry 1989: 7). This, of course, is standardly taken as being partially definitive of social contract theories. The justice as impartiality view and the mutual advantage view have, of course, a different conception of why people are trying to reach agreement. Indeed, when we see what these conceptions are with their differing rationales, we will recognize that they are deeply different theories. The mutual advantage view says that the motive for justice is the pursuit of individual advantage. People in societies such as ours, and more generally in societies in what Hume and Rawls regard as the circumstances of justice (circumstances of limited material resources and conflicting interests or goals), pursue justice, they claim, for mutual advantage. In the circumstances of justice, which are the actual conditions of human life or at least for most human life, people can expect to advance their interests most efficiently through co-operating with other members of society rather than living with them in conditions of conflict. On such a view, rational people will agree on certain constraints – say the ones Gauthier specifies – as the minimum price that has to be paid in order to obtain the co-operation of others.

By contrast the motive for behaving justly in the justice as impartiality view is not reducible to even a sophisticated and indirect self-interest. Rather, the correct motive for behaving justly, in that view, is the belief that what happens to other people matters in and of itself. This being so, people should not look at things from their own point of view *alone*, but should seek to find a basis for agreement that is acceptable from all points of view (Kymlicka 1990). People, as Rawls puts it in a Kantian vein, are all self-originating sources of valid claims. We accept their claims because we think their interests are as important as our own and indeed that their interests are all equally important. We do not just, or perhaps even at all, take their interests into account because we are trying to promote our own interests. For the impartiality approach, at least on some of its formulations, justice would be the content of an agreement that would be reached under conditions that do not allow for bargaining power to be translated into advantage. By contrast, on the mutual advantage theory, justice can obtain even when people make agreements that are obtained by bargaining under conditions where the bargainers stand in differential power relations and have differential bargaining power. Indeed, where people are so differentially situated any agreement they come to for mutual advantage must reflect that fact. Such an approach is inescapable if appeal to self-interest is the motive for behaving justly. As Barry puts it in characterizing that position, 'If the terms of agreement failed to reflect differential bargaining power, those whose power was disproportionate to their share under the agreement would have an incentive to seek to upset it' (Barry 1989: 9). They would have no sufficient reason for sticking with the agreement. By contrast, the impartiality approach uncouples justice from bargaining power, since it does not require that everyone find it in their advantage to be just. They can have good reasons for being just even when being just is neither in their short-run nor their long-run advantage.

Given this difference in orientation, the kind of agreements for the impartialist that could count as just agreements do not allow bargaining power to be translated into advantage. Indeed, they specifically prohibit it. Both Barry and Kymlicka argue that the mutual advantage approach does not even count as a theory of *justice*. While the mutual advantage approach may generate some basic principles of social co-operation, these will not yield just agreements, since they allow as 'just agreements' agreements for mutual advantage obtained under differential power situations. The resulting system of co-operation, with its resulting system of rights and duties, lacks one of the basic properties of a moral system, namely, the property of giving equal weight to the interests of all the parties to the agreement. So while it articulates a system of social co-operation, it is not a moral theory and it is not a theory of justice.

On the mutual advantage account some persons can fall outside the system of rights altogether. Unlike the Kantian impartiality approach, it holds that those without bargaining power will fall beyond the pale of morality. Not every individual will have an inherent moral status. Some, on such an account, can be treated as a means only. This would be true of young children and of the severely retarded and it would be true of future generations (if they are to be spoken of as persons at all). All these people lack bargaining power for they have no way of retaliating against those people who harm them or fail to take into consideration their well-being.

Those are the extreme cases, but sometimes at least the powerful in our class-divided and stratified societies can treat the weak without moral concern: they can exploit them and push them against the wall. Where the dominant class is very secure, as for a time it sometimes is, it can rationally proceed in this way knowing that the dominated class has no effective means of fighting back. If indeed some gain an irresistible, effectively unchallengeable power, then they have with such power, on Hobbes's account, as well as for contemporary Hobbesians, something which 'justifieth all actions really and properly in whomsoever it is found' (quoted in Riley 1982: 39). But in a world so ordered the constraints of justice would have no place. We could have perhaps (given the circumstances) a rational system of co-operation and co-ordination. But we would not have a morality. There is no reasoning here in accordance with the moral point of view (Nielsen 2001: 1141–44). Where the strong can and do enslave or exploit the weak to the advantage of the strong we have something which is paradigmatically unjust. Barry puts the point thus:

> This gives us the defining characteristic of the second approach, namely, that justice should be the content of an agreement that would be reached by rational people under conditions that do not allow for bargaining power to be translated into advantage.
>
> (Barry 1989: 10)

Mutual advantage theory perhaps provides a good analysis of what genuinely rational, purely self-interested people would do. If we are going to engage in amoral *Realpolitik* this is perhaps how we should proceed but it does not provide us with anything that even looks like a method of moral justification. A cluster of practices which could be correctly characterized as just practices could not be a set of practices which would sustain or even allow those with greater bargaining power to turn it into such an advantageous outcome that the weak would be killed, die of starvation or live in intolerable conditions of life when that could be avoided. Such practices are paradigmatically unjust practices. If they are not unjust then nothing is.

A mutual advantage theorist might respond that her/his theory could never allow those things to obtain, for, no matter how severe the power differentials, such things (as a matter of fact) would never be to the mutual advantage of the parties (neither the weak nor the strong). But that is clearly a rather chancy empirical claim.[4] Faced, under severe and relatively secure power differentials, with the possibility of starvation, the weak might rationally settle for subsistence wages. Faced with a very marginal subsistence living, families might find it to their advantage (including the children's advantage) to opt for child labour under harsh conditions. With one's back against the wall, one might even find it to one's advantage to sell oneself into slavery or to agree to play a kind of Russian roulette where one might be killed. It is itself a rather chancy empirical claim to say that none of these things would be to the advantage of people in positions of power because the likelihood of the weak sticking with such harshly driven bargains would be too slim. That this would be so in all realistic conditions is far from evident. We can hardly be very confident that positions of power might not be so secure that it would be to the advantage of the powerful to drive such hard bargains. But whatever is in fact the case here about mutual advantage, we can know, impartiality theorists claim, that such bargains are unjust. Thus even if they do turn out to be mutually advantageous, they remain morally unacceptable. To respond 'Well, maybe they won't be mutually advantageous' is not to meet the challenge to mutual advantage theory.

Let us now consider impartiality theories. They take several forms, but whether or not they require the postulation of an original position or a state of nature, such theories view moral reasoning not as a form of bargaining but as a deliberation between agents who share a commitment to impartiality or at least, in Rawls's case, to reciprocity, to the giving of equal weight to the interests and needs of all. Put differently, they are people who are deliberating about which principles should be acceptable to all points of view. That, as Barry has it, is the basic idea of impartiality. Impartiality theorists such as Rawls, Hare, Sumner, Baier, Nielsen, Barry, Scanlon and Dworkin disagree over which principles of social justice are to be adopted, but they all in some sense are egalitarians and argue (*pace* Hayek) that justice as impartiality requires (where possible) the elimination of morally arbitrary inequalities, namely those inequalities arising from differences in social circumstances or natural talents. How fundamentally such an approach differs from the mutual advantage approach can be seen from the fact that an underlying rationale for appealing to impartial agreement is that it substitutes a moral equality for a physical or intellectual inequality. As Kymlicka well puts it, the two views are, morally speaking, a world apart: 'From the point of view of everyday morality, mutual advantage is an alternative to justice, not an alternative account of justice' (Kymlicka 1990: 103).

Appealing here to everyday morality, and not to something more abstract such as the moral point of view, begs the question with mutual advantage theorists, for they are willing to jettison much of everyday morality for a streamlined morality they regard (correctly or incorrectly) as more rational. There are on Hobbesian accounts no natural duties to others, no real moral difference between right and wrong which all persons must respect. There is, as well, no natural moral equality underlying our physical inequality. To the liberal appeal to moral equality (the life of everyone matters and matters equally) the Hobbesian can ask (as James Buchanan does), 'Why care about moral equality?' (Buchanan 1975: 54; see also Gauthier 1986).

Hobbesians, to continue the mutual advantage theorist's counter to impartiality theory, will respond to impartialists that they do not push questions of justification to a deep enough level. They do not realize that a person only has a reason to do something if the action the person contemplates doing satisfies some desires of that person, so that if something's being just is to count as a good reason for doing it, justice must be shown to be in the interest of the agent (Barry 1989: 363). Keeping this in mind we frame the Hobbesian question of why people possessing unequal power should refrain from using it in their own interests.

To this the impartialist can in turn respond in good Kantian fashion that morality needs no external justification. Morality itself provides a sufficient and original source of determination within us that is no more and no less artificial than the Hobbesian self-interested motivation. People can be motivated to act morally simply by coming to appreciate the moral reasons for doing so.

Hobbesians with their instrumentalist conception of rationality will find this impartialist acceptance here artificial and perhaps evasive. But they in turn must face Barry's claim that to equate rationality with the efficient pursuit of self-interest is a view which rests on pure assertion. Rational egoism is not an inconsistent view. There is no showing that to be consistent one must be an impartialist. But there is no good reason to believe that the very meaning of 'rational' is such that if one is rational one must be an egoist. The acceptance of the formal criterion of universalizability together with a recognition that others are fundamentally like us in having needs and goals and indeed in having, generally speaking, some of the same needs and goals, gives us powerful reasons for accepting the claims of an impartial morality (Barry 1989: 273, 285).[5] A person is not being inconsistent if she/he does not care about the needs and goals of others; she/he does not violate the criterion of universalizability, but, as Barry put it, 'the virtually unanimous concurrence of the human race in caring about the defensibility of actions in a way that does not simply appeal to power' (Barry 1989) suggests that this appeal to impartiality and to moral equality are very deeply embedded, considered convictions to some extent held across cultures and over time. To say that such persons act irrationally, if so acting is not in their individual self-interest, or even act in a way that is less than optimally rational, is to utilize what is in effect an arbitrary *persuasive* definition of what it is to be rational.

All constructivist contractualist theories of justice, and of morality more generally, whether mutual advantage theories or impartiality theories, construe justice as those principles and that set of practices on which everyone at least in principle could reach agreement. Barry as much as Rawls construes justice as impartiality in terms of agreement. But there are those who are justice-as-impartiality theorists but who reject construing justice in terms of agreement (Kymlicka 1989, 1990). Barry gives us a sense of what the stress on agreement would come to:

> [T]he function of justice is to provide a rational basis for agreement among people who do not simply look at things from the point of view of their own interests but seek to take due account of the interests of all. Justice, on this conception, is what can be justified to everyone.... It is inherent in this conception that there is a distinctively moral motive, namely, the desire to behave in accordance with principles that can be defended to oneself and others in an impartial way.
>
> (Barry 1989: 272)

Following Scanlon, Barry takes the underlying moral motive to be 'the desire to be able to justify one's actions to others on grounds they could not reasonably reject' (ibid.: 284). Conceptions of this sort are widely held, but Kymlicka among others thinks that they are fundamentally mistaken (Kymlicka 1990: 110–12). Perhaps such a conception would work if we were only considering moral relations between competent adults. But there are as well moral relations between us and children and the mentally disabled. It is senseless to talk about impartial agreement with infants or giving the mentally disabled grounds they could not reasonably reject. Considerations of justice are very stringent between them and us but there is no room for talk of justice coming to what they and we could come to an agreement about.

> If someone is incapable of being a party to an agreement with us, that certainly does not mean we lack any moral motive for attending to his or her interests. The emphasis on agreement within impartiality seems to create some of the same problems that the emphasis on bargaining power creates within mutual advantage theories: some people will fall beyond the pale of morality, including those who are most in need of moral protection.
>
> (Kymlicka 1990: 110)

It is a mistake to claim, as Scanlon does, that morality 'only applies to a being if the notion of justification to a being of that kind makes sense' (Scanlon 1982: 113–14 and Scanlon 1998).

Scanlon maintains in defence of his thesis that the fact that a being can feel pain shows that that being has a centre of consciousness and, because of this, that the notion of justification to such a being makes sense. It is because of this, Scanlon claims, that pain is so often taken as a relevant criterion for moral status. But it is false that if a being can feel pain, justification can be addressed to that being and that we can in principle at least attain agreement with her/him. Agreement requires the being not just to be able to feel pain and to be a centre of consciousness, but comprehension as well, and while infants and the severely mentally disabled can feel pain they cannot comprehend things so that they could enter into agreements with us, so the notion of justification would not make sense to them. Yet surely they have moral status. That we cannot address justification to a baby does not mean the baby lacks moral status. We give moral status to an infant not because we can address justification to it or to its moral trustee. We give moral status to it because it can suffer or flourish, because the lives of such beings 'can go better or worse, and because we think their well-being is of intrinsic importance' (Kymlicka 1990: 111). Some beings we can address justification to and some we cannot; what 'makes them all moral beings is the fact that they have a good, and their well-being matters intrinsically' (ibid.: 111). But to so argue is to break with the contractarian tradition, including its impartialist versions. But it would seem at least morally arbitrary not to do so.

Kymlicka argues that we should construe justice as impartiality not in the manner of the contractualist as based on some kind of agreement, but that we should simply take impartiality as a criterion that, with or without agreement, gives all interests equal weight. Our moral motivation is not in reaching agreement but in responding to legitimate interests. We simply come to recognize, if we are moral beings, that others have legitimate claims to have their interests taken into account. The thing is to try to find or articulate principles of justice that give equal weight to everyone's interests. Agreement, Kymlicka claims, drops out.

We have clear obligations to those who are powerless to defend, represent or even recognize their own interests. In this vein, and abstracting a little, our clearest obligations are, Kymlicka claims, not to try to reach agreement but to take people's interests into account and to give equal weight to the interests of all human beings. This is the clear claim of justice as impartiality. Our principles of justice are justified when they do that. If they do not give such equal weight to the interests of all, whether we agree about these principles or not, this agreement does not justify them. This commits us to the substantively egalitarian view that the interests of all human beings matter and matter equally. Where that is not our guiding conception we do not, at least on modern conceptions of justice, have justice. Agreement is, of course, of vital epistemological and political import. But at the foundational level, as Kymlicka has it, it does not apply; that is to say, it does not apply where we are saying what justice is and what the foundations of a just society are (Kymlicka 1990: 113). 'At the deepest level', Kymlicka continues, 'justice is about equal consideration of our legitimate interests, and the many virtues of agreement are assessed by reference to that underlying idea, not vice versa' (ibid.: 112). And, even if we are coherentist anti-foundationalists and we reject foundationalist claims or even foundationalist metaphors, we can still quite properly say that crucially and fundamentally justice, in the very primitive sense it has for us, is about the equal consideration of legitimate interests.

There is plainly something right about Kymlicka's argument here, but there may be something wrong as well which gives morals by agreement another inning. What justice as impartiality substantively comes to is giving the interests of all equal weight such that everyone's interests matter and everyone's interests matter equally. Proper names are not relevant in determining whose interest has pride of place when they conflict and both interests cannot be satisfied. Still, in such a situation we must depart from simple equality, and it is there that the careful articulation of principles of social justice such as we find in Rawls, Scanlon and Barry becomes vital. But in making such a differential weighting, such as to proceed by benefiting the worst off maximally in ways that are compatible with retaining autonomy and fair equality of opportunity for all, we should start from a position where we give equal consideration to the interests of all and where we start by giving an initial equal weighting to all interests. It is only when we recognize that not all interests can be satisfied equally that we look for impartial and fair ways of departing from simple equality. But that does not gainsay the point that justice is about the equal consideration of our legitimate interests. This obtains whether or not there is anything that everyone competent to make such judgements and bent on being reasonable would agree on. So far things seem at least to cut against contractarians.

However, let us now ask: how do we know that is so? How do we know that this is what justice is and that this is what justice requires such that we must act in this way if we would be just and that for there to be just social institutions our social practices must be so structured? It is here that agreement may come in by the back door.

Kymlicka writes as if we could just intuit or directly recognize that this is so, that we could just see that these claims are true. But if there are any accounts that are by now widely recognized to be non-starters, it is intuitionism and natural law theories where we in some mysterious way must just have direct access to the truth – indeed, even on some accounts, the certain truth – of certain moral propositions.

How then does Kymlicka know, and how can we know, that his fundamental substantive moral claims, claims not subject to agreement, are true or justified? Perhaps they are (though Kymlicka does not claim that for them) *conceptual* claims such that we can know that they are true by having a grasp of the concept of justice, where to have a grasp of the concept of justice is to know how to use 'justice' or cognate terms correctly. Perhaps the following conceptual chain holds: to be just is to be fair, to be fair is to be impartial, and to be impartial is to give equal consideration to the interests of all human beings. If this is so we could know the truth of Kymlicka's claims by coming to have a good understanding of the use of 'justice'. But that may not give us a way of meeting mutual advantage theories at all. Gauthier, for example, understands perfectly well the ordinary use of 'just' and 'justice' and what it commits us to, if we would stick with it, but he will for his theoretical purposes modify that use until it is compatible with a set of principles that are rationally sustainable and that rational people will agree to be rationally sustainable when these people are reasoning carefully. We cannot go very far in sustaining substantive claims and substantive principles of justice through being clear about the use of 'just' and allied terms. Such considerations may undermine certain absurd claims, but they leave many competitors for what is just in the field.

It may, that is, give us something like the first word but it will not carry us very far beyond that. But then how does Kymlicka know that his substantive claims about justice are justified? He leaves this mysterious. Rawls, Daniels and Nielsen explicitly, and others implicitly, have in such contexts appealed to considered judgements or convictions in wide reflective equilibrium (Rawls 1971: 19–21, 48–51, 577–87; 1975; Daniels 1979, 1996; Nielsen 1987, 1988). It has been mistakenly thought that this is a thinly disguised form of intuitionism with all its difficulties plus even more evident worries about ethnocentrism. However, these charges are mistaken, given the kind of coherentism involved in the appeal to considered judgements in wide reflective equilibrium. It starts from our firmest considered convictions of a rather specific sort, such as to enslave people is wrong, racial prejudice is evil, religious intolerance is unacceptable, and it tries to have a consistent cluster of such beliefs. But it also seeks to show how such specific considered convictions can be derived from and are explicable by more general moral principles, some of which themselves may be considered judgements. 'The interests of all human beings are of equal importance' is one such principle which is also such an abstract considered judgement. We seek by a reciprocal adjusting of many elements, sometimes modifying or abandoning a specific considered judgement or sometimes modifying or even abandoning a more general principle or sometimes by coming to articulate a new one with a powerful rationalizing power, until we get what we can recognize to be a consistent and coherent cluster of beliefs. We do this by sometimes trimming, sometimes expanding, our cluster of considered judgements and principles, but always adjusting this *mélange* of convictions and beliefs. We do this until we have something which we have good reasons to believe forms a consistent and coherent cluster. So far we have nothing more than what is given by ethical intuitionism, though there need be, and indeed should be, no claim to a bizarre epistemic status or a truth capturing power for the moral beliefs and principles. Indeed we can, following Rawls, avoid making any claim about the epistemic status of our principles of justice or our various moral claims.

Where wide reflective equilibrium clearly goes beyond ethical intuitionism, which is a narrow reflective equilibrium, is in its stress that other things besides specific moral beliefs and moral principles must be appealed to in gaining the coherent web of belief and conviction that would constitute a wide reflective equilibrium. The consistent set we seek is not only of specific moral convictions and more general principles, but of whole theories of morality, conceptions of the function of morality in society, factual beliefs about the structure of society and about human nature, beliefs about social change (including beliefs about how societies will develop or can be made to develop) as well as specific historical and sociological beliefs about what our situation is. The equilibrium we seek is one in which all these elements are put into a coherent whole. In narrow reflective equilibrium a specific considered conviction might be abandoned because it conflicted with many equally weighty specific considered convictions or a more general moral principle. But in wide reflective equilibrium they might be rejected as well because they were incompatible with some well-established empirical facts about society or human beings or our particular situation or because they made demands which, given what we know about the world, could not be realized or were beliefs which had moral alternatives which made much more sense in the light of some carefully elaborated social or moral theories or theories about the function of morality in society. There is here a considerable range of considerations, including empirical considerations, that are relevant to our decisions about what to do or how to live. We start with specific considered convictions but they are correctable by a whole range of empirical and theoretical convictions as well as by moral principles or moral theories, though sometimes in the case of moral principles and theories it will go the other way and the principles or theories will be correctable by the specific considered judgements. This yields a critical morality that lacks the dogmatism and what in effect, though not in intention, is the conventionalism and subjectivism of moral intuitionism. Moreover, that critical morality also functions as a guard against ethnocentrism. Some of the specific judgements we start with may be ethnocentric but by the time we have got them into wide reflective equilibrium the ethnocentrism will be winnowed out.

So if Kymlicka would avail himself of such a procedure he at least arguably would have a method of reasoning for his fundamental claims of justice and he need not just assert them, somehow taking them to be natural laws or basic intuitions recoverable on reflection. The method of wide reflective equilibrium could, of course, be used, as well, to argue against an account like Kymlicka's. Its advantage, whichever way it is used, is that we do not need to just assert or to rely on intuition but can appeal to a method that is very like the method used in science and in other domains.

However, in doing this he would be implicitly appealing to some agreement, to some consensus, for it is *our* considered convictions that we seek to get into wide reflective equilibrium. This means we are in effect appealing to convictions of a specific people, a specific community with its traditions situated in a determinate cultural space and time. We rely on a consensus in such a community though the shared considered convictions need not be, and typically will not be, only the shared convictions – the considered judgements – of that community. They might in some instances be quite pan-human. But for them to be *our* considered judgements they must rest on a consensus in our community and this, of course, implies an agreement. Thus (*pace* Kymlicka) agreement enters in at a very fundamental level. To show that his impartiality account of justice is justified, he must show that its principles and claims can, relying on considered judgements, be placed in wide reflective equilibrium. But this need not mean that it appeals to the agreement of everyone to whom it is addressed.

Some of the philosophers appealing to wide reflective equilibrium, and in doing so relying very fundamentally on considered convictions (Rawls most prominently), are also constructivists and contractarians and take the method of wide reflective equilibrium and their contractarianism to form a coherent whole. For Rawls, for example, in deciding on how thick the veil of ignorance is to be or how the original position is to be characterized, we at crucial junctures rely on considered convictions as we do in deciding on what it is reasonable to accept. But in turn, in deciding on whether we have for a time achieved a reflective equilibrium, we would need a conception of justice which would be acceptable to the parties under certain idealized conditions. So again, at a very fundamental justificatory level, agreement is appealed to. It is not that the substantive principles and claims of social justice are not what Kymlicka says they are or that justice is what we can agree on in certain idealized situations, but that, if we are to show that Kymlicka's or anyone else's substantive claims of justice are justified, we must show that there is such agreement.

We should note in this context that justice is like truth. Truth is not what researchers investigating under ideal conditions and over a considerable time would agree is the case. But that may be the best test for truth. Similarly justice is not what would be agreed to in the original position but that may be the best test for what is just. We have carefully to distinguish what truth and justice mean and what they are from how we ascertain what is true or just.

I want now to consider a way, a rather weak way I am afraid, in which the impartiality approach to justice and the mutual advantage approach *might* be shown to be compatible. The impartiality approaches show us what justice is, how we have to be in order to be just persons of moral principle, what just institutions would look like, and what principles of justice people, reasoning carefully from the moral point of view, would find to be most justified and why. We are asking for moral reasons here which only *per accidens* may sometimes also be reasons of self-interest. Assuming there is something called the moral point of view (one property of which is the impartial consideration of the interests of all), people of moral principle will reason in accordance with it (Nielsen 2001). They will hope and reasonably expect that most of the time their interests will not be hurt by doing so, but they will not think they are justified in doing so only when doing so answers to their own interests or at least does not go against their interests. Their motive for pursuing justice is not the pursuit of individual advantage. What happens to other people matters in and of itself. But we can still ask, and they can ask, '*Why be just?*' Can we give reasons of a broadly prudential sort which will show why a purely self-interested person, if thoroughly rational and clear about the non-moral facts, will do, though out of self-interest, what a just person will do?[6] Kant distinguished between a person of good morals (something an egoist could be) and a morally good person (someone genuinely committed to the moral point of view). Can we show that rational, purely self-interested people, if they were also persons of good morals, would, if they were thoroughly rational, do what just people do, or even do roughly what just people do, though not, of course, for the same reasons? We should recognize in pressing that question that 'Why ought we to be just?', 'Why be fair?', 'Why ought we to do what is right?' or 'Why should we be moral?' are questions that we could not ask from a moral point of view. To ask them is like asking 'Why ought we do what we ought to do?' (Nielsen 1989c; 2001).

However, as the extended discussion of 'Why be moral?' has brought out, we can ask: 'Why take the moral point of view at all?' (Baier 1958; Frankena 1980; Nielsen 1989c; Gauthier 1988). From the moral point of view, moral reasons by definition override non-moral reasons, but why take that point of view at all? From the point of view of individual self-interest, from class interests or from the point of view of a group of constrained maximizers bent on co-operation for mutual advantage, moral reasons are not the overriding reasons or at most they are only contingently overriding (Wood 1985, 1984). From the moral point of view they are necessarily overriding but not from these points of view. But why take the moral point of view? Justice, fairness and morality requires it. But so what?

Hobbesian theory can be taken as a powerful attempt to show that we have very strong prudential reasons for being, as the world is and will continue to be, persons of good morals. We have in terms of long-term self-interest the best of reasons to support the continued existence of moral constraints, including just practices. (We could not – logically could not – have moral institutions, at least where the circumstances of justice obtain, that did not include just social practices.) Rational persons, the claim goes, will not be morally good, but they will be persons of good morals.

The impartialist arguments, such as we have seen Barry and Kymlicka articulating, show, I believe, that Hobbesians (pure mutual advantage theorists) cannot get justice out of purely self-interested reasoning, including constrained maximization, which in the end is itself purely self-interested reasoning.[7] Indeed, it is true, as some modern Hobbesians have powerfully argued, that people can expect to advance their interests most effectively by co-operating and in doing this by agreeing to accept certain constraints on their direct individual utility maximization. By moderating their demands and by co-operating with others they will, as the world goes, in the long run do better. David Gauthier makes a powerful case for that (Gauthier 1986).[8] But these forms of co-operation will not give us morality, will not give us a system of justice, where the interests of all count equally, where what happens to other people matters in and of itself, where the reasons for action must not just be acceptable from the point of view of the agent doing the reasoning but from all points of view. For a social practice to be just it must not only answer to the interests of some individual or some class or elite but it must also answer to the interests of all. But, as we have seen, there can be all kinds of situations (class differentials, caste systems, hierarchical strata, adults and children, the mentally competent and the mentally disabled, developed cultures and non-literate ones) where there are differential power structures and where, by pursuing mutual advantage intelligently in certain circumstances, the powerful would exploit the weak and not for all of that be acting unintelligently or irrationally. It could, as we have seen, very well in such circumstances be in the mutual advantage of everyone involved. Justice cannot allow differential bargaining power to be translated into advantage: that is, it cannot allow exploitation. People in such circumstances, given their weakness, have reason to co-operate with the strong for otherwise they will be still worse off. And in societies as we know them these circumstances are not infrequent (Cohen 1992). So, given the differential power situation and the determination of the powerful to do the best they can for themselves, the weak have prudential reasons to co-operate even though they are exploited. But they are not being treated justly; the resulting system of co-operation, though rational, is not moral; it is not even in a Rawlsian sense reasonable. Indeed such treatment of people is immoral. We do not reach morality from Hobbesian premises and thus we do not reach justice. The impartialist does not ask why be just but shows what justice is; the Hobbesian asks why be just and tries to show that we should be just because justice pays. What has been shown is that it is not true that justice *always* pays. Some form of social co-operation always pays, but the form of social co-operation people engage in may be very different from justice. The Habermasian has not shown that the enlightened egoist or the intelligent and informed constrained maximizer must, to be thoroughly rational, be just. But the Hobbesian has not shown that we can get justice out of enlightened egoism.

To this the Hobbesian might reply that a good bit of morality is irrational. The moral point of view requires the equal consideration of interests but it is irrational, or at least it is not required by rationality, for an individual or a group to do so when it is not in their interests. What is rational to do is determined by the interests of the individual who is doing the acting. Where parts of morality do not so answer to individual interests they should, the Hobbesian can claim, be jettisoned and what is kept as a system of social co-operation, though considerably less than morality as it has been traditionally conceived, is the rational critical core of morality.

This purely instrumentalist conception of rationality, as we saw Barry arguing, is pure assertion. That it is just this that rationality comes to is not established through an examination of the use of 'rationality'. To give equal weight to the interests of all is not irrational. To say it is a rational thing to do is no more or no less rooted in the use of 'rational' than is the claim that to be rational is always to give self-interested reasons pride of place.

We can appeal to theoretical considerations to support such an instrumentalist conception of rationality, but there are other conceptions of rationality answering to different theoretical purposes. Given Hobbesian purposes we can use that Hobbesian conception of rationality, but, given Habermasian or Aristotelian purposes or the purposes of impartialism, we can use instead these quite different conceptions of rationality. There seem to be no good reasons external to these particular purposes to accept one of these purposes rather than another; and to say that the Hobbesian ones are the really rational ones is plainly question begging. Moreover, the Hobbesian conception is subject to *reductio* arguments. *If* it fits the interests of one class to enslave another class and work them to the edge of starvation, that would, on such a Hobbesian account, would, if their grip on things was reasonably stable, not only be what reason *permits*; it would be what reason *requires*, but a theory of rationality that had that implication would not only be morally repugnant, it would be groundless and thoroughly implausible.[9]

Notes

1 Nozick (as do many other libertarians) takes himself to be a genuine descendant of Locke. This has been impressively challenged by Virginia Held (1976) and Shadia Drury (1979).

2 Gauthier's position is the canonical one here. Narveson's far cruder politically committed work seeks to follow Gauthier. It is a question worth pursuing to ask how much, if any, of Herzog's trenchant critique of Narveson rubs off on Gauthier.

3 The latter claim is Habermas's and, unlike Rawls, he is not loath to make meta-ethical claims. However Rawls, with his method of avoidance, does resolutely set aside meta-ethical claims.

4 This is reminiscent of utilitarian arguments to ward off *reductio* arguments against utilitarianism.

5 To say that something is universalizable is to say that, if X is good for Y or is something Y ought to do, it is something that is good for anyone else or something anyone else ought to do if that someone is relevantly like Y and is relevantly similarly situated. 'Relevantly' here needs to be cashed in contextually. See Nielsen (1989b).

6 I am inclined to think 'non-moral facts' is pleonastic but that belief is contentious.

7 Gauthier remarks 'my discussion assumes rational, utility-maximizing individuals who are not mistaken about the nature of morality or, more generally, who recognize that *the sole rationale* for constraint must ultimately be a utility-maximizing one' (Gauthier 1988: 182).

8 The work of Will Kymlicka has deeply influenced me in the writing of this essay. His influence, my criticisms to him to the contrary notwithstanding, is particularly evident in the last third of this essay.

9 This contention about rationality is elaborated and defended in Nielsen (1991).

References

Baier, K. (1958) *The Moral Point of View*, Ithaca, NY: Cornell University Press.

Barber, B. (1988) *The Conquest of Politics*, Princeton: Princeton University Press.

Barry, B. (1989) *Theories of Justice*, Berkeley: University of California Press.

Bell, D. (1979) 'On meritocracy and justice', in D. L. Schaefer (ed.) *The New Egalitarianism*, Port Washington, NY: Kennikat Press.

Buchanan, J. (1975) *The Limits of Liberty: Between Anarchy and Leviathan*, Chicago: University of Chicago Press.

Cohen, G. A. (1989a) 'Are freedom and equality compatible?', in J. Elster and K. O. Moene (eds) *Alternatives to Capitalism*, Cambridge: Cambridge University Press.

—— (1989b) 'On the currency of egalitarian justice', *Ethics* 99 (4): 906–44.

—— (1992) 'Incentives, inequality, and community', in G. Peterson (ed.) *The Tanner Lectures on Human Values*, Salt Lake City: University of Utah Press.

—— (1995) *Self-Ownership, Freedom and Equality*, Cambridge, UK: Cambridge University Press.

Daniels, N. (1979) 'Wide reflective equilibrium and theory acceptance in ethics', *Journal of Philosophy* 76: 256–82.

—— (1996) *Justice and Justification*, Cambridge, UK: Cambridge University Press.

Drury, S. (1979) 'Robert Nozick and the right to property', in A. Parel and T. Flanagan (eds) *Theories of Property*, Waterloo, Ont.: Wilfred Laurier University Press.

Dworkin, R. (1985) *A Matter of Principle*, Cambridge, MA: Harvard University Press.

Frankel, C. (1971) 'Equality of opportunity', *Ethics* 81 (3): 191–211.

Frankena, W. (1980) *Thinking about Morality*, Ann Arbor: University of Michigan Press.

Gauthier, D. (1985) 'Justice as social choice', in D. Copp and D. Zimmerman (eds) *Morality, Reason and Truth*, Totowa, NJ: Rowman & Allenheld.

—— (1986) *Morals by Agreement*, Oxford: Clarendon Press.

—— (1988) 'Morality, rational choice and semantic representation', *Social Philosophy and Policy* 5 (2): 182.

Gilbert, A. (1990) *Democratic Individuality*, Cambridge: Cambridge University Press.

Habermas, J. (1983) *Moralbewußtsein und kommunikatives Handeln*, Frankfurt am Main: Suhrkamp Verlag; pub. in English (1990) as *Moral Consciousness and Communicative Action*, trans. C. Lenhardt *et al.* Cambridge, MA: MIT Press.

Hare, R. M. (1978) 'Justice and equality', in J. Arthur and W. Shaw (eds) *Justice and Economic Distribution*, Englewood Cliffs, NJ: Prentice-Hall.

Hayek, F. (1960) *The Constitution of Liberty*, London: Routledge; Chicago: University of Chicago Press.

Held, V. (1976) 'John Locke on Robert Nozick', *Social Research* 43: 169–95.

Kain, P. J. (1988) *Marx and Ethics*, Oxford: Clarendon Press.

Kymlicka, W. (1989) *Liberalism, Community and Culture*, Oxford: Clarendon Press.

—— (1990) 'Two theories of justice', *Inquiry* 33 (1): 81–98.

Locke, J. (1970) *Two Treatises of Government*, ed. P. Laslett, Cambridge: Cambridge University Press.

MacIntyre, A. (1988) *Whose Justice? Which Rationality?*, Notre Dame: University of Notre Dame Press.

Marx, K. (1962) *Critique of the Gotha Programme*, ed. C. P. Dutt, New York: International Publishers.

Miller, R. (1981) 'Marx and Aristotle: a kind of consequentialism', in K. Nielsen and S. Patten (eds) *Marx and Morality*, Guelph: Canadian Association for Publishing in Philosophy.

Nagel, T. (1979) *Mortal Questions*, New York: Cambridge University Press.

—— (1991) *Equality and Partiality*, Oxford: Oxford University Press.

Narveson, J. (1988) *The Libertarian Idea*, Philadelphia: Temple University Press.

Nielsen, K. (1985) *Equality and Liberty: A Defense of Radical Egalitarianism*, Totowa, NJ: Rowman & Allenheld.

—— (1987) 'Searching for an emancipatory perspective: wide reflective equilibrium and the hermeneutical circle', in E. Simpson (ed.) *Anti-foundationalism and Practical Reasoning*, Edmonton: Academic Printing and Publishing.

—— (1988) 'In defense of wide reflective equilibrium', in D. Odegard (ed.) *Ethics and Justification*, Edmonton: Academic Printing and Publishing.

—— (1989a) *Marxism and the Moral Point of View*, Boulder, CO: Westview Press.

—— (1989b) 'Justice, equality and needs', *Dalhousie Review* 69 (2): 211–27.

—— (1989c) *Why be Moral?*, Buffalo, NY: Prometheus Books.

—— (1989d) 'Equality of condition and self-ownership', in Guy Le France (ed.) *Ethics and Basic Rights*, Les Presses de l'université d'Ottawa.

——(1991) 'Can there be justified philosophical beliefs?', *Iyyun* 12: 69–94.

—— (2001) 'The moral point of view', in L. G. Becker and C. B. Becker (eds) *Encyclopedia of Ethics*, 2nd edn, vol II, London: Routledge.

Nozick, R. (1974) *Anarchy, State and Utopia*, New York: Basic Books.

Rawls, J. (1971) *A Theory of Justice*, Cambridge, MA: Harvard University Press.

—— (1978) 'The basic structure of the subject', in A. Goldman and J. Kim (eds) *Values and Morals*, Dordrecht: Reidel.

—— (1980) 'Kantian constructivism in moral theory', *Journal of Philosophy* 77: 515–72.

—— (1985) 'Justice as fairness: political not metaphysical', *Philosophy and Public Affairs* 14 (3): 223–51.

—— (2001) *Justice as Fairness: A Restatement*, ed. Erin Kelly, Cambridge, MA: Belknap.

Riley, P. (1982) *Will and Political Legitimacy: A Critical Exposition of Social Contract Theories in Hobbes, Locke, Rousseau and Hegel*, Cambridge, MA: Harvard University Press.

Roemer, J. (1988) *Free to Lose*, Cambridge, MA: Harvard University Press.

—— (1998) *Equality of Opportunity*, Cambridge, MA: Harvard University Press.

Sandel, M. (1982) *Liberalism and the Limits of Justice*, Cambridge: Cambridge University Press.

Scanlon, T. (1982) 'Contractualism and utilitarianism', in A. Sen and B. Williams (eds) *Utilitarianism and Beyond*, Cambridge: Cambridge University Press.

—— (1988) *What we Owe to Each Other*, Cambridge, MA: Belknap.

Shklar, J. (1986) 'Injustice, injury and inequality', in F. Lucash (ed.) *Justice and Equality Here and Now*, Ithaca, NY: Cornell University Press.

Taylor, C. (1985) *Philosophical Papers*, vol. II, Cambridge: Cambridge University Press.

Walzer, M. (1983) *Spheres of Justice*, Oxford: Basil Blackwell.

Wood, A. W. (1984) 'Justice and class interests', *Philosophica* 3 (1): 9–32.

—— (1985) 'Marx's immoralism', in B. Chavance (ed.) *Marx en Perspective*, Paris: Éditions de 1'École des Haute Études en Sciences Sociales.

Further reading

Aristotle (1975) *The Nicomachean Ethics*, Cambridge, MA: Harvard University Press.

—— (1977) *Politics*, Cambridge, MA: Harvard University Press.

Baier, K. (1995) *The Rational and the Moral Order*, Chicago, IL: Glen Court Publishing.

Barry, B. (1991) *Liberty and Justice*, Oxford, UK: Clarendon Press.

—— (1995) *Justice as Impartiality*, Oxford, UK: Clarendon Press.

Clayton, Matthew and Williams, Andrew (eds) (2000) *The Ideal of Equality*, New York: St Martin's Press.

Cohen, G. A. (2000) *If You're an Egalitarian How Come You're So Rich?* Cambridge, MA: Harvard University Press.

Dworkin, R. (2000) *Sovereign Virtue: The Theory and Practice of Equality*, Cambridge, MA: Harvard University Press.

Elster, J. (1984) 'Exploitation, freedom and justice', in J. R. Pennock (ed.) *Marxism, Nomos*, vol. 26, New York: New York University Press.

Gauthier, D. (ed.) (1970) *Morality and Rational Self-Interest*, Englewood Cliffs, NJ: Prentice-Hall.

Hampshire, S. (1989) *Innocence and Experience*, Cambridge, MA: Harvard University Press.

—— (2000) *Justice Is Conflict*, Princeton, NJ: Princeton University Press.

Hardin, R. (1988) *Morality within the Limits of Reason*, Chicago: University of Chicago Press.

Hayek, F. (1973) *Law, Legislation and Liberty*, 3 vols, Chicago: University of Chicago Press.

Heller, A. (1987) *Beyond Justice*, Oxford: Basil Blackwell.

Herzog, D. (1990) 'Gimme that old-time religion', *Critical Theory* 4 (1, 2): 74–85.

Kelly, Paul (1998) *Impartiality, Neutrality and Justice: Re-Reading Brian Barry's Justice as Impartiality*, Edinburgh: Edinburgh University Press.

Levine, A. (1984) *Arguing for Socialism*, London: Routledge & Kegan Paul.

—— (1998) *Rethinking Liberal Equality From a 'Utopian' Point of View*, Ithaca, NY: Cornell University Press.

—— (2002) *Engaging Political Philosophy from Hobbes to Rawls*, Malden, MA: Blackwell.

Mandle, J. (2000) *What's Left of Liberalism? An Interpretation and Defense of Justice as Fairness*, Lanham, MD: Lexington Books.

Miller, R. (2002) 'Too much inequality', *Social Philosophy and Public Policy* 19 (1): 275–313.

Nielsen, K. (1988) 'Radically egalitarian justice', in A. F. Bayefsky (ed.) *Legal Theory Meets Legal Practice*, Edmonton: Academic Printing and Publishing.

——(1994) 'Rights-based ethics: A critique and replacement', *Windsor Yearbook of Access to Justice* 14: 162–94

—— (1996a) *Naturalism Without Foundations*, Amherst, NY: Prometheus Books.
—— (1996b) 'Radical egalitarianism revisited: On going beyond the difference principle', *The Windsor Yearbook of Access to Justice* XV: 121–58.
Okin, S. M. (1989) *Justice, Gender and the Family*, New York: Basic Books.
Peffer, R. (1990) *Marxism, Morality and Social Justice*, Princeton: Princeton University Press.
Pogge, T. W. (1989) *Realizing Rawls*, Ithaca, NY: Cornell University Press.
Rawls, J. (1975) 'The independence of moral theory', *Proceedings and Addresses of the American Philosophical Association* 47: 7–10.
—— (1996) *Political Liberalism*, New York: Columbia University Press.
—— (1999) *Collected Papers*, ed. Samuel Freeman, Cambridge, MA: Harvard University Press.
Reiman, J. (1990) *Justice and Modern Moral Philosophy*, New Haven: Yale University Press.
Roemer, J. (1988) *Free to Lose*, Cambridge, MA: Harvard University Press.
Schofield, M. and Sorabji, R. (eds) (1977) *Articles on Aristotle: 3 – Ethics and Politics*, London: Duckworth.
Sumner, W. (1987) *The Moral Foundation of Rights*, Oxford: Oxford University Press.
Tully, J. (1982) *A Discourse on Property: John Locke and his Adversaries*, Cambridge: Cambridge University Press.

6

CONCEPTIONS OF HUMAN NATURE

Leslie Stevenson

Theories or assumptions about human nature are explicit or implicit in political philosophies, social programmes, ethics and religions. There has been disagreement about whether we are essentially different from other animals; about how far humans differ from each other individually, racially, or culturally; and about whether human nature is basically good and in need only of appropriate sustenance, or innately defective and in need of transformation. According to some conceptions, human nature can be altered given sufficiently radical educational or political or economic programmes (or perhaps religious conversion); but other views assume an unchangeable core in human biology and psychology.

The multiple ambiguity of the word 'nature' should be noted straightaway. In asking about human nature we usually have in mind human dispositions and behaviour as we know them, in the society we live in. But some thinkers have made assumptions about how human 'nature' would be if there were no state, no government or politics, perhaps even no education or culture. Other theorists say that since human beings are fundamentally social creatures, there can be no meaningful conception of human nature except in some sort of society.

Another important ambiguity is about whether the supposed 'natural' state of humanity is to be preferred or avoided. In contemporary discourse, what is 'natural' is often implied to be good (e.g. in talk of 'natural' food, colourings, and babycare), and the 'unnatural' is condemned as bad. Rousseau (especially his eloquent eighteenth-century treatise on education, *Émile*) has been influential in fostering this assumption that what is 'natural' must be best; but it is highly contentious. Consider, for example, feeding infants on formula, adults drinking cows' milk, innoculation, office work, air travel, body jewelry, heart surgery, celibacy, and contraception. Each of these may be described (by someone) as 'unnatural' in some sense or other – but it does not follow that they are wrong. Conversely, it is often claimed that it is natural for human beings to be aggressive towards other tribes or nations, and for everyone to be selfish – but it does not follow that these are morally right. It is quite consistent to approve a practice that is admitted to be in some sense unnatural, and conversely to say that we have some natural tendencies which we need to overcome.

This essay will provide a brief overview of some of the most politically influential conceptions of human nature, noting how normative views can be concealed within apparently factual theories, and comparing them on the issue of constancy versus changeability, and on the question of the objectivity of values.

Plato

The Greek philosopher Plato set out his conception of human nature and an ideal society in his lengthy dialogue, *The Republic* (*c.*380 BCE), which ranges widely over psychology, theory of knowledge, metaphysics, moral philosophy, government, education, the arts, and the role of women. His theory of individual human nature finds three mental factors at work in us – Reason (intellect or rationality), Spirit (personality or emotional character, especially courage, self-assertion, and ambition), and Appetite (the bodily based desires). Plato remarks that children show 'Spirit' before they display reason. Depending on which of these elements is dominant we get three kinds of people, whose main desire is, respectively, for knowledge, reputation, or material gain: Plato describes them as philosophic, victory-loving and profit-loving. The three factors each have their proper part to play, but they sometimes conflict, and what is needed for human flourishing is a harmonious combination. Reason should, however, be in overall control, for Plato argues at length that by the use of our intellect we can come to know what is real and what is good for us. It is 'Reason' that gives us reliable knowledge of objective, unchanging realities – what Plato called 'the Forms', including at their head the Form of the Good. He believed that questions of value about what is best for individuals and for human societies can be matters of knowledge, just as much as mathematics.

Plato recognized that we are ineradicably social beings. Individuals are not self-sufficient, we each have many needs which we cannot meet by ourselves. A lone human would be hard put to it even to find enough food, and would miss out on the distinctively human activities of language, co-operative work, friendship, play, art, politics, learning, and reasoning. The problems of human individuals are therefore intimately related to those of human societies, and so Plato's main proposal in *The Republic* is an ambitious programme of social engineering. He lays great stress on appropriate education as the most important way to produce harmonious, well-balanced, moral or 'just' people, and he has in mind not just formal schooling, but all the social influences on human development. This requires both a clear conception of what is aimed at – an account of human flourishing – and elaborate social organization and resources. Thus Plato is led to a programme for the radical reform of government.

In Plato's view, people have different innate strengths of Reason, Spirit, and Appetite, so there is no natural equality between individuals. He was sceptical about the democratic tendency in Athens, and he argues that just as the reasoning part of the soul ought to direct and control the individual, so those people with the most highly developed 'Reason' (which includes moral and political wisdom) ought to rule society. He proposes a threefold class division affecting lifelong duties and status, paralleling his theory of the human mind. There are to be 'Guardians' (the ruling elite), 'Auxiliaries' (the state-functionaries including soldiers and police), and Workers (who provide the economic basis in farming and crafts). Plato goes against Greek convention in allowing the Guardian class to include women (but they will not be allowed any family life – children are to be brought up communally). A stable, well-ordered, 'just' society will be one in which each class is restricted to its own function. There is a totalitarian air about this ideal republic, revealed also in Plato's recommendation of strict censorship of the arts, to prevent any destabilizing ideas gaining currency.

Plato prescribed a detailed and lengthy education (restricted to those with sufficient talent) by which the future 'philosopher-kings' are to be trained. But he can offer no guarantee that even the best-educated elite will govern for the good of society as a whole rather than in their own interest, and he offers no mechanism for changing rulers, or for resolving disputes between them. His proposal is remarkably unpolitical and impractical. It is a timeless, other-worldly conception, with no allowance for such basic human dispositions such as pair-bonding and love of one's own children, no provision for individual failures to fit into the social functions he allots, and no recognition of variations between different societies.

Plato's great successor Aristotle provides a more realistic, this-worldly analysis of human nature and human society in his *Nicomachean Ethics* and *Politics* (c.300 BCE). But his conception, for all its philosophical depth, is also limited by his experience of the *polis*, the small Greek city-state. He assumes a rigid class-structure, the unfitness of women for political roles, the existence of humans who are slaves 'by nature', and the inferiority of 'barbarian', non-Greek peoples.

Religious conceptions

Religious traditions tend to conceive of the most important aspect of human nature as lying in the area of will and moral character rather than intellect. Greek thought put its hopes in our ability to attain rational knowledge; and the highest human fulfilment was thought to be open only to those who are able to gain such intellectual knowledge of theoretical and moral truth. The Semitic religions – Judaism, Christianity and Islam – teach that human goodness is something which is open to all, independently of intelligence. A different tripartite division of mental faculties that has become standard is intellect, emotion and *will*, with the latter being seen as crucial.

In common with Plato, religious views see the only firm foundation for human goodness in our relation to something transcendent. Some religious traditions (Hinduism and Buddhism) see the transcendent as impersonal. But the three monotheist religions interpret this as a relationship with a personal God who is Creator, Saviour and Judge. Fundamental to the Biblical and Koranic understanding of human nature is the notion of human freedom and responsibility, conceived of as the choice between obedience to God's will or disobedience, self-will, pride and faithlessness. The diagnosis of what is wrong with humankind follows. We misuse our God-given free will, we choose evil rather than good, we thus disrupt our relationship to God and are infected with sin. The Fall need not be thought of as a particular event (the story of Adam and Eve can be read as parable rather than history), it is a symbol of the fact that we are all imperfect, that there is a flaw in our nature. Throughout the Biblical history of the children of Israel there are repeated denunciations of their unfaithfulness to God. According to St Paul, we are mired in sin – we can recognize what we ought to do, but we find great difficulty in doing it – so we stand in need of redemption, something beyond our own powers.

Much religious thought thus tends to see human fulfilment as depending on individual acceptance of divine salvation. If society is to be transformed in accordance with divine purposes, this must happen primarily through the transformation of individuals. Some traditions, however, give a special social authority to religious institutions or individual leaders, and extreme versions have supported theocracy, the exercise of political power by a priestly class, a Pope, an imam, or a guru. But although there is a standing temptation for religious enthusiasts to claim the infallible authority of God for imposing their beliefs and practices on others, another kind of religious attitude sees *all* human beings as finite, fallible, and imperfect before God – which suggests humility, tolerance, and respect for universal human rights.

Hobbes

Thomas Hobbes wrote his *Leviathan* (1651) in the era of the rise of physical science and of the English civil war. He starts from an uncompromisingly materialist conception of human beings as consisting of nothing more than matter in motion. And he assumes a bleak perspective in which there is no objective good for human existence to aspire towards, we are simply intelligent animals with desires for survival and ease. Each individual is purely self-interested, seeking the satisfaction of his/her own desires: what anyone calls 'good' is only what he/she desires.

'Natural', i.e. pre-political, human life is very insecure, because of the constant danger of fighting over vital resources. In such a 'state of nature', with no government, there is competition between people of approximately equal strength and intelligence, and no co-operation unless it serves individual self-interest. Those with possessions will live in fear of robbery; and this gives them reason to make preemptive strikes against others, extending their power in order to increase their security. Thus Hobbes writes: 'I put for a general inclination of all mankind, a perpetual and restless desire of power after power, that ceaseth only in death'. So without any 'common power to keep them all in awe', there is little incentive for any longer-term projects like agriculture, industry or science. There can be no justice, rights, property or law, and the life of man is 'solitary, poor, nasty, brutish, and short' (Hobbes [1651] 1962: ch. XI, 123, ch. XIII, 143).

In Hobbes's view, this gives each person overwhelming reason to accept a social contract by which everyone agrees to be subject to the supreme authority of a 'sovereign'. Thus the State comes into being: but this need not be thought of as a historical event, the point is to show why everyone has good reason to accept the authority of government. And Hobbes argues that for security to be achieved, the sovereign (whether an individual, or a corporate body) must have absolute authority over the subjects.

Locke

A few decades later, in 1690, Locke painted a less bleak picture of human nature. For him, the pre-governmental 'state of Nature' already contains a moral obligation (which he calls a 'law of Nature') to the effect that mankind 'being all equal and independent, no one ought to harm any other in his life, health, liberty, or possessions' (Locke [1690] 1965: 20). And Locke backs this up by appeal to God – saying that we are 'the workmanship of one omnipotent and infinitely wise Maker' (he even says we are 'His property'). But he is not so naive as to suppose that everyone will obey the law of Nature, and he maintains that in the pre-political state there is a right to punish transgressions and to take reparations. Locke conceives of people in the state of Nature as being free and equal, in that nobody has more power or authority than any other, but he differs from Hobbes in holding that it can be a state of 'peace, goodwill, mutual assistance and preservation'. And he posits a pre-political notion of property, with the distinctive rights of use and disposal: whenever a person 'mixes his labour with' something, e.g. plucking wild fruit, cultivating crops, or digging ore – in such quantity as for his own use – the result becomes his private property. But when there is scarcity of vital resources, forcible competition is likely to ensue, and so Locke recommends civil government as 'a proper remedy for the inconveniences of the state of Nature'. His thought strongly influenced the writing of the American constitution.

Is it because Hobbes and Locke differ in their conceptions of pre-political human nature that they diverge in political philosophy? Or is it because they have opposing political views (Hobbes favouring absolute authority, and Locke wanting checks on state power), that they propose different theories of human nature to justify these views? It looks as if what they present as factual descriptions of 'the state of nature' conceal normative preconceptions – and this is a possibility to which we must be alert in all theories of human nature.

Rousseau

Hobbes and Locke used the state of nature as a device to illuminate the advantages of political society. But Rousseau argued (against the optimistic mood of the Enlightenment) that society had introduced all sorts of unnatural practices and unjust inequalities. In his thought the conception of a 'state of nature' serves as a critique of crucial features of existing society, and thus his ideas were used to support radical reform in the era of the French revolution.

In his *Discourse on Inequality* (1755) Rousseau offered a speculative account of the stages by which society has developed, referring to some of the evidence about primitive cultures which was becoming available. He speculates about how human language might have evolved out of instinctual cries. He accuses Hobbes of reading back into the 'state of nature' motives like pride which can only exist in society; and he claims that humans have an innate repugnance against seeing a fellow creature suffer, which moderates competition. Rousseau implausibly depicts 'the noble savage' as 'wandering in the forests, without work, without speech, without a home, without war, and without relationships', and thus 'without any need of his fellow men and without any desire to hurt them'.

Rousseau suggests that the golden age was when there were families living together in houses, with some interfamilial socialization into communities, so that property rights for the immediate necessities of life were recognized, and offences against these punished. This was 'the true youth of the world', and he interprets all so-called progress since then as steps towards 'the decrepitude of the species'. He blames the division of labour (especially in agriculture and metallurgy) for starting the rot, making it necessary for many people to work under the direction of others, allowing some to amass huge property, hence the economic and social inequality of which he was so painfully conscious. His analysis is a tragic one: that the economic progress due to human intelligence has corrupted an originally good human nature. But one has to suspect that his revulsion from the society he knew led him to idealize his speculative 'golden age'.

In that work Rousseau did not offer any alleviation of the unhappy condition which he diagnosed in society. But in *The Social Contract* (1762) he took a more positive view, arguing that human beings can after all find their most complete fulfilment in civil society. As in Hobbes and Locke, people in the state of nature are supposed to reach a stage where they find it to their advantage to enter into a contract with everyone else. But in Rousseau's version the power is granted not to an absolute sovereign, nor to an elected government, but to the community as a whole. This involves his mysterious notion of the 'general will', which is always for the good of everyone, and yet cannot be identified with the actually expressed will of the citizens (it seems to be what people *ought* to want, rather than what they actually want). Such a notion tempts those who are actually in power to claim that they embody 'the general will', i.e. they know better than the people what is good for them.

Kant

According to Kant's 'critical philosophy' of the late eighteenth century, we have both theoretical and practical reason, i.e. we recognize the facts of the world by perception and we explain them scientifically, and we are also agents who act in the world and make changes in it. In both respects, we transcend the animals: they perceive and behave, but they do not have concepts of what they see and do, nor do they have reasons for their beliefs or actions.

Humans, by contrast, always have reasons for their actions. Some reasons for action appeal only to the agent's own desires (and factual beliefs) – I am doing A because I want B, and I believe that A will be the best way to bring about B – this is what Kant calls a 'hypothetical imperative'. But some reasons for action are moral, based on an obligation, a universal 'ought', which holds irrespective of self-interested desires, and may go against them: we recognize a 'categorical imperative' of the form 'I ought to do C, whatever my own inclinations may be'. For Kant, the objective basis for such universal ethics lies in the principle of respect for persons, i.e. for all beings endowed with reason, as 'ends in themselves'. He thus provides a secular basis for the recognition of universal human rights.

Kant was a firm believer in human freedom and moral responsibility. He sees us as rational beings who are able (at least sometimes) to act on moral reasons, not just on selfish desires. He distinguished two points of view, by which we can regard ourselves as belonging both to the perceptible world of material bodies and to the intelligible world of reasons for action, including moral laws. Kant offers a distinctively practical defence of freedom. In any situation where one is deciding what to do, one cannot think of one's decision as predetermined, for there is no escaping the necessity to make up one's mind what to do. Whether or not an omniscient observer could predict one's choice, one has to act 'under the idea of freedom' – so from the practical point of view we are free.

Kant strongly emphasizes the distinction between self-interested inclinations and moral duty. He contrasts our human nature with the animals on one side, and with the conception of a 'holy will' on the other. Animals do not have any tension between desires and obligations, for they do not have the concept of obligation. Conversely, a rational being without desires would not be subject to temptation, and would always do the right thing. But we are midway between animals and angels: we are finite creatures with bodily appetites, and desires for love, approval, status or power, yet we also recognize moral obligations.

How are virtuous dispositions to be cultivated? In his late work on religion, Kant offered a theory of the 'radical evil' in human nature. He acknowledges the frailty of our nature – our difficulty in doing what we ought to do, and our 'impurity' – i.e. our tendency to confuse or adulterate moral reasons with other motives. What is evil is not our naturally given desires, but the 'depravity' of the human heart – the freely chosen *subordination* of duty to inclination. Kant suggests that radical evil is a result of human development under social conditions. In this he was influenced by Rousseau: what Kant calls the 'unsocial sociability' of human beings is our need and desire to be members of society, combined with our tendency to be selfish and competitive. His thesis that we are by nature evil amounts to much the same thing as Rousseau's assertion that we are naturally good. For the term 'nature' is used by them in different ways: Rousseau means 'prior to society', whereas Kant doesn't accept that there is such a thing as pre-social *human* nature. (There was a related debate within the Confucian tradition in China: see Stevenson and Haberman 1998.)

Kant's answer to the problems of human nature shares the ambiguity of his diagnosis. He is deeply concerned about the relation between virtue and happiness. He argues that there is more to morality than the performance of right actions: there must be a final end of all our striving – the 'highest good' – which is a combination of virtue and happiness for everybody. Virtuous actions do not always lead to happiness in the world as we know it. Yet we need to assume that doing the right thing is not pointless. In invoking God and immortality at this point, Kant endorses the common hope for justice and reward in a life after death, yet for him morality is prior: religion is the seeing of moral duties as God's commands.

Kant also entertained this-worldly hopes, expressed in his essays on history and politics, which paved the way for the historical philosophies of Hegel and Marx in the nineteenth century. He envisioned the possibility of gradual emancipation of people from poverty, war, ignorance, and deference to traditional authorities. In all this Kant was arguably the deepest thinker of the Enlightenment, for he also had a realistic sense of the dark side of human nature, our potentiality for evil – which has been amply confirmed since his time. His philosophy leaves us with this combination of hope for gradual, intermittent social progress, and a religious viewpoint which sees our individual hope in divine grace, in so far as we acknowledge our finitude and our faults, and resolve to be better human beings (see Wood 1999, especially Part II, Anthropological Applications; Stevenson and Haberman 2004).

Marx

Karl Marx, writing in the nineteenth century when ideas of historical evolution were all the rage, presents a sweeping theory of the development of human society through a series of economic stages, from ancient cultures through the feudalism of the Middle Ages to capitalism, to be superseded (he predicted) by a revolutionary change to communism. According to Marx, we are essentially social beings, we do not merely find our subsistence in the world, we have to work for it – domesticating animals, growing crops, building houses, making tools and manufacturing commodities. His crucial claim is that apart from merely biological characteristics, human nature depends on the prevailing type of human society, which is defined by the mode of production of the necessities of life. Marx presented this 'materialist theory of history' as a scientific analysis of the laws governing the development of human cultures. As the economic basis of society changes, laws, politics, morals, ideology and religion will change too. For example, he would dismiss Locke's theory of a pre-social right to private property as merely an expression of the bourgeois concept of property characteristic of early capitalism, rather than a universally valid philosophical principle.

Marx was not just a theorizer, he was keenly aware of the human costs of the unregulated early capitalism of his day. He longed for the predicted transition to communism, in which he idealistically believed that a system of common ownership of the means of production would allow, for the first time in history, the free development of the potential of all human beings. Although the communist revolution could not happen until economic development made the time ripe, those with a scientific understanding of the situation could prepare the way by organization and propaganda, and when the chance came, they could seize power, as Lenin did in Russia in 1917. About society after the revolution Marx was optimistic but vague; he foresaw the need for a 'dictatorship of the proletariat' for a transitional period, but he thought that the state could eventually 'wither away' and the era of true human freedom would begin. Twentieth century experience has shown quite the reverse happening: under Lenin, Stalin, and Mao, dictatorships of the communist party (the self-appointed representatives of the proletariat) attempted social engineering on a huge scale, and extended state power into almost every feature of life, often involving totalitarian terror. The Marxist conception of human nature tends to ignore the persistence of certain kinds of human behaviour – the enjoyment of power and privilege by ruling groups, the rivalries engendered by ethnicity and nationalism, and the desire to profit from one's own enterprise.

From Darwin to socio-biology

Kant wrote before Darwin, and Marx arrived at his main ideas before the publication of *The Origin of Species* in 1859, but there is nothing to prevent the integration of evolutionary theory into their thought. Such an integration of ideas would yield a view with (i) an a priori philosophical account of what distinguishes human beings as rational thinkers and moral agents; (ii) a scientific biological theory of how these faculties of perception, inference, emotion, and agency have evolved in the human species; and (iii) a historical and anthropological account of how human society has developed through various cultural and economic changes. Such a comprehensive explanatory account is precisely what certain socio-biologists claim for their theories.

Marx welcomed Darwin's theory as consonant with his historical materialism. But in stark contrast to the socialist or communist ideal, the movement called 'Social

Darwinism' enshrined economic competition as both inescapable and desirable in human society. Darwin cannot be held responsible for this view – the theory of evolution is a scientific explanation of the diversity of species, not a political philosophy. However, since the time of Herbert Spencer in England and W. G. Sumner in the USA (see Jones 1980; Rose *et al.* 1984), social theorists who favour the least possible control by the state over economic activity have often appealed to Darwinian ideas to justify the 'free market economy'. They interpreted the phrase 'survival of the fittest' not in the factual sense that those individuals best fitted to the prevailing environment will leave more progeny, but in the normative sense that it is a *good* thing that the less fit should not survive or reproduce. This is a political ethic that suits the successful capitalist very well, for it seems to justify the ruthless elimination of rivals, to bless economic success with 'virtue', and to discourage any redistribution of resources through taxation. But it leaves out of consideration all tendencies to co-operation between people, it treats individuals or families as isolated units without acknowledging their membership in larger social groups which have profound effects on their identities, obligations and rights. At its extreme, it asserts the manifest falsity that 'there is no such thing as society'.

In the twentieth century there was a neo-Darwinian revolution in biology, in which genetic theory was said to supply the missing biochemical mechanism for natural selection (see Dawkins 1976). And this has been vigorously promoted as offering new insights into human nature. Konrad Lorenz (1966), for example, offered a controversial diagnosis of human aggressive tendencies on the basis of his theory of 'intraspecies aggression' drawn from observation of a variety of animal species. According to Lorenz, male aggression in humans is due to a built-in 'drive', manifested in the distinctly intercommunal (ethnic, nationalist, religious) nature of human carnage, which reflects the evolutionary remnants of selective pressures of survival organized among competing tribes.

In the last chapter of his book *Sociobiology* (1975) E. O. Wilson claimed that the application of his evolutionary approach to human beings would revolutionize the social sciences. In subsequent books (1978 and 1998) Wilson offered to explain specific categories of human behaviour such as aggression, sex, altruism, ethics and religion in evolutionary terms. For example, Wilson suggests that contemporary sexual practices reflect certain evolutionary imperatives, i.e., the selective pressure on males to spread their genes around as widely as possible explains 'male promiscuity', while evolutionary pressures on females to select their partners cautiously for genetic fitness and for likelihood of providing resources for children explains women's preference for monogamous relationships. Wilson's account has been faulted on a number of fronts. His account of sexuality is permeated by the 'ideology of reproduction' (Barrett 1980), the notion that all sexual practices are heterosexual and inherently linked to species reproduction, a notion that is singularly at odds with the range and diversity of erotic practices documented by sex researchers such as William H. Masters and Virginia E. Johnson. Some biologists have hotly criticized both the 'scientific claims' of sociobiology and what they saw as its reactionary social and political implications (Rose *et al.* 1984). Because of those controversies, the term 'evolutionary psychology' has come to replace 'sociobiology' in certain academic disciplines – yet debate still continues about the validity and implications of the evolutionary approach to human nature.

In recent years there has been quite an explosion of 'evolutionary psychology' (Wright 1994; Ridley 1996; Pinker 1997; Boyer 2001). Much of this writing has a popular appeal, because it promises some explanation and diagnosis of the human predicament, and perhaps some implications for practical policy – but it is morally, politically and philosophically controversial for just this reason. Evolutionary psychology offers a wider ranging analysis of 'genetically based predispositions' in human nature, which interact with the social environment or culture in subtle ways in the production of human personality and behaviour. The emphasis is very much on 'innate tendencies', seen as the result of a long history of natural selection, whose detailed development and expression may depend on culture and individual develop-ment and learning. Yet much of what evolutionary psychologists say about human nature remains controversial, for at least two reasons – because it is so difficult to separate the contributions of heredity and upbringing, and because of the normative involvements of the whole topic of human nature and behaviour (O'Hear 1997; Richards 2000).

We here touch on the matter of 'ideology' – moral, political, religious views about what we are and what we ought to be, that reflect the ideas and interests of partic-ular groups. Every human way of life presupposes some beliefs of this kind, and people typically resist changing their fundamental assumptions, especially when they are involved in practice. Many social scientists and campaigners for social change have made questionable assumptions about the plasticity of human nature in different human cultures. But on the other side, whenever supposedly scientific evidence is adduced for claims about our 'evolutionary nature', or about 'innate differences' between human races, sexes, or social classes, we must be alert to the possibility that such assertions may serve the interest of certain social groups rather than others. Factual evidence can only show how people have so far behaved in certain forms of society, which we may want to change. For example, feminist theo-rists have raised important questions about whether existing differences between men and women are a matter of innate, biological, 'natural' tendencies, or whether they have been produced by forms of cultural conditioning which have served the interests of men (Mill [1869] 1970; Jaggar 1983).

Recent critiques of canonical conceptions of human nature

In taking up questions of human nature, philosophers have claimed to identify the *differencia specifica* – that which all members of the human species share and that which distinguishes humans from all other species. Yet careful examination of the canonical works on human nature indicates that the 'defining characteristics' identi-fied by particular philosophers were typically ascribed to a very small sample of the human population, i.e., to an elite group of men. Thus while enshrining rationality as the *differencia specifica* and devising a universal educational system to enable those governed by reason to achieve rulership within his ideal Republic, Plato did not believe that many would succeed in the forty plus years of education requisite for the Guardian class. And he was quite convinced that some were far less likely to succeed than others: 'The one sex is, so to speak, far and away beaten in every field by the other' (*Republic* V 455d2–3). Indeed, according to Plato, 'human nature being two-fold, the better sort was that which should thereafter be called "man"'

(*Timaeus* 42e). Aristotle was so convinced that women were 'defective males', i.e., that their rationality 'lacked authority' that he barred them altogether from participation in political life (*Politics* 1259b).

Inspired by the frequency with which male philosophers have argued that women are not wholly human, feminist political philosophers have undertaken a systematic review of canonical accounts of human nature. Their interrogations of the classic texts have documented a profound reification of gender 'difference' that has legitimated male dominance. Ignoring what men and women share in common, philosophers have articulated various misogynous conceptions of femininity, which they have then attributed to 'Nature', 'Divine Ordination', or 'Biology', and used to justify inequitable distributions of social burdens and benefits, as well as sex-specific roles, responsibilities, and rights (Bishop and Weinzweig 1979; Clark and Lange 1979; Elshtain 1981; Mahowald 1978; Osborne 1979).

In addition to demonstrating how philosophers have produced accounts of gender difference while claiming merely to describe the natural or divine order, feminist theorists have also raised important questions about the degree to which particular constructions of human nature and the political reflect peculiarly gendered concerns. Jean Elshtain, for example, questions the rigid bifurcation of public and private spheres in Western political thought, suggesting that it reflected men's overriding concern to insulate themselves against the 'tug of the private, the lure of the familial, against evocations of female power...ideas that must be fended off in order to deal with perceived threats and dangers' (Elshtain 1981:15). Wendy Brown argues that the conceptions of human nature advanced by Aristotle, Machiavelli, and Weber sustained conceptions of politics 'saturated with problematic and dangerous ideals and practices of manhood' (Brown 1988:12). Christine DiStefano (1991) has suggested that the notion of autonomy so central to modern political thought (e.g., Hobbes, Locke, Kant) reflects peculiarly masculine concerns with self-creation and individuation, which mask processes of birth, nurturance, and socialization in which women figure so prominently.

The import of feminist critiques of classic conceptions of human nature lies not only in clear demonstrations of particular (male) experience masquerading as universal (human), but also in the possibility they raise that women's historic (and continuing) exclusion from politics may not be accidental. Indeed several feminist political theorists (Elshtain 1981; Brown 1988; Di Stefano 1991; Pateman 1988; Zerilli 1994) have argued that male constructions of politics presuppose and require the exclusion of women even when male theorists advance claims about equality, liberty, and justice (cf., Hobbes, Locke, Rousseau, Kant, Marx).

Feminist scholars have been joined by critical race theorists, postcolonial theorists and queer theorists in advancing trenchant critiques of the classic conceptions of human nature and political order advanced by Western philosophers (Butler 1990, 1993; Mills 1997; Sedgwick 1990; Spivak 1999). Under the guise of systematic reflection on human nature, Western philosophers have naturalized and normalized racial hierarchy, imperial domination, and heterosexism. Theorists critical of classic accounts of human nature suggest that Western political theorists, like contemporary sociobiologists, are guilty of far more than intellectual error. For they have fabricated and fixed sex, gender, race, ethnic, and class boundaries that have no basis in nature. Their 'naturalizations' of these suspect classifications have helped produce a world of marked inequities and injustices. And their insistence in attributing the origins of such differences to nature, divine will, biology or evolutionary imperatives helps make these social artifacts particularly impervious to social change.

The stakes in discussions of human nature remain high. At issue are not simply a record of past and continuing injustices ensconced in the centre of political life, but the prospects for justice in the future.

References

Aristotle (1975) *The Nicomachean Ethics*, Cambridge, MA: Harvard University Press.

—— (1977) *Politics*, Cambridge, MA: Harvard University Press.

Barrett, Michèle (1980) *Women's Oppression Today*, London:Verso.

Bishop, Sharon and Weinzweig, Marjorie (eds) (1979) *Philosophy and Women*, Belmont, CA: Wadsworth Publishing.

Boyer, P. (2001), *Religion Explained: The human instincts that fashion god, spirits and ancestors*, London: Heinnemann.

Brown, Wendy (1988) *Manhood and Politics*, Totowa, NJ: Rowman and Littlefield.

Butler, Judith (1990) *Gender Trouble*, New York and London: Routledge.

—— (1993) *Bodies That Matter*, New York and London: Routledge.

Clark, Lorenne and Lange, Lynda (eds) (1979) *The Sexism of Social and Political Theory: Women and Reproduction From Plato to Nietzsche*, Toronto: University of Toronto Press.

Dawkins, R. (1976) *The Selfish Gene*, Oxford: Oxford University Press.

Di Stefano, Christine (1991) *Configurations of Masculinity: A Feminist Perspective on Modern Political Theory*, Ithaca: Cornell University Press.

Elshtain, Jean B. (1981) *Public Man, Private Woman: Women in Social and Political Thought*, Princeton: Princeton University Press.

Hobbes, T. (1651) *Leviathan*, ed. J. Plamenatz, London: Collins, 1962.

Jaggar, A. (1983) *Feminist Politics and Human Nature*, Brighton: Harvester.

Jones, G. (1980) *Social Darwinism and English Thought: The Interaction between Biological and Social Theory*, Brighton: Harvester.

Kant, I. (*c*.1780–95), *Kant's Political Writings*, edited with an introduction and notes by Hans Reiss, trans. H. B. Nisbet, London: Cambridge University Press, 1970.

Locke, J. (1690) 'Second Treatise on Government', in *Locke on Politics, Religion, and Society*, ed. M.Cranston, New York: Collier Books, 1965.

Lorenz, K. (1966) *On Agression*, trans. from German Marjorie Latzke, London: Methuen.

Mahowald, Mary (1978) *Philosophy of Women: Classical to Current Concepts*, Indianapolis: Hackett Publishing.

Marx, K. (*c*.1843–75) *Selected Readings in Sociology and Social Philosophy*, eds T. Bottomore and M. Rubel, London: Penguin, 1963.

Mills, Charles W. (1997) *The Racial Contract*, Ithaca: Cornell University Press.

Mill, John Stuart. ([1869] 1970) *The Subjection of Women*, Cambridge, MA: MIT Press.

O'Hear, A. (1997), *Beyond Evolution: Human Nature and the Limits of Evolutionary Explanation*, Oxford: Oxford University Press.

Osborne, Martha (1979) *Women in Western Political Thought*, New York: Random House.

Pateman, Carole (1988) *The Sexual Contract*, Cambridge: Polity Press.

Plato (*c*.380 BCE) *The Republic*, trans. R. Waterfield, Oxford and New York: Oxford University Press, 1993.

Pinker, S. (1997) *How the Mind Works*, New York: W. W. Norton.

Richards, Janet R. (2000) *Human Nature after Darwin*, London: Routledge.

Ridley, M. (1996) *The Origins of Virtue*, New York: Viking.

Rose, S., Lewontin, R. C. and Kamin, L. J. (1984) *Not in Our Genes: Biology, Ideology and Human Nature*, London: Penguin.

Rousseau, J.-J. (1755) *Discourse on Inequality*, trans. Maurice Cranston, Harmondsworth: Penguin, 1984.

—— (1762) *Emile*, Paris: Editions Sociales, 1974.

—— (1762) *Of the social contract, or, Principles of political right, and Discourse on political economy*, trans. Charles M. Sherover, New York, London: Harper & Row, 1984.

Sedgwick, Eve Kosofsky (1990) *Epistemology of the Closet*, Berkeley: University of California Press.

Spivak, Gayatri (1999) *A Critique of Postcolonial Reason: Toward a History of the Vanishing Present*, Cambridge, MA: Harvard University Press.

Stevenson, L. and Haberman, D. (2004) *Ten Theories of Human Nature* (4th edition), New York: Oxford University Press.

Stevenson, L. and Haberman, D. (1998) *Ten Theories of Human Nature*, New York: Oxford University Press

Wilson, E. O. (1975) *Sociobiology: the new synthesis*, Cambridge, MA: Harvard University Press.

—— (1978) *On Human Nature*, Cambridge, MA: Harvard University Press.

—— (1998) *Consilience: the Unity of Knowledge*, London: Little, Brown and Company.

Wood, A.W. (1999) *Kant's Ethical Thought*, Cambridge: Cambridge University Press.

Wright, R. (1994) *The Moral Animal*, New York: Pantheon Books.

Zerilli, Linda (1994) *Signifying Woman: Culture and Chaos in Rousseau, Burke, and Mill*, Ithaca: Cornell University Press.

7

CONCEPTIONS OF LEGITIMACY

Mattei Dogan

Why do people voluntarily follow and obey their rulers? Why do people accept and maintain authorities and institutions? In authoritarian regimes people obey involuntarily, by fear. But, as Xenophon already knew, the power of tyrants is not based uniquely on material force and constraints. Even the most tyrannic rulers try to justify their reign. The key concept for understanding the need of such justification is legitimacy, because only legitimacy can transform brutal power into recognized authority.

Legitimacy has always been in the mind of political thinkers. Plato's idea of justice bears on the problem of legitimacy, as well as Aristotle's distinction between monarchy, aristocracy and democracy. In his analysis of the nature of government, Locke displaced the source of legitimacy, replacing the divine right of kings by the consent of the people. No discussion of the concept of power could be complete without reference to legitimacy. For contemporary political systems in which participation of the people is a criterion of political worth, legitimacy is a fundamental concept.

Definitions of legitimacy

The concept of legitimacy and its definition have changed significantly since the emergence of democratic governments. Current definitions of legitimacy dissolve legitimacy into belief (Schaar 1981). If people hold the belief that existing institutions are appropriate or morally proper, then those institutions are legitimate. Such a reference to beliefs becomes even clearer when we consider the widely accepted definition formulated by Lipset: 'the capacity of the system to engender and maintain the belief that the existing political institutions are the most appropriate ones for the society' (Lipset 1959: 77). It is also clear in Merkl's definition: 'a nation united by a consensus on political values...a solemnly and widely accepted legal and constitutional order of democratic character' (Merkl 1988: 21).

Juan Linz proposes as a 'minimalist' definition, 'the belief that in spite of shortcomings and failures, the political institutions are better than any other that might be established, and therefore can demand obedience' (Linz 1988: 65). The concept of 'diffuse regime support' developed by David Easton is another way to define legitimacy (Easton 1965).

Legitimacy is particularly important in democracies since a democracy's survival is ultimately dependent on the support of a majority of its citizens. Hence, without the granting of legitimacy by the people, a democracy would lose its authority. In dictatorships, while the granting of support or legitimacy by the people may be an asset, it is not of ultimate importance since authority is based on force.

Authoritarian regimes may lack legitimacy but they still feel a need to acquire it. The subtitle of Michael Hudson's book on Arab politics is very significant: *The Search for Legitimacy*.

> Whether in power or in the opposition, Arab politicians must operate in a political environment in which the legitimacy of rulers, regimes and the institutions is sporadic and, at best, scarce. Under these conditions seemingly irrational behaviour, such as assassinations, coups d'état and official repression, may in fact derive from...the low legitimacy accorded to political processes and institutions.
>
> (Hudson 1977: 2)

The best-known definition of legitimacy was formulated by Max Weber, who distinguished three types of legitimacy: traditional, charismatic and legal-rational (Weber 1978). This typology has been meaningfully applied in many historical studies: 'Since Weber, we have been busy putting the phenomenon into one or another of his three boxes and charting the progress by which charismatic authority becomes routinized into traditional authority, which...gives way in turn to rational legal authority' (Schaar 1981: 15).

Anachronism of the classical Weberian typology of legitimacy

Historically, traditional authority and charismatic power are rooted in authoritarian regimes. The implication is that some authoritarian regimes can be legitimate. Among the contemporary countries with rational-legal authority some are legitimate, particularly the pluralist democracies, but most are not, particularly the authoritarian regimes. Thus, the Weberian typology does not cover directly the relationship between legitimacy and democracy.

Throughout the centuries, until the American and French Revolutions, the governments of independent countries, with the exception of Switzerland, were based on traditional legitimacy. During the nineteenth century all but two of the European countries were ruled by monarchs. At the turn of the century Pope Leo XIII proclaimed in his encyclical *Immortale Dei* that 'the authority of those who govern derives from God's power and so has more than human dignity'. But two decades later four emperors – one Catholic, one Protestant, one Orthodox and one Muslim – fell almost simultaneously from their thrones, having lost their legitimacy. Today, in the monarchies that still survive, the throne fills a symbolic, mythical or ceremonial function, the most interesting case being the Japanese emperor. Among the democratic regimes only in Spain and Belgium did the monarch have an opportunity to play, at certain moments, a political role – one that could have been, also, assumed by a president. True traditional legitimacy still exists for a significant part of the population only in a handful of countries (Morocco, Saudi Arabia, Nepal).

Since the traditional dynasties, legitimacy of divine right represents a vanishing form of authority: the Weberian typology is losing one of its 'boxes'. In the contemporary world this type of legitimacy is rare.

Few words in the sociological literature have been as blessed as the word 'charisma'. Some scholars abuse it. Today the most frequent phenomenon is not the charismatic leadership, but the personalization of power, which can take extreme forms – such as the cult of personality or the engineering of political idolatry.

In the distant past the charismatic leadership was always rooted in religious grounds – Moses, David and Muhammed being the archetypes. The concept of charisma borrowed by Max Weber from the canonist Rudolph Sohn has a religious connotation and for this reason is inappropriate for contemporary secularized societies, even if it remains important as an 'ideal type' in historical studies.

The nineteenth century (1814–1918) offered few cases of charismatic leadership because Europe had been dominated by monarchs who embodied political legitimacy. The accomplishments of heroes like Garibaldi or of great statesmen such as Bismarck, Disraeli or Gladstone have in fact reinforced the monarchical legitimacy.

The building of new nation-states after the Second World War in Asia and Africa saw the appearance of founding fathers, most of whom soon became armed prophets, political priests or plebiscitarian dictators; India was a clear exception. But this historical period of the emergence of new nation-states that idolized their founding fathers – Bourguiba being a notable example – has almost ended because there remain few nations that are deprived, as in Kurdistan, of independent status. Today, the most frequent phenomenon in Third World countries is authoritarian-bureaucratic rulership, in some cases of a military nature. These regimes born from *coups d'état* have a very low potential for legitimation.

The legitimacy of most leaders who were initially charismatic has been eroded. Biographical studies written after their fall or their death explain their success not in terms of charisma but by taking into consideration a multiplicity of factors that reduce charisma to a congruence between the image of a personality and the aspirations of the masses – the best example being Nasser – or interpreting it as organized political religion. Yesterday's subjugation remains a historical fact, but it is necessary to stress that the degeneration of transient charismatic leadership into an idolatrous cult and tyrannical rule has been more frequent than the routinization of charisma into new institutions. For the twentieth century the notion of charisma is helpful only for a handful of political leaders. Its application to a satrap such as Stalin or to a 'commediante' such as Mussolini is misleading. The limited number of modern genuinely charismatic leaderships – Gandhi, Ataturk, Khomeini, and a few others – makes the charismatic type of legitimacy a residual one. For many leaders in the last decades the appropriate concept is engineering idolatry.

At the beginning of the twenty-first century there remains only one full 'box' in the Weberian typology: the legal–rational–bureaucratic legitimacy. A typology which in empirical research shrinks to such an extent is no longer fruitful: it becomes an inadequate tool, even though it remains a useful guide in historical sociology. The fact that we need several words to designate this 'box' – legal-rational-bureaucratic – suggests that it is very heterogeneous, amalgamating many varieties.

In this amalgam we can distinguish at least four varieties. First we have the advanced pluralist democracies accepted by most of their citizens as basically legitimate. Depending on the definition we adopt, we can count in 2000 between 30 and 45 advanced pluralist democracies that have enjoyed a substantial legitimacy for more than a full generation.

The second variety represents the so-called authoritarian bureaucratic systems where civil rights are partially respected and which have civilian rulers. They may have some legitimacy in the eyes of part of the population. There is, obviously, a great diversity among these authoritarian regimes. The right question to ask is not whether or not they are legitimate but, avoiding such a dichotomy and using Easton's (1965) terminology, how much 'diffuse support' they enjoy.

The third variety includes dictatorial, tyrannical or totalitarian regimes rejected by the large majority of the population, even if it cannot denounce publicly such an illegitimacy. Absence of revolt does not imply adhesion to the regime. Revolt is possible only in certain historical circumstances, when a regime is obliged to start a process of liberalization. In totalitarian regimes attempts to revolt can be suicidal. The Chinese communist establishment, by repressing revolt in Tienanmen Square, wanted to stop the incipient liberalization movement. The number of *coups d'état* is the most visible measure of illegitimacy, for instance in Africa in the last four decades of the twentieth century, and earlier in Latin America. This criterion has been adopted by a number of scholars, but we should not assume that in a given country legitimacy exists simply because the regime is not openly contested.

The fourth variety refers to the countries where there is neither acceptance nor rejection of rulership and for which discussion of legitimacy becomes meaningless (Hertz 1978: 320). Most of these countries are among the poorest in the world. In many rural areas of Africa and Asia, identified by the World Bank, and in the shantytowns of giant metropolises, the issue of legitimacy of the regime is absent from the minds of most people. Their poverty is not perceived as resulting from the behaviour of current rulers, it is attributed to some god or nature. In these countries tyrants are often perceived as a fatality. Where violence is absent, legitimacy is not necessarily present. The concept of legitimacy is not adequate for perhaps one out of every four developing countries.

This simple account shows that the majority of political regimes are deprived of legitimacy, and consequently are not covered by the Weberian typology. Many other categories are needed: the quasi-legitimate type, the illegitimate type and so on. Today it is more difficult than in the past to make clear-cut classifications, because the legitimacy of a regime can be based on more than one type of authority. American democracy is not based exclusively on the constitution. How much rationality and how much tradition is there in the contemporary Indian democracy? Max Weber has implicitly accepted this idea of mixed legitimacy by discussing the dynamics of the process of legitimation and delegitimation. The ideal types that he constructed are antagonistic only in theory. In reality, all traditional systems have some features of legality: the Chinese emperors or the Russians tsars both respected some rules of the game.

Briefly stated, the Weberian typology of legitimacy appears anachronistic for the contemporary world. It is no longer appropriate because only a few countries today have a traditional authority, while the charismatic phenomenon is extremely rare; Khomeini is the latest example. Two of the three boxes of Weberian typology are, for the contemporary world, almost empty. In the third box we have to lodge almost all independent nations – about 200 – mixing a wide variety of regimes. Weber's definition of legitimacy needs an updated reformulation by taking into consideration the neighbouring concepts of confidence, trust, popularity and effectiveness.

Operationalizing the concept of legitimacy

Scholars and politicians have the tendency to adopt the dichotomy: legitimate versus illegitimate. Since the reality is much more varied, legitimacy must come in degrees. Ranking regimes on an imaginary axis from a minimum to a maximum degree of legitimacy is a promising way for the comparative analysis of political systems. Many scholars have felt the need of such scaling: 'Legitimacy runs the scale from complete acclaim to complete rejection, ranging all the way from support, consent, compliance through decline, erosion and loss. In case of conscious rejection we may speak of illegitimacy' (Hertz 1978: 320).

As Juan Linz stresses, 'no political regime is legitimate for 100 per cent of the population, nor in all its commands, nor forever, and probably very few are totally illegitimate based only on coercion' (Linz 1988: 66). Legitimacy never reaches unanimity, nor do groups and individuals ever recognize equally the authority of the political power. There are apathetic popular strata and rebellious subcultures, pacifist dissidents and armed terrorists, and between these extremes many who are only partially convinced by the pretensions of legitimacy claimed by the rulers. The support of the majority is generally considered as a test of legitimacy, but as David Easton observes, it is also necessary to consider the substance and intensity of the popular support. Easton argues that the 'ratio of deviance to conformity as measured by violation of laws, the prevalence of violence, the size of dissidence movements or the amount of money spent for security would provide indices of support' (Easton 1965: 163). But it is difficult in empirical research to measure 'violations of laws' or 'dissident movements'.

Can the legitimacy of a political system be judged in terms of subjective adherence of the people? Obviously, confidence is a subjective phenomenon, that can be analyzed objectively. But in countries that do not allow freedom of speech, it is difficult to measure by survey the adherence to the regime.

The main problem with any study of legitimacy is the difficulty in measuring it accurately. Opinion polls attempting to measure a regime's legitimacy often measure things related to legitimacy without measuring legitimacy directly. For example, support of leaders and policies, or willingness to fight for the country's defence, are all easily measured by such polls and may be related to legitimacy, but none are real measures of legitimacy itself. Support of a leader and his/her policies does not always include the granting of legitimacy to the larger systems, and lack of support for a specific leader or policy does not always imply a lack of overall legitimacy. In spite of all these difficulties it is possible to consider legitimacy as an evaluable trait of political systems, and to state if a particular country is more or less legitimate than another. Legitimacy is a concept that can be empirically tested. Only the empirical approach can avoid the tautological circle which too often traps the discussion of legitimacy.

The lower the degree of legitimacy, the higher is the amount of coercion. Therefore, in order to operationalize the concept of legitimacy it is advisable to take into consideration some indicators of coercion, such as the absence of political rights and of civil liberties. These indicators are based on evaluation of freedom of expression, of association, of demonstration, the degree of military intervention in the political arena, fair elections, freedom of religious institutions, independent judiciary, free competition among parties, absence of government terror, and so on. Raymond Gastil in his *Freedom in the World*, has attempted, in collaboration with many experts, to rank countries according to these criteria. Such a ranking is an acceptable substitute for scaling legitimacy more directly.

A high level of corruption is one of the best symptoms of delegitimation (Dogan 2002). The fall of political regimes is often accompanied by a generalized corruption – the most notable historical examples being the fall of the Chinese imperial dynasty, of the reign of the Iranian Shah, and of the Soviet *nomenklatura*. Numerous testimonies and dozens of books denounce institutionalized corruption, at all levels of public administration, in most African and Asian countries. The judiciary often represents a regime's last bastion against corruption. When judges are also contaminated there is no more hope for the ordinary citizen. Then we can predict a crisis of legitimacy, brought about in reality by a *coup d'état*, revolt or revolution.

Paradoxically, scandals are not symptoms of delegitimation, because they can occur only where there is some freedom of speech. On the contrary, we may be certain that a regime where scandals occur is not totally illegitimate. In some exceptional cases, the scandal may appear as an irrefutable test of the democratic functioning of the regime. The Dreyfus affair and the Watergate affair are superb monuments honouring the French and American democracies. Few countries in the world have a democracy sufficiently well-rooted as to oblige the president to resign.

Legitimacy and trust

The distinction between legitimacy and trust appears in the possible replies to a very simple question: 'Should a police officer be obeyed?' The reply 'The officer should be obeyed because his/her order is right', implies legitimacy *and* trust; 'This particular police officer is wrong, and an appeal to a higher authority should be made, but for the moment he/she should be obeyed because he/she represents authority' indicates legitimacy without trust. The police as an institution can be perceived as legitimate even if a particular police officer may not be trusted. If too many police officers are corrupt or unnecessarily brutal the legitimacy of the police, as an institution, is contested. The mistrust of police officers can be tested empirically, as can the loss of confidence in the police as an institution. If many other institutions are mistrusted (the army, the political parties, the civil service), the regime itself could become illegitimate.

While the concept of legitimacy refers to the whole political system and to its permanent nature, the concept of trust is limited to the rulers who occupy the power in a transitory way. This distinction between the legitimacy of the regime and confidence in particular institutions or office-holders is appropriate for most countries. Obviously no political system, not even a democratic one, is perfect. No institution can escape criticism from some segment of society. Unanimity is a ridiculous pretension of totalitarian regimes.

Survey research done during the last two decades has revealed a gap of confidence in major institutions. The ubiquity of this loss of confidence in almost all advanced democracies raises important questions concerning the theory of democracy (Dogan 1996, 2002). Is the decline of public confidence in institutions a manifestation of a deeper loss of legitimacy or only a ritualistic cynicism? S. M. Lipset and W. Schneider, after having analysed a large amount of American survey data (Lipset and Schneider 1983), ask frankly: 'Is there a legitimacy crisis?' An identical question should be asked of all democracies. The diagnosis reached by Lipset and Schneider is that:

> People lose faith in leaders much more easily than they lose confidence in the system. All the indicators that we have examined show that the public has been growing increasingly critical of the performance of major institutions. There has been no significant decline in the legitimacy ascribed to the underlying political and economic systems.
>
> (Lipset and Schneider 1983: 378–9)

Their conclusion is 'that the decline of confidence has both real and superficial aspects. It is real because the American public is intensely dissatisfied with the performance of its institutions. It is also to some extent superficial because Americans have not yet reached the point of rejecting those institutions' (Lipset and Schneider 1983: 384). Already in early 1974 Jack Citrin argued that we should not confuse a crisis of confidence with a crisis of legitimacy (Citrin 1974).

An examination of the results of surveys conducted in 1981 by the European Value Systems Study Group and repeated in 1990 and 2000 leads us to similar conclusions. At the question 'How much confidence do you have in each of the following institutions?' the majority of Europeans replied that they had 'a great deal' or 'quite a lot' of confidence in the police, the armed forces, the judiciary, the educational system and the church. The proportion is lower for the parliament (43 per cent), the civil service (39 per cent), the press (32 per cent), and labour unions (32 per cent). The astonishingly low confidence in the parliament is a serious strain on legitimacy, particularly in Italy, although even in Britain only 40 per cent of the respondents replied positively (Harding *et al.* 1986: 78, 95; see also Halman 2001: 185–211).

A significant part of the population may manifest a low confidence in specific institutions, but only a small minority replied that 'they are unsatisfied or not at all satisfied with the way democracy is functioning in [their] country', and only a fringe minority declared themselves in favour of 'radical or revolutionary change' of the system. The vast majority has faith in the democratic system.

Legitimacy and effectiveness

The relationship between legitimacy and the effectiveness of a political system is of crucial importance. Lipset defines effectiveness as the actual performance of the government or the 'extent to which the system satisfies the basic functions of government' (Lipset 1959: 77). When faced with a crisis of effectiveness, such as an economic depression, the stability of the regime depends to a large extent on the degree of legitimacy that it enjoys.

This is illustrated in the Lipset matrix, crossing legitimacy and effectiveness, showing the dynamics. If a regime finds itself in box A, with both a high degree of legitimacy and effectiveness, in a moment of crisis it should move to box B, showing a loss of effectiveness but the maintenance of legitimacy. Once the crisis has passed it should then move back to its original position in box A.

This idea that legitimacy, once obtained, can be more easily preserved has also been argued by others. For example, Eckstein (1966) stresses that legitimacy produces a reservoir of support guaranteeing the co-operation of the citizens even in the case of quite unpopular policies. Legitimacy creates a reservoir of goodwill on which the authorities can draw in difficult times and increases considerably the willingness of the people to tolerate shortcomings of effectiveness. By contrast, if a regime finds itself in box C, with a high degree of effectiveness but a relatively low degree of legitimacy, a crisis in effectiveness would move the regime from box C to box D. The regime would then be likely to break down.

The relationship between these two concepts can be further understood through an analysis of historical examples. During the Great Depression of the 1930s a major crisis in effectiveness seriously affected European as well as American economies. We can contrast the effects of the Depression on the USA and Britain, which had a high level of legitimacy, with the effects on Germany and Austria, where legitimacy was low. In the two first countries, the crisis of effectiveness did not encourage anti-democratic movements and did not bring the regime's legitimacy into question. The people required a change in leadership, not of the regime. In Germany and Austria, however, the crisis of effectiveness led to the collapse of the democratic regime. The unemployment rate and the vote for the National Socialist Party were intimately related.

Movement from box C to box A is also possible since long-term effectiveness can give a regime the chance to build its legitimacy. The rulers in Singapore, South Korea and Taiwan have gained enough legitimacy by their economic success to enable them finally to organize free elections. But the most famous examples are Japan and the Federal Republic of Germany, where democracy was born, or implemented, during a military occupation in a climate of suspicion and scepticism. Their economic miracles raised these two regimes from total absence of legitimacy and from deep national humiliation to the forefront of the most legitimate pluralist democracies.

The same period has seen the collapse of the Soviet Union, not because of a military defeat, but because of a complete failure in effectiveness. The Soviet Union not only had a revolutionary ideology for decades but also had the technological capacity to penetrate and control society in an enormous and relatively rich land. The speed of the breakdown of the communist system in the Soviet Union and in its Eastern European satellites since 1989 demonstrates how the economic ineffectiveness of a regime can ruin its legitimacy.

Italy and Argentina are good recent examples of the move from box A to box B. The Italian democracy has experienced a serious crisis of inefficiency in the 1990s, but the democratic regime has not lost its legitimacy (Dogan 2002). The Argentinian democracy was severely shaken in June and July 2002, after several years of economic decline and financial difficulties. The country has been at a certain moment (in the years after the Second World War) one of the richest countries. But because of the incompetence and irresponsibility of the political class the standard of living of the population, particularly of the middle classes, has fallen to a very low level. None the less the belief of the people in democracy has remained solid, nourished by the reservoir of rooted values.

The role of elites in the legitimation process has attracted the attention of many authors. When the intellectual elites are confident in the regime, an optimistic future for the regime could be predicted. But when, on the contrary, the civil elites are those that oppose the regime, that regime's legitimacy seems more fragile. In China, in the spring of 1989, it was the most educated segment of the society that protested. The students represented less than one per thousand of the Chinese society, but they succeeded in shedding light on the illegitimacy of the regime.

In a comparative analysis of the factors in the revolutionary movements in Puritan England, in the USA at the time of Washington, in France in 1789 and in Russia in 1917, Crane Brinton (1965) stresses the importance of the intellectual ferment, which subsequently led to the spread of the new ideas to a large part of the population, engendering a crisis of legitimacy. Other social strata have attracted attention, such as the working class in the Marxist analysis. The clergy have also played an important historic role, as in the Protestant countries in the past, and with the Liberation theology in some Latin American countries more recently. The army has been the most visible actor of delegitimation in dozens of developing countries.

The strains on legitimacy and the loss of trust can be explained in part by the difficulty to govern, to steer society. There are two opposite kinds of ingovernability: either the government is overloaded with demands from a very complex society, is doing too much as in the advanced democracies called welfare states, or is not doing enough because the state is economically too weak and lacks the resources required to affect society.

In most contemporary regimes, political leaders seek to base their power on trust rather than on coercion. Almost all countries, even authoritarian regimes, feel obliged to pay lip-service to the institution of elections, which are considered as the source of legitimacy. It is for this reason that today the concept of legitimacy is used in electoral rhetoric.

Power, legitimacy, trust and effectiveness do not have identical meanings in London and Jakarta, or in Washington and Cairo. The ambition to encapsulate these concepts in definitions of universal validity may be a 'sin' of Western cultural ethnocentrism.

References

Brinton, C. (1965) *The Anatomy of Revolution*, rev. and expanded edn, New York:Vintage Books.

Citrin, J. (1974) 'The political relevance of trust in government', *American Political Science Review* 68: 973–8.

Dogan, M. (2002) 'Dissatisfaction and mistrust in West european democracies', *European Review* vol. 10, 1, 91–114

Dogan, M. (1996) 'La Crise de confiance dans les democraties pluralistes', *Encyclopedia Universalis, Universalia*, 112–17

Easton, D. (1965) *A Systems Analysis of Political Life*, New York: John Wiley.

Eckstein, H. (1966) *Division and Cohesion in a Democracy: A Study of Norway*, Princeton: Princeton University Press.

Gastil, R. D. (1980–9) *Freedom in the World, Political Rights and Civil Liberties*, 6 vols, New York: Freedom House.

Halman, L. (2001) *The European Values Study: the Third Wave*, Tilburg: Tilburg University Press.

Harding, S., Philips, D. and Fogarty, M. (1986) *Contrasting Values in Western Europe*, London: Macmillan.

Hertz, J. (1978) 'Legitimacy, can we retrieve it?', *Comparative Politics* 10: (3): 317–43.

Hudson, M. C. (1977) *Arab Politics. The Search for Legitimacy*, New Haven: Yale University Press.

Linz, J. (1988) 'Legitimacy of democracy and the socioeconomic system', in M. Dogan (ed.) *Comparing Pluralist Democracies: Strains on Legitimacy*, Boulder: Westview Press.

Lipset, S. M. (1959) *Political Man, The Social Basis of Politics*, New York: Doubleday.

Lipset, S. M. and Schneider, W. (1983) *The Confidence Gap, Business, Labor and Government in the Public Mind*, Baltimore: Johns Hopkins University Press.

Merkl, P. H. (1988) 'Comparing legitimacy and values among advanced countries', in M. Dogan (ed.) *Comparing Pluralist Democracies: Strains on Legitimacy*, Boulder: Westview Press.

Schaar, J. H. (1981) *Legitimacy in the Modern State*, New Brunswick: Transaction Books.

Further reading

Dogan, M. (ed.) (1988) *Comparing Pluralist Democracies: Strains on Legitimacy*, Boulder: Westview Press.

Habermas, J. (1973) *Legitimation Crisis*, Boston: Beacon Books.

Miller, A. H. (1974) 'Political issues and trust in government 1964–1970', *American Political Science Review* 68 (3): 951–72.

Nye, J. S., Zelikov, P. D. and King, D. C. (1997) *Why People Don't Trust Government*, Cambridge, MA: Harvard University Press.

Pharr, S. and Putnam, R. (2000) *Disaffected Democracies, What's Troubling the Trilateral Countries?*, Princeton: Princeton University Press.

Sternberger, D. (1968) 'Legitimacy', *International Encyclopaedia of Social Sciences*, New York: Macmillan Free Press.

Weber, M. (1978) *Economy and Society*, eds G. Roth and C. Wittich, vol I, Berkeley: University of California Press, particularly the sections on 'The types of legitimate domination', 'Domination and legitimacy', 'Charisma and its transformation'.

8

POSTMODERNISM AND THE REPUDIATION OF GRAND THEORY

Renee Heberle

> I mistrust all systematizers and avoid them.
> The will to a system is a lack of integrity.
> Friedrich Nietzsche (1889) *Twilight of the Idols*

Postmodernism describes an approach to theorizing that itself criticizes and resists the impulse to categorize. Thus, writing an essay meant to capture the meaning of postmodernism is somewhat of a paradoxical venture. As well, most theorists specifically identified with the postmodern turn in theory do not acknowledge the term as an appropriate or even helpful description of their work. In fact some suggest that the term itself has come to be one of convenience allowing for easy appropriation or dismissal of an otherwise discordant set of theorists without engaging their particular arguments (Butler 1995; Cornell 1995). Keeping this in mind, I offer what follows as a descriptive cartography of some highlights of contemporary theoretical work that travels, often unwillingly, under the sign of postmodernism.

The term postmodernism was originally used in the 1950s in the fields of art and literary criticism. It signalled a critical recognition of the failures of modernist art forms to resist absorption into commodified culture. It then came to be used as a descriptive term for an aesthetic style that announced itself as unmoored from unnecessarily reified modernist distinctions between high art and popular culture (Huyssen 1990). Since about the middle of the 1970s, however, postmodernism has lost its specificity as a term referring to the art world or aesthetic sensibilities. It has migrated into social and political theory. In the context of social and political inquiry, postmodernism signals a critique of the Enlightenment that suggests Enlightenment thinking has not only failed to live up to its own promises of human emancipation, but that those failures are immanent to the very terms on which Enlightenment seeks to emancipate.

A concise, commonly accepted account of the project of Enlightenment is found in Immanuel Kant's essay 'What is Enlightenment?' (1784). Kant says simply Enlightenment is 'man's emergence from his self-imposed immaturity' (1983: 41). For Kant, Enlightenment describes the capacity to use one's own understanding free of the undue influence of authority or power. This difference from a state of willful ignorance will be gradually but irrevocably and progressively realized in human history. Kantian Enlightenment suggests a faith in reason and the human

120

capacity for self-understanding, in scientific inquiry and the virtues of disinterested inquiry, and ultimately in the potential coherence and stability of moral truths waiting to be discovered through philosophical inquiry. Jean-François Lyotard identifies these as 'metanarratives' of Enlightenment. At the most general level of description, Lyotard characterizes postmodernism as 'incredulity' toward these metanarratives (1979: xxiv).

Our particular concern here is with postmodernism and the status of grand theory as it informs the project of political inquiry. With respect to political philosophy, the category of grand theory includes those thinkers for whom the chaotic sweep of human history can and should be systematically captured through philosophical inquiry. Sheldon Wolin asserts in *Politics and Vision* (1960) that no political theorist ultimately advocates disorder in the realm of human affairs but rather seeks out the most just order of things. He describes political philosophy as a field of inquiry that explores human nature, the qualities of the good life, and the workings of power, always with an eye toward establishing the most just terms of ordering human interactions. Hobbes's Leviathan, Locke and Rousseau's social contract, Marx's communism, Mill's marketplace of ideas, and Rawls's original position are each representations of a state of affairs in which human beings can best make sense of their world and aspire to justice.

This explicitly normative approach to political inquiry is commonly viewed in contradistinction to behaviouralist, empirical approaches. The development of these approaches dates approximately to the 1950s. The empirical study of human behaviour prioritizes questions about what people do rather than speculating about what they should do, and thus claims a closer relationship to reality than normative theory. Developing the best methods for measuring empirical phenomena related to the question of 'who gets what, where, when, why and how' has gradually become the mainstream objective of political science. Empiricists critique political philosophy as a mode of inquiry for its apparent distance from the real, lived stuff of historical reality and human behaviour. Seen from the perspective of postmodern critique, however, these apparently divergent modes of inquiry rely on similar metanarratives of Enlightenment about the sufficiency and reliability of the project of human self-examination as a means to the ends of justice. They each ultimately seek closure on certain questions about the proper objects, procedures, and ends of politics.

Influenced by Lyotard, Michel Foucault and Jacques Derrida, among others, postmodern political theorists seek to unsettle and disrupt these efforts to bring closure. They do so through exploring spaces, identities, actions, and concepts typically obscured or ignored in the name of marking and proscribing the boundaries of the political. Their goal is not thus disorder, anarchy, or chaos, but an attunement to what Bonnie Honig has called 'the remainders of politics' (1993: 4), that which stubbornly prevents politics from being a closed system or a stable means to predictable ends. Further, postmodern theorists argue that the dichotomies worked out (albeit in very different ways) by Enlightenment thinkers, such as the public/private, reason/desire, subject/object, and appearance/reality, are not universal and necessary, but can be shown to do work in the service of particular historical projects of legitimation and certain historical configurations of power.

The term postmodernism is often used to refer to several different but overlapping currents in theoretical inquiry, namely, poststructuralism, genealogy, deconstruction.

Poststructuralism is literally the critique of the structuralist movement identified with thinkers like Louis Althusser and Ferdinand de Saussure. It suggests that 'power pervades the very conceptual apparatus that seeks to negotiate its terms, including the subject position of the critic....To establish a set of norms that are beyond power or force is itself a powerful and forceful conceptual practice that sublimates, disguises, and extends its own power play through recourse to tropes of normative universality' (Butler 1995: 39). Genealogy describes a practice that critiques the search for origins or determinant causes and effects in historical inquiry. It seeks instead to articulate the conditions of possibility through which truths about human nature, the terms of morality, or the virtue of scientific knowledge, for example, become self-evident or naturalized. Deconstruction signals an interpretivist approach to reading the world as text. In doing so it rejects dualistic distinctions, for example, that between an objective factual world that is available to logical analysis and a subjective textual world that is available to the vagaries of imagination and interpretation. Deconstruction calls into question all such Enlightenment dualisms, including that between reason and desire, arguing that they are regulatory fictions that unduly circumscribe in advance what counts as legitimate knowledge. In what follows I will elaborate on the insights made available to political inquiry by these approaches.

With respect to the question of the 'post' in postmodernism, it does tend to suggest that the field of inquiry understands itself as standing beyond the terms of the Enlightenment. However, in sustaining an attitude of 'incredulity' I suggest the thinkers I will discuss seek not simply to repudiate metanarrative, as if we can simply brush off the detritus of the Enlightenment and progressively assume the indeterminacy of meaning. Rather I think it is more accurate to say that they seek to elaborate how questions that become legitimate through the Enlightenment open up but also, and as importantly, constrain and proscribe possibilities for inquiry. Foucault explicitly admonishes us that there is no standing for or against the Enlightenment. Indeed, he calls that a simplistic and authoritarian kind of intellectual blackmail. Rather, he says:

> It seems to me that Kant's reflection [on Enlightenment] is even a way of philosophizing that has not been without its importance or effectiveness during the last two centuries. The critical ontology of ourselves has to be considered not, certainly, as a theory, a doctrine, nor even as a permanent body of knowledge that is accumulating; it has to be conceived as an attitude, an ethos, a philosophical life in which the critique of what we are is at one and the same time the historical analysis of the limits that are imposed on us and an experiment with the possibilities of going beyond them. ...I do not know whether it must be said that the critical task still entails faith in Enlightenment; I continue to think that this task requires work on our limits, that is, a patient labor giving form to our impatience for liberty.
>
> (Foucault 1984a: 50)

Critics often miss the point that those identified with postmodernism do not treat the Enlightenment as a kind of monolith from which one must escape (see McGowan 1991). On the contrary, in as much as postmodern theorists understand 'the knowing subject' to be constituted in and through the Enlightenment, they insist that we remain attuned to that which must be subordinated, silenced, or excluded in order for the truths of Enlightenment to function as such, to the remainders identified by Honig. This does not require us to seek out an alternative truth that is to be found in these excesses. However, there is a positive project to be found in this critical practice. In exposing the inherent instability in categories otherwise taken for granted and thus rendered impermeable by or immune to politics, postmodern critique opens alternative spaces for political contestation and, as Foucault would have it, experimentation with otherwise unforeseen possibilities.

In what follows I elaborate on the work of particularly influential thinkers who are commonly identified with the postmodern turn in political inquiry. I start by further elaborating Lyotard's thinking about what he identifies as the crisis of legitimacy suffered by knowledge forms that rely on metanarrative. Then, following an interlude that introduces Nietzschean challenges to Enlightenment thinking, I turn to Foucault's theory of genealogy and Derrida's work on deconstruction. My discussion will ultimately turn to debates in feminist political theory about the significance of the postmodern turn. This discussion could address any subdiscipline of Political Science; the intellectual influence and challenge of postmodernism is far reaching. However, feminist political theory brings into sharp relief the risks and benefits of postmodern forms of critique and their significance for political inquiry.

Grand theory and postmodern scepticism

Postmodern theorists show how Enlightenment forms of theorizing and knowledge production naturalize the grounds of their own legitimacy, thus placing those grounds off-limits to inquiry. It is a complicated and often apparently esoteric task as the legitimacy of the impulse to deny the contingent and accidental quality of human affairs through philosophical and scientific knowledge has been, for most part, unchallenged since the dawning of the age of Enlightenment. However, given the systematic and highly technological and innovative forms human dominance over humans and nature has taken in late modernity, it is worth asking whether the drive to Enlightenment, to self-understanding, rationalized forms of identity, and technological progress, is itself complicit with the contemporary forms of violence inflicted by totalitarian states, unchecked systems of capitalist exchange, and high-tech weapons of mass destruction. Theorists identified with postmodernism take various positions with respect to these kinds of questions, but they are all profoundly sceptical of the stories Enlightenment thinkers tell about the inevitably progressive effects of reason as it guides human relationships and understanding.

Jean-François Lyotard is one of a few contemporary theorists who acknowledge the term 'postmodern' as having meaning in itself. In an essay entitled *The Postmodern Condition: A Report on Knowledge* (1979), he argues that the apparently distinct projects of normative and behavioural approaches to political inquiry are interrelated in that they both rely for legitimacy on reference to metanarrative, which Lyotard identifies with examples such as 'the dialectics of Spirit, the hermeneutics of meaning, the emancipation of the rational or working subject, or the creation of wealth' (Lyotard 1979: xxiii) As noted above, postmodernism is a problematic that was named during the late 1950s with reference to aesthetic form and critique. Lyotard's analysis deploys the term more broadly to describe a crisis in the legitimacy of Enlightenment metanarratives about the pursuit of unitary truth and the linear quality of human progress. For Lyotard, the pursuit of knowledge in postmodern culture has been cast off its moorings in metanarrative, and dispersed into a necessarily pragmatic project of legitimation *games*. It is the impact of 'incredulity' toward metanarrative that distinguishes postmodernity from modernity. This incredulity is both a cause and a symptom of the postmodern condition.

Lyotard suggests several important historical premises in his description of the postmodern. Postmodernism maps onto the emergence of a postindustrial society in the Occident, or Western world. It thus coincides with the emergence of a new internationalized division of labour. This division of labour organizes not only material production but intellectual and cultural production. The commodification of knowledge in the information driven economy signals the emergence of postmodern incredulity and subsequent legitimacy contests.

For Lyotard, postmodernism has both spatial and temporal aspects. It is a condition of disintegration and opportunity as it signals a legitimacy crisis in the epistemological, cultural and political life of 'highly developed' societies. For Lyotard, as for Richard Rorty, postmodernism suggests a shift to a pragmatic approach to knowledge and to political inquiry that will be more appropriate to the present condition than transcendental or empirical approaches. This pragmatism is described by Rorty:

> When they [pragmatists] suggest that we not ask questions about the nature of Truth and Goodness, they do not invoke a theory about the nature of reality or knowledge or man which says that 'there is no such thing' as Truth or Goodness. Nor do they have a 'relativistic' or 'subjectivist' theory of Truth or Goodness. They would simply like to change the subject. They are in a position analogous to that of secularists who urge that research concerning the Nature, or the Will, of God does not get us anywhere. Such secularists are not saying that God does not exist, exactly; they feel unclear about what it would mean to affirm His existence, and thus about the point of denying it. Nor do they have some special, funny, heretical view about God. They just doubt that the vocabulary of theology is one we ought to be using.
>
> (Rorty 1982: 2)

Poststructuralism, genealogy, and deconstruction

Lyotard and Rorty's reading of the postmodern condition relies on critical insights made available in large part through the recuperation and rereading of the work of Friedrich Nietzsche since the late 1950s. Nietzsche directly and aggressively engaged in a critique of grand theory, understood as the effort to order and manage the internal and external nature of human beings. It is from Nietzsche that Foucault develops a genealogical approach to history, to knowledge, and to power and Derrida a deconstructive approach to interpretation. Before addressing their work, we should look more specifically at how Nietzsche challenged some basic premises of Enlightenment thinking.

Nietzsche's claim that God is dead and that man has killed him is perhaps his signature challenge (1974: 181, 279). By this he does not mean that man is no longer a believing creature. Nor is he advocating the death of God. Rather, he is announcing the displacement of God by truth claims that deny their own status as belief systems. Thus, for example, empiricism expresses a will to know that which is given as if it can reveal the truth with no imprint of interpretation from the author or reader. Nietzsche's observation does not suggest that belief has receded from the human world. Rather, belief in God and divine revelation as a source of truth and morality has been displaced by belief in science, evolutionary progress, and ultimately in the autonomy and transparency of human knowledge. This belief and the humanist principles that attend it, obscure the violence intrinsic to the discovery of Man as such, of subjectivity, and of the invention of moral principles. For Nietzsche, two thousand years of Judeo-Christian acculturation has resulted in the bloody triumph of reason over instinct, of Man over nature, and of the domesticated guilty conscience over the active will to power.

The concept of ressentiment, developed in *Beyond Good and Evil* (1973) and *On The Genealogy of Morals* (1967), captures much of what Nietzsche argued was damaging to the human spirit within the context of Judeo-Christian culture. In these texts Nietzsche tells the story of the emergence of ressentiment as the moral code for man who has become self-conscious. He asks how the 'good' is conceived by the man of ressentiment.

> That lambs dislike great birds of prey does not seem strange: only it gives no ground for reproaching these birds of prey for bearing off little lambs. And if the lambs say among themselves: 'these birds of prey are evil; and whoever is least like a bird of prey, but rather its opposite, a lamb–would he not be good?' There is no reason to find fault with this institution of an ideal, except perhaps that the birds of prey might view it a little ironically and say: 'we don't dislike them at all, these good little lambs; we even love them: nothing is more tasty than a tender lamb'.
>
> (Nietzsche 1967: 44–5)

It is the reactive quality of the judgement by the lambs that Nietzsche names the slave mentality, or ressentiment.

Nietzsche by no means dismissed the logic of ressentiment; rather he argues that it is with this move to internalize the will, to instill the guilty conscience, that man becomes an interesting creature. For Nietzsche, no historical figure is more clever than the priest who succeeds in rendering human instinct accountable to the soul. For Nietzsche this reflects the tragedy of the contemporary order: that man has willfully sacrificed his capacity for independent action in the name of social welfare and security, all the while telling himself the humanist story of the individual as imbued with sacred and heroic meaning.

A question introduced by Nietzsche and taken up by what is now identified as postmodern thinking is that of the impact of this form of reactive moral judgment on relationships between self and other. This is not in itself an original question. For example, a century before Nietzsche, Rousseau argued that civilization is founded upon our loss of radical independence and the development of a corrupted form of dependence upon others for self awareness. Civilized consciousness is shown as developed only through comparative judgment with others. The radically independent individual imagined by Nietzsche and Rousseau runs into his/her chains through the civilizing process. For Rousseau, the project of Enlightenment was to transform this corrupt form of interdependence into one that could express the otherwise rational and virtuous nature of man. As Nietzsche sees it, however, the man of ressentiment is victorious; he is not a passing figure in historical time. There may be a future beyond the slave mentality but there is not a teleological vision to be found in Nietzsche.

Nietzsche's work suggests the very difficult, perhaps unanswerable, question of what it would be like to live without the foundational categories of good and evil as a means by which to know how to act and judge. He demands we recognize our reliance on historical constructions of good and evil that ultimately disallow the healthy discharging of instinctual aggression, but also of instinctual love and generosity. For Nietzsche, ressentiment comes to inhabit the modern self, conditioning it to *react* in the vengeful spirit of the slave. Starting from the idea that the being of man emerges through historical relationships, and is not grounded in an eternal essence or nature, post-Nietzschean scholarship has struggled with questions about relationships of self to other that will not rely on naturalized and thus unspoken and unacknowledged forms of moral judgment (see Connolly 1991; Coles 1997). The notion that we are consistently progressing toward the realization of the good is yet another means by which we obscure the reactive and vengeful response to otherness, captured in the concept of ressentiment, upon which our presumably civilized selves are founded.

Another crucial Nietzschean insight is in his articulation of 'perspective seeing'. In the *Genealogy* he warns philosophers to:

> be on guard against the dangerous old conceptual fiction that posited a 'pure, will-less, painless, timeless knowing subject;...let us guard against the snare of such contradictory concepts as 'pure reason', absolute sprituality', 'knowledge in itself' these always demand that we should think of an eye that is completely unthinkable, an eye turned in no particular direction, which the active and interpreting forces through which alone seeing becomes seeing something, are supposed to be lacking;...There is only a perspective seeing, only a perspective 'knowing' and the more affects we allow to speak,...the more complete will our 'concept of this thing', our 'objectivity' be.
>
> (Nietzsche 1967: 119)

For Nietzsche, to eliminate the will in the project of knowledge production is to castrate human intellect.

This interpretivist approach to social and political theory can be traced to thinkers before Nietzsche. However, unlike Hegel, for example, whose dialectical method suggests the conflictual quality and incomplete status of human understanding, Nietzsche has no teleological aspirations of finally transcending the limits of human understanding, of this perspectival seeing. Instead he points to the dangers implicit in efforts to transcend the all-too-human limits of understanding. According to Nietzsche universalizing claims about transcendence are always only legitimated through what for him is a self-willed violent renunciation of self. These efforts renounce the heterogeneity and plurality of the self and of the human condition, privileging instead perspective that thinks it can ultimately grasp the totality of human experience.

Nietzsche critiques the dualisms of good and evil, self and other, subject and object, without which, it is claimed by thinking imbued by Enlightenment values, legitimate knowledge of history and the purpose of life cannot be had. In questioning such apparently fundamental and structuring features of knowledge production, he is said by some to be advocating a kind of moral relativism. Another way of reading his project, however, suggests that he simply wants to know to what uses morality, as structured through those dualisms, is put at certain historical junctures. Foucault captures the spirit of Nietzsche's project as follows:

> If interpretation were the slow exposure of the meaning hidden in an origin, then only metaphysics could interpret the development of humanity. But if interpretation is the violent or surreptitious appropriation of a system of rules, which in itself has no essential meaning, in order to impose a direction, to bend it to a new will, to force its participation in a different game, and to subject it to secondary rules, then the development of humanity is a series of interpretations. The role of genealogy is to record its history: the history of morals, ideals, and metaphysical concepts, the history of the concept of liberty, or of the ascetic life; as they stand for the emergence of different interpretations, they must be made to appear as events on the stage of historical process.
>
> (Foucault 1984b: 86)

Foucault deploys this approach in studies of medical perception (1973), madness (1965), punishment (1977), and sexuality (1978). Like Nietzsche, in these studies he does not pretend to seek the origin of these modern developments in the scientific approach to the 'normal' subject, nor does he seek to draw conclusions about the well-being of Man in light of these developments. He treats them as symptomatic rather than as expressive of the ethos of Enlightenment; he historicizes them as made possible, or legitimate, by particular relations of power specific to particular contexts.

It is in part due to his conceptualization of power that Foucault makes a radical departure from the project of grand theory. If most Enlightenment narratives treat power as a kind of substance to be possessed, or wielded, or traded, from centralized sovereign locations (the King, the state, the self), Foucault treats power as 'exercised from innumerable points, in the interplay of nonegalitarian and mobile relations'. He continues:

> Relations of power are not in a position of exteriority with respect to other types of relationship (economic processes, knowledge relationship, sexual relations), but are immanent in the latter; they are the immediate effects of the divisions, inequalities, and disequilibriums which occur in the latter, and conversely they are the internal conditions of these differentiations; relations of power are not in superstructural position, with merely a role of prohibition or accompaniment; they have a directly productive role, wherever they come into play.
>
> (Foucault 1978: 94)

127

In a manner reminiscent of Lyotard but more explicitly concerned with power, Foucault suggests that what he calls the figure of the universal intellectual, 'the man of justice, the man of law, who counterposes to power, despotism and the abuses and arrogance of wealth the universality of justice and the equity of an ideal law' has been displaced by the figure of the specific intellectual who derives from the privileging of science, particularly biology and physics. '[The intellectual] is no longer the rhapsodist of the eternal, but the strategist of life and death' (Foucault 1980: 128–9). Importantly then, Foucault has a significantly different approach to truth than metaphysicians and empiricists. Truth is not something that exists outside of power, something to be captured through detached contemplation or disinterested objectivity. Rather, 'Truth is a thing of this world: it is produced only by virtue of multiple forms of constraint. And it induces regular effects of power. Each society has its regime of truth, its general politics of truth...' (Foucault 1980: 131).

Foucault's work encourages what some have called a radical constructivist approach to politics and to the problem of freedom. For example, following Foucault, affects deemed by the most progressive of the modern political philosophies to be essentially expressive of the true or authentic self, such as individuality (liberalism), sexuality (feminism), racial identity (anti-colonialism), class positioning (Marxism), could be argued to be in themselves effects, or symptoms of particular relationships of power. I will discuss this further when I consider feminist debates about Foucault's ideas. For now I will note that Foucault insisted that there is no 'beyond' to power, no expression of individuality or sexuality, and no authentic racial or class identity that exists outside of relations of power specific to time and place.

Derrida's work is also indebted to Nietzschean insights, but develops by way of a critique of the phenomenological movement, most importantly, by way of critical readings of Edmund Husserl and Martin Heidegger. Heidegger was inspired by, but ultimately diverged from Nietzsche. He was similarly critical of the unquestioned Cartesian foundations of philosophical inquiry. He was not interested in the way foundations are built, or in the timing of the construction, or in showing that they are poorly put together. Rather, he was concerned with destructing (sic) the imperative to have a foundational basis on which to build philosophical knowledge. Heidegger introduces the concept of *Dasein* to encourage the doubling back of philosophic thinking on itself. *Dasein* refers to the being that questions the meaning of being. More importantly for our purposes, *Dasein* questions the a priori claims about being made by traditional philosophy emphasizing instead its essential relatedness and condition of being in the world, or its *worldliness*.

Put in the most simple terms, deconstruction brings to the forefront of theoretical inquiry the notion that any asserted presence (Being) *requires* an absence, or a disavowal of the otherness necessary to draw the boundaries of selfhood. Derrida addresses the violence immanent to this disavowal of otherness. He draws critically on the work in the psychoanalytic tradition inspired by Sigmund Freud and Jacques Lacan, in which ideas about the developmental movement toward autonomy and selfhood in infants figure prominently, to develop the project of deconstruction. Deconstruction asserts the essential relatedness of the human subject and suggests a consequential instability as built into selfhood.

Derrida coined the term '*différance*' to capture the simultaneous movement of differentiation and deferral experienced as the infantile self emerges into the realm of the symbolic, or language, wherein personhood becomes possible. Psychoanalytic theory argues that an infant moves through stages of separation from his mother as he establishes his wholeness and distinctness of self. Further, as desires such as food and or touch are not immediately gratified, he necessarily develops a capacity to defer satisfaction. These experiences of differentiation and deferral signal the overcoming of, but never a total emancipation from, the semiotic, identified in psychoanalytic theory as the forces of the Mother but more generally for purposes of deconstruction, as that other, object, or boundary that defines the limits of subjectivity and the self.

Différance designates the deconstructive move beyond structuralist theories of language inspired by Ferdinand Saussure which posit that no word has meaning except in the context of the differential network of meaning. For Saussurian structuralism, 'There is no self-evident or one-to-one link between "signifier" and "signified", the word as spoken or written vehicle and the concept it serves to evoke. Both are caught up in a play of distinctive features where differences of sound and sense are the only markers of meaning' (Norris 1991: 24–5). *Différance*, designating the simultaneity of difference and deferral in the construction of meaning, disrupts the modern dream of narrative closure through systematic and cumulative knowledge of that which is not yet understood.

Nancy Holland writes 'What differance tells us is that these oppositions [form/matter, subject/object, rational/irrational, light/dark, male/female, true/false] have meaning only because of the posited difference between the two terms and, therefore, that neither of the terms has any meaning in and of itself, but always defers its final referent along the trajectory of the series' (Holland 1997: 5–6). In Enlightenment thought, these dualisms are structured such that the second term is always already understood to be properly subordinate to the claims of the first. Deconstruction shows how this obscures the radical interdependence of the terms and the subsequent indeterminacy of the meaning of either.

Derridean deconstruction identifies the slippage between the signifier and the signified, between language and that which it claims to represent, as a potential space of politics, rather than as something politics, as the voice of reason, must clean up. For Derrida, the clean-up is itself an act of violence, of dominance, of the assertion of an ever-elusive mastery.

In what follows I briefly explore a particular field of discourse, feminist political theory, as a case study for identifying what is at stake, in this case, for women and gender politics, in adopting these critical insights about and approaches to grand theory.

Feminist political theory and postmodernism

Postmodern feminist critique suggests some versions of feminism as a critical, transformative project may be self-defeating in that they share with their masculinist Enlightenment protagonists assumptions about power, identity, the universality and immutability of male/female as a dichotomous relation, and the liberating potential of a revelatory search for the truth (in this case, in women's articulations of their own experiences). I will refer to Catharine MacKinnon's work by way of example as it has been profoundly influential in the development of feminist analysis, both as an inspiration and as a focal point for critique.

MacKinnon argues that feminism should give up its efforts to critically engage masculinist theories (in this case, Marxism and Liberalism) and travel under its own sign, radically autonomous from the fatherly paradigms of Enlightenment thought. To drive home this point she titled her book, *Feminism Unmodified* (1987). It is this desire for a space uninflected by patriarchal norms, values, and insitutions, that defines the current in feminism commonly called Radical feminism. Radical feminism attempts to isolate gender as a category of analysis and the identity of woman as a univocal point of departure for critical theory. It identifies male power as the cause and women's oppression as the effect of gender relations of inequality.

Postmodern feminist critics have suggested that this approach ultimately places feminism in the position of claiming itself to be outside of or immune to the politics of representation. Postmodern critics suggest that when feminism obscures its positioning within a politics of representation, through reference to the immutable 'reality' of women's suffering, or the universality of women's condition within a patriarchal order, it prematurely forecloses on political contest within feminism (see Butler and Scott 1993; Brown 1995). It thus renders the very existence of feminism dependent upon an anti-democratic impulse. It assumes that in order to have a politics we must seek to agree in advance, or outside of the space of politics, about the meaning of women's experiences, the origins and causes of inequality between males and females, indeed, that we know what woman is and what she wants.

Further, it has been noted that every effort to assert a univocal truth about women's experiences, like MacKinnon's, has generated multiple protests and resistances (Butler 1990: 7). It is this history that causes some to suggest there is an elective affinity between postmodernism and feminism. That feminist ideas and practices have proliferated into the wide-ranging and discordant field of discourse it is today can be attributed to the conflict among self-identified feminists in addition to their refusal to stand down before those who assert women and gender are not the proper stuff of political inquiry. In other words, feminism, as an essentially contested concept and set of practices, itself performs as a critique of the impulse of grand theory to unify and seek closure on the meaning, in this case, of women's positioning and gender identity.

For MacKinnon, in particular, the universality, or fundamental sameness, of the experience of women's suffering at the hands of men, no matter what differences might be manifest, must be put off-limits to inquiry if feminism is to have a presence at all in the world. Other feminists who are sceptical of the postmodern turn argue that while MacKinnon's universalism may be overreaching, there remain some important reasons feminism should keep its distance from postmodernism.

Feminists raise important questions about the significance of the fact that postmodern critiques of the subject of Enlightenment humanism emerged just as those persons historically denied the standing of subjects, women, people of colour, sexual minorities, and colonized others, are speaking out as such. Nancy Hartsock comments 'Somehow it seems highly suspicious that it is at the precise moment when so many groups have been engaged in "nationalisms" which involve redefinitions of the marginalized Others that suspicions emerge about the nature of the "subject", about the possibilities for a general theory which can describe the world, about historical "progress"' (1990: 163). Hartsock questions whether a Foucauldian theory of power wherein power is said to be everywhere (and therefore, perhaps, nowhere) is helpful to the transformative projects of feminist theory and activism. Similarly, Nancy Fraser and Linda Nicholson (1990) worry that postmodern theory throws the baby of social criticism of general patterns of dominance out with the bathwater of grand theory. In other words, in critiquing the manner in which Enlightenment knowledge legitimates its claims to truth with claims about objectivity, or what Fraser and Nicholson call 'the view from nowhere', postmodernism may leave us instead with an uncritical 'view from everywhere'.

The very capacity of social critics to name the problem, in this case, male domination and exploitation of women is said to be at stake in these debates. The category 'woman' has come under scrutiny from those who critique feminists' tendency to allow the experience of white, middle-class, heterosexual women stand in for the experience and understanding of all women. But this insight, these critics suggest, should not deprive us of the category once and for all as a salient category of identity and analysis.

Postmodern feminists argue that relying on the assumption that the category 'women' exists prior to what it is we say about it, or to its discursive production, paradoxically depoliticizes the category. It presumes that such an identity exists somewhere outside of the framing apparatuses made possible by certain configurations of power. For postmodern feminists, gender and sexual difference are discursively produced within the context of certain relations of power and symbolic configurations. To say anything less would be to agree with the phallocentric constructions of Enlightenment thinking that put certain questions about gender and the nature of masculinity and femininity off-limits to inquiry in the name of political stability. For example, reading psychoanalytic theory through a postmodern lens that emphasizes interpretation and language has offered feminism 1) a way of thinking about how we are psychically and socially acculturated through language as sexed and gendered figures and 2) how we might resist the heteronormative imperatives that follow from assumptions about the immutability of gendered and sexed identities within the political and social order (see for example, Irigaray 1985; Butler 1990; 1997; Cornell 1995).

In general critics of postmodernism suggest it is overreaching in its critique of humanist discourses and its reliance on linguistic constructionism for understanding human experience. Similar questions have been raised in debates about postmodernism in the fields of anti-racist theory and post-colonial theory. Further, the eurocentric quality of postmodern theory should be noted. Psychoanalytic theory, structuralism, Marxism, and other discourses which postmodern theory takes as critical points of departure are particular to a certain historical setting. Arguments about postmodernism should take this into account in considering whether and how its varied insights are ultimately helpful in understanding and transforming global relationships of domination and exploitation. Lyotard's 'incredulity' toward meta-narrative may itself be, as much of his essay does suggest, salient only within certain historical conditions. Postcolonial theorist Homi Bhabha notes:

> if the interest in postmodernism is limited to a celebration of the fragmentation of the 'grand narratives' of postenlightenment rationalism then, for all its intellectual excitement, it remains a profoundly parochial exercise...The wider significance of the postmodern condition lies in the awareness that the epistemological 'limits' of those ethnocentric ideas are also the enunciative

boundaries of a range of other dissonant, even dissident histories and voices
– women, the colonised, minority groups, the bearers of policed sexualities.

(Bhabha 2001: 139)

Conclusion

That grand theory should be 'repudiated' remains a highly contentious claim. Most
contemporary students of politics continue to argue that the task of theory is to seek
to articulate universal principles of rationality, justice, morality, and truth. The term
most commonly used to describe those who criticize that impulse is 'relativist'. The
concern is that if one does not assume and subsequently make aspirational claims
about certain values, including but not limited to morality, human rights, basic
human needs, the dignity of persons, liberal pluralism, alleviating material suffering
and class/race/gender/sexual oppression, then one must be indifferent to those
things. There are numerous statements of concern in scholarly and popular writings
about postmodernism as it appears to be guided by amoral and even nihilistic
impulses. It appears at times to be theory for the sake of theory.

However, it should be noted that what travels under the designation postmodernism has opened up valuable debate about Enlightenment and post-Enlightenment
modes and principles of political inquiry. Further, these thinkers challenge assumptions about the proper objects of political inquiry. They have contributed to opening
the discipline of political science to interdisciplinary inquiry and thereby invigorated
debates about power and representation. In exploring 'postmodernism' it should be
remembered that some who are identified with the term find little particularly
helpful about it in describing their approaches to the task of critical inquiry.
However, at the very least they have in common that they argue that grand theory
and the metanarratives of Enlightenment are no longer adequate to the task of interpreting the workings of politics.

Acknowledgements

I am indebted to the guidance and help of Elizabeth R. Wingrove and William D.
Rose in developing this essay.

References

Bhabha, Homi K. (2001) 'Locations of Culture: The Postcolonial and the Postmodern' in
    Postmodern Debates, Simon Malpas (ed.) New York: Palgrave.
Brown, Wendy (1995) *States of Injury*, Princeton: Princeton University Press.
Butler, Judith (1995) 'Contingent Foundations' in *Feminist Contentions*, New York: Rout-
    ledge.
—— (1990) *Gender Trouble: Feminism and the Subversion of Identity*, New York: Routledge.
—— (1997) *The Psychic Life of Power: Theories in Subjection*, Stanford, CA: Stanford
    University Press.
Butler, Judith and Scott, Joan (eds) (1993) *Feminists Theorize the Political*, New York: Rout-
    ledge.
Coles, Romand (1997) *Rethinking Generosity, Critical Theory and the Politics of Caritas*,
    Ithaca: Cornell University Press.

Connolly, William E. (1991) *Identity/Difference, Democratic Negotiations of Political Paradox*, Ithaca: Cornell University Press.

Cornell, Drucilla (1995) 'What is Ethical Feminism?' in *Feminist Contentions*, New York: Routledge.

Derrida, Jacques (1976) *Of Grammatology*, trans. Gayatri Spivak, Baltimore: Johns Hopkins University Press.

Foucault, Michel (1965) *Madness and Civilization*, New York: Random House Books.

—— (1973) *The Birth of the Clinic: An Archeology of Medical Perception*, New York: Pantheon Books.

—— (1977) *Discipline and Punish: The Birth of the Prison*, New York: Vintage Books.

—— (1984a) 'What is Enlightenment?' in *The Foucault Reader*, Paul Rabinow (ed.) New York: Pantheon Books.

—— (1984b) 'Nietzsche, Genealogy and History' in *The Foucault Reader*, Paul Rabinow (ed.) New York: Pantheon Books.

—— (1978) *The History of Sexuality*, New York: Random House Books.

—— (1980) 'Truth and Power' in *Power/Knowledge, Selected Interviews and Other Writings*, Colin Gordon (ed.) London: Harvester Press.

Hartsock, Nancy (1990) 'Foucault on Power: A Theory for Women?' in *Feminism/Postmodernism*, Linda Nicholson (ed.) New York: Routledge.

Holland, Nancy (1997) *Feminist Interpretations of Jacques Derrida*, Nancy Holland (ed.) State College: Pennsylvania State University Press.

Honig, Bonnie (1993) *Political Theory and the Displacement of Politics*, Ithaca: Cornell University Press.

Huyssen, Andreas (1990) 'Mapping the Postmodern' in *Feminism/Postmodernism*, Linda Nicholson (ed.) New York: Routledge.

Nietzsche, Friedrich (1967) *On the Genealogy of Morals*, trans. Walter Kaufmann, New York: Vintage Press.

—— (1973) *Beyond Good and Evil*, trans. R. J. Hollingdale, New York: Penguin Classics.

—— (1974) *The Gay Science*, trans. Walter Kaufmann, New York: Vintage Press.

Irigaray, Luce (1985) *This Sex Which is Not One*, trans. Catharine Porter, Ithaca: Cornell University Press.

Kant, Immanuel (1983) 'What is Enlightenment?' in *Perpetual Peace and Other Essays*, trans. Ted Humphrey, Indianapolis: Hackett Publishing Company.

Lyotard, Jean-François (1979) *The Postmodern Condition: A Report on Knowledge*, Minneapolis: University of Minnesota Press.

McGowan, John (1991) *Postmodernism and Its Critics*, Ithaca: Cornell University Press.

Nicholson, Linda and Fraser, Nancy (1990) 'Social Criticism Without Philosophy: An Encounter Between Feminism and Postmodernism' in *Feminism/Postmodernism*, Linda Nicholson (ed.) New York: Routledge.

Norris, Christopher (1991) *Deconstruction, Theory and Practice*, London: Routledge.

MacKinnon, Catharine (1987) *Feminism Unmodified*, Cambridge: Harvard University Press.

Rorty, Richard (1982) *The Consequences of Pragmatism*, Minneapolis: University of Minnesota Press.

Wolin, Sheldon (1960) *Politics and Vision*, Boston: Little, Brown and Company.

Further reading

Benhabib, Seyla (1992) *Situating the Self: Gender Community, and Postmodernism in Contemporary Ethics*, New York: Routledge.

Cornell, Drucilla (1992) *The Philosophy of the Limit*, New York: Routledge.

Dean, Jodi (ed.) (2000) *Cultural Studies and Political Theory* Ithaca: Cornell University Press.

Deleuze, Gilles (1983) *Nietzsche and Philosophy*, trans. Hugh Tomlinson, New York: Columbia University Press.

Deleuze, Gilles and Guattari, F. (1983) *Anti-Oedipus: Capitalism and Schizophrenia*, Minneapolis: University of Minnesota Press.

Derrida, Jacques (1987) *The Post-card: From Socrates to Freud*, trans. Alan Bass, Chicago: University of Chicago Press.

—— (1989) *Of Spirit: Heidegger and the Question*, trans. Geoff Bennington and Rachel Bowlby, Chicago: University of Chicago Press.

Fuss, Diana (1989) *Essentially Speaking: Feminism, Nature, and Difference*, New York: Routledge.

Gordon, Avery F. and Newfield, Christopher (1996) *Mapping Multiculturalism*, Minneapolis: University of Minnesota Press.

Jameson, Frederic (1991) *Postmodernism or The Cultural Logic of Late Capitalism*, Durham: Duke University Press.

Koelb, Clayton (ed.) (1990) *Nietzsche as Postmodernist: Essays Pro and Contra*, Albany: State University of New York Press.

Lubiamo, Wahneema (ed.) (1997) *The House that Race Built: Black Americans, US Terrain*, New York: Pantheon Books.

Natoli, Joseph and Hutcheon, Linda (eds) (1993) *A Postmodern Reader*, Albany: State University of New York Press.

Omi, Michael and Winant, Howard (1986) *Racial Formation in the United States from the 1960s to the 1980s*, New York: Routledge.

Rajchman, John (ed.) (1995) *The Identity in Question*, New York: Routledge.

Young, Iris (1990) *Justice and the Politics of Difference*, Princeton: Princeton University Press.

PART III

CONTEMPORARY IDEOLOGIES

9

LIBERALISM

R. Bruce Douglass

Liberalism presents itself today as a coherent body of theory and practice with a well-defined place in the affairs of our time. Its proponents see themselves, typically, as an extension of a long-standing tradition of moral and political reflection that is the source of what has turned out to be the authoritative interpretation of the meaning and significance of the political experience of the West in the modern era. At a time when most of the plausibility has evaporated from the competitors with which it used to do battle, it is cast as a survivor that has stood the test of time and come away vindicated, in the main, by the course that events have taken.

This was not always so. In fact, for much of what is now commonly character-ized, retrospectively, as the history of liberalism, the course of events would in no way have supported such a conclusion. Indeed, for much of the period in question, there scarcely was any such thing, at least not in the minds of those who lived through it. John Locke, for example, whose articulation of the political aspirations of the Whigs in their struggle with the Stuart monarchy in seventeenth-century England is now conventionally treated as a major contribution to the founding of the liberal tradition, hardly thought of himself as such. Nor is there much evidence to suggest that Kant, Locke's counterpart on the Continent a century later, was much different in this regard. Even though Kant can be appropriately looked upon as the source of some of the most influential ideas with which liberalism has come to be associated, he did not intend them as such. He, too, was a voice for a developing current of thought (and practice) well before it crystallized into anything like the full-blown partisan doctrine with pretensions of universal validity that it has subse-quently become.

Nor, once such crystallization did in fact begin to take place, would it have been thinkable to construe the resulting body of ideas as anything other than one point of view among others. For by the time it made sense for those who found themselves thinking in such terms to begin identifying themselves as liberals, it made just as good sense for others to define their politics in very different (and competing) terms. Even as, with the political coming of age of the rising 'middle' class, the process of emancipating individuals to live their lives as they chose, which was at the heart of what the liberal project was about, came into its own as a historical force, it was still manifestly very much in compwatition with other alternative visions that chal-lenged root and branch most of what it entailed. Precisely because, in fact, it was so clearly identified with the sweeping change that accompanied the economic revolution that the entrepreneurial class pioneered, it met with active opposition from more than one quarter, and it could not help but be seen, in turn, as the reflection of a distinctly partisan response to the events in question.

Even its identification with change, moreover, had its limits. In the heyday of its ascendency it was not uncommon for adherents to speak as though what it represented was synonymous with all that was progressive. The success that liberals enjoyed in putting their stamp on English society in the middle years of the Victorian era in particular inspired such confidence. But even then it was not difficult to see that there were events in the making that liberals were not at all likely to embrace and, indeed, that they would be predisposed actively to resist. It was no accident, for example, that once the case for the expansion of the franchise to include the middle class had been successfully made, the initiative in advocating further democratization tended to fall to others (most notably, representatives of the working class), and liberals were inclined to greet that prospect with ambivalence at best.

So, too, with the laying of the foundations of the welfare state. Even as the conditions that industrialization brought virtually required the assumption of some degree of collective responsibility for the provision of social welfare (public health and sanitation, for example), the liberal presumption was against it. In particular it was against the assumption of any sort of role by those exercising public power to determine social outcomes. Thus the lead in the creation of social insurance and modern social services was taken by others, and it made sense, especially at a time when working-class parties were coming into their own as a political force, to think of what was emerging in this respect, too, as the fruit of currents of thought and practice other than those that found expression in liberalism (Flora and Heidenheimer 1981).

Moreover, the more momentum the movement in this direction gained, the more uncertain the liberal prospect tended to become. Even as imaginative adaptations to the emerging new realities were undertaken by a whole series of 'new' liberals (Freeden 1978), they themselves had to wonder whether they were not holding on to a fossil that had essentially done its work and was on its way to being superseded. The precipitous decline in electoral fortunes that even the more resourceful liberal parties (most notably, the British Liberal Party) tended to suffer when confronted with any sort of sustained competition from working-class parties could easily be read as a portent of things to come. The longer this went on, the harder it became to think that it represented anything other than a reversible trend.

This was the case even more after the onset of war in 1914 and the several decades of ongoing social and political upheaval that it set in motion, particularly as the experiments in constitutional government that followed the war succumbed to crisis in one country after another and movements espousing militantly illiberal sentiments came to the fore. The impression that the world that was in the making was one in which liberal thinking simply no longer fitted was powerfully reinforced.

In fact, with the coming of the depression in the 1930s, it was not at all uncommon for liberals themselves to hold liberal ideas responsible for the vulnerabilities that were being exposed, and to wonder, in turn, whether effective protection could be found without turning sharply in another direction. The pull of events was almost inexorably in the direction of the 'end of *laissez-faire*', as Keynes aptly characterized what was taking place (Keynes 1926). As it became evident that the continuing influence of liberal thinking was in large measure responsible for the societies in question finding it difficult to make the necessary adaptations, questions were inevitably raised about the continuing viability of liberalism even as a guide to the making of economic policy.

Nor did the Allied victory in the Second World War altogether relieve the uncertainty. For, as the process of reconstruction got underway, liberals themselves could scarcely help but wonder whether the old problems would not reappear. The likely economic prospect was for a long, protracted period of rebuilding that was destined to be fraught with uncertainty, particularly in view of the devastation caused to the European heartland, and there was no guarantee that the course events had taken after the previous war would not be repeated. Nor was the political prospect much different. For all of the widespread desire to reconstitute democratic government on a more secure basis in the countries where it had failed to take root successfully, it could not be taken for granted that the old sources of instability would not reassert themselves. The success of the democratic recovery was anything but assured, especially in view of the popular following that the communists enjoyed in a number of countries.

At the same time, however, as the apprehensions that these conditions inspired were making themselves felt, the ground was being prepared for a very different mood to emerge in its stead. It soon became evident that the prolonged austerity that had been anticipated was not going to materialize. Indeed, within scarcely a decade it was clear that an economic 'miracle' was in the making. One fear after another dissolved as the effects of the resulting affluence began to be felt, and it did not take long before the appropriate conclusions began to be drawn. Liberals in particular began to speak with an optimism and assurance that had not been heard in decades.

It was not just, of course, the mere fact of affluence *per se* that was responsible for the recovery of nerve that liberals experienced in the post-war era. The sheer magnitude of the growth experienced by much of Western Europe in particular was impressive by any standard and could not help but catch the imagination of the people who were expecting much less. However, it was the fact that the growth was as sustained as it was that really made the difference in altering the tenor of liberal thinking. There was scarcely any historical precedent for the continuous, ongoing expansion of output, consumption, investment and employment that took place, and it could not escape attention that the governments of the societies in question had devoted themselves to the active management of economic life in ways that had shown themselves to be conducive to this result. A 'new' capitalism was in the making (Shonfeld 1965), born of a difficult learning experience that had taught invaluable lessons about the pursuit of stable prosperity, and the longer the growth persisted, the more of an inclination there was to assume that the economic problems of the past had been effectively solved.

Every bit as impressive, too, was the fact that the prosperity that was being achieved was not being purchased at the price of deprivation for the majority of the population. Quite the contrary. The benefits of prosperity were spread widely. High levels of employment and steadily expanding consumer demand were treated as essential to economic progress. As Galbraith in particular emphasized (Galbraith 1958), what was distinctive about the threshold that was being crossed was that affluence for the many was coming to be an economic as well as a political necessity. If production was going to be maintained at the desired level, consumption had to be cultivated as a way of life.

Social policy underwent a comparable development, too, as the welfare state truly came into its own as a guarantor of entitlements. Under the impact of the common hardships (and resulting mobilizations) imposed by both the depression and the war, the prejudice against collective provision had faded, and in its place emerged a belief in ensuring each citizen freedom from 'want' as a matter of right. Nor was it just the avoidance of poverty that was intended. The state was to see to it that no one was denied access to basic goods and services, from 'cradle to grave', as a famous liberal apologist for the English version of this development was to characterize its purpose (Beveridge 1942). As tax revenues multiplied and the idea of equality of opportunity caught on, there was an increasing tendency to think in terms of guaranteeing a certain quality of life as well.

There was no mistaking, either, the contribution that liberals and their ideas, from Beveridge to Keynes, had made to these developments. They were hardly alone, and the collaboration of socialists in particular was no less important in setting events on the course they were taking (Crosland 1956). But the active endorsement and even sponsorship of the emerging mix of public and private arrangements that the drift toward planning in post-war liberalism represented went a long way toward explaining the appeal it enjoyed. Much of the thinking that went into the policies in question reflected the prior development of liberal thought and practice over the previous half-century, and the fact that liberals were increasingly inclined to take credit for these policies, and assume their necessity, contributed greatly to the perception that they constituted the foundation of an emerging agreement about how to govern industrial democracies that was on its way to eclipsing any and all of its competitors.

Yet for all the support they received from other quarters, it is not difficult to see why these measures appealed to liberals. An ideological convergence of sorts was indeed in the making, but it was clearly on terms that liberals above all had reason to endorse. Economic planning, social services, social insurance and the rest of what went into the making of the emerging 'public household', to use Daniel Bell's apt term (Bell 1976), were undeniably steps in a collective direction, but by design they were almost always implemented in a way that fell well short of anything like a serious challenge to the liberal presumption in favour of private economic power. The resulting economies might reasonably be characterized as 'mixed', but there could be no question about their essentially capitalist character.

Nor could there be much doubt about the concessions made by the other parties involved. From the socialists' increasingly frank disavowal of nationalization to the Christian Democrats' renunciation of the confessional state, the pattern, in one Western European country after another, was for the adherents of competing currents of thoughts that were at all serious contenders for power to abandon, in effect, much of what historically had put them at odds with liberalism. In the name of one or another kind of *aggiornamento*, they gave up, for all practical purposes, a good part of what previously had given them their identity, and in the process they did away, too, in large measure, with the rationale for any sort of principled opposition to what liberalism represented. Indeed, the accommodation that they made tended to be such that what remained often had the appearance of being little more than a series of variations on liberal themes.

This was especially so with respect to the value placed on civil and political liberties. After the trauma of totalitarianism, their worth tended to be appreciated more widely – and deeply – than ever before, and the more evident it became that their realization could be reconciled with both political stability and economic progress, the harder it became to discover any sort of principled opposition to what they represented. Aside from the occasional cavil from one or another radical critic about 'repressive tolerance', the days were over when their proponents had to contend with suggestions that they were instruments of one or another partisan purpose. In their place emerged a climate of opinion in which, if anything, they were taken for granted as the necessary point of departure for any politics that were to stand a chance of achieving legitimacy.

A premium on toleration was also part of the same climate. With the social and cultural conditions that gave rise to the old ideological combat fading, and the aspiration to the all-out victory they fostered discredited by events, toleration took on an appeal that it had not had since the religious wars occasioned by the Reformation. With groups from Catholics to Communists going out of their way to declare their allegiance to respecting diversity, pluralism came to acquire such significance that, in fact, it began to take on the status of one of the principal defining features of the societies in question. Their 'openness' in this sense became one of the major qualities on which they prided themselves, and the more experience they had with it, the more self-conscious its practice tended to become.

It could therefore only be a matter of time before the trend this represented found theoretical expression. For a brief period it was inhibited by the inclination of many liberals to go along with the suggestion that what was taking place was the transcendence of ideology (Bell 1960–1), and to refrain from giving any elaborate philosophical expression to the ideas that were really at stake. This was particularly the case when the very possibility of moral and political philosophy was called into question by the influence that positivism enjoyed. But once Rawls showed that it was possible – and necessary – to join anew the philosophical issues at stake (Rawls 1971), it quickly became evident that a different construction was needed on what was underway. For as the renaissance of liberal theory that followed showed, liberals themselves clearly were not about to concede that the tradition they represented was finished. Just the opposite. With Rawls leading the way, the view that permeated their writings was that after years of struggle against one competitor after another, liberalism was finally on its way to claiming its rightful place as *the* public philosophy of the West.

Nor, for all the effort that has been put into making the result out to be a common ground capable of accommodating the legitimate interests of other contenders (Rawls 1987), has there ever been much question about the partisan character of what was intended. In fact, the more fully the logic of the turn that liberal reasoning has taken in this latest mutation has come to be revealed, the more obvious its partisan edge has tended to be. For the interpretation that is put on the experience(s) in question is, for all of the talk about neutrality, in no sense a neutral one, and it is not in the least neutral in its practical implications either. As the recurring (albeit highly selective) invocation of Kantian premises reveals, one rather specific way of understanding what has taken place is presupposed, and it is accompanied, predictably, by a preference for a particular way of conceiving of its promise as well.

What in particular is thrown anew into sharp relief in this relation is the distinctiveness of the priority – and meaning – that liberals are inclined to attach to liberty. For it is by no means just as one good among others that it figures in what they have to say. Building on the special significance that personal autonomy has come to acquire as a result of the events of the last century, they would have it understood to be the fundamental good, the realization of which is above all what the recent experience of the West has been about. More than anything else, they insist, the opportunity for individuals to be self-determining – to function, as Rawls puts it, as moral agents, choosing one's own conception of the good and living life accordingly – is what the societies in question have learned is important in the conduct of public affairs, and their achievement, in turn, has been to show how this can be successfully pursued as a way of life.

Nothing has contributed more to this result, moreover, in the account that tends to be favoured by the current generation of liberal theorists, than the growing awareness of the limits of the human capacity to prescribe how life ought to be lived. In marked contrast to the days when liberal arguments were distinguished by the boldness with which they affirmed the power of reason, they now tend to be predicated on an equally dedicated epistemological modesty (Spragens 1981), and it is to the increasingly widespread acceptance of the sense of restraint this entails that they are inclined to attribute the success that the 'liberal' democracies have come to enjoy. There is no way, virtually every liberal thinker of consequence now asserts matter-of-factly, that we can know with any sort of objective certainty what 'God's will' or the 'laws of history' dictate, and it is because this 'fact' is increasingly taken for granted by the peoples in question that they have come to be able to live as they do. Through long (and sometimes bitter) experience they have learned the futility of assigning a public role to what are essentially private visions, and in the process they have come to appreciate, too, the impropriety of doing so as well. Indeed, more: the experience they have had with toleration has taught them, increasingly, to look upon it as the only appropriate response to the challenge posed by the heterogeneity of the good that human beings are prepared to seek.

What they have also learned, it is said, is the value of the resulting diversity. It is not just that they have become accustomed to accommodating beliefs and values different from their own, but that they have also come to appreciate the promise such a practice holds. For the more consistently and deliberately it is pursued, the more evident it becomes that the effect, almost inescapably, is to enlarge steadily the opportunities for individuality to flourish. Instead of their lives conforming to one or another pre-existent pattern, people are virtually invited to experiment and innovate in keeping with their own distinctive tastes and inclinations, with the result that life takes on an increasingly varied and fluid character. So the richness of the variety of which human beings are capable is experienced as never before, and the way is open for it to be explored as an end in itself.

To make the case for embracing this possibility as a matter of principle is, in turn, above all what liberalism has come to stand for (Ackerman 1980; Dworkin 1977–8), and it is clear from virtually everything about the way this is done that it is assumed that the fact that such an opportunity now presents itself to the societies in question represents a historical accomplishment of the first magnitude. For even as they speak in increasingly historicist terms and make a point of avoiding any sort of explicit metaphysical commitments (Rawls 1985), there is no mistaking the presumption that pervades the arguments advanced by Rawls and those who have followed his lead that the way of life to which they seek to give expression amounts to more – much more – than just one more chapter in history's ongoing succession of different ways of ordering human relations. Indeed, just the opposite. If anything, the tendency, as the Cold War has faded away and ideas championed by liberals have been embraced as symbols of liberation in one popular insurgency after another, has been to revive with a vengeance the old liberal conceit that what the liberal vision represents is the definitive conclusion of the quest for the good society, beyond which further progress is neither necessary nor possible (Fukuyama 1989).

Precisely, however, because of the increasingly historicist character of so much of the reasoning to which liberals have been given of late, this is a claim that is much more easily made than defended. Indeed, philosophically its defence becomes positively anomalous. All along, to be sure, there has been something of an anomaly about the doctrinaire universalism of a creed so firmly committed to making a virtue of toleration. But in the days when liberals were capable of backing up the claims that they made in this regard with bold generalizations about human nature whose merits they were prepared to argue, what they said at least had the appearance of epistemological consistency. Now, however, as any sort of owning up to metaphysical commitments (much less arguing their merits) is dismissed as obsolete (Rorty 1989) and liberal theorists are reduced to appealing to nothing more than (their version of) the considered experience of the West, even that appearance of consistency is gone, and all that remains is a presumption in favour of treating the experience in question as authoritative.

That such a presumption can be taken for granted so matter-of-factly in serious theoretical arguments is a tribute, of course, to the confidence liberals now have that history can be counted on to vindicate what they espouse. But it is also, no less, a reflection of the silences to which they have been reduced. For even as they feed on the good fortune that ideas deriving from their tradition now enjoy, it can scarcely be ignored that they do so as much out of necessity as choice. At a time when they have all but abandoned any pretence of an objective warrant for the practices they favour (Rorty 1989), they are hardly in a position to enter seriously into arguments about their merits in principle. Aside from stipulating what they themselves (as self-conscious Westerners) prize, 'history' is all they have to go on.

As long as the returns that history brings continue to be congenial, this may, of course, as a practical matter suffice. There is nothing, after all, like the confirmation of events to make critical questions seem beside the point. But equally there is nothing like a reversal of fortune to give them fresh relevance, and to expose, in turn, the vacuity of answers that are grounded in nothing but convention. For what is 'self-evident' when things are going smoothly can all too easily turn out to be anything but when they are not.

If the confidence that liberals now tend to have that a corner has been turned and what is in the making is a world in which, for all practical purposes, the triumph of their way of thinking can be treated as an accomplished fact, then this is an eventuality which, presumably, will never need to be confronted. History will indeed settle the issue, and in a manner that makes further argument permanently irrelevant. But if the talk that we are now hearing about the 'end of history' itself turns out to be just one more ideological illusion, just the opposite could occur. This is especially likely if the economic stability and vitality that support the way of life that liberals now take for granted proves to be something less than permanent. In particular, in the event that growth stalls (and/or is seriously challenged), questions that are now being swept under the rug can almost certainly be expected to come surging back into the forefront of public life, and in a form that liberals could well find themselves less prepared than ever to confront. Precisely because they have become so accustomed to taking for granted things that do not deserve at all to be taken for granted, they could well be hard put, in fact, even to make sense of what they are up against.

Even in the present environment, moreover, there are definite limits to the plausibility of the claims liberals want to make on the terms they prefer to make them. Especially is this evident in the things they have to say about the relevance of their ideas and ideals to other parts of the world. For they can hardly engage the rest of the world successfully without appealing to something more than just Western experience. If they were prepared to turn inward and give up the global ambitions liberals have had in the past, that would not be necessary, of course. But they have shown little inclination to take that step. In fact, one of the more interesting things that has happened to liberal thought in the period since the end of the Cold War is that its better-known proponents have turned their attention more directly to the wider world, and as they have done so, they have become increasingly explicit about their conviction that liberal ideals apply in principle everywhere.

This could conceivably mean, of course, that they were prepared to accept the cultural diversity that now exists in the world and to affirm the right of other peoples to organize themselves and conduct their affairs as they choose, even if that meant departing from the example set by the West. It might mean a turn toward toleration on a global scale, in other words. But that is hardly ever what the people making such claims have in mind. Virtually every liberal thinker of any consequence who has discussed this matter in recent years has taken just the opposite tack. Not only have they assumed that they have a right (if not a duty) to stand in judgement on regimes based on other beliefs, but they have also made it clear that they believe the desirable state of affairs for every nation is to have a liberal regime (eventually, at least). Even Rawls, who has been relatively cautious in dealing with this matter because he has recognized the impropriety of insisting on toleration in the internal affairs of Western nations if one is not prepared to extend it to their relations with other peoples, ultimately ends up saying that the liberal objective should be for all the nations of the world to be governed in a liberal manner (Rawls 1999).

It is impossible to provide anything like an adequate justification of this idea, however, if one is committed to remaining on the level of argument that Rawls has appropriately characterized as the 'philosophical surface' (Rawls 1985). For the implication of all such claims is clearly that a certain approach to life (which unmistakably is the fruit of one particular civilization) should be privileged at the expense of the alternatives, and the obvious question is why anyone who is not a liberal should be expected to accept it. It does not suffice as a reply, moreover, to keep citing, as liberals typically do, the qualities of liberal regimes that appeal to those who have already been convinced of the value of the goods they deliver. Only arguments designed to address the concerns of those who have a *different* outlook from the one(s) favoured by liberals stand any chance of even appearing to satisfy the justificatory challenge that is posed by such a global project. But arguments of that kind are precisely what is precluded once it is assumed that it is inappropriate to get into any sort of serious consideration of life's meaning and purpose. Ironically, therefore, liberals tend to find themselves today in the odd position of wanting to take actions vis-à-vis other peoples that can only be properly justified by getting into an examination of matters that most of them are unprepared to discuss.

Not only is this situation most unsatisfactory philosophically, but it invites the inference that liberalism is (still?) nothing more than an ideological justification for pursuing the interests of certain groups who have enough power to believe that they have a right to impose their will on everyone else. It is a situation that also invites, moreover, just the kind of reaction from those who are subjected to such behaviour that makes it plausible to think that what may now await us is a new 'clash of civilizations' that will be in its own way every bit as dangerous as the Cold War (Huntington 1996). Clearly, therefore, this is a subject on which more work is needed, and not just for the sake of the internal coherence and plausibility of liberalism, either.

References

Ackerman, B. (1980) *Social Justice in the Liberal State*, New Haven and London: Yale University Press.

Bell, D. (1960–1) *The End of Ideology*, New York: Free Press/London: Macmillan.

—— (1976) *The Cultural Contradictions of Capitalism*, New York: Basic Books.

Beveridge, W. (1942) *Social Insurance and Allied Services* (Report of the Inter-Departmental Committee on Social Insurance and Allied Services), London: Macmillan.

Crosland, C. A. R. (1956) *The Future of Socialism*, London: Jonathan Cape.

Dworkin, R. (1977–8) *Taking Rights Seriously*, Cambridge: Harvard University Press.

Flora, P. and Heidenheimer, A. (eds) (1981) *The Development of the Welfare State in Europe and North America*, New Brunswick and London: Transaction Books.

Freeden, M. (1978) *The New Liberalism*, Oxford: Clarendon.

Fukayama, F. (1989) 'The end of history?', *National Interest* 16: 3–18.

Galbraith, J. (1958) *The Affluent Society*, Boston: Houghton-Mifflin.

Huntington, Samuel P. (1996) *The Clash of Civilizations*, New York: Touchstone.

Keynes, J. (1926) *The End of Laissez-Faire*, London: L. and Virginia Woolf.

Rawls, J. (1971) *A Theory of Justice*, Cambridge: Harvard University Press.

—— (1985) 'Justice as fairness: political not metaphysical', *Philosophy and Public Affairs* 14: 223–51.

—— (1987) 'The idea of an overlapping consensus', *Oxford Journal of Legal Studies* 7: 1–25.

—— (1999) *The Law of Peoples*, Cambridge: Harvard University Press.

Rorty, R. (1989) *Contingency, Irony and Solidarity*, Cambridge: Cambridge University Press.

Shonfeld, A. (1965) *Modern Capitalism*, London/Oxford/New York: Oxford University Press.

Spragens, T., Jr (1981) *The Irony of Liberal Reason*, Chicago: University of Chicago Press.

Further reading

Bentham, J. (1948) *A Fragment on Government* and *The Introduction to the Principles of Morals and Legislation*, ed. W. Harrison, Oxford: Oxford University Press.

Dewey, J. (1935) *Liberalism and Social Action*, New York: G. P. Putnam's Sons.

Halevy, E. (1955) *The Growth of Philosophical Radicalism*, Boston: Beacon.

Hamilton, A., Madison, J., and Jay, J. (1961) *The Federalist* ed. J. Cooke, Middletown, CT: Wesleyan University Press.

Hartz, L. (1955) *The Liberal Tradition in America*, New York: Harcourt, Brace and World.

Hobhouse, L. (1964) *Liberalism*, Oxford: Oxford University Press.

Kant, I. (1970) *Kant's Political Writings*, ed. H. Reiss, Cambridge: Cambridge University Press.

Keynes, J. M. (1931) *Essays in Persuasion*, New York: Macmillan.

Locke, J. (1952) *A Letter on Toleration*, ed. A. C. Fraser, Oxford: Oxford University Press.

—— (1960) *Two Treatises of Government*, ed. P. Laslett, Cambridge: Cambridge University Press.

Mill, J. (1937) *An Essay on Government*, ed. E. Barker, Cambridge: Cambridge University Press.

Mill, J. S. (1962) *On Liberty*, London: Everyman's Library.

Popper, K. (1966) *The Open Society and Its Enemies*, 2 vols, Princeton: Princeton University Press.

Rawls, J. (1971) *A Theory of Justice*, Cambridge University Press.

Rorty, R. (1993) 'Human Rights, Rationality and Sentimentality', *The Yale Review*, v. 81, 1–20.

Ruggiero, G. de. (1927) *The History of European Liberalism*, Oxford: Oxford University Press.

Smith, A. (1976) *The Wealth of Nations*, ed. W. B. Todd, Oxford: Clarendon Press.

10

CONSERVATISM AND NEO-LIBERALISM

Kenneth R. Hoover

As a philosophical orientation, as an ideology, and as a political movement, a version of conservatism has come to set the terms for policy debates in the major nations of the West. In its ascent to primacy, however, conservatism has taken on the characteristics of an ideology – an ideology quite at odds with the original impulses of conservative forebears.

An understanding of the divergent tendencies within conservatism requires a broad analysis of historical definitions as well as a sense of contemporary political forces. What began in the eighteenth century as an orientation against change and rationalist ideas such as egalitarianism has become, at the beginning of the twenty-first century, an ideologically based movement intent on reordering society, politics and the economy. We shall begin by characterizing contemporary conservatism and shall then turn to its historical roots to discover how institutional traditionalists were overtaken by libertarians with their distinctive version of individualism.

Contemporary conservatism

The common theme of political conservatism is an acceptance of differences and inequalities among individuals. What characterizes conservatives of all kinds is a sense that the differences between people are more important than the similarities. It is in these differences that conservatives locate the keys to the problems of social order, on the one hand, and productivity, on the other. Whereas liberals have thought that people should be moved toward greater equality of status and opportunity, conservatives have been more impressed with the need for institutional accommodations of individual differences, or, more recently, for simply leaving individuals to their differing devices thereby to learn how to become productive – and moral – citizens (Hayek 1960; Joseph and Sumption 1979).

Having accepted the fact of inequality, there is a major division in conservative thought on what to do about it. The rival tendencies may be labelled 'individualist' (or libertarian) and 'traditionalist' (or paternalist) (Nash 1996; Green 2002). Individualist conservatives argue that, since there are such manifest differences in individual abilities, talents, and knowledge, society will best be served by maximizing individual freedom. If people are left free to pursue their own talents and interests without governmental interference, they will learn to be responsible for

149

their own behaviour, and they will be encouraged, especially in a free-market society, to develop abilities that involve the production of goods and services that are in demand by the society. Sometimes labelled neo-liberals, individualist conservatives borrow arguments from liberals about the importance of freedom, however they leave aside the liberal regard for the equalization of access to power and opportunity. Constitutional limits on government are deemed essential.

By contrast, traditionalist conservatives generally argue that, given the limitations of human nature and the inequality that results, the key problem is how to organize the institutions that will constrain and guide individual behaviour so that a measure of order and social cohesion can be achieved. These institutions must be bound by a due regard for customs and mores, and to a moderate approach to change.

For individualist conservatives, the question of initiative and particular knowledge is paramount in establishing differences between people; for traditionalists, it is a matter of character and innate ability. These rationales for inequality overlap in some respects, but there are important differences that have profound political consequences. Initiative and particular knowledge are qualities that individualist conservatives imagine to be a matter of volition, and within reach of all people. Character and innate ability, on the other hand, are shaped by heredity, breeding and the civilizing power of institutions – and they are sure to be tested in a world that is made disorderly by the weaknesses of human nature. The political consequence is that individualist conservatism leads to the market-place as the premier institutional form, whereas traditional conservatism points toward institutions such as the family, the church and the government.

Freedom as a political value is perceived quite differently by individualists and traditionalists. The former adopt the classical liberal position on the centrality of individual liberty, while rejecting most of the community-regarding limits liberals have placed upon it (Friedman 1962). Individualist conservatives would reject what Locke said about restraints on accumulation, Mill on qualitative judgements of utility, or Green on rationality as a guide to true freedom. Libertarianism is the version of freedom congenial to the individualist conservative position, and the logic of material self-interest is its calculus (Buchanan and Tullock 1962; Downs 1965). For these reasons, neo-liberalism is a misnomer for the movement that has come to power in the West.

Traditional conservatives have a more complicated view of freedom. They argue that real freedom is only possible within a proper structure. Without limits, licence is the result, not liberty. Institutional limits create spaces within which choice may be prudently exercised, and such freedom as is beneficial to humans may be exercised responsibly. In the USA, paleo-conservatives have turned this argument toward a plea for the preservation of Judeo–Christian moral values in opposition to an increasingly secular world. A more militant variant are the religious conservatives who draw upon fundamentalist versions of the Christian faith to promote the censorship of pornography, school prayer, and opposition to homosexual rights.

The market is the chosen social device of individualist conservatives because it rewards effort, 'free' choice (in terms of perceived material self-interest) and entrepreneurial skill. Traditionalists have always been chary of the market per se, although they have justified the institution of private property as a vital adjunct of other institutional bases for the society: the family, the bourgeois state, the church, and the corporation. It is the propensity of the market-place to disrupt settled patterns of institutional life that worries traditional conservatives.

These two tendencies have opposed each other on issues such as the desirability of minimum social provision for the disadvantaged. Traditional conservatives believe that the lower classes should be dealt with responsibly (Wills 1979). Individualist conservatives regard redistributive activities as coercion. Such governmental programmes are regarded simply as interferences with the process of free volition and individual choice that should be allowed to determine the 'true' distribution of rewards according to effort.

Education, abortion and the environment are other issues that divide the two tendencies. Traditional conservatives see the provision of support for education as a critical means of transmitting the moral code and cultural patrimony of Western civilization. Education helps to establish the hierarchies of ability even while it reproduces the values of civilization itself. For individualists, the educational system should resemble a market-place where people can pay for what they would like. Vouchers for educational services provide a means of using this principle while retaining public taxation as a financial basis for the system. The diversification of schooling systems, coupled with a decentralization of control in the hands of parents, places policy-making where individualist conservatives think it should be.

Abortion poses a direct opposition between the use of government power to enforce a moral code, a view taken by religious conservatives, and the assertion that individuals should be able to choose their own approach to reproduction. Environmental issues create similar difficulties within conservatism. Traditionalists favour conservation through public control where necessary; individualists are likely to support freedom of action or market incentives that reward preservation.

The movement containing these contradictory tendencies may be called conservative capitalism (Hoover and Plant 1989). It is a movement that contains a considerable internal tension between an institutionalist approach and an individualist regard for the sanctity of free choice. The latter is a product of capitalist doctrine as it has come to be conceptualized in the West; the former reflects historic commitments to customary practices.

Conservative capitalism thus marks a period of politics that is distinct from the liberal capitalism characterized by the pre-Thatcherite social democratic consensus in Britain, and the general agreement on reform liberal principles that characterized American politics from the New Deal until the fall of the Carter presidency in 1980. In the concluding section of this essay, the future of this coalition will be explored, but first a brief historical survey will provide necessary background.

The European roots of conservatism

In the classical scholarship on conservatism, the defining theme is the orientation toward change. According to the Oxford English Dictionary, conservatism first appears as a political term in 1835 in Matthew Arnold's letters, and its meaning has to do with preserving traditional social and political forms. Shortly thereafter, in Disraeli's *Coningsby* (Disraeli 1844), conservatism is described as a sceptical attitude towards secular doctrines of salvation.

Resistance to change had, besides its obvious advantages as a ploy for the preservation of the position of the elite, a philosophical basis in two rather different traditions: the doctrines of natural law, on the one hand, and epistemological scepticism on the other. The former proposed a constancy to human affairs that could be used to deny the possibility of innovation, while the latter undermined the basis upon which proposals for change could be grounded.

The belief in a natural order is as old as philosophy, and the political form given to this belief in the Middle Ages embraces a version of hierarchy that is congenial to those who accept divisions of society on the basis of class or of religious commitment. Just as an acorn grows into an oak tree, there is a natural order in society that, when brought to full maturity through the appropriate institutions, will lead to as much order and justice as human beings are capable of.

While scepticism can be used to undermine custom and tradition, it also has its conservative uses. David Hume (1711–76) opened the way to a devastating critique of the institutional inventions of classical liberalism by alternately exposing the evident rudeness of political arrangements, and deriding the pretensions of theorists who would dignify power with formulas based on consent. Deprived of rationalist certainty, liberalism remains only a speculative system from which a few observations on justice may be derived for the benefit of evolving institutions of law and order (Hayek 1960; Oakeshott 1962, 1975).

Natural law is the philosophical well-spring of traditional conservatism, while scepticism remains the touchstone of individualist conservatism. There is no necessary opposition between them, as sceptics of human inventions can blend with pessimists who place justice outside the bounds of human achievement. Yet there is a version of scepticism that erodes the basis of traditional society, as well as the pretensions of the new liberal order. This is the spirit in which Adam Smith approaches political economy (Hirschman 1977), and through his analysis the basis was laid for new variations of liberalism as well as conservatism.

Smith presented classical liberalism with the market-place as the economic analogue of democracy. Here was an opening to mass participation in economic affairs on the basis of labour, if not of capital itself. The enemy of the market was misguided government policy – a government of the privileged – that found through its mercantilist policies a doctrine that justified a powerful state and the enrichment of political allies simultaneously. In the spirit of 1776, Smith was the ally of the masses.

There was a moral strain to Smith's thought as well. He was preoccupied with the problem of moral behaviour. For Adam Smith, it is the search for respect that guides the invisible hand, not material self-interest per se. In *The Theory of Moral Sentiments* (Smith 1759), Smith laments the misguided search for respect through materialist self-seeking, however he sees the market, as contrasted with state monopolies and tariffs, as a way of enabling the spread of prosperity. A judicious government might be able to encourage sensible public policies, but it cannot command virtue nor can it direct economic activity efficiently.

The extension of this institutional analysis in *An Inquiry into the Nature and Causes of the Wealth of Nations* (Smith 1776) demonstrates that the market, by harnessing the power of respect-seeking through the price system, will yield a measure of self-discipline and community benefit in the interest of obtaining the best possible return on investment whether of labour or capital. For Smith, the main problem was the conversion of destructive behaviour into socially useful energy (Hirschman 1977). At that, he held out no hope of perfection. Rather, he wished to avoid harm, increase productivity, and at least allow room for the play of higher motives (Rothschild 2001).

The specifically political intent of conservatism has to do with a resistance to the use of government to further, most significantly, equality. The resistance is predicated, in the writings of Edmund Burke (1729–97), the premier articulator of traditional conservatism as a philosophical orientation, upon a distrust of rationalist abstractions, a positive valuation of custom and tradition, and a fundamental acceptance of human differences as the basis of civil order (Burke 1976). This conservative orientation did not uniformly require a disavowal of change, for Burke could accept the American colonial revolt as an assertion of traditional English rights by disenfranchised citizens. At the same time, he rejected the French revolution as a murderous exercise in the imposition of the abstractions, liberté, egalité, fraternité. Burkean conservatism amounted to a faith in a plurality of authoritative institutions that operate to produce an 'organic society' characterized by moderation, discipline and a recourse to spiritual solace in the face of the vicissitudes of life (Burke 1976; Kirk 1962; Nisbet 1986).

Simultaneously, in late eighteenth-century Germany, conservatism acquired a range of meanings clustering around the defence of the status quo, reform and reaction (Epstein 1966). The defining criterion for the orientation to change had to do with how best to maintain differentiations of status, authority and rank that fitted with conservative conceptions of human nature. For some the best course involved simple resistance to innovation, for others a careful moderation of the forces of change, and for the least practical, the revival of the past.

For both English and German conservatives, nationalism provided a palpable political form for these philosophical yearnings. While the state was viewed with some suspicion, the nation offered, at least in the abstract, the hierarchies of meaning and authority that accommodate a conservative political analysis. The state, as distinct from the nation, may be the vehicle of progressives, liberal reformers or radicals. The nation, while founded in a revolt against medieval imperialism, by the late eighteenth century came to represent the qualitative and spiritual principle that could be opposed to the quantitative and rationalist axioms of classical liberalism and its radical offspring. The fateful alliance of conservatism and nationalism was born of this union of doctrine and politics.

French conservatives such as Joseph de Maistre (1753–1821) mingled nationalism with Christianity to produce a reactionary form of conservatism that took aim at all of the inventions of classical liberalism and radicalism: the social contract was a fiction, the possibility of improving on 'the state of nature' a dangerous illusion, and democracy itself a reproach to divine law. While this sort of recourse to the ancien régime limited the appeal of conservatism, the link made between nationalism and Christianity gave a populist opening to conservatism which reappears in contemporary conservative movements.

An ideology may be defined as a world view that contains a programme of political action. An ideology de-contests the ambiguities in political ideas and assigns them a definite meaning, the better to activate followers and define a political platform (Freeden 1996). Conservatism became an ideology when it took the form of a partisan credo during the political combat of the nineteenth century. The traditional conservative world view has roots in stoicism and medieval Christian pessimism about human nature. It centres on the need for hierarchy, the consequences of human limitations, and the inescapable role of spiritual faith. What gave conservatism a modern political presence was the evolution of the Tory party in the hands of Disraeli, Alexander Hamilton's creation of a Federalist party in the USA, and the ferment of rightist partisanship on the Continent. In each arena, traditionalist conservatism became an active ideological force.

While there is resistance to characterizing conservatism as anything more than a set of orientations to change (Rossiter 1982; Huntington 1957), the development of a political program can be clearly identified. Disraeli countered the utilitarianism of his age with prescriptions for the maintenance of distinctions and the celebration of customary arrangements that went well beyond caution to resolute affirmation. The struggles over the Reform Bills and the alliance with Victorianism defined a distinctively Tory political program.

The alliance of conservatism, nationalism and imperialism brought Britain to the apogee of its power and influence in world affairs by the turn of the century. The foundations of this power within the conservative class system and the economic relations that flowed from imperialism were shaken to the core by the social and physical devastation of the First and Second World Wars. Churchill's evocation of Britain's 'finest hour', testimony as it was to the power of nationalist symbolism, also marked the beginning of the end of traditional conservatism in British society. The Conservatives lost power decisively for the first time at the end of the Second World War, and the initiative shifted to the left with the installation of a Labour government in 1945.

While the socialists commanded the rhetorical heights in the ensuing four decades, no small part of the institutional innovations of the social democratic consensus involved a regard for conservative institutional preferences. The distribution of services may have been democratized, but the institutions of the British welfare state retained a substantial measure of hierarchy within and autonomy without. This made more palatable the accommodation that the Conservative Party was led to make through the 1950s, 1960s and 1970s up until the advent of the first Thatcher government.

The result was an entitlement-driven bureaucracy that found itself by the 1970s increasingly isolated and declining in public esteem (Niskanen 1973; Brittan 1983). In an economic environment characterized by rising expectations, shrinking resources and the increasing power of the means of collective action through union control of the Labour Party, the British welfare state came to its great crisis. That the Conservatives could not capitalize on this crisis sooner was partly due to their complicity in it, and to the discredited traditionalism that underpinned their doctrinal approach. It was the development of Margaret Thatcher's distinctive combination of social traditionalism and individualist conservative economic policy that supplied a resolute conservative capitalist program with which to confront a divided left. It was the unpopularity of such doctrinally driven measures as the poll tax that dismantled this combination and led to the downfall of Thatcher as prime minister.

North American conservatism

The story of the demise of traditional conservative orthodoxy is different in the American context, though the result was remarkably similar. In the newly independent colonies, Alexander Hamilton brought together a formidable group of notables intent on creating a strong national political and commercial system that could confront the rising power of democrats and debtors. His conceptual framework relied on the notion of an elite so composed as to balance contending forces: between those who, in the pursuit of fame, must cultivate public regard, and those who seek dominion and are led to exploit the forces of production (Dolbeare 1984). He envisioned an elite characterized by noblesse oblige who would command the apparatus of a powerful federal union in extending the benefits of the new society across the continent.

Hamilton's project foundered in the battle with the democratizing forces led by Thomas Jefferson, and suffered a major institutional blow when Andrew Jackson vetoed the rechartering of the Bank of the United States in 1832. It is ironic that Jackson undid this conservative institution in the name of *laissez faire* which was to become, 150 years later, the doctrinal basis for a renovated conservatism.

Conservatism as a political credo in the USA suffered its second major blow in the defeat of the South in the Civil War. While many conservative citizens were for the Union, the intellectual basis of the confederate cause comprised a full program of conservative principles from the reverence for traditional institutions through to the stratification of the population on the grounds of race, gender and class. The victory of the Union abetted the spread of democratic radicalism, and its extension ultimately to movements for full civil rights for minorities and women.

While conservative institutionalism was the declining cause of nineteenth-century American politics, conservatism as a firm defence of the limited basis of the constitutional contract remained in place until the New Deal. Though considerably weakened by the democratization of the political process arising from populist, progressive and socialist initiatives, the policy constraints of constitutional conservatism were not truly broken until the Supreme Court acquiesced in the policy innovations of the Roosevelt administration in the late 1930s.

From that point forward, traditional conservatism went slowly into the political night, kept alive only by its opposition to communism during the Cold War. It took the admixture of a new individualist interpretation, and a complex crisis within liberal capitalism, to revive the label and bring conservatism to the forefront of public attention in presidential campaigns, beginning with Barry Goldwater's unsuccessful candidacy in 1964 and culminating in Ronald Reagan's victory in 1980 (Piven and Cloward 1982). Reagan's triumph was even more clearly a case of coalition building between traditionalists and individualists, though contests over policies and priorities were usually decided in favour of the latter. His victory was abetted by the revisionist sociology of intellectuals who renounced the left in favour of a new conservatism that promised a stronger defence of individual freedom than the reformist left had delivered (Steinfels 1979; Kristol 1983; Nash 1996).

The Canadian pattern diverges from the British and American in that the 'Red Tory' tradition was an assertive force in shaping institutions of political economy (Taylor 1982). The idea that governmentally based national and provincial economic institutions in banking, transportation, communications and mineral extraction should lead the way in forming a distinctive identity for Canadian culture was the work of traditionalist conservatives with a penchant for institutional innovation. The objective of these efforts was not at variance with the desires of populists and even liberals for much of Canada's history, though there was plenty of room for partisanship in the allocation of influence and control within this institutional framework.

The introduction of *laissez-faire* terminology into the Canadian conservative lexicon was inhibited by the persistence of classical liberalism in the opposing party and the delicacy of devolutionist politics in a fragile federation. It was once more the economic burden of the welfare state in the readjustments following the oil embargo and the divisions on the left between establishment liberals and Western populists that created an opening for a new kind of conservatism.

The Mulroney government (1984–93) represented a departure for Canadian conservatism. Free trade and a minimalist role for the state were its hallmarks. The Free Trade Agreement tests the cultural and economic solidarity of Canada in a manner that will directly confront the residual traditionalism and nationalism of conservatives. The program runs the risk of jeopardizing the future of Canada as a sovereign entity, though, by the axioms of modern economics, there is little choice but to do so if there are to be gains in the gross national product comparable to other industrialized nations. Whether such gains will materialize given the disparities of economic power between Canada and its principle trading partner may well determine the future of conservative political fortunes. Whether conservatism can survive a loss of cultural cohesion and national identity in the name of economic ambition is being tested by the Canadian experience.

Continental-European conservatism

In continental-European politics, the strengths of traditionalist conservatism were also the sources of its weaknesses, though an amelioration of the extremes through the development of Christian democratic parties preserved conservatism as a powerful rival to the left in much of Europe. The appeals of nationalism and of its combination with Christian religious identifications led to a complicity, dating from the late nineteenth century, between chauvinist attitudes and aristocratic forms. Charles Maurras (1868–1952) brought to fruition the anti-semitic pro-fascist potential of this alliance in France during the Second World War and was condemned for it by a court of law when the Vichy regime fell.

Houston Stewart Chamberlain (1855–1927) provided a link between British, German and Austrian Aryan nationalism of the kind that nurtured Adolf Hitler. Hitler rapidly outstripped any real link between Nazism and a recognizable conservatism. Anti-semitism became a genocidal fixation that no Christian could justify, plebiscitary rule a substitute for traditional authority, and Hitler's fantasies of Aryan supremacy an excuse for the wholesale destruction of human life. While fascism itself can be intellectually separated from conservatism, the early complicity of some conservative intellectuals, literati and politicians in its rise to power contributed to the decline in the credibility of conservative parties.

Only in Franco's Spain, however, did the union of religion, nationalism and social conservatism reach its institutional peak and survive for an extended period of time. While there is an intellectual basis for a moderate version of Spanish conservatism in the writings of José Ortega y Gasset (1883–1955), the Franco regime went far beyond Ortega's admonitions concerning the masses to institutionalize a repressive hierarchy. The reactionary nature of the combination was fully revealed in the systematic violation of human rights, and in the refusal to consider elementary programs of social justice of the kind that helped to modernize the rest of Europe in the post-war period. Franco, El Caudillo, became an icon of modern conservative politics, and his likeness could be seen all too often in the regimes of Latin America.

The use of police state tactics by governments claiming to be conservative gave the increasingly educated masses a reason to reject the right and, for those with a commitment to solving the world's injustices, grounds to embrace the left. The links between the conservative peasant parties of eastern and central Europe and proto-fascist attitudes of anti-semitism provided a pretext for the Russian annexation of Latvia, Lithuania, and Estonia at the outset of the Second World War, and the subjugation of eastern Europe in the post-war period. While there were many powerful factors at work in these situations, it is apparent that conservative excesses contributed to the extremes of political confrontation that set the stage for both the Second World War and the Cold War.

In the post-war period, however, a more benign face of conservatism appeared and reclaimed a legitimate place in the politics of the Western democracies. Konrad Adenauer in the Federal Republic of Germany and Charles de Gaulle in France provided models of conservative rule that, especially in the former case, made good the claim that conservatism and democracy can co-exist. In their stout resistance to communism, Continental conservatives, and to a lesser extent American conservatives, were able to raise the credibility of the right whenever it ebbed away from an accommodationist left (Diggins 1975). By emphasizing the themes of cultural solidarity, traditional social values and Christian moral commitment, Adenauer and de Gaulle restored a measure of confidence to the European right.

While Continental conservatives could not respond effectively to the distributive demands of an increasingly potent labour movement, or the social innovations of an affluent middle class, they did succeed in holding together the core of a national identity in an increasingly secular and materialistic culture. If distributive equity remains the lesser theme of contemporary European politics, and the struggle for national identity remains significant, the basis for an enduring conservative presence may have been laid. However, there are new sources of tension affecting all of the conservative movements of the West, and these may well determine its survival.

Conservative capitalism: lines of cleavage

The contest between the individualist and communitarian elements in conservative capitalism has been made evident in the struggles over income security, education, the devolution of central political authority, and many other issues. What has become increasingly apparent is that there are cross-cutting splits that divide each tendency along lines of class attitude, if not of class itself.

Within traditionalist conservatism, there is a split between establishment conservatives based in the customary institutions of Western society, and moralist conservatives who base their politics in evangelical churches, single-cause organizations and patriotic associations. Both favour the use of governmental authority to shape individual behaviour by limiting certain freedoms. There is, however, a considerable difference of degree and of moral purpose separating these points of view.

While establishment conservatives are supporters of a moderate accommodation with the welfare state as a matter of sustaining social stability, moralist conservatives are more inclined to think of government provision as a means of fostering dependency and personal laxity. Where establishment conservatives find government programs of population control acceptable, moralists wish to use government policy to restrict abortion, require prayers in schools and censor pornography. Establishment conservatives are inclined to restrain licence in individual behaviour, while moralists tend toward the imposition of discipline as a means of moral improvement.

Moralist politics in the USA were a prominent factor in securing Republican control of the US House of Representatives in 1994 and of the US Senate on and off in 2000. The first Bush presidency brought together an establishment conservative and a vice-president, Senator Daniel Quayle of Indiana, who had strong ties to the moralist wing of the party. The second Bush presidency has courted religious conservatives with major appointments and significant policy initiatives in line with their agenda.

On the individualist side of conservative capitalism, there is a similar class division between populist conservatives and corporate conservatives. Populism has a long history in American politics of both left and right. On the right, populism has been associated with nativism and nationalism. In its new incarnation, the populism of the right is concerned with threats to individual freedom arising from government regulation as well as the collusion of the major financial and commercial concerns in an elite politics that threatens small business people, independent entrepreneurs, farmers, non-union workers, and those who believe in the pure theory of the free market. Populist conservatives tend to be wary of major corporations, and especially multinationals. In the re-fashioning of civil liberties protections after the terrorist strike of 11 September, some populist representatives in Congress have been found among those protesting the extension of government surveillance and arrest powers.

Those conservatives who are based in the corporate-banking sector and whose interests are tied to the largest units of production also claim allegiance to the free market. Their orientation is to economic development as a solution for social problems, but there is also a willingness to make government an active agent in promoting economic freedom and protecting capitalist interests against internal regulation and external encroachment. By co-operating at the elite level, corporate conservatives see the government as a useful asset in the struggle to maintain the mobility and independence of capital. They are to be found supporting the World Trade Organization, the International Monetary Fund, and other trade liberalization organizations.

Populist conservatives would quite willingly divorce the government from its role in monetary regulation, for example, while corporate conservatives see monetary regulation as a principal means of influencing economic policy in a manner favourable to their interests. The appeal of populism has historically been to the smaller commercial interests, while major corporations have operated with a substantial level of security and continuity. Recent large scale corporate bankruptcies and accounting scandals have sharpened the division between corporate conservatives and populists.

These internal tensions in conservative capitalism are not yet as consequential as the splits within the left that have permitted conservatives to acquire power in many parts of the Western world. They may, however, have prevented the consolidation of that power. President Reagan's conservative agenda was stymied fairly effectively by Congressional opposition from 1983 on, some of which came from moderate Republican resistance to the violation of customary understandings concerning income security policy, among other issues. Democrats briefly regained control of the Senate because of the defection of a moderate Republican. In Britain, Prime Minister Thatcher faced several rebellions from traditionalists in her own party prior to being unseated by a challenge based in that faction. John Major was able to hold the coalition together for several more years, but his successors have seen internal factions undermine the party's electoral viability.

It is in the nature of politicians to build coalitions, and the most likely result of these splits is that the challenge of conservative politics will lie more in maintaining coalitions among rival tendencies than in mobilizing any sector in its pure form. At the same time, reform liberals in the USA may be seen to have adopted some of the moralist conservative policies by advocating strong anti-drug initiatives, prosecuting pornographers, or endorsing the death penalty as a way of outflanking the political appeal of the conservative movement.

There is also the possibility of using the contradictory elements of conservative capitalism as mutual reinforcing explanations. The plight of the poor can be attributed to bad personal choices in a free market, rather than to the perpetuation of inequities in the distribution of life chances. These opportunities for rationalization within the broader ambit of conservative capitalism may override the effects of inconsistent policies on the loyalties of those who vote conservative.

There are several alternatives to the classification scheme suggested in this essay that centre on distinctions between what is new and what is old in conservatism, for example: neo-conservatism vs. conservatism (Kristol 1983), and the New Right vs the 'old right' (King 1987). The problem with these labels is that there is little agreement as to what it is that is new, possibly because neither the traditionalist nor the individualist stream represent new thinking. Some see the New Right as a combination of moralist and populist conservatism as against the coalition of establishment and corporate conservatism that characterized conservative parties prior to the mid-1970s. This classification captures the sense in which electoral victories have been based on a coalition that has never before had such success.

Others see the New Right as a name for individualist conservatism as against traditional conservatism. What is presented as new here is the arrival in the conservative camp of advocates for a minimalist version of classical liberalism. The problem with either variant is that attention is directed away from both the historical basis and the enduring power of the larger conservative frame of reference (Hoover 1987; King 1988). There is also the implication that this is a united movement, when in fact it is not. Indeed, some pre-eminent thinkers cited frequently by conservatives, such as Friedrich Hayek, disavow the conservative label entirely (Hayek 1960). To refer to conservative capitalism is to suggest the hybrid nature of the movement and to retain the critical conceptual references to its historical roots.

Conservative capitalism has succeeded in reshaping the agenda of Western politics, though it has not yet developed a substructure of the same durability as that of the New Deal in the USA, or the postwar expansion of social services in Britain. While traditional conservatives may be able to address the increasingly significant issues of the environment and human development, the individualist tendency has few solutions to offer. The ever more visible disparities between rich and poor may undercut the legitimacy of unrestrained capitalism. The threat of terrorism, or perhaps the yearning for national identity, may provide a common focus for conservatives to replace anti-communism. Otherwise, conservative capitalism as a political movement is in danger of losing its way among its own internal divisions.

References

Brittan, S. (1983) *The Role and Limits of Government: Essays in Political Economy*, London: Smith.

Buchanan, J. and Tullock, G. (1962) *The Calculus of Consent: Logical Foundations of Constitutional Democracy*, Ann Arbor: University of Michigan Press.

Burke, E. (1976) *Reflections on the Revolution in France*, ed. C. C. O'Brien, London: Penguin.

Diggins, J. (1975) *Up From Communism*, New York: Harper & Row.

Disraeli, B. (1844) *Coningsby*, London: Penguin.

Dolbeare, K. (1984) *American Political Thought*, Chatham, NJ: Chatham House.

Downs, A. (1965) *An Economic Theory of Democracy*, New York: Harper & Row.

Epstein, K. (1966) *The Genesis of German Conservatism*, Princeton: Princeton University Press.

Freeden, M. (1996) *Ideologies and Political Theory*, Oxford: Oxford University Press.

Friedman, M. (1962) *Capitalism and Freedom*, Chicago: University of Chicago Press.

Green, E. H. H. (2002) *Ideologies of Conservatism: Conservative Political Ideas in the Twentieth Century*, Oxford University Press.

Hayek, F. (1960) *The Constitution of Liberty*, London: Routledge; Chicago: University of Chicago Press.

Hirschman, A. (1977) *The Passions and the Interests: Arguments for Capitalism Before Its Triumph*, Princeton: Princeton University Press.

Hoover, K. (1987) 'The rise of conservative capitalism: ideological tensions within the Reagan and Thatcher governments', *Comparative Studies in Society and History* 29 (2): 245–68.

Hoover, K. and Plant, R. (1989) *Conservative Capitalism in Great Britain and the United States: A Critical Appraisal*, London and New York: Routledge.

Huntington, S. (1957) 'Conservatism as an ideology', *American Political Science Review* 51: 454–73.

Joseph, K. and Sumption, J. (1979) *Equality*, London: John Murray.

King, D. (1987) *The New Right: Politics, Markets, and Citizenship*, London: Macmillan.

—— (1988) 'New right ideology, welfare state form, and citizenship', *Comparative Studies in Society and History* 30 (4): 792–803.

Kirk, R. (1962) *A Program for Conservatives*, Chicago: Regnery.

Kristol, I. (1983) *Reflections of a Neoconservative: Looking Back, Looking Ahead*, New York: Basic Books.

Nash, G. (1996) *The Conservative Intellectual Movement in America: Since 1945*, New York: Basic Books.

Nisbet, R. (1986) *Conservatism*, Minneapolis: University of Minnesota Press.

Niskanen, W. (1973) *Bureaucracy – Servant or Master?: Lessons from America*, London: Hobart Publications.

Oakeshott, M. (1962) *Rationalism in Politics*, London: Methuen.

—— (1975) *On Human Conduct*, Oxford: Oxford University Press.

Piven, F. F. and Cloward, R. (1982) *The New Class War*, New York: Pantheon.

Rothschild, E. (2001) *Economic Sentiments: Adam Smith, Condorcet, and the Enlightenment*, Cambridge, MA: Harvard University Press.

Rossiter, C. (1982) *Conservatism in America: The Thankless Persuasion*, New York: Viking.

Smith, A. (1759) *The Theory of Moral Sentiments*, Indianapolis: Liberty Press, 1969.

—— (1776) *An Enquiry into the Nature and Causes of the Wealth of Nations*, ed. by R. H. Campbell and A. S. Skinner, Oxford: Oxford University Press.

Steinfels, P. (1979) *The Neoconservatives*, New York: Simon and Schuster.

Taylor, C. (1982) *Radical Tories: The Conservative Tradition in Canada*, Toronto: House of Anansi Press.

Wills, G. (1979) *Confessions of a Conservative*, London: Penguin.

Further reading

Anderson, M. (1978) *Welfare*, Palo Alto, CA: Hoover Institution Press.

Behrens, R. (1980) *The Conservative Party from Heath to Thatcher: Policies and Politics 1974–1979*, London: Saxon House.

Blumenthal, S. (1988) *The Rise of the Counter-establishment*, New York: Harper & Row.

Dolbeare, K. and Dolbeare, P. (1976) *American Ideologies: The Competing Political Beliefs of the 1970s*, 3rd edn, Chicago: Rand McNally.

Ebenstein, A. (2001) *Friedrich Hayek: a Biography*, New York: Palgrave.

Gamble, A. (1981) *Britain in Decline: Economic Policy, Political Strategy and the British State*, Boston: Beacon Press.

Gilmour, I. (1969) *The Body Politic*, London: Hutchinson 1969.

—— (1992) *Dancing with Dogma: Britain under Thatcherism*, London; New York: Simon & Schuster.

Gottfried, P. and Fleming, T. (1988) *The Conservative Movement*, Boston: Twayne.

Gray, J. (1998) *Hayek on Liberty*, 3rd edn, London: Routledge.

Hall, P. (1986) *Governing the Economy: The Politics of State Intervention in Britain and France*, New York: Oxford University.

Hayek, F. (1976) *Law, Legislation and Liberty*, London: Routledge & Kegan Paul.

Hoover, K. (2001) *Ideology and Political Life*, New York: Harcourt.

—— (2003) *Economics as Ideology: Keynes, Laski, Hayek and the Creation of Contemporary Politics*, Lanham, MD and Oxford: Rowman and Littlefield.

Kirk, R. (1986) *The Conservative Mind: From Burke to Eliot*, 7th edn, Chicago: Regnery.

Krieger, J. (1986) *Reagan, Thatcher, and the Politics of Decline*, New York: Oxford University Press.

Lawson, N. (1980) *The New Conservatism*, London: Centre for Policy Studies.

Machan, T. and Johnson, M. (1983) *Rights and Regulation: Ethical, Political, and Economic Issues*, New York: Ballinger.

Moynihan, D. (1988) *Came the Revolution: Argument in the Reagan Era*, New York: Harcourt Brace Jovanovich.

Murray, C. (1984) *Losing Ground*, New York: Basic Books.

Nisbet, R. (1962) *The Quest for Community*, New York: Oxford University Press.

Novak, M. (1982) *The Spirit of Democratic Capitalism*, New York: Simon and Schuster.

O'Sullivan, N. (1976) *Conservatism*, New York: St Martin's Press.

Palmer, J. and Sawhill, I. (1986) *Perspectives on the Reagan Years*, Philadelphia: Urban Institute.

Phillips, K. (1982) *Post-Conservative America: People, Politics, and Ideology in a Time of Crisis*, New York: Vintage.

Reichley, A. (1981) *Conservatives in an Age of Change: The Nixon and Ford Administrations*, Washington, DC: Brookings Institution.

Ropke, W. (1971) *A Humane Economy*, Chicago: Regnery.

Scruton, R. (1980) *The Meaning of Conservatism*, London: Macmillan.

Shklar, J. (1969) *After Utopia*, Princeton: Princeton University Press.

Sowell, T. (1984) *Civil Rights: Rhetoric or Reality*, New York: William Morrow.

Stockman, D. (1986) *The Triumph of Politics*, New York: Harper & Row.

Thatcher, M. (1976) *Let Our Children Grow Tall*, London: Centre for Policy Studies.

Tocqueville, A. de (1981) *Democracy in America*, New York: Random House.

Vigurie, R. (1983) *The Establishment vs. the People: Is a New Populist Revolt on the Way?*, Chicago: Regnery.

11

MARXISM AND SOCIALISM

Mark Neocleous

The French Revolution has for over two centuries served as a deeply ambiguous symbol, with different political traditions taking their stands over its meaning and legacy. The conservative tradition is to treat Edmund Burke's *Reflections on the Revolution in France* (1790), with its sweeping attack on revolutionary 'Reason', as one of the doctrine's founding texts. Fascism likewise sets itself against all the principles which the Revolution claimed to represent. In contrast, certain doctrines see themselves as the legitimate heirs of the Revolution and the broader Enlightenment project of which it is understood to have been a part. Liberalism is one of these doctrines; Marxism and socialism the other two.

One of the reasons Marxism and socialism tend to be treated together is because they occupy what is known as the 'Left' of the political spectrum. In the immediate aftermath of the French revolution, the National Assembly divided spatially: on the left hand side sat the 'progressives', seeking reform; on the right were those opposed to the revolutionary momentum, aiming instead to conserve the existing order or to engage in a negative reaction to the revolution. Out of this a language of 'Left' and 'Right' has emerged: conservatives and fascists are considered to occupy the terrain of the Right, Marxists and socialists on the Left, with the liberals holding the center. In such language, Marxism and socialism are politically affiliated, assumed to possess something in common, something that unites them as 'the Left'; indeed, many would argue that socialism is the Left, and that Marxism is merely one of the many varieties of socialism. The outcome is that 'the Left' is often thought of as a homogeneous and coherent grouping. There are therefore good historical and theoretical reasons why Marxism and socialism might be treated together. On the other hand, there are many reasons why the two doctrines might be understood as distinct.

One of the key inheritances from the Revolution, for both Marxism and socialism, is the idea that a radical critique of the existing order is both necessary and possible. The idea that government should be of the people, for the people and by the people is taken seriously, giving rise to a critique of, for example, the limitations of the franchise (not until the early-twentieth century did developed nations allow for a universal franchise equal between adult men and women), hereditary power (as Tom Paine put it, the idea of a hereditary ruler is as silly as the idea of a hereditary hairdresser or mechanic), or unelected officials. This critique has continued to this day, in the demand for further democratization of political institutions and processes, such as through increased participation on the part of the people and greater accountability of those holding office.

163

But to treat socialism and Marxism in these terms alone would limit their radicalism to a critique of political arrangements; this would make them seem very much like liberalism. What distinguishes Marxism and socialism from liberalism is their stance on private property. Where many thinkers had considered the evils of society to stem from human nature (selfish, greedy, egotistical) or from bad (i.e. interfering) government, for Marxism and socialism it is the existence of private property which gives rise to the fundamental problems affecting society. In other words, socialism and Marxism are doctrines concerned with the social and political implications of economic organization. Exploring these implications allows a sense of what Marxism from socialism have in common, as well as a sense of Marxism's distinctiveness.

In the 1859 'Preface' to his *Critique of Political Economy*, Marx outlined his intellectual and political development. Claiming that he had been developing an approach to understanding 'the anatomy of civil society' which had come to serve as the 'guiding thread' to his work, he writes that

> in the social production of their life, men enter into definite relations that are indispensable and independent of their will, relations of production which correspond to a definite stage of development of their material productive forces. The sum total of these relations of production constitutes the economic structure of society, the real basis, on which rises a legal and political superstructure... The mode of production of material life conditions the social, political and intellectual life process in general.
>
> (Marx 2000: 425)

Relations of production (the kind of relations which humans can enter into on the basis of the kind of productive system that exists) 'correspond' to a stage in the development of the productive forces (the kind of technology and industry in existence). This Marx calls the 'economic structure of society' or 'material base'. Upon this economic structure or material base there arises a set of legal and political relations, or what Marx calls the 'superstructure'.

This 'guiding thread' is what Marx describes as 'the materialist method of history' (or what is generally called 'historical materialism'). As a philosophical doctrine materialism argues that reality is ultimately material. On this basis it follows that immaterial phenomena (such as God) either do not exist, or they exist only as products of a material process. Whether Marx was a materialist in this sense is open to debate (he probably was, but whether he was or not doesn't get to the point about historical materialism). Marx's 'materialist' approach does not constitute a matter–consciousness dichotomy, in the way that some commentators suggest. Rather, it is materialist in the sense that it treats the *material* forces as the foundation (or *base*) of society as a whole. At the same time, the method is 'historical' because it aims to show that this material base has changed throughout history. The method assumes that to understand a society *as a totality* one needs to start with the material economic base; it is the way that the means of production are organized that determines the character of society as a whole.

Now, so long as it is left like this there is nothing truly distinctive about Marxism, for the idea that the nature of a society is rooted in that society's economic/material base is an argument found in many of the eighteenth-century Enlightenment thinkers such as Adam Smith, David Hume and Adam Ferguson. These writers all believed that with 'civilization' – by which they meant a system founded on private property – one gets more political and civil liberties. In other words, a certain kind of economic base – capitalism – will generate a certain kind of political and legal 'superstructure' (though they never used this term) with, for example, individual liberty and a general right to private property. Marx's originality lies less in the development of the base–superstructure argument and more in the way he thought that historical change came about, an argument that takes us to the core of his doctrine: classes and their struggles.

For Marxism, history is the history of class struggles. Class struggle is the motor of history, in the sense that it is the struggles that take place over the productive forces which generate new forms of society. For Marxism, capitalism has simplified the class system, to the extent that it is only meaningful to speak of two classes: bourgeois and proletariat. These classes are defined according to their relationship to the means of production. The bourgeois class owns the means of production; the proletariat owns nothing other than labour power, which workers sell for a wage. This does not mean, as is sometimes assumed, that Marx thought that there were only two classes. Far from it: he often talks about the peasantry, the aristocracy, the petty-bourgeoisie, and many others. But for Marx these classes are dying out and, because they are dying out, they are no longer historical agents. For example, where the aristocracy may once have been the ruling class, it has been usurped in this role by the bourgeois class. The aristocracy may still exist (in varying degrees in different countries) but as a historical agent – a class that can act on and change history – it is dead.

Class, then, is one of Marxism's central categories of analysis. Moreover, the way Marxists use the category tends to distinguish them from all other political positions, including many socialist ones. For despite the fact that many socialists still talk about class, there is often a major difference between their understanding of class and Marx's.

Many of the early socialists took their cue from liberal political economists such as Locke and Smith, who regarded labour as the source of wealth. The socialist reading of this was to say that if labour was the source of wealth, then the unequal 'share' of this wealth going to the capitalist class must surely be unfair. The labouring class must be entitled to the whole of this product – had not Locke himself argued that there was a natural right to the fruits of one's own labour? Thus many socialists argued – and continue to argue – that society should be founded on the principle of a more equal exchange. Equalizing the distribution of wealth and income would create a fairer or more just society. The result is an argument for the redistribution (i.e. growing equalization) of wealth and income from one class to another (or, as socialists sometimes prefer to say, from the wealthy to the poor).

But for Marx, such an argument makes the mistake of treating the exploited and alienated condition of the worker as an effect of an unequal or unfair distribution of the total social product. He points out that seen from the bourgeois principles embedded in the market system the distribution is perfectly 'fair'. He asks rhetorically: 'Do not the bourgeois assert that the present-day distribution is "fair"? And is it not, in fact, the only "fair" distribution on the basis of the present-day mode of production?' This is in part what Marx means when in the 'Critique of the Gotha Programme' (1875) he attacks the principle of 'equal wages for equal work' adopted by the German socialists, since this evaluates the workers by only one aspect of their existence (Marx, 2000: 612–16). This is thus a bourgeois formula for perpetuating inequality.

What Marx tries to show is that what is wrong with the system of private property is not the 'unequal' or 'unfair' *distribution* but the way *production* is organized under the rule of capital. Marx's most important work, *Capital* (1867), shows that because capitalists seek to receive back from their market transactions a greater sum of money than they spend, they have to find on the market a commodity which could create value. The only commodity that can do this is labour power. Capitalist society thus requires the existence of a class whose members sell their labour for a wage. And for this to happen, such a class must have no means of subsistence other than the sale of its labour power. Its members must live in absolute poverty, in the sense that they must live with no means of subsistence other than the wage. (Note that Marx is here using a conception of absolute poverty radically different to that used by sociology.) In other words, capitalism presupposes the existence of a class with nothing other than its labour power for sale. This is one reason why Marx's reading of political economists such as Locke and Smith varies from the socialist reading. Instead of seeing in Locke and Smith's account of labour the basis of an argument for a fair and equal distribution, what struck Marx was that such writers drew no distinction between the buying and selling of ordinary commodities and the buying and selling of human labour power. Marx was at pains to show that labour is not just another commodity but the essential life activity of human beings *qua* human beings. When humans sell their labour power, they are engaged in a process of alienating themselves: from other human beings, from the tools used, from the products they produce, and from the human species as a whole. They are in the process, in other words, of seeing themselves and others as little more than commodities.

Now, in the context of capitalist production the major interest of the worker lies in working only for as long as it takes to provide to the capitalist the wages he has paid out. This may not overcome the debilitating effects of alienation, but it at least provides for a living wage. But if all the capitalist receives back is the equivalent of the wages they have paid out they will have made no profit. The capitalist class thus has an interest in ensuring that the workers produce commodities the value of which is more than the total amount of wages paid out. In other words, the capitalist class has an interest in making sure the workers produce surplus value.

What Marx is pointing to with this argument is the fact that there is a fundamental conflict of interest at the heart of the production process. It is a conflict between those pursuing higher wages and those pursuing greater profit – between workers and capitalists. It is thus a conflict between classes. The fundamental source of conflict in bourgeois society is therefore not over how 'equal' the distribution of the surplus product is, but rather is over how the surplus is produced. The class basis of the production process means not simply that distribution is 'unfair' or 'unequal', but that human beings are exploited and alienated in the exercise of their human capabilities. More to the point, one class of human beings is exploited by another class. This is why the concept of class and class struggle is so central to Marx's understanding of society and history, for it is this struggle over the means of production that drives historical change.

A greater sense of the importance of Marx's contribution here might be achieved by situating it in a broader account of class. As a concept 'class' can appear very abstract and indeterminate; it is for this reason that many political theorists have said that we should do away with it as a conceptual tool. In contrast to the supposedly far more concrete and determinate categories such as gender, 'class' is said to be a highly limited conceptual tool on the grounds that there are simply too many ways of talking about it. Does it mean income, status, wealth? Is it more cultural than economic, or subjective rather than objective? Does it not mean different things in different societies? Add to this the prevalent idea that we live in a 'classless society' or that 'we are all middle class now' and it becomes clear that as a concept 'class' is bandied around in all sorts of ways. But in fact there are really only two ways of thinking about class: one is to see it as a structural location; the other is to see it as a form of social relation.

The first of these can be found in the work of a broad spectrum of writers. It is a classical sociological approach but, importantly, it is also found in the work of many socialists. The second is the specifically Marxist view. The differences between the approaches provide us with the overall distinctiveness of the Marxist position.

The first approach treats class as a form of social stratification or a layer in a hierarchical structure, and differentiates between these layers according to economic criteria such as income, 'market chances' or occupation. In contrast, the second approach is a socio-historical conception which sees class as a relation between appropriators and producers, a relation determined by the specific form in which surplus labour is pumped out of the direct producers. In the case of the first approach, the central issue is 'inequality', which it determines by comparing people on the structural hierarchy. In contrast, for classical Marxism the focus is on the social relation itself, the dynamic of the relation between appropriators and producers, the contradictions and conflicts which account for social and historical processes. In the Marxist conception class is understood as a social process of collective domination and exploitation and not a system which generates inequality between individuals located variously across a particular social scale.

These two approaches can be presented schematically as follows:

Class: Two Approaches

Approach	
Class as structural location	Class as social relation
Found in	
Classical sociology, political administration, many socialists	specifically Marxist
Key assumptions	
Class is a form of social stratification	Socio-historical conception of a class as a relation between appropriators and producers
Class as a layer in a hierarchical structure, differentiated according to economic criteria e.g. income, 'market chances', occupation	Class determined by the specific form in which a surplus is pumped out of the direct producers
Focus	
Central focus is inequality, based on a comparison of individuals placed on a structural hierarchy	Focus on the social relation itself, the dynamic of the relation between appropriators and appropriated; the contradictions and conflicts which account for social and historical processes

Of course, thinking about class as a form of structural location is the common-sense way of thinking about class, and has wide appeal. But thinking about class as a form of social relation and process, in the way Marx does, has three significant advantages.

First, it stresses that objective relations to the means of production are significant because they establish societal antagonisms and generate conflicts and struggles. Bearing in mind that the historical materialist method aims to show how the nature of the economic base of society conditions the whole of that society, what this means is that the whole of modern society is determined by the existence of classes within it – not only the material base but also the legal and political superstructure. This is why Marx and Engels suggest that the modern state is but a committee for managing the affairs of the whole bourgeois class. Second, it stresses that these conflicts and struggles shape social experience, and that they therefore shape it in 'class' ways. In other words, that these relations impose their logic on social and cultural processes. And third, it recognizes that the process of class is a process of domination and exploitation; this fact is not apparent from the idea of class as inequality.

This tells us something important about Marxism, which is that inequality is not a driving feature of the Marxist conceptual framework. This is important not only because 'equality' is one of the central concepts in political thought, but also because it is perhaps the central concept in socialist politics. As Bernard Crick puts it, 'Anyone who can honestly call themselves a socialist must agree that equality is the basic value' (1987: 88). Many people argue that one of the central problems in today's world is the drastic inequalities that exist: between individuals, nations, or even classes. At the same time, many writers also feel that the distinction between Left and Right centers on the idea of equality: that the Left is committed to eradicating inequality (or achieving an 'equal' society) where the Right accepts the existing of inequality as a natural extension of differing abilities (whether between individuals, nations, or classes).

Socialists therefore make a great deal out of the fundamental antagonism in bourgeois society between the aspirations to equality and the impossibility of their fulfilment under capitalism. Their response is to point to the necessity for state intervention to achieve greater 'equality of outcome' as well as 'formal equality' and 'equality of opportunity'. The offshoot is that Marxism is lumped together with socialism as being committed to equality. The assumption tends to be that because Marx criticizes capitalism so much, he must be criticizing it along the same lines as others. Since socialists criticize capitalism on the grounds of the inequalities it generates, then Marx must be making the same sort of claims. Or, to put the point another way, many think that Marx criticized capitalism because of its inequalities and that what Marx wants is a 'truly' or 'fully' equal society.

If all that is meant by 'equality' is something intrinsic to humans by virtue of their existence as humans and their capacity to feel, suffer, enjoy, and so on, then Marx would no doubt accept it. But if, as is usually the case, 'equality' is taken to refer to something associated with rights and opportunities, then Marx should be understood as operating at a critical distance from the socialist position. For Marx nowhere condemns capitalism on the grounds that it generates inequality. Rather, he makes a very different set of claims.

One way to understand bourgeois society is to recognize that whatever material inequalities exist, the society as a whole is nonetheless founded on equality. That is not to say that everyone is equal; it is to say that it is founded on the idea of equality. Bourgeois society is a society of equals in the sense that it purports to recognize no privilege due to birth or caste (this was the basis of the French Revolutionary demand for equality as against the aristocratic regime of unequal rank). Rather, bourgeois society treats people as equals insofar as they have an equal right to dispose of themselves and their property. This is why Marx describes the market as 'the exclusive realm of Freedom, Equality, Property'. Freedom because 'both buyer and seller of a commodity...are determined only by their own free will'. Property 'because each disposes only of what is his own'. And equality 'because each enters into relation with the other...and they exchange equivalent for equivalent' (2000: 492). So the very thing that many socialists think is the realm of inequality, the market, Marx describes as a realm of equality. Why? Because when commodities are exchanged they are exchanged as equivalents. The market thus treats capitalist and worker as equal insofar as they are owners and traders of commodities. The relation between capital and worker is one of equality in the way that the relation between slave-owner and slave or lord and serf is not. Marx therefore follows Aristotle in sensing that aspirations to equality are in fact secreted by a system based on generalized commodity production. Aristotle had argued that the concept of 'human equality' can acquire the widespread acceptance it has only in a society where the dominant social relation is the relation between men as possessors of commodities. Marx understands that in terms of the political economy of bourgeois society this requires that human labour takes the form of a commodity.

On the other hand, when Marx says that the capitalist market is a realm of equality he is also speaking ironically. He knows full well that capital and labour do not meet as equals in terms of their social power: the wage relation is highly coercive, not least because it rests on the absolute poverty of the producers. What Marx seems to be suggesting, then, is that the idea of equality has historically served as a crucial vehicle for bourgeois society. Socialists may formulate notions of equality which are more favourable to the socialist ideal of redistribution, but at the end of the day they are using a bourgeois ideal; they are rooted in a bourgeois theoretical framework. The radicalization of the demand for equality on the part of socialists may point to the boundary of bourgeois society, but it cannot point beyond it.

What seems to follow from this is that if one argues against capitalism on the grounds of the inequalities it generates then one will lose the fight, because bourgeois ideologists will insist that the market is indeed a sphere of equality. For Marx, the fight against capitalism should not be done in the name of equality. Marx's desire is for a classless society – an end to the social process of class exploitation and domination. Rather than frame his conception of a classless society in terms of any goal of equality, Marx avoids all such language. As Engels comments in a letter to Bebel in March 1875, 'the notion of socialist society as the realm of equality is a superficial French idea resting upon the old "liberty, equality, fraternity"'. The idea of 'doing away with all social and political inequality' is a highly questionable phrase in place of 'the abolition of all class differences'.

This is why when Marx does talk about a future communist society, he does so in terms different to the future society described by many socialists. Again, Bernard

Crick provides an useful formulation: in every form of socialism, he suggests, 'it must be believed, however practice disappoints, that every adult human being is capable of making an equal contribution to the common good and should be treated equally' (1987: 97). In contrast, when in the 'Critique of the Gotha Programme' Marx describes a future communist society, he does so in terms of the following slogan: 'from each according to his ability, to each according to his needs' (2000: 615). He does so partly because his concept of human being is founded on the notion of need. For Marx human needs are constitutive of our essence as human beings. Not just the need to eat, drink and so on, but the need to work, gain recognition from others, and realize one's potential. The need, in other words, to flourish as a human being. The satisfaction of and generation of new needs is considered as the foundation of emancipation. (This is a view which contrasts quite starkly with the main tradition of western thought which views needs as somehow antithetical to our essence as 'free' beings or as a limit of our possibilities.) But the phrase 'from each according to his ability, to each according to his needs' also points to the fact that needs and abilities are, by definition, unequal, and necessarily so. Thus any society founded on the satisfaction of existing needs and development of new needs, on the one hand, and the realization of human abilities on the other, must by definition be a society which in some sense is unequal. Quite what such a society might look like is less important than the general point here: that 'equality' is, of its essence, a category within bourgeois society. In other words, the demand for equality has no place in the political discourse of communism.

If the view that 'equality' is a superficial idea and that a better society would do without the notion strikes us a startling, it is a sign of the extent to which the notion of equality has seeped into our everyday consciousness. Or, to put that another way: it is a sign of the extent to which the idea of equality has become part of ruling class ideology. And for Marx, the extent to which socialists try to use the idea as part of their critique of capitalism is indicative of the limitations of socialism.

This point returns us briefly to the legacy of the French Revolution. For the most part socialists think the Revolution important because of the abstract principles which it sought to realize: the Revolutionary slogan 'liberty, equality, fraternity' became transformed into foundational principles for many socialists. For Marxism, in contrast, the French Revolution is of historic importance not because of the principles which it sought to realize, but because it represents a willed transformation of society in the interests of an economically ascendant class, the political destruction of an outmoded social order and the beginning of a new one. This is a major difference: the importance lies not in whether the principles are 'good' ones, but in whether a class is willing to take its stand on the world historic stage. This is also why Marx and Engels's *Manifesto of the Communist Party* (1848), a text which sets out the arguments for a proletarian revolution against the bourgeoisie, begins by heaping enormous praise on the bourgeois class and its achievements. The bourgeoisie 'has been the first to show what man's activity can bring about. It has accomplished wonders far surpassing Egyptian pyramids, Roman aqueducts, and Gothic cathedrals; it has conducted expeditions that put in the shade all former exoduses of nations and crusades' (Marx 2000: 248). It has established modern industry and the world market, globalized production and consumption, conquered political power, civilized the world, torn away the religious and sentimental veil which shrouded exploitation, abolished the idiocy of rural life. In other words, the bourgeoisie has created a world after its own image. In this process an historically revolutionary political moment such as the French Revolution assumes an importance not because of the abstract ideals on which it was founded, but because it represented the political action of a united class. What Marx and Engels wish for is for the proletariat to ape that action, not to march under the banner inscribed with its principles.

The discussion thus far suggests that Marx's critique of bourgeois society rests heavily on a rejection of the basic categories of that society, such as equality and rights, and that in so doing Marxism becomes distinguishable from socialist positions which aim to radicalize such bourgeois ideas. This is why the *Manifesto of the Communist Party* has a long section on 'Socialist and Communist Literature'. Marx and Engels categorize the forms of socialism as follows: 1) Reactionary Socialism, 2) Conservative or Bourgeois Socialism, and 3) Critical-Utopian Socialism and Communism.

The defining characteristic of reactionary socialism is its desire to restore past social forms. One type, 'feudal socialism' holds up past forms of exploitation as somehow better than present. As such, the feudal socialists often join forces with classes for which feudalism was most suited, namely the landed aristocracy. The second type, 'petty-bourgeois socialism' wishes to reinvigorate corporate guilds as the basis for manufacture and therefore aims at 'restoring the old means of production and exchange, and with them the old property relations, and the old society'. The third type, 'German, or "True", Socialism' results in the tendency to obliterate theoretically the question of class in its concern for 'Human Nature' or 'Man'. In doing so it too is reactionary because it serves the class of philistines, the petty-bourgeoisie.

In contrast to reactionary socialism, conservative socialism aims more at the maintenance of existing property relations but without the revolutionary potential within them. It therefore seeks a reform of the mechanisms by which bourgeois property is administered. Rather than propose a radical rejection of modern conditions on the basis of a reactionary return to feudal or semi-feudal social structures, conservative socialism prefers to contemplate the possibility of 'the existing state of society minus its revolutionary and disintegrating elements' (2000: 267). That is, it desires a bourgeoisie without a proletariat. In this context it is worth noting that Marx and Engels's heading for this section is 'Conservative, *or Bourgeois,* Socialism'.

Critical-Utopian Socialism has the advantage of recognizing the proletariat and its sufferings. But it sees the proletariat *only* as a suffering class rather than a class with the power to change society. The critical-utopians thus use such suffering to appeal to 'society at large', on the grounds of such principles as the general public good. In so doing they necessarily stand apart from class struggle and reject all revolutionary action. Worse, they end up appealing to the ruling class.

This brief sketch does little justice to either the positions Marx and Engels are describing, or to their own position. But it allows us to draw out two themes from Marx and Engels's comments which identify what from the Marxist position is wrong with a whole range of socialist positions. The first theme is the question of class alliance. Marxism sets itself firmly on the side of the proletariat against the bourgeoisie. Any other classes are either historically insignificant or will come over to the side of one of these two classes. Other socialist positions often recognize the condition of the proletariat yet either ignore it in some kind of universal appeal to all classes, or believe that the solution to the condition of the working class lies in the action of some other class. But for Marx and Engels the working class and the working class alone will be the agent which emancipates the working class. (The idea that the working class needs a revolutionary political party to lead it into the future because left to its own devices it is simply too passive or disorganized is an idea developed by the German Social Democrats and the Bolsheviks in Russia during the early twentieth century. It is an idea which is much closer to mainstream socialist assumptions about the working class than it is to Marxism.)

The second issue concerns the question of historical social form. For Marx and Engels, too many socialists think that the solution lies either in the return to a past social form, for example in the 'unity' of feudalism, or in an attempt to maintain the status quo. Such socialists are either reactionary, in that they aim to retrieve some kind of ideal past, or they are conservative in that they want the present society but without the class struggle. In other words, part of what is at stake in Marx and Engels's criticisms of various socialist positions is a politics of time. In this politics Marx and Engels are vehemently turned towards the future – they see communism as transcending capitalism in the future. Facing the future is of course also a feature of critical-utopian socialism. But the critical-utopians fail to base their vision of the future on the revolutionary potential of the proletariat; rather, they have visions of the future which they think the proletariat should follow and, because the proletariat fails to do so, they become either conservative or reactionary.

One of the implications of these last comments is that it should be clear about where Marx and Engels think the future lies: in the conjunction of the revolutionary potential within capitalist society, and a revolutionary class willing to realize that potential. This is not the case for all forms of socialism, many of which disregard the proletariat as a revolutionary force (or even an effective political force at all). In doing so they often appeal not to the need to realize the revolutionary potential within capitalism which would bring an end to class domination and exploitation, but to general slogans along the lines of 'humanity', 'liberty', or 'human rights'. Marx is highly critical of such ways of thinking, for however radical they appear they are often based on a misunderstanding of their political origins and thus often play a role in ideologically glossing over the nature of class society. Where many socialists, for example, criticize capitalism on the grounds that it persistently infringes the human rights of citizens, Marx points out in *Capital* that the market is in fact the 'very Eden of the innate rights of man': the demands for the rights to liberty and equality can be traced to the defense of private property (2000: 492). The general idea of the 'rights of man' has its roots in a bourgeois conception of man – a conception of man as an egoistical and property-owning individual: 'None of the rights of man go beyond man in bourgeois society', Marx comments in 'On the Jewish Question' (1843, in Marx 2000: 60). The consequence is that while the demand for the 'rights of man' may constitute the grounds for a positive move in terms of political emancipation, such as the right to vote, the demand manifestly fails to do anything about the socio-economic domination of capital. It is for this reason that we find that unlike many socialists, Marx nowhere condemns capitalist society for its violation of people's rights.

Moreover, Marx points out that 'moralistic terminology' such as 'humanity' is more often than not a way of avoiding talking about classes, even when spoken by socialists. In an 1847 essay on 'Moralizing Criticism' he argues that terms such as 'humanism' and, by extension, 'humanistic socialism', become little more than catch-phrases, ways of saying nothing in particular but which have the effect of masking the realities of class domination. As Marx put it (2000: 234), all classes are somehow expected to 'melt away before the solemn concept of "humanity"'. (Similarly, there is a strand of Christian socialism with ideas such as the 'brother-hood of man', 'human fellowship', and so on. In contrast, there can be no such thing as a 'Christian Marxist'. It is a contradiction in terms. The essential character of Marxism is its materialism; the essential character of Christianity is its idealism.)

What this means is that although Marxism and socialism share some important ground concerning the detrimental effects of private property on the lives of the bulk of the population, there are many conceptual and thus political issues which keep them apart. If we are to think of Marxism as a form of socialism, then, we should think of it as *revolutionary proletarian* socialism, as opposed to *non-revolutionary non-proletarian* socialism.

References

For the student the best selection of Marx's works in one volume remains Karl Marx, *Selected Writings*, ed. David McLellan, Oxford: Oxford University Press, 1977; 2nd edn 2000. This has been used to provide the references for the entry above.

Crick, Bernard (1987) *Socialism*, Milton Keynes: Open University Press.

Further reading

Avineri, Shlomo (1968) *The Social and Political Thought of Karl Marx*, Cambridge: Cambridge University Press.

Cleaver, Harry (1979) *Reading 'Capital' Politically*, Brighton: Harvester.

Cowling, Mark (ed.) (1998) *The Communist Manifesto: Contemporary Interpretations*, Edin-burgh: Edinburgh University Press.

Dunn, John (1984) *The Politics of Socialism: An Essay in Political Theory*, Cambridge: Cambridge University Press.

Kay, Geoff (1979) *The Economic Theory of the Working Class*, London: Macmillan.

Lichtheim, George (1975) *A Short History of Socialism*, London: Fontana.

Miliband, Ralph (1977) *Marxism and Politics*, Oxford: Oxford University Press.

Miliband, Ralph (1995) *Socialism for a Sceptical Age*, Cambridge: Polity Press.

Wood, Allen (1991) *Karl Marx*, Cambridge: Cambridge University Press.

12

FASCISM

Stanley Payne

Fascism has been one of the most controversial political phenomena of the twentieth century, first of all because of the complete absence of any general agreement about the definition of either the term itself or the broader political developments to which it refers. Fascism is frequently employed as a derogatory epithet and applied to widely varying political activities. At one time or another it has been attached by critics to nearly all of the major movements, particularly the more radical ones, whether of the right or left.

Historically, the term originated with the radical nationalist movement of the Fasci Italiani di Combattimento, organized by Benito Mussolini and others in 1919. *Fascio* in Italian means 'bundle' or 'union' and was a common name given to varying types of new political groupings, particularly those of more radical character. The Fasci Italiani di Combattimento were in turn reorganized two years later, in 1921, as the Partito Nazionale Fascista, or Fascist Party for short, converting the original substantive into an adjective. In October 1922 the Fascist leader Mussolini became prime minister of Italy, and in 1925 converted his government into a one-party dictatorship, thus creating the first, and prototypical, 'fascist regime'.

As early as 1923, however, there developed a growing tendency to generalize beyond the Italian example and apply the term fascist or fascism to any form of right-wing authoritarian movement or system. In the broadest sense, therefore, the trend was to identify any form of non-leftist authoritarianism as fascist, while competing left-wing groups, particularly Soviet Stalinists, began to apply the term to leftist rivals. By the 1930s the term fascist had sometimes become little more than a term of denigration applied to political foes, and this categorical but vague connotation has remained to the present day.

Despite the vagueness, a limited consensus has emerged among some of the leading scholars in the study of fascism, who use the term to refer to the concrete historical phenomena of a group of radical nationalist movements which emerged in Europe between the two World Wars, first in the Italian Fascist and German National Socialist movements and then among their numerous counterparts in other European countries. This consensus is that specific movements bearing the same characteristics did not exist prior to 1919 and have not appeared in significant form in areas outside Europe or in the period after 1945. None the less, disagreement persists among scholars as to whether the various reputedly fascist movements of inter-war Europe can be linked together as a generic and common phenomenon, or whether they so differed among themselves that they can accurately be discussed only as individual phenomena. The weight of opinion now tends to fall on the side of the former argument, viewing fascism not merely as an Italian or German political form but as a more general phenomenon.

A successful definition of fascism as a generic entity must be able to define common unique characteristics of all the fascistic movements in Europe during the 1920s and 1930s while also differentiating them from other political phenomena. Such an understanding must comprehend basic features such as:

1   the typical fascist negations;
2   fascist doctrine and goals; and
3   the relative uniqueness of fascist style and organization.

Fascism postulated a unique new identity and attempted to occupy a new political territory by opposing nearly all the existing political sectors, left, right and centre. Thus it was anti-liberal, anti-communist (and anti-socialist at least in the social democratic sense) and also anti-conservative, though fascists proved willing to undertake temporary alliances with rightist groups, and to that extent diluted their anti-conservatism.

In terms of ideology and political goals, fascist movements represented the most intense and radical form of nationalism known to modern Europe. Their aim was to create new nationalist and authoritarian state systems that were not merely based on traditional principles or models. Fascist groups differed considerably among themselves on economic goals, but had in common the aim of organizing some new kind of regulated, multi-class, integrated national economic structure, which was varyingly called national corporatist, national socialist or national syndicalist. All fascist movements aimed either at national imperial expansion or at least at a radical change in the nation's relationship with other powers to enhance its strength and prestige. Their doctrines rested on a philosophical basis of idealism, vitalism and voluntarism, and normally involved the attempt to create a new form of modern self-determined secular doctrine (although several of the minor fascist movements were remarkably religious in ethos).

Fascist uniqueness was particularly expressed through the movement's style and organization. Great emphasis was placed on the aesthetic structure of meetings, symbols and political choreography, relying especially on romantic and mystical aspects. All fascist movements attempted to achieve mass mobilization, together with the militarization of political relationships and style, with the goal of a mass party militia. Unlike some other types of radicals, fascists placed strong positive evaluation on the use of violence, and stressed strongly the principle of male dominance. Although they espoused an organic concept of society, they vigorously championed a new elitism and exalted youth above other phases of life. In leadership, fascist movements exhibited a specific tendency toward an authoritarian, charismatic, personal style of command (the *Führerprinzip*, in German National Socialist terminology).

The Italian Fascist movement was first organized in Milan in March 1919 by a small group of military veterans, ex-socialists and former revolutionary syndicalists, and Futurist cultural avant-gardists. At first it failed to attract significant support, adopting at that time an advanced 'leftist' nationalist programme. Fascism became a mass movement only towards the end of 1920 when it spread into the north Italian countryside, gaining wider backing by its assault on the Socialist Party in rural areas. Fascists at first criticized the Socialists for their internationalism and not for their economics, but the movement soon moved to the right on economic issues as well. Fear of socialism made the Fascists seem attractive to conservatives as shock troops, and the Fascists in turn made an appeal to nearly all sectors of society as the only new national movement not bound by the past or by class interests. After the parliamentary system became stalemated, Mussolini led the so-called 'March on Rome' in October 1922 that convinced the King to appoint him as constitutional prime minister. The following two years were a time of growing authoritarianism, but also of uncertainty as to what form a Fascist government should take. Only after some hesitation did Mussolini install a direct political dictatorship in January 1925.

The new Fascist regime was then constructed between 1925 and 1929. It adopted the myth of the 'totalitarian state', yet the Mussolini regime was far from a total dictatorship. Its control was limited in large measure to the political sphere. The King, not Mussolini, remained head of state, and many aspects of the Italian Constitution remained in force. Elite sectors of society remained unmolested, the economic system enjoyed considerable freedom, the military remained partially autonomous in administration, censorship in culture was comparatively limited, and a new concordat was signed with the Roman Catholic Church. A system of national syndicates, later termed national corporations, was organized and administered by the government to regulate economic affairs, but in practice industry and management enjoyed wide autonomy. Parliament itself was replaced in 1928 with a new 'corporate chamber', composed of representatives chosen not by direct nomination and vote but by government and economic groups. During most of the 1920s the economy prospered, and Italian society seemed to accept the new regime which hailed itself as the alternative to the conventional left and right.

Fascists also proclaimed themselves revolutionaries and empire builders, but Mussolini showed little inclination to carry out a full-scale social or institutional revolution. The Fascist Party itself was reduced to a limited bureaucracy and subordinated to the regular government administration, rather than being placed in complete control of it, as in the Soviet Union. The Fascist regime thus functioned as a limited or semi-pluralist dictatorship rather than as a truly totalitarian system. When the Depression of the 1930s brought economic distress, Mussolini did not rely on the new national corporations to rescue the economy so much as on the extension of state administrative agencies. Despite mass propaganda, there was no revolution in the educational system, either.

Mussolini was well aware that he had failed to effect a true revolution, but was none the less increasingly overcome by a kind of megalomania and his own myth of the 'Duce' (leader). He became convinced that Fascism would become great by creating a new African and Mediterranean empire, using the conquest of Ethiopia in 1935 as the beginning of this expansion. He believed that after the construction of a new empire another generation of Fascist dominance in Italy would somehow create a new Fascist culture and the Fascist 'new man'.

Though Italian Fascism created the original terminology, when many commentators speak of 'fascism' they refer primarily to Adolf Hitler's National Socialist movement in Germany, whose character and history were in key respects strikingly different. Whereas Italian Fascism was converted into a major mass movement in scarcely more than two years, the same process in Germany required more than a decade. Hitler's original National Socialist German Worker's Party (NSDAP in German) had to compete with numerous other small radical nationalist and rightist groups. After one brief bid for power in 1923, it had to devote ten years to building up a strong party organization and mass following. Its great opportunity came with the major political and economic crisis provoked by the Depression, which threatened German society with further chaos after the disasters of the First World War and the immediate post-war period.

By 1932 the 'Nazis', as they became known after the pronunciation of the first two syllables of 'National' in German, had become the largest single party in Germany, primarily by promising all manner of things, however contradictory, to diverse sectors of German society. They portrayed themselves as the only strong national force able to bring unity and restore security and prosperity to a divided, languishing country. Adolf Hitler became Chancellor (the equivalent of prime minister) on 30 January 1933, through legal constitutional processes, just as had Mussolini, with a parliamentary majority of Nazis and rightists in support.

Hitler moved to establish a complete political dictatorship within only six months, also becoming legal head of state by taking over the German presidency in mid-1934. A general *Gleichschaltung* or 'co-ordination' of most German institutions was carried out to extend Hitler's control. The German dictatorship became both more efficient and more thoroughgoing than that of Italy, but in Germany the emphasis also lay on government political power rather than on thorough institutional or social revolution. The Nazis proclaimed a new 'people's community' of common interest, with nominal equality of status but with differentiation and subordination of social functions. Most of the country's social and economic structure remained intact and the principle of private property was generally honoured, as in Fascist Italy.

Yet whereas Mussolini had great difficulty creating a fully coherent programme or even defining his own goals, Hitler had certain basic ends in view from the early 1920s onwards. Hitlerian doctrine was grounded in the racial principle of Aryanism or Nordicism, which reduced all values and achievements to racial criteria and the inherent superiority of the Nordic race. In Hitler's thinking, the true Nordic master race could only develop if it were also given 'space', and that meant conquest of *Lebensraum* (space for living) in eastern Europe. Only after a successful war to dominate most of Europe could the true Nazi revolution take place, which in Hitler's view was neither a social or economic revolution, nor even a cultural revolution, but an actual racial and biological revolution to rid the German race of inferior elements and create the new breed of 'supermen'. Economic and political doctrines were secondary to this peculiar ideology grounded in race and war, a kind of international social Darwinism. Thus for Hitler war must precede revolution, for only a successful war could create the conditions for racial revolution.

During the first years of Hitler's regime, in 1933–4, relations with Italy were rather tense. Fascists were well aware of the extremist racial tendencies in Nazi doctrine and of the inferior place of south Europeans in such an ideology. Hitler, however, was the only major European leader to support Italy's conquest of Ethiopia and looked to Mussolini as the only kindred spirit directing one of the larger European countries. His view was that Italy and Germany were natural allies, since Italy was interested in the Mediterranean and Africa, neither of them primary targets of German expansion.

In 1936 Italy and Germany both intervened on the side of the right-wing Spanish Nationalists in the Spanish Civil War. In October of that year they first established the 'Rome–Berlin Axis', a loose understanding aimed at mutual consultation and co-operation. By 1937 Mussolini had fallen under Hitler's spell, his attitude toward Germany fuelled by a combination of fear and envy. Convinced that a militarily powerful Germany would soon dominate Europe, he carried out a partial and super-ficial 'Nazification' of Italian Fascism in 1938, introducing the goose step and a new doctrine of 'Italian racism'. The latter was a feeble attempt to create a special place for the Italian 'race' in the new racial order, though this belated doctrine defined the Italian race as the product of history and culture, rather than mere biology as in the Nazi scheme.

Mussolini entered the Second World War only in June 1940, shortly before the fall of France. He then endeavoured to launch his own 'parallel war' in Africa and the Balkans to create an autonomous Italian sphere of power. This soon met shattering defeat, and by 1941 Mussolini had become a satellite of Hitler. As the war came directly home to Italy in July 1943, he was overthrown by a coalition of the Italian Crown, the military and dissident Fascists. Rescued by German commandos, Mussolini ruled a new 'Italian Social Republic' in German-occupied northern Italy during 1944–5 in an unsuccessful attempt to rally support for a return to the semi-collectivist doctrines of early radical Fascism.

Hitler's own goals aimed at the domination of nearly all continental Europe, after which Germany could complete the racial revolution and eventually dominate the entire world. After France fell, Hitler turned in 1941 to his principal rival, invading the Soviet Union, declaring a special 'war of racial extermination' for the final conquest of *Lebensraum*.

This also coincided with the most sinister of Nazi policies, the 'Final Solution' for the liquidation of European Jewry. In Hitlerian doctrine, the arch-enemy of the Nordic race, and of all true races, was held to be the Jews, defined as a malevolent 'anti-race' of parasites devoted to racial pollution and the destruction of all true culture. In this paranoid nightmare, Hitler came to believe that the world could only be made safe for the creation of a master race by the total extermination of Jews, a process that had begun as early as 1939–40, but finally took the form of mass exter-mination camps two years later. By the end of the war and the destruction of Nazism, nearly six million Jews had been liquidated, the greatest single act of delib-erate genocide in all human history. (Italian Fascism, by contrast, had not originally discriminated against Jews. The proportion of Jewish members of the Fascist Party in the 1920s was greater than that of Jews in Italian society as a whole, and Fascist officials had publicly lauded Jews. When the first legal measures of discrimination were adopted in 1938 in imitation of Germany, they were unpopular both with the general Italian populace and even with many Fascists themselves.)

German Nazism was by far the most powerful and influential variant of what historical analysts sometimes call 'generic fascism', but fascist-type movements existed in nearly all European countries during the 1930s, as well as in other parts of the world. The great majority of these fascist-type movements were complete fail-ures, for in most countries and under most conditions the extremist doctrines of fascism had little appeal. By the late 1930s, in Europe as a whole, there were consid-erably more anti-fascists than fascists.

None the less, at least four other fascist movements gained considerable popular support and merit brief attention. For example, the only other fascist-type movement to rival German National Socialism in popular support was the Hungarian Arrow Cross movement. Whereas the Nazis gained 38 per cent of the popular vote in Germany in 1932, the Arrow Cross may have held nearly 35 per cent in the Hungarian elections seven years later. There were proportionately more different fascistic parties and movements in Hungary than in any country in the world, in part because of the trauma of the First World War and because the loss of territory and population was proportionately greater in Hungary than anywhere else. Aggrieved nationalism was, if anything, even keener than in Germany. The Arrow Cross movement of Ferenc Szalasi appealed especially to workers and poor peasants, and espoused a greater degree of social collectivism and economic reorganization than did many other fascistic movements. Szalasi's goal was a 'Greater Danubian Federation' led by Hungary, but he himself did not endorse war and violence to the same extent as Hitler and Mussolini. The Arrow Cross was strongly anti-Semitic, however, and was finally placed in power by Hitler in 1944 after the German military had taken over Hungary. The few fleeting months of Arrow Cross rule that followed prior to the Soviet military conquest did not provide time to create a genuine new system, though radical political and economic changes were imposed.

In Romania, the Legionary, or Iron Guard, movement led by Corneliu Zelea Codreanu became a major force in the late 1930s. Although Romania was one of the victors in the First World War, it was economically backward and politically divided. The Legionary movement was built on the support of university students and eventually developed considerable backing among poor peasants. Iron Guardists were distinct from most fascists in their emphasis on religiosity – Romanian Orthodoxy being strongly endorsed as essential to the life of the nation. Yet the Legionaries did not have a genuine programme; their goal was the '*Omul nou*', the new man, to be created by radical nationalist and religious culture. The existing government and elite were to be swept away in favour of the interests of the common Romanian people, even though it was not clear how these interests were to be articulated and structured. Codreanu and the top Legionary leaders were murdered by the government police in 1938, but the movement was eventually brought into the government in 1940 when General Mihai Antonescu overthrew the monarchy and established a new dictatorship. The Guardists then made a desperate attempt to seize sole authority in January 1941, but were easily defeated by the Romanian army, a blow from which they never recovered.

In Croatia a radical new fascist-type movement, the Ustasi (Insurgents), became influential among young nationalists during the 1930s. After his military conquest of greater Yugoslavia in 1941, Hitler divided the country into zones, making most of Croatia autonomous under the Ustasi leader Ante Pavelic. The Ustasi regime of 1941–4 was the only other fascist-type regime to rival that of Hitler in sheer gruesomeness. It carried out its own liquidation of native Jewry and then attacked the sizable Serbian population living in southern and eastern Croatia, resulting in possibly 300,000 wanton murders.

The Spanish Nationalist dictatorship of General Francisco Franco that came to power in the Spanish Civil War of 1936–9 also at first contained fascistic features. In 1937 Franco took over the native fascist party, Falange Española (Spanish Phalanx), and made it his official state party, adopting its Twenty-six Point programme (based generally on that of Fascist Italy) as the official ideology of his new state. The Falange enjoyed considerable political influence particularly during 1939–42, when Franco cultivated close relations with Nazi Germany.

The Franco regime, however, was also based on Spanish Catholicism and cultural traditionalism, and carried out a sweeping new right-wing neo-traditionalist revival. Many Catholics and rightists were strongly anti-Falangist, and Franco was careful to limit the influence enjoyed by the new state party. By 1943, when it had become doubtful that Hitler would win the war, Franco initiated a tentative 'defascistization' of his regime. This was rapidly expanded at the end of the war in 1945, when the Falange was drastically downgraded and the regime refurbished as a 'Catholic corporatist' system of 'organic democracy'. Defascistization became, in fact, a continuous and ongoing feature of the regime, which progressively transformed itself in chameleon fashion. An attempt by moderate Falangists to make a comeback was defeated in 1956, and by 1958 the Twenty-six Points had been replaced by nine anodyne 'Principles of the Movement', a series of platitudes about the nation, its unity and familial values. By the time that Franco died in 1975, the quasi-fascist aspects dating from the origins of his regime had long since disappeared.

The dual rightist/fascist character of the early Franco regime presents a striking example of both the potential alliance and disharmonies of fascist groups and the radical right. Although the two sectors had much in common, they were also distinct and marked by significant differences in almost every European country. Radical rightist groups shared some of the fascists' political goals, just as revolutionary leftist movements exhibited some of their stylistic and organizational characteristics. The uniqueness of the fascists compared with the radical right, however, lay in their rejection of the cultural and economic conservatism, and the particular social elitism of the radical right, just as they rejected the internationalism, egalitarianism and materialist socialism of the left. The historical uniqueness of fascism can be better grasped once it is realized that significant political movements sharing all – not merely some – of the common characteristics of fascism existed only in Europe during the years 1915–45.

During the 1930s efforts were made to imitate fascism outside Europe in China, Japan, southern Asia, South Africa, Latin America and even in the USA. None of these extra-European initiatives gained mass support or enjoyed any political success. The peculiar combination of extreme nationalism together with cultural and social radicalism that made up fascism could grow neither in the soil of non-European democracies nor in more backward and traditionalist societies elsewhere. During its great war effort of 1937–45, imperial Japan adopted only a few of the features of fascism. The legal institutional order of the country was scarcely altered, and comparatively normal parliamentary elections were held in 1942. No single-party system was ever installed in Japan, where leadership was provided by traditional elites and the military.

Fascists claimed to represent all classes of national society, particularly the broad masses. Marxists claimed conversely that they were no more than the tool of the most violent, monopolistic and reactionary sectors of the bourgeoisie. Neither of these extreme interpretations is supported by empirical evidence. In their earliest phase, fascist movements often drew their followers from among former military personnel and small sectors of the radical intelligentsia, in some cases university students. Though some fascist movements enjoyed a degree of backing from the upper bourgeoisie, the broadest sector of fascist support, comparatively speaking, was provided by the lower middle class. Since this was one of the largest strata in European society during the 1920s and 1930s, the same might also have been said for various other political groups. In both Italy and Germany a notable minority of party members were drawn from among urban workers. In Hungary and Romania, primary backing came from university students and poor peasants, and there was also considerable agrarian support in some parts of Italy.

A bewildering variety of theories and interpretations have been advanced since 1923 to explain fascism. One of the most common sets of theories are those of socio-economic causation, primarily of Marxist inspiration, which hold that this phenomenon was the product of specific economic forces or interests, or of specific social groups, such as big business, the bourgeoisie or the petite bourgeoisie. A second set of concepts emphasizes psychocultural motivations, related to certain kinds of personality theories or forms of social psychology. Another approach has been derived from modernization theory, which posits fascism as intimately related to a specific phase in modern development. Theorists of totalitarianism, on the other hand, sometimes include fascism as one major aspect of the broader phenomenon of twentieth-century totalitarianism. The most flexible and effective approaches, however, are historicist in character, employing multi-causal explanations in terms of the major dimensions of European historical development, and especially its key variations in different countries, during the early twentieth century.

A historicist approach would account for fascism by attempting to isolate key historical variables common to those national circumstances in which significant fascist movements arose in various countries. These variables should identify key differences in the areas of national situation, political problems, cultural tendencies, economic difficulties and social structure. The common variable with regard to national circumstance was generally one of status deprivation or severe frustration of nationalist ambitions. In terms of strictly political circumstances, strong fascist movements arose in certain countries when they were just beginning, or had only recently begun, the difficult transition to direct democracy. (Conversely, neither advanced and experienced democracies nor very backward countries not yet introduced to democracy were susceptible.) The key variable of cultural milieu probably had to do with the degree of acceptance of rationalism and materialism, as distinct from idealism and vitalism, the latter currents being much more propitious to fascism. Fascism also developed significantly only in countries experiencing major economic difficulties, but the exact character of those difficulties differed enormously, from highly industrial Germany to very backward Romania. Probably the most common feature of the economic variables involved was a general belief that problems were national in scope yet somehow vaguely international in origin. In terms of social mobilization, differing syndromes may be encountered, but the most common variable concerned widespread discontent among the young and among the lower middle classes generally, though this discontent had to some extent to spread more broadly into the lower classes for fascist movements to develop a strong mass basis. Again, no one or two or even three of the aforementioned variables sufficed to produce a significant fascist movement. Only in those few countries where all five variables were present at approximately the same time were conditions propitious.

That fascism temporarily became a major force in Europe was due above all to the military expansion of Nazi Germany, for the purely political triumphs of fascist movements were very few. Similarly, the complete defeat of Germany and Italy in the Second World War condemned fascism to political destruction, making it impossible for fascist movements to emerge as significant political forces after 1945. Above all, the identification of fascist-type policies not so much with Fascist Italy as with the militarism and mass murder wrought by Nazi Germany fundamentally discredited them for following generations.

Nevertheless, fascism did not completely die in 1945. Efforts to revive fascism have been rather numerous, and literally hundreds of petty neo-fascist grouplets have emerged during the second half of the twentieth century, usually each more insignificant than the next. These groups have been concentrated in western Europe, but are also found in North and South America, as well as in other parts of the world. Neo-fascist parties are usually movements of extreme protest, operating far outside the political mainstream and unable to mobilize support. Extreme racism has been a prime characteristic of such groups in the USA and in some European countries such as France, one recent example being the 'skinhead' white racist movement of the late 1980s. In Germany itself, the only movement that tried to some extent to build on the Nazi heritage failed to mobilize 2 per cent of the vote. The most successful neo-fascist movement, however, has been the 'Italian Social Movement' (MSI), principal Italian successor to the original Fascist Party. The MSI has tried to modernize and revise fascist doctrine in a more moderate and sophisticated direction, and in a few areas of Italy has garnered 6 per cent or more of the vote in local elections.

Does fascism have a future? Worried foes sometimes fear so, but it is doubtful if the specific forms of early twentieth-century European fascism can be successfully revived. Broad cultural, psychological, educational and economic changes have made the re-emergence of something so murderous as Nazism in a large industrial nation almost impossible, just as the late twentieth-century era of international interdependence seems to rule out war among the major European and industrial countries. The prevailing culture of materialism and consumerism militates against extreme positions, and any appeal to mass vitalist and irrationalist politics.

Movements and regimes with most similarities to certain aspects of fascism during the second half of the twentieth century have been much more important in some countries of the Third World than in the West. There nationalist regimes of one-party dictatorship have not been uncommon, and more than a few governments in Afro-Asian countries have preached their own versions of national socialism or national corporatism, also relying on elitism and violence, as well as ideologies of mysticism and idealism, in certain instances. There too the 'cult of personality' and charismatic dictatorship has sometimes been powerful, so that more of the specific features of fascism have assumed prominent roles in Africa and Asia than in the Western world in recent decades. None the less, it is not possible to refer to more than specific features and tendencies, for the nationalist movements and dictatorships of the Third World have also developed unique identities and profiles of their own, and in no case have literally copied or revived European fascist movements and regimes.

When some commentators speculate about the 'return of fascism', they are referring not so much to revival of the specific forms of early twentieth-century European fascism and Nazism as to the emergence of new forms of authoritarianism and dictatorship, which is a rather different question. The 'authoritarianism temptation' in varying forms is present in diverse kinds of extremist politics. While the development of new modern dictatorships in major Western countries is not likely, it cannot be ruled out in all forms. Any new authoritarianism in the twenty-first century would however, have to develop particular characteristics appropriate for its own times and could never be a literal revival of the past.

Further reading

Birken, L. (1995) *Hitler as Philosophe: Remnants of the Enlightenment in National Socialism*, Westport, CT: Praeger.

Cassels, A. (1975) *Fascism*, New York: Thomas Y. Crowell.

Gregor, A. J. (1969) *The Ideology of Fascism*, New York: The Free Press.

—— (2000) *The Faces of Janus: Marxism and Fascism in the Twentieth Century*, New Haven: Yale University Press.

Griffin, R. (1990) *The Nature of Fascism*, London: Pinter.

—— (1995) *Fascism*, Oxford: Oxford University Press.

—— (1998) *International Fascism*, London: Arnold.

Knox, M. (2000) *Common Destiny: Dictatorship, Foreign Policy, and War in Fascist Italy and Nazi Germany*, Cambridge: Cambridge University Press.

Laqueur, W. (ed.) (1976) *Fascism: A Reader's Guide*, Berkeley and Los Angeles: University of California Press.

—— (1996) *Fascism: Past, Present and Future*, New York: Oxford University Press.

Linz, J. (2000)*Totalitarian and Authoritarian Regimes*, Boulder: Lynne Rienner.

Larsen, S. U., Hagtvet, B. and Myklebust, J. (eds) (1980) *Who were the Fascists? Social Roots of European Fascism*, Bergen-Oslo: Universitetsforlaget.

Milza, P. (1985) *Les fascismes*, Paris: Imprimerie Nationale.

Mühlberger, D. (ed.) (1987) *The Social Basis of European Fascist Movements*, London: Croom Helm.

Nolte, E. (1966) *Three Faces of Fascism*, New York: Holt, Rinehart and Winston.

Payne, S. G. (1980) *Fascism: Comparison and Definition*, Madison: University of Wisconin Press.

—— (1995) *A History of Fascism 1914–1945*, Madison: University of Wisconin Press.

Rees, P. (1984) *Fascism and Pre-fascism in Europe: A Bibliography of the Extreme Right, 1890–1945*, Brighton: Harvester.

Spielvogel, J. J. (2001) *Hitler and Nazi Germany: A History*, Englewood Cliffs, NJ: Prentice-Hall.

13

FUNDAMENTALISM

Bassam Tibi

Fundamentalism has become such a loose term in public debates that some scholars have suggested that it no longer be used in serious writings. In Germany, for instance, journalists distinguish between 'dogmatic' and 'open-minded' green ecologists, labelling the first fundamentalists while viewing the latter as realists. To acknowledge the importance of the issue and to move beyond spurious references to fundamentalism, it is critical to resuscitate the original meaning of the term. Fundamentalism is a reference to religion and to a particular use of religion in response to challenges in politics and society. Thus fundamentalism combines political concerns with religious legitimation.

The challenge of modernity is the starting point for fundamentalists. Since the Christian Reformation and throughout the ensuing centuries, responses to this challenge have included adjustment and accommodation to a process of secularization (Habermas 1987). The contemporary crisis of modernity, however, has provoked a resurgence of religion, transforming religion from a phenomenon under challenge to a systemic challenge to secular order. De-secularization is the new challenge, a religious fundamentalist response to secularization (Tibi 2000). While Islamic fundamentalism is today the most prominent manifestation of this challenge, the origin of the phenomenon can be traced back to American Protestant fundamentalism (Ammerman in Marty and Appleby 1991: 1–65).

Fundamentalism is an indication of a fight: 'fundamentalists see themselves as militants...they react, they fight back...next they fight for...they fight with particularly chosen repository of resources...they fight against others...they also fight under God' (Marty and Appleby 1991: ix–x). All varieties of fundamentalism claim to be a revival of religion, but these fundamentalisms are foremost an indication of a political phenomenon. Since the publication of Rousseau's *Social Contract*, popular sovereignty has been the foundation of democratic government and politics, but fundamentalisms are opposed to democracy as government of people by the people (Tibi in *Encyclopedia of Democracy* 1995a: vol. II). Indeed, fundamentalists seek to challenge democracy by acting as the 'Defenders of God' (Lawrence 1989). As the Islamic variety of this phenomenon makes clear, the ultimate goal to be achieved is '*hakimiyyat Allah* (God's rule)'. This chapter will introduce and explain the meaning of fundamentalism for government and politics, focusing primarily on Islamic fundamentalism as a global phenomenon.

Introduction: What is fundamentalism?

Akin to the basic character of the contemporary world as a 'global formation' (Chase-Dunn 1989), fundamentalism, in what it fights for and what it fights against, is also a global phenomenon that occurs in all world religions (Marty and Appleby 1991–5, 5 volumes). European expansion constitutes the background against which this global phenomenon emerged. The expansion of the international society in the aftermath of the Peace of Westphalia 1648 (Bull and Watson 1984) established the foundation to which fundamentalism as a global formation is opposed. Central to this expansion was not only the real structural and institutional globalization of the secular nation-state (Tilly 1985: 45; Giddens 1987: ch. 10), but also a universal process of Westernization (Laue 1987). Fundamentalisms in non-Western civilizations are directed against this globalization of the Western secular model and against the universalization of its values, in particular with regard to government and politics.

Globalization heralds a shrinking of the globe, but this shrinking does not entail an even-handed process of spreading Western structures and related value systems. Globalization has not been – as believed – a process of standardization of the world, a generic spreading of 'McCulture'. It is too simple to see it this way, and such simplistic notions fail to grasp important aspects of fundamentalism. Fundamentalism is much more a sort of 'jihad versus McWorld' (Barber 1995). As Hedley Bull rightly observes, while the depicted shrinking of the world, 'has brought societies to a degree of mutual awareness and interaction that they have not had before, it does not in itself create a unity of outlook and has not in fact done so' (Bull 1977: 273). Quoting Brzezinski's formula, Bull notes that 'humanity is becoming simultaneously more unified and more fragmented'. To capture the complexity of this phenomenon, it is critical to think in terms of the 'simultaneity of structural globalization and cultural fragmentation' (Tibi 1998: chs I and V). With the 'European expansion' structures emanating from the new international system first established in Europe have been globalized, but this process of globalization is not matched by a parallel process of universalization of Western values. In short, the 'Idea of the West' (Gress 1998) has not become universal with the globalization of the Western model of the secular nation state.

The rise of fundamentalism is one significant manifestation of the process of unfolding cultural fragmentation, i.e. the increasing decline in consensus (Tibi 1998: ch. V). Although fundamentalism existed during the East–West conflict, as Raymond Aron in his 'Paix et guerre entre les nations' – published at the height of the Cold War in 1962 – put it, bipolarity 'veiled the heterogeneity of civilizations', hiding the global political conflict lying beneath (Aron 1962). With the end of the Cold War the ongoing global return of religion, of which fundamentalism is one manifestation, became so obvious that it could not be overlooked or denied. Secularization is being challenged by fundamentalism. Of course, the increasing role and relevance of religion in global politics (Haynes 1998: 7) is a much broader phenomenon than fundamentalism is, but the rise of religious fundamentalism in the context of a politicization of religion is the most significant aspect in this process to government and politics. To be sure, at issue is not a renaissance of religion, but rather an emerging new totalitarianism (see my critique of Habermas, Tibi 2002c).

As already noted, all fundamentalisms have grown from a fight of 'Defenders of God' against secular modernity. The major streams of fundamentalism involve a revolt against the modern nation-state thriving in non-Western civilizations launched by those belonging to particular religious communities. 'The revolt Against the West' is a major drive of fundamentalism (Bull in Bull and Watson 1984: ch. 14). The fight against cultural modernity becomes anti-Western not only due to the hegemony of the West, but also because this civilization has been the only one that underwent a secularization. In the study of fundamentalism, the Islamic case has always been the most prominent case for demonstrating de-secularization. Students of Islamic civilization dealing with political and social-scientific issues have long been familiar with the rise and growth of political Islam, understood both as an Islamic fundamentalism and a variety of the revolt against the West.

Prior to the shattering assault of September 11, 2001 the application of the notion of religious fundamentalism to the politicization of Islam was nevertheless highly disputed – even among those scholars engaged in Islamic studies and thus professionally familiar with Islam and its civilization. It was considered 'politically incorrect' to look at political Islam as a threat to international security. In the academic literature such concerns were belittled: those raising the issue were accused of being trapped between myth and reality (Esposito 1992), or worse, they were accused of 'Orientalism'. Some Western academics even accused Islamic scholars who were themselves Muslim, descendents of the Islamic nobility (*ashraf* of Damascus), of 'Orientalism' because they addressed political Islam as a threat to international security. It is true that the media coverage of political Islam complicated the matter by unwittingly providing evidence for the suspicion that treatments of religious radicalism in non-Western cultures too often depict 'alien' cultures within a framework of enmity. Nonetheless to shatter myths, it is important to distinguish between Islam and Islamism, 'sensational terms', perhaps, but terms that mark a crucial distinction (Lawrence 1998).

When it comes to political Islam we are clearly dealing with a variety of fundamentalism, i.e. not merely with respect to image, but with respect to reality itself. The Fundamentalism Project of the American Academy of Arts and Sciences was long an exception and a breakthrough in establishing the political and social-scientific study of religious fundamentalism on global grounds. This phenomenon is not restricted to Islam as some biased media coverage had suggested. The findings of this project, published subsequently in five volumes in the years 1991–5 smoothed the way for distinguishing between world religions as a system of belief and the politicization of those religions resulting in religious fundamentalism (Marty and Appleby 1991–5). The findings made clear that the study of fundamentalism is a serious approach dealing with an existing reality, definitely not a constructed one. Despite such cogent arguments, it was deplorable to see many 'politically correct' minded students of Islam dismiss these findings as well as the Fundamentalism Project itself and to see how little impact these five volumes had on Islamic studies in the West.

The situation has changed radically in the light of September 11, although some continue to argue Islam has nothing to do with the pending threat. On this view, the issues to be addressed are fundamentalism and terrorism not touching on Islam as a world-religion. Other authors have insisted that an understanding of Islam is essential to a full comprehension of Islamism. Egytian Professor Hasan Hanafi (1989), for example, argued that *al-usuliyya al-Islamiyya* (Islamic fundamentalism) is precisely the term needed for addressing Islamic revival. Hanafi's usage of the term, fundamentalism/*usuliyya*, has become authoritative in Arabic. In contrast to Hanafi, I see no revival of religion, arguing instead that fundamentalism is an indication of the politicization of Islam in a crisis-ridden age. Others, addressing the issue on global grounds, characterize fundamentalism as the articulation of political opposition to existing political rule and as an indication of the drive to de-Westernize the world within the framework of a 'Revolt against the West' (Bull and Watson 1994, 217–28).

The crisis out of which all fundamentalisms arise – including the Islamic variety – is both a crisis of meaning and a crisis related to political and socio-economic constraints. Dealing with fundamentalism as an outgrowth of the crisis of meaning is a matter of cultural analysis and thus goes beyond the confines of this article. Fundamentalism as a matter of government and politics is the focus of the present article. With respect to Islamic fundamentalism as an expression of a definitely political Islam, I will argue that toppling existing orders is the concern of the fundamentalists. In subscribing to historical sociology the subject matter is being addressed in general as a global phenomenon, but the chapter concentrates on the most significant case of Islamic fundamentalism, a case integrally connected to the predicament of Islam, as a civilization, with modernity (Watt 1988).

In generally depicting religious fundamentalism in a few phrases one can state that fundamentalism results from the politicization of religion and it is based on a claim for establishing a political order on the grounds of divine precepts. Thus, reading of the religious scripture matters for understanding the worldview of the fundamentalists. However, the scriptural reference by the fundamentalists is always highly selective and it projects modern issues into the text. In this understanding of religious fundamentalism as a political and social phenomenon, the subject matter falls within the scope of the study of government and politics in the post-bipolar age. To be sure, in the case of Islam the rise of fundamentalism precedes the fall of the Berlin Wall and the end of bipolarity. This supports the contention made earlier at the outset, namely that the role of religion in global politics and the rise of fundamentalism herald a process much older than the unfolding of post-bipolarity itself.

The case of Islamic fundamentalism

Islamic fundamentalism is the most significant case among all contemporary fundamentalisms. The emergence of Islamic fundamentalism precedes the end of the East–West Conflict and its Cold War and can be traced back to the year 1928 when the first fundamentalist movement in the world of Islam, The Society of the Muslim Brothers, was established (Mitchell 1969). This politicization of Islam included not only the adaptation of general Islamic beliefs in order to develop the concept of Islamic order/government/*Nizam Islami*, but also the specific religious doctrine of jihad.

In his *risalat al-jihad* (essay on jihad) the founder of the Muslim Brotherhood, Hasan al-Banna, lays down the foundations for a new interpretation of jihad as an irregular war conducted as terrorism (al-Banna 1990). No doubt, the concept of jihad as one of irregular war is much older than al-Banna (Kelsay 1993: ch. 5), but linking jihad to terrorism is a new interpretation. In the camps of Bin Laden's al-Qaida in Afghanistan the cited essay of al-Banna was an essential part and parcel of the teaching and training in Islamic jihad against the West and its civilization. The internal al-Qaida manual of jihad, the fundamentalist manifesto, includes this essay.

Between 1928 and 1967 the movement of the Muslim Brotherhood was able to grow the seeds of political Islam and spread them far beyond the boundaries of its country of origin, Egypt. However, prior to 1967 the fundamentalists failed to become a significant mass movement. Given the great appeal of secular ideologies, like Nasserism and Ba'thism, in the Arab world, virtually the core of Islamic civilization, fundamentalism had to remain on the fringe. Like Gamal Abdel Nasser in Egypt other secular Muslim leaders such as Ahmed Sukarno in Indonesia, enjoyed great popularity during this period. Only after the shattering defeat of all Arab armies against the state of Israel in the Six-Day-War of 1967 (Tibi 1998a: chs 3, 4) did political Islam succeed in flourishing (ibid. ch. 12). It presented itself as the ultimate alternative to the *anzimat al-hazima* (regimes of defeat) i.e. to the secular orders of nation-state as the dominant order in the entire world of Islam. In other words: the rise of political Islam (Ayubi 1991) as a variety of the global phenomenon of religious fundamentalism has been related to the call of de-secularization (Tibi 2000) and de-Westernization (Tibi 1995: ch. 6). Both of these processes are closely intertwined.

Hasan al-Banna coined the term *al-Nizam al-Islami* (Islamic system). His contemporary and co-combatant Sayyid Qutb, an intellectual of much higher profile and calibre, established a more powerful understanding of Islam as a proposal for government construed as *hakimiyyat Allah* (God's rule). Qutb prescribes for all Muslims the pursuit of this rule in his book *Ma'alim fi al-Tariq* (*Sign Posts along the Road*). Literally Qutb is providing sign posts for all Muslims within the framework of what he terms a 'World Revolution of Islam' to free the world of *jahilliyya* (pre-Islamic ignorance), a symptom of Western rule (Qutb repr. 1989: 5–10, 201–2). Euben, an expert on fundamentalism, has noted that 'Qutb's prominence seems an accepted fact…Qutb's influence is undisputed' (Euben 1999: 54–5).

Those who decouple Islam and Islamic civilization from Islamism, i.e. the Islamic variety of fundamentalism, insist that theologies in terms of belief in God have nothing to do with politics and government. They suggest that fundamentalists abuse religion, in this case Islam, using it as a pretext for furthering their political and economic concerns only superficially presented as an Islamic agenda. Of course, Islamism is not Islam, but it is misleading to present Islamic fundamentalism as an issue utterly remote to Islam. As all other fundamentalisms, the Islamic variety of this global phenomenon is based on a belief in religion and it is a very influential and powerful interpretation of it. In my survey of the worldview of Islamists (Tibi 1993), I found in interviews with Islamic fundamentalists in a variety of Islamic countries that there is no cynicism involved at all; I was speaking to and dealing with religious people who believe that they, and only they themselves are the 'true believers'. In short, religion is intrinsic to the mind of fundamentalism and not on its surface. Therefore, the argument concerning 'abuse of religion' by fundamentalists is superficial and it does not hold.

Fundamentalism as a quest for a new divine order in opposition to the secular nation-state

Basically every religious fundamentalism is a quest for establishing a new order believed to be the true government of God based on divine precepts. The study of fundamentalism leads to the insight that at issue is a competition between religious and secular order (Juergensmeyer 1993). If we look at the writings of major fundamentalists – for instance in the Islamic case – we see the religious-cultural underpinning of their political argumentation. In Islamic fundamentalism, government is the pivotal issue (al-Awwa 1983; Fahmi 1981). In the politico-religious ideology of Islamic fundamentalists we basically find a concept of order envisaged to challenge and subsequently replace the prevailing Westphalian order of sovereign states, which was created in the aftermath of the Peace of Westphalia 1648 (Watson 1992: ch. 17). According to pre-eminent historian, Charles Tilly: 'over the next three hundred years the Europeans and their descendents managed to impose that state system on the entire world. The recent wave of de-colonization has almost completed the mapping of the globe into that system' (Tilly 1985: 45).

Five years later, Tilly noted that 'Something has changed in the extension of the European state system to the rest of the earth': 'Europeans created a state system that dominated the entire world. We live within that system today. Yet the world outside Europe resembles Europe no more than superficially' (Tilly 1990: 191).

Nation-states in non-Western civilizations are no more than nominal nation-states (Tibi 1990). During the expansion of the West presented as an expansion of international society most parts of Asia and Africa were first colonized. In the course of de-colonization those colonies developed nominally to nation-states. In the world of Islam – being a civilization itself – Islamic provinces succumbed to this process. After the dissolution of the former Ottoman Empire its provinces engaged themselves in an effort at an accommodation to this new environment, that is the international system of nation-states. The Arab regions re-emerged in the shape of a number of nation-states designed along the Western model. The new states were committed to secular Arab nationalism, but they were never free from the existing tension between Islam and the nation-state (Tibi 1997). By applying the term 'nominal nation-state' to these states, I attempt to capture the lack of most of the basic requirements for the formation of a substantial nation-state. In the various regions of Islamic civilization the new states can be adequately described in this manner.

The defeat in the Six-Day-War in 1967 triggered a variety of crises the most important of which has been the crisis of the nation-state. The nominally secular state is being challenged by Islamic fundamentalism. The background of all fundamentalisms in other parts of the world is a similar one. In the Arab part of the Muslim world the existing nation-states have been ridiculed as 'tribes with national flags'. The symbols of the nation-state have been there, but the substance continues to be utterly lacking. Today, the successor of al-Banna and Sayyid Qutb is also an Egyptian: the Muslim Brother Yusuf Qaradawi. This person maintains the tradition of keeping the roots of political Islam in Egypt, but he is now acting in a Gulf state. Rich families of these states use oil-wealth to support fundamentalism financially. It is Qaradawi who first systematically dismissed the introduction of the nation-state into contemporary Islamic civilization as one of the misleading *hulul-mustawrada* (imported solutions). Qaradawi blamed these *hulul mustawrada* (imported solutions) for the defeat of 1967. Since the 1970s he keeps calling for the return of Islam, arguing that only the Islamic solution/*al-hall al-Islami* can provide the needed way out of the impasse of the crisis. In his view, the solution can only be the divine Islamic order (Qaradawi repr. 1980)

As already argued, the roots of Islamic fundamentalism go back to 1928 and the dissemination of the related ideology can be seen as an accompanying phenomenon to the Arab defeat in the Six-Day-War in terms of spill-over effects. Since then Islamic fundamentalism has moved into the entire world of Islam. It is neither Arabo-centric nor a belittling of the impact of the Islamic revolution in Iran to trace Islamic fundamentalism back to a Sunni-Arab state, Egypt. These are the facts. In Turkey, Southeast Asia and also in West Africa I was able to verify the spread of political Islam in combination with the dissemination of the writing of Sayyid Qutb. No doubt, the Iranian revolution contributed to establishing the political belief that the world of the future will be ordered along the line of Islamic precepts. It has successfully demonstrated that Islamists are able to topple a powerful existing order and then establish an Islamic one as 'The government of God' (Benard and Khalilzad 1984). The impact of the Iranian Revolution can be seen mushrooming across most parts of Islamic civilization. As illustrated in the case of North Africa, François Burgat states: 'The revolution of Khomeini breathed life into Islamist movements everywhere' (Burgat 1993: 185). To be clear, breathing life means reinforcing an ongoing process, not causing life in it. The Islamic Revolution in Iran reinforced the unfolding of Islamic fundamentalism but did not cause it.

In my research I confine the impact of the Iranian Revolution to 'demonstration effects'. In addition to confusing causes and effects, Western experts in world affairs often have difficulties in distinguishing between the Sunni and Shi'a parts of Islamic civilization, i.e. between the majority and minority among Muslim peoples. Those scholars of Islamic studies familiar with this distinction are mostly philologists and cultural anthropologists not trained in the study of Politics and International Relations and thus not able to understand what was going on, not to speak of the reluctance of the Orientalists among them to acknowledge the rise of fundamentalism as an expression of a distinctly religio-political Islam. Due to a lack of needed knowledge, the Islamic revolution of Iran was immensely overrated. There were only a few scholars able to understand the failure of political Islam (Roy 1994) as well as the of failure Shi'i-fundamentalists to export the Iranian model of government of God (Tibi 1999a). In the scholarly literature we encounter many interpretive strains among which is the contention of an end of Islamism (Kepel 2000), as well as the mere culturalistic interpretation of what is termed 'Islamic politics' (Eickelman and Piscatori 1996). These views cannot explain Islamic fundamentalism nor its meaning for government and politics. 'Islamic Politics' is not a matter of cultural anthropology.

It is certain that as long as the factors underlying the global rise of fundamentalism continue to be there, the phenomenon itself will be flourishing further. It may be at times combined with setbacks of fundamentalist movements, but these do not indicate the end of the phenomenon nor that it is subsiding. When it specifically comes to Islamic fundamentalism, I maintain:

1   It is not in decline, and therefore strongly disagree with Gilles Kepel (Kepel 2000; see Tibi, introduction to the new 2002 edition of 1998).
2   It continues to grow globally under the impact of its Sunni-Arab origins (Qutb, al-Banna, Qaradawi, Bin Laden and whoever his successors may be).
3   Fundamentalism continues to flourish within what is called the 'New Cold War' (Juergensmeyer 1993) against the secular nation-state, i.e. it is an indication of a quest for a new pattern of government.
4   Islamic fundamentalism matters to the West not only on global grounds, but also through Islamic migration to Europe and North America – to the West itself (Tibi 2001, 2002a). In other words: Fundamentalism matters to the politics of multiculturalism (Tibi 2002b).

Issue areas in the study of Islamic fundamentalism and their historical background

Having addressed fundamentalism as a global phenomenon, outlined it in general, and clearly looked at it on the Islamic case both in world historical and world political terms, it is now imperative to concretely depict its substance. By this I mean what is called an *hall-Islami* (Islamic solution) with regard to government and politics. Islamists raise the issue on a global scale. For a preliminary understanding of this worldview as well as the revival and politicization of Islamic doctrines and precepts, an outline of the historical background often denied by the 'politically-correct' minded scholars is needed. By this I mean the tensions between Islam and the West arising in particular from different and rival understandings of how political order has to be shaped.

The pending tensions have their historical grounds and without taking them into account the meaning of Islamic fundamentalism relevant to government and politics cannot be understood properly. All fundamentalisms (Jewish, Hindu, etc., see Marty and Appleby, vols I and III) claim an order, but only Islamic fundamentalism, being based on a politicized universalism, claims a world order. It was Islam and no other civilization before the West that triggered a process of a – even though not fully fulfilled – globalization. The 'Islamicate' (Hodgson 1974: vol. I) was considered to be the order of the world. In this pursuit, Arab Muslims first engaged themselves in the *Futuhat* (i.e. openings) wars of jihad from the 7th century onwards. The goal was to expand their civilization (Hodgson 1974: vol. I). The Turks continued this endeavour after the Arab decline. They were however stopped by the rise of the West and its military revolution 1500–1800 (Parker 1988; Tibi 1999: chs 1, 4 and 6).

There is a clear link between the presented history and Islamic fundamentalism of the present day. Islamic fundamentalists blame Christianity and the West for the decline of the Islamic jihad and set out in a new effort to resume the Islamization of the world. They make clear that a world in peace and prosperity can only emerge under an Islamic rule. Therefore Sayyid Qutb called for an Islamic world revolution (Qutb reprinted 1992: 172) to free humanity from the ill-designed rule of the West.

In their endeavour, Islamic fundamentalists revive some Islamic concepts, but give them, in terms of 'Invention of Tradition' (Hobsbawm 1983), an utterly new meaning. The Islamicate was a dominant civilization, but definitely not a world order. This is clearly a modern concept being read into the Islamic history. The concepts that are currently used by Islamic fundamentalists and accorded a new meaning include:

- Islamic order/*Nizam Islami*
- *Sharia*/divine law or moral code
- War and peace (world order)
- Jihad/self exertion or an Islamic war of expansion in its Koranic understanding, but currently used to mean terrorism legitimized as jihadism.

Means of politics in an Islamist agenda

In this section I shall briefly outline the basic goals of Islamism, the Islamic variety of fundamentalism. The concepts pursued by Islamists came from the Islamic past, but their present meaning is much different. In contrasting both, i.e. traditional understanding and the new meaning an effort will be made to shed light on the tactics and policies employed in the agenda of Islamic fundamentalism.

Islamic order: The caliphate or what else?

Foremost among the concerns covered by the formula *al-Islam huwa al-Hall* (Islam is the solution), ranks the claim for a *nizam Islami* (Islamic system of government). This however is the only Islamist concern not underpinned by any earlier Islamic tradition. Within traditional Islam, 'the Islamicate' (Hodgson 1974) is similar to the caliphate (Arnold 1924), the expression of an Islamic order headed by a successor of the prophet, i.e. by a caliph. A caliph leads the *umma* not only as a religious, but also as a political Imam (Tibi 1996a). Contemporary Islamic fundamentalists acting as Islamists do not use this language, but instead coin a neo-Islamic term: *Nizam Islami*/Islamic system of government in neo-Arabic, or *hukumat-e-Islami* in Farsi. This government is committed to the *Sharia* and runs an Islamic state.

The early language of contemporary political Islam also developed the neo-Arabic formula, *al-Islam din wa daula* (Islam is a unity of state and religion), which supports the claim for an Islamic state representing an Islamic system of government. Although the Koran includes the term *hakamah*, in the old meaning of 'to judge', it contains no notion at all of government/*hukumah*, or state/*daula* or system/*nizam*. These Arabic terms do not occur in the Koran nor are they common in classical Arabic. W. C. Smith notes that the term *nizam* or system 'does not occur in the Koran, nor indeed does any word from this root....The explicit notion that life should be...ordered according to a system...and that it is the business of Islam to provide such a system seems to be a modern idea' (Smith 1978: 117). At issue is an *invention* of tradition.

In fact, exactly on this issue we are in a position to distinguish between common Muslims and Islamic fundamentalists. We can identify where a Muslim stands depending on the answer given to the question whether or not Islam provides a political system for the rule and for ordering all aspects of public life. In short, Islamism is not the religion of Islam, but a concept of government based on politicizing Islam, i.e., a variety of religious fundamentalism. This concept is modern, an invention of tradition, which does not even make use of the traditional language of the caliphate, the classical Islamic order. All other varieties of fundamentalism do share a similar concern, i.e. the establishing of a political order.

Sharia

In monotheist religions and also in those with a written heritage (e.g. the place of the *Veda* in neo-Hinduism), the fundamentalist ideology makes a strong reference to the concept of *divine law*. This is paramount in Islamic fundamentalism. The only verse in the Koran in which the term *Sharia* occurs is in *al-Jathia* (sure 45, verse 18) with the phrasing *thumma ja'alnaka ala Sharia mina al-amr fa attabi'uha* (and we have shown you a path of conduct you ought to follow). This is not a concept of law *per se*, and in an open-minded interpretation, this *Sharia* would mean no more and no less than a moral code in the Koranic sense of forbidding evil and enjoining good. In my view, the Koran does not include a legal system; any such claim involves a reading into the Koran of contemporary concerns. In fact, the interpretation of *Sharia* as a divine legal system is post-Koranic, emerging in the eighth century, i.e. almost one century after the conclusion of Islamic revelation. This interpretation developed within the framework of the rise of the *Madhabib* (Islamic legal schools) diversifying *Sunna*-Islam (Coulson 1964: ch. 3). Again, these historical facts support the view that the *Sharia* is a post-Koranic construction. At any rate and regardless of whether or not the *Sharia* is a legal system, it is true that in Islamic history there is a tradition of divine law on which fundamentalists draw. We have however to distinguish between two different variations:

First: The concerns of the *Sharia*-judges/Kadis revolved around issues of civil law, such as marriage, divorce, inheritance and the like. With very few exceptions, the foremost of which are Ibn Taimiyya and al-Mawardi (Tibi 1996a: ch. 5), we find no political interpretation of the *Sharia*. The greatest authority in the study of Islamic law, Joseph Schacht, makes clear that in Umayyad and Abbassid Islam (seventh to thirteenth century) there was a separation between *Siyasa* in the meaning of state administration, and *Sharia* in the meaning of sacred law. Schacht states: 'As a result of all this, a double administration of justice, one religious and exercised by the Kadi on the basis of *Sharia*, the other secular and exercised by the Siyasa, has prevailed in practically the whole of the Islamic world' (Schacht 1964: 54–5).

Second: In the call for *tatbiq al-Sharia* (implementation of *Sharia*) pronounced by Islamic fundamentalists, we see the entire Islamic history of separating *Siyasa* and *Sharia* being fully disregarded. The return to Islam as *al-Hall* ('the solution') is cast as a 're-implementation' of the *Sharia* believed to be suspended by the incursion of Western civilization into the world of Islam, as if Islamic rulers had always complied with the *Sharia*, which they never did. The claim to de-Westernization (Tibi 1995 and 1995b) is articulated as the call for *tatibiq al-Sharia*, a very concrete prescription to abolish positive law and all patterns of human legislation, because God/*Allah* is the only legislator.

The Islamic reformer Mohammed Said al-Ashmawi has uncovered the confusion between the *fiqh* (sacred law) designed by Islamic scribes and *Sharia* (conduct prescribed by God) (Ashmawi 1983). Conflating these two concepts, Islamic legal scholars present their views as God's rules. Similarly, Islamic fundamentalists conflate these terms when they preach the establishment of an Islamic state as God's will. In recent history such fundamentalist appeals to sacred law have surfaced equally in Shi'i Iran, Sunni Sudan, as well as predominantly Sunni Afghanistan when it was under the rule of the Taliban. In the judgement of experts each of these *Sharia*-states are to be viewed as a new pattern of religious dictatorship, definitely not as legal order. Elsewhere I have shown that the revival of the *Sharia* along with its politicization as state law and the re-establishment of Islamic learning are major instruments of Islamic fundamentalism (Tibi 2001: chs 7, 8).

It is impossible to escape the conclusion that Islamic fundamentalism is an expression of a religiously legitimized dictatorship. This is also true for all other varieties of fundamentalism (Jewish, Hindu, etc.). Thus fundamentalism stands in opposition to 'modern democracy...i.e., democracy of the nation-state' (Huntington 1991: 13). Inasmuch as all varieties of fundamentalism are directed against the nation-state and its secular order (Tibi 1998: chs 5, 8; Juergensmeyer 1993), fundamentalist governments that come into being keep their countries outside the third wave of democratization.

War and peace

In contrast to the Kantian vision of a democratic world peace, fundamentalists promote the clash of civilizations through their understanding of war and peace. Islam views itself as a religion of peace. Indeed, the abode of Islam is characterized as *dar al-salam* (house of peace). In contrast, however, non-Islamic territory is considered to be *dar al-harb* (the abode of war). The term *harb* applies only to non-Muslims, for Muslims wage jihad not war. Although Islam invokes a distinction between jihad and war, within a broader frame jihad is war, because every use of force is war. To support this argument, it is important to note several points.

1   While it is true that the terms, war and peace, have particular referents in Islam, these technical meanings have nothing to do with jihadist fundamentalism of our time.
2   Students of international relations and history define the use of force on an international level as war. Thus as a matter of historical record, the Islamic expansion between the 7th and 17th century is classified as a chapter in the history of war (Tibi 1999), even though Muslims do not view this expansion as a war, but rather as a *futuhat*/opening the world for Islam's vision of world peace under the Islamic banner (Tibi 1996).

Before I explain the relevance of this classical understanding of war and peace in Islam for efforts to deal with fundamentalism, I have to denote a third realm in Islamic thought on war and peace: *dar al-Ahd* (abode of contract). In the case of Islamic weakness, Muslims are entitled to make a peace contract with their enemies, however, not an enduring peace and only on a temporary basis. This division of the world in three areas of peace, war and temporary contract has never been revised by a recognized Islamic authority, although it has always been inconsistent with existing realities in history and in the present. As the Islamic scholar Armanazi has noted, there have been pragmatic adjustments to realities, but no conceptual revisions (Armanazi 1930). More importantly, however, these Islamic concepts do not apply at all to the practices of contemporary Islamic states.

Formally, all 56 existing Islamic states grouped in the Organisation of Islamic Conference (OIC) adjust themselves to the prevailing Westphalian system of states and do not challenge this order. In contrast to the ruling Islamic elites in these 56 states, the emerging counter-elites of Islamic fundamentalists (Tibi 1999b) revive the Islamic concept of peace and war and view the relationship between Islam and the West in terms of a state of war. We not only find this rhetoric in the pronouncements of Bin Laden and al-Qaida (Bergen 2001; Bodansky 1999), but references to the use of force in terms of 'irregular war' or *jihadism* surface in all kinds of Islamisms (see the new introduction of 2002 to Tibi 1998). The assault of September 11 was not the first, but rather the most prominent act of irregular war in the name of Islam, i.e. jihad-Islamism. This leads us to the final fundamentalist new interpretation of classical Islamic concepts.

Jihad

The Koran distinguishes between jihad in the understanding of self-exertion and *qital* (fight) – use of force, but ranks the latter also within the overall concept of jihad. This means that the Koran allows violence, but it establishes clear limitations on the use of violence (Tibi 1996). Among the prohibited violence is any ambush fighting. It follows then that 'fundamentalist terrorism' (O'Balance 1997) cannot be legitimized as jihad. Nevertheless, Islamic fundamentalists view their terrorism as being an act of Islamic jihad. We should therefore distinguish between classical jihad in Islam and jihadism in the present. The latter is clearly terrorism.

Classical jihad was not only religious exertion of Muslims, but also wars of expansion for the spread of Islam. Therefore, the Islamic early *futuhat* (openings) were a war of jihad. However, the new concept of jihad as jihadism means terrorism. As earlier shown this can be traced back to the essay of al-Banna already cited. The most prominent contemporary case is the jihadism of Bin Laden and his al-Qaida.

Not only for fairness, but also because this article is on fundamentalism in general, it is imperative to note that we also find in all other fundamentalisms the combination of religion and violence. It is an expression of Islamophobia to describe Islam as a religion of violence while overlooking this combination in other religious fundamentalisms. Mark Juergensmeyer (2000) has coined the term 'Terror in the Mind of God' and documented this mindset in different religions. Thus, Islamist jihadism as resort to violence and use of force in an irregular war, is only a case in point. It sustains efforts to establish an Islamic order first on domestic ground and later on an international level. The remote goal is an Islamic world order. This concept is a new reading of Islamic order in that jihadism conveys a new, utterly untraditional understanding of jihad. Despite similarities among various forms of fundamentalism with respect to the combination of religion and violence, however, it is clear that this internationalism is unique to Islamic fundamentalism and distinguishes it from all other varieties. All terrorist groups in the world of Islam appeal to jihad in many ways in their rhetoric and the scope for their jihadism is Islamic internationalism.

Conclusions

Among the signs of the post-bipolar stage of world politics is the return of religion and the challenge of de-secularization heralding a post-secular and anti-Western development (Haynes 1998 and *Millennium* issue, vol. 29, 3/2000). These new developments are heralded by the rise of many varieties of fundamentalisms basically in non-Western civilizations, but also in Western Christianity. The Islamic case is the most serious variety of this politicization of religion, for Islam is – like Christianity – a universal world religion (see Sharma 1993: ch. Islam). Given the fact that Western civilization is the only secular one among world civilizations (Braudel 1994), we need to relate the return of religion as a factor in global politics (Haynes 1998) to the return of civilizations to world politics (Tibi 1995; Huntington 1996). However, civilizations do not occur as actors in world affairs, they are embedded in the existing system of sovereign states. There are only a few fundamentalist governments in the world. Fundamentalists primarily act as non-state actors (e.g. al-Qaida).

In summarizing the findings of the present article it can be stated that fundamentalism is an issue of government and politics and not an indication of a renaissance of religion. It is Islamic fundamentalists – and not common Muslims as Prof. Huntington (1996: 209–18) suggested – who are calling for a clash of civilizations.

Unlike Jewish or Hindu fundamentalists, who restrict their political visions to their call for a Jewish (Erez-Israel) or Hindu (Hindustan) state, Islamic fundamentalists reject the present international system and view the envisioned Islamic state only as a step on the way towards a universal Islamic world order. Consequently, the clash of civilizations not only takes place between politicized Islam and the Western world order, but within the Islamic civilization itself. Islamic fundamentalists are a minority, though a very vocal, well organized, and violent one, within Islamic civilization. The political battle is on-going within Islamic civilization (e.g. in Turkey between Kemalists and Islamists).

In dealing with fundamentalism the pending issue pertinent to all varieties of the phenomenon is: What government and what politics for the future? Kant's vision of a world peace suggests that only democratic governments are in a position to engage themselves in what is called a 'democratic peace' (Russet 1993). All varieties of religious fundamentalism share the opposition to the secular democratic nation-state and envisage a divine order for the future. In recalling history, we are reminded that it was only the secular Peace of Westphalia (Miller 1990: ch. 2) that ended wars of religions in Western Europe. Keeping this fact in mind, it is foreseeable that the victory of Islamic, Jewish, Hindi, Buddhist, Sikh or other fundamentalisms would lead to governments of religious dictatorship like the one in Iran. Claiming to be based upon divine politics, such regimes draw stark divisions between the godly and the ungodly and in so doing shut down any option for a democratic peace. In the long run, we will see fundamentalisms creating a version of 'The Coming Anarchy' (Kaplan 2000).

The case of Islam clearly shows that fundamentalism is a threat not only to world peace, but also to Muslims themselves. (Tibi 2000). Clearly, opposition to and rejection of the policy preferences and government options of fundamentalists are not an indication of xenophobia. In the case of Islamic fundamentalism it is neither Islamophobia nor an instance of Orientalism to look at this issue with a critical mind. The late Ernest Gellner was among the few Western scholars who understood fundamentalism properly. Before he passed away, Gellner took great pains to revive Enlightenment against the challenge of fundamentalism. In his last book Gellner wrote: 'Religious fundamentalism…gives psychic satisfaction to many…It is at present quite specifically persuasive and influential within one particular tradition, namely Islam' (Gellner 1992: 84).

Gellner argued that Islamic fundamentalism, like all other fundamentalisms, is based on the idea of a divine message as a solution to the crisis of modernity and as an alternative to the nation-state in the realms of politics and government. To the extent that the fundamentalist message 'declares itself to be authoritative, final and self-confirming …'., Gellner suggested that this message is 'morally as well as intellectually unacceptable' (Gellner 1992: 84, 96). For this reason, he called for 'a rival counter-model', based on reviving Enlightenment on new grounds.

A dialogue between fundamentalism and Enlightenment rationalism is not possible, much as a dialogue between neo-absolutism and relativism is not feasible. Mistaken notions of reconciliation between such opposed conceptions of government and politics illuminate what the Dutch Erasmus-Foundation called 'The Limits of Pluralism' (1994). Fundamentalism and democratic government are incompatible. For this reason, the acceptance of fundamentalism in the name of tolerance is seen by the French writer, Jean-François Revel as an indication of what he calls 'democracy against itself', an altogether inadequate stance in dealing with the threat posed by fundamentalism (Revel 1993: ch. 12). In conclusion, it is not Islam or any other religion, but religious fundamentalisms that create a threat to world peace resulting from the clash of civilizations.

References

Armanazi, Najib (1930) *al-Shar' al-Duvali fi al-Islam* repr. as *International Law in Islam*, London: El-Rayyes Books, 1990.

Arnold, Thomas, Sir (1924) *The Caliphate*, London: repr. 1965.

Aron, Raymond (1962) *Paix et guerre entre les nations*, Paris: Calmann-Lévy.

Ashmawi, Mohammed Said (1983) *Usul al-Shari'a* (Origins of the Sharia), Cairo: Madbuli.

al-Awwa, Salim (repr. 1983) *Fi al-Nizam al-Siyyasi lil-dawla al-Islamiyya* (On the Political System of the Islamic State), Cairo: al-Makthab al-Misri al-hadith.

al-Awwa, Mohammed (1983) *fi al-Nizam al-Siyasi lil al-Dawla al-Islamiyya* (On the Political System of Islamic State), 6th edn, Cairo.

Ayubi, Nazih (1991) *Political Islam*, London: Routledge.

al-Banna, Hasan (1990) *Majmu'at Rasail al-Imam al-Shahid*/collected essays of the martyr Imamm Cairo: Dar al-Da'wa. Herein the essay on jihad, pp. 271–92.

Barber, Benjamin R. (1995) *Jihad vs. McWorld*, New York: Ballantine Books.

Bergen, Peter (2001) *Holy War Inc. Inside the Secret World of Osama bin Laden*, New York: Free Press.

Bernard, Cheryl and Khalilzad, Zalmay (1984) *The Government of God. Iran's Islamic Republic*, New York: Columbia University Press.

Bodansky, Yossef (1999) *Bin Laden. The Man who Declared War on America*, Rocklin, CA: Forum.

Braudel, Fernand (1994) *A History of Civilizations*, London: Penguin Books.

Bull, Hedley (1977) *The Anarchical Society. A Study of Order in World Politics*, New York: Columbia University Press.

Bull, Hedley and Watson, Adam (1984) (eds) *The Expansion of International Society*, Oxford: Clarendon Press.

Burgat, François (1993) *The Islamic Movement in North Africa*, Austin, TX: The University of Texas.

Chase-Dunn, Christopher (1989) *Global Formation*, Cambridge, MA: Basil Blackwell.

Coulson, N. J. (1964) *A History of Islamic Law*, Edinburgh: University of Edinburgh Press.

Eickelman, Dale and Piscatori, James (1996) *Muslim Politics*, Princeton, NJ: Princeton University Press.

Erasmus Foundation (1994) *The Limits of Pluralism. Neo-Absolutisms and Relativism*, Amsterdam: Praemium Erasianum Foundation – with contributions by E. Gellner, G. Geertz and B. Tibi.

Esposito, John (1992) *The Islamic Threat. Myth or Reality*, New York: Oxford University Press.

Euben, Roxanne (1999) *Enemy in the Mirror. Islamic Fundamentalism and the Limits of Modern Rationalism*, Princeton: Princeton University Press.

Fahmi, Mustafa Abu Zaid (1981) *Fan al-Hukm fi al-Islam* (The Art of Government in Islam), Cairo: al-Maktab al-Masri al-Hadith.

Gellner, Ernest (1992) *Postmodernism, Reason and Religion*, London: Routledge.

Giddens, Anthony (1987) *The Nation-State and Violence*, Berkeley: University of California Press.

Gress, David (1998) *From Plato to NATO. The Idea of the West and its Opponents*, New York: Free Press.

Habermas, Jürgen (1987) *The Philosphical Discourse of Modernity*, Cambridge, MA: MIT-Press.

Hanafi, Hasan (1989) *al-Usuliyya al-Islamiyya* (Islamic Fundamentalism) Cairo.

Haynes, Jeff (1998) *Religion in Global Politics*, London: Longman.

Hobsbawm, Eric and Ranger, Terence (eds) (1983) *The Invention of Tradition*, Cambridge, UK: Cambridge University Press; repr. 1996.

Hodgson, Marshall G. S. (1974) *The Venture of Islam. Conscience and History in a World Civilisation*, 3 vols, Chicago: Chicago University Press.

Huntington, Samuel P. (1991) *The Third Wave: Democratization in the Twentieth Century*, Norman and London: University of Oklahoma Press.

—— (1996) *The Clash of Civilizations*, New York: Simon & Schuster.

Juergensmeyer, Mark (1993) *The New Cold War? Religious Nationalism Confronts the Secular State*, Berkeley: University of California Press.

—— (2000) *Terror in the Mind of God. The Global Rise of Religious Violence*, Berkeley: University of California Press.

Kant, Immanuel (repr. 1979) *Entwurf eines demokratischen Friedens*, Frankfurt: Suhrkamp Verlag.

Kaplan, Robert D. (2000) *The Coming Anarchy*, New York: Random House.

Kelsay, John (1993) *Islam and War*, Louisville, KY: John Knox Press.

Kepel, Gilles (1994) *A l'Ouest d'Allah*, Paris: Editions du Seuil.

—— (2000) *Jihad. Expansion et Déclin de l'Islamisme*, Paris: Gallimard.

Laue, von Theodore (1987) *The World Revolution of Westernization*, New York: Oxford University Press.

Lawrence, Bruce (1989) *Defenders of God. The Fundamentalist Revolt against the Modern Age*, San Francisco: Harper & Row.

—— (1998) *Shattering the Myth. Islam beyond Violence*, Princeton, NJ: Princeton University Press.

Marty, Martin and Appleby, Scott (eds) (1991–5) *The Fundamentalism Project*, 5 volumes [vol. I (1991) *Fundamentalism Observed*, vol. II (1993) *Fundamentalism and Society*, vol. III (1993) *Fundamentalism and the State*, vol. IV (1994) *Accounting for Fundamentalism*, vol. V (1995) *Comprehending Fundamentalism*] Chicago: Chicago University Press.

Miller, Lynn H. (1990) *Global Order*, Boulder, CO: Westview Press.

Mitchell, Richard P. (1969) *The Society of the Muslim Brothers*, London: Oxford University Press.

O'Ballence, Edgar (1997) *Islamic Fundamentalist Terrorism. The Iranian Connection 1979–95*, New York: New York University Press.

Parker, Geoffrey (1988) *The Military Revolution and the Rise of the West 1500–1800*, Cambridge, UK: Cambridge University Press.

al-Qaradawi, Yusuf (repr. 1980) *al-Hulul al-Mustawrada* (The Imported Solutions), Beirut: al-Risalah.

Qutb, Sayyid (repr. 1989) *Ma'alim fi al-Tariq* (Road Signs) Cairo: Dar al-Shuruq.

—— (repr. 1992) *al-Salam al-Alami wa al-Islam* (World Peace and Islam) Cairo: Dar al-Shuruq.

Revel, Jean-François (1993) *Democracy Against Itself*, New York: Free Press.

Roy, Olivier (1994) *The Failure of Political Islam*, Cambridge, MA: Harvard University Press.

Russet, Bruce (1993) *Grasping the Democratic Peace. Principles for a Post-Cold War World*, Princeton, NJ: Princeton University Press.

Schacht, Joseph (1964) *An Introduction to Islamic Law*, Oxford: Clarendon.

Scharma (ed.) (1993) *Our Religions*, San Francisco: Harper & Row.

Smith, Wilfried C. (1978) *The Meaning and End of Religion*, San Francisco: Harper & Row.

Tibi, Bassam (1990) 'The Simultaneity of the Unsimultaneous. Tribes and Imposed Nation-States', in Khoury and Kostiner (eds) *Tribes and State Formation in the Middle East*, Berkeley: University of California Press.

—— (1993) 'The Worldview of Sunni-Arab Fundamentalists', in Marty and Appleby (eds), *The Fundamentalism Project*, vol. II, *Fundamentalism and Society*, 73–102.

—— (1995) 'Culture and Knowledge. The Fundamentalist Claim to De-Westenization', in *Theory Culture and Society*, vol. 12, issue 1: 1–24.

—— (1995a) 'Fundamentalism', in *Encyclopedia of Democracy*, Washington DC: vol II: 507–10.

—— (1995b) *Krieg der Zivilisationen*, Hamburg: Hoffmann & Campe Verlag, new enlarged edition as paperback München: Heyne-Verlag.

—— (1996) 'War and Peace in Islam', in Terry Nardin (ed.) *The Ethics of War and Peace*, Princeton, NJ: Princeton University Press; repr. 1998.

—— (1996a) *Der wahre Imam*, Munich: Piper Verlag; repr. 1998 and 2001.

—— (1997) *Arab Nationalism: Between Islam and the Nation-State*, 3rd enlarged edn, New York: St Martin's Press.

—— (1998) *The Challenge of Fundamentalism*, Berkeley: University of California Press, updated edn 2002 with new introduction on September 11.

—— (1998a) *Conflict and War in the Middle East. From Interstate War to New Security*, 2nd edn, New York: St Martin's Press.

—— (1999) *Kreuzzug und Djihad. Der Islam und die christliche Welt*, München: Bertelsmann Press; paperback edn Goldmann Verlag, 2001.

—— (1999a) 'The Failed Export of Islamic Revolution', in Frederic Grare (ed.) *Islamism and Security*, Geneva: PSIS Special Studies, vol. 4: 63–102.

—— (1999b) 'The Fundamentalist Challenge to Secular Order in the Middle East', in *The Fletcher Forum*, vol. 23, issue 1: 191–210.

—— (2000) 'Secularization and De-Secularization in Islam', in *Religion, Staat und Gesellschaft*, vol. 1, issue 1: 95–117.

—— (2000a) *Fundamentalismus im Islam. Eine Gefahr für den Weltfrieden*, Darmstadt: Primus Verlag.

—— (2000b) 'Post-Bipolar Order in Crisis: The Challenge of Politicised Islam', in *Millennium*, vol. 29, issue 3: 843–59.

—— (2001) *Islam between Culture and Politics*, New York: St Martin's Press.

——(2002a) *Muslim Migrants in Europe*, in N. Al-Sayyad and M. Castells, *Muslim Europe or Euro-Islam*, Lanham and Berkeley: 31–52.

——(2002b) *Islamische Zuwanderung. Die gescheiterte Integration*, Munich.

——(2002c) Habermas and the Return of the Sacred, in: *Religion, Staat, Gesellschaft*, vol.3 (2002), issue 20.

Tilly, Charles (ed.) (1985) *The Formation of the National States in Western Europe*, Princeton, NJ: Princeton University Press.

—— (1990) *Coercion, Capital and European States*, Cambridge, MA: Basil Blackwell.

Watt, W. M. (1988) *Islamic Fundamentalism and Modernity*, London: Routledge.

Watson, Adam (1992) *The Evolution of International Society*, London: Routledge.

PART IV

CONTEMPORARY POLITICAL SYSTEMS

14

LIBERAL DEMOCRACIES

G. Bingham Powell

Liberal democracies are identified by an implicit bargain between the representative governments and their citizens and by a specific arrangement that regulates that bargain. The bargain is that the government's legitimacy, its expectation of obedience to its laws, is dependent on its claim to be doing what the citizens want it to do. The organized arrangement that regulates this bargain of legitimacy is the competitive political election.

In competitive political elections voters can choose from among alternative candidates. In practice at least two organized political parties that have some chance of winning seem to be needed to make choices meaningful. The people are allowed basic freedoms of speech, press, assembly and organization so that they can form and express preferences about public policies. Using these freedoms, all citizens can participate meaningfully in the competitive elections that choose the policy-makers. Such electoral participation means that the people participate indirectly in the general direction of the public policies of the society. Participation in policy-making by the people is the fundamental meaning of democracy (Cohen 1971: ch. 1).

A number of liberal democracies also make some occasional use of direct citizen involvement in policy-making through the referendum, a popular vote on a proposed law (Butler and Ranney 1978). However, even in Switzerland, where the device is used more frequently than elsewhere, most legislation is made through the representative institutions.

The term 'liberal' in 'liberal democracy' draws attention to two related features of these political systems. First, their claim to democracy rests on responsiveness to the wishes of the citizens, not to some vision of citizens' best interests as defined by the rulers or by some ideological system. Second, the wishes of a majority are not to override all the political and civil rights of the minorities. At a minimum these rights include the political freedom to organize and participate. They may also include rights of due process, privacy and personal property, although liberal democratic theorists are less unanimous on the boundaries of these rights. The 'liberal' and the 'democratic' elements in liberal democracy may be in tension if citizen majorities favour policies that curtail political and civil rights. More often the two elements support each other; each is an essential component of liberal democracy.

Historical and contemporary examples of liberal democracy

Liberal democracy is primarily a phenomenon of the twentieth century. In the nineteenth century, only the USA, France and Switzerland had approached universal manhood suffrage by the 1870s; the vote for women came even later. Using quite loose standards of voter eligibility, there were about nine democracies among forty-eight independent nations in 1902. After the First World War internal pressures from social groups and international emulation led to a spread of both representative assemblies (Gerlich 1973: 94–113) and the suffrage (Rokkan 1961: 132–52). By the mid 1920s there were perhaps twenty-two democracies among the sixty-five independent nations then in existence. Some of these, most notably Weimar Germany, collapsed in the turmoil of the worldwide economic depression of the subsequent decade. Others were seized by the aggressive dictatorships in 1938–42, further reducing the proportion of democracies. Following the victory of the allied powers in the Second World War and the break-up of the European colonial empires, there was a new surge of liberal democratic practices.

The number of liberal democracies waxed and waned from the 1950s through the 1970s, although gradually increasing with the number of independent states. Many newly independent Third World nations (such as Nigeria, Ghana and Pakistan) began as democracies, but were unable to stabilize their political systems. Some well-established democracies were overthrown (Chile and Uruguay in 1973, for example), while some authoritarian regimes were replaced by democracies (for example Spain in 1977). Several states (such as Greece, Turkey and Argentina) experienced both democratic and authoritarian interludes. Various analyses of the 1960s and 1970s placed the number of stable contemporary democracies between thirty and forty, somewhat less than one-quarter of the world's independent national governments (Dahl 1971; Powell 1982a). In the 1980s a 'third wave' of democratization (Huntington 1991) brought increasing freedom of information, organization and electoral competition to Latin America, Eastern Europe and the Pacific rim.

In 1989 a spectacular movement towards full liberal democracy took place in the previously tightly controlled regimes of Poland, Hungary, East Germany and Czechoslovakia. The break-up of the Soviet Union in 1991 encouraged liberalization and democratization in many of the successor states particularly in the Baltic region, eventually extending the proportion of fully free liberal democracies to more than a third of the nations of the world and contributing to the presence of formally competitive, but variously flawed, electoral regimes in another 40 per cent (Karatnycky 2001). In the 1990s no region of the world was completely untouched by continuing democratization, but the failures of electoral regimes in states such as Pakistan and Peru, as well as in many African states, limited the aggregate results.

Studies of the processes of liberal democracy have been dominated by analyses of the nations of Western Europe and North America (including Costa Rica and the English-speaking Caribbean), Japan, Australia, New Zealand, India and Venezuela, plus scattered small states. However, the last decade has seen an explosion of analyses of the introduction and stabilization (or failure) of liberal democracy in Latin America, Eastern Europe and Asia.

206

Major variants of liberal democracy

The detailed arrangements by which contemporary liberal democracies choose policy-makers and make policies are varied and complex. Various analysts focus on different features in constructing 'variants' of liberal democracies: majoritarian or inclusive policy-making rules, presidential or parliamentary executives, single member district or proportional representation election laws, two-party or multi-party competition, corporatist or pluralist interest groups.

Constitutional organization: decision rules

In stable democracies there is agreement on a 'constitution' (whether a single written document or a set of practices and statutes) that specifies how laws must be made (the 'decision rule') and how the makers are to be chosen. The most fundamental conceptual property of any stable decision rule is its degree of inclusiveness: what part of the membership must agree before a policy is accepted. In a pure dictatorship, the decision rule would be that one individual (the dictator) decides all the policies. In a majoritarian system, the decision rule is that 50 per cent plus one must agree on a policy before it is accepted. In a completely consensual system, the decision rule is unanimity: everyone must agree to a policy before it can be adopted.

Democratic theorists agree that dictatorships and all decision rules requiring the assent of only a small minority are not compatible with the concept of democracy. Most would agree that complete unanimity is impractical if any policies are to be made. They are divided, however, on whether a simple majority or some more inclusive rule is preferable (Dahl 1989, chs 10, 11.) In theory, we expect that the majoritarian form would be more efficient at making policy, but the consensual form would be more protective of the rights of minorities (Buchanan and Tulloch 1962).

The fused executive and legislative power in a basic parliamentary system, such as that of Britain, is in many ways the simplest form of decision rule; a government in control of the lower house of parliament need not share power with other institutions or political opponents. However, most democracies embed their basic decision rules in varied and complex constitutional arrangements, which can be understood as requiring the policy-makers to secure in various ways the consent of more than a simple majority of citizens (Dahl 1989: chs 10–11; Lijphart 1999.)

Many democracies explicitly require application of a more inclusive decision rule for changing the constitution itself (Lijphart 1999: 216–23). Such rules range from a two-thirds vote in the national legislature to elaborate ratification by regional units, as in the American requirement of ratification by three-quarters of the states. Others may require more inclusive support for some particular legislation, such as treaty approval (the USA) issues given explicit constitutional status (such as ethnic or religious relations), or even raising new taxes (Finland).

Moreover, even in the case of ordinary legislation, a variety of kinds of institutional arrangements are widely used, individually or in combination, to increase the inclusiveness of the policy-making process. Among these are strong legislative committees, bicameralism, judicial review, and federalism. Strong committee systems that give committees power in drafting laws and require proportional sharing of committee chairs with opposition parties usually make it necessary for government majorities to take greater account of minority oppositions (Strom 1990; Powell 2000: ch. 2.) Constitutional rules that share power between two legislative houses imply wider bargaining if policies are to be made when different parties control different institutions. Judicial review has become an increasingly widely used, although sometimes controversial, process through which governing majorities may be restrained by special constitutional courts or councils. Power may also be dispersed through federalism, in which policy-making power is shared between a national government representing the citizens as a whole and representatives of geographic subunits. Federalism and bicameralism may be combined, and sometimes further supported by judicial review, if one of the legislative houses primarily represents the regions or regional governments, as in Australia, Germany and the USA (Lijphart 1999: chs 10–12).

The best-known and most fiercely disputed empirical distinction in democratic constitutions is between parliamentary and presidential variants. These alternatives specify the relationship between the assembly, which represents the people and has primary authority to make the laws, and the executive, which has authority to carry out the laws. In the parliamentary systems of most West European nations, the chief executive, the prime minister, is chosen by the legislature and can be removed by it in a vote of confidence. These arrangements encourage party cohesion in the legislature (Huber 1996; Bowler, Farrell and Katz 1999). The executive may dominate the legislature through control of a disciplined majority of legislators, but the two are closely fused. In presidential systems, such as those of the USA and most Latin American nations, the legislature and the chief executive, who is also head of state, are independently elected and have separate resources for shaping decision making. The balance between them will depend on the specific powers of each, as well as interconnections of party control (Shugart and Carey 1992; Carey and Shugart 1998). When party control is divided, these systems will become less majoritarian and require broader coalitions. France and Finland provide cases of mixed 'semi-presidential' regimes (Duverger 1980), which have also been widely emulated in the new democracies of Eastern Europe. These systems feature a directly elected head of state with substantial policy-making powers, but also a prime minister responsible to the legislature; their functioning depends on both the partisan balance of the legislature and the powers of the president.

Constitutional organization: election rules

A second critical feature of democratic constitutions specifies the rules by which the representatives who make policy are selected. As Riker (1982b) has pointed out, it was already suspected in the nineteenth century that the type of election rules known as first-past-the-post would tend to lead to exclusion of smaller parties and creation of single party majorities. Much later, French sociologist Maurice Duverger (1954) stated the 'law' that such rules tend to create two-party systems. Duverger proposed that the dualism is supported both by 'proximate' or 'mechanical' effects in the aggregation of votes and by 'distal' or psychological effects as voters and politicians anticipate the mechanical effects. Empirical research (Rae 1967; Riker 1982b; Lijphart 1994; Cox 1997) has discovered evidence of both mechanical and psychological effects, but the former seem to dominate in most cases.

The 'first-past-the-post' election rule, in which a country is divided into single-representative constituencies and the candidate with the most votes (plurality) wins each district, is used today in Britain, the USA, and many nations once under British domination, such as New Zealand (until 1996), Jamaica, Canada, and so forth. The British general elections since 1983 have produced typical examples of the mechanical effects, in which smaller parties with votes evenly distributed across districts do badly, and legislative majorities have been created for parties winning less than 45 per cent of the popular vote. Occasionally, such election rules produce legislative majorities for even smaller parties (35 per cent of the vote won by the National Party in New Zealand in 1993) or for a party finishing second in the popular vote (generally, see Powell 2000: ch. 6). Single member district variants such as the alternative vote (Australia) or majority run-off (France) have somewhat different implications for party competition and alliances, but similar mechanical representation effects.

The major alternative form of election rule is proportional representation (PR). Favoured by most of the nations of continental Europe and Latin America, PR provides for multi-member legislative districts, with parties represented in proportion to their voting support in the district. The size and complexity of the districts, the exact rules for distributing 'remainder' votes and the presence of 'cut-off' rules eliminating parties below a certain size can shape the working of the systems (Rae 1967; Taagepera and Shugart 1989; Lijphart 1994). Moreover, the experiences with PR in the new democracies of Eastern Europe have shown that even a fairly low cut-off rule can leave many voters unrepresented if too many parties compete in the election, as in Poland in 1992 and Russia in 1995. (On the effect of the number of parties generally, see Cox 1997.) But in systems such as those of the Netherlands or Denmark, the presence of PR allows a substantial number of small parties to form, compete, and obtain legislative representation with only a few per cent of the national vote. It is difficult for single parties to gain legislative majorities under PR rules.

Post-Second World War Germany pioneered and popularized a 'mixed' electoral system that combines single-member districts and proportional representation. Some part of the legislature (half in Germany) is elected in single-member districts and the remainder by PR, with each citizen casting two ballots to choose district and party/PR representatives. Many sub-variants have emerged, linking the two ballots in various ways or with varying proportions from each. These systems have been adopted in many new democracies and also have replaced more traditional electoral systems in countries such as New Zealand, Japan, Italy and Venezuela.

Competitive party systems: critical linkage

Competitive party systems shape the critical electoral linkages between citizens and policy-makers. Bryce's observation eighty years ago holds true today: no large democracy has been able to do without political parties as the vehicle for organizing and structuring elections (Bryce 1921: vol. 1, 119). Without such organization the ability of citizens to have an impact through elections is extremely limited.

Moreover, parties are one means through which constitutional arrangements, especially the election rules, shape democratic policy-making and, sometimes, a means through which constitutional arrangements can be overcome. Party competition is affected by the historic social and political cleavages of the society (Lipset and Rokkan 1967; Kitschelt *et al.* 1999; Rogowski 1989) and its cultural values, as well as by the constitutional arrangements and by the strategies of politicians (Downs 1957; Cox 1997). Party systems also have autonomous influence of their own and, usually, substantial ability to sustain themselves over time (Lipset and Rokkan 1967; Inglehart 1984; Lijphart 1994).

The literature on party systems and party competition is voluminous. (See, for example, discussions in Cox 1997; Dahl 1966; Downs 1957; Duverger 1954; Epstein 1967; Lipset and Rokkan 1967; Mainwaring and Scully 1995; Neumann 1956; Powell 1982a: ch. 5; Sartori 1976: ch. 6; Strom 1985, 1990; Ware 1988). Two major distinctions dominate much of the analysis. The first of these distinguishes two-party, or at least majority electing, systems from multi-party systems. Theorists and observers who favour clarity of responsibility and the power to implement promises (Schattschneider 1942; Ranney 1962), and/or the pre-election aggregation of citizen preferences (Lipset 1960; Epstein 1967; Pinto-Dushinsky 1999) that seem to go with majoritarian government naturally prefer two-party systems. Those who favour explicit representation of social and political factions in policy-making and elaborately consultative political processes tend to prefer multi-party systems (Nordlinger 1972; Lehmbruch 1974; Lijphart 1977, 1999).

A second major distinction between party systems focuses on the degree or type of political conflict that they express. Many party system theorists hold that highly polarized party systems, in which there is a great gap between the espoused policy packages (ideologies) of major parties, or in which 'extremist' parties that challenge the basic ground rules of the society gain substantial strength, endanger the continued performance of democracy (e.g. Duverger 1954: 419–20). Sartori's influential analysis of polarized pluralism (Sartori 1976: ch. 6) argues that the polarized systems enhance the ideological intensity of policy debate, encourage a pattern of irresponsible 'outbidding' by extremist parties, and discourage turnovers of power that could keep incumbent parties responsible to citizens (see also Powell 1987). Substantial research suggests that polarized or extremist party systems tend to promote instability of party governments, and perhaps mass turmoil as well (Taylor and Herman 1971; Hibbs 1973; Powell 1982a, 1986a; Warwick 1994).

The two distinctions are often associated in argument, as many theorists have explicitly or implicitly linked multi-partism and polarization. It seems to be true that the constitutional arrangements that encourage multi-party legislative representation will also allow extremist party representation if discontent emerges. The new 'right radical' parties in Western Europe, whose support reflects intense unhappiness over immigration, European integration, and the slow response of traditional parties to new concerns, illustrate such extremist expressions (Kitschelt and McGann 1995). However, there is less empirical support for the argument that multi-partism as such encourages or exacerbates political conflict (Powell 1982a: ch. 5, 1987).

Interest group systems

While the 'major variants' of liberal democracy have traditionally been defined by constitutional and party systems, political scientists have also focused considerable attention on the ability of certain systems of interest group arrangements to deal more effectively than others with national economic problems. A set of such arrangements called 'democratic corporatism' has included a relatively centralized and comprehensive system of interest groups, continuous political bargaining between groups, political parties and state bureaucracies, and a supportive ideology of national 'social partnership' (Katzenstein 1985: 32; Lijphart 1999: ch.9). These systems contrast with the more fragmented, decentralized, and loosely organized 'pluralist' interest group systems. The countries having the regularized democratic corporatist relationships (among them Austria, the Netherlands, Norway and Sweden) had better inflation/unemployment performance in the difficult years of the mid-1970s and early 1980s than did systems with more pluralist interest group and party relationships, such as Britain, Canada, France and the USA (Schmitter 1981; Katzenstein 1985; Golden 1993). While research to date has concentrated primarily on labour and industrial relations, investigation of the consequences of various systems of interest group relations in other policy areas and at other times is underway in many countries.

Patterns of liberal democracy

Lijphart's empirical study of structural arrangements and political processes in 36 democracies suggests two general patterns of deviation from democratic concentration of political power (1999: ch. 14). One dimension is reflected especially by the party system, with multi-party legislatures, proportional election outcomes, multi-party and minority cabinets and their instability, and corporatist interest group systems all correlated. The second dimension associates federalism, bicameral legislatures, judicial review, rigid constitutions, and central bank independence. The first dimension seems to reflect shared power within the same policy-making organizations, while the second involves divided power across different policy-making organizations.

Citizen influence in different variants of liberal democracy

From the point of view of citizen influence, many details of constitution, party and interest group systems can be simplified theoretically into a single dimension of majoritarianism and consensualism. Where the constitutional arrangements, party and interest group systems work together to elect controlling government majorities, able to make and implement policy without further elaborate bargaining, it should be easier for citizens to assess policy responsibility and hold incumbents accountable. If policy outcomes are unsatisfactory, the incumbents can be ejected and the opposition(s) brought to power. Citizens should frequently get the policies they want without an elaborate process of search and rejection, because incumbents desiring re-election, or contenders seeking to displace them, will anticipate citizens' desires (Downs 1957; Pennock 1979: ch. 7; Powell 2000: ch. 3). (However, for difficulties in this connection, see Powell 2000: ch. 8.)

Such majoritarian governmental systems can also promote mandate processes (Ranney 1962; Birch 1972; Powell 2000: ch. 4). If the parties offer alternative policy choices to citizens and keep their promises when elected, citizens can use elections to set the basic policy agenda for the future. Such alternative promises may be an important way for options to be widened and policy change desired by citizens to come into focus. Moreover, the clarity of responsibility in the majoritarian system should make it easy for voters to punish incumbents who fail to keep their promises.

The difficulty for citizen control posed by the majoritarian variant lies particularly in the bluntness of the electoral weapon under conditions of many different political issues. Unless all these issues can align citizens the same way, forming a single 'dimension', there will be different possible majorities of citizens on different issues. Citizens in the majority on one issue will be in the minority on another. The tendency of the pure majoritarian variant to 'freeze' into policy all the promises of the party winning office will result in some policies that do not have majority support. (British politics provides various examples of this, such as Labour's nationalization of the steel industry after the 1966 election, or the Conservative government's privatization of utilities after the 1987 election. Both policies were carried out as 'mandates'; both were clearly opposed by citizen majorities.) Furthermore, the presence of multiple issue dimensions creates difficulties for simple accountability of incumbents as well. Apart from the multidimensionality problem, situations where dominating government majorities are created by the operation of the electoral laws on less than a majority of the votes (the typical situation in democracies, as shown by Rae 1967: 74; Powell 2000: chs 4, 6) are normatively uncomfortable for the concept of democratic control.

The consensual variant of democracy avoids some of these difficulties. Inclusive decision rules or election rules that help bring into power a variety of parties that represent many configurations of voter opinion will open up the possibility of forming different governing coalitions on different issues (King 1981). First, the parties must negotiate parliamentary coalition governments that will have positions corresponding more complexly to the variety of clusters of voter preference, and which may change before the next election. Alternatively a 'minority' government may gather support from different parties outside the government on different issues. Second, the party government will have to negotiate with individuals or parties that have resources from committee positions (Strom 1990), the other legislative house, the regional governments, and so forth (Powell 2000: chs 5, 9). 'Early elimination' of possible majorities (Riker 1982a) will be less frequent.

But the consensual version has the difficulties of its virtues. The complex stages of bargaining make it difficult for voters to see connection between their choices and government policy. The absence of connection can be frustrating even for those not wedded to a strict mandate model, as Dutch voters emphasized over thirty years ago in their support for the (then) protest party D66. Even more fundamentally, it can be difficult to assess responsibility for policy. American voters facing divided presidential–congressional control, shifting party factions and strong committees in Congress, significant state government authority, and an intrusive Supreme Court may well find it impossible to know whom to blame for policy failure. Similarly, short-lived coalitions, frequent minority governments, and strong committees can make responsibility equally hard to pin down in Belgium, Italy or Norway. It is harder to use elections to express fundamental democratic dissent by throwing out the incumbents when the potential alternative policy-makers are also contaminated by power-sharing.

There may be no variant of democracy that guarantees the most effective single approach to citizen influence. Rather, each of the major variants and combinations has its strengths and weaknesses (Powell 2000: ch. 10). (But see Lijphart 1999: ch. 16.) The importance of each type of weakness may depend on the number and intensity of the issues that divide (or unite) the citizens, as well as on the qualities that citizens most value.

Citizen participation in liberal democracy

Whatever the possibilities for control created by the different democratic variants, it remains up to the citizens to make use of them. Effective citizen control will require employment of both electoral and non-electoral channels to supplement the blunt, but essential, voting instrument with forms of participation capable of conveying citizens' desires more clearly and completely (Verba and Nie 1972: 322–7).

Voting participation

It is clear that voting is both the most widely used and most equally used form of citizen participation in liberal democracies (Verba, Nie and Kim 1978; Barnes, Kaase *et al.* 1979; Dalton 2002). It is also clear that levels of citizen voting participation differ systematically across the liberal democracies. Voter turn-out in national elections ranges from around 50 per cent of the citizens of voting age in Switzerland, the USA and Poland to about 90 per cent in Australia, Austria, Belgium and Italy. Average turn-out in nations without compulsory voting provisions is slightly under 80 per cent (Powell 1986b; Franklin 2001). While turn-out does vary from election to election, usually turn-out within each nation is relatively consistent compared to the striking cross-national differences. Differences in rates of political participation are in part a consequence of differences in the attitudes and characteristics of the citizens (education, interest, confidence, party commitment). Even more important are differences in the institutional context, such as compulsory voting, registration laws, nationally competitive election districts, and, somewhat less certainly, other features of policy-making and party competition (Powell 1986b; Jackman 1987; Franklin 2001; Norris 2002).

Campaign and communal participation

The importance of institutional setting applies to participation in campaign activity as well as to voting. It is clear that in some countries election activities, such as working for parties and candidates, are dominated by small numbers of dedicated activists or by party members rewarded by patronage. In other countries, such as the USA, decentralized but extensive organizations of party and candidates mobilize more citizens into campaign activities (Barnes, Kaase *et al.* 1979: 541–2; Verba *et al.* 1978: 58–9). In a variety of modern societies, however, citizen participation in campaigns seems to be declining, although general political interest does not. Campaigns seem to be becoming more of a spectator activity (Dalton, McAllister and Wattenberg 2000: 56–9).

None the less, participation studies (Verba, Nie and Kim 1978; Barnes, Kaase *et al.* 1979; Dalton 2002: 47–54) suggest that the individual characteristics of citizens, such as education, interest, socio-economic resources and partisanship, are more important in explaining who participates in election campaigns or community activity than in explaining who votes. The combination of a relatively educated and organized citizenry and significantly independent local governments have led, for example, to impressive amounts of communal participation in the USA; it is, however, participation more frequently from the better-off citizens in the society (Verba and Nie 1972). The participatory advantages of citizens with more social and economic resources can be countered in part, but only in part, by deliberate efforts of unions and labour parties to organize and mobilize the disadvantaged. (See Verba, Nie and Kim 1978: 94–142, on the connections between socio-economic resources, organizational systems, and degree and equality of political participation in different democracies.)

Interest groups and citizens in liberal democracies

The conditions of freedom of organization and communication found in liberal democracies naturally encourage the formation of interest groups of many kinds. As societies become more complex and organizationally differentiated, and as individual citizens become better educated and informed, these groups proliferate. Some of them are formed explicitly to articulate political demands; even more are pressed into political service when the group's interests encounter a potentially political issue. However, for both historical and socio-economic reasons democracies vary substantially in the density of interest group organization, as well as in the connections between groups and political parties. Citizen participation in voluntary associations seems to be high in the USA and Austria, even higher in Sweden and some other Scandinavian countries (Pestoff 1977: 65; Verba, Nie and Kim 1978: 101). Despite further complex changes across different types of groups, there is some evidence of further increases in the density of citizen group involvement in West Europe (Dalton 2002: 43–6; but see Putnam 2000). In Eastern and Central Europe a vigorous civil society is emerging gradually from 40 years of stifling suppression by the Communist parties and the government bureaucracies.

Some scholars have seen such activity on the part of autonomous labour unions, consumer and environmental groups, churches, business and professional associations, recreational groups, civic associations and so forth as essential to liberal democracy. One line of thought emphasizes conflict mediation. 'Cross-cutting' multiple group affiliations can tie individuals together and encourage taking account of multiple views (Truman 1951; Lipset 1960; Pestoff 1977). Another line of thought focuses on group activity that can mediate between the citizen and the state (Kornhauser 1959), helping citizens to develop and clarify their own desires, interpret them politically and cooperate for participate in politics beyond the electoral arena (Almond and Verba 1963: 300–22; Cohen and Arato 1992; Putnam, Leonardi and Nanetti 1993: 86–113). The group activity can articulate the wants of individual citizens to policy-makers with far more clarity and targeted precision than the crude linkage of party and election. Organized groups can bring to bear more resources than can the citizen acting alone. Even if organized initially or primarily for some other purpose, a developed civil society can solve many of the problems of organizing and mobilizing faced by discontented, but scattered, individuals (Olsen 1965; Verba, Nie and Kim 1978; Putnam, Leonardi and Nanetti 1993), creating social capital.

Other democratic theorists have regarded interest groups (pressure groups) suspiciously, stressing that the special demands and advantages of such groups may be contrary to the public interest or the interests of the less well organized, who are also commonly the less educated and well-off members of the society. Schattschneider, for example, wrote of 'the pressure group' as 'a parasite living on the wastage of power exercised by the sovereign majority' (Schattschneider 1942: 190) and later argued that 'the business or upper-class bias of the pressure system shows up everywhere' (Schattschneider 1960: 30). (See also McConnell 1966.)

In a general sense, competitive elections should help check the tendency of policy-makers to respond to the more frequently articulated interests of the better-off and the organized, just as they should check the tendency for policy-makers to follow their own desires. In practice, problems of citizen attention, information and competing issues limit the electoral constraint. Hence the importance of interest group organization for all parts of the citizenry.

Conditions for sustaining liberal democracy

Given a certain degree of autonomy and desire on the part of the citizens, it is possible to introduce and sustain a liberal democracy in any society. Certain conditions of the social setting are, however, much more conducive to liberal democracy and provide better prospects for its survival than others. Moreover, political theorists have long believed that certain variants have greater survival capacity than others.

As a first condition, the international setting will have important effects on the prospects for liberal democracy. In the extreme case, such penetrated societies as those of Eastern Europe from 1945 until 1989 may not be allowed to develop liberal democracy, whatever the desires of their citizens. Moreover, the financing of internal rebellions by outside governments, or the perception by an internal minority that they might be part of a majority in another state, can fuel internal conflict and weaken a would-be democracy. Less directly, international conditions can give a strong argument for or against internal proponents of democracy. The victories of (at least partially) democratic forces over authoritarian ones in World War I and World War II not only imposed democracy on the losers, but greatly enhanced the prestige of the democratic models for new states. More recently, as Huntington remarks, 'By the late 1980s the major sources of power and influence in the world – the Vatican, the European Community, the USA and the Soviet Union – were actively promoting liberalization and democratization' (1991: 86).

Second, the level of modernization of the society will affect its prospects for sustaining democracy. The greater wealth and income of economically developed societies make it possible for them to deal with internal conflict, especially economic conflict, in a greater variety of ways. Closely associated, the higher levels of literacy, the more dense communication media, and the more complexly developed patterns of associational life all encourage a citizenry able to deal successfully with democratic participation (Huntington 1991: 59–72; Putnam, Leonardi and Nanetti 1993).

The complex dispersal of power in such societies may contribute to resistance to authoritarian overthrow from within (Dahl 1989: 251–4; Vanhanen 1990). Przeworski *et al.* find the level of economic development by far the strongest factor affecting the durability of democratic regimes between 1945 and 1990 (2000: ch. 2). Democracy has been supported in some relatively poor and economically undeveloped societies, such as India, but it is more fragile there. Short-term economic performance, such as growth and inflation, plays a significant additional role in sustaining or undermining democratic regimes in the less modernized societies. The level of modernization has also been strongly associated with development of an autonomous middle class and an organized working class, which have historically been important democratizing forces (for debate about their respective roles, see e.g. Rueschemeyer, Stephens and Stephens 1992).

Third, the degree of internal social and ethnic fragmentation is likely to affect the prospects for stable and successful liberal democracy (Hibbs 1973: ch. 5; Powell 1982a: 42–7). Nations with divisions of religion, language, ethnicity, race and other demographic characteristics that involve the deep personal identity (and identifiability) of individuals and groups are likely to have a more difficult time in achieving political stability under any system. They often face public policy issues that are particularly difficult to resolve through compromise and partial measures. Situations involving simple divisions of the society into majority and minority ethnic groups can be even more difficult to resolve than multiple groups with no majority. Moreover, the threat to the identity of individuals and social groups makes for great intensity of feeling and easy development of fear and distrust. Once internal ethnic conflicts are mobilized and fear and grievances accumulated, they may long defy the most imaginative efforts at democratic reconciliation.

It is also likely that the cultural traditions and values of a society can work for or against liberal democracy. As France has demonstrated to the rest of Europe for two hundred years, historical political cleavages and conflicts can haunt a nation's political life and make democratic conflict resolution more difficult. The general association between a Protestant religious heritage and early democratic development has frequently been noted; particular difficulties for democracy in Confucian and Islamic nations have been suggested, although also challenged (Huntington 1991: 298–311). The presence of such citizen attitudes as social trust, subject and participant competence, social cooperation (Almond and Verba 1963: 504; Inglehart 1990), and 'norms and networks of civic engagement' (Putnam, Leonardi and Nanetti 1993: 116) seem to enhance the stability and performance of liberal democratic systems.

Theorists of the consequences of liberal democratic constitutions and party systems have been seriously divided over the merits of each major variant for sustaining democracy. Under conditions of general citizen agreement on the basic procedures and policies of the society, any of the approaches will probably survive. In his study of liberal democracies stable since the Second World War, Lijphart (1999) found examples both of highly majoritarian types (Britain, New Zealand) and highly consensual ones (Switzerland, Belgium), as well as various mixes. On the other hand, under conditions of extreme pressure any of them may fail.

Nor is it obvious whether or not intense polarization of citizen opinion is better dealt with through enforced incorporation within two-party, majoritarian politics than through proportional representation and consultation. Supporters of majority government stress its ability to make policy rapidly and decisively, and suggest that this capacity can be critical in times of great stress. At least since the fall of the Weimar Republic, many writers have seen multi-party systems as fatefully unable to deal with major internal crisis (for example, see Bracher 1964; Dahl 1971: 173). A contradictory view is that majoritarian politics is destabilizing in the presence of intense opinion conflicts (Lehmbruch 1974; Lijphart 1977, 1999; Nordlinger 1972). Majoritarianism tends to lead to suppression of minorities and/or too much threat for incumbents to yield power; therefore, societies divided by ethnicity or other sources of intense disagreement must move to non-majoritarian, consultative arrangements. Another suggested element in the situation (Powell 1982a, 1986a) is that multi-party or consensual arrangements may not exacerbate conflict but do tend to move turmoil from the streets (protests and riots) to the constitutional arena (less durable coalitions).

Debate over the durability of variants of democracy has also swirled about the presidential-parliamentary distinction. Scholarly research has tended to argue the greater durability of parliamentary systems over presidential ones (e.g. Linz and Valenzuela 1994). The greater flexibility and legitimacy of executive-legislative fusion seemed to contrast favourably with the dangers of confrontation between strong presidents and their assemblies. Although these inferences have been based in part on the favourable experience with parliamentarism in Western Europe and unfavourable experience with presidentialism in Latin America, the controlled analyses of Przeworski *et al.* also support the greater fragility of presidential systems in less economically developed societies (2000: 128–36). However, in many new democracies the constitution-makers have chosen presidential forms, perhaps because they offer more executive stability when undeveloped or polarized party systems seem unlikely to sustain parliamentary governments through negotiation.

If democratic failure occurs, it may well take different forms in the different democratic variants. Majoritarian systems are more likely to succumb to the temptation of the strong government (of either presidential or parliamentary type) to constrain civic freedom or even competition in the name of stability, or to do away with elections entirely in the name of security. Consensual systems are more likely to become immobilized, unable to address serious policy issues, lose citizen confidence and open the path to military intervention (see Powell 1982a: 170–4) But there is no magic formula that applies to all cases; rather it is up to the elites in the society to devise ways of overcoming the weaknesses and taking advantages of the strengths that reside in their variant of liberal democracy (Lijphart 1977; Powell 1982a: 218–24). It is the essence of liberal democracy that ordinary citizens must also have the attentiveness and wisdom to support the efforts to sustain democracy and freedom.

Performance of liberal democracies and non-democracies

Despite the democratization and liberalization of the last twenty-five years, supported by generally favourable international and economic trends, a majority of the world's citizens still live in regimes that do not fully qualify as liberal democracies. Worse, Freedom House classifies a quarter of the contemporary regimes, especially in Asia, Africa and the Middle East, as clearly 'unfree' (Karatnycky 2001).

Nothing guarantees that liberal democracy will not suffer new reversals. Therefore, it seems appropriate to conclude with a few words of comparison between liberal democracies and the non-democratic alternatives.

The easiest area in which to document relatively superior performance of democracy is in sustaining civil rights and personal freedom from elite abuse. Reviewing the yearly studies of political rights and civil liberties by Freedom House (Gastil 1978, 1988; Karatnycky 2001) makes this association quite clear. Some authoritarian governments permit substantial civil freedom. Some electoral democracies restrict press freedoms and civil rights, abuse the positions of minorities, or suffer from debilitating corruption that renders citizen influence less meaningful. But the general intertwining of electoral competition and political rights with civil freedom is obvious. Moreover, statistical studies of repression of human rights strongly support the positive effects of democracy in constraining states' abuse of their citizens (Poe and Tate 1994.) Studies of genocide indicate that liberal democracy inhibits this most terrible misuse of state power (Rummel 1995).

There is also some evidence that democracy restrains political violence. This evidence would probably be more compelling if we had better data on deadly violence in authoritarian systems. But Hibbs's careful analysis of mass political violence on a worldwide scale found that elite restraint when confronted with citizen protest and turmoil helped prevent the escalation of internal war (1973: 186–7). Moreover, at the international level many empirical studies have shown that democracies, although hardly immune to international conflict, very seldom, if ever, have gone to war against each other (e.g. Maoz and Russett 1993).

Studies of economic growth, income equality, and corruption reveal more mixed consequences of democracy. Different associations between democracy and average growth levels appear in different time periods and different settings, with little systematic pattern. One consistent connection seems to be that democracy seldom engenders either the most spectacular economic successes or the most devastating economic failures (Przeworski *et al* 2000: 176–8). Once account is taken of the social and economic setting, there seems to be little relationship between current democracy of the regime and perceived levels of corruption, although long-term, continuous democratic experience is associated with somewhat reduced corruption (Triesman 2000: 433–5).

Welfare policies and their consequences are hard to distinguish from the broad socio-economic setting and the shifting incumbent commitments. Both democratic and non-democratic regimes show wide variations in their policy patterns (Powell 1982b: 386–8). Studies of wage and income equality yield mixed results (Gasiorowski 1997: 245, 266; Przeworski *et al.* 2000: 168–76), although perhaps favouring the democracies. Przeworski *et al.* find average spending on welfare and health policies substantially higher in democracies, with significantly positive consequences for lower death rates, especially for infant mortality, and longer life expectancies (2000: 235–41). Their analyses point to a discouraging picture of women under dictatorships: 'They participate in gainful activities at the same rates as they do in democracies and, as workers, they get lower wages. But they also have more children, see more of them die, and are themselves more likely to die in childbirth' (Przeworski *et al.* 2000: 271). Finally, Dreze and Sen (1989) argue that no democracy has ever experienced a major famine, perhaps because of the 'early warning system' of a free society.

As a new millennium began, it was perhaps too easy to be optimistic about the prospects for liberal democracy and the performance of liberal democracies compared to authoritarian systems. The fading of communism seemed to leave democracy with few ideological challengers in the modern world, religious fundamentalism posing the most serious threat. Yet, democracy has been hard to stabilize in the less modernized societies and electoral democracies facing hard conditions of internal violence or persistent corruption have too often yielded to the temptation to constrain liberties. The imperfections of liberal democratic regimes, from elite domination or deadlock to ill-judged citizen choices, are manifest. Minorities and women remain particularly at risk; competitive elections are a limited tool for controlling elite policy-makers; the appeals of extremism to those whose livelihood or values are threatened by globalization cannot be ignored. Relative superiority of the average democracy to the average dictatorship leaves vast room for improvement. Yet, Churchill's judgement stands:

> Many forms of government have been tried and will be tried in this world of sin and woe. No one pretends that democracy is perfect or all-wise. Indeed, it has been said that democracy is the worst form of government except for all those other forms that have been tried from time to time.
>
> (Churchill 1950: 200)

References

Almond, G. and Verba, S. (1963) *The Civic Culture: Political Attitudes and Democracy in Five Nations*, Princeton: Princeton University Press.

Barnes, S. H., Kaase, M. *et al.* (1979) *Political Action: Mass Participation in Five Western Democracies*, Beverley Hills: Sage Publications.

Birch, A. H. (1972) *Representation*, London: Macmillan.

Bowler, S., Farrell, D. M. and Katz, R. S. (1999) *Party Discipline and Parliamentary Government*, Columbus: Ohio State University Press.

Bracher, K. D. (1964) 'The problem of parliamentary democracy in Europe', *Daedalus* 93: 178–98.

Bryce, J. (1921) *Modern Democracies*, 2 vols, New York: Macmillan.

Buchanan, J. and Tullock, G. (1962) *The Calculus of Consent*, Ann Arbor: University of Michigan Press.

Butler, D. and Ranney, A. (1978) *Referendums: A Comparative Study*, Washington, DC: American Enterprise Institute.

Carey, J. M. and Shugart, M. S. (eds) (1998) *Executive Decree Authority*, Cambridge: Cambridge University Press.

Churchill, W. S. (1950) *Europe Unite: Speeches 1947 and 1948*, ed. R. S. Churchill, Boston: Houghton Mifflin.

Cohen, C. (1971) *Democracy*, New York: Free Press.

Cohen, J. and Arato, J. (1992) *Civil Society and Political Theory*, Cambridge: M.I.T. Press.

Cox, G. W. (1997) *Making Votes Count: Strategic Coordination in the World's Electoral Systems*, Cambridge: Cambridge University Press.

Dahl, R. A. (ed.) (1966) *Political Oppositions in Western Democracies*, New Haven: Yale University Press.

—— (1971) *Polyarchy: Participation and Opposition*, New Haven: Yale University Press.

—— (1989) *Democracy and Its Critics*, New Haven: Yale University Press.

Dalton, R. J. (2002) *Citizen Politics: Public Opinion and Political Parties in Advanced Industrial Democracies*, New York: Chatham House.

Dalton, R. J., McAllister, I. and Wattenberg, M. P. (2000) 'The Consequences of partisan dealignment', in R. J. Dalton and M. P. Wattenberg, *Parties without Partisans*, Oxford: Oxford University Press.

Downs, A. (1957) *An Economic Theory of Democracy*, New York: Harper & Row.

Dreze, J. and Sen, A. (1989) *Hunger and Public Action*, Oxford: Oxford University Press.

Duverger, M. (1954) *Political Parties: Their Organization and Activity in the Modern State*, New York: John Wiley.

—— (1980) 'A new political system model: semi-presidential government', *European Journal of Political Research* 8: 165–87.

Epstein, L. D. (1967) *Political Parties in Western Democracies*, New York: Praeger.

Franklin, Mark (2001) 'Electoral participation', in L. LeDuc, R. G. Niemi and P. Norris (eds) *Comparing Democracies 2*, London: Sage Publications.

Gasiorowski, M.J. (1997) 'Political Regimes and Industrial Wages', in M. I. Midlarsky (ed.) *Inequality, Democracy and Economic Development*, Cambridge: Cambridge University Press.

Gastil, R. D. (ed.) (1978) *Freedom in the World: Political Rights and Civil Liberties*, New York: Freedom House and G. R. Hall.

—— (1988) *Freedom in the World: Political Rights and Civil Liberties 1987–88*, New York: Freedom House.

Gerlich, P. (1973) 'The institutionalization of European Parliaments', in A. Kornberg (ed.) *Legislatures in Comparative Perspective*, New York: David McKay.

Golden, M. (1993) 'Dynamics of trade unionism and national economic performance', *American Political Science Review* 87: 439–54.

Hibbs, D. A. (1973) *Mass Political Violence*, New York: John Wiley.

Huber, J. D. (1996) 'The Vote of confidence in parliamentary democracies', *American Political Science Review* 90: 269–92.

Huntington, S. P. (1991) *The Third Wave: Democratization in the Late Twentieth Century*, Norman: University of Oklahoma Press.

Inglehart, R. (1984) 'The changing structure of political cleavages in Western society', in R. Dalton, S. Flanagan and P. A. Beck (eds) *Electoral Change in Advanced Industrial Democracies*, Princeton: Princeton University Press.

—— (1990) *Culture Shift in Advanced Industrial Society*, Princeton: Princeton University Press.

Jackman, R. (1987) 'Political institutions and voter turnout in the industrial democracies', *American Political Science Review* 81: 405–24.

Karatnycky, A. (2001) 'The 2000–2001 freedom house survey of freedom', in *Freedom in the World*, downloaded from *www.freedomhouse.org*, June 2002.

Katzenstein, P. (1985) *Small States in World Markets*, Ithaca, NY: Cornell University Press.

King, A. (1981) 'What do elections decide?', in D. Butler, H. Penniman and A. Ranney (eds) *Democracy at the Polls*, Washington, DC: American Enterprise Institute.

Kitschelt, H. with McGann, A. J. (1995) *The Radical Right in Western Europe*, Ann Arbor: University of Michigan Press.

Kitschelt, H., Mansfeldova, Z., Markowski, R. and Toka, G. (1999) *Post-Communist Party Systems*, Cambridge: Cambridge University Press.

Kornhauser, W. (1959) *The Politics of Mass Society*, Glencoe: Free Press.

Lehmbruch, G. (1974) 'A non-competitive pattern of conflict management in liberal democracies', in K. D. McRae (ed.) *Consociational Democracy*, Toronto: McCelland & Stewart.

Lijphart, A. (1977) *Democracy in Plural Societies*, New Haven: Yale University Press.

—— (1994) *Electoral Systems and Party Systems*, Oxford: Oxford University Press.

—— (1999) *Patterns of Democracy: Government Forms and Performance in Thirty-Six Countries*, New Haven: Yale University Press.

Linz, J. and Valenzuela, A. (eds) (1994) *The Failure of Presidential Democracy*, Baltimore: The Johns Hopkins University Press.

Lipset, S. (1960) *Political Man*, Garden City, NY: Doubleday.

Lipset, S. and Rokkan, S. (1967) *Party Systems and Voter Alignments*, New York: Free Press.

Mainwaring, S. and Scully, T. R. (1995) *Building Democratic Institutions: Party Systems in Latin America*, Stanford: Stanford University Press.

Maoz, Z. and Russett, B. (1993) 'Normative and structural causes of democratic peace', *American Political Science Review* 87: 624–38.

McConnell, G. (1966) *Private Power and American Democracy*, New York: Knopf.

Mueller, D. C. (1979) *Public Choice*, Cambridge: Cambridge University Press.

Neumann, S. (1956) *Modern Political Parties*, Chicago: University of Chicago Press.

Norris, P. (2002) *Democratic Phoenix: Political Activism Worldwide*, New York: Cambridge University Press.

Nordlinger, E. (1972) *Conflict and Conflict Management in Divided Societies*, Cambridge, MA: Harvard Center for International Studies.

Olson, M. (1965) *The Logic of Collective Action*, Cambridge, MA: Harvard University Press.

Pennock, R. (1979) *Democratic Political Theory*, Princeton: Princeton University Press.

Pestoff, V. A. (1977) *Voluntary Associations and Nordic Party Systems*, Stockholm: Liber Tryck.

Pinto-Duschinsky, M. (1999) 'Send the rascals packing!', *Representation* 36: 117–26.

Poe, S. C. and Tate, C. N. (1994) 'Repression of human rights to personal integrity in the 1980s', *American Political Science Review* 88: 853–72,

Powell, G. B., Jr. (1982a) *Contemporary Democracies: Participation, Stability and Violence*, Cambridge, MA: Harvard University Press.

—— (1982b) 'Social progress and liberal democracy', in G. Almond, M. Chodorow and R. H. Pierce, *Progress and Its Discontents*, Berkeley: University of California Press.

—— (1986a) 'Extremist parties and political turmoil: two puzzles', *American Journal of Political Science* 30: 357–78.

—— (1986b) 'American voter turnout in comparative perspective', *American Political Science Review* 80: 17–44.

—— (1987) 'The competitive consequences of polarized pluralism', in J. Holler (ed.) *The Logic of Multiparty Systems*, Dordrecht: Martinus Nijhoff.

—— (2000) *Elections as Instruments of Democracy: Majoritarian and Proportional Visions*, New Haven: Yale University Press.

Przeworski, A., Alvarez, M. E., Cheibub, J. A. and Limongi, F. (2000) *Democracy and Development: Political Institutions and Well-being in the World, 1950–1990*, Cambridge: Cambridge University Press.

Putnam, R. (2000) *Bowling Alone: The Collapse and Renewal of American Community*, Princeton: Princeton University Press.

Putnam, R. with Leonardi, R. and Nanetti, R. Y. (1993) *Making Democracy Work: Civic Traditions in Modern Italy*, Princeton: Princeton University Press.

Rae, D. W. (1967) *The Political Consequences of Electoral Laws*, New Haven: Yale University Press.

Ranney, A. (1962) *The Doctrine of Responsible Party Government*, Urbana: University of Illinois Press.

Riker, W. H. (1982a) *Liberalism Against Populism*, San Francisco: W. H. Freeman.

—— (1982b) 'The two-party system and Duverger's law: an essay on the history of political science', *American Political Science Review* 76: 753–66.

Rogowski, R. (1989) *Commerce and Coalitions: How Trade Affects Domestic Political Alignments*, Princeton: Princeton University Press.

Rokkan, S. (1961) 'Mass suffrage, secret voting and political participation', *Archives Européennes de sociologie* 2: 132–52.

Rueschemeyer, D., Stephens, E. H. and Stephens, J. D. (1992) *Capitalist Development and Democracy*, Chicago: University of Chicago Press.

Rummel, R. J. (1995) 'Democracy, power, genocide and mass murder', *Journal of Conflict Resolution* 39: 3–26.

Rustow, D. A. (1967) *A World of Nations: Problems of Political Modernization*, Washington, DC: Brookings Institution.

Sartori, G. (1976) *Parties and Party Systems*, New York: Cambridge University Press.

Schattschneider, E. E. (1942) *Party Government*, New York: Holt, Rinehart & Winston.

—— (1960) *The Semi-Sovereign People*, Hinsdale: Dryden Press.

Schmitter, P. (1981) 'Interest intermediation and regime governability', in S. Berger (ed.) *Organizing Interests in Western Europe*, New York: Cambridge University Press.

Shugart, M. S. and Carey, J. M. (1992) *Presidents and Assemblies*, Cambridge: Cambridge University Press.

Strom, K. (1985) 'Party goals and government performance in contemporary democracies', *American Political Science Review* 79: 738–54.

—— (1990) *Minority Government and Majority Rule*, New York: Cambridge University Press.

Taagepera, R. and Shugart, M. S. (1989) *Seats and Votes: The Effects and Determinants of Electoral Systems*, New Haven: Yale University Press.

Taylor, M. and Herman, V. (1971) 'Party systems and party governments', *American Political Science Review* 65: 28–37.

Treisman, D. (2000) 'The Causes of Corruption: A Cross-National Study', *Journal of Public Economics* 76: 397–457.

Truman, D. (1951) *The Governmental Process*, New York: Knopf.

Vanhanen, Tatu (1990) *The Process of Democratization*, New York: Crane Russak.

Verba, S. and Nie, N. H. (1972) *Participation in America*, New York: Harper & Row.

Verba, S., Nie, N. H. and Kim, J. (1978) *Participation and Political Equality: A Seven-Nation Study*, New York: Cambridge University Press.

Ware, A. (1988) *Citizens, Parties and the State*, Princeton: Princeton University Press.

Warwick, P. V. (1994). *Government Survival in Parliamentary Democracies*, Cambridge: Cambridge University Press.

15

COMMUNIST AND POST-COMMUNIST SYSTEMS

Leslie Holmes

Until the 'anti-communist' revolutions of 1989–91, approximately one third of the world's population lived in systems claiming to be building communism; such systems can be called communist. Even as of late 2002, almost 1.4 billion people lived in five still putatively communist systems, although most of these five – the People's Republic of China (PRC, or China), Cuba, Laos, the Democratic People's Republic of Korea (DPRK, or North Korea) and Vietnam – are likely to become 'post-communist' in the next few years. Indeed, many commentators now question China's claim still to be communist, since its economic and social systems are increasingly capitalist. The first part of this essay is concerned with communist states as they were up until 1989 (with occasional references to the remaining communist states), while the second part focuses on the so-called 'post-communist' states. Despite the continued existence of a small number of communist states, the past tense will be used for the analysis of actual communist systems, except where reference is explicitly to one or more of the remaining five; for the most part, the present tense is used for the more abstract, general parts of the discussion of communist systems.

Communist systems

None of the communist states ever claimed to have reached communism. According to their official spokespersons, most were at various stages of socialism. This has led some commentators to argue that the use of the term 'communist' is inappropriate. The two most popular alternative terms are 'state socialist' and simply 'socialist'. However, there are two major reasons why the term 'communist' remains a better label than any other. First, even the person seen by some as the 'father' of communism, Karl Marx, argued that communism refers to two phenomena – an ideal towards which society moves, and the political movement that abolishes an existing state of affairs so as to create the conditions for the movement towards the ideal (Marx and Engels 1970: 56–7). Indeed, Marx further made it clear that the latter (i.e. the political movement) was closer to what he meant by communism than was the former (the ideal). Second, there are and have been a number of systems (states) in the world that claim or have claimed to be socialist, but which are not organized in the same way as communist states, and which do not claim to be building a

Marxist-style communism; examples include Libya, Tanzania, Nicaragua and Burma (or Myanmar). In order to avoid confusion with such states, it is appropriate to call the latter socialist and the former communist.

There has been a major debate in the field of comparative communism on the question of whether or not self-ascription is acceptable in determining whether or not a particular country should be classified as 'communist'. Harding (1981: 33) argues that it would be wrong to characterize a regime as communist – or Marxist, as he would prefer to call it – simply in terms of the goals it professes. For him, there have to be the appropriate means and preconditions for their realization. The problem with this argument is that none of the existing communist or post-communist systems – with the possible, partial exceptions of Czechoslovakia and what was, until October 1990, the German Democratic Republic (GDR, or East Germany) – had the preconditions necessary for the building of socialism when the communists took power. Harding argues (1981: 33) that if a regime does not have the proper level of development, for instance, 'Marxism may well become merely a convenient rhetoric of legitimation for Jacobins, populists, nationalists or tyrants'.

In fact, there were few if any communist systems that had not been led at least part of the time by 'Jacobins, populists, nationalists and tyrants', and it is unclear which actual regimes could be included using Harding's approach. In fairness to Harding, it seems at times (e.g. 1981: 21) that he wishes to distinguish Marxist from communist regimes. However, on other occasions (ibid.: 23) he appears to use the term Marxist to apply to at least many of the regimes most observers would choose to call communist, so that the reader is ultimately uncertain as to whether Harding is actually pleading for the use of the term 'Marxist regime' only as an ideal-type, or whether he does in fact wish to use it as an alternative label to 'communist'. It is therefore worth considering another approach.

One of the more provocative analyses of what constitutes a communist state is provided by John Kautsky. In a 1973 article, he argued that none of the variables others have used to identify communist systems is unique to such systems. Kautsky maintains that the only variable that distinguishes them is their symbols, and that symbols are insufficient as a distinguishing criterion. There are two main problems with this argument. First, as semioticians tell us, symbols can be very important, especially if the actual organization of society is closely related to such symbols. Second, whilst one can certainly isolate each of the variables Kautsky identifies – such as a nationalist component in the ideology, an authoritarian political structure, state intervention in the economy, etc. – and find examples of non-communist systems that have a similar approach to the communist systems' on these, the particular *configuration* of variables is reasonably distinctive in communist states. Thus, while Kautsky is justified in arguing that communist systems should not be treated as if they are totally different from all other kinds of system (especially non-communist developing countries), he goes too far in suggesting that they are indistinguishable from many other systems.

In one of the most popular introductions to communist systems, the authors maintain that these have four defining characteristics (White, Gardner, Schöpflin and Saich 1990: 4–5). First, communist states all base themselves upon an official ideology, the core of which is Marxism–Leninism. Second, the economy is overwhelmingly publicly rather than privately owned, and is organized on the basis of a central plan; communist systems have 'administered' or 'command' economies rather than market economies. Third, communist states are typically ruled by a single or at least dominant communist party, within which power tends to be highly centralized, and organized according to the principle of 'democratic centralism'. Finally, institutions that are more or less independent of the political authorities in liberal democracies (e.g. the press, trade unions and the courts) are in communist states effectively under the direct control of the communist party, exercising its 'leading role'. This is a useful summary of the distinguishing features of a communist system. Although it will be argued below that the communist states were dynamic, and that some of these features were less pronounced by the 1980s than they once were, the question then arises as to whether or not this dynamism eventually steered these states away from communism. For now, assuming that this four-fold analysis is more or less valid, each of the variables can be examined in more detail.

The term 'Marxism–Leninism' as a label for communist ideology appears to have been used first by the Soviet dictator, Josef Stalin (in power 1929–53). The ideology is a materialist one, meaning that its adherents believe that matter – the material world around us – determines the way we think. In this sense, they differ fundamentally from idealists, of whom Hegel is a prime example, who believe that ideas constitute reality, and that the world around us is merely a reflection of such ideas. Marxism–Leninism is also based on a dialectical approach to the world; expressed crudely, this holds that everything is in a constant state of flux, and that change occurs as a result of the interaction of various factors. For Marxist–Leninists, as for Marxists generally, the most important is class struggle, which in turn reflects changes in the nature and ownership of the means of production. Marxist–Leninists believe that there are observable laws to such developments, and hence claim that their ideology is 'scientific'. The first Soviet leader, Vladimir Lenin, added two particularly important components to this Marxist base. First, he developed the notion of a tightly-knit, centralized and elitist political party. This concept was originally expounded in *What is to be Done?* (1902), before the Russian Revolution of October 1917; subsequently, in 1921, he reiterated the need for a tight-knit party, in which factionalism would not be tolerated even following a socialist revolution. This constitutes the origins of the Marxist–Leninist emphasis on the monolithic and centralized party. Second, Lenin produced a major analysis of imperialism. Whilst many of his ideas on this have been discredited, a number of revolutionaries in the developing world have been inspired by Lenin's arguments. This is largely because they have accepted his view that the world is basically divided into imperialist countries and colonies, and because he appeared to them to have demonstrated how, largely through a tightly organized and centralized political system, a group of domestic communists would be able to develop their country independently of the imperial powers.

The above analysis of Marxism–Leninism is highly truncated, and readers are strongly advised to consult both the chapter on 'Marxism and socialism' on pp. 163–73 and the sources cited at the end of this essay (especially Harding 1983; McLellan 1995 and 1998). Here, it should be pointed out that some communist states have added phrases to 'Marxism–Leninism' to describe their particular ideology. The best-known example is the People's Republic of China (PRC), which at the time of writing still officially described its ideology as 'Marxism–Leninism and Mao Zedong Thought'. The Chinese, more explicitly than many other communists, clearly distinguish between the 'pure' ideology of Marxism–Leninism and the 'practical' ideology of Maoist thought. In this approach, Marxism–Leninism is primarily a mode of analysis, a general way of interpreting the world – whereas the 'practical' component of the ideology has to apply this general methodology to the concrete situation in a given country at a particular period, and devise policies, etc. on the basis of this. One important element often found in the 'practical' ideology, but which in a real sense contradicts the 'proletarian internationalism' of classical Marxism, is official nationalism. A prime example of this can be found in North Korean ideology, which is described as 'Marxism–Leninism and Juche'; Juche is very much a nationalist ideology.

The level and nature of public ownership and central planning of the economy varied considerably across communist states. At one end of the spectrum were countries in which there was (and in some cases still is) very little private ownership and a high level of directive planning; Albania, North Korea and Cuba are examples. At the other end were countries in which private enterprise was not merely tolerated but even encouraged, and in which central planning was not only less comprehensive than in other communist states, but also largely indicative (i.e. it tended to be more in the form of suggestions than orders). Examples of this type of economy were former Yugoslavia, Hungary, increasingly the USSR during the 1980s, and the PRC.

Although all communist states were ruled by a dominant communist party, two common misconceptions need to be dispelled. The first is that all communist systems were clearly one-party states. Whilst the communist party (which may or may not have had the word 'communist' in its formal title) did typically dominate, a number of communist states *formally* had a bi- or multi-party system; examples include Bulgaria, the GDR, Poland, the PRC, and Vietnam (the last two still have such an arrangement). It must be appreciated, however, that the minor parties did not usually play a significant role in these countries until the transition to post-communism was underway. Second, in some of the non-European communist states – such as Cuba and Ethiopia – the communist party played little or no role in the early years of communist rule, in some cases simply because it did not exist. In such cases, the country would be called communist primarily because of the formal commitment of the leaders to Marxist–Leninist ideology and communism as an end goal – although, strictly speaking, some leaders such as Castro did not even commit themselves to these ideas until some time after they had seized power. This is one of the reasons why analysts sometimes disagree on whether or not to classify a particular system as 'communist'.

As mentioned above, communist parties were structured according to the principle of 'democratic centralism'; in fact, by the 1970s, many other political agencies in communist systems, including much of the state itself, were formally organized on this basis. According to Article 19 of the Statute of the Communist Party of the Soviet Union (CPSU) adopted in 1986, democratic centralism within the party entailed the following:

1   election of all leading Party bodies, from the lowest to the highest;
2   periodic reports of Party bodies to their Party organizations and the higher bodies;

3   strict Party discipline and the subordination of the minority to the majority;
4   the binding nature of the decisions of higher bodies on lower bodies;
5   collective spirit in the work of all organizations and leading Party bodies, and the personal responsibility of every Communist for the fulfilment of his/her duties and Party assignments.

It is important to note that the noun in this basic political principle is 'centralism', the adjective 'democratic'. In other words, 'democracy', however defined, is only meant to act as a check on a centralized system, not to constitute the basis of the system itself.

The ways in which communist parties exercised their 'leading role' in society, and in particular over other institutions such as the media and trade unions, were several, and it is beyond the scope of this essay to elaborate these fully. The single most important lever was the so-called *nomenklatura* system. This was exercised in various ways, depending on the country and period; but the basic concept was common. The communist party was organized hierarchically, and at each level a secretary or secretariat had a list of posts, the *nomenklatura*. The party was required to play a role in hiring and/or firing individuals to/from these key posts; in some cases, the party was directly involved in this process, in other cases only kept informed. The important point is that the *nomenklatura* included all the most politically powerful and sensitive posts at a given level, not merely party posts. Thus a city-level *nomenklatura* typically included the editorships of the city's newspapers, the directorships of many of the major enterprises, the headships of the city's colleges, etc. Not everyone appointed to a *nomenklatura* post was a member of the party, though most people in most communist states were.

Using the above criteria, it is possible to identify more than twenty states in four continents that were communist until 1989; listed alphabetically, they were Afghanistan, Albania, Angola, Benin, Bulgaria, Cambodia (Kampuchea until 1989), China, Congo, Cuba, Czechoslovakia, Ethiopia, East Germany, Hungary, North Korea, Laos, Mongolia, Mozambique, Poland, Romania, Soviet Union (the Union of Soviet Socialist Republics or USSR), Vietnam, South Yemen (the People's Democratic Republic of Yemen or PDRY) and Yugoslavia.

However, many of these countries experienced overt systemic crises in the years following 1989, so that by the mid-1990s, only five (listed earlier) still qualified *relatively* clearly as communist. All the others were post-communist, although the nature of this varied considerably from country to country. Several communist states had disintegrated altogether. Thus Czechoslovakia had become two countries (Czechia; Slovakia), while Yugoslavia was now five (Bosnia and Herzegovina; Croatia; Republic of Macedonia; Slovenia; Yugoslavia, comprising Montenegro and Serbia). The former USSR had by then been transformed into fifteen sovereign states (Armenia; Azerbaijan; Belarus; Estonia; Georgia; Kazakhstan; Kyrgyzstan; Latvia; Lithuania; Moldova; Russia; Tajikistan; Turkmenistan; Ukraine; Uzbekistan); of these, Russia and Ukraine had the largest populations. Conversely, two other formerly communist states had united with culturally similar neighbours during 1990 and had thus ceased to exist as sovereign states (GDR, PDRY). In order to understand how this all happened, it is necessary to analyse the dynamism of communist states; what follows must necessarily be presented in a highly abbreviated and generalized form, and individual communist states will approximate more or less closely to the pattern outlined.

Communists typically take (as well as lose!) power in crisis situations. The crises most commonly occur either during or following a major international war. In the case of the world's first communist state, Russia (the USSR from 1922), the crisis of 1917 was partly a result of the country's poor performance in the First World War. Between 1917 and the mid 1940s, only one other country – Mongolia – came under communist rule (1924); in this particular case, the system was in crisis less because of war than because of domestic factors. But in the aftermath of the Second World War, a spate of new communist states came into being. Thus, between 1945 and 1950, communists came to power in eight East European states, as well as in mainland China, northern Korea and parts of Vietnam (though the Vietnamese process was protracted; Vietnam as a whole did not come under communist rule until 1975). The circumstances varied in each. But in all of them an old regime had collapsed or was collapsing, and in many the Red (Soviet) Army and/or other forms of Soviet involvement assisted indigenous communists to take power. There was only one new communist state in the 1950s (Cuba – 1959), and in a sense even this is questionable, since Castro did not formally commit himself to Marxism–Leninism until 1961; he came to power not in the aftermath of an international war, but primarily as a result of the corruption and widespread unpopularity of the Batista regime. Nor were the 1960s a period of major expansion in the communist world; in the view of many analysts, communists took power in Congo (Brazzaville) in 1968 and in South Yemen in 1969. The second major wave of communist expansion (i.e. after the period 1945–50) occurred in the early-to-mid 1970s. In this case, the major factors leading to crisis were communist success in an international war (in the case of the three Indochinese states of Vietnam, Laos and Cambodia), and the further collapse of various European empires, notably the French and the Portuguese. Thus communists took power in the ex-French colony of Benin in 1972, while Angola and Mozambique rapidly came under the control of the MPLA and Frelimo respectively following the overthrow of the Caetano regime in Portugal in September 1974 and the subsequent Portuguese abandonment of its centuries-old empire. In the cases of the two other countries that came under communist control in the 1970s – Ethiopia (1974) and Afghanistan (1978) – the crisis that led to the revolutionary change was primarily related to the unpopularity and general decline of legitimacy of the regimes of Emperor Haile Selassie and General Daoud respectively.

Communists do not generally assume power in economically developed countries (so that Marx failed to predict the emergence of actual communist systems). One ramification of this is that the new leaders have sought to transform their societies rapidly and fundamentally; they often set about this following their consolidation of power, the duration of which varies considerably from country to country. This desire for rapid transformation can be explained both in terms of their country's need to reach a level of industrialization and general economic development that is, in Marxist terms, appropriate and necessary for the creation of a truly socialist and eventually communist society, and to demonstrate the superiority of the Marxist–Leninist development model over other possible paths – notably capitalism. This commitment to a rapid 'revolution from above' typically involves socialization of the means of production and collectivization of agriculture, which frequently engenders widespread hostility to the communists. This in turn promotes a violent clampdown by the communists, and it is common for this top-down transformation to be accompanied by widespread state terror. Terror has been a salient feature of several communist states, notably the USSR in the 1930s (Stalin's so-called 'Great Terror'), most of Eastern Europe in the late-1940s/early-1950s, Cambodia in the mid-to-late-1970s, Afghanistan at the end of the 1970s, and several of the African communist states in the late-1970s and into the 1980s. In some of the Asian communist states, there was a mixture during the transition phase of overt physical terror and less draconian 'thought reform'. In the latter, many deemed by the regime to be openly hostile, or merely insufficiently positive, towards communism were sent to 're-education camps'. In most cases, these were essentially prison-camps in which internees were subjected to intensive 're-socialization techniques' (i.e. brainwashing). China, Vietnam, Laos and North Korea made extensive use of such camps (for further details on communist terror see Dallin and Breslauer 1970).

It will be clear from the above that, in the consolidation and rapid transition phases, communist states typically exercise power primarily in the coercive mode. But as time passes, leaders change, and the disadvantages of the predominantly coercive mode (e.g. it discourages initiative, and frequently alienates much of the population) become increasingly obvious. Hence communist leaderships normally seek to place less emphasis on coercion and more on legitimation. At least seven domestic modes of legitimating systems and regimes – old traditional, charismatic, teleological (also known as goal rational), eudaemonic, official nationalist, new traditional, and legal-rational – and three external modes (formal international recognition; informal support; existence of an external role model) can be identified. To a limited extent, the salience of each of these can be related to the different development stages of communist states. Expressed differently, the significance of each mode varies according to time, place and situation.

In the earliest stages, one of the main tasks of a new communist regime is to discredit its non-communist predecessor, to undermine old traditional legitimation. Many older people, in particular, may still believe in the divine right of monarchs, and hence find it difficult to develop allegiance to the new type of power system. As part of their attempts to destroy old values and attitudes, and quite possibly at the same time as coercion becomes the dominant form of power, communists often seek to create the impression that their top leaders are superhuman, and have made extraordinary efforts and personal sacrifices to serve the people. This is an attempt to legitimate in terms of leadership charisma, and can be seen in the personality cults communist propagandists promoted around leaders such as Lenin (USSR), Mao (PRC), and Ho Chi Minh (Vietnam); in the 1980s, the most extreme personality cults were of Kim Il Sung in North Korea and Nicolae Ceauşescu in Romania. While some of these cults are based on the genuine popularity of leaders, there is no question that propagandists seek to enhance them.

But charismatic legitimation, like coercive power, usually becomes less effective as educational standards rise and the secularizing effects of communist power spread. Communists therefore begin to seek other modes of legitimation. Typically, the transition from power exercised primarily through coercion towards more legitimation-based power begins at about this time. An emphasis on teleological (or goal rational) legitimation often emerges; communists begin to seek authority largely by reference to their all-important role in leading society towards the distant end-goal (or *telos* – hence teleological) of communism (on this see Rigby 1982). The publication of the CPSU Programme in 1961 is a prime example of this attempt at teleological legitimation.

For several reasons – including the growing popular cynicism generated by years of coercion, new leaders criticizing the faults of their predecessors, and economic shortages; and leadership doubts about the practicality of achieving goals rapidly enough to act as a stimulus to people – goal rational or teleological legitimation eventually fades into the background. In its place, normally, is a form of legitimation that is less ambitious and more geared to satisfying the immediate demands of the consumer. This can be called eudaemonism (here meaning 'conducive to happiness'), since it seeks to satisfy citizens through regime performance. This was characteristic of many European communist states in the late-1960s and the 1970s, when there was a simultaneous emphasis on 'realistic socialism' (as distinct from the more idealistic socialism implied in teleological legitimation) and the better satisfaction of consumer demands. At that time, such states introduced economic reforms that were designed, *inter alia*, to meet these requirements. China introduced a somewhat similar but more radical plan at the end of the 1970s, whilst Vietnam also moved in this direction in the 1980s.

Unfortunately, the economic reforms are often relative failures (the Chinese were a notable exception), so that legitimation in the eudaemonic mode becomes problematic. There are various responses to this. One is a new emphasis on official nationalism, whereby communist leaders seek to gain support for the system by appealing to the population's nationalist feelings. This attempt may hark back to a glorious pre-communist past (Ceauşescu did this in Romania), or it may emphasize contemporary national achievements (e.g. the GDR's focus on sporting success in the Olympic Games). Such nationalism contains dangers, however. Excessive emphasis on the distant past can undermine the relatively new and radical ideas of communism, while official nationalism can trigger unofficial nationalism among ethnic minorities. Another regime response can be called 'new traditionalism'. In this, communist leaderships emphasize the advantages of earlier periods of communism, and either implicitly or explicitly suggest that current difficulties would be reduced were there to be a return to some of the traditional communist values. Examples of this include Gorbachev's emphasis on the positive aspects of the Lenin era (including Lenin's economic policies from 1921) and, from the middle of 1989, the Chinese leadership's increasingly favourable re-assessment of the Maoist era (1949–76). Once again, there can be problems with this form of legitimation. Contemporary conditions will often be very different from those pertaining in the earlier period, for instance, so that leaders need to be careful in choosing from their predecessors' policies; many would be quite inappropriate.

Partly because of the problems of official nationalism and new traditionalism as legitimation modes, many communist leaders either avoid them, or else limit their use of them. Instead, there emerged in several communist states in the 1980s an emphasis on legal-rational legitimation. According to Max Weber and a number of more recent political theorists (e.g. Poggi 1978), this form of legitimation is the only one appropriate to the 'modern' state, and there were certainly signs of moves towards Western-style modernity in countries such as Hungary, Poland and the USSR even before 1989. One of the salient features of legal-rationality is an emphasis on the rule of law and, as a corollary, the depersonalization of politics and economics. Signs of this development include not only verbal commitments, such as references in communist politicians' speeches to the rule of law, but also more concrete manifestations. Among the latter are the limiting of tenure for political office-holding; granting citizens the right to bring legal charges against officials at any level; genuinely contested elections; and greater tolerance of investigative journalism (for a more detailed comparative analysis of the communists' moves towards legal-rationality see Holmes 1993: esp. 274–91). In the USSR, these changes were closely associated with Mikhail Gorbachev (in power 1985–91), and were manifest in his emphasis on political and economic restructuring (*perestroika*), greater openness and honesty (*glasnost*) on the part of the authorities, and more political rights to the citizenry (*demokratisatsiya*).

Many communist leaders took these steps towards legal-rationality largely because other modes of legitimation had proved disappointing. In particular, the late-1980s' encouragement of citizens to criticize corrupt, inefficient or arrogant party and state officials can be seen on one level as a method by which leaders hoped to be able to ensure proper implementation of the economic reforms. Prior to this, communist leaders had often adopted policies designed to improve economic performance, only to see their own officials sabotage these policies out of fear that the proposed changes would undermine these officials' positions. Thus, both Deng (PRC) and Gorbachev – in different ways and to different extents – employed moves towards legal-rationality, including mass involvement in campaigns against corrupt officials, as one method for improving economic performance. The motive for such an approach was probably less a commitment to a genuine rule of law as generally understood in the West, than a means for improving such performance. It is likely that the leaders' ultimate aim was to be able to return to a form of eudaemonic legitimation – only this time, based on a genuine improvement in the economy and thus in living standards. Deng was considerably more successful than Gorbachev in achieving this objective.

But developments in the late-1980s suggested that communist leaders cannot control (i.e. limit) the moves towards legal-rationality that they themselves feel compelled to initiate. The measures taken towards more open politics and privatization (an economic dimension of the general move towards legal-rationality, since it represents a depersonalization and deconcentration of the running of the economy) often encourage citizens to demand and expect more than the communists can and/or are willing to provide. This tension became very visible in the USSR, in China and in several East European states at the end of the 1980s. One response is to move back towards coercion; the Beijing massacre of June 1989 and its aftermath typifies this. But some communist countries – notably most of the East European states – proved incapable of reversing the trend. Many communist leaderships found themselves and their system in a fundamental identity and legitimacy crisis. The more they accepted elements of legal-rationality into the system, the more the communist system began to resemble what the leaders themselves had for so many years portrayed as the arch-enemy, the liberal-democratic capitalist system. Even worse, the new hybrid appeared to incorporate many of the worst aspects of both types of system, rather than the best. On the one hand, the communists were now accepting unemployment, inflation, and growing inequality. On the other hand, citizens had still not been granted high levels of freedom of speech, freedom of assembly, freedom of travel – or the living standards of the West.

In addition to this basic dilemma, the leaderships of many communist states began to lose faith in what they were doing, as the leader of their role-model (i.e. Gorbachev in the USSR) acknowledged that his country was in crisis and uncertain of its future direction. Hence, even this form of external legitimation (i.e. existence of an external role-model) was failing. It was in this situation of fundamental contradictions, pressure from below, and loss of their principal role-model, that many communists realized by 1989–90 that the very dynamism of communist power had brought them to a point at which that power and system had run its course. One after another, and in different ways, most communist systems collapsed. What followed is commonly known as post-communism.

Post-communism

At this point, three questions need to be addressed. First, what does the term post-communism mean, and is it still a useful and valid concept? Second, why have countries gone in different directions since exiting communism? Finally, are there any salient features of post-communist systems and, if so, what are these? Each of these questions is large, and only introductory answers can be provided here.

More than a decade since the collapse of communist power in CEE (Central and Eastern Europe) and the FSU (Former Soviet Union), analysts still cannot agree on a definition of post-communism. At least four approaches can be discerned. The narrowest is one favoured by several scholars in CEE, and refers to periods since 1989 in which successor parties to the former communist parties are in power. According to this definition, for instance, Poland has been post-communist not for the entire period since 1989, but only 1993–7, and then again from 2001. Such scholars perceive their countries as basically in transition to democracy, and therefore prefer to use a label they believe focuses too much on the past and insufficiently on the future *only* when communist successor parties dominate the government.

At the other end of the spectrum are two very broad definitions that refer to the state of the whole world since the collapse of communist power. One is primarily concerned with changes in the state of international relations. It refers to a world in which there are no longer two major superpowers, one of which is communist. Instead of this essentially bi-polar world, there is, according to which analyst one reads, either a world dominated by just one superpower (the USA, with more or less support from its allies), or an increasingly multi-polar world. Again depending on the analyst, such scenarios can be described as the New World Order, the New World Disorder, or 'the West versus the Rest'. But their common focus on changes in the international setting since the collapse of communist (esp. Soviet) power suggests that this development is better described as 'post-Cold War' than post-communism.

The second very broad approach – our third overall – focuses on changes in attitudes towards political theories and ideologies; it is a more abstract approach than the previous one. As Richard Sakwa (1999: esp. 1–3) points out, one of the salient features of recent years is that grand theories and ideologies (nowadays often called metanarratives) have been largely discredited, and politics almost everywhere has become ever more pragmatic and discursive. The collapse of communist power is seen as one of the major watersheds in this demise of ideology. Although this collapse was undoubtedly a major contributory factor to the declining faith in teleological ideologies, the phenomenon described here can be seen as part of a general questioning of modernity that started well before 1989. For this reason, it is better seen as a component of post-modernity than as post-communism.

This leaves us with the fourth and final definition of post-communism. It is unquestionably the one in most common usage, and refers in an aggregated way to the recent developments in the countries that were previously under communist rule, but that have now moved on. Most basically, then, a post-communist state is a transitional one that has in the past been ruled by communists, but in which the communists have now lost their politically privileged position. The remainder of this essay will adopt this interpretation.

Graeme Gill (2002: esp. 201–3) has argued that our fourth approach remains too vague, and he distinguishes between post-communism as a system, a condition, and a situation. In his view, the first of these implies 'considerable uniformity across all post-communist countries', which is one reason he does not favour its use. While, for Gill, the conception of post-communism as a condition implies less integration and uniformity than does the notion of a system, it still suggests greater homogeneity than he believes is to be found across the range of countries usually described as 'post-communist'. Hence, his own preferred interpretation is what he calls the 'minimalist' one of 'the period following the collapse of communism'. But he also makes it clear that he is referring to the experiences only of the formerly communist states, not the whole world – and in this sense is still using our fourth ('most popular') approach.

For some writers, the diversity Gill identifies particularly in his discussion of post-communism as a system had by the late-1990s become so great that it was no longer appropriate to use the term post-communism (see e.g. Rupnik 1999). There is no question that the term is often applied to a wide range of systems and societies, from virtual dictatorships in many of the Central Asian states and Belarus through to essentially consolidated democracies such as Poland, Hungary and Slovenia. It is also true that there have been very divergent views across (and even within) all of these countries on the nature, pace and direction of change that is desirable and/or feasible. Rupnik's position is therefore understandable. Nevertheless, the post-communist states had similar legacies to overcome in an essentially similar international context, and simply because they have dealt with their pasts and their transitions in such different ways does not alter the fact that they all had much in common at the beginning of the 1990s. Moreover few, if any, had been accepted yet as 'Western' by the turn of the millennium. Hence, many authors continue to use the generic term 'post-communism', at the same time as they highlight and attempt to explain the significant differences that exist between the numerous countries to which this term is applied (see e.g. Mandelbaum 1996; Anderson et al. 2002). Even when the synchronic applicability of the term does eventually appear to have become redundant – as it surely will vis-à-vis several CEE states once they are admitted to the European Union – it will still be used in the social sciences to describe a significant historical phenomenon, just as fascism is. Moreover, it is highly probable that countries such as Cuba and Vietnam will one day be 'post-communist'. Therefore, despite all its shortcomings, it would be inappropriate to jettison the term.

Answering our second question – i.e. concerning the very different paths taken by post-communist countries since the beginning of the 1990s – is difficult, and too big to address adequately here. Among the many factors to be considered in any comprehensive attempt at explanation are political culture; level of economic development; types and levels of ethnic conflict; the nature of early post-communist institutions and the reasons for them; geographical proximity to the West; awareness of what is occurring elsewhere in the world – and, apparently, the way in which the communists came to power. Concerning the last of these, there appears to be a reasonably clear pattern whereby countries in which communism was essentially installed by a foreign power moved more rapidly to post-communism, and experienced fewer problems, than countries in which native communists assumed power largely by their own efforts. For example, Poland and Hungary were by the mid 1990s at a more advanced stage of transition than former Yugoslavia, Albania or the former USSR.

Whether or not there is a causal relationship here is particularly difficult to answer; while this point does not pertain to Albania, the more troubled exits from communism in both former Yugoslavia and the former Soviet Union could well relate more to the greater ethnic diversity in those countries compared with the East Central European states, for example. In the case of the former USSR, moreover, its multiple losses – of its inner and outer empires; of the Cold War; of its role as a superpower; and of its role as the model socialist state – meant that, unlike the initial elation many central and east Europeans experienced in the immediate aftermath of the collapse of communism and Soviet domination, many former Soviet citizens had decidedly mixed feelings. This was particularly true of the Russians. While there were unquestionably differences between Hungarians, Poles, Czechs, etc. in terms of their views on the optimal path forward, a common sense of liberation provided a level of social cohesion that did not exist among Russians.

Numerous scholars have attempted to classify the post-communist states in terms of the extent to which they have moved towards democracy. For adherents of the Schumpeterian minimalist approach to democracy, the measures taken at the beginning of the 1990s towards both competitive electoral politics and capitalist economic systems were sufficient for such countries to be classified as democracies. Thus John Mueller argues that:

> It is the central contention of this chapter that most of the postcommunist countries of central and eastern Europe have essentially completed their transition to democracy and capitalism: what they now have is, pretty much, it. They are already full-fledged democracies if we use as models real Western countries (as opposed to some sort of vaporous ideal).
>
> (Mueller 1996: 102)

and suggests that analysts should stop seeing post-communist states as 'transitional'.

But this view is a minority one, and most scholars have conceived of post-communist states as a particular type of transitional state (see e.g. Linz and Stepan 1996). This said, there has been a heated debate on the extent to which it is appropriate to compare the post-communist countries with other transitional states, such as those in Latin America (see e.g. Schmitter and Karl 1994; Bunce 1995a; Karl and Schmitter 1995; Bunce 1995b). More recently, the debate has focused on the problems of determining when the 'trailblazer' states can be said to have consolidated democracy – at which point they cease to be classified as post-communist, which is a descriptor for countries still reacting to the past, and typically undergoing rapid and significant change.

This is not the place to rehearse the complex and sometimes precious arguments developed in these debates on transition and consolidation in the post-communist world. Suffice it to note that most commentators have drawn a reasonably sharp distinction between the paths taken by the CIS – Commonwealth of Independent States – countries (i.e. all FSU states except for the Baltic states of Estonia, Latvia and Lithuania) and the post-communist states of Central and Eastern Europe. The latter are widely seen to have been more successful in their moves towards both democracy and the market. However, it should be noted that a number of observers draw a further distinction between the East Central European states (the Baltic States, Czechia, Hungary, Poland, Slovakia and Slovenia) and the South East European, or Balkan, states. The latter are considered to have experienced greater problems in their transitions than have the former, though both groups are seen by most commentators to have been more successful in their democratization processes than the CIS states have been. Some analysts have linked this to the fact that most CEE states opted for more parliamentary arrangements, whereas many CIS states developed presidential and even 'superpresidential' systems. Unfortunately, this is a chicken and egg issue, since it then needs to be asked why some states adopted or later transferred to one arrangement, while other states chose and retained the other (for a sophisticated analysis of the differences, and an interesting thesis on the reasons for this, see Fish 2002).

One way to conceptualize transition and consolidation is to examine whether a country is primarily dealing with the past or focusing more on the future. In this approach, the transition phase is seen as comprising two parts – transformation and consolidation – corresponding to the two different emphases. Thus transformation is mainly concerned with rejecting the past and overcoming the legacy of the communist era, including 'foreign' (mainly Soviet or Russian, but also Serbian in former Yugoslavia) domination, and high levels of coercion, elitism, corruption, mendacity, hypocrisy and incompetence. It also involves dealing with the sorry state of the economy in almost all formerly communist systems. At this stage, policies are often adopted quickly and without sufficient deliberation, although it is understandable *why* this happens in the revolutionary circumstances. As time passes, flaws and gaps in legislation become obvious, and people begin to think less of the past and more of the present and future. In this consolidation phase, there is more focus on the quality of laws and policy implementation; the situation is relatively calmer, while patterns of political behaviour and affiliation begin to crystallize. Political discourse is less about fundamentals, and more about improvement within increasingly accepted parameters.

The third question is also difficult to answer satisfactorily, especially in a short essay. As already noted, there are by now significant differences between post-communist states, in terms of structures and success-rates. Yet all had to overcome the communist legacy – which is a feature unique to post-communist states – and all were doing so in a basically similar global context. The latter variable distinguishes them from Latin American transition states, which began their moves away from dictatorship at different times, and hence in different international contexts. The

South European transition states of the mid 1970s (Greece, Portugal and Spain) *did* all commence their transitions in essentially the same international climate, although this was different from that of the late-1980s/early-1990s.

Moreover, while some post-communist states have in recent years been back-tracking on the initial democratization moves they took in the early-1990s (Turkmenistan is the only one not to have had even some sort of competitive election, although there have been irregularities in many other post-communist elections), almost all had putatively similar goals in the earliest phases of post-communism. These included Western-style democratization; marketization; privatization; and a reorientation of their international allegiances. The *range* of transitions relative to these objectives has been broader in post-communist countries than in other transitional states. The existence of rapid, multiple and simultaneous transitions is thus one of the most significant distinguishing features of post-communism. Most other transitional states have undergone major political transitions, but already had significant elements of a privatized and marketized economy at the time of the collapse of their previous systems.

Another feature common to most if not all post-communist countries is the pattern of dramatically changing public attitudes. Thus, there was a widespread and overwhelming sense of euphoria and liberation in the earliest days after the collapse of communist power. But this honeymoon period was soon replaced by a sense of profound disappointment, as the hardships of early post-communism impacted upon citizens. In the early-1990s, unemployment and inflation rates soared throughout the post-communist world. In a real sense, the effect of these on popular attitudes was greater there than elsewhere, since citizens were not used to either. The problems were further compounded by the sorry state of welfare systems in the post-communist states. The situation had begun to improve somewhat in many post-communist countries by the late-1990s, so that a third era – of sober realism – emerged.

In the earlier discussion of conceptions of post-communism, it was noted that some commentators have seen its emergence as reflective of the rejection of metanarratives. However, while the evidence suggests that 'grand theories' such as Marxism have been discredited in the eyes of most, there were signs by the late-1990s that teleological legitimation was not yet dead. For many CEE countries, the new *telos* became membership of the European Union (EU). These countries were still suffering economically, albeit to very differing degrees; as they looked at the success of countries such as Ireland, Portugal and Spain since joining the EU, the CEE applicants for EU membership believed they could see light at the end of their own tunnels.

Future membership of the EU, including the likely impact of this on the consolidation of democracy and the market, has become one of the most significant divisions between post-communist states. Not only does this factor have implications for the *future* further consolidation of democracy and the market, but meeting current requirements in order to qualify for membership has also forced the pace and direction of change in the applicant states. Moreover, together with NATO and the Council of Europe, the EU has encouraged resolution of a number of disputes in CEE that might otherwise have festered or even intensified had it not been for external pressure. Such disputes mostly relate to the position of minorities within post-communist countries, and sometimes territory; examples of successful resolution include the Hungarian-Slovak and Hungarian-Romanian Treaties of the mid-1990s.

To conclude this brief consideration of post-communism, it is worth noting that while the *structures* of the former communist systems have been decisively rejected almost everywhere, some of the *values* of communism remain or have become attractive to many citizens. Such values include a commitment to limiting inequalities; state subsidization of basic foodstuffs, housing, and transport; a well-developed state-run welfare system; and full or near-full employment. Thus, the communists have been the single largest party in the Russian parliament (*Duma*) since the mid 1990s, while communist successor parties have fared well in many other elections, including the Lithuanian of 1992, the Polish of 1993 and 2001, the Hungarian of 1994 and 2002, the Mongolian of 2000, and the Moldovan of 2001. But in almost all cases, the communist successors have distanced themselves from much of the communist era, and mostly represent a radical version of social democracy. Thus they overwhelmingly support a basically market-oriented economy and the notion of contested elections (as of mid-2002, there were doubts about the Moldovan government's commitment to both of these). This attraction to what may be seen as communist values is far more common in post-communist systems than in other transitional states.

Second, the fate of the existing post-communist countries has had implications for the few remaining communist systems. Certainly for the first decade, the post-communist systems as a whole were perceived to represent little if any real improvement on communism, which provided communists still in power with an opportunity to prolong their rule. Many post-communist countries were so severely troubled that violence was a key dimension of everyday life, whether in the form of actual wars (esp. in former Yugoslavia) or turf warfare between organized crime gangs. Moreover, as questionable – often corrupt – privatization processes in several post-communist states appeared in practice to benefit former communists (this is usually called '*nomenklatura* privatization') and even criminals more than anyone else, it began to look as if post-communism might be worse than communism, greater freedom of speech and to travel notwithstanding. However, these delaying factors will bring only a temporary respite for the remaining communist systems. The dynamism of communism in power is such that democratic centralism, the *de facto* one-party state and the centrally planned national economy eventually become outdated and are replaced – suddenly or gradually; violently or peacefully; from below, above or outside, depending on the particular circumstances. Communism is often a relatively effective system for modernizing societies; but it is incompatible with law-based, pluralist modernity or post-modernity. Thus, despite the severe teething problems of early post-communism, the growing success of even a handful of countries (mostly in East Central Europe) will help to enhance post-communism's image, and hence its attractiveness in countries still under communist control.

References

Anderson, R., Fish, S., Hanson, S. and Roeder, P. (2002) *Postcommunism and the Theory of Democracy*, Princeton, NJ: Princeton University Press.

Bunce, V. (1995a) 'Should Transitologists be Grounded?', *Slavic Review*, 54 (1): 111–27.

—— (1995b) 'Paper Curtains and Paper Tigers', *Slavic Review*, 54 (4): 979–87.

Dallin, A. and Breslauer, G. (1970) *Political Terror in Communist Systems*, Stanford, CA: Stanford University Press.

Fish, S. (2002) 'The Dynamics of Democratic Erosion' in Anderson *et al.*, 2002.

Gill, G. (2002) *Democracy and Post-Communism*, London: Routledge.

Harding, N. (1981) 'What Does It Mean to Call a Regime Marxist?', in B. Szajkowski, *Marxist Governments – A World Survey*, Vol. 1, London: Macmillan.

—— (1983) *Lenin's Political Thought*, London: Macmillan.

Holmes, L. (1993) *The End of Communist Power*, Cambridge: Polity Press.

Karl, T. and Schmitter, P. (1995) 'From an Iron Curtain to a Paper Curtain: Grounding Transitologists or Students of Postcommunism?', *Slavic Review*, 54 (4): 965–78.

Kautsky, J. (1973) 'Comparative Communism versus Comparative Politics', *Studies in Comparative Communism*, 6 (1–2): 135–70.

Linz, J. and Stepan, A. (1996) *Problems of Democratic Transition and Consolidation*, Baltimore: Johns Hopkins University Press.

Mandelbaum, M. (ed.)(1996) *Post-Communism: Four Perspectives*, New York: Council on Foreign Relations.

Marx, K. and Engels, F. (1970) *The German Ideology – Part One*, London: Lawrence and Wishart.

McLellan, D. (1995) *The Thought of Karl Marx*, London: Pan.

—— (1998) *Marxism After Marx*, London: Macmillan.

Mueller, J. (1996) 'Democracy, Capitalism, and the End of Transition' in Mandelbaum 1996.

Poggi, G. (1978) *The Development of the Modern State*, London: Hutchinson.

Rigby, T. H. (1982) 'Introduction: Political Legitimacy, Weber and Communist Mono-organisational Systems', in T. H. Rigby and F. Feher (eds) *Political Legitimation in Communist States*, London: Macmillan.

Rupnik, J. (1999) 'The Postcommunist Divide', *Journal of Democracy*, 10 (1): 57–62.

Sakwa, R. (1999) *Postcommunism*, Buckingham: Open University Press.

Schmitter, P. and Karl, T. (1994) 'The Conceptual Travels of Transitologists and Consolidologists: How Far to the East Should They Attempt to Go?', *Slavic Review*, 53 (1): 173–85.

White, S., Gardner, J., Schöpflin, G. and Saich, T. (1990) *Communist and Postcommunist Political Systems*, London: Macmillan.

Further reading

Hammond, T. (ed.) (1975) *The Anatomy of Communist Takeovers*, New Haven: Yale University Press.

Holmes, L. (1986) *Politics in the Communist World*, Oxford: Oxford University Press.

—— (1997) *Post-Communism*, Cambridge: Polity Press.

Szajkowski, B. (ed.) (1981) *Marxist Governments: A World Survey*, 3 vols, London: Macmillan.

Westoby, A. (1983) 'Conceptions of Communist States', in D. Held *et al.*, *States and Societies*, London: Martin Robertson.

White, S. and Nelson, D. (eds) (1986) *Communist Politics: A Reader*, London: Macmillan.

16

AUTHORITARIAN REGIMES

Catharin E. Dalpino

In the post-Cold War era, roughly the decade of the 1990s, authoritarianism was frequently viewed as the default position for democracy. At the height of the Third Wave, a democratizing bias was often evident in both policy-making and scholarship. Nondemocratic nations were assumed to be moving toward democracy, however distant the goal and slow the pace; accordingly, authoritarianism was explained as a delay in that inevitable movement, and authoritarian systems were seen as incomplete or transitional forms of democracy. Authoritarian regimes were often assumed to be the only factor holding back reform-minded societies, and political oppositions to these regimes were almost always assumed to be democratic. An exception to the latter generalization was made in countries where the primary or sole opposition was based in political Islam. Indeed, in the early 1990s 'the Algerian dilemma', in which a rightist authoritarian regime was deemed tolerable if it prevented an Islamist party from coming to power, presaged a new Cold War, this one between polarized civilizations rather than ideologies (Quandt 1998).

Measurements were similar to those on the democratic spectrum, albeit in reverse: authoritarian systems were defined by the absence of democratic features. In the early 1990s, for example, Huntington (1993: 12) drew a rough dividing line between democratic and authoritarian systems at elections: nondemocratic regimes were those which did not permit electoral competition or grant widespread (if not universal) franchise. This dichotomy did not anticipate authoritarian regimes that use democratic institutions as the very means of preserving political power. By the end of the decade, several states exhibited formal democratic processes which were technically correct; however, in a cynical phrase often heard in these countries, they resembled 'a level playing field on which the government always wins.'

In the new decade, much of this intellectual framework remains, but the assumption of democratic inevitability is waning. To be sure, substantial gains in the worldwide movement toward democracy have been realized in the past several years. At the same time, the number of countries under authoritarianism has risen as well. From 1991 to 2001, the number of liberal democracies (as measured by the Freedom House ratings) has climbed from 76 to 85. Those under authoritarian rule have increased from 42 to 48 (Freedom House 2001). The 59 'partly free' countries occupy a middle ground more difficult to classify. Many of these are democratizing countries. However, at least an equal number are states in which some political and civil rights are observed, and might even be strengthening, but in which authoritarian regimes have devised new ways of preserving power. In an era of consolidation, democratic and authoritarian rule are both consolidating.

As a result of these mixed trends, scholars are showing renewed interest in the study of authoritarianism in its own right, an inquiry that had been abandoned for much of the 1990s. The spectrum of authoritarian systems is becoming wider and more diverse, and the perception of a democratic continuum is weakened as a result. Through much of the 1970s Linz and Stepan endeavoured to break through a simplistic dichotomy in prevalent analysis which paralleled broader Cold War thinking. Their mission was fuelled by large-scale reversals in Second Wave countries in the face of the continuing pitched competition between the world's two major political blocs. They identified authoritarianism as a mid-point between democracy and totalitarianism, the ideological poles of the Cold War, and argued that it warranted examination as a separate phenomenon (see, for example, Linz and Stepan 1978). However, this earlier body of work, albeit ground-breaking, was based largely on countries – primarily in Latin America – which had suffered reversals from democratic experiments, and so offered analysts some democratic reference points. The focus on this group of countries intensified in the 1980s under the lead of the Reagan administration's Kirkpartick Doctrine, which maintained that repressive regimes on the left (i.e., communist ones) were incapable of evolving into more benign forms and that right-wing regimes offered greater hope for political reform (Dalpino 2002: 22).

In contrast to the political spectrum three decades ago, the present field of examination contains several authoritarian countries with virtually no prior democratic experience. Moreover, in a clear departure from predominant assumptions of the 1990s, the salient features of current authoritarian systems are open to new interpretation. Linz is now inclined to view democratic processes in otherwise authoritarian states as diminished authoritarianism – or even signs of new types of authoritarian systems – rather than the harbingers of imminent democratization (Linz 2000).

Totalitarianism: going, but not gone

Although this new attention is focused on authoritarian regimes on the liberal or liberalizing end of the spectrum, those which occupy the other end deserve scrutiny as well. The number of totalitarian regimes decreased dramatically with the liberation of Eastern Europe in the late 1980s and the dissolution of the Soviet Union a few years later, and most studies have since folded those that remain into an expanded category of authoritarianism. This is the opposite of the conceptual framework which Linz and Stepan sought to counter during the Cold War. It would be useful not to abandon this category altogether, and even to amend it *ex post facto*. During the Cold War, when Leninist regimes were largely out of reach for close study by Western academics, it was commonly assumed that they uniformly followed the Soviet model in architecture, if not always in political allegiance (Gasiorowski 1991). However, the years since the end of the Cold War have revealed that Soviet-style totalitarianism was easier to surmount than its Asian counterpart.

As with authoritarianism, concepts of totalitarian rule are varied and incomplete. However, many analysts adhere to a two-pronged definition of totalitarianism. First, citizens in a totalitarian society are not only denied civil and political rights, but usually lack personal rights as well. Totalitarian regimes have customarily regulated citizens' employment, housing and travel. Many, particularly communist totalitarian regimes, have often reached down into families and the most basic levels of social organizations. Second, totalitarian regimes seek to reorganize societal as well as government institutions, usually prohibiting or repressing voluntary organizations and substituting them with government-organized and run mass organizations. Most regimes which might be classified as totalitarian meet some but not all of these criteria, making such labels controversial. In the post-Cold War era, regimes which are retained under this category tended to fall into two groups: those which seek to enforce theocracy, and hold-over regimes from earlier eras.

The concept of totalitarianism has been divorced from Cold War ideology in most academic communities (although not in some political quarters), but it cannot be said that no competing ideology exists to engender new totalitarian regimes. The Taliban revolution in Afghanistan in the 1990s, which occurred at a time when democracy appeared to be making headway in nearly every region, was an unsettling reminder of this possibility. Indeed, it bears mention that totalitarianism was a distinctly modern phenomenon, scarcely appearing before the twentieth century. The tools of modernization – improved technology, and broader and more personalized systems of communication, which are presently touted as the strengths of globalization – were used to their own advantage by totalitarian leaders in past decades. We cannot assume that they could not be similarly employed by future totalitarian regimes under certain circumstances.

Just as contemporary authoritarian regimes may require new indicators, so should we look more closely at the markers for totalitarianism. For most of the twentieth century, gross human rights abuse, genocide in particular, was associated with totalitarian regimes: those of Hitler, Stalin, Mao, and Pol Pot. In the post-Cold War era, however, large-scale genocide has tended to arise more from countries which were in the earliest stages of democratization, such as Bosnia and Rwanda. This may be because most of the gross human rights violations in the Cold War were based on communist ideology (Soviet Union, China, Cambodia) and even on anti-communist reaction (Indonesia in 1965–66). In contrast, post-Cold War gross abuse has tended to target specific groups within a society.

During the Cold War, governments were assumed to be the architects and sole caretakers of totalitarian systems, with civil society co-opted and ultimately destroyed by state domination and persecution. Society was seen as totally oppressed by the state. The contemporary prospect of religious fundamentalist regimes, however remote, suggests a much larger gray area, and a somewhat different arrangement between state and society. In post-Shah Iran, under the rule of the Ayotollah Khomeni, as well as in the Taliban era in Afghanistan, the government and a significant segment of society (religious administration) shared responsibility for enforcing totalitarian rule.

A disproportionate amount of attention has focused on the prospects for future Islamist totalitarian regimes, there being none at present which qualify. However, the handful of remaining totalitarian regimes fall into the hold-over category and represent both the extreme left and right of the political spectrum. These may include Burma, Cuba, Libya, North Korea, Saudi Arabia, Syria and

Turkmenistan. Although there is no one common variable, save their extreme levels of repression, a slim majority of these countries have been in isolation – international or self-imposed – for decades. This isolation enables regimes to limit the consequences of their mistakes. If a regime's hold on a captive population slips for any reason, it can be easily restored. One clear, even astonishing, example of this was the 1990 national election in Burma, in which a totalitarian regime allowed a political opposition to contest for power in a relatively free election. When the election did not return the expected result (victory for the ruling power), the regime was able to nullify the results and return Burma to its prior totalitarian state.

Liberalizing, with limits

In the post-Cold War era, a greater number of totalitarian countries, particularly former communist ones, have developed authoritarian systems which at least grant greater personal freedoms to their citizens. Some are making strides toward democracy, with expanded civil and political rights. In the former Soviet Union and Eastern Europe, the collapse of communism helped to catapult several countries into electoral democracies. In other regions, the exit from totalitarianism was found not in rupture but in more gradual reform. The progress of these countries, which might be labelled as liberalizing authoritarian regimes, is more subtle; indeed, it is often indiscernible to the outside observer for some time. This is due to the dual nature of liberalization, in which the regime may consent to, or even initiate, reforms which simultaneously enable them to retain power while they loosen the reins on citizens. These regimes often do the 'right' thing for the 'wrong' reason, and their reforms are usually met with confusion and scepticism from the West (Dalpino 2002: 25). Thus, China's village elections and the democratic characteristics of Khatami's Iran give conflicting signals on the likely path of political change in these countries.

Liberalizing authoritarian regimes are best identified by the unevenness of the liberalization process, labelled by some as the 'reform tango.' This often reflects a growing spectrum within the regime itself. A surge too far forward will be pulled back, either by ruling hardliners or by moderates within the regime seeking to prevent a backlash which would harm reforms. Conversely, a move toward greater openness may be prefaced by a period of increased control, to assure the regime (and remind reformers) of its continued power. These regimes are also uneven in their distribution of the benefits of liberalization: they depend upon disconnects or gaps. The most that is usually tolerated is an enclave of openness, in the informal system or in civil society. Thus, village elections are permissible in China because the villagers' committees are not a formal part of the Chinese political system, and there is less chance of their sparking demands for a bottom-up democratization process.

Liberalizing authoritarian regimes are often invested in reforming rubber stamp institutions, rather than establishing new structures. This is the safest way of expanding reforms beyond the regime itself. For this purpose, legislatures or their equivalent are often the targets of such experiments. Assemblies are becoming slightly more assertive in China and Vietnam, and in some traditional Middle

Eastern states. In the latter region, the prototypes for legislatures in many of these countries are privy councils or other informal deliberative bodies, in which members of the extended royal family or other representatives of the privileged class are invited to venture opinions on public issues.

In countries where formal legislatures exist, their rubber stamp character is still present but is eroding. Although these assemblies usually continue to approve draft laws submitted by the executive branch, they may do so with thinner margins or stronger debates.

When a liberalization process in the state is allowed to continue, however halting and modest it may be, it will usually cross over into civil society at some point. In these systems, however, there is usually the thinnest of spaces between state and society, making it relatively easy for the regime to control and co-opt reforms for its own purposes. As in the formal system, regimes often attempt first to reshape totalitarian structures into more open ones. Mass organizations previously established by the state may be encouraged to reconsider their roles as 'transmission belts' for regime policy and dedicate themselves to social service, making society rather than the regime their primary client (Cook 1994). Regimes may also allow the formation of voluntary organizations and other citizens groups, so long as they remain apolitical and pursue goals defined, or at least approved, by the regime.

Although these reforms are uniformly modest, they can represent profound shifts in relations between state and society. For a more active civil society to emerge in post-totalitarian systems, state and society must agree on new definitions of citizenship. In these systems, the initial step is often in forging a concept of society as a collection of individual citizens rather than an indivisible 'mass'. This has implications for the citizen's relationship to other citizens and to the state. In China, for example, the establishment of a universal system of taxation introduced the concept of citizens as taxpayers, with some means to hold government accountable for the use of public funds. In this sense, citizens have shifted from their role as servants of the party to 'creditors' of the government (Dalpino 2002: 56)

On the political spectrum, liberalizing authoritarian regimes are the first rung on the ladder of performance legitimacy. Like all but the most totalitarian strongmen, in the post-Cold War era all regimes (including liberal democratic ones) are increasingly subject to pressure to improve the lives of everyday citizens, usually through economic development and more extensive social services. And, as in countries on the democratizing end of the spectrum, the impetus for liberalization is often a crisis in regime legitimacy, originating in economic failure and felt both within the regime and in the general population. In its quest to re-legitimate itself, the regime usually loosens controls slightly while it attempts to improve its economic performance. The two are often related. For example, citizens may be given the freedom to choose their own jobs and residences in order to free the state from the cost of providing employment and furnishing housing. The regime itself may be expanded to include technocrats to whom economic policy may be shifted. This liberalization process can radiate out in several directions, but it does not extend to allowing political competition with the regime. Thus, although citizens in many liberalizing authoritarian systems may see quantum leaps in personal rights, and may even participate in very circumscribed polls, comprehensive elections to achieve transfer of power are beyond their reach.

Electoral authoritarianism

When authoritarian regimes accede to elections but manage to retain power, their political systems begin to resemble hybrids and their labels often acquire hyphens. Judgment on regime type becomes more difficult, and these systems are frequently categorized as either semi-authoritarian or semi-democratic. Despite such theoretical hedging, electoral authoritarianism is unmistakable in its heavy manipulation of electoral processes and the invariable outcome in favour of the regime. Nevertheless, this form of authoritarianism represents a major step up from liberalizing authoritarian regimes. Two features are present in the former which the latter prohibit. The first is the conduct of formal elections and the promise, if not the execution, of open contests. The second is the very existence of a political opposition, much less one that is permitted to contest for power.

Diamond (2002) points out that such regimes are not new. Electoral autocracies, as he calls them, have existed since the 1960s and the 1970s, when the list included Mexico, Singapore, South Africa, Malaysia and Taiwan. From this era only Singapore and Malaysia have survived their hybrid form. However, their ranks have been swelled with later entrants in the post-Cold War period: from the former Soviet Union (e.g., Azerbaijan, Kazakhstan, Tajikistan), Africa (Uganda, Angola and several others), and the Middle East (Kuwait, Jordan, Egypt).

Schedler (2002) lists several tactics employed by these regimes to hobble and effectively neutralize elections. One of the oldest is that of incomplete elections, in which selected levels of government are open to contestation while others are closed. In semi-authoritarian systems, elections are typically permitted at the local level but withheld for national government. (By contrast, in democratizing systems elections may begin at the national level, to install a democratic government. Local elections often follow behind, as the new government attempts to democratize the system more fully.)

Another common strategy is to schedule elections and to exclude the opposition from any significant participation by a variety of means. These range from banning opposition parties and disqualifying candidates to physical intimidation that can run to murder. Opposition parties may also be denied access to media, denied space for public address, and otherwise prevented from waging political campaigns.

Although legal disenfranchisement of voters is usually no longer practiced by authoritarian regimes that hold elections, informal disqualification of citizens who are likely to support the opposition is common. Lastly, numerous techniques of electoral fraud may be employed which introduce bias into electoral administration or misrepresent the results. In the post-Cold War era, the conduct of election fraud has become more subtle and sophisticated. Vote-buying now takes place weeks before the election and miles from the polls. Into the late 1980s, ballot boxes were physically snatched from polling places and stuffed with fraudulent ballots on site. By the mid 1990s, the fraud of choice was manipulation of computerized registration lists.

Authoritarianism is often sustained in these systems because the political culture is at odds with electoral processes. Ottaway (2003: 16) points out that power is opaque in such systems, resulting from relationships established among individuals rather than open and established procedures. Because these relationships are not institutionalized, they are difficult to map and do not lend themselves to public accountability. These regimes negate popular Western beliefs that elections are a catalyst for democratic reform in authoritarian systems. Absent other factors which encourage or compel these regimes to commence democratization, or to yield to leaders that will, elections are a theatrical device for regime re-legitimatization.

The dilemma of competitive authoritarianism

Huntington's dividing line between democracy and authoritarianism – the conduct of free elections – still holds to a significant degree. It is easily discerned in the three regimes types discussed thus far. However, in the least repressive form of authoritarianism, which Levitsky and Way (2002) have termed competitive authoritarianism, the line is blurred. Democratic institutions are held to be meaningful, if subverted. In these systems, elections are held regularly and are generally free of massive fraud. They are also, however, the primary mechanism for sustaining the incumbent regime in power. The seeming contradiction in this lies in the more sophisticated form of electoral abuse these regimes practice. Bribery and co-optation are favoured over voter intimidation. Although opposition politicians are seldom murdered, they may be unfairly taxed. They may find themselves in prison not for their opposition of the regime but for more technical (and often trivial) violations of law. Levitsky and Way cite a growing number of such regimes: Russia under Putin, Peru under Fujimoro, and Malaysia under Mahathir.

In contrast to electoral authoritarian systems, the results of elections under competitive authoritarian regimes are not a foregone conclusion. Enough democratic legitimacy is present in the system to make the regime's manipulation of the system a calculated risk. In competitive authoritarian systems, manipulation of the process alone is not enough to ensure political longevity. Leaders must win some measure of genuine public support. Once results are in, regimes are generally expected to abide by them. For example, Prime Minister Mahathir and his ruling party (United Malays National Organization) were forced to honour the outcome of the 1999 elections in which the opposition Islamic party won two provinces. Moreover, too blatant attempts at electoral manipulation may backfire in these systems and set off a chain of events which force the regime from power. More than opposition from the West and his indictment as a war criminal, the central cause of Slobodan Milosevic's removal was his attempts to falsify the results of Serbia's 2000 election, precipitating a regime crisis.

Levitsky and Way also identify another distinguishing factor of competitive authoritarian regimes. Because the political system is more open, regimes have a greater number of areas in which they must face opposition. Foremost among these are legislatures which, although far weaker than their counterparts in democracies, are often the natural focal points for political opposition. In several authoritarian countries, legislatures have served as both launching pad and shield in opposition attacks against the regime. Judiciaries are another venue for contest in competitive authoritarian systems. Some incumbents harass and even remove their political opponents through the judiciary, and regimes usually attempt to subordinate the courts through intimidation or co-optation. However, even 'caged' judiciaries in competitive authoritarian systems have succeeded in defending the opposition and themselves against total regime domination upon occasion. Lastly, the media in these authoritarian systems is usually itself a hybrid. Typically, the broadcast media is under heavy government control, while the print media is more independent. Thus, the freer elements of the media may function as a watchdog on regime tactics and even serve as a surrogate opposition. Although they must fight on an increasing number of fronts, several regimes are able to maintain control by playing these elements off against one another and by keeping their manipulations as discreet as possible. However, in a multiplicity of contests, the odds that the regime will make a fatal miscalculation go up significantly.

In the post-Cold War era, competitive authoritarian systems have been a growth industry. No doubt, the steady increase in international pressure on regimes to democratize in the 1990s forced regimes to adopt some, but not enough, democratic practices. Some faltering or failed democratic experiments in the Third Wave regressed to competitive authoritarian regimes. They may be relatively short-lived (Thailand in the 1980s) or endure for generations (Malaysia for the past three decades). Those who embrace theories of the democratic imperative believe that competitive authoritarian regimes stand at the threshold of democratization. This may indeed be the case, but the majority of these incumbents have no intention of crossing that threshold. Many of them have succeeded, even in nations in which there is clear popular support for democracy. Leaders in competitive authoritarian systems are often, by definition, highly organized in their manoeuvers to retain power. Political opposition particularly in nondemocratic systems, is often extremely disorganized, not only because of interference from the regime but also because of internal splits and general inexperience. As Caspar and Taylor (1996) observe, authoritarian regimes often win wars of attrition.

Enabling environments: authoritarianism and society

In the post-Cold War era, popular caricatures of authoritarian systems have painted democratically-minded (but ineffectual) societies being held hostage by authoritarian leaders. This strong state–weak society model attempts to divorce the regime from underlying social structures. The notion of a conquered society has roots in several historical periods, when leadership was imported from other countries or territories and imposed by force upon the population. Quandt (1998) recounts how successive periods – ranging from the Ottoman empire to Western colonialism – prevented a ruling class from emerging from society. In these times, order was maintained and diverse language or religious groups were sometimes allowed to live in relative freedom so long as they did not challenge the prerogatives of the state. External masters quickly learned the principles of 'divide and rule', and pit social groups against one another. This social engineering in order to maintain control was arguably a precursor for modern totalitarian systems.

Centuries later, authoritarian regimes (and some democratizing ones) still exhibit many of the same disconnects or gaps. Ottaway (2003) attributes the tenacity of authoritarianism in many modern nations to the failure of elites to embed themselves in the society. Authoritarian elites have no overwhelming need to do so, since they can control the population through means other than popular support. However, democracy-minded elites in these countries have also failed to integrate with society; to some degree, this failure keeps democracy at bay. Ironically, this may be one of the things they have most in common with their authoritarian counterparts (and antagonists).

In many cases, however, authoritarian leaders have become more embedded in societies than have democrats by allying themselves with nationalist, nativist or populist movements. The break-up of the former Yugoslavia in the 1990s and the subsequent carnage was fuelled by authoritarian leaders with strong ethnic identification, who were able to wrest (or withhold) power from new democrats. Such episodes lay bare the role that society itself can play in promoting or sustaining repression. The Yugoslavia example stands in stark contrast to the image of that same region only a few decades before, of populations held captive behind an Iron Curtain of communism and Soviet domination. At the same time, the 'Algeria dilemma' – in which the social phenomenon of Islamic extremism threatened security – presented itself in North Africa and the Middle East.

A few years later Fareed Zakaria (1997) offered an intellectual chapeau to this seemingly new danger with his description of 'illiberal democracies'. If Zakaria did not necessarily intend his thesis to condemn democratization outright or in all cases, it offered new justification for authoritarian leaders who promised 'stability' in return for the right to rule without submitting themselves to genuine political competition. Warnings of the dangers of 'illiberal democracy' were incorporated into the 'Asian values' debate, which ran the course of the 1990s and was only slowed by the 1997–98 Asian economic crisis. In the post-September 11 era, policymakers are focused almost myopically on the terrorist threat that some societies, or elements within them, present.

Out of this concern is arising a new dilemma, of balancing political openness and individual freedoms with internal security. Authoritarian regimes have seized on this to advance a new justification for their continued rule, or at least for delaying democratic reforms indefinitely. The established democracies have not as yet attempted to counter this justification with the vigour they demonstrated for democracy promotion in the early years of the post-Cold War era.

In the late twentieth century, authoritarianism lost ground to democracy, but it has hardly disappeared. On the contrary, new sources and varieties of authoritarian rule have emerged. The ability of policymakers and scholars to affect the course of political development in authoritarian countries will depend in great part upon their willingness to recognize and examine these forms of government as phenomena in their own right, proceeding at their own pace.

References

Casper, G. and Taylor, M. R. (1996) *Negotiating Democracy: Transitions From Authoritarian Rule*, Pittsburgh: University of Pittsburgh Press.

Cook, J. (1994) *The Rise of Non-Governmental Organizations in China: Implications for Americans*, New York: National Committee on US–China Relations.

Dalpino, C. (2002) *Deferring Democracy: Promoting Openness in Authoritarian Regimes*, Washington, DC: Brookings Institution Press.

Diamond, L. (2002) 'Thinking About Hybrid Regimes', *Journal of Democracy* 13: 21–35.

Freedom House (2001) *The 2001–2002 Freedom House Survey of Freedom*, New York: Freedom House.

Gasiorowski, M. J. (1991) 'The Political Regimes Project', in Inkeles, A. (ed.) *On Measuring Democracy: Its Consequences and Concomitants*, New Brunswick, NJ: Transaction Publishers.

Huntington, S. P. (1993) *The Third Wave*, Norman: University of Oklahoma Press.

Levitsky, S. and Way, L. A., (2003) 'The Rise of Competitive Authoritarianism', *Journal of Democracy* 13: 51–65.

Linz, J. J. (2000) *Totalitarian and Authoritarian Regimes*, Boulder, CO: Lynne Rienner Publishers.

Linz, J. J. and Stepan, A. (1978) *The Breakdown of Democratic Regimes*, Baltimore: Johns Hopkins University Press.

Ottaway, M. (2003) *Democracy Challenged: The Rise of Semi-Authoritarianism*, Washington, DC: Carnegie for International Development.

Quandt, W. B. (1998) *Between Ballots and Bullets: Algeria's Transition from Authoritarianism*, Washington, DC: Brookings Institution Press.

Schedler, A. (2002) 'The Menu of Manipulation', *Journal of Democracy* 13: 36–50.

Zakaria, Fareed (1997) 'The Rise of Illiberal Democracy', *Foreign Affairs* 76: 22–43.

Further reading

Alagappa, M. (ed.) (1995) *Political Legitimacy in Southeast Asia: The Quest for Moral Authority*, Stanford, CA: Stanford University Press.

Bertrand, J. (1996) 'False Starts, Succession Crises and Regime Transition: Flirting with Openness in Indonesia', *Pacific Affairs* 69: 319–40.

Chua, B. H. (1995) *Communitarian Ideology and Democracy in Singapore*, London: Routledge.

Dawisha, K. and Parrott, B. (1997) *Democratic Changes and Authoritarian Reactions in Russia, Ukraine, Belarus and Moldova*, New York: Cambridge University Press.

Fowler, W. (ed.) (1996) *Authoritarianism in Latin America Since Independence*, Westport, CT: Greenwood Press.

Garfinkle, A. and Pipes, D. (eds) (1991) *Friendly Tyrants: An American Dilemma*, New York: St Martin's Press.

Guo, S. (2000) *Post-Mao China: From Totalitarianism to Authoritarianism?* Westport, CT: Praeger.

Jalal, A. (1995) *Democracy and Authoritarianism in South Asia: A Comparative And Historical Perspective*, New York: Cambridge University Press.

Kalathil, S. and Boas, T. C. (2003) *Open Networks, Closed Regimes: The Impact of the Internet on Authoritarian Rule*, Washington, DC: Carnegie Endowment for International Peace.

Munro-Kua, A. (1996) *Authoritarian Populism in Malaysia*, New York: St Martin's Press.

Nelson, D. N. (ed.) (1995) *After Authoritarianism: Democracy or Disorder?*, Westport, CT: Greenwood Press.

O'Donnell, G. (ed.) (1999) *Counterpoints: Selected Essays on Authoritarianism and Democratization*, Notre Dame, IN: University of Notre Dame Press.

O'Donnell, G. and Schmitter, P. (1986) *Transitions from Authoritarian Rule: Conclusions About Uncertain Democracies*, Baltimore: Johns Hopkins University Press.

Ottaway, M. (1999) *Africa's New Leaders: Democracy or State Reconstruction?*, Washington, DC: Carnegie Endowment for International Peace.

Steinberg, D. I. (2001) *Burma: The State of Myanmar*, Washington, DC: Georgetown University Press.

Twohey, M. (1999) *Authority and Welfare in China: Debates in Historical Perspective*, New York: St Martin's Press.

Wekkin, G. D. (ed.) (1993) *Building Democracy in One-Party Systems: Theoretical Problems and Cross-Nation Experiences*, Westport, CT: Praeger.

17

MILITARY RULE

Talukder Maniruzzaman

Any student of the military and politics cannot but be struck by the fact that civil–military relations in developing countries from the 1950s to the present have been closely linked to changes in the international environment and more particularly to the foreign policy of the USA. Over the past half-century American foreign policy has undergone two distinct phases. The first phase supported a large number of military coups in many Third World countries. The second phase, starting from the late 1970s and continuing to the present time, endorsed military withdrawals from politics. It is rather intriguing that in both diametrically opposed foreign policy phases, the US government's philosophy of international relations synchronized with two different types of literatures produced by American political scientists.

Soon after the end of the Second World War, George Kennan, in his famous 'X' article in *Foreign Affairs* advocated a 'long term, patient, firm and vigilant containment of the Soviet pressure against the institutions of the Western World'. Kennan suggested that Soviet expansionism could be contained by 'the adroit and vigilant application of counter force at a series of constantly shifting geographical and political points' (quoted in Girling 1980: pp. 153–4). In accordance with the containment doctrine, US foreign policy supported *coups d'état* in Latin and Central America, Africa, and Asia.

One of the earliest US scholarly articles to argue for an expanded role in Southeast Asia was written by Guy Pauker (1959: 325–45) and it advocated this technique of mobilizing the organizational strength and coercive capacity available to societies so that they might fight communism (Maniruzzaman 1987: 11). American political scientists such as L. W. Pye, S. P. Huntington, Morris Janowitch, J. Johnson and others developed theoretical models depicting the military as a highly modern force capable of transferring its organizational and technical skills to the field of government and administration (see for example, Pye 1962: 68–9; Halpern 1962: 277–313; Daadler 1962; Johnson 1964). Encouraged by the support of academe, successive American Presidents began to arm the military regimes of developing countries. The US government also formed military pacts (SEATO, CENTO etc.) with 'Friendly Tyrants' so that they could stamp out the communists in the states with strategic importance (Sayeed 1995: 22).

With the end of Cold War in 1988–9 and the collapse of the Soviet Union and its satellite states in Eastern Europe, American scholarship and government policy makers retreated from their earlier theoretical formulations. The idea that autocracy and military dictatorship fostered economic and political development, which sustained the containment doctrine, was suddenly discarded. Instead, theories of democratic rule and competitive politics were heralded as the best means to promote economic transformations to market systems. In the 1990s, political scientists such as S. P. Huntington and many others argued that 'democracy is good in itself and it has positive consequences for individual freedom, domestic stability and international peace' (Huntington 1993: xv). Moreover, it was suggested that replacement of military regimes by liberal democracies would open up 'new economic frontiers' and accelerate both political and economic growth.

The correlation between changing academic paradigms and changing US foreign policy objectives raises important ethical questions about predictions concerning the future of military dictatorships. But any effort to assess those issues requires fuller explication of the distinctive nature of military rule; the origins and growth of military rule from the early twentieth century until 1988–9; strategies of rulership by military dictators; the effects of military rule as well as the consequences of the withdrawal of military rule. This chapter will consider each of these issues in turn.

Defining military rule

Oliver Cromwell is reported to have said, 'Nine citizens out of ten hate me? What does it matter if that tenth alone is armed?' (Fried 1966: 87–8). This short statement by the first and the last military dictator in modern English history sums up much of the substance of military dictatorship. Military dictatorship means the rule by a military officer or a military junta who takes over the state power through a military *coup d'état* and rules without any accountability as long as the officer or the junta can retain the support of the armed forces.

Some scholars working on military rule argue that military governments usually have a large civilian component – bureaucrats, managers, politicians and technocrats. So the dichotomy between military and civilian rule can hardly be sustained. For example, Amos Perlmutter states, 'modern military regimes are not purely military in composition. Instead they are fusionist, that is, they are military-civil regimes' (Perlmutter 1981: 97). Military dictators usually bring civilian technocrats and political renegades into their governing councils, but that does not blur the distinction between military and civilian regimes. The civilian counsellors joining the military government hold office on the sufferance of the military dictator. Moreover, under the military rule it is the military ruler and his advisers from the armed forces who play the predominant role in all 'decisions of decisive consequences'. Thus military dictatorship emerges as a distinct sub-type of authoritarianism. (To avoid excessive repetition we have used the phrases 'military regime', 'military ruler', 'military politician', 'military leadership', 'soldier ruler' as synonyms for 'military rule'.)

Military dictatorship differs from other forms of authoritarianism in terms of origin, legitimacy, range of governmental penetration into the society, or a combination of all these factors. The present-day military dictatorship is often compared to the absolute monarchies of seventeenth- and eighteenth-century Europe, but the differences between the two types of governments are quite pronounced. First, as force does not automatically create right, any government of military provenance suffers from an innate sense of lack of legitimacy. On the other hand, the origin and rule of the European absolute monarchies were clothed in powerful traditional legitimacy. The European monarchs extended the direct control of the central government over the whole, more or less, of culturally homogeneous, state-territories by creating a civil administration, particularly through the apparatus of tax collection (Tilly 1985). Present-day military dictators in the Third World usually resort to repressive measures to manage the problem of national integration of states divided on primordial loyalties. As we shall see later, military leaders only aggravate the problems of nation building after taking over power from the civilian political leaders.

Military dictators also differ from the *caudillos* that flourished in the institutionally decomposed societies of post-independence Latin America. The *caudillos* were not professional soldiers. They were adventurers and warriors utilizing violence for political ends, but they lacked institutionalized armed forces to support their regimes (Rouqui 1987: 39–71).

Military dictators are different from the civilian autocrats in their sources of legitimacy. The civilian dictators in the Third World derive their legitimacy from their leadership in the independence struggle or from the leadership of the single parties founded by them or from some rigged election. They retain their power by maintaining 'a vertical network of personal and patron-client relations' (Jackson and Rosberg 1984: 421–2), a strategy of rulership also resorted to by military dictators.

Military dictatorship differs from totalitarian dictatorship on three counts. First, totalitarian dictators claim legitimacy on the basis of their ideologies, which, they state, are higher and nobler forms of democracy. Military dictators do not generally espouse elaborate and guiding ideologies; they have only, to use the phrase of Juan Linz, 'distinctive orientations and mentalities' (Linz 1975: 264). Second, unlike military dictators, totalitarian dictators seize power by organizing armed political parties. Once in power, totalitarian dictators establish the supremacy of their parties over all organizations, including the armed forces. Third, while military dictators allow 'a limited, not responsible, pluralism' (Linz 1975: 264), totalitarian dictators try to control the whole society through the single-party system and widespread use of terror.

Military rule is also different from 'War Lordism'. War Lordism is a function of failed states. In these failed states tribal leaders divide the territory along lines of ethnicity and tribal identity. War Lordism is also different from the *caudillos* that flourished in Latin American countries in the nineteenth century. While *caudillos* depended on primitive weapons, War Lords have access to modern sophisticated arms and ammunitions and carry on fighting among themselves killing thousands of innocent men, women and children (e.g., Somalia, Sierra Leone, Belgian Congo, Rwanda, Algeria and Burundi). In these states diverse War Lords divide the territories on the basis of ethnicity and tribal identities. Some of these War Lords are getting support not from the USA or European countries but from their neighboring countries. The growth of War Lords has been attributed to generic failure of the political system.

The word dictator is derived from the early Roman constitution. This constitution provided for the election of a magistrate as dictator for six months with extraordinary powers to handle some unforeseen crises. This constitutional dictatorship degenerated into military dictatorship when the post-constitutional rulers of the Roman Empire used the Praetorian Guards as the main base of their power. More recently a few

European states – Spain (1920s and 1930s), Portugal (1920s and 1970s) and Greece (late 1960s and mid 1970s) underwent military dictatorships. However, it is in the post-Second World War states belonging to the Third World that military dictatorship has emerged as 'a distinctly and analytically new phenomenon, restricted to the developing and modernizing world' (Perlmutter 1981). Burma (Myanmar), which has been under military rule since 1962, approximates this model of military rule (Fink 2001; Maung 1989).

Growth of military rule

Several schools of thought have evolved to explain military intervention and the growth of military rule in developing states. The first school, the organizationalists, focus on the special characteristics that are generally attributed to professional Western military organizations – such as centralized command, hierarchy, discipline and cohesion – to explain military intervention. As Morris Janowitz writes, 'the organizational format designed to carry out the military functions as well as experience in the "management of violence" is at the root of these armies' ability to intervene politically' (Janowitz 1964: 32). However, it is not the organizational strength of the military but rather the military's organizational decay that often creates conditions for various factions within the military to launch sudden and swift raids on the government (Decalo 1976: 14–15).

The organizationalists, whether they speak of the military's organizational strength or decay, place more emphasis on the organizational dynamics within the army than on forces outside the barracks to explain the political behaviour of soldiers. After studying African *coups* since 1967, Clause Welch argues that 'organizational variables are far better predictors of success than are sociopolitical or environmental variables' (see Kelleher 1974: ix).

A second group of scholars places more emphasis on society as a whole to analyse the reasons for military rule. According to S. E. Finer, military intervention results from the 'low or minimal political culture of the society concerned' (Finer 1969: 110–39). Samuel P. Huntington argues that: 'Military explanations do not explain military interventions. The reason for this is simply that military interventions are only one specific manifestation of a broader phenomenon in under-developed societies: the general politicization of social forces and institutions' (Huntington 1969: 194).

The third group are the sceptical behaviouralists, who stress the internal dynamics of military hierarchies, cliques within the army, corporate interests, personal ambitions, and idiosyncracies of particular military men in explaining the political behaviour of the army (Decalo 1976: 7–22).

Some of the very prominent Latin American scholars, particularly Guillermo O'Donnell, have tried to explain the rise of military ('bureaucratic-authoritarian') dictatorship in Latin America from the 1960s to the mid 1980s in terms of interactions between world economic forces and the indigenous economic trends of relatively more developed countries, such as Argentina, Brazil, Chile and Uruguay. O'Donnell (1978: 19) argues that these bureaucratic–authoritarian regimes arose at 'a particularly diaphanous moment of dependence' of the countries concerned. This 'historical moment' was created by the 'exhaustion' of import-substitution industries as a means of expanding the domestic economy and by the weakening of the international market for Latin American primary exports. The result was economic crisis marked by rising inflation, declining GNP and investment rates, flight of capital, balance of payments deficits, and the like. This crisis in turn activated the popular sector in Latin American countries. This was perceived as a threat by other social classes. Military officers, as we shall discuss later, already indoctrinated in the ideas of 'national security' and afraid of Cuban-style revolution that would mean the end of the army as an institution, stepped in to create bureaucratic–authoritarian regimes in collaboration with civilian technocrats.

Some scholars argue that one of the basic reasons for military intervention in the developing countries is that, unlike the soldiers in the formative phase of the growth of the standing armies in Europe, the soldiers in developing countries face a situation of 'military structural unemployment' (Barros and Coelho 1981: 341–9). The European states developed standing armies between the sixteenth and eighteenth centuries. This was also the period when Europe was a constant theatre of interstate wars. Where are the wars today in the Third World? Our research shows that the median length of wars in Europe during the period 1415–1815 was four years, while the median length of wars during the period 1946–84 was less than two months. Even if we multiply the median length of wars in the Third World countries by nine to make the time span of comparison similar for both areas, the median length of Third World wars comes to one and a half years, about one-third of the length of European wars (Maniruzzaman 1987: 113–15).

While the European armies between 1495 and 1815 were almost continuously engaged in war, the armies in the Third World are only engaged in 'barrack sittings'. Third World armies easily become alienated from society because these organizations, having a monopoly on the instruments of violence, fail to find a meaningful role in society due to the absence or infrequency of war and lack of facilities for proper training. This estrangement from society predisposes them to role expansion. Because of the endemic and 'cumulative crisis' in Third World states, alienated armies easily find opportunities to intervene. As a former chief justice of Pakistan stated sometime after the military take-over in Pakistan in 1958, the valiant armed forces of Pakistan had nothing to do and therefore subjugated their own people (Razzak 1981: 17).

Empirical studies on military intervention

Present-day social scientists would reject any single master paradigm and argue that no single method of approach can by itself provide a comprehensive understanding of a complex social and political phenomenon (Needler 1978). It is the confluence and interaction of several of the variables discussed above that explains the occurrence of the military *coup d'état* and growth of military dictatorship in any particular country. The crucial question is the relative weight of each variable in the process of interaction. Statistical tools can be used to understand the particular 'mix' of the variables involved in the process of military take-over of powers of the state.

Of the several empirical studies done on military interventions, two stand out – Jackman's 'The predictability of *coups d'état*: a model with African data' (Jackman 1978) and Londregan and Poole's 'Poverty, the *coup* trap, and the seizure of executive power' (Londregan and Poole 1990). These two studies are well-grounded in theoretical structure and use sophisticated statistical models to explain military *coups d'état*. Jackman's study shows that military *coups d'état* are a function of structural factors (social mobilization, cultural pluralism, party dominance and electoral turn-out) almost in a deterministic pattern, and idiosyncratic factors emphasized by Zolberg (1968: 7) and Decalo (1976: 22) account for only one-fifth of the variance in *coups d'état* (Jackman 1978: 1273).

In their recent study covering 121 countries for the period 1960–82, Londregan and Poole construct a statistical model enabling them to use income level, economic growth rate, past history of *coups,* and interdependence of *coups* and economic growth as independent variables, and the military *coup d'état* as the dependent variable. They find that both high level of income and high level of economic growth as separate factors inhibit *coups d'état*. According to their study, the incidence of *coups d'état* is twenty-one times more likely in the poorest countries than among the wealthiest. More interesting is their 'compelling evidence of a "*coup*-trap"; once a country has experienced a *coup d'état*, it has a much harder time avoiding further *coups...Coups* spawn countercoups' (Londregan and Poole 1990: 175, 178).

Although no grand theory has yet emerged, the theoretical and empirical studies discussed above have greatly increased our understanding of the occurrence of the military *coup d'état*. This understanding, however, is not enough. The way that military dictators rule and the policies they pursue condition much of later social, economic and political development of *coup*-affected states. Let us now discuss the methods generally used by military dictators to perpetuate their rule.

Strategies of rulership by military dictators

The first strategy of rulership by military dictators is to manage their 'constituency', i.e. to keep their hold on the armed forces. In countries with non-professional armies divided on ethnic or religious lines, this strategy often means the establishment of dominance over the whole army by the group led by the military dictator. The establishment of this dominance often requires the use of crude and ruthless violence to suppress the opposition factions within armed forces and to terrorize the civilian population into total submission.

One of the most notorious military dictators in this regard is Mengistu of Ethiopia, who physically liquidated his rivals among the officer corps and used 'red terror' against civil revolutionaries on such a massive scale that even the initial supporters of the military *coup* were not only disenchanted but appalled (Halliday and Molyneux 1983: 122–7). Idi Amin, Bokassa and Mobutu were no less ruthless 'in eliminating and annihilating opposition within the military and outside it' (Perlmutter 1981: 16).

The sub-Saharan military dictators are not the only ones to use violence to keep their hold on the army. In Syria (between 1946 and 1970), officers drawn from two minority communities, the Alawis and the Druze, eliminated officers drawn from the Sunnis (the majority community) through successive *coups* and counter-*coups*. Finally, the Alawis purged the Druze officers through a *coup* in 1970. Hafiz al Assad, an Alawi, seized power and ruled Syria until his death, at which time his son, Bashar al Assad, assumed rulership. Paralleling the Alawis in Syria, Iraqi officers belonging to the Sunni minority community drawn from the small town of Takrit gradually eliminated their opponents, and through the *coup d'état* in 1968 established their absolute control over the armed forces (Maniruzzaman 1987: 32–41).

Developments in the Bangladeshi army followed the common pattern. The army was divided into two groups – those who participated in the liberation war of 1971 and those who had been in West Pakistan and later joined the Bangladeshi army. After several *coups* and counter-*coups* the 'repatriates' from Pakistan established their dominance over the armed forces through the *coup* of 1982 and ruled until 1990 (Maniruzzaman 1989: 216–21).

In countries such as Argentina, Brazil, Pakistan and Peru with professional and disciplined armies, military *coups d'état* become more or less systematic and disciplined operations. This is because unlike the soldier in non-professional armies who is loyal only to himself or at best to his faction, the professional soldier is amenable to the discipline of the army as an institution. Professional armies tend to factionalize at the highest echelon at the time of intervention. The senior officers soon develop a formula for sharing power among themselves and close their differences. Because the power struggle remains limited to upper levels of the hierarchy, discipline among the officers and rank and file remains unaffected.

However, the difference between military dictators coming to power through successive *coups* and counter-*coups* and military dictators seizing power with the help of professional armies is one of degree rather than kind. In Brazil between 1964 and 1985 torture became 'an intrinsic part of the governing process' (Stepan 1971: 262). In Argentina between 1976 and 1983 the military rulers killed between 6,000 and 30,000 Argentines in their 'dirty war' against the leftists (Schumarcher 1984: 1076). In Pakistan, the military government of Zia-ul Huq physically eliminated the nation's first elected prime minister, Zulfiquar Ali Bhutto, on the basis of a judgement given by what has been called 'rigged benches' of the High Court in Lahore and the Supreme Court of Pakistan (Quereshi 1979: 920).

As repression becomes a part of the strategy of rulership, military dictators develop an elaborate network of intelligence services. In his latest work, *Rethinking Military Politics: Brazil and the Southern Cone*, Alfred Stepan (1988) points out how the military intelligence services in Brazil became a formidable threat to the ruling junta itself. As Stepan argues, it was the need for civilian support against the intelligence community that led the Brazilian military to start the process of liberalization, which ultimately led to the withdrawal of the military from power. General Zia-ul Huq of Pakistan, to give another example, developed an Inter-Service Intelligence Directorate with 100,000 employees as one of the most influential military and internal security agencies in the Third World for surveillance of politicians as well as officers.

Violence and intelligence surveillance are, however, negative strategies of rulership. A more positive way of keeping the armed forces satisfied is the raising of salaries and other allowances and perquisites of the members of the armed forces. Military rulers almost invariably increase the defence budgets soon after a take-over. Once raised, defence allocations usually remain at high levels in subsequent years. For the decade of the 1960s, the average annual expenditure on defence compared with total state budgets in Asia, sub-Saharan Africa and Latin America was almost double for military governments compared with non-military governments (Kennedy 1974: 163). The rate of growth for defence expenditure in developing countries is surpassing the growth rate in the developed nations (Janowitz 1977: 48). As most of the defence budget in developing countries is spent on buying sophisticated weapons in hard currency from developed countries, such expenditures do not have multiplier effects on national economies.

Another strategy of rulership adopted by military dictators is to depoliticize and control the participation of the masses. To this end, the Latin American military dictators usually resort to the system of corporatism. Under this system the military regimes try 'to eliminate spontaneous interest articulation and establish a limited number of authoritatively recognized groups that interact with the government apparatus in defined and regularized ways' (Malloy 1977: 4). Some military dictators – especially those in the Middle East and sub-Saharan Africa – established one-party systems as the structural mechanism of organizing and controlling participation. In Syria the Ba'ath Party has been subjugated by the army wing of the party since 1966. In Iraq, however, the military and the Ba'ath Party seem to have a symbiotic relationship. The parties created from above by military dictators such as Mobutu in Zaire, Eyadema in Togo and Kerekou in Benin do not seem to have much influence on the policy-making process and are not likely to decide the succession of the present military dictators. These parties are merely appendages of the military regime. Writing in 1966, Aristide R. Zolberg asserted that single parties founded in West Africa are usually paper organizations (Zolberg 1966: 25, 33–4, 128–50). Bienen seems more to the point when he argues that the single-party system is more like US political machines as far as distribution of patronage is concerned (Bienen 1970: 99–127). Indeed, the African one-party system, often headed by the military dictator himself, is part of an overall strategy of ruling through patrimonialism. Mobutu in Zaire provides the most typical example in this regard. In November 1973 Mobutu took over about 2,000 foreign-owned enterprises and distributed these as 'free goods' among the politico-commercial class. Mobutu himself and the members of the politburo of the single party, the Popular Revolutionary Movement, partook of this largesse (Young and Turner 1984: 714–49).

Modernization and the role of military regimes: some empirical findings

It seems that in order to make their studies of policy relevant, political scientists in the West, particularly the USA during the 1950s and 1960s, tried to over-estimate the role of the military in the modernization of Third World countries. A number of respected scholars developed theoretical models depicting the military as a highly modern force, capable of transferring its organizational and technical skills to fields of government and administration (see for example Pye 1962: 69–89; Halpern 1962: 227–313; Daadler 1962; Johnson 1964).

These theoretical formulations were, to use the facetious phrase of Henry Bienen, 'unencumbered by empirical evidence', but later empirical research on the actual performance of military regimes has largely belied these early theoretical expectations. Indeed, a study by Eric A. Nordlinger (1970: 1131–48), drawing on an analysis of cross-national data from seventy-four non-Western and non-communist countries, found negative and zero-order correlations between the political strength of the military and social and economic modernizations. In another cross-national aggregate study of all independent, non-communist countries with a population greater than one million, covering the period from 1951 to 1970, R. D. McKinlay and A. S. Cohan concluded that 'there is no profound effect on economic performance produced by military regime when MR (Military Regime) and CMR (period of civilian rule in countries that have experienced military regimes) are compared with CR (low income countries who have experienced only civilian rule)' (McKinlay and Cohan 1975: 1–30). Another study based on data covering the period from 1960 to 1970 for seventy-seven independent countries of the Third World reported: 'In short military intervention in politics of the Third World has no unique effect on social change, regardless of either the level of economic development or geographic region' (Jackman 1976: 1096). In the latest empirical study, Londregan and Poole conclude: 'Despite the dramatic effect of economic performance on the probability of *coups*, the reverse is not true: a country's past *coup* history has little discernible effect on its economy. We find no evidence that either the recent history of *coups* or the current propensity for a *coup d'état* significantly affect the growth rate' (Londregan and Poole 1990: 153).

Military rule and the circle of political underdevelopment

The performance of military regimes has been even more disappointing in the sphere of political development than in the sphere of economic development. It is often argued that since most of the new nations are divided on ethnic, religious, linguistic and regional lines, the military alone can bring about the national integration that is a prerequisite for political development.

The performance of military rulers to date does not support this hypothesis. It was the military dictators Ayub Khan and his successor Yahiya Khan who, following a 'policy of blood and iron' in Pakistan, produced the first successful secessionist movement in the Third World. In a similar fashion the process of Nigerian disintegration started after the *coup* of 15 January 1966, when Nzeogwu and his cohorts launched a ruthless attack on prominent military and political figures. The military leadership presided over the civil war in Nigeria for two years with combat deaths running into hundreds of thousands.

Likewise, the Sudanese military rulers have been fighting the guerrillas in the southern part of the country from 1958 up until the present day.

As a matter of fact, in most cases military intervention creates a vicious circle that perpetuates the conditions of political underdevelopment, which initially brought about the imposition of military rule. As Huntington has argued (Huntington 1965: 421–7), the key factor in political development is the growth of durable political institutions. The primary resources for developing political institutions in any country are the political skills of its politicians. The political skills needed for developing a viable and self-sustaining political system involve, among others, ideological commitment, the capacity to respond to new challenges, and the arts of administration, negotiation, representation and bargaining. These skills can be acquired only in the hard school of public life. (See Morris-Jones 1957: 49, 57, 71; 1978: 131–43; Weiner 1967: 11–16; Kochanek 1968: xix–xxv.)

Because of their 'military minds' and perspectives, soldier-rulers, from Ayub Khan in Pakistan to Acheampong in Ghana or Castello Branco in Brazil, fail to see the functional aspects of the great game of politics. They severely restrict the free flow of the political process and force would-be politicians into a long period of hibernation. The period of military rule is usually a total waste as far as the development of political skills is concerned. Because about two-thirds of civil and military governments fall victim to military *coups d'état*, the opportunity for people once under a military regime to gain political skills is likely to be continually postponed with the arrival of every new military regime.

Only one-third of the military governments that have existed in the Third World have been succeeded by civilian governments. In some cases of civilian restoration, newly incumbent civilian leaders soon demonstrate their inability to match their official performance with the expectation of the people. This is not unnatural: first, because of general intractability of the problems faced by the developing nations; and second (and more important), because of the lack of political skills in the civilian leaders resulting from the preceding period of military rule. Military officers waiting in the wings then depose the civilian regime in response to even a modest manifestation of public discontent against the civilian government and assert the vindication of their self-fulfilling prophecy of the 'inevitable failure of the self-seeking politicians. Thus the period of waste for political growth begins anew' (Maniruzzaman 1987: 6–7).

Role expansion of the military and defence vulnerability

As the army begins to 'patrol the society', the frontiers of state remain utterly vulnerable. Since the 1960s several armies have been compromised by their political role expansion and suffered humiliating defeats at the hands of other armies encouraged only to excel in professionalism. In the Arab–Israeli War of 1967, the Syrian army's performance suffered immeasurably because of fratricidal feuds among its officers, which resulted in an inability to mount a serious offensive against the Israeli army. The Iraqi army was similarly debilitated by internal political strife (Brown 1967: 269–71).

Egypt's total fiasco in the 1967 war is also attributed to the political role expansion of the Egyptian armed forces. The Egyptian air commanders committed 'monumental neglect of the most elementary rules of protecting aircraft on the ground'. The result was that a large part of the Egyptian air force was completely incapacitated by an Israeli pre-emptive attack on the first day of the war. The Egyptian army disintegrated in less than a week (Brown 1967: 269–71).

Thirteen years of political involvement similarly impaired the fighting edge of the Pakistani armed forces in the 1971 war with India. One could reasonably argue that the Pakistani forces in former East Pakistan, denied all logistical support from West Pakistan because of an Indian blockade, were not in a position to give stiff resistance to the Indians. But the failure of the Pakistani forces to mount a significant challenge to Indian forces on the western front can not be explained by any other terms than inadequate morale and fighting skills of the Pakistanis (Morris-Jones 1972: 188–9).

Another example of how the political role of the armed forces corrodes military vitality is provided by Idi Amin's armed forces in Uganda, which first acted as an instrument of Idi Amin's terror and brutality and then simply disintegrated when faced with poorly equipped Tanzanian troops and a Ugandan exile force in April 1979. In the early 1980s an Argentine military spoiled by politics was easily defeated by Great Britain in the Falklands/Malvinas War.

Failure of the 'new professionals'

Nowhere has the claim of superior rule by the military leaders over the politicians been more dramatically and poignantly disproved than in Latin America. Military leaders seized power in Brazil (1964), Argentina (1976), Peru (1968) and Chile (1973) for unlimited periods to effect fundamental transformation in social, economic and political structures. They developed the 'doctrine of national security' to justify their rule (Stepan 1976: 240–60; O'Donnell 1976: 208–13). According to this doctrine, the governments in Latin America were engaged in an internal war with the communist revolutionaries. The days of the 'old professional' soldier who fought conventional wars with external enemies were almost over. The 'new professional soldier', trained in fighting a 'total war' with the internal enemy on military, social, economic and political fronts, was the prime need. Because civilian leaders did not have requisite skills and organizations to fight the new war, it became the manifest destiny of the 'new professional soldiers' to establish control over all aspects of society, bring about rapid socio-economic development, and win the glory of defeating the great threat to Western civilization.

Brazil was the test case for implementation of the doctrine of national security and national development; Brazil had the best soldiers and materials in the whole of Latin America, and the 'new professionals' of Brazil held power for two decades to show their mettle. Yet the economic and political reforms effected by the new professional soldiers proved illusory. The military regimes were bedevilled by the growth of factionalism within the armed forces and conflicts between military governments and military institutions. The result was frequent instability (changes in government personnel, including the president of the nation) and policy incoherence. The strategy of growth followed by the soldier-rulers not only accentuated social and regional cleavages but also led to a debt burden of over US$90 billion by the early 1980s. Popular discontent mounted, and the military governments 'deepened the revolution' by resorting to more and more terror and torture (Maniruzzaman 1987: 11).

The developments in Argentina (1976–83) under the new professionals followed closely the pattern in Brazil (1964–85). The Argentine economy plunged into deep recession, and foreign debt increased fourfold from US$9.8 billion in 1978 to US$38 billion in 1982. As resistance to government increased, the Argentine military rulers used terror and torture on a scale much larger than those applied by their Brazilian counterparts (Sanders 1983: 2–3).

It was Peru's 'armed intellectuals' who tried to play the most revolutionary role. They nationalized petroleum, fishing and other natural resources, introduced the system of worker participation in industrial plants, decreed new land reforms, enacted new education policy, and organized mass participation in national interest group associations. The 'revolution from above', however, aborted; Peruvians showed an utter disinterest in the soldier-rulers' reforms. The military-sponsored, radical reform measures, on the other hand, dislocated the national economy further (Sanders 1981: 77; Malloy 1982: 4). It was ironic that the Peruvian voters in 1980 forced the ruling army elite to hand power back to the very civilian politician (Fernando Belaúnde) from whom the officers snatched political power in 1968 (Handelman 1981: 132–5).

From the discussion so far certain conclusions emerge. Soldier-politicians seem incapable of furthering major socio-economic development in the countries they rule. The military's performance in the field of political development has been even more dismal. Military regimes accentuate the problems of political development with which the civilian regimes were initially faced, and they deprive the civilian politicians of the opportunity to acquire much-needed political skills, thus perpetuating the chain of political underdevelopment. Finally, role expansion of the military creates both internal and external security vulnerabilities. The study of military withdrawal from politics thus seems imperative.

Military withdrawal from politics

The nature and duration of military withdrawal from politics are, in part, a function of organizational aspects of the armed forces. Factionalism within non-professional armies creates the syndrome of abrupt intervention–withdrawal–reintervention until one faction comes to dominate the whole army and impose a longer period of military rule.

Military dictators – Ayub Khan (1958–69), Zia-ul Huq (1977–88), military juntas in Brazil (1964–85), Argentina (1966–73) and Peru (1968–80), to mention only a few – who were supported by professional armies usually ruled for longer periods relative to a short duration of rule of the officers leading non-professional armies. Some of the officers coming to power with the support of professional armies withdrew from politics because of sheer exhaustion of ruling the problem-ridden Third World countries (Brazil, Argentina and Peru). Some military dictators are forced to withdraw by spontaneous mass upheavals – for example Bolivia (1946), Sudan (1964), Pakistan (1969), Thailand (1973) and El Salvador (1979). These multi-class upheavals, however, cannot install stable civilian governments and usually military juntas resume control (Maniruzzaman 1987: 80–2, 164–5).

One way of preventing the growth of military dictatorship is to create a consensus among the political parties against military rule. This deprives the military juntas of the 'civilian constituency' which according to some scholars is often a prerequisite for a military *coup d'état*. In Venezuela (1958) and Colombia (1957) the leading political parties entered into a political pact for sharing power among themselves for twenty years, eliminating support for army intervention. This coalition of dominant political parties against army rule has enabled these two countries to maintain civilian rule for nearly three decades (Karl 1981; Kline 1979).

The methods of military withdrawal from politics discussed above belong to superstructural architectonic levels and cannot break the cycle of intervention–withdrawal–intervention. Durable and long-term military withdrawal is the function of social revolution: the process of replacing one social class by another as the ruling class, and the cataclysmic social structural transformation wrought in the process. The two archetypical social revolutions – bourgeois and proletarian – consolidated the class rule of bourgeoisie and the proletariat, respectively, and brought the armed forces under the control of the hegemonic classes.

The few cases of long-term withdrawal that have taken place in the Third World states point to the same conclusion. Whether it is a revolution of the Jeffersonian farmers and the middle classes as in Costa Rica in 1948, or a revolution under a coalition of classes – professional middle class and peasant class – as in Mexico (1911–17), or a socialist revolution led by the scions of upper and middle classes in Cuba (1959) and Nicaragua (1979), or peasant-supported revolution in Venezuela (1958), or reactivated upper classes in Columbia (1957), the cathartic effect is the same – 'politics in command'. Revolution is primarily an intellectual event and only secondarily a military phenomenon. The revolution defines the role of the armed forces in the new society. The fresh political formula with a new scheme of distributing power sanctified by the revolution gives precedence to the role of ideas over arms, to policy over instruments and to politics over guns. In this respect the aftermath of contemporary social revolution is the same as that of the two archetypical social revolutions – bourgeois and proletarian (Maniruzzaman 1987: 212).

Conclusion: future of military rule

The period of military withdrawals or transitions from military rule to liberal democracies has been labelled the *Third Wave of Democracy* by S. P. Huntington, the most quoted political scientist of the contemporary world (Huntington 1993). In a subsequent celebrated publication, *The Clash of Civilizations and the Remaking of World Order*, Huntington (1996) suggested that the new wave of democratization may be replaced by the clash of Western civilization versus Islamic civilization cum Confucious civilization, which could be more devastating than the Second World War.

Francis Fukuyama (1992), on the other hand, prophesied in *The End of History and the Last Man* that '"Liberal Democracy", which has by now swept almost the whole world may constitute the end point of mankind's ideological evolution and final form of government'.

By contrast our conclusion about the future of the military rule would be prosaic rather than apocalyptic. While of 190 nations of the world (all members of the United Nations), only eight countries – Burma (Myanmer), Pakistan, Egypt, Algeria, Sudan, Syria, Iraq, Libya – are now under military rule, the new wave of democracy might not be a continuous phenomenon. Indeed, some of the liberal democracies have already been transformed into 'illiberal democracies' (Zakaria: 1997). Some others have degenerated into 'hybrid regimes committed to effective governance and real economic development but not Western style democracy' (Barkan and Gordon 1999). Moreover, as the horrendous and the fateful event of September 11, 2001 has shown, catastrophic and cataclysmic events could prevent any unidirectional course of history.

References

Barkan and Gordon (1999) 'Democracy in Africa: No Time to Forsake It', in *World Politics 99/00*, Guilford, CT: Dushkin/McGraw-Hill (http://www.dushkin.com/annualeditions/).

Barros, A. S. C. and Coelho, E. C. (1981) 'Military intervention and withdrawal in South America', *International Political Science Review* 2 (3): 341–9.

Bienen, H. (1970) 'One-party systems in Africa', in S. Huntington and C. H. Moore (eds) *Authoritarian Politics in Modern Society*, New York: Basic Books.

Brown, N. (1967) 'The third Arab–Israel war', *World Today* 23: 269–71.

Daadler, H. (1962) *The Role of the Military in Emerging Countries*, The Hague: Mouton.

Decalo, S. (1976) *Coups and Army Rule in Africa: Studies in Military Style*, New Haven: Yale University Press.

Finer, S. E. (1969) *The Man on Horseback: The Role of the Military in Politics*, London: Pall Mall Press.

Fink, C. (2001) *Living in Silence: Burma Under Military Rule*, Dhaka: University Press Limited.

Fried, R. C. (1966) *Comparative Political Institutions*, London: Macmillan.

Fukuyama, F. (1992) *The End of History and the Last Man*, New York: Penguin Books.

Girling, John L. S. (1980) *America and The Third World: Revolution and Intervention*, London: Routledge & Kegan Paul.

Halliday, F. and Molyneux, M. (1983) *The Ethiopian Revolution*, London: Verso.

Halpern, M. (1962) 'Middle Eastern armies and the new middle class', in J. J. Johnson (ed.) *The Role of Military in Underdeveloped Countries*, Princeton: Princeton University Press.

Handelman, H. (1981) 'Postscript', in H. Handelman and T. Sanders (eds) *Military Government and Movement Toward Democracy in South America*, Bloomington: Indiana University Press.

Huntington, S. P. (1965) 'Political development and political decay', *World Politics* 7 (3): 386–430.

—— (1969) *Political Order in Changing Societies*, New Haven: Yale University Press.

—— (1993) *The Third Wave: Democratization in the Late Twentieth Century*, Norman and London: University of Oklahoma Press.

—— (1996) *The Clash of Civilizations and the Remaking of World Order*, New York: Simon & Schuster.

Jackman, R. W. (1976) 'Politicians in uniform: military government and social change in the Third World', *American Political Science Review* 70 (4): 1078–97.

—— (1978) 'The predictability of *coups d'état*: a model with African data', *American Political Science Review* 72 (4): 1262–75.

Jackson, R. H. and Rosberg, C. G. (1984) 'Personal rule: theory and practice in Africa', *Comparative Politics* 16 (4): 421–42.

Janowitz, M. (1964) *The Military in the Development of New Nations*, Chicago: University of Chicago Press.

—— (1977) *Military Institutions and Coercion in Developing Nations*, Chicago: University of Chicago Press.

Johnson, J. J. (1964) *The Military and Society in Latin America*, Stanford: Stanford University Press.

Karl, T. (1981) *Petroleum and Political Pacts: The Transition to Democracy in Venezuela*, Working Paper no. 107, Washington, DC: Woodrow Wilson International Center for Scholars, Latin American Program.

Kelleher, C. McA. (ed.) (1974) *Political-Military Systems: A Comparative Perspective*, Beverly Hills: Sage Publications.

Kennedy, G. (1974) *The Military in the Third World*, London: Duckworth.

Kline, H. F. (1979) 'Colombia: modified two-party and elitist politics', in H. J. Wiarda and H. F. Kline (eds) *Latin American Politics and Development*, Boston: Houghton Mifflin.

Kochanek, S. A. (1968) *The Congress Party of India*, Princeton: Princeton University Press.

Linz, J. (1975) 'Totalitarian and authoritarian regimes', in N. Polsby (ed.) *Handbook of Political Science*, vol. 3, London: Addison-Wesley.

Londregan, J. B. and Poole, K. T. (1990) 'Poverty, the *coup* trap, and the seizure of executive power', *World Politics* 42 (2): 151–83.

McKinlay, R. D. and Cohan, A. S. (1975) 'A comparative analysis of political and economic performances of military and civil regimes: a cross national aggregate study', *Comparative Politics* 8 (1): 1–30.

Malloy, J. M. (1977) *Authoritarianism and Corporatism in Latin America*, Pittsburg: Pittsburgh University Press.

—— (1982) *Peru's Troubled Return to Democratic Government*, Report no. 5, Hanover: Universities Field Staff International.

Maniruzzaman, T. (1987) *Military Withdrawal From Politics: A Comparative Study*, Cambridge, MA: Ballinger Publications Company.

—— (1989) 'Politics: Bangladesh', in *The Cambridge Encyclopedia of India, Pakistan, Bangladesh, Sri Lanka, Nepal, Bhutan and Maldives*, Cambridge: Cambridge University Press.

Maung, S. L. (1989) *Burma: Nationalism and Ideology: An Analysys of Society, Culture and Politics*, Dhaka: University Press Limited.

Morris-Jones, W. H. (1957) *Parliament in India*, London: Longmans Green.

—— (1972) 'Pakistan post-mortem and roots of Bangladesh', *Political Quarterly* 43: 187–200.

—— (1978) 'India's political miracle', in *Politics Mainly India*, New Delhi: Longman Orient.

Needler, M. C. (1978) 'The logic of conspiracy: the Latin American military coup as a problem in social sciences', *Studies in Comparative International Development* 13 (3).

Nordlinger, E. A. (1970) 'Soldiers in mufti: impact of military rule upon economic and social change in non-Western states', *American Political Science Review* 64 (4): 1131–48.

O'Donnell, G. (1976) 'Modernization and military coups: theory, comparisons and the Argentine case', in A. Lowenthal (ed.) *Armies and Politics in Latin America*, New York: Holme & Meir.

—— (1978) 'Reflections on patterns of change in the bureaucratic-authoritarian state', the *Latin American Research Review* 13 (1): 3–38.

Pauker, G. J. (1959) 'South East Asia as a problem area in the next decade', *World Politics* 11 (12): 325–45.

Perlmutter, A. (1981) 'The comparative analysis of military regimes: formations, aspirations and achievements', *World Politics* 33 (1): 96–120.

Pye, L. W. (1962) 'Armies in the process of political modernization', in J. J. Johnson (ed.) *The Role of Military in Underdeveloped Countries*, Princeton: Princeton University Press.

Quereshi, S. A. (1979) 'An analysis of contemporary Pakistan politics: Bhutto versus military', *Asian Survey* 19 (9): 910–20.

Razzak, A. (1981) *Bangladesh: State of the Nation*, Dhaka: Dhaka University Press.

Rouqui, A. (1987) *The Military and the State in Latin America*, Berkeley: University of California Press.

Sanders, T. G. (1981) 'The politics of transition', in H. Handelman and T. G. Sanders (eds) *Military Government and the Movement Toward Democracy in South America*, Bloomington: Indiana University Press.

—— (1983) *Argentina's Return to Democracy: Political Economic Perspectives*, Report no. 29, Hanover: Universities Field Staff International.

Sayeed, K. B. (1995)*Western Dominance and Political Islam: Challenge and Response*, Karachi, Oxford University Press.

Schumarcher, E. (1984) 'Argentina and democracy', *Foreign Affairs* 62 (5): 1070–95.

Stepan, A. (1971) *The Military in Politics: Changing Patterns in Brazil*, Princeton: Princeton University Press.

—— (1976) 'The new professionalism of international warfare and military role expansion', in A. F. Lowenthal (ed.) *Armies and Politics in Latin America*, New York: Holmes & Meir.

—— (1988) *Rethinking Military Politics: Brazil and the Southern Cone*, Princeton: Princeton University Press.

Tilly, C. (1985) 'War and the power of warmakers in Western Europe and elsewhere, 1600–1980', in P. Wallenteen, J. Galtung and C. Portales (eds) *Global Militarization*, Boulder: Westview Press.

Weiner, M. (1967) *Party Building in a New Nation: The Indian National Congress*, Chicago: University of Chicago Press.

Young, C. and Turner, T. (1984) 'The rise and decline of the Zaire state', unpublished manuscript.

Zakaria, Fareed (1997) 'The Rise of Liberal Democracy', *Foreign Affairs*, November/December.

Zolberg, A. R. (1966) *Creating Political Order: The Party-States of West Africa*, Chicago: Rand McNally.

—— (1968) 'Military intervention in the new states of Africa', in H. Bienen (ed.) *The Military Intervenes: Case Studies in Political Development*, New York: Russell Sage.

18

THE ISLAMIC STATE

M. A. Muqtedar Khan

Islamic state as cultural and political independence

Since the 1979 Islamic revolution in Iran, which established the Islamic Republic of Iran, the idea of an Islamic state has become an important if not a contentious issue in world politics (Esposito 1990). There are perhaps two important reasons for this state of affairs. First, some of the so-called Islamic states, such as the Islamic Republic of Iran and the Islamic Emirates of Afghanistan (Afghanistan under the Taliban regime), have been hostile to the West, and the USA in particular; and some of the prominent theoreticians and ideologues of the Islamic states, such as Ayatollah Ruhollah Khomeni of Iran and Syed Qutb of Egypt, have also been virulent polemicists against the West. (For a review of their ideas, see Rahnema 1994.) Second, except in the Muslim world, liberal democracy has been acknowledged everywhere as the most efficient and legitimate form of government and is increasingly becoming the system of choice globally. It is only in the Muslim world that popular sentiment is in search of an alternative principle or process for self governance. Thus the idea of an Islamic state represents not only a rejection of liberal democracy in its moment of triumph but also a means to register opposition to the global hegemony of the West (Bin Sayeed 1995).

Before the Iranian revolution the idea of an Islamic state was merely rhetorical and theoretical. Its potentiality as a transformative agent – transformative of the global regime through a radical foreign policy, and of domestic society through an aggressive socio-political campaign – remained imaginary. But after the Iranian revolution most Islamists realized that this dream of acquiring a coercive instrument for socio-political change was possible and their activism became more purposeful and even more fruitful. Since then several states have claimed to have become Islamic, including Sudan and Afghanistan (Esposito and Piscatori 1990).

As Islamic revivalist movements, primarily *Jamaat-e-Islami* (Islamic Society) in South Asia, and *Ikhwan al-Muslimeen* (Islamic Brotherhood) in the Arab World, gained momentum and led to a greater awareness of Islam in Muslim societies, the call to create Islamic states gained more and more momentum. Islam became the alternative to the cold war dichotomy, which presented the world with only two alternatives, the Capitalist West or the Communist East. For Muslims seeking authenticity the slogan, 'Islam is the solution', had great appeal. Just embracing this concept was liberating in experience as it implied that by advocating Islam, one was not only free of Western global ideologies of capitalism and communism; but was

265

also free from the internal colonization by secular Westernized elites who used authoritarian means to subjugate Muslims in their own countries. Thus the rejection of Western ideas and ideologies was a mark of rebellion against imperialism as well as internal colonialism (Ayubi 1991; Esposito 1997).

The key to understanding the antecedents to the concept of an Islamic state are the multiple roles of the Prophet Muhammad as religious founder, political leader, head of state and spiritual guide, and his unparalleled success in establishing his religion as the foundation of a state and society in a little over a decade. In AD 622 just 12 years after he declared his Prophethood, Muhammad migrated from Mecca to Medina, and established an Islamic society and state at the invitation of the various tribes that lived in Medina (then known as *Yathrib*). His state was based on a treaty or social contract referred to as the *Dastur-Al-Madinah* (Constitution of Medina) (Ayubi 1991; Haykal 1976; Khan 2002b). The Constitution of Medina establishes the importance of consent and cooperation for governance. According to this compact Muslims and non-Muslims are equal citizens of the Islamic state, with identical rights and duties. Communities with different religious orientations enjoyed religious autonomy, which amounted to essentially choice of legal system based on their religion. Jews were judged by the Torah, Christians by the Gospel, and Muslims by the Koran. This idea of freedom was much wider in scope than the modern idea of religious freedom. The Constitution of Medina established a pluralistic state, a community of communities. It promised equal security to all and all were equal in the eyes of the law. The principles of equality, consensual governance and pluralism were upheld by the compact of Medina (Khan 2002b).

This prophetic precedence has made the inseparability of religion and politics an enduring aspect of Islamic thought and practice. The status of Muhammad as the Prophet of God as well as the ruler of Medina has established the significance of religion in statecraft and the role of religious identity in shaping the character and identity of the political community. The objective of forming a political community is also seen in terms of religious needs and religious obligations. Thus when contemporary political theorists talk of an Islamic state, they imagine it as an ideological instrument designed for the explicit purpose of advancing an Islamic religious agenda; even though the very objectives of the Islamic constitution (*maqasid al-Sharia*) are widely understood as those guiding principles, which enable the individual and the community to live a virtuous life in a society determined to establish social justice and public welfare (Chapra 1992; Osman 1994).

The idea of an Islamic state is a highly contested and even nebulous conception within contemporary Muslim political thought. It needs historical as well as analytical clarification. There are at least two prominent types of discourses about the Islamic state: one from classical thinkers who lived and wrote when Islamic civilization was dominant and before much of the Muslim world was colonized; and the other in the postcolonial era when the pain of subjugation was still felt strongly and the power and influence of former imperial powers was still palpable. I distinguish between the two by calling pre-colonial theories, *Islamic theories of the state*, and postcolonial theories, *theories of the Islamic state*.

Islamic theories of the state are basically the discussion of the nature of the state in the limited political theory developed by Muslims prior to the colonial era. There are primarily four major theorists of this era including Al Farabi (870–950), Al

Mawardi (974–1058), Ibn Taymiyyah (1263–1328) and Ibn Khaldun (1332–1406). Theories of the Islamic state are contemporary attempts at imagining the utopian ideal of the just and dominant Islamic state. The major contributors to this discourse are Jamaluddin Afghani (1837–97), Maulana Maududi (1903–79), Ayatollah Khomeini (1902–89), Syed Qutb (1906–66) and Taqiuddin an-Nabbhani (1909–77). (For histories of Islamic political thought and practice, see Ahmad 1986; Black 2001; Enayat 1991; Watt 1968.)

Islamic theories of the state

While Islamic thought is multilayered and very rich, the tradition of political theory and philosophy remains underdeveloped (Khan 1997). Perhaps this could be explained by the hegemonic nature of Islamic legal thought which has always sought to colonize Islamic thinking at the expense of metaphysics, mysticism, philosophy and literature (Khan 2001). Even contemporary Islamic legal scholars often tend to equate Islam itself with Islamic legal thinking as if there is nothing outside law (and the study of *Sharia*). Nevertheless the pre-colonial era did witness several political thinkers of whom Al Farabi, Al Mawardi, Ibn Taymiyyah and Ibn Khaldun remain very prominent. Al Farabi's approach was philosophical, Al Mawardi's legalistic, Ibn Taymiyyah's theological, and Ibn Khaldun's sociological.

Al Farabi on state, governance and democracy

Abu Nasr Al Farabi is widely recognized as one of the most important Islamic philosophers. His debt is acknowledged by both the Western as well as Islamic philosophical and political traditions. In his *Mabadi ara al-madinat al-fadilah*, (Opinions of the Citizens of the Excellent City), Al Farabi develops his ideas linking metaphysics and cosmology with social ethics and political community. He develops a typology of polities and discusses how a sense of collective purpose, informed by a consciousness of the divine, can enable human beings to develop virtuous cities and polities which will not only be governed in a just and noble fashion but will also enable their citizens to work toward the perfection of the self (Al Farabi 1998; see also, al-Ma'sumi 1963; Black 1996).

While reading Al Farabi one is immediately stuck by the contemporary relevance of his theories. Al Farabi conceived of the possibility of establishing ideal polities at three levels – global, national and city. He actually thought that political unity and ethical governance was possible not only at the level of a city state but also on a global scale. Three elements can be identified as crucial to Al Farabi's vision of an ideal state: a knowledgeable population, the presence of choice or freedom, and the role of a philosopher or philosophers. Al Farabi clearly believed that whatever a city became, virtuous or ignorant or even wicked, it must do so through free choice of its people. Thus in a sense freedom of conscience more than anything else or rather the freedom to choose or eschew an ethical path was important for Al Farabi and it is a lesson that contemporary Islamists must not ignore. A state where citizens are coerced into pursuing an ethical path would be meaningless since the virtue of virtue is in its independent realization as a result of knowledge and communion with the divine (in Al Farabi's terms with the active intellect) (Al Farabi 1998: 231).

Al Farabi imagined the state as a cooperative effort of free and willing citizens seeking a common purpose, ultimate happiness through contact with the active intellect. In essence the state for Al Farabi, whatever the collective goal, existence or perfection, was an instrument to solve collective action problems. In his discussion of the nature of a state he anticipates two important contemporary theories, namely, systems theory, and the Weberian conception of the modern state as a product of rationalization, division of labour, and specialization. Al Farabi compares the state to a human body and argues that just as each organ through perfecting its own function and integrating with the whole creates a functional body; so should various elements of society perfect their roles and integrate to create the state. It is in the rationalization of the state and in treating it as a system that Al Farabi sneaks in his Platonic Republicanism by talking of hierarchical individuals and hierarchical roles from the noble to the ignoble. He places the philosopher or philosophers on top of the hierarchy. He argued that their knowledge, wisdom and nobility were necessary for any city to achieve a virtuous status (Al Farabi 1998).

Unlike contemporary political theory where the emphasis is on perfecting structure and process, Al Farabi concentrates on the nature and character of the governors in arguing for the possibility of realizing virtue in society. It is when virtuous individuals govern that we have a virtuous society. Social virtue for Al Farabi is a personality effect and not a systemic effect (Khan 2002a: 111–14). Needless to say, contemporary theorists who live in far more complex societies would disagree with this premise. But we must remember that Al Farabi's work was only the beginning of Islamic political theorizing.

According to Al Farabi the key to virtue and happiness is knowledge. The categories of knowledge that he insists rulers and citizens of a virtuous city must have will appear as esoteric and even ascetic to those of us who live in contemporary times. But the first item on his list remains important. He claims that rulers and ruled must have the knowledge of the first cause and it is here that Al Farabi reveals his Islamic stripes: the citizens of the virtuous city must have God consciousness and it is also here that politics and faith become inseparable (Al-Ma'sumi 1963: 704–9). Virtuous governance and virtuous polities happen when politics is guided by those who have knowledge of the divine origins of being. The Koran frequently describes such people as those who know (*Arifeen*).

Al Farabi was the first Muslim thinker to explore the virtues of democracy. Al Farabi places democracy in the category of ignorant cities. Ignorant cities are those cities which collectively are not aware of God (the first cause). They also do not have a single purpose. He recognizes that since democracies are free societies there will be multiple objectives that the citizens of a democracy will seek. He also suggests interestingly that if people who seek security dominate the polity, a democracy can become a national security state (Al Farabi talks in terms of cities of war and peace). But he also makes a very interesting observation which is perhaps the most important lesson contemporary Muslim thinkers can take from him. Al Farabi suggests that because democracies are free societies and are also non-homogenous, there will be people who will excel in good as well as people who will excel in evil. But the fact that one can find the pursuit of perfection present within a democracy, a democracy has the best chance of all ignorant cities of becoming a virtuous city (Al Farabi 1998: 315). This is a cautionary but powerful endorsement of democracy when the options available to societies largely fall in the ignorant category, which includes monarchies as well as dictatorships. (For discussion of Farabi's conception of democracy, see Mahdi 1987: 2001.)

Al Mawardi in defence of the Caliphate

The tenth to the twelfth century saw the steady decline of the power of the Abbasid Caliphate. Warlords and independent rulers gained more power and the role of the Caliph himself began to shrink and was ultimately reduced to ceremonial purposes only. In the early eleventh century, when the Sunni theorist Al Mawardi was working for the Abbasid caliph, the Buwayhid tribe and their warlords not only gained control over the central lands of the empire but also exercised *de facto* sovereignty over Baghdad. The Buwayhid like the Fatimids, who then had control over Cairo and much of the southern parts of the Islamic lands and claimed religious leadership over the entire *Ummah*, were *Shiites*. Thus the Sunni Caliph of Baghdad had neither direct nor any religious control over the Islamic empire. It was in this period that Al Mawardi, who worked for the Caliph and was trying to preserve and restore the institution of the Caliphate, wrote his famous *Al Ahkam as-Sultaniyyah, The Ordinances of the Government* (Watt 1968).

Al Mawardi wrote his now famous treatise between 1045–58, a crucial time when there appeared the possibility that through an alliance with the rising Seljuks, the Abbasid Caliphate could regain its past glory and power. Although much of Al Mawardi's work is empirical and deals mostly with practical aspects of governance and public administration, a small part of his work deals with the theory of the Caliphate. It is a mixture of legalistic manipulation and political theology with the clear objective of assigning exclusive religious legitimacy to the Caliph and working to restore his socio-political status and legal authority (Qamaruddin 1963).

Al Mawardi's *Ahkam* is not a theory of the state in any sense of the term. It does not offer any conception of what the ultimate purpose of political community is, or why states exist, and what are just and good states. His entire focus is advancing a theoretical argument to legitimize the claim of the Abbasid Caliphate to legitimate power over the entire Muslim community to the exclusion of all other rulers, regimes and claims. In one sense his theory of the Caliphate is a repudiation of the *Shiite* claims. This political objective becomes clearer in one particular claim that he advances with regard to who can be the Caliph. Al Mawardi argues that if there is more than one person qualified to become the Caliph, then it is not necessary that the best one should become the Caliph. It is acceptable for anyone to be chosen as the Caliph. The Electoral College, which can consist of even one individual (he does not advocate universal franchise as advocated by the *Kharijites*, for example), does not need to offer an explanation as to why they chose the inferior candidate over the superior candidate. This is clearly a *Sunni* defence against the *Shiite* claims that no one was more superior to the descendents of the Prophet when it came to religious legitimacy. This gift from Al Mawardi and other Sunni jurists to this day remains an excuse for the incompetent rulers who have plagued the Muslim world (for an excellent critique of Al Mawardi, see Khan 1963).

Al Mawardi's methodology was rather simplistic. He basically studied the history of the early Caliphate and based his theories on this early Islamic period. The first four Caliphs are considered as the rightly guided Caliphs by Muslims generally. Even though this claim is not based on the Koran or any explicit tradition of the Prophet, it is so widely accepted by Islamic scholars that it has become a religious canon. Since the early Caliphs were considered as righteous, many of their practices and actions are also taken as principles. Thus Al Mawardi's theory of the Caliphate is an articulation of selective historical episodes as theoretical principles of Islamic government (Al Mawardi 2000; see also Brown 2000).

Al Mawardi also insisted on some rather dubious criteria in his theory of the Caliphate (see Black 2001). For example, he insisted that only a member of the tribe of Quraish can become a Caliph. This stipulation was to exclude the *Buwayhids*, the *Fatimids* and the *Seljuks* from usurping the title of the Caliph. It did not matter to him that it was completely in contradiction to the universalism characteristic of the message of Islam. It also did not matter to him that he was reducing Islamic political theology to crass tribalism and parochialism. (In his last sermon, considered his last will and testament, which Muslims must uphold, the Prophet specifically instructed his followers not to distinguish between an Arab and a non-Arab. Making tribal distinctions for purposes of legitimacy was clearly self serving [for the Quraish and the Abbasids who belonged to the Quraish tribe] and antithetical to the Message of Muhammad. [See Siddiqui 1991]). After all, he was a court scholar and he served his master the Abbasid Caliph in exemplary fashion. It is apparent from his other works in the field of jurisprudence and even in sociology that Al Mawardi was an excellent thinker and scholar. But his inability to rescue his political theology from his partisan politics demands that his contribution, regardless of its popularity with contemporary Islamists, be viewed with caution .

Ibn Taymiyyah and the primacy of the Sharia

Ibn Taymiyyah lived at a time when the Muslim world experienced some degree of insecurity. The Tartars and the Crusaders were threatening the integrity of Muslim lands and many new religious practices inspired by eclectic mysticism and neo-Platonic philosophers were in Ibn Taymiyyah's view, threatening the integrity of Islam as a faith. Just as Al Mawardi's theory of the Caliphate was inspired by the threats to the Caliphate, Ibn Taymiyyah's ideas of the state were also inspired by a deeply felt insecurity about the future of Islam as a faith and Islam as a civilization or empire. It is important to remember that while Al Farabi and later Ibn Khaldun's attempts to theorize the state were inspired more by intellectual curiosity than temporal politics, the theories of Al Mawardi and Ibn Taymiyyah were firmly embedded in the politics of their time and were clearly designed to advance their partisan positions. While Al Mawardi sought to restore the glory of the Caliphate, Ibn Taymiyyah sought to restore the global dominance of the Islamic civilization and domestic domination of Islamic *Sharia* (Black 2001; Khan 1982; Ibn Taymiyya 1985).

Ibn Taymiyyah's approach was a significant departure from traditional scholarship. His methodology was a mixture of selective use of tradition and past scholarship and a direct use of the Koran in contrast to Al Mawardi who relies primarily on the traditions and historical narratives about the early period of Islam. One of the reasons why Ibn Taymiyyah's rather ideological and stark conceptualization of the purpose of the state has so much appeal for so many is the raw nature of his discourse. He relies on direct and literalist use of the Koran and his selection of Koranic verses gives a quality to his discourse which his followers find compelling. After all if he is using so many words of God, then it stands to reason that his discourse must be more authentic than others whose discussions are corrupted by their reason and interpretation. Ibn Taymiyyah also makes the most systematic analysis of the need, the nature and the ideological objectives of the state, and this clarity of discourse adds to his appeal and influence even today. While Al Mawardi's limitations are easily apparent, Al Farabi's and Ibn Khaldun's analyses have an erudite quality, which easily alienates simplistic readers. The two make intellectual demands of their reader, especially Al Farabi whose writings are complex and philosophical. But Ibn Taymiyyah is clear, dogmatic, and simple.

Ibn Taymiyyah was convinced that Islamic duties, such as encouraging good and forbidding evil, could not be fulfilled without state power. He also felt that several Islamic obligations such as *Jihad* (struggle) against sin and disobedience to God, enforcement of Islamic law, and even fulfillment of collective obligations such as establishing social justice needed the power and machinery of the state. Arguing that religion needed the state to realize itself, Ibn Taymiyyah provided for the first time the argument for a religious necessity of the state. Thus unlike previous Muslim thinkers like Al Farabi, who believed that religious knowledge was necessary for political excellence, Ibn Taymiyyah argued that political power was necessary for religious excellence (Khan 1982: 23–51).

Ibn Taymiyyah's enduring and to some extent problematic characterization of the Islamic state as one that enforces the *Sharia* is his most distinct contribution to the conception of the Islamic state. Today this has become the defining characteristic of the Islamic state for most thinkers and nearly all Islamic movements. Today Muslim states and politicians use the symbolic application of the *Sharia* (which is often operationalized as the application of stringent Islamic laws known as *hudud*, laws against adultery, theft, murder and apostasy), along with banning of interest as a litmus test to determine the Islamic nature of states (Khan 1982: 23–51).

Ibn Taymiyyah also emphasized the importance of security and military functions of the Islamic state. It is in this arena that he departs considerably from the Koranic injunction that 'there is no compulsion in religion' (*Koran* 2: 256); and essentially sees the state as a coercive means to expand and spread Islam beyond its borders, while maintaining the doctrinal purity of Islamic practice within its borders. He brought a severity to the business of establishing Islam, and this approach to religion without compassion has become the trademark of neo-conservative movements such as the *Salafi* movement and the *Wahhabi* movement, which see Ibn Taymiyyah as a great reviver and resuscitator of purity in Islam. Clearly Ibn Taymiyyah's Islam is one which is deeply motivated by insecurity and fear that the faith and its polity are under siege and about to be destroyed. This insecurity more than anything else is the cause for his imagination of the state as an Islamic *Leviathan* that exercises absolute power within and ferociously attacks threats from without.

Ibn Khaldun and the state as an engine of civilization

Ibn Khaldun's approach was unique and far more empirical than any of the three theorists considered so far. While Al Farabi, Al Mawardi and Ibn Taymiyyah were all normative and prescriptive, Ibn Khaldun was empirical, historical and descriptive in his analysis of the origin and decline of states and societies. He was less interested in describing desirable qualities in states and was rather occupied in understanding the natural laws that shaped the origin, growth and declines of cultures and civilizations. The state was a constitutive element of this civilizational life cycle. In a curious way Ibn Khaldun's state has a dual character (somewhat like Anthony Giddens's (1984) structuration theory, which is essential to constructivism in contemporary international relations theories); it is both the medium as well as the product of civilization (Ibn Khaldun 1969; see also Mahdi 1957, 1963; Lakhsassi 1996; Black 2001: 165–82).

Ibn Khaldun's key concept was the idea of *asabiyyah* or solidarity. He, like Al Farabi, also saw the state as an expression of a group's collective desire to achieve a singular goal. The necessary convergence of interests that leads to the recognition of a common goal comes from the emergence of group solidarity or tribal kinship, *asabiyyah*. Ibn Khaldun's theory of the state is essentially a discussion of how tribes, which live in rural and nomadic conditions, band together under the relations and rules of kinship, and when this *asabiyyah* is territorialized through conquest, they establish a state. The emergence of cities and urban lifestyle is the beginning of the establishment of culture and civilization which lead to the stages of contentment and corruption and the collapse of solidarity and the state. Ibn Khaldun argued that the development of the state had five stages:

1   Emergence of solidarity in tribal and nomadic people leading to territorial conquest.
2   The capture of territory and the establishment of the state with the tribal head as the leader.
3   Consolidation of power and sovereignty and the establishment of cities.
4   Emergence of culture, civilization and the state of contentment as citizens of the city enjoy the fruits of civilization and conquest.
5   Decline of solidarity, the decline of the state, and the emergence of threats on the outskirts of the city as alternate tribes, freshly rejuvenated by the emergence of their own solidarity, seek to establish their own state.

Ibn Khaldun suggested that while tribal identity and kinship may work as *asabiyyah* in formative and rural stages, religion was the only cement that could keep a civilization alive and thriving. The solidarity that is so necessary to maintain the territorial integrity and the cultural momentum of the civilization could come only from religion. Thus he too, like Al Farabi, posits religion as a necessity for the state (for a discussion of the continuing relevance of Ibn Khaldun, see Ahmad 2002; Cox 1992). It is interesting to note that not only did the rise and decline of the Islamic civilization follow the life cycle described by Ibn Khaldun; the modern state of Saudi Arabia too seems to be following it. What is not clear is whether the present day Saudi Arabia is in stage 3, 4 or 5.

It is important to note that all the four prominent classical Muslim political thinkers saw religion playing an important role in the formation, maintenance, governance and sustenance of the state. For Al Farabi religion brought a foundational and epistemological quality to the polity, for Al Mawardi it was a legitimizing principle, for Ibn Taymiyyah state was necessary for religion itself and for Ibn Khaldun religion was the cement that kept the state and society intact. Needless to say none of these theorists have advanced a decisive treatise on the state. They are all remarkably similar in one way and that is that they are all formative approaches to studying the state from different perspectives; political socio-cultural, legal and theological. It is one of the limitations of Islamic political thought that very little work has been done subsequently to pursue the philosophical and sociological approaches to the state that were initiated by Al Farabi and Ibn Khaldun. It is also an indication of the insecurity of contemporary Muslim thought that Al Mawardi and Ibn Taymiyyah, play such a prominent role in the theories of the Islamic state that are being advanced in the postcolonial era.

Theories of the Islamic state

Muslims not only wished to organize and govern their own societies but also wished to do so in the authentic traditions of their own civilization. This search for organizational and political authenticity is unique to the Muslim world primarily because like the contemporary West the Islamic civilization too was a globally dominant one in more than a military sense. The Islamic world had its own civilization, which means that it had its own way of organizing state and society and this had worked for it for over a millennium. Many Muslims, intellectuals and lay people, believe that it was the departure from the 'Islamic way' which was the cause for the decline of the Islamic civilization and a return would once again herald the reawakening of Islamic civilizational glory. The Islamic state has been envisioned as the vehicle of change that would realize these aspirations (Ayubi 1991; Asad 1981; Enayat 1991; Ahmad 1986).

There have been three distinct theoretical directions that Muslim thinkers have sought to shape the Muslim world's postcolonial reality. The first and the most dominant one was by secular Muslims who basically sought only political freedom while culturally and intellectually embracing the West. Many of these Westernized secular elites replaced foreign colonization with internal colonization and in effect continued with the same regimes as the past. These secular elites over the years have proven to be corrupt, more inclined to sell out national interests in pursuit of power and wealth, and in spite of their Western intellectual allegiance, extremely authoritarian and undemocratic. Much of the Muslim world today is ruled by these Western secular authoritarian elites. The limits of their vision and the poverty of their commitment is perhaps one of the major causes of the present crisis in the Muslim world.

Reviving the Caliphate

The second and the third directions that Muslims are pursuing are both Islamic and non-secular in nature. They are the efforts to either establish an Islamic state or revive the old institution of the Caliphate. The Islamic state and the Caliphate though similar are actually mutually exclusive ideas. It was the recognition by leading Muslim thinkers such as Rashid Rida that the possibility of reinstituting the Caliphate was impossible, which led them to settle for a limited Caliphate accepting the postcolonial order of nation-states and advancing the idea of the Islamic state. The theory of the Islamic state in principle accepts the world of nation-states and is also an abandonment of the utopian goal of global political integration of the Muslim world.

The most prominent theorist with some contemporary influence in advocating the revival of the Caliphate was Taqiuddin an-Nabhani, the founder of *Hizb ut-Tahrir*. An-Nabhani has provided the Caliphate (*Khilafah*) movement the intellectual framework for their ideology. He produced a grand narrative about the virtues of the Caliphate far removed from historical reality. He believed that until the British and the Turks destroyed the institution of the *Khalifah*, the entire Muslim world was under one rule. Details such as the presence of three simultaneous Caliphs, the Abbasids in Baghdad, The *Fatimids* in Egypt, and the *Ummayyads* in Spain during the tenth and eleventh century, or the long wars between Muslim empires, and the presence of numerous dynasties such as the Mughals in India or the Safavids in Iran, are irrelevant to his claim that a unified Caliph ruled uninterrupted from the first successor to Prophet Muhammad until 1922. He seems to be labouring under a simplistic belief that all Muslims have to do is declare the *Khilafah* and Islam and Islamic civilization will regain its lost glory. He obviously does not bother to explain how, if *Khilafah* alone is the panacea of all problems, this glory was lost in the first place even while the *Khilafah* existed (an-Nabhani 1996).

An-Nabhani's book, *The Islamic State*, is full of historical inaccuracies, confusion between description and prescription, and is more an expression of anger and frustration at the Muslim condition than a systematic theory of an Islamic polity. This confusion is further heightened by using the term Islamic state interchangeably with the global Caliphate. He does advance a sample constitution, however, which is a confused mixture of liberal democratic ideas and Islamist rhetoric. This itself is a departure from the practice of the original Caliphate, which was never a constitutional polity. An-Nabhani's idea is now advanced mostly by disenfranchised and disgruntled Muslim youth who use it to express their frustration with modernity and the powerlessness of the *Ummah* in the face of Western domination.

Characteristics of the Islamic state

The third and the more enduring and partially successful response to Muslim postcolonial reality is the idea of the Islamic state. The idea of the Islamic state is essentially a postcolonial expression that rejects Western cultural and geopolitical domination of the Muslim world. It must be understood within the context of Muslim self-conception and Muslim political aspirations under colonial occupation. The first modern call for a political revival of the Muslim community was raised by Jamaluddin Afghani whose most important goal in life was to decolonize Muslim lands and Muslim culture. He wanted Muslims to become independent of the West politically as well as culturally, and he envisaged an Islamic polity that would act as this beacon of freedom from Western occupation. Even though Afghani did not actually talk of an Islamic state, his ideas of political independence from the West remain key foundations for the subsequent call for an Islamic state made by Maududi and Iqbal in South Asia and echoed in Egypt by Rashid Rida, Hassan al-Bannah and Syed Qutb (Rahnema 1994; Esposito and Voll 2001).

Afghani and his disciples such as Muhammad Abduh were basically Islamic modernists. They accepted several aspects of modernity such as the importance of rational thought and science. Afghani and Abduh succeeded to some extent in reviving the rationalist tradition of the early *Mutazzalites*. But Afghani's most important impact was his ability to incite Muslim nationalism and awaken the desire for political freedom. But even at this time, late nineteenth century and early twentieth century, Muslim intellectuals were still talking of the *Ummah*, of the Muslim community as one global political entity and they hoped to unite them all under one banner. This call for a global political unity became temporarily more urgent and popular in the late 1920s after the British forced the Ottomans to dissolve the institution of the Caliphate. Until then the Caliphate had served as a symbol of Muslim political unity and with its dissolution, the dream of a unified free *Ummah* ended (Keddie 1983).

The earliest articulation of the Islamic state was made in South Asia by Maulana Maududi, the founder of *Jamaat-e-Islami*, a movement seeking to revive Islamic civilization through the establishment of an Islamic state, and by Muhammad Iqbal who is considered the intellectual architect of Pakistan. The independence movement in India had generated a sense of insecurity among Muslims who feared that they would be marginalized and dominated by the Hindu majority in the region after independence. This insecurity and the mishandling of Muslim fears by India's Hindu leaders led to the call for a separate state for Muslims in South Asia. Pakistan was thus conceived as a safe haven for Muslims, a Muslim homeland. Both Iqbal and Maududi, however, hoped not just to create a Muslim homeland but also an Islamic state.

For Iqbal, an Islamic state was the expression of the Muslim spiritual self that sought to excel morally in all spheres including the political arena. He envisaged the Islamic state as a culmination of the Muslim pursuit of perfection and also submission to the will of God. He saw it as a vessel of Muslim identity and manifestation of Islamic civilization (Esposito 1983). Maududi, however, imagined the Islamic state as an ideological instrument that sought to establish the 'sovereignty of God' (*Al-Hakimiyyah*) on earth. This was the first and also the most sophisticated theorization of an Islamic state. For Maududi the objective of the Islamic state was to enforce the will of Allah and this was to be operationalized by applying the *Sharia* as the law of the land (Maududi 1992; see also Hasan 1984; Nasr 1997). Both Iqbal and Maududi accepted the territoriality of the Islamic state as opposed to the globality of the *Ummah* and they also were in favour of democracy with some adjustment. Iqbal sought to limit the franchise to those who were intellectually developed and knowledgeable and Maududi sought to make democracy ultimately subordinate to the *Sharia*. In essence they were willing to embrace the democratic process but not the democratic spirit.

There are five important characteristics that are common to all these theorists:

1   They saw the Islamic state as an ideological actor seeking to rescue the Muslim *Ummah* from Western domination. For most of these theorists the concept of a malevolent, imperial, Judeo-Christian and anti-Islamic West was the threat against which the Islamic state was expected to emerge and resist.
2   For the first time Islamic political theorists felt the need to assert that religion and politics are not separate. Thus the Islamic state became a vehicle to reject secularism and secular humanism.

3 The Islamic state was represented as a political arrangement wherein God and God alone was sovereign and legislator. Once again this was conceived in opposition to Western democracies where it was assumed that human will was sovereign, thereby denying the possibility of politics guided by moral absolutes.

4 The ideological purpose of the Islamic state was seen as applying the *Sharia* within its borders and a commitment to *Jihad* (struggle) to spread Islam abroad.

5 Finally nearly all theorists of the Islamic state including Maududi, Qutb, Iqbal, Rida and Khomeini, their criticism of democracy notwithstanding, advocated the embrace of democratic procedures in selecting rulers and legislators, even advocating collective decision-making.

It is obvious that except for an-Nabhani who is a modernized replica of Al Mawardi, most other theorists of the Islamic state are modern versions of Ibn Taymiyyah in their conception of the application of the *Sharia* as the definitive characteristic of an Islamic state. They too like Ibn Taymiyyah were living in times when Muslims felt insecure about their borders from Western imperialism and the dilution of their Islamic identity from the globalization of Western culture. The added dimension – that in an Islamic state God alone is sovereign – is merely another way of registering their resistance to Western domination, which still continuous even after decolonization. When Islamist theories say God is sovereign, what they basically mean is that *Sharia* is applied and Western influences must be resisted.

Conclusion

It is ironic that the discourse on the Islamic state is at once a rejection of Western modernity, as well as a consequence of and a simultaneous embrace of Western modernity. Several constitutive elements of modernity, the nation-state, territorial sovereignty and democratic procedures have been incorporated into the idea of the Islamic state. What is rejected is the idea of secularism. The idea of the Islamic state is more useful for discursive purposes, than for developmental purposes. It is a useful tool to rescue Muslims from the yoke of Western intellectual domination, but is of little value in generating socio-political change in the real sense. Wherever the so called Islamic states have emerged, they have only brought defeat, isolation, sanctions and criticism from the rest of the world and very little support from the rest of the Muslim world. It is only through more practical experience that Islamic political theory can advance beyond the ideological state in which it currently exists. The present struggle for more freedom in Iran which promises to reshape the fundamental premises of the Islamic revolution of 1979, and the experience that Islamists may gain by running a secular democracy in Turkey may provide some of the practical lessons, which could eventually help reformulate contemporary theories of the Islamic state.

References

Ahmad, A. (2002) 'Ibn Khaldun's Understanding of Civilizations and the Dilemmas of Islam and the West Today', *Middle East Journal*, 56, 1.

Ahmad, M. (ed.) (1986) *State Politics and Islam*, Indianapolis, IN: American Trust Publications.

Asad, M. (1981) *The Principles of State and Government in Islam*, Gibraltar: Dar Al-Andulus.

Ayubi, N. (1991) *Political Islam: religion and politics in the Arab world*, London: Routledge.

Black, A. (2001) *The History of Islamic Political Thought: from the Prophet to the present*, London: Routledge.

Black, D. L. (1996) 'Al-Farabi', in S. H. Nasr and O. Leaman (eds) *History of Islamic Philosophy I*, London: Routledge.

Bin Sayeed, K. (1995) *Western Dominance and Political Islam: challenge and response*, Albany, NY: State University of New York Press.

Brown, L. C. (2000) *Religion and State: the Muslim approach to politics*, New York: Columbia University Press.

Chapra, M. U. (1992) *Islam and the Economic Challenge*, Herndon, VA: International Institute of Islamic Thought and The Islamic Foundation.

Cox, R. (1992) 'Towards a post-hegemonic conceptualization of world order: reflections on the relevancy of Ibn Khaldun', in J. Rosenau and E. Czempiel (eds) *Governance without Government: order and change in world politics*, Cambridge: Cambridge University Press.

Enayat, H. (1991) *Modern Islamic Political Thought*, Austin, TX: University of Texas Press.

Esposito, J. L. (1983) 'Muhammad Iqbal and the Islamic State', in J. L. Esposito (ed.) *Voices of Resurgent Islam*, New York: Oxford University Press.

—— (ed.) (1990) *The Iranian Revolution: its global impact*, Miami, FL: Florida International University Press.

—— (1997) *Political Islam: revolution, radicalism or reform*, Boulder, CO: Lynne Rienner Publishers.

Esposito, J. L. and Piscatori, J. (1990) 'The Global Impact of the Iranian Revolution', in J. L. Esposito (ed.) *The Iranian Revolution: its global impact*, Miami, FL: Florida International University Press.

Esposito, J. L. and Voll, J. O. (2001) *Makers of Contemporary Islam*, New York: Oxford University Press.

Al Farabi, A. N. (1998) *Mabadi ara ahl al-madinat al-fadilah*; trans. R. Walzer as *On the Perfect State*, Chicago, IL: Great Books of the Islamic World.

Giddens, A. (1984) *Title*, Place of publication: Publisher.

Hasan, M. (1984) *Sayyid Abul A'ala Maududi and His Thought*, Lahore: Islamic Publications.

Haykal, M. H. (1976) *The Life of Muhammad*, trans. I. R. al Faruqi, New Delhi: Crescent Publishing Company.

Ibn Khaldun (1969) *Muqaddimah*, trans. F. Rosenthal, Princeton, NJ: Princeton University Press.

Ibn Taymiyya (1985) *Public Duties in Islam: the institution of the Hisbah*, trans. M. Holland, Leicester: The Islamic Foundation.

Keddie, N. R. (1983) *An Islamic Response to Imperialism: political and religious writings of Sayyid Jamal ad-Din 'al-Afghani'*, Los Angeles, CA: University of California Press.

Khan (1963) *Title*, Place of Publication: Publisher.

Khan, M. A. M. (1997) 'Islam as an Ethical Tradition of International Relations', *Islam and Christian-Muslim Relations*, 8, 2: 173–88.

—— (2001) 'Political Philosophy of Islamic Resurgence', *Cultural Dynamic*, 13, 2: 213–31.

—— (2002a) *American Muslims: bridging faith and freedom*, Beltsville, MD: Amana Publishers.

—— (2002b) 'The Compact of Medina and its Democratic Foundations', in *American Muslims: bridging faith and freedom*, Beltsville, MD: Amana Publishers.

Lakhsassi, (1996) *Title*, place of publication: publisher

Mahdi, (1963) *Title*, place of publication: publisher

Mahdi, M.S. (1957) *Ibn Khaldun's Philosophy of History*, Chicago, IL: Chicago University Press.

—— (1987) 'Al Farabi', in L. Straus and J. Cropsey (eds) *History of Political Philosophy*, Chicago, IL: University of Chicago Press.

—— (2001) *Alfarabi and the Foundation of Islamic Political Philosophy*, Chicago, IL: University of Chicago Press.

al-Ma'sumi, M. S. H. (1963) 'Al-Farabi', in M. M. Sharif (ed.) *A History of Muslim Philosophy I*, Karachi: Royal Book Company.

Al Mawardi, A. H. (2000) *The Ordinances of Government*, trans. W. H. Wahba, New York: Ithaca Press.

Maududi, S. A. A. (1992) *Islamic Law and Constitution*, Lahore: Islamic Publications.

an-Nabhani, T. (1996) *The Islamic State*, Walnut, CA: The Islamic Cultural Workshop.

Nasr, S. V. (1997) *Maududi and the Making of Islamic Revivalism*, New York: Oxford University Press.

Osman, F. (1994) *Sharia in Contemporary Society*, Los Angeles, CA: Multimedia Vera International.

Qamaruddin Khan, M. (1963) 'Al-Mawardi', in M. M. Sharif (ed.) *A History of Muslim Philosophy I*, Karachi: Royal Book Company.

—— (1982) *The Political Thought of Ibn Taymiyyah*, New Delhi: Adam Publishers.

Rahnema, A. (ed.) (1994) *Pioneers of Islamic Revival*, London: Zed Books.

Siddiqui, A. H. (1991) *Life of Muhammad*, Des Plaines, IL: Library of Islam.

Watt, W. M. (1968) *Islamic Political Thought*, Edinburgh: Edinburgh University Press.

PART V

POLITICAL INSTITUTIONS

19

EXECUTIVES

Jean Blondel

National executives are universal. Every country has an executive, a 'government' in the strict sense of the word, as indeed does every other social organization, from the most simple to the most complex. In all these cases there is always a body, normally relatively small, which has the task of running the organization. Indeed, since the third quarter of the twentieth century, independent governments have come to rule practically the whole of the planet: as a result, the number of national executives has more than doubled since the 1940s. The executive is manifestly a focal point, if not *the* focal point, of political life. This remains true even if doubts are sometimes expressed about the ability of executives to affect markedly the course of events, let alone alter drastically the social and economic structures of their countries. At least they have, more than any other body, an opportunity to shape society; it is indeed their function to do so.

National governments are at the centre of political life; they are also rather compact bodies, whose views and pronouncements are usually well-publicized. Parties and even legislatures are more amorphous; their 'will' is less clear. Because national governments are relatively small and very visible, it is easier to think of them as groups that have a common goal and indeed act as teams, although they may be disunited and their differences may even come out into the open.

Governments do differ markedly from each other, however. They vary in composition, in internal organization, in selection mechanisms, in duration, in powers – both formal and informal. There are autocratic governments and governments which emanate from the people and from their representatives; there are egalitarian governments and hierarchical governments; there are governments which seem to last indefinitely and ephemeral governments; finally there are strong and weak governments.

It is difficult to define governments as their boundaries are somewhat unclear. They are composed of a number of 'vertical' layers. At the top one finds the leader (and sometimes more than one leader), typically a president or a prime minister and less and less so a monarch (since there are by now few ruling monarchs, although there are still a number of 'symbolic' monarchs, as in Britain). 'Below' the leaders are the ministers, often formally designated as 'secretaries' in presidential systems (as the Secretary of State, in the USA, who is in effect the foreign minister). Below the 'ministers' or 'secretaries' one finds often 'junior' ministers or 'under secretaries', regarded as members of the government as they are appointed by ministers and leave office at the same time as them; yet others who are not formally in the government also fulfil identical functions, such as the personal staff of ministers, who need therefore more than occasionally to be taken into account, since these may play an important part in decision-making, especially, but not exclusively, the personal staff of the leader. While governments may have a clear nucleus, composed of the leader(s) and at least many ministers, a 'grey zone' whose boundaries are not precise form, so to speak, the 'tail' of these governments.

It might seem easier to define a national executive by the functions that it fulfils. Yet these, too, are somewhat unclear. Governments are expected to 'run the affairs of the nation', but they do so only up to a point, since they are 'helped' or 'advised' by groups, by parties, by the legislature, and, above all, by the very large bureaucracy that all states have now developed. One can distinguish three functions that governments have to fulfil. First, they have to elaborate policies and to elaborate policies that are realistic in the sense that they can both be implemented and be politically acceptable (if necessary by using compulsion). An agricultural, industrial or social policy will be developed on the basis of the perceived 'needs' of the country as well as on the basis of the impression of what the citizens are prepared to 'live with'. There is thus a function of *conception*. Second, governments have a function of *implementation*, at least in so far as they must find the means by which policies can become reality: they must therefore appoint and supervise a bureaucracy that is able to put the policies in operation. This twofold function can create tensions, as there are profound differences between those who 'dream' and those who 'manage'; this means that members of the government must have a combination of different skills. Yet there is also a third function which may be viewed as intermediate, that of *co-ordination*. An important element of the process of policy elaboration consists in ensuring that the policies do not go against each other but that they, ideally, develop harmoniously. Moreover, policy elaboration entails making choices or at least establishing priorities, both for financial reasons and because of constraints in human resources. As not all can be done simultaneously, a timetable has to be drawn up; but such a timetable must take into account the interrelationships between policies and the internal logic of policy development (Blondel 1982: 23–5).

Conception, co-ordination and direction of implementation are therefore the three elements of governmental action. These elements are analytically distinct: it is the government's duty to combine them. This combination inevitably raises problems, however: depending on circumstances, conception, coordination and implementation will be given a different emphasis. It is not surprising that the development of governmental structures in the contemporary world should have been the result of a variety of *ad hoc* experiments which have been more or less successful; not surprisingly, too, the conflict between the three goals or functions of government has been solved only to a rather limited extent.

The evolution of governmental arrangements

Contemporary governmental arrangements reflect the diversity and increasing complexity of the tasks that are being undertaken by executives. The variations in the structure of these executives are not a new phenomenon: the oligarchical structure of the Italian republican cities of the Renaissance was at great variance from the structure of the absolute monarchies which began to emerge in sixteenth-century Europe and even more from the theocratic and despotic governments which existed in other parts of the world at the same time.

Nineteenth-century developments have endeavoured to 'domesticate' governmental arrangements and give them a less haphazard and more rational character. Two constitutional systems have dominated the European and North American scene for a century (Lijphart 1992). On the one hand, the *cabinet system*, which originated in England and in Sweden, is based on the notion that the head of the government, the prime minister, has to operate in the context of a collegial system in which a group of ministers fully participates in the decision-making process, while also being in charge of the implementation of the decisions in a particular sector. Cabinet government gradually extended to western European countries. In central and eastern Europe, meanwhile, the remnants of absolutism were gradually undermined, to the extent that the cabinet system seemed likely at one point to replace old absolutist and authoritarian governmental structures everywhere.

In contrast to the cabinet system, the *constitutional presidential system* was first established in the USA and extended gradually to the whole of Latin America. In this model, the executive is hierarchical and not collective: ministers, who, as we noted, are typically named 'secretaries' in this system, are subordinates of the president and responsible only to him or her. Although this formula is closer to that of the monarchical government than to that of the cabinet system, it does imply some demotion for both the head of state (who is elected for a period and often not permitted to be re-elected indefinitely) and for the secretaries (as these typically have to be 'confirmed' by the legislature). The formula has proved, for a long time at least, unsuccessful in Latin America, as many presidents have been uncomfortable with the limitations of their position, leading to *coups*, and the installation of authoritarian and even 'absolute' presidential governments (Shugart and Carey 1992).

At least one of the two constitutional formulas had already encountered difficulties prior to the First World War. The problems multiplied afterwards, with the communist system in Russia and authoritarian governments of the fascist variety in Italy and later in much of southern, central and eastern Europe; after the Second World War, moreover, numerous 'absolute' presidential systems, civilian and military, have ruled many parts of the Third World, in the wake of the 'decolonization' process. These developments occurred in the wider context of the emergence or re-emergence of strong leaders, a phenomenon which constitutional systems had sought to diminish, and the consequential decline of the idea, fostered by cabinet government, of collective or at least collegial government. Yet this period was also characterized by the 'invention' of a new form of executive structure which was consequential on the development of parties but which had not been brought to its ultimate limits in either of the two constitutional systems, the intrusion of the single party in the machinery of government. This type of arrangement was perfected by communist regimes which were to play a major part in twentieth-century political life, but it was also practised in other regimes of both Right and Left, in parts of Europe and in the Third World, although another form of authoritarian regime, to be found essentially in the Third World, was non-party military government (Blondel 1982).

Types of governmental structures in the contemporary world

Above all, governments can be classified depending on the extent to which they are collective or hierarchical, a distinction which is continuous and not merely dichotomous. *Cabinet government* is nominally collective and egalitarian: as decisions have to be taken by the whole body, neither the prime minister nor any group of ministers is formally entitled to involve the whole government. The counterpart of this provision is 'collective responsibility', which stipulates that all the ministers are bound by cabinet decisions; in its most extreme form, the rule suggests that ministers are also bound to speak in favour of all the decisions taken by the cabinet.

These principles are markedly eroded in practice in nearly all the countries which operate on the basis of cabinet government, i.e. in western Europe, in central Europe and much of the Balkans, in many Commonwealth countries (Canada, Australia, New Zealand, India, Malaysia, Singapore, most ex-British Caribbean and Pacific islands), Japan and Israel (Blondel and Muller-Rommel 1997: 14–16; Blondel and Muller-Rommel 1993). In the first instance, following British practice, collective decision-making in many of these countries applies only to members of the cabinet *stricto sensu*: the government can be much larger (in Britain, for instance, it comprises a hundred members or more), because of the existence of substantial numbers of 'junior' ministers. The latter are bound by the principle of collective responsibility, but do not share in the collective decision-making process. Second, the number and complexity of decisions are such that the cabinet cannot physically, during what are normally short meetings of two or three hours a week, discuss all the issues which have to be decided on. As a result, while the cabinet ratifies decisions, many of these are *de facto* delegated to individual ministers (when they are within the competence of their department), to groups of ministers sitting in committee (the number of which has increased markedly in many cabinet governments) or to the prime minister and some of the ministers (McKie and Hogwood 1985: 16–35).

Cabinet governments vary markedly. An important distinction has been made between 'adversarial' or 'Westminster' cabinet systems (when government and opposition are pitted against each other) and 'consensual' cabinet systems (when, in a broad coalition, most parties are represented in the government) (Lijphart 1999): there are many intermediate cases, however, especially among coalition governments. Perhaps the more fundamental distinction is between cabinets which are truly collegial and those which are not. As a matter of fact, the only truly collective government is probably the Swiss federal council, which is not strictly based on a cabinet arrangement in that its members are elected independently, albeit simultaneously, by the two chambers of the parliament; the Commission of the European Union is appointed in a somewhat similar manner by the European Council and subsequently endorsed by the European parliament. Many cabinets form 'teams', rather than strictly collective bodies, whether they are composed of a single party only or of a coalition (Browne and Dreijmannis 1982; Strom 1990). In 'team' cabinets, the ministers have often worked together for a number of years in parliament and have broadly common aims and even a common approach. There is much delegation to individual ministers and to committees of the cabinet but there is a spirit of common understanding. Yet other cabinets are or are close to being of a 'prime ministerial' type, however: this occurs when ministers are markedly dependent on the head of the government, perhaps because he or she is 'charismatic' and won decisive election victories or created the ruling party, the regime or even the country. Such cases have been frequent in Third World cabinet governments of the 1960s, 1970s and 1980s; they have occasionally been found in Western Europe, in France or Germany, for instance. The relationship between ministers and prime minister becomes then almost hierarchical.

The large majority of the other governments are indeed *hierarchical*, in that the secretaries or holders of other ministerial or junior ministerial positions are wholly dependent on the head of the government and/or the head of state. They are appointed and dismissed at will; their decisions are taken by delegation of the head of the government and they play no formal part in policies which do not affect their department. These arrangements were traditionally those of monarchical systems: the constitutional presidential model did not alter this structure. The many authoritarian presidential systems which emerged in the Third World after the Second World War also adopted a formula of this kind. Thus, while perhaps sixty or seventy countries are ruled by a cabinet, many more are governed by hierarchical executives, whether traditional monarchical (for instance in the Middle East), authoritarian presidential (for instance in Africa and in parts of Asia including in the Middle East) or constitutional presidential (typically in the Americas) (Neustadt 1960; Shugart and Carey 1992).

There are variations in the extent to which these governments are hierarchical, however. In traditional monarchical systems, members of some families may be very influential; in civilian or military presidential systems, some individuals may have helped the successful head of the government to come to power. Indeed, the president of the USA is freer in this respect than most other constitutional presidents, who are more closely dependent on party support. Moreover, the complexity of issues, especially economic and social, obliges many heads of government not merely to appoint some well-known managers or civil servants, but to pay attention to their views to such an extent that these may exercise influence well beyond their own department. Indeed, for this and other reasons, it is difficult to regard the US executive as truly hierarchical: it is more accurately described as atomized. Departments are vast and therefore naturally form self-contained empires. Moreover, any vertical relationships which might exist between departmental heads and the president are undermined by the horizontal relationships existing between each department and Congress and especially the committees of Congress relevant to the departments, as these want to ensure that they obtain the appropriations which they feel they need and the laws which they promote. Finally, the links which develop between departments and their clientele (the various interest groups that gravitate around each department) tend to reduce further the strength of the hierarchical ties between departments and president. Admittedly, presidents since Franklin D. Roosevelt in the 1930s have appointed increasingly large personal staffs in order to ensure that presidential policies are carried through (Heclo 1977: 166–8). This has meant, however, that it has become difficult to discover what constitutes the 'real' government of the USA. By becoming gradually a government at two levels, the American government thus resembles in part the 'dual' arrangements which prevail in some countries and which prevailed in particular in Communist states in the second half of the twentieth century.

The governments that we have considered so far are concentrated in one body: indeed, traditional analysis always assumed that governments formed one body. Yet this view is questionable. It is questionable in the context of the modern USA. It was even more questionable in the case of communist states, as, in these, the government was closely supervised by the party and in particular by the top leadership of the party. In the Soviet Union, for instance, especially from the 1950s and up to its disintegration in the early 1990s, four distinct bodies could be regarded as constituting the government: one was the Politburo of the party, which was primarily in charge of policy elaboration; it was helped by its Secretariat; a third body was the Presidium of the Council of Ministers, which was in charge of coordination; finally the Council of Ministers dealt with implementation. The links between these bodies were achieved through some of the more important ministers and the prime minister (who normally was not the secretary of the party) belonging at the same time to the Politburo of the party, to the Presidium and, of course, to the Council of Ministers.

Multi-level governments have also existed in some non-communist single party systems and in a number of military regimes. Supreme Military Councils or Committees of National Salvation have been created to ensure that the regular government (often composed of civil servants) carried out the policies of the military rulers. This formula, which originated in Burma in 1962, was adopted by many African states (for example by Nigeria, for a period); it also existed for some years in Portugal after the end of the dictatorship in 1974. These arrangements have had a varying degree of longevity and of apparent success: they typically have been less systematically organized than they were in communist states (Blondel 1982: 78–93, 158–73).

Governmental leadership

Executives are fashioned by the role of their leaders. Political leadership is highly visible, much talked about and complex to assess. The visibility of leadership has been markedly enhanced by the development of the mass media, in particular television, but it has always been prominent: great leaders of Antiquity, of the Renaissance and of the modern period were all well known to their contemporaries, despite the fact that they could only be seen and heard by relatively few numbers. Their qualities and defects were probably the subject of many conversations; scholarly work was at any rate devoted to them. Indeed, the studies of historians were primarily concerned with the description of their actions, while the concept of leadership began to be analysed.

Leaders can be judged to be good or bad, heroes or villains; but leaders are also seen as more or less successful, more or less effective. The distinction has been made, in this respect, between *leaders*, in the strong sense of the word and mere 'power-holders' or, perhaps more accurately, office-holders (Burns 1978: 5; Kellerman 1984). It seems intuitively correct to claim that many rulers – probably the large majority – are not very influential, as they appear to do little to modify the course of events, while only a few are great 'stars' who, at least ostensibly, affect profoundly the destiny of humanity. A further distinction has been made in terms of 'great' leaders who shape their society entirely, who 'transform' its character, and of those who are primarily concerned with the functioning of society and who make compromises and 'transactions' while accepting the framework within which economic, social and political life takes place (Burns 1978). Such a distinction should not be viewed as a dichotomy, but as two poles of a continuous dimension dealing with the 'extent of change' which leaders wish to bring about (Blondel 1987: 10–26). It is in a somewhat similar context that Max Weber introduced the notion of 'charisma', a concept which has come to be devalued by comparison with the rather strict conception of Weber, but which has played a major part in the contemporary world. This is particularly because, in the new countries, alongside the other Weberian categories of traditional and bureaucratic-legalistic rule, personal rule has been widespread in order to help to maintain regimes and indeed states lacking basic support (Weber 1968: 214).

The scope of activities of leaders is strongly regulated in the context of two types of rulers only, the prime ministers of parliamentary or cabinet systems and the constitutional presidents; the constitutional monarchs who comprise a third category now usually have a purely symbolic role. The position of prime minister is, ostensibly at least, less prestigious than that of president (Elgie 1995): it exists normally in conjunction with that of a symbolic monarch (as in Britain, most Scandinavian countries or the Low Countries) or of a symbolic president (as in Germany, Italy or India). Although these heads of state have few real powers, they exercise ceremonial functions which give them a large authority that is denied to prime ministers; this is indeed the reason why a number of Third World prime ministers, in particular in Black Africa, brought about constitutional changes a few years after independence to allow them to become presidents (as in Kenya, Zambia or the Ivory Coast, for instance) (Jackson and Rosberg 1982).

Prime ministers have ostensibly limited power because they exercise it in the context of the cabinet which must concur in all decisions but, as we have already noted, there are substantial differences in their influence. The power of presidents is also very varied, although, because they run hierarchical governments, presidents by and large exercise major influence. This is particularly the case in authoritarian presidential systems, which constitute the majority of cases, despite the growth in the number of liberal democratic governments in the course of the last decades of the twentieth century. As a matter of fact, apart from that of the USA, constitutional presidencies have only had a limited success. Authoritarian presidents, and in particular military rulers, whose numbers have diminished, one hopes not temporarily, in the last decades of the twentieth century, either operate without any constitution or devise constitutions designed to suit their ambitions. They are sometimes allowed to be re-elected indefinitely and are even occasionally appointed for life. They are allowed to dissolve the legislature if one exists and the government depends entirely on them. The spread of these 'absolute' presidencies has coincided with attainment of independence by many countries, especially in Africa, and many countries of the Middle East. Many authoritarian presidents were the first leaders of their country: they were able to build political institutions and to shape these in the way they wished. Some were close to being 'charismatic' in the full sense that Weber delineated (Weber 1968: 214–15). In the main they relied on strong popular support as well as on authoritarian practices; they were the 'fathers' of their countries and often remained in office for two decades or more, thereby forming a disproportionately large number of the long-serving leaders in the contemporary world. The successors of these first leaders generally found it more difficult to rule in such a 'paternal' and absolute manner: in some cases, in Senegal for instance, the result has been a more 'domesticated' presidency, but this is far from being universally the case.

Among authoritarian rulers one must not forget the leaders of the remaining communist regimes as well as the rulers of ex-communist regimes which have changed the ideological, but not the form of their rule: except for Castro's Cuba, these regimes are all in Central and East Asia, China, North Korea, Vietnam and Laos being the only countries of the region which still maintain a communist ideology on the political, if not necessarily, in the case of China and even Vietnam, on the economic plane. Given the size of the Chinese population, it is clearly rather exaggerated, or at any rate premature, to consider communist regimes – and their authoritarian practices – a vestige of the past.

An interesting form of executive leadership is constituted by dual leadership, one form of which has typically been referred to as 'semi-presidentialism' as both president and prime minister share the leadership (Lijphart 1992: 62–72; Elgie 1999). Single-leader rule is often considered as the norm: yet there are many cases where it does not obtain. There are examples of government by council, to which the cabinet system is only partly related; there are 'juntas', in particular among provisional Latin American governments, in which a small number of military officers (often drawn from the three branches of the services) rule the country for a period: above all there are a substantial number of cases of dual leadership.

Dual leadership has existed at various moments in history: for example, Republican Rome was ruled primarily by two consuls. Its modern development arose in the first instance from the desire (or the need) of kings to share a part of their burden with a first or prime minister. This occurred partly as a result of popular pressure, but it took place also in highly authoritarian states, from the early seventeenth century in France with Richelieu to the nineteenth century in Austria with Metternich and in Germany with Bismarck. It results both from legitimacy difficulties (when the king has to associate a 'commoner' to his power) or as a consequence of administrative necessities.

This is why countries as diverse as France or Finland, on the one hand, and communist states on the other, the kingdoms of Morocco and Jordan at one extreme and the 'progressive' states of Tanzania, Algeria or Libya at the other, have adopted dual leadership at various points in time. The system has existed in both liberal and authoritarian systems, in conservative and non-conservative systems, in communist and non-communist systems, although, in communist systems, the distinction between party secretary and prime minister has been particularly sharp as it corresponds to the division between 'party' and 'state' which has traditionally characterized that type of political system.

Systems of dual leadership are often viewed as transitional, but enough examples have lasted for many decades to raise doubts about the 'natural' character of single leadership: perhaps a quarter of the nations of the world are ruled by a system of dual rule and in most of these that system has operated in a stable manner. The two leaders may not be equal: indeed, this is often quite the contrary, as the distinction between a leader embodying the national legitimacy and a leader embodying the administrative legitimacy suggests, but the complexity of the modern state is such that it is far from surprising that leadership should often have to be shared in order to be effective.

Thus leaders can play very different parts: it is clear that not all these differences stem from the character of the regime. The role of personal characteristics also appears intuitively to be large, but seems to elude precise measurement and even broader assessment (Bass 1981: 43–96). Studies have begun to analyse the impact of personality characteristics on national leadership, though much still remains vague. Intelligence, dominance, self-confidence, achievement, drive, sociability and energy have appeared correlated with leadership in a substantial number of studies undertaken by experimental psychologists. Attention has also been paid to revolutionary leaders, who have been shown to have a number of traits in common, such as vanity, egotism, narcissism, as well as nationalism, a sense of justice and a sense of mission. They are also characterized by relative deprivation and status inconsistency; it was also found that these leaders had marked verbal and organizational skills (Rejai and Phillips 1983: 37–8). Overall, two factors, drive or energy (labelled 'activity' or 'passivity') and satisfaction with the job (a 'positive' or 'negative' approach) appear essential, as has been shown in the context of American presidents (Barber 1977: 11–14). Although it is difficult to assess the extent to which, under different conditions, leaders can modify the institutions that they need to exercise their power and although the part that they play in this respect is often overshadowed by the durable and even ostensibly permanent character of these institutions, it is clear that personal factors account markedly in the development of leadership.

The impact of leaders and of governments

The career of leaders, ministers and secretaries is short: it lasts on average only four or five years; very few stay in office for ten years or more, although duration was traditionally longer in communist states and in traditional monarchies than elsewhere (Blondel 1985). Such short periods in office make it difficult to measure the realizations of governments. First, one needs to distinguish between what would have occurred 'naturally' and what occurred because of what the government decided. Second, it is often not possible to relate particular outcomes precisely to particular governments: this can be because the duration of some governments is very short (a year or less), because governments 'slide' into one another, so to speak, as with coalitions and with reshuffles, and because of the 'lag' between policy elaboration and implementation. Thus, not surprisingly, conclusions about the impact of governments have remained rather imprecise; they have concerned certain broad characteristics of whole classes of executives rather than individual cabinets. It has been possible to establish that social democratic governments do have, at least in many respects, an impact on social and economic life, despite the views sometimes expressed that no difference could be detected any longer among governmental parties (Castles 1982; Rose 1984). It also seems established that, contrary to what some had claimed, Third World military governments do not perform better economically than civilian governments. On the other hand, some generalizations often made about governments have not so far been confirmed: in particular, it has not been proved that the instability of ministerial personnel has the negative consequences for social and economic development that it is often said to have (though it may have a negative impact on the regime's legitimacy). (See Hook 1955.)

291

Nor is it easy to establish fully, for the same reasons, the impact of leaders. 'Great' revolutionaries appear to make a major impact; yet they are helped by the fact that the demand for change in their society is strong and provides opportunities that are denied to those who rule a society whose members are satisfied with the *status quo*. Thus the efforts of Lenin or Mao were helped by the turmoil prevailing in Russia and China at the time. The impact of leaders must therefore be assessed not only by examining the policies elaborated and implemented by these leaders, but by examining the demands made by the population and in particular by its more vocal elements (Blondel 1987). Rulers who administer the system as it is and who do not aim at altering policies may be regarded as having very little impact, even though they may be very influential by thwarting a substantial demand for change. Meanwhile, rulers who introduce changes on a relatively narrow front need not necessarily have less impact than those who embark on policies designed to alter their society fundamentally. The role of leadership must therefore be assessed by relating the rulers to the ruled and the characteristics of personalities to the climate among the population. It must also be assessed over time: indeed, it may never be fully determined, as it may be exercised on generations as yet not born. It can also fluctuate, as what has been done by a leader can be undone by his or her successors. For example, Mao's policies have been profoundly modified, even overturned by those who followed him. Thus the impact of the founder of the communist regime in the world's most populated country does not appear as great at the beginning of the twenty-first century as it was in the 1970s.

It may seem paradoxical to ask if governments matter when so much emphasis is placed on national executives by the media, organized groups and large sections of the public. This paradox is only one of the many contradictory sentiments that governments appear to create. Perhaps such contradictory views are understandable: governments and their leaders both attract and repel because they are at least ostensibly powerful and give those who belong to them an aura of strength, of *auctoritas*, which fascinates, tantalizes, but also worries and, in the worst cases, frightens the subjects as well as the spectators of political life. Yet there are also other contradictions and paradoxes of governments, from the great complexity of the tasks to be performed to the often ephemeral character of the members, from the many ways in which they can be organized to the ultimate paradox – namely that it is almost impossible to know how much they affect the destinies of humanity.

References

Barber, J. D. (1977) *The Presidential Character*, Englewood Cliffs, NJ: Prentice-Hall.

Bass, B. M. (1981) *Stogdill's Handbook on Leadership*, New York, NY: Free Press.

Blondel, J. (1982) *The Organisation of Governments*, London and Los Angeles: Sage.

—— (1985) *Government Ministers in the Contemporary World*, London and Los Angeles: Sage.

—— (1987) *Political Leadership*, London and Los Angeles: Sage.

Blondel, J. and Muller-Rommel, F. (eds) (1993) *Governing Together*, Basingstoke, Hampshire: Macmillan

—— (1997) *Cabinets in Western Europe*, Basingstoke, Hampshire: Macmillan.

Browne, E. C. and Dreijmannis, J. (eds) (1982) *Government Coalitions in Western Democracies*, London: Longman.

Burns, J. McG. (1978) *Leadership*, New York, NY: Harper and Row.

Castles, F. C. (ed.) (1982) *The Impact of Parties*, London and Los Angeles: Sage.

Elgie, R. (1995) *Political Leadership in Western Democracies*, Basingstoke, Hampshire: Macmillan.

—— (1999) *Semi-presidentialism in Europe*, Oxford: Oxford University Press.

Ham, C. and Hill, M. (1993) *The Policy Process in the Modern Capitalist State*, Hemel Hempstead, Herts: Harvester Wheatsheaf.

Heclo, H. (1977) *A Government of Strangers*, Washington, DC: Brookings Institution.

Hook, S. (1955) *The Hero in History*, Boston, MA: Beacon Press.

Jackson, R. H. and Rosberg, C. G. (1982) *Personal Rule in Africa*, Berkeley, CA: University of California Press.

Kellerman, B. (ed.) (1984) *Leadership*, Englewood Cliffs, NJ: Prentice-Hall.

Lijphart, A. (1992) *Parliamentary Versus Presidential Government*, Oxford: Oxford University Press.

—— (1999) *Patterns of Democracy*, New Haven, CT: Yale University Press.

McKie, T. T. and Hogwood, B. W. (eds) (1985) *Unlocking the Cabinet*, London and Los Angeles: Sage.

Neustadt, R. (1960) *Presidential Power*, New York, NY: Wiley.

Rejai, M. with Phillips, K. (1983) *World Revolutionary Leaders*, London and Los Angeles: Sage.

Rose, R. (1984) *Do Parties Make a Difference*, London: Macmillan.

Shugart, M. S. and Carey, J. M. (1992) *Presidents and Assemblies*, New York, NY: Cambridge University Press.

Strom, K. (1990) *Minority Government and Majority Rule*, New York, NY: Cambridge University Press.

Weber, M. (1968) *Economy and society*, (3 vols) New York: Bedminster Press.

20

LEGISLATURES

G. R. Boynton

It is the century of the legislature. Before and after the Second World War, as colonialism failed and nations grew in number, constitutions incorporating a national legislature replaced extant governing institutions throughout the world. In the late 1980s, the political transformation of Eastern Europe was propelled by the rejuvenation of legislative institutions. Instead of control by the communist party, elections for membership in parliament were held in the first free elections since the Second World War. Legislative institutions have spread throughout the world and their influence appears to be on the rise in the twenty-first century.

The viability of legislatures during the second half of the twentieth century was mixed, however. In democracies with a longer history, legislatures maintained or even increased their importance within the governing institutions of the country. In some new democracies legislatures were stable, important institutions of governing. In many new democracies legislatures suffered a different fate. In Korea, for example, a thirty-five-year period of Japanese colonial occupation was followed by a national election in 1948 to establish the first National Assembly. The president elected under the new constitution soon turned autocratic and suppressed political opposition. A student revolt in 1960 overturned the Syngman Rhee government, and was followed by free elections for the National Assembly. The new government lasted less than two years before it was overthrown by a military junta. Two years later the military junta held elections and had themselves elected to political office (Kim *et al.* 1984). This pattern of military government punctuated by return to democratic elections (principally elections for the National Assembly) continued in South Korea until almost the end of the century, and was prevalent in other new nations as well. Pakistan is another example of punctuated military rule; the army ruled Pakistan for twenty-four of the first forty-three years of independence. Then electoral democracy was resuscitated at the end of the century only to be overthrown once again.

This exceedingly brief excursion into legislative history is designed to make two points. First, legislative stability is as puzzling as is the instability of legislative institutions in some of the newer democracies. Even though stability may seem the natural course of affairs for those of us living in relatively stable systems of governing, we are reminded of the presence of something here by its absence elsewhere. The puzzle is: what is present and absent that yields stability in one case and instability in another? The second point worth noting is that elections and legislatures have become the fall-back position. When the generals or colonels find themselves so divided that they cannot rule or when they weary of ruling, as has happened at times in Latin America, it is elections and legislatures to which the country returns. Legislatures rarely control the guns, but they became remarkably resilient in the second half of the twentieth century (Mezey 1985). This change in the fall-back position is a major change in world history. Around the world, legislatures have been elevated to the position that they have held for roughly two hundred years in Europe.

How elections matter

Some are born to office, some rise through military or civilian bureaucracies, and some are elected to office. Election is a distinctive route into the political elite; it is an avenue that distinguishes legislators from most other members of a nation's political elite. An important question to ask about legislatures is how they differ from other governing institutions of a nation because their members are selected by election.

Who is elected?

Are members of legislatures drawn from segments of society different from those that produce other political elites? This question has been more thoroughly investigated and can be answered more confidently than any other question about legislatures. The answer is no. Most legislators are educated, wealthy men from the higher status sectors of society. Donald Matthews (1985) has drawn together the very large body of research on the social background of legislators and discovered that, in the USA, in Western Europe, in the communist nations, in Latin America, Asia and Africa the results are the same: members of the legislature are drawn from the advantaged classes of society. There are only two variations on this theme. In less developed countries with very small elite populations and large populations of poor, the status gap between legislators and electors is greater than in the more developed countries in which the income distribution is more equal. Only in Scandinavia (Skard 1981) and in some communist nations (Hill 1973) do women approach 50 per cent of the membership of legislatures (Fox, Lawless and Feeley 2001). Perestroika has halved the percentage of women in the Supreme Soviet; before the election of 1989 women held approximately 33 per cent of the seats in the Supreme Soviet, but in the 1989 election they won only 17 per cent of the seats (Mann, Monyak and Teague 1989).

Legislators are drawn from the very same sectors of society from which other elites are drawn (Matthews 1954; Bell, Hill and Wright 1961; Putnam 1976; Button and Hedge 1996). Elections produce a legislature that is quite different in its social experiences from the social experiences of the electorate, but legislators are not, in this respect, distinctive from other political elites. Elections may facilitate circulation of the elite, but it is the elite that is being circulated. The impact of elections must be sought elsewhere.

Legislators and the concerns of constituents

In August 1990, the US military was suddenly mobilized to put a large contingent of troops into Saudi Arabia. A young Michigan couple, planning to be married, was separated when he was transferred to South Carolina in transit to Saudi Arabia. Senator Carl Levin of Michigan, a member of the Armed Services Committee and running for re-election, used his good offices to help the couple arrange to be married at the base where the soldier was temporarily stationed. Senator Levin, the couple and the wedding were featured on television in Michigan and on network news. The story is worth recounting as a reflection on the following statement about legislatures:

> Because in many non-Western cultures the political realm is not as well differentiated from the nonpolitical, Third World legislators have had to deal with requests that their Western counterparts seldom confront.... In Thailand, legislators reported that they were asked to act as go-betweens in arranging marriages.
>
> (Mezey 1985: 743)

Whether in the USA or in the Third World, elections focus legislators' attention on the concerns of their constituents. If the concern is arranging marriages, legislators become involved when only they have the stature required to provide the assistance.

In Tanzania, legislators said bringing the needs of their constituents to the attention of the government was one of their most important tasks (Hopkins 1970). Members of the Colombian Congress said helping their constituents deal with government offices, identifying regional problems and making them public problems, and working as a broker between their constituency and the government were among their most important tasks as legislators (Hoskin 1971). Chilean legislators invested much effort in assisting constituents with a bulky social security bureaucracy and getting local projects into the budget (Valenzuela and Wilde 1979). Legislators in Kenya, Korea and Turkey said they had been effective in channelling resources to their districts (Kim *et al.* 1984). The picture does not change for the USA (Olson 1967; Fiorina 1977) or Western Europe (Barker and Rush 1970; Cayrol, Paroid and Ysmal 1976).

Two themes characterizing constituents' concerns are found in the research. One theme is bureaucratic indifference. Getting the social security bureaucracy to acknowledge and deal with the special circumstances of a constituent is as much a part of the working life of members of the US Congress as it is for the Chilean legislator (Freeman and Richardson 1996). The second theme is local economic development. Local development may be an access road or a well in Kenya (Barkan 1979) or Colombia (Ingall and Crisp 2001) or it may be a nuclear fuel reprocessing plant or military bases in the USA (Rundquist, Lee and Rhee 1996). Whether Kenya or the USA, the best possible site is the concern of planners, but the economic development of the constituency is the concern of the elected legislator.

It is plausible that elections predispose legislators to focus on the concerns of constituents to a greater degree than do other political elites, but an unusual feature of the Korean constitution provides more direct evidence on the point. For a brief period the Korean constitution stipulated that two-thirds of the members of the National Assembly would be elected to their offices and one-third would be appointed. The provision virtually guaranteed that the party of the president would have a substantial majority in the National Assembly. It also made it possible for Kim and Woo (1975) to examine differences in the actions of elected and appointed members of the National Assembly. Elected legislators were substantially more likely to engage in constituency service activities than appointed legislators. Elections matter by focusing legislators' attention on the concerns of constituents.

For whom you speak; to whom you speak

Representation is the Anglo-American way of framing this subject. The Legislative System (Wahlke *et al.* 1962), which traced its roots directly back to Edmund Burke, was the influential starting point for two strands of research on the connection between elections and government action. The basic conception is representation as the function by which the views of citizens are mapped into public policy; the views of citizens are represented in the policy-making process. One strand of research based on this conception examined the congruence between constituents' opinions and the voting of legislators. The most straightforward statement of this line of research was 'Congress and the public: how representative is one of the other?' (Backstrom 1977). The theme was most systematically carried through in a set of studies employing sample surveys of the electorate and voting in legislatures (Barnes 1977; Converse and Pierce 1986; Miller and Stokes 1963). The second strand followed Wahlke *et al.* (1962), who did not have access to surveys of citizens, by investigating more fully the representative role orientation of legislators. Since this second research strategy could be employed in countries where survey data were not available, a broader range of countries was included in the research (see for example, Hopkins 1970; Hoskin 1971; Kim 1969; Kim and Woo 1975; Mezey 1972).

The result of the research is an understanding of the weaknesses of this way of framing the relationship between elections and governing. There have been many critiques and attempts at reformulation (Boynton and Kim 1991; Eulau and Karps 1977; Pitkin 1967). Three criticisms are particularly important. First, legislators do not seem to play the role in policy making assumed in the theory; this was one finding of the second strand of research. Second, citizens do not do their part; they do not carry around well-formulated views on the broad range of policy matters governments must handle; this was one finding of the first strand of research. Third, when constituents agree it is easy for legislators to represent agreement. When constituents disagree 'representation' is no assistance in specifying what a legislator will or should do, and constituents disagree more than they agree. What is needed is a reformulation that refocuses the importance of elections and that is more descriptively adequate.

The reformulation can begin by noticing that the arguments of elected officials about what the government should do are always made facing in two directions. They address each other; simultaneously they address the electorate. In addressing each other and the electorate they remember who supported them in the last election and they seek additional supporters in the next election. Instead of representation this formulation focuses on appeal for support. Instead of acting out the will of the electorate it is acting to create a will in the electorate. Frank Baumgartner (1987) argues for this understanding of policy arguments in the French parliament. By reframing issues, issues framed by the government as technical matters, in terms of equality, French cultural heritage and other important symbols in French politics, opposition parties change the focus of the debate, criticize the government, appeal to their supporters and appeal for new supporters. Boynton (1991) showed that even highly technical argument plays a role in forming views in the arguments about clean air. Shanto Iyengar (1990) showed that the framing and reframing of communication can have a substantial impact on how citizens respond. The important point is not the reframing, however. Reframing is rather rare, but it is a striking example of what elected officials do all the time in appealing to voters from the floor of the chamber. And citizens do respond (Lipinski 2001; Bishin 2000). Elections are held, and in wealthier societies there are interest group organizations and public opinion polls which fill in between elections. Thus, conversation – the appeal of the official and the response of the electorate and the appeal of the electorate and the response of officials – is a better formulation than representation. Elections are important because they engage politicians in conversation with their constituents (Boynton 1990).

How electoral systems matter

In asking how elections matter the organization of elections has not yet been taken into account. There are substantial differences in electoral systems and the differences have consequences for who the constituents are who receive the attention of legislators and for the conversations between legislators and electorates. Three features of electoral systems are particularly important: the rule for determining a winner; the geographic unit for candidates' election; and control of nominations (Duverger 1963; Rae 1971). The three features are combined in many different ways in the nations of the world, but the most important consequences of the three can be treated independently.

Three criteria are widely used in determining the winner of an election. A candidate may need a majority of the votes cast, or a plurality of the votes cast, or parties may be allocated seats based on the proportion of the vote received in the election. Systems requiring a majority or a plurality of votes result in the parties that receive the largest percentage of the votes nationally receiving a larger percentage of the seats in the legislature than their percentage of votes. Parties that receive smaller percentages of votes in the election receive an even smaller percentage of the seats in the legislature. Allocating seats on the basis of the percentage of votes received in the election, known as proportional representation, is less biased in favour of large parties and against small parties in translating votes into seats. The consequence of the counting procedure is reducing or increasing the number of conversations. Small parties do not survive in majority and plurality systems, and the ensuing conversations are limited to the few that do survive.

At one extreme the country may be divided into geographic units with a single legislator elected from each geographic unit; this requires a majority or plurality rule for determining the winner. The other extreme is using the entire country as the geographic unit for counting votes; this requires some form of proportional allocation of seats based on votes. Who the legislators' constituents are is altered by the geographic unit used for counting votes. Constituents will be geographically contiguous residents in one case. In this case local implies geography. If the nation is the geographic unit used, constituents and local have quite different meanings. For example, constituents might become everyone in the nation who is concerned about the state of the environment, wherever they live.

One cannot be elected without first being nominated. Political parties control nominations in almost every country, but there is great variation in how much control is exercised. It is relatively easy for a party organization to control nominations if the electoral system uses proportional representation because that system requires a national list of candidates. Who gets on the list and the placement on the list become very important for election. Election systems based on smaller geographic units, especially if a primary election is used, minimize the control of nomination by parties. This reduces or increases the number of conversations. When parties exercise tight control the legislator who disagrees with the party is easily replaced in the next election, and the number of conversations is reduced. When parties exercise little control the number of conversations proliferate as individual candidates appeal to different groups in the electorate.

Legislatures and the argument about what we should do as a nation

Politics is the ongoing argument about what we should do as a nation and how it should be done, where the rules by which we argue may themselves become part of the argument. Legislatures, then, are part of the rules by which we argue. A legislature establishes a privileged status in the argument for a subset of the total population – the legislators. They speak in arenas where others cannot and their arguments are attended to in a way that the arguments of others are not. In becoming legislators they speak and listen where others do not go.

Characterizing legislatures as part of the arrangements by which we conduct arguments may thus seem rather odd. After all, it might be said, legislatures pass laws; legislators should busy themselves passing legislation rather than spending their time arguing. It is certainly true that, with few exceptions, constitutions establishing legislatures stipulate that legislation must be passed by the legislature to become law. In this formal sense legislatures throughout the world pass laws. However, if one expects those laws to be initiated by legislators, to be written by legislators, to be substantially modified during consideration and passage by legislators, or that legislators will fail to pass legislation that is initiated and written elsewhere, the expectation does not match what legislatures do. There is a consensus among legislative scholars that legislatures play only a modest role in initiating and writing legislation (Mezey 1985). Distinctions can be drawn, of course. The US Congress is substantially more influential in formulating policy than are other legislatures. The Costa Rican legislature was found to be more important in the formulation of legislation than the Chilean legislature (Hughes and Mijeski 1973). The German Bundestag is more influential in formulating legislation than the British House of Commons, and both are substantially more influential than the legislature of Kenya (Loewenberg and Patterson 1979). But these distinctions are drawn within a very narrow range. What is needed is a different formulation of the role of legislatures in political life of a country; one that is more descriptively adequate.

The earlier discussion of how elections matter leads to thinking about legislatures as the last election, legislators appealing for support from the floor, and the next election – in other words, the argument about what we should do as a nation and how we should do it (Kahn and Kenney 2001). In contrast, thinking about the legislature as a law-writing body de-emphasizes elections and the argument. Then scholars and other observers are surprised when 'politics', the next election, intrudes itself into law writing or not law writing in the legislature (Rockman 1985).

Legislatures and the current state of the argument

An election registers the current state of the argument. All parties argue their position on what the nation should do and how it should be done, which in elections becomes who should do it. The current state of the argument, who is persuaded by whom, is registered when voters go to the polls, and the outcome is embodied in persons in offices. How the offices are arranged, particularly the relationship between the legislature and the executive, is important in how the current state of the argument becomes laws.

In some countries the executive, usually called the president, is selected separately from the election of the legislature, but in other countries the executive, usually called prime minister and cabinet, may, or in some cases, must, be members of the legislature. In a survey of fifty-six legislatures Herman and Mendel (1976) found that fourteen prevented members of the legislature from serving in executive offices, seventeen required some or all of the top executive officers to be drawn from the legislature, and that most did not require the executive to be drawn from the legislature.

Embodying the current state of the argument in persons in office is straightforward in a country with a president and an electoral system that produces few political parties in the legislature. The president is elected and appoints his or her administrative officers – cabinet, heads of ministries, etc. – and the executive is in place. Legislative elections usually produce a majority that organizes the legislature. The majority party in the legislature may or may not be the same as the party of the president, but the current state of the argument is registered in a set of officials to continue the argument. In a country in which the executive comes out of the legislature and with an electoral system that produces many political parties in the legislature there is another step in the argument. A government must be created by forming a coalition in the legislature. Only after a coalition government is established is the current state of the argument fully registered in persons in office. These are two widely used organizations of offices. The USA is a notable presidential system. Many of the European democracies are parliamentary systems with the configuration of offices described. But there are many variations on these themes. In Great Britain, for example, the prime minister and cabinet are drawn from parliament, but the electoral system produces few parties in parliament; thus, there is normally a majority party in parliament and the majority party forms the government without the necessity of forming a coalition.

Research on coalition governments provides evidence for the contention that elections register the current state of the argument by embodying that state in offices.

The early research, which traced its roots to Riker's (1962) theory of coalitions, assumed that office seeking was all that was at stake in forming the coalitions. From this perspective, the second step in forming a government would reflect the current (electoral) state of the argument only indirectly – only by establishing the distribution of seats before bargaining over the distribution of the spoils of office. But this conception of coalition formation proved inadequate. The inadequacy of the theory was clearest in failing to account for minority coalitions. If office was the major motivation in forming coalitions, the majority of legislators not in the coalition should have formed a government and split the offices between themselves rather than letting a minority have them. Thirty per cent of the cabinets studied were minority cabinets. There is now general agreement among scholars that forming a coalition government is, at least in part, a continuation of the argument about what the nation should do and how (Browne and Franklin 1986; Budge and Laver 1986; Peterson and De Ridder 1986).

Research on coalition governments also provides evidence that the argument is ongoing, that the argument – within and without the legislature – about what the nation should do does not stop with elections. There is great variation in the length of time coalitions survive; some last only a few months and most last fewer than fifty-two months (Dodd 1976). First, researchers attempted to explain the survival of a coalition based on its characteristics when it was formed. From this perspective, the state of the argument at the time of the election would explain how long a coalition lasted. After the election, governing would be a matter of passing laws representing the state of the argument at election time. This cannot be completely discounted, but it is, at best, a partial explanation. More recently researchers have used post-election events to improve their explanations of coalition durability (Browne, Frendreis and Gleiber 1986; Cioffi-Revilla 1984). Events occur subsequent to the election, the argument continues, and the governing coalition is re-formed registering a new state of the argument.

The research on coalition governments is useful in establishing what happens in all legislatures. The need to form coalitions and the breakdown of coalitions puts in public view the processes going on in all legislatures. Go to any legislature and what you will find is ongoing argument about what the nation should be doing and how it should be done – on the floor, in the corridors, in committees or wherever legislators meet.

The level of detail in the arguments

'We can have clean air and a sound economy.' That is one level of detail in an argument about the health effects of air pollution and the economy; it is roughly the level of detail found in headlines reporting political campaigns. Saying that vehicles are a major source of pollution that causes health problems for persons with asthma and other lung ailments adds more detail to the arguments about the extent of pollution due to vehicles and how debilitating the pollution is for how many people. More detail can be added by specifying the harmful chemicals emitted by vehicles, how much the chemicals would have to be reduced to reduce health effects to an acceptable level, the determination of an acceptable level, how much emission reduction is provided by current catalytic converters, how far emissions could be further reduced with improved catalytic converters, how much improving catalytic converters will cost, how the chemicals that escape in the sale of petrol contribute to the problem, how the pumps could be redesigned and at what cost, how vehicle petrol tanks could be redesigned to reduce the escape of the harmful chemicals, and so on.

The point is simple. Arguments can be, and are, carried on at all of these levels of detail. Laws can be characterized at all of these levels of detail, but law cannot be written at all of the levels of detail. A law that said 'Henceforth there will be clean air' would not tell anyone, vehicle manufacturers for example, what they must do to conform to the law. Laws are full of details that most citizens and most legislators do not know about and do not know enough to evaluate.

The level of detail in the argument is an idea that can be used to integrate the conception of legislatures as arenas of ongoing argument, the institutional arrangements for formulating legislation, and legislators' attention to the concerns of constituents.

Voters may be convinced it is important to clean the air even if it means some additional cost for vehicles or they may be convinced that the health effects do not warrant the costs to the economy, but it is an extremely rare voter who wants to learn about the chemistry of air quality and its regulation in full detail. The arguments in election campaigns are carried on at a modest level of detail, and votes are cast for the party and candidate who seems most likely to do something.

When a government is formed the argument at one level of detail must be transformed into argument at the much more detailed level of legislation. In most countries this is done by the executive and the experts working for government departments. The executive presents the law to the legislature and the majority party members in the legislature or the majority of members who form a coalition vote yes – most of the time. Legislators, generally, do not have the expertise to evaluate the law in detail. The US Congress is unusual because in the permanent committees members develop enough expertise on a subject to argue about the detail (Boynton 1991; Loewenberg and Patterson 1979). Most of the interaction between Congress and the administration takes place in the committee consideration of the legislation. When legislation moves to the full legislature in the USA, as in other countries, the level of argument returns to the level of detail at which elections are conducted. And the prospects of passage of a bill reported by the committee is as high, 85 to 98 per cent depending on the committee, as in other legislatures (Lewis 1978).

Permanent committees also provide the chairman of the committee considering clean air legislation an opportunity to interject the concerns of the vehicle manufacturers in his Michigan constituency into the legislation. It should be noted, however, that the action of the Michigan congressman is not different in kind from the action of the Kenyan legislator who negotiates special arrangements for his district (Barkan 1979), even though the US Congress is taken to be a strong legislature and the Kenyan legislature a weaker one. Many concerns of constituents are in the detail. When that is the case legislators become involved in detail.

Conclusion

Politics is the ongoing argument about what we should do as a nation and how we should do it. Elections of legislators matter because elections focus the attention of legislators on their constituents and the arguments that are convincing to constituents. Legislatures are a continuation of the argument at a different level of detail.

The arguments that are elections and the arguments that are legislatures are not idle matters. They are arguments that have major consequences for nations and the individuals and organizations that comprise them. Losing an argument may be exceedingly costly. Vehicle manufacturers in the USA, therefore, are prepared to pay as handsomely as the law allows to assist the member of Congress who takes their concerns seriously in his or her re-election campaigns. In other places guns are used to guarantee winning the argument. Bullets beat votes every time – at least in the short-run. Weapons have been used to win arguments throughout human history. What is unusual about this half-century is the spread of substituting votes for bullets in determining the winners and losers of the argument.

References

Backstrom, C. H. (1977) 'Congress and the public: how representative is one of the other?', *American Politics Quarterly* 5: 411–36.

Barkan, J. D. (1979) 'Bringing home the pork: legislative behavior, rural development, and political change in East Africa', in L. D. Musolf and J. Smith (eds) *Legislatures in Development*, Durham, NC: Duke University Press.

Barker, A. and Rush, M. (1970) *The British Member of Parliament and His Information*, Toronto: University of Toronto Press.

Barnes, S. H. (1977) *Representation in Italy*, Chicago: University of Chicago Press.

Baumgartner, F. R. (1987) 'Parliament's capacity to expand political controversy in France', *Legislative Studies Quarterly* 12: 33–54.

Bell, W., Hill, R. J. and Wright, C. R. (1961) *Public Leadership: A Critical Review*, San Francisco: Chandler.

Bishin, Benjamin G. (2000) 'Constituency Influence in Congress: Does Subconstituency Matter?, *Legislative Studies Quarterly* 25: 389–415.

Boynton, G. R. (1990) 'Our conversations about governing', unpublished paper.

—— (1991) 'When senators and publics meet at the Environmental Protection Subcommittee', *Discourse and Society* 2: 131–56.

Boynton, G. R. and Kim, C. L. (1991) 'Legislative representation as parallel processing and problem solving', *Journal of Theoretical Politics* 3 (4).

Browne, E. C. and Franklin, M. (1986) 'New directions in coalition research', *Legislative Studies Quarterly* 11: 469–83.

Browne, E. C., Frendreis, J. P. and Gleiber, D. W. (1986) 'The process of cabinet dissolution: an exponential model of duration and stability in Western democracies', *American Journal of Political Science* 30: 628–50.

Budge, I. and Laver, M. (1986) 'Office seeking and policy pursuit in coalition theory', *Legislative Studies Quarterly* 11: 485–506.

Button, J. and Hedge, D. (1996) 'Legislative Life in the 1990s; A Comparison of Black and White State Legislators', *Legislative Studies Quarterly* 21: 199–218.

Cayrol, R., Paroid, J.-L. and Ysmal, C. (1976) 'French deputies and the political system', *Legislative Studies Quarterly* 1: 67–99.

Cioffi-Revilla, C. (1984) 'The political reliability of Italian governments: an exponential survival model', *American Political Science Review* 78: 318–37.

Converse, P. E. and Pierce, R. (1986) *Political Representation in France*, Cambridge, MA: Belknap Press.

Dodd, L. C. (1976) *Coalitions in Parliamentary Government*, Princeton: Princeton University Press.

Duverger, M. (1963) *Political Parties*, New York: John Wiley.

Eulau, H. and Karps, P. D. (1977) 'The puzzle of representation: specifying components of responsiveness', *Legislative Studies Quarterly* 2: 233–54.

Fiorina, M. P. (1977) *Congress: Keystone of the Washington Establishment*, New Haven: Yale University Press.

Fox, Richard L., Lawless, Jennifer L. and Feeley, Courtney (2001) 'Gender and the Decision to Run for Office', *Legislative Studies Quarterly* 26: 411–35.

Freeman, Patricia K. and Richardson, Lilliard E. (1996) 'Explaining Variation in Casework Among State Legislators', *Legislative Studies Quarterly* 21: 41–56.

Herman, V. and Mendel, F. (eds) (1976) *Parliaments of the World*, London: Macmillan.

Hill, R. J. (1973) 'Patterns of deputy selection to local Soviets', *Soviet Studies* 25: 196–212.

Hopkins, R. (1970) 'The role of the MP in Tanzania', *American Political Science Review* 64: 754–71.

Hoskin, G. W. (1971) 'Dimensions of representation in the Colombian National Legislature' in W. H. Agor (ed.) *Latin American Legislatures: Their Role and Influence*, New York: Praeger.

Hughes, S. W. and Mijeski, K. J. (1973) 'Legislative–Executive Policy-Making: The Case of Chile and Costa Rica', Sage Research Papers in the Social Sciences, *Comparative Legislative Studies Series* no. 90–007, Beverly Hills: Sage Publications.

Ingall, Rachael E. and Crisp, Brian F. (2001) 'Determinants of Home Style: The Many Incentives for Going Home in Colombia', *Legislative Studies Quarterly* 26: 487–512.

Iyengar, S. (1990) 'Framing Responsibility for Political Issues: The Case of Poverty', *Political Behavior* 12: 19–40.

Kahn, Kim Fridkin and Kenney, Patrick J. (2001) 'The Importance of Issues in Senate Campaigns: Citizens' Reception of Issue Messages', *Legislative Studies Quarterly* 26: 573–97.

Kim, C. L. and Woo, B.-K. (1975) 'Political representation in the Korean National Assembly', in G. R. Boynton and C. L. Kim (eds) *Legislative Systems in Developing Countries*, Durham, NC: Duke University Press.

Kim, C. L., Barkan, J., Turan, I. and Jewell, M. (1984) *The Legislative Connection: The Politics of Representation in Kenya, Korea, and Turkey*, Durham, NC: Duke University Press.

Kim, Y. C. (1969) 'Role orientations and behavior: the case of Japanese prefectural assemblymen in Chiba and Kanagawa', *Western Political Quarterly* 22: 390–410.

Lewis, A. L. (1978) 'Floor success as a measure of committee performance in the House', *Journal of Politics* 40: 460–7.

Lipinski, Daniel (2001) 'The Effect of Messages Communicated by Members of Congress: The Impact of Publicizing Votes', *Legislative Studies Quarterly* 26: 81–100.

Loewenberg, G. L. and Patterson, S. C. (1979) *Comparing Legislatures*, Boston: Little, Brown & Co.

Mann, D., Monyak, R. and Teague, E. (1989) *The Supreme Soviet: A Biographical Directory*, Washington, DC: Center for Strategic and International Studies.

Matthews, D. R. (1954) *The Social Background of Political Decision-Makers*, New York: Random House.

—— (1985) 'Legislative Recruitment and Legislative Careers', in G. Loewenberg, S. C. Patterson and M. E. Jewell (eds) *Handbook of Legislative Research*, Cambridge, MA: Harvard University Press.

Mezey, M. L. (1972) 'The functions of a minimal legislature: role perceptions of Thai legislators', *Western Political Quarterly* 25: 686–701.

—— (1985) 'The functions of legislatures in the Third World', in G. Loewenberg, S. C. Patterson and M. E. Jewell (eds) *Handbook of Legislative Research*, Cambridge, MA: Harvard University Press.

Miller, W. E. and Stokes, D. E. (1963) 'Constituency influence in Congress', *American Political Science Review* 57: 45–56.

Olson, K. G. (1967) 'The service function of the United States Congress', in A. de Grazia (ed.) *Congress: The First Branch of Government*, Garden City, NY: Doubleday.

Peterson, R. L. and De Ridder, M. M. (1986) 'Government formation as a policy-making arena', *Legislative Studies Quarterly* 11: 565–81.

Pitkin, H. (1967) *The Concept of Representation*, Berkeley: University of California Press.

Putnam, R. D. (1976) *The Comparative Study of Political Elites*, Englewood Cliffs, NJ: Prentice-Hall.

Rae, D. W. (1971) *The Consequences of Electoral Laws*, New Haven: Yale University Press.

Riker, W. (1962) *The Theory of Political Coalitions*, New Haven: Yale University Press.

Rockman, B. A. (1985) 'Legislative–executive relations and legislative oversight', in G. Loewenberg, S. C. Patterson and M. E. Jewell (eds) *Handbook of Legislative Research*, Cambridge, MA: Harvard University Press.

Rundquist, Barry, Lee, Jeong-Hwa, and Rhee, Jungho (1996) 'The Distributive Politics of Cold War Defense Spending: Some State Level Evidence', *Legislative Studies Quarterly* 21: 265–81.

Skard, T. (1981) 'Progress for women: increased female representation in political elites in Norway', in C. F. Epstein and R. L. Coser (eds) *Access to Power: Cross-National Studies of Women and Elites*, London: Allen & Unwin.

Valenzuela, A. and Wilde, A. (1979) 'Presidential politics and the decline of the Chilean Congress', in L. D. Musolf and J. Smith (eds) *Legislatures in Development*, Durham, NC: Duke University Press.

Wahlke, J. C., Eulau, H., Buchanan, W. and Ferguson, L. C. (1962) *The Legislative System*, New York: John Wiley.

Further reading

Boynton, G. R. and Kim, C. L. (eds) (1975) *Legislative Systems in Developing Countries*, Durham, NC: Duke University Press.

Fenno, R. F. (1966) *The Power of the Purse: Appropriations Politics in Congress*, Boston: Little, Brown & Co.

Fiorina, M. (1977) *Congress: Keystone of the Washington Establishment*, New Haven: Yale University Press.

Kim, C. L., Barkan, J., Turan, I. and Jewell, M. (1984) *The Legislative Connection: The Politics of Representation in Kenya, Korea, and Turkey*, Durham, NC: Duke University Press.

Loewenberg, G. L. and Patterson, S. C. (1979) *Comparing Legislatures*, Boston: Little, Brown & Co.

Loewenberg, Gerhard, Squire, Peverill and Kiewiet, D. Roderick (eds) (2002) *Legislatures: Comparative Perspectives on Representative Assemblies*, Ann Arbor, Michigan: University of Michigan Press.

Loewenberg, G., Patterson, S. C. and Jewell, M. E. (eds) (1985) *Handbook of Legislative Research*, Cambridge, MA: Harvard University Press.

Matthews, D. R. (1960) *US Senators and Their World*, Chapel Hill: University of North Carolina Press.

Mayhew, D. R. (1974) *Congress: The Electoral Connection*, New Haven: Yale University Press.

Musolf, L. D. and Smith, J. (eds) (1979) *Legislature in Development*, Durham, NC: Duke University Press.

Polsby, N. (1968) 'The institutionalization of the US House of Representatives', *American Political Science Review* 62: 144–68.

Rae, D. W. (1971) *The Consequences of Electoral Laws*, New Haven: Yale University Press.

Wahlke, J. C., Eulau, H., Buchanan, W. and Ferguson, L. C. (1962) *The Legislative System*, New York: John Wiley.

21

COURTS

Kanishka Jayasuriya

A broad range of 'styles of reasoning' have been applied to the study of courts as political institutions, thereby exemplifying the multiple ways in which social scientists have sought to explain the dynamics of judicial institutional change and conflict. Understanding these various styles of reasoning and methodologies used to analyze courts provides an insight into the diverse ways in which courts have been conceptualized, especially in the way they are applicable to emergent transnational juridical regimes. A caveat: in this article no attempt is made to provide anything like a comparative overview of courts; rather, the ambition is to provide, in the light of recent trends in the study of new transnational juridical regimes, some sense of the flavour and diversity of approaches to the study of legal institutions. (For a comparative introduction to the study of the politics of courts, see, for example, Shapiro 1981; Jacob *et al.* 1996; and Damaška 1986.)

The study of courts may be classified under three main approaches or styles of reasoning:

1 An *attribute approach* which identifies a formal set of attributes that in one way or another strip down courts to some essential functioning.
2 A *constitutive approach* which locates courts within a specific legal discourse and is more broadly mapped into conceptions of the polity.
3 A *terrain of conflict approach* which regards courts as being shaped by underlying structures of power and conflict within society.

The attribute approach

In this style of reasoning, legal institutions are described and explained in terms of some underlying set of attributes. Courts are stripped down and reduced to bare essential elements, the dynamics of which are largely invariant across countries and time. One influential line of argumentation within this 'attribute' framework attempts to identify the origin and evolution of courts by their fundamental function, or in terms of legal institutions, as a 'triadic' system of dispute resolution, that is, two disputants and an impartial third party arbitrator. Martin Shapiro's (1981) valuable study exemplifies this broad approach to the study of legal institutions. Conflict resolution is not the only function of courts; various other functional attributes such as 'social control' and the generation of political legitimacy have also been identified as defining attributes (see Jacob *et al.* 1996). However, for

Shapiro (1981) these other functions follow from the fundamental attribute of legal institutions as mechanisms for conflict resolution.

The structure of this conflict resolution argument takes the following form: whenever two people enter into an exchange, conflicts may arise over the precise nature of obligation entered into; therefore, a common way of resolving these conflicts is to appoint a third party to determine either the method of resolution or an outcome of the particular issue at conflict, and this evolves over time into a body of settled principles and procedures that regulate exchange. Of course, as Sweet and Burnell (1998) point out, in this triadic model, institutions such as legislatures can come to specialize in the generation of legal norms, but the judiciary itself can generate rules through its own processes of interpretation.

One of the strengths of the triadic model of conflict resolution is that 'court'-like functions can be taken on by a range of non state rules and bodies. Indeed, in this respect the substitution of public office and law for private enforcement can be seen as an evolutionary process. In medieval times, associations of merchants were allowed to conduct fairs with specific regulations, establish courts, and determine methods of enforcement. The term 'law merchant' (*lex mercatoria*) is applied to these various practices, principles and regulations which were derived from this mode of 'law making' (Berman and Kaufman 1978; Cremades and Plehn 1984; Milgrom, North and Weingast 1990).

Identifying courts in this manner, i.e., as a formal institution for conflict resolution is closely allied to an influential body of theory relating to the evolution and dynamics of legal institutions, which has come to be known as 'rational choice institutionalism' (North 1981; North and Weingast 1989). Scholars working within this tradition use the tools of economic analysis to explore the design and evolution of legal institutions. Three main features can be identified in rational choice institutionalism: i) the institutional market assumption, ii) the efficiency assumption, and, iii) the strategic rationality assumption.

The institutional market assumption

Legal institutions are conceptualized in terms of the supply and demand of institutions where institutions are regarded as a set of arrangements which function to reduce transaction costs associated with an intensification of economic exchange and activity. This is clearly evident in the emergence of the institution of the law merchant and underlines the manner in which the growing complexity of market exchange drove the demand for conflict resolution mechanisms and enforcement procedures to stabilize and regularize economic exchange (Milgrom, North and Weingast 1990).

From this perspective, the substitution of public office and law for private enforcement can be conceived as a stage in an evolutionary process. However, this is not an unlinear evolutionary process because there is a renewed interest in the role and function of the institution of the recent adaptation of the 'law merchant' in the form of international arbitration of commercial disputes (Dezalay and Garth 1996). Arbitration with its distinctive institutions, procedures, and methods of enforcement, harking back to the medieval notion of the law merchant (Cutler 1999; Cremades and Plehn 1984) is becoming increasingly important in the context of an expanding globalized economy, particularly in the development of new transnational legal institutions.

In related vein, Sweet and Brunell (1998), using the triadic model of conflict resolution have applied the institutional market assumption to the process of dispute resolution in the European community. Accordingly, they suggest that the growth of transnational economic activity in Western Europe has generated a demand for conflict resolution mechanisms which in turn have been satisfied by the creation of Europe-wide institutions such as the European Court of Justice (ECJ). Supportive evidence comes from the case load of the ECJ, much of which is driven by direct reference from various national EU courts in response to private litigation. This is a clear sign that many features of the new European institutions are governed by imperatives to resolve conflicts generated by transnational economic activity. The 'supply' of these institutions in turn deepens transnational integration and generates greater demand for transnational institutions. With the deepening of global economic activity this argument has broader implications for the growth of global juridical activity, as for example, in the dispute resolution mechanisms of the World Trade Organization (WTO) (Petersmann 1997).

The efficiency assumption

Rational choice institutionalism is characterized by the *efficiency assumption*, highlighting the fact that legal institutions provide the most effective means of reducing transaction costs. This 'efficiency' argument is clearly illustrated in the Milgrom, North and Weingast (1990) analysis of the role of the 'law merchant' in the evolution of this type of legal institution, as an efficient solution to the high transaction costs created by the absence of conflict resolution arrangements. More recently, Posner (1992), though challenged by others such as Tullock (1980), has argued that the common law is economically efficient as an effective tool of market economics. These efficiency arguments have tended to provide the analytical engine which has led to new thinking under the rubric of the 'law and economic movement'. This has spawned a large literature that explores how legal doctrines and the design and operation of judicial institutions contribute (or do not contribute) to efficiency. Nevertheless, the concept of efficiency – problematic, even with regard to the assessment of market transactions – is even more difficult to apply to judicial organizations and structures. This is mainly because efficiency in these contexts is assessed not in terms of outcomes but in terms of the *degree* to which the behaviour of judicial actors and institutions is consonant with a prior model of economic behaviour.

The strategic interest assumption

Rational choice institutionalism makes a series of assumptions about the nature of strategic action and interests in political and social interaction between people (the strategic rationality assumption). Central to this triadic model is the assumption that the parties involved – judges and litigants – in the process of conflict resolution act in a strategic manner that best maximizes their interests. It is this set of assumptions, generally known as the *methodological individualism argument* that has informed much of the recent work amongst political scientists and economists studying law and economics – all of whom are working within rational choice theory. What is distinctive of the analytical engine of these theories is the idea that institutional dynamics of courts are best understood in terms of the strategic interests and actions of *individuals* operating within these institutions. Not unexpectedly, this has led to an emphasis on identification and analysis of strategic actions of judicial office holders who depend on 'internal institutional rules', external constraints, as well as interaction with other actors, in order to maximize their judicial objectives which may be related to the pursuit of certain policy goals (Maltzman, Spriggs and Wahlbeck 1999).

Much of this strategic interest model has been tested in the US context (for a review see Gillman and Clayton 1999; Epstein and Knight 1997, 1998). For instance, one of the main strategic constraints in the US Supreme Courts lies in getting cases on to the Court docket for which at least four judges must agree. A number of studies have explored the determinants of the certiorari process and suggest, amongst other things, that the grant of a certioria decision depends not just on the policy preference of the individual judge, but equally on a calculation of the strategic preferences of other judges (e.g., Maltzman, Spriggs and Whalbeck 1999; Epstein and Knight 1998). Others have explored the assignment of opinion writing which is critical in influencing legal doctrine and is shaped by a variety of strategic considerations. As Maltzman, Spriggs and Wahlbeck (1999) note:

> Given the importance of court opinions, it is not surprising that each justice attempts to shape the majority opinion with his or her policy objectives. Opinions contain legal rules that establish referents for future behavior and thus have an impact beyond the parties in the litigation.
>
> (Maltxman, Spriggs and Wahlbeck 1999: 55)

In short, it is clear from these studies that judges seek to pursue their policy preferences in a context where both institutional rules and external constraints push them towards strategic interaction with other agents within and outside legal institutions.

Ramseyer (1994) and Ramseyer and Rosenbluth (1993) extend this framework of methodological individualism to a comparative study of judicial independence. Ramseyer points out that in Japan, the judiciary, while nominally independent, is more open to political interference than in the USA, mainly because Japan has a civil law system in which Japanese judges sit for special exams and are recruited to the bench in their twenties. Their careers are controlled by the Supreme Court secretariat which can reward or punish judges through assignment to favourable or unfavourable positions. However, over the post war period, the composition of this secretariat was determined indirectly by Japan's long dominant ruling party, the Liberal Democratic Party (LDP) which had the responsibility for appointing judges to the Supreme Court (Ramseyer and Rosenbluth 1993).

Within this context, Ramseyer's (1994) explanation for the lack of Japanese judicial independence relies heavily on an electoral model of judicial independence, and entails the likelihood that where the ruling party like the LDP has been in power more or less continuously, there will be little or no incentive to provide for an independent judiciary. By contrast, in a system where political power alternates between parties – such as in the United States – there is more incentive to provide for judicial independence because parties are desirous of protecting the legislation they pass into law for as long as possible even if they lose office. Therefore, in such competitive systems Ramseyer (1994) argues that strong political incentives prevail for less political interference within the judiciary; in these terms judicial independence can be explained by the strategic interests of political actors.

These strategic rationality approaches and more broadly, the identification of conflict resolution as a defining attribute of legal institutions, are not without difficulties. First, this type of analysis tends to assume that 'strategic interests' are all determined exogenously. There is scant attention paid to the way interests are shaped by broader contextual forces. This is a point that we will examine in more detail in the next section but it will suffice to note that within conflict resolution models, interests and preferences are undertheorized and taken as 'given'. Second, these approaches – because they are intent on identifying a broad common set of attributes amongst courts – attenuate differences in institutional design and organization of legal institutions. Finally, there is a problematic functionalist streak in many of the approaches that seek to employ a strategic approach. More often than not, these approaches often settle for rational accounting of a range of existing institutional practices rather than provide a casual analysis of institutional dynamics.

The constitutive approach

As with the attribute approach to courts, the constitutive style of reasoning on courts encompasses a range of theoretical perspectives and methodologies. However, these diverse theories are linked by a common focus on the way legal institutions and strategies of actors in these institutions are situated within the broad compass of social and economic institutions, prevailing ideas of authority, and more especially the understanding of the 'institutional mission of courts'. Adopting such a constitutive perspective means that there can be no 'essentialist' definition of courts or legal institutions. At root, constitutive perspectives differ from attribute theories of legal institutions in departing from a narrow view of rationality as the maximization of self-interests (even if these are seen in terms of the pursuit of policy goals) towards a more complex understanding of rationality as embedded in the broader mission of the institutions. Judges and other actors within institutions are embedded within a legal discourse that is often specialized and organized with its own routines, and therefore rationality can only be assessed in terms of the background assumptions of actors within legal institutions (Gillman 1999). These debates over rationality replay arguments between an understanding of rationality as strategic actions governed by instrumental considerations and a more communicative mode of rationality governed by 'value' considerations (Habermas 1979).

Smith (1998) offers a forceful defence and advocacy of these constitutive approaches on the grounds that research in the area of public law must take more cognisance of the manner in which various legal traditions influence the overriding sense of the institutional purpose, particularly if research is to move beyond an agenda dominated by strategic and instrumentalist forms of rationality. The persuasiveness of Smith's argument lies in drawing attention to the need for a proper acknowledgment of the 'relative autonomy' of legal ideologies or traditions as well as institutional practices. He notes that:

> The role of institutions, moreover, goes well beyond providing the rule governing decision making situations in the manner Riker stresses. It influences the relative resources and the sense of purpose and principles that political actors possess. And sometimes, at least, those purposes and principles may be better described as conceptions of duty or inherently meaningful actions than as egoistic preferences.
>
> (Smith 1998: 95)

Though this assumption of 'relative institutional autonomy' does not in itself preclude the impact of a range of external social and economic forces on judicial decision-making, Smith suggests that these structural contexts tend to press on institutional routines and traditions only at critical junctures. A clear inference to be drawn from this is that identifying these critical junctures is a key issue for empirical research in the area of politics and courts.

Since Smith's work in the late 1980s, a number of studies in the US context have attempted to develop further the constitutive theory of courts. (See the subsequent work of Smith (Smith 1997) as well as several chapters in Gillman and Clayton (1999) for a good overview of this research.) Notwithstanding Smith's point about critical junctures one general problem arising from this literature is the question of how broader changes in patterns of social and economic activity are causally related to changes in legal doctrine and ideology. A notable exception, however, is the work of Orren (1991, 1995) in the US context. Orren argues that constitutional developments have been inexplicably connected with the issues of labour relations, but these changes have been processed within the established framework of property relations. According to Orren, 'American constitutional development has required, above all, the inclusion of society's essential work tasks within the core principles of liberalism' (Orren 1995: 377). This valuable analysis links the changes in the notion of property within the legal doctrine to broader changes in the nature of work relations.

Nevertheless, theories falling within the domain of constitutive approaches remain broader in scope than a narrow focus on institutional goals and traditions and encompass the more fundamental principles that govern the way the polity is organized. In this respect, one of the most important contributions has been the comparative study of legal institutions and processes undertaken by Damaška (1986) who proposes a typology of legal institutions (which goes beyond the usual common/civil law distinctions) on the basis of two criteria:

1   The division of the structure of governmental authority between a highly *hierarchical structure* where a professional cadre of officials, applying highly technical standards, is organized in a hierarchical fashion, and a *coordinate structure* of authority characterized by non professional decision makers. This differentiation results in a more horizontal distribution of authority and less tendency to rely on rigorous application of technical standards.

2   The relationship between the dominant view of the role of the state within society and its legal processes suggests two distinct sub-types – one termed *reactive state* and the other *activist state*. The 'reactive state' provides the broad framework of

order and facilitates the resolution of disputes by individuals. It suggests a model of conflict resolution procedures – much akin to what Shapiro (1981) sees as the essence of all legal institutions – where the state both facilitates and provides a means of resolving conflicts between members of civil society. On the other hand, an 'activist state', because it 'espouses a theory of the good life, [uses it] as a basis for a conceptually all embracing programme of material and moral betterment of its citizens' (Damaška 1986: 80). An 'activist state' leads to a distinct set of legal processes, a policy-implementing type of legal institutions where state interests and goals have primacy over the allocation of rights; the purpose of legal institutions is to produce accuracy of outcome – outcomes that reflect substantial goals or objectives of the state.

The value of Damaška's contribution here is in pinpointing the relationship between various aspects of the legal process – including the relationship between litigants and the judiciary, rule of evidence, procedural rules – and the constitutive rules of the polity. An illustrative example is Jayasuriya's (1999) study of judicial independence in East Asia, which demonstrates the extent to which judicial independence is shaped by the statist nature of legalism where legal institutions are seen to be enabling of broad state ends or objectives. This argument provides a neat example of Damaška's 'policy implementing' type of legal institutions or Oakeshott's (1975) 'enterprise association'. For example, the core of the relationship between the judiciary and the executive takes a corporatist form, not in the conventional theoretical understanding of corporatism (i.e., as denoting a system of interest representation) but as a system of concertation or collaboration between the executive and the judiciary. Judicial-executive relations can be characterized as conforming to a corporatist pattern in that judicial autonomy exists within the executive structures of the state as a division of responsibility within the executive rather than as a separate power operating outside of the executive structures. From this vantage point, the distinction between a *division of power* and a *separation of power* captures the East Asian judicial condition of both simultaneous autonomy and dependence (Jayasuriya 1999). In a similar vein, Haley's (1991) innovative analysis of judicial authority in Japan appeals to the importance of understanding courts in terms of the broader political vocabulary of the state. Indeed, ideas such as judicial independence within Japanese court organization cannot simply be analyzed within a framework of strategic rationality (such as that provided by Ramseyer 1994). Instead, it needs to be placed in the context of the broader interaction between legal institutions and the constitutive principles of the polity that is located within a framework of communicative rationality.

Yet, the constitutive framework remains problematic for a variety of reasons. If we take seriously the argument that legal institutions are in some way constituted by the broad structuring principles of the polity, how does one account for the way laws and new institutional ideas are transplanted into specific 'local' contexts and traditions? This is not merely an academic argument because one of the most important effects of globalization has been the increasing importance of legal transplants in areas outside North America and Western Europe. To be relevant, constitutive theories must provide an adequate account of this complex interaction between legal transplants and local conditions.

Teubner's (1998) account of legal transplants provides one possible way of understanding these changes in legal transplants. In many ways, Teubner's innovative explanation of transplants extends the earlier work of Kahn-Freund (1978) by arguing that transplanting law and institutions does not automatically lead to a global convergence of law or legal institutions, and instead it is more likely to produce new forms of differentiation as transplanted laws and institutions adapt and collide with 'local rationalities' of legal discourse and structures of power. Teubner's interesting suggestion here is that transferred rules or institutions can only act as irritants on the law as well as the broader social structures to which law is connected. On the legal side, the transplants can be adapted to prevailing categories of legal interpretation, and on the social side it will be reconstructed in terms of the dominant pattern of meaning, and I would add, power, within the social field. What is at stake here is the fact that transplants do not lead to simple convergence or uniformity but act as irritants to dominant rationalities.

One key area where transplants have played an important role is in the extension of the institutions of judicial review as explored by Ginsburg (2001) in Korea and Taiwan. In Taiwan, Ginsburg (2001) notes that the Grand Council of Justices of Judicial Yuan – whose job it is to interpret the constitution – has been active in extending the scope of judicial review in dismantling much of the authoritarian political structure built by the Kuomintang (KMT). In seeking to bolster its power and legitimacy, the Grand Council of Justices have often used foreign cases and structural principles borrowed from other constitutional courts such as giving local courts the power to directly refer constitutional questions. In all of this, foreign transplants have proved to be an important factor in securing the increasing legitimacy of the Grand Council of Justices. At the same time, what the emergence of judicial review 'involves is great sensitivity on the part of the court to the preferences of the highest political authority' (Ginsburg 2001: 44), which also reflects a form of 'Confucian constitutionalism'. In these terms, the transplantation of the judicial review was an 'irritant' – in the sense that Teubner uses the term – that produced new styles of judicial review as existing institutional rationalities were accommodated with new 'transplanted' rationalities.

Clearly, the constitutive model of courts has a number of strengths, the foremost being the ability to locate institutional dynamics in the context of the normative vocabulary of legal institutions and the broader polity. In comparison with the attribute model of courts, the constitutive approach remains historically much more nuanced. Nevertheless, these approaches remain somewhat problematic because they cannot easily account for the impact of issues of power and conflict on institutional dynamics. Consequently, these approaches remain somewhat problematic in so far as they obscure the way in which issues of power and conflict are mapped on to the terrain of legal institutions.

The terrain of conflict approach

Legal institutions, and the law more generally, are influenced by deep-seated changes in the social and political structures. Take the example of globalization – an important and fertile area for scholars of legal institutions – which raises critical issues for analysts of law and courts. These relate mainly to the impact of globalization on the creation of new forms of legal adjudication (such as international arbitration), new actors (such as multinational corporations) and new legal ideas (such as giving standing to private parties in forums like the WTO dispute resolution mechanisms). In essence, courts are more appropriately the juridical arena and do not simply act as a mirror to broader societal conflicts; they are themselves a terrain of conflict and competition. This style of reasoning, when applied to the analysis of legal institutions underscores the 'relationality' of courts and institutions to social actors and other institutions.

One powerful exposition of this understanding of courts as 'terrains of conflict' is to be found in the work of Pierre Bourdieu (1987) with his notion of a *juridical field*. Although there are substantial similarities between Bourdieu's notion of a field and the constitutive theories, critically, for Bourdieu, courts and judges cannot be simply disentangled from other actors such as lawyers and legal academics. All of these actors operate within a social field, in this case the juridical field. A 'field' provides the terrain for struggle and competition for control and in turn this struggle for control leads to a certain hierarchy of power within the field – a kind of division of labour. For example, labour lawyers and equal opportunity lawyers may have less prestige and power than others such as corporate lawyers within the terrain.

But even within the institution of courts, new juridical institutions and processes are in constant competition for dominance, and the institutional strategies need to be understood within this struggle for competition. On this score, there is considerable overlap between strategic theories of rationality and the theory of the juridical field. For example, one of the principle mechanisms in the consolidation of the institutions of judicial review has been the institution of a system of direct reference from lower courts to higher (constitutional) courts. This has been a factor of some importance in consolidating the position of both the European Court of Justice (Sweet and Brunell 1998) and the Grand Council of Justices in Taiwan (Ginsburg 2001). But the more general point here is to see courts themselves as engaged in a web of competitively structured social relations within the 'field' of judicial activity.

At the same time, actors within the juridical field are constantly engaged in competition to keep outsiders from gaining entry into the field. As Bourdieu points out:

> In reality, the institution of a 'juridical space' implies the establishment of a borderline between actors. It divides those qualified to participate in the game and those who, though they may find themselves in the middle of it, are in fact excluded by their inability to accomplish the conversion of mental space – and particularly of linguistic stance – which is presumed by entry into this social space.
>
> (Bourdieu 1987: 828)

The establishment of this monopoly of representation is to a great extent accomplished by the control of symbolic capital embodied in the very profession of training and legal knowledge which is tightly controlled. Again, the emphasis is on the way the entry to an organization of the juridical field or terrain is controlled by the organization and structure of symbolic capital. Hence for Bourdieu (1987), competition within the social field is often over access to the structures of symbolic capital. This is particularly relevant in an area such as human rights law, and associated institutions such as human rights commissions. At one level, the establishment of these institutions has meant the development of specialized techniques and knowledge of human rights law which becomes a new form of symbolic capital, creating insiders and outsiders. But, at another level it has meant that these new sites compete with more established and entrenched sites within the juridical arena (Woodwiss 2002). But the general point to be made here is that this approach places courts in a broader relationship with others both inside and outside the juridical terrain.

Dezalay and Garth (1996) have used this notion of a 'juridical field' in a study of international arbitration, which attempts to examine the internationalization of the rule of law as manifested in the growth and power of international arbitration. What is worthy of note here is the emergence of a new juridical field with transnational actors, opportunities, and struggles. In sum,

> [their] concern is to identify the ways in which internationalization, and in particular, international commercial arbitration, reveals and contributes to the reorganization and reshuffling of hierarchies of position, modes of legitimate authority, and structures of power.
>
> (Dezalay and Garth 1996: 18)

The competition involves a struggle around various national approaches, focusing considerable attention on the role of law by large US law firms in transforming the character of international arbitration. The precise details of this remain outside the brief of this article, but what stands out for our purposes is the way in which the legal field is conceptualized as a set of competitive relations between various actors organized around a competition for symbolic capital.

One of the problems raised by this conflict approach for the study of courts is that, if as Bourdieu as well as number of other scholars (see e.g., Luhmann 1985) grant the autonomy (albeit relative) of the juridical arena, how does one explain the impact of broader social and economic changes on the legal field? Bourdieu's answer to this is interesting. He argues that it is the very formalization, universality and neutrality which courts render to conflicting social interests that represent its particular social power. The essence of this neutralization is to produce a form of symbolic domination as underlying conflicts of interests are naturalized through their transformation in the juridical arena. There is here a partial convergence between Shapiro's ideas of courts as mechanisms for conflict resolution (Shapiro 1981) and Bourdieu's notion of neutralization, but the major difference lies in the fact that for Bourdieu, what is significant is not conflict resolution *per se*, but its symbolic representation.

There is indeed much value to be gained in using this framework to examine the increasing trend toward the extension of judicial forms to new areas of social and economic life. As noted previously, in many new democracies there has been a significant increase in the use of the institutions of judicial review as well as other rights instruments (Epp 1998; Sweet 2000). A similar move towards an emergent economic constitutionalism exists where major economic decisions and policy-making move from discretion to rule-based policy-making (Jayasuriya 2001). This is reflected, for example, in the emergence of independent regulatory agencies and networks. Reinforcing this trend towards the increasing judicialization of politics is the emergence of specialized policy-making courts such as drug courts. Certainly, the notion of neutralization and the naturalization of social conflict by its transformation into the juridical arena captures a key driving element of this process of the judicialization of politics.

Nevertheless, it still does not account for why this trend toward growing judicialization of politics has become an increasingly prominent feature of contemporary politics in industrializing and newly industrializing countries. One factor, certainly, is the importance of globalization and the consequent decentering of the state. However an equally important motor driving this process is the fact that modern society has become so complex that 'political steering' is often ineffective and problematic. Eventually this leads to an increasing fragmentation of both social life and public power as reflected in the high levels of autonomy for various specialized judicial and regulatory arenas ranging from trade policy to drug policy. This fragmentation also means that the role of representative and legislative bodies in the production of law has become less relevant as judicial arenas not only become arenas of conflict resolution but have also tended to take on a policy-making role much more in line with Damaška's (1986) model of policy implementing legal institution.

Conclusion: New agendas for research

The discussion so far has explored with illustrations of the ways in which the complex process of globalization are creating new forms and types of courts that challenge our received wisdom of a monistic legal order that all essentials overlap with the territorial boundaries of the state. Globalization does not, as is sometimes erroneously assumed, diminish the powers of the state. Rather, globalization tends to restructure our traditional models of government, fragmenting and creating multiple legal sites or orders, some of which increasingly rely on private regulation (Jayasuriya 1999a). Developments in international economic law lead to construction of new transnational legal institutions such as the WTO dispute resolution mechanisms. Increasingly, there are regional juridical institutions such as the European Court of Justice which have significant ramifications for the operation of domestic institutions. The impact of these developments is to impel us to acknowledge how the changing architecture of power – both globally and within the state – serves to rupture and fragment the institutions and process of governance. From this perspective, globalization is as much an internally as an externally driven process. In short, the most important effects of globalization are to be felt within the boundaries of what is usually regarded as the domain of domestic institutions, thereby disturbing the settled boundaries between domestic and international domains.

In this context the impact of a number of contemporary trends including – but not limited to – globalization is the creation of a multiple set of legal orders and this raises a host of important issues which are likely to shape the future direction of the study of courts and politics. For example, there is an assumption shared across the various styles of reasoning that the national courts, organized hierarchically, have a monopoly on the determination of legality. But the emergence of new transnational legal fields such as the European Court of Justice, juridical regimes such as the WTO dispute resolution system, and the role of private, non state institutions such as international arbitration, all point to the weakening of the traditional notion of an internal monistic legal order. Instead, this review of the study of courts demonstrates, importantly, that there is an increasing fragmentation of public power and juridical regimes. In fact, part of this fragmentation occurs along specific kinds of market sectors, so that not everyone is included in a particular juridical regime. For example, the system of courts as understood in international arbitration in many developed countries is very specific to the export sector; other sectors belong to different types of legal regimes. But this emerging fragmented legal order is not just confined to the transnational legal activities. Even within the confines of the national state, one can observe the emergence of new forms of regulatory activity – ranging from industry self regulation to the creation of hybrid forms of regulation such as environmental monitoring mechanisms. This raises a profoundly important question for the students of legal institutions, namely: what is a court? If we are to abandon the traditional notion of a monistic legal order – as I think we need to do – this becomes an issue of considerable importance.

Along with this fundamental rethinking we need to recognize the importance of a new range of actors within new juridical regimes. As mentioned earlier, Dezalay and Garth (1996) have noted the importance of large legal firms in international arbitration. Woodwiss (2002) points to the important role played by international human rights organizations in promoting new rights regimes; multinational legal firms and multilateral agencies have been active in promoting judicial reform in developing countries. What is clear is that the emergence of new transnational juridical regimes has produced in its wake new actors and organizations who have an active role in promoting certain forms of – to use Bourdieu's term – symbolic capital.

The agenda for the study of courts as political institutions is evidently in the midst of a significant transformation. However, at the same time it is clear that the various styles of reasoning outlined here will continue to be relevant to this new agenda. The agenda may change, but the styles of reasoning that we have identified in this essay will still remain central to answering some of the puzzles posed by new judicial institutions at both the national and the transnational level.

References

Berman, Harold and Kaufman, Colin (1978) 'The Law of International Commercial Transactions (Lex mercatoria)', *Harvard International Law Journal* 19(1): 221–77.

Bourdieu, Pierre (1987) 'The Force of Law: Towards a Sociology of the Juridical Field', 38 *Hastings Law Journal*: 805–53.

Cremades, Bernado M. and Plehn, Steven L. (1984) 'The New Lex Mercatoria and the Harmonization of the Laws of International Commercial Transactions', *Boston University International Law Journal* 2 (3): 317–48.

Cutler, Claire (1999) 'Public Meets Private: The international unification of and Harmonization of Private International Trade Law', *Global Society* 13 (1): 30–33.

Damaška, Mirjan (1986) *The Faces of Justice and Stat Authority: A Comparative Approach to the Legal Process*, New Haven: Yale University Press.

Dezalay, Yves and Garth, Bryant G. (1996) *Dealing in Virtue: International Commercial Arbitration and the Construction of a Transnational Legal Order*, Chicago: University of Chicago Press.

Epp, Charles (1998) *The Rights Revolution: Lawyers, Activists, and Supreme Courts in Comparative Perspective*, Chicago: University of Chicago Press.

Epstein, Lee and Knight, Jack (1997) 'The New Institutionalism', Part II *Law and Courts* 7: 4–9.

—— (1998) *The Choices Justices Make*, Washington: CQ Press.

Maltzman, Forrest, Spriggs, James F. and Whalbeck, Paul J. (1999) 'Strategy and Judicial Choice: New Institutionalist Approaches to Supreme Court Decision-Making', in Howard Gillman and Cornell W. Clayton (eds), *Supreme Court Decision-Making: New Institutionalist Approaches*, Chicago: University of Chicago Press.

Gillman, Howard (1999) 'The Court as an Idea, Not a Building (or a Game): Interpretive Institutionalism and the Analysis of Supreme Court Decision Making', in Howard Gillman and Cornell W. Clayton (eds), *Supreme Court Decision-Making: New Institutionalist Approaches*, Chicago: University of Chicago Press.

Gillman, Howard and Clayton, Cornell W. (1999)*Supreme Court Decision-Making: New Institutionalist Approaches*, Chicago: University of Chicago Press.

Ginsburg, Tomas (2001) 'Confucian Constitutionalism: Globalisation and Judicial Review in Korea and Taiwan', Illinois Public Law and Legal Theory Research Paper *Series Research Paper* No: 00–03 (University of Illinois: College of Law). Paper available at: <http:/papers.ssrn.com>

Habermas, Jurgen (1979) *Communication and the Evolution of Society*, London: Heinemann Educational.

Haley, John (1991) *Authority without Power: Law and the Japanese Paradox*, Oxford: Oxford University Press.

Jacob, Herbert *et al.* (1996) *Courts, Law and Politics in Comparative Perspective*, New Haven: Yale University Press.

Jayasuriya, Kanishka (1999) 'Corporatism and Judicial Independence within Statist Legal Institutions in East Asia', chapter 8, in K. Jayasuriya (ed.), *Law, Capitalism and Power in Asia: the Rule of Law and Legal Institutions*, London: Routledge.

—— (1999a) 'Globalization and Law: Authoritarian Legalism in the Global Order', *Indiana Journal of Global Legal Studies* 6 (2) (Spring) 425–55.

—— (2001) 'Globalisation, Sovereignty, and the Rule of Law: From Political to Economic Constitutionalism?', *Constellations*, 8 (4): 442–60 (Special Issue on 'Globalisation and Law').

Kahn-Freund, Otto (1978) *Selected Writings*, London: Stevens.

Luhmann, Niklas (1985) *A Sociological Theory of Law*, London: Routledge and Kegan Paul.

Milgrom, Paul, North, Douglass and Weingast, Barry (1990) 'The Role of Institutions in the Revival of Trade: The Law Merchant, Private Judges and the Champagne Fairs', *Economics and Politics* 2 (1): 1–23.

North, Douglass C. (1981) *Structure and Change in Economic History*, New York: Norton.

North, Douglass C. and Weingast, Barry R. (1989) 'Constitutions and Commitment: the Evolution of Institutions Governing Public Choice in Seventeenth-Century England', *The Journal of Economic History* XLIX (4), 803–32.

Oakeshott, Michael (1975) *On Human Conduct*, Oxford: Clarendon Press.

Orren, Karen (1991) *Belated Feudalism: Labour, the Law and the Liberal Development in the United States*, Cambridge University Press.

—— (1995) 'The Primacy of Labour in American Constitutional Development' *American Political Science Review* 89 (2): 377–88.

Petersmann, Ernst-Ulrich (1997) *The Gatt/WTO Dispute Settlement System: International Law, International Organizations and Dispute Settlement*, Boston: Kulwer Law International.

Posner, Richard (1992) *Economic Analysis of Law*, 4th edn, Boston: Little, Brown.

Ramseyer, Mark (1994) 'The Puzzling (In)dependence of Courts: A Comparative Approach', *Journal of Legal Studies* 23: 721–47.

Ramseyer, Mark and Rosenbluth, Frances MaCall (1993) *Japan's Political Marketplace*, Cambridge, MA: Harvard University Press.

Shapiro, Martin (1981) *Courts: A Comparative and Political Analysis*, Chicago: University of Chicago Press.

Smith, Rogers (1997) *Civic Ideals: Conflicting Visions of Citizenship in US History*, New Haven: Yale University Press.

—— (1998) 'Political Jurisprudence, the "New Institutionalism" and the Future of Public Law', *American Political Science Review* 82 (1): 89–108.

Sweet, Alec Stone (2000) *Governing with Judges: Constitutional Politics in Europe*, Oxford: Oxford University Press.

Sweet, Alec Stone and Brunell, Thomas L. (1998) 'Constructing a Supranational Constitution: Dispute Resolution and Governance in the European Community', *American Political Science Review* 92 (1): 63–81.

Teubner, Gunther (1998) 'Legal Irritants: Good Faith in British Law or How Unifying Law ends up in New Divergences', *Modern Law Review* 21 (1): 11–32.

Tullock, Gordon (1980) *Trials on Trial: The Pure theory of Legal Procedure*, New York: Columbia University Press.

Woodwiss, Anthony (2002) 'Human Rights and the Challenge of Cosmopolitanism', *Theory, Culture and Society* 19 (1–2): 139–55.

22

BUREAUCRACIES

Ferrel Heady

Bureaucracies are large-scale organizations that are common in both the public and private sectors of contemporary society.

Origins

The word 'bureaucracy' was coined fairly recently, but it is derived from much older Latin and Greek sources; Fritz Morstein Marx (1957: 17–18) states that the first half of the word can be traced to *burrus*, meaning in Latin a dark and sombre colour, and that in Old French *la bure* was a related word referring to a certain kind of cloth covering for tables, especially those used by public officials. The word *bureau* was first applied to the covered table, then to the surrounding room or office. Eventually, the word *bureaucratie* was created by combining *bureau* with a Greek suffix referring to type of rule. This usage is credited to an eighteenth-century French minister of commerce, Vincent de Gournay, who presumably intended the word to be a way of describing government as rule by officialdom. Soon it took the form *Bürokratie* in German, and later appeared in many other languages.

Meanings

This evolution explains the pejorative connotation commonly and popularly given to 'bureaucracy' when it is used as a way of expressing disapproval of the actions of government officials or objection to the procedures required in large organizations that are alleged to be cumbersome and inefficient. The term 'bureaucracy' also has, however, a less negative and more neutral meaning in the social sciences, referring to organizational arrangements of a distinctive type characteristically found in modern societies. Bureaucratic organizations, in this sense, are those that have attributes identified in the writings of the German social scientist Max Weber (1864–1920) and his successors. Bureaucracies of Weber's 'ideal-type' model are marked by traits such as hierarchy, specialization, professional competence, separation of the office and the incumbent, full-time occupational commitment, fixed monetary salaries and written regulations specifying internal relationships and procedures to be followed in bureaucratic operations (Weber 1922; Bendix 1960; Hall 1962).

Ambiguity of meaning in the use of 'bureaucracy' and 'bureaucracies' is unavoidable. The stress here is put on the identification of attributes that distinguish between bureaucratic and other types of organizations, with neither positive nor negative implications as to organizational outcomes. This is the Weberian meaning, as opposed to Harold Laski's use of the term as applying 'to a system of government the control of which is so completely in the hands of officials that their power jeopardizes the liberties of ordinary citizens' (Laski 1930: 70). Even Weber, while emphasizing the superior capabilities of bureaucracies over earlier organizational types, expressed concern late in his career because of the 'overtowering' power position of fully developed bureaucracies. More recently, Henry Jacoby (1973) has argued that bureaucracies are necessary but dangerous, with a strong potential for the usurpation of political power. His interpretation is that modern all-encompassing bureaucratic organizations are the culmination of a long process of centralization and accumulation of power begun long ago, when historical civilizations found it necessary to create and then to rely on the prototypes of present-day bureaucracies. The resulting paradox for our time is that bureaucracy is necessary and indeed inevitable but is at the same time dangerous and potentially usurpative. Contemporary societies simultaneously demand, depend on, and deplore the apparatus of bureaucracy. This outlook is basically pessimistic as to future prospects.

Another manifestation of this negative orientation is the tendency by Merton (1952: 361–71) and others (Morstein Marx 1957: 25–8; Crozier 1964: 4–5) to highlight as typical behaviour in bureaucracies traits that are 'dysfunctional', pathological, or self-defeating, tending to frustrate the realization of organizational goals. Red tape, buck passing, rigidity and inflexibility, over-secretiveness, excessive impersonality, unwillingness to delegate, and reluctance to exercise discretion are all identified as behavioural orientations typical of the 'trained incapacity' of bureaucrats. Undoubtedly, such behaviour occurs frequently within bureaucracies, but so does a range of other kinds of behaviour with more positive implications for attainment of organizational objectives. Some students of bureaucracies, including Friedrich (1963: 471) as a prime example, stress traits such as objectivity, precision, consistency and discretion, describing them as 'desirable habit or behaviour patterns' which are usually followed by members of bureaucratic organizations (Friedrich 1968: 44–5).

In contrast to these differences in describing dominant bureaucratic behavioural traits, there is considerable agreement as to the basic structural characteristics of bureaucratic organizations. A compact formulation is that of Victor Thompson (1961: 3–4), who says that such an organization is composed of a highly elaborated hierarchy of authority superimposed upon a highly elaborated division of labour. Friedrich (1963: 468–70) asserts that the pivotal structural characteristics can be reduced to these three:

- hierarchy;
- differentiation or specialization; and
- qualification or competence.

Bureaucracies with such structural characteristics are prevalent in what Robert Presthus (1978) calls today's 'organizational society'. No contemporary nation-state, for instance, can be viable without a public bureaucracy as one of its major political institutions (Heady 2001: 77; Riggs 1970: 388). Hence an understanding of the distinctive internal features of different nation-state public bureaucracies and of the relationships between these bureaucracies and other institutions in the political system is crucial both to the analysis of particular polities and to comparisons among them. One aspect of such study needs to be consideration of the negative possibilities in bureaucratic operations already mentioned, including the self-defeating proclivities of patterns of bureaucratic behaviour that undermine achievement of policy goals, and the dangers of encroachment by public bureaucracies on the appropriate roles of other political institutions.

Structural variations

Patterns of differentiation among national public bureaucracies as to their organizational features have received much attention, and there is considerable consensus about appropriate categories. Among the more developed countries, three such basic groupings emerge (Bendix 1968; Heady 2001; Rowat 1988). One group consists of the democracies on the European continent in an arc from Scandinavia through western and southern Europe, plus perhaps other examples geographically widely scattered such as Ireland, Israel, and Japan. A second group includes Great Britain, the USA and other former British colonies such as Canada, Australia and New Zealand. The third group consists of the Soviet Union and other nations in Eastern Europe included in the Soviet bloc since the Second World War.

Despite significant individual differences, the public bureaucracies in each of these groups share some basic similarities. Members of the first group, typified by Germany and France (with historical roots in Prussia and the French *ancien régime*), are sometimes referred to as 'classic' systems, conforming most closely to Weber's 'ideal-type' bureaucracy. The present public service can usually be traced to an earlier royal service that was itself highly professionalized. Members of the bureaucracy are recruited on a career basis according to educational attainment; mobility upward within the bureaucracy from one level to another is relatively limited; higher-ranking bureaucrats are intimately involved in the policy process, are allowed to engage in political activity, often have opportunities for second careers in either the public or private sectors, and generally enjoy high prestige in the society.

Countries in the second group have in common a 'civic culture' with widespread citizen participation in governmental affairs. A public service based on selection by competence or merit is relatively recent, with civil service reform having occurred after the middle of the nineteenth century in both Great Britain and the USA and even later elsewhere. Although educational background is increasingly important, entry points into the bureaucracy are more varied and internal mobility is greater. Higher-level bureaucrats are also heavily involved in policy making, but in a manner that varies from country to country. They are often subjected to severe restrictions as to partisan political activity, and the career paths of politicians and career bureaucrats are generally distinct and separate. Public service careers, especially in the more egalitarian former British colonies, do not rank as high in societal prestige as in the 'classic' systems.

The communist bloc countries were in the past the most highly bureaucratized, both in the apparatus of the dominant party and of the state. A 'public' bureaucratic career of some type was the only choice for most individuals, because of the enormous range of party and state activity. Educational and professional qualifications gradually gained over loyalty considerations as factors in bureaucratic selection and promotion, so that the backgrounds and career paths of higher bureaucrats in these countries differed less markedly in the USSR during its later years than earlier from their counterparts elsewhere. The dramatic and unforeseen changes which took place in these systems during the decade of the 1990s tended toward greater similarity, rather than increasing divergence, between the communist bloc (including what was the USSR and countries of Eastern Europe) and other developed nations with regard to the societal role of bureaucratic organizations. However, it is doubtful that any of the countries that were formerly in the communist bloc should be regarded as currently in the more developed category. It is probably more realistic to consider them as belonging in a second tier grouping as to level of development. The Russian Federation, as the largest and most important remnant of the USSR, seems to fit here, after moving down from the higher ranking generally given to the USSR before its decline. The People's Republic of China, meanwhile, has moved or is moving upward into this category.

The public bureaucracies of developing countries (in what in the past has often been labelled the Third World) are usually lumped together as a fourth major category, but with wide variations among them in their degree of competence, and in the educational backgrounds, career prospects, degree of participation in the making of public policy and societal power status of members of the bureaucracy. Generalizations are difficult to make, beyond noting the impact of inherited colonial public service patterns, the general lack of security in bureaucratic careers, the importance of the public sector in societal decision making generally, and the frequent ascendency of military bureaucrats over both civil bureaucrats and politicians.

Behavioural variations

In contrast to organizational or structural distinctions, the identification and classification of distinctive national patterns of bureaucratic behaviour is as yet at an early stage of sophistication. Clearly cultural factors are basic to such efforts. Some useful analyses of specific cases have been made by knowledgeable scholars who are themselves products of the culture described. A notable example is the examination by Crozier (1964) of behavioural traits in the French bureaucracy. He traces these traits to more general French cultural characteristics, stressing the qualities of rationality, impersonality and absoluteness. He views France as essentially a 'stalemate society', with the bureaucratic system providing a means of reconciling two deep-seated but contradictory attitudes. One is an urge to avoid as much as possible direct face-to-face authority relationships, and the other is a prevailing view of authority in terms of universalism and absolutism. The bureaucratic system combines an absolutist conception of authority with the elimination of most direct dependence relationships, hence solving the basic French dilemma about authority as indispensable but hard to endure. At the same time, the system suffers from deficiencies in co-ordination, in the decentralization of decision-making, and in adjusting to change.

More systematic comparative studies are dependent on advances in cultural analysis at a variety of relevant levels – societal, political, administrative and organizational. Some progress is being made at each of these levels. Hofstede (1980) has identified four value dimensions as accounting for a major proportion of cultural differences among societies. These are:

1 individualism–collectivism;
2 uncertainty avoidance, relating to attitudes toward risk-taking and ambiguity;
3 power distance, concerned with attitudes towards patterns of power distribution; and
4 masculinity–femininity, having to do with the extent that dominant values are 'masculine' in terms of assertiveness, advancement and acquisition of material goods.

Hofstede, after analysing data from forty countries showing various combinations of these value dimensions, identified eight country clusters with distinctive patterns in their value systems differentially affecting behaviour in these social groupings.

Almond and Verba (1963) undertook pioneering work in exploring the concept of political culture for differentiating among national polities. Building on their foundation, Nachmias and Rosenbloom (1978) have proposed a model for the more restricted concept of bureaucratic culture as a means of studying orientations toward the public bureaucracy as a sub-unit of political systems. Retaining the cognitive, affective and evaluative cultural orientation sub-types suggested by Almond and Verba, they concentrated on two dimensions – orientations of citizens or the general public toward the public bureaucracy, and orientations of the bureaucrats themselves toward the bureaucracy. In addition, they were interested in assessing the congruence of these two sets of dimensions.

More recently, Schein (1985) and others (Frost *et al.* 1985) have used the concept of organizational culture to focus on specific organizations, mostly in the private sector. Organizational culture is defined by Schein as:

> a pattern of basic assumptions – invented, discovered, or developed by a given group as it learns to cope with its problems of external adaptation and internal integration – that has worked well enough to be considered valid and, therefore, to be taught to new members as the correct way to perceive, think, and feel in relation to those problems.
>
> (Schein 1985: 9)

Clearly this definition recognizes that organizational culture is significantly influenced by cultural characteristics at more inclusive levels in the society.

Among these studies, the bureaucratic culture model appears to offer most promise for systematically profiling the characteristics of different national bureaucratic systems. However, it has been applied only to Israel, and any application on a multinational basis would require a massive effort of data accumulation and analysis.

More has been accomplished in the comparative treatment in a variety of settings of the relationships between public bureaucracies and other political institutions. An assumption commonly made is that political modernization or development requires a balance between the public bureaucracy and institutions (such as chief executive officials, legislatures, political parties, courts and interest groups) in the 'constitutive' system (Riggs 1973: 28–9), so that the public bureaucracy is subjected to effective external controls from these other political institutions, and thus plays an instrumental role in the operation of the political system rather than usurping political power and taking over as the dominant political elite group.

Two factors have received most attention in the analysis of various patterns of relationships between public bureaucracies and the 'constitutive' political institutions. The first is the role of the 'state' or the degree of 'stateness' in the polity, and the second is the nature of the existing political regime.

A recent trend in comparative political studies has been a renewed interest in political institutions and a lessened interest in political functions. This 'neo-institutionalism' has emphasized the importance of the 'state' as distinct from both 'society' and 'government', and has advanced the notion of degree of 'stateness' (referring to the relative scope and extent of governmental power and authority) as a tool for making cross-societal comparisons (Nettl 1968). Metin Heper and a group of associates (Heper 1987) have undertaken to distinguish four ideal types of polity based on their degree of 'stateness', and to identify six types of bureaucracy corresponding to these polity types. 'Personalist' and 'ideological' polities rank high in 'stateness'; 'liberal' and 'praetorian' polities rank low. A one-to-one relationship between polity type and bureaucracy type is suggested in three instances: 'personalist' with a 'personal servant' bureaucracy, 'liberal' with a Weberian 'legal–rational' bureaucracy, and 'praetorian' with a 'spoils system' bureaucracy. The 'ideological' polity can produce any one of three types of bureaucracy, depending on whether the high degree of 'stateness' is linked with a ruler ('machine model' bureaucracy), the bureaucracy itself ('Bonapartist' or 'Rechtsstaat' bureaucracy), or a dominant party ('party-controlled' bureaucracy). The application of this framework for analysis by Heper and his associates includes case examples that are both historical (ancient Rome, Prussia, nineteenth-century Russia) and contemporary. The authors do not directly address the issue of balance between the bureaucracy and other institutions, but the implication is that the 'Bonapartist' or 'Rechtsstaat' bureaucracy in the 'ideological' polity would present the most unbalanced situation in favour of the bureaucracy, followed by the 'spoils system' bureaucracy in a 'praetorian' polity. The other linkages of polity and bureaucracy indicate that sufficient effective external control over the bureaucracy is provided by a ruler, a party, or some other source or combination of sources. The contemporary case studies (dealing with the USA, Great Britain, France, Germany, Turkey and Indonesia) seem to fit this assessment. At any rate, presumably some degree of 'stateness' can be detected in any polity, with consequences for bureaucratic behavioural characteristics and the role of the bureaucracy in the operation of the political system.

Another variable always present and likely to be highly significant for characterizing and comparing public bureaucracies is the type of political regime existent in the polity (Heady 2001: 89–90). Western democracies (whether unitary or federal, parliamentary or presidential, two-party or multi-party) are balanced in the sense that their public bureaucracies, although participating in major decisions as to public policy, are ultimately answerable to and controlled by various extra-bureaucratic political institutions (Dogan 1975; Aberbach et al. 1981). Distinctive national features do exist that affect bureaucratic behaviour enough to justify description and analysis on a case-by-case basis, but in their fundamental characteristics they are basically similar political regimes. European one-party communist bloc political regimes, exemplified in the past by the Soviet Union, also were balanced in this same sense, but the source of control over the official state bureaucracy was concentrated in the dominant party, and this continued even after *perestroika* reforms opened up the political arena somewhat to other parties or political groupings, leading to additional channels for maintaining bureaucratic accountability.

Developing countries are numerous enough and diverse enough to require groupings into broad categories of political regimes for comparative purposes. Numerous classification schemes have been proposed (Heady 2001: 293–8), with variations mainly in terminology rather than in essentials.

Some developing democratic regimes with competitive party systems closely resemble Western democracies, but their legitimacy and stability are more subject to challenge, and they are often short-lived. Evidence indicates that vulnerability may be greater for countries that have adopted the presidential model of democracy rather than the parliamentary one. Only a few of these countries have had a lengthy record of open competition among two or more parties and of peaceful political transition after free elections. Costa Rica is a leading example. Many developing countries have moved to single-party systems (usually communist or oriented towards some variety of Marxism-Leninism, as in China, Cuba, and numerous countries in Africa and the Middle East), with political competition from outside the party either prohibited or severely restricted. In other instances (as in India, Malaysia and Mexico), party competition is allowed, but a dominant single party has been in power either continuously or for most of the time, in some cases since independence. The presumption in these regimes is that the dominant party can be replaced peaceably after an electoral defeat. This possibility has now been demonstrated several times in India, and once in Mexico as a result of the 2000 election. All of these developing nations have what can be described as 'party-prominent' political regimes, with the public bureaucracies (including the military segments) playing secondary political roles.

Much more common in the developing world are 'bureaucratic-prominent' regimes, with military and/or civil bureaucrats wielding political power either directly or behind the scenes. Even in the declining group of traditional regimes with monarchical or religious leaders (such as Morocco, Saudi Arabia or Iran), a loyal and minimally competent bureaucracy is crucial for regime survival. The most prevalent regime type among developing countries is a personalist or collegial bureaucratic elite with one or a group of professional bureaucrats (usually military professionals) clearly dominating the political system. Examples are numerous among developing nations in every geographical region of the world. When not so openly in control, high-ranking military bureaucrats are often crucially influential behind the scenes, or are in a position to intervene to replace a civilian government in nations with a political record of pendulum-like swings between bureaucratic elite and civilian competitive regimes (Turkey, Nigeria and Brazil are representative cases from different regions). The overall picture is thus one of imbalance rather than balance in the relationship between public bureaucracies and the other political institutions that are generally considered to have a more legitimate claim to the exercise of ultimate political power.

Controls over public bureaucracies

The acknowledged tendency in most countries for the public bureaucracy to assume increasing importance in the formulation and implementation of public policy at the expense of executive officials and legislators, and the undeniable fact of political dominance by professional bureaucrats in numerous developing countries have together activated various efforts to curb the excesses of bureaucracies or even to replace them with other forms of organization.

Attempted reforms by chief executives have included the creation or strengthening of managerial units with budgetary and personnel controls over administrative agencies, the expansion in numbers of political appointees in the upper leadership levels of agencies, and greater involvement in the placement of high-ranking career bureaucrats. Legislatures and legislative committees have often greatly expanded their staff capabilities in an attempt to match the expertise of bureaucratic professionals in a variety of programme areas, and have tried to strengthen their capacity to conduct investigations of administrative actions and to carry out corrective measures. Numerous countries have initiated programmes of 'equal opportunity' or 'affirmative action' to increase the proportions in the public bureaucracy of previously under-represented groups such as women and ethnic minorities. 'Sunshine' laws have allowed greater access to the proceedings of public bodies and to public documents. In the USA and other countries, courts have experienced a rapid growth in administrative law cases, and have begun to intervene more frequently to overturn or alter administrative decisions. As a remedial instrument for citizens, the Scandinavian institution of *ombudsman* has been widely imitated elsewhere to protect the public against administrative abuses or inadequacies (Rowat 1985).

This is a sampling of the measures designed to bring public bureaucracies under better control without drastic changes in their characteristics or the role they play in modern societies. Evaluations as to the results are mixed. The usual attitude is one of continuing concern, as expressed by R. E. Wraith that:

> the growing impact of government and governmental agencies on everyday life has brought a more than corresponding increase in public administration which, both by its ubiquity and its sheer size, appears to 'feed on itself' and which could grow to a point when it became virtually beyond political control.
>
> (Wraith 1982: 139)

However, Donald C. Rowat has more recently concluded that the net effects of these reform efforts are likely to be that 'the influence of senior officials will more nearly represent the interests of society', that 'the bureaucracy will be supervised and controlled more closely', and that bureaucratic influence will be reduced by 'increasing the political input into policy-making' (Rowat 1988: 457)

Alternatives to bureaucracies

Some critics of bureaucracies propose to go further, either by restricting the bureaucracies' scope of operation, or by replacing them with other organizational forms.

Ramos (1981) and other advocates of 'social systems delimitation' and a 'new science of organizations' recognize a continuing need for bureaucracies with their hierarchical and coercive attributes for dealing with market-centred activities, but urge the recognition and encouragement of other institutional arrangements in which members of the organization are peers or are subject to minimal formal controls, contending that such non-bureaucratic organizational forms are more appropriate for 'social settings suited for personal actualization, convivial relationships, and community activities of citizens' (Ramos 1981: 135). The functioning of bureaucracies would thus be sanctioned but limited as compared to the present.

A more drastic reorientation is called for by proponents of substitute and presumedly more suitable organizational forms to take the place of contemporary bureaucracies (Bennis 1973; Thayer 1973). Much as Weber claimed earlier that bureaucracies were most efficient for meeting the needs of a society recognizing the legitimacy of a 'legal-rational' pattern of authority, the argument is that societal needs now are for a predominant type of organization that is post-bureaucratic, even though its exact characteristics remain to be clarified.

Organizational evolution is likely and probably desirable, but whatever its timing and shape, bureaucracies are likely to remain the most prevalent form of organization for the foreseeable future. Hence attention must continue to be focused on how to maximize the positive while minimizing the negative influences of bureaucracies as they operate in contemporary society.

References

Aberbach, J. D., Putnam, R. D. and Rockman, B. A. (1981) *Bureaucrats and Politicians in Western Democracies*, Cambridge, MA: Harvard University Press.

Almond, G. A. and Verba, S. (1963) *The Civic Culture*, Princeton: Princeton University Press.

Bendix, R. (1960) *Max Weber: An Intellectual Portrait*, Garden City, NY: Doubleday.

—— (1968) 'Bureaucracy', in *International Encyclopedia of the Social Sciences*, vol. 2, New York: Macmillan Free Press.

Bennis, W. G. (1973) *Beyond Bureaucracy*, New York: McGraw-Hill.

Crozier, M. (1964) *The Bureaucratic Phenomenon*, Chicago: University of Chicago Press.

Dogan, M. (ed.) (1975) *The Mandarins of Western Europe: The Political Role of Top Civil Servants*, New York: John Wiley.

Friedrich, C. J. (1963) *Man and His Government*, New York: McGraw-Hill.

—— (1968) *Constitutional Government and Democracy*, 4th edn, Boston: Blaisdell Publishing Company.

Frost, P. J., Moore, L. F., Louis, M. R., Lundberg, C. C. and Martin, J. (1985) *Organizational Culture*, Beverly Hills: Sage Publications.

Hall, R. H. (1962) 'Intraorganizational stuctural variation: application of the bureaucratic model', *Administrative Science Quarterly* 7 (3): 295–308.

Heady, F. (2001) *Public Administration: A Comparative Perspective*, 6th edn, New York: Marcel Dekker.

Heper, M. (ed.) (1987) *The State and Public Bureaucracies: A Comparative Perspective*, New York: Greenwood Press.

Hofstede, G. (1980) *Culture's Consequences: International Differences in Work-Related Values*, Beverly Hills: Sage Publications.

Jacoby, H. (1973) *The Bureaucratization of the World*, Berkeley: University of California Press.

Laski, H. J. (1930) 'Bureaucracy', in *Encyclopaedia of the Social Sciences*, vol. 3, New York: Macmillan.

Merton, R. (1952) *Reader in Bureaucracy*, New York: Free Press of Glencoe.

Morstein Marx, F. (1957) *The Administrative State: An Introduction to Bureaucracy*, Chicago: University of Chicago Press.

Nachmias, D. and Rosenbloom, D. H. (1978) *Bureaucratic Culture*, London: Croom Helm.

Nettl, J. P. (1968) 'The state as a conceptual variable', *World Politics* 20: 559–92.

Presthus, R. (1978) *The Organizational Society*, rev. edn, New York: St Martin's Press.

Ramos, A. G. (1981) *The New Science of Organizations*, Toronto: University of Toronto Press.

Riggs, F. W. (ed.) (1970) *Frontiers of Development Administration*, Durham, NC: Duke University Press.

—— (1973) *Prismatic Society Revisited*, Morristown, NJ: General Learning Press.

Rowat, D. C. (ed.) (1985) *The Ombudsman Plan*, rev. 2nd edn, Lanham, MD: University Press of America.

—— (ed.) (1988) *Public Administration in Developed Democracies*, New York: Marcel Dekker.

Schein, E. H. (1985) *Organizational Culture and Leadership: A Dynamic View*, San Francisco: Jossey-Bass.

Thayer, F. C. (1973) *An End to Hierarchy! An End to Competition!*, New York: Franklin Watts.

Thompson, V. A. (1961) *Modern Organization*, New York: Knopf.

Weber, M. (1922) 'Bureaucracy', in H. H. Gerth and C. W. Mills ed. and trans., *From Max Weber: Essays in Sociology*, New York: Oxford University Press, 1956.

Wraith, R. E. (ed.) (1982) *Proceedings, XVIIIth International Congress of Administrative Sciences, Madrid 1980*, Brussels: International Institute of Administrative Sciences.

Further reading

Aberbach, J. D., Putnam, R. D. and Rockman, B. A. (1981) *Bureaucrats and Politicians in Western Democracies*, Cambridge, MA: Harvard University Press.

Almond, G. A. and Verba, S. (1963) *The Civic Culture*, Princeton: Princeton University Press.

Bennis, W. G. (1973) *Beyond Bureaucracy*, New York: McGraw-Hill.

Crozier, M. (1964) *The Bureaucratic Phenomenon*, Chicago: University of Chicago Press.

Dogan, M. (ed.) (1975) *The Mandarins of Western Europe: The Political Role of Top Civil Servants*, New York: John Wiley.

Heady, F. (1959) 'Bureaucratic theory and comparative administration', *Administrative Science Quarterly* 3: 509–25.

—— (2001) 'A focus for comparison', chap. 2 in F. Heady, *Public Administration: A Comparative Perspective*, 6th edn, New York: Marcel Dekker.

Heper, M. (ed.) (1987) *The State and Public Bureaucracies: A Comparative Perspective*, New York: Greenwood Press.

Heper, M., Kim, C. L. and Pai, S.-T. (1980) 'The role of bureaucracy and regime types', *Administration and Society* 12: 137–57.

Jacoby, H. (1973) *The Bureaucratization of the World*, Berkeley: University of California Press.

Merton, R. (1952) *Reader in Bureaucracy*, New York: Free Press of Glencoe.

Morstein Marx, F. (1957) *The Administrative State: An Introduction to Bureaucracy*, Chicago: University of Chicago Press.

Nachmias, D. and Rosenbloom, D. H. (1978) *Bureaucratic Culture*, London: Croom Helm.

Peters, B. G. (1984) *The Politics of Bureaucracy*, 2nd edn, New York: Longman.

—— (1988) *Comparing Public Bureaucracies*, Tuscaloosa: University of Alabama Press.

Presthus, R. (1981) *The Organizational Society*, rev. edn, New York: St Martin's Press.

Ramos, A. G. (1981) *The New Science of Organizations*, Toronto: University of Toronto Press.

Rowat, D. C. (ed.) (1988) *Public Administration in Developed Democracies*, New York: Marcel Dekker.

23

FEDERALISM AND INTERGOVERNMENTAL RELATIONS

Grant Harman

Introduction

This article discusses federalism and federal political systems, and intergovernmental relations in both federal and unitary political systems. Federal political systems are based on political and social theories about federalism, a concept whose origins go back to the ancient world. Such systems have existed in various forms over the ages but their popularity increased greatly following agreement on the US constitution in 1787, followed by establishment of the Swiss, Canadian and Australian federations, and extensive post Second World War federal experiments. Of approximately 180 sovereign nations in 1999, 24 were federations that together accounted for a total population of about two billion people, or 40 per cent of the world's population (Watts 1999: 4). Intergovernmental relations have rapidly become key aspects of federal systems but such relations are also of increasing concern in unitary states, especially in terms of relations between central and local government.

In essence, federalism is an organizational mechanism of partnership employed to achieve a degree of political unity within populations whose characteristics demonstrate diversity and variety. Under this arrangement, separate regional political units (often referred to as states or provinces) are combined for limited, specified purposes under an overarching administration, but in such a way that the government of each separate regional unit maintains its integrity and substantial autonomy. Both levels of government have the ability to pass laws, levy taxes and relate directly to the people. Usually there is explicit constitutional demarcation of powers and functions between central and regional governments, as well as specified procedures for resolving conflicts and disputes between central and regional governments, and also between two or more regional governments. As Elazar points out, partnership implies the distribution of real power among several centres that must negotiate cooperative agreements with one another in order to achieve common goals (Elazar 1984: 2).

Intergovernmental relations refer to activities or interactions occurring between governmental units of all types and levels within federal or unitary political systems. Wright (1974: 1–16) identifies a number of distinct characteristics of contemporary intergovernmental relations, including: the multiplicity of relationships between all types of government bodies; the importance of interactions between individuals, especially public officials (both politicians and administrators); the prevalence of continuous, day-to-day and informal relations; the political nature of relationships; and the strong focus on substantive policies, especially financial issues such as who raises what amount and who spends it for whose benefit with what results. In many unitary states, there is considerable debate about how best to organize local government units to provide services, and about the extent of decentralization that is desirable and politically possible (Rhodes 1992). Within federal systems, intergovernmental relations are often even more complex as illustrated in the case of countries such as the USA, Canada, Germany and Australia where highly complex sets of machinery have been developed to achieve cooperation and joint activity between governmental bodies at three or more different levels. Both unitary and federal political systems are characterized by high degrees of interdependence between all levels of government.

Conceptual issues

Discussions of federal systems and intergovernmental relations within political systems are often plagued with problems of definition. This is particularly so in the case of the three key terms 'federalism', 'federal' and federation', but it also applies to other terms used in discussion of the distribution of power and responsibilities.

In its broadest sense, the word federalism refers to the linking of people and institutions by mutual consent for a specified purpose, without sacrifice of their individual identities. The term federal was coined by Bible-centred federal theologians of seventeenth-century Britain and New England to refer to a system of enduring covenants between God and human beings, which lay at the foundations of their world view (Elazar 1968: 353–4). The word federal was derived from the Latin word *foedus*, meaning covenant. This conception of federal was taken up by nineteenth-century social theorists and used in the development of various ideas about social contracts. As a political device, however, federalism can be viewed more narrowly as a form of organization in which power is dispersed as a means of safeguarding individual and local liberties. In federal political systems, a wide range of political organizations generally take on a distinctive character, including interest groups and political parties as well as formal institutions of government (Truman 1951).

Federalism also has been conceptualized as a means to achieve particular political and social purposes. Two particular purposes stand out. First, federalism has been seen as a means to unite people already linked together by bonds of nationality. In such cases, the political units brought together are seen as a part of a national whole. Essentially, this is the US view of federalism, which today has become the generally accepted one. An alternative view is that federalism is a means to unify diverse peoples for important but limited purposes, without disrupting the primary ties to their existing governments. Within this arrangement, the federal government is much more limited in scope and powers, and the particular structures used are often referred to as a confederation.

Federal systems differ from other related forms of political organization. True federal systems are different in conception from dual or multiple monarchies, where union between political units exists only through the sovereign and the exercise of his or her executive power. Such legislative unions are closely similar to federal systems, except that the terms of the union allow retention of particular non-centralizing elements. Federal systems also are different from decentralized unitary states, in which local administration is usually limited and subject to supervision and overall control by central authorities. In such politics, local autonomy can be reduced by the central government. Many of the governments of South America which purport to be federal have in practice combined devolution of power to regional governments with an overriding authority exercised by the central governments (Watts 1966).

The word federal is used in a variety of ways in political discussions. As a rule, the adjective 'federal' has been applied to constitutions and to forms of government, although some writers (Laski 1941; Livingston 1956) have talked of federal societies and others of federal ideologies (King 1982). Livingston sees federal government as 'a device by which the federal qualities of the society are articulated and presented.... If [the diversities] are grouped territorially, i.e. geographically, then the result may be a society that is federal. If they are not grouped territorially, then the society cannot be said to be federal' (Livingston 1956: 2).

Discussions about federalism and intergovernmental relations also often are plagued by confusion about terms used in analysis of power relationships and the distribution of responsibilities between different levels and types of government. The term 'decentralization' refers to the distribution of power to lower levels in a territorial hierarchy, whether the hierarchy is one of governments within a state or offices within a large-scale organization (Smith 1985: 1). The term encompasses both political and bureaucratic decentralization, federal and unitary states, and multiple decentralization or decentralization between levels of government and within each type of government (Rhodes 1992: 317). The term 'delegation' refers to transfer 'of decision-making and management authority for specific functions to organizations that are not under the direct control of central government ministries' (Rondinelli and Cheema 1983a: 20). Such organizations are referred to variously as parastatal organizations, non-departmental public bodies and quangos (quasi-autonomous non-governmental organizations). The term 'devolution' refers to the exercise of political authority by lay, primarily elected, institutions within areas defined by community characteristics (Smith 1985: 11).

Essential characteristics of federal systems

Federal systems differ considerably in terms of their formal constitutions and division of powers, how they operate, and which particular federal principles they emphasize. Nevertheless, political theorists and researchers involved in empirical studies of federalism and federal systems have found it useful to try to specify those characteristics that are essential to a truly federal system.

Watts emphasizes the notion of dual sovereignty, with central and regional governments acting side by side, 'each possessing powers delegated...by the people through a constitution, and each empowered to deal directly with the citizens in the exercise of its legislative, administrative and taxing powers, and each directly elected by the citizens' (Watt 1999: 8). Generally, although not necessarily, the division of authority should be specified in a written constitution and an independent judiciary must be created to interpret the supreme constitution and to act as a guardian of the constitutional division of powers.

Much earlier, K. C. Wheare (1946), whose writings had a major influence on the post-Second World War experiments with federal structures for new nations in Asia, Africa and the Middle East, discussed at some length what he understood by federal government. He saw the division of powers between central and regional government as being a central element. But the central government, according to Wheare, must not be thought of as subordinate to regional governments, as it was with the post-revolutionary association of American colonies, but rather each level within its sphere is independent and autonomous. 'By the federal principle', he wrote, 'I mean the method of dividing powers so that the general and regional governments are each, within a sphere, co-ordinate and independent' (Wheare 1946: 11).

A decade later, A. W. Macmahon listed the essential attributes of federalism as follows:

> (a) a federal system distributes power between common and constituent governments under an arrangement that cannot be changed by the ordinary process of central legislation...(b) the matters entrusted to the constituent units...must be substantial and not merely trivial; (c) [the] central organs are to some extent directly in contact with individuals, both to draw authority from them through elections and also for the purpose of exacting taxes and compliance with regulations...(d) the member states have considerable leeway in devising and changing their forms of government and their procedures...(e) A further essential is the equality of the constituent states, absolute as to legal status but at best relative as to such matters as size, population and wealth.
>
> (Macmahon 1955: 4–5)

Daniel J. Elazar, a leading American scholar of federalism, defines the essential elements of federalism as a written constitution (the federal relationships must be established through a perpetual covenant of union embodied in a constitution which specifies the terms by which power is divided), non-centralization (the authority for state and federal governments to exercise powers cannot be withdrawn without mutual consent), a real division of power (the area of authority of the constituent units is territorially based), direct contact with the people (thus providing a powerful mechanism to maintain the union) and mechanisms to maintain non-centralization (such as permanent boundaries of constituent units, and effective ways of combining units of different size), and the federal principle (such as both the central governments and state governments having a substantially complete set of governing institutions). According to Elazar, viewed theoretically,

> these patterns of behavior and the arguments advanced to justify them serve to reaffirm the fundamental principles that (1) the strength of a federal polity does not stem from the power of the national government but from the authority vested in the nation as a whole; (2) both the national government

and the governments of the constituent politics are possessed of delegated powers only; and (3) all governments are limited by the common national constitution.

(Elazar 1968: 361)

In recent years, there has been far less interest amongst scholars in specifying the essential characteristics of federalism and federal systems, except for discussions of topics such as devolution in Britain to Scotland and Wales (McKay 2000; Peters 2001) and the character of bodies such as the European Union (Davis 1995: 177–220) where a major issue is to what extent they should be regarded as true federations rather than confederations.

Federalism and federal systems

Generations before the invention of the term federal, both political systems and political organizations had evolved embodying elements of federal principles. In the ancient Greek world, for example, federal arrangements were first articulated in religious, tribal and city–state alliances. The classic example was the Achaean League (251–146 BC), which was an alliance or super polis to provide military protection. About the same time, the Israelite political system provided an example of a union of constituent politics, based on a sense of common nationality.

In medieval times, elements of federalism were seen in feudalism and in the leagues of self-protection established by the commercial towns of central Europe. Later quasi-federal arrangements developed in Spain and Italy under a system of multiple monarchy. In the sixteenth and seventeenth centuries, biblical scholars of the Reformation began to apply federal principles to state-building; such ideas provided an organizational basis for the federation of the United Provinces in the Netherlands in the late sixteenth century, while the Swiss soon after created a loose confederation of cantons.

The first modern formulations of federal ideas were associated with the rise of the nation-state in the sixteenth and seventeenth centuries (Forsyth 1981). In this situation, federalism provided an attractive means of dealing with problems of national unity. But it was not until immediately following the American revolution that the ideas of British and continental thinkers combined to create the first modern federal system – that of the USA in 1787. This development and its success have had a major influence on ideas about federalism internationally since then.

The founders of the USA had distinct advantages over others who had experimented earlier with federal ideas. Theirs was a post-feudal society with a relatively short history. Once established, the USA was a relatively isolated nation, with only minor external pressures until the twentieth century. Moreover, Americans were concerned above all else with the practical aspects of making federalism work. The creation of a theoretical framework for the American experiment took place in the debates over ratification of the constitution and in the formulations in *The Federalist*. The end result was a compromise between those who wished the federal government to be supreme and those who wished for the states to have the leading role. In essence, the model adopted was that the business of State is 'divided' between two popularly elected governments, a national government embracing the whole territory of the nation and a regional government for each of the lesser territories; that each government will possess the basic facilities to make, manage, and enforce its laws 'like any ordinary government'; that subject to the provisions of the constitution, each government is 'free' to act 'independently' of, or in concert with, the other, as it chooses; that jurisdictional disputes between the national government and the governments of the lesser territories will be settled by judicial arbitration; that the principle of national supremacy will prevail where two valid actions, national and regional, are in conflict; that the instruments of national government, but not necessarily the lesser territories, are set forth in a written constitution; that the national legislature is a bicameral system in which one house, the 'first branch', is composed according to the size of the population in each territory, while each territory has equal representation in the 'second branch'; lastly that the constitution is fundamental law, changeable only by a special plebiscitary process.

(Davis 1978: 121–2)

The US constitution provided the popular archetype to which scholars continued to turn. Writing immediately after the Second World War, Wheare asserted that 'since the USA is universally regarded as an example of federal government, it justifies us in describing the principle, which distinguishes it so markedly and so significantly, as *the federal* principle' (Wheare 1946: 11). Similarly, Sawer commented: 'Federal Government, as that expression is now usually understood, was devised by the Founders of the Constitution of the United States of America in 1787–8' (Sawer 1969: 1).

The federal constitutions of Canada and Australia were considerably influenced by American experience. Other nations also experimented with federalism in Latin America (Argentina, Brazil and Mexico), while federal principles were adopted in the constitution of the German Weimar Republic and used by the United Kingdom in an attempt to accommodate the Irish. However, the major push towards federal systems was a post-Second World War phenomenon, springing out of post-war reconstruction efforts in Europe (Austria 1945, Yugoslavia 1946, Germany 1949) and building new nations in Asia (India 1950, Pakistan 1956), Africa (Libya 1949, Nigeria 1954), and the Middle East (the United Arab Emirates 1971). Britain was by far the most prolific creator of post-colonial federations.

Some of these post-war federal attempts soon collapsed while others experienced major economic and social difficulties. Somewhat later, three important federations in Europe collapsed – Czechoslovakia, the Soviet Union and Yugoslavia. On the other hand, many post-war federations continue to be remarkably successful; examples include Germany, Austria, Malaysia, Nigeria, India and Pakistan. The long established federations of the USA, Canada and Australia have continued as stable democracies, despite recent threats from the province of Quebec to secede from Canada (Rocher and Smith 1995). Moreover, since the early 1990s, there has been some revival of interest in federal solutions. Belguim adopted a federal constitution in 1993, South Africa in 1996 confirmed its interim constitution of 1994 with both federal and unitary features, while the United Kingdom adopted new devolutionary features for Scotland, Wales and Ireland.

The lasting popularity of the federal form of government has surprised many. Scholars such as Harold Laski over sixty years ago had concluded that federalism was obsolete, and outmoded for the modern world. Writing in 1939, he declared: 'I infer in a word that the epoch of federalism is over' (Watts 1966: 5). But, especially in the process of building new nations in North America, Australia and Canada, in decolonization, and in reconstruction efforts in parts of Europe, federalism has provided a convenient model for creating political systems of reasonably large size, for achieving some degree of transcending unity in geographic areas of ethnic diversity, and as means of power sharing between major ethnic groups. In such situations, where the forces for integration and for separation have been at odds with each other, the federal solution has proved a popular formula. Today's federal systems, as Watt has observed, demonstrate that

> the application of the federal idea has taken a great variety of forms. The degrees of centralization and decentralization differ across federations as do their financial arrangements, the character of their federal legislative and executive institutions, insitutional arrangements for facilitating intergovernmental relations, judicial arrangements for umpiring internal conflicts, and procedures for constitutional amendments.
>
> (Watts 1999: 6)

Elazar (1968: 365) admits that federalism does not suit all political cultures, but argues that it appears to fit particularly well with Anglo-American societies, with their strong commitment to constitutionalism and a distinct preference for non-centralization. These propositions are open to debate, but certainly the successful operation of federal systems requires a particular kind of political environment, conducive to popular democratic government and with strong traditions of political cooperation and self-restraint that minimize the need for coercion. Apart from this, federal systems appear to work best in societies with sufficient overriding shared interests to provide continuing reason for federal combination and a willingness to rely on a large measure of voluntary cooperation.

Federal systems, admittedly, are not without their problems and particularly some forms of intergovernmental relations invariably involve frustrations, tensions, conflicts and a certain degree of managerial inefficiency. In most modern federal systems, there are often ongoing discussions about ways in which to improve or change the existing division of constitutional powers, and to overcome perceived problems. Still, defenders of federal systems argue that, despite the costs involved, federalism provides net advantages, especially compared with alternatives such as micro-nationalism among small neighbouring countries.

The study of federalism

With the development of political science as a discipline in the late nineteenth and early twentieth centuries, the study of federalism shifted from being concerned with normative theory to empirical research. Such scholars as Bryce and Dicey studied federalism as part of an interest in political systems. Yet, with a few exceptions, the study of federalism was generally neglected for many years.

Renewed interest in federalism developed in the late 1930s and the immediate post-Second World War period, stimulated by problems in intergovernmental relations within the USA and by a period of active nation building. Beginning in the 1930s, a new generation of political scientists began to raise questions about the particular characteristics of federal systems and how federal structures influence the development and operation of other components of political systems, such as interest groups and political parties. By the 1960s, federalism was attracting the attention of students of comparative politics and the politics of developing countries, as well as scholars interested in public administration.

Two major topics were of particular importance in the early post war period. The first concerned motivations behind the creation of federal structures, or why populations chose federal constitutions. Two important hypotheses were developed by W. K. Riker in *Federalism: Origins, Operation and Significance* (1964) and R. L. Watts in *New Federations: Experiments in the Commonwealth* (1966). Riker's study was in the quasi-scientific style of the 'behavioural movement', attempting to develop testable generalizations, while Watt's work was in the tradition of the historically oriented comparative study concerned with the search for significant patterns.

Riker's argument was that federalism is a bargain between prospective national leaders and officials of constituent governments for the purpose of aggregating territory. The parties favour such a bargain by the existence of two circumstances, the desire to expand territorial control or to meet an external military or diplomatic threat. Riker examined examples of the establishment of federations and concluded that military and the expansion conditions are necessary to the occurrence of federalism (Riker 1964).

Watts examined six new federal experiments (India, Pakistan, Malaya and Malaysia, Nigeria, Rhodesia and Nyasaland, and the West Indies) and identified a number of social factors and motives that operated, with each being potentially either unifying or separating. He concluded that, while dominant motives varied in each case,

> two features stand out in common to them all. First, there was a geographical distribution, at least to some degree, of the diversities within each of these societies, with the results that demands for political autonomy were made on a regional basis. Secondly, in each of the recent federations, as in the older ones, there existed at one and the same time powerful desires to be united for certain purposes, because of a community of outlook or the expectation of common benefits of union, and deep rooted desires to be organized under autonomous regional governments for others, because of contrasting ways of life or the desire to protect divergent interests. The result in each was a tension between the conflicting demands for territorial integration and for Balkanization.
>
> (Watts 1966: 93)

The second important debate related to how federal systems change over time, and the operation of conflicting pressures towards integration and decentralization.

Research initially concentrated particularly on factors that promote integration and decentralization, on whether pressures for integration or decentralization are dominant, and whether pressures for integration tend to lead to the eventual modification of federal systems in favour of unitary structures while decentralization will lead to disintegration. Many researchers pointed to the strongly centralizing tendency within many federal systems. Davis, for example, saw a centralizing trend as being dominant in federal systems in all complex societies. In such societies, he argued, to talk of independent action by either federal or regional governments is meaningless 'when two governments, whether from love or necessity, become so wedded to each other in the common bed of nationalized politics that neither can turn, talk, or breathe without immediately affecting the other' (Davis 1978: 148). In such situations, strong tendencies operate for central governments to take a commanding role, especially in terms of fiscal relations.

A decade earlier Livingston took a different approach arguing that, instead of employing legal/formal or jurisprudential approaches to understanding federalism, research should focus on the social configuration of society, particularly the types of interests which compose it, their diversity, and their geographic distribution. According to Livingston, every society 'is more or less closely integrated in accordance with its own peculiar historical, cultural, economic, political and other determinants' (Livingston 1967: 37).

A somewhat similar theoretical approach was adopted by Friedrich, who saw federation essentially as a process of federalizing. He explained:

> an emergent federal order may be operating in the direction of both integration and differentiation; federalizing being *either* the process by which a number of separate political units...enter into and develop arrangements for working out solutions together...*or* the reverse process through which a hitherto unitary political community, as it becomes differentiated into a number of separate and distinct political subcommunities, achieves a new order in which the differentiated communities become capable of working out separately and on their own decisions and policies on problems they no longer have in common. Federalism refers to this process, as it does to the structures and patterns this process creates.
>
> (Friedrich 1968: 176–7)

More recently the debate on integration and decentralization has taken a variety of different approaches. Some efforts have concentrated particularly on the mechanisms for change in federal arrangements. Brown-John (1988), for example, argues that in recent years in federal systems there is generally less use of constitutional amendments than in the past, and more use of agreements between governments, often negotiated by public officials. At the same time, many of the old themes continued to be debated, particularly in the USA in relation to the relative balance of federal and state powers (Dye 1990; Zimmerman 1992).

Since the early 1980s, the main thrusts of scholarly research on federalism have changed dramatically. Research has attracted a growing number of scholars leading to a major expansion in the research literature. This has been facilitated by the establishment of specialist research centres on federalism and intergovernmental relations, and specialist journals (such as *Publius* that was founded in 1970) and newsletters. Research has also attracted a more diverse group of scholars, drawn not only from political science, public administration and law but also from disciplines including economics, public finance, public policy, sociology and geography. Comparative studies have become more common as have studies of how federalism and the character of intergovernmental relations impact on particular policy areas such as health, education, transport and communications. Other problems that have attracted attention include whether or not federalism is a force of conservatism, whether federal structures facilitate social and political change, and whether federalism promotes or undermines human rights (Tarr and Katz 1996). Research in many federal nations has been given considerable stimulus by the work of various government commissions and committees of inquiry appointed to review particular arrangements in intergovernmental relations and recommend modifications.

While various publications have provided international surveys of federal systems (Elazar 1994; Watts 1999), the main research attention has been directed to the operation of American, Australian and Canadian federalism, comparative studies of federal structures and issues particularly in these three countries, and studies of new forms of economic and social confederations such as the European Union. By far the largest amount of published work has come out of the USA where research effort has covered an impressive range of diverse topics. Particularly important have been assessments of new directions in American federalism under different US Presidents, studies of constitutional issues and the role of the Supreme Court, detailed studies of intergovernmental relations, and an ongoing debate about the foundations and character of American federalism and its links to American nationalism and identity. Possibly one of the most important recent contributions has been from the distinguished political scientist, Samuel H. Beer (1993), whose book, *To Make a Nation: The Rediscovery of American Federalism*, provides a comprehensive analysis of the origins of American federalism and its links to liberalism. Beer argues that American federalism is based on the establishment and integration of a single American population, rather than being a compact among the states, and that American nationhood is based on the ideals of a federal democracy.

Australian and Canadian research has been much more focused on a limited range of topics. The main attention in Australia has been given to the study of particular intergovernmental agencies and to the impact of federalism on particular policy domains such as education (Harman and Smart 1983), health and environment. A recent study by Painter (1998), for example, documents recent changes in federal-state relations towards a much more collaborative form of federalism. Particularly important has been creation in the early 1990s of the Council of Australian Governments, which today provides an important forum for bargaining and negotiating between the Commonwealth and the states. This Council has facilitated new forms of cooperation and joint action such as with regard to road transport reform and the National Competition Policy Agreement. In contrast, Canadian federalism has exhibited more conflict and over the past two decades the Canadian nation has been concerned to a major degree with repatriation of the constitution and constitutional issues, and efforts by the province of Quebec to secede. These developments not surprisingly have attracted the interests of Canadian students of federalism (Simeon and Robinson 1990; Rocher and Smith 1995; and Watts 1999).

Research on new regional forms of economic federalism has particularly centred on the European Union. A survey by McKay (2000) uses Riker's rational bargaining theory and argues that the European Union is moving gradually towards a new species of federation while Elazar (1995) sees a move towards a new paradigm under which existing states will not disappear but rather they will be overlaid by a variety of federal arrangements of a confederal character.

Intergovernmental relations

Intergovernmental relations is of increasing concern today in both federal and unitary political systems as various pressures operate to change the balance of power in multi-level government situations and to achieve new forms of cooperation between different governmental bodies. While federalism demands a measure of interdependence between federal and state/provisional governments, until more recent times each level was able to operate with a substantial measure of independence, having agreed areas of responsibility. This situation, however, has changed dramatically in recent years, with increasing degrees of overlapping responsibilities, demands for a variety of new services, resource pressures and strong conflicting pressures towards both centralization and decentralization. Similar pressures now operate in many unitary political systems, making intergovernmental relations of increasing and often crucial importance, especially in terms of maintenance of high standards of government service delivery.

Current tensions today in many federal systems raise the question of how relationships actually operated in the early stages of federal systems. Elazar, for example, argues passionately that American federalism was always marked by cooperation between governments at different levels and that 'virtually all the activities of government in the nineteenth century were shared activities, involving federal, state and local government in their planning, financing and execution' (Elazar 1969: 84). But his argument needs to be seen in the context of his defence of the role of the states in the American system, and his belief that effective federalism means a real partnership and balance of power between central and regional levels of government.

Whatever the merits of the debates about the precise nature of federal arrangements in their formative stages, it is clear that today in major federal systems such as the USA, Canada, Australia and Germany highly complex sets of machinery have evolved in order to facilitate intergovernmental relations. In the USA, for example, cooperation takes place through a variety of mechanisms including interstate compacts, uniform state laws, reciprocity statutes, administrative agreements and regular meetings of federal and state officials (Zimmerman 1996: 1–15). Important roles are also played in America by the courts in resolving constitutional disputes. In Australia, intergovernmental relations involve a large number of special purpose institutions including the Council of Australian Governments (previously called the Premiers Conference), the Loan Council and specialist councils of federal and state ministers for each major overlapping policy domain (Galligan, Hughes and Walsh

1991). The extent of the current network of interrelating units of government is vast; in the USA it includes approximately 80,000 separate governmental units, comprising federal, state, county, municipal and special-district jurisdictions. Their powers and responsibilities overlap and there is a considerable degree of competition in providing services to the public.

O'Toole (1985) sees the key distinguishing features of intergovernmental relations in modern federal systems as complexity and interdependence – complexity in the sense that the intergovernmental network is large and highly differentiated, and inter-dependence in the sense that intergovernmental relations exhibit an amalgamated pluralism, with power and responsibility being shared among the branches and layers of government even within a single policy domain. This situation developed in response to various external pressures, such as major wars and international inci-dents, recessions and depressions, but also of great importance have been internal problems related to social welfare, crime, education, transport and the needs of cities. In addition, there have been special and highly sensitive problems such as racial segregation in the USA and ethnic and cultural diversity in Canada.

Not surprisingly fiscal relations are of great concern in federal systems, especially on matters such as how income is raised through taxation and charges and by whom, and how such resources are shared and distributed. Federal governments use a number of different strategies to allocate resources to regional and local govern-ments and to the public. These include intergovernmental transfers by block grants and by tied or special purposes grants, shared funding between governments on agreed formulas, and direct allocations to individuals and groups (Grewal, Brennan and Mathews 1980; and Grewal and Matthews 1997). In Australia for example, all proceeds from a Goods and Services Tax levied by the Commonwealth Government since 1 July 2000 have gone to the states and territories that, in return, have agreed to discontinue various forms of taxes regarded as being anti-business, such as stamp duty levied on the sale of stocks and shares, and a financial duties tax levied on financial transactions. Various mechanisms frequently operate to make the resource base of regional units more equitable; for example, in Australia for many years a higher proportion of federal taxation reimbursements has been allocated to the less well-off states through the Commonwealth Grants Commission established in 1933 (May 1971; and Galligan, Hughes and Walsh 1991).

In unitary political systems, important debates and conflicts have centred on the roles of central and local government, and the desirable balances between central-izing and decentralizing pressures. There is considerable variety between different nations in the distribution of responsibilities, revenue generation and resource allo-cation procedures, and the degree of both political and bureaucratic decentralization within central government (Rhodes 1992: 317–35). After comparing central–local relations in seven European unitary states, Page and Goldsmith (1987b: 156–62) conclude that there are clear differences between North European and South European states. In North European states, a category which comprises Norway, Denmark, Sweden and Britain, local authorities have more functions and there is a clearer division of labour between centre and locality. Local government in France, Italy and Spain, by contrast, spends a much smaller proportion of total public expenditure. There are also differences in the forms of control, with North

European states preferring statutory regulation while in South European states the preferred method is administrative regulation or detailed state approval of local actions. Page and Goldsmith (1987b: 163–8) identify a variety of possible explanations for this pattern including the experience of Napoleonic states in South Europe and in North Europe social-democratic regimes committed to the development of welfare state services using local government to deliver those services.

Two major trends that were particularly important in intergovernmental relations in European countries in the 1970s and 1980s were reorganization and decentralization (Page and Goldsmith 1987a: 1–2). Reorganization was concerned with how best to organize local government units to provide services. Reform efforts included both structural reform and changes affecting the number of governmental units (e.g. amalgamations of municipalities as in Britain and Sweden, creation of regional tiers as in France and Italy, and participatory local service delivery agencies such as in Norway and Spain); and organizational reforms in the internal structure of local government, usually to achieve efficiency (e.g. corporate planning in Britain). Decentralization related to what should be the powers and capabilities of local government in modern states. In some cases such as Britain and Norway, reductions in the level of grants to local government work towards centralization while in other cases such as in Italy and France measures aimed at decentralization were deliberately introduced by central governments. Associated with these tends in many cases were financial pressures, with an increasing gap between local taxes and grants on the one hand, and local expenditure on the other.

In developing countries, decentralization was the favoured model in the 1960s. It was seen as a way of surmounting the limitations of national planning by getting closer to problems, cutting through red-tape and meeting local needs of the poor. Also the decentralization model was seen as achieving improved central 'penetration' of rural areas, thereby spreading knowledge of, and mobilizing support for, the plan and bypassing obstructive local elites. But generally the expectations of decentralization for local government fell far below expectations (Smith 1985: 188) and, in many cases, the powers allocated to local government were severely limited.

There are markedly different interpretations of the constraints on decentralization in developing countries. The interventions of the centre are often seen as responses to poor local living standards and the need to control scarce resources. The centre also is said to be technically and administratively more competent, monopolizing an urban, educated, economically powerful elite and leaving only a restricted pool of talent in local government where morale is often low and discipline is poor (Wallis 1989: 132). More important, local government faces stiff competition from traditional ruling authorities, from established castes and classes of landowners defending their sectional interests, and from modern governing elites striving to control national resources (Mawhood 1987: 17). Further still, there is also considerable confusion between the ideas of effective local government and decentralization within central government departments.

Current trends and prospects

In the short term, current federal systems seem likely to continue along existing lines, with even greater interest in reviewing detailed arrangements and addressing particular problems in intergovernmental relations. The extent to which federal principles may be used in the rearrangement of existing political systems is difficult to predict, but certainly there have been some important recent examples of successes. Moreover, it appears likely that federal principles will be adopted increasingly as convenient means of linking sovereign states for limited economic and regulatory purposes (Norrie, Simeon and Krasnick 1986).

In terms of scholarship, there is probably more uncertainty than ever about the future directions of federalism research, despite the significant contributions of recent decades. There are so many different perspectives, so many different approaches. But it seems reasonable to expect that in the future there will be less interest in defining federalism and discussing the extent to which different politics exhibit federal characteristics and much more interest in analysis of the changing nature of federal systems, in their adaptability to meet new needs, and in the complexities of intergovernmental relations associated with federal systems.

The future of intergovernmental relations in unitary systems seems likely to be characterized, at least in the short term, by increased centralization, associated in many cases with declining accountability and certainly with increased turbulence and uncertainty. While commentators agree that there is a clear trend towards greater centralization in both developed and developing countries, at the same time, central government in many countries is becoming more fragmented, and so centralization and differentiation co-exist though somewhat uneasily.

References

Beer, Samuel H. (1993) *To Make a Nation: The Rediscovery of American Federalism*, Cambridge: Harvard University Press.

Brown-John, C. L. (ed.) (1988) 'Centralizing and Decentralizing Trends in Federal States', in C. L. Brown-John (ed.) *Centralizing and Decentralizing Trends in Federal States* Lanham: University Press of America.

Davis, S. R. (1978) *The Federal Principle*, Berkeley: University of California Press.

—— (1995) *Theory and Reality: Federal Ideas in Australia, England and Europe*, St Lucia: University of Queensland Press.

Dye, T. (1990) *American Federalism: Competition Among Governments*, Lexington: Lexington Books.

Elazar, D. J. (1968) 'Federalism', in D. S. Sils (ed.) *International Encyclopedia of the Social Sciences*, New York: Macmillan/Free Press.

—— (ed.) (1969) *Cooperation and Conflict*, Ithaca, IL: Peacock.

—— (1984) *American Federalism: A View from the States*, 3rd edn, Cambridge: Harper & Row.

—— (1994) *Federal Systems of the World: A Handbook*, 2nd edn, London: Longman.

—— (1995) 'From Statism to Federalism: A Paradigm Shift', *Publius*, 25 (2), 5–18.

Forsyth, M. (1981) *Unions of States: The Theory and Practice of Confederation*, Leicester: Leicester University Press.

Friedrich, C. J. (1968) *Trends of Federalism in Theory and Practice*, New York: Praeger.

Galligan, B., Hughes, O., and Walsh, C. (eds) (1991) *Intergovernmental Relations and Public Policy*, North Sydney: Allen & Unwin.

Grewal, B. S., Brennan, G. and Mathews, R. L. (eds) (1980) *The Economics of Federalism*, Canberra: Australian National University Press.

Grewal, B. S. and Matthews, R. (1997) *The Public Sector in Jeopardy: Australian Fiscal Federalism from Whitlam to Keating*, Melbourne: Centre for Strategic Economic Studies, Victoria University.

Harman, G. and Smart, D. (eds) (1983) *Federal Intervention in Australian Education: Past, Present and Future*, Melbourne: Georgian House.

King, P. (1982) *Federalism and Federation*, London: Croom Helm.

Laski, H. J. (1941) *A Grammar of Politics*, 4th edn, London: Allen & Unwin.

Livingston, W. S. (1956) *Federalism and Constitutional Change*, Oxford: Clarendon Press.

—— (1967) 'A note on the nature of federalism', in A. Wildavsky (ed.) *American Federalism in Perspective*, Boston: Little, Brown & Co.

McKay, D. (2000) *Federalism and the European Union*, Oxford: Oxford University Press.

Macmahon, A. W. (ed.) (1955) *Federalism, Mature and Emergent*, New York: Doubleday.

Mawhood, P. (1987) 'Decentralization and the Third World in the 1980s', *Planning and Administration* 14: 11–22.

May, R. J. (1971) *Financing the Small States in Australian Federalism*, Melbourne: Oxford University Press.

Norrie, K., Simeon, R. and Krasnick, M. (1986) *Federalism and the Economic Union in Canada*, Toronto: University of Toronto Press.

O'Toole, L. J. (ed.) (1985) *American Intergovernmental Relations: Foundations, Perspectives, and Issues*, Washington, DC: CQ Press.

Page, E. C. and Goldsmith, M. J. (1987a) 'Centre and locality: functions, access and discretion', in E. C. Page and M. J. Goldsmith (eds) *Central and Local Government Relations*, London: Sage Publications.

—— (1987b) 'Centre and locality: explaining cross national variations', in E. C. Page and M. J. Goldsmith (eds) *Central and Local Government Relations*, London: Sage Publications.

Painter, M. (1998) *Collaborative Federalism: Reform in Australia in the 1990s*, Cambridge: Cambridge University Press.

Peters, B. G. (2001) 'The United Kingdom becomes the United Kingdom? Is federalism imminent, or even possible?', *British Journal of Politics and International Relations*, 3 (1): 71–83.

Rhodes, R. A. W. (1992) 'Intergovernmental Relations', in M. Hawkesworth and M. Kogan (eds) *Encyclopedia of Government and Politics*, London and New York: Routledge, 316–35.

Riker, W. H. (1964) *Federalism: Origins, Operation and Significance*, Boston: Little, Brown & Co.

Rocher, F. and Smith, M. (1995) *New Trends in Canadian Federalism*, Toronto: Broadview Press.

Rondinelli, D. A. and Cheema, G. S. (1983a) 'Implementing decentralization policies: an introduction', in D. A. Rondinelli and G. S. Cheema (eds) *Decentralization and Development*, London: Sage Publications.

Sawer, G. (1969) *Modern Federalism*, London: C. A. Watts.

Simeon, S. and Robinson, I. (1990) *State, Society and the Development of Canadian Federalism*, Toronto: University of Toronto Press.

Smith, B. C. (1985) *Decentralization*, London: Allen & Unwin.

Tarr, E. and Katz, G. A. (eds) (1996) *Federalism and Rights*, London: Rowman & Littlefield.

Truman, D. B. (1951) *The Governmental Process: Political Interests and Public Opinion*, New York: Knopf.

Wallis, M. (1989) *Bureaucracy: Its Role in Third World Development*, London: Macmillan.

Watts, R. L. (1966) *New Federations: Experiments in the Commonwealth*, Oxford: Clarendon Press.

—— (1999) *Comparing Federal Systems*, Montreal: McGill-Queen's University Press.

Wheare, K. C. (1946) *Federal Government*, London: Oxford University Press.

Wright, D. S. (1974) 'Intergovernmental relations: an analytical overview', *Annals of the American Academy of Political and Social Science* 416 (November): 1–16.

Zimmerman, J. F. (1992) *Contemporary American Federalism: The Growth of National Power*, Leicester: Leicester University Press.

—— (1996) *Interstate Relations: The Neglected Dimension of Federalism*, Westport: Praeger.

PART VI

POLITICAL FORCES
AND POLITICAL PROCESSES

24

PERSONALITY AND POLITICS

Fred I. Greenstein

The personalities of political actors impinge on political affairs in countless ways, often with great consequences. Political life regularly generates such contrary-to-fact conditionals as 'If Kennedy had lived, such-and-such would or would not have happened'. Counterfactual propositions are not directly testable, but many of them are so compelling that even the most cautious historian would find them persuasive. Most historians would agree, for example, that if the assassin's bullet aimed at President elect Franklin D. Roosevelt in February 1933 had found its mark, there would have been no New Deal, or if the Politburo had chosen another Leonid Brezhnev, Konstantin Chernenko or Yuri Andropov rather than Mikhail Gorbachev as General Secretary of the Communist Party of the Soviet Union in 1985, the epochal changes of the late 1980s and early 1990s would not have occurred, at least not at the same time and in the same way.

The seemingly self-evident effects of many changes in leadership, including changes of a much lesser order in lesser entities than the national governments of the USA and the Soviet Union, along with the innumerable other events in the political world that are difficult to account for without taking cognizance of the actors' personal peculiarities, lead the bulk of non-academic observers of politics, including journalists, to take it for granted that personality is an important determinant of political behaviour. Yet political scientists typically do not make personality and politics a principal focus of investigation. They tend instead to focus on impersonal determinants of political events and outcomes, even those in which the participants themselves believe personality to have been significant. Or, if they do treat individual action as important, they posit rationality, defining away personal characteristics and presuming that the behaviour of actors can be deduced from the logic of their situations (compare Simon 1985).

Personality and politics as a field of academic study is controversial and poses formidable methodological challenges, but many of the controversies can be turned to constructive intellectual purposes and important phenomena demand study, even if they pose methodological difficulties. There is controversy among scholars even about such a seemingly simple matter as the definition of the terms 'personality' and 'politics', and there are more fundamental disagreements about the extent to which personality can, in principle, be expected to influence political behaviour. Reservations have been expressed about the utility of studying the personalities of political actors on the grounds that:

351

1   political actors are randomly distributed in roles and therefore their personalities 'cancel out';

2   political action is determined more by the actors' political environments than by their own characteristics;

3   the particular stratum of the psyche many political scientists equate with *personality*, psychodynamics and the ego defences, does not have much of a political impact;

4   the social characteristics of political actors are more important than their psychological characteristics; and

5   individuals are typically unable to have much effect on political outcomes.

On analysis, each of these reservations or disagreements proves to have interesting substantive ramifications for the study of personality and politics.

Definitional questions

Narrowly construed, the term *politics* in *personality and politics* refers to the politics most often studied by political scientists – that of civil government and of the extra-governmental processes that more or less directly impinge upon government, such as political parties and interest groups. Broadly construed, it refers to politics in all of its manifestations, whether in government or any other institution, including many that are rarely studied by political scientists – for example, the family, school and workplace. By this broader construction, the common denominator is the various referents of *politics*, including the exercise of influence and authority and the diverse arts of interpersonal manoeuvre such as bargaining and persuasion connoted by the word 'politicking', none of which are monopolized by government.

Personality also admits of narrow and broad definitions. In the narrow usage typical of political science, it excludes political attitudes and opinions and often other kinds of political subjective states as well (for example, the ideational content associated with political skill) and applies only to non-political personal differences, or even to the subset of psychopathological differences that are the preoccupation of clinical psychology. In psychology, on the other hand, the term has a much broader definition – in the phrase of the personality theorist Henry Murray (1968), it 'is the most comprehensive term we have in psychology'. Thus, in their influential study of *Opinions and Personality*, the psychologists M. Brewster Smith, Jerome Bruner and Robert White (1956: 1) use an expression one would not expect from political scientists, describing opinions as 'an integral part of personality'.

Although usage is a matter of convention and both the narrow and the broad definitions encompass phenomena worthy of study, this seemingly semantic controversy has a significant bearing on what scholars study. As Lasswell (1930: 42–4) argued long ago, there are distinct advantages to adopting the broader definition. A perspective that transcends governmental politics encourages the study of comparable phenomena, some of which may happen to be part of the formal institutions of governance and some of which may not. Browning and Jacobs (1964), for example, compared the needs for power, achievement and affiliation (friendship) of business people and public officials in highly diverse positions that imposed sharply divergent demands. They found that the public officials were by no means all cut from the same psychological cloth, but that there were important similarities between certain of the public officials and business people. The underlying principle appears to be that personality tends to be consistent with the specific demands of roles, whether because of preselection of the role incumbents or because of in-role socialization.

The distribution of individuals in roles

If the first of the reservations sometimes expressed about the value of studying personality and politics – the claim that individuals are randomly distributed in political roles and therefore their impact is somehow neutralized – is empirically sound, that is by no means a reason not to study personality and politics. If one visualizes political processes as analogous to intricately wired computers, political actors can be viewed as key junctures in the wiring, such as circuit breakers, for example. If anything it would be *more*, not less, urgent to know the performance characteristics of the circuit breakers if their operating properties were random, with some capable of tripping at inappropriate times, losing valuable information, and others failing to trip, exposing the system to the danger of meltdown.

In the real political world, events sometimes do more or less randomly assign individuals with unanticipated personal styles and proclivities to political roles, often with significant consequences. This was the case of two of the national leaders referred to in the opening of this chapter: neither Franklin Roosevelt's nor Mikhail Gorbachev's contemporaries anticipated the innovative leadership they displayed in office. As the Browning and Jacobs (1964) study suggests, however, people do not appear to be randomly distributed in political roles, though the patterns of their distribution appear to be complex and elusive. Ascertaining them and examining their political consequences is an important part of the intellectual agenda for the study of personality and politics.

Personality and environment

The second reservation about the study of personality and politics – that environment has more impact than personality on behaviour – and the other three reservations need to be considered in the context of a general clarification of the types of variables that in principle can affect personality and politics and their possible interconnections. An important example of such a clarification is M. Brewster Smith's well-known 'map for the study of personality and politics' (Smith 1968). (See also Stone and Schaffner's (1988: 33) depiction of 'political life space'.) The representation that I will employ (Greenstein 1975) is introduced in segments in Figures 24.1 and 24.2 and set forth in its entirety in Figure 24.3.

The most fundamental distinction in the map is the rudimentary one that, as Kurt Lewin put it, 'behaviour or any kind of mental event...depends on the state of the person and at the same time on the environment (Lewin 1936: 11–12). Figure 24.24.1 shows the links between the two broad classes of behavioural antecedent Lewin refers to and behaviour itself, using the terminology of Lasswell and Kaplan (1950: 4–6), who ground an entire conceptual framework for the analysis of politics on the equation that human response (R) is a function of the respondent's environment (E) and predispositions (P): $E \rightarrow P \rightarrow R$. Here again, terminology is a matter of convenience.

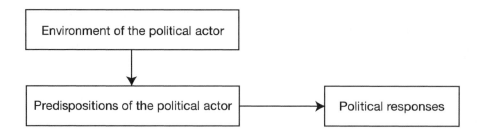

Figure 24.1 Basic antecedents of political behaviour: E→P→R

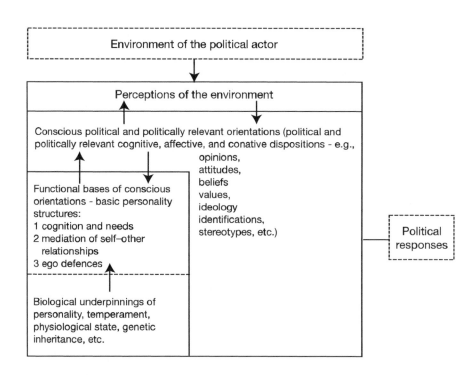

Figure 24.2 Predispositions of the political actor

Instead of *predispositions*, it would have been possible to use many other of the eighty terms Donald Campbell (1963) enumerates in his account of the logic of studying 'acquired behavioural dispositions'. Such terms as *situation*, *context* and *stimulus* are common alternative labels for all or part of the environment of human action.

The E→P→R formula provides a convenient way of visualizing the fallacy in the claim that behaviour is so much a function of environments that individuals' predispositions need not be studied (reservation two). In fact, environments are always mediated by the individuals on whom they act; environments cannot shape behaviour directly, and much politically important action is not reactive to imme-diate stimuli. Indeed, the capacity to be *proactive* (Murray 1968) and transcend

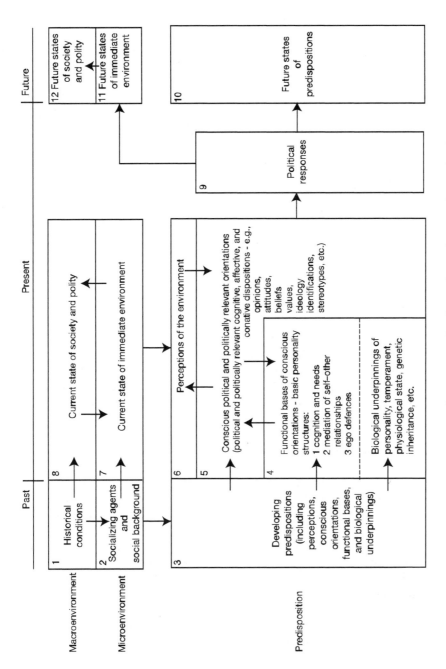

Figure 24.3 A comprehensive map for the analysis of personality and politics

existing perceptions of what the environment dictates is at the core of effective leadership. But the debate about whether environments determine political behaviour is a reminder of the endless interplay of individuals and the political contexts in which they find or place themselves.

Some contexts are indeed associated with the kind of behaviour that leads social determinists to be skeptical about the need to study personality. Informed of the impending collapse of a building, everyone – irrespective of temperament and personality type – will seek to leave it. Other contexts illustrate Gordon Allport's aphorism that 'the same heat that hardens the egg, melts the butter' (Allport 1937: 325). Still others are virtual ink blots, leading individuals with varying characteristics to project their inner dispositions onto them.

The connection between personality and context is so integral that this relationship has become the basis of an important approach to personality theory known as interactionism (Magnusson and Endler 1977; Pervin and Lewis 1978; Endler 1981). By systematically analyzing personality and politics in interactional terms, the analyst is sensitized to the kinds of contingent relationships that make the links between personality and politics elusive.

A good example of a contingent relationship in which the impact of personality is mediated by the environment is to be found in the work of Katz and Benjamin (1960) on the effects of authoritarianism in biracial work groups in the north and the south of the USA. Katz and Benjamin compared white undergraduates in the two regions who scored low and high on one of the various authoritarian personality measures to see how they comported themselves in interracial problem-solving groups. They found that in the south authoritarianism (which previous studies showed to be associated with racial prejudice) was associated with attempts of white students to dominate their black counterparts, but that in the north the authoritarians were more likely than the non-authoritarians to be *deferential* to blacks. The investigators' conclusion was that the socio-political environment of the southern authoritarians enabled them to give direct vent to their impulses, but that the liberal environment of the northern university led students with similar proclivities to go out of their way to avoid conflict with the prevailing norms.

The relative effect of environment and personality on political behaviour varies. Ambiguous environments – for example, new situations and political roles that are only sketchily defined by formal rules (Budner 1962; Greenstein 1969: 50–7) – provide great latitude for actors' personalities to shape their behaviour. Structured environments – for example, bureaucratized settings and contexts in which there are well-developed and widely known and accepted norms – tend to constrain behaviour. The environment also is likely to account for much of the variance in political behaviour when strong sanctions are attached to certain possible courses of action.

The dramatic reduction of political repression in the Soviet Union and Eastern Europe in the late 1980s led to an outpouring of political action. Just as the absence of authoritarian rule leads individuals in the aggregate to express their personal political proclivities, its presence magnifies the effects of leaders, assuming that the authoritarian system is one in which the individual or individuals at the top have more or less absolute power (Tucker 1965). The striking capacity of leaders' personalities to shape events in an authoritarian system was evident in the leeway

Gorbachev appears to have had at the time of the initiation of *glasnost* and *perestroika*, if not later when the forces of pluralism began to bedevil him.

Just as environments vary in the extent to which they foster the expression of individual variability, so also do predispositions themselves. There is an extensive literature on the tendency of people to subordinate themselves to groups and consciously or unconsciously suppress their own views when they are in the company of others. Some individuals, however, are remarkably resistant to such inhibitions while others have compliant tendencies (Asch 1956; Allen 1975; Janis 1982; 't Hart, Stern, and Sundelius 1997). The intensity of psychological predispositions promotes their expression. Most people suppress their impulses to challenge the regimes of authoritarian systems, but those with passionate convictions and strong character-based needs for self-expression or rebellion are more likely to oppose such regimes. (In doing so, they alter the environment, providing social support for their more compliant peers to join them.)

Psychopathological and other political motivation

One of the ways in which humans vary is in the extent to which they manifest emotional disturbance and ego defensiveness. Equating all of personality with the psychological stratum that traditionally concerns clinical psychologists, some students of politics voice the third of the reservations about the study of personality and politics, arguing that the links between psychopathology and politics are rare and unimportant. A specific exploration of the general question of whether ego-defensive motivation is common in politics can be found in the extensive empirical literature on the student political protest movements of the 1960s. Some research findings appeared to indicate that protest was rooted in 'healthy' character traits, such as an inner strength to stand by one's convictions and the cognitive capacity to cut through propaganda, whereas other reports suggested the possible influence of the kinds of neurotic needs that might, for example, arise from repressed resentment of parents or other authority figures from everyday life.

In order to consider the general issue of the role of psychopathology in politics and the specific issue of the roots of protest, it is necessary to elaborate the E→P→R formula. Figure 24.2 expands the personality panel in Figure 24.1. The panel is constructed so as to suggest, in a metaphor common in personality theory (Hall and Lindzey 1970), 'levels' of psychic functioning. The level closest to the surface and most directly 'in touch' with the environment is the perceptual. Perceptions can be thought of as a cognitive screen that shapes and structures environmental stimuli, sometimes distorting them, sometimes reflecting them with considerable verisimilitude. In the 1970s and 1980s there was a burgeoning of inquiry into political perception and cognitive psychology more generally (Lau and Sears 1986; Jervis 1976; Jervis, Lebow and Stein 1985; Vertzberger 1990). Also at the surface, in the sense that they are conscious or accessible to consciousness, are political orientations such as attitudes, beliefs and convictions. Psychologists commonly conceive of dispositions at this level as composites of the more basic processes of cognition (thought), affect (emotion) and conation (proclivities toward action). (For an important work on political affect see Marcus, Neuman, and MacKuen 2000.)

The sub-panel of Figure 24.2 labelled 'functional bases of conscious orientations' and, more or less synonymously, 'basic personality structures', represents the level of psychic activity that political scientists often have in mind when they speak of personality. Different personality theorists emphasize the importance of different underlying personality structures, but most of them distinguish (in varied terminology) three broad classes of inner processes – those bearing on thought and perception, on emotions and their management (including feelings of which the individual may have little conscious understanding) and on the relation of the self to significant others. The terms used for these processes in Figure 24.2 are cognition, ego defence and mediation of self–other relations. Figure 24.2 also includes a sub-panel identifying the genetic and acquired physical states that contribute to personality and diffuse into political behaviour (Masters 1989; Park 1986).

Both the broad question of whether psychopathology manifests itself in political behaviour and the narrow question of what motivates political rebels can be illuminated by reference to Figure 24.2. One way of thinking about political attitudes and behaviour is in terms of the functions they serve for the personality (Smith, Bruner and White 1956; Pratkanis, Breckler and Greenwald 1989) – hence the use of the phrase 'functional bases of conscious orientations'. What might on the surface seem to be the same belief or class of action, may serve different functions in the motivational economies of different people. For one individual a certain view – for example, a positive or negative racial stereotype – may result from the available information in the environment, mainly serving needs for cognitive closure. For another, it might be rooted in a need to take cues from (or be different from) significant others. For a third, it might serve the ego-defensive function of venting unacknowledged aggressive impulses. (More often than not, a political behaviour is likely to be fuelled by more than one motivation, but with varying mixes from individual to individual.)

The incidence of psychopathological and other motivational bases of political orientations needs to be established by empirical inquiry. Just as some environmental contexts leave room for the play of personality in general, some are especially conducive to the expression of ego defences. These include stimuli that appeal to the powerful emotional impulses that people are socialized to deny, but that remain potent beneath the surface. For example, there is an especially steamy quality to political contention over issues like abortion and pornography that bear on sexuality. Nationalistic issues such as flag burning and matters of religious doctrine also channel political passions (Davies 1980), for reasons that have not been adequately explained. Extreme forms of behaviour are also likely (though not certain) to have a pathological basis, as in the behaviour of American presidential assassins such as Ronald Reagan's would-be killer, John Hinckley, Jr (Clarke 1990).

The circumstances under which psychopathology and its lesser variants find their way into politics are of great interest, as are those under which the other motivational bases of political behaviour come into play. Depending upon the basic personality systems to which a given aspect of political performance is linked, differences can be expected in the conditions under which it will be aroused and changed, as well as in the detailed way it will manifest itself. Opinions and actions based in cognitive needs will be responsive to new information. Those based on social needs will respond to changes in the behaviour and signals provided by significant others. Those based on ego defences may be intractable, or only subject to change by extensive efforts to bring about self-insight, or by certain manipulative strategies such as suggestion by authority figures (Katz 1960).

The functional approach to the study of political orientations provides a useful framework for determining whether and under what circumstances political protest has motivational sources in ego-defensive needs. There is much evidence bearing on this issue, at least as it applies to student protest. A remarkable number of empirical studies were done of student protest activity of the late 1960s and early 1970s in the USA and elsewhere, no doubt because that activity occurred in contexts where numerous social scientists were available to conduct research. A huge literature ensued, abounding in seemingly contradictory findings, many of which, however, appear to fit into a quite plausible larger pattern, once one takes account of the diversity of the institutions in which protest was studied and of the particular periods in the cycle of late 1960s and early 1970s student protest in which the various studies were conducted.

The earliest student protests of the 1960s occurred in colleges and universities with meritocratic admissions policies and upper middle-class student bodies. The first studies of this period, those by Flacks (1967) of University of Chicago students, suggested that student protest was largely a cognitive manifestation – the response of able students to the perceived iniquities of their political environment. Later analyses of data collected in the same period on similar populations (students at the University of California, Berkeley) suggested a more complex pattern in which some of the activists did seem to have the cognitive strengths and preoccupations that Flacks had argued were the mark of *all* of them, but others appeared to be channelling ego-defensive needs (based in troubled parent–child relations) into their protest behaviour. The students who the later analysts concluded had ego-defensive motivations and those who they concluded were acting out of cognitive needs showed different patterns of protest behaviour, the first directing their activity only on the issues of national and international politics, the second taking part in local reform activities (Block, Haan and Smith 1969).

The psychological correlates of student activism changed over time in the USA, as activism developed from the actions of a few students in the 'elite' universities to a widespread form of behaviour, which at the time of the Nixon administration's incursion into Cambodia and the killing of student protesters at Kent State University manifested itself in the bulk of American college and university campuses. Studies conducted at that time found little in the way of variation in the characteristics of protesters (Dunlap 1970; Peterson and Bilorusky 1971).

Personality, historical context and social background

Variation according to historical context and change over time are so important in determining how personality becomes linked with politics that the map around which this article is organized needs to be expanded, as it is in Figure 24.3, which encompasses the time dimension and differentiates the immediate and remote features of the political environment. Figure 24.3 suggests that the fourth reservation about the utility of studying personality and politics – the claim that social backgrounds are more important than psychological characteristics – is grounded in a confusion which can be readily dissolved. The social backgrounds of political actors (panel 2 of Figure 24.3) influence their actions, but only as mediated by the individual's developing predispositions (panel 3) and the different levels of personality they shape (panels 4, 5 and 6). Thus, to take a final example from the literature on student protest in the 1960s, it was fallacious (as Block, Haan and Smith 1969, pointed out at the time) for Lipset (1968) to argue that because so many student activists were young, middle-class Jews, personality was not an important determinant of activism. To the extent that Jewish background was connected with activism, it had to be part of a causal sequence in which developmental experiences specific to Jews contributed to their psychological orientations. The latter, not Jewish background *per se*, would have been the mediator of behaviour.

The study of how ethnicity, class and other of the so-called background characteristics affect political behaviour is important and highly relevant to (but no substitute for) the study of personality and politics. To the extent that a characteristic becomes part of an actor's personal make-up, it is no longer 'background' – it is an element in the psyche. But evidence of whether background experience distinguishes members of one social group from those of others is grist for political psychologists. Lipset may have been correct in sensing that Jewish political activists of the 1960s had some distinctive qualities that were important for their behaviour, but the observation that many student protesters were Jewish not only fails to prove this, it also forecloses systematic inquiry.

An appropriate programme of inquiry into Lipset's claim would entail specifying the precise psychological dynamics that ostensibly make Jewish protesters distinctive and comparing Jewish and non-Jewish protesters with comparable non-protesters in order to determine whether the imputed patterns existed. If they did, one would want to know whether they resulted from particular developmental histories, whether they had predictable consequences for political behaviour, and why some Jews protested and some did not. Whether a distinctly Jewish psychology of political protest exists is an empirical question, and is part of a broader set of questions that can be asked about how group membership affects personality and political behaviour.

The impact of personality on events

The last of the reservations about the study of personality and politics derives from the view that individuals are not likely to have much impact on events. Such a premise underlies many theories of history. In the nineteenth century the question of whether historical actors have an impact on events was the basis of a fruitless grand controversy, with such social determinists as Herbert Spencer denying the efficacy of historical actors and such 'Great Man' theorists as Thomas Carlyle proclaiming their overriding importance (Kellerman 1986: 3–57). Contemporary leadership theorists typically describe themselves as interactionists, emphasizing the interdependence of leaders and their environments and the contingent nature of the leader's impact on larger events (Burns 1978).

The debate about whether actors can shape events is about the causal chain from personality (panels 4–6 of Figure 24.3), through political responses (panel 9), to future states of the immediate and more remote political and social environment (panels 11 and 12). Claims that particular actors did or did not have an impact on events usually prove to be claims about actor dispensability and action dispensability (Greenstein 1969: 40–6) – that is, about whether the actions of the individuals in question were necessary for the outcome to have occurred or whether the actions were ones that any similarly placed actors would have taken. The second issue is one I have already explored under the heading of personality and environment, but the first requires clarification.

The capacity of actors to shape events is a variable, not a constant. The sources of variation parallel the determinants of success in the game of pool. The number of balls a player will be able to sink is in part a function of the location of the balls on the table. The parallel in politics is the malleability of the political environment (Burke and Greenstein 1989: 24). The second determinant of success in the pool room is the position of the cue ball. This is analogous to the actor's position in the relevant political context. Roosevelt and Gorbachev could not have had an impact from lower-level administrative positions. The third class of variable has the same labels in the games of pool and politics – skill, self-confidence and the other personal requisites of effective performance.

Kinds of personality-and-politics analysis

Every human being is in certain ways like all other human beings, in certain ways more like some human beings than others, and in certain ways unique (Kluckhohn and Murray 1953). Each of these resemblances is reflected in a different kind of personality-and-politics analysis. The universality of human qualities is explored in writings that seek in some broad way to make the connection stated in the tide of Graham Wallas's *Human Nature and Politics* (1908). Sigmund Freud's *Civilization and its Discontents* (1930), Fromm's *Escape from Freedom* (1941), Norman O. Brown's *Life Against Death* (1959) and Herbert Marcuse's *Eros and Civilization* (1966) are notable contributions to this tradition. At their best such works provide fascinating and provocative perspectives on the human condition. Many of them are rich in insights that suggest testable hypotheses.

Because they seek to explain the variable phenomena of political behaviour with a constant, such efforts are not themselves subject to confirmation or disconfirmation. In contrast, it *is* possible to conduct systematic, replicable inquiries into political actors' unique qualities (single-case analysis) and the qualities that make them more like some individuals than others (typological analysis). The ways in which individual and typical political psychology affect the performance of political processes and institutions (aggregation) can also be studied systematically.

Single-case personality analysis is more important in the field of personality and politics than it has come to be in personality psychology generally, because students of politics are concerned with the performance of specific leaders and their impact on events. There have been noteworthy personality-and-politics studies of leaders as diverse in time, culture and the circumstances of their leadership as Martin Luther (Erikson 1958), Louis XII (Marvick 1986), Woodrow Wilson (George and George 1956), Kemal Ataturk (Volkan and Itzkowitz 1984) and Josef Stalin (Tucker 1973), as well as many others. There also have been valuable single-case psychological analyses of figures whose political importance derives from their impact on leaders – for example, George and George's analysis of the influence of Colonel Edward House on Woodrow Wilson (George and George 1956) and Kull's of US defence policy advisers (Kull 1988). In addition, there is a tradition in the field of personality and politics of single case analyses of 'faces in the crowd' – people who are without policy influence but who illustrate in depth the psychological process that can only be examined more superficially in surveys (Riesman and Glazer 1952; Smith, Bruner and White 1956; Lane 1962).

Typological study of political and other actors is of potentially great importance: if political actors fall into types with known characteristics and propensities, the laborious task of analyzing them *de novo* can be obviated, and uncertainty is reduced about how they will perform in particular circumstances. The notion of a psychological *type* can be stretched to include all efforts to categorize and compare the psychology of political actors, even straightforward classifications of the members of a population in terms of whether they are high or low on some trait such as ego strength, self-esteem, or tolerance of ambiguity. The more full-blown political psychology typologies parallel diagnostic categories in medicine, including psychiatry. They identify syndromes – patterns of observable characteristics that reflect identifiable underlying conditions, result from distinctive developmental histories and have predictable consequences.

Of the many studies that employ the first, simpler kind of psychological categorization, the studies by Herbert McClosky and his students are particularly valuable because of their theoretical and methodological sophistication and the importance of the issues they address (McClosky 1967; Di Palma and McClosky 1970; Sniderman 1974; McClosky and Zaller 1984). Political personality typologies of the second, more comprehensive variety go back at least to Plato's account in the eighth and ninth book of *The Republic* of the aristocrat, the democrat, the timocrat and the tyrant – political types that Plato believed were shaped in an intergenerational dialectic of rebellion of sons against their fathers' perceived shortcomings. (For a gloss on Plato's account see Lasswell 1960.) Latter-day typologies that have generated important bodies of literature are the authoritarian, dogmatic and Machiavellian personality classifications (Adorno *et al.* 1950; Rokeach 1960; Christie and Geis 1970). Within political science the best-known personality typology is James David Barber's classification of the character structures of American presidents (Barber 1985). For an alternative approach that focuses on the psychological traits of presidents see Greenstein 2001. (See also George and George 1998: chs 2 and 5.)

Single-case and typological studies alike make inferences about the inner quality of human beings (panels 4, 5 and 6 of Figure 24.3) from outer manifestations – their past and present environments (panels 1, 2, 7 and 8) and the pattern over time of their political responses (panel 9). They then use those inferred constructs to account for the very same kind of phenomena from which they were inferred – responses in situational contexts. The danger of circularity is obvious, but tautology can be avoided by reconstructing personality from some response patterns and using the reconstruction to explain others.

The failure of some investigators to take such pains contributes to the controversial status of the personality-and-politics literature, as does the prevalence of certain other practices. Some biographers, for example, impose diagnostic labels on their subject, rather than presenting a systematic account of the subject's behaviour in disparate circumstances (George 1971). Some typological analysts categorize their subjects without providing the detailed criteria and justifications for doing so. Some analysts of individuals as well as of types have engaged in the fallacy of observing a pattern of behaviour and simply attributing it to a particular developmental pattern, without documenting causality, and perhaps even without providing evidence that the pattern existed. Finally, some analysts commit what might be called the psychologizing and clinical fallacies: they explain behaviour in terms of personality without considering possible situational determinants, or conclude that it is driven by psychopathology without considering other psychological determinants, such as cognition. Both fallacies are evident in the body of literature attributing the high scores of poor blacks and other minorities on the paranoia scale of the Minnesota Multiphasic Personality Inventory (MMPI) to emotional disturbance. The scores appear actually to have reflected cognitively based responses to the vicissitudes of the ghetto environment (Gynther 1972; Newhill 1990).

It is not surprising that some personality-and-politics studies are marked by methodological shortcomings. Certain of the inferences mapped in Figure 24.3 pose intrinsic difficulties. Claims about the determinants of personality characteristics (that is, of the connections between panels 1 and 2 and panels 3–6) are unlikely to be conclusive. Characterizations of personality structures themselves are never wholly persuasive, if only because of the absence of uniformly accepted personality theories with agreed-upon terminologies. Fortunately, the variables depicted in Figure 24.3 that *can* be characterized with great confidence are those closest to and therefore most predictive of behaviour: the environments in which political action occurs (panels 7 and 8) and the patterns that action manifests over time (panels, 9, 10, etc.). Those patterns are themselves variables, and they can be treated as indicators of an important further dimension of personality and politics – *political style*.

Two examples of political biographies that provide impressively comprehensive accounts of the precise patterns of their subjects' behaviour are Walter's (1980) study of the Australian Prime Minister Gough Whitlam and Landis's (1987) of Senator Joseph McCarthy. Richard Christie's studies of the types of people who manifest the Machiavellian syndrome (Christie and Geis 1970) – the characterological proclivity to manipulate others – provide a model of careful measurement and theoretically sophisticated analysis in which contingent relationships are carefully explored. People who score high on tests of Machiavellianism do not differ in their behaviour from non-Machiavellians in all contexts, only in contexts in which their manipulative impulses can be effective – for example, in situations that permit improvisation and in situations requiring face-to-face interaction.

Personality is likely to interest most political scientists only if it has aggregate consequences for political institutions, processes and outcomes. The literature on the aggregate effects of personality on politics is varied because the processes of aggregation are varied. Broadly speaking, political psychology affects the performance of political systems and processes through the activities of members of the public and the deliberations and decision-making of leaders. The impact of mass publics on politics, except through elections and severe perturbations of public opinion, is partial and often elusive. The political impact of leaders and others in the active political stratum is, on the other hand, more generally direct, readily evident, and potentially momentous in its repercussions.

The first efforts to understand the psychology of mass populations go back to the accounts by writers in the ancient world such as Tacitus of the character of the members of remote tribes and nations. Such disquisitions are an antecedent of the vexed post-Second World War national character literature in which often ill-documented ethnographic reports and cultural artifacts such as child-rearing manuals, films and popular fiction were used to draw sweeping conclusions about modal national character traits. That literature came to be known to students of politics mainly because of its methodological shortcomings, but it anticipated later, more systematic studies of political culture (Inkeles and Levinson 1968–9; Inkeles 1983).

By the 1950s, there was broad scholarly consensus that it was inappropriate simply to attribute psychological characteristics to mass populations on the basis of anecdotal or indirect evidence. Direct assessment of publics through survey research became the dominant mode of studying mass populations. Studies like those of McClosky and his associates (McClosky 1967; McClosky and Zaller 1984) provided survey data on basic personality processes such as ego-defences and cognitive styles and how they affect political opinion. But basic personality processes have not been persuasively linked to the aspect of mass behaviour that most clearly and observably has an impact on political institutions and processes – electoral choice. Most members of the general public appear to be too weakly involved in electoral politics for their voting choices to tap deeper psychological roots, and many of those who are involved appear to take their cues from party identifications formed in their early years and from short-run situational stimuli.

If what is commonly thought of as personality is not linked to electoral choice, attitudinal political psychology most definitely is. The literature on electoral choice (Niemi and Weisberg 1984) is too vast to begin to review here, but the research of Kelley (1983) is of particular interest in that it is explicitly aggregative; it reveals the precise distributions of attitudes and beliefs about issues and candidates that were associated with post-Second World War American election outcomes. So is the research of Converse and Pierce (1986), who have convincingly linked certain attributes of the French political system to the distinctive ways members of that nation's electorate orient themselves to political parties.

In contrast to the ambiguous links between mass publics and political outcomes other than in elections, the connections between political decision makers and political outcomes are direct and palpable. Nevertheless, many historical reconstructions of political decision-making are insufficiently specific about which actors in what precise contexts took which actions with what consequences. Sometimes the historical record does not contain the appropriate data. Often, however, the difficulty lies not with the record but with the way in which it has been analyzed.

The questions the analyst needs to ask of the historical record are suggested by the analytic distinctions of *actor* and *action dispensability*: Were the actions a decision maker took those that any individual placed in a comparable context would have taken? That is, were they imposed by the actor's situation? Did those actions make a difference? That is, would the outcome have been the same if they were not taken? Questions of actor dispensability call for examination of the contexts in which the decision makers act. Questions of action dispensability call for reconstructions of the determinants of particular outcomes and assessment of the part particular actors played in them.

A good example of a reconstruction that addresses both questions is the analysis by George and George (1956) of Woodrow Wilson's role in the crisis over ratification of the Versailles Treaty. The intense, uncompromising qualities of Wilson the man, at least in certain kinds of conflicts, are an essential part of any account of the ratification fight. There is abundant evidence that the political context did not impose a course of action on Wilson that would have kept him from achieving his goal of ratification. All that was required was that he accept certain nominal compromises that his supporters urged upon him, pointing out that they had no practical significance. Moreover, Wilson's actions are necessary to explain the outcome. Wilson's supporters were lined up for a favourable ratification vote, but were unprepared to act unless he authorized them to accept mild qualifying language. This he refused to do.

The explanatory logic of propositions about whether an individual's actions and characteristics were consequential in some episode is that of counter-factual reasoning. This is the only available alternative in analyses of single events to the quantitative analysis that would be called for if data existed on large numbers of comparable episodes. Counter-factual reasoning is not falsifiable, but it can be systematic. To be so it must be explicit and addressed to bounded questions – not conundrums about remote contingencies. 'Was Lyndon Johnson's action necessary for the 1965 American escalation in Vietnam to have occurred?' is an example of a question that is susceptible to investigation (Burke and Greenstein 1989). 'If Cleopatra's nose had been an inch longer, how would world history have been changed?' is an example of one that is not.

Personality and political psychology more generally affect political processes not only through the actions taken by leaders more or less on their own, but also through group processes such as the collective suspension of reality testing manifested in what Irving Janis (1982) has characterized as groupthink. Groupthink occurs in highly cohesive decision-making groups. The members of such groups sometimes become so committed to their colleagues they more or less unconsciously suspend their own critical faculties in order to preserve group harmony. Janis, who is scrupulous about setting forth the criteria for establishing whether a group has engaged in groupthink, analyzes a number of historical episodes (the most striking example being the Bay of Pigs) in which a defective decision-making process appears to have led able policy makers to make decisions on the basis of flawed assumptions and defective information. To the extent that groupthink is a purely collective phenomenon, emerging from group interaction, it is a manifestation of social psychology rather than personality psychology. But, as Janis suggests, personality probably contributes to groupthink in that some personalities are more likely than others to suspend their critical capacities in group settings.

Concluding remarks

Political institutions and processes operate through human agency. It would be remarkable if they were *not* influenced by the properties that distinguish one individual from another. In examining that influence, this article has emphasized the logic of inquiry. It does not constitute a comprehensive review of the literature. For a variety of useful reviews and compendia, readers should consult Greenstein and Lerner (1971), Knutson (1973), Stone (1981), Herman (1986) and Simonton (1990).

To the extent that this article brings out possible pitfalls in studies of personality and politics, its message to cautious scholars may seem to be: find pastures that can be more easily cultivated. Even daring scholars might conclude that the prospects for the systematic study of personality and politics are too remote to justify the investment of scholarly time and effort. Nothing in this article is meant to support such conclusions. In a parable on the shortcomings of scientific opportunism, Kaplan (1964: 11, 16–17) relates the story of a drunkard who lost his keys in a dark alley and is found searching for them under a street lamp, declaring, 'It's lighter here'. The drunkard's search is a poor model. If the connections between the personalities of political actors and their political behaviour are obscure, all the more reason to illuminate them.

References

Adorno, T. W., Frenkel-Brunswick, E., Levinson, D. J. and Sanford, R. N. (1950) *The Authoritarian Personality*, New York: Harper.

Allen, V. L. (1975) 'Social support for nonconformity', *Advances in Social Psychology* 8: 1–43.

Allport, G. W. (1937) *Personality: A Psychlogical Interpretation*, New York: Holt.

Asch, S. E. (1956) 'Studies of independence and conformity: "A minority of one versus a unanimous majority"', *Psychological Monographs* 70: 9.

Barber, J. D. (1985) *The Presidential Character: Predicting Performance in the White House*, 3rd edn, Englewood Cliffs, NJ: Prentice-Hall.

Block, J. H., Haan, N. and Smith, M. B. (1969) 'Socialization correlates of student activism', *Journal of Social Issues* 25: 143–77.

Brown, N. O. (1959) *Life Against Death*, Middletown, CT: Wesleyan University Press.

Browning, R. P. and Jacobs, H. (1964) 'Power motivation and the political personality', *Public Opinion Quarterly* 24: 75–90.

Budner, S. (1962) 'Intolerance of ambiguity as a personality variable', *Journal of Personality* 30: 22–50.

Burke, J. P. and Greenstein, F. I. (1989) *How Presidents Test Reality: Decisions on Vietnam, 1954 and 1965*, New York: Russell Sage Foundation.

Burns, J. M. (1978) *Leadership*, New York: Harper & Row.

Campbell, D. T. (1963) 'Social attitudes and other acquired behavioral dispositions', in S. Koch (ed.) *Psychology: A Study of a Science*, vol. 6, New York: McGraw-Hill.

Christie, R. and Geis, F. L. (1970) *Studies in Machiavellianism*, New York: Academic Press.

Clarke, J. W. (1990) *On Being Mad or Merely Angry: John W. Hinckley Jr and Other Dangerous People*, Princeton: Princeton University Press.

Converse, P. E. and Pierce, R. (1986) *Political Representation in France*, Cambridge, MA: Harvard University Press.

Davies, A. F. (1980) *Skills, Outlooks and Passions: A Psychoanalytic Contribution to the Study of Politics*, Cambridge: Cambridge University Press.

Di Palma, G. and McClosky, H. (1970) 'Personality and conformity: the learning of political attitudes', *American Political Science Review* 64: 1054–73.

Dunlap, R. (1970) 'Radical and conservative student activists: a comparison of family backgrounds', *Pacific Sociological Review* 13: 171–81.

Endler, N. S. (1981) 'Persons, situations, and their interactions', in A. I. Rabin, J. Aronoff, A. M. Barclay and R. A. Zucker (eds) *Further Explorations in Personality*, New York: John Wiley.

Erikson, E. H. (1958) *Young Man Luther: A Study in Psychoanalysis and History*, New York: Norton.

Flacks, R. (1967) 'The liberated generation: an exploration of the roots of student protest', *Journal of Social Issues* 25: 52–75.

Freud, S. (1930) 'Civilization and its Discontents', in J. Stratchey, *The Standard Edition of the Complete Psychological Works of Sigmund Freud*, vol. 17, London: Hogarth Press.

Fromm, E. (1941) *Escape from Freedom*, New York: Rinehart.

George, A. L. (1971) 'Some uses of dynamic psychology in political biography: case materials on Woodrow Wilson', in F. I. Greenstein and M. Lerner (eds) *A Source Book for the Study of Personality and Politics*, Chicago: Markham.

George, A. L. and George, J. L. (1956) *Woodrow Wilson and Colonel House: A Personality Study*, New York: John Day (reprinted by Dover, 1964).

—— (1998) *Presidential Personality and Performance*, New York: Westview Press.

Greenstein, F. I. (1969) *Personality and Politics: Problems of Evidence, Inference and Conceptualization*, Chicago: Markham; Princeton University Press 1987.

—— (1975) 'Personality and polities', in F. I. Greenstein and N. W. Polsby (eds) *The Handbook of Political Science: Micropolitical Theory*, vol. 2, Reading, MA: Addison-Wesley.

—— (2001) *The Presidential Difference: Leadership Style from FDR to Clinton with an Afterword on George W. Bush*, Princeton, NJ: Princeton University Press.

Greenstein, F. I. and Lerner, M. (1971) *A Source Book for the Study of Personality and Politics*, Chicago: Markham.

Gynther, M. (1972) 'White norms and Black MMPIs: a prescription for discrimination', *Psychological Bulletin* 78: 386–402.

Hall, C. S. and Lindzey, G. (eds) (1970) *Theories of Personality*, 2nd edn, New York: John Wiley.

Herman, M. G. (ed.) (1986) *Political Psychology*, San Francisco: Jossey-Bass.

Inkeles, I. (1983) *Exploring Individual Modernity*, New York: Columbia University Press.

Inkeles, I. and Levinson, D. J. (1968–9) 'National character: the study of modal personality', in G. Lindzey and E. Aronson (eds.) *The Handbook of Social Psychology*, vol. 4, 2nd edn, Reading, MA: Addison-Wesley.

Janis, I. L. (1982) *Groupthink: Psychological Studies of Policy Decisions and Fiascos*, 2nd edn, Boston: Houghton Mifflin.

Jervis, R. (1976) *Perception and Misperception in International Politics*, Princeton: Princeton University Press.

Jervis, R., Lebow R. N. and Stein, J. (1985) *Psychology and Deterrence*, Baltimore: Johns Hopkins University Press.

Kaplan, A. (1964) *The Conduct of Inquiry: Methodology for Behavioral Sciences*, San Francisco: Chandler.

Katz, D. (1960) 'The functional approach to the study of attitudes', *Public Opinion Quarterly* 24: 163–204.

Katz, I. and Benjamin, L. (1960) 'The effects of authoritarianism on biracial work groups', *Journal of Abnormal and Social Psychology* 61: 448–56.

Kellerman, B. (ed.) (1986) *Political Leadership: A Source Book*, Pittsburgh: University of Pittsburgh Press.

Kelley, S. K., Jr (1983) *Interpreting Elections*, Princeton: Princeton University Press.

Kluckhohn, C. and Murray, H. A. (1953) 'Personality formation: the determinants', in C. Kluckhohn and H. A. Murray (eds) *Personality in Nature, Society and Culture*, 2nd edn, New York: Knopf.

Knutson, J. N. (1973) *Handbook of Political Psychology*, San Francisco: Jossey-Bass.

Kull, S. (1988) *Minds at War: Nuclear Reality and the Inner Conflict of Defense Policymakers*, New York: Basic Books.

Landis, M. (1987) *Joseph McCarthy: The Politics of Chaos*, Cranbury, NJ: Associated University Presses.

Lane, R. E. (1962) *Political Ideology: Why the Common Man Believes What He Does*, New York: Free Press of Glencoe.

Lasswell, H. D. (1930) *Psychopathology and Politics*, Chicago: University of Chicago Press.

—— (1960) 'Political character and constitution', *Psychoanalysis and Psychoanalytic Review* 46: 1–18.

Lasswell, H. D. and Kaplan, A. (1950) *Power and Society: A Framework for Political Inquiry*, New Haven: Yale University Press.

Lau, R. R. and Sears, D. O. (eds) (1986) *Political Cognition*, Hillsdale, NJ: Lawrence Erlbaum Associates.

Lewin, K. (1936) *Principles of Topological Psychology*, New York: McGraw-Hill.

Lipset, S. M. (1968) 'The activists: a profile', in D. Bell and I. Kristol (eds) *Confrontation: The Student Rebellion and the Universities*, New York: Basic Books.

McClosky, H. (1967) 'Personality and attitude correlates of foreign policy orientations', in J. N. Rosenau (ed.) *Domestic Sources of Foreign Policy*, New York: Free Press of Glencoe.

McClosky, H. and Zaller, J. (1984) *The American Ethos: Public Attitudes Toward Capitalism and Democracy*, Cambridge, MA: Harvard University Press.

Magnusson, D. and Endler, N. S. (eds) (1977) *Personality at the Crossroads: Current Issues in Interactional Psychology*, Hillsdale, NJ: Lawrence Erlbaum Associates.

Marcus, G. E., Neuman, R. and MacKuen, M. (2000) *Affective Intelligence and Political Judgement*, Chicago: University of Chicago Press.

Marcuse, H. (1966) *Eros and Civilization*, rev. edn, Boston: Beacon.

Marvick, E. W. (1986) *Louis XII: The Making of a King*, New Haven: Yale University Press.

Masters, R. D. (1989) *The Nature of Politics*, New Haven: Yale University Press.

Murray, H. A. (1968) 'Personality: contemporary viewpoints: components of an evolving personological system', *International Encyclopedia of the Social Sciences*, vol. 12, New York: Macmillan.

Newhill, C. E. (1990) 'The role of culture in the development of paranoid symptomatology', *American Journal of Orthopsychiatry* 60: 176–85.

Niemi, R. and Weisberg, H. E. (1984) *Controversies in Voting Behavior*, 2nd edn, Washington, DC: Congressional Quarterly Press.

Park, B. E. (1986) *The Impact of Illness on World Leaders*, Philadelphia: University of Pennsylvania Press.

Pervin, L. A. and Lewis, M. (eds) (1978) *Perspectives on Interactional Psychology*, New York: Plenum.

Peterson, R. E. and Bilorusky, J. A. (1971) *May 1970: The Campus Aftermath of Cambodia and Kent State*, New York: Carnegie Foundation for the Advancement of Teaching.

Pratkanis, A. R., Breckler, S. J. and Greenwald, A. G. (eds) (1989) *Attitude Structure and Function*, Hillsdale, NJ: Lawrence Erlbaum Associates.

Riesman, D. and Glazer, N. (1952) *Faces in the Crowd: Individual Studies of Character and Politics*, New Haven: Yale University Press.

Rokeach, M. (1960) *The Open and the Closed Mind: Investigations into the Nature of Belief Systems and Personality Systems*, New York: Basic Books.

Simon, H. A. (1985) 'Human nature in politics: the dialogue of psychology with political science', *American Political Science Review* 79: 292–304.

Simonton, D. K. (1990) 'Personality and polities', in L. A. Pervin (ed.) *Handbook of Personality: Theory and Research*, New York: Guilford.

Smith, M. B. (1968) 'A map for the study of personality and polities', *Journal of Social Issues* 24: 15–28.

Smith, M. B., Bruner, J. S. and White, R. W. (1956) *Opinions and Personality*, New York: John Wiley.

Sniderman, P. M. (1974) *Personality and Democratic Politics*, Berkeley: University of California Press.

Stone, W. F. (1981) 'Political psychology: a Whig history', in S. L. Long (ed.) *The Handbook of Political Behavior*, vol. 1, New York: Plenum.

Stone, W. F. and Schaffner, P. E. (1988) *The Psychology of Politics*, 2nd edn, New York: Springer Verlag.

Tucker, R. C. (1965) 'The dictator and totalitarianism', *World Politics* 17: 555–83.

—— (1973) *Stalin as Revolutionary, 1879–1929: A Short Study in History and Personality*, New York: Norton.

'T Hart, P., Stern, E.K, and Sundelius, B. (1997) *Beyond Groupthink: Political Group Dynamics and Foreign Policy*, Ann Arbor, MI: University of Michigan Press.

Vertzberger, Y. Y. I. (1990) *The World in their Minds: Information Processing, Cognition, and Perception in Foreign Policy Decisionmaking*, Stanford: Stanford University Press.

Volkan, V. D. and Itzkowitz, N. (1984) *The Immortal Ataturk: A Psychobiography*, Chicago: University of Chicago Press.

Wallas, G. (1908) *Human Nature and Politics*, 3rd edn, New York: Crofts, 1921.

Walter, J. (1980) *The Leader: A Political Biography of Gough Whitlam*, St Lucia, Queensland: University of Queensland Press.

25

INTEREST GROUPS

Ivar Bleiklie

Definitions

In modern, complex societies a great variety of organizations links the individual to public institutions. Interest groups may be defined as groups that consciously try to move public policy in particular directions. This distinguishes them in the first place from groups whose members share certain attitudes, but are not concerned with public policy. The concept of interest group is defined broadly and it encompasses corporations, foundations, business and professional associations, labour unions, as well as environmental and consumer groups. It covers not only what one might call interest groups proper, which have as their purpose the enhancement of the interests of their members. The concept also covers collectivities that have a more general outlook and seek to promote values or the interests of society at large. Typical representatives of the former type are business associations and labour unions, whereas typical representatives of the latter are environmental and consumer groups. Nevertheless, interest groups can be distinguished from other social collectivities that mediate citizen preferences to policy makers such as political parties and social movements. Since many of these collectivities, e.g. corporations and foundations, have no members and are not really groups, some prefer the term 'organized interests' to 'interest groups'. Although interest groups often have informal or formal connections with **political parties** (pp. 381–98), they are different from political parties in that they do not nominate their own candidates in order to run the government. Compared to **social movements** (pp. 616–27) they have a higher degree of formal organization. However, in practice the difference between these three types of collectivities is gradual.

Types of interest groups

Interest groups in a modern sense have, under a variety of labels, at least two kinds of roots. One is ideological and based on the narrowing down of the concept of interests by the eighteenth century philosophers of the enlightenment to material and rational interests, as opposed to and counteracting the passions (Hirschman 1977). The second root is the proliferation of voluntary associations that started in the Western world from the beginning of the nineteenth century following the American and French revolutions.

Although democratization made legally possible the establishment of most voluntary associations that today make up the modern systems of interest media-

370

tion in the Western world, other processes were important triggering factors. Industrialization, urbanization and rising state interventionism of the emerging social and welfare states in the nineteenth and twentieth centuries brought with them a combination of new alignments of economic interests, new social problems, new perceptions of such problems as ones that demanded and lent themselves to some kind of action, and new capacities for dealing with the problems, be it through state intervention or voluntary organization. Waves of establishment of associations concerned with broad social issues, protection of single interests, and economic and professional interests thus followed. Some of the new organizations grew out of previous organizational forms such as premodern guilds or professional associations. In any case the proliferation meant that the absolute number of organizations grew, that the scope of the organizations increased from municipalities and regions into national level organizations. During the last decades of the twentieth century there has been an increasing number of interest organizations established on a transnational, even global level, in areas such as disaster relief and environmental protection (Brown *et al.* 2000). In the area of global economic policy, the anti-globalization movement that evolved at the last turn of century has so far been more engaged in social protest than in interest group politics.

Very crudely one may distinguish between at least six categories of interest groups depending on what kind of interests they organize.

1   Organizations of business, commerce and industry, and   2   labour unions are the two major interest groups of the industrial societies. Many of these organizations have developed out of earlier commercial guilds or professional associations of craftspeople and workers. Their development into efficient labour unions depended on their ability to overcome traditional fragmentation along lines of regions as well as trades, and establish themselves as national unions. This took place from the late nineteenth and into the twentieth century, but the outcomes varied considerably. However it also made a difference whether they finally evolved one coordinating peak association (Scandinavia, UK) or whether there were two (e.g. Spain) or an even more fragmented situation like in the USA. The formation of employers' associations was often a direct response to unionizing and institutionalization of labour relations in order to coordinate negotiations with labour unions. Later with the rise of a service economy, employees and employers in banking, insurance, small business and public administration have organized separately.

3   Agricultural interest groups were in most cases organized during the last half of the nineteenth century. Although defending agricultural interests against industry and the adverse effects of the development of a market based agricultural economic sector, agricultural interest groups normally reflected in various ways the divisions between crop sectors and regions of the agricultural economy. Usually the interests of larger producers dominated compared to those of the smaller ones. In countries with a greater number of dependent small peasants and farm labourers agricultural interests have also been organized in labour unions and social movements.

4   Professional associations make in many ways the most classical examples of interest groups. They often cater to functions that previously were taken care of by guilds, brotherhoods, estates or clubs, particularly in regulating access to key professions. Medical associations, bar associations, associations of civil engineers make classical examples of professional associations. During the twentieth century occupational groups like teachers, nurses and social workers have organized professional associations, particularly if they did not unionize within the labour movement, as has been the case in several southern European countries.

5   What is here labelled single interest groups covers a wide variety of organized interests. The nature of such single interests varies according to: a) the extent to which they are advancing the personal interests of its own members or are contributing to the public good and b) the extent to which the group legitimizes its activities in terms of some overarching ideology or not. In the category that focuses on member interests one may for instance put sports associations and other groups – such as automobile or hunting associations – that struggle for exclusive or commercialized interests of their members. One category that has been gaining strength in the last decades includes a rising number of groups promoting the interests of patients with particular diagnoses and thus reflects the expansion, growing importance and growing financial needs of modern health care. Among public interest groups we may find groups fighting for civil liberties, human rights, the environment and general consumer interests. Among the more ideologically based groups we may find everything from temperance organizations, feminist groups, anti-abortion and pro-choice groups or human rights groups. In practice it is often difficult to distinguish clearly between interest groups along the lines indicated above. Groups that by others are regarded as protectors of their members' interests may claim that they are defending or at least contributing to the public good. Whether a group is ideological in the sense that the term is used above may depend on the degree to which the interests that are promoted have a high degree of legitimacy and are taken for granted or are controversial and therefore need to be justified in terms of an overarching set of ideas. Groups that combine the ideological motivation and promote public interest have made themselves felt at the transnational level from the late twentieth century on. Amnesty International and Greenpeace make typical examples here.

6   Welfare associations also make up a heterogeneous category. They often combine professional interests with those of public authorities (mostly cities and counties), religious interests of churches, religious communities and other private agents in the welfare arena. Early examples of this category were organizations or charities that in the nineteenth century started to provide relief for the poor. As the role of the welfare state has been questioned since the 1980s and doubts have been raised both with regard to its efficiency, its affordability and its future, the voluntary sector has emerged as an increasingly important actor in welfare provision and politics (Kuhnle 2000). The increased importance of NGOs has not only taken place in the national welfare sectors. Both in national development aid programs and in connection with international

relief operations national and transnational NGOs, such as Red Cross/Red Crescent, Caritas and Médecins sans Frontières, are important players.

Functions

From a political science perspective the crucial question about interest groups is what kind of link it is that they provide between citizens and government. First, do they represent a valuable addition to the regular democratic institutions or an alternative to and possibly a threat against them? Second, what kind of citizens and interests do interest groups represent? Do they represent a cross-section of society or do they act on behalf of the privileged few? The answer to the first question is that interest groups are engaged as intermediaries in a two-way process of communication. They articulate interests and provide information that helps politicians design public policies; they also seek to persuade politicians to choose a preferred course of action. But interest groups also keep their members informed about what government is doing, educating them about the political process and cultivating support. In practice it is often difficult to distinguish clearly between these different functions – between the provision of information and attempts at persuasion, and between promotion of member interests in the political system and helping government in educating and persuading group members to accept government policies.

The answer to the second question is tightly related to the first. One important issue concerns membership and turns on the proportion of the citizenry that belongs to an interest group. A much higher proportion of the citizenry is organized in the Scandinavian countries where most employees belong to some union or professional association, than in Greece or Italy. Another issue turns on what kind of interests are articulated. A citizen may be concerned about public policy in a number of different capacities or roles; be it as a taxpayer, a consumer of public services (health, education), member of a local community, as employer or employee or as law-abiding citizen. Although membership in interest groups may generally be equitably distributed in a society, it does not follow that the groups automatically raise the issues that most citizens consider important (Wilson 1995). However, one of the arguments raised in favour of interest groups emphasizes that they are an important supplement to political parties. Because major political parties often have programs that are based on broad compromises between a wide range of different interests, interests groups serve an important function in that they both broaden the range of interests and represent specific interests more efficiently than the major parties are able to do. Finally, interests change over time and the degree of permeability of the political system to new interests may be important to its capacity to act efficiently on the preferences of its citizens as they develop and change (Olsen 1983). Thus interest groups may enter into close alliances with government agencies and establish a coalition that exercises a virtual monopoly over policy making in certain sectors and thereby make it highly resistant to change of any kind whether it be new points of view or new actors that are affected by the policies in question. Business associations and trade unions have thus been important in the formulation of economic policies in many countries since the middle of the twentieth century, particularly in Scandinavia. Conversely interest groups, such as environmental organizations, may be effective vehicles for bringing new issues on the political agenda and weakening existing coalitions.

The actual functions of interest groups vary across sectors as well as across nations with regard to how numerous and active they are, how they relate to the political system and their own members. There is also considerable cross-national variation with regard to how integrated or fragmented systems of interest representation are. Austria and Sweden are the classical examples of integrated and centralized systems. In contrast business associations in Netherlands are divided along religious lines, whereas in Belgium, business associations are divided along regional lines and unions along religious and political lines. Different types of interest groups vary also as to their relative strength and political power. Business associations and labour unions, particularly in highly centralized systems have usually considerably more resources and possibilities to influence policies than other types of interest groups, such as, for instance, single interest groups. Yet it is probably a common characteristic of most democratic countries that groups representing economic producer interests in one way or another are well represented, be it through peak associations, associations representing certain sectors of the economy, branches of industry or through individual corporations.

Patterns of interest group organization

Political science literature on the role of interest groups in the policy process is of a relatively recent date. In the first half of the twentieth century American political scientists wrote on the impact of 'pressure groups' whereas European studies of interest groups first started after the Second World War. Although European studies of interest groups at first were clearly influenced by American predecessors, the European experience with interest groups was different from the American one with considerable variation across Europe. Studies of European interest groups therefore led to a perspective that differed from the traditional American one. The differences between the perspectives had to do with the fact that interest groups interact with one another and with the different legislative and executive branches of government in nationally distinct ways. These patterns of interest mediation are usually presented in the literature in terms of two main models that make opposite poles between which actual systems oscillate. The poles are liberal market-orientated pluralism and corporatism or neo-corporatism, as opposed to the authoritarian state-corporatism that characterized fascist political systems between the two World Wars. A pluralist system is one in which membership in interest groups is voluntary and where several groups compete for members and access to government agencies in the various policy sectors. Pluralists assume therefore that power is widely distributed and that different centers of power keep one another in check (Dahl 1961). In contrast, corporatists assume that there are a few, small groups of power holders who determine political outcomes in society (Schmitter and Lehmbruch 1979; Cawson 1983; Grant 1985). As defined by Philippe Schmitter corporatism is a system where one organization is granted a monopoly to represent the interests of an affected party in a policy sector, where membership (*de facto* or *de jure*) is compulsory and where groups are organized in a hierarchy so that, e.g. a union representing workers within a branch of industry is a subunit of the bigger union that represents all industrial workers, which again is a subunit of the general workers' union. In exchange for the representational monopoly interest groups have to accept certain limitations in their selection of leaders and in terms of what kinds of demands and support they express in relation to government (Schmitter and Lehmbruch 1979).

The pure models of pluralism as well as of corporatism hardly exist in the real world. What can be observed in actual politics are systems in which characteristics of both models are present to varying extent. The predominance of pluralistic or corporatist patterns of interest mediation varies not only across nations, but also across policy sectors. The United States, particularly during the Progressive Era around the late nineteenth and early twentieth century, has been held up as an example of a pluralist system. However, Robert Dahl's study of local democracy in the USA during the 1950s still serves as a classical rendition of pluralist democracy (Dahl 1961). Sweden and Austria are counted as classical examples of neo-corporatist systems. However, the form of corporatism which has characterized Western European countries after 1945, has been portrayed as a form of pluralist politics, and concepts like 'corporate pluralism' (Rokkan 1966) and 'social pluralism' (Schmitter 1974) have been coined to indicate situations where major interest organizations like labour unions and business associations have access to important decision arenas, but where no one organization has a monopoly on power so that a measure of competition between organizations exists. Additionally, although there may exist a strong pressure for workers or businesses within a particular sector to join the major organizations, membership is usually voluntary at least in principle. If the systems in most European countries are characterized by a certain amount of pluralism, the American system is vice versa characterized by certain corporatist characteristics. The concept of 'iron triangles' has been used to pinpoint situations where subcommittee legislators, bureaucratic agencies and interest groups control the policy process in a certain area in a pattern of interest mediation that comes close to the classical 'tripartite' arrangements between industry, labour and the state in corporatist systems. Such triangles have been observed in the USA until the 1990s (McCool 1994).

The two patterns usually have been associated with different types of interaction between government and interest groups. Pluralist patterns have tended to be characterized by relatively fluid relations and lobbying, directed more often than not towards legislators. Corporatist patterns have been made up by more stable, regular, and sometimes semi permanent committees and other forms of consultation with actors who are considered legitimately affected parties. These structures have served as arenas for representatives from bureaucratic agencies and interest groups. Whereas lobbying first and foremost seeks to influence policy decisions, committee participation and other forms of consultation involve both agenda setting and policy formulation as well as policy implementation.

Pluralism reached a peak in the USA a century ago, and corporatism culminated in the Scandinavian and other European countries during the 1970s. After a period of growth in corporate arrangements and a growing influence of labour unions and employers' associations in a number of countries in central Europe (Austria, Germany) and Scandinavia, the trend was reversed during the 1980s. The rise of neo-liberalism and managerialism after 1980 has been taken as an indication that the role of corporatist arrangements and the influence of employee interests were weakening. However, the actual role played by corporate arrangements can safely be assumed to vary considerably both cross-nationally and cross-sectorally. The differences between a presumably pluralist USA and corporatist European countries seem to have diminished. The growing importance of the European Union furthermore represents a new level of interest group politics where lobbying plays a prominent part. These observations suggested to many in the 1980s both the possibility of some kind of convergence and more variation and fluidity in interest group mediation than what the two models of pluralism and corporatism could accommodate. This meant that further conceptual development was called for.

The term 'policy network' was accordingly originally coined in order to account for a situation that seemed to be characterized by less stability and clear-cut patterns in the forms of interest mediation. It acts as a metaphor, a generic label so to speak, for the different types of state/interest group relationships that exist in the policy process (Dowding 1995; Raab 1994; Jordan and Schubert 1992; Rhodes and Marsh 1992). There is still much confusion, and no consensus, as to exactly what the different types of relationships are. In addition, the range of network members conducting these relationships is wide, including governmental and nongovernmental actors and organizations. A number of attempts have been made in order develop typologies or taxonomies of policy networks. Reviewing the policy networks literature Van Waarden (1992) found 38 characteristics that could be used to identify 11 different types of policy networks. The characteristics have proved extremely difficult to apply in empirical analysis however, and Rhodes and Marsh's (1992) suggestion to conceptualize different types of policy networks along a continuum, with 'policy community' and 'issue networks' at the two opposing ends, has gained wider acceptance. The criteria used in their analysis are membership, integration, resources and power. A 'policy community' is thus characterized by its limited membership, frequent interaction, shared basic values, all participants having a resource base and the ability to deliver their members' support, and a relatively equal power distribution among the network members. On the opposite end of the continuum is the 'issue network', characterized by a large and/or wide range of affected interests, fluctuations in contacts, access, and level of agreement, unequal resource distribution combined with varying abilities to deliver member support, and unequal power distribution among the group members. Corporatist arrangements lean towards the 'policy community' side of the Rhodes and Marsh continuum. The loosely coupled networks of decision makers in 'issue networks' constitute a pattern that resembles more the pluralist pattern of interest mediation. Although seen by many as a promising theoretical development, the policy network concept is still more of a metaphor than a precisely defined theoretical concept. Considering both the variations across countries and the way in which the relationship between state and interest groups has changed, an approach that allows for greater variety in the organizational expressions of such relationships seems to be called for. It still remains to be seen to what extent the concept can add theoretically to the analysis of interest mediation.

Theoretical assumptions

Theoretical assumptions about interest group behaviour and interest mediation in political science have mainly been of two types and one may distinguish crudely between the following explanatory models. One is the 'rational model' and the other the 'natural system' model (Wilson 1995). The rational model assumes that organizations are collectively orientated to the attainment of a specific purpose; its ends are given or can be identified, its internal processes turn on decision-making, and its performance is judged by standards of efficiency and effectiveness. Its ideal form is the classical model of the business enterprise as portrayed by Olson (1965). The natural system model assumes that the organization operates like a social system in which goal attainment may be one of several functions. System maintenance or organizational survival is a central objective and determines what objectives an organization seeks to reach (Scott 1981). One version of this perspective is developed further in political science by neo-institutionalists. Their emphasis is on organizations as normative orders where behaviour is guided by deeply entrenched perceptions of reality and shared systems of norms and habits (March and Olsen 1989).

In order to illustrate the assumptions the models make about interest mediation one may distinguish between two main classes of ideas that, can be applied to the topic (March and Olsen 1989, 1994). With exchange theories and theories of rational choice, one may assume that interest group behaviour is the outcome of interest maximizing and exchange relationships. Interest mediation and its effect on public policy may thus be traced back to conscious design and purposive action. Interest group behaviour is accordingly understood as adaptation to changing environments and as determined by exogenous factors. Different environments typically explain why outcomes vary, and internal processes become of less importance. How such processes actually are triggered is, by the same token, given little attention as the answer is implied by the analysis. Changing resource bases and strategies would be the key to understanding interest group behaviour and its influence on public policy.

By contrast, norm-orientated institutional approaches assume that behaviour is rule driven rather than preference driven. Action is understood in terms of whether it is perceived as appropriate or not. The emphasis is thus on whether or not action conforms to formal or informal rules and whether it undermines or reinforces group identities (March and Olsen 1989, 1994). Although interest group behaviour according to this latter perspective might be the result of adaptation to changing environmental conditions, there are several reasons why it often is better understood in different terms. One main reason is that the concepts of organization and environment tend to be ambiguous and fuzzy. Therefore, it is often difficult to establish the clear, unambiguous concepts of 'organization' and 'environment' that are presumed by the rationalist kind of analysis. If for instance policies are run by 'iron triangles' (politicians, top civil servants and interest group leaders) there is no self evident answer to the question of who the actors are: the triangle itself or the participating organizations. When the causal knowledge of ends and means is uncertain, one must be open to the possibility that policy making may be driven by rule-orientated as well as calculating goal-orientated behaviour. According to this perspective the following proposition is particularly relevant. Interest group behaviour and interest mediation are not so much a question of adaptation to changing environmental conditions, as an outcome of changing beliefs about the nature of a given policy field and the way in which it relates to the rest of society. The production and diffusion of such beliefs thus make an important focus of the analysis.

Still, the most common assumption about interest mediation is that it is characterized by rather static, structural arrangements and by goal-orientated behaviour
(Atkinson and Coleman 1992; John and Cole 1997; Knoke *et al.* 1996; Raab 1994;
Rhodes and Marsh 1992; Richardson 1997). However, these presumptions do not
necessarily apply to interest groups, or to policy networks. It has been suggested to
combine the two main approaches within more eclectic frameworks that accommodate a variety of motives and a more dynamic conceptualization of interest
mediation. This requires a broader conception of 'interest' to include both economic
and non-economic interests and a broader conception of organizations that includes
both the instrumental rational aspect and its function as a normative order.

The implications of these models as to how interest mediation is shaped by organizational behaviour are straightforward. If rational action is the driving force of the
policy process, the assumption follows that interest mediation takes place under
conditions where it is the outcome of power plays among actors who are involved in
the process. The outcome depends on the positions they hold, the resources they
control, the coalitions they make and the bargains they are able to strike. Policy
variation across policy sectors, nations and over time can be explained in this
perspective as the outcome of how the preferences of the members of the dominant
coalition determine the outcome.

If institutionally shaped norm-orientated behaviour drives the policy process, the
model assumes that interest mediation is the result of a process of adaptation
between existing norms and values and new arrangements. The outcome thus
depends on what values and norms the actors identify with and feel obliged by.
Furthermore it depends on what the prevailing authority patterns are like, how the
actors adapt their behaviour to conform with current norms in a mutual process of
adaptation and how they reinterpret their values in order to accommodate new
arrangements mandated by current policies. Policy variation can be explained as the
outcome of what the shared norms are that define the community of decision
makers.

Bearing this in mind, two kinds of processes may explain variation in patterns of
interest mediation: a) the constellation of actors and thereby the policy preferences
of those actors who make up a policy regime; and b) hegemonic values and normative conceptions that are shared by all (or at least the dominant coalition of) actors
in question. *Actor-preference* driven processes and *value-structure* driven processes
are not mutually exclusive. An eclectic approach assumes that actual interest group
behaviour usually does not fall clearly into one of those two categories, but that
some peculiar mix characterizes each process and makes individual processes distinguishable from one another. This should not be taken to mean that the two kinds of
drivers are alternatives in the sense that strong preferences come at the expense of
normative strength and vice versa. Actual interest mediation may be characterized
by a combination of strongly preference-driven and strongly value-driven processes.
Rather than arranging themselves neatly along one dimension, therefore, we are
likely to find that unique combinations of characteristics measured along a number
of dimensions can distinguish specific processes of interest group mediation.

Combining the major approaches to better understand interest group behaviour
may be helpful to empirical research in two connections. It should be helpful to
understanding changes in systems of interest mediation and interest group behaviour

and it should help to understand differences in interest group processes comparatively in order to identify policy variation over time, between policy areas or even different polities.

An eclectic framework thus recognizes the coexistence and potential tension between the rational and the norm-orientated models and takes into account that both may be operating at the same time. It emphasizes, therefore, the tension between what Becher and Kogan (1992) call organic growth and radical change. Furthermore it suggests that, changes in patterns of interest mediation that are the product of consciously designed policies that result in radical change are not the only form of change that needs to be explained. The alternative possibility is a process of gradual change where new structures and values result in new behavioural patterns that are grafted onto established arrangements in a process of meandering and sedimentation (Bleiklie 2000). These two explanatory foci may also supplement one another, *ceteris paribus*, in the following sense. The more macroscopic the scope and the longer the time frame, the more relevant will the relatively stable structural arrangements be for explaining patterns of behaviour. The more microscopic the scope and the shorter the time frame, the more relevant will choices and strategies made by individual actors be for explaining the outcome of a given policy process.

References

Atkinson, M. M. and Coleman, W. D. (1992) 'Policy Networks, Policy Communities and the Problems of Governance' *Governance*, 5 (2): 154–80.

Becher, T, and Kogan, M. (1992) *Process and Structure in Higher Education* (2nd edition). London: Routledge.

Bleiklie, I. (2000) 'Policy Regimes and Policy Making', in M. Kogan, M. Bauer, I. Bleiklie and M. Henkel (eds) *Transforming Higher Education. A Comparative Study*, London and Philadelphia: Jessica Kingsley.

Brown, L. D., Khagram, S., Moore M. K. and Frumkin P. (2000) 'Globalization, NGOs, and Multisectoral Relations', in J. S. Nye and J. D. Donahue (eds) *Governance in a Globalizing World*, Washington DC: Brookings Institution Press.

Cawson, A. (1983) 'Functional Representation and Democratic Politics', in G. Duncan (ed.) *Democratic Theory and Practice*, Cambridge: Cambridge University Press: 178–98.

Dahl, R. A. (1961) *Who Governs?* New Haven and London: Yale University Press.

Dowding, K. (1995) 'Model or Metaphor? A Critical Review of the Policy Network Approach', *Political Studies*, vol. 42, no.1: 136–58.

Grant, W. (ed.) (1985) *The Political Economy of Corporatism*, New York: St Martin's Press.

Hirschman, A. O. (1977) *The Passions and the Interests: Political Arguments for Capitalism before its Triumph*, Princeton NJ: Princeton University Press.

John, P. and Cole, A. (1997) 'Networks or networking? The importance of power, position and values in local economic policy networks in Britain and France', Paper prepared for delivery at the 1997 Annual Meeting of the American Political Science Association, Washington, August 28–31.

Jordan, G. and Schubert, K. (1992) 'A preliminary ordering of policy network labels', *European Journal of Political Research*, 21: 7–27.

Knoke, D., Pappi, F. U., Broadbent, J. and Tsujinaka, Y. (1996) *Comparing Policy Networks. Labor Politics in the U.S., Germany and Japan*, Cambridge Studies in Comparative Politics. Cambridge: Cambridge University Press.

Kuhnle, S. (ed.) (2000) *Survival of the European Welfare State*, Routledge/ECPR studies in European political science 14, London: Routledge.

March, J. M. and Olsen, J. P. (1989) *Discovering Institutions*, New York: The Free Press.

—— (1994) 'Institutional Perspectives on Governance', in *Systemsrationalität und Partialinteresse: Festschrift für Renate Mayntz/Hans Ulrich Derlien*, Baden-Baden: Nomos Verlagsgesellschaft.

McCool, D. (1994) *Command of the Waters: Iron Triangles, Federal Water Development and Indian Water*, Phoenix: University of Arizona Press.

Olsen, J. P. (1983) *Organized Democracy*, Bergen: Universitetsforlaget.

Olson, M (1965) *The Logic of Collective Action*, Cambridge: Harvard University Press.

Raab, C. (1994) 'Theorising the Governance of Education', *British Journal of Educational Studies*, vol. 42, no. 1, March.

Rhodes, R. A. W. and Marsh, D. (1992) 'New Directions in the Study of Policy Networks', *European Journal of Political Research*, vol. 21: 181–205.

Richardson, J. (1997) 'Interest Groups, Multi-Arena Politics and Policy Change', Paper prepared for delivery at the 1997 Annual Meeting of the American Political Science Association, Washington, August 28–31.

Rokkan, S. (1966) 'Norway: Numerical Democracy and Corporate Pluralism', in R. A. Dahl (ed.) *Political Oppositions in Western Democracies*, New Haven: Yale University Press.

Schmitter, P. (1974) 'Still the century of corporatism', in F. Pike and Th. Strich (eds) *The New Corporatism*, Notre Dame: University of Notre Dame.

Schmitter, P and Lehmbruch, G. (eds) (1979) *Trends Toward Corporatist Intermediation*, Sage: Beverly Hills.

Scott, W. R. (1981) *Organizations: Rational, Natural and Open Systems*, Englewood Cliffs, NJ: Prentice Hall.

Van Waarden, F. (1992) 'Dimensions and Types of Policy Networks', *European Journal of Political Research*, vol. 21: 29–52.

Wilson, J. Q. (1995 [1974]) *Political Organizations*, Princeton, NJ: Princeton University Press.

26

POLITICAL PARTIES

Joseph LaPalombara and Jeffrey Anderson

Political parties are about power. In democracies, they are the principal instrument employed by segments of the population to compete for control of elective institutions, and through them to influence public policies. Everywhere, including in dictatorial regimes, elites try to legitimize their rule via this same instrument. In recognition of the basic link between political parties and power, V. O. Key once remarked that they 'provide a good deal of the propulsion of the formal constitutional system' (Key 1964: 154).

It is not simply that parties are central to elections and to policy-making, or that they make and break governments, administer patronage, and make decisions that deeply affect a nation's welfare. Under their aegis, mass publics have been mobilized for good and evil, revolutions fomented, dissidents arrested, tortured and killed, and ideologies transformed into moral imperatives. Not only democracies, then, but political systems of every conceivable variety seem unable to function without the presence of one or more parties. Beginning in the late 1980s, the scramble to form political parties across Central and Eastern Europe, in anticipation of the first free elections held in these countries in a half century or more, provided a most vivid confirmation of the continuing and universal relevance of parties.

The ubiquity of parties suggests that they perform important political functions independent of the level of economic development or of the type of regime. In other words, the British Conservative Party, the Chinese Communist Party, and Iraq's Baath Party all carry out comparable tasks as 'organizational instrumentalities' (LaPalombara 1974: 515). Among other things, each organizes public opinion, transmits demands from society to its governors and vice versa, recruits political leaders, and engages in oversight of the implementation of public policies.

Admittedly, some would deny the comparability of democratic and totalitarian parties (Friedrich and Brzezinski 1966). Neumann, a noted scholar of parties, virtually rules out comparisons altogether, arguing that 'a party's character can be spelled out only in time and space' (Neumann 1956: 396). Our premise is that we can in fact compare political parties and make certain generalizations about them. In order to clarify what these organizational entities have in common, and how such characteristics have evolved and changed, we require a working definition of the political party itself.

A definition

Political parties are not quarks. That is, they are visible and easily recognized in the wild. Despite these tangible qualities, the scholarly literature has struggled to arrive at a consensus definition of party. One long-standing disagreement centres on the glue that binds together a party: public interest or private gain. Edmund Burke is perhaps the first and certainly the most eloquent spokesperson for public interest. 'Party is a body of men united, for promoting by their joint endeavors the national interest, upon some particular principle upon which they are all agreed' (Burke 1839: 425–6). Joseph Schumpeter, the best-known antagonist of the public interest school, counters with the following definition of party, full of the grit of power and political gain:

> A party is a group whose members propose to act in concert in the competitive struggle for power.... Party and machine politicians are simply the response to the fact that the electoral mass is incapable of action other than in a stampede, and they constitute an attempt to regulate political competition exactly similar to the corresponding practice of a trade association.
>
> (Schumpeter 1976: 283)

E. E. Schattschneider, an early political scientist who minced no words about the power-centred nature of politics, promotes this narrowly instrumental view of parties in even more forceful terms (Schattschneider 1942: 35). For him, the essence of party is the urge to gain and keep power.

Such conceptual disunity should not surprise us. Parties occupy the main intersections of the political process – conflict regulation, integration, public opinion formation, policy formulation. They are therefore complex, multi-faceted aspects of the political system. As nothing more than a working definition, we offer the following: a party is any political group, in possession of an official label and of a formal organization linking centre and locality, that presents at elections, and is capable of placing through elections (free or non-free), candidates for public office.

There are numerous advantages to this formulation, an amalgam of LaPalombara and Weiner (1966) and Sartori (1976). By stressing both free and non-free elections, it preserves comparability across regime-type. Moreover, unlike the Burkean and Schumpeterian definitions, it addresses several broader considerations (Sartori 1976: 58–64). First, the definition delimits parties from other actors that are or have been involved in the rough and tumble of politics: court factions, parliamentary clubs, mass movements, interest groups, bureaucracies, church organizations and the military. As the only organizations to operate formally in the electoral arena (Panebianco 1988: 6; Schlesinger 1965: 767), political parties are distinctive. Second, the definition is minimal. That is, it contains only those elements necessary for delimitation, and it leaves all other properties as hypotheses subject to empirical verification. Too often, parties are defined in functional terms, which makes it almost impossible to disprove that the putative functions are in fact carried out by parties (King 1969: 116). Finally, our working definition avoids any identification of parties with party systems, a common confusion that often leads to the conclusion that parties found in dictatorial settings are aberrations.

The origins of political parties

The arguments of Madison and Tocqueville – namely, that parties emerge wherever there exist salient differences of interest among the public (Madison 1961: 77–84; Tocqueville 1969: 174) – are clearly incomplete. The presence of conflicting interests is a necessary but not sufficient condition for the emergence of parties. Were this otherwise, parties would surely number among the oldest forms of social organization. Instead, parties are a phenomenon of the last 150 years, and as such are creatures of modernity.

There are three distinct explanations of the recent origins of parties (LaPalombara and Weiner 1966: 8–21):

1   institutional theories that stress the transformation of parliaments;
2   historical theories that emphasize systemic crises tied to the nation-building process; and
3   theories of modernization and political development.

While each successive approach seeks to embed political parties in progressively more inclusive theories of social and political change, they all acknowledge a common determining factor in the appearance of parties: social mobilization, or the entry of the masses onto the political stage. Once politics could no longer be confined to a small circle of aristocratic elites, parties emerged as the instruments to link the centre of political power with the masses. In this parties proved consistently indispensable, whether the transformation of politics was induced by competition among elites or by pressures from the masses below.

Parties and the evolution of parliaments

Institutional theories, informed primarily by the Western experience, locate the origins of political parties in the gradual extension of suffrage and the resulting transfiguration of parliamentary bodies. Scholars credit Duverger with the seminal contribution, though Weber is often mentioned in the same breath (Duverger 1954: xxiii–xxxvii; Weber 1946: 102–7). Duverger suggests three stages in the development of parties: the birth of parliamentary groups, the formation of local electoral committees, and the creation of permanent links between the two. The expansion of the electorate and the responses of elites in and outside the parliamentary arena drive the process.

Under a restricted suffrage, politics is very much an elite intramural affair. Factions and other loose associations of notables form within assemblies, but these are often ephemeral groupings. Even where they endure, they display little continuity of purpose, and no institutionalized connections to the extra-parliamentary environment. Disrupting this cosy state of affairs, the initial expansion of the suffrage prompts and indeed compels like-minded notables to create local electoral machinery to woo the new electors, and to organize them as reliable supporters. Disraeli's efforts on behalf of the Conservative Party in mid-nineteenth-century Britain represent perhaps the classic example of this dynamic. As the electorate expands still further, and party notables begin to face competition from emergent

383

parties outside of parliament (see below), they seek to improve the integration of the national and local levels, both vertically and horizontally. The result is a modern mass political party. Whatever the specific circumstances of its origins, the party emerges to deal with the incorporation of unprecedented numbers of persons into the political process.

The preceding describes the genesis of political parties created by the legislators themselves. Classic examples include the British Conservative and Liberal Parties, the Democratic and Republican Parties in the USA, the National Liberal Party of Wilhelmine Germany, and the Liberals of nineteenth-century Italy. Duverger distinguishes these 'internally created' parties from those that originate outside the established representative institutions, and that typically present ideological and electoral challenges to the ruling elites. Externally created parties also derive their sustenance from an expanded electorate, yet they seek to enter the corridors of power to pursue the interests of previously excluded groups, or even to transform the political system itself. The vehicle is again a mass political party. Typical examples in the European context are socialist parties, communist parties, christian democratic parties, as well as parties of agrarian defence.

Although Duverger's analysis retains a certain plausibility where the Western experience is concerned, its limited reach is all too apparent. The theory is space-bound; it does not connect with the experience of colonial regimes or developing nations, where parliamentary assemblies – centre stage for Duverger – were either non-existent or excluded the indigenous population, and yet political parties emerged nevertheless. The theory is also time-bound, in that it does not illuminate the process by which new parties form in places where universal suffrage has been the norm for many decades. The emergence of ecological and environmental parties, and of new-style right-wing parties, in Western democracies during the 1980s and 1990s, is a prime example. The recent proliferation of political parties in countries that were once dominated by a single Communist party would be another example. To correct these deficiencies, scholars have offered more complex theories to explain the origins of parties.

We must now add to the above the emergence of what we might call the 'instant party' or 'lightning party'. The most striking example of this potential new breed would be the *Forza Italia* (Go Italy!) Party led by Silvio Berlusconi. Born largely out of the will, energy, charisma and financial capital of one man, this party, within the incredible short space of four months, became the largest in Italy, and captured the national government. To prove that this was not a fluke, of the Pierre Poujade French experience of the 1950s, Go Italy! improved its electoral fortunes in 2002, and seems destined to prevail for some years.

Two points about this phenomenon are germane to this essay. First, organizationally, although seemingly yet another of the externally-created mass parties, it does not really resemble any of them. The party leader intends to avoid, if possible, that local or regional party organizations should become challenges to his own charisma-based powers. Second, the key to Go Italy! electoral success was the systematic application, through the mass media, of marketing strategies that have so often underlain the market prowess of commercial organizations, also tightly controlled at the center.

The 'lightning party', too, if it persists in Italy and/or spreads to other advanced industrial countries, will tax the theoretical inventiveness, especially of those who are loath, as are we, to think about this phenomenon as either a passing aberration or as something unique to Italian society and politics.

Parties and the nation-state

As political elites cope with the economic, social, political, military and administrative problems that typically accompany the nation-building process, they create institutions that endure long after earlier moments of crisis, despair and euphoria have passed. The rise of parties accompanies certain types of crises, in particular those relating to national integration, the nation's legitimacy, and demands for increased participation. More importantly perhaps, the content and sequencing of these crises will determine the pattern of evolution that parties will follow. In Europe and in developing countries in the past, in the former Eastern bloc countries at the present, and in places like China in the future, we can and will discern how intimately related are legitimacy, integration and participation, on the one side, and the nature of political parties on the other.

According to proponents of this approach, legitimacy crises explain the emergence of some of the earliest examples of political parties, both on the European continent and in the developing countries. Duverger's internal parties formed at a time when the legitimacy of existing representative institutions was placed in doubt. In the post-colonial era, which saw an effervescence of new nations, political parties emerged from nationalist movements that questioned the legitimacy not just of representative institutions, but of the state itself. The rise of fascist and communist parties in the twentieth century also reflected legitimacy crises in liberal democracies. Ironically, these crises were engendered to some degree by the malfunctioning and negative repercussions of party pluralism (Sartori 1976: 39).

Participation demands prove to be even more closely linked to the formation of political parties. The timing, as well as the nature, of elite responses to them will tend to influence not only the parties' organizational forms and political behaviour but their ideologies as well. The incorporation of new social groups into the political system typically requires extended suffrage. As nations develop along this particular participatory dimension, the creation of political parties is the natural outcome. As a rule then, almost all externally created parties are formed either along with system-expanding crises of electoral participation, or with more or less sweeping attacks on the inadequacies of the extant system.

The most dramatic examples of this last impulse to the creation of new parties occurred in recent years in all of the countries that once constituted parts of the Soviet bloc. Public revulsion against former one-party rule, and the conditions of near anarchy that accompanied the disintegration of the Soviet Empire brought dozens, sometimes hundreds, of new parties into being. It will be years before anything like a more stable configuration of parties materializes in these places. Nor are we to know, before that occurs, what organizational forms these East European parties will take.

Parties and modernization

A broader formulation is that mass parties are the products of societal modernization. New social groups seek more direct access to the political process owing to 'increases in the flow of information, the expansion of internal markets, a growth in technology, the expansion of transportation networks, and, above all, increases in spatial and social mobility' (LaPalombara and Weiner 1966: 20). Other factors associated with modernization, like secularization of values, the emergence of voluntaristic collective action and improvements in the means of communication, also facilitate the emergence of the political party as the prime form of political organization.

Samuel Huntington goes so far as to argue that the political party – not public bureaucracy, not parliament, not election – is *the* distinctive institution in the modern polity (Huntington 1968: 89). Modern society is everywhere mass society and, as such, requires an institution (the party) to organize the inclusion and integration of mass publics into the system. Others pursue a less deterministic line, but nevertheless associate the emergence of political parties with the effects of industrialization. In this vein, Daalder states, 'the modern political party ... can be described with little exaggeration as the child of the Industrial Revolution' (Daalder 1966: 52). As Marx anticipated, the concentration of workers in industrial urban centres carried political consequences. He did not fully appreciate, however, that the political party would emerge to mobilize these masses not for revolution but rather for quite routine and indeed productive and system-reinforcing forms of electoral participation. Yet whatever the aims of power-seeking elites they have found the political party of extraordinary instrumental utility.

Industrialization also generates substantial costs for traditional social groups like artisans, small shopkeepers and farmers, and thereby spurs the creation of political parties whose purpose it is to defend these threatened groups. The agrarian parties of Scandinavia, as well as the fascist parties elsewhere in Europe, are examples of such reactions to modernization. Later in the modernization process, the accumulation of negative externalities generated by industrial activity poses a major threat to the environment, leading to another wave of party formation around 'green' issue agendas.

Modernization theory also has its shortcomings. Most obvious among these is that we have not yet clearly delineated alternative paths to modernity or nation building. For this reason, there is little that can be said with confidence as to when, under what circumstances and with what probable consequences particular kinds of political parties will in fact materialize. With this caveat in mind, we turn to some additional observations regarding these important institutions.

Party origins: so what?

One might well suppose that a party's origins would affect its organizational structure, internal dynamics, functions and ideological principles. Duverger offers an unalloyed statement to this effect: 'It is the whole life of the party which bears the mark of its origins' (Duverger 1954: xxxv). According to him, internally created parties are less ideologically coherent and disciplined, less centralized, open to greater influence by their parliamentary wings, and more likely to place supreme emphasis on the parliamentary arena of political conflict than are other parties.

Similar, though not as deterministic in tone, are propositions that derive from those who associate the advent of parties with modernization or national development. For example, parties that are associated with crises of legitimacy of older orders, or that are involved in the dismantling of the latter, will rely on ideology as a means of cementing relationships among party members, motivating them and others to action, and establishing the legitimacy of the new order. Such parties also develop hierarchical and secretive organizational structures to protect themselves against penetration by opponents. The 'vanguard party' outlined by Lenin is the classic example (Lenin 1969). Emphasis on mass membership, self-conscious attention to ideology, and political activism are presumably characteristics of parties that have their origins in demands for expanded participation. Only the modernization school seems to be reluctant to ascribe political party characteristics to the circumstances that surround their birth.

These arguments or propositions are neither wholly implausible nor incorrect. For example, Duverger's distinctions between elite-based parties and mass-based parties are reasonable and interesting (Ware 1987: 6). As formulated, however, they are static and therefore ill-equipped to help us understand changes in the structure, ideology and functions of parties that may have occurred since their birth. Preconditions and context will certainly leave their imprint. Yet it stands to reason that these effects eventually will fade; in any case, parties that survive do so because they manage to adapt as they encounter alterations in their larger environments. The graveyards of history are strewn with political parties that failed to respond to such challenges.

Two attempts to grapple with these shortcomings are worthy of mention. Von Beyme, pursuing the line of inquiry begun by Duverger, ascribes the often complex relationship between a party's parliamentary and extra-parliamentary wings neither to the parties themselves nor to their origins, but rather to other aspects of the political system (Von Beyme 1983). His work amplifies the arguments of scholars like Mckenzie who assert that the organization and behaviour of political parties tend to adapt to structural and configurative dimensions of the systems in which they operate (Mckenzie 1963). He cites as particularly important the type and institutional position of the governmental executive, the role of interest groups, and the professionalization of politicians. Unlike Duverger, Von Beyme does not see the two party wings locked into a zero-sum relationship. He suggests instead that twentieth-century developments of the kind mentioned have simultaneously strengthened both groups (Von Beyme 1983: 392).

Another striking application of organizational theory to political parties (Panebianco 1988) takes as its starting point the work of Michels, who proposed the Iron Law of Oligarchy for political parties (Michels 1962). Panebianco suggests a three-phase model of party development, namely, genesis, institutionalization and maturity. Over time, a party's internal hierarchy, its objectives, and even its principles are determined by the changes in the needs and power positions of party elites and rank-and-file members (Panebianco 1988: 18). His work is an intriguing answer to those who lament the lack of theories that address the internal workings of parties (Daalder 1983: 22).

Party functions

Theories of course can be hopelessly abstract, and nowhere is this more apparent than in the many efforts to delineate the functions of political parties. More often than not, these functions are simply imposed on the parties by theoretical or logical fiat, without regard to what parties do in practice. Yet as Sartori reminds us, 'What parties are – that is, what their functions, placement, and weight in the political system are – has not been designed by a theory but has been determined by a concurrence of events' (Sartori 1976: 18). With this admonition in mind, we can ask what specific functions parties have carried out, whether these vary (in space or time), and which are shared with other actors in the political system. If we can specify party functions, we may also ask how well and in what circumstances they perform them.

Leadership recruitment

Wherever they exist, parties are a critical aspect of the structure of political opportunity (Schlesinger 1966). They serve the interests of ambitious men and women. They help to cull from society individuals who assume positions endowed with considerable power and authority. In the system within which political elites operate, parties are powerful 'gatekeepers' (Putnam 1976: 49–61). Given our definition of the political party, it would be a real puzzle were this not the case.

Recruitment is far from a simple matter; to understand its nuances requires more detail than is typically provided in the literature. Analysis in depth is required of such things as 'the motives that lead individuals to seek or accept political roles or inhibit them from doing so; the "catchment pools" from which the political classes are drawn...; the criteria by which they are selected; and the characteristics and aims of those selecting them' (King 1969: 129). Another critical question is the extent to which the political parties monopolize the recruitment of persons to key political positions. Were parties to share this responsibility widely with other organizations (like interest groups) or actually fall into their shadow, they would lose a principal *raison d'être* (Daalder 1966: 75; Katz 1980: 4).

It goes without saying that, in pluralist democracies, parties do share this particular function with other organizations, including the military, the public bureaucracy, the court, the academic community, trade unions, business enterprises and a wide variety of other interest groups. All of them represent competing channels through which individuals enter the leadership stratum of a given society. In practice, then, the weight of parties in the selection of lawmakers and bureaucrats, and in some places judges as well, will vary. The USA, even in the era of Jacksonian Democracy, would be at one extreme. At the other, we might place Austria during the heyday of *Proporz*, when the two leading parties enjoyed cartel-like control over access to elite positions in the polity.

Even where parties are strong, however, it is useful to think about them in part as 'an abstraction – a label under which a number of organized groups compete for a share of the elective offices to be filled' (LaPalombara 1974: 546). In many developing countries, weak party organizations take a back seat to the military or the civil bureaucracy in the recruitment of the political elite. Only in established one-party states of the fascist or communist type is political recruitment performed on a virtually exclusive basis by parties. These dictatorial parties by definition seek to negate pluralism. Even there, however, party monopoly of recruitment may have its negative side, encouraging the creation of a narrowly based, conservative, and even reactionary leadership stratum. Lenin understood this danger, as did Mao, whose 'mass line' campaigns were explicitly designed to loosen the party bureaucracy's hold on recruitment.

Formation of governments: the ruling function

According to Katz, the key function of the party is 'to rule and to take responsibility for ruling' (Katz 1987: 4). This is the truly distinctive function of the party, one which sets it apart from other organizations. In short, it intends to capture control of the political system under its own name, exclusively if possible or, failing that, in coalition with another party or parties. Bagehot commented on the close connection between party and government in his pathbreaking nineteenth-century treatise on the English constitution (Bagehot 1963: 158). The modern literature also highlights this critical aspect of the political party (Schattschneider 1942: ix; Neumann 1956: 400). Daalder identifies the spectacular collapse of the Weimar Republic in 1933 and its tragic aftermath as the principal source of the overwhelming scholarly concern with effective party control of the apparatus of government (Daalder 1983: 6).

The notion of 'grasp' is one way of conceptualizing a party's capacity to form governments, to rule, and to be responsible for rulership itself (King 1969: 132). We know that the capacity varies – from country to country, within the same country, and, indeed within the same political party over time. This last type of variation signals why parties, as opposed to party systems, should be studied in their own right, as complex organizations that may be well or poorly endowed with leadership, well or poorly managed, and so on. Panebianco's work provides important evidence that these capacities are strongly influenced by the circumstances that surround not the birth but, rather, the institutionalization of each political party, and by the type of party, i.e. 'mass bureaucratic' or 'electoral professional', that emerges (Panebianco 1988: part II and ch. 14).

Examples of extensive party grasp would be Austria during the period of the Red–Black coalition (1945–66), the *Parteienstaat* in the Federal Republic of Germany, the established one-party governments in the pre-Gorbachev Soviet Union, and today's People's Republic of China. One source of a party's capacity to penetrate a system is its ability to dominate the elite recruitment process. Presumably, the greater the number and diversity of positions a party is able to fill with its supporters – the military, the judiciary, the public economic sector, the bureaucracy – the more likely it is to forge an effective and purposeful government.

Extensive grasp may facilitate the formation of government, but it does not automatically produce effective rulership. One reason for this is, again, to be sought within the party itself. Parties are not necessarily coherent organizations, and even more rarely are they the monoliths that we sometimes imagine. Thus, in their respective primes the Italian Christian Democrats and the Japanese Liberal Democrats were both dominant, hegemonic parties whose grasp in the sense just described was extensive, even all-encompassing. But both were also faction-ridden; they encompassed fluid and shifting internal coalitions of 'notables', each of which represents a somewhat autonomous power base (LaPalombara 1987; Calder 1988; Zuckerman 1979). Even the Soviet Communist Party, despite its domination of the instruments of government, faced formidable internal obstacles to its effective rule; witness the ability of lower-level party functionaries to thwart Gorbachev's economic reform programme. Similar obstacles stand in the way of the Chinese Communist Party's continuing efforts to govern that vast country, monolithically from Beijing.

In thinking about parties, rather than impute to them certain 'functions' of the kind we review here, we should ask what it is they actually do or achieve. Where the formation of government and rulership are concerned, we must not only ask what are the capacities of individual parties to do these things; we must also probe to establish whether these represent the mission of the parties, that is, the *intentions* of those who control them (Katz 1987: 7–11). Theories of democracies and of one-party governments suggest that parties exist to provide political direction to the institutions of government. In practice, however, parties often cede the field to the bureaucracy, the military or interest groups. The typical result is policy drift, or a segmentation of political authority exercised by narrow coalitions of interest that colonize the governmental apparatus. Moreover, if rulership or 'party government' implies the formulation of coherent, distinctive and purposive public policies, the empirical evidence suggests that the impact of political parties remains at best contingent. The position of a given country in the world economy, or the strength of its labour unions, strongly conditions and limits party performance (Hibbs 1977; Cameron 1984).

Political identity and the vote

Parties are also described as instruments that structure a person's political identity and that channel the popular vote (Schattschneider 1942: 52; Key 1964: 314). This particular function, unlike the others so far discussed, requires an electoral market in which more than one party competes for political currency, that is, for the citizen's vote. To encourage loyal customers who will stay with the party over the longer course, parties utilize techniques that range from official labels and symbols to party platforms and complex ideologies, from propaganda and educational programmes to a vast apparatus of auxiliary party organizations. For many parties, election day is simply a recurring opportunity to display how well their efforts to instill a particular political party identity in the voter have proceeded. This matter is so obviously vital to the survival of the party that it is given the highest priority, even by parties in dictatorships that face no electoral opposition at all. George Orwell chillingly captures the extremes to which these parties will go in pursuit of this goal (Orwell 1949).

Parties of course will also seek to shape public opinion in the broader sense that encompasses the identification of public issues, the assignment of valence to them, and the specification of policies designed to deal with them. In one-party systems, the party line will be handed down from on high and disseminated by the party faithful. The phenomenon of 'agitprop' under Stalin and of the 'mass line' under Mao are good examples of this approach. In more open and democratic systems, not only do party lines compete with each other for the voter's support, but other volun-taristic organizations, as well as the mass media, compete with the parties to register the same effect.

It is self-evident that the grasp of the party – that is, how far and deeply it can actually penetrate a society – will bear directly on its capacity to structure political identities and to attract voters at the polls. The relationship, however is not linear; absolute monopoly control by the party of the instruments of communication and of political socialization does not translate into equal success in the moulding of citizen identity and voter support. This was apparent in the Soviet Union and its East European sphere of control even before the fall of the Berlin Wall. Since then, we have witnessed a veritable explosion in the formation of new parties, each of which is frenetically in search of strong (even weak!) adherents.

In fact, not even in totalitarian systems does the single party ever really monopo-lize all of the institutions and channels of communication that mould public opinion. Schools, churches, village markets, the factory, the halls and labyrinths of the bureaucracy, the military and even the units of the party itself become places where information is exchanged – and where subversive thoughts are born, matured and disseminated. Furthermore, advances in literacy and the untrammelled transmis-sion of sound and visual images across space make it unlikely that one party can successfully impose an Orwellian Newthink or Newspeak on a national population.

Therefore, on this matter of moulding and reinforcing the citizen's political iden-tity and structuring his or her vote, the party must come to terms with the realities of modern societies, where pluralism is increasingly the rule. This implies that infor-mation relevant to politics is both widely produced and instantly transmitted to participants in the electoral and other political processes. In these pluralistic contexts, it's not just that potential voters do a lot of shopping around before selecting a party to support. Easy access to information also tends to stack the cards against strong party identification, and the knee-jerk support that this type of loyalty is expected to produce in the voter. Indeed, the advent of the electronic revo-lution, and the political salience of the media, have raised in some minds the thought – not entirely reassuring for any democratic society – that the political party could go the way of the dinosaur.

Mobilization and integration

This leads us to inquire whether parties may be especially salient in circumstances involving mass mobilization and/or the integration of national political systems. The mobilization of masses of people has typically been associated with single party systems in both developed and developing nations (Friedrich and Brzezinski 1966: 47). This is obviously too narrow a view. As complex organizations driven by persons with great ambitions to exercise power and influence, parties tend to be opportunistic everywhere. Thus if they are unable to have their way through the regular and orderly procedures of governmental institutions, they may easily shift to mass mobilization techniques. In the West, left-wing parties have not hesitated to use their affiliated trade unions or youth organizations to bring hundreds of thousands of persons into the streets and squares. Similarly, right-wing political parties use forms of mass mobilization as one of the weapons in their political arsenal. Indeed, as the suffrage is extended to include earlier non-participants, the process (with the party situated typically at the very centre) whereby these persons are incorporated is itself described as 'social mobilization' and 'political development' (Huntington 1968: 32 ff., 132–7; LaPalombara and Weiner 1966: 400–7).

In recent years, parties like the Greens in Germany and the Radicals in Italy have deliberately combined both parliamentary and extra-parliamentary forms of political intervention and opposition. Furthermore, events of the late 1960s in the West showed that the line between 'normal' political participation and forms of mobilization ranging from mass demonstrations to riots and acts of terrorism can be very thin indeed. Historically, political parties have served as models for every conceivable type of political intervention, including mobilization.

Parties may not be the only organizations in society that lean in this direction, but they are certainly those from which we *normally* expect such efforts to emanate. Indeed, one way to gauge the stability of any democratic system is to weigh the relative frequency with which mobilization of the masses for political ends is at the hands of movements and organizations that are *not* primarily interested in linking citizens to governmental institutions or to the policy-making process (Lawson 1980; Barnes and Kasse 1979). The still-growing 'No Global' movements of very recent vintage are prime examples of this phenomenon.

Mobilization of this kind, outside party channels, implies a challenge to existing political institutions and authority, and may actually represent a direct assault on the political system *in toto*. The 1926 General Strike in Britain, student revolts of the late 1960s followed by waves of terrorism in some countries, the rise of Solidarity in Poland after 1980, the Chinese June 4 Movement, the awesome display of people power in the Eastern Bloc during 1989 and after, and today's radical Islamic sects and movements are prime examples. Where such events emerge, existing parties, including previously dictatorial single parties, scramble to catch up with these outbursts of collective action and new manifestations of the public mood.

Where parties do succeed in becoming and remaining the main linkage between citizen-voters and ruling office holders, they clearly contribute to the integration of the overall political system. Psychological and social affinities to the party, at least where the latter are not clearly of the anti-system variety (Sartori 1976: 132–4), serve as an integrative mechanism that brings the individual more meaningfully into a political regime, thus indirectly benefiting the latter as well (Kirchheimer 1966: 188–9).

Political parties that lead successful revolutions, as well as nationalist movements that overthrow colonial rule and then assume party form, may also be described as aiding the effective integration of new regimes. The earliest example of both of these phenomena is the USA (Lipset 1963). Parties in established liberal democracies perform an integrative function too. For example, the British Conservative Party, with its intimate ties to the Church of England, the Royal Family and other symbols of British nationality, accomplishes similar ends. Indeed, even in the case of allegedly anti-system parties, like the communist parties of Western Europe, active involvement in the normal and constitutional types of political mobilization and participation up through the 1980s had the effect of reinforcing the legitimacy as well as the integration of the same systems these parties ostensibly were seeking to overthrow.

In some cases, the principal beneficiaries of integration are the party itself and a social order yet to be realized. Neumann speaks of parties of 'social integration', typically on the left and engaged in 'permanent revolution', that seek to envelop the individual in an all-encompassing ideology and a self-contained network of social, political and economic relationships (Neumann 1956: 404). These integrative efforts often, but not always, challenge the principles and values of the existing political order. Islamic parties, even when they come to power through democratic elections, as in Turkey in 2002, may also lean in a similar de-stabilizing direction.

National integration is one of those important but elusive concepts for which precise empirical indicators are hard to specify. This being so, it is even more difficult to show whether parties are any more effective than other organizations or institutions in bringing about minimum or higher levels of integration (King 1969: 124–6). Indeed, far from winning much praise on this particular score, parties are often condemned as the principal reason why so many modern societies seem to wallow in deep-seated crises – evidenced by citizen apathy, mass alienation and antisocial behaviour. As important as that particular allegation may be, it addresses the political party *system* and not the political parties that are our prime concern in this essay.

Political parties: facing the future

Bagehot, writing in 1867, predicted that parties would change the face of British parliamentary politics, substituting an unstable and even dangerous form of 'Constituency Government' for the more virtuous 'Parliamentary Government' (Bagehot 1963: 161). His gloomy assessment was echoed loudly and frequently by others writing in the twentieth century. The recurring message has been that mass-based, disciplined parties are not necessarily healthy for democracy (Ostrogorski 1902; Beer 1966). Schattschneider attributes the 'plebiscitary presidency' in the USA to political parties, which 'took over an eighteenth-century constitution and made it function to satisfy the needs of modern democracy in ways not anticipated by the authors' (Schattschneider 1942: 2). And Joseph Schumpeter (1976) too, whose classic defence of political parties argues that they are essential to the electoral competition required of large-scale democracies, did not anticipate the extent to which, over time, they would become much more than this.

Thus, essentially from the beginning, students of parties echo one unassailable fact: parties, the product of expanded suffrage, quickly transcended election-oriented tasks and arrogated to themselves responsibilities and authority belonging to other, more formal, institutions. As complex and effective organizations, parties triumphed over older and less specialized competitors. In doing so, they transformed the struggle for power itself, and in ways that the framers of older regimes and constitutions neither anticipated nor intended. As the key instrumentality designed to give substance to the concepts of participation and representation (Huntington 1968; Schumpeter 1976), or to provide linkage between the electorate and the formulation and execution of public policy (Lawson 1980: 3–24), the advent of parties represents a quantum change in the nature of the polity.

Nevertheless, after less than two centuries, we encounter claims that these same organizations are now of dubious relevance as components of modern political systems. If they are not on the verge of extinction, so one argument goes, they risk losing the centrality they once enjoyed. In less developed countries, they have tended to give way to military or other forms of dictatorship that do not tolerate party organizations – at least not those they are unable to control. In developed countries, the claim is that technological advances in communication and information-processing have undercut their role as the principal links between governors and governed. In addition, new social movements, particularly among the young and the emerging professional middle classes, have emerged apart from and even in open hostility toward parties.

There is more. In advanced industrial society, a growing *lumpenproletariat* – unskilled, illiterate, and increasingly isolated – is said to be impervious to direction from parties. The complexities of a vast, interdependent and volatile world economy are said to privilege organized capital and labour at the expense of parties and even parliaments in the policy-making process (Berger 1981; Schmitter and Lehmbruch 1979). In this framework, it is easy to conclude that parties are indeed institutional has-beens, whose time has come and gone.

In fact, almost all such formulations offer at best half-truths. One reason, as a seasoned observer points out, is that parties are often victims of the inflated expectations of those who theorize about them (King 1969). As scholars looked more closely at reality, party myths had to be recast. These second looks have produced much more reasonable statements as to what these organizations are and what they can or cannot do.

Of course, literacy, the electronics revolution and the advent of new modes and norms of collective behaviour will have an impact on the parties too. Generally speaking, parties today are not what they were even as recently as a generation ago. Party membership (as opposed to electoral support or identification) is in decline every-where, and more and more parties are managed by paid professionals, not activist volunteers. Coupled with the rapid growth in public funding for political parties, this places added empirical and theoretical emphasis on the changing relationship between parties and the state on the one hand, and parties and society on the other. Put another way, the tightening embrace of the state coincides with a loosening of the typical party's roots in society; the disintegration of the Christian Democratic and Social Democratic social milieus throughout Western Europe carry profound organizational and program-matic implications for these quintessentially 'external' political parties.

Despite these transformations, rumours of the atrophy or demise of political parties are greatly exaggerated. On the contrary, they remain the only organizations that operate on the electoral and governmental scenes in the sense we have described. Until this changes, parties will rightly continue to occupy the attention of journalists and politicians, citizens and academic researchers. The sophisticated treatment of parties as organizations (Panebianco 1988) marked a welcome return to earlier modes of studying these institutions. For decades now, research has centred on parties as seen from the vantage point of the individual citizen and voter, or alternatively, as the components of the party system itself. Thus, in certain respects, the newer trend brings us full circle, back to the focus suggested by writers like Michels (1962), Ostrogorski (1902), and Duverger (1954). Equipped with new analytical techniques and better data than, we can explore new avenues of research such as the relationship between parties and the particular configuration that a variety of political systems now in transition might eventually assume.

Developments after 1990 in the former Soviet bloc conspired to create a most opportune time to return to the study of parties as organizations. In almost all of these countries, communist parties, once the monopolizers of power, were compelled to adapt to electoral competition. New parties literally emerged by the dozen, alongside trade union movements like Solidarity in Poland or intellectual circles like Civic Forum in Czechoslovakia. In all of these countries, one encountered seemingly unlimited opportunities to observe parties that were born anew or that sought to reconstitute themselves from a past that only a handful of persons could remember as part of an earlier and different experience.

If, as some scholars have claimed, the unions, the bureaucrats and the plant managers are the 'natural' components of corporatist systems of policy-making, we have to explain why there has been such a veritable explosion of political parties in this part of the world. It may very well be that the establishment of the market is a necessary condition for the eventual emergence of democracy. Yet it seems self-evident that, long before the economic market was established or reemerged, all of these countries were confronted with the critical issue of the *political* market, and of the degree and kind of competition that can take place within it without causing additional and unwanted upheaval. Now, a decade a more down the road, many of these political parties in Central and Eastern Europe and the former Soviet Union appear to have connected in stable and recurring ways with their mass electorates. Empirical research suggests that where competitive elections are held regularly in this region (e.g. Russia), citizens have formed meaningful partisan attachments and perceive programmatic differences among parties in a consistent and uniform manner, all within in a remarkably short period of time (Miller and Klobucar 2000).

Based on the outcomes of these transitions to democracy as well as those underway in other parts of the world, we can predict with confidence that the political party as a complex organization will play a major role, and perhaps *the* central role, in these processes. Not only is this prospect intellectually exciting in its own right, but it will also provide the opportunity to test a wide range of propositions about the nature of political development, and the precise role of the political party in settings where degrees of tolerance of organized efforts to win control of the machinery of government, and/or to oppose those who succeed in this undertaking, now vary markedly.

In dealing with the political party, it is essential to avoid all forms of sociological reductionism of the kind suggesting that the form, meaning and function of political institutions are the abject dependent expressions of much deeper societal determinants. The more accurate reality, as Panebianco (1988: 275–6) has reminded us, is that the political party was and remains prominent among the *political* institutions that shape the configuration and plot the direction of social institutions, as well as the destinies of humankind. They richly deserve to be studied in this vein, and in their own right.

References

Bagehot, W. (1963 [1867]) *The English Constitution*, Ithaca, NY: Cornell University Press.
Barnes, S. H. and Kasse, M. (eds) (1979) *Political Action: Mass Participation in Five Western Democracies*, Beverly Hills: Sage Publications.

Beer, S. (1966) *British Politics in the Collectivist Age*, New York: Knopf.

Berger, S. (ed.) (1981) *Organizing Interests in Western Europe*, New York: Cambridge University Press.

Burke, E. (1839) 'Thoughts on the cause of the present discontents' (1770), in *The Works of Edmund Burke*, vol. 1, Boston: Little, Brown & Co.

Calder, K. (1988) *Crisis and Compensation*, Princeton: Princeton University Press.

Cameron, D. (1984) 'Social democracy, corporatism, labor quiescence, and the representation of economic interest in advanced capitalist society', in J. Goldthorpe (ed.) *Order and Conflict in Contemporary Capitalism*, Oxford: Clarendon Press.

Daalder, H. (1966) 'Parties, elites, and political developments in Western Europe', in J. LaPalombara and M. Weiner (eds) *Political Parties and Political Development*, Princeton: Princeton University Press.

—— (1983) 'The comparative study of European parties and party systems: an overview', in H. Daalder and P. Mair (eds) *Western European Party Systems: Continuity and Change*, Beverly Hills: Sage Publications.

Duverger, M. (1954) *Political Parties*, New York: John Wiley.

Friedrich, C. and Brzezinski, Z. (1966) *Totalitarian Dictatorship and Autocracy*, New York: Praeger.

Hibbs, D. (1977) 'Political parties and macroeconomic policy', *American Political Science Review* 71: 1467–87.

Huntington, S. (1968) *Political Order in Changing Societies*, New Haven: Yale University Press.

Katz, R. S. (1980) *A Theory of Parties and Electoral Systems*, Baltimore: Johns Hopkins University Press.

—— (ed.) (1987) *Party Government: European and American Experiences*, Berlin: de Gruyter.

Key, V. O. (1964) *Politics, Parties, and Pressure Groups*, New York: Thomas Y. Crowell.

King, A. (1969) 'Political parties in Western democracies: some skeptical reflections', *Polity* 2: 112–41.

Kirchheimer, O. (1966) 'The transformation of the Western European party systems', in J. LaPalombara and M. Weiner (eds) *Political Parties and Political Development*, Princeton: Princeton University Press.

LaPalombara, J. (1974) *Politics within Nations*, Englewood Cliffs, NJ: Prentice-Hall.

—— (1987) *Democracy Italian Style*, New Haven: Yale University Press.

LaPalombara, J. and Weiner, M. (1966) 'The origin and development of political parties', in J. LaPalombara and M. Weiner (eds) *Political Parties and Political Development*, Princeton: Princeton University Press.

Lawson, K. (ed.) (1980) *Political Parties and Linkage: A Comparative Perspective*, New Haven: Yale University Press.

Lenin, V. I. (1969 [1902]) *What is to be Done?*, New York: International Publishers.

Lipset, S. M. (1963) *The First New Nation*, New York: Basic Books.

Mckenzie, R. (1963) *British Political Parties*, New York: Praeger.

Madison, J. (1961) 'No. 10', in A. Hamilton, J. Madison and J. Jay (eds) *The Federalist Papers*, New York: New American Library.

Michels, R. (1962) *Political Parties: A Sociological Study of the Oligarchical Tendencies of Modern Democracy*, New York: Free Press; translation of (1911) *Zur Soziologie des Partei-wesens in der Modernen Demokratie*, Leipzig: Klinghardt.

Miller, A. and Klobucar, T. (2000) 'The Development of Party Identification in Post-Soviet Societies', *American Journal of Political Science* 44: 667–86.

Neumann, S. (1956) 'Toward a comparative study of political parties', in S. Neumann (ed.) *Modern Political Parties*, Chicago: University of Chicago Press.

Orwell, G. (1949) *Nineteen Eighty-Four*, New York: Harcourt Brace.

Ostrogorski, M. (1902) *Democracy and the Organization of Political Parties*, 2 vols, London: Macmillan.

Panebianco, A. (1988) *Political Parties: Organization and Power*, New York: Cambridge University Press.

Putnam, R. D. (1976) *The Comparative Study of Political Elites*, Englewood Cliffs, NJ: Prentice-Hall.

Sartori, G. (1976) *Parties and Party Systems*, New York: Cambridge University Press.

Schattschneider, E. E. (1942) *Party Government*, New York: Farrar & Rinehart.

Schlesinger, J. A. (1965) 'Political party organization', in J. March (ed.) *Handbook of Organizations*, Chicago: Rand McNally.

—— (1966) *Ambition and Politics: Political Careers in the United States*, Chicago: Rand McNally.

Schmitter, P. and Lehmbruch, G. (eds) (1979) *Trends Toward Corporatist Intermediation*, Beverly Hills: Sage Publications.

Schumpeter, J. (1976 [1942]) *Capitalism, Socialism, and Democracy*, New York: Harper & Row.

Tocqueville, A. de (1969) *Democracy in America*, Garden City, NY: Anchor Books.

Von Beyme, K. (1983) 'Governments, parliaments, and the structure of power in political parties', in H. Daalder and P. Mair (eds) *Western European Party Systems: Continuity and Change*, Beverly Hills: Sage Publications.

Ware, A. (1987) 'Introduction: parties under electoral competition', in A. Ware (ed.) *Political Parties: Electoral Change and Structural Response*, Oxford: Basil Blackwell.

Weber, M. (1946) 'Politics as a vocation', in H. Gerth and C. W. Mills (eds) *From Max Weber: Essays in Sociology*, New York: Oxford University Press.

Zuckerman, A. (1979) *The Politics of Faction: Christian Democracy in Italy*, New Haven: Yale University Press.

Further reading

Baerwald, H. (1986) *Party Politics in Japan*, Boston: Allen & Unwin.

Barnes, S. (1967) *Party Democracy: Politics in a Socialist Federation*, New Haven: Yale University Press.

Blondel, J. (1978) *Political Parties: A Genuine Case for Discontent?*, London: Wildwood House.

Budge, I. Crewe, I. and Farlie, D. (eds) (1976) *Party Identification and Beyond*, New York: John Wiley.

Butler, D. and Stokes, D. (1969) *Political Change in Britain*, New York: St Martin's Press.

Castles, F. (1979) *The Social Democratic Image of Society*, London: Routledge & Kegan Paul.

—— (ed.) (1982) *The Impact of Parties: Politics and Policies in Democratic Capitalist States*, Beverly Hills: Sage Publications.

Chambers, W. N. (1963) *Political Parties in a New Nation: The American Experience 1776–1809*, New York: Oxford University Press.

Coleman, J. S. and Rosberg, C. G. (1964) *Political Parties and National Integration in Tropical Africa*, New Haven: Yale University Press.

Dahl, R. (ed.) (1966) *Political Oppositions in Western Democracies*, New Haven: Yale University Press.

Downs, A. (1957) *An Economic Theory of Democracy*, New York: Harper & Row.

Epstein, L. (1975) 'Political parties', in F. Greenstein and N. Polsby (eds) *Handbook of Political Science*, vol. IV, Reading, MA: Addison-Wesley.

Esping-Anderson, G. (1985) *Politics against Markets: The Social Democratic Road to Power*, Princeton: Princeton University Press.

Irving, R. E. M. (1979) *The Christian Democratic Parties of Western Europe*, London: Allen & Unwin.

Jowitt, K. (1978) *The Leninist Response to National Dependency*, Berkeley: Institute of International Studies, University of California at Berkeley.

Lipset, S. and Rokkan, S. (eds) (1967) *Party Systems and Voter Alignments*, New York: Free Press.

Maisel, L. and Cooper, J. (eds) (1978) *Political Parties: Development and Decay*, Beverly Hills: Sage Publications.

Paterson, W. E. and Thomas, A. H. (eds) (1977) *Social Democratic Parties in Western Europe*, London: Croom Helm.

Pizzorno, A. (1981) 'Interests and parties in pluralism', in S. Berger (ed.) *Organizing Interests in Western Europe*, New York: Cambridge University Press.

Powell, G. B. (1982) *Contemporary Democracies*, Cambridge, MA: Harvard University Press.

Rokkan, S. (1966) *Citizens, Elections, Parties*, Oslo: Universitetsforlaget.

Rose, R. (1969) *The Problem of Party Government*, Harmondsworth: Penguin.

—— (1980) *Do Parties Make a Difference?* New York: Chatham House.

Scarrow, S. (1996) *Parties and their Members: Organizing for Victory in Britain and Germany*, New York: Oxford University Press.

Schapiro, L. (1971) *The Communist Party of the Soviet Union*, New York: Random House.

Weiner, M. (1967) *Party Building in a New Nation: The Indian National Congress*, Chicago: University of Chicago Press.

27

CAMPAIGNS, ELECTIONS
AND ELECTORAL SYSTEMS

Paul Webb

Elections have, broadly speaking, drawn political scientists into investigation of three types of question: first, the nature and impact of electoral institutions, systems and administration; second, issues of electoral participation and behaviour; and third, matters of electoral campaigning and political communication. This article focuses in turn on each of these distinct, but inter-connected, strands of inquiry, after discussing issues of definition and scope as a necessary preliminary.

Elections: definition and scope

An election is a formal process of selecting a person for public office or accepting or rejecting a political proposition by voting. Elections thus provide a legitimate means of making political choices. For an election to be meaningful, the voter should have a free and genuine choice between at least two alternatives. In a purely formal sense, most of the world's political systems hold 'elections', but in probably only a third or so of these do more or less competitive contests take place; elsewhere the situation tends to be more ambiguous (thanks, for instance, to practices such as deliberate gerrymandering of constituency boundaries, voter intimidation and manipulation of vote counts), or restricted to one-party elections.

The widespread use of elections in the modern world has its origins in the gradual emergence of representative government in Europe and North America since the seventeenth century. Once governments were expected to seek the consent of the governed, the definition of an eligible elector gradually became more inclusive in democratizing states. Across Western Europe and North America manhood suffrage was ensured almost everywhere by 1920, though in one or two cases women's suffrage followed somewhat later (for example, 1929 in Britain, 1945 in France and 1949 in Belgium). In post-colonial regimes in Africa and Asia, universal adulthood suffrage emerged in the post-war era.

There are various types of election. Most commonly, they are a means of political recruitment, since they facilitate the legitimate selection of public office-holders. Moreover, by granting officials the authority to make public-policy decisions, they legitimize those decisions. Thus, any electoral mandate resulting from such a process does not entail the implementation of the abstract preferences of the majority of citizens, but rather the introduction of the policy of those leaders who come to power. In this rather loose and implicit sense, we may conceive of democratic rule as

399

embodying the 'will of the people'. Only in referenda on specific issues does an explicit popular will on particular policy questions become apparent (see below).

It should be added that most officeholder elections are interpretable only in terms of the role of political parties in the political process. Because of the difficulty in fixing individual responsibility for the actions of modern governments, political parties, rather than individual representatives, have largely become the vehicles of democratic accountability. Parties perform a number of important political functions, including the provision of a pool of talent from which candidates for elective office are drawn, the simplification and organization of electoral choices, the mobilization of electors during registration and election campaigns, the aggregation and articulation of social interests, the political education of citizens, and the organization and direction of government (Webb, Farrell and Holliday 2002). In recent decades, however, the significance of party has become more muted in many democratic elections where the emergence of 'candidate-centred' politics has rendered campaigning and accountability more personalized (Wattenberg 1991); this is equally true in parliamentary as well as presidential regimes (Poguntke and Webb, forthcoming).

Other types of election found throughout the democratic world include – increasingly – referenda and initiatives (Magleby 1984; Cronin 1989). These are elections in which the preferences of the community regarding particular issues are assessed; whereas the former are instigated by those in government, the latter are initiated by groups of electors. Referenda usually concern the raising and spending of public money, although they are occasionally used to decide major constitutional issues which are deemed to require the express consent of the people, or moral issues in which the elected bodies are deemed to possess no special competence. They may be legislatively binding, or merely consultative, but even consultative referenda are likely to have the force of legislative mandates. Referenda and initiatives are most heavily used at national level in Switzerland and Italy, and in a variety of countries at sub-national level, notably the USA and Germany.

Electoral systems and institutions

The first post-war political scientist of note to investigate the impact of electoral systems was Maurice Duverger (1954). Duverger's so-called 'law' – that single-member plurality systems tend to spawn stable two-party patterns of politics – generated considerable criticism and debate (see especially Rae 1971), and academic interest has become prominent once more since the mid-1980s (see, for instance, Taagepera and Shugart 1989; Lijphart 1994a; Katz 1997; Shugart and Wattenberg 2000). It is important to emphasize that such debates are not merely the obscure rituals of academic self-indulgence: they involve politicians, bureaucrats and the media and impact directly on the institutional and cultural frameworks of politics. Thus, a number of countries have introduced significant electoral reforms for national, sub-national or European elections in recent years, including Italy, New Zealand, Japan, and the United Kingdom.

In practice, the democratic world's electoral systems can be classified into three broad categories: majoritarian (including plurality systems); proportional; and semi-proportional. The simplest system for counting and converting votes into representative office is the *plurality* rule. To win, a candidate need only poll more votes than any other single opponent; s/he need not, as required by the majority formula, poll more votes than the combined opposition. Thus, the more candidates that contest an elective office under this system, the greater the probability of the winning candidate receiving less than 50 per cent of the vote. The plurality formula is or has been used mainly in the national elections of countries whose political development has been influenced by Britain (such as the USA, Canada, India and, until recently, New Zealand).

Under the *majority* rule, the party or candidate gaining more than 50 per cent of the vote in a constituency wins. Variants of the majority formula are employed in Australia (where the Alternative or Preferential Vote is used in lower house elections) and France (where Double Ballot systems operate in lower house and presidential elections). An unusual version known as the Supplementary Vote is used in mayoralty elections in the UK. Majority formulas are usually applied only within single-member electoral constituencies, though multi-member plurality voting is occasionally used (for instance, in some local government constituencies in the UK).

Neither the majority nor the plurality formulas distribute legislative seats in proportion to the share of the popular vote won by the competing parties. Both formulas tend to reward the strongest party disproportionately and to handicap the weaker parties, though small parties may escape the inequities of these electoral systems if they have regionally concentrated bases of support. The plurality formula usually, though not always, distorts the distribution of seats more than the majority system. By contrast, *proportional representation* (PR) requires that the distribution of offices be broadly proportional to the distribution of the popular vote among competing political parties. It seeks to overcome the disproportionalities that result from majority and plurality formulas and to create a representative body that reflects the distribution of opinion within the electorate. Because of the use of multi-member constituencies in proportional representation, parties with neither a majority nor a plurality of the popular vote can still win representative office.

While PR systems, unsurprisingly, usually achieve more proportional outcomes than plurality or majoritarian systems, a number of factors can generate disproportional outcomes even under PR. The major single factor is 'district magnitude', or the number of seats per constituency: the larger the electoral district in terms of the number of seats it contains, the more proportional the outcome will be (Lijphart 1990). A further important factor is the specific type of proportional formula used, the main distinction being that between the Single Transferable Vote (STV) and list PR systems.

Developed in the nineteenth century, STV employs a ballot that allows the voter to rank the competing candidates in order of preference. When the ballots are counted, any candidate receiving the necessary 'Droop' quota (Farrell 2001: 127) of first preference votes is awarded a seat. In the electoral calculations, votes received by a winning candidate in excess of the quota are transferred to other candidates according to the second preference marked on the ballot. Any candidate who then achieves the necessary quota is also awarded a seat. This process is repeated, with subsequent surpluses also being transferred, until all the remaining seats have been awarded.

Although it is the preferred option of influential bodies such as the Electoral Reform Society in the UK, STV is in fact little used by the world's democracies: it has been deployed in Northern Ireland, the Republic of Ireland, Malta and in the upper houses of Australia and South Africa. The characteristic of STV which distinguishes it from other proportional representation formulas is its emphasis on candidates rather than parties: the party affiliation of the candidates has no bearing on the computations, and voters may choose to cast preferences for candidates from different parties. This imposition on party control – along with the dubious argument of some critics that it is a more complex form of PR than the alternatives – probably explains the limited take-up of STV around the world.

Under list-PR electoral systems voters choose between party-compiled lists of candidates, rather than between individual candidates. Although certain versions of list system also permit voters to express individual candidate preferences, seats are principally awarded in respect of party rather than candidate totals. The seats that a party wins are allocated to its candidates in the order in which they appear on the party list. Several types of electoral formulas are used to decide the precise allocation of seats to which each party is entitled, although they fall into two broad categories: highest average and largest remainder formulas. Highest average systems are more widespread, being used in countries such as Austria, Belgium, Finland, and Switzerland, while largest remainder systems operate in Israel, Luxembourg and in some elections in Denmark.

Research suggests that the largest remainder Droop formula is the most proportional of the list systems, while the d'Hondt highest average is the least proportional (Farrell 2001: ch. 4, 161). A further factor which can dilute the proportionality of outcomes under PR is the imposition of electoral thresholds. These are national vote minima which parties must achieve if they are to be awarded any representation at all in parliaments. Designed to limit the political progress of small extremist parties, such thresholds can constitute significant obstacles, notably in the cases of Sweden (where a 4 per cent threshold exists) and Germany (where it stands at 5 per cent).

The choice of majority and plurality or proportional systems is, of course, not simply a matter of pure theory. Different methods of counting, just as different conceptions of representation, usually reflect cultural, social and political circumstances in a particular context. Majority or plurality systems are most likely to be acceptable in relatively stable and homogeneous societies. In such cultures, the 'winner-takes-all' implications of these formulas do not risk excluding from power for a prolonged period significant social groups. Proportional representation, on the other hand, is more likely to be found in societies with traditional ethnic, linguistic or religious cleavages or in societies experiencing pervasive class and ideological conflicts. In such contexts it is a vital institutional component of 'consensus democracy', since it tends to facilitate the sharing of power between different socio-political groups (Lijphart 1984, 1999).

An increasingly common variant of the systems discussed is the Mixed Member Proportional (MMP) or Additional Member System (AMS). This is a category which is in itself quite diverse, though all MMP systems elect some representatives by proportional representation and the remainder by a non-proportional formula (Shugart and Wattenberg 2000). The classic archetype of such a system is the

German Bundestag model, which uses regional list-PR to elect 50 per cent of the country's national parliamentarians and simple plurality voting in single-member constituencies to elect the remainder. A growing number of other countries have adopted Mixed Member systems in recent years, including Italy, New Zealand, some of Eastern Europe's new democracies and the UK's devolved assemblies in Scotland and Wales. Japan offers a somewhat different semi-proportional system – the Single Non-Transferable Vote (SNTV) – in which voters cast their votes and, as under plurality rules, candidates with the most votes are elected; however, voters can only select one candidate in multi-member constituencies.

Finally, it should be noted that problems of 'apportionment' can have a dramatic bearing on the fairness of electoral outcomes, especially in single-member systems. These problems stem from an inability to reconcile the territorial and population bases of representation, and result in electoral 'malapportionment' that defies the one-vote, one-value principle of equal representation. This failure usually occurs because of population shifts. For instance, under modern conditions of urbanization, failure to redraw constituency boundaries to take account of population changes has often benefited rural electoral districts. More recently, the shift of city people to suburbs or rural areas has reversed the problem. In addition to malapportionment, patterns of 'tactical' voting by electors can serve to introduce 'electoral bias' into a country's electoral system, such that two parties achieving the same share of the national popular vote would not be rewarded with remotely similar levels of representation in the national legislature. This has become a problem of alarming proportions in recent UK general elections (Johnston *et al.* 2002).

Problems of malapportionment help to explain why the administration and regulation of elections has continued to develop across the democratic world. Bodies of electoral law have increasingly been accompanied by the development of regulatory and supervisory organs charged with functions such as the registration of voters, the drawing and re-drawing of constituency boundaries, and the publication and control of campaign income and expenditure by candidates. One of the least regulated of the world's leading democracies until recently was the United Kingdom: however, the *Political Parties, Elections and Referendums Act 2000* established a new regulatory framework and national Election Commission which came into effect shortly before the general election of June 2001 (Webb 2001).

Electoral participation and behaviour

The second major stream of electoral studies concerns the behaviour of voters. Two broad questions have found particular prominence: why do citizens vote? And why do they vote the way they do? The former is a question which greatly exercises academics, journalists and politicians alike in the democratic world, for low electoral turnout by voters is widely regarded as a phenomenon which threatens to delegitimize democracy itself. Studies have consistently suggested that a number of factors influence the decision to vote.

The first of these is the electoral system, in that proportional systems provide incentives for electors because they know that their individual votes are likelier to 'count' in affecting the outcome of constituency contests. Certainly the empirical evidence is consistent with this, for PR systems are associated with a significantly higher average voter turnout than plurality systems (Lijphart 1994b, 1999; Farrell 2001: 203–4). The second factor that matters is the 'personal resources' at the disposal of the individual voter, in that the more affluent and educated an individual, the greater the likelihood that he or she will vote (Verba, Nie and Kim 1978; Parry, Moyser and Day 1992). In addition, it is universally true that young people who have recently been enfranchised are less likely to vote than people who are middle-aged. This often generates a misperception that democratic legitimacy is destined to suffer in the future, but since low turnout among young voters is usually a life-cycle effect, it need not necessarily be so: the uncertain and disengaged young citizens of today frequently turn into the concerned and reliable participants of tomorrow. That said, recent evidence from a number of countries suggests that a generational effect may be occurring which sets current cohorts of young (non-)voters apart from their predecessors (Blais 2000). Whether this is a purely temporary or more enduring phenomenon remains to be seen.

A third factor which undoubtedly affects turnout is the (perceived) closeness of the electoral contest. When voters feel that a race for elective office is likely to be close, they tend to conclude that their individual voting decision is likelier to have some bearing on the outcome. This explains why turnout is systematically higher in 'marginal' seats than in 'safe' seats under single-member plurality voting rules (Denver and Hands 1985). A fourth consideration is the perceived importance of the office being competed for, since this clearly seems to make a difference to the voter's decision about whether or not to participate in an election. 'First-order' elections for national political office (legislative or presidential) generally attract greater rates of participation than 'second-order' state, local or European parliamentary elections (Reif and Schmitt 1980). Finally, partisan motivation has an impact on turnout in as much as citizens with strong affinities to particular parties are more likely than non-partisans to feel it a matter of importance to make the effort to support 'their team'. Though it remains a matter of dispute, some researchers feel that a down-turn in turnout at national elections has occurred in Western democracies since the 1970s (Wattenberg 2000); in so far as evidence can be mustered to support this view, it seems most likely that such a decline is consequent upon a process of 'partisan de-alignment' and the erosion of social cleavages based on class and religion (see below).

When people do decide to participate in elections, their electoral choices appear to be influenced by a range of factors. The study of electoral behaviour developed as part and parcel of the behaviouralist revolution in the social sciences during the 1950s. Especially prominent in the field was the seminal work of the 'American Voter' scholars based at the University of Michigan (Campbell *et al.* 1960). They pioneered a social–psychological approach which became known as the 'partisan identification' model. This drew largely upon two important concepts imported from psychology and sociology. First, *identification*, which refers to a persistently held affective attachment to some group-object in the social environment – such as a political party. The party then acts as a reference point by which other objects in the social and political environment may be evaluated; in short, it becomes a source of cues for interpreting the political world. Hence, for the Michigan researchers political parties structured the 'individual's cognitive and affective map of politics', helping to shape interpretations of issues and candidates. The second core concept they drew upon was *socialization*. Rooted in the 'deep-seated human desire for conformity' (Franklin 1985: 50), this process leads to mimicry of attitudes and values in humans who engage with each other on a regular basis. In particular, people may well be first induced to adopt a partisan identification during childhood, before they have any well-developed cognitive understanding of politics. This initial family socialization experience may be reinforced by other primary and secondary group links so that partisan identification actually tends to harden with age. In addition, voters are to some extent susceptible to the influence of more short-term and contingent factors such as campaign events, issues and candidate appeals. However, with its emphasis on habitual partisan loyalties, the strength of the Michigan model lay in its capacity to explain enduring patterns of electoral alignment. Allied with the classic work of S. M. Lipset and Stein Rokkan (1967) on the social and historical bases of electoral support in Europe, this provided a persuasive account of stable – even 'frozen' – party systems.

By the middle of the 1970s, however, scholars were beginning to observe that a process of 'partisan de-alignment' was reducing the proportion of voters in Western democracies who retained their long-term partisan identities (Dalton 2000). In conjunction with the declining impact of social group influences (Franklin *et al.* 1990), this seemed to open the way for voter choice to be more heavily affected by short-term factors relevant to specific election campaigns, whether these might be issue assessments, candidate evaluations or judgements on aspects of performance of governing parties. This shift from long-term predisposition to short-term evaluation seems to have been facilitated in part by the phenomenon of 'cognitive mobilization', a supposed enhancement of the political independence and intelligence of voters who are both better educated than earlier generations and, thanks to the development of the mass media, better informed on public affairs (Barnes and Kaase 1979; Dalton 1996). Initially, the evidence of partisan de-alignment, electoral instability (Pedersen 1979) and cognitive mobilization encouraged the rational choice school of political scientists to place emphasis on the growing significance for the voting decision of specific issue assessments by voters (Downs 1957; Alt, Sarlvik and Crewe 1976; Himmelweit, Humphreys and Jaeger 1981). Later, however, it became evident that such narrowly conceived issue voting models did not perform well in explaining electoral behaviour and outcomes (Dunleavy and Husbands 1985; Heath, Jowell and Curtice 1985; Sanders 1992), and alternatives based on voter assessments of the governing performance of parties – especially in respect of macro-economic management – and the personal qualities of candidates came to assume greater prominence (Fiorina 1977; Enelow and Hinich 1982; Lewis Beck, Norpoth and Lafay 1991; Alesina and Rosenthal 1995; Mughan 2000). More recently, an attempt has been made to salvage issue voting models by substituting 'directional' variants for the classic 'proximity' models derived from the pioneering work of Anthony Downs. Whereas the latter suggest that voters offer their support to the candidates or parties whose policies are perceived to lie closest to their own preferences in one-dimensional space, the former propose that voters will opt for candidates or parties who promise to shift public policy in the direction they (the individual voters) prefer (Matthews 1979; Rabinowitz and MacDonald 1989). It is interesting and important to note, however, that the most successful models all tend to propose accounts of individual-level voting behaviour which incorporate a blend

405

of long-term predispositional factors and contingent, short-term assessments (Merrill and Grofman 1999: 167). While the sophistication and detail of such models vary considerably, in essence this leaves the study of electoral behaviour remarkably close to the intellectual framework developed by the Michigan scholars in the 1950s.

Campaigning and political communication

The notion that voters may be more susceptible to the influence of relatively short-term developments implies that what candidates and parties do in the course of their election campaigning may matter more for electoral outcomes than the rather static Michigan model seemed to imply. It is not surprising, therefore, that academic interest has grown in campaigning and the growing sophistication with which politicians seek to communicate with voters (for overviews see Bowler and Farrell 1992; Butler and Ranney 1992; Swanson and Mancini 1996).

This literature tends to show party organizations as highly adaptive, investing heavily (in time and resources) in the new campaign technologies, professionalizing (and centralizing) their organizations (particularly around their top leaderships), and paying far more attention to 'image' and specific campaign issues (as opposed to traditional ideological standpoints). Increasingly the tendency is less one of 'selling' themselves to voters, but rather one of designing an appropriate 'product' to match voter needs – in short, a switch to a 'marketing' approach.

At the risk of over-simplification, the professionalization of election campaigning can be broken down into three broad stages of development (Farrell and Webb 2000). The first stage was characterized by a number of features, including: relatively limited preparation; communication through party press, posters, mass rallies and canvassing; reliance on traditional party bureaucrats and volunteer activists; a focus on the local campaign with little centralization or coordination; dependence on the political intuitions of party strategists and activists rather than on systematic opinion research; the use of the party leaders in public rallies and whistle-stop tours to boost the campaign efforts of the local politicians; the targeting of fixed social groups of voters, with a resulting emphasis on the mobilization of known supporters, rather than the attempted persuasion of non-partisans; and finally, campaign communications consisting primarily of propaganda, 'a one-directional communication process in which passive audiences found themselves subjected to the sometimes manipulative appeals of political elites' (Wring 1996a: 102).

The second stage of campaign professionalization was driven by the arrival of television. The ensuing emphasis on television as the major means of communication generated a more self-consciously professional approach to public relations, advertising and the media training of leaders and candidates. It also inspired more detailed long-term campaign preparation based on specialist campaign committees, and the professionalization of party personnel (Panebianco 1988), including more pervasive use of media and marketing specialists, and the use of campaign consultants and agencies; this coincided with a nationalization of campaigning in which power and resources were concentrated at the centre. There was, moreover, a growing emphasis on party leaders, and a tendency to standardize national campaigns by coordinating the messages broadcast by candidates and local party organizations. All of this coincided with the development of 'catch-all' electoral strategies in which (major) parties sought to broaden their electoral appeals (Kirchheimer 1966). Although some attempt was made to test the market, the goal remained one of selling a more or less sacrosanct product (Scammell 1995: 9).

The third stage of campaign professionalization has coincided with the arrival of new telecommunications technology since the 1980s (such as cable and satellite technology, and more recently the Internet). These developments have helped spawn the arrival of 'the permanent campaign', with greater emphasis on targeted communication via cable television and the Internet. This 'narrowcasting' is complemented by a growing reliance on opinion research designed to adapt the message to suit the audience. Inevitably, this approach renders the campaign specialist yet more prominent, and may provoke tensions with traditional party bureaucrats. Some have argued (see, for instance, Wring 1996b; Scammell 1995), that the growing consumer-orientation of campaign communications implies that it is now the *product* rather than the voter which is regarded as 'malleable'. If so, this would seem to imply a model of party competition which is overwhelmingly preference-accommodating rather than preference-shaping, though it should be said that even here there must be some limits to the malleability of the product. For party policy appeals to remain credible, programmatic adaptation should remain within the bounds of enduring party policy reputations (Laver 1997: 136), or such pledges are likely to be discounted by sceptical voters.

A summary such as this is inevitably a gross over-simplification, but it is a useful heuristic device. Thus, the three stages can be regarded as developmental ideal-types which constitute a linear continuum along which campaign organizations are moving, from a 'premodern' pole to an 'advanced-modern' pole. Not all countries or campaign organizations move smoothly from one end of the continuum to the other in an orderly logical sequence. For instance, many of the new East European and Latin American democracies appear to have skipped much of the first stage (Jakubowicz 1996; Mickiewicz and Richter 1996; Rospir 1996; Angell *et al.* 1992). There are a number of factors in national environments which influence the development of campaigning styles, some institutional (such as campaign laws, and the governmental or electoral systems), others cultural.

Conclusion

Studies of electoral institutions, campaigns and voting behaviour have become mainstream components of contemporary political science and it is virtually inconceivable that this will not continue to be the case for many years to come. Resurgent interest in electoral systems has been driven by a number of factors, including the intellectual fashion in favour of the 'New Institutionalism' which emerged in the late 1980s, and the very real need for effective and practical expert advice on constitutional design (Sartori 1994); this in turn was given new impetus by the democratization of the former Soviet bloc countries after 1989, and the widening and deepening of European integration at about the same time. The widespread desire for the transparency and regulation of all aspects of electoral competition in order to stave off the potentially delegitimizing effects of corruption has further rein-forced this.

The study of electoral behaviour has been a constant and growing element of political science for nearly half a century now, and its global spread has been facili-tated by the steady development of (primarily survey-based) national election studies that emulate, to some extent or other, the American National Election Study. Once again, the democratization of Eastern and Central Europe has played its part in facilitating research of this nature (see, for instance, White *et al.* 1996). Indeed, such large-scale studies of mass opinion and behaviour have spread beyond national boundaries, with the development of the EU-wide *Eurobarometer* survey and the multinational *World Values Survey*, both of which have been directed by the eminent US political scientist Ronald Inglehart (see, for instance, Inglehart 1997).

One of the principal findings to emerge from the study of voter behaviour – the phenomenon of partisan de-alignment – has fuelled the desire to understand election campaign dynamics, methods and effects. Hence the burgeoning literature on the professionalization of political communications, and on the interaction between candidates and the media. Technological developments which may lie at the root of partisan de-alignment are also central to changing styles of political communication, and virtually ensure that such changes are irreversible.

Inevitably, challenges remain for scholars in all three areas. Students of electoral systems will continue to seek to refine their understanding of the precise incentives and impacts of the myriad variants which exist, under the diverse conditions in which they operate; those studying electoral behaviour must go further in developing models which blend dispositional, spatial and contingent factors; and research into political communications has to track, describe and explain the developments which flow from the constantly changing interactions between voters, campaign and media profes-sionals. The growing specialization of political science in contemporary democratic societies means that these challenges are sure to be taken up.

References

Alesina, A. and Rosenthal, H. (1995) *Partisan Politics, Divided Government and the Economy*, Cambridge: Cambridge University Press.

Alt, J. E., Sarlvik, B. and Crewe, I. (1976) 'Partisanship and Policy Choice: Issue Preferences in the British Electorate', *British Journal of Political Science*, 6.

Angell, Alan, D'Alva Kinzo, M. and Urbaneja, D. (1992), 'Latin America' in D. Butler and A. Ranney (eds), *Electioneering*, Oxford: Clarendon.

Barnes, S. and Kaase, M. (1979) *Political Action: Political Participation in Five Democracies*, Thousand Oaks, CA: Sage.

Bartolini, Stefano and Mair, Peter (1990) *Identity, Competition and Electoral Availability: The Stabilisation of European Electorates 1885–1985*, Cambridge: Cambridge University Press.

Blais, A. (2000) *To Vote or Note to Vote? The Merits and Limits of Rational Choice Theory*, Pittsburgh: University of Pittsburgh Press.

Bowler, Shaun and Farrell, David (1992) *Electoral Strategies and Political Marketing*, Basingstoke: Macmillan.

Budge, I. (1996) *The New Challenge of Direct Democracy*, Oxford: Polity Press.

Butler, D. and Ranney, A. (1992) *Electioneering*, Oxford: Clarendon.

—— (1994) *Referendums Around the World: The Growing Use of Direct Democracy*, Washington: American Enterprise Institute.

Campbell, A., Converse, P., Miller W. E., and Stokes, D. (1960) *The American Voter*, New York: John Wiley.

Crewe, I. and Denver, D. (1985) *Electoral Change in Western Democracies: Patterns and Sources of Electoral Volatility*, Beckenham: Croom Helm.

Cronin, T. E. (1989) *Direct Democracy: The Politics of Initiative, Referendum and Recall*, Cambridge, MA: Harvard University Press.

Curtis, G. (1988) *The Japanese Way of Politics*, New York: Columbia University Press.

Dalton, R. J. (1996) *Citizen Politics* Chatham, NJ: Chatham House.

—— (2000) 'The decline of partisan identifications' in R. J. Dalton and M. P. Wattenberg (eds), *Parties Without Partisans: Political Change in Advanced Industrial Democracies*, Oxford: Oxford University Press, 19–36.

Dalton, R. J., Flanagan, S. and Beck, P. A. (1984) *Electoral Change in Advanced Industrial Societies: Realignment or De-alignment?* Princeton, NJ: Princeton University Press.

Denver, D. and Hands, G. (1985) 'Marginality and turnout in general elections in the 1970s', *British Journal of Political Science*, 15: 381–8.

Downs, A. (1957) *An Economic Theory of Democracy*, New York: Harper & Row.

Dunleavy, P. and Husbands, C. (1985) *British Democracy at the Crossroads*, London: Allen & Unwin.

Duverger, M. (1954) *Political Parties*, London: Methuen.

Enelow, J. M. and Hinich, M. (1982) 'Non-spatial candidate characteristics and electoral competition' *Journal of Politics*, 44: 115–30.

Evans, G. (1999) *The End of Class Politics?* Oxford: Oxford University Press.

Farrell, David (1996), 'Campaign Strategies and Tactics' in L. LeDuc, R. Niemi and P. Norris (eds), *Comparing Democracies*, Thousand Oaks, CA: Sage.

Farrell, D. M. (2001) *Electoral Systems: A Comparative Introduction*, Basingstoke: Palgrave.

Farrell, D. M. and Schmitt-Beck, R. (2002) *Do Political Campaigns Matter? Campaign Effects in Elections and Referendums*, London: Routledge.

Farrell, D.M. and Webb, P. D. (2000) 'Political parties as campaign organisation' in R. J. Dalton and M. P. Wattenberg (eds), *Parties Without Partisans: Political Change in Advanced Industrial Democracies*, Oxford: Oxford University Press, 102–28.

Fiorina, M. P. (1977) 'An Outline of a Model of Party Choice', *American Journal of Political Science*, 21.

Franklin, M. N. (1985) *The Decline of Class Voting in Britain: Changes in the Basis of Electoral Choice, 1964–83*, Oxford: Clarendon Press.

Franklin, Mark N., Mackie, T. T. and Valen, H. (1992) *Electoral Change: Responses to Evolving Social and Attitudinal Structures in Western Countries*, Cambridge: Cambridge University Press.

Heath, A., Jowell, R. and Curtice, J. (1985) *How Britain Votes*, Oxford: Pergamon.

Himmelweit, H., Humphreys, P. and Jaeger, M. (1981) *How Voters Decide*, Milton Keynes: Open University Press.

Inglehart, R. (1997) *Modernization and Post-Modernization: Cultural, Economic and Political Change in 43 Countries*, Princeton, NJ: Princeton University Press.

Jakubowicz, K. (1996) 'Television and Elections in Post-1989 Poland' in David Swanson and Paolo Mancini (eds), *Politics, Media, and Modern Democracy*, Westport, CT: Praeger.

Johnston, R., Pattie, C., Dorling, D. and Rossiter, D. (2002) *From Votes to Seats: The Operation of the UK Electoral System Since 1945*, Manchester: Manchester University Press.

Katz, R. S. (1997) *Democracy and Elections*, Oxford: Oxford University Press.

Kirchheimer, O. (1966) 'The Transformation of Western European Party Systems' in J. LaPalombara and M. Weiner *Political Parties and Political Development*, Princeton: Princeton University Press.

Laver, M. (1997) *Private Desires, Political Action: An Invitation to the Politics of Rational Choice*, Thousand Oaks and London: Sage.

Lewis Beck, M., Norpoth, H. and Lafay, J. D. (1991) *Economics and Elections: The Calculus of Support*, Ann Arbor, MI: University of Michigan Press.

Lijphart, A (1984) *Democracies: Patterns of Majoritarian and Consensus Government in 21 Countries*, New Haven, CT: Yale University Press.

—— (1990) 'The political consequences of electoral laws, 1945–85', *American Political Science Review* 84: 481–96.

—— (1994a) *Electoral Systems and Party Systems: A Study of 27 Democracies, 1945–90*, Oxford: Oxford University Press.

—— (1994b) 'Democracies: Forms, performance and constitutional engineering', *European Journal of Political Research* 25: 1–17.

—— (1999) *Patterns of Democracy: Government Forms and Performance in 26 Countries*, New Haven: Yale University Press.

Lipset, S. M. and Rokkan, S. (1967) *Party Systems and Voter Alignments: Cross-National Perspectives*, New York: Free Press.

Magleby, D. B. (1984) *Direct Election: Voting on Ballot Propositions in the U.S.*, Baltimore: Johns Hopkins University Press.

Matthews, S. (1979) 'A simple direction model of electoral competition', *Public Choice*, 34: 141–56.

Merrill, S. and Grofman, B. (1999) *A Unified Theory of Voting: Directional and Proximity Spatial Models*, Cambridge: Cambridge University Press.

Mickiewicz, E. and Richter, A. (1996) 'Television, Campaigning, and Elections in the Soviet Union and Post-Soviet Russia' in David Swanson and Paolo Mancini (eds), *Politics, Media, and Modern Democracy*, Westport, CT: Praeger.

Miller, W. E. and Merrill Shanks, J. (1996) *The New American Voter*, Cambridge, MA: Harvard University Press.

Mughan, A. (2000) *Media and the Presidentialization of Parliamentary Elections*, Basingstoke: Palgrave.

Panebianco, A. (1988), *Political Parties: Organisation and Power*, Cambridge: Cambridge University Press.

Parry, G., Moyser, G. and Day, N. (1992) *Political Participation and Democracy in Britain*, Cambridge: Cambridge University Press.

Pedersen, M. (1979) 'The dynamics of European party systems: changing patterns of electoral volatility', *European Journal of Political Research* 7: 1–26.

Poguntke, T. and Webb, P. D. (Forthcoming) *The Presidentialization of Democracy: A Study in Comparative Politics*, Oxford: Oxford University Press.

Popkin, S. L. (1994) *The Reasoning Voter: Communication and Persuasion in Presidential Campaigns*, Chicago: University of Chicago Press.

Rabinowitz, G. and MacDonald, S. E. (1989) 'A directional theory of issue voting' *American Political Science Review* 83: 93–121.

Rae, Douglas (1971) *The Political Consequences of Election Laws*, New Haven, CT: Yale University Press.

Reif, K. and Schmitt, H. (1980) 'Nine second-order national elections: A conceptual framework for the analysis of European election results', *European Journal of Political Research*, 8: 3–44.

Rospir, Juan (1996) 'Political Communication and Electoral Campaigns in the Young Spanish Democracy' in David Swanson and Paolo Mancini (eds), *Politics, Media, and Modern Democracy*, Westport, CT: Praeger.

Sanders, D. (1992) 'Why the Conservative Party won – again' in A. King (ed.), *Britain at the Polls*, Chatham, NJ: Chatham House, 171–222.

Sartori, G. (1994) *Comparative Constitutional Engineering: An Inquiry into Structures, Incentives and Outcomes*, Basingstoke: Macmillan.

Scammell, Margaret (1995) *Designer Politics: How Elections are Won*, Basingstoke: Macmillan.

Shugart, M. S. and Wattenberg, M. (2000) *Mixed-Member Electoral Systems: The Best of Both Worlds?*, Oxford: Oxford University Press.

Swanson, David and Mancini, Paolo (1996) *Politics, Media, and Modern Democracy*, Westport, CT: Praeger.

—— (1996a) 'Politics, Media and Modern Democracy: Introduction' in David Swanson and Paolo Mancini (eds), *Politics, Media, and Modern Democracy*, Westport, CT: Praeger.

Taagepera, R. and Shugart, M. S. (1989) *Seats and Votes: The Effects and Determinants of Electoral Systems*, New Haven, CT: Yale University Press.

Verba, S., Nie, N. H. and Kim, J. (1978) *Participation and Political Equality: A Seven Nation Comparison*, Cambridge: Cambridge University Press.

Wattenberg, M. (1991) *The Rise of Candidate-Centred Politics: Presidential Elections in the 1980s*, Cambridge, MA: Harvard University Press.

—— (2000) 'The decline of party mobilization' in R. J. Dalton and M. P. Wattenberg (eds), *Parties Without Partisans: Political Change in Advanced Industrial Democracies*, Oxford: Oxford University Press, pp. 64–77.

Webb, P. D. (2001) 'Parties and party systems: Modernisation, regulation and diversity' *Parliamentary Affairs*, 54: 308–21.

Webb, P. D., Farrell, D. M. and Holliday, I. (2002) *Political Parties in Advanced Industrial Democracies*, Oxford: Oxford University Press.

White, S., Rose, R. and McAllister, I. (1996) *How Russia Votes*, Chatham, NJ: Chatham House.

Wring, Dominic (1996a) 'Political Marketing and Party Development in Britain' *European Journal of Marketing*, 30: 100–11.

—— (1996b) 'From Mass Propaganda to Political Marketing' in C. Rallings, D. Farrell, D. Denver and D. Broughton (eds), *British Elections and Parties Yearbook 1995*, London: Cass.

Further reading

Farrell (2001) provides a readable, up-to-date and comprehensive overview of contemporary electoral institutions, while the impact of electoral systems on party systems is analysed in detail in Rae (1971), Taagepera and Shugart (1989), and Lijphart (1994a). The significance for democratic theory of electoral arrangements is considered in depth in Katz (1997), and the recent development of mixed-member electoral systems is the focus of Shugart and Wattenberg (2000). Analyses of referenda and direct democracy can be found in Magleby (1984), Cronin (1989), Butler and Ranney (1994) and Budge (1996). Classic perspectives on voting behaviour and electoral participation can be found in Downs (1957), Campbell *et al.* (1960), and Lipset and Rokkan (1967). The debate about electoral change is covered in major publications such as Crewe and Denver (1985), Dalton *et al.* (1984), Bartolini and Mair (1990) and Franklin *et al.* (1992). More recent developments in voting behaviour are dealt with in Popkin (1994), Miller and Shanks (1996), Evans (1999), and Merrill and Grofman (1999). Overviews of campaigning and marketing developments are provided by Bowler and Farrell (1992), Swanson and Mancini (1996) and Farrell and Schmitt-Beck (2001).

Articles on all aspects of electoral processes regularly appear in the leading national and international general political science journals, but a number of specialist journals are also worth noting. *Representation* specializes in the study of electoral systems and administration, while *Electoral Studies* focuses on voting behaviour; the leading journal focusing on political marketing and communications is the *Harvard Journal of Press and Politics*, while *Party Politics* covers all three fields.

28

POLITICAL PARTICIPATION AND VOTING BEHAVIOUR

W. L. Miller

Insightful though they have been, too many studies of participation and voting have tended to present a highly individualistic account that overstates the very real but also rather limited significance of voters' choices. There is no such thing as a free choice even in democratic politics. Voters' participation and choices are (unconsciously) *conditioned* by the social and political context in which they live. Moreover, their behaviour must be distinguished from their preferences, because voters are consciously *constrained* (or *mobilized*) by institutions – by the electoral system and by the limited range of voting options available to them.

Voting may be compulsory. Or particular groups may be excluded from the franchise – like conscientious objectors after the First World War in Britain for example, or women in Spain before 1977. But many institutional constraints and incentives are more psychological than legal in origin and less predictable or even visible in their consequences. The power of electoral systems to influence voters' choices only becomes fully obvious when the electoral system is changed or when several systems operate simultaneously within the same country – though cross-national comparisons may provide a partial substitute for within-country variation. Similarly, the dependence of voters' choices on the range of options (parties, politicians, programmes) available to them only becomes fully obvious when voters are offered a new choice or when they are offered different choices at different levels of government. As long as the electoral system and the range of political options remain fixed, the potential for voter volatility will be underestimated and the individual component of the voter's decision-making will be overestimated. Conversely, changes in participation or voting behaviour may not reflect 'changing voters' so much as 'changing constraints' (Crewe 1992).

Participation

In their classic study of political participation, Verba, Nie and Kim argued that there is a universal tendency for citizens with higher levels of 'socio-economic resources' to be more willing to participate in politics (Verba, Nie and Kim 1978: 63–79). By socio-economic resources they meant, primarily, education and income. These resources provide the skills, the stimulation and the capability to participate in many kinds of political activity.

413

However, the influence of these personal resources is likely to vary with the particular type of activity, and with the particular institutional context. They distinguished three 'modes' or kinds of political participation: (i) voting, (ii) electoral campaigning and (iii) non-partisan lobbying. These three kinds of participation differ in terms of the degree of institutional conflict implied, and the amount of individual initiative and effort required. Activities that involve the most individual effort and the least institutional conflict should be the least affected by institutional incentives and constraints. Those that involve the most institutional conflict and the least individual effort should be the most susceptible to institutional influence.

The act of voting requires very little effort by the individual but it involves a great deal of institutional conflict. So the natural propensity for individuals with high resources to participate more than others should be least evident in the case of voting. Parties will be both willing and able to mobilize relatively apathetic citizens into such an important (for the parties) but easy (for the citizen) form of participation.

In general Verba, Nie and Kim's evidence confirmed this theory. Within a wide range of countries there was a uniformly high correlation (averaging 0.36) between citizens' socio-economic resources and their psychological involvement with politics – that is their interest in politics and their inclination to discuss political questions. But there was a much lower and more variable correlation between citizens' socio-economic resources and their actual, physical participation. The correlation with *voting* was particularly low overall (averaging only 0.08), though it ranged from almost nothing at all in some countries up to 0.24 in the USA. This suggests that powerful institutional forces generally, but not always, work to prevent the pattern of psychological involvement being reflected in actual voting.

Indeed, more recent research across 40 countries shows that the cross-national variation in voting participation far exceeds the variation within countries. On this aspect of political participation at least, the impact of diverse institutional constraints and incentives far outweighs the impact of personal characteristics. Even if everyone in the USA had a university degree, turnout would still not reach 'even the levels found in medium-turnout countries such as Britain' (Franklin 2001: 151).

Cross-nationally, compulsory voting increases turnout by around 7 per cent in national elections, postal voting by 6 per cent and weekend voting by 6 per cent also. The cumulative impact of this trio of legal incentives is large. Proportional electoral systems, in which 'wasted vote' arguments do not apply to supporters of locally weak (or locally hegemonic) parties, achieve turnout levels up to 10 per cent greater than under FPTP (First Past The Post). But although it is extremely difficult to define with clarity, the most powerful cross-national influence on turnout seems to be 'electoral salience': in countries where national elections have clearly visible and important policy consequences turnout is far higher than where it does not (Franklin 2001: 158). For the same reason, turnout in many countries is far less in Local Government and European Parliament elections than in national elections: these 'second order' elections simply do not matter so much to the electorate.

Institutional incentives that lead to *extremely* high levels of turnout almost inevitably reduce the scope for socio-economic bias in participation. But there is no guarantee that institutional incentives and constraints will always offset the influence of personal resources on political participation. They can amplify the effects of personal resources. It all depends upon whether institutions mobilize the poor and exclude the rich, or exclude the poor and mobilize the rich.

Some citizens may be discouraged from participation because they cannot legally form a party to represent their interests (though they are legally entitled to vote), or because politics in their country is dominated by a set of parties, none of which represents their particular interests and values. Conversely, citizens can be mobilized into active participation not just by legal pressure but also through psychological identification with a party that does represent their interests and values. The match between citizens and parties has a much less obvious and mechanical effect upon participation than legal requirements or exclusions, but it nonetheless exerts significant influence.

Socialist, social democrat and trade-union parties are committed to mobilizing the poor. Where they have been strong they have tended to ensure that the poor turned out to vote even though they were uninterested in politics. Less obviously, some religious-based parties have appealed to religious groups that just happen to be poor. (Rural peasant communities tend to be both poor and religious.) So these religious-based parties also tended to mobilize the poor and offset personal deficiencies. But where socialist parties are virtually non-existent, and where religion mobilizes the well-off more than the poor, institutional factors amplify the tendency of the rich and well-educated to participate disproportionately. Thus, in the USA especially, the rich and well-educated are not just more interested in politics than the poor, they actually participate much more.

Biased turnout is far more deadly than low turnout. Electoral participation in the USA fails the test of representative democracy not because turnout is low but because it is so unrepresentative. If a mere thousand well-chosen respondents in an opinion poll can reasonably substitute for an electorate of millions then a 50 per cent turnout is more than adequate – but only if it is a representative 50 per cent, not if it is extremely biased in terms of race, gender, class or ideology.

Lobbying provides a particularly sharp contrast with voting. Voting involves the most institutional (i.e. party) conflict, lobbying the least. Voting requires the least personal initiative, lobbying the most. So we should expect that the citizens with the highest levels of education and income would be prepared to lobby most actively and that this tendency would be relatively unaffected by all but the most draconian of institutional incentives or constraints. That seems to be the case. The correlation between personal resources and lobbying is moderately high – much higher than for voting.

The three kinds of participation discussed by Verba, Nie and Kim have been christened 'conventional' or 'elite-directed' to distinguish them from 'unconventional', 'protest' or 'elite-challenging' modes of participation such as demonstrations, strikes, damage to property or violence against people. But citizens tend to see at least some of these options as supplements rather than alternatives to voting, campaigning and lobbying. Few express support for outright violence. So most of the empirical findings refer to protest activity that goes no further than demonstrations and sit-ins – which is very much a part of conventional democratic activity and should not be confused with terrorist activity (Miller *et al.* 1982). There is a moderately sized *positive* correlation between support for such (peaceful) protest activity and 'conventional' participation such as voting and electoral campaigning (averaging 0.24: see Marsh and Kaase 1979: 93).

But there are some differences in the patterns of elite-directed and elite-challenging participation. The young are much more inclined than the old to support demonstrations and occupations, but less inclined than the old to vote. However, the highly educated and strong partisans are more likely than others to engage in all kinds of political activity – protest activity as well as electoral activity (Dalton 1996a: 58–61 and 80).

There is a great irony here. Western democracies provide responsible government but not, in general, representative government – at least not socially representative. Elected bodies are notoriously unrepresentative in the social sense. The US Congress is a congress of lawyers, the German parliament is a parliament of civil servants. But even at much lower levels of participation than holding elective office, political activists are socially unrepresentative. They are drawn disproportionately from those who are adding the advantage of political influence to the advantages of income and education. Young elites may challenge old elites, but even protest activity fails to compensate for the unrepresentative nature of political activists.

Voting has been by far the most socially representative aspect of political participation. In the future however, voter turnout may become less representative even outside the USA. Though the dramatic drop in turnout at the British General Election of 2001 was exceptional, the trend in many countries is towards somewhat lower turnout (Franklin 2001: 164). That makes bias possible. And the repositioning of European Socialist parties towards the centre makes it more difficult for them to play their historic role of mobilizing the poor into participation. Ironically, by mobilizing the poor and uneducated, extremist parties may contribute towards more democratically representative participation even as they erode liberal democratic values.

Voting choice

Voting choice, like participation, is not just a matter of personal inclination. Obviously voters are more likely to vote for a party that they like than one they dislike. But their likes and dislikes are influenced and conditioned by a variety of outside forces – in particular by their social and family background and by the way the parties are portrayed in the media. And institutional constraints may prevent them converting their preferences into votes. Irrespective of their likes or dislikes, voters cannot vote for a party that does not put forward a candidate in their constituency. And even when their preferred party does contest the election, voters may be reluctant to vote for it if they feel it has no chance of winning locally or no chance of making an impact nationally. Conversely, in 'second-order' elections – by-elections, local elections or European Parliament elections – voters may feel free to cast a vote precisely because they are sure it will have only a limited impact. 'Protest' voters may vote against the government in order to 'send it a message' without threatening its hold on power. But whatever the voters' calculus, it makes little sense to discuss voting without paying attention to the situation of the voter and the circumstances of the election.

Individual preferences: long- and short-term influences

But ignoring for the moment the impact of conditioning and constraint, what personal factors might explain individual preferences? Conventionally, they have been divided into *long-term predispositions* and *short-term factors*.

Predispositions: interests, values and identifications

Rational if narrowly self-interested voters might vote for policies and parties that further their group's interests – the centre or the periphery, urban or rural areas, rich or poor, men or women, public or private sector workers, religious, racial or ethnic groups. And Lipset and Rokkan (1967) suggested that historic socially defined voting cleavages might remain, indeed had remained, 'frozen' long after the clash of real interests had faded. If so, the ice has now broken. Social cleavage voting has declined significantly since Lipset and Rokkan advanced their theory. On average, the religious versus secular cleavage is now the strongest, while class, sectarian, urban/rural and regional cleavages are significantly weaker (Dalton 1996b: 325). Data from 20 Western countries over the half-century 1945–1990 suggest that levels of class voting have declined, and declined most where they had originally been greatest (Nieuwbeerta and Ultee 1999:147).

This decline of class voting is not in dispute, but there is too much cross-national variation in the shape and timing of trends for it to be explained in terms of some process of social change. Voting options are defined by political elites – and not just in terms of the available parties but also in terms of the programmes put forward by those parties. And the decline of class voting reflects the changing character of the parties as much as the changing sensitivities of the voters (Evans 1999).

The decline of social cleavage voting is neither universal nor inevitable. Circumstances and politicians can stimulate new voting cleavages or reinvigorate old ones. In Britain, Canada, and Spain, voting for secessionist parties has increased, at least in regional elections. In the world's largest democracy, India, the BJP (Bharatiya Janata Party) which was a sectarian fringe party with around 10 per cent of the vote until the 1980s, had advanced to around 30 per cent by 1998 (Mitra and Singh 1999). And immigration into western Europe has not only prompted the growth of anti-immigrant parties but increased the significance of the immigrant vote (Van der Brug, Fennema and Tillie 2000).

Ideology or values provide a second basis for long-term predispositions. In its simplest form ideology can be expressed in terms of the voter's position on a single *left/right* value-dimension. But that may be too simple. First, it ignores the increasingly important *nationalist/cosmopolitan* dimension. Second, it compounds two distinct dimensions: an *egalitarian/free-market* dimension and a *liberal/authoritarian* dimension – both of which are often labelled *left/right*.

In the absence of strong social cleavages or long-established partisan identities, values provide a particularly significant foundation for voting choice in new democracies (Toka 1998, 607; Miller and White 1998). But even in Britain, Labour/ Conservative voting preferences are strongly related to both the liberal/authoritarian and the egalitarian value dimensions, though more strongly to the latter. More important, once both these value dimensions have been taken into account, social cleavages have little or no additional impact on voting preferences (Miller, Timpson, and Lessnoff 1996: 438).

Psychological identifications provide a third basis for long-term predispositions. Identifications reflect a sense of closeness, ownership, sympathy, belonging, even 'self-image'. They may be pure irrational emotion, devoid of content but potent nonetheless. Religious, ethnic and national identities can be particularly powerful political motivations however tenuous the 'objective' basis for them. Indeed, what appears on the surface to be interest-based cleavages between social groups is often more identity-based than interest-based. Even class cleavages increasingly reflect mere class identity. Voters identify with the occupational class of the parents or their neighbourhood. Retired voters identify with the occupational class of their middle-age. Ambitious students who work in bars and burger-outlets to get through college most certainly do not see their current occupation (or lack of it) as defining their class.

But one identification, *party identification*, originally proposed as the political equivalent of religious identification, has had a special place in voting studies since the 1950s. We are increasingly aware that there are other objects of political identification than parties. In the new democracies of eastern Europe or Asia where politicians, particularly incumbents, last much longer than their parties or their policies, voters may identify (positively or negatively) with familiar and charismatic politicians or long-established governments. But in most mature democracies, parties last so much longer than personalities that parties rather than politicians constitute the natural focus for political identification, and party identification remains the most significant form of political identification even if its significance is declining.

Levels of party identification appear to be increasing from a low base in the new democracies of the EU (Portugal, Greece, and Spain) (Schmitt and Holmberg 1995: 107) and, less clearly, in East–Central Europe. In the former Soviet Union (FSU) party identification has remained low, particularly with any party other than the Communists. Considerably more FSU voters can point to a party which 'best represents their views' (Miller *et al.* 2000: 462, 486–7) but that lacks the emotional and supra-rational quality of identification.

In mature democracies there is widespread evidence of slowly declining levels of party identification (from a very high base). But there is disagreement over the cause – as there is with explanations of declining turnout. The sociological explanation argues that post-industrial society is producing 'newly independent and resourceful postmaterialist citizens' who need parties less than the citizens of traditional mass societies. The political explanation argues that such 'general macro-sociological explanations' cannot explain the variety of country-specific findings. Instead Schmitt and Holmberg (1995: 121–3) conclude that the degree of party identification depends on the degree of political polarization and ideological conflict between the parties. Thus the level of party identification – like so much else – owes as much to the behaviour of institutions and elites as to the spontaneous feelings of voters.

Short-term factors: 'events', leaders, candidates, economic trends and campaigns

There can be no doubt that 'enduring' long-term factors play an important role in voting decisions. But short-term factors have been underrated, if not by journalists and politicians then by academics. They fit the mould of the journalistic mind so much better than the academic. They are too disparate for tidy analysis, but too important to ignore.

An international crisis, a high-level corruption scandal, or a change of leaders can have a dramatic effect in the short and medium term. Leaders can have a significant role in defining what a party means: Tony Blair even rebranded his party as 'New Labour' with visible effects on Labour support.

Truly 'candidate effects' also exist and should be distinguished from 'leader effects'. It is at this level that the USA differs most clearly from western Europe and has much in common with post-communist Russia – or at least with elections for that half of the Russian Duma elected by territorial constituencies. Russian and American candidates differentiate themselves from their parties even if they have a nominal affiliation, they fight candidate-centred campaigns, and they score personal victories or suffer personal defeat to a degree that is without parallel in western Europe (White, Rose and McAllister 1997: 120–9; Wattenberg 1991).

Because transient issues and events are so variable, it has been surprisingly difficult to generalize about their influence on voter behaviour. But the state of the economy has been found to be widely influential. Yet here again, institutions intervene. In responding to economic up-turns and down-turns, voters are sensitive to the degree of control that the government can exert over economic policy in their particular country (Lewis-Beck 1997; Powell and Whitten 1993: 398; Stokes 1996: 505).

Conditioning

Even though they may have the freedom to choose between parties or candidates, voters' choices are unconsciously conditioned by barely visible influences of various kinds. Two very different but equally invisible influences are the media – outside the confines of its explicit advertising and editorializing which are, of course, easily visible – and the socio-geographic context within which the voter lives.

Early media studies replaced intuitive notions of an all-powerful mind-conditioning media with a 'minimal effects' model in which the media did little other than reinforce existing public opinion. But later the notion of 'agenda-setting' allowed some role for media-conditioning (Semetko et al. 1991). And when combined with the theory of 'issue-ownership' (Petrocik 1996) – the idea that particular parties are widely accepted as the best able to handle particular issues – this notion of 'agenda-setting' points to potentially powerful media effects (Kleinnijenhuis and de Ridder 1998). Indeed there is now some 'new support for the discredited idea of massive media impact' (Zaller 1996).

Moreover – and this gets closest to the notion of *media-conditioning* – even apparently objective phenomena are not free of media influence. Economic conditions, for example, are often observed indirectly through media reports. While the media are to some extent neutral reporters of uninterpreted statistics or simply the mechanism for transmitting experts' opinions (MacKuen et al. 1992; Zaller 1992, ch. 12), they also inject an independent element into the news (Sanders, Marsh and Ward 1993; Nadeau and Niemi 1999; Nadeau, Niemi, and Amato 2000). Media influence is likely to be most insidiously effective where the media develop a consensus about how the facts should be interpreted. Thus Dunleavy and Husbands

(1985: 110) complain that 'we should be less concerned about trying to gauge the political impact achieved by any one media source – such as a single newspaper – and focus attention instead upon the overall climate of media influence to which people have been exposed'. That presents severe problems for analysis though it has an intrinsic plausibility.

The evidence for *context-conditioning* is less ambiguous and its effects are large. An initial effect of context is the socialization of young people by their parents. Despite possibly weaker inter-generational ties than in the 1950s, young people still very often share partisan tendencies with their parents. In later life, the impact of this early socialization experience may fade, only to be replaced by the ongoing influence of friends, neighbours, colleagues in the work-place, leisure-associates, and partners. At no stage in the life-cycle is it realistic to view voters as isolated individuals insulated from their social environment.

The local environment has a particularly significant impact on voting patterns because it tends to intensify partisan choice whenever people of the same type live and work in close proximity. It intensifies left-wing partisanship in working-class areas that would already be inclined towards the left, and intensifies right-wing partisanship in more affluent areas that would already be inclined towards the right. And the effect is large – enough to double the natural class-polarization of constituency voting patterns (Butler and Stokes 1974: 130–7; Miller 1978; McAllister *et al.* 2001)

The existence of such contextual effects has long been obvious. But whether these effects were caused by inter-personal communications or by some statistical artifact was less obvious. But questions about 'conversational partners', which have been included in recent election studies, now provide direct evidence about the impact of 'discussion networks' (frequent discussion-partners), 'party networks' (patterns of interactions with party members), 'social class networks', and residential or 'neighbourhood networks' (Zuckerman, Kotler-Berkowitz and Swaine 1998; see also Lalljee and Evans 1998; Pattie and Johnson 2001). These new studies conclude that the powerful impact of context is no statistical artifact, but a reflection of the power of 'discussion networks' which 'rival party identification' as influences upon vote choice (Zuckerman *et al.* 1998: 291).

Constraint

Irrespective of voters' preferences, their choices are constrained by the number and nature of the available options (parties, candidates, programmes). In normal conditions, voters can exert little influence over these options. The 'start-up' costs of inventing new political parties are high. So the main source of innovation in the political market-place consists of new or revised models from old entrepreneurs – new parties that emerge from elite-level party splits, or just revised policy programmes from old parties. Consequently, except in the long term, the available options determine voters' choices, not the other way round.

Parties can have a dramatic effect upon voting choice simply by changing the number of seats they contest. The British Liberal Party took roughly the same share of the vote in seats that it contested at elections in 1951 and 1997. But it contested six times as many seats in 1997. Less mechanically, parties affect voters' choices by shifting to the left or the right, by entering or leaving coalitions, or by emphasizing or de-emphasizing particular policy differences between them.

Although public unrest may occasionally produce a change in the electoral system, voters' influence over electoral systems is normally even less than their influence over the range of available party options. Electoral systems remain unchanged for long periods, or are changed to satisfy the ambitions of the governing elite. So, it is usually the electoral system (or elite-imposed changes in it) that determines voters' choices, not the other way round

FPTP: tactical voting and demobilization

The first-past-the-post system (FPTP) has well-understood implications for turnout and choice. Supporters of parties that are expected to come third in a local constituency are thought to be 'wasting' their votes if they 'vote their preference'. They would do better to vote tactically, casting their vote for whichever of the top two parties they find more acceptable or less distasteful. The same argument has implications for parties as well as voters. Parties that are likely to come third may withdraw their candidates, discreetly hint that their supporters abandon them in favour of a coalition partner, or simply avoid over-exerting themselves. Conversely, a party that is expected to win a seat by a large majority should not waste resources unnecessarily. It would do better to neglect its 'core' areas and shift resources to marginal seats where the outcome is less certain – even if its core voters in its core areas are left feeling neglected and apathetic. The consequence is that turnout in FPTP elections is depressed and votes differ significantly from preferences. Questions about whether the party with most votes in the country should have the most seats in parliament are inappropriate for example: aggregate national voting figures have no real meaning.

If voters have a strong preference for a single party then 'tactical' voters may feel they have been pressured to vote against their preferences. However parties in multi-party systems can be viewed as allies as well as enemies. And if voters have a 'dual preference' – or even a 'dual party identification' of some kind – then they may view tactical voting as an opportunity as well as a constraint.

Multiple-vote systems: ticket-splitting

In complete contrast to FPTP, multiple-vote systems clearly widen voters' choices because they can, if they wish, vote for more than one party. In the American phrase, they can 'split their ticket'. Various kinds of split-ticket voting are made possible by presidential elections, bicameral legislatures, mixed-member electoral systems, and multi-level governance.

Where *government is split* between two separately elected Houses, or between directly elected executives (usually presidents, occasionally prime ministers) and legislatures, voters will often cast two or more votes simultaneously – as occurs in the USA and in many Latin American countries. Under *mixed-member systems*, voters are required to cast two votes for a single legislative body. The best known example is the German AMS (Additional Member System) for electing the Bundestag, but mixed-member systems have been growing rapidly in popularity and are now used in at least 29 countries covering over a fifth of the world's population – including Japan, New Zealand, post-communist Russia and (for regional assemblies) post-devolution Britain (Massicotte and Blais 1999; Wattenberg and Shugart 2000). Finally, *multi-level governance* typically requires voters to cast votes (not usually simultaneously) for 3 or 4 levels of government – national, regional or state, local, and (in Europe) supra-national.

Because of this variety, split-ticket voting has very different magnitudes, sources, and meaning in different countries. In complete contrast to the USA, split-ticket voting in Germany for example has nothing to do with the personal attractions of candidates and mostly depends on coalition preferences.

The new electoral system adopted for the Italian Chamber of Deputies after the 'tangentopoli' scandal provides a good example of system-liberated but party-constrained split-ticket voting. The new electoral system lifted constraints on voters by giving each voter the opportunity to cast two votes instead of one: one for a single-member constituency MP, one for a party list in a wider area. But at the same time, party elites imposed new constraints on voters by arranging 'cartel' (i.e. coalition) deals to field joint candidates in territorial constituencies (Bartolini and d'Alimonte 1996: 111). So voters could vote their preference with their 'list' vote, but had to switch to their party's coalition partner for their 'constituency' vote.

Apart from coalition pressures and cartel deals, other factors constrain voters' choices in multiple-vote systems. Typically one vote is counted under majoritarian rules, and the other under proportionate (PR) rules. So one choice is constrained by tactical considerations while the other is not. In Germany, Japan, Australia, and Scotland ticket-splitting typically helps the smaller parties in the PR vote but the larger parties in the majoritarian vote though this effect has been less evident in New Zealand and Wales.

Multi-level governance: dual party-identities?

Ticket-splitting under some systems, notably the German AMS, hints at a 'dual party identification' founded on *support for a coalition*. But multi-level governance produces a different kind of ticket-splitting, that hints at a very different kind of dual partisanship based on *support for opposing parties* and explicable only by theories of 'issue-ownership'.

Voters in ethnic regions of Spain, Britain, and Canada consistently and consciously prefer different parties for regional and national elections, giving more support to the regional party in regional elections, and more support to national parties in national elections. Averaging across all Spanish elections between 1977 and 1997 for example, regional parties won twice as many votes in regional elections as in national or European elections. In Catalonia, regional parties have averaged 58 per cent in regional (Catalan) elections but only 32 per cent in national (Spanish) elections. Moreover, Catalans tend to vote leftist (PSOE) in national elections yet for a conservative regional party (CiU) in regional elections (Hamann 1999: 123) – which makes the discrepancy between their regional and national voting choices all the more remarkable.

In Scotland since devolution, monthly opinion polls have recorded a Labour lead over the SNP that is on average 17 per cent greater for Westminster (British) Parliament elections than for Holyrood (Scottish) Parliament elections. (The monthly polls ask three questions about voting preferences – for the British Parliament, for the territorial seats in the Scottish Parliament, and for the AMS party-list seats in the Scottish Parliament.) And actual elections have been consistent with this long-term difference.

Where discrepancies between voting preferences for regional and national elections are so large and consistent over time, it makes little sense to regard votes at one level as a reflection of voters' party identifications while treating their votes at the other level as temporary deviations in a 'second order' election. It seems more reasonable to infer that significant numbers of voters may even have developed a 'dual party identification' based on 'issue-ownership' – that is, they feel one party is suited to represent them in the national parliament on national issues but another in the regional parliament on more local issues.

The best direct evidence of such multi-level 'dual party identification' comes from a series of Canadian surveys (Stewart and Clarke 1998). Between 1974 and 1993 the number of Canadians who self-consciously identified with different parties for regional and national elections rose from 17 to 31 per cent. Meanwhile, the number who identified with the same party at both levels declined from 64 to 52 per cent (the rest failing to identify with a party at one or both levels.)

Such findings suggest that not only votes themselves, but also more psychological identifications may be constrained (or liberated) by changes in electoral and party systems. The more votes, for important but different purposes, that the system permits the greater the incentive to abandon a purely mono-party identification and perhaps develop a dual-party identity based on issue-ownership. Similarly, the closer parties are locked into quasi-permanent coalition arrangements, the greater the incentive for voters to view them as a composite whole and develop a dual party-identity or even identify with the coalition itself rather than its components. (Extreme examples might be 'Labour and Cooperative' or 'Conservative and Liberal Unionist' which by the 1950s had degenerated into mystifying anachronisms rather than permanent coalitions.)

Debates over the extent of party identification, including the question of whether it is increasing or decreasing, are merely quantitative. But the concept of dual party identification, whether based on coalition support or issue-ownership, is qualitatively different from party identification as originally defined (Campbell *et al.* 1960) in American election studies.

Conclusion

There are calls for more attention to be given to context and institutions as determinants of voter choice (Scarbrough 2000). Context and institutions were never entirely neglected, but they have become more obviously significant as participation and voting have been studied over a longer time-scale and from a more global perspective – in which the constraints on voters vary more widely and reveal their power more clearly. The 'third wave' of democracy has also focused attention on new as well as mature democracies, and on institutions as variables rather than constants. Indeed in this new world even mature democracies no longer have very stable institutions. Institutional change, reform, and decay have been infectious and voters have responded to it.

References

Bartolini, Stefano, and d'Alimonte, Roberto (1996) 'Plurality competition and party realignment in Italy: the 1994 parliamentary elections', *European Journal of Political Research* 29: 105–42.

Butler, David, and Stokes, Donald (1974) *Political Change in Britain: The Evolution of Electoral Choice*, 2nd edn, London: Macmillan.

Campbell, Angus, Converse, Philip, Miller, Warren and Stokes, Donald (1960) *The American Voter*, New York: John Wiley.

Crewe, Ivor (1992) 'Changing votes and unchanging voters', *Electoral Studies* 11: 335–45.

Dalton, Russell J. (1996a) *Citizen Politics: Public Opinion and Political Parties in Advanced Industrial Democracies*, 2nd edn, Chatham, NJ: Chatham House.

Dalton, Russell J. (1996b) 'Political cleavages, issues, and electoral change', in Lawrence LeDuc, Richard G. Niemi and Pippa Norris *Comparing Democracies,* (eds) Thousand Oaks, CA: Sage.

Dunleavy, Patrick, and Husbands, Christopher T. (1985) *British Democracy at the Crossroads: Voting and Party Competition in the 1980s*, London: Allen and Unwin.

Evans, Geoffrey (1999) 'Class and vote: disrupting the orthodoxy', in Geoffrey Evans (ed.) *The End of Class Politics? Class Voting in Comparative Context*, Oxford: Oxford University Press.

Franklin, M. N. (2001) 'The dynamics of electoral participation', in Lawrence LeDuc, Richard G. Niemi and Pippa Norris (eds) *Comparing Democracies 2: Elections and Voting in Global Perspective*, 2nd edn, London: Sage Publications, 148–68.

Hamann, Kerstin (1999) 'Federalist institutions, voting behavior, and party systems in Spain', *Publius: The Journal of Federalism* 29: 111–37.

Kleinnijenhuis, Jan, and de Ridder, Jan A. (1998) 'Issue news and electoral volatility: a comparative analysis of media effects during the 1994 election campaigns in Germany and the Netherlands', *European Journal of Political Research* 33: 413–37.

Lalljee, Mansur, and Evans, Geoff (1998) 'Political talk and the stability and consistency of political orientation', *British Journal of Social Psychology* 37: 203–12.

Lewis-Beck, Michael S. (1997) 'Who's the Chef? Economic voting under a dual executive', *European Journal of Political Research* 31: 315–25.

Lipset, Seymour Martin, and Rokkan, Stein (1967) 'Cleavage structures, party systems and voter alignments', in Seymour Martin Lipset and Stein Rokkan (eds) *Party Systems and Voter Alignments*, New York: Free Press.

Marsh, Alan, and Kaase, Max (1979) 'Measuring political action', in S. Barnes and M. Kaase (eds) *Political Action*, Beverly Hills: Sage Publications.

Massicotte, Louis, and Blais, Andre (1999) 'Mixed electoral systems: a conceptual and empirical survey', *Electoral Studies* 18: 341–66.

McAllister, Ian, Johnston, Ron J., Pattie, Charles J., Tunstall, Helena, Dorling, Danny F. and Rossiter, David J. (2001) 'Class dealignment and the neighbourhood effect', *British Journal of Political Science* 31: 41–59.

MacKuen, Michael, Erikson, Robert S. and Stimson, James A. (1992) 'Peasants or bankers? The American electorate and the U.S. economy', *American Political Science Review* 86: 597–611.

Miller, Arthur H., Erb, Gwyn, Reisinger, William M. and Hesli, Vicki L. (2000) 'Emerging party systems in post-Soviet societies: fact or fiction?', *Journal of Politics* 62: 455–90.

Miller, William L. (1978) 'Social Class and Party Choice in England: a New Analysis', *British Journal of Political Science* 8: 257–84.

Miller, William L., Brand, Jack, Jordan, Maggie, Balsom, Dennis, Madgewick, Peter and van Mechelen, Dennis (1982) *Democratic or Violent Protest?* Studies in Public Policy, no. 107, Glasgow: Centre for the Study of Public Policy, University of Strathclyde.

Miller, William L., and White, Stephen (1998) 'Political values underlying partisan cleavages in former communist countries', *Electoral Studies* 17: 197–216.

Miller, William L., Timpson, Annis May and Lessnoff, Michael (1996) *Political Culture in Contemporary Britain: People and Politicians, Principles and Practice*, Oxford: Oxford University Press.

Mitra, Subrata K., and Singh, V. B. (1999) *Democracy and Social Change in India*, Delhi: Sage.

Nadeau, Richard, and Niemi, Richard G. (1999) 'Rating the Chancellors and their budgets', *Political Studies* 46: 857–76.

Nadeau, Richard, Niemi, Richard G. and Amato, Timothy (2000) 'Elite economic forecasts, economic news, mass economic expectations and voting intentions in Great Britain', *European Journal of Political Research* 38: 135–70.

Nieuwbeerta, Paul, and Ultee, Wout (1999) 'Class voting in western industrialized countries 1945–1990', *European Journal of Political Research* 35: 123–60.

Pattie, Charles, and Johnston, Ron (2001) 'Talk as a political context: conversation and electoral change in British elections 1992–1997', *Electoral Studies* 20: 17–40.

Petrocik, John R. (1996) 'Issue-ownership in Presidential elections', *American Journal of Political Science* 40: 825–50.

Powell, G. Bingham, and Whitten, Guy D. (1993) 'A cross-national analysis of economic voting: taking account of the political context', *American Journal of Political Science* 37: 391–414.

Sanders, David, Marsh, David and Ward, Hugh (1993) 'The electoral impact of press coverage of the British economy, 1979–87', *British Journal of Political Science* 23: 175–210.

Scarbrough, Elinor (2000) 'The British election study and electoral research', *Political Studies* 48: 391–414.

Schmitt, Herman, and Holmberg, Sören (1995) 'Political parties in decline?' In Hans-Dieter Klingemann and Dieter Fuchs (eds) *Citizens and the State,* Oxford: Oxford University Press.

Semetko, Holli A., Blumler, Jay G., Gurevitch, Michael and Weaver, David H. (1991) *The Formation of Campaign Agendas: A Comparative Analysis of Party and Media Roles in Recent American and British Elections*, Hillsdale, NJ: Lawrence Erlbaum.

Stewart, Marianne C., and Clarke, Harold D. (1998) 'The dynamics of party identification in federal systems: the Canadian case', *American Journal of Political Science* 42: 97–116.

Stokes, Susan C. (1996) 'Public opinion and market reforms – the limits of economic voting', *Comparative Political Studies* 29: 499–519.

Toka, Gabor (1998) 'Party appeals and voter loyalties in new democracies', *Political Studies* 46: 589–610.

van der Brug, Wouter, Fennema, Meindert and Tillie, Jean (2000) 'Anti-immigrant parties in Europe: ideological or protest vote?', *European Journal of Political Research* 37: 77–102.

Verba, S., Nie, N. H. and Kim, J. (1978) *Participation and Political Equality*, New York: Cambridge University Press.

Wattenberg, Martin (1991) *The Rise of Candidate-Centered Politics: Presidential Elections of the 1980s*, Cambridge: Harvard University Press.

Wattenberg, Martin P., and Shugart, Matthew (2000) *Mixed-member Electoral Systems: The Best of Both Worlds?*, Oxford: Oxford University Press.

White, Stephen, Rose, Richard and McAllister, Ian (1997) *How Russia Votes*, Chatham, NJ: Chatham House.

Zaller, John, R. (1992) *The Nature and Origins of Mass Opinion*, Cambridge: Cambridge University Press.

Zaller, John R. (1996) 'The myth of massive media impact revisited: new support for a discredited idea', in Diana C. Mutz, Paul M. Sniderman, and Richard A. Brody (eds) *Political Persuasion and Attitude Change*, Ann Arbor: University of Michigan Press.

Zuckerman, Alan S., Kotler-Berkowitz, Lawrence A. and Swaine, Lucas A. (1998) 'Anchoring political preferences: the structural bases of stable electoral decisions and political attitudes in Britain', *European Journal of Political Research* 33: 285–321.

Further reading

Barnes, Samuel and Kaase, Max. (eds) (1979) *Political Action*, Beverly Hills: Sage.

Dalton, Russell J. (1996a) *Citizen Politics: Public Opinion and Political Parties in Advanced Industrial Democracies*, 2nd edn, Chatham, NJ: Chatham House.

LeDuc, Lawrence, Niemi, Richard G. and Norris, Pippa (eds) (2002) *Comparing Democracies 2: Elections and Voting in Global Perspective*, 2nd edn, London: Sage Publications.

Harrop, Martin and Miller, William L. (1987) *Elections and Voting: A Comparative Introduction*, London: Macmillan.

Verba, Sidney, Nie, Norman H. and Kim, Jae-On (1978) *Participation and Political Equality*, New York: Cambridge University Press.

Wattenberg, Martin P., and Shugart, Matthew (2000) *Mixed-member Electoral Systems: The Best of Both Worlds?*, Oxford: Oxford University Press.

29

POLITICAL SOCIALIZATION IN A DIVIDED SOCIETY AND DANGEROUS AGE

Stanley Renshon

Almost fifty years ago, Herbert Hyman (1959) used the term political socialization in the title of his study on the psychology of political behaviour. He did so to call attention to the fact that political orientations could be productively analysed as learned behaviour, a view that, though obvious now, represented a new departure at the time. In doing so, he laid the groundwork for an interdisciplinary field combining psychological theories of learning with political theories of regularity and change (Turiel 1989: 48).

That foundation also corresponded with a paradigmatic change in one of the field's three major disciplinary sources: political science (Dahl 1961). The behavioral paradigm in political science emphasized four major points in studying political process: the importance of the individual in the functioning of political institutions and processes; the importance of interdisciplinary political theory; the use of systematic measurement strategies; and the development of generalizable theories regarding political behaviour and its causes. The result of these congruent trends in political socialization and political science was an outpouring of theory and research.

The field of political socialization was attractive to political scientists for two reasons. First, it attempted to link socialization processes to the development of politically relevant views and activities, and second, it attempted to link the development of individual citizens with the functioning of the larger political system. Much of the early research in the area was generated by the attempt to document these links, as well as to establish the nature of the mechanisms that shaped the process.

Several questions now arise from these efforts. A first set of questions concerns whether political socialization has successfully demonstrated the validity of its premises. In over four decades of study, has the field accumulated empirically supported theory that links the development of individuals with their political functioning and to that of the larger political system?

A second and related set of questions concerns the state of political socialization, its prospects and the various prescriptions that have been offered for ensuring its future. There is no doubt that the pace of research and publication in the field has slowed (Cook 1989; Merelman 1989; Allen 1989; Turiel 1989). This has led some critics to suggest that the field, 'has not fulfilled its promise' (Rosenberg 1985: 715). On the other hand, Dennis (1985: vii) writes that, 'While the science of political socialization is far from the ideal of a cumulative, fully codified body of knowledge, we have made considerable strides towards being able to give a systematic account of these processes and of their products since the late fifties'. So, does the slowing of political socialization theory and research reflect a hiatus, a failure, or paradoxically can it be considered a reflection of its success?

Lastly, political socialization was born in the behavioural revolution during the 1950s, matured in the dynamic political period of the 1960s, and seemed to have reached a conceptual and empirical plateau by the late 1980s and early 1990s. In some respects the field of political socialization and the questions that arose within it were partially related to the times during which it developed and matured. In the 1950s it sought to explain consistency and continuity in the development of political orientations. In the 1960s and 1970s it was forced to account for change and development. In the 1980s and 1990s it addressed identity politics. The question naturally arises then: What questions might need to be addressed in our contemporary political period – one characterized by the end of the cold war, an era of mass migration and one punctuated by the devastating terrorist attack of 11 September (9/11)?

The rationale for studying political socialization

There are several plausible rationales for studying political socialization. The first and most general is based on the fact that socialization is a central part of every society's social process. According to Allen, 'it is a phenomenon taking place continually in every organized society' (Allen 1989: 4). Part of this process concerns learning about authority and rule-making institutions. In this formulation therefore, the field of political socialization can lay claim to legitimacy on the basis of centrality, universality, and the fact that the content of socialization has substantial political implication.

A second rationale stems from a 'concern with the proper development of offspring – with their acquisition of needed skills, the curbing of aggressive tendencies, the directing of their feet to paths of righteousness' (Clausen 1968: 20). In this formulation, the importance of socialization and the nature of its impact are assumed, and study is directed at the best method(s) of bringing about desired ends. Theories of socialization found in Plato's *Republic*, Machiavelli's *The Prince*, and Rousseau's *Social Contract*, to name three of many, are reflective of this rationale.

Finally, a third and somewhat more direct theoretical and political rationale for political socialization rests on its posited effects on the continuity, change and persistence of political systems (Easton and Dennis 1969). In this view, early political socialization, especially in relation to authorities and the public's understanding of citizenship roles, provides leaders and policy makers with a cushion of 'diffuse support'. This cushion represents the range of policy latitude available to elites in pursuit of (their understanding of) the national interest, and allows them to occasionally take unpopular but necessary steps.

None of these has provided an untroubled rationale for the field. The first rationale, for example, falters on the grounds of generality. It fails to differentiate sufficiently between the process of socialization and its outcomes. Research to be examined in this essay strongly supports the view that there is no one political socialization process, but rather a variety of processes at work.

The second rationale, which stems from a concern with attempting to socialize citizens into the 'good citizen' role, raises the basic question of whose views of that role should be paramount. Dowse (1978: 409), among others, questions the wisdom of this approach as the basis for political socialization, however laudable it may appear. He points out that political alienation, for example, may be a perfectly rational response to real powerlessness. In such cases he argues, political education cannot reverse the effects of structural disadvantage, and may in fact end up reinforcing them.

The third rationale proposes a specific link between political socialization and the operation of the political systems. However, this linkage, while intuitively plausible, has proved difficult to establish. Part of the problem is the measurement of outcomes such as 'stability', 'change', 'continuity', etc., but this is only part of the problem. Because the best evidence for the systemic effects would come from the kinds of large-scale research efforts that have been comparatively rare in the social sciences, the logic of support has rested on the accumulation of inferences from small-scale studies.

Imperfect as they have proved, each rationale provides some justification for taking the concerns of political socialization seriously. It is true, after all, that infants are not born with politically relevant adult characters, beliefs and skills. A logical corollary therefore must be that these characteristics develop over time. It is this fundamental insight, the 'developmental hypothesis', which forms the basis of Lasswell's early observation that political analysis must try to 'discover what developmental experiences are significant for the political traits and interests of the mature' (Lasswell 1930: 8), and which functions as a continuing rationale for the field.

Political socialization as an interdisciplinary field: problems and prospects

The study of political socialization rests primarily on three major disciplinary foundations, political science, psychology and sociology, along with a somewhat smaller major contribution from anthropology (but see Almond and Verba 1963 and Pye 1968 for the linkage between political socialization and political culture). Of the three, political science has been concerned for the shortest time with three central concepts of the field: socialization, learning and development. As a result, political socialization has borrowed many models, theories and concepts from the other two core disciplines, psychology and sociology.

There are advantages to borrowing from other disciplines. Concepts and theories not yet developed in the interdisciplinary field can be borrowed when needed. In the case of political socialization, borrowing was not only attractive but also necessary. Concepts such as learning, maturation, development, identification, etc., were central to the processes being researched in the field, but had little history of theoretical development within political science. More importantly, without theory to guide research linking these processes with political socialization, the field could not seriously address questions relevant to its premises.

However, while borrowing may be necessary it is not without costs. There is, for example, the problem of paradigmatic compatibility. It is one matter for researchers to deal with a discipline's major paradigm, but quite another when there are three or more paradigms involved. Consider in this respect some aspects of the basic paradigms of sociology and psychology. Wrong (1961) pointed out some time ago that sociology tended to view individuals as products of social forces, while downplaying the role of individual agency. Psychology on the other hand, has a long history of concern with individuals, whether with the psychology of individual differences or, more recently, with life histories. These two views of psycho-social process are not necessarily irreconcilable, but they do not automatically point researchers in the same direction. For example, in discussing the different views of sociology and psychology, Rosenberg argues that:

> The distinguishing characteristic of systematic sociology is a focus on the collective dimension of human activity. A central assumption is that social reality constitutes a domain which exists between and beyond individuals...which is understood to determine individual-level phenomena.... [T]he sociological conception of political activity renders any consideration of individual-level phenomenon inappropriate and uninteresting.
>
> (Rosenberg 1985: 716–17)

The problem of paradigmatic compatibility is made somewhat more complicated by the fact that at least one of political socialization's core disciplines, psychology, has several paradigms rather than just one that is dominant. Cognitive psychology is certainly prominent within psychology (Gardner 1987), but the behaviouralist, developmental and psychoanalytic paradigms continue to maintain a strong disciplinary presence. As a result, problems of theoretical and paradigmatic integration are more complex.

Paradigmatic integration is one of several issues that using interdisciplinary theory raises. These issues make interdisciplinary research more demanding and difficult in some respects than traditional disciplinary research. Greenstein recognized one reason for this in his early analysis of the 'personality and politics' literature. In that analysis, Greenstein noted that when researchers in the field of personality and politics look to psychology to borrow meanings of such terms as 'personality' they find that:

> Rather than finding a psychological science on which to draw for insight, [they find] congeries of more or less competing models and frames of reference, with imperfect agreement on the nature of man's inner dispositions, on the appropriate terms for characterizing them, and on the methodologies for observation.
>
> (Greenstein 1967: 12–13)

Greenstein's point was that the term 'personality' had different meanings that were tied to theoretical views. Trait theorists, psychoanalytic theorists, developmental theorists, and so on, defined and researched personality in very different ways. Therefore one could not simply adapt a definition of personality and apply it without being aware of the controversies surrounding the concept in its home discipline.

The same dilemma confronts political socialization theory and research. On one hand, political socialization theorists needed to examine other disciplines for knowledge about processes central to the field's premises. On the other hand, detailed knowledge, for example, of the concept of development – from either a cognitive or psychoanalytic theoretical perspective – is no small undertaking, since each of these theories has its own historical development and theoretical controversies.

Clearly there is a balance to be struck here. Yet it appears difficult, particularly in the early stages of interdisciplinary research and field development, to integrate fully a borrowed theory's range and complexity into research designs. One result is that the full range of a theory's possible contributions is rarely adequately explored. For example, by the 1960s psychoanalytic theory had developed rich and diverse models of psychological functioning that went well beyond unconscious impulse and childhood. Yet early political socialization theorists made use of only a limited aspect of the theory ('fear of authority' as the basis for political identification).

This continues to be a problem for interdisciplinary work in general and for political socialization. Turiel (1989: 49) notes, for example, that, although the use of developmental theories to explain political socialization has become more sophisticated, they are still narrowly applied. What most researchers using development models have done, for instance, is directly apply Piaget's (1965) model of stages to political thinking. This has been productive, but in Turiel's view it does not exhaust the range of potential applications of these developmental theories. Turiel proposes expanding the application of Piaget's model to include the epistemological analyses of the definitions and classifications of the substantive domains of politics.

However, even being more fully conversant with the range of a discipline's major theories and applications may no longer be sufficient in interdisciplinary research. As an interdisciplinary field like political socialization develops, it may become necessary to be more fully conversant with a range of theories and applications *within* a discipline, as well as with theoretical applications across disciplines. Consider, for example, the question of whether social learning or developmental theory provides a better model to explain political learning. Being conversant with, and even empirically testing, one model does not necessarily resolve all the researcher's problems.

Moore (1989) (see also Moore, Lare and Wagner 1985) argues that some aspects of political learning conform to social learning theory, an argument he bases on assessments of increased exposure to political stimuli. But as Turiel points out in this connection, 'both social learning and cognitive developmental approaches expect greater exposure to influence learning, but by different processes' (Turiel 1989: 47). In other words, the empirical findings linking exposure with political learning do not necessarily resolve the question of which theory more fully accounts for the data.

These examples suggest that the conduct of interdisciplinary research raises difficult, complex theoretical issues. In the sections that follow, we will examine some of these with a view towards laying out, even if not fully resolving, the questions raised at the beginning of this essay. We begin with an overview of the field, its framework of definitions and early studies.

Political socialization: early definitions and frameworks

Political socialization attracted social scientists because it promised a pay-off in explaining the functioning of political institutions and processes. The framework that most clearly articulated that rationale was systems theory (Easton 1965). The political theory of political socialization derived from that framework (Easton and Dennis 1969; Hess and Torney 1969) provided researchers with an agenda as well as a rationale.

Since political systems were stable and persisted because institutions socialized citizens into providing political authorities with diffuse support, one major item on the research agenda was to see how particular agents (the word itself reflects a view of institutions as surrogates for political authorities) inculcated the relevant 'norms'. Thus a number of studies examined various agents to analyse how they shaped political development. (For an early summary of such research see Renshon (1977), which includes chapters on: the comparative analysis of agents (Beck 1977); the family (Davies 1977); schools (Patrick 1977); peers (Silbiger 1977); media (Chaffe 1977), and so on.)

Since political authorities could hardly afford to wait until adulthood to generate diffuse support, research was also oriented towards finding the origins of adult support in childhood. The number of studies examining the political orientations of children, and later 'youth', led one researcher (Greenstein 1970) to include the study of children as one basic definition of the field. These twin related pillars, the moulding of citizens to norms (in reality those of the political regime and particular political authorities) and the focus on children, were the basis of much of the research undertaken in the field.

The understanding of 'socialization' as a conservative process has a long intellectual history. Clausen (1968: 21) notes that as early as 1828 the term appeared in the *Oxford English Dictionary* with the meaning 'to render social, to make fit for living in society'. Early definitions in the field followed this lead and stressed the child's accommodation to the adult world, particularly the normative values of the society. Hyman's view that 'humans must learn their political behaviour early and well and persist in it' (Hyman 1959: 17) was echoed in many theories. Sigel's observation that 'political socialization refers to the learning process by which the political norms and behaviors acceptable to an ongoing political system are transmitted from generation to generation' (Sigel 1961: 1) was one of several influential views of the process that took this position.

This view has persisted, although not unchallenged, to the present. For example, Allen, in introducing a symposium on 'Children's political socialization and cognition' in *Human Development* (Allen 1989: 2), defines the process as 'an individual's adaptation to the political environment'. Less emphasis has generally been given to the ways in which individuals selectively accept, develop and shape political orientations. Similarly, insufficient attention has been given to the ways in which individuals may influence and shape the very social and political systems that supposedly socialize them to regime support.

From the beginning there has been dissatisfaction with the view that individuals are generally passive accommodators to institutional norms. Reservations about this view were expressed quite early in the field's development (Connell and Goot

1972–3) and continued to be expressed periodically (Sears 1975; Renshon 1977). Criticisms of this view took several forms.

Connell and Goot (1972–3) argued that the forced-choice format of the research methodology imposed a structure on the children's answers which tended to suppress the expression of their full range of understandings. He pointed out that Greenstein and Tarrow's study of children using semi-projective and open-ended questions (Greenstein and Tarrow 1970) had revealed that children know more about 'political realities' than they could express in a typical forced-choice format. Sears (1975: 95) pointed out that socialization models tended to overlook the child's idiosyncratic growth, while Renshon's analysis of the basic assumptions behind models of political learning (Renshon 1977: 22–40) detailed exactly why this criticism was well taken.

The most telling argument by far against the conformity to social norms model, however, was the rise of student activism in the 1960s and 1970s by the very same cohorts who had provided researchers with evidence of early support for political authorities. Clearly something had changed. Early research (for example, Greenstein 1965; Hess and Torney 1969) had found that children, especially those in the political and economic mainstream, had a 'positivity bias' in favour of authority. While there was some controversy about whether these findings were an artefact of method (see the discussions in Sullivan and Minns 1976; Greenstein 1976; and Maddox and Handberg 1979), the general consensus was that these findings tended to support the view of the socialization process as developing 'diffuse support', although there were some research caveats to these general findings.

Research on children who were not integrated into the economic and political mainstream, for example American children in economically depressed Southern rural areas (Jaros, Hirsch and Felron 1968), found that they were substantially less supportive of the political authorities and more alienated from the political and social system. In some cases, economic or political marginality did not lead to wholesale alienation from the political system. Greenberg (1970), for example, found that, while black children were less likely to support political leaders and some governmental institutions than were a comparative sample of white children, they were still generally supportive of the Supreme Court, a finding which the authors plausibly argue reflected the court's long involvement in civil rights. This study is not only important because it examined black children, but in addition because it showed that even among children learning could be selective.

A similar dynamic was uncovered in studies of children's responses to the Watergate crisis. Atherton (1975), for example, found that children's positive evaluations of political leaders and institutions were negatively influenced by the Watergate scandals. This finding was supported by Meadow's two-wave panel study, which uncovered a decline in children's support for the President (Meadow 1982) as more damaging evidence became public. These findings should have made the unexpected activism of the 1960s and 1970s less mysterious, since it suggested that even children who began by supporting the government could and did respond to changes in the political environment.

In retrospect, it seems clear that students of political socialization erred in focusing primarily on explaining political stability and continuity. This was a plausible and understandable focus given the politics of that period, but socialization theory paid a price for its failure to place that particular period in American politics within a larger historical context. Had that been done, stability (although not necessarily continuity) might have been seen as less of a rule and more the product of a particular set of historical and political circumstances, which themselves were in need of analysis.

As noted, the focus on childhood was dictated in part by the theory of the origins of diffuse support, but this is not the only reason. The focus on childhood was probably influenced as much by the lack of alternative models of development after childhood as it was by the theoretical requirements of systems theory. Although Erikson's eight-stage theory of psychological development, extending from childhood through adulthood, had been published in 1950, its implications for political socialization were not appreciated or integrated for many years. The same could be said of other models of development in adulthood (Levinson 1978; Gilligan 1982). In the first major review of the topic of 'adult political socialization', Sigel wrote that 'there does not exist as yet a theory of adult political socialization' (Sigel 1977: 261). Twelve years later, the first major book on adult political socialization had been published with its editor, Sigel, noting:

> Attention to political socialization over the entire life span – especially attention to adult development – broadly defined – is still the exception rather than the rule. While we do have much information about how adults at a given moment act or react...we lack systematic knowledge of whether such behaviour is a carry-over from values learned during childhood or whether it has arisen in response to changed social or personal circumstances not anticipated in childhood.
>
> (Sigel 1989: x)

The absence of alternative theories and the implications of the political theory of political socialization led research to focus on childhood. The numerous studies of this period of political development uncovered basic and previously unknown information about the process, but ran into several difficulties. At first, large numbers of studies concentrated on uncovering the dynamics of children's attitudes towards authority (in keeping with the theory of diffuse support). However, questions were soon raised about whether children had attitudes at all. Vaillancourt (1973) found so much variability in children's responses over time that she questioned whether political attitudes were the appropriate level of childhood socialization analysis. Others had doubts too. Knutson (1974) suggested that rather than attitudes, 'prepolitical ideologies' might be the appropriate unit of childhood analysis, while Renshon (1974) argued that analysis of children's 'basic beliefs' about the nature of the social and political world might prove productive.

But there was a more basic problem to be addressed. Meadow's panel study (Meadow 1982) suggested that even when one could reliably measure political attitudes in children there was evidence that these attitudes could change and develop. These changes were not related to the failure to develop and consolidate attitudes, as Vaillancourt had suggested was true for her younger panel sample, but rather because there was a dynamic relationship between the child's views and his/her understanding of and reaction to external political events.

The importance of this finding is that it underscores the fact that the *political* theory of political socialization put forward as the most important rationale for the field had, paradoxically, failed to take into account the importance of actual political events. These research findings further suggested that in addition to trying to find models which linked childhood learning with adult political activity, one would need to account, independently of that objective, for changes and development in childhood itself. This is still an area in need of exploration.

Political socialization: controversy and development

The general question of impact

At the core of the political socialization debate are questions about the impact of the process. One must, at the beginning, distinguish between potential and actual impact. The fact that some children's books, for example, may contain 'anti-authority' messages (Cook 1983) does not in and of itself confer importance. Children may not read such books, or, if they do, they may remain unaffected by them. Thus the question of impact can only be answered by establishing some relational connection. Establishing this connection has frequently been approached through the analysis of correspondence, that is the extent to which various relational permutations (for example, parent–child, person–institution, etc.) correspond.

One can conceive of at least three possible levels of impact. The first, an individual level, would look for the impact of socialization on the development of a person's individual orientations. The second, the group/institutional level, would look to small aggregates of individuals to see how particular clusters of individuals developed politically. This level might also seek to tie such group development to the operation of specific contexts or aspects of institutional functioning. Lastly, we can examine the functioning of the polity itself for evidence of socialization effects.

As noted above, the promise of political socialization for many political scientists was to be found in its ability to document a set of causal relationships between political socialization and systematic functioning. This has proved difficult to accomplish. Aside from difficulties in terminology, definition and operationalization of the main terms involved (for example, 'stability', 'persistence', etc.), the fundamental dilemma of linking the field's accomplishment to this particular requirement has been the daunting level-of-analysis problem. This problem is not unique to political socialization theory, but it is more central to its premises. The question, briefly put, is how can studies, most of which are done at the individual level of analysis, be aggregated to account for systemic effects?

Even when we examine some of the nationally representative samples that have been very influential and informative in political socialization, questions of systemic effects are not unambiguous. Himmelweit, for example, in discussing the Jennings and Niemi panel study points out that stability at the aggregate level may occur either 'because people's views haven't changed or because people's views have changed but in different ways with the result that changes at the aggregate level cancel each other out' (Himmelweit 1983: 247). And of course, the empirical determination of stability and change in a sample is not necessarily synonymous with the use of these terms to characterize the operation of political systems.

Problems in this area have proved difficult given that a majority of studies in the field are neither nationally representative nor designed as panel studies. Inference in these cases therefore becomes tricky. Do we simply sum up the results of the survey or other research findings and generalize them across the whole system? Is there some kind of step level, or critical mass function, which will accelerate the effects we uncover? Is the impact of the various dynamics uncovered interactive? And what is to be done with issues of individual and collective change over time, and in response to changes in circumstance? Simply to state these questions underscores the enormous complexity of the problems involved. That these problems have not been solved by political socialization is not surprising. Other areas of social science inquiry have fared no better.

One by-product of the attempt to forge aggregate linkages has been that less attention has been paid to making individual or 'mid-range' (Merton 1968) linkages. These are effects that might be felt at the institutional level, without necessarily having dramatic effects on the overall functioning of the system. For example, a rise in the level of sceptical reactions to political leaders after political experiences like Watergate might lead to an emphasis on 'honesty' and 'integrity' as campaign themes. This, in turn, might even result in somewhat more actual political behaviour of this kind. However, it is probably too much to require of socialization theory that in order to prove its worth all or most political leaders must become dramatically more honest in response to more sceptical socialization. Would the effect of greater honesty be less of an impact than a step-level change in the behaviour of all political office-holders? Of course. Is there no discernible or important socialization effect in this example because the latter has not occurred? I think not.

Finally, in addition to the aggregate and institutional level of political socialization effects, there is the impact of socialization on individuals. Of course, discussions of impact at both the societal and institutional level assume individual-level impact. But it is at this level of analysis that research documenting the effects of political socialization is the most substantial and convincing.

Research demonstrating individual-level effects has actually proceeded along two tracks. The first is simply the basic documentation of the fact that children do have a wide range of political orientations. This fact, first demonstrated in the early studies of Greenstein (1960), Hess and Easton (1960) and others, is now taken for granted, but its implications are important and worth pausing a moment to consider. If children as young as four and five have the beginnings of political understandings (however much they may evolve) and if these understandings are not innate, then a strong logical case has been made for the reality of political learning. This is important because whatever debates there are in the field, and there are many (who learns what, how, when, under what circumstances and to what degree), there is empirical evidence that there is something to explain.

The empirical demonstration that political learning exists, as important as it is, is but a first step. The next steps are to gain an appreciation of the areas affected by the process as well as to understand the nature of the process itself. In the first of these two areas, especially, the empirical demonstration of effects in a variety of areas and contexts has been significant. For example, there is by now a large body of evidence to support the proposition that parents do have an impact on the political views of their children (Jennings and Niemi 1968; Gundy 1982), an indication of impact being a correlation between the political orientations of different family members when these orientations are independently sampled. But these are not the only kinds of studies that have documented individual-level impact. Chapman (1987), studying a sample of women candidates for political office in Scotland, found that having been part of a women's group was the strongest and best predictor of these candidates' political orientations. Using a causal model she concludes that 'there is no doubt that the effect we are measuring is that of experience on consciousness, and not the other way around' (Chapman 1987: 323).

Finally, Zaslavsky and an unnamed (for reasons of personal safety) colleague (Zaslavsky and Z. 1980) studied Soviet workers' support for their country's invasion of Czechoslovakia. They found that workers in 'closed enterprises' (industries that produce something deemed strategically important by the government) were much more likely to support the invasion than those who worked in relatively 'open' industries. Related to workers in 'closed' industries were party membership, past military service, higher pay and special status. They interpreted their findings in terms of 'embeddedness' in the regime, a concept that is consonant with the cumulative effects model of socialization that we will discuss below.

Overall, these and numerous other empirical studies have documented the existence of socialization effects. However, these effects have been more effectively documented at the individual and group/institutional levels. Documented effects at the social level remain largely inferential.

Specification: the maturing of political socialization models

It may well be one hallmark of social science fields that in the beginning they put forward rather global and relatively undifferentiated theories and models. These may take the form of general if–then propositions, inference from smaller studies to larger effects, or simply a set of models which purport to describe general processes but which in hindsight and on the basis of accumulated research experience are shown to be much more complex and differentiated than originally posited.

Specification, then, is a process by which these original formulations of a field are modified on the basis of research findings. To the sceptical, such a process looks as if the original formulations have been found wanting (they have – but not in a necessarily adverse way for the field's development), and that therefore the whole enterprise is suspect. A different view is put forward here. Specification of process to take account of context, individual and developmental differences, and so on, represents a maturing of social/political theory, not its failure. We will illustrate this process in political socialization theory in this section by looking more closely at the question of impact and the models that have been developed to account for it. We begin with an examination of the question of the persistence of socialization effects over time.

The necessity to develop models of persistence stem from the logical requirements imposed by systems theory and the fact that politics is most frequently the province of adults. Some have put the matter forcefully. Dowse argues, for example, that political socialization research 'makes sense *only* if the child is father to the man' (Dowse 1978: 403). Still, it is true that, while children's political learning may be of interest in and of itself, it becomes more important for research and analysis if it can be shown to influence or shape adult political behaviour (not necessarily the operation of the political system) in some ways. Therefore, the effects of socialization must be found not only to originate early in the life cycle, but also to persist in some form over it.

These requirements are the basis of two of the most well-known models of impact in the literature: the primacy principle (Searing, Wright and Rabinowitz 1976) and the structuring principle (Searing, Schwartz and Lind 1973). Taken together, these principles suggest: (a) that crucial political learning takes place in childhood; (b) that this early learning is a filter through which subsequent political learning passes (hence it also structures subsequent political learning); and (c) that these crucial behaviours, acquired in childhood, persist into adulthood to influence adult political behaviour. These are basic principles which Searing and his colleagues note 'everyone subscribes to...in varying degrees' (Searing, Schwartz and Lind 1973: 415).

As noted, political socialization research has found pervasive evidence that assumption (a) is correct. Children do begin to develop political attitudes, political information and policy opinions, and identifications with political parties, prepolitical ideologies, basic beliefs, and so on. But whether, and especially to what degree, these orientations structure subsequent learning and persist through time are questions to which there are diverse answers.

The fates of these two principles suggest the ways that failures to substantiate early, generally formulated theoretical assumptions can lead to developments in theory specification. Consider in this regard one empirical test of the structuring principle. Searing and his colleagues tested the structuring hypothesis with cohort data by seeing whether political attitudes acquired in childhood could predict later political opinions. They did not. From this they concluded 'that the primacy principle is surely overstated' (Searing, Wright and Rabinowitz 1976: 94). In this they are no doubt correct. Yet the question should be asked: Does 'approval of police officers', or 'approval of conservatives' – questions that they used to test the 'basic orientations' discussed in the literature really do so? And is there some compelling reason why approval of police officers should be correlated with an individual's position on admission of China into the United Nations (Searing, Schwartz and Lind 1973: 423)?

The emphasis on attitudes is one that political scientists find particularly comfortable and has been the basis for much early work in political socialization. Even Hess and Torney (1969), who argue that the main product of early socialization is a generalized attachment to the political system, state their case in terms of attitudes. But why should we expect attitudes to be the key element of what is learned in childhood? It makes much more intuitive sense, and appears to fit better with the findings of political learning, to suggest that more global beliefs (Knutson's 'pre-political ideologies' (1974) or Renshon's 'basic beliefs' (1974) for example) and the feelings and understandings associated with them, would be the building blocks of subsequent political orientations. And if 'ideology', with its implications of a coherent, interrelated system of beliefs, appears too cognitively and developmentally advanced, one could begin to use the concept of 'schema', to address questions raised by the primacy and structuring principles (Peterson and Somit 1981–2: 325–6).

In some respects, however, the concept of structuring does not go directly to the heart of the question at the core of political socialization's research premises, that of persistence itself. If what is learned during childhood does not persist to shape adult politics, a basic premise of the field has proved untenable. Yet, for a concept so central to the field's rationale and development, early models of persistence were surprisingly general in their formulation.

Early political learning was simply expected to persist relatively unchanged through adulthood. In this form the theory is relatively undifferentiated. It does not specify exactly which orientations learned in childhood are expected to persist and which are not. Nor does it go very far in distinguishing the many possible meanings of persistence: it is possible that orientations may persist in most important respects, but not remain static. Sears, for example, suggests such a possibility in his review of some data on the transmission of racism from fathers to sons. He cites evidence that suggests that 'a latent racism had been passed on and retained over the years, but was manifested in different forms' (Sears 1990: 84).

In retrospect, the model of 'unchanging persistence' was a theoretically naïve expectation, and the fact that it has not fully held up should come as no great surprise. One source of this expectation can be traced to a selective reading of psychoanalytic theory. In that theory, unconscious childhood conflicts were theorized to persist relatively unchanged into adulthood, resulting in wide ranges of adult behaviour.

The only problem with borrowing this formulation is that unconscious conflicts are not a suitable model of political orientations. Most of the latter, unlike the former, are conscious, relatively unconflicted, and clearly responsive to changes in individual development and situational dynamics. The 'repetition compulsion' familiar to psychoanalysts hardly describes the evolution of the child's political world in which cognitive development; modelling and learning from experience (to name just three mechanisms of political learning and change) are the rule, not the exception. Moreover, it doesn't even describe very well the various ways in which unconscious early conflicts can develop and unfold in adulthood.

Not unexpectedly, findings that political learning and development take place throughout the life cycle have forced the refinement of this theory. Connell (1971) interviewed 119 children aged from five to sixteen in Australia and found that between ages five and seven is a period of 'intuitive thinking' about politics, with children moving somewhat freely between political fact and fantasy. Between seven and nine a stage of primitive realism develops, between nine and twelve the children actually begin to construct their political world; and between twelve and sixteen they become able to engage in abstract political thought. Based on these findings, Connell argues that the political world of the young child is too much in a process of development to expect that it will 'persist' through adulthood.

Moore and his colleagues (Moore, Lare and Wagner 1985) reported the results of a longitudinal study of American children. They began their study with children in kindergarten and then reinterviewed them every year up until the fourth grade and reported their results. The authors demonstrated clearly that children do develop their political views over time. Indeed, they found evidence of a clear cognitive progression of children's political understanding, as suggested by Piaget's general model. Yet they did not find evidence for some of that theory's general hypotheses regarding children's thinking, namely that they are unable to think abstractly before about the fourth grade.

In Britain, Himmelweit *et al.* (1981) reported the results of an extended panel study begun with a group of adolescents in 1951 when they were 13–14 years old, and then reinterviewed again in 1962, 1964, 1966, 1970 and 1974. That study was centred on voting, but also collected enormous amounts of data about a variety of political and social views. They found 'many of the attitudes to be remarkably stable over the eight-year period', but surprisingly this did not extend to the act of voting. Of interest to us here is that only 31 per cent of the sample voted the same way on all six occasions (Himmelweit 1983: 241). Himmelweit's model of socialization and voting preference gives more weight to situational determinants of such choice, a view in keeping with political learning as having an important situationally specific dimension.

Finally, Jennings and Marcus (1984) analysed the results of a three-wave panel study conducted in the years 1965, 1973 and 1982 and focused on party identification and electoral choice. They found much more variability in the younger cohorts compared to their parents, yet, in the years between 1973 and 1982 partisan stability among the younger group increased dramatically. Jennings and Marcus put forward 'a political experience' model in which as a person gathers political experience his/her political orientations tend to crystallize.

These and other studies have all documented what appears to be a fundamental fact of the socialization process, variability *within* and *across* stages of development. This leads to a view of the political socialization process as 'development in progress'. The rule at each stage of development and for each set of orientations seems to be 'incompleteness', rather than completion. No agency, or set of agencies, has been documented in the USA or any other country (including authoritarian regimes) to fully form or shape political orientations.

These findings raise a more general issue concerning the need to develop models that explain change and development, and not just correspondence. It is therefore one sign of theoretical development in political socialization that continuing questions about undifferentiated theories of impact have prompted a whole new generation of models. Sears (1990), for example, discussed three new models of persistence, which he compares with the traditional mode that asserts that 'the residues of early socialization are relatively immune to change in latter years'. One new model is the *life-long openness* model, which asserts that 'age is irrelevant for attitude change'; a second model, the *life-cycle* view, suggests that 'persons are particularly susceptible to adapting particular dispositions at certain life stages'; and a third model, the *impressionable years* model, suggests that 'any dispositions are unusually vulnerable in late adolescence and early adulthood given strong enough pressure to change' (ibid.: 77).

The importance of these models may ultimately be not in their mutually exclusive accuracy, but in their attempts to come to grips with the problems of persistence and change in the political socialization process. Even these 'second generation' models contain some ambiguities, which suggest the need for further specification. Sapiro, for example, in reviewing these models, finds some ambiguity in the use of the term 'life-cycle' (Sapiro 1990: 4). She points out that this term may have two different (but not necessarily unrelated) meanings, with different implications for studies of persistence and change: one would imply that change is a natural consequence of ageing itself; the other that it is a consequence of socially constructed 'expected' life events. A question that arises given this differentiation is what specific kinds of orientations are expected to change in each model.

Other models of persistence and impact have been put forward. One of the best of these is the 'cumulative effects' model put forward by Langton (1984). Langton reanalysed the Almond–Verba five-nation study and also presented data of his own from a random sample of interviews with 494 workers in the central Andes in Peru. His strategy was to assess the impact of family, school and jobs, not to see which contributes most to socialization but to see what effects continuity and discontinuity of experience had on the development of particular political orientations like political efficacy.

Not surprisingly perhaps, he found that similar experiences in home, school and work tended to have a cumulative effect. That is, growing up in a non-repressive family, and then attending a school which encouraged participation, and then going into a job in which independence was valued tended to result in individuals having the highest levels of political confidence. When respondents were reared in a repressive home (associated with low political efficacy), but then went on to a school setting which encouraged efficacy, their efficacy scores increased by 17 points. However, when this same group was then subjected to a repressive work environment, their efficacy scores plunged 35 points. Clearly consistency of experiences affects persistence.

New models alone, however, while crucial to the field's continuing development, will not fully address the needs of political socialization theory and research by themselves. There must be new data too. This is said with the knowledge that the behavioural movement in political science has been criticized for its emphasis on data collection, measurement and statistical analysis. This movement has also been criticized for being ahistorical, non-contextual, and too concerned with drawing generalized 'laws' from data and subjects that do not support that pursuit.

Many of these concerns, especially as evidenced in the early years of the behavioural movement, have some validity. On the other hand, a concern with the representativeness and generalizability of results, asking questions in a systematic way, and a concern with uncovering and explaining patterns of behaviour would seem to be no drawback for the development of any field, including political socialization. This would appear to be as true for case studies as it is for more traditional survey designs.

Just what well-designed studies can do to refine the theories of the field can be seen in the landmark University of Michigan socialization studies conducted by Jennings and his colleagues (Jennings and Niemi 1968). They drew a representative sample of high school seniors and one or another of the adolescents' parents who completed an interview schedule in 1965. Eight years later 81 per cent of the students and 76 per cent of the parents who were originally interviewed were re-interviewed. That study and the analyses drawn from it are a prime example of the way in which second generation research studies facilitate the specification of relationships originally framed in a general, relatively undifferentiated way. Consider, for example, the effects of the family on the transmission of political orientations. The family has long been regarded as the most important agency for transmitting political orientations (Hyman 1959: 69) by many theorists in the area, but the Jennings and Niemi (1968) study was able to test not only *if*, but *when* it was the case.

Jennings and Niemi analysed parent–child correspondence in several areas including party identification, four political issues, and the sense of political cynicism. Briefly, the strongest correspondence they found was in the area of party identification (Tau b = 0.47), although there were some indications of a decline in such identifications. On policy issues, Jennings and Niemi found only moderate overlap in parent–child views, and they did not find much overlap on feelings towards certain political groups in the country (for example, labour unions, negroes, big business, etc.). Finally, on the political cynicism measure, the parent sample was much more cynical than the high school senior sample.

Next, Jennings and Niemi (1968) examined the impact of several factors that might influence the transmission process. They examined the effects of parent–student sex combinations (mother–daughter, father–son, etc.), feelings of closeness among family members, power and authority relationships in the family, and the level of family politicization. Most of these factors had only modest effects on the degree of correspondence, but the level of family politicization did affect the degree of correspondence in the cases of party identification and political cynicism (Jennings and Niemi 1968: 182).

Jennings and Niemi sum up their findings by observing that 'any model of socialization which rests on assumptions of pervasive currents of parent-to-child value transmissions of the types examined here, is in serious need of modification' (Jennings and Niemi 1968: 183) And that is precisely the point. The Jennings–Niemi study is a good representative example of the ways in which theories can be specified for particular factors within a given context.

It is important to keep in mind that Jennings and Niemi did not examine the kinds of basic orientations and consensual attachments to the political system (support of the regime, political institutions, etc.) that others like Hess and Torney (1969) had argued were the foundation of the family's influence. Nor did they examine the more basic political/psychological/philosophical frameworks (for example, 'pre-political ideologies', 'basic beliefs', etc.) that others have suggested are an important area of family impact. Their study assumed that these attachments were in place (Jennings and Niemi 1968: 172).

Even leaving aside these matters, did the Jennings and Niemi study negate the role of the family in the political socialization process? Not really; it specified it. Does the fact that the family appears to have a more limited role in the transmission of some political orientations than previously thought call into question the existence or impact of socialization processes? No, but it does point researchers toward other factors and time frames needed to specify further what gets acquired when.

Carefully drawn studies can not only be used to specify theoretical relationships but can also help in making comparative assessments of different theoretical approaches to the same phenomenon. A longitudinal study by Moore, Lare and Wagner (1985), begun with children in kindergarten and extending four years, was designed to assess the explanatory power of social learning and cognitive development theories. They found that although social learning theory could explain knowledge acquisition (recognition of political symbols, understanding policy issues, etc.), a capacity to move from concrete to abstract thinking was also involved. Thus the findings here seem to support the idea of theoretical complementarity, at least as far as mechanisms of early childhood political learning are concerned.

Another exemplar of this possibility is the Jennings and Niemi study described above. In addition to the parent–child interviews (panels) conducted in 1965 and 1973, they also collected data from a sample of all senior classes in 97 schools in both 1965 and 1973. This data set therefore consists of three panels (i.e. the parent's panel, the youth panel, and the 1965 and 1973 senior classes), which combine both cross-sectional and longitudinal designs. With this vast array of data, Jennings and Niemi (1981) were able to distinguish empirically between life-cycle effects (youth panel converges with parent panel, youth cohorts remain the same), life-cycle effects mixed with generational effects (youth panel converges with parent panel, youth cohorts diverge), and period effects (generations begin the same move congruently over time).

In reporting the results of the parent–child panel study described above, Jennings and Niemi also used the data specifically to address the persistence question. They found substantially more persistence in the adult panels than in the youth panels in both political and non-political domains. Yet overall they found that political orientations were far from stable for both groups, although there were differences in specific areas. This led them to favour the life-long openness model.

In sum, the hallmark of young fields and disciplines is unspecified theory, while field maturity is reflected in part by studies that can address comparative theoretical questions. There is an important relationship between theory and data: not only can data be used to test theory, but also data can function to generate theory. Incompatible, anomalous findings are an important aspect of the search for sounder theory. In all of these respects political socialization, while it has not answered most of the field's major questions fully, has certainly developed knowledge enough to be considered a solidly established, matured field whose basic premises have gone from controversy to conventional wisdom. And that paradoxically is both the good and the bad news.

Political socialization: prescriptions and possibilities

This essay began with two general questions. First, has political socialization theory demonstrated the validity of its premises? Second, what is the status of the field's development and what are its prospects for the future? Let us turn briefly to summarize each before making some observations on future directions in the field.

The question of whether the field has demonstrated the validity of its premises rests, as noted, on a view of what these premises are. Two general positions have been advanced on this matter. One locates the importance of the field in demonstrating linkages between political learning and systemic functioning. The other, not unrelated position locates the importance of political socialization in its impact on the individual's political development.

It seems clear that the four plus decades of research in the area have conclusively demonstrated the validity of the fundamental political socialization axiom, namely the 'developmental hypothesis'. That is, there is political learning over time to be explained, and there is little doubt that theories of socialization impact have helped to explain them. There are now numerous studies tracing the development of a range of political orientations, attitudes, beliefs, feelings, values, policy positions, and so forth, most of which have tried to ascertain which factors are instrumental in shaping them. That there is not full agreement about the latter should not obscure the gains in understanding derived from the former.

The attempt to link political socialization with systemic functioning has proved more difficult for reasons already discussed. This linkage makes intuitive sense, and is probably accurate in the general sense, but the size and complexity of the political systems for which it is proposed are simply too large and complex for anything but inference. Having said this, it must be noted that there is more direct evidence and correspondingly less inference involved in seeing the effects of political learning on the functioning of particular aspects of the political system. The combination of period effects (Watergate, Vietnam, etc.) and life-cycle effects on political cynicism found in the Jennings and Niemi (1981) study, and the relationships of those sets of variables to political participation, suggest one way in which theories of political socialization can be plausibly linked to one aspect of systemic functioning. This is a more modest linkage than 'system persistence' or 'system continuity', but perhaps a more realistic one.

Questions about the current state of political socialization are subject to different interpretations. While there is evidence of a decline in the amount of published research, this does not, I think, reflect a decline of interest and intellectual vitality. On the contrary, the decline in published research may well reflect the field's success, not its failure.

There are several reasons to advance this view. First, many of the basic models and concepts of the field (for example, learning, development, etc.) have been incorporated into cognate research fields such as political behaviour (Sapiro 1990) and comparative political analysis (Arian 1989). Sapiro provides an illustration of this phenomenon in noting the dearth of political socialization and development studies which focus specifically on adults. She observes, however, that one can 'develop a considerable bibliography of studies of partisanship, political behaviour and public opinion [which] considers "life-cycle" explanations for change or the impact of specifically adult experiences and settings on people's orientations and behaviour' (Sapiro 1990: 15). In other words, a measure of a field's success may be not only the number of studies published within a field but the degree of conceptual transfer of its ideas and theories to other arenas. This is a dimension which critics of the political socialization field have failed to consider.

Second, many of the concepts and models of political socialization have also been integrated into the mainstream of the various 'foundation disciplines', particularly political science. This can be seen by reading through the *American Political Science Review* and other major disciplinary journals, but it can be seen in its most dramatic form by noting the presidential address to the American Political Science Association in 1981 by Charles Lindblom, whose research and publications have not been in the field. In that address he noted that the question of political learning and political socialization was 'as important a question for political science as can be examined' (Lindblom 1982: 17). This is not a reflection on a field whose intellectual importance is in decline.

Finally, the core elements of political socialization theory have migrated laterally to new subfields that are clearly and directly in the 'political socialization' domain – although not ordinarily labelled as such. Consider in this regard the concept of identity. It is at its core both a psychological and developmental construct – two key socialization elements. When one adds to this the four plus decades of 'identity' and ethnic politics the term is clearly within the *political* socialization domain. A look through the journals such as *Psychology of Women Quarterly* or the *Journal of Black Psychology* will reveal a robust empirical and theoretical set of papers on various aspects of woman and black identity in relationship to topics of traditional interest to political socialization (cf., Banerjee 1986; Phinney 1987; Smith and Jackson 1989; and Hill 1999). One can even find the beginnings, in the aftermath of 9/11 (Schildkraut 2002; Renshon 2002; – but to some degree even before; cf., Citrin, Reingold and Green 1990; Renshon 2001) – of growing interest in American national identity and its development and political implications and the possible European-wide new identity (Blank and Schmidt 2003). In all these respects, the field of political socialization is alive and well. One merely needs to know where to look.

Since the number of publications is only an indirect indicator of field vitality and development, it is worth commenting briefly on some of the new developments that these publications represent. First, there has been a dramatic shift away from a focus on childhood to a concern with political socialization through the life cycle. This has been spurred by anomalous findings and also by the integration of 'newer' theories of adult development into political socialization research. This, in turn, has opened up new vistas of analysis.

One indication of this is the development of new and more refined models of impact, and its counterpart persistence. Political socialization now has a competing set of models in each of these important areas rather than the few relatively undifferentiated ones that characterized the early stages of the field's development. That these more differentiated theories have generated their own controversies may also be read as a sign of intellectual ferment (one possible reflection of vitality) rather than a lack of erudition.

The range of adult experience is much wider than those of most children. Thus, in addition to the familiar litany of childhood agents (for example, family, school, peers, media, etc.), there are whole new contexts to explore, such as the work environment (Lafferty 1989), military service (Lovell and Stiehm 1989), careers in politics (Renshon 1989, 1990) and international political administration (Peck 1979), experiences connected with movement politics (Morris, Hatchett and Brown 1989), and immigration and acculturation (Lamare 1982).

The integration of theories of adult development into political socialization research has also been partially responsible for new efforts to collect data relevant to these theories. We have already noted the Himmelweit *et al.* (1981) and Jennings and Niemi (1968, 1981) studies, but there are others too. Whalen and Flacks (1989), Braungart and Braungart (1990a, 1990b), Bermanzohn (1990), and Fendrich and Turner (1989) have all re-interviewed selected groups of political activists to chart the course of their political lives from early radicalism through adulthood.

In examining the developments of the last several decades, a word is also in order about the developing sophistication of the research designs and data analysis. I do not mean by this more and better statistical techniques, but rather research which incorporates several different data gathering modalities, and which is designed to assess the comparative value of different socialization theories. As an example of the first, the Moore, Lare and Wagner panel study (1985) used a combination of open-ended and closed questions and gathered all the data in face-to-face interviews, thus bypassing the problems associated with the administration of closed-ended survey instruments to large groups of individuals. As an example of the second point, the Jennings and Niemi (1968, 1974, 1981) studies were designed to allow comparisons of different models of persistence and change.

Finally, in assessing the development of the field one must also note the introduction and examination of other models of psychological development and functioning. Social developmental models associated with Piaget, Kohlberg and others have received more attention over the past decade, and several recent books have directly addressed the contribution of these theories to political socialization (Rosenberg 1985; Rosenberg *et al.* 1988).

A somewhat newer development on the theoretical horizon is the application of other cognitive theories, most particularly those associated with schema analysis (Torney-Purta 1990) to political socialization theory. Schema analysis is addressed as much to the issue of how political understanding gets organized in individuals' minds as it is to the particular content involved (although the latter is important also). Schemata may be thought of as mental filing systems that are organized in both socially conventional and idiosyncratic ways.

Torney-Purta (1990: 113) notes that a major question at this point is how useful schemata will prove in helping to understand important aspects of political life. The structure of schemata may tell us something about how individuals organize their political world, and by what rules political experiences through the life cycle are assigned to different intra-psychic categories. This, in turn, may help to explain variations in response to similar political experiences. These would seem to be useful additions to knowledge about the political socialization process. Moreover, if schema theory does prove useful, questions of acquisition and development over the life cycle will come to the fore.

The development and application of new models of individual functioning in political socialization theory, coupled with the refinement of the more 'traditional' models of the past, underscore an important point about the relationship of models to the phenomenon that the field of political socialization studies. One can argue that the increase in the number of new and old competing models in the field reflects either a state of robust intellectual vigor or a failure to fully test and discard those theories that do not pull their own explanatory weight.

Some criticisms of the field have appeared to adopt the second view. Cook (1985) argues that the decline (as he sees it) of political socialization is directly related to the 'misunderstood psychological theories'. While his critique of the 'invariant persistence' model is well taken, his suggestion that the field reorientate itself on the basis of Vygotsky's model of cognitive development is not likely to prove of decisive help. So too, Rosenberg's call to reorientate the field by fully developing a psychological approach, which he defines as a person's subjective understanding of the political world, runs the risk of equating and confounding socialization with perception (Rosenberg 1985: 725).

The problem with these calls for reorientation is not that political socialization would fail to benefit from further model development. Rather the problem is that given the complexity and diversity of the processes the field covers, no one model is likely to be decisive. Do children learn according to principles of social learning theory? Yes. Do children go through, in some form, the developmental stages that Piaget and others described? Yes. Is affectively charged political experience important in shaping political orientations both in childhood and adulthood? Yes. However, if the answer to all these, and similar questions that could be raised, is affirmative, then the road to further progress in the field will not lie in finding a single master theory of the process.

One of political socialization's needs is to develop *integrative* models. To give one example, individual-level theories of cognitive functions are presented as if affect and cognition are unrelated in actual practice. Given that feelings about leaders, for example, have come to be the single best predictors of voting choices, this would appear to be a serious omission indeed. So too, integration must also be maintained between sociologically orientated and psychologically orientated theories. Politics does not take place solely in the psyche, nor do many external political 'realities' go uninterrupted.

Political socialization and identity in a dangerous age

Political socialization theory, like other theories, is embedded in its social and political contexts. In the 1950s it attempted to account for persistence and regularity. In the 1960s and thereafter, it struggled to account for change. In the 1980s and 1990s it focused on the elements of identity politics. It should therefore not be surprising that at least two new developments – globalization and the rise of catastrophic terrorism – have raised important new questions for the field as well as having recast some older ones. Among the major implications of each of these new developments are questions of identification and belonging – subjects that have echoes in the field's past and which I think are critical to its future.

The essence of globalization is the extraordinary worldwide fluidity of information, markets, and people. This raises questions, not so much as is commonly said, about the future of the nation state, but of its basis. Unprecedented international migration flows from East to West and from South to North have raised basic questions of inclusion, identification and accommodation for the liberal democracies that are the goal of most of this migration. At the same time, the rise of catastrophic terrorism[1] associated with the regions and countries from which most migration originates adds to the profound dilemmas of liberal democracies. I would like to briefly examine the implications of these twin trends for political socialization theory and research in three primary areas:

1   the implications of 9/11 for the political cultures of the USA;
2   questions of immigration and integration of new communities; and
3   questions of citizenship and civics training.

American political culture and the implications of 9/11

When highjacked planes demolished the World Trade Towers and part of the Pentagon, they did more than destroy buildings, they assaulted a core belief of American psychology – its sense of exceptionalism (it can't happened here) and some would say, its exuberant optimism. On surface many things appeared the same.

447

Religious attendance that had risen dramatically after 9/11 returned to pre-attack levels. Overt manifestations of patriotism, like displaying flags, did the same. Domestic political concerns began to draw increasing attention in the period before the 2002 Congressional and State elections. Life went on – as it must.

Yet, in other respects the USA was transformed from a country that before 9/11 had worried more about shark attacks than about national and domestic security. In the aftermath of 9/11, the President declared that America was at war with an enemy that had the desire and the intention – if they could – to unleash chemical, biological or nuclear weapons against the USA and on US soil. Fortress America had ceased to be a barrier to destruction during the cold war, and likewise deterrence in the form of mutual assured destruction ceased to be such a barrier with the 9/11 attacks.

Political socialization, which had in the past studied the impact of discrete events like the Watergate scandals, or the assassination of John F. Kennedy, now has before it an event of the most enormous magnitude to examine. It is one that has political implications not only for the many groups that were and are affected by the events of 9/11 and their aftermath, but also for the society and its institutions more generally. What happens in a democratic society used to framing its activities through the lens of *laissez-faire* politics when it must now reframe itself through the lens of domestic national security?

What happens to the core foundations of national character and psychology? If it can no longer realistically ignore the threat to its way of life and perhaps its existence in what ways must the USA change and what are the forces – of psychology, politics, and culture – that affect its capacity to do so? Political socialization, as noted, has had some difficulty measuring and documenting systematic change through the aggregation of individual developmental experiences. The tragic events of 9/11 provide an opportunity to examine the consequences of system-wide political experience and learning from a reverse perspective. Rather than using the more traditional socialization approach of individuals–development–political institutions and culture, it may now be more possible, given the scope of 9/11, to document the connection in the opposite direction.

Immigration and integration

As noted, the essence of globalization is the extraordinary worldwide fluidity of information, markets, and people. Here I would like to focus on the last of these three. Among the most profound challenges to Western democracies in North America and Europe are those that arise from immigration. The numbers are immense. From 1961 to 1997, the USA took in almost 22 million legal immigrants. That flow has averaged about 800,000 legal immigrants a year, with an estimated 8 million illegal immigrants now estimated to be living in the USA. Recent census figures show that the number of legal and illegal immigrants living in the USA has almost tripled since 1970, rising from 9.6 million to 26.4 million today (Escobar 1999; Rodriguez 2000).

No other country equals the USA in either the absolute numbers or geographical diversity of its immigrant stream. Yet many countries – Canada, Great Britain, Australia, and the countries of Western Europe – all face similar dilemmas. The question basically is the following.

In an age when immigrants come from diverse cultural, religious, psychological and political traditions; where they can and often do retain emotional, political and other ties to their home countries, and are increasingly encouraged to do so by them, how is it possible to honor both the immigrants' wish to retain these ties and the necessity to integrate large numbers of immigrants from diverse traditions into an on-going society and culture without threatening either the immigrants' self and group identity on one hand or the national identity and practices of the countries to which they immigrate?

This is no minor or easy matter. The traditional model of assimilation was based on the expectation that immigrants would learn the language, culture, and civic traditions of the countries in which they choose to live (Salins 1997). Moreover, since immigrants ordinarily had substantial personal reason to emigrate – be it to increase their freedom, opportunity, or both – it followed that they would feel some level of emotional connection with their new country as a place that offered them what they sought. This foundation, in turn, would be the basis for further identification and attachment as immigrants put down roots and their new country becomes more fully – emotionally and experientially – theirs. This model was important not because of its conceptual and theoretical stature, but rather because it provided a successful method by which millions of new immigrants could and did become substantially integrated and emotionally connected citizens.

Like many other aspects of American culture, the concept of assimilation and more importantly, its practice has come under heavy criticism from some quarters (Glazer 1993). Critics in the USA and elsewhere question whether immigrants should accommodate to their new home or vice versa. They ask whether the country should not become more multilingual rather than putting the onus on immigrants to learn English. And they see nothing problematic, indeed they encourage, new immigrants to retain and extend their financial, cultural, political and psychological ties to their 'home countries'.

These are not just theoretical or definitional questions, they have the most profound political and civic consequences. There are for sample now over 90 countries that allow and encourage their nationals to hold multiple citizenships. From 1961 to 1997 over 75 per cent of American immigrants came from dual citizenship allowing countries. What is the effect of having so many new immigrants retain and build on their ties to their home countries?

Rubin Rumbaut conducted one of the largest surveys of immigrant socialization. He found (1994: 764, table 2) that among second-generation Mexican-American adolescents almost half choose a racial or pan-ethnic identity and that another 8 per cent choose an identity that was wholly allied with their country of national origin. These are the children of immigrants and yet over half choose an identity that was specifically exclusionary of an American element in their identity (as in for example Mexican American).

Is it possible, and even if possible, is it preferable to have unprecedented numbers of new citizens with active and ongoing loyalties to their home countries or who don't identify as Americans? Political socialization, has always been embedded in social and political contexts as it has sought to answer the field's most pressing questions. Surely these are questions worth answering.

449

Civic learning: clarifying ideals, losing ground

From its inception, a major focus of the political socialization field has been the effort to understand and encourage good citizenship. The link between the nature and requirements of good citizenship and the continued vitality of a democratic republic had been obvious since Plato. Yet, at first, theorists focused on the impact of the schools – did they influence politically relevant attitudes and behaviours. Generally, they did – but not as much, it turned out, as family and even peer experiences. Still, given that most family political socialization was *laissez-faire*, schools remained the one place where one could see actual evidence of intentional efforts to develop political awareness and so it was very natural to try and measure impact. Did joining in extracurricular activities have an effect? Yes. Did taking part in student government have an effect? Yes. Did these, or other elements of school experience produce informed, reflective and involved citizens? Apparently not.

Voting rates continued to decline – and were never very high among 18–24 year olds. Nor were young people particularly attuned to information that would help to make them informed citizens. In 1997, The Pew Research Center for the People and the Press reported that in the 1996 elections '25 per cent of those they surveyed said they learned about the presidential campaign from the likes of [Jay] Leno and David Letterman, a figure rising to 40 per cent among those under 30' (Cited in Kurtz 1999, A01; see also Della Carpini and Keeter 1999).

Not surprisingly perhaps in view of the above, the schools appeared to be losing ground in what might well be considered the most basic element in preparing young persons for their role as citizens – having a foundation of knowledge about the country in which they live and the political institutions that are the foundations of its freedom and way of life (cf., Patrick 1977; Bahmueller and Quigley 1991; Torney-Purta, 1995a, 1995b; Niemi 1999). A national survey conducted by the National Constitution Center (cited in Branson 1998), found 'only 6 per cent can name all four rights guaranteed by the First Amendment; 62 per cent cannot name all three branches of the Federal government; 35 per cent believe the Constitution mandates English as the official language; and more than half of Americans don't know the number of senators'.

The 1990 National Assessment of Educational Progress (NAEP) Report Card in Civics, a major test of subject knowledge for 4th, 8th, and 12th graders, revealed that (Branson 1998) 'students have only a superficial knowledge of civics and lack depth of understanding'. For example, only 38 per cent of 8th graders knew that Congress makes laws; and nearly half of high-school seniors did not recognize typical examples of the federal system of checks and balances.

The 1998 national surveys and 'civics report card' (National Assessment of Educational Progress 1999: 40) divided scores on knowledge and proficiency into four groups: Below Basic, Basic, Proficient, and Advanced. At each of the three grade levels tested (4th, 8th, and 12th), Basic was defined as having 'partial mastery and skills that are fundamental to proficient work at each grade', while Proficient was defined as representing 'solid academic performance'. So how many students at each grade level were 'proficient' or even better 'advanced'? Not many. In 4th grade, only 25 per cent scored as proficient or advanced, which means of course that 75 per cent did not reach proficiency. In 8th grade the figures were 24 per cent for proficiency or advanced competence, and in 12th grade the figures were 30 per cent for the two categories. These are composite scores and do not directly report the disparities by race and ethnicity that are, if anything, even more troubling.

Lest this be seen as an issue affecting only public schools with their mixed record of academic performance, the results of a survey conducted at America's most elite colleges is instructive. A recent report by the American Council of Trustees and Alumni (Martin and Neal 2000; see also Veale 2000), a group that supports liberal arts education, recently asked a series of high-school level multiple choice questions to a randomly selected group of graduating seniors at Harvard, Princeton and Brown. The results were dismal. Among the best students in the USA, 71 per cent did not know the purpose of the Emancipation Proclamation and 78 per cent were not able to identity the author of the phrase 'of the people, by the people, for the people', Seventy per cent could not link Lyndon Johnson with the passage of the historic Voting Rights Act of 1965. Yet, 90 per cent could correctly identify the rap singer Snoop Doggy Dogg.

The implication of these data should be clear and troubling. Americans do not have and are not acquiring the levels of basic information and proficiencies that are essential to living in and supporting a democratic republican form of government. These deficiencies apparently extend from the most average students to the 'best and brightest'. They raise severe questions about whether American children will have the tools to shoulder the responsibilities of living in and helping to guide the USA through dangerous and difficult times. Equally significant questions emerge in relation to the schools' critical role in helping to integrate millions of new immigrants.

Political socialization developed and thrived as a field because it asked the most basic and profound question of political life: how does an understanding of the political world develop. It has always been framed by large questions, even as its strategy to accumulate knowledge was of necessity more tailored. As my essay above makes clear, the field is again facing some very large questions indeed. Is political socialization a field in decline? I think not. Is it a field with enough solid knowledge accumulated over forty plus years to be in a position to address the most pressing political and socialization issues we now face. Let us hope so.

Note

1   The term catastrophic terror simply reflects the rise of terrorists groups with the will, the desire and, if they can acquire the means, the intention to unleash chemical, biological, or nuclear weapons against the sworn enemies – primarily the USA – but more generally the Western democracies.

References

Allen, G. (1989) 'Introduction' (Special topic: Children's political socialization and cognition), *Human Development* 32: 1–4.

Almond, G. and Verba, S. (1963) *The Civic Culture*, Princeton: Princeton University Press.

Arian, A. (1989) 'A people apart: coping with national security problems in Israel', *Journal of Conflict Resolution* 33: 605–31.

Atherton, F. C. (1975) 'Watergate and children's attitudes towards political authority revisited', *Political Science Quarterly* 90: 477–96.

Bahmueller, C. F. and Quigley, C. N. (eds) (1991) *CIVITAS: A Framework for Civic Education*, Calabas, CA: Center for Civic Education.

Banerjee, B. G. (1986). *Socialization: An Ethnic Study*, New York: Stisous/Advent Books

Beck, P. A. (1977) 'The role of agents in political socialization', in S. A. Renshon (ed.) *Handbook of Political Socialization: Theory and Research*, New York: Free Press.

Bermanzohn, S. (1990) 'Survivors of the Greensboro massacre; ten years later', paper presented to the International Society for Political Psychology, Washington, DC.

Blank, T. and Schmidt, P. (eds) (2003) 'Special Issue: National Identity in Europe', *Political Psychology*, 24:1.

Branson, M.S. (1998) *The Role of Civic Education*, Los Angeles, CA: Center for Civic Education <http://www.civiced.org/articles_role.html>

Braungart, M. M. and Braungart, R. G. (1990a) 'The life course development of left- and right-wing youth activist leaders from the 1960s', *Political Psychology* 11: 243–82.

—— (1990b) 'Studying political youth: a reply to Flacks', *Political Psychology* 11: 293–308.

Chaffe, S. H. (1977) 'Mass media in political socialization', in S. A. Renshon (ed.) *Handbook of Political Socialization: Theory and Research*, New York: Free Press.

Chapman, J. (1987) 'Political socialization and out-group politicization: an empirical study of consciousness-raising', *British Journal of Political Science* 17: 15–40.

Citrin, J., Reingold, B. and Green, D. (1990) 'American identity and the politics of ethnic change', *Journal of Politics* 52: 1124–54

Clausen, J. (ed.) (1968) *Socialization and Society*, Boston: Little, Brown & Co.

Cook, T. E. (1983) 'Another perspective on political authority in children's literature: the fallible leader in L. Frank Baum and Dr Seuss', *Western Political Quarterly* 36: 326–36.

—— (1985) 'The bear market in political socialization and the costs of misunderstood theories', *American Political Science Review* 79: 1079–93.

—— (1989) 'The psychological theory of political socialization and the political theory of child development: the dangers of normal science', *Human Behavior* 32: 24–34.

Connell, R. W. (1971) *The Child's Construction of Politics*, Carlton: Melbourne University Press.

Connell, R. W. and Goot, M. (1972–3) 'Science and ideology in American political socialization research', *Berkeley Journal of Sociology* 27: 323–33.

Crosby, T. L. (1984) 'Gladstone's decade of crisis: biography and the life course approach', *Journal of Political and Military Sociology* 12: 9–22.

Cummings, S. and Taebel, D. (1978–9) 'The economic socialization of children: a neo-Marxist analysis', *Social Problems* 26: 198–210.

Cundy, D. (1982) 'Parents and peers: dimensions of political influence', *Social Science Journal* 19: 13–23.

Dahl, R. (1961) 'The behavioral approach in political science: epitaph for a monument to a successful protest', *American Political Science Review* 55: 69–81.

Davies, J. C. (1977) 'Political socialization: from womb to childhood', in S. A. Renshon (ed.) *Handbook of Political Socialization: Theory and Research*, New York: Free Press.

Della Carpini, M. X. and Keeter, S. (1999) *What Americans Know About Politics and Why It Matters*, New Haven, CT: Yale University Press.

Dennis, J. (1985) 'Foreword', in S. W. Moore, J. Lare and K. A. Wagner, *The Child's Political World: A Longitudinal Perspective*, New York: Praeger.

Dowse, R. (1978) 'Some doubts concerning the study of political socialization', *Political Studies* 26: 403–10.

Easton, D. (1965) *A Systems Analysis of Political Life*, New York: John Wiley.

Easton, D. and Dennis, J. (1969) *Children in the Political System*, New York: McGraw-Hill.

Erikson, E. E. (1950) *Childhood and Society*, New York: Norton.

Escobar, G. (1999) 'Immigrants' Ranks Tripled In 29 Years', *The Washington Post*, January 9; A01.

Fendrich, J. M. and Turner, R. W. (1989) 'The transition from student politics to adult politics', *Social Forces* 67: 1049–57.

Gardner, H. (1987) *The Mind's New Science: The History of the Cognitive Revolution*, New York: Basic Books.

Gilligan, C. (1982) *In a Different Voice: Psychological Theory and Women's Development*, Cambridge, MA: Harvard University Press.

Glazer, N. (1993) 'Is assimilation dead?', *The Annals of the American Academy of Political Science* 530: 122–36.

Greenberg, E. S. (1970) 'Children and government: a comparison across racial lines', *Midwest Journal of Political Science* 14: 249–79.

Greenstein, F. I. (1960) 'The benevolent leader: children's images of political authority', *American Political Science Review* 54: 934–43.

—— (1965) *Children and Politics*, New Haven: Yale University Press.

—— (1967) *Personality and Politics*, New York: Markham.

—— (1970) 'A note on the ambiguity of "political socialization": definitions, criticisms, and strategies of inquiry', *Journal of Politics* 32: 969–78.

—— (1976) 'Item wording and other interaction effects on the measurement of political orientations', *American Journal of Political Science* 20: 773–9.

Greenstein, F. I. and Tarrow, S. (1970) *Political Orientations of Children: The Use of a Semi-projective Technique in Three Nations*, Sage Comparative Politics Series 1: 479–558, Beverly Hills: Sage Publications.

Hess, R. D. and Easton, D. (1960) 'The child's changing image of the president', *Public Opinion Quarterly* 24: 632–44.

Hess, R. D. and Torney, J. (1969) *The Development of Political Attitudes in Children*, Chicago: Aldine.

Hill, S. A. (1999). *African American Children: Socialization and Development in Families*, New York: Corwin Press.

Himmelweit, H. T. (1983) 'Political socialization', *International Social Science Journal* 35: 237–56.

Himmelweit, H. T., Humpreys, P., Jaeger, M. and Katz, M. (1981) *How Voters Decide*, London: Academic Press.

Hyman, H. (1959) *Political Socialization*, Glencoe, IL: Free Press.

Jaros, D., Hirsch, H. and Felron, F. J. (1968) 'The malevolent leader: political socialization in an American sub-culture', *American Political Science Review* 62: 564–75.

Jennings, M. K. and Marcus (1984) 'Partisan orientations over the long haul: results from a three-wave political socialization panel study', *American Political Science Review* 78: 1000–18.

Jennings, M. K. and Niemi, R. G. (1968) 'The transmission of political values from parents to child', *American Political Science Review* 62: 169–84.

—— (1981) *Generations and Politics*, Princeton: Princeton University Press.

Knutson, J. N. (1974) 'Pre-political ideologies: the basis for political learning', in R. Niemi (ed.) *The Politics of Future Citizens*, San Francisco: Jossey-Bass.

Kurtz, H. (1999) 'Americans Wait for the Punch Line on Impeachment as the Senate Trial Proceeds, Comedians Deliver the News', *The Washington Post*, January 26; A01.

Lafferty, W. M. (1989) 'Work as a source of political learning among wage-laborers and lower level employees', in R. S. Sigel (ed.) *Political Learning in Adulthood*, Chicago: University of Chicago Press.

Lamare, J. W. (1982) 'The political integration of Mexican-American children: a generational analysis', *International Migration Review* 16: 169–88.

Langton, K. (1984) 'Persistence and change in political confidence over the life-span: embedding life-cycle socialization in context', *British Journal of Political Science* 14: 461–81.

Lasswell, H. D. (1930) *Psychopathology and Politics*, Chicago: University of Chicago Press.

Levinson, D. (1978) *The Seasons of a Man's Life*, New York: Knopf.

Lindblom, C. (1982) 'Another state of mind' (APSA presidential address, 1981), *American Political Science Review* 76: 9–21.

Lovell, J. P. and Stiehm, J. H. (1989) 'Military service and political socialization', in R. S. Sigel (ed.) *Political Learning in Adulthood*, Chicago: University of Chicago Press.

Maddox, W. S. and Handberg, R. (1979) 'Presidential effect and chauvinism among children', *American Journal of Political Science* 23: 426–33.

Martin, J. L. and Neal, A. D. (2000) 'Loosing America's Memory: historical Illiteracy in the 21st Century', Washington, DC: American Council of Trustees and Alumni. <http://www.goacta.org/linksframeset.htm>

Meadow, R. G. (1982) 'Information and maturation in children's evaluation of government leadership during Watergate', *Western Political Quarterly* 35: 539–51.

Merelman, R. (1972) 'The adolescence of political socialization', *Sociology of Education* 45: 134–66.

—— (1986) 'Revitalizing political socialization', in M. G. Hermann (ed.) *Political Psychology*, San Francisco: Jossey-Bass.

—— (1989) 'Commentary' (Special topic: Children's political socialization and cognition), *Human Development* 32: 35–44.

Merton, R. K. (1968) *Social Theory and Social Structure*, New York: Free Press.

Moore, S. (1989) 'The need for a unified theory of political learning: lessons from a longitudinal project', *Human Development* 32: 5–13.

Moore, S., Lare, J. and Wagner, K. A. (1985) *The Child's Political World: A Longitudinal Perspective*, New York: Praeger.

Morris, A. D., Hatchett, S. J. and Brown, R. E. (1989) 'The civil rights movement and black political socialization', in R. S. Sigel (ed.) *Political Learning in Adulthood*, Chicago: University of Chicago Press.

National Assessment of Educational Progress (1999) *1998 CIVICS Report Card for the Nation*, Washington, DC: US Department of Education. <http://nces.ed.gov/nationsreportcard/civics/>

Niemi, R. (1999). *Civic Education: What Makes Students Learn?* New Haven, CT: Yale University Press.

Patrick, J. (1977) 'Political socialization and political education in schools', in S. A. Renshon (ed.) *Handbook of Political Socialization: Theory and Research*, New York: Free Press.

Phinney, J. S. (ed.) (1987). *Children's Ethnic Socialization: Pluralism and Development*, Thousand Oaks, CA: Sage Press.

Piaget, J. (1965) *The Moral Development of the Child*, New York: Free Press.

Peck, R. (1979) 'Socialization of permanent representatives in the United Nations: some evidence', *International Organization* 33: 365–90.

Peterson, S. A. and Somit, A. (1981–2) 'Cognitive development and childhood political socialization: questions about the primacy principle', *American Behavioral Scientist* 25: 313–34.

Pye, L. (1968) *The Spirit of Chinese Politics*, Cambridge, MA: MIT Press.

Renshon, S. A. (1974) *Psychological Needs and Political Behavior: A Theory of Personality and Political Efficacy*, New York: Free Press.

—— (1977) 'Assumptive frameworks in political socialization theory', in S. A. Renshon (ed.) *Handbook of Political Socialization: Theory and Research*, New York: Free Press.

—— (1989) 'Psychological perspectives on theories of adult development and the political socialization of leaders', in R. S. Sigel (ed.) *Political Learning in Adulthood*, Chicago: University of Chicago Press.

—— (1990) 'Educating political leaders in a democracy', in O. Ichilov (ed.) *Political Socialization, Citizenship Education and Democracy*, New York: Teachers College Press.

—— (2001) 'American character and national identity: The dilemmas of cultural diversity', in S. Renshon and J. Duckitt, *Political Psychology: Cultural and Cross Cultural Foundations*, New York: Macmillan, pp. 285–310.

—— (ed.) (2002) *One America? Political Leaders, National Identity, and the Dilemmas of Diversity*, Washington, DC: Georgetown University Press.

Rodriguez, C. (2000) 'Latino Influx Boosts number of US Immigrants to all-time High', *Boston Globe*, September 12; A1.

Rosenberg, S. W. (1985) 'Sociology, psychology and the study of political behavior: the case of research on political socialization', *Journal of Politics* 47: 715–31.

—— (1988) *Reason, Ideology and Politics*, Princeton: Princeton University Press.

Rosenberg, S. W., Ward, D. and Chilton, S. (1988) *Political Reasoning and Cognition: A Piagetian View*, Durham, NC: Duke University Press.

Rumbaut, R. (1987) 'The crucible within: Ethnic identity, self-esteem, and segmented assimilation among children of immigrants', *International Migration Review* 28:4, 748–94.

Salins, P. (1997) *Assimilation American Style*, New York: Basic Books.

Sapiro, V. (1990) 'What do we know about political socialization during adulthood?' paper prepared for delivery at the Annual Scientific Meeting of the International Society for Political Psychology, Washington, DC, July 11–14.

Schildkraut, D. (2002) 'The more things change...American identity and mass and elite response to 9/11', *Political Psychology*.

Searing, D. D., Schwartz, J. J. and Lind, A. B. (1973) 'The structuring principle: political socialization and belief systems', *American Political Science Review* 67: 415–32.

Searing, D. D., Wright, G. and Rabinowitz, G. (1976) 'The primacy principle: attitude change and political socialization', *British Journal of Political Science* 6: 83–113.

Sears, D. O. (1975) 'Political socialization', in F. I. Greenstein and N. Polsby (eds) *Handbook of Political Science*, vol. 4, Reading, MA: Addison-Wesley.

—— (1990) 'Whither political socialization research: the question of persistence', in O. Ichilov (ed.) *Political Socialization, Citizenship Education and Democracy*, New York: Teachers College Press.

Sigel, R. (1965) 'Assumptions about the learning of political values', *Annals of the American Academy of Social and Political Science* 361: 1–9.

—— (1977) 'Perspectives on adult political socialization: areas of research', in S. A. Renshon (ed.) *Handbook of Political Socialization: Theory and Research*, New York: Free Press.

—— (ed.) (1989) *Political Learning in Adulthood: A Sourcebook of Theory and Research*, Chicago: University of Chicago Press.

Silbiger, S. (1977) 'Peers and political socialization', in S. A. Renshon (ed.) *Handbook of Political Socialization: Theory and Research*, New York: Free Press.

Smith, J. O. and Jackson, C. E. (1989) *Race and Ethnicity: A study of Intercultural Socialization Patterns*, New York: Kendall/Hunt publishing.

Sullivan, J. L. and Minns, D. R. (1976) 'The benevolent leader revisited: substantive finding or methodological artifact?', *American Journal of Political Science* 20: 673–772.

Torney-Purta, J. (1990) 'From attitudes and knowledge to schemata: expanding the outcomes of political socialization research', in O. Ichilov (ed.) *Political Socialization, Citizenship Education and Democracy*, New York: Teachers College Press.

—— (1995a) 'Psychological theory as a basis for political socialization research: Individuals' Construction of Knowledge', *Perspectives on Political Science* 24: 23–33.

—— (1995b) 'Education on multicultural settings: Perspectives from global and international education programs', in W. D. Hawley and A. W. Jackson (eds) *Toward a Common Destiny: Improving Race and Ethnic Relations in America*, San Francisco: Jossey-Bass, pp. 341–70.

Turiel, E. (1989) 'Commentary' (Special topic: Children's political socialization and cognition), *Human Development* 32: 45–64.

Vaillancourt, P. M. (1973) 'Stability of children's survey's responses', *Public Opinion Quarterly* 37: 373–87.

Veale, S. (2000) 'History 101: Snoop Doggy Roosevelt', *New York Times*, July 2, wk 5.

Whalen, J. and Flacks, R. (1989) *Beyond the Barricades: The Sixties Generation Grows Up*, Philadelphia: Temple University Press.

Wrong, D. (1961) 'The oversocialized concept of man in modern society', *American Sociological Review* 26: 183–93.

Zaslavsky, V. and Z. (1980) 'Adult political socialization in the USSR: a study of attitudes of Society workers to the invasion of Czechoslovakia', *Sociology* 15: 407–23.

Further reading

Bilu, Y. (1989) 'The other as nightmare: the Israeli–Arab encounter as reflected in children's dreams in Israel and the West Bank', *Political Psychology* 10: 365–90.

Braungart, R. G. and Braungart, M. M. (1984) 'Life course and generational politics', special issue *of Journal of Political and Military Sociology* 12: 1–207.

Flacks, R. (1990) 'Social basis of activist identity: comment on Braungart article', *Political Psychology* 11: 283–92.

Ichilov, O. (ed.) (1990) *Political Socialization, Citizenship Education and Democracy*, New York: Teacher's College Press.

Kearney, R. N. (1984) 'The mentor in the commencement of a political career: the case of Subhas Chandra Bose and C. R. Das', *Journal of Political and Military Sociology* 12: 37–48.

Shernick, S. K. (1984) 'Politics and opportunity in the post-revolutionary generation: the cases of Nazi Germany, Stalinist USSR and Maoist China', *Journal of Political and Military Sociology* 12: 113–36.

Sidanius, J. and Lau, R. R. (1989) 'Political sophistication and political deviance: a matter of context', *Political Psychology* 10: 85–110.

Wagner, J. (1990) 'Rational constraint in mass beliefs systems: the role of developmental moral stages in the structure of political beliefs', *Political Psychology* 11: 147–76.

30

POLITICAL COMMUNICATION

Denis McQuail

All political institutions depend on communication for the symbolic representation of authority and the exercise of power. Modern democratic political processes presume the participation of informed citizens in the choice of representatives and thus on extensive and complex communication networks and flows. Political communication is both about the flow of information and ideas and also about many kinds of interactions ranging from conversations to crowds and demonstrations. It includes actions and non-verbal forms of expression as well as linguistic texts. As a result the terrain covered by the term 'political communication' is very broad and diverse. In a short overview, little more can be done than to introduce and explain the main contemporary issues and topics that are of shared interest to students of both politics and communication. Trends in political communication practice and also in theory and research will be identified.

The press and the rise of democracy

The central focus in the study of political communication has nearly always been the relation between democracy and the available or dominant means of public communication. Modern democracy found its first clear expression in eighteenth-century Europe and North America. Before that time, from the early sixteenth century at least, printed books, pamphlets and letters were the main means by which new political ideas were disseminated and change advocated. In response, the use of printing presses was strictly controlled by authorities of church and state, who used the same means in defence of the 'old order'. Print media were also much used by rulers and governments as instruments in dynastic and national conflicts. The modern notion of 'propaganda' is well represented in the communication activities of proponents and opponents of power and privilege in the early modern period.

In the day-to-day political struggle for or against democratic ideas, the newspaper was the primary form of political communication. It originated in the mercantile states of North Western Europe in the course of the seventeenth century. It served to report events of political significance as well as the proceedings and outcomes of assemblies; it provided a platform for political opinion and a weapon in factional conflict. Later it also adopted the role of watchdog and critic of government as well as a means of political organization and mobilization. In all periods it has offered a channel of information and influence from government to people (and vice versa). These essential political functions of the press have not greatly changed although the balance between them and the form they take has.

The importance of the press for democracy is well attested by the attention given to it in early statements of political rights and democratic constitutions. The essential point was that the press should be free of government control or censorship in advance. Although freedom of the press gained its first constitutional guarantee in Sweden in 1766, the most famous clause is to be found in the 1791 First Amendment to the US constitution which states that 'Congress shall make no law...abridging the freedom of the Press'. Freedom of the press was part and parcel of other communicative rights, including those of expression, assembly and religious belief. Historically, the press has always played a key role in popular revolutions, including the American and French Revolutions (1776 and 1789), the 1848 Central European Revolution and the Russian Revolution of 1917. However on these occasions its role was mainly confined to disseminating new ideas amongst an elite and aiding radical minority agents of change rather than directly stimulating the mass of the population to overthrow its rulers. It is also of interest that the most recent examples of popular revolution, those that toppled the Communist regimes of Central and Eastern Europe were not notably stimulated by a press (or by other media) advocating change, since no such press existed. However, in other parts of the world, there is evidence of various media, especially underground or alternative publications, having played a significant role in radical social and political change (Downing 2001).

Less dramatically, but more important for democracy in the long run, was the essential service provided by the press to reformist political parties and to radical and labour movements during the later nineteenth and early twentieth centuries, when our present system of electoral and representative democracy was largely forged. During this period, the newspaper press acquired its sobriquet of 'Fourth Estate' (initially with ironic intent), meaning a power in the land of equal weight with other estates (in Britain, the Crown, Lords and Commons). Elsewhere it was known as the 'Fourth Branch' of government. The role of the press in this concept is primarily one of independent information, commentary and critique concerning the actions of government (Schultz 1998). This is close to the ideal of objective professional journalism on the Anglo-American model.

An alternative concept, with equal claim to democratic credentials, is that of a partisan and advocacy press that takes sides, advances its own chosen causes and pursues an active role in politics. This alternative model has been in gradual decline since the start of the twentieth century, undermined by changes in media systems as much as by the supposed decline of ideology in 'post-industrial' society. One major change was the rise of television broadcasting as a politically neutral and widely trusted medium. In respect of the newspaper press, trends towards 'massification' and 'commercialization' did not sit easily with high levels of partisanship. While contemporary political journalism is dominated by values of 'objectivity' (including both independence and reliability), the alternative model is still to be found and is still needed in a vital democracy.

Theory of press and politics

During the last century there have been a number of successive or competing theoretical formulations of the role of the press in the political life of societies. Most familiar and enduring is that of the press as Fourth Estate as described above, which is favoured by the press itself. In the early twentieth century, a critique of the press was first formulated, especially in the leading industrial democracies of the USA and Britain, pointing to the debasement of the press in pursuit of profit and its loss of independence due to the wealth and right-wing affiliations of monopolistic propri-etors. The use of the press for nationalistic propaganda during the First World War and then its subordination to the aims of communist or fascist propaganda tarnished its reputation still more. Socialists denounced the new forms of control of the masses. More sophisticated 'mass society' theory formulated after the Second World War portrayed the press and other media (film and broadcasting especially) as tools employed by ruling classes, elites or cliques to control and manipulate mass opinion, belief and behaviour (Mills 1955). The media collectively were dedicated, in this view, to promoting political passivity, social conformity, consumerism and more or less voluntary subordination to the centralized state (Marcuse 1964).

Mass society theory gave way to a more politically pointed version of 'critical theory', in line with the radical neo-Marxist thinking of the 1960s and beyond. Critical theory specifically identified mass media as collective means of hegemonic control, upholding the power of state bureaucracies and capitalism, resisting the liberating changes that were waiting to happen. Theory favoured diverse, small scale and uncontrolled use of all new communication technologies, promoting social and cultural as well as political change. The expectations of critical theorists were over-taken before being fulfilled by a less favourable intellectual climate in the late twentieth century. Postmodern relativism and neo-conservatism between them displaced Marxist certainty and an end of ideology was widely proclaimed. In the world of political events, conservative governments came to power and free enter-prise solutions were favoured over state welfare and planning. The implosion of communism in the East served to reinforce the same tendencies. The exploitation of new communication technologies of computers, satellites and telecommunications was pursued for industrial and commercial rather than social or cultural ends.

The most widely cited contemporary theory to express norms for the proper rela-tion between media and politics is that of 'the public sphere', a quite venerable notion given fresh life mainly by the late translation into English of Jorgen Habermas's orig-inal 1972 essay entitled *Strukturwandel der Öffentlichkeit*. Public sphere theory envisages a role for the media in 'civil society' of providing an agora or open space for the free expression and circulation of opinions and beliefs. This notional 'space' is also one that intervenes between institutions of the state and the private sphere of personal and family life. It is occupied not only by the media but also by numerous and diverse voluntary or professional associations and activities in which individuals interact with each other and participate in everyday social life outside the home. For the media to play a proper role in this concept of a 'civil society' they need to be numerous and diverse in type and content, free from state or economic domination and serving a range of informational, expressive and integrative roles (Dahlgren 1995).

While hardly a theory in the same sense, we can also piece together what might be called an enduring 'functional' theory of political communication in the sense of a set of roles that need to be fulfilled if the democratic political institution is to work. The main functions can easily be identified by observation of actual practice. In the terms used by Seymour-Ure (1974) there is a *horizontal* as well as a *vertical* dimension to political communication, the former referring to inter-communication across different levels or strata, ranging from political elites through groups and organizations to the mass of citizens who may meet or discuss politics. The vertical dimension of communication connects governments and elites 'downward' to followers and citizens and also in the reverse direction (by various means, including 'feedback' from opinion polls, personal contacts, demonstrations and of course elections). The mass media generally facilitate these contacts and flows and especially help to *mediate* the relations between those separated by distance, power or status. A fuller version of the range of functions of political communication would include a reference to the following:

- Providing a wide range of information to enable citizens (voters) to participate in political life and to make rational choices between candidates, parties and policies.
- Providing a forum for the expression of a full (or representative) range of opinions, ideas and beliefs current in the society.
- Publishing criticism of and commentary on actions of governments and politicians.
- Providing the means for competing candidates and parties to campaign for office and contest elections.
- Enabling individuals to connect with each other and also address concerns and views to political representatives.
- Providing the means for informed participation in civic life.
- Enabling political movements, minorities and interest groups to organize, express their aims and seek to influence political outcomes.

The language of politics

Although there is no particular theory of political language, an important line of investigation into political communication has been pursued by way of linguistic analysis. Attention is paid to the symbolic forms in which political ideas are expressed and to the forms of discourse that embody political processes. The origins of this approach lie in Aristotle's study of rhetoric and it has been pursued especially by close examination of the way words and other signs are used to achieve particular effects, especially in propaganda and persuasion, but also in the formulation and dissemination of ideology (Edelman 1977) and in analysing political speech. George Orwell's *Animal Farm* is an early imaginative reflection on the devices by which language can be misused and distorted to reverse the truth. All political movements seek, consciously or not, to establish uses of words and symbols that suit their own purposes and to delegitimate the key words of others. As Graber (1981: 195) has remarked 'Politics is largely a word game'. The same author (Graber 1976) made an inventory of different functions of political language under five headings. The first is 'informational' – the giving of facts, always selectively. Second there is 'agenda-setting', in which a communicator seeks to become identified with an important issue (see below). Third is 'interpretation and linkage', where positive connotations are invoked by phrases such as 'welfare state' or 'founding fathers'. Then there is 'projection to past and future' and finally 'action stimulation' (the mobilizing and activating function of language).

Modern communications media trends

While the above statement of 'functions' of communication for politics remains valid, there have been changes in the available systems of communication that are having a potentially large effect on the relationship between media and politics. Despite its resonance and broad reference to most forms of (political) journalism, the term 'press' has for some time no longer adequately described the full range of relevant means of political communication. By some criteria, the newspaper press has lost its leading role as the primary means of political communication. From the late 1960s onwards it was generally supplanted by television as the medium that was perceived to be the main source of political news by most people and also the most trusted source. There is some evidence of a gradual decline in the perceived status of the press as an institution and of the newspaper in particular, along with a parallel decline in newspaper reading.

The most likely explanation does not lie in the intrinsic virtues of television as a medium (although it is believed by its audience to make reality more directly observable) nor in its wide popularity as a medium for all purposes. Rather, it lies in the fact that television has been obliged (and expected) in most democratic countries to meet higher standards of objectivity (fairness and truthfulness especially) than the newspaper. These remarks apply at least to the central institution of national broadcast (or network) television news that many countries had developed in the heyday of broadcasting (between 1960 and 1990). Broadcasting was not only regulated by government and unusually accountable for its performance, but it was also assigned some positive tasks for society and for politics in particular, especially in its public service variant. The conditions vary from place to place, but typically broadcasting has been obliged to give access on a fair basis to contenders for office, especially during election campaigns and not to favour one side over another in controversial matters.

Since the peak period of television's reputation and popularity there have been trends towards multiplication of channels and fragmentation of audiences, reducing the central and unifying role of the television institution. Neither television nor any single medium reaches a large mass of the population at the same time with the same message, except on rare occasions of national crisis (or celebration). There has also been a possible decline in standards in the matters just discussed, brought about by deregulation and intense competition for audiences and for advertising revenue. The role of television in political life has become less 'sacerdotal' and dutiful and more pragmatic in its approach to political coverage and access. There may be less political coverage and what there is less searching, substantial or deep (see below). In this it may simply be responding to a parallel trend amongst the public. It is not a return to bias and partisanship, but it may be an opening to the sensation-seeking traditions of popular journalism (sometimes referred to as 'tabloidization').

Television has proliferated on the basis of new technologies of distribution, especially cable and satellite. There is more of it and it is less within the power of government to control. It is being used in new ways for political communication, that go beyond its original tasks of providing reliable information and platforms for political voices and the voice of government. Political advertising has increased and is gradually spreading from its main breeding ground in the USA to other countries (Swanson and Mancini 1996). New formats, involving entertainment, audience participation and interactivity are being adapted to political campaign purposes (see p. 465). There are other changes in media systems that may have an impact on politics. Not least is the trend towards globalization which helps to diffuse formats and ideas of political communication internationally and may undermine local norms and practices. Of relevance is also the trend to *convergence* of different media (press, broadcasting, cable, telecommunications, etc.), driven by digitalization. This has decreased the difference between different regulatory regimes of media and also the difference in political function between different media.

More important than this is the rise of the Internet as a new medium that seems well suited to fulfilling a number of the political communication functions indicated earlier. The advantages of the Internet as a medium of political communication have been widely remarked on (Axford and Huggins 2001; Hacker and van Dijk 2000). Beyond a certain point of development there is a high level of access for individual receivers and unlimited opportunities for individuals, groups and major institutions to express their views and pass on information. The basic interactivity of the technology seems to secure extra benefits by comparison with the one-way (one-to many) traffic of traditional mass media or the slow and limited possibilities for non-computer-mediated personal communication. The ideal goal of bringing rulers and ruled closer together and answerable to each other seems open to fulfilment by way of the new media technologies. The opportunities are widely sought out and used although experience and early research has already damped much of the optimism about a new dawn of active, participant citizenship and open and responsive government.

The points that have been made in this section are intended to underline the fact that both the practices of politics and the possibilities of communication are continually, even rapidly, evolving and interacting with each other. The relationship is also mediated by institutional features of media systems that are partly under political control by way of national media or communication policies. The traditional view of the role of the press as informant and guide in a rational process of decision-making is now being actively challenged by changing social norms and life-styles in which institutional politics has a less central place. There are new kinds of party formations and logics, driven by various social movements or the rewards of office rather than by ideology. They are also stimulated by an emerging array of new means of public communication, with varying possibilities for incorporation into political strategies.

Changing relations between media, government, public and political parties

There are several possible and observable models of linkages media and their other main 'partners', as indicated. The earliest model historically is one in which government sought to use the publishing institution for its own ends of control. Political opponents did the same in the search for influence, with the balance of power decidedly in favour of government. The voice or interest of a 'public' in the modern sense barely existed.

462

This version of the relationship was transformed when democratic rights to a free press were obtained from the eighteenth century onwards. The power of government to use or control the press was much reduced. The public acquired an identity and rights of expression and politicians spoke and acted in its name and on its behalf and addressed it through available means of publication.

The 'massification' and 'commercialization' of the press from the late nineteenth century onwards promoted two new variants of a relationship: one of a neutral, non-partisan high quality press independent of government serving the informational needs of the emerging middle class and the political elite; the other of a popular press aiming to amuse and mobilize the masses, supported by advertising and owned by rich proprietors whose own political leanings led them to support conservative governments.

The maturing of broadcasting into a main mass medium in mid twentieth century, along with the post-war reformist politics of the time established a new dominant model of relations between media, government and politicians. In this model, the media carry out a professional task of information and enlightenment, independent of the state and politically neutral, but with responsibilities to serve the public (good) and the basic democratic process. Government has no control but is granted certain unwritten rights of access in recognition of its legitimate communication needs. In principle much the same applies to established political parties, more or less according to their representativeness of the public. Access to media channels has to be earned by anyone else either on grounds of clear public interest or on editorial judgements made by professional journalists. This arrangement is generally agreeable to political elites and media are rewarded by policy in various ways (e.g. concessions for broadcasting, protection from competition for newspapers).

This is being modified yet again, although the new version is not yet clearly apparent. Requirements of service to the public interest are being reduced and the expanding free media market is expected to satisfy requirements of information and diversity by way of its own competitive dynamic. It is too early to assess the political consequences of media liberalization, but some strains are already apparent. These include an alleged depoliticization of content and a reduction in informational quality as well as revival of fears of political bias and interference in less direct forms. The audience is treated less as a body of citizens than as another consumer market. Trends towards media and cross-media concentration are still apparent and the gradual decline of public broadcasting has reduced democratic control over access.

This short account is intended to underline the fact that there is a permanent flux in the relationship between the main actors. Government, politicians and media all need the public, and the first two need the media to reach the public. The media, under conditions of free market operation have less need for governmental or political assistance. The general trend over the democratic era seems to have been for the media to have increased their independence relative to government and politics and to have increased their power of control over the essential channels of political communication. At the same time, they have also become more beholden to economic interests.

Propaganda as political communication

The modern field of political communication virtually began with the study of propaganda as a response to the uses made of press and film during the First World War to promote patriotism amongst mass publics. The early equation of political communication with propaganda was reinforced by the example of Soviet Russia and Nazi Germany, both of which used their monopoly of mass media (to which radio had been added) for their own projects of social control and transformation. Between the two World Wars and later during the Cold War, increasing efforts were made by many governments to use various media for international propaganda efforts (Jowett and O'Donnell 1999).

The term 'propaganda' has always had a negative connotation, stemming from its origins in papal Counter-Reformation campaigning. Jowett and O'Donnell define propaganda (1999: 6) as 'the deliberate, systematic attempt to shape perceptions, manipulate cognitions, and direct behaviour to achieve a response that furthers the desired intent of the propagandist'. It is always manipulative, often concealed as to origin and aims, deceptive even if not lying directly. The practice of state propaganda does not seem to have diminished, but it has become more sophisticated, especially by co-opting trusted sources of communication, such as news media, in the effort. In recent cases of regional and international conflict (the Gulf War, the Israel–Palestine conflict, the Kosovo campaign, the attack on Afghanistan, etc.) there was much evidence of propaganda practices being widely used by democratic governments to influence national and international opinion, taking advantage of control of sources and tendencies of media to respect government intentions. In the kind of situations referred to, propaganda is engaged in without much evidence of its effectiveness or even potential counter-productivity. But the same has always been true and to some degree it has to be considered part of the political ritual associated with states going to war or engaging in any controversial action.

Political action as communication

In the contemporary period, the main examples of political action with communicative intent have taken the form of street demonstrations or acts of 'terrorism'. The former often aim for effect through their massive character and can be overtly peaceable or aggressive, depending on circumstances and objectives (Halloran, Elliott and Murdoch, 1970). Terroristic acts, often with civil rather than military targets, have always had a symbolic character, although this has been increasingly recognized and taken into account in the response of authorities who seek to control the communication environment in which they occur (Schmid and de Graaf 1982). Terror in the form of hijacking, bombing and hostage-taking usually aims primarily at causing fear and alarm, but it is often an attempt to draw attention to a cause, much as do demonstrations. Both forms of symbolic political action have been adapted to and possibly even stimulated by the availability of modern mass media, with their typical news values and predictable logic of operation. These are essential to the amplification of the message and actions are planned so as to secure maximum media (in effect, television) coverage. Demonstrations and terrorist acts without publicity are largely pointless. This presents a challenge to authorities that would like to be able to manage the publicity that terrorist acts receive, although the possibilities for control-ling such publicity are quite limited.

Political communication as propaganda: election campaigns

Political campaigning has become primarily identified with competitive election campaigning, ever since the first true social scientific study of an election, that for the US presidency in 1940 (Lazarsfeld, Berelson and Gaudet 1944). The systematic study of election campaigns was made possible by advances in the techniques for measuring attitudes and opinions and in methods of multivariate statistical analysis. An extensive research industry into all aspects of political campaigning has flourished ever since, extending to nearly all countries and serving the appetite for scientific knowledge of political communication processes as well as the practical needs of campaigners (Swanson and Mancini 1996). Modern elections are inconceivable without extensive research activities that are geared to planning persuasive campaigns, monitoring their progress and adapting tactics and strategies on a day-to-day basis. Research (mainly in the form of polling) has become an essential part of the election ritual and a key ingre-dient of media coverage as well. Sometimes research can also yield some explanation for particular outcomes or an understanding of the underlying processes involved.

The impulse to conduct research derives in part from the greater centrality of mass media in modern political campaigns and the belief that they hold the key to success or failure. The more that campaigning and communication have become professionalized and taken over by communication experts rather than being governed by political intuition or belief, the more the media tend to 'wag the dog' of politics and the more attention, in turn, is paid to research. The model of commer-cial advertising and marketing has increasingly guided political campaigns, despite attempts to restrict campaign financing. There is a widespread belief that it is the 'image' of the candidate or party rather than the substance of politics that matters most. This belief happens also to suit the requirements of 'media logic', which holds that the audience is more interested in following the political 'horserace' and the fate of various personalities involved than in hearing (over again) the details of policy proposals and party standpoints on issues (Capella and Jamieson 1997). Campaigning politicians are inclined to accept the media recipe for gaining attention from a less than enthralled electorate and may not have power to do otherwise, given the strength of the media position in the communication chain.

In advance of the following section on the effects of political communication, it can be said that the election campaign trends referred to have proceeded without much reference to findings of campaign effectiveness. As with commercial adver-tising, it sometimes works and sometimes doesn't and it is still impossible to predict when it will or won't. The trends described have been driven by a belief in the power of the media in general and television in particular which has the character of a self-fulfilling prophecy. Parties and politicians cannot afford not to do their best to use the media. An undesirable side-effect of the developments described is the greater advantage that goes to the well-funded contender.

Research into election campaigns has shed light not only on the needs of media, political parties and candidates, but also on the needs of voters and on their motives for following campaigns. This confirms the traditional view that campaigns serve the democratic function of providing necessary information about candidates, issues and politics for voting choices to be made. They help otherwise politically detached electors to catch up with issues and events, to remind them of their own values and beliefs. In addition, research has confirmed that for many, elections are also like (second rank) sporting events or beauty contests, with some entertainment value (Blumler and McQuail 1968). They are also a source of dislike and negative feelings, often provoked by the contents and means of campaigning as much as by any intrinsic lack of interest in politics. A full understanding of the political campaigning and informational process needs to be gained from the perspective of the voter as well as from that of the campaigner (Graber 1988).

The trends in election campaigning that have been described have been increasingly linked to several negative tendencies in modern democracies, amounting to what has been called a 'democratic deficit'. Others have spoken of a 'crisis of public communication' (Blumler and Gurevitch 1995). The main elements or symptoms of this crisis have been a steady decline in voting and other forms of political participation, the declining reputation of politicians, a greater cynicism or disillusionment about the whole political institution and an erosion of civic engagement, with a large minority effectively detached from the whole democratic process. These trends have been highlighted in the USA but several of them have shown up in other societies, in Europe and elsewhere. The media are said to be implicated in several ways: by highlighting policy failures and personal scandals; by failing to provide political information of any value or substance (more 'tabloidization' and 'infotainment'); by lending themselves to the propaganda strategies of political campaigners in return for rewards; by not properly carrying out their role as defenders of the public interest. Although criticism of the media has been vocal, none of the trends described are likely to have occurred without some 'connivance' by politicians or against the will of the people. There is a collective responsibility, which makes it unwise to see the media as a primary cause.

Political communication as information management

As this account of electioneering trends implies, there has been considerable development in strategies and techniques by those who want to exert influence either on the public or on governments and other institutions. The would-be agents of influence include, besides governments and political parties, many special interests of an economic, social or even cultural character. There is nothing new in itself in using communication to gain advantages and objectives, but the type and scale of informational activities of this kind have changed. There are more means available, more expertise and experience and in some respects more opportunity and necessity in a more open and competitive environment for engaging in such activities. There is also a great deal of money to be spent, despite attempts to control campaign spending.

The main relevant types of activities can be classified either as lobbying, where special interests seek to influence government policy on their own behalf, or information management, used by all organizations to control their relations with the outside world. The basic aim is to manage the release of information in such a way that it will effectively achieve the objectives of the organization, and also present it in a favourable light, maintaining or improving its 'image'. Governments are especially active in this area because of the large information flows they engender and the potentially sensitive or conflict-laden character of much of that information. In addition to the activities mentioned there is scope for would-be communicators to stage so-called 'pseudo-events', if only in the form of press conferences, designed to capture favourable media attention especially within the context of news reporting. Governments in office have more chance than contenders to do this effectively.

Attention has focused on the role of 'spin-doctors', public relations specialists who are widely used to intervene between politicians and people and make the best (for their clients) of whatever information is available. Not surprisingly, this has led to much criticism and suspicion of the motives behind it. If nothing else, it raises the spectre of deceptive propaganda and can backfire for that reason alone. In general people prefer to hear political leaders and responsible officials speak directly for themselves. But it is journalists and the media in general that are most incensed by the developments described. They see their own role of information intermediary being taken over or restricted by the new professional communicators and are themselves blocked from obtaining raw information from the sources that matter. More generally, the activities described have been associated with the alleged public disillusion and cynicism in relation to organized politics described above. Political parties can hardly offer solutions to this problem, since they use the same methods themselves.

Effects of political communication

The question most often asked in respect of political communication concerns the effects of the mass media, rather than what are the effects of the rise of communications media on political life, although in the long run that is what matters. Most of the research carried out until recently has centred on the former question, with limited and mixed results (McGuire 2001). We can still not predict the probable effect of any given media input into a campaign, and even after the event, it is unusual to be able to make any clear statement about the contribution of any aspect of the media campaign to the outcome. There are some good reasons for this. First, an actual outcome of an election (in political terms) has many causes, often entirely contingent and derived from underlying political realities. Second, the typical contribution of media to an overall outcome is almost certainly quite small, when all kinds and directions of effect are taken into account (see, e.g. Norris *et al.* 1999). Third, elections are still won or lost by the actions of voters, who are not typically easy to brainwash or unable to make up their own minds. Even when small margins count for a lot, it is unlikely that media will 'make elections', however much they are the main vehicle for manifesting the election process and event. Elections take place in open and fluid situations where deep convictions and issues of fundamental importance may be at stake.

The less 'good' reasons for the low explanatory or predictive power of election campaign research include the continued inadequacy of methods of research and basic ineffectiveness of the campaigns themselves. Most campaigns are usually run on the basis of a mixture of hunches and inadequate social science. Available theories of political influence and information processing are also often inadequate, inconsistent and flawed. The target audience of political campaigns is not well-conceived of as a single mass, but is composed of innumerable sub-audiences with different expectations, needs and potential for influence. Despite the increased possibility for targeting specific sub-groups and shaping messages accordingly, the process of matching message with potential audience is not well developed and faces severe obstacles.

Types and conditions of communication effect

Despite this negative conclusion about the yield of political communication research, quite a lot can be said about various kinds and degrees of effect. Campaigns have multiple (sometimes inconsistent) objectives, which have to be disentangled in the research process and are not easy to reassemble as an overall effect, or one that can be labelled as 'persuasion'. Certain generalizations can be made about types of effect. Both cognitive (informational) and affective (attitudinal and image) effects are more likely to occur on previously unfamiliar or more distant objects, issues or persons, than on matters on which attitudes are already formed or where there is already much information. There is much more evidence of campaigns having cognitive effects (e.g. increased knowledge) than causing attitudinal or behavioural change. At the same time, a reinforcement of existing opinion or attitude and a mobilization of support is easier to achieve than any real conversion effect.

As far as conditions of effects are concerned, we have a number of indications. First, monopoly control of sources or the consonance and repetition of messages do contribute to achieving results in the expected direction. This means that consistent 'bias' in communication is likely to work for its intended beneficiary, while minority voices and views are at a disadvantage, unless gaining a critical mass of media support. Second, the status, attractiveness and personal appeal of a communicator do matter. Third, the conditions for an effect, of whatever kind, are more likely to be found in the receiver than in the sender or message. These include the degree of interest, positive disposition, previous level of knowledge and also the social factors that lie in turn behind these. Fourth, effects are very much influenced by personal relationships and social location. The support of relatives, friends and influential persons ('opinion leaders') has been shown to matter for anchoring or weakening opinions and behaviour (Lazarsfeld, Berelson and Gaudet 1944). In a sense, people are typically protected from direct mass media influence, more so than they would be from face-to-face contact or public oratory, especially in crowd situations. Finally, the various motives for attending to political communication (as noted above) also play a part in determining the kind and degree of effects, promoting some but inhibiting others.

Political communication research has developed and followed certain specific lines of inquiry about the nature of effects. The most prominent of these are described under the following headings.

Agenda-setting

The so-called 'agenda-setting' hypothesis had its origin in early election campaign research that appeared to show media having little or no direct effect on party preferences or voting behaviour, but nevertheless influencing opinions on what were the main issues of the day (McCombs and Shaw 1972). In general the amount of attention and prominence given by news media to different political issues tends to be strongly correlated with the rank order of importance assigned to the same issues by electors. Such findings have often been replicated, suggesting a media effect of some importance. It opens the way for parties to manipulate opinion by concentrating attention on these issues on which they are likely to be favourably rated or with which they are traditionally associated. Despite the plausibility of this particular hypothesis, it has never been conclusively demonstrated that the media are the real cause of change. The media do not only take their cue from political parties in assembling their 'agenda', but also use their own judgement and consult the interests of the public, which they then reflect. Political parties are also constrained to follow what they believe to be public opinion in choosing issues. In short, there is a complex interplay between a party agenda, a media agenda and a public agenda, which cannot be untangled easily to reveal the independent contribution of mass media. Even so, this remains one of the most plausible types of media effect, especially where the less involved members of an electorate are concerned.

Framing

The concept of framing has been used to apply to different stages of the political communication process. Essentially framing is a matter of selective presentation that makes new facts easier to understand in terms of other familiar information, but has several side effects. Entman defines framing as the selection of 'some aspects of perceived reality [so as to] make them more salient in a communicating context, in such a way as to promote a particular problem definition, causal interpretation, moral evaluation, and/or treatment recommendation' (1993: 52). There is a sequence involved. News sources frame their input into news to conform to journalistic news values. Journalists then frame their 'raw material' in such a way as to fit their own requirements for news processing and to anticipate audience interests. Third, the audience fits incoming information (already framed) into its own available stock of knowledge and its outlook and values. At each stage there is some change, but nevertheless there is considerable scope for media (according to their own media logic) to impose meaning on events and help shape public opinion and understanding. Original communicators also have scope for manipulating impressions received.

The spiral of silence

There are several theoretical perspectives on how the individual opinions that go to make up 'public opinion' can be shaped by mass media. Much emphasis, as noted, has been placed on the social and group context. One perspective that emphasizes the role of mass media in combination with the social groups has been given the name 'spiral of silence' by its originator (Noelle-Neumann 1984), who traces it back to some observations made by de Tocqueville about the conformist tendencies he found in early nineteenth-century America. The foundation of the concept is that most people have a psychological need to avoid the discomfort and isolation of seeming to think differently from others around them. They consequently seek to avoid expressing deviant opinions. However, in a modern society the mass media have become the main source of knowledge of what the consensus actually is. The views most often expressed and least contested in the media are taken to be what the great majority actually hold. Those who hold other views tend to remain silent and the dominance of the supposed consensus actually increases, hence the 'spiralling' effect referred to. Noelle-Neumann applied this theory to the supposed leftwing bias of the German media in the 1960s and the surprise of the Christian Democrat election victory in 1976. However, it has some general application and plausibility but has received rather mixed validation from research in other countries. For the process to operate as indicated there have to be very monopolistic, consensual tendencies in the mass media. Although critics have often assumed this to be the case, it is not a universal condition and is fairly exceptional in open societies, except where a few fundamental values are concerned.

The 'power of the media': a note

The question most often asked about the media and politics (e.g. Paletz and Entman 1981; Iyengar and Reeves 1997), looks for a global assessment of media power. It should be clear from what has already been discussed that no simple answer is likely to be forthcoming. If we speak of short-term effectiveness of media in elections, we might conclude that the power of media is very limited for reasons given above. We should also keep in mind that 'the media' have no legitimate claim to exercise power and in general do not seek to have power, although particular media do want to influence particular events. Nevertheless, taking a larger view of influence, the evidence suggests that the mass media, in post-industrial societies, have become more central to the nexus of relations within which power is exercised. They own the principal means available to influence the general public and because of this, agents of power come closer to the media without, in free and open societies, being able to dominate them fully.

The means of influence possessed by media are of several kinds. One is their control over the flow of public information, even if this is not exercised purposefully for any political end. Second, the media have the means of 'making public' and selectively amplifying what is otherwise hidden or unknown. They can produce fame and also infamy, both of which are valuable resources in politics. Third, there is the fact that the public largely depends on media for its stock of politically relevant ideas, information and impressions. Fourth, and in connection with this, the 'reality' of world events is initially largely interpreted and made sense of by the media, even if not in a uniform way. They are in some sense primary definers of what is taken for reality. Fifth, most of the relations between politicians, leaders and the public are in one way or another mediated through the channels of mass communication, which means they are subject in some degree to the requirements of media systems. If a summary statement it is possible it would be to the effect that the power of the media depends on the success with which others who seek power or its benefits manage to use the media for these ends. The potential for influence by the media still depends, however, not only on their reach and volume but also on their reputation for reliability and the respect they earn from their own audiences, based on experience of their performance.

Research issues and trends in political communication

Most of the fundamental themes of political communication research remain unchanged, especially insofar as they relate to persuasion during and outside election campaigns as well as to political participation, interest and 'learning' about politics and political events. The latter embraces the topic of political socialization amongst the young. Many matters to do with the formation and expression of public opinion also remain central to the field (Glynn *et al.* 1999). In continuing the mainstream tradition of research an important place is still occupied by attention to media news and to the various ways in which media construct or frame perceptions of reality.

It is easier to indicate trends by naming the central issues of concern, which in one way or another have already been mentioned. The field seems dominated at present by the very large issue of the quality of democratic life in a mass media age, with generally somewhat pessimistic prediction of the consequences of increased 'mediatizaton' of politics (Bennett and Entman 2000). The concerns have two focal points. One is that the quality of political communication is being debased as a result of commercializing trends in the media, as noted earlier. Second, there is a fear that increased orientation to the requirements of the media ('media logic') is hollowing out the political substance of the message and stimulating negative, distrustful and cynical feelings amongst the public.

Both these trends give a central place to the nature and tendencies of the mass communication system itself and identify it as an important object of inquiry in its own right (see Blumler and Gurevitch 1995; and Blumler and Kavanagh 1999). Additionally, between them, the concerns translate into a political problem of a poorly informed citizenry, a loss of interest, low participation and a decline in the status of politics generally.

Another topic of interest has less negative associations. It concerns the potential of the Internet and other new media to re-invigorate political communication (Axford and Huggins 2001; Hacker and van Dijk 2000). The new media have enormous capacity, offer open access without barriers to all who wish to communicate, have a high interactive capacity and can connect citizens with each other and with movements and ideas, without dependence on the traditional mass media and without limits of national frontiers. They offer a possible solution to excessive 'mass mediatization' of politics and to the growing individualization and isolationism of civic life. Early research findings are less positive in their conclusions than the expectations and there are fears that 'new media' may go the way of old media and never fulfil the potential of the technology.

Attention already centres on one of the old problems of political communication, that of structured 'knowledge gaps' that separate the informed and participant from the information-poor and uninvolved. Television at one time seemed to close this gap, but it is no longer seen in this light. The new problem is identified as a 'digital divide' referring to the seemingly unbridgeable gap between those who have resources and skills to access and use the new media and the large minority at least who do not.

All in all, it seems that political communication research and theory is very much engaged with issues of considerable moment in political life and in relation to changing technology and social conditions. It is also characterized by an internationalism and drive to do comparative research. As far as methods are concerned, the principal means are those of surveys and content analysis, but there are increasing signs of experimentation being adapted to the testing of political communication hypotheses (Iyengar and Simon 2000).

References

For current developments in research, consult the journal *Political Communication*.

Axford, B. and Huggins, R. (eds) (2001) *New Media and Politics*, London: Sage.

Bennett, W. L. and Entman, R. E. (2000) *Mediated Politics: Communication in the Future of Democracy*, Cambridge: Cambridge University Press.

Blumler, J. G. and Gurevitch, M. (1995) *The Crisis of Public Communication*, London: Routledge.

Blumler, J. G. and McQuail, D. (1968) *Television and Politics: Its Uses and Influence*, London: Faber and Faber.

Blumler, J. G. and Kavanagh, D. (1999). 'The third age of political communication: influences and features', *Political Communication*, 16: 209–30.

Capella, J. N. and Jamieson, K. H. (1997) *The Spiral of Cynicism: The Press and the Public Good*, Oxford: Oxford University Press.

Dahlgren, P. (1995) *Television and the Public Sphere*, London: Sage.

Downing, J. D. (2001) *Radical Media: Rebellious Communication and Social Movements*, London: Sage Publications.

Edelman, M. J. (1977) *The Symbolic Uses of Politics*, Urbana, IL: University of Illinois Press.

Entman, R. (1993) 'Framing: Towards clarification of a fractured paradigm', *Journal of Communication*, 43: 51–8.

Glynn, C. J., Herbst, S., O'Keefe, G. J. and Shapiro, R. Y. (1999) *Public Opinion*, Boulder, CO: Westview Press.

Graber, D. A. (1976) *Verbal Behavior in Politics*, Urbana, IL: University of Illinois Press.

—— (1981) 'Political language' in D. Nimmo and K. Sanders (eds) *Handbook of Political Communication*, Beverly Hills: Sage Publications.

—— (1988) *Processing the News*, 2nd edn., White Plains: Longman.

Habermas, J. (1972) *Strukturwandel der Öffentlichkeit*, trans. as *Structural Transformation of the Public Sphere*, Cambridge: Polity Press, 1989.

Hacker, K. L. and van Dijk, J. (eds) (2000) *Digital Democracy. Issues of Theory and Practice*, London: Sage Publications.

Halloran, J., Elliott, P. and Murdock, G. (1970) *Demonstrations and Communications*, Harmondsworth: Penguin.

Iyengar, S. and Reeves, S. (1997) *Do the Media Govern? Politicians, Voters and Reporters in America*, Thousand Oaks, CA: Sage Publications.

Iyengar, S. and Simon, A. (2000) 'New perspectives and evidence on political communication and campaign effects', *Annual Review of Psychology*, 51: 149–69.

Jowett, G. S. and O'Donnell, V. (1999) *Propaganda and Persuasion*, Newbury Park, CA: Sage Publications.

Lazarsfeld, P. F., Berelson, B., and Gaudet, H. (1944) *The People's Choice*, New York: Columbia University Press.

McCombs, M. and Shaw, D. L. (1972) 'The agenda-setting function of the mass media', *Public Opinion Quarterly*, 36: 176–87.

McGuire, W. J. (2001) 'After half a century of election studies: whence, where and whither?', in E. Katz and Y. Warshel (eds) *Election Studies: What's Their Use?* Boulder, CO: Westview Press: 15–57.

Marcuse, M. (1964) *One Dimensional Man*, London: Sphere Books.

Mills, C. W. (1955) *The Power Elite*, New York: Oxford University Press.

Noelle-Neumann, E. (1984) *The Spiral of Silence*, Chicago: University of Chicago Press.

Norris, P., Curtice, J., Scammell, M., Sanders, D. and Semetko, H. A. (1999) *On Message: Communicating the Campaign*, London: Sage.

Paletz, D. and Entman, R. (1981) *Media, Power, Politics*, New York: Free Press.

Schultz, J. (1998) *Reviving the Fourth Estate: Democracy, Accountability and the Media*, Cambridge: Cambridge University Press.

Schmid, A. P. and De Graaf, A. P. (1982) *Violence as Communication*, London: Sage.

Seymour-Ure, C. (1974) *The Political Impact of Mass Media*, London: Constable.

Swanson, D. L. and Mancini, P. (1996) (eds) *Politics, Media and Modern Democracy*, New York: Praeger.

Further reading

Altheide, D. L. (1985) *Media Power*, Newbury Park, CA: Sage Publications.

Graber, D. A., McQuail, D. and Norris, P. (eds) *The Politics of News: News of Politics*, Washington DC: CQ Press.

Gunther, R. and Mughan, A. (eds) (2000) *Democracy and the Media: A Comparative Perspective*, Cambridge: Cambridge University Press.

Katz, E. and Warshel, Y. (eds) (2001) *Election Studies: What's Their Use?* Boulder CO: Westview Press.

Norris, P. (2000) *A Virtuous Circle. Political Communications in Postindustrial Societies*, Cambridge: Cambridge University Press.

31

ELITE RECRUITMENT

Gwen Moore

Hereditary succession to elite positions is rare in the contemporary world. In societies with hereditary rulers, the question 'Who rules?' is easily answered. By contrast, in most contemporary societies, the selection of the few who lead from the many who do not is a process of concern to citizens and leaders alike. In his influential 1976 book *The Comparative Study of Political Elites*, Robert Putnam wrote: 'Political recruitment refers to the processes that select from among the several million socially favored and politically motivated citizens...those several thousand who reach positions of significant national influence' (1976: 46). Political elites are persons holding authoritative positions that allow them to regularly influence public policy and state activities (Burton and Higley 1987; Putnam 1976). Construed broadly, the political elite includes not just governmental officeholders but also leaders of other groups with significant national power, such as economic, media and voluntary-sector elites (Bachrach 1967; Putnam 1976).

Elite recruitment studies, like all elite analysis, have been controversial, at least partly due to the close connection to the classical elite theorists of the late nineteenth and early twentieth century who are often seen as anti-democratic (Nagle 1992). The classical elite theorists – Vilfredo Pareto (1848–1923), Gaetano Mosca (1858–1941) and Robert Michels (1876–1936) – sought to offer a realistic political theory in contrast to Marxian and democratic theories (Parry 1969; Burton and Higley 1987). Pareto, Mosca and Michels agreed in declaring the inevitability of elites in society, although their explanations for this fact varied.

Gaetano Mosca, an Italian political theorist and later politician, wrote:

> In all societies – from societies that are very meagerly developed and have barely attained the dawnings of civilization, down to the most advanced and power societies – two classes of people appear – a class that rules and a class that is ruled. The first class, always the less numerous, performs all political functions, monopolizes power and enjoys the advantages that power brings, whereas the second, the more numerous class, is directed and controlled by the first.
>
> (Mosca 1939: 50)

Mosca and Michels attributed elite power in part to the minority's superior organization (Mosca 1939; Michels 1962). Its small size and extensive control of resources facilitate the development of organization and cohesion among elite members. Mosca (1939) described elites as drawn primarily from the privi-leged classes, with some talented members of the middle classes moving into elite positions.

Vilfredo Pareto defined elites as persons with the highest achievements or capaci-ties in their field (1935: 1422–32). Yet he too saw elites as drawn largely from the upper classes (Pareto 1991: 59). Pareto distinguished two groups of elites, the governing elite and the non-governing elite, contrasting both to the non-elite who are the great majority of the citizenry. According to Pareto, elites can maintain their strength and quality only by recruiting the most able members of the non-elite lower classes and by shedding their own less able members. He depicted the governing elite as 'always in a state of slow and continuous transformation' (Pareto 1991: 49). In Pareto's view, elites must recruit talented outsiders if they are to maintain their power.

C. Wright Mills, writing in the mid-1950s on elite power in the USA, extended and revised elite theory (1956). He portrayed a 'power elite' in the post-Second World War USA, comprised of the top position-holders in the military, corpora-tions and the executive branch of the federal government. The power elite exerted power over both the middle and mass levels of American society. Elite power, he wrote, rested in major institutions and the officials occupying their command posts (Mills 1956). Power resides in control of key institutions rather than in classes or families. Without a command position an individual holds little power. Mills described the 'higher circles' as based on the psychological and social unity and coincidence of interests of the leaders of the economic, political and military hierarchies (1956: ch. 1). Although the American elite was not derived from an aristocracy and was not a ruling class, Mills did agree with earlier elite theorists that it derived chiefly from the upper classes (1956: 277–80). Further, members of the power elite were typically college-educated men drawn primarily from native-born Protestant families (Mills 1956: ch. 12). In this view, the American power elite consisted disproportionately of officials from the privileged classes, status groups, and sex (Mills 1956).

These theorists thus portrayed a political elite closely tied to but not synonymous with the upper classes. The far larger group of non-elites in the lower classes was seen as nearly powerless and uninvolved in governing. Michels declared that 'effec-tive power is…in inverse ratio to the number of those who exercise it' (1962: 880). To him the masses lack expertise, organization and will. He declared 'Though it grumbles occasionally, the majority is really delighted to find persons who will take the trouble to look after its affairs' (1962: 88). Still, as Pareto emphasized, most elite groups recruit some talented and ambitious members of the lower classes, both to maintain their strength and to forestall organized opposition among the masses (Pareto 1991; Michels 1962). Elite theorists see the majority of the population who hold no leadership positions as having little impact on key decisions made in the economic, political or civil society sectors (Pareto 1991; Mosca 1939; Michels 1962; Mills 1956).

Both Mosca and Pareto declared that they sought to develop a science of politics, rather than a political ideology (Parry 1969). Although elite theories are not inher-ently ideological, they have often been seen as prescriptive (e.g., Bottomore 1993). Mosca and Pareto did intend to 'demolish the myths of democracy', contending that democracy is neither possible nor fully desirable (Parry 1969). Such views and these theorists' pro-fascist sympathies led to their description by later scholars as conservative and anti-democratic. By contrast, Mills, who is often classified as a radical elite theorist, was highly critical of the concentrated power of elites and the increasing passivity and powerlessness of the American masses, while remaining pessimistic that elites could be held accountable to the public (1956).

Elite theory's division between the few – the elite – and the many – the masses – is problematic for the theory of democratic rule (e.g., Bottomore 1993; Lasswell 1936; Etzioni-Halevy 1993). If elites are powerful and largely self-perpetuating, what is the role of other citizens in a democratic society? To what extent is the political elite open, both to upward mobility from the masses and to downward mobility for its less effective members? How cohesive is the elite? Stated differently, is the elite a meritocracy or a plutocracy? Both elite and democratic theories propose answers to these questions, but empirical evidence is necessary to test such logical arguments. Investigations of processes and outcomes of elite recruitment in various nations and historical eras can help answer these questions.

Elite recruitment – or, put more simply, who rules? – has broad importance and impact in societies. For instance, study of elite recruitment addresses these questions: To what extent is social inequality reproduced in political inequality in elite positions? Which groups enjoy privileged access to the pinnacles of power? Which groups are largely excluded from such positions? In a discussion of Harold Lasswell's writing on elites and democracy, Eulau described political equality as not power shared by all but rather power that is equally *accessible* to all citizens (Eulau 1976).

Approaches and findings of elite recruitment studies

Extensive research has examined the recruitment and functioning of elites in the modern world. Varied methods have been used to locate and study elites, with the positional, decision-making, and reputational methods the most common. Some studies have focused on the outcomes of controversial issues: the leaders involved and the decisions reached (e.g., Dahl 1961). In this approach elites are those active in decision-making, with a wide variety of elites participating in different issues (Dahl 1961; Polsby 1963). Many of these decision-making studies have been at the local level, such as Robert Dahl's influential study of New Haven, Connecticut *Who Governs?* (1961). A typical finding of decision-making studies is that distinct elite groups with varying backgrounds and positions are active in the community over time, with no group dominant on all issues. The decisional method has been extensively critiqued, especially for its exclusive focus on the visible phase and end result of policy-making, the omission of possible power behind-the-scenes, and omission of 'non-decisions', the ability of elites to keep controversial issues off the public agenda (Lukes 1974; Bachrach 1967).

Rather than looking at the groups involved in decision-making on important issues, studies using the reputational approach – typically at the community level – look at informal power that is not necessarily held by the formal occupants of leading positions. Key informants are asked to name or select from a list the most powerful people in the community (Hunter 1953; Domhoff 2002). This method, infrequently used now, has often found that an economic elite, with privileged social origins, has the highest reputation for power. Critics argue that this method is biased and often omits individuals who exert significant influence over community issues (e.g., Polsby 1963).

A third and widely used method of studying elites is the institutional or positional method. Powerful institutions, those with authority over wide-ranging policies, are first identified. Individuals holding the most senior authority posts in these institutions are the elites to be studied. Using the positional method to identify elites, researchers use quantitative or qualitative methods – such as surveys, focused interviews or public documents – to examine elite recruitment, structure, actions, and attitudes (see Moyser and Wagstaffe 1987 on elite research methodology; for examples of elite research, see Porter 1965 on Canada; Barton, Denitch and Kadushin 1973 on Yugoslavia; Barton 1985 and Domhoff 2002 on the USA; Higley, Deacon and Smart 1979 on Australia; Zapf 1965 and Hoffman-Lange 1992 on West Germany).

Most often, research on elites is narrow in time and scope. Scholars frequently study a single elite group, such as business or political leaders (e.g., Useem 1980; Kadushin 1974). Especially useful for understanding elite recruitment are longitudinal and comparative studies that can uncover patterns of elite recruitment and behavior across time and space. An example is a comparative study (discussed below) during the 1970s that investigated the social origins, ideology, roles, and behavior of senior bureaucrats and politicians in six West European countries (Britain, France, Germany, Italy, the Netherlands and Sweden) and the USA (Aberbach, Putnam and Rockman 1981; also see Dogan 1989).

From his analysis of numerous studies of elite recruitment up to the mid-1970s, Robert Putnam declared that political, economic and administrative leaders in most countries are disproportionately drawn from privileged family backgrounds, from the highly educated who hold high-status occupations, and from majority ethnic and racial groups (Putnam 1976: 22–36; also see Prewitt and Stone 1973; Barton 1985). Indeed, the frequency of such personal characteristics increases as the level of the position held increases, an instance of 'the law of increasing disproportion' (Putnam 1976: 33–6). The representation of privileged groups steadily decreases from the narrow apex of the pyramid of power to its broad base in the citizenry. For instance, Presidents and Prime Ministers generally have higher social origins than Members of Parliament do (Putnam 1976). Further, Putnam states that women are the most underrepresented of all groups in political elites and that this gender disparity varies little across nations (Putnam 1976: 32–3; also see Blondel 1980).

A comparative study of government bureaucrats and politicians in European countries in the late 1970s showed that individuals from blue-collar families were greatly underrepresented (Aberbach, Putnam and Rockman 1981). As one example, nearly 80 per cent of the Italian working population at that time were in manual occupations, while just one-third of parliamentarians and three per cent of civil servants shared these social origins (Aberbach, Putnam and Rockman 1981: Table 3.3). Hoffmann-Lange's study of West German elites in the economic, political and civil society sectors in 1981 revealed that 13 per cent had working-class origins, far less than the 45 per cent of the population (1992).

Camp's study of political elite recruitment in Mexico for the period 1884 to 1991 also found that officeholders came overwhelmingly from middle- and upper-class backgrounds throughout the period, with a sharp increase in middle-class officeholders after 1970 (Camp 1995: 172–81). Since 1970 the proportion of officials from working-class families had declined sharply (Camp 1995: 172–81). But the presence of officeholders with upper-class backgrounds had also shrunk to less than five per cent (Camp 1995: 172–81). In state socialist nations in Central and Eastern Europe up to the 1970s, a relatively high proportion of party leaders and state officials had working-class or peasant origins, but those from more privileged families still enjoyed advantaged access to top political positions (Putnam 1976: 23–6).

Women in elite positions

Researchers have studied the key channels to and credentials for elite positions, as well as processes and patterns of elite recruitment across nations and regime types. I turn now to Putnam's statement that women are the most underrepresented group in elite positions throughout the world. Since Putnam wrote on comparative elites in the 1970s, much attention has been paid both within nations and in global organizations such as the United Nations to women's rarity in top decision-making positions in societies. The International Labor Organization, the Inter-Parliamentary Union, the United Nations, and other organizations track women's representation in high-level positions in the political and economic sectors in all nations. The United Nations declared the Decade of Women beginning in 1975. Since then the UN has sponsored regular world meetings on the status of women, most visibly the Beijing Conference in 1995.

The Beijing Declaration and Platform for Action states: 'We are convinced that: women's empowerment and their full participation in the decision-making process and access to power, are fundamental for the achievement of equality, development and peace' (UN 2000). Many nations and institutions – though far from all – accept the goal of gender equality in public life. Women have the right to vote in most nations, though in some such as Switzerland, Angola, and Jordan women's suffrage was granted less than thirty years ago (UN 1995). At the start of the Decade for Women (1975) the Convention to Eliminate All Forms of Discrimination against Women (CEDAW) was adopted by the General Assembly of the United Nations. More than 150 nations – excluding the USA and about two dozen others – have since ratified this convention, pledging to pursue public policies to eliminate gender discrimination (Seager 1997; United Nations 2000).

Is the goal of the elimination of gender disparities in decision-making positions being realized? The overwhelming male predominance in elite positions has declined slightly since Putnam wrote in the mid-1970s. In most nations economic and political elite posts remain overwhelmingly male.

One indicator of women's access to power is their presence in national parliaments. In 1975, the UN Year for Women, 11 per cent of parliamentary seats were held by women (InterParliamentary Union 2002). Women's representation in national parliaments has gradually increased since then, to nearly 15 per cent in 2002.

Women in national parliaments

Year	All nations
1975	10.9%
1985	12.0%
1995	11.6%
2002	14.7%

Source: InterParliamentary Union web site

This average figure masks patterns within regions and countries. In Eastern Europe, where gender quotas assured women's representation in the largely power-less socialist legislatures, there was a precipitous decline in women's seats in parliaments in the 1990s. For instance, Bulgaria and Poland had approximately 22 per cent women parliamentarians in 1987, a figure that fell to 13 per cent by 1995 (UN 2000). By 1999 women's proportion of parliamentary seats in the former socialist states of Central and Eastern Europe at ten per cent was closer to the world average.

Large increases in women's parliamentary representation occurred in many nations between 1975 and 2002. Examples include Mexico (from 5 per cent to 16 per cent), Costa Rica (5.3 per cent to 31.6 per cent), Sweden (21.4 per cent to 42.7 per cent), Japan (1.4 per cent to 7.3 per cent), France (1.6 per cent to 12.3 per cent). But nowhere outside of Sweden does women's representation in the national legislature approach their proportion of the national population. The Scandinavian countries head the list of the proportion of parliamentary seats held by women, with each having more than one-third women members (InterParliamentary Union 2002). As is well known, parties and public policies in the Scandinavian countries strongly support gender equality, including women's election to parliament. Many European parties have quotas for women on their electoral lists. Other nations, for instance Argentina and South Africa since the 1990s, assure women's representation in elec-toral politics by legislation or in their constitutions, and the results are clear, with women comprising about thirty per cent of both national legislatures in 2002.

Twenty-eight out of 180 countries have had a woman head of state or head of government since 1990 (UN 2000). Worldwide the proportion of women govern-ment ministers increased from 1987 to 1999, from 3 per cent to 8 per cent. Still, in 1998 45 countries had no women ministers and at least eight nations had parlia-ments comprised entirely of men (UN 1995; UN 2000; Inter-Parliamentary Union 2002).

Leading posts in the business sector are even more male-dominated, though specific, comparable data are sparse (UN 2000). Without pressure from parties, constitutions, or legislation for gender equity, almost no large business organizations in any nation are headed by women. Even in the Scandinavian countries, men hold most top business posts. A 1998 study of five top banks in each European Union-member state – including Denmark, Finland and Sweden – found that none reported a female president of its board of directors or executive management committee and just one had a woman as vice president of the board of directors (*Women in*

Decision-Making: Women in Banking 2002). A 1995 German study reported that men held 97 to 99 per cent of top executive and director posts in large businesses (UN 2000: 131). A census of the top seven titles in the 500 largest US corporations found 5.1 per cent of these titles held by women in 1999 and 3.4 per cent of like positions in Canada in 2000 (Catalyst 2000). Even lower proportions of women in leading business posts have been reported for Brazil, Sweden, and Japan (Wirth 2001: 38–40). Still, as in elected politics, women's representation in top business posts has been increasing. For example, the figure in the USA has more than doubled since 1995, when it was 2.4 per cent (Catalyst 2000). To an even greater degree than in the political sector, top leaders in major business organizations are men.

As is true for elite men, women elites generally come from high-status families with well-educated, upper or upper middle-class parents (e.g., Dye 1995; Zweigenhaft and Domhoff 1998; Liddle and Michielsens 2000). Studies of men and women elites in the political, economic and civil society sectors of Australia, West Germany and the USA in the 1970s to early 1980s found that the tiny number of women in such elite positions had higher social class and status origins than did their male counterparts, though both groups generally shared privileged family backgrounds (Moore 1988). An analysis of the class and status origins of 1500 top position holders in the economic and business sectors of 27 industrialized democracies during the mid-1990s confirmed these findings (Liddle and Michielsens 2000). This cross-national study included 21 European nations, and six others (Australia, Canada, Israel, Japan, New Zealand, and the USA). Liddle and Michielsens examined several dimensions of social class, based chiefly on parents' education and occupation, and found that on most of these dimensions of class women had higher rankings than did men in their sectors and country grouping. The gender–class relationship was strongest in the 'full capitalist' countries and weaker in the social democratic and post-communist countries of northern and eastern Europe (Liddle and Michielsens 2000). They conclude: 'Class, in whatever way we wish to define it, is central to women's challenge to men's monopoly on public power at the global level' (Liddle and Michielsens 2000: 34).

Putnam's claim made more than a quarter of a century ago that women are the most underrepresented group in political elites still has much validity, but not everywhere. In the Nordic countries, in particular, and in some others, including Costa Rica, Argentina, and South Africa, women have increasingly moved into leadership positions in elected politics. Overall, the progress toward gender equality in the political sector has been slow. Women remain a tiny minority of top leaders in the economic sector throughout the world.

Social background and education of elites

Not only women are underrepresented in senior leadership positions. Members of ethnic and racial minorities are also rare in top positions in the public and private sectors. Putnam (1976: 32) reported that lower status ethnic and religious minorities are usually underrepresented in political elites, citing Canada, the USA, and Yugoslavia as examples. To illustrate, in an analysis of the ethnic and racial origins of American elites in the economic, political and voluntary sectors in the early 1970s, Alba and Moore concluded that WASPs (Protestants with ancestors from the British Isles) held nearly half of the elite positions studied, a far larger proportion than in the general population (1982). Also, members of racial minority groups comprised less than four per cent of the elites (Alba and Moore 1982).

Elite researchers rarely report the ethnic and racial composition of leadership groups, making investigation of this topic difficult. In some cases, the issue of the homogeneous ethnic makeup of the elite seems taken for granted. Camp, for example, does not mention it in his extensive analyses of Mexican elite recruitment (1995). Norris and Lovenduski (1995) for MPs in Britain and Zweigenhaft and Domhoff (1998) for political and business leaders in the USA have investigated trends in the ethnic and racial composition of these groups. Norris and Lovenduski (1995: ch. 6) report a gradual increase in ethnic minority candidates in both major parties from 1970 (eight candidates) to 1992 (17 candidates). From no MPs from ethnic minority groups before 1987, the number rose to four in that year and six in 1992 (Norris and Lovenduski 1995: Table 6.4). Still, Norris and Lovenduski conclude that the number of black members of the House of Commons is far lower than would be expected based on their proportion of the British population (1995: 106).

Zweigenhaft and Domhoff reported that the number of African American executives and business directors, as well as Cabinet officials, in the USA began to increase in the late 1960s as a result of the Civil Rights Movement (1998). Yet African Americans remained underrepresented in these positions in 1995, with just 3.6 per cent of seats on the major corporate boards and roughly 13 per cent of the population (Zweigenhaft and Domhoff 1998). The legislative branch, especially the House of Representatives, has also seen an increase in ethnic and racial minority officeholders since the 1970s. In 2002 Hispanic Americans, African Americans and Asian Americans held 15 per cent of the seats in the House of Representatives. The Senate remained overwhelmingly white (and male), with one Asian American and one Native American member. In the USA, the economic and political sectors have become less overwhelmingly white than they were thirty years ago. Still, at the pinnacles of power – chief executive officers of major corporations, the presidency and the vice presidency, and the US Senate – little has changed.

Have the pathways to top positions – especially the need for higher education and a career in an administrative or professional field – changed in recent decades? In the period 1945 to 1975 Blondel (1980) found high levels of education and high status occupational backgrounds for the large majority of heads of government throughout the world. The state socialist countries were the sole exception, with a university education for just under half of their heads of government (Blondel 1980). Blondel also found that world leaders in this period came overwhelmingly from professional and managerial occupations (1980: 123–4). In most regions a tiny proportion of leaders had previously been manual workers – between zero and five per cent. Again, the state socialist countries differed, with 30 per cent of their leaders coming from manual occupations (Blondel 1980).

Evidence suggests that these educational and occupational credentials are even more essential now than they were in the previous century (Putnam 1976). The trend toward increasing homogeneity in elites' educational and occupational credentials is widely prevalent. A study of political elite recruitment in Britain illustrates this point (Norris and Lovenduski 1995). Examining the occupations of Conservative and Labour MPs from 1918 to 1992, Norris and Lovenduski found

481

that the proportion of workers among Conservative MPs declined from four per cent to zero per cent over the period, while those in the Labour Party went from 72 per cent to 22 per cent (1995: ch. 6). By 1992 MPs from both parties had far lower proportions from manual occupations than in the British population (43 per cent) (Norris and Lovenduski 1995: ch. 6).

A similar pattern is evident for trends in higher education among British MPs (Norris and Lovenduski 1995: ch. 6). Increasing proportions of MPs and the general population had achieved a university education throughout the century. The gap between population and MPs remained great in 1992: about 12 per cent of Britons, over 60 per cent of Labour MPs, and about 75 per cent of Conservative MPs had university education (Norris and Lovenduski 1995: 101).

Camp's analyses of political elite recruitment in Mexico over two centuries are also valuable for tracing patterns in elites' education (1995). In the late 1800s Mexican presidents and their administration officials had high levels of education, with at least two-thirds attending the university (Camp 1995: Table 4.1). In recent decades this proportion has risen even further until the two final presidents in the study had administrations with 87–100 per cent university credentials (Camp 1995: Table 4.1).

Less has been published on the education of business elites, but the qualification of university education is widespread. In a US study of top position holders in large corporations in the 1980s, Useem and Karabel found that more than 85 per cent had at least a bachelor's degree (1986). Not only is education itself important. In many countries – including France, the USA and Mexico, among others – attendance at one of a small number of highly prestigious schools paves the route to an elite position (Useem and Karabel 1986; Camp 1995; Birnbaum *et al.* 1978; Suleiman 1978; Putnam 1976). Useem and Karabel found that US business leaders from elite undergraduate or graduate schools were far more likely than others to be named chief executive officer of their corporation (1986). In France, attendance at a highly selective *grande école* is a path to the top in government, business and other sectors (Suleiman 1978; Birnbaum *et al.* 1978; Kadushin 1995). Camp describes the importance of the National University in the education of twentieth-century Mexican leaders (1995: ch. 4). Over half of the administrative officeholders were educated at the National University. Indeed, many had been professors before entering politics (Camp 1995). Attendance at one of the small number of channelling educational institutions in France, Mexico, the USA, the United Kingdom, Japan and elsewhere is often a road to elite recruitment not only because of the quality of education obtained but also due to powerful interpersonal connections made there.

Elite recruitment in post-socialist Central and Eastern Europe

The transitions from state socialism to democracy in Central and Eastern Europe during the 1990s have drawn scholars' attention to the topic of elite circulation or reproduction in those countries. With membership in the Communist Party no longer a prerequisite for elite positions, scholars have asked whether the rapid and extensive social transformations in these countries have included new pathways to power. Numerous researchers have examined elite continuity or replacement since 1989, comparing elites in the late socialist period to those in the early transition years (e.g., Szelenyi 1995; Higley and Lengyel 2000; Wasilewski 1998; Beyme 1996). Such studies have typically focused on the extent to which party and government leaders from the state socialist period have maintained influential positions in the new democratic state or economy.

In writing on elites after state socialism, Higley and Lengyel distinguished two aspects of elite circulation, its scope (breadth and depth) and its mode (speed) (2000: 4–7). Scope refers to the breadth of positions affected and to the depth of recruitment from lower levels of the political and social hierarchies (Higley and Lengyel 2000). While the mode of elite replacement in former state socialist nations varied little in its rapidity, the scope of elite circulation differed across the countries of Central and Eastern Europe. Surveying the transition to democracy in Eastern Europe, von Beyme found that in most countries top leaders from the state socialist period lost their positions, while middle and lower-level officials, including some from the state security apparatus, remained in the administrative, political or economic elite (1996; see also Lane and Ross 1999 on Russia). Other former communists – in Bulgaria, Poland, Lithuania and Hungary, among others – reentered the political system as members of newly formed socialist parties (Nikolov 1998; Beyme 1996).

Wasilewski (1998) examined the fate of the nomenklatura elites in Russia, Hungary and Poland during the transition period. Comparing position held in 1988 to that in 1993, he traced routes taken by nomenklatura elites during that period. The patterns in Hungary and Poland were similar, with nearly 40 per cent of the nomenklatura elites moving to business or state sector positions by 1993 (Wasilewski 2000). Wasilewski concluded that in these two countries the state, party, and economic nomenklatura elites of the late 1980s formed the core of the new capitalist class (2000: 165). Less movement had occurred in Russia by 1993, with large proportions of the former political and economic elite maintaining their 1988 positions (Wasilewski 2000; also see White and Kryshtanovskaya 1998).

Iglič and Rus (2000) analysed the dynamics of change in Slovenian elite positions and networks in business, politics and civil society from 1988 to 1995. Only 17 per cent of the 1988 elite had lost their positions by 1995, an indicator of high elite reproduction (2000). Yet their findings on changes in elite contacts led to the conclusion that this old elite was highly adaptable to new circumstances. 'The 1995 elite was predominantly old in composition but its contacts were mostly new' (2000: 184). Iglič and Rus contend that although the personnel in Slovenian elite positions were generally not replaced, their worldviews, political objectives, and interpersonal contacts adapted effectively to the new democratic and market reform policies (2000).

The breadth of elite recruitment, and thus of circulation or reproduction of elites, varied across the post-socialist nations in the 1990s. I turn now to the second component of the scope of elite circulation, the depth of changes in the social and political origins of top leaders in these countries.

Often the level of social origins – measured by parents' educations or occupations – among economic and political leaders in the transition period increased in comparison to the preceding state socialist years. For instance, in studying Czech elites before and after the transition, Machonin and Tucek found large differences in the occupational origins of politicians in the two periods (2000: 37): a majority of state socialist politicians had begun their careers as workers, while virtually none of their successors in the 1990s had working-class origins. In a study of Hungarian bankers and managers in 1990 and 1993, Lengyel and Bartha found a decline in working-class origins even during that short period (2000). The proportion of managers with working-class fathers declined from 33 per cent to 23 per cent, and bankers from blue-collar origins shrank from 55 per cent to 38 per cent (Lengyel and Bartha 2000). Educational credentials also increased among bankers and managers during this period (Lengyel and Bartha 2000).

In a study of Bulgarian economic elites from 1990 to 1998, Kostova found high levels of education throughout the period, even reaching 100 per cent with a university degree in 1998 (2000). A 1994 study of Bulgarian elites in many sectors and Wasilewski's 1998 study of Polish elites also showed that the large majority had tertiary education (Toneva 1997; Wasilewski 2000). This suggests that higher education credentials might have become even more important in most of the transition countries during the 1990s (see Sekulic and Sporer 2000 for an exception in the Croatian business elite).

In accord with Machonin and Tucek's results for Czech politicians, Kostova found that working-class origins became increasingly rare among Bulgarian business leaders during the 1990s, while previous professional or managerial experience characterized most Bulgarian economic leaders in the mid 1990s (2000: 203–7). A 1999 study of members of the Bulgarian Parliament revealed that many parliamentarians also had privileged family origins, as measured by parents' education, with over half of their fathers and 42 per cent of their mothers obtaining education beyond the secondary level (Moore and Muharska (2002) unpublished).

The Bulgarian Parliament study in 1999 also revealed high levels of education among elected politicians (Moore and Muharska (2002) unpublished). Virtually all parliamentarians had completed at least a university degree (96 per cent) and most listed professional or managerial occupations. Although the educational attainment of the MPs is far higher than in the Bulgarian population (15 per cent with tertiary education), it is difficult to know how much change this represents in parliament, since Kostova (2000) reports that university education was also common for elites during the state socialist period. In the Bulgarian Parliament elected in 1997, fewer than two per cent of members reported their occupation as worker, while more than two-thirds (68.1 per cent) fall into one of these occupational categories: engineer, medical professional, economist, and teacher/professor.

In Bulgaria, as elsewhere in newly democratic Central and Eastern Europe, high status social origins, advanced educational credentials and specialized occupational experience – in addition to male gender – are important criteria for movement into economic and political elite posts. There and elsewhere in nations with newly developed competitive political systems, educational and experiential credentials have overtaken party credentials as channels of elite recruitment.

Concluding remarks

A related but crucial issue, not addressed in studies of elite recruitment, is: what difference do social background and recruitment patterns make for elite actions and policy? Many scholars argue that individuals' life experiences, including social origins, form a worldview that affects beliefs and actions (e.g., Bottomore 1993; Domhoff 2002). Others counter that structural constraints limit the options for elites' behavior, especially in democratic systems (e.g., Weber 1947). Studies of elite recruitment seek to understand the paths to the top, not the consequences. Still, this essential issue in studies of elite structure and action must be examined.

Attention to the recruitment and structure of trans-national elites is also essential. The European Union, the International Monetary Fund, the World Bank, and transnational corporations exert influence throughout much of the world today. With processes of globalization, future research on elite recruitment must consider not only powerful positions at the national level but also in supra-national organizations.

Pareto and Mosca argued that a small minority of the population rules in every society. This rule by the few occurs in regimes of all types, not just totalitarian or authoritarian ones. Recruitment to elite positions is nowhere equally open to all citizens. Men from socially privileged families, with advanced education, and a professional or managerial occupation enjoy far easier access to elite positions in the political, economic and non-profit sectors than do other citizens. Beyond these general facts of elite recruitment, many variables such as history, culture, and political structure shape the channels to leading positions, the credentials required, and the circulation of elites.

References

Aberbach, J. D., Putnam, R. D., Rockman, B. A. with the collaboration of Anton, T., Eldersveld, S. J. and Inglehart, R. (1981) *Bureaucrats and Politicians in Western Democracies*, Cambridge, MA: Harvard University Press.

Alba, R. D., and Moore, G. (1982) 'Ethnicity in the American elite', *American Sociological Review* 47: 373–82.

Bachrach, P. (1967) *The Theory of Democratic Elitism: A Critique*, Boston: Little, Brown and Co.

Barton, A. H. (1985) 'Background, attitudes and activities of American elites', in G. Moore (ed.) *Studies of the Structure of National Elite Groups. Volume 1 of Research in Politics and Society*, Greenwich, CT: JAI Press.

Barton, A. H., Denitch, B. and Kadushin C. (eds) (1973) *Opinion-Making Elites in Yugoslavia*, New York: Praeger.

Beyme, K. von (1996) *Transition to Democracy in Eastern Europe*, New York: St Martin's Press.

Birnbaum, P., Barucq, C., Bellaiche, M. and Marié, A. (1978) *La Classe Dirigeante Française: Dissociation, Interpénétration, Intégration*, Paris: Presses Universitaires de France.

Blondel, J. (1980) *World Leaders: Heads of Government in the Postwar Period*, London: Sage Publications.

Burton, M. and Higley, J. (1987) 'Invitation to élite theory. The basic contentions reconsidered', in G. Domhoff and T. Dye (eds), *Power Élites and Organizations*, Newbury Park, CA: Sage Publications.

Camp, R. A. (1995) *Political Recruitment across Two Centuries: Mexico, 1884–1991*, Austin, TX: University of Texas Press.

Catalyst (2000) 'Catalyst expands into Canada', Catalyst Perspective, Available online, <http://www.catalystwo.org> (accessed 19 September 2001).

Dahl, R. A. (1961) *Who Governs?*, New Haven, CT: Yale University Press.

Dogan, M. (ed.) (1989) *Pathways to Power: Selecting Rulers in Pluralist Democracies*, Boulder, CO: Westview.

Domhoff, G. W. (2002) *Who Rules America? Power and Politics*, 4th edn, Boston: McGraw Hill.

Dye, T. R. (1995) *Who's Running America? The Clinton Years*, 6th edn, Englewood Cliffs, NJ: Prentice-Hall.

Etzioni-Halevy, E. (1993) *The Elite Connection: Problems and Potential of Western Democracy*, Cambridge: Polity Press.

Eulau, H. (1976) 'Elite analysis and democratic theory: the contribution of Harold D. Laswells', in H. Eulau and M. Czudnowski (eds) *Elite Recruitment in Democratic Polities: Comparative Studies Across Nations*, New York: Sage Publications.

Higley, J., Deacon, D. and Smart, D. (1979) *Élites in Australia*, London: Routledge & Kegan Paul.

Higley, J. and Lengyel, G. (eds) (2000) *Elites After State Socialism: Theories and Analysis*, Lanham, MD: Rowman and Littlefield.

Hoffmann-Lange, U. (1992) *Eliten, Macht und Konflikt in der Bundesrepublik*, Opladen: Leske Budrich.

Hunter, F. (1953) *Community Power Structure: A Study of Decision Makers*, Garden City, NY: Anchor Books.

Iglic, H. and Rus, A. (2000) 'Elite networks in transition: the dynamics of change in personal networks of Slovenian elites', in J. Frentzel-Zagórska and J. Wasilewski (eds) *The Second Generation of Democratic Elites in Central and Eastern Europe*, Warsaw: Institute of Political Studies, Polish Academy of Sciences.

InterParliamentary Union (2002) *Women in Parliaments*. Online. Available online: <http://www.ipu.org> (accessed 15 August 2002).

Kadushin, C. (1974) *The American Intellectual Elite*, Boston, MA: Little, Brown and Co.

—— (1995) 'Friendship among the French Financial Elite', *American Sociological Review*, 60: 202–21.

Kostova, D. (2000) 'Bulgaria: economic elite change during the 1990s', in J. Higley and G. Lengyel (eds) *Elites After State Socialism: Theories and Analysis*, Lanham, MD: Rowman and Littlefield.

Lasswell, H. D. (1936) *Politics: Who Gets What, When, How*, New York: McGraw-Hill.

Lane, D. and Ross, C. (1999) *The Transition from Communism to Capitalism: Ruling Elites from Gorbachev to Yeltsin*, New York: St Martin's Press.

Lengyel, G. and Bartha, A. (2000) 'Hungary: bankers and managers after state socialism', in J. Higley and G. Lengyel (eds) *Elites After State Socialism: Theories and Analysis*, Lanham, MD: Rowman and Littlefield.

Liddle, J. and Michielsens, E. (2000) 'Gender, class, and public power', in M. Vianello and G. Moore (eds) *Gendering Elites: Economic and Political Leadership in 27 Industrialised Societies*, London: Macmillan Press.

Lukes, S. (1974) *Power: A Radical View*, London: Macmillan.

Machonin, P. and Tucek, M. (2000) 'Czech Republic: new elites and social change', in J. Higley and G. Lengyel (eds) *Elites After State Socialism: Theories and Analysis*, Lanham, MD: Rowman and Littlefield.

Michels, R. (1962) *Political Parties: A Sociological Study of the Oligarchical Tendencies of Modern Democracy*, New York: Free Press.

Mills, C. W. (1956) *The Power Elite*, New York: Oxford University Press.

Moore, G. (1988) 'Women in elite positions: insiders or outsiders?', *Sociological Forum*, 3: 566–85.

Moore, G. and Muharska, R. (2002) 'The Bulgarian parliament study.' Unpublished manuscript.

Mosca, G. (1939) *The Ruling Class*, ed. and rev. by A. Livingston, New York: McGraw-Hill.

Moyser, G. and Wagstaffe, M. (eds) (1987) *Research Methods in Elite Studies*, London: Allen & Unwin.

Nagle, J. (1992) 'Recruitment of elites', in M. Hawkesworth and M. Kogan (eds) *Encyclopedia of Government and Politics*, London: Routledge.

Nikolov, S. E. (1998) 'Bulgaria: a quasi-elite', in J. Higley, J. Pakulski and W. Wesolowski, (eds) *Postcommunist Elites and Democracy in Eastern Europe*, Basingstoke: Macmillan.

Norris, P. and Lovenduski, J. (1995) *Political Recruitment: Gender, Race and Class in the British Parliament*, Cambridge: Cambridge University Press.

Pareto, V. (1935) *The Mind and Society*, New York: Harcourt, Brace.

—— (1991) *The Rise and Fall of Elites: An Application of Theoretical Sociology*, New Brunswick, NJ: Transaction Publishers.

Parry, G. (1969) *Political Elites*, New York: Praeger.

Polsby, N. W. (1963) *Community Power and Political Theory*, New Haven, CT: Yale University Press.

Porter, J. (1965) *The Vertical Mosaic: An Analysis of Social Class and Power in Canada*, Toronto: University of Toronto Press, 1969.

Prewitt, K. and Stone, A. (1973) *The Ruling Elites: Elite Theory, Power and American Democracy*, New York: Harper & Row.

Putnam, R. D. (1976) *The Comparative Study of Political Elites*, Englewood Cliffs, NJ: Prentice-Hall.

Seager, J. (1997) *The State of Women in the World Atlas*, London: Penguin.

Sekulic, D. and Sporer, Z. (2000) 'Croatia: managerial elite circulation or reproduction', in J. Higley and G. Lengyel (eds) *Elites After State Socialism: Theories and Analysis*, Lanham, MD: Rowman and Littlefield.

Suleiman, E. N. (1978) *Elites in French Society: The Politics of Survival*, Princeton: Princeton University Press.

Szelényi, I. (ed.) (1995) 'Circulation and reproduction of elites during the post-communist transformation of Eastern Europe', special issue, *Theory and Society*, 24.

Toneva, Z. (1997) 'Research on economic and political elites in Bulgaria in the period 1990–1995', in H. Best and U. Becker (eds) *Elites in Transition: Elite Research in Central and Eastern Europe*, Opladen: Leske Budrich.

United Nations (1995) *The World's Women 1995: Trends and Statistics*, New York.

—— (2000) *The World's Women 2000: Trends and Statistics*, New York.

Useem, M. (1980) 'Which business leaders help govern?', *Insurgent Sociologist*, 9: 107–20.

Useem, M. and Karabel, J. (1986) 'Pathways to top corporate management', *American Sociological Review*, 51:184–200.

Wasilewski, J. (1998) 'Hungary, Poland, and Russia: the fate of nomenklatura elites', in M. Dogan and J. Higley (eds) *Elites, Crises, and the Origins of Regimes*, Lanham, MD: Rowman and Littlefield.

Weber, M. (1947) *The Theory of Social and Economic Organization*, New York: Free Press.

White, S. and Kryshtanovskaya, O. (1998) 'Russia: elite continuity and change', in M. Dogan and J. Higley (eds) *Elites, Crises, and the Origins of Regimes*, Lanham, MD: Rowman and Littlefield.

Wirth, Linda (2001) *Breaking Through the Glass Ceiling: Women in Management*, Geneva: International Labour Office.

Women in Decision-Making: Women in Banking (2002) Online. Available online: <http://db-decision.de/Banken/Banken_E.htm> (accessed 1 August 2002).

Zapf, W. (1965) *Wandlungen in der Deutschen Elite: Ein Zirkulationsmodell Deutscher Führungsgruppen 1919–1961*, Munich: Piper.

Zweigenhaft, R. L. and Domhoff, G. W. (1998) *Diversity in the Power Elite: Have Women and Minorities Reached the Top?* New Haven, CT: Yale University Press.

Further reading

Higley, J. and Lengyel, G. (2000) *Elites after State Socialism: Theories and Analysis*, Lanham, MD: Rowman and Littlefield.

Norris, P. and Lovenduski, J. (1995) *Political Recruitment: Gender, Race and Class in the British Parliament*, Cambridge: Cambridge University Press.

Pareto, V. (1966) *Vilfredo Pareto: Sociological Writings*, New York: Praeger.

PART VII

CENTRIPETAL AND CENTRIFUGAL FORCES IN THE NATION-STATE

32

POLITICAL CULTURES

Shiping Hua

Political culture, the idea that the character or *ethos* of the people is integrally related to the type of regime ruling a polity, was first explored by Plato and Aristotle in ancient Greece and later discussed by Machiavelli and Montesquieu. The study of political culture resurfaced in the twentieth century, an era marked by enormous social upheavals and technological advances (Almond 2000: 7–8). Scientific inquiries are rarely conducted in a social vacuum.

In the first half of the twentieth century, the study of political culture was noted for its methodological emphasis on a synthesis of psychoanalytic ideas and cultural anthropology. Led by Harold Lasswell, Ruth Benedict, Margaret Mead, and Erich Fromm, this approach was noted for its studies of the 'national character' of nations embroiled in the Second World War. The failure of the Enlightenment spirit as demonstrated in the irrational behaviour in the war coupled with technological advances, especially the use of computer and survey techniques, prompted not only a surge of political culture study but also a strong emphasis on rigorous testing and statistical measurements in the two decades after the Second World War. The most significant breakthrough in political culture studies during this period was made by Gabriel Almond and Sidney Verba in *The Civic Culture* (1963), which involved a comparative survey of the civic cultures in five nations. In a departure from previous political culture studies which had relied largely on impressions, their study shifted the focus to testable propositions (Inglehart 1988).

Political culture study suffered setbacks in the late 1960s and 1970s when it was attacked by neo-Marxists and by proponents of rational choice theories. 'The study of political culture is based on the implicit assumption that autonomous and reasonably enduring cross-cultural differences exist and that they can have important political consequences' (Inglehart 1988: 1205). In this era of global radicalism, some Marxists criticized the political culture theoretical assumption concerning the autonomy of political consciousness, arguing that people's relations to the ownership of the means of production was the key to understanding their political consciousness. The rational choice group, on the other hand, criticized political culture theory by arguing that short term self-interest was the determinant of people's behaviour, not cultural traditions.

Other criticisms of political culture study also surfaced. It was suggested that:

1   The direction of causality is more complex than political culture studies often suggest. While political culture influences political institutions, political institutions influence political culture too.
2   It may not be possible to separate political attitudes from political behaviour as distinctly as the scientific testing of political culture would require (Almond 2000: 11).
3   The unit of analysis in political culture study is not clear. Does political culture refer to the beliefs, values, and attitudes of a person, a population, or a nation?
4   Political culture studies failed to examine variations within specific cultures.
5   Political culture study is insensitive to change (Ross 2000: 56–61). The cumulative effect of such criticisms produced a lag in political culture studies during the 1970s.

A number of factors contributed to renewed interest in political culture studies in the 1980s and 1990s. The elections of Margaret Thatcher in Great Britain in 1979 and Ronald Reagan in the USA in 1980, as well as the fall of the Berlin Wall in the late 1980s seemed to suggest massive changes in political culture in comparatively short periods (Almond 1994: ix–xii). In addition, as political culture study developed through the years, later studies in the field have avoided some of the problems pointed out by political culture critics. Many scholars are keenly aware that people in different regions and people within different social strata have different political cultures and these cultures are constantly changing. The factors that shape political culture include not only tradition, but also contemporary socialization and socio-economic determinants (Hua 2001).

The reemergence of political culture studies was also connected with the changing context of contemporary international affairs. The impressive growth of East Asia in the last three decades of the twentieth century and the terrorist attack on the World Trade Center Towers in New York City on September 11, 2001 cannot be fully understood without making cultural references. The heated debate generated by Samuel Huntington's *The Clash of Civilizations* (1993) is a living testimony to the importance of political culture study.

In spite of such recent developments, political culture has not received the attention it deserves. There are currently only 35–40 books, about 100 journal articles, and about 1,000 citations about political culture (Almond 2000: 9). In the words of Marc Howard Ross, '[f]ew graduate students [in political science] take culture very seriously, and if one peruses the annual list of dissertations in comparative politics over several years, it is difficult to place cultural analysis in the trinity of comparative politics' (Ross 2000: 40). Political culture is not a concept with which most political scientists are comfortable. Indeed, some critics continue to maintain that political culture is one of the most controversial and confused concepts in the political lexicon (Elkins and Simeon 2000: 22).

In addition to being subject to the vicissitudes of social change and technological advance, political culture study has its inherent problems as a concept of scientific inquiry. Many political scientists consider political culture an epi-phenomenon to be explained away rather than to be incorporated into theories and explanations; and many who do invoke culture define it so thinly that they do not develop analyses of cultural dynamics (Ross 2000: 43). Few other words in the social sciences have a greater variety of uses than 'political culture' (Verba 1965: 513). Thus, political culture is generally considered to be an illusive concept (Pye 1972: 287).

Political culture study, like culture studies in general, generates debates in the following areas: (1) What is it? – the definitional problem. (2) How to study it? – the methodological problem. (3) What does it do? – the functional problem (Geertz 1973). Each will be addressed in turn.

The definitional problem

Traditionally, the concepts central to 'political culture' were defined in a broad and general way by political philosophers. Rousseau conceived political culture in terms of the morality, customs and public opinion of a particular people. Tocqueville referred to political culture as 'the habits of heart', the whole moral and intellectual condition of a people (Almond 1990: 77). When political scientists attempted to operationalize political culture in the mid twentieth century, definitional problems became increasingly significant (Almond 1956: 391–409). Generally speaking, there have been three major approaches to the definition of political culture. It has been defined as (1) political psychology; (2) public opinion; or as (3) political ideology. Although each of these approaches has specific ontological and methodological implications, most political culture theoreticians do not endorse just one of these three approaches (Hua 1999). In turning to the study of political culture, many scholars conflate people's deep sentiments towards politics, public opinion, and political ideology. For instance, Gabriel Almond defined political culture as consisting of the set of subjective orientations to politics in a national population or subset of a national population. As such, political culture has cognitive, affective and evaluative components. It includes knowledge and beliefs about political reality, feelings with respect to politics, and commitments to political values (Almond 1990: 144). Lucian Pye defined political culture as the set of attitudes, beliefs and sentiments, which give order and meaning to a political process, and which provide the underlying assumptions and rules that govern behaviour in the political system. In this sense, political culture encompasses both the political ideals and the operating norms of a polity. It is thus the manifestation in aggregate form of the psychological and subjective dimensions of politics (Pye 1968: 218). Political culture includes 'public opinion, political ideology, national ethos and the basic consensus, values, and constitutional integrating sentiments of a people' (Pye 1972: 287). Views such as those of Almond and Pye might be considered an all-inclusive approach to political culture.

A narrow approach, on the other hand, defines political culture mainly as public opinion. Some behavioural political scientists argue that any attempt at scientific development of the concept of political culture required a clear empirical referent (Stern, Dobson and Scioli 1973: 499). Lowell Dittmer, for example, argued that the key to operationalizing political culture is to determine precisely the empirical variables to be analysed and to separate political culture variables clearly from political structure and from political psychology. He complained that the failure to define the empirical variables of political culture resulted in an unhelpful drift between microanalysis and macro-analysis (Dittmer 1977: 552–3). For proponents of this narrow approach to political culture, only public opinion studies could meet the criterion of 'objective testability' (Chilton 1988: 419–45).

In contrast to the all-inclusive and the narrow approaches, some political scientists have attempted to define political culture as political ideology. According to Roy Macridis, political culture appears synonymous with political ideology (Macridis 1992: 2). James Townsend uses the term of 'elite political culture' to cover what is understood to be political ideology (Townsend 1984: 385). Richard Wilson defines political culture as a dominant ideology justifying compliance with a society's institutional system (Nathan 1993: 931).

Although these three approaches to the definition of political culture have existed since the term was first introduced in 1956, within the discipline of political science the momentum has 'moved in the direction of making it clearer and more usable as a focus for empirical hypothesis testing' (Stern, Dobson and Sciolo 1973: 493). Thus positivist approaches have dominated political culture studies: public opinion has received more attention, often at the expense of in-depth analysis of 'the habits of heart' and ideological persuasions; quantitative methods have been accorded greater legitimacy, often at the expense of qualitative ones (Isaak 1985).

The perplexity in defining political culture is rooted in the nature of the research object. *People's subjective orientations towards politics*, the simplest and broadest constituent of political culture, are multi-dimensional. Some subjective orientations towards politics are conscious, others are not conscious; some are coherent, others are not coherent. Based on an understanding of this complexity, three dimensions of political culture can be identified, which roughly correspond to the three major approaches to the definition of political culture. (1) Fathomable to political psychology, which is attuned to subconscious aspects of political culture, the first dimension encompasses people's deepest sentiments towards politics. On this view, a Chinese peasant can behave like a Confucianist or a Buddhist without ever reading a single word of the Confucian or the Buddhist texts. The political culture engrained in the psyche 'remains below the threshold of consciousness', because members of a polity seldom encounter individuals who take for granted quite different assumptions (Almond 2000: 23–4). (2) Captured in public opinion polls, the second dimension of political culture may be conscious, although it may be far from systematic. For instance, a Democrat in the USA may be conscious of his or her party affiliation, while holding contradictory political commitments, favouring increasing welfare for everybody, but voting against any measures to raise taxes. (3) As suggested by the notion of political ideology, the third dimension of political culture is not only highly conscious but also coherent and systematic. Marxism, Liberalism, or Confucianism, for example, are highly coherent and systematic doctrinal systems, which may be expressly embraced by members of a political community.

While some analysts have found it helpful to conceptualize political culture along the vectors of conscious/unconscious and coherent-systematic/incoherent-unsystematic, a number of alternative schemes have also been suggested for categorizing aspects of political culture. As previously mentioned Gabriel Almond construes political culture in terms of three dimensions, the cognitive, the evaluative and the affective. The cognitive dimension refers to people's knowledge about the polity; the evaluative captures their assessment of how well political or economic institutions perform; and the affective attempts to grasp their deepest political attachment to or disaffection with the political system. Sidney Verba advanced a four-fold classification for understanding political culture, which included (1) national identity, (2) identification with one's fellow citizens, (3) beliefs about government policy and (4) beliefs about decision-making processes (Verba 1965: 526–43). Edward W. Lehman argued political culture could best be studied when classified according to 'participational and institutional dimensions' (Lehman 1972: 363–4). J. R. Townsend suggested that an accurate understanding of political culture required separate analyses of elite political culture and mass political culture (Townsend 1984). As part of an on-going discussion among scholars, surely there will be more ways to analyse the dimensions of political culture advanced in the years ahead.

The perplexity in defining political culture is not only connected to the fact that political culture is multi-faceted and can be analysed fruitfully according to various dimensions. It is also connected to the complex ways in which research traditions are linked to the particular cultural traditions of particular nations. For scholars of China, for example, it is inconceivable to study China without discussing China's official ideology. Indeed, China scholars typically are introduced to the study of China through the systematic study of China's official ideology (Pye 1992: 14–31). This is because China in the last two thousand years has relied on official ideologies, whether Confucianism or Marxism, to remould the Chinese consciousness. Studies of Western nations, by contrast, may make reference to the role played by religion in shaping people's political consciousness in pre-modern times, but it is taken as given that there is no official ideology guiding people's political consciousness in modernity. The Liberalism that undergirds central political tenets in Western nations is taken to be 'non-ideological'. The 'market place of ideas', to borrow J. S. Mill's language, is said to structure a political arena in which different ideas, neither comprehensive nor coherent, contest with each other. The insistence on the non-ideological nature of Western political culture is especially prevalent in the USA, where the two main political parties eschew the ideological commitments of their West European counterparts. Although some commentators dating from Tocqueville have argued that liberal individualism is the dominant ideology in the USA, such interpretations are given short shrift in comparison with claims about the political culture of a communist country where a comprehensive official ideology is deemed essential for the stability of the polity.

Because political ideology is frequently associated with communism, fascism, or Islamic fundamentalism, it is viewed negatively in the West among scholars as well as among the populace. One consequence of this Western distaste for ideology is that certain parts of the world are said to have political ideologies, while others allegedly do not. Political culture studies that encompass political ideology seem to acquire a particular regional flare. For those who study China or the Middle East, political ideology will be reviewed as an important part of political culture, while in the West, the study of political ideology may not carry as much weight and may therefore be overlooked.

In addition to the multi-dimensional nature of political culture and cultural idiosyncrasies across nations, historical conditions and positivist assumptions about the requirements for scientific investigation have also limited approaches to political culture study in specific nations. For instance, until the 1980s, it was not possible to study Chinese political culture by focusing on public opinion surveys. This was not only due to the government's authoritarian control of society, but also to China's backward technological situation at that time. By contrast, the openness of Western societies and technological advances in the West helped public opinion surveys to flourish in the study of Western political culture. Thus the conceptualization of Chinese political culture *qua* political ideology and US political culture *qua* public opinion may be determined by complex historical, political, and technological forces, as well as the methodological commitments of particular scholars.

In undertaking the study of particular political cultures, then, scholars have had to juggle the competing demands of theoretical aspirations and pragmatic possibilities. Specific studies bear the marks of such tensions. Although Almond's definition of political culture is a broadly inclusive one, for example, his positivist reliance on survey research as the key means of documenting comparative political cultures in five Western democracies produced findings in *The Civic Culture* far narrower than his comprehensive definition would lead one to expect. Lucian Pye, on the other hand, was criticized for his 'unscientific approach' to the study of Chinese political culture (Pye 1992), yet he has since been commended for his insistence on maintaining objective standards for testing political cultural hypotheses on a general level (Chilton 1988: 424). Definitional questions intersect with methodological concerns in the context of pragmatic research possibilities.

The methodological problem

The definitional problem and the methodological problem in the study of political culture are intimately related. Some political scientists disagree about what political culture is, because they cannot agree about the appropriate methods for its study. For those concerned with the scientific study of politics, the complexities of culture complicate issues of evidence, transforming hopes of rigorous analysis into 'just so' accounts that fail to meet widely held notions of scientific explanation. Culture, according to these scholars, defies easy operationalization and raises serious unit of analysis problems for which there are no simple answers (Ross 2000: 40).

The methodological approaches that have dominated political culture studies can be put into two camps, the positivist and the interpretative. The positivist approach accredits itself as 'scientific', while deriding alternative methodologies as interpretative or unscientific. For those who believe that the only legitimate methodological approach is the positivist one, public opinion is conflated with political culture, because that is the dimension of political culture that can be studied through survey research. Although the positivist approach, when applied properly, has the advantage of being rigorous and systematic, it also severely restricts the study of political culture. Some important aspects of political culture are omitted because they are not amenable to quantification. For instance, it is hard to study elite political culture using public opinion methodologies. Even under optimal conditions survey research may limit the scope of claims about political culture. Capturing a frozen moment in time, survey research cannot illuminate the past or the future. Thus it cannot account for the dynamics of change within the political culture of a particular nation. Critics have also suggested that survey questions simplify complex cultural attributes. And in cases of cross-national comparisons, surveys designed to capture the same phenomena cross-culturally may be unable to identify attributes that are culturally unique (Nathan and Shi 1993: 97). Clifford Geertz has labelled cultural generalizations based on survey data 'thin description', insisting that 'thick description' of culture requires hermeneutic or interpretive methods (Chilton 1988: 423).

Interpretative approaches are designed to unearth the beliefs and values that underlie political discourses, customs, and traditions. Attuned to the symbol systems that have been developed within particular cultures, interpretative analyses may 'decode' important political messages through the textual analysis of popular novels, films, and idioms (Pye and Leites 1982: 1150–1). Interpretative approaches may be sensitive to changing historical, psychological, and ideological dimensions of political culture (Nathan *et al.* 1993: 96; Townsend 1984). They may also be uniquely appropriate for analyses of elite political culture, which depends upon in-depth analysis of the tacit assumptions and operational codes that inform the principles guiding political behaviour (Pye 1965: 16; Putnam 1971: 653). Interpretative methods also have their limitations, however. Some interpretations may seem idiosyncratic, relying more on the interpreter's analytic lens than on the political culture under investigation. For large, heterogeneous nations, interpretative methods may not be well suited to map the complexities of mass political culture.

Given the limitations of both positivist and interpretative methodologies, sophisticated analysts will tailor their methods to the aspect of political culture under investigation. Those who wish to probe the subconscious dimensions of political culture whether in the domain of political psychology or political ideology will of necessity devise interpretative-hermeneutic approaches. For those who wish to tap the conscious cognitive, evaluative and affective dimensions of political culture, surveys of public opinion may be adequate to the task.

The functional problem: what does political culture contribute to politics?

What functions does political culture perform in human societies? Does it perform any functions at all? Political scientists disagree about this question as well. Rational choice scholars generally dismiss culture as insignificant in shaping political behaviour. Arguing that individuals are rational and as such their political action is determined by calculations of short term interest, proponents of rational choice insist that there is no need to invoke additional explanatory variables to account for political behaviour (Rogowski 1974). Although they recognize the relevance of culture to human behaviour, Marxists argue that political culture itself is derivative of economics. On this view, political interests and political action depend on an individual's class position. Members of the proletariat who do not possess the means of production should manifest different political sentiments than capitalists who own the means of production. Moreover, because economic power drives political outcomes, the laws governing the political system reflect the class interests of the capitalists. Thus law as well as political culture more broadly can be understood as part of the 'superstructure', which is profoundly shaped by 'the economic base' of particular societies.

In contrast to the dismissive view of rational choice scholars and the derivative view of Marxist scholars, some political observers have argued that political culture is very important in influencing not only politics but economics as well. Alexis de Tocqueville, for example, argued that Islam is incompatible with democratic ideals, while Christianity sustains them (Tocqueville 1961). Max Weber suggested that the particular values fostered by Protestantism were the key to capitalist development in the West (Weber 1930). In a similar vein, Tu Wei-ming (1990) has argued that particular cultural values explain the rise of East Asia as an economic power house in the last few decades of the twentieth century.

Many scholars view the relationship between political culture and other parts of the social system as a matter of interaction effects. That is to say that emphasis on the importance of culture in a polity does not imply that other political and economic factors are not important. For example, Samuel Huntington's thesis (1993) that twenty-first century world politics will largely be determined by cultural factors, i.e., 'the clash of civilizations', rather than ideological and economic factors, depends on a particular interpretation of the collapse of communism in the early 1990s. To Huntington, culture emerges as the most important factor in world politics precisely because ideological and economic problems have been 'settled'.

A brief comparison of two concrete studies, *The Civic Culture* (Almond and Verba 1963) and *Chinese Political Culture* (Hua 2001) helps to illuminate a range of claims about the role that political culture plays in the political system. In their classic study of political culture in five liberal democratic nations (the UK, the USA, Germany, Italy, and Mexico), Almond and Verba sought to identify the cognitive and affective beliefs and values of citizens that sustain a stable liberal democracy. Examining citizens' views about the effectiveness of the political and the economic system, levels of trust in government, levels of participation, and perceptions of 'freedom' within their political systems, Almond and Verba suggested that the UK and the USA had a more developed 'civic culture' than Germany, Italy, and Mexico. Defining 'civic culture' as 'a pluralistic culture based on communication and persuasion, a culture of consensus and diversity, a culture that permitted change but moderated it', Almond and Verba (1963: 8) claimed that one of the most central values to stable liberal democracy was 'apathy'. A gap between citizens' sense of political efficacy (i.e., the belief that they could influence their government if they chose to do so) and their actual levels of political engagement (never mobilizing to try to influence government policy) was characteristic of a 'stable' liberal democracy. On this view, greater levels of political activism, anomic as well as electoral, on the part of citizens in Germany, Italy, and Mexico contributed to greater 'instability', characterized by more frequent and more radical changes in political regimes.

Questions concerning the direction of causality remain unresolved by this study, however. Does the political culture produce political instability in these three nations or did unstable political systems in Germany, Italy and Mexico in the first half of the twentieth century produce 'less civic culture'? Although the answer is unclear, Almond and Verba emphasize the importance of the interaction between political culture and political system: attitudes influence citizens' participation, which influences the political system, which in turn influences citizens' participation (Almond and Verba 1963: 480, 504). In advancing an account of how citizens come to have particular beliefs and values in liberal democracies, however, Almond and Verba emphasize the role of education rather than direct government 'indoctrination' or dissemination of ideas. Thus despite clear evidence of the direction of causality, Almond and Verba reinforce the view that liberal democracies do not mould political culture in a direct way.

Chinese Political Culture (Hua 2001) undertakes comparative investigations of political culture in mainland China, Hong Kong, and Taiwan. The values governing electoral competition in China are different from those in liberal democracies. In a study of the dynamics of Chinese village elections conducted in minority areas, Chih-yu Shih found in the 1990s that the governing value was not competition, but rather a seeking of harmony among the villagers (in Hua 2001: 247–75). Providing evidence for the critical role of the government in shaping political culture, Wenfang Tang found that the Chinese government's efforts to reduce religiosity had been effective in that mainland China is now much less religious than Taiwan (in Hua 2001: 298–319). Investigating the complex dynamics between government and media, Jonathan J. H. Zhu and Huixin Ke found that exposure to Hong Kong television leads to an increase in 'fact-based' knowledge among the population in Hong Kong, while exposure to the government-controlled media in the People's Republic of China reinforces subjective knowledge among the people on the mainland (in Hua 2001: 188–218).

In contrast to Almond and Verba's claims about the absence of active governmental efforts to mold political culture in liberal democracies, the impact of the Chinese government in molding political culture is more direct and more obvious. Specifically, the official ideologies of nationalism, neo-Maoism, and conservatism, actively promoted by governmental agencies and the official media, all impact on Chinese political culture in some important ways.

How effective are governments in producing a political culture that sustains the regime? A comparison of *The Civic Culture* and *Chinese Political Culture* on this question generates interesting results. Through surveys of people in the People's Republic of China, Hong Kong, and Taiwan, Yun-han Chu and Yu-tzung Chang discovered that people on the mainland have a stronger affinity with the state than do the people in Hong Kong and Taiwan, suggesting that the Chinese government has been quite successful in inculcating supportive beliefs and values (Hua 2001: 320–48). Ironically, however, Almond and Verba also found that the people in the USA and Britain experienced a greater impact of national government on their beliefs and values than people in Germany, Italy and Mexico (Almond/Verba 1963: 80–1), despite their claim that liberal democratic governments do not directly shape the political culture.

The political system is not the only force that shapes political culture. Cultural traditions also play an important part. Yet, historical analysis is very thin in Almond and Verba's study, a result of reliance on survey research, which generates data bound to the particular historical moment of the study. Perhaps, for a country like the USA, which is relatively young and whose values are closely linked to the dominant Western heritage, this deficiency poses less of a challenge in interpreting political culture. For a country like China, however, historical analysis is often indispensable. In the words of Lucian Pye, China is a 'civilization, not an ordinary nation-state'. As such the influence of Confucianism can be traced over centuries. To illustrate this pervasive influence, Kam Louie argues in *Chinese Political Culture* that while a 'Confucian gentleman' in ancient China was a scholar-official, it is now possible to interpret Confucianism in such a way that a 'Confucian gentleman' can be a businessman (in Hua 2001: 21–41). Indeed Roger Ames suggests that such evolving interpretations are made possible because Chinese philosophy is biographical, which distinguishes it in a variety of ways from the more analytical orientation of Greek philosophy (in Hua 2001: 70–102).

Efforts to trace the impact of political culture upon the political system in China, Taiwan, and Hong Kong reveal another important difference between political cultures in the East and the West. In contrast to the free and open expression of political values, including criticism and dissent, which Almond and Verba identify as a hallmark of civic culture, the expression of political values is indirect in *Chinese Political Culture*. While people's apathy and cynicism have been and continue to be expressed in literature and other artistic works, public demonstrations of such feelings are hard to detect (Moody in Hua 2001: 161–87).

While the study of political culture raises a variety of definitional and methodological challenges, recent scholarship in this area suggests that an understanding of political culture is vital to a full grasp of contemporary politics. With the simultaneous emergence of Islamism as a global political force and the 'third wave' of democratization in nations around the globe coexisting with the evolving mix of nationalism, neo-Maoism and Confucianism in China, the most populous nation, the stakes in this quest for knowledge of political culture grow larger every day. It remains to be seen whether political scientists will rise to the challenge.

References

Almond, G. A. (1956) 'Comparative Political Systems', *Journal of Politics*, 18.

—— (1994) 'Foreword: A Return to Political Culture', in Diamond, L. (ed.) *Political Culture and Democracy in Developing Countries*, Boulder, CO: Lynne Rienner.

——(2000) 'The Study of Political Culture', in Crothers, L., and Lockhart, C. (eds) *Culture and Politics: A Reader*, New York: St Martin's Press.

Almond, G. A. (with Sidney Verba) (1963) *The Civic Culture: Political Attitudes and Democracy in Five Nations*, Princeton: Princeton University Press.

Chilton, S. (1988) 'Defining Political Culture', *The Western Political Quarterly*, 3: 419–45.

Dittmer, L. (1977) 'Political Culture and Political Symbolism: Toward a Theoretical Synthesis', *World Politics* 4: 552–81.

Elkins, D. J. and Simeon, R. E. B. (2000) 'A Cause in Search of Its Effect, or What Does Political Culture Explain?' in Crothers, L. and Lockhart, C. *Culture and Politics: A Reader* New York: St Martin's Press.

Geertz, C. (1973) *The Interpretation of Cultures*, New York: Basic Books.

Hua, S. P. (1999) 'Definition and Methodology of Political Culture Theory: A Case Study of Sinology', *Asian Thought and Society* 70: 23–41.

—— (2001) (ed.) *Chinese Political Culture (1989–2000)*, Armonk, NY: M. E. Sharpe.

Huntington, S. (1993) 'The Clash of Civilizations?' *Foreign Affairs* 3.

Inglehart, R. (1988) 'The Renaissance of Political Culture', *American Political Science Review*, 82: 1203–30.

Isaak, A. C. (1985) *Scope and Methods of Political Science*, Belmont, CA: Wadsworth Publishing Company.

Lehman, E. W. (1972) 'On the Concept of Political Culture: A Theoretical Reassessment', *Social Forces*, 50: 361–70.

Macridis, R. C. (1992) *Contemporary Political Ideologies: Movements and Regimes*, New York: HarperCollins Publishers.

Nathan, A. (1993) 'Is Chinese Culture Distinctive?' *The Journal of Asian Studies*, 4: 923–36.

Nathan, A. with Shi, T. (1993) 'Cultural Requisites for Democracy in China: Some Findings from a Survey', *Daedalus*, 2.

Putnam, R. D. (1971) 'Studying Elite Political Culture: The Case of "Ideology"', *The American Political Science Review*, 3: 651–81.

Pye, L. W. (1968) in Sills, D. L. (ed.) *International Encyclopedia of the Social Sciences*, New York: Macmillan Co. and the Free Press: 218–24.

—— (1965) 'Introduction: Political Culture and Political Development', in Pye, L. W. and Verba, S., *Political Culture and Political Development*, Princeton, NJ: Princeton University Press.

—— (1972) 'Culture and Political Science: Problems in the Evaluation of the Concept of Political Culture', *Social Science Quarterly*, 2: 283–96.

—— (1992) *The Spirit of Chinese Politics*, Cambridge, MA: Harvard University Press.

Pye, L. W. and Leites, N. (1982) 'Nuances in Chinese Political Culture', *Asian Survey*, 12: 1147–65.

Rogowski, R. (1974) *Rational Legitimacy*, Princeton, NJ: Princeton University Press.

Ross, M. H. (2000) 'Culture and Identity in Comparative Political Analysis', in Crothers, L. and Lockhart, C. (eds) *Culture and Politics: A Reader*, New York: St Martin's Press.

Stern, L. N., Dobson, L. D. and Scioli, F. P. (1973) 'On the Dimensions of Political Culture: A New Perspective', *Comparative Political Studies*, 493–509.

Tocqueville, A. de (1961) *Democracy in America*, New York: Schocken Books.

Townsend, J. R. (1984) 'Politics in China', in Almond, G. A. and Powell, G. B. Jr. (eds) *Comparative Politics Today: A World View*, Boston: Little, Brown and Company.

Tu, W. (1990) *'Rujia ziwo yishi de fansi (Self Reflection on the Sense of Self Awareness of Confucianism)*, Taipei: Lianjing chubanshiye gongsi.

Verba, S. (1965) 'Comparative Political Culture', in Pye, L. W. and Verba, S. *Political Culture and Political Development*, Princeton, NJ: Princeton University Press.

Weber, M. (1930) *The Protestant Ethic and the Spirit of Capitalism*, trans. T. Parson, New York: Charles Scribner's Sons.

Further reading

Almond, G. A. (1990) *A Discipline Divided: Schools and Sects in Political Science*, Newbury Park, CA: Sage Publications.

Chilcote, R. H. (1981) *Theories of Comparative Politics: The Search for a Paradigm*, Boulder: CO: Westview.

Crothers, L. and Lockhart, C. (2000) (eds) *Culture and Politics: A Reader*, New York: St Martin's Press.

Hauss, C. (2000) *Comparative Politics: Domestic Responses to Global Challenges*, 3rd edn, Belmont, CA: Wadsworth.

Hua, S. P. (1995) *Scientism and Humanism: Two Cultures in Post-Mao China (1978–1989)*, Albany, NY: The State University of New York Press.

Johnson, J. B. and Joslyn, R.A. (1995) *Political Science Research Methods*, Washington, DC: CQ Press.

Kuhn, T. S. (1962) *The Structure of Scientific Revolutions*, Chicago: University of Chicago Press.

Leites, N. (1948) 'Psycho-Cultural Hypotheses about Political Acts', *World Politics*, 1: 102–19.

Manicas, P. (1987) *A History and Philosophy of Social Sciences*, Oxford: Basil Blackwell.

Plamenatz, J. (1970) *Ideology*, New York: Praeger.

Pye, L. W. (1976) *Mao Tse-tung – The Man in the Leader*, New York: Basic Books.

—— (1988) *The Mandarin and the Cadre: China's Political Cultures*, Ann Arbor, MI: Centre for Chinese Studies.

Sartori, G. (1969) 'Politics, Ideology, and Belief Systems', *American Political Science Review*, 63.

33

RELIGION AND POLITICS

Robin Lovin

Religion is a powerful motivating force in human life, including political life. The narratives, rituals, moral expectations, and philosophical formulations of religious traditions provide a comprehensive conception of the world and a motivation for action that seems grounded in enduring realities, rather than transitory interests (Geertz 1973: 90).

The political relevance of religious ideas, motives, and movements has become more apparent in recent years. With the end of the Cold War and the decline of ideological tensions between Marxism and liberal democracy, new attention has been focused on the dangers of civil strife and international conflict resulting from religious differences. While the long history of many of these conflicts has linked religion to ethnic identity, nationalistic aspirations, and class conflict, religion itself has an important, sometimes dominant role in defining the identity of the parties and sustaining their commitment to the conflict. At the same time, religion has claimed a larger role as a trans-national force, connecting persons across boundaries and motivating work for peace, human rights, and the relief of suffering. Religion may also connect the parties in local or regional conflicts to a wider global network of co-religionists who thus acquire a stake in the outcome of those conflicts.

Religious beliefs are not, however, only relevant to conflict and political change. Religion may also contribute to the legitimacy and stability of political systems by connecting them to sacred origins or moral purposes. Japanese mythology links the imperial dynasty to the sun goddess Amaterasu, while the Chinese emperors derived their power from a 'mandate of heaven'. Puritan colonists in North America saw divine providence in the success of their political commonwealth, while others, notably the Baptists, saw the religious neutrality of a non-sectarian government as a high moral achievement.

The historical relationships between religion and politics thus include both legitimation and resistance, both close identification between political power and divine will and sharp differentiation between secular and sacred authority. The purpose of this chapter is to review some of the theoretical frameworks in which these changing relationships have been understood. We will consider both functionalist and secularization theories, which provide the most general terms in which social scientists have understood the role of religion. We will then consider some of the limitations of

502

functionalism and secularization as accounts of the role of religion in political life, indicating ways in which religion may sustain communities and systems of belief which are neither simply reflections of the social order nor subject to the demands of secular rationality. Alternative religious communities and beliefs may form a differentiated centre of religious authority within a more comprehensive social and political framework, or they may attempt to isolate themselves from society's corrupting influences, but in either case the actions and beliefs of religious people will have political consequences in the wider society as a whole. Finally, increasingly in today's world, a religious community that finds its social context hostile to its faith and values may attempt a political transformation or overthrow of the wider society. With this full range of observed possibilities in mind, this chapter will conclude with a typology which suggests a pluralistic approach to the connections between religion and politics.

Functionalism

The widespread tendency of rulers and governments to draw on the legitimating power of religion suggests a functionalist account of religion's social role. Religions inspire the attitudes and commitments that politics require, and any substantial transformation of the political order necessarily overthrows the religious regime as well. A new political order requires a new religion, and every political system will eventually generate a religious affirmation of its basic beliefs and requirements.

Functionalist accounts of religion appear early in the modern era. Hobbes understood a 'Christian commonwealth' as one in which the sovereign controls religious ritual and doctrine with the same absolute authority that determines civil law. Here, the marks of a true prophet are the doing of miracles and 'not teaching any other Religion than that which is already established' (Hobbes 1968: 412). Rousseau provided for a 'civil religion' (*la religion civile*) as an essential feature of a society that would offer both individual freedom and social solidarity (Rousseau 1973: 268–77). Auguste Comte drew up plans for what he called 'positivism', a humanistic religion complete with nine 'social sacraments' (Comte 1891: 90).

The functional religion that Comte provided as part of his programme of religious and political reform appeared to some later social theorists as a feature of any stable social system. For Emile Durkheim, Catholicism had in an earlier age served the social purposes that Rousseau and Comte anticipated for civil religion and positivism (Durkheim 1965: 475). Historical changes may diminish the authority of a particular religion, or sweep it aside completely, but history cannot eliminate the need for a centre of devotion and enthusiasm that sustains moral unity in a people. Talcott Parsons draws on Durkheim's understanding of religion in his theoretical delineation of the role of religion in social systems (Parsons 1952: 368). Robert Bellah utilizes the concept of a 'civil religion' existing alongside and independent of organized religious traditions to explain the elements of religious aspiration and commitment that have characterized politics in the USA (Bellah 1967).

From this perspective, the politically relevant religion is just whatever system of beliefs provides this unifying, inspiring, and, for Bellah, self-critical and self-correcting function (Bellah 1975: 162). Alternative beliefs, even if they are related to a religious tradition, will either be rendered politically quiescent by the prevailing civil faith, or they will form communities of retreat and withdrawal for those who do not participate in political life. When social conditions change dramatically and people no longer adhere to the beliefs of their ancestors, traditional religions may shed little light on what is happening in society and politics. This does not mean, however, that religion has disappeared. It is necessary rather to probe for the 'invisible religion', the pervasive, persistent, but often unarticulated beliefs that provide the necessary foundation for shared social commitments (Luckmann, 1970).

Secularization

As an alternative to identifying a social function that describes religion's political role, other theorists have sought to trace a general pattern of historical development that links the fate of all religions in a variety of cultural contexts. Here, too, the roots of the argument lie early in modern social thought. Hume hypothesized that monotheism developed from a polytheism based in primitive humanity's vulnerability to the forces of nature (Hume 1927: 269–73). In the nineteenth century, James Frazer and Edward Tylor argued that a rational, scientific world view developed out of the failures of primitive magic and superstition (Evans-Pritchard 1965: 24–9). For these observers, the history, and perhaps the eventual disappearance, of religion was conditioned by the development of rationality.

Early in the twentieth century, Max Weber (1958, 1964) traced the impact of rationality on religion in social terms. Weber's views grew out of his study of the emergence of modern European capitalism and its relationship to the ethics of Protestant Christianity, but he later developed a general theory of history and of religion. In developed industrial society, religion has a far less important role than in the pre-modern world of Protestant piety. The disciplines which once depended on faith are now imposed by the bureaucratic and economic structures on which we all depend for a livelihood, structures which create, in Weber's grim image, an 'iron cage' in which we are all confined, and where we shall remain 'until the last ton of fossilized coal is burnt' (Weber 1958: 181).

Religion in such a society undergoes a process of secularization. Religion persists, at least in the sense that its ethics are incorporated into the *saeculum*, the order of the world itself; but the beliefs, institutions and authorities of such a religion become irrelevant. They lose their power to shape events or to mitigate the demands of economic rationality.

Later developments of secularization theory moderate Weber's tendency towards economic determinism, but they continue to stress the demands that rationality makes on all ways of thinking, including moral and religious thought. Ideas can be used only to the extent that they shed their pre-rational, affective orientation towards the world and make sense in terms of this modern understanding. Religious traditions may enhance our understanding of human aims and our appreciation of human dignity, but they can make these contributions only if they give up their historical particularities and the mythic presentations of their truth for the formulation of a rational morality (Horkheimer 1972: 129–31; Habermas 1984: 43–74).

Secularization theories call attention to important changes in the place of religion in modern society as contrasted to earlier ages and traditional cultures. The differentiation of artistic, economic and educational organizations from religious institutions reduces the importance of specific religious texts and symbols in intellectual and creative life, and religious leadership, like all leadership, becomes more specialized and professionalized. The prestige and authority once concentrated in religious institutions as centres of education and culture are now distributed among schools, museums, theatres and publishers, and the religious ceremonies that once provided generally shared opportunities for renewal and inspiration now serve the specifically religious needs of a limited number of worshippers.

Differentiation

Functionalist and secularization theories suggest that religions must inevitably either reinforce loyalty to the social group or yield to prevailing forms of rationality. Those tendencies are no doubt very strong, but it is important also to note the capacity of religion to create its own social organizations and to sustain systems of belief and ways of thinking that differ from the social standard.

Religious change may, of course, effect a revolution in the whole society, creating new political systems and educational institutions, reorganizing commerce, and redirecting military power while it generates new scriptures, rituals, and forms of devotion. In these cases, the socially creative power of religion overwhelms existing beliefs and practices and creates a new culture. While the predecessor culture is never completely obliterated, the transformation is so complete, and often so sudden, as to lead observers to see the result as a whole new society. The rise and rapid spread of Islam is a notable example of this kind of transformation (Hourani 1991: 7–79).

In other cases, a new religious movement enters an environment already dominated by strong political institutions. Such movements may be quickly crushed or domesticated, but they may also assert themselves as new and independent centres of authority. If they succeed, the result will be a differentiation within the society between moral or religious authority on the one hand and political authority on the other. Buddhism and Christianity, like Islam, spread widely in their early centuries, but Buddhism and Christianity counselled obedience to the established political powers. At the same time, however, they both created highly structured religious organizations that resisted coercion and began to exercise their own influences on the rulers. The *Sangha*, the order of Buddhist monks, provided counsellors to the princes of India and Southeast Asia and generated an important literature on the ideals of Buddhist rulership (Tambiah 1976: 32–3). Christian bishops formed a network of leadership that rivalled the organization of the Roman Empire (Drake 2000: 72–110).

This differentiation of religious from political authority is not inevitable, but once in place, it tends to persist, even when subsequent developments once again produce close links between religious and political powers. Christianity had a pervasive influence on the political institutions of medieval Europe, but the theologians still distinguished between spiritual and temporal authority. Once religious and political authorities have become clearly differentiated, even their cooperation is marked by an inherent tension, and the possibility of religious delegitimation or political coercion is always present. The threat of conflict colours even those moments when the two sources of authority enjoy the closest harmony and agreement.

There were distinctions between religious and secular authority and debates about their appropriate relationships in both Buddhism and Christianity long before secularization. Indeed, the earlier differentiation of spiritual and temporal authority may have contributed to the differentiation and rationalization of social functions in the modern age. Religious organizations which have adapted to this differentiation have an authority which resists secularization and which may survive enormous political changes. Consider, for example, the role of the Roman Catholic Church in Europe over the course of the twentieth century, or the persistent influence of Buddhism in Southeast Asia (Spiro 1982).

Such religious organizations have a more complex role in politics than functionalist theories assign them, and they are not as irrelevant as secularization theories would suggest. Religious organizations sustain beliefs and values that may shape political choices even where the political realm is overtly 'secular'. Religious ideas are politically relevant because they inform the choices which some citizens will make (Greenawalt 1988), and because they contribute to the whole society's discussion of human aims and purposes. While the public role of religion in many modern democracies often suggests a 'civil religion' joining the general celebration of values and loyalties that everyone shares, there is also a place for 'public religion' that articulates the more specific convictions of a religious tradition within the framework of public discourse (Thiemann 1996: 121–44). Such a religion need not be uncritical of prevailing laws and mores, but neither need it demand universal acceptance of its own doctrines to make its political choices intelligible.

Withdrawal and resistance

Precisely because religion provides a comprehensive explanation of reality and powerful motives for action, religion has unusual power to sustain organized communities, even where the religion is ignored, rejected, or persecuted. Such communities often begin with the aim of transforming the whole society, or with an apocalyptic expectation of the imminent end of the world. What is interesting about them sociologically is their ability to sustain themselves, often for a very long time, after the disappointment of their initial expectations.

Christian monasticism has been the paradigm case. Beginning with the withdrawal of individuals to a desert life of prayer and asceticism, monasticism developed into organized communities that often had a powerful impact on the economic and political environment from which they had ostensibly turned away. The process was repeated in Western Christianity at the time of the Protestant Reformation, as radical Protestants first demanded a social transformation in accordance with their religious ideals of freedom and equality, and then formed sectarian communities where they could live by their own rules in isolation from the wider society whose values they had rejected. These Christian communities, though never large, continue in existence to this day, and the idea of a sectarian group that sustains itself by strict internal discipline and explicit renunciation of the thoughts, values, and practices of the world around it has been has been elaborated as a sociological and anthropological model, applicable across a wide range of cultures and religious traditions (Wilson 1967; Douglas 1982: 114–24).

Sectarian groups have been studied more for their sociological and anthropological interest than for their political importance. Because they are small and readily identifiable, they are susceptible to persecution and control by government authorities, and their beliefs often reject political activities such as voting or holding public office. Even with these constraints, however, they may become significant advocates for minority groups of all sorts and exercise political power through the influence of their witness on a wider public. The vigilant, worldwide efforts of the Seventh-Day Adventists, linking their apocalyptic theology to campaigns for religious freedom and human rights, offer one instance of the political significance of sectarian religious ideas in secular contexts. For some Christian theologians, a sectarian rejection of the values of an individualist, consumption-orientated society built on the political use of force and violence marks an appropriate contemporary Christian stance (Yoder 1984). Similar movements can be found among contemporary followers of ascetic 'forest saints' in Southeast Asian Buddhism (Tambiah 1984). The political importance of these alternative organizations and belief systems may be large, even when their followers are relatively few in number.

The impact increases, however, when the religious groups take a stance of active opposition to values and practices in the wider society. This may include suppression of conduct that the group considers immoral, reform of educational systems in accordance with religious beliefs, or even overthrow of governments perceived as immoral or anti-religious. A religious group that goes beyond withdrawal from society to an active resistance to prevailing beliefs and practices usually holds the belief that the wider society is not merely indifferent to true religion, but actively hostile to it. Thus, fundamentalist groups which have emerged in recent decades in a wide variety of religious traditions in different parts of the world often believe that modern scientific thought and secular educational and political institutions have been devised specifically to undermine religion and prevent training in religious beliefs and practices. (Marty and Appleby 1991). The differentiation of religious, political, and educational institutions that typically accompanies modernization becomes suspect, and aggressive political action may be taken to assert religious control over all aspects of life. Such responses are likely to be even stronger if the modernization was imposed by a colonial power or results from adaptation to global economic changes. In recent years, such fundamentalist movements have initiated revolutions or offered major political challenges to governments across the Islamic world.

Secularization and persistence: a typology

Both functionalist and secularization theories tell us much about religion and politics. At the same time, the persistence of differentiated religious organizations and beliefs in modern societies reminds us that more complex relationships between religion and politics are possible, and the rise of fundamentalism warns us that the power of religious movements to influence political events may be much larger than either functionalism or secularization theory would lead us to predict. Over-reliance on these theories may cause both political leaders and political scientists to overlook significant groups and individuals who neither provide functional support for the political order nor yield to the requirements of modern, rationalized social and economic life.

The principal reason why the relations between religion and society and the political impact of religion cannot be reduced to a single model is the persistence of religious ideas themselves. Formed in a religious context, ideas about personal morality, obligations to family and associates, the acquisition and use of wealth, and the legitimacy and limits of power have remarkable tenacity in the face of changing ideas about productive rationality or political expedience. Confronted with material circumstances or political opposition, the leaders and communities who are the bearers of these ideas may adapt and modify them to fit the new conditions, or they may resist and create alternative forms of community and belief that will allow them to maintain traditional values. Either way, political possibilities will be altered by the specific norms that are given importance in the new social context, or by the presence of groups that challenge the functional social consensus.

Understanding the political implications of religious ideas thus requires a number of different models for the interaction. This has been well understood by historians, theologians and sociologists who have tried to understand the social thought of Christianity across the centuries (Troeltsch 1976) or to interpret the complexity of denominational Christianity in the USA (Niebuhr 1965; Roof and McKinney 1987). Ernst Troeltsch saw the history of Christian social teaching as the development of two basically different types of relationship between Christian teaching and social life, types he identified as 'church' and 'sect'. To those forms, he also added a distinctly modern 'mystical' type, which fails to take the institutionalized forms characteristic of church and sect (Troeltsch 1976: 729–802). H. Richard Niebuhr adapted this typology for constructive theological purposes, expanding Troeltsch's three types to a more differentiated five (Niebuhr 1956).

The need now, however, is for a typology that can be used for comparative purposes beyond the boundaries of Western Christianity. While Christianity provides us with important lessons in religion's adaptation to modernity, an account that draws the possibilities from Christianity alone will leave much out. The following typology is therefore offered as a scheme for organizing understandings of the relationships between religion and politics which may have some validity for other traditions and histories, as well as for Western Christianity. It suggests five principal forms which the relationship may take, though as with all such schemes, the types will be found in many variations, and the boundaries between different types may in practice be difficult to determine.

Legitimating religions offer consistent support and confer sacred authority on the political order. These religions may have existed in some form from the very beginnings of an ethnic or national history, and they continue to provide a distinctive sense of identity for a people as a whole. Traditional forms of Hinduism and Shinto, despite extensive changes through history, thus relate to the politics of India and Japan. In other cases, religious changes in historical times have taken place with such completeness that the events also represent a new political foundation. The expansion of Islam after 633 CE provides an example, as does, perhaps, the conversion of the Slavic peoples to Byzantine Christianity after c.860. In many of these cases, religious identity becomes closely associated with ethnic or national identity, and the ruler assumes some religious authority. At the same time, the religious tradition may set strong expectations about how the political authority is supposed to behave and what sort of justice the community may expect.

Differentiated religions acknowledge important distinctions between religion and other aspects of social life, such as government, economics, family life and education. While religious norms and values may permeate the whole society, differentiated religions place limits on religious authority and religious law. Concepts of natural law or moral consensus may allow for cooperation with members of other religious groups on issues of justice and social welfare, without requiring religious unanimity. Indeed, where the differentiations between religion, law and morality are well-developed and long-standing, it may be difficult to determine whether a specific normative position is or is not based on religious convictions. Western Christianity, particularly in modern liberal democracies, provides the clearest examples of differentiated religion. Buddhism, however, has often taken differentiated forms as it has moved into new contexts and, as with Christianity, Buddhism's capacity for differentiation and its relationship to a variety of political systems partly accounts for its success as a missionary religion. It is possible for at least some adherents of these religions to speak of a 'Christian society' or a 'Buddhist society' in terms of how the society treats the poor and/or how it uses military and judicial force, without a necessary connection to a particular form of political organization or a specific political role for religious authorities.

Sectarian religions maintain religious norms and values in the face of hostility or indifference from civil powers, or in dissent from the religious ideas of a dominant religious authority. Religious conceptions of the proper ordering of human life can adapt to a wide variety of circumstances, as differentiated religions demonstrate, but the religious ideas are not infinitely flexible. At some point, religious communities and leaders will see themselves in insurmountable opposition to the prevailing political or religious system, and they may at that point seek to preserve the possibility of religious life as an alternative community. Characteristically, sectarian religions withdraw from politics, eschewing both the burdens and the benefits of citizenship and often striving to maintain economic self-sufficiency. While the religious community may itself remain politically inactive, preferring even persecution to a political defence of its interests, sectarian religions none the less pose unavoidable questions for political life about how far the claims and obligations of citizenship extend and what the limits of conscientious dissent from societal norms will be.

Fundamentalist religions arise when religious groups with strong moral expectations and distinctive beliefs find themselves confronting beliefs that appear to them to be actively hostile to their own discipline and values. Often, these religions appear when a new set of dominant beliefs and values is imposed from outside, or when traditional believers are drawn into a new industrialized or urban environment. In fundamentalist religions, the difficulties posed by the new context patterns inspire a systematization of belief and ethics and coercive enforcement of the newly formulated requirements on members of the religious community, as well as attempts to make the standards normative for society as a whole. Contemporary Hindu and Islamic fundamentalists agitate for a return to traditional social patterns in which religion is central, and they sometimes take violent action against religious sites or social institutions that are perceived to represent the incursion of alien religions or of modern, secular ideas.

Individualist religions exist primarily in modern liberal societies that place a high value on individual freedom and may encompass many different religious traditions in the same state. Individualist religions thus reflect Troeltsch's observation that an individualistic 'mystical' type is the characteristically modern form of religious social organization, distinguished precisely by the fact that it does not create large, permanent religious institutions. While sectarian religions find the religious and moral neutrality of the modern secular state inimical to their religious life, individualist religions see it as a sphere of freedom in which persons can follow their own religious consciousness without seeking to impose it on others or making it conform to authoritative doctrines and practices. Because individualist religions usually accept the differentiation of religious beliefs from systems of law, government, and even from the basic norms of social morality, their political activity and impact is generally limited to support for norms of individual choice and religious freedom.

In each of these types – legitimating, differentiated, sectarian, fundamentalist, or individualist – religion provides the comprehensive explanations and orientations that enable people to understand their place in the political order as part of the ultimate reality in which they live and act. Because religious traditions hold definite ideas about that reality, the forms they can take and the politics they can support are limited, and specific traditions may become closely identified with a particular type. Because major traditions endure through history and take root in a variety of cultures, however, each of them will assume nearly every one of the characteristic types at one time or another.

Understanding the political dimension of a religious tradition begins by comprehending the affinities between its basic orientation toward life and the world and the types of relationships to politics outlined here, and identifying the ways of relating to social order and political power that are most congenial to the conception of ultimate order and power that this particular tradition holds. Estimating the political impact of religious belief, by contrast, requires attentiveness to the new or unusual types of relationships to politics that a religious tradition may take on in changing economic and cultural circumstances. In the last few centuries in the industrialized countries of the West, those circumstances have largely favoured Protestant Christianity and other traditions which have historically tended toward the differentiated type of religion. Other traditions, notably Judaism, that found themselves in those circumstances have developed previously uncharacteristic differentiated types. Social theory, which emerged simultaneously with these developments, has charted them well, but has also lent a certain sense of inevitability to the rise of differentiated and individualist types of religion. As our attention widens to include more of the world's religious traditions, and as the material circumstances that marked the rise of modern industrialism shift dramatically, our understanding of religion must also expand to include other religious types and to anticipate their impact on politics.

References

Bellah, R. N. (1967) 'Civil religion in America', *Daedalus* 96 (Winter): 1–21.
—— (1975) *The Broken Covenant*, New York: Seabury Press.
Comte, A. (1891) *The Catechism of Positive Religion*, London: Kegan Paul.
Durkheim, E. (1965) *The Elementary Forms of the Religious Life*, New York: Free Press.
Douglas, M. (1982) *Natural Symbols*, New York: Pantheon Books.
Drake, H. A. (2000) *Constantine and the Bishops: The Politics of Intolerance*, Baltimore: Johns Hopkins University Press.

Evans-Pritchard, E. E. (1965) *Theories of Primitive Religion*, Oxford: Oxford University Press.

Geertz, C. (1973) 'Religion as a cultural system', in C. Geertz (ed.) *The Interpretation of Cultures*, New York: Basic Books.

Greenawalt, K. (1988) *Religious Convictions and Political Choice*, New York: Oxford University Press.

Habermas, J. (1984) *Theory of Communicative Action*, vol. 1, trans. T. McCarthy, Boston: Beacon Press.

Hobbes, T. (1968) *Leviathan*, ed. with intro. C. B. Macpherson, Baltimore, MD: Penguin.

Horkheimer, M. (1972) *Critical Theory*, trans. M. J. O'Connell, New York: Continuum.

Hourani, A. H. (1991) *A History of the Arab Peoples*, Cambridge, MA: Harvard University Press.

Hume, D. (1927) 'The natural history of religion', in C. W. Hendel (ed.) *Hume: Selections*, New York: Charles Scribner's Sons.

Luckmann, T. (1970) *The Invisible Religion: The Problem of Religion in Modern Society*, London: Macmillan.

Marty, M. E., and Appleby, R. S. (eds) (1991) *Fundamentalisms Observed*, Chicago: University of Chicago Press.

Niebuhr, H. R. (1956) *Christ and Culture*, New York: Harper & Row.

—— (1965) *The Social Sources of Denominationalism*, Cleveland: World Publishing.

Parsons, T. (1952) *The Social System*, London: Tavistock Publications.

Roof, W. C. and McKinney, W. (1987) *American Mainline Religion*, New Brunswick: Rutgers University Press.

Rousseau, J.-J. (1973) *The Social Contract and Discourses*, rev. edn, London: J. M. Dent & Sons.

Spiro, M. (1982) *Buddhism and Society: A Great Tradition and Its Burmese Vicissitudes*, 2nd edn, Berkeley: University of California Press.

Tambiah, S. J. (1976) *World Conqueror and World Renouncer*, Cambridge: Cambridge University Press.

—— (1984) *The Buddhist Saints of the Forest and the Cult of Amulets*, Cambridge: Cambridge University Press.

Thiemann, R. (1996) *Religion in Public Life: A Dilemma for Democracy*, Washington, DC: Georgetown University Press.

Troeltsch, E. (1976) *The Social Teaching of the Christian Churches*, trans. O. Wyon, 2 vols, Chicago: University of Chicago Press.

Weber, M. (1958) *The Protestant Ethic and the Spirit of Capitalism*, trans. T. Parsons, New York: Charles Scribner's Sons.

—— (1964) *The Sociology of Religion*, trans. E. Rischoff, Boston: Beacon Press.

Wilson, B., (ed.) (1967) *Patterns of Sectarianism*, London: Heinemann Educational Books.

Yoder, J. H. (1984) *The Priestly Kingdom: Social Ethics as Gospel*, Notre Dame, IN: University of Notre Dame Press.

Further reading

Barth, K. (1960) *Community, State, and Church: Three Essays*, Garden City, NY: Doubleday.

Bellah, R. N. (1965) *Religion and Progress in Modern Asia*, New York: Free Press.

—— (1967) 'Civil religion in America', *Daedalus* 96 (Winter): 1–21.

Fingarette, H. (1972) *Confucius: The Secular as Sacred*, New York: Harper & Row.

Gutiérrez, G. (1973) *A Theology of Liberation: History, Politics and Salvation*, Maryknoll, NY: Orbis.

Hauerwas, S. (1985) *Against the Nations: War and Survival in a Liberal Society*, Minneapolis: Winston Press.

Lewis, B. (1988) *The Political Language of Islam*, Chicago: University of Chicago Press.

Locke, J. (1983) *A Letter Concerning Toleration*, ed. H. Tully, Indianapolis: Hackett Publishing.

Marty, M. E. and Appleby, R. S. (eds) (1993) *Fundamentalisms and the State: Remaking Politics, Economics, and Militance*, Chicago: University of Chicago Press.

Milbank, J. (1990) *Theology and Social Theory: Beyond Secular Reason*, Oxford: Blackwell.

Martin, D. (1978) *A General Theory of Secularization*, New York: Harper & Row.

McBrien, R. P. (1987) *Caesar's Coin*, New York: Macmillan.

Niebuhr, H. R. (1956) *Christ and Culture*, New York: Harper & Row.

Niebuhr, R. (1960) *The Children of Light and the Children of Darkness*, New York: Charles Scribner's Sons.

Tambiah, S. J. (1976) *World Conqueror and World Renouncer*, Cambridge: Cambridge University Press.

Tinder, G. (1989) *The Political Meaning of Christianity*, Baton Rouge: Louisiana State University Press.

Troeltsch, E. (1976) *The Social Teaching of the Christian Churches*, 2 vols, trans. O. Wyon, Chicago: University of Chicago Press.

Walzer, M. (1987) *Exodus and Revolution*, New York: Basic Books.

Watt, W. M. (1968) *Islamic Political Thought: The Basic Concepts*, Edinburgh: Edinburgh University Press.

Yoder, J. H. (1984) *The Priestly Kingdom: Social Ethics as Gospel*, Notre Dame, IN: University of Notre Dame Press.

34

THE POLITICS OF RACE AND RACISM

Shamit Saggar

When the writer and sometime Pan African activist, W. E. B. DuBois, wrote that 'the problem of the twentieth century is the problem of the colour line', it would be fair to say that he did not have the emerging research priorities of political science in mind. Throughout the course of the century, the relationship between race and politics has always tended to occupy a fairly esoteric status within the established political science literature. Whilst it would be misleading to claim that race has been ignored by the discipline, it is certainly the case that the interest of scholars in race-related issues has been led by other areas of concern. Racial conflict and related policy issues have not occupied a major strand within academic writing; however, the research that there has been in this field has been primarily focused on major – and more familiar – questions of political science and political philosophy such as democracy, representation and power. An illustration of this conditional interest can be seen in Myrdal's 1944 study of race relations in the USA, *An American Dilemma*, which clearly sought to address itself to the application of democracy in the first democratic nation (Myrdal 1944). Indeed, the more one examines the literature in this field, the more one is struck by the extent of scholars' interest in the subject matter for broader purposes.

Notwithstanding the latent motives underscoring academic research in this field, it is important to note that *specifically* political analyses of race and racism remain relatively sparse and underdeveloped compared with other disciplines of social enquiry. Chief amongst this larger and longer developed literature has been the contribution of sociology and, to a lesser degree, social psychology and social anthropology (see for example Park 1950; Cox 1948; Barth 1969; Hechter, Friedman and Applebaum 1982; Weinreich 1986).

The aim of this essay is to explore the contribution of political studies of race and racism. A cursory glance at writing in this field will reveal a preponderance of research on, *inter alia*, the electoral participation of racial and ethnic minorities, state immigration policy, public policy governing minority–majority relations, race and class, and autonomous black political thought and activity. The attention of empirical political scientists has tended to fall on the former two areas, whilst the emphasis of recent theoretical debates has been centred around the latter areas.

An essay such as this must be selective in its approach and coverage. As a survey it cannot hope to be comprehensive and, therefore, certain themes and debates are given greater attention than others. The purpose is to draw together and discuss several central themes found in the literature, and to evaluate the broad trends in the volume of research. The interests of researchers, however, have tended to be patchy and clustered around several major topics and approaches.

The main body of this discussion comprises six parts. First, a number of preliminary points are considered that serve to shape the nature of our survey of the literature. Second, an overview is presented of some of the substantial findings of research on race and politics. Third, the dominant institutional and behavioural framework of research in this field is examined. Fourth, attention is given to the largely neglected debate on race and political power. Fifth, the commonly overlooked work of students of comparative race politics is explored. Finally, the article concludes with a brief discussion of trends and priorities in the future agenda of research on race and politics.

Maps and compasses

It is worth pausing to consider some of the reasons why race has become an interesting subject of study in terms of politics. We cannot merely assume that the literature represents a uniform and consistent approach to race issues in political affairs. It does not. Moreover, a number of theoretical, conceptual and empirical approaches have characterized the study of race and politics.

First, explicit racial conflict has frequently been presented as a factor guiding research interest. Illustrations can be found in the writing on the US civil rights movement, non-white immigration to western Europe, and South African race relations (see for example Preston, Henderson and Puryear 1982; Miles 1982; and Wolpe 1970; Hansen 2000, respectively). Whilst much of this material has proved to be illuminating, the theoretical basis for it has varied considerably. One such dominant theoretical approach has been the Parsonian functionalist tradition that purports an often unwieldy and rather deterministic societal-level explanation for racial conflict and its underlying causes. The specifically race-related aspects of racial conflict appear to hold little interest, and the overall thrust of this approach is weakened as a consequence.

Second, much of the research has been governed by the familiar reductionist themes and principles of academic scholarship. Much sociological writing for instance, notably within the Marxist and Weberian traditions, seeks to account for and explain the relationship between race and politics in terms of detached and unbending theoretical criteria. Consequently it is rarely found embracing a multiplicity of explanatory approaches (see for example the Centre for Contemporary Cultural Studies 1982; Rex 1981). The result is that research is peculiarly handicapped by the lack of multi-theoretical approaches. Political scientists have been afflicted by such theoretical narrowness no less than their sociologist counterparts.

This leads to a third factor involved in this field of study: unlike the volumes of sociology or social policy literature, the political analysis of race and racism remains comparatively atheoretical. By this it is not meant that political scientists have been entirely unconcerned about theoretical questions to do with race, but rather that their efforts have tended to be fairly empirically led and less noticeably bogged down in sectarian disputes of theory (so often a hallmark of the volume of sociological writing in this field). The problems encountered in the political analysis of race have undoubtedly been confounded by the relative absence of deep theoretical foundations. Political science research has consequently tended to become highly empirical in purpose and content, and rests heavily upon the much stronger theoretical foundations of sociological race research. For example, Katznelson's comparison of the experiences of racial politics in Britain and the USA, *Black Men, White Cities* (Katznelson 1976), although heavily theoretical in its scope and aims, appears to take its cue from a number of essentially non-political science debates. In noting the dearth of comparative studies of race and politics, Katznelson correctly emphasizes the obvious, yet often absent, centrality of politics to studies of race:

> By themselves, the physical facts of race are of little or no analytical interest. Racial-physical characteristics assume meaning only when they become criteria of stratification. Thus studies of race inescapably put politics – which, fundamentally, is about organized inequality – at the core of their concern.
>
> (Katznelson 1976: 14)

Fourth, the study of racial tensions and conflicts has a number of obvious implications for political stability. Banton cites the example of Enoch Powell's critical contribution to debates in British politics on the question of nationhood in a multiracial society (Banton 1986: 51–2). Claims about the supposed racial and ethnic building-blocks of the modern nation-state and worries about political stability were clearly at the core of Powell's message. Sensing an underlying concern for the viability of British nationhood in a rapidly transformed multiracial society, Powell argued that:

> Our response has been to attempt to force upon ourselves a non-identity and to assert that we have no unique distinguishing characteristics.... A nation which deliberately denies its continuity with its past and its rootedness in its homeland is on the way to repudiate its own existence.
>
> (quoted in Banton 1986: 52)

Finally, political scientists, in common with social scientists at large, have turned their attention to race with at least one eye on the need to formulate universal truths. In a number of cases they have failed to do so and the result has been a preponderance of over-generalizations about the link between race and politics. A further associated fault has been the extent of unrefined approaches to, and claims made about, racial and ethnic minority political action. To be sure, at the basic yet critical level of nomenclature, writers concerned with describing non-white political behaviour (all too) frequently speak of 'the black community' or 'black politics' and similar terms. The difficulty with doing so is that these overarching terms may deny the tremendous degree of internal diversity within such minority populations (Modood and Werbner 1997). In Britain, for instance, a strong debate has been generated on this theme, with several commentators at pains to stress the deep running yet historically smothered distinctions which exist between not merely African and Caribbean and South Asian-origin groups but also between sub-groups within these larger groups (see for example Banton 1977; Smith 1989; Robinson 1986).

Within government, the internal differentiation among different black and Asian groups is now openly acknowledged as a tool for informing policy. Moreover, a recent Cabinet Office study of the labour market accepted that Britain was characterized by both high and low achieving ethnic minority groups and that a number of circumstantial factors to do with housing, mobility, education, and social networks all played a role in this outcome (Cabinet Office 2002). The distinctions found in the labour market ensure that the notion of 'ethnic minorities' is an increasingly obsolete concept for evidence-based policy-making. The labour market experiences of a typical first generation female immigrant of Pakistani origin living in the north of England appear to bear little or no resemblance to those of a second generation Indian origin male located in suburban London. The upshot is that empirical social science needs to be better grounded not just in these fairly obvious variations but also in the political and policy ramifications to which they are likely to point.

The argument is largely one concerned with preserving and resurrecting the notion of ethnicity in both practical and analytical terms. It is claimed that the distinction and precision of ethnic identity lies at the heart of the experience – and therefore politics – of these minority groups. Although it is indeed the case that the bulk of the literature stands collectively guilty of such myopia, we should none the less be cautious in our abandonment of the traditional race categories and relationships of social science enquiry. For one thing, the persistence of racially exclusionary policies, practices and routines, both by public agencies as well as by private groups and individuals, suggests that the emphasis should continue to rest with established racial umbrella categories, albeit at the risk of over-generalization (Blumer and Duster 1980; Husbands 1983; Smith 1989). Further, social science students of race need always to guard against the temptation of allowing their research strategies and priorities to be guided solely by the dicta of so-called grassroots action research. As Mason notes in relation to one example of such a research strategy (Ben-Tovim *et al.* 1986), 'what may result...is not so much research in the service of the oppressed as manipulation of researchers by minority interest groups or the rule of the mob' (Mason 1986: 14).

Racial conflict and political processes

Many of the substantive studies of the race–politics nexus have tended to concentrate on a number of important questions about political behaviour. These have included, for example, the relationship between racial groups and levels and forms of political participation, single-issue interest group activity, and group mobilization towards areas of political protest and/or violence. Starting from this perspective, it is possible to see the different ways in which race has shaped not merely formal political processes but also a wide range of underlying social tensions including, *inter alia*, differential public service delivery and competition for scarce resources in urban political environments. Of course, the question that much of this research leads to is the extent to which race plays either a determining or conditioning role. Or put another way, do black people – and indeed other less or non-racialized ethnic minority groups – in a society such as the USA differ from their white counterparts in terms of the level and type of public service consumption or political participation as a result of their racial background or because of other factors such as economic or educational status? Of course, the most immediate rejoinder to this kind of question is to acknowledge that it is the degree to which race-specific or related characteristics condition behaviour that really matters. Indeed, precisely because of very strong patterns of conditioning – as seen in say the Democratic Party's domination of the black vote – that it is easy to miss the vital influence of other factors. The use of multivariate analysis has been one particularly useful technique in casting light on these kinds of influence. Race, as many US electoral observers have commented, does undoubtedly trump class in the voting patterns of the black electorate but, crucially, this does not deny the impact and significance of class-based political outlooks and behaviour. In terms of the research that has been carried out on this broad question, it seems that, whilst a certain amount of correlation between race and political behaviour has been established, the task of demonstrating causal explanation has proved more difficult.

The significance of race as a concept frequently stems from its potential as an exclusionary variable. Thus its capacity to give focus to shared values and backgrounds cannot be underestimated, since, unlike other similar variables, it usually operates in an unambiguous, dichotomous manner. Social class, ethnic group, regional origin, generational cohort and other familiar variables of political analysis differ from race in that they exhibit various degrees of internal overlap and conceptual imprecision. In contrast, the political impact of race, whilst regularly burdened by theoretical and empirical confusion with that of collective ethnic group action, has been analysed in rather clearer and more tangible terms. To take the well-documented example of residential segregation between black and white communities in the USA, researchers have encountered *relatively* few methodological difficulties in assigning individual behaviour to forms of group cohesion. The difficulty that arises is being able to account for political action based on such cohesion, particularly in the absence of external constraints fuelling racially specific shared interests such as legally sanctioned force (as in South Africa since the early 1960s) or technical obstacles to electoral participation (as in parts of the USA until the mid-1960s). It is not sufficient to suppose that discrimination alone will result in collective political action on the basis of race, although there is plenty of scope for it do so. The processes behind such action, if it is to occur, are commonly more complex and involve a wide range of social interaction between, and political integration of, different racial groups (Verba and Nie 1972: 149–73; Saggar 2000).

The voting behaviour of ethnic minority groups in advanced industrial states appears to confirm this point. Studlar (1983), Williams (1982), St Angelo and Puryear (1982) and Saggar (2000) have all pointed to variance in black and other ethnic minority voting patterns in Britain and the USA. They show that black voters do *not* respond uniformly to their shared experiences as subjects of discrimination or exclusion. However, what is equally important is the generally high level of similar voting patterns among ethnic minority groups. Using survey data from 1997 and 2001, Saggar has written about the 'iron law' of black and Asian voting in the UK whereby, for almost thirty years, four in five of all black and Asian votes that were cast went to the Labour Party. The importance of this is not to be understated since it showed the loyalty or stickiness of the party's support from one section of the electorate regardless of Labour's wider standing with the electorate at large.

Of course, racial differences are not only significant in terms of their impact on formal political participation, but are also closely intertwined with the distribution of power. Indeed, in several polities that have been characterized by overt legal discrimination on racial grounds, underlying power relations have served to exclude certain groups from key social and economic resources. In doing so, the skewed picture of control and influence below the level of formal participation served to reflect what was already apparent at the level of mass party politics. Moreover, as Wilson reminds us, the power relationship between racial groups is invariably uneven: 'Differential power is a marked feature of racial-group interaction in complex societies; the greater the power discrepancy between subordinate and dominant racial groups, the greater the extent and scope of racial domination' (Wilson 1978: 18). But why should domination necessarily extend beyond the political realm? The response to this question must point to sociological and historical understanding of power as a multi-faceted concept which goes further than the use of coercive force in the face of interest confrontation. Economic and cultural dependency, for example, are both key forms through which domination has occurred 'and facilitated the emergence of still another, more sophisticated form of control: psychosocial dominance' (Baker 1983: 80). This historical process was exemplified by the former white-dominated South African and Rhodesian cases, but it is important to note that, despite great emphasis placed on coercive and structural dominance, it has perhaps been the psychosocial that has had the most enduring consequences (Baker 1983: 81). The counter-forces of black African nationalism have been conspicuous by their diluted impact in both these societies compared with numerous other post-colonial African states. Moreover, as many writers have commented, white hegemony in terms of cultural awareness and discussion of inter-race power relations has transcended the nominal southern African divide, and is manifest in several diverse multi-racial societies. For example, the adoption of European-based parliamentary systems by a number of black African states following post-war struggles for independence has inevitably shaped political development in ways that have sometimes been in conflict with local circumstances.

The relative inability of these states to reform their political infrastructures – beyond that associated with large-scale political violence – is perhaps further testimony to the persisting dominance of European, Enlightenment-based philosophical assumptions concerning representation and individual rights. Moreover, as Smith (1986: 223–5) notes, considerable problems of political instability have occurred in many black African states owing to their diverse plural compositions and structures; in a number of cases such as Nigeria, Sierra Leone, Uganda, Ethiopia and Chad this mismatch has been closely linked to the colonial legacies of past European-imposed constitutional–legal settlements (Davidson 1983). Elsewhere, a succession of civil rights leaders in the USA have observed, and constructed quasi political issues over, the lexicon of race in political debate. In the 1960s radical black leaders in the USA fashioned a new rejectionist philosophy of anger leading to positive mobilization of black communities. Central to their analysis was opposition to perceived white-dominated cultural categories that had historically viewed black thought and contributions as marginal to mainstream society. In this context a campaign was launched for black self-awareness in which it was declared, 'I am a man – I am somebody', a cry echoed during the 1980s by the Rev. Jesse Jackson's call for the hyphenated term 'African-American' to displace 'black' as the collective reference for the black minority he (then) sought to lead.

Some of the sharpest and most interesting political conflicts based on race have been the product of inequalities in public service provision. The policy process, whilst rather neglected as a focus of empirical investigation outside the USA, serves as a useful arena of study for those interested in questions ranging from the formation of policy agendas through to evaluation of programme outcomes. Studlar and Layton-Henry's important essay (1990) highlighted the comparatively limited resources of black and Asian citizens to affect the agenda of race policy. Rather, the agenda has been highly crisis-led, *ad hoc* in treatment of specific race-related issues, and atomized in the formation of clearly identifiable policy networks or communities. Saggar (1991) has argued that the origin of many of these problems can be traced back to the liberal settlement in British race relations which served to constrain public policy debate away from overt discussion of racial inequality and instead placed a premium upon the attainment of short-term racial harmony.

Policy-orientated research in the USA has been fairly substantial. But even here it seems, researchers are aware of the problems associated with examining modes and scales of participation in isolation from wider political analyses of power and influence. In their major study of political participation in the USA, Verba and Nie (1972: 172–3) concluded that sharp black–white disparities were apparent, particularly in the area of the establishment and maintenance of direct contact(s) with government officials. However, the blocking of black citizens from a key channel of influence occurred in the context of generally poor and ineffective black participation; but the race factor itself, they argued, appeared to provide a major, often underutilized factor around which group consciousness could be 'a great resource for political involvement' (ibid.).

Sharp disparities in black–white experience in employment, education and housing in the USA have been confirmed by empirical evidence. US evidence shows that black members of the labour market suffered widespread discrimination in applying for vacancies as well as in attaining similar status and remuneration to their white counterparts once in work. For example, whilst the period 1964–79 shows there to have been a one-third improvement in the representation of black male graduate managers, they still remained under-represented in relation to their white counterparts by a factor of one-quarter. Research by the UK Cabinet Office (2002) has pointed to more recent similar patterns in both the UK and US labour markets. Despite continuing significant levels of labour market discrimination against black workers, the scale of reduction in discrimination achieved since the 1964 Civil Rights Act has impressed some commentators. One such commentator, William Wilson, has viewed this process as part of an irreversible absorption of black Americans into the mainstream class structure. In his landmark study, *The Declining Significance of Race*, he argues that:

> Race relations in America have undergone fundamental changes in recent years, so much so that now the life chances of individual blacks have more to do with their economic class position than their day-to-day encounters with whites.
>
> (Wilson 1978: 1)

This important thesis has been generally greeted with controversy in the debate on black–white relations in the USA. For one thing, it appeared to challenge the established view that saw black political participation in purely or largely racial terms. Moreover, it provided the groundwork for a neo-conservative attack on existing perceptions of racism hindering the socio-economic progress of black Americans. Wilson's alternative explanation for lower black performance in economic competition with white Americans claimed that such differential attainment was broadly in line with differences in educational and other skills associated with the promotion of individual life chances. Certainly Wilson has not stood alone in advancing such a neo-conservative perspective and was joined by the publication of David Kirp's *Doing Good by Doing Little* (1979) and *Just Schools* (1982). In these books Kirp contended that both British and US educational policy makers (Kirp 1979 and 1982 respectively) ought to return to so-called 'colourblind' approaches to publicly funded school programmes. He emphasized in particular three factors working against the use of racially determined public education programmes in the USA: first, since their high water mark in the early 1970s, there had been a general decline in the public's faith in government intervention to ensure integration; second, the period had also witnessed a secular fall-off in public perceptions of government having a strong role to play in many aspects of society; and third, and most crucial of all, the black constituency itself reported increased disillusionment with the prospects for, and necessity of, an integrated system of public education.

Institutional and behavioural politics

In common with the major trends in political science since the 1950s, specialist studies of race and politics have tended to follow mainly institutional and behavioural frameworks of enquiry. That is to say, the rise of racially plural societies – most notably in European and north American countries – has had a number of important consequences for the operation of different political systems. These consequences, commonly impacting on areas such as party competition, labour migration and civil rights policies, have captured the attention of researchers and have been at the forefront of research in this field (see for example Welch and Secret 1981; Layton-Henry and Rich 1986; Welch and Studlar 1985; Pinderhughes 1987; Saggar 2000; Ali and O'Cinneide 2002). Institutional and behavioural approaches have thus dominated investigations of the race–politics nexus and, to that extent, the literature does not present us with any new or particularly novel questions for the understanding of this topic.

This guiding framework includes a number of specific areas of study involving the political impact of race. An example of one such area has been that of state immigration policy, which has resulted in a veritable trove of research on the Western European experience in particular (Rogers 1985; Freeman 1979; Castles, Booth and Wallace 1984; Brubaker 1992; Hollifield 1999; Hansen 2000). The policies of various national governments to fill domestic labour shortages through foreign recruitment in the 1950s and 1960s came to have an increasingly politicized dimension by the 1970s and 1980s. The popular-cum-electoral politicization of these policies came about not least because of the non-European origin of much of the labour force involved in this process, and the negative anti-immigrant backlash it provoked in many receiving countries. A number of writers have emphasized the economically related aspects of such immigration policies and their eventual reversal during the 1970s and 1980s. Writing on the former West German case, Katzenstein argued that the appearance of the immigration issue in domestic politics compelled 'policy makers to confront the social consequences of decisions made largely for economic reasons' (Katzenstein 1987: 213). Elsewhere the electoral spoils of explicit anti-immigrant platforms have been seen most vividly in Britain (during the 1970s) France (beginning in the 1980s and peaking in the 2002 presidential run-off), Denmark (where a far right, anti-immigration party made up part of the governing coalition after 2001), The Netherlands (where anti-immigrant political sentiment reached a peak in 2002) and Austria (whose national political landscape has been scarred by such sentiment since the late 1990s). The *Front National* run-off against Chirac in the French presidential contest, the inclusion of far right parties in the Austrian and Danish centre-right coalitions, and the anti-immigrant zeal of the Berlusconi first and second administration in Italy, are all cases in point.

Writers have not limited themselves to state immigration policy in a narrow sense but have also extended their interest to matters concerning the processes underlying and resulting from the politicization of immigration. Interest has grown, for example, in areas such as the political rights of immigrant workers (Layton-Henry 1989), the experience of racism and racially exclusionary public policies (Castles, Booth and Wallace 1984), and the anti-immigrant backlash of the right (Husbands 1989). However, the thrust of this literature has emerged from within the conventional lines that have shaped the discipline and, in general, has not attempted to challenge or reach beyond them. The interpretations of political scientists and commentators were thus able to note and dispense with the politics of race with comparative ease. Underlying conflicts and issues of power relations involving race have been largely neglected for the same reason that such broader critical approaches to political analysis were themselves overlooked and relegated to the fringes of the discipline for so long. For example, almost two decades ago, writers on British politics such as Dearlove and Saunders (1984) have argued that preoccupations with narrow views of politics will preclude fuller understanding not only of British politics as a whole but also of key interlocking aspects of the broader picture (such as divisions of race, gender, and so on). The political analysis of race has usually taken as its frame of reference an unsatisfactorily narrow view of politics and, in doing so, has merely replicated the dominant scholastic frameworks of the discipline, but on a smaller scale.

Race and political power

Researchers have broadened their theoretical and conceptual starting points for the understanding of race and politics in important and exciting ways. At least part of this process can be attributed to underlying shifts of emphasis within the discipline away from the strong institutional and behavioural preoccupations of the past. The political analysis of social divisions and inequalities has been one area of renewed interest, reflecting the major reappraisals within the discipline that occurred during the 1970s. Undoubtedly, the most voluminous and significant research in the field of race and politics emanated from the USA in the half-century after the 1930s. The main driver of interest has been questions pertaining to US democracy and, in the last thirty years, the location of power in the mosaic of social, political and economic relationships which are to be found in US cities (Myrdal 1944; Glazer and Moynihan 1963; Greenstone and Peterson 1973; Pinderhughes 1987).

Borrowing heavily from the findings of studies of social policy, a handful of political scientists have turned to examine the political causes and consequences of racial inequality stemming from discrimination and disadvantage. For example, Glazer and Young (1983) present a timely comparative exposition of the public policy considerations in the old (Britain) and new (USA) worlds. One of the more interesting conclusions of this comparison is the extent to which policy content and substance are shaped by underlying dominant philosophies and belief systems. The predisposition found in the USA towards the practice of making groups the principal subjects of public policy (in contrast to Britain where policy discussion (then) remained stalled at the definition of policy subjects as geographic areas), is held to be one of the most significant factors explaining the differences in experience of race policy. Furthermore, Glazer notes that the US political system contains many more separate points at which policy can be created and carried out than in Britain; the result, he reports, is that US policy makers possess something of a head start in the development of issues of racial and ethnic pluralism in the policy process (Glazer 1983: 1–7). In the more recent times there is evidence to support the claim that Britain's race policy agenda has shifted in the direction of long-standing US debates. The publication of the MacPherson Report in 1999, followed by the enactment of the 2000 Race Relations (Amendment) Act, both served to establish a much stronger group rights political culture in Britain. With these critical concepts now firmly on the domestic political agenda, it remains to be seen as to how far questions of race and racism have penetrated the mainstream of domestic policy-making (Griffith and Leonard 2002).

The transatlantic contrasts do not stop there. Indeed, they have been an important source of comparison for researchers interested in the underlying influence of political culture on policy choices and dilemmas involving race. Debates have taken place at several levels, ranging from the theoretical discussion of liberal democratic power structures to empirically based policy studies. For example, Gordon observes the constraining influence – and indeed clash – of value systems between 'the principles of equal treatment and individual meritocracy [and] principles that call upon group compensation for undeniable past injuries' (Gordon 1981: 181). The evolving pluralist tradition within the discipline has been a dominant and attractive paradigmatic starting point for writers such as Glazer who have somewhat over-celebrated the capacity of

> Anglo-Saxon political tradition…to accept a remarkable degree of pluralism, not only in culture and society, but also in politics. It offers hope that we may yet manage to contain these problems of ethnic and racial diversity and to become richer societies as a result.
>
> (Glazer 1983: 6)

The restatement of the liberal, pluralist ideal of a multi-racial society that this view embodied is, of course, a familiar feature of the literature not merely on race and politics but also on the distribution of political power. The inclusion of wider questions to do with power structures and relations underpinning pluralist views of the politics of race have generally been overlooked, although students of power in

US cities have been keen to redress this imbalance (see for example the landmark analysis of racial power relations in city politics by Bachrach and Baratz 1970: 3–16). In seeking to explore behind the political structures inherent in cosy pluralist orthodoxies, they cite the following important remarks of Schattschneider:

> All forms of political organization have a bias in favour of the exploitation of some kinds of conflict and the suppression of others because *organization is the mobilization of bias*. Some issues are organized into politics while other are organized out.
>
> (Schattschneider 1960: 71)

The pluralist interpretation contains important conceptions of the context and framework shaping public policy. These involve conceptualization of the relationship between race and politics at a very general level and issues of race in the policy process more precisely (Banton 1985; Saggar 1991). There are at least four major problems associated with the pluralist approach to these questions. First, as Bachrach and Baratz (1970) are at pains to point out, the unchallenged and comprehensive inclusion of race issues into urban politics and policy process cannot be taken for granted. Indeed, on the basis of their evidence from a medium-sized US city, the opposite seems to be the case. Urban politics may be conducted within a guiding framework that, put simply, leaves out race. This may be done through a combination of two processes. Policy makers may refuse to give explicit legitimacy to issues of race and ethnicity or, as is more usually the case, they may routinely absorb and effectively deflect such issues into the otherwise common 'colour-blind' approach of public agencies. Another related difficulty emerges from the concept of 'non-decision-making' in urban politics. The maintenance of 'colour-blindness' constitutes a major mobilization of bias away from open recognition of the legitimacy of race issues and conflicts. In failing to give such recognition, urban policy makers can be said to be engaging in the 'suppression or thwarting of a latent or manifest challenge to [their] values or interests' (Bachrach and Baratz 1970: 44). Of course, the validity of this view remains to be empirically tested and it may be that the evidence suggests that non-decision-making has given way to a new phase of highly active decision-making which serves to incorporate formally the race dimension into the policy process. However, even here, a third problem can be identified whereby forms of co-option and participatory democracy, as Selznick put it, 'gives the opposition the illusion of a voice without the voice itself and so stifles opposition without having to alter policy in the least' (quoted in Coleman 1957: 17). Finally, recent research reveals that race-related policy debate has been focused towards questions of direct discriminatory behaviour at the expense of subtler questions to do with the indirect discriminatory impact of the routines, procedures and established norms of public policy. The primary factor responsible for this narrow conceptualization of race in the policy process, argues Saggar (1991), has been the 'liberal policy framework' of British race relations established in the 1960s. Racial harmony presided as the chief policy goal of this framework, something which Hill and Issacharoff (1971: 284) remind us is by no means the same thing as – and may be detrimental to – racial equality. Writing about London local politics, Saggar reports that policy discussion remained restricted to comparatively 'safe' issues and ensured that:

direct [race] conflicts often failed to see the light of day and many issues were labelled 'off limits' even before they were discussed. It [was] often easiest to disarm rivals or challengers by claiming that they [did] not support the legitimate 'ground-rules' of the existing policy framework.

(Saggar 1991: 26)

These interpretations suggest that the explanatory emphasis should turn to focus more sharply on the factors that develop and sustain competing value systems – or the mobilization of bias as this variable is more commonly known. The routine and successful influence of such systems in politics and policy processes is, after all, an area that has gained greater exposure in the discipline in recent years. In short, these and other studies in the same vein represent an abandonment of the narrow institutional and behavioural concerns of political scientists interested in race. Recent studies of the policy process in particular have given political science a model for deeper and broader exploration of the relationship between race and politics. At least one result of this change has been to dissuade researchers from even further attention being placed on narrowly conceived and somewhat familiar questions about formal participatory politics. A greater degree of intellectual pluralism can now be observed in the literature and within the ambit of mainstream political debate.

Comparative race politics

As already mentioned, comparisons between the experience of the politics of race in Western European countries and with the US case have been familiar features of research activity. However, what of race and politics beyond this narrowly and hemispherically defined context? In one obvious sense it is worrying that consideration of what must surely be an important topic is so sharply compartmentalized – and even segregated – from the other themes of this essay. This is undesirable for a number of reasons, not least because of the opportunities it misses for comparison across the developed and developing world. Furthermore, it still remains an open question as to whether the guiding themes of research have been shaped by the priorities and developments within a modern discipline that has emerged from, and to this day is heavily concentrated upon, the study of Western industrial democracies. The debates surveyed earlier concerning participation, power and class – to name just three – have of course been closely rooted to Western political sociology, but this does not mean that their relevance or input ends there. It has been suggested that the broad brush approach of research in the developed world may be left conceptually and theoretically wanting in the context of studies of the developing world. Smith, for example, pointedly criticizes the tendency of most (Western-orientated) academics to jumble up what are considered to be distinct analytical categories:

To understand [racial and ethnic] relations…it is essential to distinguish them clearly as objects of study, and not to conflate them, as is now the dominant fashion among white 'experts' on race and ethnic relations, who treat inter-racial and inter-ethnic relations as one and the same for purposes of documentation, analysis and comparison.

(Smith 1986: 191)

However, in another sense the choice of, and demarcation between the themes of this essay can be defended as a fair reflection of the literature in this field. The leading debates within many developing nations about race and racism have been the subject of a body of literature largely separate from that discussed previously (Kuper and Smith 1969; Davidson 1983). For instance, there is an absence of studies of racialized state immigration policies, a topic that has preoccupied many scholars of European societies and governments in recent years.

Furthermore, the theme of race in urban politics has largely emerged in the context of the development of the discipline in developed countries such as the USA. It is hard to spot a similar debate in studies of developing countries that compares with the seminal works of Bachrach and Baratz (1970) and Key (1949). This literature in fact largely developed as part of a debate within the political science of industrial democracies concerning the distribution of power in these societies. The broader contextual setting of urban politics, however, may enable scholars to pursue similar questions about the location of power in developing countries. It would seem that, despite the seeming distinctiveness of much of this literature, there are clear and urgent comparisons to be made across the developed and developing world about the impact of race upon the conceptual understanding of political power. Indeed, these types of questions have been the mainstay of cross-national comparative work within the discipline in the developed world and there is little reason to suggest that they are any less relevant in Africa or Asia. Moreover, such comparative work is commonplace in the area of race and political behaviour, uncovering, for example, interesting distinctions between the experience of black African-Americans in the USA and lower caste Harijans in India (Verba, Bashiruddhin and Bhatt 1971). Finally, parallel bodies of literature exist on long-standing Marxist questions concerning race and class structures, making it much easier to draw together research findings both from the developed and developing world. The location of the Apartheid South African case in all of this undoubtedly presents difficulties of classification, but the work of Wolpe (1987) has highlighted the complex interrelationship between race and class factors in that country.

Shaping future research themes

The future research agenda of race and politics is likely to move beyond the traditional, strait-jacketed institutional and behavioural focus as illustrated by the recent growth of policy studies devoted to the so-called 'race dimension' in matters of mass public service delivery. These studies have served to shift the emphasis towards new areas of research and have concomitantly promoted the development of a more theoretically driven analysis. Interest has moved to examining the impact of race in the policy process and, building on the impressive developments in the discipline in this field, a theoretical debate has begun on the problems of establishing coherent and sustainable race policy. Indeed, a central debate has emerged as to what is meant by state race policy. Factors that mobilize bias against, and deny full legitimacy to race issues in public policy-making have been of particular interest. In this respect, the discipline has played an important part in developing the theoretical literature on race and political power. The theoretical understanding of the relationship between race and politics can only benefit from this development rooted in the policy studies branch of the discipline.

Questions relating to political stability have previously played a significant part in research on race and politics and are likely to continue to do so. Racial and ethnic conflicts have never been far from the core of studies of nation building, particularly in post-colonial Asian and African states. The issue of stability – or the avoidance of overt, race-related conflict – has been of considerable relevance in various Western industrial states where the political consequences of labour migration, past and present, have produced new tensions and conflicts. With recent developments across Europe and North America in particular highlighting the long-term, underlying distinctiveness of these immigrant-descended communities, it is likely that the attention of researchers will return to basic questions about social integration, cultural pluralism and political stability (Hing and Lee 1996; LEAP 1993).

Finally, in whatever way the research agenda of race and politics evolves, future work is likely to be increasingly underscored by the conceptual heterogeneity of race. The political significance and presumed impact of race, as successive scholars have found, is not a single and easily identifiable phenomenon. Instead, the politics of race and racism has many facets, which suggests that explanation will be aided by a multi-theoretical, multi-disciplinary strategy. Unfortunately, so much of the existing research has tended to box itself into one narrowly defined approach or another. The result has been that the many complex facets of the phenomena have not been fully appreciated or explored in a way that genuinely informs our understanding of the political society at large.

References

Ali, R. and O'Cinneide, C. (2002) *Our House? Race and Representation in British Politics*, London: Institute for Public Policy Research.

Bachrach, P. and Baratz, M. (1970) *Power and Poverty: Theory and Practice*, New York: Oxford University Press.

Baker, D. (1983) *Race, Ethnicity and Power: A Comparative Study*, London: Routledge & Kegan Paul.

Banton, M. (1977) *The Idea of Race*, London: Tavistock.

—— (1985) *Promoting Racial Harmony*, Cambridge: Cambridge University Press.

—— (1986) 'Epistemological assumptions in the study of racial differentiation', in J. Rex and D. Mason (eds) *Theories of Race and Ethnic Relations*, Cambridge: Cambridge University Press.

Barth, F. (ed.) (1969) *Ethnic Groups and Boundaries*, Bergen: Universitetsforlaget.

Ben-Tovim, G., Gabriel, J., Law, I. and Stredder, K. (1986) 'A political analysis of local struggles for racial equality', in J. Rex and D. Mason (eds) *Theories of Race and Ethnic Relations*, Cambridge: Cambridge University Press.

Blumer, H. and Duster, T. (1980) 'Theories of race and social action', in *Sociological Theories: Race and Colonialism*, Paris: UNESCO.

Brubaker, R. (1992) *Citizenship and Nationhood in France and Germany*, Cambridge, MA: Harvard University Press.

Cabinet Office (2002) *Improving the Labour Market Achievements of Ethnic Minorities*, interim analytical report, London: Strategy Unit

Castles, S. and Kosack, G. (1985) *Immigrant Workers and Class Structure in Western Europe*, London: Oxford University Press.

Castles, S., Booth, H. and Wallace, T. (1984) *Here for Good: Western Europe's New Ethnic Minorities*, London: Pluto Press.

Centre for Contemporary Cultural Studies (1982) *The Empire Strikes Back: Race and Racism in 70s Britain*, London: Hutchinson.

Coleman, J. (1957) *Community Conflict*, New York.

Cox, O. (1948) *Caste, Class and Race*, New York: Monthly Review Press.

Crewe, I. (1983) 'Representation and the ethnic minorities in Britain', in N. Glazer and K. Young (eds) *Ethnic Pluralism and Public Policy: Achieving Equality in the United States and Britain*, London: Heinemann.

Davidson, B. (ed.) (1983) *Africa South of the Sahara*, London: Europa Publications.

Dearlove, J. and Saunders, P. (1984) *Introduction to British Politics*, Oxford: Polity Press.

Freeman, G. (1979) *Immigrant Labour and Racial Conflict in Industrial Societies: The French and British Experience, 1945–75*, Princeton, NJ: Princeton University Press.

Glazer, N. (1983) 'Introduction', in N. Glazer and K. Young (eds) *Ethnic Pluralism and Public Policy: Achieving Equality in the United States and Britain*, London: Heinemann.

Glazer, N. and Moynihan, D. (1963) *Beyond the Melting Pot*, Cambridge, MA: MIT Press.

Glazer, N. and Young, K. (eds) (1983) *Ethnic Pluralism and Public Policy: Achieving Equality in the United States and Britain*, London: Heinemann.

Gordon, M. (1981) 'Models of pluralism: the new American dilemma', *Annals of the American Academy of Political and Social Science* 45: 178–88.

Greenstone, J. and Peterson, P. (1973) *Race and Authority in Urban Politics: Community Participation and the War on Poverty*, New York: Russell Sage Foundation.

Griffith, P. and Leonard, M. (2002) *Reclaiming Britishness: Living Together After 11 September and the Rise of the Right*, London: The Foreign Policy Centre.

Hansen, R. (2000) *Citizenship and Immigration in Post-war Britain*, Oxford: Oxford University Press.

Hechter, M., Friedman, D. and Appelbaum, M. (1982) 'A theory of ethnic collective action', *International Migration Review* 16: 412–34.

Hill, M. and Issacharoff, R. (1971) *Community Action and Race Relations*, London: Oxford University Press.

Hing, W. and Lee, R (1996) *Reframing the Immigration Debate*, Los Angeles: Leadership Education for Asian Pacific/UCLA Asian American Studies Centre.

Hollifield, J. (1999) 'Ideas, institutions and civil society: on the limits of immigration control in liberal democracies', *IMIS-Beiträge*, 10: 57–90

Husbands, C. (1983) *Racial Exclusionism and the City*, London: Allen & Unwin.

—— (1989) *Race and the Right in Contemporary Politics*, London: Pinter.

Katzenstein, P. (1987) *Policy and Politics in West Germany: The Growth of a Semi-Sovereign State*, Philadelphia: Temple University Press.

Katznelson, I. (1976) *Black Men, White Cities: Race, Politics, and Migration in the United States, 1900–30, and Britain, 1948–68*, Chicago: University of Chicago Press.

Kirp, D. (1979) *Doing Good by Doing Little*, London: University of California Press.

—— (1982) *Just Schools: The Idea of Racial Equality in American Education*, Berkeley: University of California Press.

Key, V. (1949) *Southern Politics in State and Nation*, New York: Random House.

Kuper, L. and Smith, M. (eds) (1969) *Pluralism in Africa*, Berkeley: University of California Press.

Layton-Henry, Z. (ed.) (1989) *The Political Rights of Migrant Workers in Western Europe*, London: Sage Publications.

Layton-Henry, Z. and Rich, P. (eds) (1986) *Race, Government and Politics in Britain*, London: Macmillan.

LEAP (1993) *The State of Asian Pacific America: Policy Issues to the Year 2020*, Los Angeles: Leadership Education for Asian Pacific/UCLA Asian American Studies Centre.

Mason, D. (1986) 'Introduction: controversies and continuities in race and ethnic relations theory', in J. Rex and D. Mason (eds) *Theories of Race and Ethnic Relations*, Cambridge: Cambridge University Press.

Miles, R. (1982) *Racism and Migrant Labour: A Critical Text*, London: Routledge & Kegan Paul.

Modood, T. and Werbner, P. (eds) (1997) *Debating Cultural Hybridity: Multicultural Identities and the Politics of Anti-racism*, London: Zed Books.

Myrdal, G. (1944) *An American Dilemma*, New York: Harper Brothers.

Park, R. (ed.) (1950) *Race and Culture*, New York: Free Press.

Pinderhughes, D. (1987) *Race and Ethnicity in Chicago Politics*, Chicago and Urbana: University of Illinois Press.

Preston, M., Henderson, L. J., Jr., and Puryear, P. (eds) (1982) *The New Black Politics: The Search for Political Power*, New York: Longman.

Rex, J. (1981) 'A working paradigm for race relations research', *Ethnic and Racial Studies* 4: 1–25.

Robinson, V. (1986) *Transients, Settlers and Refugees. Asians in Britain*, Oxford: Clarendon Press.

Rogers, R. (ed.) (1985) *Guests Coming to Stay: The Effects of European Migration on Sending and Receiving Countries*, Boulder: Westview Press.

Saggar, S. (1991) *Race and Public Policy: A Study of Local Politics and Government*, Aldershot: Avebury.

—— (2000) *Race and Representation*, Manchester: Manchester University Press

St Angelo, D. and Puryear, P. (1982) 'Fear, apathy and other dimensions of black voting', in M. Preston, L. J. Henderson Jr. and P. Puryear (eds) *The New Black Politics: The Search for Political Power*, New York: Longman.

Schattschneider, E. (1960) *The Semi-Sovereign People*, New York.

Smith, M. G. (1986) 'Pluralism, race and ethnicity in selected African countries', in J. Rex and D. Mason (eds) *Theories of Race and Ethnic Relations*, Cambridge: Cambridge University Press.

Smith, S. (1989) *The Politics of 'Race' and Residence*, Cambridge: Polity Press.

Studlar, D. (1983) 'The ethnic vote, 1983: problems of analysis and interpretation', *New Community* 11: 92–100.

Studlar, D. and Layton-Henry, Z. (1990) 'Non-white minority access to the political agenda in Britain', *Policy Studies Review* 9 (2): 273–93.

Verba, S., Bashiruddhin, A. and Bhatt, A. (1971) *Caste, Race and Politics: A Comparative Study of India and the United States*, Beverly Hills: Sage Publications.

Verba, S. and Nie, N. (1972) *Participation in America: Political Democracy and Social Equality*, New York: Harper & Row.

Weinreich, P. (1986) 'The operationalisation of identity theory in racial and ethnic relations', in J. Rex and D. Mason (eds) *Theories of Race and Ethnic Relations*, Cambridge: Cambridge University Press.

Welch, S. and Secret, P. (1981) 'Sex, race and political participation', *Western Political Quarterly* 34: 5–16.

Welch, S. and Studlar, D. (1985) 'The impact of race on political behaviour in Britain', *British Journal of Political Science* 15: 528–40.

Williams, E. (1982) 'Black political progress in the 1970s: the electoral arena', in M. Preston, L. J. Henderson Jr. and P. Puryear (eds) *The New Black Politics: The Search for Political Power*, New York: Longman.

Wilson, W. J. (1978) *The Declining Significance of Race: Blacks and Changing American Institutions*, Chicago: Chicago University Press.

Wolpe, H. (1970) 'Race and industrialism in South Africa', in S. Zubaida (ed.) *Race and Racialism*, London: Tavistock.

—— (1987) *Race, Class and the Apartheid State*, London: James Currey.

Further reading

Banton, M. (1987) 'The beginning and the end of the race issue in British politics', *Policy and Politics* 15: 39–47.

Hammar, T. (ed.) (1985) *European Immigration Policy*, Cambridge: Cambridge University Press.

Omi, M. and Winant, H. (1983) 'By the rivers of Babylon: race in the United States', *Socialist Review* 71: 31–65 and 72: 35–69.

Phizacklea, A. and Miles, R. (1980) *Labour and Racism*, London: Routledge & Kegan Paul.

Rex, J. and Mason, D. (ed.) (1986) *Theories of Race and Ethnic Relations*, Cambridge: Cambridge University Press.

Rex, J. and Moore, R. (1967) *Race, Community and Conflict*, London: Oxford University Press.

UNESCO (1980) *Sociological Theories: Race and Colonialism*, Paris: UNESCO.

Wilson, W. (1980) *The Declining Significance of Race*, Chicago: University of Chicago Press.

35

CLASS AND POLITICS

Barry Hindess

Two of the most influential political movements of the last hundred years, communism and European social democracy, were built on the idea that classes and the relations between them are fundamental elements in the life of any complex society. While it is impossible to understand contemporary politics without taking the impact of these movements into account, this fact alone tells us little about the political significance of class. Not only is there considerable disagreement over the concept of class and the role it should play in a general understanding of society but developments in the latter part of the twentieth century have brought into question the very understanding of society in class terms on which the earlier successes of these movements appear to have been based: notably, the collapse of communism in Europe and its accommodations with capitalism in other parts of the world, and the final shedding of class-based political appeals by social democracy and its adaptation to the demands of neo-liberal economic and social agendas.

On the conceptual issue we can distinguish two broad approaches, both of which have been influential in Western social democratic and labour movement politics. The first approach treats classes and the conflicts between them as characteristic of certain types of society, and of modern capitalist societies in particular. According to this view classes and the most significant relations between them arise out of basic structural features of society and they inevitably have major social and political consequences. This approach to class has been influential in the politics of communist parties throughout the world and on the left wing of labour and social democratic movements. While there are different views as to the precise conceptualization of class, there is nevertheless a common insistence on the importance of classes and class relations for the understanding of politics in capitalist societies. Marxism provides the best-known example of this type of approach, but there are also influential non-Marxist versions.

At the other extreme is a treatment of classes as categories of persons (usually identified by reference to occupational characteristics) that may or may not prove useful for the purposes of distributional analysis. Here class is used, along with sex, age, ethnicity, union membership, or housing tenure, as one of a number of variables that may be related to the social distribution of income, health, attitudes and values. In this approach class is often regarded as relevant to politics either because it relates to the social distribution of political attitudes and values, and thus to voting behaviour, or because of its consequences for education, life expectancy, and other aspects of the life chances of the population that are thought to be politically important on normative grounds. Here too there are competing views as to how classes themselves should be identified, giving rise to competing accounts of the political significance of class.

While the distinction between these two approaches is not always as clear-cut as this brief summary suggests, it is nevertheless important to recognize that one approach does not necessarily imply the other. In Marxist analysis, class would be regarded as an important part of politics in capitalist society even if class differences did not show up in the pattern of voting behaviour (Gibson-Graham, Resnick and Wolff 2001). On the other hand, the fact that the class variable has significant distributional implications in Britain and other capitalist societies does not establish that classes must themselves be regarded as social forces. Differences between the south of England and the north-west also have significant distributional implications but no one would regard those regions as social forces in the way that classes have often been seen.

This essay considers the idea of classes as social forces before moving on to consider the idea of class as a social category that may, or may not, be related to the distribution of political attitudes and behaviour. The former has had greater significance in the modern period and will be given correspondingly greater attention here. On both accounts the practical political implications of class may vary over time and from one society to another but there are important differences between them in the way these changes are evaluated. In one, changes in the apparent significance of class are seen either as relatively superficial, masking a deeper underlying continuity, or else as representing a major change in the character of the society in question. In the other, they are a straightforward empirical matter, the consequences, as the case may be, of changes in the occupational structure, the character of party competition or other features of the society in question. All of these responses can be found in attempts to make sense of the changing fortunes of what were once class-based political movements. These are examined in the third section of this essay.

Classes as social forces

There are many different versions of the claim that classes are social forces generated by the fundamental structure of society, but perhaps its best-known formulation can be found in the opening section of *The Communist Manifesto*, first published in 1848:

> The history of all hitherto existing society is the history of class struggles. Freeman and slave, patrician and plebeian, lord and serf...[I]n a word, oppressor and oppressed, stood in constant opposition to one another, carried on an uninterrupted, now hidden, now open fight, a fight that each time ended, either in a revolutionary re-constitution of society at large, or in the common ruin of the contending classes.
>
> (Marx and Engels 1948: 35–6)

In Marx's view, classes are the main contending forces in society and the relations between them are the key to the understanding of politics and, in particular, to the identification of the forces promoting or resisting progressive social change. Class struggle may be open or it may be hidden, but it will make its presence felt for as long as classes themselves exist. The German Social Democratic Party (SPD), the largest and most successful of nineteenth-century socialist parties, was strongly influenced by Marxism and accordingly took the view that the socialist transformation of society would be brought about primarily by the political action of the working class. Socialists disagreed about how this transformation should be pursued: one side arguing that it could be achieved through a process of peaceful and constitutional reform – essentially by establishing political majorities in elected parliaments and using these to bring about social and political change; the other insisting that more radical political action, a revolution, would also be required. The SPD generally supported the former view, as did the majority Menshevik faction of the much smaller Russian Social Democratic Party. Significant minorities in both parties favoured revolution, arguing that the state was an instrument of the ruling class and therefore that serious social change could be brought about only if the state itself were to be overthrown. Otherwise, they insisted, attempts at social and political reform would amount to little more than superficial meddling which, by giving the misleading impression that significant changes could be brought about by peaceful means, tended in fact to reinforce the power of the ruling class.

These disputes turned in part on radically different perceptions of representative government: one side insisting that it served merely to obscure the underlying class character of the state and the other tempted by the liberal view of constitutional rule, believing that it provided conditions in which the working class and its allies could use their electoral strength and mobilizing capacity to overcome the resistance of the ruling class. They were further complicated by bitter divisions within the socialist movement over whether to support the war aims of their respective national governments during the First World War, and again over their responses to the Bolshevik seizure of power in the second Russian Revolution of 1917. This event radically transformed these disputes by forcing supporters of the conflicting views into implacably opposed camps: communists and other revolutionaries in one camp and social democracy as a movement of reform in the other. While both sides have had considerable successes, at least in their own terms, developments in the latter part of the twentieth century have not been kind to either of them. The collapse of communism in Europe in the latter part of the twentieth century and its accommodations with capitalism in other parts of the world suggested to many observers that, far from transforming the class character of society, socialist revolution was simply one of the more uncomfortable routes between capitalism and capitalism. European social democracy, on the other hand, has had many achievements, culminating in the welfare states established in Western Europe, North America and Australasia during the post-Second World War era, but it has abandoned its earlier commitment to fundamental social change and its welfare institutions are gradually being wound back under the impact of neo-liberal reforms. It survives as a movement of cautious and progressive reform in Western Europe and a few states elsewhere, but only by adapting its policies to the demands of neo-liberal economic and social agendas.

The treatment of classes as social forces is most commonly associated with Marxist thought, although Marx insisted that he was not the first to discover either 'the existence of classes in modern society or the struggle between them' (Marx 1968). Max Weber (1978) was highly critical of Marx's treatment of class relations, but he too took the view that classes could be important social forces. Thus, Weberian political analysis has often been concerned with the identification of classes and the relations between them because of their potential significance as social forces. John Goldthorpe, for example, takes care to distance himself from Marxism in his discussion of the implications of social mobility for the prospects of egalitarian social change in Britain. Nevertheless, he argues, to 'this extent at least we would agree with Marx: that if class society is to be ended – or even radically modified – this can only be through conflict between classes in one form or another' (Goldthorpe 1987: 29; see also Dahrendorf 1959; Parkin 1979). For these non-Marxist authors, conflict between classes is not an inescapable feature of modern society, as it is in Marx's argument: rather, it exists only to the extent that classes have developed into collective actors capable of a significant degree of common action. Social mobility is therefore important in Goldthorpe's argument, for example, because of its supposed effects on the development of the class identification and the ties of solidarity which he regards as necessary for the formation of classes as collective actors.

There is no space here to consider the differences between the various Marxist and non-Marxist forms of class analysis. For present purposes it is more important to concentrate on what they share: namely, an insistence on the importance of classes and class relations for the understanding of capitalist societies. The treatment of classes as social forces usually draws on at least one of the following two beliefs: first, that classes can be seen as collective actors and, second, that class interests are objectively given to individuals by virtue of their class location, thereby providing members of the one class with a basis for action in common. Both beliefs are problematic. The suggestion that classes, in this sense, play a fundamental role in politics involves the further claim that crucial features of political life can be understood in terms of the actions or the interests of classes themselves. We consider each of these issues in turn.

The problem with the idea that classes can be regarded as collective actors is simply that even the most limited concept of actor involves some means of taking decisions and of acting on them. Human individuals are actors in this sense, and so too are capitalist enterprises, political parties, trade unions, states and international agencies. There are other collectivities, such as classes and societies, which have no identifiable means of taking decisions – although it is not difficult to find those who claim to take decisions and to act on their behalf. Actors' decisions play an important part in the explanation of their actions – and that is the most important reason for restricting the concept of actor to things that are able to take decisions and act on them. To suggest, for example, that the neo-liberal transformations of Western welfare states in the last quarter of the twentieth century could be explained in terms of the actions of *classes* (Esping-Anderson and Korpi 1984) is to construct a fantastic allegory in which the factions, parties, international organizations and other agencies involved and their often confused and conflicting objectives are reduced to the actions of a few collective actors. Such allegories appear to simplify our understanding of the state of affairs in question while thoroughly obscuring the question of what can or should be done about it.

What of the belief that the interests which individuals share by virtue of their class position provide the basis for action in common, thereby constituting classes as actual or potential collective actors? On this view, class interests are determined by the structure of relations between classes, and the parties, unions and other agencies of political life are then to be seen as more or less adequate representations of these interests. Two features of this concept of interests are particularly significant.

One is that it appears to provide an explanatory link between the behaviour of individuals and their position in the structure of society: interests provide us with reasons for action, and are determined by our position as members of a particular class, gender or community. Marxist class analysis suggests, for example, that the working class has an objective interest in the overthrow of capitalism in favour of a socialist society. The difficulty here, of course, is that the vast majority of those who are thought to have an objective interest in socialism rarely acknowledge those interests as their own. Far from providing an effective explanatory link between the structure of capitalist society and political behaviour, the idea of structurally determined class interests generates a host of explanatory problems. A considerable part of Marxist political analysis has been devoted to considering why the working classes in the capitalist West have not pursued their objective interests in socialism.

The other significant feature of this concept of interests is that it seems to allow us to combine a variety of discrete relationships and conflicts into a larger whole. In Britain, for example, the 1984–5 miners' strike, industrial action by transport workers, and the defence of the National Health Service against cuts were regarded by many commentators on the Left as instances of a wider struggle between one class and another on the grounds that the same set of class interests was ultimately at stake in each of these conflicts. The invocation of class interests as a means of bringing together a variety of distinct relationships and conflicts suggests that the participants in each case be regarded as standing in for the classes whose interests are supposed to be at stake. It brings us back, in other words, to the allegory of classes as collective actors.

This brings us to the third issue: the claim that crucial features of political life can be understood in terms of the actions or the interests of classes themselves. No serious advocate of class analysis, Marxist or non-Marxist, maintains that the analysis of class relations tells us all we might want to know about the political forces at work in the modern world: many insist, for example, on the independent significance of gender, ethnicity and environmental issues. The allegory of classes as collective actors is nevertheless intended to provide us with one of the most important keys to the understanding of political life: this is precisely the point of the passage from *The Communist Manifesto* quoted earlier.

John Goldthorpe's study of social mobility in modern Britain provides a clear non-Marxist example of this device. We have seen that he regards class conflict as necessary to bring about significant social change. He therefore proceeds to examine the implications of social mobility for the patterns of 'shared beliefs, attitudes and sentiments that are required for concerted class action' (Goldthorpe 1987: 265) – as if those implications could be identified quite independently of the actions of political parties, the media, or state agencies. What is involved here is a failure to take seriously the consequences of movements, organizations and their actions, both for political forces and the conditions under which they operate, and for the formation of the political interests and concerns which bring them into conflict. Political attitudes, beliefs and behaviour may then be treated as if they reflect other social conditions, in this case the strength and consciousness of the contending classes. The implication is that these other conditions are in some sense more real than the political phenomena that reflect them.

This example brings out a general feature of the idea that classes provide the key, or one of the keys, to an understanding of political life. This type of approach claims to bring together two distinct but related levels of analysis. At one level are the factions, parties, ideologies and the like that constitute the political life of society. At the other level is the allegory of classes as collective actors, which is presented as if it provided the key to our understanding of the mundane. Unfortunately, there is at most a gestural connection between these two levels. The class analysis of politics, in other words, combines an insistence on the irreducibility of political phenomena with the explanatory promise of reductionism. How the trick is done, of course, remains obscure.

Class and political behaviour

If the socialist movements of the nineteenth and early twentieth centuries drew on the image of classes as social forces, then the split in socialism following the Russian Revolution led Western social democracy to focus on the electoral and industrial significance of these forces. Labour or Social Democratic parties on the one side and trades unions on the other were often described as the two wings of the Labour Movement. The influence of class on voting behaviour and the role of trades unions in Labour and social democratic parties then came to be seen as central features in the relationship between class and politics.

In the period between the end of the Second World War and the late 1950s, it seemed clear to most commentators on British politics that the division between the working class (that is, manual workers and their families) and the rest of the population was the single most important influence on voting behaviour. Electoral politics were strongly polarized between the Labour and Conservative Parties, with only about a quarter of the electorate abstaining or voting for minor parties. Roughly two-thirds of working-class voters supported the Labour Party and the evidence of opinion polls suggested that most of them did so because they regarded it as being in some sense the party of the working class. Labour, it seemed, was the natural political home of the working class, and only the deviant, Conservative-voting minority posed a particular problem of explanation. The middle and upper classes were overwhelmingly Conservative, with only a deviant minority supporting Labour.

The class polarization of British politics was widely regarded as providing the clearest example amongst the larger Western democracies of the influence of class on political behaviour (Rokkan 1970). Robert Alford (1963) devised an index of class voting, which was calculated by subtracting the percentage of non-working class voters who supported left-wing parties from the percentage of working-class-voters who supported these same parties. This index suggested that in continental Europe the class polarization of political behaviour was complicated by the influence of religious parties, significant regional and cultural differences, and divisions within the organized labour movement. In the USA, the absence of a major socialist party was seen as resulting in a somewhat weaker relationship between class and political behaviour.

By the end of the 1950s, however, there were indications that this picture of the class character of British politics might be too simplistic. Some commentators had already noted signs of the slow but steady erosion of support for the Labour Party which continued, with minor variations, throughout the rest of the century (Abrams, Hinden and Rose 1959; Crosland 1960). Some years later a major study of political attitudes and voting behaviour found a marked weakening in the class alignment of electoral politics throughout the 1960s. It also suggested that the image of politics as a matter of conflicting class interests was most widely accepted amongst those who entered the electorate during and immediately after the Second World War. 'But such an image was accepted less frequently among Labour's working class supporters who entered the electorate more recently' (Butler and Stokes 1974: 200–1). Subsequent studies, both in Britain and elsewhere, found both that party allegiances within the electorate were becoming weaker and that the relationship measured by the Alford Index between class and party affiliation was declining (Sarlvik and Crewe 1983; Franklin, Mackie and Valen 1992; Nie, Verba and Petrocik 1981). Rather than continue to vote on class lines, it seemed to many commentators that important sections of the working class were making a more pragmatic, hard-headed assessment of where their interests lay and changing their vote accordingly.

The class polarization of British politics in the 1950s had been seen as reflecting a relationship between class and political behaviour that was characteristic of the larger Western democracies, and the erosion of that polarization was accordingly seen as part of a broader international development. Jan Pakulski and Malcolm Waters (1996a) argue that the old relationship between class and politics, which dominated the electoral politics of Western democracies up to the 1970s, has now broken down.

However, it would be misleading to close the discussion of class and electoral behaviour at this point. Critics of these studies have suggested that the declining significance of class in British politics and in Western politics more generally is more apparent than real. The argument is that the traditional working-class/middle-class dichotomy provides too simple a model of class structure, and that a more refined model, taking account of significant changes in the occupational structure since the 1950s, would show that the relevance of class to politics is not declining (Goldthorpe and Marshall 1992; Brooks and Manza 1999). The relevance of class, then, would appear to depend on the manner in which classes themselves are defined. Against that view Richard Rose and Ian McAllister insist that, however classes are actually identified, 'most British voters do not have their vote determined by occupational class' (Rose and McAllister 1986: 50).

This more refined version of class analysis nevertheless shares with the traditional view the idea of a natural affinity between classes and political parties such that changes in the relative size of one invariably leads to corresponding shifts in the political fortunes of the other. However, the comparative success of social democratic and labour parties in parts of northern Europe and in Australasia throughout the 1980s appears to show that these parties may have greater sources of potential support than the pessimistic sociological determinism of this approach would suggest. This point has been used to argue that the relationship between class and politics may well depend on the conduct of parties themselves.

Prospects for labour and social-democratic politics

Both communism and European social democracy have been based on some version of the idea that classes and class relations are fundamental aspects of the political life of modern societies. Supporters of both movements have been disappointed in their expectations. It is beyond the scope of this essay to consider the fate of communist regimes, but what of the responses of the labour and social democratic parties of the capitalist West?

Social democratic attempts to come to terms with the failures of their expectations can be divided into two broad clusters. On the one side there is the 'revisionist' response that class in either of the above senses has become less relevant to politics in the modern world and that labour and social democratic parties must therefore broaden their appeal if they are to succeed – that is, they must modernize and revise their doctrines and objectives to take account of the effects of social and economic change. The opposite view is that the political salience of class is, to a considerable extent, a consequence of the policies pursued by social democratic parties themselves and by the broader labour movement. The declining salience of class in Britain and many other Western democracies would then be seen, at least in part, as a consequence of the failure of their labour or social democratic parties to pursue an appropriate form of class politics.

The revisionist response operates at two levels. One involves the general claim that classes are becoming less relevant as a consequence of economic development, at least in the democratic societies of the modern West. Towards the end of the nineteenth century, the German socialist Edward Bernstein argued that capitalist economic development had brought about a situation in which 'ideological, and especially the ethical factors, [had] greater space for independent activity than was formerly the case' (Bernstein 1961: 15). The revisionist argument here assumes a hierarchy of human needs: once material needs have been satisfied then people will turn their attention to non-material values. The appeal to class interests may have been important in the earlier stages of capitalist development, but it must now be replaced by a politics organized around the ethical appeal of socialist values.

A closely related argument about the effects of economic growth was set out in Tony Crosland's *The Future of Socialism* (1956) and his Fabian pamphlet *Can Labour Win?* (1960). While class was once the main determinant of voting behaviour, he argues that, 'as material pressures ease and the problem of subsistence fades away, people become more sensitive to moral and political issues' (Crosland 1960: 22). More recently, the literature on what are often called 'new' social movements has given a new twist to the old revisionist argument by suggesting that conflict between classes has been displaced by feminist, environmentalist and other new forms of politics in the more advanced societies of the modern world (Inglehart 1990; Giddens 2000).

This general argument in favour of developing a non-class political appeal is often supplemented by a second, more pragmatic level of revisionist argument. Bernstein used German census material to argue that the peasantry and the middle classes were far from disappearing, as orthodox Marxism appeared to suggest, and that the working class was far from being an overwhelming majority of the population. The implication, at least for the foreseeable future, was that there would always be a substantial part of the electorate, neither capitalist nor working class, whose votes could significantly affect the chances of achieving any major socialist objective. The social democratic party needed therefore to dilute its sectional appeal to the interests of a single class if it was to have any hope of winning power.

Similarly, Crosland's *Can Labour Win?* (published in 1960, following the Labour Party's third successive post-war election defeat) maintains that long-term social changes have eroded the significance of class differences in British politics, with the result, first, that a growing proportion of the electorate no longer votes on the basis of class identification and, second, that the Party's working-class image is a wasting electoral asset. Crosland argued that economic development was producing changes in the occupational structure. The relative size of the manual working class fell throughout the 1950s (by about 0.5 per cent a year) and it has continued to do so. Assuming a straightforward association between class position and voting behaviour, such a fall in the relative size of the working class entails a corresponding fall in the Labour Party's class-based support. Labour's difficulty is compounded, Crosland suggests, by the gradual breakdown of that association as a result of increasing affluence, social and geographical mobility and the breakup of old working-class communities. In the more prosperous sections of the working class, people had 'acquired a middle class income and pattern of consumption, and sometimes a middle class psychology' (Crosland 1960: 12). This inexorable erosion of class as a basis for the Labour Party's electoral support means, in his view, that the party has to concentrate on other determinants of electoral behaviour, particularly on its image and performance in office.

The revisionist argument, then, is that the analysis of politics in class terms has become less informative as other, non-class forms of politics have come to the fore. Here the contrast between a past in which socialist politics could be conducted in class terms, and a present and future in which it cannot, serves as a rhetorical device. It is a means of arguing against the analysis of politics in class terms without directly confronting the conceptual weaknesses of class analysis.

In fact, the revisionist account of the implications of economic change is open to challenge on a number of points. First, many of those recruited into the expanding middle-class occupations came from working-class backgrounds. It is far from clear that they would be repelled by the Labour Party's class identification. Nor is it clear why working class affluence should be expected to result in Conservative voting. Academic critics have shown that what might seem to be the most plausible mechanisms linking improved living standards with right-wing voting behaviour have little empirical foundation (Goldthorpe *et al.* 1968).

More seriously, the traditional revisionist argument reproduces many of the problems noted above with regard to the analysis of classes as social forces. In particular, it treats the political concerns and orientations of the electorate as if they were formed independently of the political activities of parties and other political agencies, and ultimately as if they were a function of changes in the economy. The anti-revisionist case attempts to incorporate this point into its class analysis of society by arguing that, while politics is ultimately a matter of class struggle, the apparent significance of class in the political life of a capitalist society will itself depend on the strength of the working class in that society. Where the working class is strong it will be in a position both to force an accommodation on the ruling capitalist class and to insist on the class content of the political disputes in which it is engaged. Where it is weak, the class content of politics will be less apparent.

Thus Gosta Esping-Anderson and Walter Korpi (1984), taking Sweden in the 1970s and 1980s as an exemplary case in point, argue that classes develop parties, unions and other organizations in order to further their collective interests and that they will attempt to shape public institutions in their favour. In the area of social policy, for example, they suggest that the primary concerns of the working-class parties have been to reduce workers' dependence on market forces by developing a system of basic citizenship rights and maintaining full employment:

> Among the Western nations since 1973, it is only the three with the most powerful labour movement – Sweden, Norway and Austria – which have utilized macro-economic, wage or labour-market policies in order to hold unemployment at relatively low levels.
>
> (Esping-Anderson and Korpi 1984: 205)

In contrast, the capitalist class with its interest in limiting the political and economic strength of the working class favours decentralized wage bargaining and forms of social policy that promote sectional divisions – for example, by separating manual workers from other employees and fostering the growth of private pensions and insurance schemes. This argument suggests that, where working-class politics are relatively unsuccessful, the class itself will be divided, class solidarity will have limited political appeal and working-class parties will then be vulnerable to the revisionist temptation of seeking electoral support on non-class grounds – thereby reducing the appeal of class politics even further. In the British context, for example, Lewis Minkin and Patrick Seyd (1977) suggested that the declining salience of class was partly a result of the Labour Party's all too successful attempts to manipulate its image and electoral appeal in line with the recommendations of Crosland's (1960) *Can Labour Win?*

In fact, it is far from clear that the comparative performance of Swedish social democracy and the British labour movement in the 1970s and 1980s can be interpreted as resulting from the relative strengths of different classes in these two countries. The anti-revisionist point that the relative strength of class-based forms of politics in, say, Sweden and Britain, cannot be explained without reference to the conduct of parties themselves is well taken, but it hardly implies that politics must ultimately be understood in class terms. Pakulski and Waters (1996a, 1996b) develop its implications in precisely the opposite direction, arguing that the class politics of Britain and other Western democracies throughout much of the twentieth century was not the cause but rather the consequence of the successful development of trades unions and employers associations and of political parties campaigning on the basis of class-based ideologies and appeals to broadly defined material interests. Since the end of the post-Second World War economic boom, they suggest, 'these politically-organized, nationalized, and mass-ideologically constructed forms of class have started to decompose' (1996b: 676) under the influence of new patterns of employment, economic globalization and the emergence of new social movements.

This last point suggests that the survival into the twenty-first century of what had once been class-based Labour and Social Democratic Parties can hardly be seen as reflecting the continued political significance of class. What it indicates, rather, is the ability of parties to adapt to new conditions, in part through a successful process of 'cartelisation' (Mair 1997) in which established parties cooperate to secure state funding for themselves and to make life difficult for newly emerging competitors.

References

Abrams, M., Hinden, R. and Rose, R. (1959) *Must Labour Lose?*, London: Penguin.

Alford, R. (1963) *Party and Society*, Chicago: Rand McNally.

Bernstein, E. (1961) *Evolutionary Socialism*, New York: Schocken.

Brooks, C. and Manza, J. (1999) *Social Cleavages and Political Change: Voter Alignments and US Party Coalitions*, New York: Oxford University Press

Butler, D. and Stokes, D. (1974) *Political Change in Britain*, 2nd edn, London: Macmillan.

Crosland, C. A. R. (1956) *The Future of Socialism*, London: Cape.

—— (1960) *Can Labour Win?*, Fabian Tract no. 324, London: Fabian Society.

Dahrendorf, R. (1959) *Class and Class Conflict in Industrial Society*, London: Routledge & Kegan Paul.

Esping-Anderson, G. and Korpi, W. (1984) 'Social policy as class politics in post-war capitalism', in J. Goldthorpe (ed.) *Order and Conflict in Contemporary Capitalism*, Oxford: Clarendon Press.

Franklin, M., Mackie, T. and Valen, H. (1992) *Electoral Change: Responses to Evolving Social and Attitudinal Structures in Western Countries*, Cambridge: Cambridge University Press.

Gibson-Graham, J. K., Resnick, S. and Wolff, R. (2001) *Re/Presenting Class: Essays in Postmodern Marxism*, Durham: Duke University Press

Giddens, A. (2000) *The Third Way and its Critics*, Cambridge: Polity

Goldthorpe, J. H. (1987) *Social Mobility and Class Structure in Modern Britain*, 2nd edn, Oxford: Clarendon Press.

Goldthorpe, J. H., Lockwood, D., Bechofer, F. and Platt, J. (1968) *The Affluent Worker*, Cambridge: Cambridge University Press.

Goldthorpe, J. H. and Marshall, G. (1992) 'The promising future of class analysis', *Sociology*, 26: 381–400

Inglehart, R. (1990) *Culture Shift in Advanced Industrial Society*, Princeton: Princeton University Press

Mair, P. (1997) *Party System Change*, Oxford: Oxford University Press

Marx, K. (1968) Letter to Weydemeyer, 5 March 1852, in K. Marx and F. Engels, *Selected Works*, p. 679, London: Lawrence & Wishart.

Marx, K. and Engels, F. (1968) 'The Communist Manifesto', in K. Marx and F. Engels, *Selected Works*, London: Lawrence & Wishart.

Minkin, L. and Seyd, P. (1977) 'The British Labour party', in W. E. Patterson and A. H. Thomas (eds) *Social Democratic Parties in Western Europe*, London: Croom Helm.

Nie, N., Verba, S., and Petrocik, J. (1981) *The Changing American Voter*, 2nd edn, Cambridge, MA: Harvard University Press

Parkin, F. (1979) *Marxism and Class Theory: A Bourgeois Critique*, London: Tavistock.

Pakulski, J. and Waters, M. (1996a) *The Death of Class*, London: Sage

—— (1996b) 'The reshaping and dissolution of social class in advanced society', *Theory and Society*, 25 (5): 667–91

Rokkan, S. (1970) *Citizens, Elections, Parties*, Oslo: Universitetsforlaget.

Rose, R. and McAllister, I. (1986) *Voters Begin to Choose*, London: Sage Publications.

Sarlvik, B. and Crewe, I. (1983) *Decade of Dealignment*, Cambridge: Cambridge University Press.

Weber, M. (1978). *Economy and Society. An Outline of Interpretive Sociology*, Berkeley: University of California Press.

Further reading

The clearest accounts of what was once the standard view of the relation between class and political behaviour in Western democracies are Alford (1963) and Rokkan (1970). T. N. Clark and S. M. Lipset (eds) *The Breakdown of Class Politics* (Baltimore: Johns Hopkins University Press, 2001) is a recent survey of shifting patterns of electoral support in Western politics. There are numerous treatments of the apparent decline in the salience of class in British elections: see especially, Butler and Stokes (1974), Franklin, Mackie and Valen (1992) and Rose and McAllister (1986). The last two provide useful discussions of the implications of different definitions of class for the analysis of electoral behaviour. The idea of classes as social forces once generated an enormous literature, but this has declined significantly in recent years. Marxist and non-Marxist versions are discussed in B. Hindess, *Politics and Class Analysis* (Oxford: Blackwell, 1987). P. Calvert, *The Concept of Class* (London: Hutchinson, 1982), is still the most useful historical survey of various understandings of the concept. The claim that class politics have become less significant as a result of economic development can be found in the writings of socialist revisionism (Bernstein 1961; Crosland 1956, 1960) and, in a slightly updated form, in the literature on post-materialism and 'new social movements' (Ingelhart 1990; Giddens 2000). The most thoroughgoing critique of the contemporary relevance of class is Pakulski and Waters 1996a. A shorter version of their argument together with some critical responses appears in 'Symposium on class', *Theory and Society*, 25 (5), 1996. Variants of the contrary argument, that what seems to be the limited salience of class is really a consequence of the political strategies pursued by left-wing parties and their opponents, can be found in Brooks and Manza (1999) A. Przeworski, *Capitalism and Social Democracy* (Cambridge: Cambridge University Press, 1985), and several contributions to J. H. Goldthorpe (ed.) *Order and Conflict in Contemporary Capitalism* (Oxford: Clarendon Press, 1984).

36

ETHNICITY AND POLITICS

T. David Mason and David Galbreath

Since the end of the Second World War, the world has witnessed the revival, intensification and stubborn persistence of ethnicity as an issue in politics, as a focal point of popular political mobilization, and as a source of domestic and interstate conflict. No region of the world nor any type of political system – from democracies to Marxist-Leninist states to military regimes to patrimonial dictatorships – has been immune to the bloody consequences of ethnic strife. The political salience of ethnicity has endured not just in the former colonial territories of the Third World but also in the advanced post-industrial democracies of Western Europe and North America, as well as in the major communist and post-communist nations of the People's Republic of China, the Soviet Union, Yugoslavia, and the rest of Eastern Europe. The US civil rights movement of the 1950s and 1960s became, arguably, the most politically significant social movement of the twentieth century in that nation (see McAdam 1982; Chong 1991). It was accompanied by waves of ethnically based riots in the 'long, hot summers' of 1965–1971 (see Feagin and Hahn 1973). The coincidence of ethnicity and geography in the Soviet and Yugoslav federal systems was the critical centrifugal force that led to the dissolution of those two nation-states into their constituent republics (see Bunce 1999). Ethnicity was the source of identity around which anti-colonial movements in Asia and Africa mobilized in the immediate aftermath of the Second World War, and ethnic identity has served as a source of identity for mobilizing Third World revolutionary and secessionist movements in the years following decolonization (see Gurr 2000; Horowitz 1985; Young 1976).

The structural conditions that give rise to ethno-regional politics, the immediate causes that catalyse ethnic conflict, and the forms that ethnically based conflict assume differ markedly both across and within the three worlds. What is apparent, however, is that neither the penetration of 'modernity' into all regions of the world nor the often heralded process of 'globalization' has led to the 'withering away' of ethnicity as a source of political conflict; indeed, its salience appears to have grown as a consequence of the diffusion of modernity and globalization.

What is perhaps most striking about the study of ethnicity and politics is that, during the Cold War, the resurgence of ethnicity as a political force was, with a few notable exceptions, largely ignored in much of the mainstream academic literature on comparative social change and political development. It remained the purview of a relatively small number of scholars who achieved an impressive degree of consensus on structural theories of ethnic conflict and individual participation in those events. Especially noteworthy among these were the works of Walker Connor (1972), Robert Bates (1974), Michael Hechter (1974, 1975, 1978; also Hechter and Levi 1979; Hechter, Friedman, and Appelbaum 1982), Donald Horowitz (1971, 1973, 1981, 1985) and Crawford Young (1976). Thirty years ago, Walker Connor (1972: 319–20) noted that, among a sample of ten works that would now be regarded as classics of the political development literature, none of them contained a section, a chapter, or even a major subheading on ethnicity. Six of the ten contained not a single reference to ethnic groups, ethnicity, or minorities in their indexes, and the remaining four made only passing references to the subject in an occasional isolated passage.[1]

Equally striking has been the dramatic rise in the salience of ethnicity as a focus of political inquiry since the end of the Cold War, a trend that is reflected in the sheer volume of published books, monographs, and journal articles on ethnic politics (and especially ethnic conflict) over the course of the last fifteen years. My own brief scan of four major journals in international and comparative politics[2] revealed that they published more articles on ethnic politics in the 1990s than in the previous two decades combined.

To some extent, the earlier relegation of ethnicity to the theoretical periphery of international and comparative political science is attributable to, first, the paradigmatic competition between modernization and Marxist schools of social development. Both depicted ethnic identity as a primordial sentiment whose relevance would diminish with the expansion and penetration of modern industrial society into the former colonial territories of the Third World. For the modernization school ethnicity was regarded as a set of 'residual loyalties from an earlier phase of social development' that inevitably would be displaced by economic rationality as the motivational basis of people's behaviour (Birch 1978: 325). Authors such as Parsons and Smelser (1956), Lipset and Rokkan (1967) and Butler and Stokes (1969) argued that 'extensions in the scope and centrality of the market would lead to the erosion of ethnic attachments' because ethnic identities have no direct relevance to the transactions of the marketplace and, therefore, should lose their social meaning (Leifer 1981: 24–5). The expanded spatial mobility of labour, capital, and goods and services should likewise discourage the geographic concentration of any ethnic group and thereby facilitate the assimilation of its members into a more universal social order (Hechter and Levi 1979: 266).

From the Marxist perspective, both nationalism and ethnic identity are examples of false consciousness. The true source of one's identity is class identity. One's relationship to the means of production – a relationship that is shared with others of one's class – is what defines one's true interests and the group with whom one has shared interests. Nationalism and ethnic identity are used by elites to manipulate the proletariat in the service of the dominant class's interests and to the detriment of the proletariat themselves. To the extent that people identify themselves by the nationality or ethnicity, they have failed to achieve true proletarian consciousness. Conversely, as capitalist relations of production diffused to all corners of the world, Marxists predicted that ethnic identity would wither away, to be replaced by class identity.

Contrary to the expectations of both Marxists and modernizationists, however, we have not witnessed the waning of ethnic identity or ethnic politics. Quite the contrary, the world has experienced a resurgence of ethnic politics at precisely that point in time when the waning of the ideological struggle between East and West, the penetration of the global political economy, and the diffusion of the 'modern' or 'global' culture into all corners of the world should have led mainstream analysts of the Cold War era to anticipate the imminent demise of ethnicity as an issue nexus for politics within and between nations. The continued salience of ethnicity as a force even in advanced societies posed an anomaly for both Marxists and modernization theorists alike. Rogowski and Wasserspring (1971: 9–10) argued that, contrary to modernization theory, greater interaction does not increase the 'cognitive problem' of placing people by particularistic criteria; indeed, it may serve to crowd out *all but* ascriptive criteria. Amid the cognitive overload that inevitably accompanies the transition from tradition to modernity, race and ethnicity often become more salient as determinants of people's behaviour because they are identification mechanisms that have a low cost of information. The increasing complexity of modern society, and the accompanying difficulty of distinguishing potential allies from potential rivals in the competitions that characterize it, reinforce the tendency toward ethnic solidarity because it is easier to distinguish allies from rivals on the basis of ethnicity than on the less obvious (and hence more costly to determine) criteria of occupation, class, political preferences, or other non-ascriptive criteria. The contemporary globalization school echoes this argument in its account of the continued salience of ethnicity as a source of identity at a time when globalization is rendering national boundaries ever more porous.

A second factor in the earlier marginalization of ethnicity as a variable in comparative politics was the predominance of Cold War paradigms in academia and in public discourse concerning armed conflict. Cold War paradigms often obscured the ethnic basis of many conflicts in the Third World by depicting them as little more than proxy wars in the geopolitical struggle between the USA and the USSR. Leaders in both the Soviet Union and the USA used the cloak of Cold War rhetoric to characterize these conflicts not as internal struggles between competing ethnic communities but as manifestations of the global struggle between capitalism and communism. Thus, the USA characterized of the civil war in Angola as a struggle between Jonas Savimbi's 'democratic' UNITA 'freedom fighters' and the Soviet/ Cuban-backed Communist regime of the MPLA.[3] Similarly, the African National Congress (ANC) in South Africa was depicted by some in the USA as an agent of Soviet expansionist ambitions in southern Africa and the white minority regime of the Republic of South Africa as the only bastion of Western resistance against communism in the region. With the end of Cold War and the waning of Cold War rhetoric, scholars and policy makers alike could recognize these conflicts for what they were and always have been: armed conflicts between groups divided by racial, linguistic, religious, and cultural chasms that are the substance of ethnic identity.

Third, after the Cold War ended ethnic conflict erupted in regions of the globe other than the Third World. Kal Holsti (1992: 41) noted that between 1945 and 1989, only 176,000 of the 21,809,000 civilian and military casualties resulting from interstate and civil wars perished on European soil. Since 1989, however, Europe's immunity to armed conflict has apparently evaporated. Of the 111 instances of armed conflict that Wallensteen and Sollenberg identified as occurring between 1989 and 2000, 21 occurred in Europe and nine of these reached the level of 'intermediate armed conflict' or 'war'. Nineteen of the 21 European conflicts were ethnically based (Wallensteen and Sollenberg 2001: 637). Most of those conflicts were in the republics of the former Soviet Union or Yugoslavia. However, low level conflicts persisted in Northern Ireland and the Basque region of Spain, to name but two. The spread of violent ethnic conflict to Europe – the heart of the 'central powers system' – implies that the major powers can no longer simply write off ethnic strife as insignificant (to the major power system) squabbles in the backwaters of the Third World that bear no significance to the vital interests of the major powers themselves. This trend has compelled the global community to seek some understanding of the origins and dynamics of ethnic conflicts.

Thus, we are presented with the questions that will serve as the focus of this essay. Why has ethnicity remained such a powerful focus of political identity in the contemporary global community? Why has the diffusion of global political culture, economic institutions and modernization processes not led to the anticipated decline in the salience of ethnicity in politics? Indeed, has globalization perhaps even intensified the political relevance of ethnicity as a source of political identity? What are the different forms that ethnic political mobilization assumes, and what structural, cultural, and individual factors account for differences in the probability, form, and issue focus of ethnic collective action?

This essay presents an overview of some of the more compelling themes in recent research on ethnic politics. By describing the theoretical principles upon which this body of research is grounded, this essay can perhaps illustrate the extent to which this research has been integrated theoretically into the broader paradigmatic terrain of the politics of collective action, including both institutionalized politics (democratic and otherwise) as well as extra-institutional forms of conflict, including ethnically based social movements and violent ethnic conflict. In this manner, we can perhaps highlight the relevance of research on ethnicity and politics to the evolution, refinement and elaboration of the major research traditions dealing with social change and political development.

Dimensions of ethnicity and ethnic conflict

When one realizes that ethnic heterogeneity is the norm among the nations of the contemporary global community, it should not be surprising that ethnicity has remained such a powerful ingredient in the domestic politics of so many nations. Observing the international system thirty years ago, Walker Connor (1972: 320) pointed out that less than 10 per cent of the nation-states in existence at that time were essentially ethnically homogeneous, while about one-fifth had one ethnic group that accounted for more than 90 per cent of the population, and another fifth had one group that accounted for between 75 and 90 per cent of the population. In almost one-fourth of the nation-states, the largest ethnic group comprised only 50 to 74 per cent of the population, and in another thirty per cent the largest single ethnic group accounted for less than half of the population. In forty per cent of the nations the population was divided among more than *five* significant groups.

The proliferation of new nation-states in the last thirty years has not resulted in any decrease in the multi-ethnic character of the nations that make up the international system. Ten years ago David Welsh noted that '[o]f the approximately 180 states that exist today, fewer than 20 are ethnically homogeneous, in the sense that ethnic minorities account for less than 5 percent of the population' (Welsh, 1993: 45). Ted Gurr (2000) and his colleagues at the Minorities at Risk project identified 233 ethnopolitical groups that, during the 1980s, could be defined as being 'at risk', in the sense of being subject to any of several forms of discrimination and repression. As of 1998, the Gurr team had identified 275 minorities at risk in 116 different countries, constituting 17.4 per cent of the world's population (Gurr 2000: 9). In view of what Connor termed 'the remarkable lack of coincidence...between ethnic and political borders', it should not be surprising to find that ethnicity remains a focal point of political organization and competition throughout the world.

The evidence on the extent of ethnic violence testifies to the intensity with which ethnic issues are prosecuted in the political arena. Since the end of the Second World War, there have been three waves of ethnopolitical violence. The first coincided with the decolonization process. Independence movements in most colonial territories were by definition ethnically based: indigenous peoples engaging in violent and nonviolent collective action aimed at compelling European colonial powers to withdraw from their territory and grant them independence as fully sovereign nation states. As Horowitz (1985) points out, however, the anti-colonial movements were not always representative of all of the ethnic groups within a given colonial territory. Accordingly, gaining independence did not bring an end to civil war and ethnic conflict. Instead, indigenous ethnic and tribal hostilities supplanted colonial domination as the dominant issue driving the continuing diffusion of revolution and secessionist war throughout Asia and Africa.

Thus, a second wave of ethnically based conflicts arose in the aftermath of decolonization. The focus of contentious politics shifted from the external target of the colonial power to internal issues of national identity and ethno-nationalist autonomy. Nationalist leaders who had led the struggle for colonial independence found their efforts to build a new sense of national identity thwarted by the strength of long-standing ethno-regional identities. For example, Nigeria faced a secessionist revolt by the Ibo that lasted from 1967–70. Ethiopia faced protracted secessionist conflict with Eritrea, and Pakistan was forced to concede the secession of East Pakistan, which became the nation of Bangladesh. In some cases ethnic fragmentation was manifested in the ethnic basis of parties and party competition in the newly independent states. Sri Lanka's post-independence party system coalesced along ethnic lines, and when majority Sinhalese parties began enacting legislation mandating the use of Sinhalese language and limiting minority Tamil access to civil service positions and university admissions (among other things), a secessionist guerrilla movement eventually arose among Tamil youth. In other cases, the conflict between long-standing ethnic identities and the newly created national identity produced tensions that erupted into revolutionary civil war. The conflicts in Angola, Uganda, and Rwanda were ethnically based but revolutionary rather than secessionist in their goals.

Ethno-regional movements could have been anticipated in some of the multiethnic nation-states of Asia and Africa in the aftermath of independence from colonial rule. In many cases an explicit component of the colonial power's 'divide and rule' strategy was to preserve intact the cultural autonomy of the various ethnic groups. Upon achieving independence, the institutions of the newly formed state posed no immediate threat to this patchwork of ethnically distinct social subsystems left over from the colonial era. However, as the central state increased its capacity to regulate society and extended its authority into the ethno-regional enclaves, the isolation that had allowed ethnically distinct subsystems to retain their autonomy under colonial rule gradually dissolved. All too often, the resultant challenges faced by ethnic groups evoked in them an almost xenophobic 'reactive ethnicity' characterized by the resistance of previously autonomous ethnic enclaves to the potentially corrosive and exploitive penetration of the modern state's institutions and authority (Blanton, Mason and Athow 2001; Connor 1972: 329; Hechter and Levi 1979: 263; Nielsen 1985: 134). Many of these conflicts involved the efforts of ethno-regional minorities to gain their own independence. Others involved the efforts of revolutionaries from subordinate ethnic groups to seize control of the state from a dominant ethnic group. In both forms of civil strife, ethnicity provided a powerful and perhaps critical basis for popular mobilization. Hence, we have witnessed secessionist warfare in Burma, Bangladesh, the Sudan, Nigeria, Morocco, Iraq, Ethiopia and the Philippines, ethnically based civil wars in Lebanon, Zaire, Angola and Afghanistan, interstate war between Ethiopia and Somalia over the Ogaden region and between India and Pakistan over Kashmir, ethnic riots in India, Sri Lanka, Malaysia, Zaire and Guyana, attacks by an army of one ethnic group against civilians from another ethnic group in Rwanda, Burundi, Uganda and Zimbabwe, and the expulsion of Asians from Uganda, and of Beninese from the Ivory Coast and Gabon (Horowitz 1985: 3; see also Gurr 2000 for a list of ethnic groups and conflicts).

This second wave of ethnic conflicts became inextricably intertwined in Cold War politics, as the two rival superpower blocs chose sides in many of these conflicts. As with the end of decolonization, however, the end of the Cold War did not mean an end to ethnic conflict. Instead, the world witnessed a third wave of ethnic conflict marked by the eruption of long-suppressed ethnic tensions in many of the newly independent republics of the former Soviet Union and Yugoslavia. In addition, Third World conflicts that had been suppressed directly or indirectly by the major powers in the interest of Cold War stability erupted into violence as the major powers no longer had a stake in containing conflicts within their former client states. The dissolution of the Soviet Union and Yugoslavia demonstrated the impact of ethnic politics in its most potent form: ethno-nationalism. The establishment of exclusive republics in Estonia and Latvia, the Russian Federation's continued struggle with Chechnya, war between Armenians and Azerbaijanis in the disputed region of Nagorno-Karabakh, the civil war in Tajikistan, and the violence in the Trans Dniester area of Moldova reveal the extent to which ethnic tensions in the Soviet successor states could erupt into armed conflict once the control mechanisms of the Soviet state dissolved (see Snyder 2000). Likewise, the inter-ethnic warfare in the former Yugoslavia, the issue of Hungarian minorities in Romania, Slovakia, and Slovenia, and the failure of the People's Republic of China to eradicate independence sentiments among Tibetans and the Turkish peoples in Xinjiang Province attest to the pervasiveness of ethnic loyalties and identities among the peoples of Eastern Europe and Asia (see Goldhagen 1968; Laitin 1991, 1998; Motyl 1995; Smith 1996; Tishkov 1997; King and Melvin 1998; Beissinger 1999). The adoption of Marxist-Leninist ideology in Eastern Europe clearly did not immunize those nations against ethnically based internal conflict (Kemp 1999).

Explaining the persistence of ethnic politics

In order to appreciate the role of ethnicity as an political issue axis, we must first give a proper theoretical foundation to its meaning. What is ethnicity as an identity construct and how does it affect intra- and inter-group interactions? *Ethnicity* is a part of every person's identity construct and defines the 'permissible constellations' of statuses an individual may have (Barth 1969). Jenkins (1995: 198) argues that ethnicity is situationally defined rather than a fixed aspect of one's identity. Therefore, the salience of ethnicity among members of a particular group is variable. In most cases, ethnicity is subordinate to most other statuses such as class, tribal, or familial. However, ethnicity is most salient when defined in terms of group dynamics. Put simply, ethnicity becomes important when groups make their decisions in response to the actions of other groups on the basis of ethnic distinctions or ethnic issues.

For many scholars, ethnic boundaries are the key to explaining relations between ethnic groups (Barth 1969; Barth and Noel 1972; Hannan 1979; Banton 1983, 1998; Olzak 1992). Ethnic boundaries represent those characteristics that are recognized as distinguishing groups from each other, but do not necessarily represent the entire array of cultural characteristics that define a group's shared identity. Thus, the continuity of the group as a cultural entity depends on the maintenance of the ethnic boundary. Anthony Smith (1991) defines an *ethnic group* with six characteristics that constitute such a boundary:

1   a collective proper name of the group;
2   a myth of common ancestry;
3   shared historical memories;
4   one or more differentiating elements of common culture, e.g. language;
5   an association with a specific 'homeland', and
6   a sense of solidarity for significant sectors of the population.

According to Smith, these characteristics allow ethnic groups to be treated as another social unit. Groups are continually re-evaluating their status in society in terms of their hierarchical positioning relative to other groups. Richard Jenkins (1995: 198–201) argues that this evaluation is based on internal and external definitions of the group's status in relation to the other group(s). Internal definitions are characteristics that define the 'self'. Alternatively, external definitions are characteristics that define the 'other'.

The definition of the 'self' and 'other' are easily contained in what Donald Horowitz (1985: 46) refers to as ethnic markers. These are shared characteristics that distinguish one ethnic group from another. They can range along a continuum from the visible to the nonvisible. For Rogowski (1974: 71) this continuum of markers is defined by how easily detected the markers are and how costly they are to alter. Visible cues that are 'birth determined and bodily, such as color, physiognomy, hair color and texture, height and physique' are the most easily detected and the most costly to alter (Horowitz 1985: 46). Next are those that are not birth determined but are also bodily, including 'circumcision and earring holes…and…scarification'. Next are those that are visible but behavioral (and not determined by birth), such as dress, grooming, and gestures. Finally, there are nonvisible cues, many of which are derived from language, such as accent, syntax and differences in names. The more easily detected and costly to alter an ethnic marker, the more easily group membership can be determined by others, the more difficult assimilation into other groups will be, the more persistent will be perceptions of group differences, and the more likely group solidarity is to emerge.

Combined with Smith's definition of ethnic boundaries, ethnic markers are important in determining the strength and persistence of ethnic groups' shared identity. As ethnic group dynamics vary, the salience of some markers is not necessarily common across groups, nor is their salience always static within groups. Ethnic boundaries and markers do not necessarily determine the degree of cleavage and competition between groups. Rather, it is during times of conflict that these markers become most important in differentiating between groups, lending themselves to the rhetoric of aggressive behaviour. Those markers that are more recognizable and more difficult to alter will induce ethnic groups to remain separated. On the other hand, those markers that are more easily changed, such as dress and language, allow members of one ethnic group to assimilate into another group. If the conflict conditions become more acute, it becomes more important for members of a group to locate those cues that differentiate the largest number of members within their own group

Ethnicity has had its greatest effect on politics through nationalist movements. (See Connor 1978; Gellner 1994.) In fact, the notion of 'nation' itself heavily overlaps that of ethnicity. Bernard Yack (1999) argues that, in particular, there is no substantial difference between 'civic' and 'ethnic' nationalisms. Rather, one set of identities is no less an inherited cultural artifact than the other. Through this perspective, we can look at several approaches to the analysis of ethno-nationalism in order elucidate the importance of ethnicity and its relationship to collective action. In other words, why is ethnicity a natural issue axis around which groups of individuals join together to influence the state, its policies and its policy makers?

Cultural constructionists argue that there is a natural tendency to organize around certain cultural characteristics such as language and religion (see especially, Anderson 1991; Greenfeld 1990). Anderson refers to these groups as 'imagined communities'. The typical response of critics of cultural constructionism is that it fails to address the inter-group dynamics that lead to the defining of the 'self' in the first place.

Social-psychological treatments of ethno-nationalism look at the psychology of ingroup-outgroup dynamics (see especially, Haas 1986; Wilder 1986, and Tajfel and Turner 1979, 1986). In essence, ethnicity exists as just one component of an individual's multi-faceted social identity. Under contentious circumstances, it is a natural tendency for the survival of the 'self' to create an ingroup and an outgroup in relation to the characteristics of the situation. Therefore, the salience of ethnicity depends on the nature and strength of the perceived threat. Although the social-psychological approach offers an explanation of how individuals naturally coalesce around ethnicity as a survival strategy, it does not address the causal mechanisms attributed to group dynamics that motivate members of a group to act collectively.

Finally, *structuralists* argue that the structure of the multi-ethnic system determines the salience of an individual's ethno-nationalist identity (see especially; Gellner 1983, 1994; Nagel and Olzak 1982; Olzak 1989, 1992; Hechter 1975, 1978, 1987;

Horowitz 1985). Rather than a natural tendency to organize, structuralists claim that an individual's reaction to the structure of inter-ethnic relations will cause him or her to seek security by attaching to others of similar ethnic background. In particular, different structures of ethnic stratification produce varied opportunities and constraints on collective action.

From this perspective, it becomes possible to conceive of ways in which social and economic development or any other form of social change could reinforce ethnic identity and inter-ethnic conflict. First, development creates benefits and costs, both public and private in nature. These benefits must be allocated among different constituencies in society. Ethnicity is one way by which constituencies can be distinguished from each other in that it is relatively easy to allocate benefits and costs differentially according to ethnic criteria. In this manner, the opportunity structure and the changes in it that are generated by social change and economic development may be biased in favour of one ethnic group over another.

Classifying ethnic groups

How and why ethnic groups mobilize for collective action varies with the make-up of the group, its relationship to other groups in the nation, the institutional configuration of the state as it defines the opportunities for collective action and the means by which policy decisions are made and scarce resources allocated (Gurr and Harff 1994: 18–23). Ted Gurr has developed a five-fold typology of ethnic groups based on these and other factors. Those types are:

1   *Ethnonationalists* are defined as large, regionally concentrated ethnic groups that live within the boundaries of one state or of several adjacent states. Ethnonationalist have organized leadership and occupy substantial territory. Indeed, they are typically concentrated in territorial enclaves. While they may be a minority in the nation, they are often a majority within that enclave. Social movements that arise among ethnonationalists usually form around demands for greater autonomy from the central state or, *in extremis*, independent statehood. Since the Second World War, at least thirty of these groups have fought protracted wars for national independence or for unification with kindred in other nations. Secessionist wars by Ibos in Nigeria, Eritreans in Ethiopia, and Tamils in Sri Lanka follow this pattern.

2   *Indigenous peoples* are also concerned with autonomy issues but they differ greatly from ethnonationalists in terms of their relative size and their ambitions with regards to the state. Indigenous peoples include the original inhabitants of conquered or colonized regions, and other relatively small groups that were subjugated without their consent. Most are subsistence farmers, herders, or hunters. They live in isolated territorial enclaves that are not well-integrated into the national economy or the national social system. They are subject to discrimination by more technologically advanced groups, a condition that tends to reinforce their ethnic identity and provide them with incentives to mobilize for defensive collective action. However, the goal of their collective action is not usually secession or revo-

lution, for they typically lack the numbers or the resources to sustain an armed rebellion against the state. Instead, they seek to protect their culture and their way of life from the threat of *ethnocide* represented by the prospect of forced assimilation into the culture of the larger nation in which they are contained. The Zapatista movement in southern Mexico fits this image of a movement of indigenous people.

3   *Communal contenders*, like ethnonationalists, are relatively large ethnic groups. However, unlike ethnonationalists, their main goal is not autonomy or secession but a greater share of power in the existing state. Where a multi-ethnic nation is governed by a multi-ethnic coalition, an *advantaged* group may come to dominate the coalition. Under these circumstances conflict occurs when other members of the coalition – communal contenders – seek to improve their standing at expense of others. Conflicts between Hutu and Tutsi in Rwanda and Burundi fit this pattern.

4   *Ethnoclasses* are minorities who occupy distinct social strata within a society and have specialized economic roles. Unlike ethnonationalists, they do not typically live in distinct territorial enclaves but instead are intermixed throughout society with other ethnic groups. In Third World nations, they often began as immigrant groups. In some cases, these immigrant classes were advantaged social strata, disproportionately represented among the merchant, civil service, or professional classes. In other cases, they were brought in to fulfill a demand for cheap labour in some critical economic sector, such as export agriculture. Accordingly, they are usually dispropor-tionately concentrated in lower status occupations. Many ethnoclasses are subject to political restrictions such as Chinese in Southeast Asia or Indians and Lebanese in Africa. Ethnoclasses resemble communal contenders in that they want to improve their status within existing political system. However, as long as they are not concentrated in a territorial enclave, they are not generally secessionists; instead, they seek an end to the discrimination that confines them to low status roles in society.

5   *Dominant minorities* are a subclass of culturally distinct ruling groups, such as Afrikaners in South Africa or Tutsi in Burundi. They use the power of their status to maintain their advantage by keeping other groups subordinate.

6   *Religious minorities* are groups whose religious beliefs and practices are distinct from those of the dominant group in society. Religious differences intensify conflicts between already ethnically divided groups.

Ethnicity and politics: theoretical approaches

With a typology of ethnic groups, we can explore the question of how one explains variations in the conditions under which each type of group is likely to engage in collective action and in the form that collective action takes. An important initial step, discussed earlier, was to define ethnicity in terms that allow its integration as a concept into existing theoretical frameworks on social change, political development and collective action. Rogowski's (1974: 71) and Horowitz's (1985: 46) definitions of ethnic markers as any identifying characteristics that have low cost of detection and a high cost of conversion has proven to be theoretically rich in that they provide us with access to the conceptual tools with which to explore the different ways in which ethnicity and other ascriptive characteristics affect individual political behaviour and participation in collective action.

From this perspective, it becomes possible to conceive of ways in which modernization or any other form of social change could reinforce ethnic identity and inter-ethnic conflict. First, modernization creates benefits and costs, both public and private in nature. These benefits must be allocated among different constituencies in society. Ethnicity is one way in which constituencies can be distinguished from each other in that it is relatively easy to allocate benefits and costs differentially according to ethnic criteria. In this manner, the opportunity structure and the changes in it that are generated by modernization and other forms of social change may be biased in favour of one ethnic group over another (Brass 1976; Melson and Wolpe 1970; Bates 1974; for an alternative view see Horowitz 1985: 103).

The differential distribution of the benefits of modernization may occur for a number of reasons. Largely serendipitous environmental factors may advantage one ethnic group over another when, for instance, one group happens to occupy territory in which rare minerals are located or the soil and climate are more appropriate for a particularly valued cash crop. The discovery of oil in the traditional homeland of the Ibo in Nigeria, for instance, no doubt added to their incentives for secession. In other cases, geography affords one group earlier and more frequent contact with the outside world and thereby gives that group a developmental 'head start' over other ethnic enclaves that are more isolated from global contacts. Some cultural groups may be more predisposed than others to take advantage of the new opportunities presented by the advent of modernization and to compete for the benefits of modernization (Melson and Wolpe 1970: 1115–16; see also Bates 1974: 464–6). In some cases this cultural predisposition may be a function of the niche occupied by that group in the pre-modern 'cultural division of labour'. For instance, an ethnic group that traditionally was denied access to land and therefore became concentrated in commercial activity as merchants may find itself favourably positioned to take advantage of the changes in the indigenous economy and social structure brought on by its integration into the global economy. Alternatively, that advantage may be conferred on it by a colonial power. The Tamil minority in Sri Lanka were disproportionately represented in the British colonial administration. After independence, the Sinhalese majority used its dominance in parliament to reverse the Tamil advantages and, indeed, to confer advantages on Sinhalese and disadvantages on Tamils in the markets for jobs and educational opportunities. If the benefits of modernization are distributed according to ethnic criteria, then the structural relationship between different ethnic groups becomes significant for explaining whether disadvantaged groups will engage in collective action to remedy these inequities and, if so, what form that collective action will assume. Structural approaches to ethnic politics are based on a fundamental distinction between vertical and horizontal differentiation, or between 'ranked' and 'unranked' systems of ethnic stratification.

Ranked systems of ethnic stratification

In a vertically integrated or 'ranked' system of inter-ethnic relations, stratification is synonymous with ethnicity in the sense that the status hierarchy is characterized by one ethnic group being subordinate to the other. Because ethnicity and class coincide, social mobility is restricted by ascriptive criteria (Horowitz 1971: 232; 1985: 23–5). Generally, the several ethnic groups are intermixed geographically so that interaction between members of the different ethnic groups is a routine feature of everyday social life. However, the relations between groups are governed by clearly recognized norms of superordinate and subordinate status. Behavioural norms governing inter-group relations in ranked systems typically have ritualized modes of expressing the subordinate group's deference and the superordinate group's dominance. In short, interactions approximate the etiquette of a caste system (Horowitz 1985: 26).

Despite the rigidity of ranked systems, relations between dominant and subordinate ethnic groups are usually characterized by some measure of social cohesion and shared expectations in addition to the coercion that preserves what Hechter has termed the 'cultural division of labor'. The dominant modality of interactions between members of the subordinate and dominant groups is that of a clientelist exchange: members of the subordinate group seek protection and subsistence security from their patrons in the dominant group in exchange for providing those patrons with personal services, loyalty, deference and a share of their economic output in what amounts to the extraction of rents by the dominant group (Horowitz 1985: 26). To challenge the system is to jeopardize one's subsistence security, and such an extreme risk is not undertaken lightly. Thus, we witness the persistence of ethnically ranked social structures in many Third World nations (and in the southern United States prior to the civil rights movement) despite the rather obvious and severe inequities that characterize them.

Ranked systems of ethnic stratification are subject to erosion by what Horowitz (1971: 236) terms the 'diffusion of universalistic norms' that accompanies modernization. The exchange relationship between ethnic groups breaks down as a result of changes in the local political economy induced by the nation's increasing integration into the global political economy. This process alters the local markets for land, labour and capital in such a way that elites in the dominant group find it profitable to divert resources away from production for local consumption and towards production for world markets. Under such circumstances, the cost of insuring their clients against the risks of subsistence crisis begins to appear less attractive compared to the returns they could accrue from diverting those resources into additional production for global markets. Consequently, they begin displacing clients from land and reducing their labour costs. At the same time, integration into the global economy also brings to the local economy new employers and occupational alternatives to agriculture. As a consequence, members of the subordinate group become less exclusively dependent on the dominant group for their subsistence. The rationale for continued deference to the dominant group erodes, and the other forms of discrimination that are embedded in the old cultural division of labor come to appear intolerable. At this point members of the subordinate group are subject to mobilization for collective action.

Unranked systems of ethnic stratification

The alternative to ranked systems is the 'unranked' or horizontally integrated system of ethnic stratification. Here, each ethnic group has its own stratification system internal to the group and distinct from that of all other groups. Different ethnic groups co-exist as parallel social hierarchies, with each group organized effectively as an incipient whole society. Indeed, in many cases groups in unranked systems were formerly constituted as more or less autonomous whole societies (Horowitz 1985: 24). In unranked systems, relations among members of different ethnic groups are characterized by a lack of mediating national authority that can establish a high level of reciprocity premised on equality in interactions between members of different groups (ibid.: 28). In this respect relations between groups take on the character of international relations (Horowitz 1971: 234).

Horowitz (1985: 35) argues that unranked systems have more ability to survive the changes and dislocations that accompany modernization and development because, within each ethnic group, there are opportunities for upward mobility, and the exploitation of these opportunities does not necessarily lead to inter-ethnic conflict. When inter-ethnic conflict does occur in an unranked system, it usually aims not at social transformation but at the exclusion from power of one group by another and the desire to revert to some ethnically homogeneous *status quo ante* (Horowitz 1971: 235). For this reason, violent inter-ethnic conflict in an unranked system is more likely to take the form of a secessionist revolt than a social revolution.

Van de Berghe (1967) sees the 'ranked' structure as being the most likely form of ethnic stratification to evolve in multi-ethnic societies. John Furnivall (1944) argues that ethnic systems can be broken down even further. He refers to ethnically heterogeneous societies as 'poly-ethnic social systems'. Relying on Furnivall, Fredrik Barth (1969) presents four forms of poly-ethnic social systems. First, ethnic groups may control separate niches and have minimal competition for resources, both economic and political. Second, ethnic groups may monopolize separate territories and compete for resources. Third, there may be a symbiotic relationship between groups whereby they provide important goods and services for each other. However, they may also compete if the goods and services provided by each group are obtained through the monopolization of different means of production. Finally, ethnic groups may partially compete within the same niche. Overtime, one group will displace the other or assimilation will occur.

Ranked and unranked systems create two rather distinct bases for ethnic competition and conflict. However, conflict of interests does not necessarily lead to collective action. Cultural divisions of labour and competitive ethnicity are far more pervasive than ethnic conflict or ethnic collective action. Theories of ethnic relations must address the question of how mobilization along ethnic lines is achieved. With ethnicity as the basis of shared interests, what are the obstacles to collective action in pursuit of those interests and what role does ethnicity play in overcoming those obstacles to collective action?

Reactive ethnicity versus ethnic competition

The implications of this distinction between ranked and unranked systems has been elaborated theoretically in the juxtaposition of Michael Hechter's 'internal colonialism' model of inter-ethnic relations with the emerging 'ethnic competition' model of such relations. Internal colonialism explores the social and behavioural implications of ranked structures of inter-ethnic relations while the ethnic competition model can be seen as an elaboration of the social and political implications of unranked structures of ethnic relations.

Central to Hechter's internal colonialism model is the concept of a 'cultural division of labour' (CDL). This refers to a pattern of structural discrimination such that 'individuals are assigned to specific types of occupations and other social roles on the basis of observable cultural traits or markers' (Hechter 1974: 1154). From this perspective, the structure of relations between subordinate and superordinate ethnic groups corresponds to the sort of exploitation that characterizes relations between peripheral and core nations in neo-colonial patterns of international relations (hence the term 'internal colonialism'). Ethnic boundaries coincide with lines of structural differentiation, and as a consequence ethnic solidarity is intensified (Nielsen 1985: 133). Where the stratification system links ethnic identity and economic status, it confers a meaning to ethnic identity that persists so long as this linkage between status and ascriptive traits remains. Ethnic solidarity is reinforced as a reaction of a culturally distinct periphery against exploitation by the centre. Hence, a number of scholars have referred to this consequence of CDL as 'reactive ethnicity', whereby ethnic solidarity is reinforced by the perceived exploitation of the subordinate group by the superordinate (Nielsen 1985: 133). Under these circumstances, ethnic differences do not disappear and indeed may form the basis for collective action by members of the peripheral communities against the core community because ethnic identity cannot be detached from one's economic and political interests within the system (Leifer 1981: 26; Birch 1978: 326–7).

Whereas the 'internal colonialism' argument and other reactive ethnicity variants predict that ethnic resurgence is more likely when there is a cultural division of labour, there has emerged an alternative 'ethnic competition' model that predicts that ethnic resurgence is more likely where the cultural division of labour has broken down and group inequalities have diminished (Nagel and Olzak 1982: 130–7). In an unranked system, competitive ethnicity emerges as members of different groups find themselves competing for the same resources (Nielsen 1985: 134). As culturally heterogeneous societies become industrialized, the proliferation of the market economy throughout the nation along with the increasing bureaucratization of society and other correlates of modernity should enhance the precedence of universalistic criteria that cut across the traditional ethnically based systems of ascribed status. The assignment of individuals to occupations and the distribution of societal rewards in general will increasingly be made on the basis of rational and achievement-based criteria that transcend ethnic boundaries.

However, this does not render ethnic distinctions irrelevant. The benefits of modernization are highly desired but relatively scarce. Consequently, members of different ethnic groups increasingly find themselves in a position to compete against each other for the same occupations and rewards. As these changes progress, they tend to reinforce rather than erode ethnic solidarity (Nielsen 1985: 133–4; see also Hannan 1979; Nielsen 1980; Ragin 1979; Olzak 1983). Extension of the rational labour market renders the types of interests motivating members of an ethnic group more nearly homogeneous and thereby makes the ethnic group more salient as an organizational channel for collective action (Nielsen 1985: 142). Therefore, ethnic groups persist because of their capacity to extract goods and services from the modern sector and thereby satisfy the demands of their members for the benefits of modernity (Bates 1974: 471).

The capacity of ethnic groups to extract resources from the modern sector depends upon their capacity to impose sanctions on those of their membership who do not act to advance the status of the group, especially elites who do not use their elite status to enhance their standing within their own ethnic group. Many modernized members of an ethnic group convert their success in the modern sector into status in the traditional sector of the ethnic group by using the income they have received from the modern sector to cultivate clientelist support networks among those members of their own ethnic group (Bates 1974: 472–4). If they decline to do so, they may be subject to sanctions by the membership of their own ethnic group. The likelihood of this occurring would depend on how easily they can be identified as members, how readily their non-support can be detected, and how capable the existing regime is in imposing its will on a discontented ethnic group. Hence, ethnicity becomes salient in the competition over the benefits of modernization for both elites and non-elites.

Bates (1974: 465–6) has argued that in many African nations the rise of ethnic competition is a direct legacy of colonial administration. By delineating administrative boundaries along tribal lines, colonial powers made it in the interests of their subjects to organize along ethnic lines so as to gain control over the administrative machinery with which the modernization process was managed. Local administration controlled such things as access to markets and market stalls, the regulation of crop production and animal husbandry, the construction of roads for the export of produce, and, in many cases, access to land. Local councils often acted to bias the distribution of and access to these resources in favour of the local ethnic group. Because control over the distribution of the benefits of modernity was vested in the local administration whose jurisdiction corresponded with ethnic boundaries, it was natural for local communities to coalesce into politically cohesive ethnic groupings and to utilize this solidarity to restrict the degree to which local or national administration could compel the sharing of the benefits of modernity with members of other ethnic groups (Bates 1974: 464–7).

Ethnic conflict

Stuart Kaufman (1996: 111–5) has offered a set of conditions that must be present for tensions between ethnic groups to escalate into armed conflict (see also Posen 1993). First, there must be ethnic hostility that is based in part on rationally calculated grievances but fuelled by emotional hate and fear. Second, a *security dilemma* must arise, whereby one group fears annihilation by another and arms itself in defense against that possibility. In so doing, its actions engender fear of annihilation on the part of the other ethnic group, so that its members arm themselves as well.

Thus, the contending groups begin the spiral toward ethnic violence. Finally, there must be leaders in each group who fan the flames of ethnic fear and hatred and use those fears to mobilize members of their group for violent collective action. Indeed, it is usually these leaders who instigate the fear of annihilation among the members of their own ethnic constituency and thereby create an ethnic security dilemma.

Under what conditions is an ethnic security dilemma likely to arise? Structural arguments suggest a number of factors that make ethnic tensions more or less likely to generate a security dilemma that escalates to armed conflict. The number of ethnic groups in the nation (or the degree of ethnic fragmentation) as well as the extent to which groups are dispersed throughout the territory or concentrated in geographic enclaves can affect the likelihood of ethnic conflict erupting. Often nations that are fragmented among a large number of different ethnic groups are less prone to serious ethnic strife than nations with a small number of groups (i.e., two or three) that are relatively equal in size (Melson and Wolpe 1970: 1121–2). If the nation is fragmented among a large the number of relatively small ethnic groups, each of which is geographically concentrated in a distinct enclave, there is little incentive for any one group to devote much of its time and resources to political activity beyond its own locality (Horowitz 1985: 37). It is also unlikely that any one group will enjoy suffi-cient numerical advantage to threaten hegemony over the other groups. Nor is it likely that a coalition of groups will emerge with sufficient strength to exert dominance over the other groups. In short, an ethnically-based security dilemma is less likely to emerge in a system that is fragmented among a large number of geographically dispersed groups. Inter-ethnic relations approximate a multi-polar balance of power system in international relations. In addition, the state has greater flexibility in responding to the demands emanating from the individual groups. It can often accede to the demands of one group without necessarily injuring the interests of another. Moreover, the state can deal with the demands of one group at a time, assuring the other groups that they need not fear destabilizing ethnic upheavals (Horowitz 1971: 238).

When the number of ethnic groups is relatively small (two or three) and they are concentrated in territorial enclaves, each ethnic group becomes a potential contender for control over the central state, either out of hegemonic ambitions of its own or out of a defensive desire to preempt hegemony by rival ethnic groups. Accommodating the demands of one group often comes at the expense of another (Horowitz 1971: 239). This is one set of circumstances in which a security dilemma can emerge, setting off a spiral toward ethnic conflict. The other set of circumstances that can generate a security dilemma is when there are only two or three groups that are intermixed geographically, and one or the other comes to fear annihilation by the other. If one group mobilizes to defend itself, the other group may interpret that mobilization as a threat to its existence and mobilize its members as well. In these instances, the structure of relations between the contending ethnic groups becomes critical in determining the likelihood that inter-ethnic conflict will occur and, if it does, what form it will assume.

We have discussed the ways in which variations in the strength and source of ethnic identity and in the configuration of inter-ethnic relations affect the ways in which ethnicity comes to serve as a source of shared interests. However, shared inter-ests do not automatically lead to collective action and even less often to violent ethnic conflict. Fearon and Laitin (1996) note the relative rarity of ethnic collective action and attribute this to the obstacles to such action posed by the disjunction between individual interest and collective action (see also Hechter, Friedman and Appelbaum 1982: 414). Ethnic divisions, as we have seen, are rather common features among the members of the contemporary nation-state system. Ethnic groups typically co-exist in some structural arrangement characterized by the differential distribution of societal benefits on the basis of ethnicity. If such discrimination were sufficient to induce ethnic conflict, then ethnic conflict would be far more pervasive and persistent than it is in fact. Indeed, what is striking is the relative rarity of ethnic collective action in a global system in which ethnic stratification is anything but rare.

Rational choice theory offers an explanation for why such conflict is so rare: despite the presence of shared interests defined along ethnic lines, it is still always not rational for individuals to participate in ethnic collective action to advance those interests (or redress their grievances) unless the free rider problem, as elaborated by Mancur Olson (1965) can be overcome. According to Olson, individuals have an incentive to withhold their support for or participation in group action aimed at the production of collective benefits because, should the action succeed, they will be able to partake of the collective benefits anyway and, assuming the group is large enough, their own particular contribution will not substantially affect the probability that the collective action will produce the desired public benefits. Free rider tendencies can be overcome by the provision of 'selective incentives', which are private benefits (or punishments) that are available only to those who participate (or do not participate) in the collective action. Beyond selective incentives, anything that decreases the cost of participation or increases the impact of one's own contribution on the production of collective benefits will make an individual more inclined to participate. In particular, free rider tendencies can be diminished by the presence of a leadership whose organizational skills give people the assurance that their contributions will make a difference and will not be in vain (Frohlich, Oppenheimer and Young 1971). Hence, the central issue of specifically ethnic conflict is how ethnicity facilitates the task of overcoming free rider tendencies.

According to Rogowski and Wasserspring (1971: 20–1), the necessary and sufficient conditions under which it will be rational for an individual to engage in ethnically based collective action are:

1   the individual must be a member of a stigmatized group;
2   he/she must perceive some group-specific collective good as desirable;
3   ethnic collective action must offer a 'cheaper' way of obtaining the good than does conversion out of the group;
4   the individual must believe that his/her own contribution will make at least some difference in determining whether or not the desired good is produced.

Accordingly, rational choice theory suggests that 'the position of an ethnic group in the stratification system has no direct bearing either on any member's decision to participate or on the group's propensity to engage in collective action' (Hechter, Friedman and Appelbaum 1982: 420). Instead, 'the role of stratification in collective action is indirect; it operates principally through its effects on group solidarity (that is, the member's compliance with the group's normative obligations) and organization' (ibid.: 421).

Rogowski (1985) argues that the tendency toward ethnically based collective action will differ depending upon whether the structure of inter-ethnic relations is characterized by a cultural division of labour (i.e. a ranked system) or, alternatively, a 'pillarized' structure of parallel (i.e. unranked) ethnic communities. In the former, upward social mobility effectively requires assimilation into the culture of the super-ordinate ethnic group (ibid.: 92). The ease with which they can be assimilated will be a function of the willingness of the superordinate group to accept them and the ability of the upwardly mobile to avoid negative sanctions from the subordinate group for assimilating. This, in turn, will often depend upon the strength of the ethnic markers that distinguish members of the subordinate from the dominant group. Ethnicity, as a set of markers that are relatively easy to detect and costly to alter, renders the detection and punishment of defectors relatively easy and therefore makes upwardly mobile members of a subordinate ethnic group more inclined to pursue the mobilization of their own ethnic compatriots rather than to seek assimi-lation into the dominant group.

If the dominant group resists assimilation of upwardly mobile members of the subordinate group, then eventually the subordinate group will have its own cadre of skilled leaders. Having been denied access to leadership positions in the society because of their ethnic heritage, these leaders have a powerful incentive to organize the subordinate group for collective action aimed at altering permanently the cultural division of labour in such a way as to create opportunities for themselves to assume leadership positions. The independence movement in India was led by British-educated Indians who, despite their qualifications, were denied acceptance into British society or advancement beyond middle levels of the British colonial administration. In these circumstances, free rider tendencies are overcome, first for the elite of the subordinate group by the promise of the selective incentives of leader-ship positions in the new social order that will result from collective action, and for the masses of the subordinate group by the organizational activities of these aspiring elites (Van Belle 1996). The creation by dissident elites of an effective opposition organization increases non-elites' estimate of the likelihood that their contributions, no matter how small, will be aggregated with those of others in such a way as to produce the collective benefits. In short, the creation of an organization enhances their willingness to participate in collective action by giving them greater confidence that their contributions will not be in vain (Frohlich, Oppenheimer and Young 1971). Following Rogowski (1985), then, the role of ethnicity in collective action is that it simplifies the identification of potential allies in the collective action and the detection and sanctioning of those members who attempt to free ride and/or assimi-late into the status system of the rival ethnic group.

Ethnic collective action in ranked systems is especially impeded by the difficulty subordinate groups face in developing the leadership cadre capable of mobilizing members for collective action. The stringent ethnic criteria for social mobility in ranked systems all but preclude the emergence of leaders from the subordinate group who have the organizational skills and resources to build collective action organizations. Members of the subordinate group are usually denied access to the educational or occupational opportunities that would allow them to acquire the knowledge, experience, and skills necessary to become effective organizers. Any efforts to instigate collective action are likely to be detected by the dominant group and repressed quickly and severely. Thus, despite the obvious and extreme inequities inherent in those systems, ranked systems of ethnic stratification have persisted in many nations precisely because there are such formidable obstacles to organizing dissident challenges from among the subordinate group.

Another impediment to collective action in ranked systems of ethnic stratification is that members of the subordinate group typically lack the material resources to contribute to collective action. The strict ethnic criteria that govern occupational mobility in ranked systems relegate members of the subordinate group to low income occupations. Indeed, in many ranked systems the subordinate group remains dependent on the dominant group for their very subsistence. Members of the dominant group monopolize control over land, credit, jobs, and other means of subsistence. By manipulating access to these resources, the dominant group can compel the quiescence of the subordinate group and keep them so impoverished that they do not have the time or resources to contribute to any dissident organization that might emerge from within their own ranks. As long as the dominant group can keep the subordinate group preoccupied with subsistence security, they can deter them from contributing time, money, or other resources to any dissident organization.

For all of these reasons, ethnically based collective action, especially violent collective action, is less likely to emerge in ranked systems than in unranked systems. However, when conflict does erupt in a ranked system, it is likely to be extremely violent. Indeed, ethnic violence in ranked systems takes on the character of a social revolution because the only outcome that is worth the extreme risks that accompany challenging the dominant group is the destruction of the rigidly hierarchical structure of ethnic stratification (Horowitz 1971: 234). This pattern was evident in many of the anti-colonial revolts that occurred in Africa and Southeast Asia during the process of decolonization. Colonial governments typically maintained rather stringently ranked systems of ethnic stratification, with the indigenous population being relegated to low status labor positions that supported the extractive economy created by the colonial power. Colonial administration and the commercial economy were monopolized by a European elite. When the system was challenged, either the colonial power acceded to the demands of the indigenous population and granted independence (as the British did in India and most of its African colonies), or the colonial power resisted the challenge by the indigenous population and tried to repress the groups challenging their dominance. The challengers responded by shifting to violent tactics of their own, as witnessed in French Indochina and Algeria, as well as the Portuguese colonies of Angola and Mozambique. Thus, conflict in ranked systems is rare because of the extreme risk that accompanies it; but when it does occur, it tends to be extremely violent because the outcome that subordinate group rebels seek is destruction of the ranked system of ethnic stratification.

In Hechter and Levi's (1979: 266) resource mobilization formulation of ethnic conflict, any group will engage in collective action only if it has the capacity to do so, and this will depend upon the tolerance of dissident cultural and political organization by the central state; an infrastructure of pre-existent voluntary associations; and the availability of sufficient resources to sustain organized activity (see also Tilly 1978; McCarthy and Zald 1977). In an ethnically divided society, whether ranked or unranked, traditional communal organizations typically will be ethnically based: because social benefits are distributed along ethnic lines, shared needs and grievances will likewise correspond to ethnic divisions, as will the communal organizations that emerge to address those needs

We can expect the state to be more tolerant of such organizations when they are ethnically based because to attempt their suppression would be to invite an ethnic backlash. Furthermore, in a ranked system, a central state controlled by the dominant ethnic group would prefer the emergence of local communal organizations among the subordinate groups to the necessity of the state itself having to provide the same services out of its own resources. Similarly, in an unranked system, the central state will be tolerant of ethnically based communal organizations because, by definition, each ethnic group has its own hierarchy of social strata and, consequently, will develop its own organizational infrastructure to address the needs of its members.

Indeed, for these reasons, the central state may be more tolerant of an ethnically based network of dissident political organizations in an unranked system than in a ranked one. In a ranked system, the state has a greater capacity to suppress such organizations. And in a ranked system, the constituency of such organizations would have at their disposal a smaller pool of resources to contribute to the support of opposition political organizations. Hence, ethnically based communal organizations are less likely to arise and more easily repressed in ranked than in unranked systems.

Because ethnic groups in unranked systems exist as relatively autonomous whole societies, organizing group members for collective action is not precluded in the same manner that it is in a ranked system. First, groups in unranked systems typically live in territorial enclaves, and geographic concentration makes it easier for group leaders to organize their constituents, free from interference, subversion, or intimidation by rival ethnic groups. Likewise, geographic concentration makes it more difficult for the state and rival ethnic groups to monitor dissident political mobilization by a particular ethnic group.

Second, the availability of opportunities for upward mobility within the status hierarchy of each ethnic group makes it easier for each group to cultivate its own cadre of leaders with the organizational skills to mobilize members for collective action. Ambitious and talented members of each group are not excluded from schools or jobs on the basis of ethnic criteria in the same way they would be in a ranked system of ethnic stratification. Therefore, more of them will be able to develop their talents to the point that they can fulfill the role of political entrepreneur, organizing the members of their ethnic group for collective action.

Finally, because members of each ethnic group can aspire to the full range of occupational strata, the group as a whole is more likely to have members with enough income beyond subsistence requirements to contribute materially to ethnic organizations that engage in collective action on behalf of the group. Dissident organizations that arise among aggrieved ethnic groups will have a greater pool of resources available for mobilization than is the case in a ranked system, where the inequitable distribution of resources and opportunities is enforced by the coercive capacity of the state.

This still leaves us with the question of how individual members of an ethnic group can be induced to participate in ethnic collective action generally and ethnic conflict specifically. Individuals can be induced to participate in collective action if they perceive that their participation will bring them private rewards ('selective incentives') and if they perceive that their contribution to the collective action will make some difference in the outcome (i.e. the production of the collective benefits). According to Hechter, Friedman and Appelbaum (1982: 425–7), an individual's esti-mate of the private rewards from participation in collective action will increase when: the organization has a store of resources apart from those to be gained through collective action; the organization's monitoring capacities are extensive enough that it can identify those supporters who are deserving of selective incentives and those free riders who are deserving of negative sanctions; and the organization has a proven record of justice in distribution. Following Olson (1965) they note that both the organization's ability to monitor and the individual's perception of the effi-cacy of the monitoring process will be increased when membership is small.

Ethnicity can enhance the individual's willingness to contribute to collective action in several ways. First of all, ethnicity makes the identification of potential participants easier for the leadership. They can target their recruitment efforts more efficiently by not wasting time and effort on non-members of the aggrieved ethnic group. Likewise, it is easier for the leadership to detect and sanction those who attempt to free ride. In short, as Rogowski (1985) has argued, ethnicity reduces the cost of information for the leadership in its efforts to overcome free rider tendencies.

When collective action takes the form of violent conflict, the calculus of participa-tion is complicated by the additional consideration of the risks of participation. Here, too, ethnicity can enhance the ability of leaders to overcome the tendency of group members to free ride in order to avoid the risks of participation in violent conflict. The strategy that the incumbent government adopts in dealing with ethnically based chal-lenges to its stability and legitimacy is likewise affected by the ethnic component of the conflict. Just as ethnic divisions enhance the ability of dissident leaders to identify and sanction free riders, the government can also use ethnicity as a means of identifying its actual, potential, or imagined enemies. If the government confines its repressive actions to known participants in opposition activities, the fact that those participants are from an identifiable ethnic group facilitates the government's ability to identify and punish them. So long as government is precise in targeting its repression, it can under-mine the ability of the opposition leadership to mobilize additional participants in its programme. However, if government repression escalates in scope and intensity to the point that its selection of targets for repression becomes relatively indiscriminate, then the ethnic character of the conflict can become an advantage for the opposition. When repression becomes so widespread and indiscriminate that membership in the dissident ethnic group effectively marks one as a target for repression regardless of one's partici-pation or non-participation in opposition activities, then members of the opposition ethnic group will have an incentive to join the opposition organization if for no other reason than to seek protection from indiscriminate government repression (Mason and Krane 1989). Free rider tendencies are overcome by the calculus of fear that is induced by government repression targeted indiscriminately against members of the dissident ethnic group.

Ethnicity and democracy

In addition to the proliferation of ethnic conflict, the last quarter of the twentieth century was marked by what Samuel Huntington has labelled the 'third wave of democracy'. Over one hundred nation-states made the transition from some form of authoritarian rule to political democracy. Though for many of these new regimes it remains to be seen whether they will be able to consolidate democracy, the fact that so many nations have embarked on such a profound transition is unprecedented. While the transition to democracy is the subject of other chapters in this volume, it is appropriate to consider in this chapter how ethnic divisions in a nation affect the dynamics of democratic transition and the prospects for democratic consolidation in ethnically divided democracies compared to new democracies where ethnicity is not a dominant source of identity or party formation.

Ethnic divisions pose a special set of challenges for the leaders of newly established democratic states. Societies that are deeply divided along ethnic line tend to produce party systems that exacerbate rather than moderate ethnic conflict. An ethnic party does not require exclusive command of an ethnic group's allegiance in order to survive. What matters is how *party* support is distributed, not how *group* support is distributed. A given ethnic group may split its support among several parties. However, if each *party* draws its support exclusively from one ethnic group, then ethnicity will tend to dominate party politics, and elections can degenerate into an to 'ethnic census'. Minority groups may eventually conclude that they are doomed to the status of permanent minority, with little or no prospect of ever winning enough votes to form a government or even participate in a governing coalition. If they also come to see themselves as targets of a legislative 'tyranny of the majority', they may withdraw their support from and participation in the democratic system and choose instead to pursue their interest through violent conflict.

According to Horowitz (1985: 309), the pressures toward an ethnically based party system are evident in the evolution of party systems in post-colonial Africa and Asia. Many of the parties that developed there near the end of the colonial era began as multi-ethnic social movements. Their founding leaders framed identities in terms of nationalist independence. They avoided ethno-nationalist appeals since that would have undermined popular unity in support of the goal of independence. After independence, the challenge facing these leaders was to convert their anti-colonial social movement into an equally multi-ethnic political party. Their success depended in part on how the institutional rules of the game in the new state encouraged or discouraged the growth of multiple parties. Where proportional representation (PR) rules were adopted for legislative elections, multiple parties could emerge and survive while commanding only a small proportion of the popular vote. To the extent that multiple parties proliferated, they could chip away at the multi-ethnic party's base of support by making ethnically based appeals to ethnic minorities in the electorate. Under PR rules appeals targeted to a narrowly defined segment of the population (such as an ethnic minority or even a radical segment of an ethnic minority) can win a party enough seats in the legislature to deny the dominant multi-ethnic party a majority and thereby compel that party to negotiate concessions in order to form a governing coalition.

After independence, multi-ethnic parties (now governing parties or at least competing for the right to be the governing party) often faced intensified and some-times incompatible demands from their different ethnic constituencies. To satisfy the demands of one ethnic constituency, they risked alienating supporters among other ethnic constituencies. While the party leaders may have preferred to preserve the multi-ethnic, nationalist character of the party and its platform, they were faced with the risk of losing support to ethnic activists who catered to the demands of one ethnic group. Nationalist leaders were forced to choose between becoming ethnic party leaders themselves or losing significant blocs of supporters from several ethnic groups. Transforming their own party into an ethnic party allowed them to consolidate their support among one segment of their once multi-ethnic constituency, even if it meant resigning themselves to being a permanent minority party in the legislature. Their best hope, then, was to preserve enough support among a sufficiently large single ethnic group to ensure that their party would be a valued if not necessary partner in any governing coalition.

According to Horowitz (1985: 193), the pressures for parties to coalesce around ethnic identity come from imperatives both internal and external to the party system and the parties themselves. To the extent that ethnic groups in a nation are segregated along lines of residence, language, and religion, parties are compelled to appeal for votes along ethnic lines. In such circumstances, ethnic appeals offer party elites a secure base of support: 'politicians who can count have something they can count on' (Horowitz 1985: 295). To the extent that parties come to rely on an ethnic base of voter support, the mediation of inter-group differences becomes difficult because to compromise with other ethnic parties is to be seen as compromising the interests of one's own ethnic base of support. Party leaders who pursue such a strategy leave themselves vulnerable to challengers from within their own ethnic group.

Chief among the external imperatives is that once one party organizes along ethnic lines, others are inclined to follow suit, even if this is contrary to the preferences of the party leaders themselves (Horowitz 1985: 306). Parties that attempt to ameliorate ethnic tensions in society by appealing across ethnic lines face the prospect of challengers arising who play the ethnic card in order to win a significant bloc of supporters from within their own ethnic group. As demands from constituencies within the once multi-ethnic party begin to coalesce along ethnic lines, leaders are compelled to 'go ethnic' themselves in order to preserve some base of support. Otherwise, their multi-ethnic coalition may dissolve into a collection of competing ethnic blocs, each led by a challenger who is satisfied with a committed and loyal minority of voters (Horowitz 1985: 309). Party leaders come to recognize that they cannot count on defections from other ethnic group to offset any loss of voter support from within their own ethnic base. Consequently, those leaders who, in the absence of challengers from within their own group, would prefer to build a multi-ethnic party, are compelled to consolidate their own ethnic base of support by 'going ethnic'.

Party leaders prefer strategies that result in electoral victory. In multi-party systems, leaders often must settle for strategies that lead to mere representation, as opposed to majority control of legislature. The special dilemma that party leaders face in an ethnically divided society is that, first, they are unlikely to win a clear majority of seats. Instead, they are compelled to search for electoral strategies that produce marginal gains at best in the number of seats they control. If other parties appeal to voters along ethnic lines, then they may lose seats themselves if they do not play the ethnic card. Yet if they do 'go ethnic', their ability to make even marginal gains in the number of seats they control is constrained by the relative size of the ethnic group that forms their base constituency. In effect, they face greater competitive pressures from other parties within their own ethnic group than from parties from other ethnic groups. Competition for votes tends to be *within* ethnic lines, not across ethnic lines, in what has been termed a 'segmented electoral market'. Competition within an ethnic group can be fierce and result in replacement of one ethnic party by another. Soon after independence in Sri Lanka, the predominantly Sinhalese United National Party tried to form a multi-ethnic coalition with the Tamil Congress, the largest party of the minority Tamil population. Soon the UNP faced a challenge from the Sri Lanka Freedom Party (SLFP), composed of former UNP members who had become disenchanted with what they saw as the failure of that party's leaders to defend the interest of the Sinhalese majority and the Buddhist religion against Tamil Hindu minority's dominance of the economy and the civil service. Soon the UNP was forced to abandon any efforts at multi-ethnic coalition and instead adopt much of the SLFP's 'Sinhalese only' legislative agenda. Otherwise, the UNP would likely have been eclipsed as a major party.

Once a party system has coalesced along ethnic lines, legislative politics naturally polarizes around ethnic issues as well, reinforcing rather than moderating the tendencies toward ethnic conflict. The ethnic issue axis comes to dominate the legislative agenda to the point of preempting the electoral salience of other issue axes. Any attempt by a party to introduce other issues into the electoral arena subjects that party to challenges from within its own ethnic group. As voters coalesce into ethnic voting blocs, party leaders are confronted with the reality that there are no swing voters to be won by appeals to non-ethnic interests. Party leaders have a strong incentive to take care of extremist voters within their ethnic group in order to preempt challengers from within their own group. Party leaders who try to accommodate across ethnic lines run the risk of catalyzing the radical fringe of their group to form a challenger party. This pulls the centre of the original ethnic party away from the centre of the national polity (Horowitz 1985: 346).

Once a party system has coalesced along ethnic lines, the prospects for democratic consolidation rest on how effectively ethnically based parties can cooperate in the legislature to address critical policy matters. *Coalitions of convenience* are perhaps the weakest cooperative mechanism that can emerge. These are coalitions of ethnic parties that form after the election. The parties in the coalition competed against each other in the elections and opposed each other on a number of ethnic issues. The post-election coalition is a coalition driven by convenience or necessity in the sense that the parties join forces solely for the purpose of forming a governing majority in the legislature. Coalitions of convenience are dictated often by numbers: if there are three or more parties with no one in majority, some coalition must be formed to get anything done. The major incentive for them to compromise thereafter is the simply the incentive to preserve the governing majority. Convergence on issues and moderating ethnic divisions are not motives for the formation of such coalitions. They simply agree to bargain over ethnic issues. The weakness of such coalitions is that they are not based on any shared commitment on issues. Accordingly, it is much easier for coalitions of convenience to dissolve than to form in the first place. If norms of reciprocity or the original bargain dissolve, so does the coalition.

Coalitions of commitment are also temporary. Parties in such a coalition still run for office separately and retain their own organizational identity. However, the coalition is formed not just on the basis of minimum winning criteria; partners have a shared commitment to moderate ethnic tensions. That commitment is usually reflected in parties' willingness to share seats by agreeing not to compete against each other for all seats in all districts. In this manner they enhance the prospects of one of the parties in the coalition winning each seat and they reduce the prospects of a third party not in the coalition – and, therefore, not sharing their commitment to moderating ethnic tensions – winning the seat.

The alternatives to a reasonably well-functioning coalition of ethnic parties are 1) the party system can degenerate into a one-party dominant system, or 2) one or more of the ethnic parties withdraws from parliamentary politics and reconstitutes itself as a challenger to the regime, through violence if necessary. In an environment of ethnic conflict, there is room for only one multi-ethnic party or alliance. After it is formed, all remaining electoral opportunities are at the flanks of the political spectrum. Indeed, the formation of an alliance of ethnic parties often leads to party formation at the flanks. To win any votes, flank parties must take extreme positions, which usually disqualifies them from participation in the governing coalition. These dynamics often lead to the degeneration of party politics into either a one party system or violent ethnic conflict (Horowitz 1985: 429).

Where multi-ethnic parties survive, they often do so by outlawing or severely constraining electoral competition, dissolving the opposition, or recreating by coercion their multi-ethnic base. Single party systems emerge in response to the inability of multi-ethnic parties (usually formed in opposition to colonialism) or coalitions of ethnic parties to maintain their multi-ethnic support in the face of elections (Horowitz 1985: 429). This occurs as a reaction to flanking. Flanking parties threaten to erode the constituency of the multi-ethnic party or coalition. In so doing, they can make democratic rule difficult by denying the dominant party or coalition the ability to form a governing majority. Under these conditions, legislative immobility may compel the dominant party/coalition to suspend elections and severely restrict participation in them, all in the name of preserving national unity.

One-party dominant regimes, in which the dominant party is the party of national liberation can often preempt the fragmentation of the party system along ethnic lines by shaping the electoral rules in ways that impede the easy emergence of new parties capable of challenging its dominance. Their success depends on their ability to establish and maintain a patronage machine that can consolidate a base of electoral support not based strictly on ethnic appeals. So long as the party can reward voters with tangible benefits for their continued support, it can preempt the emergence of ethnic challenger parties. One-party regimes in Kenya and Zambia, for instance, sought to moderate ethnic tensions by including powerful ethnic leaders in the central government's cabinet and legislature. These leaders were provided with patronage resources to distribute to their followers in return for dampening any tendency toward conflict among their constituents. In effect, national leaders sought to create a 'grand coalition' groups within the confines of a single national party (see Rothchild 1997: 29–30).

A third alternative for managing ethnic politics in a democracy is *consociationalism* or compromise by segregation (Lijphart 1969). This model attempts to produce a mixture of autonomy and power-sharing among ethnic groups. Group autonomy extends to the realms of culture and local governance. The key elements of consociationalism revolve around ethnic self-determination enshrined in the structure of power-sharing (i.e. federalism). Through group autonomy, as well as checks within the political process to maintain this autonomy, competing ethnic groups may be able to co-exist within the same state. Consociationalism applies best to groups that are geographically concentrated. As Kymlicka (1995) points out, the problem with self-government lies with maintaining the balance between centralization and de-centralization.

Another key element of consociational arrangements is the concentration on collective rights. Indeed, one criticism often levelled at consociationalism is that its grant of ethnic autonomy over a range of policy issues has the effect of institutionalizing ethnic boundaries. Explicit grants of group rights may allow a minority group to shield itself from the policies of a national government controlled by the dominant ethnic group. In a democratic sense, this requires that the minority ethnic group will need in some way to bargain with the dominant ethnic group for relief, possibly through a polyethnic discourse. In the second case, groups intent on maintaining their own cultural heritage must reduce the incentives of their own members to assimilate because assimilation weakens the group's claim to autonomy. Laitin (1993, 1998) argues that while maintaining group boundaries is a choice made by the group as a whole, assimilation is an individual action. Assuming that partial or complete assimilation brings with it some benefits, individuals who assimilate are likely to gain from the access to opportunities outside their own ethnic community while at the same time gaining from the group's efforts to maintain its own boundaries from external pressures. The optimal outcome for individuals is to individually assimilate while at the same time supporting group rights. One individual's assimilation will have no impact on group solidarity and claims to autonomy. However, as a classic tragedy of the commons problem, all members of the group pursuing this individually optimal strategy will eventually undermine the group's claims to autonomy and group rights.

Ethnic politics in the dissolution of Yugoslavia and the Soviet Union

The other momentous event of the last decade that was driven by ethnic politics was the dismemberment of the Soviet Union, Yugoslavia and Czechoslovakia along ethnic lines. Three nations disintegrated into 22 sovereign units. Both the Soviet Union and Czechoslovakia made the transition relatively peacefully (though the successor states of the Soviet Union have been torn by violent ethnic conflict) while a series of secessionist wars marked the dismemberment of Yugoslavia into its constituent republics. These were watershed events not just in the development of those three nations but in the evolution of the international system. Prior to this, there had been only one instance of successful secession recognized by the international community: the Bangladesh secession from Pakistan in 1971. Other secessionist wars – Sudan, Nigeria, Morocco, Iraq, Ethiopia, Sri Lanka, and the Philippines, to name but a few – had met with resistance (or at least non-support) from an international community committed to the legal sanctity of nation-states and their formal borders. Secessionist movements rarely if ever earned international recognition as legitimate claimants, no matter how egregious the disjunction between the formal borders of nation-states and the cultural boundaries of the peoples who occupied them. The dissolution of the Soviet Union in 1991 set a precedent: in the post-Cold War world, secession could be accepted by the international community. When Slovenia and Croatia declared their independence from

Yugoslavia, they immediately gained diplomatic recognition from major powers, despite the objections of the Yugoslav state.

How do we account for the disintegration of the Soviet Union and Yugoslavia, and what role did ethnic politics play in their dismemberment? Clearly, ethnic divisions were the dominant issue driving the centrifugal tendencies that led to the dissolution of the Soviet Union and the violent dismemberment of Yugoslavia. Those ethnic tensions had their roots not only in the multi-ethnic diversity of those two nations but in the institutions of federalism that defined relations between centre and periphery in both nations and the policies toward ethno-national groups that both Marxist states adopted during their early years.

As noted earlier, Marxist theory conferred no legitimacy on ethno-national identity. For Marx, ethnicity and nationalism were both false consciousness. One's true identity was class identity. To the extent that one's identity was defined in terms of nationality or ethnicity, one was subject to exploitation by elites who sought to preserve their own dominance by dividing the proletariat against itself.

Yet the realities of politics in the early days of the Soviet Union and Yugoslavia compelled Lenin and Tito, respectively, to make concessions to the multiple ethnic groups that co-existed within their boundaries. To attempt to suppress ethno-national identity would have risked a backlash that would have jeopardized the stability of the new regime. Both founders placed a higher priority on building a modern industrial economy than on the forced assimilation of ethnic minorities. Assimilation by force would have diverted resources from other priorities. Besides, the Marxist theory predicted that prosperity and economic development would erode ethnic identity in favor of class identity anyway. Therefore, both regimes built into their original constitutions concessions to ethnic and cultural autonomy.

Constitutionally, these concessions to ethno-nationalist identity were incorporated into the institutions of federalism in both nations. In both Yugoslavia and the USSR, the republics that made up the units in the federal system were ethnic republics. In the Soviet Union, each republic was an ethno-linguistic community with its own language and religion. Indeed, national identity in the USSR was defined in terms of ethnicity and language, not residence. Someone born in Moscow of Armenian parents, for instance, would be designated Armenian on their identification, even if that person had never lived in Armenia (Hough 1997: 221–7). Federalism conferred on each of these communities their own set of economic and government institutions to be staffed by indigenous elites. In the Soviet Union, Moscow's oversight of the republics was achieved by what amounted to Russian colonization: in most of the fourteen non-Russian republics Russians made up the second largest ethnic group. Usually they were concentrated in key party and state offices as well as in leadership positions in major industrial enterprises.

Both nations constituted what Philip Roeder (1991: 199) has termed *ethno-federal states*. Valerie Bunce contends that the coincidence of ethnicity and territory had the effect of creating, 'states-in-the-making' in Yugoslavia and the Soviet Union. Each republic within each of these federal systems was a proto-nation-state, 'complete with their own borders, elites, national communities, and a full array of economic, political, social and cultural institutions' (Bunce 1999: 84–5). The federal structure politicized ethno-territorial divisions, giving them economic content as well as cultural and political meaning. Bargaining over power and privilege between the centre and the periphery was given a distinctly ethno-national content. In the case of the Soviet Union, language added another dimension of ethnic unity within republics and ethnic distinctiveness between the republics. In Yugoslavia, religious differences – Eastern Orthodox in Serbia, Islam in Bosnia, Catholicism in Croatia and Slovenia – provided another reinforcing source of cleavage between republics.

The convergence of protracted leadership succession in both the Soviet Union and Yugoslavia and the declining performance of each nation's economy undermined the ability of the national Communist Party to honor the commitments to republics that had held the federal system together. The passing of Tito and Brezhnev opened debate in both nations about the continued wisdom of their respective models of state socialism. In both cases, the politics of succession weakened the centre's willingness and ability to suppress dissident challenges from the republics. In effect, the political opportunity structure was altered in both nations in such a way as to allow more space for dissident appeals and for debate about the future of the economy and the political system. Poor economic performance undermined the centre's ability to purchase the loyalty of republican leaders by bestowing upon them economic resources to distribute to their ethnic constituencies. At the same time that their own patronage resources from the centre were contracting, republican leaders were facing greater pressure from their constituencies to provide them with the means to weather the degenerating macro-economic situation confronting both nations. With the centre economically debilitated and politically paralyzed (due to leadership change), republican leaders in both nations had little reason to continuing acting as agents of the centre in their dealings with their own constituents.

In Yugoslavia, Tito's death was followed by a restructuring of the institutional ties between the centre and the republics. A substantial share of the economic decision-making power was devolved to the republican level, and republican party elites were encouraged to pursue their own strategies to revive the economy of their own republic. Some succeeded and others did not. Regardless, the hold of the central party and state leadership over the republics was severely diminished by the post-Tito institutional reforms.

The keys to Yugoslavia's dismemberment were Slovenia and Serbia (Bunce, 1999: 91). They constituted, respectively, the most economically advanced and the most populous of the Yugoslav republics. Political liberalization in Yugoslavia confronted the communist parties of both republics with strong nationalist sentiment motivated by the perception that the current Yugoslav federal structure worked against their interests. Both nationalities felt that there was a significant gap between what they deserved and what they got from the existing federal structure. Serbs constituted the largest population, but the federal structure parcelled out political power (including votes in the legislature and seats in collective presidency) more equally among the republics. Serbs favored recentralization of power to address more effectively the crisis confronting Yugoslavia as a nation. Slovenians were the wealthiest of the republics and felt that they were being forced to subsidize poorer republics. Slovenia was also the most ethnically homogeneous of the six republics. Slovenians saw their best hope for the future in greater integration with the European Community, not greater integration with the rest of Yugoslavia. Once Slovenia seceded, secessionist sentiments heightened in Croatia over the fear that Serbia would attempt to restore by force the authority of the central state, under Serbian hegemony. A brief war of secession resulted in the exit of Croatia from the Yugoslav federation. This heightened concern among Bosnian Muslims that they would no longer be able to resist Serbian hegemony, especially in the absence of Slovenian and Croatian checks on Serbian ambitions. The secessionist war in Bosnia was the bloodiest and most protracted and required international military intervention and political mediation to resolve. Macedonian secession further dismembered what remained of the Yugoslav federation, and even the Serb republic has faced secessionist conflict from the ethnic Albanian minority in the Kosovo region.

The Gorbachev political reforms provided the institutional opening for the centrifugal forces of ethno-national politics to be unleashed in the USSR. When in 1989 Gorbachev introduced competitive elections for the newly constituted Congress of People's Deputies, he provided an opportunity for ethno-national activists to take their appeal directly to constituents in their respective republics. When competitive elections were extended to the republican level in 1990, ethno-national appeals for greater autonomy from Moscow became a fertile issue position for candidates in the non-Russian republics to build a winning coalition (see, for instance, Treisman 1997). The Baltic republics were the first to carry the newly empowered ethno-nationalist sentiments to the point of enacting what amounted to secessionist legislation. When newly elected legislatures in the other republics of the Soviet Union began drafting constitutions that effectively declared their independence from the USSR, Moscow was faced with the choice of forcibly repressing these movements or conceding to them and allowing the peaceful dissolution of the Soviet Union. When Boris Yeltsin assumed the Presidency of the Russian Federation and joined the other republics in calling for greater autonomy from Moscow, Gorbachev was left with a hollowed out regime that lacked the capacity to resist the centrifugal tendencies. The Treaty of the Union was replaced by the Confederation of Independent States, and the Soviet Union ceased to exist as a sovereign entity.

Political liberalization ended the communist party's hegemony in both nations. Given the ethno-national character of the federal structure that was infused with democratic reforms, it should not have been surprising that new parties would organize around ethno-national and even secessionist sentiments among the newly enfranchised voting publics in both nations. Yugoslavia's dismemberment was much more protracted and much bloodier. But both reveal the centrifugal tendencies inherent in ethno-federalism.

Conclusion

That ethnicity remains a powerful force in the contemporary political arena cannot be denied. This essay has presented an overview of the central theoretical issues defining the study of ethnic politics and the major conceptual frameworks that have evolved from the efforts of scholars to resolve these issues. In discussing the major theoretical frameworks in the field of ethnic politics, we have tried to illustrate their grounding in existing paradigms of behavioral science, their compatibility with those paradigms, and their contributions to the elaboration of the mainstream of research traditions on social change and development. Thus, structural theories of ethnic politics allow analysts to use the tools of rational choice theory, resource mobilization theory and conflict models to explain the emergence of ethnically based

social movements and the process by which their contention with the state can esca-
lated to armed conflict. Similarly, these models of ethnic politics have allowed
scholars to derive some predictions concerning the likely course of democratic transitions in ethnically divided societies. Finally, combining the two – ethnic
mobilization and democratic transitions – has allowed us to gain some insight into
how reforms in the Soviet Union and Yugoslavia eventually resulted in an outcome
unintended by the reformers: the dismemberment of those federal states into their
constituent republics. Given the pervasiveness of ethnic divisions among the nations
of the world, we can expect ethnic politics to play a significant role in other trends
emerging in the post-Cold War global order. Perhaps this essay can point to some of
the literature that can be of use to scholars and policy makers alike in anticipated
how the ethnic variable will affect the trajectory of politics within and between
nations in this new era.

Notes

1   The works that Connor surveyed are: (1) Gabriel Almond and James S. Coleman, *The
    Politics of Developing Areas* (Princeton: Princeton University Press, 1960); (2) Gabriel
    Almond and G. Bingham Powell, *Comparative Politics: A Developmental Approach*
    (Boston: Little, Brown, 1966); (3) Gabriel Almond and Sidney Verba, *The Civic Culture*
    (Boston: Little, Brown, 1963); (4) David Apter, *The Politics of Modernization* (Chicago,
    1965); (5) Wilard A. Beling and George O. Totten, eds, *Developing Nations: Quest for a
    Model* (New York, 1966); (6) Karl W. Deutsch and William Folz, eds, *Nation Building*
    (New York, 1966); (7) Jason Finkle and Richard Gable, eds, *Political Development and
    Social Change* (New York, 1966); (8) Philip E. Jacob and James V. Toscano, eds, *The
    Integration of Political Communities* (Philadelphia, 1964); (9) Lucian Pye, ed.,
    Communications and Political Development (Princeton: Princeton University Press, 1963);
    and (10) Lucian Pye, *Aspects of Political Development* (Boston: Little, Brown, 1966).
2   The journals are *International Studies Quarterly*, *World Politics*, *Comparative Politics*,
    Journal of Conflict Resolution.
3   MPLA is the Portuguese acronym for the Movement for the Popular Liberation of
    Angola. UNITA is the Portuguese acronym for the National Union for the Total
    Independence of Angola.

References

Anderson, B. (1991) *Imagined Communities: Reflections on the Origins and Spread of
    Nationalism*, London: Verso.
Banton, M. (1983) *Racial and Ethnic Competition*, Cambridge: Cambridge University Press.
—— (1998) *Racial Theories*, 2nd edn, Cambridge: Cambridge University Press.
Barth, E. A. T. (1969) *Ethnic Groups and Boundaries: The Social Organization of Culture
    Difference*, London: Allen & Unwin.
Barth, E. A. T. and Noel, D. (1972) 'Conceptual frameworks for the analysis of race relations:
    an evaluation', *Social Forces* 50: 333–48.
Bates, R. (1974) 'Ethnic competition and modernization in contemporary Africa', *Compara-
    tive Political Studies* 6: 457–84.
Beissinger, M. (1999) 'Event analysis in transitional societies: protest mobilization in the
    former soviet union', in D. Rucht, R. Koopmans, and F. Neidhardt (eds) *Acts of Dissent:
    New Developments in the Study of Protest*, Oxford: Rowman and Littlefield.
Birch, A. H. (1978) 'Minority nationalist movements and theories of political integration',
    World Politics 30: 325–44.

Blanton, Robert, Mason, T. David and Athow, Brian (2001) 'Colonial style and post-colonial ethnic conflict in Africa', *Journal of Peace Research* 38 (4): 473–89.

Brass, P. R. (1976) 'Ethnicity and nationality formation', *Ethnicity* 3: 225–41.

Bunce, V. (1999) *Subversive Institutions: The Design and the Destruction of Socialism and the State*, Cambridge, UK: Cambridge University Press.

Butler, D. and Stokes, D. (1969) *Political Change in Britain*, New York: St Martin's Press.

Chong, D. (1991) *Collective Action and the Civil Rights Movement*, Chicago: University of Chicago Press.

Connor, W. (1972) 'Nation-building or nation destroying?', *World Politics* 24: 31–55.

—— (1978) 'A nation is a nation', *Ethnic and Racial Studies* 1 (4): 379–88.

Feagin, J. R. and Hahn, H. (1973) *Ghetto Revolts: The Politics of Violence in American Cities*, New York: Macmillan.

Fearon, J. D. and Laitin, D. D. (1996) 'Explaining inter-ethnic cooperation', *American Political Science Review* 90: 715–35.

Frohlich, N., Oppenheimer, J. A. and Young, O. (1971) *Political Leadership and Collective Goods*, Princeton, NJ: Princeton University Press.

Furnivall, J. S. (1944) *Netherlands India: A Study of Plural Economy*, Cambridge: University Press.

Gellner, E. (1983) *Nations and Nationalism*, Ithaca: Cornell University Press.

—— (1994) *Encounters with Nationalism*, Oxford University Press: Blackwell.

Goldhagen, E. (ed.) (1968) *Ethnic Minorities in the Soviet Union*, New York/London: Praeger.

Greenfeld, L. (1990) 'The formation of the Russian national identity: the role of status insecurity and resentment', *Comparative Studies in Society and History* 32: 549–91.

Gurr, T. R. (2000) *People Versus States: Minorities at Risk in the New Century*, Washington, DC: United States Institute of Peace Press.

Gurr, T. R. and Harff, B. (1994) *Ethnic Conflict in World Politics,* Boulder, CO: Westview Press.

Haas, E. (1986) 'What is nationalism and should we study it?', *International Organization* 4: 707–44.

Hannan, M. (1979) 'The dynamics of ethnic boundaries in modern states', in M. Hannan and J. Meyer (eds) *National Development and the World System: Educational, Economic, and Political Change 1950–1970*, Chicago: University of Chicago Press.

Hechter, M. (1974) 'The political economy of ethnic change', *American Journal of Sociology* 79: 1151–78.

—— (1975) *Internal Colonialism: The Celtic Fringe in British National Development*, London: Routledge & Kegan Paul.

—— (1978) 'Group formation and the cultural division of labor', *American Journal of Sociology* 84: 293–318.

—— (1987) *Principles of Group Solidarity*, Berkeley: University of California Press.

—— (1987) 'Nationalism as group solidarity', *Ethnic and Racial Studies* 10 (4): 415–26.

Hechter, M. and Levi, M. (1979) 'The comparative analysis of ethnoregional movements', *Ethnic and Racial Studies* 2: 260–74.

Hechter, M., Friedman, D. and Appelbaum, M. (1982) 'A theory of ethnic collective action', *International Migration Review* 16: 412–34.

Holsti, K. J. (1992) 'International Theory and War in the Third World', pp. 37–60 in Brian L. Job (ed.) *The Insecurity Dilemma: National Security in Third World States*, Boulder: Lynne Rienner.

Horowitz, D. L. (1971) 'Three dimensions of ethnic politics', *World Politics* 23: 232–44.

—— (1973) 'Direct, displaced, and cumulative ethnic aggression', *Comparative Politics* 6: 1–16.

—— (1981) 'Patterns of ethnic separatism', *Comparative Studies in Society and History* 23: 165–95.

—— (1985) *Ethnic Politics*, Berkeley: University of California Press.

Hough, J. (1997) *Democratization and Revolution in the USSR, 1985–1991*, Washington: Brookings.

Jenkins, J. C. (1995) 'Social movements, political representation, and the state: an agenda and comparative framework', in J. Craig Jenkins and Bert Klandermans (eds) *The Politics of Social Protest: Comparative Perspectives on States and Social Movements*, London: UCL Press.

Jenkins, R. (1994) 'Rethinking ethnicity: identity, categorization and power', *Ethnic and Racial Studies* (April): 197–223.

Kaufman, S. J. (1996) 'Spiraling to ethnic war: elites, masses, and Moscow in Moldova's civil war', *International Security* 21: 108–38.

Kemp, W. A. (1999) *Nationalism and Communism in Eastern Europe and the Soviet Union: A Basic Contradiction*, New York: St Martin's Press, Inc.

King, C. and Melvin, N. (1998) *Nations Abroad: Diaspora Politics and International Relations in the Former Soviet Union*, Boulder: Westview Press.

Kymlicka, W. (1995) *Multicultural Citizenship: A Liberal Theory of Minority Rights*, Oxford: Clarendon Press.

Laitin, D. (1991) 'The national uprisings in the Soviet Union', *World Politics* 44: 139–77.

—— (1993) 'The game theory of language regimes', *International Political Science Review* 14 (3): 227–39.

—— (1998) *Identity in Formation: The Russian-speaking Populations in the Near Abroad*, Ithaca London: Cornell University Press.

Leifer, E. M. (1981) 'Competing models of political mobilization: the role of ethnic ties', *American Journal of Sociology* 87: 23–47.

Lijphart, A. (1969) 'Consociational democracy', *World Politics* 21: 207–25.

Lipset, S. M. and Rokkan, S. (1967) *Party Systems and Voter Alignments*, New York: Free Press.

McAdam, D. (1982) *Political Process and the Development of Black Insurgency, 1930–1970*, Chicago: University of Chicago Press.

McCarthy, J. D. and Zald, M. N. (1977) 'Resource mobilization and social movements: a partial theory', *American Journal of Sociology* 82: 1212–41.

Mason, T. D. and Krane, D. A. (1989) 'The political economy of death squads', *International Studies Quarterly* 33: 175–98.

Melson, R. and Wolpe, H. (1970) 'Modernization and the politics of communalism: a theoretical perspective', *American Political Science Review* 64: 1112–30.

Motyl, A. (ed.) (1995) *Thinking Theoretically about Soviet Nationalities*, New York: Columbia University Press.

Nagel, J. and Olzak, S. (1982) 'Ethnic mobilization in new and old states: an extension of the competition model', *Social Problems* 30: 127–43.

Nielsen, F. (1980) 'The Flemish movement in Belgium after World War II: a Dynamic analysis', *American Sociological Review*, 45 (1) (Feb.): 76–94.

—— (1985) 'Toward a theory of ethnic solidarity in modern societies', *American Sociological Review* 50: 133–49.

Olson, M. (1965) *The Logic of Collective Action*, Cambridge, MA: Harvard University Press.

Olzak, S. (1983) 'Contemporary ethnic mobilization', *Annual Review of Sociology* 9: 355–74.

—— (1989) 'Analysis of events in the study of collective action', *Annual Review of Sociology* 15: 119–41.

— (1992) *The Dynamics of Ethnic Competition and Conflict*, Stanford: Stanford University Press.

Parsons, T. and Smelser, N. (1956) *Economy and Society*, New York: Free Press.

Posen, B. (1993) 'The security dilemma and ethnic conflict', *Survival*, 35 (1): 27–47.

Ragin, C. C. (1979) 'Ethnic political mobilization: the Welsh case', *American Sociological Review* 44: 619–35.

Roeder, P. G. (1991) 'Soviet federalism and ethnic mobilization', *World Politics* 43 (2): 196–232.

Rogowski, R. (1974) *Rational Legitimacy: A Theory of Political Support*, Princeton, NJ: Princeton University Press.

—— (1985) 'Causes and varieties of nationalism: a rationalist account', in E. A. Tiryakian and R. Rogowski (eds) *New Nationalisms of the Developed West*, Winchester, MA: Allen & Unwin.

Rogowski, R. and Wasserspring, L. (1971) *Does Political Modernization Exist? Corporatism in Old and New Societies*, Beverly Hills, CA: Sage Professional Papers.

Rothchild, D. (1997) *Managing Ethnic Conflict in Africa*, Washington: Brookings.

Smith, A. (1991) *National Identity* London: Penguin Books.

Smith, G. (1996) 'The ethnic democracy thesis and the citizenship question in Estonia and Latvia', *Nationalities Papers* 24 (2): 845–64.

Snyder, J. (2000) *From Voting to Violence: Democratization and Nationalist Conflict*, New York: Norton.

Tajfel, H. and Turner, J. C. (1979) *An Integrative Theory of Intergroup Conflict*, Monterey, CA: Brooks.

—— (1986) 'The Social Identity Theory of Intergroup Behavior', in William G. Austin and Stephen Worchel (eds) *Psychology of Intergroup Relations*, Chicago: Nelson-Hall Publishers.

Tilly, C. (1978) *From Mobilization to Revolution*, Reading, MA: Addison-Wesley.

Tishkov, V. (1997) *Ethnicity, Nationalism, and Conflict in and after the Soviet Union: The Mind Aflame*, London: Sage Publishers.

Treisman, D. (1997) 'Russia's "ethnic revival": the separatist activism of regional leaders in a postcommunist order', *World Politics* 49 (2): 212–49.

Van Belle, D. A. (1996) 'Leadership and collective action: the case of revolution', *International Studies Quarterly* 40: 107–32.

Van de Berghe, P. (1967) *Race and Racism: A Comparative Perspective*, New York: John Wiley.

Wallensteen, P. and Sollenberg, M. (2001) 'Armed conflict, 1989–2000', *Journal of Peace Research* 38: 629–44.

Welsh, D. (1993) 'Domestic politics and ethnic conflict', in M. Brown (ed.) *Ethnic Conflict and International Security*, Princeton: Princeton University Press.

Wilder, A. (1986) 'Social Categorization: Implications for creation and reduction of intergroup bias', in L. Berkowitz (ed.) *Advances in Experimental Social Psychology*, New York: Academic Press.

Yack, B. (1999) 'The myth of the civic nation', in R. Beiner (ed.) *Theorizing Nationalism*, New York: State University Press.

Young, C. (1976) *The Politics of Cultural Pluralism*, Madison: University of Wisconsin Press.

Further reading

Armstrong, J. (1982) *Nations before Nationalism*, Chapel Hill: University of North Carolina Press.

Bartkus, V. O. (1999) *The Dynamics of Secession*, Cambridge, UK: Cambridge University Press.

Bonacich, E. (1972) 'A theory of ethnic antagonism: the split labor market', *American Sociological Review* 37: 547–59.

Brass, P. (1991) *Ethnicity and Nationalism*, London: Sage.

Brown, M. E. (ed.) (1993) *Ethnic Conflict and International Security*, Princeton: Princeton University Press.

Brown, M. E., Coté, O.R., Lynn-Jones, S. M. and Miller, S.E. (eds) (2000) *Nationalism and Ethnic Conflict*, Cambridge, MA: MIT Press.

Connor, W. (1994) *Ethnonationalism*, Princeton: Princeton University Press.

Enloe, C. H. (1973) *Ethnic Conflict and Political Development*, Boston: Little, Brown & Co.

Esman, M. J. (1977) *Ethnic Conflict in the Western World*, Ithaca, NY: Cornell University Press.

—— (1994) *Ethnic Politics*, Ithaca, NY: Cornell University Press.

Glazer, N. and Moynihan, D. P. (eds) (1975) *Ethnicity and Experience*, Cambridge, MA: Harvard University Press.

Gurr, T. R. (1994) 'Peoples against states: ethnopolitical conflict and the changing world system', *International Studies Quarterly* 38: 347–78.

Gurr, T. R. and Moore, W. H. (1997) 'Ethnopolitical rebellion: a cross-sectional analysis of the 1980s with risk assessment for the 1990s', *American Journal of Political Science* 41: 1079–103.

Horowitz, D. L. (2001) *The Deadly Ethnic Riot*, Berkeley, CA: University of California Press.

Jenkins, J. C. (1983) 'Resource mobilization theory and the study of social movements', *Annual Review of Sociology* 9: 527–53.

Kaufmann, C. (1996) 'Possible and impossible solutions to ethnic civil wars', *International Security* 20 (4): 136–75.

Lake, D. A. and Rothchild, D. (1996) 'Containing fear: the origins and management of ethnic conflict', *International Security* 21 (Fall): 41–75.

—— (1998) *The International Spread of Ethnic Conflict*, Princeton: Princeton University Press.

Levi, M. and Hechter, M. (1985) 'A rational choice approach to the rise and decline of ethnoregional political parties', in E. A. Tiryakian and R. Rogowski (eds) *New Nationalisms of the Developed West*, Winchester, MA: Allen & Unwin.

Parenti, M. (1967) 'Ethnic politics and the persistence of ethnic identification', *American Political Science Review* 61: 717–26.

Ragin, C. C. (1977) 'Class, status, and "reactive ethnic cleavages": the social bases of political regionalism', *American Sociological Review* 42: 438–50.

Rothchild, D. (1997) *Managing Ethnic Conflict in Africa*, Washington: Brookings.

Rothschild, J. (1981) *Ethnopolitics: A Conceptual Framework*, New York: Columbia University Press.

Smith, G., Law, V., Wilson, A., Bohr, A. and Allworth, E. (eds) (1998) *Nation-Building in the Post-Soviet Borderlands: The Politics of National Identity*, Cambridge: Cambridge University Press.

Taras, R. C. and Ganguly, R. (eds) (2002) *Understanding Ethnic Conflict: The International Dimension*, 2nd edn, New York: Longman.

Tiryakian, E. A. and Rogowski, R. (1985) *New Nationalisms of the Developed West*, Winchester, MA: Allen & Unwin.

37

IDENTITY POLITICS

Gary Lehring

Identity politics historically stems from the recognition that one's deepest sense of personal identity is shaped by one's membership in groups that have been oppressed on the basis of race, class, ethnicity, gender or sexual orientation. The sense of a personal identity rooted in shared cultural oppression becomes the basis for political activity, regardless of whether groups see their shared identity as fixed and immutable or as the result of historical political struggles that have helped construct their group identity. Whether seen as biological, cultural, or political, identity politics generally involves criteria for group membership that are exclusive. These criteria are then used to help explain a kind of lived experience of discrimination that can be the basis for political demands. Identity politics is built upon the belief that one's identity as part of a minority or minoritized group makes one's social position tenuous and opens oneself to stereotyping, marginalization, exploitation, or even violence by dominant groups. Rather than organize around traditional forms of politics such as ideology, political party, or class, adherents to identity politics typically assert innovative ways of understanding their community that challenge mainstream characterizations and stereotypes.

Markers of identity have always played a role in politics and have often been used as a device to create opposition to perceived oppression. In the early nineteenth century, the labour movement used the identity 'worker' to create solidarity and union and win concessions from an exploitative capitalist class. Similarly, activists from Abigail Adams to Sojourner Truth to women suffragists, deployed 'woman' as an identity around which to politically organize. Many nationalist movements have relied upon a conception of a shared exploitation and oppression at the hands of foreigners to demand political rights and social freedoms and to resist or expel colonizers.

The term 'identity politics' is more commonly understood as a wave of political organization and contestations that came to prominence in the 1960s. Starting with black activists in the 1960s, followed by the women's movement, the gay and lesbian movements, and most recently by more conservative identity movements such as the Christian Coalition and white supremacists groups, the politics of identity has proved to be a potent force in mobilizing members of groups that feel marginalized by mainstream society. In sharp contrast to historical social movements based on class, identity politics seeks to make personal experience the basis of political goals and strategies. Identity politics can be seen as one form of a 'politics of recognition', where groups organize around socially marginalized and vilified identities, seeking to change their social or cultural status as outsiders.

In 1967, Stokley Carmichael and Charles Hamilton wrote: 'the concept of Black Power rests on a fundamental premise: Before a Group can enter the open society, it must first close ranks' (Ture and Hamilton 1992). This definition of Black Power comes close to a definition of identity politics as the construction of a cohesive group identity in prelude to political agitation and mobilization has been the cornerstone of many minority political movements. Feminists in the 1970s suggested that consciousness raising and group solidarity were important first steps toward political action. The observation that the 'personal is political' was the slogan that transformed the shared experience of the identity of 'woman' into a feminist political movement. Black lesbian activist and writer Barbara Smith makes the connection between identity and politics more explicit still. Believing that 'we have an identity and therefore a politics' she articulates the belief that not only does one's politics stem from one's identity, but that the scope and character of one's politics are dependent upon one's identity (cited in Moraga 1983: 131).

The Combahee River Collective crafted what is often seen as the definitive statement regarding the importance of identity politics, particularly for people whose identity is marked by multiple interlocking oppressions. They argued that black women needed to rely on other black women and no one else, as no other group would be as committed to their struggle. In 'A Black Feminist Statement', they wrote: 'as children we realized that we were different from boys and we were treated different – for example, when we were told in the same breath to be quiet for the sake of being "ladylike" and to make us less objectionable in the eyes of white people. In the process of consciousness raising … we began to recognize the commonality of our experiences and…to build a politics that will change our lives and inevitably end our oppression.…We realize that the only people who care enough about us to work consistently for our liberation is us.…We believe that the most profound and potentially the most radical politics comes directly out of our own identity, as opposed to working to end somebody else's oppression' (Combahee River Collective 1982: 14–15). Providing a basis for new political organization and mobilization to fight oppression, identity politics is seen by some as a progressive alternative to more traditional forms of political activity.

The belief that one's identity is the best or even a natural basis for organizing politically has come under fire in the last few decades as critics have identified the internal contradictions of 'identity politics'. Building on the work of the French philosopher Michel Foucault, critics have argued that attempts to essentialize identity may indeed be the apotheosis of a progressive politics; as such identity politics has generated much controversy. For example, the claims of a unique experience – demonstrated in the Combahee River Collective statement above – are often based on an essentialist understanding of identity that views social categories as static or fixed. These categories in turn are based on unique group characteristics that are viewed as immutable, sometimes biological. Critics argue that identity politics can have a deleterious effect on alliance or coalition building as these claims of uniqueness often become claims of exceptionalism that authorize certain voices and experiences while de-authorizing others, putting some questions beyond the traditional arena of contest and compromise that is politics.

Another criticism is that although identity politics may create new ways of under-standing oppression, it does so in ways that are flat and simplistic. Unfortunately, the Combahee River Collective example notwithstanding, identity politics offers no way to understand multiple identities simultaneously and creates a subject along a single, static, axis of identity while ignoring the multiplicity of identities that constitute subjects. In other words, one can be gay, or one can be African-American, but for the sake of politics, one cannot be both. If the goals and objectives of a politics of identity emphasize a single category of identity, it will put pressure on the members of the group to make one defining feature of their identity salient even though members understand themselves as more complex and heterogeneous, embodying multiple iden-tities and committed to multiple political objectives (Spelman 1988).

Conversely, the identity categories of a movement may well become prescriptive rather than descriptive as new members are expected to behave, if not to *be*, a certain way in order to be accepted by the marginalized group. Just as minorities were expected to integrate the norms of the more dominant groups in society, in the practice of identity politics, powerful sub-groups may seek to universalize their vision of the group's identity, forcing others to accept this vision, or leave the move-ment altogether. Still, there is no easy solution to many of these problems; to disavow all forms of identity politics may mean returning to a politics where marginalized groups have no voice whatsoever. Significantly, in feminist and sexu-ality studies, the philosophical debate over identity politics has focused on the tension between identity and difference. The scholarship in these two fields in the last fifteen years has begun to address the very difficult questions posed by identity politics.

Feminist studies

Identity politics has informed feminist theory and politics by providing both personal solidarity and a theoretical framework within which to critique many of the assumptions of liberal feminism. Second-wave feminism provides an example of a central flaw of identity politics. If members of a group are required to prioritize one aspect of their identity (such as 'woman') and subordinate other aspects (such as lesbian or Black or working class), the perspectives and concerns of one group of women will prevail. Critics of second-wave feminism maintain that feminism posited the concerns of white, heterosexual, middle-class feminists as applicable to all women, as if the experiences of these women were universal. Many women of colour, such as those in the Combahee River Collective quoted above, felt that their voices were silenced, their experiences erased, and their participation unwanted in the second wave of the feminist movement. As bell hooks has pointed out, Betty Friedan's argument that the focus of feminism should be getting women out of the house and into the workplace, had a number of embedded assumptions that many women did not share (hooks 1981; Friedan 1963). Women of colour, working-class women, and many lesbians had been working outside the home for decades. Freidan's position assumed that *all* women were middle-class housewives with professional husbands and rang untrue to many who had been juggling full or part time work with childcare and housekeeping responsibilities for years. For others who had been the sole or primary breadwinner, the model of feminist liberation that posited women's participation in the workplace as the solution to women's inequality seemed naïve. Critics charged that second-wave feminists failed to acknowledge or understand how their own situatedness reproduced power relations, specifically the power of white, heterosexual, middle-class women to construct 'the standpoint of all women'. Standpoint theorists were seen to be exercising authority defining their particular subject position as the universal one for all women, thereby asserting a race and class and sexual privilege over other women (Lugones and Spelman 1983).

The inability of second-wave feminists to recognize the specificity of their own social and political location led many other women to focus on their differences from them. Moving from the personal to the political, this critical focus inspired new theoretical directions as 'difference feminism' developed to expand and include the experiences of many women who had felt previously marginalized. As a result, feminism has been broadened to include many forms of differentiation and this has broadened the base and the appeal of feminist studies and feminist practice.

This emphasis on difference, however, has led many leftist and liberal feminists to suggest that identity politics has served to divide feminism by creating overly specific and narrow political agendas that foreclose the possibility of alliance-building based on broad coalitions. These critics suggest that by de-emphasizing things that women share, only their differences – their unique and specific claims to oppression – are emphasized in identity politics. The problem, critics charged, was that people only come to be recognized and to have access to political discourse through these categories of difference. Having given voice to experiences that differ from white, middle-class, heterosexual, feminist experience – one of the positive aspects of identity politics – identity politics nonetheless contributed to the narrowing of political discourse as it accepted that a woman's politics was reducible to and synonymous with her identity. Critics charged this led quickly to the opposite of a more inclusive movement where more voices could be heard and rather to a kind of tokenism, where giving voice to a single member of an underrepresented group was seen as equivalent to hearing from all members of the group.

Identity politics, other critics contend, fragments the voices of oppressed groups and puts them in competition with each other, creating further obstacles to coalition building. Political discourse might be limited in this scenario by the tendency of identity politics to create 'hierarchies of oppression' in which groups argue about who is most oppressed. In hierarchies of oppression, subjective experience replaces and even trumps all other arguments, political organizing for more universal issues becomes difficult or even impossible because subjective experience cannot be challenged, it is authorized by essentialist claims about the natural basis of one's identity. Political demands and political authority based on a group's perceived natural difference has been central to many of the changes feminist theory and politics have undergone in the last 40 years, but de-authorizing opinions and experiences based on anything other than this difference opens the door to charges of political correctness and an authoritarian politics. This was a 'cure' many feminists believed might well be worse than the disease.

Postmodern feminist theorists voice a different set of concerns about identity politics. The notion that identity is coherent and unified is seen by postmodernists as a part of Enlightenment ideas that enshrine the 'Sovereign Subject' as the centre of modern society and active creator of his/her own identity and destiny. Eroded by years of Marxist critique that argues that social forces help constitute one's subjectivity, the sovereign subject becomes the centre of postmodern criticism. Observing that women could no more be a unified *subject* of knowing than she a unified *object* of study, postmodern feminists argue that identity itself is little more than an effect of discourse, a historical innovation that makes individuals more susceptible to recruitment into dominant ideologies and better able to be disciplined and controlled as subjects of the state. According to this analysis, a politics based explicitly on oppressed identity is a politics that embraces its own categories of victimization, a politics that cuts off radical new ways of thinking and being, and most importantly reinforces the status quo rather than radically disrupts or alters power.

Still, many feminist adherents of identity politics remain sceptical of postmodern criticisms. Why, they ask, at the moment when women and minorities are finally making positive use of identity categories through which they have been excluded, are these very categories characterized as phantoms of the imagination and products of false consciousness? Others argue that the advances achieved through identity politics make the risks associated with essentialism worth taking in order to foster new identities and new opportunities for political agency (Spivak 1987). Indeed Fuss (1989) has argued that essentialism may be viewed as a matter of survival for relatively less powerful groups such as black and lesbian women. This notion of a 'strategic essentialism' – using essentialist notions of identity in specific contexts to further a group's agenda while explicitly realizing that the category being offered as natural is in reality a socially and politically constructed category – was a compromise many feminists were willing to make. De Lauretis (1989) has argued that essentialism may indeed be required for all feminist politics. Building on this belief that there is something essential in identity that can never be deconstructed completely, other feminists have argued that intersectionality might provide a better answer to the shortcomings of identity politics. By suggesting that the interconnections between gender, race, ethnicity, class, sexual orientation, age, and religion are central to any analysis of oppression, intersectionality suggests that one's identities are always multiple and it is impossible to separate out one from the other. For example, Catharine MacKinnon has suggested that simply because women in very different social positions may experience sexism differently, does not mean that they share nothing in common. They do all experience sexism (Mackinnon 2001). Intersectionality, seeks to provide a way to allow racialized and other particular forms of sexist oppression to be theorized and understood from within specific identity locations, thereby employing categories of identity politics but not in static or one-dimensional ways.

Kimberly Crenshaw has used the analogy of a traffic intersection to explain intersectionality (Crenshaw 1991). Race, ethnicity, class, and sexuality are the avenues of power that define the social, economic and political map. These are the routes through which 'disempowering dynamics' flow, and although often each of these avenues is considered a single and distinct axis of power, in reality they are always overlapping and intersecting, operating in relation to each other and creating interesting and complex intersections at which two or more of these axes of power meet. Because gender oppression is prevalent in so many societies, the boulevard where other axes of power intersect with gender is particularly wide, and other forms of oppression are compounded by gender, making women more vulnerable to the heavy traffic at the intersection of these axes of power. Intersectionality seeks to improve on identity politics by acknowledging that while identities matter in politics, these identities are multiple and overlapping, and not single and monolithic. While this is an important theoretical point, in practice it has proved difficult to create an analytical model that keeps all axes of power in play at once. Further, it can become difficult in practice for policy makers to take cognizance of a multiple identity model of oppression. While discrimination on the basis of race or gender might well be made illegal, courts and policy makers in the USA have been reticent to accept the intersection of race and gender, as contained in the concept 'Blackwoman' as a distinct category. For example, courts in the USA have denied African-American women the right to sue on the grounds of sex and race discrimination because they represent neither 'women' (as they cannot speak for white women) nor 'African-Americans' (as they cannot speak for black men) (Crenshaw 1998).

Today, it is often said that 'identity' is an idea in crisis in feminist thought and feminist practice and identity politics must be abandoned by feminists (Dean 1996), but the identity categories of sex–gender–race continue to serve as central analytical concepts in feminist theory, although no longer in an uncontested or unproblematic way.

GLQ studies

In the past thirty years the struggle for lesbian and gay equality in the USA and Europe has achieved ever increasing levels of recognition, attention, and understanding. In the latter part of the twentieth century, gays and lesbians have created a culture, a politics and a sense of community based upon a shared sense of self. According to a number of scholars, the strategies and techniques employed by the gay and lesbian community to realize increased levels of societal recognition and political mobilization are patterned after the identity politics of racial and ethnic minorities (Altman 1982; Escoffier 1985; Epstein 1987). But unlike racial and ethnic minorities, the gay and lesbian communities are without many of the common secondary characteristics employed by demographers to describe group similarities. Gays and lesbians come from every religious, ethnic and racial background. They come from widely divergent classes, have diverse levels of educational and occupational achievement and have no primary nation of origin. They are Republicans and Democrats, conservatives and liberals, and fall into no predictable 'gay' or 'lesbian' position with regard to most policy issues, and many have lived decades of their lives without defining themselves as gay or lesbian. For these reasons, nowhere has the politics of identity been more contested and more contentious than in the movement for lesbian and gay equality.

For all the material evidence that gays and lesbians do indeed exist, there has been great disagreement over what a sexual identity really means. There is little agreement over *why* a person is gay and in the 1980s and 1990s debates erupted over what the categories 'gay' and 'lesbian' actually describe. These questions regarding categories reveal many of the problems inherent in a politics based upon identity. For example, are these terms descriptive of something natural, something fixed, and something immutable, or are sexual identities more fluid, malleable and

hence open to social influences? Are they historical categories that come into existence at a certain time and place? Are there anthropological similarities between gay
and lesbian people today and the sexual identities and practices of people from
different cultures both ancient and modern, or do these terms really signal a late
Western identity only appearing in the last 125 years? If newly emergent, then are
modern sexual identities tied to certain levels of economic development? Finally, are
gay and lesbian identities innate and fixed, or do they include some possibility of
personal choice and change?

The belief that sexuality constitutes a stable and coherent core of one's identity
has been seriously challenged by queer politics. As with feminist studies, gay and
lesbian studies have been beset by a debate over identity politics whose academic
origin has limited the impact it has had in gay and lesbian politics and communities.
Known as the essentialist/constructivist controversy, this debate again fuelled the fire
of speculation as to the causes of homosexuality and the status of lesbian or gay
identity.

Most early lesbian and gay activists proffered a notion of gay identity as a fixed
and stable identity, no more or less authentic that their heterosexual counterparts.
Basing identity on biological or natural grounds was seen as the best avenue to end
discrimination and procure legal protections needed for gays and lesbians to live as
'normal' people with careers, legal spouses, and children. It also seemed to comport
with the lived experiences of many gay and lesbian people who argued they knew
form an early age that they were gay or lesbian, most believing to have been born gay.
This conformist line of gay activism was present from the very beginning in the US gay
rights movement. The pre-Stonewall homophile movement was made up of mostly
middle-class men, and to a lesser extent women, who argued that they were essentially
like everyone else, with one exception: their sexuality (Lehring 2003). Central to the
development of this positive gay identity was the process of 'coming out' as in coming
out of the closet. This process merged the personal with the political as individuals
were to formulate a coherent personal narrative as a gay subject in order to better
understand common and shared oppression. As with Stokley Carmichael and the
women of the Combahee River Collective, understanding one's own personal struggle,
was seen as key to building a gay and lesbian equal rights movement.

Post-Stonewall gay liberation and early lesbian feminists had a very different politics, emphasizing instead a belief that sexuality was structurally produced as an
effect of oppression and therefore heterosexuals were equally repressed if not
oppressed as everyone had the potential to experience pleasure in a multiplicity of
ways. Gay liberation would be the mechanism through which everyone could be
liberated from a restrictive and reductionist sexual identity that tried to make sexuality the basis of identity (Altman 1982; Delph 1978; Murphy 1971; Whitman
1972). The liberationists were the progenitors of the modern Queer movement, as it
shared the contemporary queer distrust of fixed and static identities.

Queer politics emerged in the USA as a result of the AIDS pandemic.
Experiencing first hand that identity could be mobilized in modern society in ways
previously unimagined, the gay community witnessed the stigma and blame that
accompanied a politics of gay identity in which the responsibility for AIDS was laid
squarely at the door of gay men. This had a radicalizing effect on the decades that
followed as many queers questioned the benefit of an essentialist gay rights agenda,

understanding for the first time what postmodernist feminists had understood before: that identity politics could easily be used as a mechanism for greater discipline and control. Michel Foucault's *History of Sexuality* (1980) provided the theoretical framework through which to understand sexual identities as historically produced, contingent effects of certain discourses and genealogies. Foucault argued that homosexuality emerged as an identity at a certain point in the nineteenth century and prior to this, sex – the way one engaged in sexual pleasure – did not form the basis of a coherent identity. He writes 'the sodomite had been a temporary aberration, but the homosexual was now a species' (Foucault 1980: 43). This transformation of sex into a form of identity politics occurred as the result of a specific constellation of forces that emerged in the late nineteenth century and, as Foucault argued, would not have been possible in an earlier era. Historicizing this process helps destabilize and reveal the forces in society that work to make sexuality appear natural and inevitable (Butler 1990).

Still, a belief that sexuality is fluid, multiple, changeable – queer – exists side by side with a modern scientific search for genetic and biological determinants of sexuality. The epistemological questions quickly take on a moral and political hue as many gays and lesbians look for irrefutable evidence that their sexuality is not a question of choice, and therefore they are no more responsible for their sexuality than are their heterosexual counterparts. Like many feminists, many gays and lesbians are willing to risk essentialism in sexual identity politics because it seems to provide some basis of protection from a homophobic society that often conflates being gay with choosing immoral behaviour. Some see the risk worth taking because if sexual identity is biological a person can be no more responsible for being gay than he or she would be for his or her race or gender. Also, if a person is born gay, attempts to 'cure' them are destined to fail and therefore will lose their rhetorical appeal.

We have learned from historical examples, however, that a biological or genetic explanation for sexuality is not likely to end homophobia. Identity can provide no safe haven from persecution. In 1951, writing in *The Origins of Totalitarianism*, political theorist Hannah Arendt documented the rise of 'racism' directed at Jews in nineteenth-century Europe. Integral to this racism was the identification of Jews as a 'race', as those *born* to a certain inescapable identity.

As far as the Jews were concerned, the transformation of the 'crime' of Judaism into the fashionable 'vice' of Jewishness was dangerous in the extreme. Jews had been able to escape from Judaism into conversion; from Jewishness there was no escape. A crime, moreover, is met with punishment; a vice can only be exterminated. The interpretation given by society to the fact of Jewish birth and the role played by Jews in the framework of social life are intimately connected with the catastrophic thoroughness with which antisemitic devices could be put to work. The Nazi brand of antisemitism had its roots in these social conditions (Arendt 1951: 87).

Arendt realized the same transformation was taking place in the arena of sexuality, arguing that 'the "vice" of Jewishness and the "vice" of homosexuality...became very much alike indeed' (Arendt 1951: 80). The transformation of criminal *acts* of sodomy into sexual *vice* and *identities*, parallels the transformation described by Arendt. A politics of identity is as likely to be used against those identified as sexual minorities as it is to provide some safe haven for them.

The promise of a queer politics has been to replace essentialist gay and lesbian identity politics with a more radical vision. A more productive 'queer politics' might seek to resist and subvert identity by constantly deconstructing and de-naturalizing it, thereby revealing the cultural power that is brought to bear to make sexual identity seem natural to many of its adherents and necessary for political organizing and community building. While intriguing in theory, this undertaking has been difficult in practice, and the perceived benefits of identity politics continues to be a strong draw for many who identify as gay or lesbian.

Conclusion

As a result of postmodern and queer challenges, identity has lost some of its force as the basis for political organizing. Our understanding of identity, however, is evolving as new groups, new technologies and new methodologies have raised interesting questions: Must identity always be subject centred? Is disability politics, a politics of identity? Can there be an identity politics of childhood? Can identity politics also be an environmental politics? Can anti-globalization movements be a politics of identity? Can transgender politics? These questions indicate how rapidly the concept of identity is evolving. As medical technologies and cosmetic procedures make physical identity increasingly mutable and fluid, one can only speculate about the future of identity politics. The very way in which politics is undertaken in the information age depends less on bodily presence and more on communication technologies. These technologies link people together in ways that allow disembodied political alliances, making the policing of identity more difficult for group members.

Despite these criticisms and challenges, identity politics persists. Perhaps its resilience is connected to its cogent critique of the notions of the universality of access to political participation in liberal democracies that historically promised equal treatment but practised discrimination and exclusion. Never successfully replacing the powerful discourse of liberal redress, identity politics nonetheless calls into question the central assumption of liberalism: all citizens must be fundamentally the same in order to receive equal rights and protections from the state. Supporters argue that identity politics need not be essentialist nor lead to separatism; rather, identity politics could inform a new kind of politics of alliance where differences are acknowledged as important and vital to one's own social and political experience and identity, even as empathy and connections to others are formed. One's experience of oppression, rather than leading to the development of a hierarchy of oppression, might lead to a politics of coalition, where ideas and political goals are understood more completely *because* of the various identity perspectives present in coalition (Benhabib 1994). Identities would serve not simply as markers of oppression, but as a new way to see and understand politics, and as the basis for producing new political agendas and social movements.

References

Altman, Dennis (1982) *The Homosexualization of America*, Boston: Beacon Press.
Arendt, Hannah (1951) *The Origins of Totalitarianism*, New York: Harcourt Brace Jovanovich.

Benhabib, Seyla (1994) 'From Identity Politics to Social Feminism: A Plea for the Nineties', *Philosophy of Education Symposium*. Published online at: <http://www.ed.uiuc.edu/EPS/PES-Yearbook/94_docs/BENHABIB.HTM>

Butler, Judith (1990) *Gender Trouble*, New York: Routledge.

Combahee River Collective (1982) 'A Black Feminist Statement', in *All the Women are White, All the Blacks are men, But Some of us are Brave: Black Women's Studies*, Gloria T. Hull, Patricia Bell Scott and Barbara Smith (eds), New York: Feminist press.

Crenshaw, Kimberly (1991) 'Mapping the Margins: Intersectionality, Identity Politics and Violence against Women of Color', *Stanford Law Review* 43:6.

—— (1998) 'A Black Feminist Critique of Antidiscrimination' in Davis Kairy (ed.), *The Politics of Law: A Progressive Critique*, New York: Basic Books, 3rd edn.

Dean, Jodi (1996) *Solidarity of Strangers: Feminism after Identity Politics*, Berkeley: University of California Press.

De Lauretis, Therese (1989) 'The Essence of the Triangle or, Taking the Risk of Essentialism Seriously: Feminist Theory in Italy, the U.S., and Britain', *Differences: A Journal of Feminist Cultural Studies* 1 (Summer): 3–37.

Delph, Edward William (1978) *The Silent Homosexual Community: Public Homosexual Encounters*, Beverly Hills, California: Age Publications.

Epstein, Steven (1987) 'Gay Politics, Ethnic Identity: The Limits of Social Constructionism', *Socialist Review* 93/94: 9–54.

Escoffier, Jeffrey (1985) 'Sexual Revolution and the Politics of Gay Identity', *Socialist Review* 15: 119–53.

Friedan, Betty (1963) *The Feminine Mystique*, New York: Norton.

Foucault, Michel (1980) *The History of Sexuality*, New York: Vintage.

Fuss, Diana (1989) *Essentially Speaking: Feminism, Nature and Difference*, New York: Routledge.

hooks, bell (1981) *Ain't I a Woman: Black Women and Feminism*, Boston: South End Press.

Lehring, Gary (2003) *Officially Gay: The Political Construction of Sexuality by the United States Military*, Philadelphia, PA: Temple University Press.

Lugones and Spelman (1983) '"Have We Got a Theory for You!" Feminist Theory, Cultural Imperialism and the Demand for "the Woman's Voice"', *Women's Studies International Forum* 6 (6): 573–81.

MacKinnon, Catharine (2001) *Sex Equality, Rape Law*, Eagan, Minnesota: Foundation Press.

Moraga, Cherrie (1983) *Loving in the War Years: Lo que nunca paso por sus labios*, Boston: South End Press.

Murphy, John (1971) *Homosexual Liberation*, New York: Praeger.

Spelman, Elizabeth V. (1988) *Inessential Woman: Problems of Exclusion in Feminist Thought*, Boston: Beacon Press.

Spivak, Gayatri Chakravorty (1987) *In Other Worlds: Essay in Cultural Politics*, London: Methuen.

Ture, Kwame and Hamilton, Charles (1992) *Black Power: The Politics of Liberation in America*, New York: Vintage Books.

Whitman, Carl (1972) 'A Gay Manifesto', in Jay and Young, *Out of the Closet: Voices of Gay Liberation*, New York: Douglas Books: 330–41.

Further reading

Blasius, Mark (ed.) (2001) *Sexual Identities, Queer Politics*, Princeton: Princeton University Press.

Connolly, William (2002) *Identity/Difference: Democratic Negotiations of Political Paradox*, Minneapolis: University of Minnesota Press.

Cruz, Jose (1998) *Identity and Power: Puerto Rican Politics and the Challenge of Ethnicity*, Philadelphia, PA: Temple University Press.

Cornell, Drucilla (2000) *Just Cause: Freedom, identity, and Rights*, Lanham, MD: Rowan and Littlefield.

Fraser, Nancy (1997) *Justice Interruptus*: *Critical Reflections on the 'Post-Socialist' Condition'*, New York: Routledge.

Hartsock, Nancy (1998) *The Feminist Studies Standpoint Revisited and Other Essays*, Boulder: Westview.

hooks, bell (1991) *Yearnings: Race, Gender, and Cultural Politics*, London: Turnaround.

Rich, Adrienne (1980) 'Compulsory Heterosexuality and Lesbian Existence', *Signs* 5:4.

Sedgwick, Eve Kosofsky (1990) *Epistemology of the Closet*, Berkeley: University of California Press.

Spivak, Gayatri Chakravorty (1990) *The Post Colonial Critic: Interviews, Strategies, Dialogues*, ed. Sara Harasym, New York: Routledge.

Torres, Maria de los Angeles (2001) *In the Land of Mirrors: Cuban Exile Politics in the United States*, Andover: University of Michigan Press.

Young, Iris Marion (1990) *Justice and the Politics of Difference*, Princeton: Princeton University Press.

38

LANGUAGE AND POLITICS

J. A. Laponce

Languages that come into contact become linked by a communication network, the density of which varies according to circumstances; but, loose or dense, communication among these languages is unavoidable. There is no example of a living language not linked by translation to at least one other living language. Bilingualism and multilingualism are thus worldwide phenomena (Edwards 1994; Mackey 2002). Humans cannot ignore humans, languages cannot ignore other languages. This seemingly trivial fact has consequences of considerable importance which have been studied by psycholinguists, sociolinguists, geographers and, more recently, by political scientists.

Bilingual and multilingual political systems (henceforth *bilingual* to simplify) are markedly affected by the kind of relations – cooperative or conflictual – associated with the transfer of information from one language to another; inversely, political systems – notably the modern state – attempt, more and more frequently, to regulate language contact by means of language planning, either corpus planning (typically to standardize the language) or status planning (typically to regulate language use).

Much confusion has resulted from the use of the single term 'bilingual' to describe a variety of phenomena ranging from the rough school-type of knowledge of a foreign language to the knowledge of different languages learned in infancy and constantly needed for communication within the family or within the surrounding community; so much confusion that, before considering the specifically political aspects of language contact, we need to distinguish various situations resulting from two languages co-existing within the mind of a given individual.

The bilingual mind

Can one say exactly the same thing in two different languages? Does the language we use shape what we think or is it on the contrary a neutral instrument under our complete control? The so-called 'Whorf–Sapir' hypothesis (Whorf 1956; Sapir 1949; Mathiot 1979), according to which language shapes thought, has fallen into disfavour among contemporary linguists who point out that any language is 'potentially' able to express what is said or written in any other language. English may not have as many words as Dene to express different types of snow but can express all these varieties by means of periphrases; Arabic is not, at present, able to describe simply and effectively the complexities of modern science but it is potentially capable of doing so; Malay still needs to develop a complex legal vocabulary before it could fully replace English in the courts of law of Malaysia. But demotic Greek created in a short time the thousands of words needed for the translation of the regulations of the European Commission into that language following the entry of Greece into the European Community. The Whorf–Sapir hypothesis, however, is far from dead. It continues to inspire research of the relation of language to culture and national identity (Coulombes 1995: ch. IV) and sustains the argument of an increased number of advocacy groups that the demise of a language signifies the death of a culture (Wurm 1996).

Whether or not different languages are wired differently in the brain and whether or not the bilingual differs from the unilingual brain (Albert and Obler 1978) it remains that, even if we are capable of learning two languages in the same context and to the same degree of fluency, in fact we practically never do so. The languages we know typically form a hierarchy of both knowledge and liking and trigger different social and psychological contexts. Different languages embody different historical experiences: the longer history of the languages themselves as well as the shorter history of the speaker will typically relate different languages to different roles and events. Mackey (1971) has shown, for example, that the associations of ideas built into French and English by means of composite words and expressions vary considerably on some of the most commonly used words (lady-killer does not convey the same meaning as its French translation *'homme à femme'*); and it is quite rare for two languages, even if learned simultaneously in infancy, not to be distinguished by remarkable specificity such as one being the language of the mother and the other that of the father or the school friends. The perfect fit of two languages – a fit measurable by such means as Osgood's Semantic Differential – is an ideal from which there are considerable variations, but an ideal that is practically never reached.

The cost of acquiring a second language – a cost measurable in terms of time, effort and frustration – and the difficulty of obtaining a perfect bilingual fit would suffice to explain that the mind tends to reject language redundancy. Rare are the individuals who, in the absence of any need to communicate with foreigners, acquire an extra language for the sole sake of having more than one. They belong to the pathological cases studied by Steyn (1972), a classic example of which is offered by Psalmanazar, who obtained an appointment at the University of Oxford in the seventeenth century to teach a language that was supposedly spoken by Formosans but was in fact a personal invention. In the absence of the need to communicate with people who speak a language other than one's own, the mind rejects language redundancy as it rejects true synonymy within a given language (Genouvrier and Peytard 1970).

Bilingualism, thought to be harmful to a child's intellectual development by most pre-Second World War educators, has subsequently been shown to have no such negative effect and in fact to facilitate what is variously called the 'Leopold effect' (Leopold 1939–49) or 'divergent thinking' – the ability to distinguish the significant from the signifier (Skutnabb-Kangas 1981).

The fact of most direct relevance to the politics of language contacts is in the finding that one can normally distinguish, even among so-called 'balanced' bilinguals (bilinguals with a seemingly equal knowledge of their two languages), a dominant language (L1) and a second or dominated language (L2). In a series of simple experiments, Dornic (1975, 1980) found that while nearly indistinguishable on simple tasks, the reaction times of bilinguals using either their L1 or their L2 increased markedly as one increased the difficulty of the problem to be resolved. Thus, in a conversation between two individuals speaking the same two languages but not having the same L1, the speaker who imposes his or her dominant language has a communication advantage over the other speaker, and the latter will often feel frustrated by his or her inability to operate at their normal level of effectiveness.

Since the knowledge of a second language is costly in terms of acquisition and maintenance time, and since the use of an L2 is less efficient than that of an L1, it follows that individuals will naturally tend to group themselves socially and geographically in such a way as to reduce the overlap among languages, unless of course they want to use more than one language to separate social functions, as in some cases of diglossia.

Bilingualism and diglossia

Ferguson (1959) coined the term 'diglossia' to refer to the use of either of two varieties of the same language, a high and a low form, in different social settings. Fishman (1967) extended the meaning of the term to distinguish two types of bilingualism according to whether the bilingual individual uses two languages across all social roles or uses one language in some specific situations and contexts while the other language is used in other cases. Calvet (1998) recommended removing the assumption of a hierarchical relation between the two forms. In agreement with Calvet, I take diglossia to refer to bilingualism by juxtaposition rather than superposition of two languages, realizing that the distinction refers to ideal types that help contrasting different kinds of language contact within the mind, different enough to require varied language policies even though the object of the policies may be the same, for example to prevent conflict and reinforce inter-ethnic cooperation.

The strong correlation between social role and language use which characterizes diglossia appears most clearly when a language such as Latin, Old Slavonic or Hebrew is used as a sacred tongue while another language – English, Russian or Yiddish, for example – is used in the secular domain. The separation is not as marked, but obvious nevertheless, when the diglossic contact is between secular languages that distinguish private from public domains and are used, the one to affirm one's local ethnicity, the other to participate instrumentally if not emotionally in the communication system of a wider community.

Unlike the Francophone Swiss who uses only standard French, the Germanophone Swiss uses two forms of German, the standard literary language that links the user to the greater German community, and a local Swiss German that is learned and spoken at home as well as in public life at the local level (Swiss German is spoken in the cantonal legislatures while standard German is used in the federal parliament; see McRae 1984). In Luxemburg, nearly all citizens speak three languages: Luxemburgese in private and either French or German in public settings, with French dominating in church and government and German (not to mention English) in the field of business. This type of diglossia is the norm in Africa and Asia where local, regional and international languages are typically associated with markedly different social roles and contexts.

Diglossic bilingualism tends to be relatively stable when the languages in contact collaborate at separating social roles that the individual wishes to keep separated (rather than conflict with each other). The more the diglossic situation is wanted by the individual concerned – as in German Switzerland, Luxembourg, Andorra or Paraguay – the more the contact between the languages concerned will be collaborative, hence stable and thereby in lesser need of intervention by the political system to either assimilate or protect one of the languages.

By contrast, instability characterizes the cases where diglossia is imposed by circumstances and is perceived as a burden by the individuals who have to know two languages – one to communicate with their parents for example, and the other to communicate with their own children, as in Brittany in the early twentieth century. In such cases diglossia fades rapidly into unilingualism (Dressler and Wodak-Leodolter 1977).

Bilingualism without diglossia is a more frequent source of individual frustrations, hence of social and political conflicts. Extending as they do to all the social roles, ready to be used in all or at least in most important social contexts, the languages are engaged in a competition for dominance.

If everyone in the community concerned preferred the same L1, then there would be no reason – internal to the group – to retain the L2. The latter would be abandoned, if not by the individuals who acquired it then at least by their children or grandchildren. This is the way most languages 'imported' into English-speaking North America keep being assimilated and would be quickly annihilated in the absence of new migrations. However, if the individuals in contact do not all have the same preferred L1, then differences between languages are very likely to become associated with differences in social and political power, differences that are likely to lead to the formation of ethno-linguistic minorities.

Asymmetrical power sharing between two language groups results in the dominant group having the power to decide how the burden of bilingualism will be borne and what language will have the greater social spread. In some rare occasions the dominant group decides to assume the cost of bilingualism. This happens when an invader, being comparatively small in number compared to the population conquered, adopts the latter's language to avoid the military and social costs of imposing its own tongue. The Roman conquerors spoke Greek in their Eastern empire and the Arabs who invaded Persia adopted Persian (Mackey 1988, 2002). In Bolivia, in the early days of Spanish colonization, the ruling group decided to learn Quechua because the natives were thought unworthy, if not incapable, of learning Castilian (Breton 1976).

More frequently the dominant group shifts the cost of bilingualism onto the ethnic minority. Flemish Belgians were and are still more likely to speak French than Walloons to speak Dutch; French Canadians are more likely to speak English than English Canadians to speak French. Switzerland is an apparent contradiction since the Germanophone majority is more likely to know French than the Francophone minority to know German; apparently because the cost of learning German is vastly increased by the diglossia (high German vs local Swiss German) that prevails throughout Alemanic Switzerland. At the level of the federal bureaucracy, which uses high German, the rule reasserts itself: the Francophones are more likely to use German than the Germanophones to use French (Laponce 1987).

If the minority accepts that its language be given subordinate status, or if it obtains satisfactory compensations (in Switzerland, for example, the weakness of French at the federal level is compensated by its uncontested dominance in the western cantons), the asymmetrical sharing of the bilingual burden may not be a source of tension. If, on the contrary, subordinate status is resented or if the compensations are thought to be insufficient, the language asymmetry characterizing bilingualism without diglossia will often be a major source of ethnic and political conflicts.

Studying and predicting language outcomes

The language strategies of individuals and groups – whether to prefer unilingualism or bilingualism and, in the latter case, what language to select as L1 and in what circumstances – are typically the result of the interplay of relatively few factors, notably communication costs, social benefits and ethnic loyalty. The importance of these factors has led some social scientists to propose the use of simple rational-choice models and two-player games to explain bilingual outcomes (Laitin 1988; Pool 1991). These powerful models will, of course, often fail to predict the actual outcome, and if they do predict accurately will sometimes do so for the wrong reasons. Nevertheless, they are one of the more promising developments in a field much in need of theoretical constructs, and even when they fail they can still be turned to profit, if only as an invitation to identify the factors that were overlooked.

Most political analysts of language contacts and conflicts have preferred the case study approach that enables the analyst to study languages within the specificity of a complex socio-historical context. Many of these studies are based on interviews with respondents who are typically asked to indicate what language they use and in what circumstances (see notably Rubin (1968) for Paraguay; Fishman (1966) and Fishman *et al.* (1971) for the USA; O'Bryan *et al.* (1976) and Corbeil and Delude (1982) for Canada; Gendron (1973) for Quebec; Laitin (1977) for Somalia. Deprez (1996) for immigrant families in France, Bissoonauth (1998) for Mauritius, Gorter, Rienmersma and Yima (2001) for the Dutch province of Friesland, Grin (1999) for Switzerland, and the Euromosaic teams for the EU's lesser used languages (<http://www.uoc.es/euromosaic>; see also interview questionnaire models in Baker 2001: ch. 2). Relatively rare are the studies, such as those of Gumperz (1971), Bourhis (1984) or Gardner-Chloros (1985) that use non-reactive measures such as the taping of conversations to produce accurate behavioural maps of language use. The technique developed by Wiegele *et al.* (1985) and Schubert (1988) to measure voice stress could be applied to the study of recorded language interactions in multilingual settings to determine the level of stress associated with the use of a second language and with the shift from one language to another.

Language compared to other ethnic definers

Can the study of the ethno-linguistic minorities created by language contact be done by means of the general typologies and theories used for the study of minority-dominant group relations? To a very large extent it is indeed possible. One may use, among others, the typology proposed by Louis Wirth (1945), who distinguishes assimilationist, pluralist, secessionist and militant minorities; or that suggested by Laponce (1960), who contrasts minorities according to whether they accept to remain as minorities for the sake of preserving their distinctiveness or are forced to retain their separateness by a dominant group refusing to assimilate them; or that of Schermerhorn (1970), who relates the respective attitudes of the minority and of the dominant group according to whether these attitudes are centripetal or centrifugal. One can also use the theory of Tajfel and Turner (1979), which posits that in order to avoid self-doubt and debasement a minority must think of itself as superior to the dominant group in at least one domain of thought or activity, a perception that may or may not be shared by the dominant group.

The fact that asymmetrical power relationships between language groups are the norm in non-diglossic situations justifies to a large extent the fact that the study of language minorities is so often subsumed under the larger study of ethnic relations, as in the study of ethnic groups in conflict by Horowitz (1985). But that should not lead one to forget or push to the background a very specific characteristic of language minorities to which geographers and political scientists have been more sensitive than sociologists and sociolinguists: the tendency of a language group, particularly so of a language minority, to form compact territorial settlements (Mc Roberts 1989; Laponce 1987, 2001).

Since in most bilingual societies the members of minority groups are more likely to know the language of the dominant group than the latter to know the minority language, and since the dominant group normally has greater power over the production of spoken and written material (from Web sites and TV programmes to internal memos and contracts), the minority, as already noted, will be at a disadvantage in an unregulated system where the languages are allowed to mix and to be chosen freely for all kinds of interactions. Thus, unless it accepts a diglossic situation that would restrict the use of its language to certain domains of activity, a minority will become all the more frustrated as the communication system grows more dense.

Unlike religions or races that can adjust their survival strategies to geographical dispersion and geographical penetration by the dominant group, a language needs a degree of spatial concentration that is commensurate with the degree of development of the society concerned.

Some Indian languages of the Canadian West Coast or the jungle of Venezuela could survive for centuries even though they were spoken by very few people. But this could happen only as long as they remained isolated from the more powerful ethnic groups that surrounded them and as long as the types of activities required for the survival of the community were limited to primitive fruit gathering, hunting, or agriculture.

A modern industrial society that needs a university to educate its elites will need a relatively large concentration of population. With only 300,000 inhabitants, Iceland cannot operate its university fully in Icelandic (although its language is protected by isolation); with only about half a million speakers, the Swedes of Finland and the Francophones of Ontario experience similar difficulties in operating a full-scale university covering the scientific as well as the other disciplines in their own languages. Languages *qua* languages need geographical concentration and, to protect themselves against the inroads of more powerful languages, linguistic minorities need linguistic territorial homogeneity. Consequently, languages pose political problems involving boundaries that non-linguistic minorities do not pose to the same extent. While non-linguistic minorities will often be satisfied with the granting of territorially transportable individual rights, linguistic minorities will typically want group rights that are territorially grounded (Laponce 1987; Kymlicka 1995; May 2001). Whether thought to be an individual or a group right, the right to language is receiving increased attention from the academic community (Skutnabb-Kangas and Phillipson 1998; Phillipson 2000) and, increasingly, it is finding a niche in international law, notably through charters and covenants such as those of the United Nations, the Council of Europe, or the European Union (de Varennes 1996).

The 'war' among languages

Writing the history of languages as one writes the natural history of animal species led to the observation (Cailleux 1953) that, until recently, the world language system had experienced a positive birth rate. That trend, probably as old as humanity, has recently been reversed. In the era of globalization and vastly more efficient communication networks, languages die more frequently than they are born (for expressions of concern about this trend, see the following web pages: <http://sapir.ling.yale.edu> maintained at Yale University; <endangered-languages-l@cleo.murdoch.edu.au> maintained at Murdoch university; and <http://www.terralingua.org> based at the Davis campus of the University of California).The stronger languages eliminate the weaker ones, sometimes violently but more often peacefully as a result of people shifting to a language with a greater purchasing power, whether the purchase is of economic, political, or cultural goods (Bourdieu 1991; Krauss 1992; Grin 1994; Breton 1999; Nettle and Romaine 2000; Crystal 2000).

Adapting Hirschman's voice-exit model (Hirschman 1970) to our subject, we note that when the voice that a language offers is no longer heard or no longer heard adequately, exit to a better language will take place, unless there be a strong enough loyalty boundary preventing such a transfer, a loyalty that will be measured typically by the strength of one's ethno-linguistic identity.

Large markets and population mobility – from countryside to cities as well as from poorer to richer and from overpopulated to low birth-rate countries – reduce the purchasing power of small languages and weaken the ethnic identity tied to these languages (Van Parijs 2001). Hence the prediction that most of the existing 7,000-odd languages spoken today in the world will disappear and that relatively few will be born (7,000 is the upper estimate given by Ferguson 1964 and Grimes 1998; other estimates are lower, notably those of Muller 1964, Burney 1966 and Breton 1976, who give estimates ranging from 2,500 to 3,500).

In the intensified 'war' among languages, what factors will favour survival and expansion? The answer varies, of course, according to whether we consider local, regional, or international contexts; and it varies also according a complex set of political, economic, social and cultural factors not easy to measure and far more difficult to predict (Mackey 2002). Projecting present trends and giving weight mostly to political and economic factors, shows English continuing to make gains as the world lingua-franca (Fishman, Cooper and Conrad 1975; Laponce 2001). Giving more weight to demographic factors shows English losing its present hegemony (Graddol 1997).

Whether to predict or simply to compare present conditions on the basis of the 'traditional' factors of language power (notably demography, education, and cultural creativity) one can rely on increasingly comprehensive statistics ranging from the language of the half million articles published each year in the field of chemistry as recorded by the *Chemical Abstracts* to the world atlases of language use produced by the *Centre de recherche en aménagement linguistique* (CIRAL) at Laval university (see among others the five volumes of McConnell *et al.* 1978–98; see also McConnell and Roberge 1994). To these traditional measures, have recently been added the internet communication statistics, such as those gathered by *Alis Technology and the Internet Society* which detail the use of the Net by language and measure the present dominance of English at roughly 80 per cent of the web sites (Maurais 2001).

Irrespective of their power and specific ranking in the world system of states (Laponce 1987; De Swaan 1993, 2001), the languages best able to survive the competition are likely to be those that have the support of a government, and better than being simply supported are also used and needed as a language of government and administration. The number of these languages has increased in the last twenty years as a result of the decentralization of power (which favours Catalan for example) and as a result of the increase in the number of independent states following the end of the cold war. But, if we discount the official languages that are official in name only (such as Gaelic in Ireland and the nine aboriginal languages made official by the post apartheid South African constitution), the number of languages effectively used in the central administration of an independent state is still below ninety. Most of them are the languages of only one state. Among the few 'multistate' languages, English prevails in terms of number and geographical distribution. It 'has' fifty-eight countries well distributed throughout the world, while French has thirty-two concentrated in Europe, Africa, and North America, Arabic twenty-five concentrated in the Middle East, Spanish twenty-one concentrated in Europe and South America, and Portuguese seven located in Europe, South America and Africa.

Most states have many more languages than those used in their central administration of government; many have an abundance of local languages. This is the case with nearly all the states of Black Africa. Why should a large number of these local languages now be threatened after having survived for so long? The prediction of the weakening and disappearance of most of them is based on the assumption that the state will modernize, hence urbanize and industrialize, and will use a state language as an instrument of mass mobilization and integration rather than use it as an instrument of segregation separating a state elite from its local constituencies (Calvet 1974).

When the state is integrative, seeking its legitimacy from the identification of the masses with their governments, and when, additionally, it is democratic, governing less by the manipulation of symbols than by means of explanations and justifications, the need to simplify the linguistic composition of the *polis* increases. In such a state the pressure towards unilingualism is great. At the time of the French Revolution of 1789, the majority of French people did not speak French; a century later most of them did so; and now, after two hundred years, French is spoken by practically all of them. Not all states of Europe have become as unified linguistically as France but they have all moved in the same direction, even Switzerland where the number of local language varieties has been markedly reduced.

The formula of the nineteenth-century school of nationalism, 'one state-one-language-one-nation' – to which 'one-religion' was sometimes added – has increasingly been simplified to a 'one-state-one-language of government' formula, henceforth made to apply to the multinational as well as to the one-nation state. The English-only movement of the 1980s in the USA is to be explained in part as an anti-foreign reaction, but it is also explainable by the fact that to some of its supporters the rate of Spanish immigration appeared to outpace the rate of assimilation (on the relation between these two rates see Deutsch 1953). The insistence on a common language could then be used by the opponents of bilingual education as concern for the preservation of a peaceful and equalitarian multi-ethnic society (Ricento 1998; Crawford 2000).

Modern states are both assimilators and protectors of languages. They tend to weaken if not destroy their weaker languages internally while protecting their own dominant languages on the international scene. However, if the democratic state finds it easier to mobilize its citizenry with a single language, it is also subject to the pressure for recognition of minority languages that can muster sufficient electoral support either through political party systems that cut across languages or, less frequently, through political parties of their own (for example the Swedish party of Finland, the Turkish Movement for Rights and Freedoms of Bulgaria, the *Bloc québécois* of Canada) – or, in the extreme case of Belgium, through a representation system where all major parties are based on language, the older parties having split into separate Flemish or French entities.

The state and language planning

State language planning takes three major forms according to whether the state attempts to affect a language's corpus, status, or usage.

Corpus planning seeks to improve the quality of the language as an instrument of communication. Such a goal was, among others, that of Richelieu when he created the French Academy in 1634, an Academy assigned the task of writing and revising a French dictionary (for a comparison of language policies in France and England, see Ager 1996); such was the goal of the Government of Quebec when it created the *Conseil de la langue française* which has among its functions that of improving the quality of the French used in Quebec; such was the goal of the Norwegian state when at various times in the twentieth century it created commissions of linguists whose task was to standardize the two versions of the Norwegian language.

The creation of many new words of science and technology and the need to standardize their meaning and application has created a competition against time that few languages can sustain if they want to be world languages. In an attempt to keep French at the level of English, as well as to facilitate communication between its two official languages, the Canadian federal government has created and maintains a terminology bank of French–English scientific and technological concepts that contains over a million terms in each language, the translation of which is accessible on line by computer from government departments and on CD rom by non-affiliated users such as university libraries.

Between the antiquated ways of the French Academy and the machine readable ways of the Canadian government, there are many means of intervention in corpus planning. Most effective are those forcing schools to use texts and examinations that act as references for the correct forms of speech and writing. Hence the importance, in the USA, of the debate over whether 'Black English' should be considered as a faulty variant of standard English or accepted as a legitimate form of the language (Sonntag and Pool 1987).

Status planning leads the state to give legitimacy or dominance to specific languages. High status is typically given to a language by recognizing it as official. That is the case, for example, of English in some American states; of French in France, of French and English at the federal level in Canada; of French, German, Italian and to a lesser extent Romansh in the Swiss Confederation; of Swedish and Finnish in Finland; of English and Gaelic in Ireland; of French and English in Cameroon, and of French and Dutch in Belgium. Sometimes the recognition as official is mostly symbolic, as in the case of the aboriginal languages of South Africa (see above p. 594).

More important than any constitutional and legal recognition is the actual practice regulating language use in schools, in parliaments, in the courts, and more generally in the providing of government information and services. The study of that practice involves considering the rules regarding speaking, writing and understanding (see Laponce 1987).

The Canadian constitution of 1867 gave French-speaking parliamentarians the right to use their language, but their right to be understood was not recognized until immediate translation was introduced in parliament, then in committees, then at cabinet meetings almost a hundred years later. Gaelic is deemed to be both the national and official language of Ireland and that country's stamps rarely use any language other than Gaelic, but the discussions at cabinet meetings are entirely in English. The laws of the Philippines are published in English but not in Pilipino, those of Singapore are published in English but not in Mandarin, Tamil, or Malay. By contrast the laws of Switzerland are published in German, French and Italian; and in Belgium, as in Canada, not only are the laws official in two languages but the meetings of the cabinet accommodate the two official languages by means of immediate translation. Sometimes, as in France, a defendant before a court of justice is merely given the right to an interpreter; in other cases – for example in Quebec and in New Brunswick – that defendant is given the right to a trial in the official language of his or her choice.

The imposition of a national language as that of the state is often used as a means of state and nation building. In the thirteenth century Alphonso X of Spain required the use of Castilian instead of Latin in the writing of government documents, and three centuries later Francis I of France imposed French on his public servants (Lapierre 1988). But state, if not nation, building is also frequently done by avoiding the use of a native language in the conduct of government. Selecting English in India or French in Senegal as the major or sole language of government had the advantage of not offending the ethnic groups that resent the use of Hindi or Woulof.

In addition to regulating the use of language in parliaments, courts, public schools and bureaucracies, the governments of multilingual societies have occasionally regulated the use of language in what is usually considered to be the private domain. Quebec requires the use of French in the writing of the contracts and internal notices of firms employing more than fifty people, and stipulates that French must be more prominent than the other language used on the bilingual signs which can be displayed within stores (Leclerc 1989; MacMillan 1998; Ricento and Burnaby 1998).

Territorial or personal solutions

When seeking to regulate the contact among languages in bilingual situations, the state has the choice of two fundamentally different solutions: *territorial* solutions of the kind used by Belgium and Switzerland; and *personal* solutions of the kind used by Estonia between the two world wars, and used also, to a lesser extent, by Finland and the Canadian federal government.

The classic example of a territorial solution is offered by Switzerland, where language boundaries separate German, Italian and French areas in such a way that unilingualism is the general rule in the operations of local government services, schools and public life. Swiss citizens are free to cross the language boundaries, but if they do they are expected to change language as would the typical immigrant to a foreign country. The political strategy guiding these stringent regulations consists of separating languages as much as possible at the regional level and restricting bilingualism or multilingualism to the central level of government; a strategy that seeks, in other words, to prevent contact in order to prevent conflict. Belgium adopted a similar system by making Flanders Flemish-speaking and Wallonia French-speaking, but it has not been able to apply fully the Swiss model because its capital, Brussels, is a predominantly Francophone city cast in Flemish territory. As an exception to the rule of territorial unilingualism the Belgian capital has been set aside as a bilingual area.

The political justification for the system of fixed language boundaries is given by the following decision of the Swiss Federal Tribunal when it rejected the claim of a businessman who had argued that a local regulation forbidding him to advertise his products in the language of his choice was in violation of the equality clause of the Federal Constitution:

> The linguistic borders of our country, once established, must be considered to be unchangeable. Safeguarding the harmonious relationship among the various segments (ethnolinguistic groups) of our country requires that each be guaranteed the integrity of the territory over which its language is spoken and over which extends its culture; and that each be given the right to prevent any encroachment.
>
> (translated from Héraud 1974: 247)

In the Swiss case, and to a lesser extent in the Belgian case, the languages are rooted territorially, and are thus given security niches of their own. The power to protect the boundaries so created is given not to individuals but to collectivities – the cantons in Switzerland, the regional and community governments in Belgium (McRae 1975, 1984, 1986; Delpérée 1996; Domenicelli 1999).

In marked contrast to the Swiss system, that used by the Baltic countries, notably in Estonia (Aun 1940), between the two World Wars allowed any ethnic group comprising at least 3,000 people to set up a nation-wide community with institutions of its own; institutions with the power to tax its members and to administer its own public and private schools. These nation-wide ethnic governments resembled local governments except in their not being territorially grounded and having extensive language rights, in particular that of selecting the language of instruction in the schools (Coakley 1994). That system – which had its forerunners in the Polish Jewish kahal and in the millets of the Ottoman empire (Laponce 1960) – did not survive the war but finds a partial revival in the *communauté* governments of the Belgian constitution of 1993 that are, together with the regional governments, pillars of the federal system (Delpérée 1996; Domenicelli 1999).

Between the extremes of the Swiss and the Estonian models, Finland offers the case of partially and temporarily grounded languages. Wherever the Swedish minority accounts for at least 8 per cent of the population of a given commune (the basic unit of local government), the public services are offered in the two official languages, Swedish and Finnish; however, a bilingual district will normally become unilingual Finnish if the Swedish population is shown by the census to have declined below the required minimum. (In the Åaland Islands, however, the Swiss system of territorial unilingualism protects the Swedish minority as a result of post-First World War agreements that regulate the status of that territory.) A variation on the Finnish system, proposed by Scott Reid (1993) for Canada would allow bilingual districts originally set within unilingual areas to contract but not expand in geographical size.

The Canadian Federal Government has by and large patterned its language policies on those of Finland rather than those of either Switzerland or Belgium, responding in so doing to the wishes of its English-speaking population but also out of fear that a unilingual French Quebec might be closer to secession than if it remained bilingual. One cannot deny that possibility (the Quebec electorate came close to voting for some form of separation in a 1995 referendum) but, interestingly, the increase in language security of the Quebecois population through the language legislation mentioned earlier (p. 595) was correlated with a lowering of separatist fervour after that legislation was introduced (McRoberts 1988: 333ff). This appears to confirm that the Swiss strategy of reducing contact between competing languages by juxtaposing unilingual areas rather than merging the languages within the same territory has the desired effect of lowering tensions – at least when the language cleavage is not reinforced by other non-linguistic cleavages that would make the ethnic groups concerned incompatible on too many grounds.

Conclusion

The rooting of political analysis into economic analysis, especially Marxian analysis, has frequently led analysts of contemporary societies to view ethnic conflicts, and language conflicts in particular, as outdated conflicts, of a type that would disappear as the state became more modern. In fact, the general lowering of class tensions in most industrial societies after the Second World War has led to reconsideration of this forecast. Unlike economic and financial resources but like religion, language does not lend itself easily to compromise, least of all when the conflict is over boundaries, whether social or spatial boundaries, and especially the latter. Languages and states are both territorial animals. Globalization may well weaken the state in the economic field, but if that weakening increases the sense of insecurity of a language community, globalization will then, very likely, strengthen the state in its role of protector of language and culture.

References

Ager, D. (1996) *Language Policy in Britain and France*, London:Cassell.

Albert, M. and Obler, L. (1978) *The Bilingual Brain: Neurophysiological and Neurolinguistic Aspects of Bilingualism*, New York: Academic Press.

Aun, K. (1940) *On the Spirit of the Estonian Minority Laws*, Stockholm: Societies Litteraturn Estonia.

Baker, C. (2001) *Foundations of Bilingual Education and Bilingualism*, Clevedon: Multilingual Matters.

Bissoonauth, A. (1998) 'La dimension francophone à Maurice et l'analyse de l'identité mauricienne', in D. Marley *et al. Linguistic Identities and Politics in France and the French-speaking World*, London: CiLT

Bourdieu, P. (1991) *Language and Symbolic Power*, Cambridge: Polity Press.

Bourhis, R. (1984) 'Cross-cultural communication in Montreal', *International Journal of the Sociology of Language*, 46 (1): 33–47.

Breton, A. (ed.) (1999) *Exploring the Economics of Language*, Ottawa: Canadian Heritage government publication.

Breton, R. (1976) *Géographie des langues*, Paris: Presses Universitaires de France.

Burney, P. (1966) *Les langues internationales*, Paris: Presses Universitaires de France.

Cailleux, A. (1953) 'L'Evolution quantitative du langage', *Société préhistorique française*, 505–14.

Calvet, J. L. (1974) *Linguistique et colonialisme, petit traité de glottophagie*, Paris: Payot.

—— (1998) *Language Wars and Linguistic Politics*, Oxford: Oxford University Press.

Coakley, J. (1994) 'Approaches to the Resolution of Ethnic conflicts: the Strategies of Territorial Autonomy', *International Political Science Review*, 15: 297–314.

Corbeil, I. and Delude, C. (1982) *Etudes des communautés francophones hors Québec et des communautés anglophones au Québec*, Montréal: CROP.

Coulombes, P. (1995) *Language Rights in French Canada*, New York: Peter Lang.

Crawford, J. (2000) *At War with Diversity: US Language Policy in an Age of Diversity*, Clevedon: Multilingual Matters.

Crystal, D. (2000) *Language Death*, Cambridge: Cambridge University Press.

de Swaan (1993) 'The Emergent World Language System', *International Political Science Review*, 14 (3): 219–26.

—— (2001) *Words of The World: the General Language System*, Cambridge: Polity Press.

de Varennes, F. (1996) *Language, Minorities, and Human Rights*, The Hague: Nijhoff.

Delpérée, F. (1996) 'Le fédéralisme forme d'adaptation de l'Etat nation: le cas de la Belgique', in C. Philip and P. Soldatos (eds) *Au delà de l'Etat nation*, Bruxelles: Bruylant.

Deprez, C. (1996) 'Politique linguistique familiale: le rôle des femmes', in C. Juillarde and J. L. Calvet, *Les politiques linguistiques, mythes et réalités*, Montréal: AUPELF, pp. 155–62.

Deutsch, K. (1953) *Nationalism and Social Communication*, New York: John Wiley.

Domenicelli, L. (1999) *Constitution et régime linguistique en Belgique et au Canada*, Bruxelles: Bruylant

Dornic, S. (1975) *Human Information Processing and Bilingualism*, Stockholm: Institute of Applied Psychology.

—— (1980) 'Information processing and language dominance', *International Review of Applied Psychology*, 29 (1): 119–40.

Dressler, W. and Wodak-Leodolter, R. (eds) (1977) 'Language death', special issue of *International Journal of the Sociology of Language*, 12 (1).

Edwards, J. (1994) *Multilingualism*, London: Routledge.

Ferguson, C. A. (1959) 'Diglossia', *Word*, 15: 325–40.

—— (1964) 'On linguistic information', *Language and Linguistics*, 201–8.

Fishman, J. A. (1966) *Language Loyalty in the United States*, The Hague: Mouton.

—— (1967) 'Bilingualism with and without diglossia, diglossia with and without bilingualism', *Journal of Social Issues*, 23 (2): 29–38.

Fishman, J. A., Cooper, R., Roxana, M. A., *et al.* (1971) *Bilingualism in the Barrio*, The Hague: Mouton.

Fishman, J. A., Cooper, R. L. and Conrad, A. (1975) *The Spread of English*, Rowley, MA: Newbury.

Gardner-Chloros, P. (1985) 'Language selection and switching among Strasbourg shoppers', *International Journal of the Sociology of Language*: 117–35.

Gendron, J. D. (1973) *Rapport de la Commission d'enquête sur la langue française au Québec*, 3 vols, Quebec: Editeur officiel.

Genouvrier, E. and Peytard, J. (1970) *Linguistique et enseignement du français*, Paris: Larousse.

Gorter, D., Reinmersma, A. and Yisma, J. (2001) 'Frisian in the Netherlands' in G. Extra and D. Gorter, *The Other Languages of Europe*, Clevedon: Multilingual Matters.

Graddol, D. (1997) *The Future of English* (1997) London: the British Council.

Grimes, B. C. and Grimes, J.(1998?) *Ethnologue: Languages of the World*, 14th edn, Dallas: Linguistics Summer Institute.

Grin, F. (1999) *Compétences et récompenses: la valeur des langues en Suisse*, Freiburg: Editions Universitaires.

—— (1994) 'The economics of language: match or mismatch', *International Political Science Review*, 15 (1): 25–42.

Gumperz, J. J. (1971) *Language in Social Groups*, Stanford: Stanford University Press.

Héraud, G. (1974) *L'Europe des ethnies*, 2nd edn, Paris: Presses d'Europe.

Hirschman, T. O. (1970) *Exit, Voice, and Loyalty*, Cambridge: Cambridge University Press.

Horowitz, L. (1985) *Ethnic Groups in Conflict*, Berkeley: University of California Press.

Krauss, M. 'The world languages in crisis', *Language*, 68: 6–10.

Kymlicka, W. (1995) *Multicultural Citizenship: A Liberal Theory of Minority Rights*, Oxford: Clarendon Press.

Laitin, D. (1977) *Politics, Language, and Thought: The Somali Experience*, Chicago: University of Chicago Press.

—— (1988) 'Language games', *Comparative Politics*, 20 (3): 289–302.

Lapierre, J. W. (1988) *Le pouvoir politique et les langues*, Paris: Presses Universitaires de France.

Laponce, J. A. (1960) *The Protection of Minorities*, Berkeley and Los Angeles: University of California Press.

—— (1987) *Languages and Their Territories*, Toronto: Toronto University Press.

—— (2001) 'Politics and the law of Babel', *Social Science Information*, 40 (2): 180–94.

Leclerc, J. (1989) *La guerre des langues dans l'affichage*, Montréal: VLB éditeurs.

Leopold, W. F. (1939–49) *Speech Development of a Bilingual Child: A Linguistic Record*, 4 vols, Evanston: Northwestern University Press.

Mackey, W. F. (1971) *La distance interlinguistique*, Quebec: Presses de l'Université Laval.

—— (1988) 'Geolinguistics: its scope and principles', in C. Williams (ed.) *Language in Geographic Context*, pp. 20–46, Clevedon: Multilingual Matters.

—— (forthcoming, 2003) 'Bilingualism and multilingualism', in U. Ammon *et al.*, *Sociolinguistics*, Berlin: Walter de Gruyter.

McConnell, G. *et al.* (1878–98) *The Written Languages of the World: A Survey of the Degree and Mode of Use*, 5 vols, Quebec: Presses de l'Université Laval.

McConnell, G. D. and Roberge, B. (1994) *Atlas international de la diffusion de l'anglais et du français*, l'enseignement Québec: Presses de l'Université Laval.

MacMillan, C. M. (1998) *The Practice of Language Rights in Canada*, Toronto: Toronto University Press.

McRoberts, K. (1989) 'Making Canada Bilingual: Illusion and delusions of federal language policy', in D. P. Shugarman and R. Whitaker (eds) *Federalism and Political Community*, Peterborough: Broadview, pp. 141–71.

—— (1988) *Quebec: Social Change and Political Crisis*, Toronto: McClelland and Stewart.

Mathiot, M. (1979) *Ethnolinguistics: Boas, Sapir, and Whorf Revisited*, The Hague: Mouton.

Maurais, J. (2001) 'Vers un nouvel ordre linguistique mondial', *Terminogramme*, 99–100, 7–34.

May, S. (2001) *Languages and Minority Rights*, London: Pearson.

McRae, K. D. (1975) 'The principle of territoriality and the principle of personality in multi-lingual states', *Linguistics*, 158 (4): 33–54.

—— (1984) *Conflict and Compromise in Multilingual Societies: Switzerland*, Waterloo, Ont.: Wilfrid Laurier University Press.

—— (1986) *Conflict and Compromise in Multilingual Societies: Belgium*, Waterloo, Ont.: Wilfrid Laurier University Press.

Muller, S. H. (1964) *The World's Living Languages*, New York: Frederick Ungar.

Nettle, D. and Romaine, S. (2000) *Vanishing Voices: the Extinction of the World's Languages*, Oxford: Oxford University Press.

O'Bryan, K. G., Reitz, J. G. and Kuplowska, O. M. (1976) *Non-official Languages: A Study in Canadian Multiculturalism*, Ottawa: Department of Supply and Services.

Phillipson, R. ed. (2000) *Rights to Language: Equity, Power, and Education*, Mahwah, NJ: Lawrence Erlbaum.

Pool, J. (1991) 'The official language problem', *American Political Science Review*, 85 (2): 495–514.

Reid, S. (1993) *Lament for a Notion: the Life and Death of Canada's Bilingual Dream*, Vancouver: Arsenal Pulp Press.

Ricento, T. (1998) 'national language policy in the United States', in T. Ricento and B. Burnaby (eds) *Language and Politics in the United States and Canada: Myths and Realities*, Mahwah, NJ: Lawrence Erlbaum.

Ricento, R. and Burnaby, B. (1998) *Language and Politics in the United States and Canada: Myth and Realities*, Mahwah, NJ: Lawrence Erlbaum.

Rubin, J. (1968) *National Bilingualism in Paraguay*, The Hague: Mouton.

Sapir, E. (1949) *Selected Writings of Edward Sapir*, in D. Mandelbaum (ed.) *Language, Culture and Personality*, Berkeley: University of California Press.

Schubert, N. J. (1988) 'Politics under the microscope: observational methods in political science', *International Political Science Review*, 9 (4): 305–26.

Schermerhorn, R. A. (1970) *Comparative Ethnic Relations: A Framework For Theory and Research*, New York: Random House.

Skutnabb-Kangas, T. (1981) *Bilingualism or Not: The Education of Minorities*, Clevedon: Multilingual Matters.

Skutnabb-Kangas, T. and Phillipson, R. (1998) 'Language in human rights', *The International Journal of Communication Studies*, 60 (1): 27–46.

Sonntag, S. K. and Pool, J. (1987) 'Linguistic denial and linguistic self-denial: American ideologies of language', *Language Problems and Language Planning*, II (1): 46–65.

Steyn, R. W. (1972) 'Medical implications of 'polyglottism'', *Archives of General Psychiatry*, 27 (2): 245–7.

Tajfel, H. and Turner, J. C. (1979) 'An integrative theory of intergroup conflict', in W. C. Austin and S. Worchel (eds) *The Social Psychology of Intergroup Relations*, Monterey, CA: Brooks & Cole.

Van Parijs, P. (2000) 'The ground floor of the world: on socio-economic consequences of linguistic globalisation', *International Political Science Review*, 21 (2): 217–34.

Whorf, B. L. (1956) *Language, Thought, and Reality: Selected Writings*, Cambridge, MA: MIT Press.

Wiegele, T. C., Hilton, G., Oaks, K. L. and Kisiel, S. V. (1985) *Leaders Under Stress: A Psycholinguistic Analysis of International Crises*, Durham, NC: Duke University Press.

Wirth, L. (1945) 'The problem of minority groups', in R. Linton (ed.) *The Science of Man in the World Crisis*, New York: Columbia University Press.

Wurm, S. A. (ed.) (1996) *Atlas of the World's Languages in Danger of Disappearing*, Paris: UNESCO.

Further reading

Beer, W. R. and Jacob, J. E. (eds) (1985) *Language Policy and National Unity*, Totowa, NJ: Rowman & Allanheld.

Fishman, J. A. (ed.) (1972) *Advances in the Sociology of Language*, The Hague: Mouton.

—— (ed.) (1978) *Advances in the Study of Societal Multilingualism*, The Hague: Mouton.

Fishman, J. A., Ferguson, C. A. and Das Gupta, J. (1968) *Language Problems of Developing Nations*, New York: John Wiley.

Haarmann, H. (1986) *Language in Ethnicity: A View of Basic Ecological Relations*, Amsterdam: de Gruyter.

Hamers, J. F. and Blanc, M. (1989) *Bilinguality and Bilingualism*, Cambridge: Cambridge University Press.

Haugen, E. (1972) *The Ecology of Language*, Stanford: Stanford University Press.

Kloss, H. (1966) 'Types of multilingual communities: a discussion of ten variables', *Sociological Enquiry*, 36: 135–45.

—— (1967) 'Bilingualism and nationalism', *Journal of Social Issues*, 23 (2): 39–47.

Mackey, (1982) *Bibliographie Internationale sur le bilinguisme*, 2nd edn, Quebec: Presses de l'Université Laval.

Mackey, W. F. and Verdoodt, A. (eds) (1975) *The Multilingual Society*, Rowley, MA: Newbury House.

Mazrui, A, and Mazrui, A. (1998) *The Power of Babel: Languages and Governance in the African Experience*, Chicago: Chicago University Press.

Rossi-Landi, F. (1975) *Linguistics and Economics*, The Hague: Mouton.

Vaillancourt, F. (1983) 'the economics of language and language planning', *Language Problems and Language Planning*, 7 (2): 162–78.

Weinreich, U. (1953) *Languages in Contact: Findings and Problems*, The Hague: Mouton.

39

GENDER AND POLITICS

Kate Bedford

Gender affects, and is affected by, politics in multiple ways. In an attempt to remain fairly attentive to the vast range of empirical concerns and analytic perspectives that interest scholars in the gender and politics field, this introductory overview is focused on three interlocking themes: the influence of gender on participation in politics; the relationship between gender, politics, and the state; and the gendered nature of the categories through which politics is defined. While far from exhaustive this tripartite approach allows attention to be focused on the scope of existing research into gender and politics, and hence should facilitate an inclusive introduction to the field.

The influence of gender on participation in multiple types of politics

Much research into gender and politics analyzes women's political participation, defined in terms of voting and involvement in government. In part this emphasis reflects a perceived need to correct distorted representations of women's political participation. Many early studies of voting behavior ignored women, for example, or made inaccurate generalizations about their inherent conservatism and candidate-oriented voting calculus (see Inglehart and Norris 2000: 443–4 for a review of such literature). In response, there is now a considerable amount of scholarship on women's voting behavior in some countries. For example, work in the UK has disproved the claim that women voters are more likely to personalize politics than men (Randall 1987). Some researchers also point to an apparent 'gender gap' in public opinion and voting that challenges assumptions of women's conservativism (Conover 1988; Carroll 1988; Lovenduski 2001). In the 1980s the gender gap was regarded as a US phenomenon, in which women were less likely to vote for Republican candidates during Presidential elections, more likely to favour gun control, less likely to support militaristic policies, and more supportive of federal government programs than men (Carroll 2001a: xiii). However in a recent overview of evidence from over 60 countries Ronald Inglehart and Pippa Norris argue that the gender gap is a global affair, with women 'moving toward the left of men throughout advanced industrial societies' (2000: 441). Inglehart and Norris explain this gender-differentiated alignment of political preferences through long-term structural and cultural trends, such as women's greater participation in the paid workforce and the breakdown of traditional gender roles. Other researchers explain the gender gap using other factors; Susan Carroll

(1988) concentrates on women's growing economic and psychological autonomy from men as a key variable, while Pamela Conover (1988) highlights the importance of feminist commitments and strong women's movements. However researchers concur that early assumptions regarding the conservative nature of women's political partici-pation are no longer valid.

Scholars have also focused on women's representation in formal politics, both to contest accounts that rendered female politicians invisible and to identify the imped-iments that exclude women from power (Randall 1987: ix). These barriers include party discrimination, fund raising inequities, gender role socialization, educational inequalities, and advantages of incumbency (Carroll 2001a: xii). Indeed scholarship on women's under-representation in formal politics has become increasingly promi-nent in recent years, in part due to growing international attention to the issue. In 1995, for example, national signatories to the Platform of Action stemming from the UN's Conference on Women in Beijing pledged that women would constitute at least one third of representatives by 2005 (Corrin 2002: 107), and between 1995 and 2000 women's representation in national legislatures increased from 10 to 12% (Karam 2000: 15). Although this level of representation is still lower than the unprecedented 14% of women in parliaments achieved in 1988, the statistics have generated considerable attention given the heightened international interest in gender and formal politics.

Some countries have achieved particularly dramatic gains through the adoption of what British analyst Karen Ross terms 'positive action strategies' (2002a: 4) to encourage women's representation. For example, in 1997 the proportion of women in the House of Commons increased from 9% to 18% (Lovenduski 2001), mostly as a result of the adoption by the victorious Labour Party of preferential selection proce-dures for women candidates to 'circumvent the reactionary proclivities of too many party members who do not believe that women are actually capable of "being" politi-cians' (Ross 2002a: 1). Such strategies were also important in increasing women's participation in the Scottish parliament and the Welsh assembly, which were 37% and 38% female at their inception (Ross 2002a; Busby and MacLeod 2002; Lovenduski 2001). Likewise 111 women entered parliament in the first free elections in South Africa, largely due to the ANC's internal quota system to support female candidates (Geisler 2001: 606). Constitutional amendments have been passed in India to reserve 30% of seats in the Panchayat system of local government for women, and as a result over 1 million women have been elected as members and chairpersons (Pal 1999: 32). Uganda's ruling National Resistance Movement has also implemented a system of reserved seats and preferential selection procedures for women at all levels of the political system (Pankhurst 2002: 127); women now hold 19% of seats in Uganda's national parliament (not all of which were reserved) and appointments to key ministerial, judicial and special commission positions (Tripp 2001).

With women's presence in formal politics increasing in some countries, analysts of women in public office have revisited early assumptions that increased numerical representation would automatically result in improved substantive representation of women's interests (Carroll 2001a: xi; Grey 2002: 19; Ross 2002: 2; Brown et al. 2002: 71). Such (re)consideration has produced complex results. Exhortations to get more women into positions of leadership can be thrown into question when one considers the record of many female leaders, for example. Many are recruited due to their relationships with men, and act as what Francine D'Amico terms 'surrogate' politicians, offering minimal disruption to stereotypes that men are the preferred political leaders (1995: 24). Examples provided by D'Amico include Corazon Aquino, Benazir Bhutto, Khalida Zia, and Violeta Barrios Torres de Chamorro. Women who rise to power within political parties may have no connection to broader women's movements, and some can actually damage women's interests. Margaret Thatcher is regarded as such a leader by many feminist observers (D'Amico 1995: 26). In another example Tansu Ciller (elected as the first female prime minister of Turkey in 1993) was recruited personally into politics by the head of the party she would take to power, and a recent analysis of her period in office notes 'her opportunistic quest for power and dismissal of women's issues' (Arat 1998: 1). As Jude Howell notes regarding the Chinese case, then, 'getting women into politics and government is not just about occupying positions of leadership. There is no guarantee that women in power promote women's diverse interests or have any commitment to feminism' (2002: 2).

If female national leaders can not necessarily be regarded as allies for women seeking greater substantive representation in particular polities, it is necessary to explore whether the same is true of female elected representatives more generally. Analysts have noted that increased numerical representation does not secure leadership roles for women within national legislatures; in South Africa, for example, nearly 30% of parliamentarians are female, but the country's national leadership is still overwhelmingly male (Ross 2002b: 197). In a similar vein critics have argued that the women serving on Panchayats as a result of India's recent constitutional amendments lack power, and often stand to enhance their husband's political ambitions (Pal 1999; Singh 1999; Prasad 1999). Attention to such factors 'problematize[s] the sometimes too facile rhetoric that of course women make a difference' (Ross 2002a: 4).

Moreover, women representatives may not support feminist policies. Sarah Childs claims that the link between increased representation of women in parliament and protection of women's interests was disproved for many British observers when only 1 of 65 new Labour women MPs rebelled against Blair's cut in lone parent allowance in 1997, a move that severely affected poor women (2002: 143). Other researchers note that women in public office are diverse, and that their impact varies considerably by context. Studies reported in a recent U.S.-focused anthology on this issue highlight the importance of multiple factors in influencing the extent to which female public officials support women-friendly policies, such as race, party and ideological affiliation, whether they are political appointees or elected officials, whether women are in conservative districts, the extent of their margin of victory if elected, whether they are operating in local councils, state legislatures or national bodies, whether they identify with feminism, and whether they can work together in a formal caucus (Carroll 2001a).

That said, however, some evidence exists to support a cautious claim in some countries that women elected to public office are more likely to prioritize legislative agendas defined as concerning women than are similarly-situated men. Susan Carroll's study of American women state legislators found clear gender differences in legislative priorities, for example, with women more likely to support bills focused on women, families, children, and healthcare. As she summarizes, 'if similarly situated men are taken as the norm against which women's behavior is measured, then many women legislators of differing party affiliations, ideological perspectives, postures toward feminism, and races can be considered agents of change – agents who are more likely than their male counterparts to act for women' (Carroll 2001b: 18). Sandra Grey's (2002) analysis of parliamentarians in New Zealand also demonstrates that women politicians are more likely to advocate for child care and parental leave than men, and that debate about these issues increased as more women were represented. This is not, however, to argue that policy priorities undergo a simple transformation as a result of women's greater representation. Rather as Karen Ross puts it in a helpful summary, 'whilst the presence of more women in the world's elected chambers undoubtedly widens the range of perspectives which are brought to bear on the development of policy through discussion and debate, a de facto shift in the policy agenda itself as an automatic consequence of women's involvement is an altogether more moot point' (2002a: 4).

Researchers in gender and politics have also considered whether a focus on formal politics (involving voting and governmental service) adequately explains gender-differentiated involvement in political struggles. On the most basic level, one can not account for women's participation in formal political structures without reference to their mobilization elsewhere. The South African case provides an important example. As Gisela Geisler notes, 'South African women's success in moving from active participation in the liberation struggle to active participation in government has been exceptional on a world scale' (2000: 605); ignoring women's early anti-state activities would give a distorted impression of how they got into parliamentary politics in the first place. Moreover, the country's Commission for Gender Equality (created to monitor gender mainstreaming in all branches of the new government) was originally headed by activists with strong ties to women's movements at the domestic and international level.

In addition, some gender and politics scholars are highly critical of the disproportionate attention given to the experiences of elite women in much research on political participation. In a particularly important volume on women and politics in the USA Cathy Cohen, Kathleen Jones and Joan Tronto note the overall failure of women elected to public office to substantively represent working-class women and women of color, and they heavily criticize the 'excessive reliance' (1997: 5) of many researchers on dominant institutions such as Congress to mark the space of legitimate politics. By treating elite women's political experiences as constitutive of the parameters of political research in this manner, scholars have neglected many alternative ways through which women engage questions of power and inequality, such as pickets, self-help projects, protest through art and music, and urban protest campaigns. In particular, a focus on non-elite forms of political participation reveals that many important episodes of gendered mobilization have occurred in social movements. Again, these episodes of political participation have been overlooked by many analysts. For example Jeong-Lim Nam (2000) argues that women's collective struggles against state violence and economic exploitation were central to the breakdown of military rule in South Korea in the late 1980s; these struggles have been ignored by scholars who do not regard women as important actors during the democratization process.

Although women have participated in a wide variety of social movements, they have been particularly prominent in peace activism, national liberation movements, ecology movements, and struggles for economic justice (Peterson and Runyan 1999:

179–207). In part this mobilization reflects the differential gendered effects of current policies at the local, state and suprastate level. Thus the dialectical nature of women's political participation becomes clear, since policies help to create the gendered constituencies that are then mobilized in social movements. For example, although there is no essential connection between women and nature to explain their heavy presence in ecological movements, women's disproportionate responsibility for securing social reproduction needs can render them particularly vulnerable to environmental destruction that destroys food sources and so on (Peterson and Runyan 1999: 201). In a similar vein Sonia Alvarez (1990) shows that Brazilian women were affected in gender-specific ways by the developmental model pursued by the military regime during the 1970s and 80s, since they had to secure family and community survival in an era of wage cuts, price rises, growing unemployment, and inadequate provision of social services. In turn women made up 80% or more of participants in the urban social movements that helped push the military out of power. Attention to such forms of political participation is crucial; it provides a more accurate insight into the relationship between gender and politics than a unitary focus on elites, and it facilitates new conversations between feminist scholars and those interested in comparative politics, social movements, international relations, and the like.

The relationship between gender, politics, and the state: a new emphasis on complexity, autonomy, and the national/global interaction

Whether one explores the patterns of gendered participation in elite or non-elite politics one is forced to consider a question central to researchers in gender and politics, regarding the ideal relationship between political action and the state. In early analyses researchers were divided between those in the liberal tradition who framed the state as a potentially neutral arbiter of competing gender interests once women were properly represented in its ranks, and those in an anti-state tradition who focused on the oppressive, patriarchal nature of state power and advised feminist disengagement wherever possible (Marshall 1997). As several more contemporary accounts point out, neither model fully captures the ambivalence of state power nor the complex relationships men and women have to state policies (Alvarez 1990; Cooper 1995; Marshall 1997; Friedman 2000). The state is a multifaceted, fluid, disconnected and occasionally erratic entity, with activists securing opportunities to seize space in some departments while proving ineffective in others. In addition, men do not have a unitary relationship to the state, given that it is implicated in multiple dimensions of social inequality including race, class, caste, religion, and sexuality. Finally the nature of the state and its relationship to feminist projects has changed over time, with some women securing opportunities to exercise state power (Piven 1990; Sarvasy 1992; Cooper 1995). Such factors prevent any assertion of the state's inherently oppressive or liberationary character.

Instead, scholars now tend to focus on the complex negotiations in which activists concerned with gender-related issues must engage to get their struggles onto the public agenda, and they increasingly recognize the importance of multiple feminist strategies, directed at the state and outside it. Indeed Louise Chappell identifies an international shift in feminist analyses away from framings of the state as either inherently oppressive or gender neutral, and towards a more context-specific focus on the interaction between gender and the state. Her own work (2000, 2002) argues that the divergent 'national political opportunity structures' available to feminists strongly influence their approach to the state. Australian 'femocrats' in public service have managed to secure more success than their counterparts in Canada or the UK, for example, in part because the Australian civil service is tolerant of advocates within the bureaucracy, and does not insist on neutrality in the Westminster tradition (2002: 90). In contrast Canadian feminists have attempted to secure more policy change through jurisprudence, in part due to the strong emphasis on constitutional rights in Canada.

Davina Cooper's study of feminist engagement with the British state also emphasizes the complex, fragmented nature of the state and the availability of space therein for activists to articulate more egalitarian social and political relationships. For example, during the 1980s gays and lesbians mobilized within the Labour-controlled Greater London Council to deploy state power themselves in an innovative way. Their actions (undertaken in an era of rightist state control) demonstrate that although total policy victories are unlikely, assumptions of absolute closure to the state are untenable (1995: 92); there are always sites within which actors can forge counter-hegemonic policies and attempt to reframe policy.

A second characteristic of contemporary gender and politics scholarship on the state is the recognition that some degree of autonomy is required for feminist movements to successfully press their demands. Aili Tripp's (2001) analysis of the Ugandan women's movement pinpointed associational autonomy from the state and the regime of semi-authoritarian ruler Museveni as key factors in its success. Although Museveni has supported women's mobilization for his own political ends, most women's organizations can freely select their leaders and are financially self-supporting, thereby ensuring distance (if not immunity) from clientelistic patronage politics. Jude Howell shares this recognition of the importance of autonomous organizational structures in her analysis of the Chinese case. While women have been mobilized repeatedly through the party-state controlled All China Women's Federation, their ability to act as 'their own agents of change' (2002: 51) with respect to unpopular policies towards population control or female migrant workers is restricted by the ACWF's limited autonomy. Although careful not to dismiss the advances women have secured through participation in what she terms 'state-derived feminism' (2002: 43), Howell also concludes that greater advances will require heightened organizational autonomy from the state.

Finally, scholars are increasingly incorporating an international dimension of analysis into their work on the state, in recognition of the importance of suprastate influences on national gender politics. In some cases activists have attempted to pressure states to change policy using suprastate mechanisms. For example, Nepali feminists took their government to court using the UN's Convention on the Elimination of All Forms of Discrimination against Women to demand the repeal of discriminatory inheritance laws (Malla 2001). In a similar move, welfare rights activists have tried to sue the US government in the Inter-American Court of Human Rights for violating the economic rights of poor people (Butts 2001). European activists have also pressured their home countries using the European Parliament, a legislative body with a higher level of female representatives than many of its member states (Freedman 2002).

Simultaneously, however, analysts have emphasized the way in which supra-national factors can influence the ability and/or willingness of some national governments to enact the political changes demanded by feminist advocates. Many highlight the effects of the debt crisis, and of neo-liberal economic restructuring policies enacted in response, in this respect. State control over some aspects of domestic policy has been reduced as indebted governments grant international agencies more influence over economic policy, for example. Moreover efforts to reduce state spending on neo-liberal terms have distinctly gendered effects (Beneria and Feldman 1992; Moser 1993; Sparr 1994; Baaker 1994). State employment in sectors such as health and education has been reduced, a move that has disproportionately affected women, and the end to state subsidies of food has led women to spend more time shopping, cooking, and preparing food than in the past. Girl children are also particularly vulnerable to being removed from school if fees are introduced.

Given this complex interaction between gender and politics at the domestic and international level, many analysts argue that discussions of the state must be attentive to the supra-national context. For example, although her analysis of the Brazilian women's movement focuses heavily on shifting domestic political opportunity structures associated with stages in the democratization process, Sonia Alvarez also notes that dependent capitalist states (such as Brazil) are far more constrained in their ability to meet feminist demands than more economically powerful states (such as the USA). In one case during the late 1980s the Brazilian state used the debt crisis as a reason not to fund a daycare program called for by feminists. Consequently, feminists who demand that the state enact such policies must also make political claims on the supra-national institutions that regulate the neo-liberal response to the debt crisis (Alvarez mentions the World Bank and the International Monetary Fund here). She thus concludes her book on Brazilian women's interactions with the state with a call for efforts to ameliorate the gendered effects of the debt crisis to enhance prospects for feminist reform in endebted nations.

Jacqui Alexander's work on the Bahamas also stresses the importance of incorporating an international component into feminist analyses of national politics. In a critique of feminist efforts to get anti-violence measures enacted by the state, Alexander (1991) notes that lesbianism and prostitution were criminalized alongside acts of male violence such as rape and incest, and she demands new approaches to violence that do not enhance state surveillance. However crucially she connects these state-level policies to the supranational realm, arguing that the state is faced with a legitimacy crisis due to its lack of control over domestic policy in the neo-liberal era of economic restructuring. In response the state eroticizes the dissolution of the nation through discourses of dread sexual diseases and perversions associated with Western decadence, while at the same time rendering the borders of the nation-state ever-more permeable for multinational corporations inline with structural adjustment imperatives.

Insights such as these highlight the Janus-faced nature of much gender and politics scholarship on the state, involving *both* attention to delicate nuances of state policy and local political fields in which specific political organizations operate (Ray 1999), *and* awareness of the international arena. Feminist research on the state is thus excellently positioned to comment on some of the most pressing issues facing scholars of politics in an era of globalization, and the failure of more mainstream researchers to utilize its insights remains perplexing.

609

The gendered nature of the categories through which 'politics' is defined

A third theme of interest to gender and politics scholars concerns the ways in which gender is embedded in the terms of mainstream political science discourse. In this research tradition, as Kathleen Jones points out, gender is understood as a cultural code of representation, or as a way to categorize behaviors and practices not necessarily connected to sex differences (1993: 30). In this way it is distinguished from research on women per se. The tradition follows Joan Scott's (1986) claim that gender is a way of signifying relations of power. As she pointed out, then, relationships between male workers and employers can be framed in gendered terms, with workers perhaps characterized as weak and subordinate, or as strong protectors of 'their' women and children.

In analyzing the gendered nature of the central organizing categories through which politics is constructed as an object of enquiry, feminists have noted that 'the terms of the dominant political discourse have structured the conceptualization of citizenship and political participation in a specifically gendered way' (Jones 1993: 30). In a profound manner, then, politics is gendered, and the ways in which one defines and researches it reflect and help perpetuate gendered inequalities. As several early analysts argued, mainstream definitions of politics rest on an unquestioning acceptance of the primacy of the public world of the economy and state, and they ignore the private world of domestic life as inherently apolitical (Pateman 1989: 3; see also Okin 1979; Elshtain 1981; Saxenhouse 1985). Yet examination of the work of early democratic political theorists illustrates that the public and private spheres were mutually inter-dependent, gendered entities. Susan Okin's investigation of the ways in which male democratic theorists framed women's relationship to politics is a classic example. She argues that the voluntary public life upon which liberal notions of citizenship rest is defined against a feminized realm of privacy, in which women's role is dictated by the functions they fulfill for male citizens. Rousseau, for example, regarded the family as a natural, indispensable part of human order, and he defined women in terms of their fulfilling family functions. As Okin points out, then, it is insufficient to argue that women be simply included in traditional definitions of liberal citizenship, without contesting the gendered nature of that discourse and the unequal social relations implicated therein.

Other scholars concerned with gender and citizenship concur. Carole Pateman, for example, argues that all classic social contract theorists (with the exception of Hobbes) believed men's natural freedom in the civic public realm rested on women's natural subjection in the private sphere. She thus frames liberal citizenship as a 'patriarchal construction' (1989: 14). In particular, she claims that men's ability to become apparently gender-neutral, disembodied public citizens through entering into a fraternal social contract with each other rested on women's coerced participation in the marriage contract, through which they exchanged their obedience, service and bodies for men's financial support and protection (1988: 163).

Wendy Brown's more recent analysis of the constitutive dualisms of liberal political discourse reinforces the feminist claim that the liberal civic subject (upon which much modern political thought in a Western context rests) is a thoroughly masculine construction. Brown examines the gendered nature of a series of value-laden binaries central to American politics, such as public/private, autonomy/dependence and individual/family to argue that liberalism itself is a discourse of male dominance (1995: 152). In this framing of politics, men are regarded as autarkic and obligated to nothing, while women are framed as already attached to men, and already obligated to children. Even though some women can enter the liberal polity on 'socially male' terms in contemporary America, the masculinized citizen's autonomy, independence, self-sufficiency and self-interestedness are still rendered oppositional to, but totally dependent upon, a feminine realm of naturalized encumbrance, responsibility for others, and selflessness. As Brown notes, then, 'the autonomous subject of liberalism requires a large population of nonautonomous subjects, a population that generates, tends, and avows the bonds, relations, dependencies and connections that nourish human life' (1995: 157). In short, it still takes two gendered entities to make one citizen (161).

Other researchers have argued that categories such as authority (Jones 1993), consent (Pateman 1988), rights (MacKinnon 1989; Williams 1991; Brown 1995), and power (Cooper 1995) are also gendered, in that they privilege men's experiences of social life and help to (re)produce a hierarchical relationship between spheres of activity rendered masculine and feminine. Rather than explore such diverse category-explorations in detail, however, it may be helpful to connect these more theoretical conversations about the gendered nature of politics to research in other areas, using the debate about citizenship noted above. Indeed feminist social policy researchers have been heavily influenced by work on gender-differentiated conceptualizations of citizenship. British analysts have examined the post-war welfare state as predicated on a breadwinner-housewife model of the nuclear family, with paid employment replacing military service as a qualification for full citizenship for men (Williams 1989; Hallett 1996; Lister 2000). Women, however, were offered a limited citizenship on different terms, requiring their normative maternity and dependence on certain men in the nuclear unit. Cohabitees, lesbians, and single and divorced women were penalised for violating these gendered assumptions about citizenship (Carabine 1996; Wilton 1995). A recognition of the importance of *normative* maternity is important here, however, since it is an over-simplification to assert that women secure citizenship through childbearing. In the British case, Black and Asian women's childbearing has been discouraged by the state (Mama 1989), as has the maternity of disabled women (Shaver 1993), poor women (Williams 1989; Hallet 1996), and teenagers (Shaver 1993; Carabine 1992). As Ruth Lister points out, then, it is important for gender and politics analysts to avoid *both* the false universalism that lurks behind the apparently gender-neutral abstract citizen, *and* the false universalism invoked in assumptions that all women are White, heteronormative, able-bodied, and middle-class (2000: 35).

US analysts have also argued that women were incorporated into state welfare projects on different terms than men, in part as a result of gender-differentiated conceptualizations of ideal citizenship. Gwendolyn Mink's exploration of the welfare provisions enacted in the Progressive Era exemplifies this type of analysis. Mink notes that dominant notions of Republican citizenship rested on the ethic of independence, understood as self-reliance, self-ownership, and autonomy (1990). This ethic was both gendered and racialized, with White male workers insisting on their rights to full citizenship on the basis of their differentiation from multiple dependent and subordinate 'others'. In arguing for state support for this dependency some women claimed citizenship rights on the basis of their potential maternity, demanding social protection for their mothering roles because of their responsibility for the future of the republic. Again this appeal to motherhood was differentiated by race; Black women's child-rearing was not considered worthy of state support, and immigrant beneficiaries of state programs were expected to conform to White middle class standards of domesticity.

Women were also assumed to be dependent on men under the New Deal (Gordon 1990), and along with many non-White and poor rural men they were denied access to the most financially rewarding, least stigmatizing forms of social provision. Nancy Fraser and Linda Gordon (1994) thus refer to a two-track welfare system, with inadequate and stigmatizing public assistance programs differentiated from the social insurance policies offered to some workers. This system institutionalized gender-differentiated notions of citizenship, with paid employment valorized for White men and dependency excused (although in a stigmatized way) for the women assumed to be dependent on them. However as several recent examinations of the US welfare state point out, in the contemporary era all adults are expected to work in the formal marketplace, with all dependency stigmatized. As Fraser and Gordon argue this shift reinforces the link between citizenship, paid employment, and independence, and it renders yet more invisible the unpaid labors and inevitable dependencies necessary to sustain human existence. One returns, then, to a central concern of Elshtain, Okin, Pateman, Brown and others regarding the masculinized conceptualization of citizenship and the neglect of social reproduction, the private realm, and subsistence concerns in mainstream definitions of politics.

Conclusion

The scope and depth of research into gender and politics necessarily renders any summarizing overview an example of oversight. While this is true of all research fields, feminist scholarship on politics is characterized by a particularly broad reach, since it draws on work from analysts in political theory, international relations, comparative politics, and American politics while remaining open to interdisciplinary insights from across the academy. By definition, then, any introductory essay on gender and politics is partial. Nevertheless, the three themes on which this chapter has focused give some sense of the diverse issues of concern to scholars in the field, and they suggest multiple ways in which mainstream research priorities could shift were the scholarship cited here taken more seriously. There is no doubt that existing research on voting behavior, political elites, representation, social movements, democratization, political economy, globalization, and state–society relations would be enhanced by attention to work in gender and politics; multiple opportunities for valuable scholarly exchange exist in these areas, and it is curious that they have not been utilized more effectively. One would also hope that taken-for-granted categories of analysis would receive greater critical attention, as researchers recognized the gendered nature of their inquiries into 'citizenship', 'participation', 'independence', 'self-interest', and the like. Perhaps the boundaries of politics would expand, as concerns with social reproduction, dependence, and subsistence received greater attention. Social policies might be designed differently; international economic policies might change; research priorities might shift.

Unfortunately such suggestions will remain conjectures until gender and politics research gains the influence to shape political analysis warranted by the depth, rigor, and scope of its existing scholarship. In this respect it is yet to be ascertained whether feminist participation in the political science project will lead to greater substantive representation of gendered concerns in the discipline as a whole.

References

Alexander, M. Jacqui (1991) 'Erotic Autonomy as a Politics of Decolonization: An Anatomy of Feminist and State Practice in the Bahamas Tourist Economy' in *Third World Women and the Politics of Feminism*, ed. Cherrie Moraga and M. Jacqui Alexander, pp. 63–100, Indianapolis, IN: Indiana University Press.

Alvarez, Sonia E. (1990) *Engendering Democracy In Brazil: Women's Movements in Transition Politics*, Princeton, NJ: Princeton University Press.

D'Amico, Francine (1995) 'Women National Leaders' in *Women in World Politics: An Introduction*, ed. Francine D'Amico and Peter R. Beckman pp. 15–30, Westport, CT: Bergin and Garvey.

Arat, Yesim (1998) 'A Woman Prime Minister in Turkey: Did It Matter?' in *Women and Politics* 19 (4): 1–22.

Baaker, Isabella (ed.) (1994) *The Strategic Silence: Gender and Economic Policy*, New Jersey: Zed Books.

Beneria, Lourdes, and Shelley Feldman (eds) (1992) *Unequal Burden: Economic Crises, Persistent Poverty and Women's Work*, Boulder, CO: Westview.

Brown, Alice *et al.* (2002) 'Women and Constitutional Change in Scotland and Northern Ireland' in *Parliamentary Affairs* 55: 71–84.

Brown, Wendy (1995) *States of Injury: Power and Freedom in Late Modernity*, Princeton, NJ: Princeton University Press.

Busby, Nicole, and Calum MacLeod (2002) 'Maintaining a Balance: The Retention of Women MPs in Scotland' in *Parliamentary Affairs* 55: 30–42.

Butts, Joy (2001) 'Poverty in the Midst of Prosperity: Organizing for Economic Rights in the United States' in *Holding on to the Promise: Women's Human Rights and the Beijing +5 Review*, ed. Cynthia Meillón in collaboration with Charlotte Bunch, pp. 107–13. New Brunswick, NJ: Center for Women's Global Leadership.

Carabine, Jean (1992) 'Constructing Women: Women's Sexuality and Social Policy' in *Critical Social Policy* 34: 24–37.

—— (1996) 'A Straight Playing Field or Queering the Pitch? Centering Sexuality in Social Policy' in *Feminist Review* 54: 31–64.

Carroll, Susan J. (1988) 'Women's Autonomy and the Gender gap: 1980 and 1982' in *The Politics of the Gender Gap: The Social Construction of Political Influence*, ed. Carol M. Mueller, pp. 236–57, Newbury Park: Sage.

—— (2001a) 'Introduction' in *The Impact of Women in Public Office*, pp. xi–xxvi, Bloomington, IN: Indiana University Press.

—— (2001b) 'Representing Women: Women State Legislators as Agents of Policy-Related Change' in *The Impact of Women in Public Office*, pp. 3–21, Bloomington, IN: Indiana University Press.

Chappell, Louise (2000) 'Interacting with the State: Feminist Strategies and Political Opportunities' in *International Feminist Journal of Politics* 2 (2): 244–75.

—— (2002) 'The "Femocrat" Strategy: Expanding the Repertoire of Feminist Activists' in *Parliamentary Affairs* 55: 85–98.

Childs, Sarah (2002) 'Hitting the Target: Are Labour Women MPs "Acting for" Women?' in *Parliamentary Affairs* 55: 143–53.

Cohen, Cathy J., Kathleen B. Jones and Joan C. Tronto (eds) (1997) *Women Transforming Politics: An Alternative Reader*, New York: New York University Press.

Conover, Pamela Johnston (1988) 'Feminists and the Gender Gap' in *Journal of Politics* 50 (4): 985–1010.

Cooper, Davina (1995) *Power in Struggle: Feminism, Sexuality and the State*, Buckingham: Open University Press.

Corrin, Chris (2002) 'Developing Democracy in Kosova: From Grass Roots to Government' in *Parliamentary Affairs* 55: 99–108

Elshtain, Jean Bethke (1981) *Public Man, Private Woman: Women in Social and Political Thought*, Princeton, NJ: Princeton University Press.

Fraser, Nancy and Linda Gordon (1994) 'A Genealogy of Dependency: Tracing a Keyword of the US Welfare State' in *Signs* 19 (2): 309–36.

Freedman, Jane (2002) 'Women in the European Parliament' in *Parliamentary Affairs* 55: 179–88.

Friedman, Elisabeth J. (2000) 'State-Based Advocacy for Gender Equality in the Developing World: Assessing the Venezuelan National Women's Agency' in *Women and Politics* 21 (2): 47–80.

Geisler, Gisela (2000) '"Parliament is Another Terrain of Struggle": Women, Men and Politics in South Africa' in *Journal of Modern African Studies* 38 (4): 605–30.

Gordon, Linda (1990) 'The New Feminist Scholarship on the Welfare State' in *Women, the State, and Welfare*, pp. 9–36, Madison, WI: University of Wisconsin Press.

Grey, Sandra (2002) 'Does Size Matter? Critical Mass and New Zealand's Women MPs' in *Parliamentary Affairs* 55: 19–29.

Hallett, Christine (ed.) (1996) *Women and Social Policy: An Introduction*, London: Prentice Hall.

Howell, Jude (2002) 'Women's Political Participation in China: Struggling to Hold Up Half the Sky' in *Parliamentary Affairs* 55: 43–56.

Inglehart, Ronald, and Pippa Norris (2000) 'The Developmental Theory of the Gender Gap: Women's and Men's Voting Behavior in Global Perspective' in *International Political Science Review* 21 (4): 441–63.

Jones, Kathleen B. (1993) *Compassionate Authority: Democracy and the Representation of Women*, New York: Routledge.

Karam, Azza (2000) 'Beijing +5: Women's Political Participation: Review of Strategies and Trends' in *Women's Political Participation and Good Governance: 21st Century Challenges*, pp. 15–26, New York: UNDP.

Lister, Ruth (2000) 'Dilemmas in Engendering Citizenship' in *Gender and Citizenship in Transition*, ed. Barbara Hobson, pp. 33–83, New York: Routledge.

Lovenduski, Joni (2001) 'Women and Politics: Minority Representation or Critical Mass?' in *Parliamentary Affairs* 54: 743–58.

Malla, Sapana Pradhan (2001) 'Using CEDAW to Fight for Women's Inheritance Rights' in *Holding on to the Promise: Women's Human Rights and the Beijing +5 Review*, ed. Cynthia Meillón in collaboration with Charlotte Bunch, pp. 89–95, New Brunswick, NJ: Center for Women's Global Leadership.

Mama, Amina (1989) 'Violence Against Black Women: Gender, Race and State Responses' in *Feminist Review* 32: 30–48.

Marshall, Sandra (1997) 'Feminists and the State: A Theoretical Exploration' in *Feminists Negotiate the State: The Politics of Domestic Police*, ed. Cynthia Daniels, pp. 95–107, Lanham, MD: University Press of America.

Mink, Gwendolyn (1990) 'The Lady and the Tramp: Gender, Race, and the Origins of the American Welfare State' in *Women, the State, and Welfare*, ed. Linda Gordon, pp. 92–122, Madison, WI: University of Wisconsin Press.

MacKinnon, Catherine (1989) *Towards a Feminist Theory of the State*, Cambridge: Harvard University Press.

Moser, Caroline (1993) *Gender Planning and Development: Theory, Practice and Training*, New York: Routledge.

Nam, Jeong-Lim (2000) 'Gender Politics in the Korean Transition to Democracy' in *Korean Studies* 24: 94–112.

Okin, Susan (1979) *Women in Western Political Thought*, Princeton, NJ: Princeton University Press.

Pal, Mahi (1999) 'Empowerment of Women through Panchayati Raj Institutions – An Assessment and Task Ahead' in *Gender Perspective: Participation, Empowerment and Development*, ed. Anil Dutta Mishra, pp. 27–46, New Delhi: Radha Publications.

Pateman, Carole (1988) *The Sexual Contract*, Oxford: Polity Press/Basil Blackwell

—— (1989) *The Disorder of Women: Democracy, Feminism, and Political Theory*, Stanford, CA: Stanford University Press.

Peterson, V. Spike, and Anne Sisson Runyan (1999) *Global Gender Issues*, 2nd edn, Boulder, CO: Westview Press.

Piven, Frances Fox (1990) 'Ideology and the State: Women, Power, and the Welfare State' in *Women, the State, and Welfare*, ed. Linda Gordon, pp. 25–264, Madison, WI: University of Wisconsin Press.

Prasad, Lokesh (1999) 'An Inquiry into the Participation of Women in the Panchayati Raj Institutions' in *Gender Perspective: Participation, Empowerment and Development*, ed. Anil Dutta Mishra, pp. 148–164, New Delhi: Radha Publications.

Randall, Vicky (1987) *Women and Politics: An International Perspective*, 2nd edn, Basingstoke: Macmillan.

Ray, Raka (1999) *Fields of Protest: Women's Movements in India*, Minneapolis: University of Minnesota Press.

Ross, Karen (2002a) 'Introduction' in *Parliamentary Affairs* 55: 1–4.

—— (2002b) 'Women's Place in "Male" Space: Gender and Effect in Parliamentary Contexts' in *Parliamentary Affairs* 55: 189–201.

Sarvasy, Wendy (1992) 'Beyond the Difference versus Equality Policy Debate: Postsuffrage Feminism, Citizenship, and the Quest for a Feminist Welfare state' in *Signs* 17 (2): 329–62.

Saxenhouse, Arlene (1985) *Women in the History of Western Political Thought: Ancient Greece to Machiavelli*, New York: Praeger.

Scott, Joan W. (1986) 'Gender: A Useful Category of Historical Analysis' in *American Historical Review* 91: 1053–75.

Shaver, Sheila (1993) 'Body Rights, Social Rights and the Liberal Welfare State' in *Critical Social Policy* 39: 66–93.

Singh, Amita (1999) 'Gender Sensitization at Grassroot' in *Gender Perspective: Participation, Empowerment and Development*, ed. Anil Dutta Mishra, pp.13–26, New Delhi: Radha Publications.

Sparr, Pamela (ed.) (1994) *Mortgaging Women's Lives: Feminist Critiques of Structural Adjustment*, London: Zed Books.

Tripp, Aili Mari (2001) 'The Politics of Autonomy and Cooptation in Africa: the Case of the Ugandan Women's Movement' in *Journal of Modern African Studies* 39 (1): 101–28.

Williams, Fiona (1989) *Social Policy: A Critical Introduction*, Cambridge: Polity Press.

Williams, Patricia (1991) *The Alchemy of Race and Rights*, Cambridge: Harvard University Press.

Wilton, Tamsin (1995) *Lesbian Studies: Setting an Agenda*, London: Routledge.

40

SOCIAL MOVEMENTS

John A. Guidry

Social movements are broad, intentional efforts by organized, collective actors who seek to alter patterns of authority, power, social values, or behaviour. Movements have formed over a variety of issues since the middle-eighteenth century and are a consistent feature of politics in the modern era. Movements are closely connected to the development of democracy as important vehicles of accountability, participation, and the institutionalization of political practice. Outside the political arena, movements emerge from and contribute to the formation of social capital and a participatory citizenship.

The most well-known movements, according to their topical content, are: *organized labour* (roots to the late eighteenth century), *abolition of slavery* (late eighteenth century), *women* (from suffrage in the middle-nineteenth century through 'second-' and 'third-wave' variants in the late twentieth century, including the pro-choice movement), *environmentalism* (from the naturalist and conservation movements of the nineteenth century to the modern 'green politics' of the present era), *liberalism/democracy* (from the French Revolution in 1789, the revolutions of 1848, and the first/second/third waves of democratization in the twentieth century), *civil rights* (especially associated with the African-American movements of 1950s in the USA, but also across the African diaspora and among ethnic minority communities in general), *anti-apartheid* (stemming from the South African state 1948–1990, but embracing a world-wide coalition), *human rights* (early twentieth century onwards), *children's rights* (including the globalized movement of street children), *professional* (from the nineteenth century onwards), *nationalism* (from the middle-nineteenth century through the anti-imperialist movements that led to the independence of much of the colonial world from the 1940s through the 1980s), *neighbourhood and community* (a growing feature of urbanization, especially in the developing world, since 1945), *gay* (a variety of sexual identity movements involving male homosexuals, lesbians, bisexuals, and transgendered persons since the 1960s), and *peace* (at different times throughout the twentieth century, especially during the Cold War and the specific conflicts over Korea in the 1950s, Vietnam in the 1960s and 70s, and the deployment of nuclear missile in Western Europe in the 1980s). In addition, a growing variety of movements have emerged in the last thirty years to challenge the progressive or left-of-centre orientation of many movements; examples include the *Right to Life* movement to curtail abortion practices, religious fundamentalist organizations such as the *Moral Majority*, and a variety of *nationalist* and *anti-immigration* movements.

This article details the main lines of *social movement theory*, the relationship of *grievances and identity formation* to movements; the *tactics of contentious politics* they employ; the *stakes* of movements in changing relationships of authority and values; relationships to the *state, civil society, and political parties*; the *scope of movement activity* and *debates over right-wing movements*; and the emergence of *globalization, neo-liberal policies, and non-governmental organizations (NGOs)* in contemporary movement analysis. In conclusion, suggested readings are listed to provide a beginning basis for students of movements to explore these issues; refer to this section for the work of individual scholars mentioned in this chapter.

Social movement theory

Movements have been analysed under four broad theoretical groupings that increasingly share some overlap as analysts begin to combine theoretical ideas in order to explain movement emergence and development. The two oldest and most influential theories are *political process/political opportunity structure* and *resource mobilization*. These two schools emerged in the 1970s to explain movements in North America and Western Europe. Process/opportunity structure explains the emergence of movements as dependent upon larger political relationships of elites, masses, and the states; movements emerge when elite alliances break down and excluded social groups perceive a new opportunity to alter their position in the political system. Resource mobilization holds that while the kinds of issues movements engage in are always present in societies, movements themselves emerge when activists are able to mobilize important resources and pre-existing social networks behind a cause.

In the 1980s, *'new social movement'* theory developed in Western Europe to explain a variety of movements – second and third wave feminist, environmentalism, peace, greens, ethnic, gay – that emerged since the 1960s. These 'new social movements' were analysed as intimately involved with identity formation and the self-realization of their constituents. Drawing from all three theoretical approaches, an important school of 'cultural framing' emerged in the 1980s to demonstrate how movements use social and political discourse to mobilize constituents and persuade authorities to take up the causes of movements. Finally, in the 1990s and beyond, a growing number of scholars began to focus on *globalization and transnational connections* involved in social movement development. As globalization became a more prominent category of political, cultural, and economic discourse after the end of the Cold War (1989), analysts began to use existing theoretical frameworks to demonstrate how movements are important actors in building a more closely-knit world. In the 'third wave of democratization', which began in southern Europe during the 1970s and has spread across the world since then, social movements have received a prominent place as carriers of democratic values and practices across national and cultural borders.

Grievances and identities

Social movements usually begin with an organized response to a grievance. The grievance might be very concrete in nature, such as working conditions in a factory, or it may have a moral or cultural aspect, such as the recognition of an identity or sexual orientation. A key factor, however, is that the kinds of grievances associated with social movements are *collectively experienced* by some *group* of persons. Where identity is related to movements, therefore, we are speaking of *collective identities*. Sometimes the initial grievance is highly local, such as the effects of exposure to hazardous waste dumped by a factory in Love Canal (New York) during the 1970s, which attaches to local issues elsewhere and helps to build a larger 'movement' of organizations and groups that have similar goals, such as the 'environmental movement'. In other cases, the grievance may be widespread and consistent across a whole society or region of the country, such as the denial of civil or voting rights to women or ethnic and religious minorities.

The relationship between grievances, identities, and movements is one of mutual cause and effect. Movements can both emerge from, as well as give rise to, *identities* that are important sources of mobilization and solidarity. Movements use identity issues to 'frame' their objectives within political and social discourse. Thus, identities can create movements: African-Americans, West Indians, women, ethnic and religious minorities, and many other groups, call upon their identities as a source of solidarity in framing the kinds of grievances they consistently experience. Sometimes grievances create identities: persons affected by toxic waste in Love Canal, victims of violent crime, mothers of persons killed in a war, persons who have suffered a particular pattern of discrimination. Finally, movements can create new identities: feminists, environmentalists, peaceniks, greens, or even national identities in colonial contexts.

We can see the overlap of these identity–grievance–movement processes, for example, in the history of the labour movement, both within countries and in its leaps across borders and oceans. From the late eighteenth century onwards, initial workplace grievances, along with associated problems of poverty and disease, helped to forge both an identity as 'working-class persons' as well as a class-based movement that used organization and mobilization to change the conditions that gave rise to the movement in the first place. At both national and transnational levels, the mobilization of labour began to grow tremendously across the nineteenth century, and by the first few decades of the twentieth century, labour movements and labour organizations had become crucial political actors in both the industrialized countries and many developing areas and colonies across South America, South Asia (India), and South Africa. As the sources of identity formation and mobilization interact and reinforce each other, social movements help to build and sustain important identities that help shape the social and political processes that define specific eras and episodes in history.

Big issues, collective action, repertoires of contention

The basis of activity for social change is in specific organizations that, taken together, form a *web of related activist networks* that we can call a *movement*. These networks are *expansive* in nature. In organizational terms, a single movement may be very diverse, involving many different kinds of organizations that may each use different tactics or follow differing ideological views in their approach to the same issue – for example, a woman's right to choose, or abortion, ecology, environmentalism, civil rights, human rights, and so forth. The process by which movements organize constituents, frame issues, and mobilize public actions is called *collective action*, to stress that movements are based in *group* issues and identities, even though the press and scholarship often focuses on the work of prominent individuals, such as Martin Luther King, Jr for the US civil rights movement.

Different social movement organizations (abbreviated as 'SMOs' in the literature) may choose strategies that work *within* the established institutions of political and social authority, or they may work outside of these through *extra-institutional* action. In the political system, for example, SMOs work through lawsuits, legislative lobbying, or electoral politics. In the social arena, SMOs may work within the established rules and structures of social institutions, civil society associations, or private firms to change a variety of social practices, such as hiring, discrimination, labour relations, etc. Through extra-institutional action, SMOs seeking change in politics or society call upon a well-known array of protest actions that include street demonstrations, boycotts, publicity stunts, public displays and advertising campaigns, traffic stoppages, labour strikes, sabotage, and other tactics that disrupt daily activities and call attention to the movement's cause. These extra-institutional activities are frequently illegal and may result in the arrest and detention of movement activists. When movement activists are aware that their actions will result in arrest and time in jail, this strategy is called 'civil disobedience'. This technique has its historical roots in the writings of Ralph Waldo Emerson, who withheld his tax payments as a protest against the Mexican-American war in the 1840s. In the twentieth century, Mohandas Gandhi and Martin Luther King, Jr used civil disobedience to successful effect in the movement for national independence in India and the civil rights movement in the American South, respectively.

Movement tactics and strategy, whether institutional or extra-institutional, develop in specific places in order to challenge local problems, but these kinds of action quickly become known and communicated throughout activist networks. Political scientist Sidney Tarrow has analysed groups of movement tactics as 'repertoires of contention' that are 'modular' and may be transferred from place to place. Thus the street blockade of the French Revolution in the eighteenth century may be equally useful to a nationalist movement in Lagos, Nigeria in the 1940s. Street protests, picketing, and parades were used in a similar manner by the women's suffrage movement in the late nineteenth century, the civil rights movement in the USA in the 1950s, and the anti-nuclear movement in Western Europe during the 1980s. Placing flowers into rifles and the barrels of tanks became important symbolic gestures in protests against the Vietnam War in the USA during the 1960s and 70s, against dictator Ferdinand Marcos of the Philippines in the 1980s, and against the authority of the Chinese state in 1989.

The international environmental movement provides a good example of how movements are expansive and diverse in their organizational, ideological, and tactical structures. Some of the largest and most well-known organizations in the environmental movement go back several decades to the emergence of the 'conservation' movement around the turn of the twentieth century – the Sierra Club and Audubon Society are prominent examples. Older ideological roots of the movement lay with the nineteenth-century 'naturalists' and thinkers such as Henry David Thoreau and Ralph Waldo Emerson. By the 1960s and 1970s, as a new era of pollution, industrial growth, and social consciousness had taken root, self-styled 'environmentalist' organizations began to emerge. Some, such as Greenpeace, became devotedly international in their outlook and linked environmentalism to the feminist, peace, and anti-nuclear movements of the Cold War era. Greenpeace militants pioneered new kinds of disruptive, prominent, and sensational 'direct actions' that often endangered the lives of their activists: rappelling off skyscrapers to leave large banners decrying the use of nuclear weapons and nuclear power, blocking drain pipes of chemical factories, surrounding military vessels in rubber dinghies, and so forth. At the same time, Greenpeace pioneered new techniques of direct mailing and newsletter correspondence that became possible with emerging computer technologies in the 1980s. While Greenpeace was considered much to the left of groups like the Sierra Club, it was also building a base in more 'passive' segments of the society concerned about the environment. Even more radical groups began to emerge in the 1970s and beyond. Earth First! is a well-known example of activists who practise 'deep ecology' and are willing to go as far as sabotage and life-risking action in order to stop loggers in the American Northwest.

The stakes: patterns of authority, power, social values, and behaviour

The changes sought by social movements affect large-scale patterns of behaviour in everyday life and political relations. Frequently, the goals of movements strike at the very core of authority, both political and social, in a society. Let us consider the women's movement as an example. Its aims would alter both power and behaviours in a variety of spaces – the home, the workplace, public spaces, and the state itself. The movement would provide a basis for public intervention in private space – either in homes with abusive husbands or partners, or in private workplaces with discriminatory practices in hiring, promotion, or workplace treatment. In different times and places, women's movements have made previously unthinkable ideas not only imaginable but also desirable: thus today it is far less contentious for women to hold political office or powerful economic positions, to vote, to work outside the home, to work in historically male categories of employment, to enjoy credit and the right to own property, or to lead religious congregations. But only 35 years ago, however, the only item on that list common to women in Western democracies was the right to vote.

Thus, movements become epoch-making as they treat the categorical distinctions that exist in human societies. These distinctions include sex and gender, race, ethnicity, religion, social and economic class, sexuality, gentility, age, and regional identity, among others. What in one era of human history is seen as a normal or 'natural' – e.g. owning another person as chattel property (slavery), the killing of an adulterous wife, or the industrial labour of children – becomes unconscionable in another era, and social movements push along important processes through which these changes occur.

The state, civil society, and private organizations

Movements may operate in arenas defined by the state, civil society, or private organizations. Our most vivid and widely known images of social movements tend to come from confrontations with political authorities and the state. On 28 August 1963, the civil rights movement in the USA mobilized over 250,000 people in the March on Washington for Jobs and Freedom, where Rev. Martin Luther King, Jr delivered a speech that changed American politics. King proclaimed, 'I have a dream', and went on to outline a future in which persons would be judged by the 'content of their character' rather than skin colour. These phrases – 'I have a dream' and 'content of their character' – have gone on to become cultural markers not only of an era but also of the promise of democracy itself, as practised in any country, including the USA. Similarly, consider the image from 1980 of Lech Walesa climbing the fence of the Lenin shipyard in Gdansk: this founding image in Poland's Solidarity movement has become an important part of labour movement iconography around the world. Even in failure, clashes between movements and states still provide us with some of the important images that speak to and help to build the courage it takes to challenge political authority: thus the 1989 photograph of one Chinese student holding his hand up to halt a file of tanks in Beijing's Tiananmen Square continues to resonate around the world even though the student movement there was violently crushed after only a few months of action.

It is important to note that movements are not always aimed at the state. Many social movements and movement activities occur within domains of civil society and culture. In the 1980s, for example, a portion of the environmental movement organized a consumer boycott of canned tunafish until the industry created new standards that prevented dolphins from becoming ensnared and killed in tuna nets. In the same era, children's and women's activists organized a boycott of Nestlé products to protest against the adverse effects of replacing breast milk with powdered infant formula, of which Nestlé is a leading producer. The movement maintained that infant formula in fact contributed to malnutrition and infant death in many poor countries and has taken the cause into legislative arenas around the world as well. In these instances and others like them, movements are engaged in civil society against other social actors, and the state may be involved in only a very limited way, if at all.

In other cases, movements arise *within organizations* in order to reform that organization. In the summer of 2000, for example, an anonymous person or group of persons wrote an open letter to the American Political Science Association (APSA) that was sent around the world over the internet. It was signed 'Mr Perestroika' and challenged the way that some schools of thought in political science have used the APSA and its control of major academic journals to act as 'gate keepers' in the discipline. The letter claimed that indirect election procedures in the APSA created a Soviet-style 'politburo' that prevented research based in ethnographic, case study, or historical methods from attaining a legitimate place in the discipline, where large-sample, quantitative survey methods and game theory predominate. In short order, hundreds of political scientists signed the letter, and by 2002 the discipline established a new journal to explore these issues and initiated several reforms in the internal organization of the APSA. The 'Perestroika Movement', as it came to be called, garnered headlines in the *New York Times* as it sought to bring 'democracy' and 'revolution' to a group of scholars who claimed these phenomena as their own domain of study! Similar movements, such as the Log Cabin Republicans or Catholics for Free Choice also challenge the dominant policies of their organizations.

Political parties

Political parties – especially those of a more 'democratic' or progressive bent – have traditionally relied upon support from social movements. The labour, women's, and civil rights movements, for example, are major parts of the Democratic Party's coalition in the USA. The relationship between movements and parties can be problematic, however, since movement activists are usually concerned to prevent the party from co-opting the movement's autonomy, especially once the party attains electoral office. After elections, movements have an important role in holding the parties they support accountable for campaign promises and platform issues.

Since the 1970s, new political parties have been born from grassroots organizing in social movements. Two examples of 'movement parties' bear mention here. The Green Party of Germany emerged in the former West Germany in the 1970s and 1980s as an expression of the political interests of three broad movements: women's, peace, and environmentalist. The party has been known for its radicalism on all three issues, and it has endured a major conflict between more radical (*Fundis*) and more conciliatory (*Realos*) sections of the party who differ on the kind of line the party should hold when in office. Over time, the more coalition-orientated 'Realo' faction has held sway, and the Green Party is now a partner in the governing Social Democratic Party–Green coalition of Germany under Gerhard Schroeder. In Brazil, the Workers' Party emerged in 1979 as an expression of new labour, community, and religious organizing that occurred during the 1970s while Brazil was in the grip of one of South America's longest-lived military regimes (1964–85). Like the Greens, the Workers' Party has confronted a series of internal divisions among more and less radical segments of the party. Since the early 1980s, the Workers' Party has grown rapidly based on a solid record of municipal administration in many of the country's largest cities. Today the Workers' Party in Brazil provides one of the few alternatives to neo-liberal policies in global politics (see below).

Contention and scope

Sidney Tarrow maintains that social movements are, by definition, *contentious* forms of social and political action. With *contention*, scholars emphasize that movements clamour for change and usually approach politics from an outsider position. This view is echoed by writers throughout the field in order to distinguish between movements and other organizations like 'special interest groups' that work within established institutional structures with the purpose of influencing specific legislation, policies, and administrative procedures. The National Association of Manufacturers (NAM), for example, which represents the interests of large, corporate, industrial concerns in the USA, has easy access to legislators and powerful politicians around the country. The NAM seeks to influence legislation and policy, but it does not engage in the kinds of *public politics* that challenge the structure of authority in the society. On the contrary, groups such as the NAM seek to reinforce the social, political, and economic power of their constituents.

The nature of 'contentious politics' and the diversity of social movements has provoked a debate among scholars and activists as to the scope and limits of the concept. This debate is fuelled especially by the emergence of 'conservative' or 'right wing' social movements in the 1980s. These kinds of groups tend to clash with the standard image of progressive, liberal, or left-leaning social movements that has emerged from the vast literature on labour, women's, environmental, peace, gay, and other movements. Analytically, the important issues are conservative groups' relationships to powerful institutions, support for traditional values and relationships, and the use of violence by more radical groups. By definition, social movements present *challenges* to power, authority, and established institutions, and many observers note that right wing or conservative movements tend to use the language and discourse of marginalization, maintaining that they are truly out-of-power in a world that is increasingly controlled by liberals and secular values. Regardless of the debate we must note that right wing groups use the same roles, discourses, framing devices, tactics, and actions as labour, women's, peace, gay, and other movements.

The Right to Life movement, which challenges feminist groups and the US Supreme Court's 1973 decision in *Roe vs Wade* that legalized abortion, is a key example. The organizations comprising the movement do exactly what is stipulated in the definition that opens this article. These groups engage in the same modular tactics – including direct mailing campaigns, demonstrations, civil disobedience, sabotage, and, on a radical fringe, open violence. The organizations that make up the movement's network are diverse and span a continuum from groups that seek common ground with pro-choice groups to those advocating violence against doctors who perform abortions and their patients. Unlike many social movements, however, the Right to Life movement is connected to powerful organizations such as the Roman Catholic Church, other large religious organizations, and conservative think-tanks that enjoy easy access to politicians. Where Republicans (and sometimes Right to Life Democrats) occupy governors' offices or the White House, Right to Life activists can count on support both through public discourse as well as in the political appointments (especially judicial) that these officials make. Other new movements, such as Mothers Against Drunk Driving (MADD), while they have no particular ideological orientation, can be traced to the words and support of conservative public officials – in MADD's case, Ronald and Nancy Reagan.

Many right wing movements are more radical than the Right to Life movement (or at least its non-violent mainstream). Skinhead, neo-Nazi, racist, and anti-immigrant groups have sprouted up across the industrialized societies of the world. These groups do not have the connections that other conservative movements do. They lack the mainstream appeal of MADD and similar campaigns. They also advocate and engage in violence, which separates them from the vast majority of more typically studied social movements. Except for a radical fringe of the labour movement (in Communist Parties and anarchist groups around the turn of the twentieth century), 'traditional' social movements are peaceful and use disruptive tactics (demonstrations, road blockages, 'direct action', etc.) in ways that do not endanger the public. Civil disobedience, while 'illegal', does not respond to, engage, or intentionally provoke public and police officials to any kind of violence, although these same police frequently employ violence against the activists. Where violence is involved, the activists take it on to themselves, as in the civil rights marches in the American South or in the independence movement in India. By contrast, so-called right wing movement organizations that involve violence usually direct that violence *against* specific targets: immigrants, non-whites, doctors who work in women's clinics, etc.

Religious fundamentalist movements also pose problems for analysts of social movements. As with other 'conservative' movements, the problem has to do with the relationship to powerful institutions and whether or not these movements really challenge authority. Fundamentalist movements do challenge, to be sure, what they perceive as a dominant pattern of secular authority, and they argue for the restoration of historical, past, or nostalgic order. Many movement scholars contend that restoring an older pattern of authority is not the same as the changing or altering of power relationships that define the nature and objectives of social movements. Like Right to Life, organizations such as the 'Moral Majority' of Reverend Jerry Falwell in the 1980s and 90s were engaged in the same movement actions, tactics, and strategies, but one could argue that their contentious politics went only so far as the world created or advocated by earlier social movements of the more typically mentioned, progressive sort. That is, many religious fundamentalist movements, including Christian, Hindu, Islamic, and other kinds, appear to be *more reactive than contentious*, even though they employ many of the methods of more contentious movement organizations.

Today, the debate over the scope of the social movement concept and how it applies to right wing or conservative movements remains open-ended. The claim to social movement status is valid – even if contested by some – for any *network of social organizations* engaged in some sort of *contention*, using roughly *similar methods* as other movements, mobilizing to *alter relationships of authority* in society or politics.

Globalization, neo-liberalism, and non-governmental organizations (NGOs)

In the post-Cold War era, scholars, movement analysts, and journalistic commentators have increasingly referred to the impact of 'globalization' on a great variety of human processes, including social movements. The reaction to globalization by movement analysts has been as varied as the movements themselves. Some scholars have embraced 'globalization' as an important factor bearing upon movements, while others have preferred to discuss simply the transnational networks that have always been important to movements since the eighteenth century. In a middle ground, some analysts make distinctions between an increasingly layered world of movement activity – with categories of local, grassroots organizations at the bottom; a variety of grassroots service, connector, and umbrella organizations in the middle; national and then international movement service, umbrella, and confederation organizations at the top. In all, it seems that the real 'debate', to the extent there is one in the movement literature, is over the concept of 'globalization' rather than movements.

But while the concept of globalization itself is somewhat varied and unsettled in its scope, there is no disagreement over the increasingly transnational nature of social movement networks. The number of social movements whose organizations rely on transnational linkages for resources and the exchange of ideas is growing at an exponential rate. Margaret Keck and Kathryn Sikkink have worked around the complications with globalization and international politics by simply referring to 'transnational advocacy networks' that build cross-border relationships for movement activists and constituents. These transnational linkages allow movement actors to swap experiences and tactics, adding to the transnational modularity of movement actions. Increasingly, both ideological and material resources cross borders as well, and countless SMOs and NGOs in the developing world rely upon grants, personnel, and other resources that originate with international NGOs, industrial corporations, private foundations, political parties, religious organizations, inter-governmental organizations (such as the United Nations and its subordinate agencies like UNESCO), and the larger movement organizations of the industrialized world (such as the AFL-CIO in North America).

The implementation of what is known as the 'neo-liberal policy model' around the world since the 1980s is one of the more important global phenomena confronted by movements. The neo-liberal model is the laissez-faire/free trade package of economic policies that came to international prominence under Margaret Thatcher in Britain (1979–90) and Ronald Reagan (1981–9) in the USA. Neo-liberalism stresses deregu-lation; free trade (and consequently low tariffs); international competition; the free flow of goods, services, financial capital, and labour (the last with great reservations in most countries); and a minimal state devoted only to economic and social infra-structure. The neo-liberal paradigm has been aggressively promoted by the International Monetary Fund and World Bank, which have together conditioned many loan and economic stabilization packages for developing countries upon compliance with a set of neo-liberal policies. While neo-liberal programmes have promised strong economic growth after an initial period of stabilization, growth results have been modest at best. The only undisputed results of neo-liberal programmes, even in developed countries, have been increased unemployment, growing income disparities, and greater social service needs at the same time as the state has withdrawn from areas of economic development and social services.

States in the developing world, which are the hardest-hit by economic crisis and have an irreplaceable role in the stabilization of basic needs (food prices, health services, education), have been placed in a serious dilemma by the IMF and neo-liberal policies. These states – shrunken and diminished by neo-liberal programmes – have in many cases dealt with their inability to meet social service needs by turning to NGOs. This has altered the once contentious relationship of states and social movements, as movement actors find themselves recruited by the state to develop civil society partnerships and NGOs that can address service needs, e.g. housing, that in the past would have been addressed directly by the state. Vast networks of NGOs around the world help movements take advantage of the new opportunity presented by neo-liberalism's impact on the state. One result of this situation is that states in the developing world now rely, more than ever, on social movements and their ties to sources of foreign aid from both other states and private foundations.

Further reading

There are several recent volumes that present the variety and scope of social move-ment theory and research. The most prominent volumes of collected papers are Morris and Mueller (1992) and McAdam, McCarthy, and Zald (1996). The papers in these volumes examine the scope of movement theory in its North American and European variants, as well contributions on the important 'cultural framing' school developed by David Snow and Robert Benford. For two influential treatments of social movements in the developing world, see Eckstein (1989) and Alvarez, Dagnino and Escobar (1998). These two volumes specialize on Latin American movements, but their conclusions can be used to examine movements elsewhere.

Tarrow (1998) is the best, sustained treatment of the whole field by a single author, including the theory of protest cycles that Tarrow developed earlier in research on Italy. Finally, the collaboration of McAdam, Tarrow and Tilly (2001) suggests a number of profitable ways we can expand from social movement studies into broader examinations of contentious politics.

The historical development of movements in Europe is explored by Charles, Louise and Richard Tilly (1975), and further by Charles Tilly (1978). Charles Tilly's work, in particular, has contributed to the *political opportunity structure* theory of movement formation and development. The *political process* approach was further developed by Doug McAdam (1999). For organizational approaches to social movements, including *resource mobilization theory*, see Zald and McCarthy (1987). For European approaches that stress identity formation and 'new social movement' theory, see Melucci (1989). Gamson (1992) provides a summary of how 'cultural framing' plays into movement discourse and mobilization.

For a wide range of perspectives on *movement-globalization relationships*, see Guidry, Kennedy and Zald (2000), and Smith and Johnston (2002). Keck and Sikkink (1998) is the most widely cited academic study in this field; it analyses movements and transnational linkages both historically and in the present with regard to human rights, women's, and environmental movements.

There are a vast number of studies that have examined particular social movements in specific times and places. These studies form the backbone of movement literature, and what follows is by no means exhaustive and should be used to lead one to other and newer sources as well. Morris (1984), together with McAdam's work cited above, are classic examples in the civil rights field. Alvarez (1990) and Bayard-de-Volo (2001) provide important discussions of women's organizing, both generally and especially in Latin American/developing world contexts. Ming-Cheng Lo (2002) and Kennedy (1991) provide analyses of how professional movements can affect larger movements for nationalism and labour organization. Waltz (1995) analyses the human rights movement in general and in the Maghrib of North Africa. Seidman (1994) provides a rare example of a cross-national study (Brazil–South Africa) that examines the political convergence of two different movements, organized labour and community-based mobilization, in the democratization of these countries. Eley (2002) provides an overview of how democracy emerged historically in both movements and political discourse. Cohen (1999) analyses how AIDS has affected the civil rights movement and the network of African-American churches that have been the backbone of that movement. In *Non-Governments* (1998), Julie Fisher shows how the growing network of NGOs are affecting both states and contentious politics around the world, especially in the developing world. Castells (1983) and Miller (2000) add space and geographic variables to the analysis of movement emergence and development.

References

Alvarez, Sonia (1990) *Engendering Democracy in Brazil*, Princeton: Princeton University Press.
Alvarez, Sonia, Dagnino, Evelina and Escobar, Arturo (eds) (1998) *Cultures of Politics/Politics of Culture*, Boulder CO: Westview Press.

Bayard-de-Volo, Lorraine (2001) *Mothers of Heroes and Martyrs*, Baltimore: Johns Hopkins University Press.

Castells, Manuel (1983) *The City and the Grassroots*, Berkeley : University of California Press.

Cohen, Cathy (1999) *The Boundaries of Blackness*, Chicago: University of Chicago Press.

Eckstein, Susan (ed.) (1989) *Power and Popular Protest*, Berkeley: University of California Press.

Eley, Geoff (2002) *Forging Democracy*, Oxford and New York: Oxford University Press.

Fisher, Julie (1998) *Non-Governments*, West Hartford, CT: Kumarian Press.

Gamson, William (1992) *Talking Politics*, Cambridge: Cambridge University Press.

Guidry, John, Kennedy, Michael and Zald, Mayer (eds) (2000) *Globalizations and Social Movements*, Ann Arbor: University of Michigan Press.

Keck, Margaret and Sikkink, Kathryn (1998) *Activists Beyond Borders*, Ithaca: Cornell University Press.

Kennedy, Michael (1991) *Professionals, Power, and Solidarity in Poland*, Cambridge: Cambridge University Press.

Lo, Ming-cheng (2002) *Doctors Within Borders*, Berkeley, CA: University of California Press.

McAdam, Doug (1999) *Political Process and the Development of Black Insurgency, 1930–1970*, Chicago: University of Chicago Press.

McAdam, Doug, McCarthy, John and Zald, Mayer (eds) (1996) *Comparative Perspectives on Social Movements*, New York: Cambridge University Press.

McAdam, Doug, Tarrow, Sidney and Tilly, Charles (2001) *Dynamics of Contention*, Cambridge and New York: Cambridge University Press.

Melucci, Alberto (1989) *Nomads of the Present*, Philadelphia: Temple University Press.

Miller, Byron (2000) *Geography and Social Movements*, Minneapolis: University of Minnesota Press.

Morris, Aldon (1984) *The Origins of the Civil Rights Movement*, New York: Free Press.

Morris, Aldon and Mueller, Carol (eds) (1992) *Frontiers in Social Movement Theory*, New Haven, CT: Yale University Press.

Seidman, Gay (1994) *Manufacturing Militance*, Berkeley: University of California Press.

Smith, Jackie and Johnston, Hank (eds) (2002) *Globalization and Resistance*, Lanham, MD: Rowman & Littlefield.

Tarrow, Sidney (1998) *Power in Movement*, 2nd edn, New York: Cambridge University Press.

Tilly, Charles (1978) *From Mobilization to Revolution*, Reading MA: Addison-Wesley.

Tilly, Charles, Tilly, Louise and Tilly, Richard (1975) *The Rebellious Century, 1830–1930*, Cambridge: Harvard University Press.

Waltz, Susan (1995) *Human Rights and Reform*, Berkeley: University of California Press.

Zald, Mayer and McCarthy, John (eds) (1987) *Social Movements in an Organizational Society*, New Brunswick: Transaction Books.

41

DEVELOPMENT

Ronald H. Chilcote

The literature on development reflects a variety of theoretical perspectives, yet fails to offer any clear conception of the meaning of the term itself. A dictionary definition suggests an evolution or gradual advance or simply growth through progressive changes. Usually development pertains to conditions within countries and between countries and the world order, whether they be characterized as advanced capitalist, command socialist, developing capitalist or socialist, or backward and less-developed cases. Thus, it is not surprising that contemporary observers (Booth 1985) may suggest that efforts to understand development are muddled by confusion and face an impasse.

The present essay deals with this dilemma by synthesizing many ways to assist the reader in understanding development. First, a multifaceted rather than unilinear process is suggested. Second, development is characterized in terms of three worlds so commonly described after the Second World War. Third, historical phases are identifiable in the evolution of developmental thinking. Fourth, schools of thought in the literature on development are evident. Fifth, development approaches in advanced capitalist, socialist, and third-world nations are delineated. Sixth, a dichotomy of strategies and issues is set forth. Finally, a synthesis of development is offered.

Dimensions of development

Although early on economists may have emphasized such aspects as per capita income or calorie intake in their calculations of development and political scientists stressed democracy in their focus, the literature has increasingly recognized the relationship of political development to economic and other facets of development. Development came to be viewed as a process involving all of society so that academic attention to development evolved from single to multi-disciplinary perspectives. Eventually, with the emergence of capitalism and socialism as predominant economic systems, theories and policies of development turned toward one or the other of these alternatives. Graphically dimensions of development can be outlined:

Dimensions	Process
Political	Representative and participatory democracy
Economic	Central and decentralized planning for improving the standard of living
Social	Provision of human needs
Cultural	Fostering of selflessness, collaboration, solidarity, political consciousness and social responsibility

Thus, the central attention of political development would be to democracy in its major forms, whereas the economic emphasis on development might be concerned with planning; the social aspect with people's basic needs such as food and shelter, health care, education and employment; and the cultural level with the building of individual outreach to others.

Three worlds of development

Characteristics of development can be portrayed according to geographical and ideological distinctions:

First World	Second World	Third World
Private capitalism	Command socialism	Human needs
Political + Economic	Economic + Social	Social + Economic

The First World of advanced capitalist societies reflects representative or formal democracy and private ownership of the means of production, usually in concert with state policy, including planning and action favouring capitalism (Sweezy 1942). The Second World of socialist societies has traditionally (until the upheavals in 1989) existed under command economies emphasizing central planning, and the provision of basic social needs, but with limited democratic space and little experimentation with representative and participatory forms of democracy (Post and Wright 1989). The Third World of less-developed and underdeveloped countries has, in the case of revolutionary situations, directed the attention of the state to resolving basic human needs and implementing centralized planning, while experimenting with representative and participatory forms of democracy in the face of domination of outside capital and the pressures of the financial and corporate world. Cultural resistance and the defence and preservation of traditional values have often been a response of indigenous peoples to colonial rule. Cultural expression has also accompanied socialist and revolutionary experiences as a means for reshaping the commitment and solidarity of people. Political culture is usually associated with development as a means of characterizing the extent people participate in the civil society.

Historical phases

The field of development has evolved through various historical phases since the Second World War. The Cold War and its obsession with communism and radical understandings tended to obscure Western attention to imperialism which since the later nineteenth century had been employed to characterize how industrializing nations exploited their colonies. The classical writers, from J. A. Hobson to Rudolf Hilferding, Rosa Luxemburg, Nilolai Bukharin, and V. I. Lenin, emphasized the negative consequences of capitalism in its financial and monopolizing impact, whereas Karl Kautsky and Joseph Schumpeter anticipated that imperialism would evolve into a peaceful form of capitalism that would deter competing nations from war. The concern with development tended to ignore these traditional perspectives on imperialism and to suggest that the experience of the advanced nations could be spread to the less-developed parts of the world. Thus, a first phase, predominant in the 1950s and 1960s, emphasized the idea that Anglo-American capital and technology could be transmitted to the rest of the world (Rostow 1960). A second phase, conspicuous in the 1960s and 1970s, embraced views from the Third World that argued that the diffusion of capitalism and technology from the advanced industrial nations tended to promote underdevelopment and backwardness in the less-developed regions of the world (Baran 1957). A third phase, evident during the 1980s, involved a reassessment of the impact of the earlier ideas on the mainstream of political science, together with a disenchantment in both capitalism and socialism, a call for a balance of resources to lessen inequality, and new policies to deal with environmental and other issues confronting the world at large (Brown *et al.* 1990). A third phase, apparent during the 1990s until the present, has argued for a rethinking of development in terms of globalization and a transnational rather than national process, and a world order that transcends the autonomy of nation-states (Hardt and Negri 2000; Harris 1998–2000; Robinson 1996; and Robinson and Harris 2000). The shifting theoretical and practical perspectives of development reflected changing relations between developing and developed countries as well as changes in the theoretical discourse.

Schools of thought

Various schools of thought are evident in the literature on development over the past half-century. A first school, based on a traditional view that growth produces development, relies on liberal democracy and capitalism (Almond and Coleman 1960). It presumes that, once the growth under capitalism is evident, policy makers will be able to allocate resources to meet social needs and mitigate differences in income and other inequalities among individuals in society. Cammack (1997) provides the best critical assessment of this idea. A second school, opposed to the view that capitalism promotes the welfare of society, embraces the perspectives of dependency and underdevelopment, advocates resistance to external influences, and favours the building of autonomous societies, premised either on capitalism or socialism (Frank 1966; Dos Santos 1970). A third school turns to the world system and to international political economy in its depiction of central, semi-peripheral, and peripheral countries evolving through centuries of capitalist influence and dominance and cycles of economic prosperity and decline (Bollen 1983; Chase-Dunn 1977; Hopkins and Wallerstein 1977; Wallerstein 1974). A fourth school emphasizes the mode of production as a means for assessing the relations people have to their work and the possibilities of transitions from pre-capitalist social formations to capitalism and socialism (Foster-Carter 1978). A fifth school identifies trends toward the internationalization of capital and labour (Palloix 1975), the rise of multinational corporations (Baran and Sweezy 1966), and the impact of late capitalism in the less-developed parts of the world since the Second World War (Mandel 1975). A sixth school incorporates old and new understandings of imperialism in its view of the world (Brewer 1980). A seventh school sees globalization as an evolving progressive process of global economic, political and cultural integration, and harmony for humanity everywhere, yet its vision has been subject to intense ideological and political debate among 'hyperglobalizers', 'sceptics', and 'transformationists' at an intellectual level (Brenner 1999; Gilpin 2002; Hirst and Thompson 1999; Mann *et al.* 2001–2) and protests at various international congresses, beginning with the World Trade Organization held in Seattle in late 1999.

Many theoretical tendencies run through these schools of development, and the task of delineating and sorting them out is complex and difficult. In an early effort, Pye (1966) set forth ten views related to economic development, industrialization, political modernization, the nation-state, administrative and legal organization, mass mobilization, democracy, orderly change, power and social change, but his review of these tendencies settled on democracy as the essential ingredient of development. In their overview of political development, Huntington and Domínguez (1975) noted three directions in the literature: the system–function approach in the work of Levy (1966), Almond and Powell (1966), and others; the social process approach of applied comparative quantitative analysis in the work of Lerner (1958), Deutsch (1961), Tanter (1967) and others; and the comparative history approach of Black (1966), Eisenstadt (1966), Moore (1966), and Huntington (1968). Chodak (1973) emphasized five approaches: evolutionary theories, macro-sociological theories of industrialization, psychological explanations, political and economic development, and modernization. Chilcote (1984) surveyed approaches in a historical synthesis of ideas on development in the developing world and drew a dichotomy between, on the one hand, reformist, nationalist and capitalist views (for example, Furtado 1964; Cardoso and Faletto 1979), and revolutionary and socialist views on development and underdevelopment (for example, Baran 1957; Frank 1966; Amin 1974), on the other. Blomström and Hettne (1984) and Hettne (1983) also moved beyond the theories on Western capitalist development to analyse dependency theory and approaches to underdevelopment in the third world. They identified new directions in Marxism, particularly in the modes of production analysis (Foster-Carter 1978) and in internationalization of capital theory (Palloix 1975). Evans and Stephens (1988) chose four areas of interest to specialists on developmental problems: the state in the process of development; the distribution of resources generated by development; the relation between industrialization and political democracy; and national development and

631

world political economy. Finally, Park (1984) and Dube (1988) offered a reappraisal of development and modernization by focusing on their weaknesses and strengths and addressing issues of the quality of life and human needs. (Other overviews are presented in Bernstein 1973; DeKadt and Williams 1974; Foster-Carter 1985; Griffin and Gurley 1985; Kay 1975, 1989; Oxaal, Barnett and Booth 1975; Roxborough 1979; Weiner and Huntington 1987.)

Given these diverse interpretations and overviews of the development literature, the reader can be guided to an understanding of different approaches through the rough classification of perspectives below. One perspective emphasizes patterns of capitalist accumulation and growth in economic development and sees formal or representative democracy as politically compatible with economic progress; it is generally reflective of developmental progress in Western advanced industrial nations and its classical theoretical inspiration likely derives from Adam Smith. The other perspective empha- sizes human needs, planned economies, and participatory or informal democracy alongside representative democratic practices; it is generally manifested in the develop- mental advances in the state bureaucratic regimes professing socialism as well as in nations that have experienced revolution and advocated transitions to socialism and equality where classical theoretical inspiration tends to stem from Marx.

Development approaches in advanced capitalist nations

A synthesis of the literature on the historical development of the advanced capitalist nations reveals many prominent approaches:

Classical growth model

W. Arthur Lewis (1955), a well-known proponent of this model, applied the classical view (that development is based on per capita growth and not distribution) to the possibility of sustainable growth in static and retarded economies of the less- developed world (particularly in the Caribbean and Africa). Although its influence has persisted, the model was largely discredited by the failure of much of this world to achieve significant growth.

Stages of growth

The notion of developmental stages is old, but its thrust has been especially influen- tial in the work of Rostow (1960), who projected a five-stage model based on economic conditions: traditional, based on lack of technology and intensive labour in agriculture; preconditions for take-off based on technological advances; take-off or self-sustaining economic growth; the drive to maturity; and mass consumption orientated to consumer goods and services. Organski's (1965) four-stage political scheme followed a similar pattern: primitive unification; industrialization; national welfare; and politics of abundance. However, stage theory is limited by its failure to account for historical conditions, particularly the relationship of underdeveloped countries with now developed countries. Frank (1971), for example, attacked the theory for assuming that underdevelopment is an original stage of traditional society rather than the consequence of European capitalist expansion.

Poles of development

The French economist, François Perroux, advocated that the activities of a new enterprise could be integrated with the economy of a region or country where a development pole could link the processing of raw materials with labour supply and productivity and be orientated to domestic producers and consumers. This approach could overcome the inequity between centres and peripheries and mitigate the negative impact of dependent relationships through central planning. Rational diffusion of capital and technology would allow for development of autonomous outlying centres which, in turn, could be integrated into a national scheme of development, ensure national control, and provide a balance between international and domestic investment. However, the idea had limited success in the less-developed countries, where domestic capital was often overwhelmed by stronger international investors and where domestic capital itself was concentrated in only a few centres, often the capital city.

Modernization

Usually associated with capitalist development, Eisenstadt (1966) understood modernization as highly differentiated political structure and diffusion of political power and authority into all spheres of society. In his early work Apter (1965) considered modernization as a particular form of development, involving a stable social system, differentiated social structures, and social skills and knowledge adaptable to a technologically advanced world. Later he described this form of modernization as the attempt of traditional societies to replicate the institutions and values of advanced industrial societies. Parallel to this was another form of modernization that takes conflict and inequality rather than integration into account (Apter 1987). These approaches, however, tend to be general, related to stages of growth from traditional to modern forms, applicable to historical development in advanced industrial societies, and for much of the third world reliant on ideal types rather than accurate descriptions of reality. Although the early theory was largely discredited, some observers (So 1990) believed that it had transcended its crisis of the late 1960s and assumed a fruitful line of inquiry two decades later.

Developmental nationalism or autonomous national development

Nationalism, essentially a late eighteenth- and nineteenth-century European idea, evolved with the rise of nation-states such as Germany and Italy and is referred to in the developmental literature as an ideological force that draws people together in common cause (Senghass 1985). Its cohesion may be based on identification of a single territory, a common language, symbols of nationhood and national heroes, but many types of nationalism appear according to various experiences. Radical nationalism, for example, is associated with the national liberation movements that fought for independence in the emerging national states of Africa, Asia and Latin America (Scalapino 1989). In the mainstream literature Deutsch (1953) linked the idea of nationalism to development, while in radical perspective Horace Davis (1967) showed the relevance of nationalism and the national question to Marxism and socialist societies. Thus, national consciousness can be orientated to the nature of society, realizing the goals of the nation-state, and ensuring broad involvement in shaping future direction. While the forces of nationalism may serve the cause of development, a theory of nationalism and development is not clearly discernible. Further, the pervasive impact of the international capitalist system in particular has tended to diminish the importance of the nationalist alternative.

Political democracy and order

The relationship of representative democracy to political development is a conspicuous theme in Pye (1966) and runs through the work of Almond (1970), Lipset (1959), Rustow (1970), Bollen (1979) and others. Political democracy becomes an ideal of consensus and bargaining in a give-and-take process. Apter (1971) emphasized that people make rational choices that relate to development and order and argued, like Hobbes, that development and order are interrelated, and that disorder may make development difficult to attain. Bates argued that 'while economic elites are behaving in ways that are economically irrational, they are behaving in ways that are politically rational' (Bates 1988: 244). They may make rational choices in seeking solutions to political problems, but sometimes at economic costs that retard development. Huntington (1965) elaborated on stability in the face of rapid social and economic changes, and advocated control and regulation of development through constraints on new groups entering politics, limits to exposure to mass media, and suppression of mass mobilization. These approaches lean toward institutional continuity and harmony rather than deep-rooted change.

Crises of development

Binder *et al.* (1971) suggested that development is the capacity of a political system to make decisions and implement policies to meet new demands and goals such as equality of opportunity, social justice and involvement while sustaining continuous change. They focused on a 'developmental syndrome' in which crises of identity, legitimacy, participation, penetration and distribution occur as the polity develops. This perspective tends to stress American political values and to divert from a theory of structural change.

Post-liberal development

Bowles and Gintis (1986) sought space for a radical democratic synthesis and posited a post-liberal democracy on the expansion of personal rights through the affirmation of traditional political forms of representative democracy and individual liberty while ensuring the establishment of innovative and democratically accountable economic freedoms in community and work. Capitalism and democracy, they argued, are incompatible, and the welfare state does not give citizens the power to make democratic decisions in the economic sphere, and democratic theory is in disarray. Their synthesis rejected many ideas of Marxism, in particular a view of class consciousness and direct democracy (ignoring Marx's advocacy of representative democracy in certain instances or his association of democracy with direct participatory activities). Their argument that Marxism reduces institutions to class terms leads to an emphasis on conflictual pluralism while obscuring class interests, diminishing the role of the state, and playing down the internal contradictions of capitalism which affect relations of production and often lead to class struggle. In capitalist society, development is also associated with decentralization of authority, routinization of bureaucratic tasks, competition among various interests for resources and power, consensus and bargaining, yet negative consequences appear with authoritarian regimes or the consolidating oligopolistic and monopolistic tendencies in the economy. In socialist society, rational planning and efficient management are expected to ensure economic growth and a more egalitarian distribution of resources to the people, but these goals are often undermined by mismanagement and lack of resources as well as failure to involve people in decisions affecting their production, basic needs, and material standards of living.

Social structures of accumulation

Focused generally on growth in the USA, this theory emphasizes the extended periods of relatively vigorous growth displayed historically by capitalist economies followed by extended periods of stagnation or sluggish growth. Kotz, McDonough, and Reich (1994) argue that the accumulation process is at the core of capitalism and that a set of institutions favourable to accumulation is necessary to ensure rapid growth. A social structure of accumulation emerges through a process of struggles, including class struggles, until it ultimately collapses due to internal contradictions that interact with the external environment of international capital, war, technological change, and so on. This is followed by the rise of a new social structure of accumulation that marks a new stage in the development of capitalism. In a case study of this process, Gordon, Weisskopf, and Bowles (1996) examine four core institutions and the post-war dominance of the USA from about 1945 to 1970.

Development approaches in socialist and Third World nations

Capitalist development of underdevelopment

The argument that capitalism fosters underdevelopment as capital and technology diffuse from the advanced capitalist to the backward nations runs through an important literature emanating particularly from Paul Baran whose *The Political Economy of Growth* (1957) was influential and popular among third world scholars and students, particularly in Latin America. Baran identified forms of economic surplus (actual, potential and planned) in an explanation of the 'roots' and 'morphology' of backwardness. He despaired that 'the colonial and dependent countries today have no recourse to such sources of primary accumulation of capital as were available to the now advanced capitalist countries' and that 'development in the age of monopoly capitalism and imperialism faces obstacles that have little in common with those encountered two or three hundred years ago' (ibid.: 16).

Among the major regional studies that analysed this theme were André Gunder Frank's *Capitalism and Underdevelopment in Latin America* (1967), Walter Rodney's *How Europe Underdeveloped Africa* (1974), Malcolm Caldwell's *The Wealth of Some Nations* (1977), and Manning Marable's *How Capitalism Underdeveloped Black America* (1983). Frank believed that national capitalism and the national bourgeoisie, unlike their counterparts in England and the USA, could not promote development in Latin America. He argued that the contradictions of capitalism had led to the expropriation of economic surplus which generated development in the metropolitan centres and underdevelopment in the peripheral satellites. Criticism of these views relates to emphasis on commercial patterns of international trade rather than to processes and relations of production. (See also Bagchi 1982; Beckford 1972; Brenner 1976; Clarkson 1972; Frank 1966; Kay 1975, 1989; Laclau 1971; Roxborough 1979; Szentes 1971.)

New dependency

Three forms of dependency appear in history: colonial dependency, evident in trade monopolies over land, mines and labour; financial–industrial dependency, accompanied by imperialism and the expansion of big capital at the end of the nineteenth century; and the new dependency, characterized by the capital of multinational corporations in industry orientated to the internal markets of underdeveloped nations after the Second World War. Dos Santos (1970) described this new form as conditioned by the relationship of dominant to dependent countries so that the expansion of the dominant country could have a positive or negative impact on the development of the dependent one. Dussel (1990) and Mohri (1979) criticized the dependency theorists for failure to root their conceptualization in the method of Marx (for other criticisms, see Brewer 1980; Caporaso 1980; Chilcote 1974; Frank 1974; Henfrey 1981; Johnson 1981; Lehman 1979; Munck 1981). Scott (1996) has argued that many understandings of dependency are rooted in the social construction of gender differences and then goes on to set forth a reconceptualization of ideas on development.

Internal colonialism

A relationship similar to the colonial ties between nations, internal colonialism involved dominant and marginal groups within a single society. For example, according to the political sociologist González Casanova (1961), internal colonialism was represented by the monopoly of the ruling metropolis in Mexico City over the marginal Indian communities. The underdevelopment of the marginal society is the consequence of its exploitation by and dependence on the developing metropolis. (See Kahl 1976 for a critique.)

Inward directed development (desarrollismo)

Advocated by the Argentine economist, Raúl Prebisch, and the Economic Commission for Latin America (ECLA), *desarrollismo* implied autonomous or domestic capitalist development through the imposition of tariff barriers, the building of an infrastructure for the local economy, and import substitution to stimulate production. Although this view reveals differences between capitalism in the advanced industrial centre and capitalism in the backward periphery, its reformist solutions to underdevelopment are usually insufficient to overcome the dominance of international capital.

Associated dependent capitalist development

Associated dependent capitalist development is defined as a situation in the periphery in which the domestic bourgeoisie ties itself to capitalism, associates with international capital, and through mediation of the state stimulates capitalist accumulation. According to Cardoso (1973) and Evans (1979), who used Brazil as an example, the accumulation and expansion of local capital thus depend on the dynamic of international capital. Socialist critics argue that this view promotes capitalist exploitation.

Unequal development

As set forth by Amin (1974), this line of thinking sees the world as comprising developed and underdeveloped societies, some of which are capitalist and others socialist, all integrated into a commercial and financial capitalist network on a world scale. Amin (1976) analysed unequal development in terms of disarticulation of different sectors of an economy, domination from the outside, and dependence caused by large foreign industrial business.

Unequal exchange

Elaborated by Emmanuel (1972) and based on David Ricardo's thesis on comparative costs and natural advantages of countries participating in commercial exchange, the theory of unequal exchange portrays capitalist production relations as penetrating a world economy whose units are distinguished by differences in specialization in the international division of labour and by unequal wage levels.

Combined and uneven development

Drawn from the thinking of Trotsky, this theory argues that the most backward and the most modern forms of economic activity and exploitation are found in variable forms in different countries, but they may be linked or combined in their development, especially under the impact of imperialism. A combined and uneven social formation is evident, for example, in the period of transition from a pre-capitalist to a full capitalist economy so that elements of feudalism and capitalism might co-exist (see Lowy 1981; Mandel 1970; Novack 1966). Lenin (1956) demonstrated how Russia in the late nineteenth century evidenced this formation.

Late capitalism

Ernest Mandel (1975) provided an overview of capitalism since the Second World War, attempting to apply the laws of the capitalist mode of production to the post-war period of boom and decline. Late capitalism is a consequence of the integrated international system which necessitates the transfer of surplus from underdeveloped regions to industrialized regions, thereby delaying the development of the former. Some less developed countries have tried to minimize this tendency by nationalizing international capital (for example, Mexican petroleum in 1938 and Chilean copper during the early 1970s).

Mode of production

Development is largely determined by the level of the forces of production – the capital and technology, labour skill and efficiency attained by society. Capital accumulation and reproduction are essential for the maintenance and expansion of capitalism (Rey 1973). Crucial in promoting the forces of production, especially in the third world, is whether capitalism itself must be strengthened *en route* to socialism or the capitalist stage skipped altogether. Amin (1976) identified precapitalist modes, including the communal mode, the tribute-paying mode, the feudal mode, and the slave-owning mode of production. This approach is sometimes deterministic in its reliance upon successive stages of development or limited by its reliance on predetermined modes that may not appear in some societies at particular historical periods (see Chilcote and Johnson 1983; Foster-Carter 1978; Taylor 1979).

Human needs development

Development can be understood in terms of meeting the basic needs of all people, a proposition emphasized by Dube (1988) and Kruijer (1987). Park (1984) identifies a fourfold structure of human needs: survival, belongingness, leisure and control. Amartya Sen has suggested a broad vision of providing 'opportunities' or 'capabilities' allowing people to enjoy the good life (1985). While it is problematic whether capitalist societies can meet such needs as health, food, shelter and employment, the politically representative character of many of them is usually viewed as a step towards development. Yet in capitalist societies large numbers of people often absent themselves from the electoral process, political participation is minimal, and grassroots political involvement may be dwarfed by electoral campaigns influenced by monied interests. Although socialist societies have generally been able to deal with basic human needs through the socialization of most means of production and planned distribution of resources, they have usually failed to establish either effective representative or participatory democracies. Thus, the welfare of all classes, groups and individuals is essential in societal development.

New imperialism and post-imperialism

Theories of imperialism were posited by J. A. Hobson (who utilized an underconsumption theory), Rudolf Hilferding (finance capital), and N. Bukharin and Lenin (monopoly capital). Contemporary analyses by Baran and Sweezy (1966), Brewer (1980), Fieldhouse (1967) and Girvan (1976), emphasized the advanced character of capitalism, especially in its monopoly form and its impact on colonial and less developed areas, while Palma (1978) carefully examined Lenin's thought for the roots of a theory of underdevelopment. These writers showed the negative consequences of the imperialist advance, yet some on the left, for example Warren (1980), have attempted to demonstrate that imperialism tends to destroy precapitalist social formations and provides for capitalist development everywhere. Chilcote (2000a, 2000b, and 2000c) argues for a return to the classical writings on imperialism in order to understand the issues and debates that have appeared in study of development.

In an effort to move beyond imperialist and dependency explanations of capitalist underdevelopment or associated capitalist development, Becker *et al.* (1987) argued that global institutions tend to promote the integration of diverse national interests on a new international basis by offering access to capital resources and technologies. This necessitates the location of both foreign labour and management in the dependent country as well as local participation in the ownership of the corporation. In such a situation two segments of a new social class appear: privileged nationals, or a managerial bourgeoisie, and the foreign nationals who manage the businesses of transnational organizations. This coalescing of dominant class elements across national boundaries suggests the rise of an international oligarchy. According to Becker *et al.*, a theory of post-imperialism serves as an alternative to a determinist Leninist understanding of imperialism and to dependency orthodoxy. However, international capital has dominated third world situations, and there is little evidence to affirm that a managerial national bourgeoisie will emerge as hegemonic and other classes will decline, nor that the national bourgeoisie will favour democracy over authoritarianism.

Sub-imperialism

Dependent capitalism, according to Marini (1978), is unable to reproduce itself through the process of accumulation. However, in some dependent countries where an authoritarian military leadership takes charge, the economy can be reorganized and the working class and opposition oppressed to allow for a project of sub-imperialism. In this case the regime facilitates foreign investment and technology and increases domestic industrial capacity, but must also seek new markets, necessitating expansion into neighbouring countries. The dependent country thus becomes an intermediary between imperialist countries and other less developed countries which are vulnerable to exploitation. Criticism of this perspective focuses on its economic determinism and its implication that only a revolutionary and not a reformist course would be necessary to overcome the ensuing exploitation.

Internationalization of capital

This theory permits an analysis of the movement of capital and class struggle on an international level, particularly the foreign investments and capital accumulation by capitalist enterprises of the centre that operate in the developing countries, and the rapid growth in the internationalization of other forms of capital such as private and public export credits, bank loans and commodity exports. This theory was elaborated by Hymer (1972) and Palloix (1975), and applied to a case study in West Africa by Marcussen and Torp (1982)

Strategies and issues

A central issue for much of the world, according to Mittelman (1988), is how to attain an investable surplus while reducing global inequality in the face of international organizations, aid agencies, technological agreements, multinational corporations and banks. He argues that underdevelopment is not inevitable in the third world, but is the consequence of three forces: capital accumulation, the state, and social classes. He delves into three general strategies of how nations could join global capitalism, retreat from the world capitalist system, and balance the bonds of dependency.

Kruijer (1987) focuses directly on the poor and the oppressed by analysing their plight in terms of the national and international wealth system of domination. He suggests a 'liberation' strategy to provide for basic needs such as education and health care, shelter and clothing, to ensure balanced development of the forces of production, orientate social values in a socialist direction; emancipate women, abolish class distinctions, establish political power with the people, and end economic relationships with the wealthy powerful capitalist world. He sees the process of change as evolving through phases: from the capitalist mode of production in which the bourgeoisie is the ruling class and dominates the state; to a transitional phase in which the capitalist mode is gradually abolished and the interests of the people are represented by the state but the people have little say; to a state-socialist phase in which private enterprise has largely disappeared and the people still have little input; to a democratic socialist phase in which the power of the state is gradually reduced and decisions are increasingly vested in the people.

Dube (1988) sums up a number of policy recommendations in the direction of rethinking the goals and strategies of development: plans for economic growth must be balanced by enriching the quality of life and meeting the basic needs of all people; eliminate all poverty, not by welfarism but by a radical altering of planning and implementation policies; instil in people recognition of their rights and responsibilities through programmes of conscientization; ensure participation in a policy of affirmative action to include all deprived sectors of society; implement administrative restructuring, renovation and innovation, and remove vestiges of colonial and Western-style democratic practices that have failed in third world countries; manage the socio-cultural environment so as to avoid counter-development; and re-examine the global context of development so as to close the bipolar gap between rich and poor worlds, find an equitable sharing of scarce resources, and improve the human condition of all peoples.

These policy issues are analysed around the notion of sustainable development in an effort to raise global consciousness about environmental degradation and the deterioration of the planet (Brown *et al.* 1990). This notion, according to the World Commission on Environment and Development, is possible when 'Humanity has the ability to make development sustainable – to ensure that it meets the needs of the present without compromising the ability of future generations to meet their own needs' (World Commission on Environment and Development 1987: 8). Goldsworthy (1988) emphasizes the politics of such policy issues, while Fuentes and Frank (1989) show the importance of popular social movements in political struggle and change. More particularly, Molyneux (1986), Sen and Grown (1987), and Scott (1996) demonstrate how both capitalist and socialist development ignore the role of women, and Redclift (1984) draws out the strengths and weaknesses of environmental movements. Some of the issues and strategies for dealing with sustainable development can be outlined as follows:

Strategies	Issues
Capitalism versus socialism	Growth or human needs
	Private or public ownership of means of production
	Market or planned economy
	Capitalist path or non-capitalist path
	One path or multilinear paths
	Physical investment (plant and equipment) or human capital investment
	Evolution versus revolution
	Growth or distribution of resources
	Reforms or radical restructuring
Endogenous versus exogenous orientation	Self reliance or interdependence
Market or planning	Industry or agriculture
	Industrial or environmental protection
	Development or non-development
Aid versus trade	Import substitution or export promotion
	Regional integration or open international exchange

Fagen, Deer and Coraggio argue for a transformation of the model of accumulation and capitalist social formation to a socialist model. They see the need for 'social ownership of the commanding heights of the economy and a relatively comprehensive system of planning' in which production and distribution are tied to basic needs of the population; forms of privilege (income, race, gender, class, etc.) are terminated; and the popular classes participate fully in determining public policy (Fagen, Deer and Coraggio 1986: 10). Their analysis is particularly concerned with uneven and under-developed capitalism on the periphery and revolutionary activity for socialism away from the advanced capitalist countries, but these socialist experiments on the periphery may also have relevance for capitalist and socialist development elsewhere.

Towards a synthesis of development

The search for an understanding of development entails a multiplicity of ideas and practices, a kind of dialectical interplay between theory and practice, and an interdisciplinary endeavour. Thus, the political dimension of development involves both representative and participatory democracy, preferably with down-up grass-roots and collective actions rather than decisions based on top-down processes of indirect decision-making. It comprises collective participation in decisions among individuals in activities extending beyond boundaries of government and political parties, including classes and groups outside and within the state. It is linked to economic and social consequences, largely dependent on the mode of production (under capitalism or socialism) and associated with the provision of basic human needs. Finally, it is a consequence of capital accumulation and distribution of its rewards in egalitarian ways.

Development, however, is unequal, uneven, and combines modes of production through history. Both progression and retrogression are possible. Sources of development relate to the economic base (largely capitalism in the contemporary world) and to state bureaucratic activity (in the capitalist and socialist countries). Development links institutions to egalitarian participation, individual and collective choice, interchange of roles (for instance, managers and workers, teachers and students, and so on), and mitigation of class divisions in society. Development involves advances in the productive forces of society (under capitalism or socialism at national and international levels) and in the drive for egalitarian participation and distribution of resources to meet basic needs and collectively raise the quality of material life of all people. Development affects individuals by eliminating vestiges of selfishness and egoism, fostering collaboration, promoting solidarity among people, raising political consciousness and social responsibility, and struggling against injustice and exploitation of person by person. The contradictions of economic and political life in the struggle for participatory and representative democracy, egalitarian distribution of resources, provision for basic needs, protection of the environment, and so on may lead to crisis and ultimately to some resolution of the issues identified above.

References

Almond, G. (1970) *Political Development: Essays in Heuristic Theory*, Boston: Little, Brown & Co.

Almond, G. and Coleman, J. S. (eds) (1960) *The Politics of Developing Areas*, Princeton: Princeton University Press.

Almond, G. and Powell, G. B. (1966) *Comparative Politics: A Developmental Approach*, Boston: Little, Brown & Co.

Amin, S. (1974) *Accumulation on a World Scale: A Critique of the Theory of Underdevelopment*, 2 vols, New York: Monthly Review Press.

—— (1976) *Unequal Development*, New York: Monthly Review Press.

Apter, D. (1965) *The Politics of Modernization*, Chicago: University of Chicago Press.

—— (1971) *Choice and the Politics of Allocation: A Developmental Theory*, New Haven: Yale University Press.

—— (1987) *Rethinking Development: Modernization, Dependency, and Postmodern Politics*, Newbury Park, CA: Sage Publications.

Bagchi, A. K. (1982) *The Political Economy of Underdevelopment*, New York: Cambridge University Press.

Baran, P. (1957) *The Political Economy of Growth*, New York: Monthly Review Press.

Baran, P. and Sweezy, P. (1966) *Monopoly Capital: An Essay on the American Economic and Social Order*, New York: Monthly Review Press.

Bates, R. H. (ed.) (1988) *Toward a Political Economy of Development: A Rational Choice Perspective*, Berkeley: University of California Press.

Becker, D. G., Frieden, J., Shatz, S. P. and Sklar, S. L. (1987) *Postimperialism, International Capitalism and Development in the Late Twentieth Century*, Boulder: Lynne Rienner Publishers.

Beckford, G. (1972) *Persistent Poverty, Underdevelopment in Plantation Economies of the Third World*, Oxford: Oxford University Press.

Bernstein, H. (ed.) (1973) *Underdevelopment and Development*, Baltimore: Penguin.

Binder, L. *et al.* (1971) *Crises and Sequences in Political Development*, Princeton, NJ: Princeton University Press.

Black, C. E. (1966) *The Dynamics of Modernization*, New York: Harper & Row.

Blomström, M. and Hettne, B. (1984) *Development Theory in Transition. The Dependency Debate and Beyond: Third World Responses*, London: Zed Books.

Bollen, K. (1979) 'Political democracy and the timing of development', *American Sociological Review* 44: 572–87.

—— (1983) 'World system position, dependency, and democracy', *American Sociological Review* 48: 468–79.

Booth, D. (1985) 'Marxism and development sociology: interpreting the impasse', *World Development* 13 (7): 761–87.

Bowles, S. and Gintis, H. (1986) *Democracy and Capitalism: Property, Community, and the Contradictions of Modern Social Thought*, New York: Basic Books.

Brenner, R. (1976) 'The origins of capitalist development: a critique of neo-Smithean Marxism', *New Left Review* 104: 24–92.

—— (1999) 'Beyond state-centrism? Space, territoriality, and geographical scale in globalization studies', *Theory and Society* 28: 39–78.

Brewer, A. (1980) *Marxist Theories of Imperialism: A Critical Survey*, London: Routledge & Kegan Paul.

Brown, L. R. *et al.* (1990) *State of the World: A Wordwatch Institute Report on Progress Toward a Sustainable Society*, New York: W. W. Norton & Co.

Caldwell, M. (1977) *The Wealth of Some Nations*, London: Zed Books.

Caporaso, J. A. (1980) 'Dependency theory: continuities and discontinuities in development studies', *International Organization* 39: 605–28.

Cardoso, F. H. (1973) 'Associated-dependent development: theoretical and practical implications', in A. Stepan (ed.) *Authoritarian Brazil: Origins, Policies, and Future*, New Haven: Yale University Press.

Cardoso, F. H. and Faletto, E. (1979) *Dependency and Development*, Berkeley: University of California Press.

Cammack, P. (1997) *Capitalism and Democracy in the Third World: The Doctrine for Political Development*, London: Leicester University Press.

Chase-Dunn, C. (1977) 'Toward a structural perspective on the world-system', *Politics and Society* 7 (4): 453–76.

—— (1974) 'Dependency: a critical synthesis of the literature', *Latin American Perspectives* 1: 4–29.

—— (1984) *Theories of Development and Underdevelopment*, Boulder, CO: Westview Press.

—— (2000a) *Theories of Comparative Political Economy*, Boulder, CO: Westview Press.

—— (ed) (2000b) *Imperialism. Theoretical Direction*, Amherst, NY: Humanity Press.

—— (ed.) (2000c) *The Political Economy of Imperialism: Critical Appraisals*, Lanham, MD: Rowman and Littlefield Publishers.

Chilcote, R. H. and Johnson, D. L. (eds) (1983) *Theories of Development: Mode of Production or Dependency?*, Beverly Hills: Sage Publications.

Chodak, S. (1973) *Societal Development: Five Approaches with Conclusions from Comparative Analysis*, New York: Oxford University Press.

Clarkson, S. (1972) 'Marxism-Leninism as a system for comparative analysis of under-development', *Political Science Review* 11: 124–37.

Davis, H. B. (1967) *Nationalism and Socialism: Marxist and Labor Theories of Nationalism to 1917*, New York: Monthly Review Press.

DeKadt, E. and Williams, G. (eds) (1974) *Sociology and Development*, London: Tavistock Publications.

Deutsch, K. W. (1953) *Nationalism and Social Communication: An Inquiry into the Foundation of Nationality*, New York: MIT Press/John Wiley.

—— (1961) 'Social mobilization and political development', *American Political Science Review* 55: 493–514.

Dos Santos, T. (1970) 'The structure of dependence', *American Economic Review* 60: 231–6.

Dube, S. C. (1988) *Modernization and Development: The Search for Alternative Paradigms*, London: Zed Books; Tokyo: United Nations University.

Dussel, E. (1990) 'Marx's economic manuscripts of 1861–63 and the "concept" of dependency', *Latin American Perspectives* 17 (2): 62–101.

Eisenstadt, S. N. (1966) *Modernization: Protest and Change*, Englewood Cliffs, NJ: Prentice-Hall.

Emmanuel, A. (1972) *Unequal Exchange: A Study of the Imperialism of Trade*, with additional comments by C. Bettelheim, New York: Monthly Review Press.

Evans, P. B. (1979) *Dependent Development: The Alliance of Multinational, State and Local Capital in Brazil*, Princeton, NJ: Princeton University Press.

Evans, P. B. and Stephens, J. D. (1988) 'Development and the world economy', in N. J. Smelsor (ed.) *Handbook of Sociology*, Newbury Park, CA: Sage Publications.

Fagen, R. R., Deere, C. D. and Coraggio, J. L. (eds) (1986) *Transition and Development: Problems of Third World Socialism*, New York: Monthly Review Press.

Fieldhouse, D. K. (1967) *The Theory of Capitalist Imperialism*, London: Longmans, Green & Co.

Foster-Carter, A. (1978) 'The modes of production controversy', *New Left Review* 107: 47–77.

—— (1985) *The Sociology of Development*, Ormskirk: Causeway Press.

Frank, A. G. (1966) 'The development of underdevelopment', *Monthly Review* 18: 17–31.

—— (1967) *Capitalism and Underdevelopment in Latin America: Historical Studies of Chile and Brazil*, New York: Monthly Review Press.

—— (1971) *Sociology of Development and Underdevelopment of Sociology*, London: Pluto.

—— (1974) 'Dependence is dead, long live dependence and the class struggle: a reply to critics', *Latin American Perspectives* 1: 87–106.

Fuentes, M. and Frank, A. G. (1989) 'Ten theses on social movements', *World Development* 17 (2): 179–91.

Furtado, C. (1964) *Development and Underdevelopment*, Berkeley and Los Angeles: University of California Press.

Gilpin, R. (2002) *The Challenge of Global Capitalism. The World Economy in the 21st Century*, Princeton: Princeton University Press.

Girvan, N. (1976) *Corporate Imperialism: Conflict and Expropriation: Transnational Corporations and Economic Nationalism in the Third World*, White Plains, NY: M. E. Sharpe.

Goldsworthy, D. (1988) 'Thinking politically about development', *Development and Change* 19 (3): 505–30.

González Casanova, P. (1961) 'International colonialism and national development', in I. L. Horowitz, J. de Castro and J. Grassi (eds) *Latin American Radicalism*, New York: Vintage Books.

Gordon, D., Weisskopf, T. E., and Bowles, S. (1996) 'Power accumulation and crisis: the rise and demise of the postwar social structure of accumulation', in Victor Lippit (ed.) *Radical Political Economy: Explorations in Alternative Economic Analysis*, Armonk, NY: M.E. Sharpe.

Griffin, K. and Gurley, J. (1985) 'Radical analyses of imperialism, the third world, and the transition to socialism: a survey article', *Journal of Economic Literature* 23: 1089–143.

Hardt, M. and Negri, A. (2000) *Empire*, Cambridge: Harvard University Press.

Harris, J. (1998–1999) 'Globalization and the technological transformation of capitalism', *Race and Class* 40 (no. 2–3), 21–36.

Henfrey, C. (1981) 'Dependency, modes of production, and the class analysis of Latin America', *Latin American Perspectives* 8: 17–54.

Hettne, B. (1983) 'The development of development theory', *Acta Sociologica* 26 (3,4): 247–66.

Hirst, P. and Thompson, G. (1999) *Globalization in Question*, Cambridge: Polity Press.

Hopkins, T. K. and Wallerstein, I. (1977) 'Patterns of development of the modern world-system', *Review* 1: 111–45.

Huntington, S. P. (1965) 'Political development and political decay', *World Politics* 17: 386–430.

—— (1968) *Political Order in Changing Societies*, New Haven: Yale University Press.

Huntington, S. P. and Domínguez, J. (1975) 'Political development', in F. I. Greenstein and N. Polsby (eds) *Handbook of Political Science*, vol. 3, Reading, MA: Addison-Wesley.

Hymer, S. (1972) 'The internationalization of capital', *Journal of Economic Issues* 6 (1): 91–110.

Johnson, C. (1981) 'Dependency theory and processes of capitalism and socialism', *Latin American Perspectives* 8: 55–81.

Kahl, J. A. (1976) *Modernization, Exploitation, and Dependency in Latin America: Germani, González Casanova, and Cardoso*, New Brunswick, NJ: Transaction Books.

Kay, C. (1975) *Development and Underdevelopment: A Marxist Analysis*, London: Macmillan.

—— (1989) *Latin American Theories of Development and Underdevelopment*, London: Routledge.

Kotz, D., McDonough, T. and Reich, M. (eds) (1994) *Social Structures of Accumulation: The Political Econmy of Growth and Crisis*, Cambridge: Cambridge University Press.

Kruijer, G. J. (1987) *Development through Liberation: Third World Problems and Solutions*, Atlantic Highlands, NJ: Humanities Press International.

Laclau, E. (1971) 'Feudalism and capitalism in Latin America', *New Left Review* 67: 19–38.

Lehman, D. (ed.) (1979) *Development Theory: Four Critical Essays*, London: Frank Cass.

Lenin, V. I. (1956) *The Development of Capitalism in Russia: The Process of the Formation of a Home Market for Large-Scale Industry*, Moscow: Foreign Languages Publishing House.

Lerner, D. (1958) *The Passing of Traditional Society: Modernizing the Middle East*, Glencoe, IL: Free Press.

Levy, M. J., Jr (1966) *Modernization and the Structure of Societies: A Setting for International Affairs*, Princeton, NJ: Princeton University Press.

Lewis, W. A. (1955) *The Theory of Economic Growth*, London: Allen & Unwin.

Lipset, S. M. (1959) 'Some social requisites of democracy: economic development and political legitimacy', *American Political Science Review* 53: 69–105.

Lowy, M. (1981) *The Politics of Combined and Uneven Development: The Theory of Permanent Revolution*, London: Verso.

Mandel, E. (1970) 'The laws of uneven development', *New Left Review* 59: 19–38.

—— (1975) *Late Capitalism*, London: NLB.

Mann, M. *et al.* (2001–2) 'The transnational ruling class formation thesis: A symposium', *Science and Society* 65 (Winter): 464–508.

Marable, M. (1983) *How Capitalism Underdeveloped Black America*, Boston: Southend Press.

Marcussen, H. S. and Torp, J. E. (1982) *The Internationalization of Capital: The Prospects for the Third World*, London: Zed Books.

Marini, R. M. (1978) 'World capitalist accumulation and sub-imperialism', *Two Thirds* 1: 29–39.

Mittelman J. H. (1988) *Out from Underdevelopment: Prospects for the Third World*, New York: St Martin's Press.

Mohri, K. (1979) 'Marx and "underdevelopment"', *Monthly Review* 30: 32–42.

Molyneux, M. (1986) 'Mobilization without emancipation? Women's interests, state, and revolution', in R. R. Fagen, C. D. Deere and J. L. Coraggio (eds) *Transition and Development: Problems of Third World Socialism*, New York: Monthly Review Press.

Moore, B. (1966) *Social Origins of Dictatorship and Democracy: Lord and Peasant in the Making of the Modern World*, Boston: Beacon Press.

Munck, R. (1981) 'Imperialism and dependency: recent debates and old deadends', *Latin American Perspectives* 8: 162–79.

Novack, G. (1966) *Uneven and Combined Development in History*, New York: Merit Publishers.

Organski, A. F. K. (1965) *The Stages of Political Development*, New York: Knopf.

Oxaal, I., Barnett, T. and Booth, D. (eds) (1975) *Beyond the Sociology of Development*, London: Routledge & Kegan Paul.

Palma, G. (1978) 'Dependency: a formal theory of underdevelopment or a methodology for the analysis of concrete situations of underdevelopment', *World Development* 6: 881–94.

Palloix (1975) *L'Internalisation du capital*, Paris: François Maspero.

Park, H. S. (1984) *Human Needs and Political Development: A Dissent to Utopian Solutions*, Cambridge, MA: Schenkman Publishing Company.

Post, K. and Wright, P. (1989) *Socialism and Underdevelopment*, London: Routledge.

Pye, L. (1966) *Aspects of Political Development*, Boston: Little, Brown & Co.

Redclift, M. (1984) *Development and the Environment Crisis. Red or Green Alternatives?*, London: Methuen.

Rey, P.-P. (1973) *Les alliances de classes*, Paris: François Maspero.

Robinson, W. I. (1996) *Promoting Polyarchy: Globalization, U.S. Intervention, and Hegemony*, Cambridge: Cambridge University Press.

Robinson, W. I. and Harris, J. (2000) 'Towards a global ruling class? Globalization and the Transnational Capitalist Class', *Science and Society* 64 (Spring): 11–54.

Rodney, W. (1974) *How Europe Underdeveloped Africa*, Washington, DC: Howard University Press.

Rostow, W. W. (1960) *The Stages of Economic Growth: A Non-Communist Manifesto*, Cambridge: Cambridge University Press.

Roxborough, I. (1979) *Theories of Underdevelopment*, Atlantic Highlands, NJ: Humanities Press.

Rustow, D. A. (1970) 'Transitions to democracy: toward a dynamic model', *Comparative Politics* 2: 337–63.

Scalapino, R. A. (1989) *The Politics of Development: Perspectives on Twentieth-Century Asia*, London: Harvard University Press.

Scott, C. V. (1996) *Gender and Development: Rethinking Modernization and Dependency Theory*, Boulder: Lynne Rienner Publishers.

Sen, A. (1985) *Commodities and Capabilities*, Amsterdam: North-Holland.

Sen, G. and Grown, C. (1987) *Development, Crises, and Alternative Visions: Third World Women's Perspectives*, New York: Monthly Review Press.

Senghaas, D. (1985) *The European Experience: A Historical Critique of Development Theory*, Dover, NH: Berg Publishers.

So, A. Y. (1990) *Social Change and Development: Modernization, Dependency, and World-System Theories*, Newbury Park, CA: Sage Publications.

Sweezy, P. M. (1942) *The Theory of Capitalist Development*, New York: Oxford University Press.

Szentes, T. (1971) *The Political Economy of Underdevelopment*, Budapest: Centre for Afro-Asian Research, Hungarian Academy of Sciences.

Tanter, R. (1967) 'Toward a theory of political development', *Midwest Journal of Political Science* 11: 145–72.

Taylor, J. G. (1979) *From Modernization to Modes of Production: A Critique of the Sociologies of Development and Underdevelopment*, New York: Macmillan.

Wallerstein, I. (1974) *The Modern World System*, vol. 1, New York: Academic Press.

Warren, B. (1980) *Imperialism: Pioneer of Capitalism*, ed. J. Sender, London: NLB.

Weiner, M. and Huntington, S. P. (eds) (1987) *Understanding Political Development*, Boston: Little, Brown & Co.

World Commission on Environment and Development (1987) *Our Common Future*, New York: Oxford University Press.